The Children of Aataentsic is both a full-scale ethnohistory of the Huron Indian confederacy and a far-reaching study of the causes of its collapse under the impact of the Iroquois attacks of 1649. Drawing upon the archaeological context, the ethnography presented by early explorers and missionaries, and the recorded history of contact with Europeans, Bruce Trigger traces the development of the Huron people from the earliest hunting and gathering economies in southern Ontario many centuries before the arrival of the Europeans to their key role in the fur trade in eastern Canada during the first half of the seventeenth century.

Trigger's work integrates insights from archaeology, history, ethnology, linguistics, and geography. This wide knowledge allows him to show that, far from being a static prehistoric society quickly torn apart by European contact and the fur trade, almost every facet of Iroquoian culture had undergone significant change in the centuries preceding European contact. He argues convincingly that the European impact upon native cultures cannot be correctly assessed unless the nature and extent of precontact change is understood. His study not only stands Euro-American stereotypes and fictions on their heads, but forcefully and consistently interprets European and Indian actions, thoughts, and motives from the perspective of the Huron culture.

The Children of Aataentsic revises widely accepted interpretations of Indian behaviour and challenges cherished myths about the actions of some celebrated Europeans during the "heroic age" of Canadian history. In a new preface, Trigger describes and evaluates contemporary controversies over the ethnohistory of eastern Canada.

Bruce Trigger is a member of the Department of Anthropology, McGill University and author of *Natives and Newcomers: Canada's "Heroic Age" Reconsidered.*

D0222036

$32.00

16

The Children of Aataentsic

A History of the Huron People to 1660

BRUCE G. TRIGGER

McGILL-QUEEN'S UNIVERSITY PRESS   Kingston and Montreal

© McGill-Queen's University Press 1976
Reprinted with a new preface 1987
First paperback edition 1987

ISBN 0-7735-0626-8 (cloth)
ISBN 0-7735-0627-6 (paper)

Legal deposit fourth quarter 1987
Bibliothèque nationale du Québec

Printed in Canada

Printed on acid-free paper

Canadian Cataloguing in Publication Data

Trigger, Bruce G.
    The children of Aataentsic: a history of the
    Huron people to 1660
    First published: Montreal: McGill-Queen's University
    Press, 1976.
    Includes index.
    Bibliography: p.
    ISBN 0-7735-0626-8 (bound) — ISBN 0-7735-0627-6 (pbk.)
    1. Huron Indians – History.   2. Indians of North
    America – Ontario – History.   3. Jesuits – Missions –
    Ontario.   I. Title.
    E99.H9T68 1987   970.004'97   C87-090208-3

Preparation of the manuscript was aided by grants from the Faculty of Graduate Studies and Research, McGill University: the first edition was published with the help of a grant from the Social Science Research Council of Canada using funds provided by the Canada Council.
    This reprint has been published with the help of a grant from the Max Bell Foundation.

To Barbara, Isabel, and Rosalyn

Contents

Illustrations

Maps

Preface to the 1987 reprinting

When *The Children of Aataentsic* was published in 1976 I doubted that, whether its reception was favourable or unfavourable, there would ever be a call to reprint this mammoth work. Indeed I had serious reservations about whether a book of this scale was worthwhile and was greatly relieved when favourable reviews started to appear, beginning with the late Walter Kenyon's "Masterwork" in *Canadian Forum*. In recent months I have received a growing number of inquiries about how copies might be obtained. It was therefore good to learn that McGill-Queen's University Press, with the generous support of the Max Bell Foundation, was planning to reprint it in a handier and more economical format.

Practical considerations alone have dictated that the text and pagination remain unchanged, although in 1982 I had produced a partially revised manuscript version of the text for translation into French. (This translation will be published early in 1988 by Libre Expression.) It is also clear that many readers wanted a copy of the original work which has become of some historical interest in relation to the development of ethnohistorical studies of the Iroquoians. A substantial updating of *The Children of Aataentsic* has already been achieved in *Natives and Newcomers* (1985) which examines more recent developments in the historical and ethnohistorical study of the native peoples of central Canada, with special emphasis on methodological problems.

In *The Children of Aataentsic* my main objective was to demonstrate that it was possible to write a history of a native people that was not focused exclusively on their relations with Europeans. In order to make this work attractive to the general reader, I sought to keep methodological discussions as brief as possible. In my introduction I limited myself to considering the importance of archaeological data for ethnohistorical research, the value of the long-established concept of interest groups for achieving parity in analyses of native and European behaviour, and the necessity of trying to understand native actions as far as possible in terms of the rational pursuit of interests in order to expose the erroneousness of long-standing claims that native people were less rational than Europeans. Unknown to me, the latter goal was simultaneously being pursued by the American historian Francis

Jennings in his remarkable book *The Invasion of America* (1975). In order to keep the introduction as brief as possible, I excised part of my discussion of rationality which I rewrote and published as "Brecht and Ethnohistory" in the journal *Ethnohistory* (1975).

In the decade since *The Children of Aataentsic* was published, the theoretical perspectives of anthropology, history, and ethnohistory have changed dramatically in some respects. In particular, there has been an increasing emphasis on understanding cultural change from what is believed to be a native point of view and explaining change in terms of altering patterns of cognition. There has also been a growing unwillingness to accept economic explanations of human behaviour. As a result of these changes, interpretations of native actions have begun to shift away from those offered in this book. This trend has influenced scholars who praised *The Children of Aataentsic* highly when it first appeared and who have since indicated no disagreement with its basic tenets. I have therefore decided to use this new preface to enunciate these tenets and to try to estimate how well my book has survived its first decade.

In *The Children of Aataentsic* I privileged a rationalist approach. My primary goal was to demonstrate that native behaviour was based on the rational pursuit of desired ends at least to the same extent as that of Europeans. I had concluded that little was to be gained by eliciting sympathy for native people (as various historians had done in the past) if it was not based on respect for their intelligence and self-discipline. I therefore sought to explain native behaviour as far as possible in terms of rational calculations of how desired ends might be achieved. In doing this I eschewed the alternative romantic approach which views the behaviour of each society as determined by its own particular cultural pattern or, as was once believed, by its own specific biological nature. In a relativistic fashion, the romantic view assumes that each culture is a closed system based on its own self-defined rules. Thus the behaviour of one group is unlikely ever to be fully comprehensible to members of another. It is this approach, with its potential for emphasizing the irrational aspects of human conduct, that in various guises has dominated the interpretation of native American behaviour from at least the time of Francis Parkman to the present. Rationalist explanations, by contrast, seek to account for human behaviour in terms of calculations that are cross-culturally comprehensible.

I had no desire, however, to commit myself in a partisan fashion to one side or the other of a simplistic debate between rationalism and cultural relativism. There is clearly not the wide range of variation in cultural behaviour that might be expected if only cultural factors shaped all aspects of human life. No society, for example, welcomes enslavement or totally ignores its own self-interest. Yet as an anthropologist I was equally aware that individuals or groups can use rational means to pursue culturally defined goals that are themselves often far from rational. The Jesuits' risking of their own lives to rescue the souls of native people from eternal damnation is one example of this. I was also keenly aware of the continuing debates among philosophers and social scientists concerning the relative importance of rational calculations and culturally defined goals as factors influencing human behaviour (see M. D. Sahlins, *Culture and Practical Reason* [1976], Ernest Gellner, *Relativism and the Social Sciences* [1985] and Dan Sperber, *On Anthropological Knowledge* [1985]). These disputes not only remain inconclusive but in many cases appear to centre on highly unproductive questions. It is frequently impossible to distinguish culturally encoded rational experience from "irrational" cultural norms. Religious prohibitions in a hunter-gatherer society may maintain conservation practices in its subsistence pattern, thereby disguising their utilitarian nature and at the same time enhancing people's willingness to practise them. Conversely, many customs that were originally non-utilitarian, if they relate to practical behaviour in any way, may be subject to long-term modification and selection that makes them more "rational." Finally, ethnologists are unable to agree whether statements such as "all men are parrots" are to be understood as intended literally or metaphorically by a particular culture.

As an Ariadne's thread to extricate myself from this labyrinth of confusion, I adopted what I believe to be the most fruitful theory of culture currently available. This theory is based on Karl Marx's assumption that "the mode of production in material life determines the general character of the social, political, and intellectual processes of life." It follows that human beings are likely to be most rational and calculating, and hence least culture-bound, with respect to those matters that relate most directly to their material well-being. Behavioural and conceptual adjustments can be made most easily in human activities such as food production, trade, and competition for material resources. On the other hand, aspects of culture that relate to social status, personal identity, and a sense of psychological well-being, including religious beliefs, values, and ethnic identity, while ultimately influenced by economic factors are by their nature likely to be much more conservative and to respond much more slowly and unpredictably to changing conditions. Traditions of these sorts are not only more tenacious but also less susceptible to rational evaluation. Two principal hypotheses or expectations can be derived from these assumptions: (a) examples of rational calculation are likely to be far more obvious in economic behaviour than in religious beliefs and cultural values, and (b) when cultures interact, accommodation and change are likely to occur more quickly and easily in economic behaviour than in other spheres. Yet, to the extent that economic change threatens a sense of identity, human groups may seek to solidify and reinforce their traditional religious beliefs and practices as a way of coping with psychological disorientation and this can, in some instances, significantly influence economic processes. Without questioning the sincere altruism with which the Jesuits perceived their missionary work, it is possible to see them as both conscious and unconscious agents of French imperialism. By trying to undermine Iroquoian religious beliefs and traditional social values, they were seeking to eliminate precisely those areas of traditional Huron culture that were most resistant to economic change and maintained the will of native people to resist European domination.

These were the ideas that guided my interpretation of Huron behaviour. Despite their materialist orientation, they are very different from the technological determinism of George T. Hunt (*The Wars of the Iroquois* [1940]) who assumed that European tools quickly and automatically transformed all other aspects of native life. They are also more akin to Alfred G. Bailey's (*The Conflict of European and Eastern Algonkian Cultures, 1504-1700* [1937]) balanced anthropological view of how native cultures responded to European contact than they are to Harold Innis' (*The Fur Trade in Canada* [1930, 1956]) economic determinism. I believe that my underlying assumptions have been evident to most anthropologists, especially those who are sympathetic to any kind of materialist approach to understanding human behaviour. Some historians, however, appear to have interpreted my detailed examination of historical events as the espousal of their own preferred "let the facts speak for themselves" approach. In my view such an approach can never be free from implicit biases which frequently assume a strongly romantic and idealist character.

Every choice has its costs as well as benefits. I cannot claim that my emphasis on rational behaviour has not involved a relative neglect (although I hope only a minor one) of culturally specific factors that shaped the Huron way of life and their responses to changing historical circumstances. Two research projects initiated in recent years are investigating subjects that promise to add significantly to our understanding of Huron behaviour.

The first of these is George Hamell's still largely unpublished analysis of the basic patterns of religious beliefs shared by the Iroquoian, Algonkian, and Siouan-speaking peoples of eastern North America. Drawing upon extensive collections of ethnographic and ethnohistorical data, he has been able, as part of this research, to demonstrate that native copper, rock crystals, and marine shells were viewed as substances associated with the supernatural underwater world and hence were believed able to confer power, health, and prosperity on their possessors. For over 6,000 years these materials were buried with the dead to enhance the welfare of their souls. Hamell argues that European metal artifacts and glass beads were seen as the equivalents of native copper and quartz crystals and that Europeans initially were viewed as spirits returning from the realms of the dead. Hence the earliest European goods appear to have been valued for their spiritual rather than for their utilitarian qualities. Metal kettles were regularly cut into pieces and fragments widely exchanged from tribe to tribe. These goods turn up far more frequently in native burials than in living sites during early decades of contact. Marine shells also began to be traded into the interior of eastern North America in far larger quantities than before as the availability of European goods stimulated burial ceremonialism and hence a demand for the full range of goods associated with such rituals (C. Miller and G. Hamell, *Journal of American History* 73 [1986]: 311-28). In *The Children of Aataentsic* I observed that in the course of the sixteenth century the arrival of European goods had an impact on Iroquoian societies that was out of proportion to their utilitarian value. What I was not able to do, not having studied native religious beliefs in the detailed and comparative fashion that Hamell is now doing, was to specify what these goods meant to native people during the earliest phases of European contact. Because of this I also failed to explain satisfactorily the fragmentary condition in which this material is found in archaeological sites and to pay as much attention as I might have done to the contexts in which it is being discovered.

Recent ethnosemantic studies by the linguist John Steckley ("The Soul Concepts of the Huron," Master's thesis, Memorial University of Newfoundland, 1978) of manuscript dictionaries, grammars, and religious texts prepared in the Huron language by French missionaries in the seventeenth and eighteenth centuries are also revealing important information about Huron culture and how the Jesuits perceived it. From these texts it is possible to learn far more about how the Hurons viewed the nature of souls than could be gleaned from seventeenth-century missionary accounts. One can also assess how much the Jesuits knew about Huron concepts of the soul at particular periods and to what degree they were linguistically capable of conveying Christian theological concepts to the Huron. More recently Steckley has used knowledge of the terminology that the Jesuits employed at different times to date the Huron carol, "Jesous Ahatonhia," to the early period of the Huron mission and hence to support the traditional attribution of its composition to Jean de Brébeuf.

In recent years the study of Huron dictionaries has helped to clarify the nature of Huron seventeenth-century clan organization and house structures as well as the meaning of place-names. It may be able to shed more light on the nature of the fur trade by revealing how the Huron categorized animal pelts and the phrases commonly used in commercial transactions with the French at different periods. These dictionaries and grammars constitute the largest corpus of relatively unstudied material relating to the Huron culture of the seventeenth century. Its systematic investigation promises to reveal much about Huron culture and how it was understood by the French at different periods. The religious texts that the Jesuits composed in the Huron language should also reveal more about how they tried, and succeeded or failed linguistically, to convey a knowledge of Christianity to the Hurons. The integration of this material into the study of Huron history should amplify and perhaps modify our understanding of many historical issues. It is important that there be more intensive study of the Huron language as a basis for the continuing investigation of these data.

Hamell and Steckley have shown how specific types of systematic study can expand our knowledge of Huron culture. In principle any new knowledge of how native people perceived the world around them and reacted to it ought to improve an understanding of how and why they behaved as they did in specific historical situations. Both approaches necessitate long and detailed study and lexical investigations require specialized linguistic skills. It also remains to be determined to what extent such studies will significantly modify an understanding of Huron history based on the sources that were used to write *The Children of Aataentsic*. The point appears to have been reached in the study of Huron history where increasing effort must be expended to recover each new item of information.

A final development in which the emphasis is on cultural specificities is the explosion in the last two decades of publications that examine how, beginning in the fifteenth century, native Americans were perceived by European scholars and colonists. This research in the field of intellectual history is of particular importance to anthropologists because it reveals in detail the cultural stereotypes, biases, and precedents that shaped the understanding Europeans had of the native peoples with whom they interacted. These studies help ethnohistorians to judge more accurately the biases that coloured European descriptions and interpretations of native peoples as well as to understand the motives that led European colonists to behave as they did. Such studies make intellectual historians such as Cornelius Jaenen (*Friend and Foe: Aspects of French-Amerindian Cultural Contact in the Sixteenth and Seventeenth Centuries* [1976]) and Olive Dickason (*The Myth of the Savage and the Beginnings of French Colonialism in the Americas* [1984]) indispensable to the study of ethnohistory.

In recent studies of the ethnohistory of eastern North America the pendulum appears to be swinging in the direction of a romantic rather than a rationalistic analysis. There is a growing tendency to reject or ignore economic interpretations of native (or European) behaviour and in their place to adopt an idealist approach. In *The Children of Aataentsic* I opposed the economic determinism of Hunt and Innis, and I continue to believe that culturally specific factors must be carefully considered in any form of historical analysis. Yet I regard the rejection of rationalist and materialist approaches as deplorable and atavistic. In particular, I deplore the failure to distinguish between ecological and economic determinism, which most social scientists — including Marxist ones — find unacceptable, and an appropriate consideration of the constraints which these factors exert on human behaviour. In my opinion the latter provides a solid framework within which to consider the operation of culturally specific factors.

It is still sometimes assumed, as was done frequently in the past, that native cultures were relatively impervious to European influences and that native peoples went on doing what they had done previously until they were overwhelmed by European settlement. The wars of the Iroquois are claimed to be a continuation of long-standing intertribal conflicts with only the scale and intensity increased as a result of the acquisition of guns. D. K. Richter (*William and Mary Quarterly* 43 [1986]: 480-3), Lucien Campeau (*La Mission des Jésuites chez les Hurons, 1634-1650* [1987]), and Conrad Heidenreich important motive for historical Iroquois warfare was the attempt to replace population losses resulting from epidemics of European diseases by capturing and incorporating other native groups in the same fashion that they had made good losses in warfare in prehistoric times. Yet it is by no means clear that this consideration was antithetical to or more important than economic ones. Francis Jennings (*The Ambiguous Iroquois Empire* [1984]), William Eccles (*William and Mary Quarterly* 43 [1983]: 480-3), Lucien Campeau (*La Mission des Jésuites chez les Hurons, 1634-1650* [1987]), and Conrad Heidenreich (*Native Studies Review* 2 [1986]: 140-7) go much further in their rejection of economic motives. They stress political considerations and suggest that the Iroquois were seeking to avenge old injuries or (in Jennings' case with British help) to build an empire in eastern North America. To varying degrees such interpretations mark a return to the position of Francis Parkman.

Eccles portrays native cultures as economically independent, resilient, and able to determine their own destinies until 1760. This is at least in part a reaction (although in my opinion an unjustifiably extreme one) against the economic determinism of Hunt and Innis which is seen as portraying native peoples as the helpless victims of impersonal economic forces. Superficially this view appears to be supported by Hamell's conclusions about the symbolic rather than the utilitarian value that Indians appear to have attached to European trade goods in the sixteenth century. It is also supported by far more contentious arguments that Indians did not seek to profit from intertribal exchanges and that European goods continued to play a minor role in their lives. Today no one disagrees that trade between native peoples and Europeans was embedded in political alliances in the same fashion as was all intertribal trade. Yet the significance of these alliances appears to have varied considerably (Daniel Francis and Toby Morantz, *Partners in Furs: A History of the Fur Trade in Eastern James Bay, 1600-1870* [1983]). Research by Arthur Ray and Donald Freeman (*"Give Us Good Measure"* [1978]) has also refuted claims by Abraham Rotstein and others that native groups did not seek to maximize returns in exchanges with other tribes and with the Hudson's Bay Company, although the ways in which they negotiated the terms of trade differed from normal European forms of market exchange. In *Natives and Newcomers* I demonstrated that these conclusions also applied to trade between the French and native groups in the early seventeenth century. Despite this, idealist historians such as Eccles continue to maintain that native people did not seek to strike favourable bargains in intertribal trade.

The claim that native people did not become dependent on Europeans is also impossible to substantiate. By the beginning of the seventeenth century the superiority of European axes, knives, and other cutting tools over their native counterparts was universally recognized by the Indians of eastern North America. These were the principal items sought by Huron traders on their long and difficult journeys to the St. Lawrence Valley. Likewise, whatever the respective firepower of bows and arrows and guns, possession of the latter weapons conferred a great military advantage. By the 1630s the Hurons explicitly recognized their dependence on French goods and that this dependence constrained their freedom to deal with French missionaries and to conclude alliances with other tribes. Not all trade was for technologically valued goods and native knowledge of traditional technology disappeared more slowly than Hunt and those who followed him believed. Yet the growing dependence of native peoples on goods they could not learn to manufacture for themselves was a major factor rendering them dependent on Europeans. Their search for furs to exchange for these goods led to the depletion of game and ultimately to spiralling intertribal warfare. This is not to say that other factors, including traditional patterns of intertribal alliances and hostilities, did not play a role in shaping the behaviour of native peoples in the historical period, although in many cases it is far from clear how far back into prehistoric times particular quarrels and alliances between native groups extended. For example, there are strong reasons to doubt that the Huron were at war with the Oneida and Mohawk prior to the seventeenth century. On the other hand, there is strong archaeological evidence of close contact, and therefore of the possibility of trade, between the Nipissing and the Ontario Iroquoians going back several centuries into prehistory. To ignore the importance of changing economic considerations is to lose sight of a key set of factors that transformed native life. It is also to ignore the intricacy of native responses to the pressures that were affecting their lives at this time. The image of Indians as impervious to European influences seems at variance not only with the facts but also with what is known about European contact with native peoples around the world (Eric Wolf, *Europe and the People without History* [1982]). While Parkman believed that Indians were too primitive and savage to change, his modern successors are romantically inclined to regard these peoples as too self-sufficient to have had to do so.

One of the most powerful manifestations of the neo-romantic bias in current ethnohistorical research is the growing importance ascribed to religious factors in bringing about cultural change. Ironically, however, most of these studies are anthropologically poorly informed, ethnocentric, and contemptuous of the spiritual resources of native cultures. W.H. McNeill in his book *Plagues and Peoples* (1976) and, far more influentially, Calvin Martin in *Keepers of the Game* (1978) have argued that major epidemics of European diseases undermined the faith that native Americans had in their traditional religions, leaving them open to spiritual conquest by Europeans. Martin also argued that the fur trade developed not as a result of native people desiring European goods but as a result of their declaring war on fur-bearing animals and seeking to exterminate them because they held animal spirits responsible for the epidemics. In *Indians, Animals and the Fur Trade* (1981), edited by Shepard Krech III, a panel of experts found little evidence to support the latter claim. This, combined with the weakness of Martin's reply, has done much to counteract widespread acceptance of his thesis of a "war against the animals."

Yet it is now widely believed that, by undermining the faith that native people had in the power of their traditional religions, early epidemics of European diseases played a major role in promoting the spread of Christianity. Christianity's emphasis on personal salvation and life after death are seen as better adapted to a calamitous mortality of this sort than were native religions with their allegedly greater emphasis on life in this world. Yet the research that I did for *The Children of Aataentsic* produced no evidence that Huron faith in their traditional religion was weakened by the epidemics of

1634 to 1640. On the contrary, this was a period of great innovation in terms of curing ceremonies. While individual rituals were abandoned when they proved ineffectual, new ones were invented which ultimately were credited with ending each of the epidemics. Despite the Jesuits' robust health, they and their teachings were not strengthened by the epidemics. The deaths of many baptised as well as unbaptised Hurons, and the missionaries' constant preaching about death, suggested that the Jesuits were sorcerers whose principal aim was to kill the Indians; hence the goal of the Hurons was to find a way to counteract their witchcraft.

The loss of many ritual specialists in the course of these epidemics may have been a serious blow to the Hurons and left them more vulnerable to ideological manipulation. Yet they were no less harmed by a loss of technical skills and political leadership. The main documentable motives for Huron conversions in the decade following these epidemics were economic ones, the promotion of alliances with the French, and the wish to obtain guns which were sold only to converts. Huron traders who were Christians received higher prices from the French for their furs and were treated with more respect than were traditionalists when they came to trade. As the Hurons turned increasingly to the Jesuits for food and protection against Iroquois attacks, many of them were baptised. Yet the Jesuits' experience among both the Huron and later the Iroquois supports A. W. Trelease's observation in *Indian Affairs in Colonial New York* (1960) that the true conversion of Indians depended "on their prior submission to the white man, with the attendant disintegration of their own culture" (p. 172). The Iroquoian data suggest the need for greater caution in assuming that native religions collapsed under the pressure of epidemics, leaving a spiritual vacuum which Christianity could fill. Native cultures appear to have been extraordinarily resilient in responding religiously and psychologically to devastating population loss.

Another trend has been to view conversion primarily as an intellectual process. Lucien Campeau (*La Mission des Jésuites chez les Hurons* [1987]) believes that already in the 1630s the Jesuits were conveying the essential meaning of Christianity to the Montagnais and the Hurons. Kenneth Morrison (*The Embattled Northeast* [1984]) and James Axtell (*The Invasion Within* [1985]) also share a belief in the intellectual and spiritual success of Jesuit conversions. Yet, however assiduously the case is argued, it is very difficult to ascertain what conversion actually meant to native people in the absence of direct documentation from the native side. It can be cynically suggested that what the Jesuits knew of their converts' thoughts and actions was generally only what the converts wished them to know. The Jesuits themselves seem to have been less sanguine about their success as missionaries than

parlovian

their modern admirers. Even in their *Relations*, which were written to encourage spiritual and financial support in France for their work, their claims of success were frequently highly qualified. They hoped that if native people could be induced through constant persuasion, rewards, and punishments to speak and act like Christians they might eventually think and believe like Christians. Yet they understood the ambiguities involved in such a process of conversion and in their more reflective moments realized that only God could distinguish between true belief and the mere appearance of it. In their missions at Kahnawake and Lorette there were many more women and children than men, and the economic dependence of these Indians on the Jesuits made them anxious to please them. Even Huron and Iroquois chiefs and traders found it politically advantageous to be perceived as Christians since this strengthened their alliance with the French. Yet the Jesuits could never be certain what these Indians did behind their backs or what they actually believed. Gossip even called into question the conduct of Kateri Tekakwitha when she left Kahnawake to accompany a winter hunting party. It is surely significant that in the history of New France no Indian was ordained as a priest and only a few native women became nuns, some on their deathbeds.

There is no agreement about how accurate an understanding of Christian teaching the Jesuits managed to convey to their early converts, although many of them were highly proficient in native languages and had well-developed pedagogical skills. In 1672 the missionary Jean de Lamberville stated that it was impossible to evangelize Indians or to teach them to think like French people because they could not reason properly as do "the Chinese and other civilized nations." The Iroquoians were born into egalitarian societies in which one human being did not have the right to give orders to another, and even parents did not command obedience from their children. Christianity, in contrast, was the creation of monarchical societies and obedience to God and to his earthly representatives within society and the family was central to its teaching. It is by no means certain that the Jesuits or any other Christian missionaries were able to make their doctrines comprehensible to people who lived in self-sufficient tribal societies. It can be argued that the meaning of Christianity only became clear to native people as they were absorbed into the lower echelons of European societies and as a result of this process learned the meaning of concepts such as authority and obedience. Anthropologists such as David Blanchard (*Anthropologica* 24 [1982]: 77-102) suggest that even after this happened the Iroquois at Kahnawake continued for a long time to perceive Christianity largely in terms of their own religious concepts rather than on its own terms. The problem remains that we do not have independent documentation of native perceptions that would permit a resolution of this problem. In the absence of such knowledge, caution against making exaggerated claims about Jesuit successes or failures seems essential.

One of the best ways available to determine what was happening is to look at the circumstances under which native people converted to Christianity. As documented in *The Children of Aataentsic* and mentioned above, these include economic necessity, the search for economic gain, a desire to secure guns not otherwise available, and a need for protection against enemies. Joseph Chihwatenha, a model convert whose activities are described in the Jesuit *Relations* of the 1630s, may have been seeking to become a sorcerer by acquiring the malevolent powers of life and death which he believed that the Jesuits, as sorcerers or supernatural spirits, possessed. This evidence strongly suggests that spiritual conviction based on an adequate understanding of what Christianity meant to Europeans was not always a primary factor in inducing native people to act as Christians. A sensitive and sensible evaluation of mission work is provided in J. W. Grant's *Moon of Wintertime: Missionaries and the Indians of Canada in Encounter since 1534* (1984).

The essence of historical scholarship is open-mindedness, but not to such a degree that every shift in academic fashion results in new interpretations of the past, whether or not these are warranted by the available data. Since I wrote *The Children of Aataentsic*, scholars such as Hamell and Steckley have pioneered analytical techniques that have produced insights that are relevant for understanding Huron culture. Yet their findings so far do not require major changes in my interpretation of Huron history. The other challenges come not from new sources of data but from changing popular views about the nature of human behaviour. For the most part these interpretations have taken the form either of examinations of specific issues, such as conversion, for specific societies or of broad surveys involving many different native societies. I would attribute what I see as the continuing strength of my interpretation of Huron history not to the theoretical assumptions that I outlined at the beginning of this preface but to my choosing to examine a single, well-documented situation in very great historical detail. In my analyses of what happened to the Huron, I tried to correlate data concerning every aspect of Huron life in an effort to develop a detailed contextual understanding of what was happening. In the course of doing this I discovered repeatedly that what from one perspective seemed to be a solid interpretation of data could not be sustained in a broader context. It is on the basis of this contextual analysis that I continue to feel equipped to defend my interpretations of Huron history against the changing academic fashions of the past decade. I do not claim that my interpretations are immune to change, but at present I do not see new data or demonstrations of flaws in my arguments that require more than minor adjustments. I further interpret this situation as independent evidence of the usefulness of the theoretical principles that have guided my work. While I believe that I was correct in rejecting the untenable concepts of ecological and economic determinism, I remain convinced of the viability of a more sophisticated materialist approach for explaining important aspects of human behaviour and, in particular, for accounting for the fundamental dynamics of contacts between European and Amerindian cultures.

Finally, one more burgeoning field of research deserves to be noted. In *The Children of Aataentsic* I considered the possibility that epidemics of European diseases had afflicted the Huron prior to 1634 but decided that there was no compelling evidence this was so; hence my estimates of pre-contact populations were based on the reports of Champlain, Sagard, and the Jesuits before 1634. Recently various individuals have challenged this conclusion. In particular Henry Dobyns (*Their Number Become Thinned* [1983]) has argued that beginning as early as 1520 epidemics of European diseases dramatically reduced the population of most of North America, including the Iroquoian region. Attempts are currently being made to determine whether or not this was so through the archaeological study of settlement patterns and the physical anthropological investigation of human remains. While no conclusive answer has emerged, the present archaeological evidence seems to suggest stability in Iroquoian population during the sixteenth century.

All books reflect the era in which they were written and to that extent are hostages to the future. It is evident that I do not regard the past decade as one of undiluted progress in social and humanistic studies. Whether this assessment is correct or I am falling victim to time remains to be determined. I hope that in the future I can continue to welcome solid new evidence, even if it contradicts my own work and the ideas that I cherish.

McGill University   B.G.T.
February 1987

Preface to the First Edition

This book is the product of nine years of intermittent study and research, followed by another five years during which almost all of my time not devoted to teaching and administration has been employed in writing it. My interest in the subject was aroused early in 1960 when, as a newly arrived graduate student at Yale University, nostalgia for Canada led me to write a long paper on French-Huron contact for a course on culture change offered by Professor E. M. Bruner. During my research, I sought to learn as much as possible about the Huron from primary rather than secondary sources. Using the facilities of the Sterling Library, I managed to survey a vast amount of literature in what now seems to have been a remarkably short period of time. The result was a paper titled "The Destruction of Huronia: A Study in Economic and Cultural Change, 1609-1650." On the kind recommendation of the late Professor T. F. McIlwraith of the University of Toronto, this paper was soon published (1960). The favourable reception it received encouraged me to continue my interest in the Huron. While further research has led me to modify many of the ideas I expressed in that paper, it constitutes a brief prototype of all but chapters 1, 3, and 4 of the present work.

During later years as a graduate student at Yale I wrote two more papers that reflected my continuing interest in the Huron. The first was on an ecological theme ("Settlement as an Aspect of Iroquoian Adaptation at the Time of Contact" [1963b]; reprinted in B. Cox, ed., *Cultural Ecology: Readings on the Canadian Indians and Eskimos*. Toronto: McClelland and Stewart, 1973, pp. 35-53) and was written for a course on the prehistory of eastern North America given by Professor Michael D. Coe; the second was "Order and Freedom in Huron Society" (1963a; reprinted in M. Nagler, ed., *Perspectives on the North American Indians*. Toronto: McClelland and Stewart, 1972, pp. 43-56) for a course on the Anthropology of Law by Professor L. J. Pospisil. Both of these papers are essentially ethnographic. About the same time, I wrote a paper on "The Historic Location of the Hurons" (1962a) in which I challenged the traditional idea that the Huron had settled in the north as refugees from the Iroquois. During this period, my awareness of the importance of ethnohistory and of developments in Iroquoian studies was strengthened by my informal contacts with William N. Fenton and Elisabeth Tooker, both of whom did much to encourage and guide me towards the present study.

Although I turned primarily to other topics in my final years as a graduate student, my interest in the Huron continued and later became more specific when I was asked to read a paper on "The Jesuits and the Fur Trade" (1965) at the Huron Symposium held in Orillia, Ontario, 30 January 1965, to mark to 350th anniversary of Champlain's visit to that region. It was while preparing the final draft of that paper that I conceived the idea of writing a book-length history of the Huron, covering the same general subject matter as the present work.

I was aware, however, that much more research was needed before such a book could be begun. I therefore welcomed the opportunity to collaborate with James F. Pendergast in a major study of the unpublished Dawson site; long alleged to be Cartier's Hochelaga. The principal outcome of this project was the publication of J. F. Pendergast and B. G. Trigger, *Cartier's Hochelaga and the Dawson Site* (1972), to which my own contribution, "Hochelaga: History and Ethnohistory", was a review of what is known about the history of the St. Lawrence Valley during the sixteenth century. This revived an earlier interest that had led to my publication of "Trade and Tribal Warfare on the St. Lawrence in the Sixteenth Century" (1962b). Before the final report appeared I published a number of papers related to this topic: "Who were the 'Laurentian Iroquois'?" (*Canadian Review of Sociology and Anthropology*, 3 [1966]: 201-13); "Archaeological and other Evidence: A Fresh Look at the 'Laurentian Iroquois'" (1968a); "Criteria for Identifying the Locations of Historic Indian Sites: A Case Study from Montreal" (1969b); as well as a general review of Iroquoian prehistory, "The Strategy of Iroquoian Prehistory" (1970). Chapter 4 and sections of chapter 3 are résumés and extensions of the work of this period.

About this time I was also persuaded to write *The Huron: Farmers of the North* (1969a), in which I attempted a functional interpretation of traditional Huron culture. I wrote that book mainly to deepen my own understanding of Huron ways. That book constitutes the basis for the briefer, but even more sharply focused, account of Huron life in chapter 2 of this book. I also published a study of Iroquoian warfare, "Settlement Archaeology—Its Goals and Promise" (1967), and another study of French-Huron relations, incorporating a significant re-interpretation of the later period, "The French Presence in Huronia: The Structure of Franco-Huron Relations in the First Half of the Seventeenth Century" (1968b). The latter paper was a pilot study aimed at planning the historical chapters of this book. During that period, a grant from the French Canada Studies Programme of McGill University permitted

Miss A. E. Clark to carry out some statistical analyses of the *Jesuit Relations* under my direction. These studies were useful in clarifying the extent of Jesuit knowledge of Huron society in each given year of the Huron mission.

Finally, in June 1968 I received sabbatical leave from McGill University and, with the assistance of a Canada Council Leave Fellowship, spent the following year in England and France reading and analysing source material. This period of study and reflection served greatly to advance my understanding of Huron history. After a further year of research, during which I wrote papers on two specialized historical topics, "Champlain Judged by his Indian Policy: A Different View of Early Canadian History" (1971*a*) and "The Mohawk-Mahican War (1624-28): The Establishment of a Pattern" (1971*c*), I began writing the present book in September 1970 and reached chapter 5 by the following summer. During the following twelve months the first draft of the remaining chapters was finished. I was aided at this time by a Killam Award of the Canada Council which permitted me to be on half-time leave from teaching duties at McGill. This allowed a degree of concentration which gave greater continuity to my draft than would otherwise have been possible. During the following year, the final draft of the text was completed.

Since my interpretations of many events in Huron history have altered in the course of writing this book, the present study should be regarded as superseding all my earlier published works whenever the two disagree. In particular, chapters 7 to 12 are not simply expansions of my major 1960 and 1968*b* papers but are often at variance with them. This is largely because of my abandonment of the McIlwain-Innis-Hunt interpretation of the wars of the Iroquois as being a struggle to control middleman positions.

The theoretical orientation of the book is discussed in detail in the Introduction and little more need be said about it here. I stress, however, that my aim has been to write a history of the Huron, not of New France or of French-Indian relations in the seventeenth century. My efforts to explain Huron history have required that I re-interpret the actions of various Europeans in eastern Canada in the sixteenth and seventeenth centuries. These, however, are only a by-product of my research.

In matters respecting the Huron, I do not apologize for detailed citing of the evidence on which I have based my conclusions. Since much of this evidence will be unfamiliar to most readers, its omission seems undesirable. Nor do I apologize for including specific information about Huron individuals whom historians might not consider to be of sufficient importance to merit such treatment. Given the limitations of the data, such information is often of great value for substantiating my arguments.

In chapters 8 to 12 I have restricted my comments about the Jesuits to what is necessary to understand the influence they exerted on the Huron. I have deliberately eschewed allowing these chapters to become a history of the Jesuit missionaries in the Huron country or enquiring into the broader aims and strategies of the Jesuit Order in international politics. Instead I have tried to understand the motives of the Jesuits who were part of the Huron mission and who were engaged in trying to influence these Indians.

Whatever merit the book has results from the presentation of familiar data from a new point of view. I have not undertaken extensive archival research, but have re-examined the voluminous published sources on the Huron, most of which have been familiar to historians for many years. To attempt to search out the small residue of unpublished documents that might shed light on the Huron would have consumed time better put to other uses and have needlessly repeated the work of skilled archivists.

The decision to write a long book was not taken lightly. Originally, I had planned to write a shorter, more popular work; however, I decided that if detailed explanations were not provided and alternative theories eliminated, the book would offer too many challenges to historians and anthropologists to engage in needless debate. There could only be a proper discussion of my work if I explained my lines of reasoning in detail. I am grateful to Robert Vogel for encouraging me to adopt the longer format and to the press for having been indulgent enough to undertake the publication of a work of this length.

Certain idiosyncrasies deserve explanation. Readers will be surprised to find that the familiar term "Huronia" has been suppressed in favour of "the Huron country." The former term has the disadvantage of implying that what was primarily a tribally constituted unit had a territorial basis. Similar toponyms are not generally applied to corresponding ethnic units among the North American Indians (except the analogous "Iroquoia" for "the Iroquois country"). I have also generally replaced the ambiguous word "chief" with the anthropological term "headman," except when referring to war chiefs. French personal names are given in the form in which they appear in the *Dictionary of Canadian Biography*, even when this departs from common usage. In the absence of a generally recognized authority on Huron phonology, I have not attempted to spell Huron personal names according to any system but have contented myself to sticking to a single form for each name, usually that preferred by the DCB or by R. G. Thwaites. For the sake of consistency I have omitted the diacritics that were sometimes used in writing Huron names, beginning in the 1640s. Where source material is published both in the original language and in English translation in the same volume, I have avoided the affectation of citing pages only in the original. This applies even to quotations, which are generally my own translation. Care has been taken to check standard translations and any significant discrepancies between them and the originals are noted in the text or notes. While every effort has been made to keep abreast of the burgeoning published literature, the size of the book has made it impossible to do this up to the time of publication. Few references were added after the completion of the final draft of the manuscript in May 1973, while active research, especially on the earlier parts, ended about a year earlier.

In keeping with internationally accepted usage, the term Iroquois refers only to the confederated Five Nations of upper New York State: the Mohawk, Oneida, Onondaga, Cayuga, and Seneca. The term Iroquoian is reserved for the broader linguistic grouping to which they, the Huron, and many other tribes belonged. Likewise, Algonkin refers specifically to the tribal grouping that inhabited the Ottawa Valley and adjacent regions early in the seventeenth century, while Algonkian refers to a more widespread linguistic grouping to which the Algonkin belonged.

For help in clarifying various issues I wish to thank C. E. Heidenreich, A. Cameron, William N. Fenton, C. Garrad, Max Gluckman, K. E. Kidd, R. Klibansky, W. Noble, J. F. Pendergast, P. P. Pratt, M. Trudel, J. A. Tuck, M. E. White, and others. For her assistance with maps and her generous hospitality I wish to thank Monique de La Roncière of the Bibliothèque Nationale, Paris. The theoretical section of chapter 3, dealing with the evolution of Iroquoian social structure, has benefited from the comments of F. G. Lounsbury and others following presentation to a seminar at Yale University 3 May 1971 and to the 1972 Iroquois Conference. For his encouragement, I also owe much to the late Robin Strachan, director of the McGill-Queen's University Press.

I wish to thank Jeanette Fernandez and Sheila Masson for the care and industry with which they typed the final version of the manuscript; H. W. Castner and the Cartographic Laboratory of Queen's University for preparing the final versions of maps; and Sylvia Haugo and A. C. Crouch of the staff of McGill–Queen's Press for editorial and production work. It remains to thank my wife (to whom along with our children this book is dedicated) for bearing patiently with the enormous demands that this book has made on my time ever since we were married.

Chapter 1  Introduction

Aims

When I began this book, I intended to write a straightforward account of the Huron Indians during the early years of their contact with Europeans. The materials for such a study are well known and have provided the basis for numerous biographical and historical accounts, many of considerable merit. These studies have concentrated largely, however, on the activities of European priests, traders, and government officials among the Huron between 1610 and 1650, rather than on the Huron themselves. I believed therefore that these materials offered an exceptional opportunity to make a detailed study of the effects that contact with Europeans had on one of the native peoples of North America. I found, however, that my objectives, although they seemed modest at first, required more work than I had anticipated. This taught me the truth of Léo-Paul Desrosiers's (1947a:8) observation that "of all types of writing, history is the one that requires the most time." It also became apparent that the network of intertribal relations that existed at the period of European contact, and which became more complex and extensive with the development of the fur trade, made it impossible to view French-Huron relations in isolation from, or even merely against the background of, events taking place in other parts of eastern North America. Nor was it possible to fill in the extra information that was required from existing historical studies.

The more I examined the relations between different tribes and different groups of Europeans, the more I became aware of the many aspects of these relationships which historians had not adequately taken into account. Hence this study has become a reassessment of the history of this whole region between 1600 and 1650. It is, however, a reassessment in which events are interpreted from a Huron perspective rather than from a French or Dutch one, as is usually the case. It also became apparent that a study of this sort requires not only the care and thoroughness of a professional historian in the use of written documents, but also new methods to tackle problems of interpretation of a sort rarely encountered by historians and to take account of kinds of data that historians usually ignore. Although the

present study is only one contribution among many to the rapidly developing field of Amerindian history,[1] in some ways it is sufficiently novel that a
general discussion of its orientation and methods seems desirable. This
Introduction is intended to provide a record of the ideas which guided me
in writing this book and of the problems I encountered.

Historians and Canadian Indians

The important role that the Indians have played in Canadian history has
long been recognized. In his influential study of the fur trade, published in
1930, the economist Harold Innis (rev. ed. 1956:392) stated that "the
Indian and his culture were fundamental to the growth of Canadian
institutions," while, the same year, his colleague in anthropology, T. F.
McIlwraith (1930:132), argued that "an accurate interpretation of the first
two hundred years of Canadian history must take cognizance of the Indian
point of view as well as that of the white man." Moving beyond his pro-
grammatic statement, Innis clearly outlined for the first time the importance of the fur trade in the development of modern Canada and investigated
the role that the Indians had played in this trade. Innis's book laid the
foundations of the so-called "Laurentian hypothesis," which was to have
the same kind of impact on Canadian historiography that F. J. Turner's
frontier hypothesis had on that of the United States. Innis viewed Canada
as a political entity originally defined by the fur trade, which had penetrated the northern interior of the continent by way of the St. Lawrence
River and its tributaries.[2]

One of the long-term benefits of this theory was that it stressed the
important role played by the Indians in the European settlement and early
growth of Canada. Historians now generally recognize that long before the
arrival of the Europeans the Indians had adapted to the harsh Canadian
environment; hence, although they lacked the iron tools and elaborate
technology of the newcomers, they were able to teach Europeans many
things. From the Indians, the French learned how to manage and later how
to construct canoes, which made travel through the north possible in
summer. From the Indians they also adopted sleds, snowshoes, and items
of clothing that permitted them to cope with the Canadian winter. Indians
taught the French how to make maple sugar, plant maize and other Indian
crops, recognize what wild plants could be eaten or used for medicine, and

to hunt animals whose habits were unfamiliar to Europeans (Trudel 1966a: 376–84). Many young Frenchmen went to live and trade with the Indians and, to the dismay of colonial officials, many of them came to prefer this to living amongst their own people.

It is also clear that relations between Indians and Europeans in early Canada were very different from those farther south. In the United States, the most coveted possession of the Indian was his land. The British government's recognition, in 1763, of Indian tribes as independent nations, and its insistence that their land could not be occupied by white settlers unless it had first been voluntarily ceded to the Crown, was one of the major grievances leading to the revolt of the American colonies. After the American revolution, the Indians over whom American hegemony extended were killed, driven westward, or herded onto reservations. Those who became despondent under white tutelage were regarded as hopeless degenerates, while those who fought to keep their land were pictured as blood-thirsty savages whom civilized men had the duty either to tame or to exterminate. For almost a century, scarcely a year went by in which the American army was not engaged in this task of subjugation (Spencer, Jennings et al. 1965: 497–506).

Canada, on the other hand, was principally a region of boreal forest, too cold to invite extensive European settlement, but rich in fur-bearing animals and laced with lakes and rivers that made the transportation of furs from the hinterland to coastal markets relatively easy. It was far easier for the white man to buy these furs from experienced Indian trappers than to hunt for them himself; hence, as long as furs remained abundant and fetched a good price on European markets, a symbiotic relationship linked the Indian hunter and the European trader. It is significant that not once was there a case of serious or prolonged conflict between Europeans and Indians living within the borders of Canada.[3] On the contrary, for a long time Indians and white men were allies in the common defence of Canada against first British, then American, invaders. This is not to say that once the Canadian Indians ceased to be a valuable economic asset, the treatment they received was any less shameful than was that meted out to Indians in the United States; one might even argue that, given the nature of earlier relations, it was worse. It is clear, however, that for a long time relations between Indians and whites in the territory on, and bordering, the Canadian Shield were very different from what they were in the United States. This difference is familiar to historians and anthropologists, but has not sufficiently been drawn to the attention of the Canadian public, whose image of the Indian has been nourished by generations of American news-papers and magazines, and, in recent times by radio, television, and imported textbooks.

Only a few historical studies have as their central theme to explain what has happened to Canadian Indians since the Europeans first arrived in the New World. In 1937, Alfred G. Bailey published his pioneering study of relations between Europeans and Algonkians in eastern Canada prior to 1700. Unfortunately this book did not receive the attention that it deserved and did not stimulate more specific historical research.[4] Professor Bailey's work on the Canadian Indians reflects an interdisciplinary point of view, which was nourished by his contacts with Innis and McIlwraith while he was studying at the University of Toronto. Another important pioneering work was Volume 1 of Léo-Paul Desrosiers's (1947*a*) *Iroquoisie*, which attempts to explain political relations between the Iroquois, the French, and the latter's Indian allies down to 1646. Even in recent decades, titles have not greatly proliferated. George F. Stanley (1952) has published an important paper on "The Indian Background of Canadian History," while Wilson Duff (1964) has published Volume 1 of *The Indian History of British Columbia*, which deals with the impact of the white man. Most recently, E. P. Patterson (1972) has published a general outline of Canadian Indian history, which he argues must be treated as a subject in its own right, rather than as an adjunct of white history.[5] Unfortunately, none of these studies has considered the major methodological problems that are associated with the investigation of Indian history, or attempted to resolve them. Because of this, Indians continue to languish on the peripheries of professional Canadian historiography.

Because so much Canadian historical writing has been in the form of biographies (Soroko 1966), historians have tended to concentrate on well-known Europeans, rather than on the small number of Indians about whom personal data have been recorded. All too often, Indians have been viewed, both collectively and individually, less as actors on the stage of Canadian history than as part of the natural setting against which this action has taken place. Unconsciously, an active role tends to be reserved for the country's European settlers. Nowhere is this tendency better illustrated than in the well-intentioned, but ill-informed and badly integrated, sketches of the Indian tribes of Canada which preface so many general studies of Canadian history. Even when individual Indians, such as Pontiac or Tecumseh, feature prominently in historical accounts, relatively little attention is paid to what motivated them, so that their actions remain incomprehensible and quixotic. Because of this, Indians who acted contrary to French or English interests are unwittingly rendered sinister and alien, while those who are treated sympathetically turn out suspiciously like the honourable, but imperfect Orientals who serve white interests in the novels of Rudyard Kipling.

Even worse, when careful research has demonstrated the falseness of certain interpretations of events in which the role of Indians has been grossly distorted to accommodate it to European stereotypes, historians often find it impossible to make the clear break with the past that these findings require. Adam Dollard and his companions now may be generally recognized by historians as having died in an effort, not to save New France, but to rob a party of Iroquois hunters of their winter catch. Yet in spite of this, historians continue to argue that this fight was "as heroic and necessary as legend has made it, for without furs New France could not live" (Morton 1963:52).

These deficiencies are not basically the fault of historians, who are accustomed to work with cultures that have long traditions of literacy. Rather, they reflect the difficulties that confront the application of conventional historical methods to the study of the Canadian Indian. These methods were devised to facilitate the use of written documents to study the past history of the society that produced them. In dealing with recent European history, the historian shares enough common cultural background with those he studies that an assessment of their hopes, aspirations, and values can usually be made on the basis of common sense. Occasionally, as, for example, in studies of European witchcraft, historians may seek theoretical guidance for their interpretations from anthropological studies of similar phenomena in contemporary societies (Macfarlane 1970), although some historians entertain doubts about this as a proper mode of analysis. Where specialized knowledge concerning technological, economic, or other matters is required, this can be derived from numerous other disciplines concerned primarily with Western civilization. Even historians who study Chinese, Hindu, or other non-Western, but literate, societies are able from the indigenous literature of these societies to acquire sufficient knowledge of them, or at least of what Robert Redfield (1956) has called their great traditions, to be able to evaluate records and behaviour in a highly informed manner.

When the historian studies the Canadian Indian, however, he is dealing with people who possessed no written records of their own and with ways of life that not only developed totally independently from those of Europe, but which also fall outside the normal range of cultural variation with which he is familiar. The native peoples of Canada were few in number and mostly lived in small, widely dispersed groupings. As in all small-scale societies, activities of a public nature lacked the highly institutionalized and hierarchical character found in technologically more complex societies. On the contrary, these activities tended to be embedded in, or were extensions of, a basic kinship system.

The differences between large-scale and small-scale societies are sufficiently great that an historian's experience and personal judgement are not enough to permit him unaided to come to terms with the ideas and values that were a part of the Indians' way of life prior to the coming of the Europeans. Unless the historian is able to acquire elsewhere sufficient knowledge of the beliefs and values of the people he is studying, he is unable to evaluate the European sources which constitute the principal record that we have of these people. Lacking such knowledge, he is further unable to transcend the prejudices and limitations of his sources and to evaluate them in the rigorous manner with which historians wish to deal with all written material. It is precisely because most historians lack such knowledge that the Indian does not come alive in their writings, no matter how sympathetic and well-intentioned they may be. The historian's dilemma is thus the lack of a technique which will permit an understanding of Indian ways without having records written by the Indians.

Indeed, in the absence of documents written by Indians, some historians have come to the fatalistic conclusion that white documents make white history. A similar, though more considered pessimism is embodied in E. S. Spicer's (1962:22) assertion that "until well into the nineteenth century the records [in the southwestern United States] are nearly mute on the subject of Indian viewpoints and feelings about the transformation being wrought in their lives." The conclusion that Indian history is not feasible has been reinforced by two further assumptions, which are to some degree interrelated.

The more romantic argument, and one that is now shared only by those who know little about the American Indian, is that Indian cultures changed so little during the centuries prior to the arrival of the Europeans that, in effect, the Indian has no history of his own. The changes that have come about since are held to be the result of white influence and therefore best discussed from the viewpoint of European history. Such ahistorical views of non-Western peoples have been held by many anthropologists, as well as historians,[6] and they have a variety of aetiologies. Anthropologists, in particular, have been prone to what may be called "the Garden of Eden syndrome"; they tend to attribute static qualities to simpler cultures and see in their equilibrium evidence of a successful adaptation to their environment, and to one another, that contrasts with the conflict and confusion of modern industrial societies. The alternative explanation blamed the static nature of Amerindian societies on the natural inferiority of the Indians. In the last century, it was widely believed that Indians were incapable of acquiring more than a thin veneer of civilization. It was even argued that they would perish under the impact of European civilization, unless they were kept on reservations where, under white supervision, a semblance of their old ways of life could be maintained.[7]

Archaeological evidence demonstrates clearly the degree to which this static view of Indian prehistory is a figment of ill-informed imaginations. Because Canadian Indians lived in one of the harshest environments in the world, they were always relatively few in number and lacked the opportunities for cultural development that in better climes culminated in the brilliant indigenous civilizations that flourished in Mexico and Peru until the Spanish conquest. It is clear, however, that even in Canada there was a gradual improvement in the Indians' adaptation to their environment. The introduction of new items of technology, such as the bow and arrow, permitted hunting bands to exploit game more effectively and the same territory to support larger numbers of people. In the far north, successive waves of Eskimo adapted themselves with remarkable skill to an extremely demanding environment, while along the coasts of British Columbia, Indians harnessed rich, but fluctuating, natural food resources to support a way of life characterized by a concern with social status, elaborate art, and ritual. In southern Ontario, in the centuries preceding the arrival of the Europeans, the Iroquoian-speaking peoples abandoned a hunting and gathering economy in favour of a sedentary way of life based on growing corn, beans, and squash. However imperfect they may be, these archaeological indices provide evidence of social change and, along with evidence of cultural diffusion and population movements, show clearly that the aboriginal cultures of Canada were far from being inherently static prior to the arrival of the Europeans.[8]

Other historians, in particular C. H. McIlwain (1915) and George T. Hunt (1940), have not specifically denied that changes went on in Indian societies prior to the arrival of the Europeans. They have argued, however, that knowledge of such changes is totally irrelevant for an understanding of subsequent events; once Indians depended on trade goods, they became entangled in a network of trading relations and intertribal competition that was fashioned by economic self-interest, rather than by any traditional modes of thought or behaviour. These new economic imperatives transformed the lives of the Indians so thoroughly and so quickly as to make any understanding of their previous behaviour unnecessary. Hunt argued that anything that the Indians did late enough to be recorded by Europeans can be interpreted in terms of the commercial logic of the fur trade.

Contact with Europeans undoubtedly quickly altered Indian life and Indian policy; on the other hand, old relationships have a powerful habit of influencing events, even when economic and political conditions are changing rapidly. Many anthropologists have objected to Hunt's "economic determinism" and have argued that traditional values and the relationships existing before the time of European contact played an important role in the development of Indian-white relations and of the fur trade (Snyderman 1948; Trelease 1960). These studies have shown many interpretations based upon Hunt's assumptions to be inaccurate and have demonstrated that traditional cultural patterns played as important a role in influencing interaction among the various groups in eastern North America as did economic self-interest. Indeed, economic interests were rarely perceived by such groups independently of these biases. Nancy O. Lurie (1959:37) has suggested that, as a general principle, Indians "made their first adjustments to Europeans in terms of existing native conditions." Recent studies have reciprocally demonstrated that the traditional values of Europeans often hindered their rational economic exploitation of Indian groups. In particular, Raoul Naroll (1969) has argued that the extreme concern of most French soldiers and administrators to safeguard their dignity was responsible for otherwise needless conflict with the Iroquois.

The inability to avoid a discussion of the important role played by the Indians in early Canadian history, combined with the lack of any method that permits this role to be studied adequately, has helped to perpetuate many unsatisfactory practices. Sometimes, well-meaning authors merely repeat the prejudices of their sources or, worse still, those of nineteenth-century commentators. Thus, the Jesuit author of a highly praised biography of Jean de Brébeuf has referred to Huron sexual behaviour as a "sewer of sexual filth" practised by "animalized savages." He also states that Huron women were "drudges from infancy," but nevertheless "were more untamed than the men, quicker to anger, more snarling in their insults, more savage in vengeance, more frenzied in times of trial" (Talbot 1956:67). These descriptions perpetuate stereotypes rather than contribute towards a genuine understanding either of the Huron or of their relations with the Jesuits.

Among the more lamentable results of such an approach is the tendency to judge tribes according to whether or not they served the interests of the particular European group the historian happens to be studying, or for whom he feels sympathy. Thus, even today, in some uncritical writings the Huron are painted as a docile, peaceful people, almost pre-formed for an exemplary Christian life, while their Iroquois opponents are driven on by an insensate fury and a lust for blood and conquest.[9] In others, particularly those whose authors are staunchly anti-French or anti-Roman Catholic, the Huron have been represented as weaklings and cowards who fell under the influence of the Jesuits, while the Iroquois, though cruel, are admired for their energy and resourcefulness (Parkman 1867). Unfortunately, because stereotypes of this sort can be absorbed so easily, they bulk large in popular histories and school texts. It is disgraceful that in influential works of this type Indian history should be so inadequately treated. Yet, until detailed studies provide the basis for a better popularization of Indian history, one can only hope to eliminate the grossest distortions of this type from such publications.

This simplistic dichotomy between good and bad, brave and cowardly is all the more pervasive because it reflects the two contrasting images of the Indian that have long dominated the white man's thinking about them. The first stereotype, that of the Indian as a bloodthirsty savage who delights in scalping and slaughter, was dominant in the minds of the land-grabbing colonists of the Atlantic seaboard, and was reinforced as the wave of American colonization spread westward. The opposite view, that of the "noble savage" can first be detected in the writings of Michel de Montaigne and, while chiefly popular in the salons of Europe, was shared by at least some of the influential Frenchmen who came to know the Indians firsthand through the Canadian fur trade. In the independence and self-reliance of the Indian, disenchanted Europeans saw a way of life untainted by the ambition, dishonesty, and self-indulgence that they had convinced themselves were the inevitable consequences of civilization (Spencer, Jennings, et al. 1965 : 595–97).

While both of these stereotypes continue to affect most writers' views of the Indian, it is perhaps indicative of the current vogue for sentimentality that today it is generally the latter view which prevails. Indeed, this is the view of the Indian past that many Indians, including Indian writers, seem to prefer (e.g., Newell 1965). Nevertheless, it must be remembered that such a view portrays the Indians of the past, not as they were, but according to the white man's ideal of what a "primitive" people should be like. Features attractive to white tastes are emphasized, while others, which are less attractive or even repugnant to them are either glossed over or suppressed. Polygamy, scalping, the torture of prisoners, and the abandonment of elderly and ailing members of a band were all customs practised by various groups of aboriginal Canadians. They are customs which, when carefully examined, prove not to have been irrational or immoral in terms of the context in which they occurred. Under the influence of white culture, many present-day Indians have been made to feel ashamed of these ancestral practices to the point that they deny they ever existed. Yet surely to ignore or distort important aspects of aboriginal Indian life to make it more acceptable to European tastes is to fail in the understanding of Indian history. The bloodthirsty savage, the noble savage, and all the corollaries that are derived from these stereotypes are products of European imagination and wishful thinking, rather than delineations of real people. While such stereotypes may at one time have been useful as propaganda for or against the Indians, neither view results in an improved understanding of them or of the role they have played in Canadian history. On the contrary, both do considerable harm, because they excuse the historian from attempting to explain the behaviour of individual Indians, or groups of them, in the same detail in which he would attempt to explain the actions of Europeans.

As early as the eighteenth century, attempts were made to explain the behaviour of Indians in biological terms. The reticence among many tribes for men and women to flirt openly, which we now know was part of a general reluctance to display emotions publicly, was once interpreted as evidence of a weak sex drive resulting from unfavourable climatic influences.[10] In the latter part of the nineteenth century there was a marked predilection for racial explanations of cultural differences (Harris 1968:80–107) and such ideas strongly influenced historians' conceptions of the North American Indians. These ideas were discounted, as early as 1862, by the Canadian anthropologist Daniel Wilson (1862, 2:327–90) and today they command no support whatsoever among reputable biologists and anthropologists. Yet in spite of this, antiquated ideas of this sort continue to contaminate historical writing in Canada. Recently, after documenting the valuable role played by the Indians in the European colonization of Canada, Gustave Lanctot (1963:330) commented that the lack of intermarriage between French and Indians during the colonial period "was probably better...for the colony, for the [French Canadian] race grew stronger being free of native cross-breeding." Since then, W. L. Morton (1963:60–61) has stated that "in settled New France there was practically no intermarriage with the Indians, and New France was spared that mixture of blood which led to so many complications in Spanish America." The downgrading of the Indians' natural abilities arises only from a crassly materialistic assessment of their way of life and hence from the inability of historians to perceive the beliefs and values that motivated them, individually and in groups. We thus return to a problem of method.

Ethnohistory and the Role of Anthropology

The problem is how information recorded by early European colonists can be used to study the history of the Canadian Indians, not merely from a white man's point of view, but with the sympathetic understanding that historians seek to bring to every situation that they investigate. It is clear that insofar as it is possible at all, given the materials at our disposal, the achievement of this kind of understanding requires an interdisciplinary approach in which both history and anthropology play a part. It is also clear that the failure to bridge this gap is largely a result of the general failure, until recently, of Canadian anthropologists to concern themselves with problems that involve using written documents. For the most part, these anthropologists have devoted their energies to the study either of Indian prehistory, by means of archaeology, or of living native peoples within Canada. Significant ethnological research began in 1884, when the British Association for the Advancement of Science appointed a committee to report on the anthropology of the tribes of British Columbia. For fourteen years, grants were provided which enabled studies to be carried out by Franz Boas, A. F. Chamberlain, and others.[11] Most of these early studies were concerned with recording aboriginal ways of life as they were remembered by old people who had grown up in more or less traditional cultures, which they had then seen fall apart as a result of European interference. Even so, their memories rarely took the anthropologist back much before 1850, by which time most Indian peoples had been considerably altered by European contact. More recent ethnological studies are concerned almost exclusively with alterations that have come about since the Indians were first studied by ethnologists, and hence cast little light on the more remote past. The result has been to leave a gap in our knowledge of the Indian between the prehistoric period, studied by the archaeologist, and the recent period, studied by the ethnologist. If either the anthropologist or the historian is to understand how Indian life has changed in the intervening years, this gap is going to have to be filled by means of historically orientated research.

Being trained in the techniques of excavation or interviewing living peoples, most anthropologists have felt themselves ill-equipped to undertake the detailed historical study of changes in Indian life since the first written records became available. They believe that such work should be done by professional historians; a view that is reinforced by the anthropologist's traditional view of himself as a "field worker" rather than a "library researcher." [12] This is especially true when it comes to locating and handling unpublished archival material, a chore that few anthropologists enjoy and even fewer have been trained to do. In addition, the anthropologist usually knows little about the complex economic and political relationships among the European powers who were in contact with the Indians, and he is thus ill-equipped to understand documentary material. When historical sources are used by anthropologists, it is usually to illustrate or support some particular point they wish to make. This, of course, is exactly the opposite of good historical method. Statements are considered without reference to their immediate context, and no effort is made to assess the biases or abilities of the recorder. The result is a mixture of arrogance and naiveté in the use of this material which frequently repels the professional historian.

Yet, if neither historians nor anthropologists have undertaken the detailed study of Canadian Indian history, it does not mean that such studies are impossible. Recent years have witnessed the development, particularly in the United States, of a new discipline called ethnohistory. [13] The precise objectives of ethnohistory are still rather uncertain. As defined by some anthropologists, the discipline aims to embrace all historical approaches in anthropology. The principal interest of ethnohistorians seems, however, to be using historical documents and oral traditions to study the history of nonliterate peoples. It can be argued quite justifiably that labelling such studies ethnohistory, as opposed to simply history, serves to perpetuate an invidious distinction between so-called primitive and complex societies. The main justification for the term seems to be that it recognizes that the methodology required to study the history of smaller-scale, nonliterate societies is different from, and in many ways more complex than, that of history proper.

The main contribution that anthropology can make to such studies is the wealth of data it provides about the ways of life of non-Western peoples. On the most superficial level, such information makes possible the more precise identification of a host of terms used in connection with Indians in early accounts. The substitution of "wampum" for "porcelain" or "longhouse" for "cabin" may be of little importance, although knowledge of the role wampum played in the northeastern part of the continent, or about the housetypes associated with particular tribes, may add considerable depth to our understanding of these accounts. On the other hand, the substitution of "chief" or "headman" for "captain" and "spirit" for "devil" not only offsets biases but also sets old descriptions of Indian life into a comparative framework. Only the anthropologist's understanding of Indian life can provide the background needed to assess and understand the behaviour of the Indians as it is recorded in historical records.

A seeming contradiction may, however, be perceived at this point. How can ethnological studies, which began in Canada less than a century ago, be useful for understanding the behaviour of Indians at a still earlier period? This question becomes particularly important when we consider the marked transformations that Indian life has undergone in response to changing conditions since the arrival of the Europeans. Nevertheless, there are many ways in which this more recent information may prove useful. For example, knowledge about the behaviour and customs of modern Indians, even those who have been greatly assimilated into the dominant culture of North America, may provide information about personality types, religious beliefs, and, in some cases, about social and economic practices, that is of value for checking and interpreting historical accounts of these people.

The reliability of such data for historical studies is difficult to establish. It is unreasonable to expect that, even among very conservative groups, prolonged European control and tutelage have not brought about many more changes than the Indians themselves are aware of. In the case of groups like the Iroquois, however, for whom written records are available beginning as early as the seventeenth century, it is possible, by checking information about present customs against progressively earlier accounts, to build up a picture of the main transformations that Iroquois life has undergone during the last three hundred years. Elisabeth Tooker's (1970a) recent study of the Iroquois Midwinter Ceremonial is an excellent example of this kind of investigation, which clearly illustrates the problems involved and the uncertainties that cloud the earlier periods, when even the fullest accounts tend to be fragmentary. This, and other studies, make ethno-historians increasingly aware of the rapid changes that have taken place in Iroquois culture during the historic period and of the dangers involved in speculatively projecting the culture of any one period farther back into the past. Since Iroquois culture is known, from archaeological data, to have been changing rapidly prior to the arrival of the Europeans, ethnohistorical studies, by themselves, are probably not very reliable for the reconstruction of this culture prior to the seventeenth century.

Indeed, there is one extreme, but in no way disreputable, point of view which maintains that every Indian culture described in early European sources must be regarded as already radically altered by European influences. T. J. Brasser (1971:261) writes, "The Indian world had been distorted already in many respects before the first notes of ethnographical value were jotted down." Developing a long tradition of such interpretation, he argues that the evolution of confederations, and even tribal structures, as these were understood in the historic period, was a response to the penetration of European commerce inland. Although building on existing patterns of kinship, these new units exceeded in scale anything known or required in pre-contact times. Brasser assumes that the Iroquoian and Algonkian emphasis on curing rituals was a response to European diseases and that family-owned trading routes among the Huron developed because of European trade. He suggests that as coastal groups were driven inland, they played an important role in disseminating traits such as splint basketry, ribbon-appliqué, and metal work among the tribes of the midwest, and also introduced prophets who undermined local magical and religious institutions. Finally, he points out that many anthropologists now regard religious institutions such as the Delaware Big House, the Ojibwa Midewiwin, and the sun dance of the Plains Indians, which at one time were believed to be purely aboriginal, as sociopolitical revitalization movements resulting from the expansion of the frontier.

In the absence of adequate historical or archaeological data, what is aboriginal and what evolved as a result of contact with Europeans remains a matter for speculation. Depending on the anthropologist's personal predilection, particular facets of Indian culture can be explained in terms of one theory or the other. In the past, too many features resulting from contact or acculturation were uncritically projected backwards into the prehistoric period; today, however, the opposite tendency appears to be in the ascendant. Attempts are made to account for the acculturative origins of many features of Indian culture previously held to be aboriginal. Much of this development is assigned to the ill-documented, and hence highly speculative, period between the arrival of the earliest European trade goods and the first Europeans who have left written records. Except in unusual cases, where pertinent archaeological or historical data are available, most of these interpretations remain at the level of unproved or unprovable hypotheses.

By contrast with the Iroquois, only a much more attenuated and poorly studied remnant of the Iroquoian-speaking tribes that flourished near the shores of Georgian Bay in the seventeenth century has survived, in the form of the Huron of Lorette and the Huron-Tionnontaté mixture, now called the Wyandot, who live in Oklahoma. Even in this case, however, the little we know about these groups helps us to reconstruct at least some aspects of Huron life that had no counterpart in European culture and therefore went unnoticed by the early French writers.[14] For example, none of the French who visited the Huron seems to have been aware of the importance of clans and lineages as units of political organization. No special terms were noted for such units and the accounts make it clear that, when the French were interacting with the Indians, they saw themselves dealing with individuals or political leaders of a European type, rather than with representatives of kinship groupings. The little that is known about Wyandot clan structure, as recorded in the last century, helps us to understand at least the broad outlines of how the Huron clan system must have functioned in the seventeenth century (Tooker 1970b). Where specific features cannot be checked out in detail, this information serves to warn anthropologists about the existence of possible lacunae in their knowledge. Finally, it allows them to see the significance of numerous details of Huron behaviour that the French recorded blindly, but which anthropologists, armed with an understanding of Huron culture, may be able to interpret from an Indian point of view.

In many cases where there are few, if any, survivors of a particular tribe, valuable insights can be gained from comparisons with tribes that are known to have had a similar way of life and which have survived. Much that we are told about the Huron makes sense when we compare it with the more substantial information concerning Iroquois culture that begins to become available only a short time after the destruction of the Huron confederacy. Because the data concerning the Iroquois are more complete and better balanced, anthropologists can observe how a culture closely related to that of the Huron functioned as a total system. This provides a framework within which the piecemeal data on Huron culture can be fitted together. There are, of course, serious dangers inherent in this method, and I have severely criticized certain Iroquoianists for treating the Huron prior to 1650 as representing merely an earlier stage in the development of Iroquoian culture generally, or for using illustrations from the Huron and the Five Nations Iroquois indiscriminately to support arguments about the latter (Trigger 1971b:186–87). Significant differences can be noted in written accounts of burial customs, torture patterns, and kinship terminology, while the archaeological record reveals differences in pottery decoration, housetypes, and fortifications, albeit within the same general pattern (Trigger 1969a:121–24). It also remains to be ascertained whether the calendrical rituals, which are now such an important feature of "traditional" Iroquois culture, were established among either the Huron or the

Iroquois before 1650 (Tooker 1960). There is little in the description of Huron religion in the early sources to suggest that these rituals had penetrated this far north prior to the destruction of the Huron confederacy. In spite of these dangers, the considerable knowledge that we have of Iroquois culture can be used, with caution, to gain better insight into the total configuration of Huron culture and hence to understand Huron behaviour as it is reported by the French.

It is also clear that many aspects of Indian life were not confined to a single tribe or even to clusters of closely related ones. Shared cultural development resulted in certain traits being common to many tribes and over vast areas, particularly when the groups involved had adapted in generally similar ways to their environment. These similarities took the form of specific games, housetypes, or rituals, shared mythological themes or a preoccupation with curing rituals, a general pattern of political organization, or similar attitudes towards child-rearing. While they are very difficult to pin down, it is not impossible that certain traits, particularly values and attitudes, may have had a pan-Indian distribution.[15] Similarities of this sort can be used, at least in a very general way, to evaluate and interpret historical records.

Comparisons with later and better documented stages of a culture's development, or with closely related cultures, and a general knowledge of the cultural patterns of aboriginal North America permit the ethnologist to assess historical records and to use them as a basis for reconstructing earlier phases in the cultural development of particular groups. This kind of historical ethnography is so basic to all other ethnohistorical research that it is usually considered to be an integral part of the discipline. Some ethnohistorians, however, choose to regard it as being merely a preliminary to ethnohistory proper, which they would define as being the study of Indian history, or that of any nonliterate people. In either case, it is agreed that as detailed knowledge of a culture as possible is required if the history of that group is to be understood.

Anthropology also contributes to the understanding of Indian history by studying the cultural contacts that have taken place between European and tribal societies during the present century in places such as Africa, New Guinea, or the Canadian Arctic. Insofar as common elements may be observed in such contacts throughout the world, an understanding of these elements may be used to interpret more fragmentary historical accounts, without slighting the obviously distinctive features that pertain to separate historical traditions. The principal danger lies in the erroneous selection of theories to interpret specific situations and the subsequent distortion of fragmentary evidence to make it conform with these theories; a mistake all too prevalent in some recent studies of Huron society.

So far, we have argued that without the knowledge of tribal life that only anthropology can provide, ethnohistory is impossible. Yet, because the ethnohistorian must deal with historical records, ethnohistory is also impossible without a command of the techniques of historiography, as these have been developed by generations of practising historians.[16] Lacking sufficient knowledge of these techniques, an ethnohistorian will remain a dilettante, however well-trained he may be in anthropology. Among the skills that must be acquired is the ability to evaluate the authenticity and accuracy of primary sources, or at least a sufficient sense of problem to seek the opinion of historians who are competent to pronounce on these matters. Where variant manuscript copies of a work survive, the history of these variations must be investigated and the amateur's sin of choosing the version most congenial to his own interpretation must be avoided. Above all, the ethnohistorian must not fall into the common anthropological error of assuming that a written document necessarily means what it says. Ambiguous wordings, mutilated or ill-copied manuscripts, improperly set type in old printed books, or the editing of manuscripts in such a way as to distort their original meaning all present serious difficulties. Where editors intervene between an eye-witness and the earliest recorded account of what he has seen, as is the case with the *Jesuit Relations*, the possible bias of these editors must be taken into account. Even when what are purported to be Indian speeches survive, they must be treated with caution. Filtered through translators, the recorder's incomprehension, and the general tendency of European authors of the time to embellish and to fabricate whole addresses, it is not always certain that such sources are reliable. All of this makes historical research a painstaking affair.

The ethnohistorian must attempt to assess the experience, ability, and above all the personal biases of the eye-witness from whom a report has been received. An observer's intelligence, his training, and fundamental aspects of his personality all affect his ability to observe the people of another culture and determine those aspects of their behaviour that interest him. Moreover, not all these variations are idiosyncratic. The difficulties encountered in understanding a culture that is radically different, not only in content but also in its basic structure, from the observer's own can result in standard biases, which are reproduced in the accounts of numerous individuals. All Frenchmen experienced difficulty in understanding the nature of Iroquoian religion, which was far more different from their own than were the non-Christian religions of the Near East, India, or East Asia.

Because the Indians lacked the pomp and hierarchy of a church, as the French understood it, their religious beliefs initially were regarded as of little consequence. Later, Indian spirits came to be seen as demons and devils, and shamans were viewed as sorcerers and anti-Christs. In spite of this, individual variations can be detected in French attitudes towards Huron religious beliefs. Some priests and laymen were convinced that the devil was constantly at work, encouraging the Indians in their religious practices, while others dismissed most of their customs as resulting from sheer ignorance. By comparing the writings of these different authors with each other, and against a knowledge of Iroquois religion derived from modern ethnographic sources, it is possible, to some degree, to see through the biases that have shaped these accounts and to extract much reliable information from them.

Self-interest and the differing circumstances under which groups of European explorers, fur traders, and rival orders of priests encountered and interacted with various Indian groups have resulted in accounts of Indian life that differ widely in their attitudes towards the Indians and the kinds of information they provide. These differences are further evidenced when accounts of a particular event were written down by men who were of rival European nationalities. A careful comparison of French and Dutch accounts of their dealings with the Iroquois invariably results in a far more detailed and more complex picture of Iroquois political and economic behaviour than could be obtained if information from only one side were available (Trigger 1971c). Comparing different accounts of a particular event, it is sometimes possible, by a process analogous to surveyors' triangulation, to arrive at some reasonable conclusions about the views of the Indian participants, even in the absence of independent Indian witnesses. Moreover, when conflicting European groups sought to justify their own policies, they occasionally noted Indian reactions to other Europeans that otherwise would have gone unrecorded. Because of the sharply divergent interests of the various groups of Frenchmen who came to Quebec in early times, some extremely unflattering Indian views of certain Europeans have been recorded. The most regrettable shortcoming of the early sources is their failure to record the experiences of the first agents who lived and traded with the Indians: such as Jean Nicollet, Etienne Brûlé, and Nicolas Marsolet. From these earliest *coureurs de bois*, who lived intimately with the Indians and must have known them better than did any other Europeans, much might have been learned about Indian attitudes towards early missionaries and the French generally. In spite of this, it is possible, by carefully comparing the available evidence, to draw reasonable inferences about the policy and motivations of certain prominent Indians or groups of Indians.

Among some Indian groups, oral traditions are of considerable value for supplementing written records. The Winnebago tribe of Wisconsin, for example, are reported to preserve memories of events that took place soon after their first encounter with a European, which probably occurred in 1634 (Lurie 1960:803). For the Huron, however, and for the Iroquoians generally, oral traditions appear to be of little historical value. The reason for this probably lies in the Iroquoians' attitude towards history. For the most part, the purpose of their traditions was not to preserve a literal memory of the past, but rather to supply them with a guide to the social, political, and moral order in which they lived. For the Iroquois of the seventeenth and eighteenth centuries this moral order was provided by the Dekanahwideh legend, which told of the founding of the Iroquois confederacy (P. Wallace 1966). Since the names of the founders of the league were passed on to future office holders, the legend of the founding of the confederacy was, in fact, a statement concerning its constitution. Apart from this legend, the Iroquois appear to have had only the vaguest traditions about their origins. These were based on a pan-Indian theme that had the first ancestors of their various clans emerging out of caves or holes in the ground (Trigger 1970:14). Early in this century, A. C. Parker (1916) noted that the Iroquois retained no memories of their aboriginal fortifications and housetypes. He also noted that many Iroquois attributed the origin of their confederacy to the religious teacher Handsome Lake, who flourished between 1800 and 1815. Even the ceremonies that had been part of Iroquois culture prior to this time were ascribed to him. Parker (1916:480–81) concluded that the Iroquois conceived of their history in terms of periods of "cultural revolution" and that each new revolution systematically blotted out the memory of a former era.

It is uncertain how far these conclusions apply to the Huron. We have no record of a myth about the founding of their confederacy, but the Jesuits imply that they had knowledge of political events going back two hundred years. Their statement that some Huron claimed to know the locations of their villages over these two centuries suggests some interest in history (Thwaites 1896–1901, 16:227). On the other hand, their inheritance of titles was similar to that of the Iroquois and Peter Dooyentate Clarke's (1870) recording of Wyandot oral history indicates that, in the nineteenth century, the latter group had only the haziest and most inaccurate memory of events prior to 1650, or even for some time subsequent to that date.[17] Hence, one seems safe in concluding that oral traditions do not provide an independent means for studying the history of Iroquoian-speaking peoples. It is of interest when oral traditions confirm other sources of information about the past, but, except when they do, they should not be used even to supplement such sources.

Ethnohistory is further distinguished from conventional history by its relatively greater reliance on data from auxiliary fields, particularly archaeology, physical anthropology, and linguistics. However, growing awareness of the contributions that colonial and industrial archaeology can make to the study of history suggests that this distinction is not as clear-cut as it used to be. Linguistic data not only provide information about the historical relationships among different ethnic groups; they can also be used to reconstruct various aspects of prehistoric Indian cultures. For example, by means of lexical studies, Wallace Chafe (1964) has provided support for Tooker's (1960) theory that shamanistic healing cults antedate the present emphasis on calendrical rites among the northern Iroquoians, and Lounsbury (1961) has done important work on reconstructing proto-Iroquoian kinship terminology. I doubt that any more productive source of information about prehistoric, or early historic, Iroquoian culture remains to be unlocked than through linguistic studies.

Archaeological data not only provide important information about the development of Indian cultures in prehistoric times, but also furnish supplementary clues about these cultures in the early historic period. Many of these data are complementary to those derived from written accounts, since they illustrate material aspects of Indian life that early accounts rarely describe in detail. Archaeological and historical data are sometimes used in combination to locate the sites of Indian communities mentioned in early historical records. While some of this work has been very slipshod, other identifications of Huron sites are models of scholarly responsibility (Kidd 1949*b*; 1953; Ridley 1947; *see also* Trigger 1969*b*). The accurate identification of such sites invariably permits archaeologists both to verify and to supplement the historical record. Archaeologists have long been aware of the potential of their discipline for investigating changes brought about in material culture by European contact, but in recent years techniques have been pioneered for also studying the social changes that result from such contact (e.g., Deetz 1965). Although still in the experimental stage, these techniques may become exceedingly valuable for studying how Indian tribes were affected by European influences prior to the time of the earliest written records.

As yet, however, the ethnohistorical approach, as practised in North America, has produced only a few major studies of Indian tribes. In my opinion, the most important published to date is E. H. Spicer's (1962) *Cycles of Conquest*, which traces in detail the impact of successive Spanish, Mexican, and American administrations upon the native peoples of northern Mexico and the southwestern United States. The principal aim of this study was, however, less to provide a history of the native peoples of that region than to examine the range of situations in which North American Indians have been influenced by their contact with Europeans. This theme was explored further by a number of anthropologists in a book edited by Spicer (1961), entitled *Perspectives in American Indian Culture Change*. In this book, the history of six widely separated Indian tribes is traced from the time of contact down to the present. Harold E. Hickerson (1962; 1970) has carefully studied the impact of the fur trade upon the Ojibwa of the upper Great Lakes region, devoting special attention to the effects that trade had upon their social and political organization. More recently, A. F. C. Wallace (1970) has published a history of the Seneca tribe which is, in fact, primarily a biography of Handsome Lake set into an extensive time-and-place description of Seneca culture and the changes it has undergone in historic times. While these studies are major contributions to understanding Indian history, in each of them historical analysis is made secondary to efforts to generalize about cultural processes. Indeed, Hickerson (1970:7) makes this quite explicit when he states that ethnohistory "employs historiographical methods to lay a foundation for the formulation of general laws: in a word, *ideographic* means to *nomothetic* ends." This also appears to be the case with Patterson's *The Canadian Indians*, which has as its main theme to demonstrate similarities between the experiences of the Canadian Indian and those of native peoples in other colonial situations, particularly in New Zealand, Australia, South Africa, and the United States (1972:3–36). While it is impossible ever to separate the explanation of particular events from generalizations about human behaviour, the relative emphasis that is given to these two processes in particular studies varies widely. The present state of ethnohistorical research appears to leave room for the development of a style of presentation in which the detailed explanation of a specific historical situation is pursued as an end that is considered worthwhile in itself.

A Statement of Methods and Assumptions

The availability of data and the willingness of the ethnohistorian to pay attention to them determines the level of specificity at which any study of

Indian-white contact is written. Early studies were generally concerned with how whole tribes responded to European contact. These studies dealt mainly with features that entire peoples had in common; what happened to individuals or to specific groups within a tribe was of interest only in relationship to the more general process of adaptation. Although attention was sometimes paid to changes in personality that resulted from these processes, the aim of such investigations was not to establish a range of individual variation, but rather to define a limited number of modal personalities which, at most, took account of differences in age, sex, and possible economic status. Such studies have contributed to our knowledge of particular tribes, as well as helping to define types of culture contact and to sharpen the understanding of this process. By their very nature, however, these studies are essentially structural rather than historical in intent and execution.

At the other end of the scale is biography, which at its best is a perceptive examination of the forces at work in a particular situation as they can be seen in relationship to the life of a well-documented individual. In recent years, American anthropologists have written biographies, or helped to write autobiographies, of Indians (Dyk 1938; Ford 1941; Marriott 1948; Simmons 1942), yet few Indians who lived in the last century, or earlier, have been the subjects of extensive biographical treatment. Most of the latter studies have been written by historians who have had only a superficial knowledge of Indian customs; hence their insights into their subjects are limited, even when the biographer wishes to be sympathetic.[18]

For the early period, a biographical approach is made difficult by the paucity of material that has been preserved concerning any particular individual. Information is available about Indians who became outstanding converts, but little of this concerns their lives prior to conversion. Of the childhood and life of these converts, as it was lived other than in the presence of the missionaries, we can learn very little. Moreover, these exemplary converts were unusual Indians and there is much about their motives and behaviour that the missionaries either did not understand or felt it inappropriate to record. For the majority of Indians whose names have been preserved, only a few isolated events are recorded and even a skeletal life history of such individuals remains beyond our grasp. That this is so can easily be ascertained from a perusal of the Indian biographies recently published in the first two volumes of the *Dictionary of Canadian Biography* (1966; 1969). We are completely ignorant, or have only the vaguest ideas about what the majority of Indians thought and felt as individuals and know little about what they did, except in their dealings with Europeans. Thus our characterization of them can rarely penetrate behind the polite facade that the Indians presented on such occasions. One must therefore accept as a limitation of the material that few studies-in-depth of individuals are possible and that there is little chance of writing large-scale biographies of the Indians who played a major role in our early history.

The weakness of the biographical approach, as far as Indians are concerned, is further illustrated by life histories of prominent explorers and missionaries. Because Indian life can be dealt with in a piecemeal fashion in such works, authors have little incentive to transcend the limitations of their subject's understanding of the Indians. Nevertheless, such ignorance exacts a higher price than might be imagined. By failing to understand those with whom the subject of his biography had dealings, the author ends up with only a partial, and often distorted, understanding of his or her motives and personality (Trigger 1971*a*).

On the other hand, enough isolated information is available concerning the behaviour of individual Indians in certain specific circumstances that a fairly detailed picture can be built up of their differing responses to these situations. Sometimes we can learn enough about the status and family affiliations of individuals that we may infer with some confidence why these Indians behaved as they did. Such data permit the ethnohistorian to steer a middle course between biographies and gross structural analysis, by studying the history of a tribe or confederacy in terms of the behaviour of groups of individuals united by certain common interests. These interest groups are not the abstract social categories established for purposes of comparative research by sociologists and ethnologists; instead, they are groupings that emerge as a result of common interests in real historical situations. Some of them were cliques that had a recognized corporate existence in their own time, others are constructs of the historian. To be a valid interest group, however, its members must have had implicitly shared common goals and supported one another in common action. It may be argued that whatever level of specificity an historian aims to work at, success ultimately must depend in large measure on his understanding of the interactions among such groups.

The nature of interest groups has been examined in detail by many sociologists. They play an important part in the theorizing of George C. Homans (e.g., 1962:182–91), one of the few historically orientated sociologists in the United States, and have been discussed in terms of historical theory in the later writings of Jean-Paul Sartre (1963). Professional historians, however, have been using this approach in a pragmatic way for a long time (Fischer 1971:216–42). One of the best examples of its application to the study of Canadian history is Gustave Lanctot's (1967) *Canada and the American Revolution*. In this study, Lanctot traces the shifting relations, between 1774 and 1783, among the French-Canadian farmers, clergy, and gentry, the British officers in Quebec, and the British merchants and American rebels in the province. The changing alliances of each group are interpreted as efforts to defend clearly defined, and largely unchanging, interests within the context of a rapidly changing situation. The influence that individual personalities such as Governors Carleton or Haldimand, or Bishop Briand, had on the conduct of affairs is by no means neglected, but it is a matter of some methodological interest to note how these men, along with less famous individuals, are treated, as far as possible, as representatives of specific interest groups.

This approach is particularly valuable for the investigation of social and economic history, especially as it concerns the lower classes. Indians stand in much the same relationship to history as do the working classes, peasantries, and other less literate members of European society in earlier times. The records that we have of both were produced by a relatively small, privileged class that had no personal experience of the ways of life of these people. It is therefore no accident that the techniques developed to study the history of less affluent Europeans resemble so closely those we propose to use for the study of the Canadian Indian.

The technique of studying social interaction in terms of interest groups provides ethnohistorians with a method of approaching as near as the data will allow to an investigation of historical events in terms of their real agents, individual human beings. In particular, it encourages a far more detailed examination of events and processes than does the study of contact as an interaction between two totally different cultural systems. In Canada, Indians and Europeans rarely constituted two homogeneous interest groups, or even lined up as two opposing teams. Groups of European fur traders, government officials, and diverse orders of the clergy often competed with each other more than with the Indians. Likewise, many Indian tribes were noted for their factionalism and internal disagreements even in periods of strength. Not infrequently, common interests gave rise to alliances that cut across ethnic lines and united various Indians and Europeans in opposition to their own people. These sorts of alliances undoubtedly were fraught with more problems than were those between members of the same society. Nevertheless, by the very act of examining how common interests could, and did, unite members of different ethnic groups, an effort is made to take account of a common humanity transcending cultural differences.

Even when this method has been accepted, however, a major problem remains unsolved. How, when all the data that we have at our disposal have been recorded by Europeans, is it possible for the work of any historian using these data not to be biased in favour of the Europeans, if not in sympathy then at least in terms of insights? Because of the nature of the historical record, we know much more about relations between specific groups of Indians and Europeans than we know about relations between one group of Indians and another. This is true even concerning the fur trade, although one might expect that European interest would have encouraged the collection of large amounts of information about intertribal relations. If so, it was never recorded. Because of this, there is an almost automatic tendency for historians to overemphasize the importance of Indian-white relations in Indian affairs generally. It is also clear that we can learn far more about the general background and personal motivations of the Europeans who are mentioned in our sources than we can about the Indians. If unchecked, the ethnohistorian's natural tendency to make the maximum use of his data can turn the best-intentioned Indian history into nothing more than a restudy of European colonization.

It is undoubtedly true that much of Indian diplomacy "had a way of reflecting" (F. Jennings 1968:23) decisions made in Europe, but to regard Indian history merely as an extension of colonial history, in the manner of some historians, is to confuse what actually happened with the manner in which Indian policy has been recorded. The historian must evaluate the impact of traditional ideas upon the conduct of Indian diplomacy and take into account the patterns of intertribal relations that existed prior to the coming of the whites and that continued to influence Indian politics for a long time afterward. Far greater attention must be paid to the references to intertribal relations that occur, often incidentally, in the historical records. It is also possible that, in the future, archaeological data will be useful in supplementing the information that historians have at their disposal.

To achieve greater equity in writing this history of the Huron, several procedures have been carefully observed. First, while not completely suppressing the individuality of historical figures, I have concentrated on those aspects of people's behaviour that reflect their roles as members of one or more interest groups. Secondly, while the motivations of the members of each interest group have been presented as clearly as possible,

I have tried to do this impartially and in such a manner that the interest of the reader focuses on the total situation rather than on the passions or problems of any one group.

This approach is necessary because, for the most part, we lack the documentation to reconstruct the psychological framework that is associated with Indian behaviour. Hence, by eliminating such considerations, as far as possible, in our evaluation of individual Europeans as well, we achieve something like parity in our treatment of both groups. Secondly, since most of our data concern the dealings of the Huron with various groups of French, by concentrating our analysis on the relationships between groups, rather than on the inner dynamics of the groups themselves, we again tend to utilize the data to best advantage for understanding the Indians.

It should not be concluded, however, that this approach has been adopted only because of the uneven nature of the data. It has also been done for more positive reasons. One can argue that the aim of an Indian history should be to make Indians sympathetic figures. Sympathy, however, does not always imply understanding and, without a clear understanding of people's motives, respect is impossible. All too much has been written about Indians that is well-intentioned and benevolent, yet most of this literature has failed to promote a genuine understanding of the Indians as people who had worthy ambitions of their own and who were, and are, able to conduct their own affairs and to interact intelligently with Europeans. I think it especially important that current ethnohistorical writing should aim to make the behaviour of Indian groups understandable. To do this, Canadian ethnohistorians must investigate, not only the economics of the fur trade, but also the cultural values of the Indians and the full range of problems they have faced. Moreover, and this many anthropologists tend to forget, if we are to understand the total situation, we must attempt to achieve a similar dispassionate understanding of the motives of European groups, such as the Jesuits, who interacted with the Indians. In the long run, this may require as much effort, and even more self-discipline, than does an understanding of the Huron.

Chapter 2   The Huron and Their Neighbours

The Huron Land and Economy[1]

NAME

Huron is not a North American Indian term but is derived from the French *hure*, meaning a boar's head. A popular tradition in New France maintained that this name was invented by French sailors, who were astonished by the bristly hair styles of the Huron warriors who began trading with the French early in the seventeenth century. Yet, this story may be no more than a folk-etymology. Long before the discovery of the New World, *huron* was a slang term meaning ruffian or rustic. No doubt, it would have seemed appropriate for the Huron, who when first encountered by Europeans on the St. Lawrence, and for a long time afterward, must have appeared outlandish by comparison with the coastal peoples, who had been trading with Europeans for over a generation and among whom European food, tools, and items of clothing already played a vital role.[2]

The Huron called themselves *Wendat*, which means "Islanders," or "Dwellers on a Peninsula."[3] This term may refer to the Huron country, which was surrounded on three sides by large bodies of water, or to Huron cosmological beliefs. The Huron imagined their country to be at the centre of the world, which in turn was an island supported on the back of a giant tortoise. *Wendat* was the name, not of a tribe, but of a confederation made up of four tribes. It is therefore analogous to the Iroquois *Hodénosaunee*, or People of the Longhouse, which was a collective term for the five tribes that made up the Iroquois confederacy.

GEOGRAPHY

The Huron country was located at the southeastern corner of Georgian Bay, on a narrow strip of land sandwiched between Matchedash and Nottawasaga Bays on the west and Lake Simcoe on the east (map 1). It was further delineated on its southern boundary by the drainage basin of the Notta-

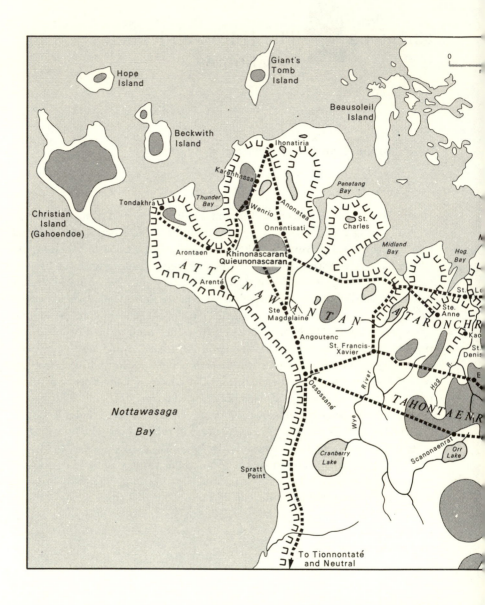

MAP 1. *The Huron Country, c. 1634, showing locations of tribes, settlements, and major trails attested by the Jesuits.*

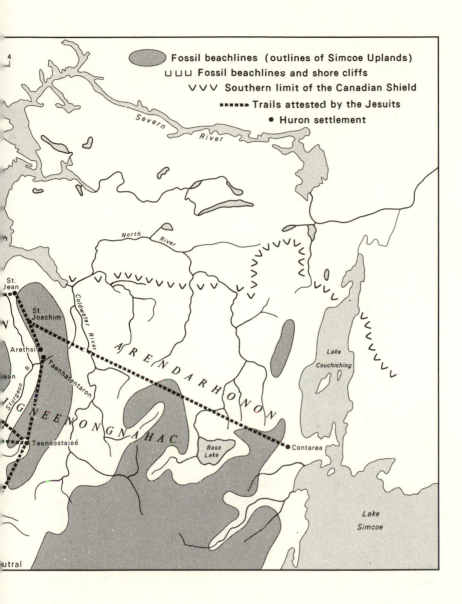

Fossil beachlines (outlines of Simcoe Uplands)
ᴗ ᴗ ᴗ Fossil beachlines and shore cliffs
∨ ∨ ∨ Southern limit of the Canadian Shield
▪▪▪▪▪▪ Trails attested by the Jesuits
● Huron settlement

wasaga River, which at that time was a vast swamp hindering communication with the south. The Huron villages were concentrated in an area that measured no more than 35 miles east to west and 20 miles north to south. The western part of this region, including the whole of the Penetanguishene Peninsula, was the tribal territory of the largest of the Huron tribes, the Attignawantan, whose name meant "the people of the Bear."[4] In the northern part of the Penetanguishene Peninsula, the land rises quickly from the lake in a series of impressive beach terraces, but, for the most part, the surface relief is only gently rolling. Much of the soil in this area tends to be rather stony and the drier soils supported large stands of oak and white pine. To the south, along the shores of Nottawasaga Bay, there were vast areas covered with sand dunes and stunted coniferous trees, now a densely populated summer resort.

Farther to the east, five short rivers flow north into Matchedash Bay: the Wye, Hog, Sturgeon, Coldwater, and North. Beyond, as the Severn River, the waters of Lake Simcoe follow a circuitous course across the Canadian Shield before entering Matchedash Bay from the north. Between each of these rivers is a ridge of high ground incised with the beach terraces of Glacial Lake Algonquin, while nearer Lake Simcoe the hills rise over 700 feet above Lake Huron. In prehistoric times, the higher ground in this area was covered with maple, beech, and basswood, while cedar and alder grew in the swampy river valleys (Heidenreich et al. 1969:123–27; Heidenreich 1971: map 20). The eastern part of the region was the territory of the Arendarhonon, whose name may signify "Nation of the Rock." The Arendarhonon appear to have been the second largest of the Huron tribes. Between the Arendarhonon and the Attignawantan lived the Attigneenongnahac and Tahontaenrat tribes. Their names have been conjectured to mean "Cord" or "Barking Dogs" and "Deer," "White Thorns," "White Canoe," or "One White Lodge" respectively.[5] Although widely used in recent publications, none of the latter etymologies is more than uncertain speculation; hence I prefer to call all of these tribes by their Huron names. A fifth group, the Ataronchronon, whose name is conjectured to mean "People of the Marshes,"[6] lived in the lower part of the Wye Valley. The existence of this group does not appear to have been recognized in the political organization of the Huron confederacy and it is possible that it was merely a division of the Attignawantan.

Everyone who visited the Georgian Bay region in the seventeenth century was struck by the contrast between the hills and plains of the Huron country, which were covered with luxuriant vegetation, and the rocky inhospitable region to the north.[7] Geographically, the Huron country is part of southern Ontario. Its bedrock of Palaeozoic limestone is overlaid with deep glacial tills, which in turn support sandy, well-drained soils. Immediately to the north, these formations give way to the metamorphic rock of the Canadian Shield which, while also wooded, is covered with only a thin, broken layer of soil. Although tribes living as far north as Lake Nipissing planted small fields of corn, the fertile soils of the Huron country marked the northern limits of effective corn agriculture in eastern Canada and of the sedentary way of life that was associated with it.

In spite of suggestions to the contrary (Martijn 1969:100 n. 7; Latta in Heidenreich et al. 1969:112), recent detailed studies have produced no evidence of significant climatic changes in this area between A.D. 1600 and the present (Heidenreich et al. 1969:123, 127). The normal frost-free period is 135 to 142 days and the growing season is 195 days. The summers are hot, as in the rest of southern Ontario, and only fourteen to sixteen inches of rain fall during the growing season. In the winter the snowfall is exceptionally heavy: 90 to 110 inches, as compared with 50 to 70 inches in the Toronto area (Heidenreich 1971:56–59; *Atlas of Canada*: maps 21, 23, 28).

Before settlement became extensive, the region must have been rich in non-migratory game, particularly deer, bear, and beaver, although these were fewer in number than in the warmer regions north of Lake Erie. Wild birds, including various kinds of aquatic fowl, were common, except for the turkey, which flourished farther south. Even more important, however, were the trout, pike, sturgeon, and other species of fish, which were spectacularly abundant in the waters that surround the Huron country on every side. Fishing constituted an economic resource for the Huron second in importance only to agriculture (Trigger 1969a:30; Heidenreich 1971:158).

From the Huron country, it was possible to travel northward along the eastern shore of Georgian Bay without ever moving out of sight of land. This water route encouraged the development of ties between the Huron and the hunting peoples of the north, which were lacking among the other agricultural peoples who lived in southern Ontario and New York State (Trigger 1962a).

POPULATION AND SETTLEMENT PATTERNS

The population of the Huron country in the early part of the seventeenth century has been variously estimated to have been between 18,000 and

40,000 people. While it is notoriously difficult to determine the size of aboriginal American populations, my investigations incline me to favour the lowest of these figures.[8] The Huron lived in eighteen to twenty-five villages. Some were very small hamlets, but about six appear to have contained forty or more multi-family dwellings and were surrounded with fortified palisades (plate 1). These large villages probably had a population of 1500 to 2000 people each, and were invariably located in naturally defensible locations which provided breaks in slope on at least two sides (Heidenreich 1971:111). The average village occupied four to six acres, although villages covering up to fifteen acres are reported (ibid. 126). The Attignawantan appear to have had two large towns, but many members of this tribe lived in about a dozen small, unfortified villages. The territories of the three other tribes were more exposed to Iroquois raids; hence their populations were concentrated in a smaller number of large, fortified villages.[9]

Most villages were located near streams, which were useful for canoe travel and close to sandy, well-drained soil that was preferred for growing corn. Especially in the eastern parts of the Huron country, soil of this type is found mostly on the sides and tops of hills, rather than in the valley bottoms. Because of this, many villages were built on old beach terraces, 200 feet or more above the valley bottom, near where springs flowed from the hillside (Heidenreich 1967:17–18). The villages were joined together by a network of narrow trails that ran roughly in a north-south and east-west direction through the forest. Extensions of these trails led southward to the territory of the Tionnontaté, near Collingwood, and to the Neutral tribes, who lived in the southwest corner of Lake Ontario. It has been estimated that there were over 200 miles of trails linking the Huron settlements (Heidenreich 1971:156–57, map 23).

DIVISION OF LABOUR

In the seventeenth century, the Huron were the northernmost of the Iroquoian-speaking peoples. They shared with their linguistic cousins to the south a way of life that was firmly based on corn agriculture and which supported many thousands of people and some of the highest concentrations of population in eastern North America.[10] Prior to their encounter with the French, the Huron knew of no culture that they had reason to believe was materially more successful than their own. They proudly contrasted the richness of their way of life with the poverty of the numeric-

PLATE 1. *Model of a Huron village based on archaeological and historical data. Courtesy National Museum of Man, National Museums of Canada.*

ally much smaller hunting bands who lived to the north. Because of their subsistence patterns, these groups not only were less sedentary than the Huron but often found themselves dependent on Huron food reserves to carry them over a bad winter. The chronic shortages and narrow margins of surplus on which these bands subsisted contrasted with the large surpluses and far less frequent food shortages that were characteristic of Huron life.

The most basic distinction in Huron society was that made between the sexes (Quain 1937; Witthoft 1959:32–36). Almost every task was considered to be either exclusively men's work or exclusively women's work, and every Huron was expected to be familiar with all or most of the tasks appropriate to his or her sex. For the most part, men engaged in tasks that required considerable physical strength, or which took them away from home for long periods. Women performed tasks of a more routine nature that kept them in, or close to, their villages. Both sexes did much of their work in teams and the differing nature of this work meant that men and women spent much of their time in the company of their own sex and apart from each other. These work habits may explain, in part, the formality and avoidance that generally characterized public relations between the sexes in Huron society.

WOMEN'S WORK

The chief task performed by women was the planting, tending, and harvesting of the crops, which accounted for perhaps three-quarters of all the food that the Huron ate.[11] These crops were limited in number. Corn was the most important by far, but beans, squash, and sunflowers were also grown.[12] Both flour and flint corn were planted, although in this northern latitude the latter was preferred as it matured in 100, as opposed to 130, days.[13] This corn had two to three cobs per stalk, each four or more inches long and bearing 100 to 650 kernels per cob (Heidenreich 1971:171–73). Assuming that corn constituted about 65 percent of the Huron diet, a woman had to produce enough to provide each member of her family with about 1.3 pounds of it per day (ibid. 163).

The Huron women worked the soil with small wooden spades, scraping it up to form hills a foot or more high and several feet in diameter, in which they planted their seeds year after year (plate 2). These hills, which may have numbered 2500 per acre, not only supported the corn stalks but prevented sheet erosion and, by trapping cold low-lying air, reduced the

PLATE 2. *Lafitau's depiction of Huron agricultural practices. This illustration from Joseph-François Lafitau's* Moeurs des sauvages amériquains *(1724) provides a striking example of the ethnographic unreliability of many of the most famous illustrations of Indian life in Canada in the early historic period. While the cornhills faithfully reproduce Lafitau's description of Indian agriculture in Canada, the human figures and their tools (but not their clothes) are copies of T. de Bry's 1591 engraving of Jacques Le Moyne de Morgues's painting of Timucua agriculture done in Florida, 1564–65. W. C. Sturtevant (American Antiquity 33 [1968]: 91 ff.) has further demonstrated that Le Moyne's hoes are of European rather than Indian type. There is no reason to accept the claim that the skyline was intended to be that of Montreal Island. Because of direct copying all the figures produced by Lafitau's artist are left-handed. Courtesy National Anthropological Archives, Smithsonian Institution.*

danger of frost damage.[14] Because only light soils could be worked and these tended to dry out easily, the Huron experienced an average of at least one serious drought every decade, as well as one or two less serious ones during that period (Heidenreich 1971:58–59). The failure of the Huron to add fresh organic matter to their fields also meant that their crops quickly depleted the fertility of the soil. It is estimated that the natural fertility of the types of soil the Huron used was sufficient to grow crops for only four to six years; however, by burning leaves and branches to add ash to the soil, and carefully weeding their fields, the Huron were able to go on using them for eight to twelve years (ibid. 180–89). As the fertility of old fields declined, new ones had to be brought under cultivation in order to maintain levels of production.[15] When nearby fields and sources of firewood had been used up, it was necessary for a Huron village to relocate. This seems to have occurred about once every ten to fifteen years.

Approximately 7000 acres would have been sufficient to feed the Huron population at any one time,[16] but, since the Huron aimed at producing surpluses to trade with other groups, the amount of land under cultivation was probably above this figure. In order to grow and harvest this much food, Huron women had to work hard. Visitors commented on the care they took to weed their fields and to chase away birds and animals that threatened their crops. In areas that were safe from attack, women frequently spent the summer living with their children in temporary cabins near their fields.

Although each woman appears to have tended her own fields, these were of small extent and there was probably a considerable amount of informal cooperation (cf. Snyderman 1951). All of the food produced by women living in the same house was either stored in the porches at either end or hung from the rafters and, while each woman may have intended to use her own, no one was permitted to go hungry as long as any food remained to the household. The corn buried in bark-lined pits either inside or near houses may have been specially protected seed corn (Heidenreich 1971:119).

In addition to growing crops, the women gathered a wide variety of wild roots, nuts, and berries, which added flavour to an otherwise bland diet. Some of the fruit was dried to preserve it for winter. Only when crops failed did wild plants become a major item in the Huron diet. At such times, in addition to the wild foods that were eaten regularly, various kinds of tree bark, mosses, and lichens were consumed. Acorns were repeatedly boiled prior to being eaten to make them less bitter.

Women were also responsible for the time-consuming tasks of cooking, sewing, and tending children. Food was cooked over an open hearth using dry, relatively smokeless wood that the women collected each spring. This wood came from the limbs of dead trees, which the winter's storms had knocked down. Most of it was a by-product of forest clearance and the depletion of nearby supplies was, as we have noted, one of the reasons for the periodic relocation of Huron villages. The ash from the hearths, along with other refuse, was dumped onto middens located on the periphery of the village. Middens have been found inside only the largest villages, but it appears that in no case did a Huron woman have to walk more than 100 feet from her house to dispose of garbage (Heidenreich 1971:147).

Although Huron cuisine is reported to have included many dishes, most of these were variations on a few themes. Their most common dish was a thin soup made of corn meal, which was ground by the women in a hollowed-out tree trunk, using a wooden pole, six or seven feet long (plate 3). Pieces of fish, meat, or squash were sometimes added to this soup. The fish were boiled whole, then mashed up without removing bones, entrails, or scales, before being returned to the pot. The Huron made unleavened bread, sometimes adding dried fruit and pieces of deer fat to the dough to give it more flavour. Meat was also roasted over the fire. The French complained about the Huron failure to wash their utensils and to observe satisfactory standards of hygiene in their cooking. They also found some Huron delicacies not to their liking; among these was *leindohy* or stinking corn: small ears of corn that had been permitted to ferment in a stagnant pond for several months before being eaten. They also objected to a special bread that was made from fresh corn, which the women masticated, spat out, and pounded in a large mortar before baking it in corn leaves. The Huron regarded both of these as party dishes.

The clothes that Huron women made were of relatively simple design. Most of them were made from the skins of animals. We know little about the preparation of these skins, except that they were fleshed with stone or bone scrapers. Men and women invariably wore loincloths and were much embarrassed by the complete male nudity that appears to have been common in the hotter months among certain neighbouring peoples, such as the Ottawa and the Neutral. In addition, Huron women wore a skirt extending from the waist partway to the knees, although in summer they left their bodies bare from the waist up, the same as men did. Men and women both wore moccasins and, in the winter, they also wore a cloak, long sleeves, and leggings, which were held in place by leather strings tied about their body. These clothes were not sufficiently warm to prevent some people from freezing to death each winter. In spite of their sense of cultural

PLATE 3. *Huron woman grinding corn. From Champlain's* Voyages of
*1619. Although these illustrations are often assumed to be Champlain's own
work, the evidence presented below (see esp. plate 21) suggests they were
drawn by a professional draftsman familiar with French and Portuguese
traditions of cartographical illustration for the southeastern United States
and tropical areas of the New World. Such a draftsman would have
attempted to give visual form to Champlain's written or verbal descriptions
of the Indians of Canada. Although nothing can be specified as incorrect
about this particular illustration, on principle none of the drawings
accompanying Champlain's publications can be regarded as having
ethnographic value independently of his written work. This engraving and
the ones that follow cannot be compared with John White's magnificent and
earlier drawings of North American Indians. Courtesy McGill University
Libraries.*

superiority, the Huron admired the clothes and camping equipment that were made by the northern hunting peoples and sought these in trade.

Crude as Huron clothes were in design and execution, they were often carefully decorated with painting and with bands of trim made from porcupine quills. Both sexes spent considerable time caring for their hair and greasing their bodies with oil and animal fat to protect them against sun, cold, and insects. On festive occasions, colours were added to these fats and the whole body was painted with representations of men and animals, or with geometrical designs. Some of these paintings were so well done that, from a distance, Europeans mistook them for suits of clothing. On these occasions, a single person might also wear up to twelve pounds of strings and plaques of shell beads. Men habitually wore tobacco pouches, which hung behind their backs and were a repository for their charms and other valued personal possessions. Many of these pouches had been elaborately decorated by the women.

Women fashioned the globular clay vessels used for cooking. These pots ranged from a few inches to a foot or more in diameter and were decorated around the lip and collar with patterns made up of incised straight lines. The Huron made only one functional type of vessel, a soup pot. Stones were used to hold these vessels in place over the hearth.[17]

Women also wove mats out of reeds and corn leaves, which were used to cover the doors and sleeping platforms of their houses. They made cord from Indian hemp (*Apocynum cannabinum*), swamp milkweed (*Asclepias incarnata*), and basswood bark (Heidenreich 1971:200–201) and used the finer cord to make scarfs, collars, and bracelets which were worn by both sexes. They also fashioned baskets out of reeds and birchbark and sewed the latter together to make dishes from which to eat and drink.

Women sometimes accompanied their husbands on the late winter hunting expeditions that travelled for several days to the south or east of the Huron country to slay deer. No doubt these women helped to butcher the game and to carry home the skins and meat. Women do not seem to have participated in the autumn hunts, possibly because warfare was still going on at that time of year, nor did they often travel outside Huron territory, especially when this involved lengthy canoe trips. Only a very few instances are recorded of women travelling between the Huron country and Quebec during the years of the French-Huron alliance. In these respects the Huron differed from the northern Algonkians, who moved as families in their annual cycle, and from the Iroquois, whose women played an important role in hunting activities and also frequently accompanied their husbands on diplomatic visits to Quebec.

Women's work was of an inward looking, familial nature. Their unit of routine association were the females who lived in a single, multi-family dwelling. Beyond that, their loyalty extended to their village, but this appears to have been the broadest focus of their loyalties. Because they did not travel abroad as men did, Huron women tended to be the guardians of family and village traditions and, possibly for this reason, were more conservative than their menfolk.

MEN'S WORK

The earliest French visitors to the Huron country judged Huron men to be the epitome of idleness. Champlain states that he found women doing most of the work, both at home and in the fields, while the men amused themselves hunting, fishing, trading, making war, dancing, and sleeping, the latter being their favourite occupation (Biggar 1922–36, 3:137). To a Frenchman of Champlain's time such a life seemed appropriate to aristocrats or to beggars, but not to common people who were supposed to earn their living by the sweat of their brow.

Such opinions reflect the difficulty that the French experienced in trying to understand even the least esoteric aspects of Huron culture. In Europe, where the fertility of fields was maintained through crop rotation, forest clearance was of minimal importance. Because of this, the French consistently failed to note the extent of this activity among the Huron. Likewise, because every Huron man performed a wide variety of tasks, he tended to organize his time in a less regular way than did contemporary Europeans, especially urban dwellers. To the French, such behaviour appeared to be further evidence of laziness.

In fact, all of the evidence indicates that Huron men worked at least as hard as Huron women did, and that their contribution to the economy was no less important. It was they who cleared new fields. With stone axes they chopped down small trees and girdled the larger ones. Then they stripped the branches off the large trees and burned these branches around their trunks in order to kill them. The women planted their crops between the remaining stumps, which were removed when they became rotten and broke apart easily.

Because the fertility of the soil was soon depleted, new fields constantly had to be cleared around a village in order to keep up with declining yields. It has been estimated that a village of 1000 people would have required at least 360 acres of cleared land to feed itself (Heidenreich 1971:213). New villages usually were located only a few miles from the old one to make it easy for fields to be cleared well in advance of the move. In addition to the extremely hard work of clearing fields, Huron men grew small quantities of tobacco for their own use, in plots of ground near their houses.[18]

Other male tasks of key importance to the Huron economy were those connected with hunting and fishing. Until recently, the importance of fishing for Huron subsistence has been greatly underestimated. Fish were taken with nets, either on the open water or at weirs constructed across streams and rivers. In the winter, nets were laid through holes cut in the ice. Fish were also caught with wooden spears or with hook and line, although the latter was not a particularly effective method, as lines tended to break easily.

Although fish were caught in great abundance at various times of the year and in different parts of Huronia, the most important fishing expeditions were those for a month or more each autumn to the islands in Georgian Bay to catch the spawning whitefish (*Coregonus culpeaformis*). Parties of fishermen built Algonkian-style round cabins on these islands and proceeded to set their nets a mile or more out in the lake each evening and leave them there overnight. Depending on the weather, the fish were either dried in the sun or were smoked, and then packed in bark containers.

Although hunting was less important than fishing from a nutritional point of view, skins were essential for clothing. Moreover, hunting was a prestigious activity much enjoyed by men. Birds were either captured in nets or shot with arrows, bears were tracked with specially trained hunting dogs, and beaver were driven from their lodges in winter and killed when forced to come up to holes in the ice in order to breathe. In addition, a variety of smaller animals were killed and eaten, including large field mice which infested Huron villages.

The Huron had no domestic animals except dogs, which they kept in great numbers. Many of these dogs appear to have been killed and eaten (Thwaites 1896–1901, 7:223; Savage 1971*a*), although some were special pets and never killed. The Huron also raised bear cubs whose mothers had been killed by hunters. When they grew older, these bears were slain and eaten in ceremonies resembling those in which dogs were sacrificed.

The principal game animal, and the one the Huron most enjoyed hunting, was the deer. Deer hunting was usually a cooperative activity, in which as many as several hundred men drove the animals into a river, or a specially constructed enclosure, where they could be slain more easily. Sometimes, converging barriers of brush, each up to nine feet high and half a mile long, were used to drive deer into these enclosures (plate 4.).

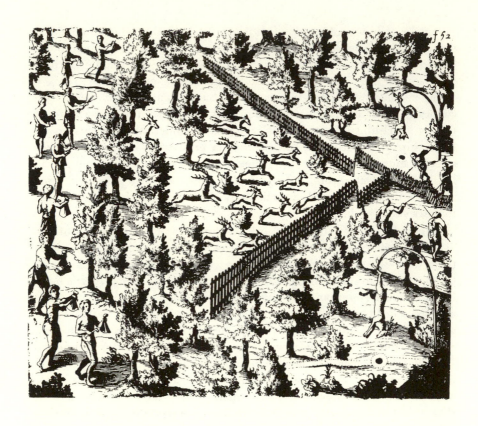

PLATE 4. *A Huron deer hunt. From Champlain's* Voyages *of 1619.
On the left hunters with bone clappers drive deer into an enclosure where
other hunters kill them with spears. The sides of the enclosure are more
elaborate and regular than Champlain describes them as well as much
shorter. Courtesy John Carter Brown Library.*

Twenty-five men could construct such a barricade in less than ten days and, by hunting every second day for five weeks, they might be able to kill 120 deer. As already noted, most of this hunting was done in the fall and late winter. This was when the deer gathered in the largest herds and hence could be hunted most easily. Because game was scarce in the vicinity of Huron settlement, deer hunting took place to the south and in the Trent Valley. The skins and fat of the deer were carefully preserved, but only a small amount of the meat could be brought back to the villages to be eaten at celebrations.[19]

The third major group of tasks performed by men was the construction carried on out-of-doors during the summer months. The most arduous activity was the erection of the multi-family longhouses. These were constructed of slabs of bark, preferably cedar, which were tied onto a wooden frame and held down by a network of saplings. Houses were located nine to twelve feet apart to minimize the danger of fire, and many had a narrow end facing into the prevailing wind, to lessen the chances of fire spreading to other houses and to prevent them from being blown down (Heidenreich 1967:18). The standard Huron house was about 90 to 100 feet long and 25 to 30 feet wide. Poles seem to have been dug into the ground along either side of the house and were tied at the top to form an arbour-shaped structure.[20] At one or both ends of the house was an enclosed porch,[21] where corn and firewood were stored, and near the centre were large poles which held racks on which the occupants placed their pots, clothing, and other possessions. A raised platform, four to five feet off the ground, ran along both sides of the house, while down the middle was a row of large hearths, each about twenty feet apart. These may have been used for heating the longhouse and smaller ones on either side used for cooking (Heidenreich 1971:118). A single family lived on either side of each of the central fires. Judging from their construction, Huron houses could have remained in habitable condition only for the average lifetime of a village. When new ones were required, all the men of the village cooperated in their construction.

Another communal activity was the construction of the palisades which protected the larger Huron villages. This work was directed by the village headmen, the labour force being provided by young men from the village and from nearby hamlets that lacked defences of their own. Huron palisades were not like those of a European fort, but consisted of several rows of wooden poles, each three to five inches in diameter and spaced six to twelve inches apart. Only if the palisade consisted of more than two rows, was one of the inner ones made of stakes up to ten inches in diameter

(Heidenreich 1971:140). The rows of stakes were reinforced by inserting large slabs of bark between them and were then woven together with smaller branches to form a kind of rough basket-weave enclosure around the village.[22] It has been estimated that as many as 24,000 poles were required to fortify the largest Huron villages (Heidenreich 1971:154). One or more gates were provided, each of which required an individual to turn several times while entering the village.[23] Watchtowers and defensive galleries were constructed on the inside of the palisades and were reached by ladders made of notched logs. For constructing both houses and palisades, small trees were preferred. The desirability of second growth for such operations was yet another reason for villages remaining in areas that had long been inhabited (Heidenreich 1971:153).

A final outdoor activity was the construction of canoes. Huron canoes, like those of the northern Algonkians, were covered with birchbark. The size of canoes varied. Large ones, which were up to twenty feet long and held as many as six men, were built for travel on Georgian Bay and the major rivers, while smaller ones were used where portages were more frequent. The building of canoes naturally required smaller work teams than did the construction of either houses or fortifications.

Men also manufactured tools and weapons. Scrapers, drills, and small triangular arrowheads were chipped from chert, some of which came from the Niagara Escarpment (Heidenreich 1971:228; Kidd 1952:72). Many tools, however, were manufactured from small nodules of chert or quartz from local glacial deposits. The bipolar technique used to work this material is more similar to that used farther north than it is to the bifacial flaking technique found among the Iroquoians to the south. This seems to reflect the similar raw material used by the Huron and the northern Algonkians (W. Fox 1971). Chisels and rectangular axes and adzes were ground mainly out of a greenish-black chlorite schist, but also out of diorite and other hard stones (ibid. 143–46). Harpoons, projectile points, awls, and needles were made of bone, and ladles were carved out of antler (Kidd 1952:73). Spoons, bowls, arrow shafts, snowshoes, sleds, clubs, and suits of armour were fashioned out of wood, using stone tools. Men also wove fishing nets out of the twine that was manufactured by the women. Many of these tasks may have been performed indoors during the winter.

Men also produced, or obtained through trade, a wide range of ornamental objects: tubular beads made out of bird bones; discoidal ones made from the ribs of imported conch shells; and stone beads, some in the shape of animals made from red slate and perhaps also from catlinite. Combs and small amulets in human form were whittled out of bone and occasionally pipes were made from stone.[24] It is uncertain whether men or women made the more common clay pipes. The bowls of these pipes were either round or flaring and some were decorated with human or animal effigies. These pipes are clearly the work of talented potters and it seems likely that a few people may have produced the pipes for an entire village.[25]

In addition to hunting and fishing, clearing land, building houses, and manufacturing tools, the major activities that men engaged in were trading, waging war, and government. These activities frequently brought men into contact with Huron from other villages and with foreigners. Particularly as a result of their trading activities, Huron men were more aware of cultural differences than Huron women were, and were accustomed to tolerating such differences. While women were the guardians of family life and its traditions, men were charged with the responsibility for safety and order, which involved maintaining their village's links with the outside world.

The Bonds of Friendship

Every human being, or group of human beings, whose existence was known to the Huron was considered to be either their enemy or friend. A man's enemies might seek to harm him in a variety of ways, and both material and spiritual assistance was necessary to combat them. Friends were those upon whom a person could rely for help under any circumstances. The principal mark of friendship was the willingness of individuals to share whatever goods they had with one another, freely and without complaint. From an enemy, whether known or unknown, one could expect only hostility, injury, or death.

KINSHIP

The basic unit of friendship and cooperation was the extended family, which lived together in a single longhouse. Although the size of longhouses varied considerably, the average one appears to have sheltered six families, each composed of a man, a woman, and their children.[26] There is little precise information about the manner in which the individual families who lived together were related to one another, but it appears that in most cases the extended family ideally consisted of a woman and her daughters,

or a group of sisters, together with their husbands and children (claims to
the contrary are discussed in chapters 3 and 6). It also seems likely, from
what is known about residence rules in other societies, that even if the
Huron preferred matrilocal residence, available space and eccentric preferences of marriage partners often resulted in this rule being ignored in
practice.

The Huron did not use kinship terms in the same way that Europeans
use them and the failure of French writers to take note of this creates
serious ambiguities in their accounts of Huron life. The Huron word for
mother (*anan* or *ondoüen*) also meant mother's sister. Sisters referred to
each other's children as sons and daughters (*ayein/eyein*), and all their
children called each other brother and sister (*ataquen/etaquen*), although
there were separate terms distinguishing older brothers and sisters from
younger ones.[27] Thus, in an ideal longhouse, all of the women of maternal
age would be called mother, and all the children were equally sons and
daughters to these women and brothers and sisters to each other. While in
no sense obliterating the identity of the nuclear family, the use of these
terms must have encouraged a more far-reaching sense of family unity
than is apparent using our own system of kinship nomenclature.

On the other hand, although brothers do not appear often to have lived
together, in a symmetrical way the Huron used a single term for father and
father's brother (*aystan* or *aihtaha*), and brothers referred to each other's
children as their sons and daughters, while these children all addressed each
other as brother and sister. The terms aunt (*harha*) and uncle (*hoüatinoron*)
were thus reserved for father's sisters and mother's brothers respectively,
and only the children of such aunts and uncles were called cousin (*earassé*).
All blood relatives of the grandparental generation, including great aunts
and great uncles, were referred to as grandfather and grandmother. Likewise, all consanguineal relatives of the second descending generation,
whether or not they were one's lineal descendants, were called grandsons
and granddaughters.

CHILDHOOD

Although children were welcomed in Huron society and were much loved,
especially by the women, the average Huron family was small by comparison with seventeenth-century French ones. They appear to have
averaged about three children. In part, this may have resulted from a high
rate of infant mortality, but births were also less frequent than in Europe

since women abstained from sexual intercourse for two or three years while they breast-fed each child. The births of girls were more rejoiced at than those of boys, because their descendants would be a source of strength to their matrilineage, whereas, once boys had married, the majority of them went to live with their wives' kindred. Yet, in spite of this preference, the Huron clearly wanted many descendants of both sexes to protect and care for them in their old age.

Pregnant women generally worked up to the time of their delivery and tried to be on their feet as soon as possible afterward. A corner of the longhouse was partitioned off for the birth, and the woman either delivered herself or was attended by an elderly female who acted as midwife. Women tried not to cry out for fear of being thought cowardly; apparently, just as a man proved his courage in battle, so a woman proved hers in childbirth. In spite of this stoical approach, a considerable number of women died in the process.[28]

Immediately after birth, a child's ears were pierced and it was given a name, which was probably the possession of an individual lineage or clan and could be given to a child only if it was not already in use. During the day, the child was swaddled in furs and tied to a cradleboard. The latter could be stood on the floor of the longhouse while the mother was working or carried around by her, either suspended against her back by a tumpline or propped up inside her dress so that the child could look forward over her shoulder. These cradleboards were often decorated with small paintings and strings of beads. At night, the child slept naked between its parents.

In view of current ideas about child rearing, it is interesting to reflect that no aspect of Huron behaviour shocked the French more than their refusal to use physical punishment to discipline their children. On general principles, the Huron considered it wrong to coerce or humiliate an individual publicly. To their way of thinking, a child was an individual with his or her own needs and rights rather than something amorphous that must be moulded into shape (Tooker 1964:124 n. 27). The Huron feared that a child who was unduly humiliated, like an adult, might be driven to commit suicide (Thwaites 1896–1901, 14:37; Fenton 1941).

Huron children received no formal training. Girls, however, began at an early age to play games that taught them how to perform household tasks and, in a short time, they were pounding corn and helping their mothers in the fields. As a result, a young girl not only acquired the skills she would need as an adult, but also became accustomed to cooperate with the women of her household, among whom she was likely to spend the rest of her life. When a girl reached puberty, she was not forced to leave the house while she was menstruating, as Algonkian women were, but henceforth she cooked and ate her food separately at such times, using small clay pots made especially for this purpose.

The training of boys was quite different. Boys were not expected to help their mothers or sisters to perform household tasks and, if asked, would refuse to do so. From an early age, however, they were trained to use weapons and spent their time out of doors shooting arrows, spearing fish, and playing ball games. These activities helped to develop a boy's sense of vision, hearing, and smell, as well as his manual dexterity. They also helped to forge strong and enduring links between boys of the same age, which in many ways became more important to them than those of family and kinship. Boys were encouraged to become brave and self-reliant and to endure misfortune with exemplary fortitude. In order to harden their bodies, they frequently went about scantily clad, even in winter. As evidence of self-control, boys were expected to learn to speak deliberately and to the point, and to curb the expression of violent emotions. Talkativeness and public displays of emotion were viewed with withering scorn as being womanly. They also learned to remember and describe places they had seen and to remember speeches, treaties, lists of names, and other information necessary to conduct business without written records.

At about the age of fifteen, at least some young men went on vision quests. They would remain in the forest without food for a fortnight or longer, until a guardian spirit revealed himself to them and foretold their future. It was also at this age that a youth had revealed to him the personal chant (in Iroquois, *adónwe'*), which he would henceforth sing in times of danger.

In the training of both sexes, much emphasis was placed on the value of good behaviour, discretion, and modesty. In their dealings with one another, Huron were expected to be gentle and considerate and to repress feelings of frustration or hostility, which could only properly be vented against a common enemy. Their repression of hostility, and reticence to express feelings in an uninhibited manner, may explain the seemingly contradictory French assertion that the Huron were cheerful and contented, but always a little taciturn.

COURTSHIP AND MARRIAGE

Men and women were expected to be restrained in each other's presence. Kissing and embracing in public were not permitted and indirect evidence suggests that even married couples tended to have sexual intercourse in the corn fields or bush outside the village.[29] In spite of such prudery, the Huron considered premarital sexual relations to be perfectly normal and engaged in them soon after puberty. To the astonishment of the French, and the horror of the more prudish of them, girls were as active as men in initiating these liasons. The French were also surprised by the lack of jealousy that characterized such relationships. Young men were required to recognize the right of a girl to decide which of her lovers she preferred at any one time. Sometimes, a young man and woman developed a longstanding, but informal, sexual relationship, in which case the girl became known as the man's *asqua* or companion. This did not prevent either partner from having sexual relations with other friends.

The Huron did not attach the same importance that we do to the distinction between married and not married. Instead, they encouraged various stages of experimentation and growing commitment that did not culminate in a stable relationship until children were born. The Huron were monogamous and are reported not to have married any relations within three degrees of consanguinity, apparently on either the maternal or the paternal sides of their families (Charlton 1968). In addition, they do not appear to have been allowed to marry any member of their own clan.

While parents could not compel their children to marry, they played an important role as marriage brokers. They provided sons with the present used to propose to a girl and approached her parents to seek their support for the match. If the consent of the girl's parents was not forthcoming, usually because they felt the boy was not a good hunter, fisherman, or warrior, the marriage could not take place. If they gave their consent, the boy offered the girl a beaver robe or a wampum necklace. If she took it, they slept together for several nights. After this, the girl was free to accept or reject her suitor, but in either case she could keep the present he had offered her. If she agreed to marry, her father provided a feast for their two families and friends. This feast served to solemnize the union. Hereafter the woman was recognized as the man's *aténonha* or wife. If a young girl who had many lovers became pregnant, it was normal for each of these men to claim the child was his and for the girl to choose from among them the man she wished to marry.

Any marriage could be terminated at the wish of either partner. Prior to the birth of a child, infidelity and divorce seem to have been common and were matters of little concern. Afterwards, couples separated only infrequently, and if they quarrelled or became estranged, friends and relatives would intervene to save the marriage. In spite of the apparent stability of these mature marriages, even elderly couples continued to take the right of divorce seriously. One of the main reasons that middle-aged men gave for not becoming Roman Catholics was their fear that if their wives left them, they would be unable to remarry.

Perhaps because of the sexual freedom of their youth, physical relations between a husband and wife do not appear to have played a vital role in holding marriages together. Adultery is not recorded as being particularly common, even though husbands spent long periods away from their wives each year.

ADULT AMBITIONS

A Huron wished above all else to be loved and respected by his fellow tribesmen. Men strove to be brave warriors, good hunters, or clever traders and to gain a reputation for giving sound advice when this was asked for. Women sought public approval by looking after their families and guests well. Generosity was an important means of winning the respect of others and, for this reason, whole families worked hard to grow the corn, obtain the meat, and accumulate the presents necessary to entertain their friends and neighbours and to be able to contribute lavishly to communal activities. A Huron's principal aim in acquiring wealth seems to have been to share it with others, social status accruing to those who dispensed their possessions unstintingly.

In particular, the Huron enjoyed giving and attending feasts, and success in any special endeavour was cause for sponsoring a celebration. Visitors were welcomed and a complete stranger had only to sit down in a longhouse in order to be fed and made to feel at home. These attitudes nourished a strong sense of responsibility towards the community. If a house and its contents were destroyed by fire, as happened not infrequently, the rest of the village helped to build a new one and presented its occupants with corn, firewood, and household utensils to repair their losses. Whenever public funds were required, families vied with one another to subscribe to them. In each case, the name of the donor and the value of his present were announced publicly. Gifts were distributed in large numbers at funerals and curing ceremonies, the extent of individual offerings again being public knowledge. A strong overt disapproval of stinginess created feelings of shame, which helped to sustain this tradition of generosity.

These attitudes towards property coloured many aspects of Huron life. There were no markets where people could gather to trade, and even ordinary barter does not appear to have been the most common means of redistributing goods within the confederacy. Instead, economic activities were largely incorporated within a system of social relations in which hospitality, gift giving, and ceremonial exchange played important parts.

The most important cleavage in Huron society, except for that between the sexes, was between young and old men. Most of the important political, economic, and ritual positions were occupied by mature men, who in their youth had proved their ability, above all as successful warriors. By contrast, young men were viewed as untried and, therefore, as unreliable: an evaluation which they much resented and which gave rise to disputes with the council chiefs.

The hereditary chiefs, in particular, had a vested interest in maintaining good relations with neighbouring tribes, both to save the Huron country from the scourge of war and to ensure that trading activities went on unhindered. In order to acquire prestige, youths were anxious to find some pretext for going to war, and often alleged that the peaceful policies of their elders were designed to prevent young men from having a greater share in the direction of village affairs. Sometimes, the desire to fight led young warriors to ignore the orders of their headmen and to attack tribes with whom the Huron were at peace. This generalized conflict was a factor that greatly complicated the foreign relations of the Huron especially since it was common to all the northern Iroquoian-speaking peoples.

DEATH

The Huron seem to have believed that they had at least two souls. One might eventually be reborn, and this explained why some children resembled their dead ancestors. The other remained with the body until the Feast of the Dead was celebrated. Death was a source of great anxiety to the Huron, who viewed it as cutting off necessary personal contact between people who loved one another. The souls of the dead were believed to be angered by this severance of familiar relationships and, for this reason, they were feared, although at the same time their memory was loved and honoured. Simply to mention a dead person's name, without using an honorific to indicate he was dead, was a serious insult to his family. This is one of the reasons why headmen quickly announced an individual's death throughout the village, and why anyone who had the same name changed it for a while. If fire broke out in a village, the first efforts were directed towards protecting the nearby cemetery.

A Huron was expected to die as bravely as he had lived. Men frequently were dressed for burial prior to death and gave an *athataion* or farewell feast, at which they partook of the best food and sang their personal chant to show that they did not fear death. Specific families, probably belonging to different phratries (or groupings of clans), were mutually responsible for burying each other's dead. As soon as someone died, those whose task it was flexed his body in a crouching position and wrapped it in the finest fur robe that his relatives possessed. Friends and relatives converged on the dead person's longhouse, bringing presents of food with them. The women of the village mourned in a stylized fashion, exciting their grief by painfully recalling the names of their own dead kinsmen. The men did not weep, but assumed a melancholy expression and sat with their heads sunk between their knees. A village notable made a speech, in which he praised the dead man and offered consolation to his relatives.

The deceased was usually buried on the third day after he died. A meal was provided at daybreak for those who had come from a distance, after which the body was carried to the cemetery. There, it was placed in a bark coffin, supported on poles eight to ten feet high (plate 5). Then presents, which had been contributed by the mourners, were presented to dry the tears of his relatives and to thank those who had buried him. Sometimes, sticks were thrown from the top of the coffin into a group of young men and women who had gathered on either side of it, and presents were given to the persons who, after a fierce struggle, gained possession of these sticks.

Not everyone was buried in the same manner. Very young children were interred under paths, in the hope that their souls might be reborn in the womb of a woman passing by. The bones of slain captives, and sometimes of other public enemies, such as witches, found their way into the village middens. Anyone who had died a violent death was immediately buried in the ground, and a small mound, with a bark hut over it, was erected on top of his grave.[30] The bodies of those who drowned or froze to death received even more bizarre treatment. These were cut up in the village cemetery and the flesh and entrails were burned, while the skeleton was buried. Failure to do this was believed to anger the sky, or the spirit of the lake, and would result in further accidents and dangerous changes in the weather.

After the funeral, the husband or wife of the deceased remained lying in a dishevelled state in their house for ten days. During this period, the bereaved spouse kept his or her face pressed against the ground and did not speak to anyone, except to say good-day to visitors. This initial period was followed by a year during which remarriage was not supposed to take place,

PLATE 5. *A Huron village cemetery. From Champlain's* Voyages *of 1619.*
A normal scaffold burial and a specialized inhumation are depicted.
The design of the poles is clearly European as are the chimneys on the
longhouse in the background. The two most elaborate hairstyles are copied
from Le Moyne's Florida illustrations. Courtesy McGill University
Libraries.

and widows and widowers neither greased their hair nor went to feasts. Women often blackened their faces and went about poorly clad and unkempt during this period.

GOVERNMENT

Among the Huron, the French encountered a system of government based on principles that were completely contrary to their own. For most seventeenth-century Europeans, authority was delegated from a divinely sanctioned king to his subordinates, who had the power to punish disobedience to his administration with fines, imprisonment, and even death. The Huron system grew out of their family structure and was so constructed that not even the smallest units were called upon to surrender any of their rights. No headman could rely on officially sanctioned power to see that his decisions were enforced; instead, he had to depend on public opinion to support his proposals. In Europe, decisions that were not made in an autocratic fashion were usually decided upon by a majority vote; among the Huron, issues were discussed until a general consensus was reached. No man could be expected to be bound by a decision to which he had not willingly given his consent.

The basic unit of Huron political organization appears to have been the clan segment.[31] A clan segment was made up of all those individuals who were members of matrilineal extended families that inhabited a single community and claimed their descent from a common female ancestor. Although there were many of these clan segments within each tribe of the Huron confederacy, each was named after one of eight creatures: Turtle, Wolf, Bear, Beaver, Deer, Hawk, Porcupine, and Snake. Members of clan segments in different villages that bore the name of the same animal recognized a symbolic affinity for one another, similar to that of kinship. Individuals were not permitted to marry either members of their own clan segment or people whose segments bore the same name. Because clan segments with the same name were found among all the Huron tribes, this symbolic kinship provided a sense of unity that cut across tribal divisions and gave additional stability to the Huron confederacy. Later evidence suggests that these clans were grouped together to form three larger divisions or phratries. These appear to have been mainly of ritual significance, although they too may have been exogamous.[32]

If a village was small, its nucleus might consist of a single clan segment. Large villages were made up of several segments, each of which appears to have occupied its own section of the village. Archaeological evidence indicates that in some villages, different clan segments, or groupings of these segments, lived in separate palisaded enclosures, which nevertheless were located in close proximity to one another.[33] If the Huron had invariably followed a pattern of matrilocal residence, all of the women and children, but none of the married men, would have lived in the part of a village that belonged to their clan segment. We know, however, that political offices were inherited matrilineally; that is, they passed to one of the incumbent's brothers or a sister's son, rather than to his own offspring. In this way, offices were retained within the same clan segment. Since it is unlikely that men would live outside the clan segment whose headmen they were, boys belonging to chiefly lineages were probably sent to live with their mother's brothers and, when they married, their wives came to live with them. Such a pattern of chiefly avunculocal residence may, in part, explain the Huron longhouses inhabited by male members of a lineage and the many women living in their husbands' villages rather than their own that are reported in the *Jesuit Relations*.[34]

Each clan segment appears to have had two headmen. One was a civil leader, who was concerned with maintaining law and order; coordinating group activities, including feasts, dances, and games; and with all dealings with other groups concerning peace. The other was a war chief, who was concerned exclusively with military affairs. The civil headmen were chosen from a particular lineage within each clan segment. Since there was no rule, such as primogeniture, to specify who this individual should be, the personal qualities of the candidates counted for a great deal. These qualities included intelligence, oratorical ability, reputation for generosity, and, above all, performance as a warrior. In order to assure that he would be able to represent the segment effectively, no one was made head of a clan segment without support from the other Huron headmen. These headmen were invited to a magnificent investiture feast to win their approval for the clan segment's nominee. At this feast, they presented the new headman with gifts on behalf of the clan segments, villages, and tribes they represented. They also symbolically drew him from the grave and conferred his predecessor's council name upon him, so that, in effect, the previous office holder was resurrected. In this manner, the names of civil headmen continued from generation to generation in the same lineage. It is unclear what role women played in the election of headmen, but it is possible that, as among the Iroquois, their opinions were important within their own clan segment.

While the mode of election of war chiefs and their role in government is not clearly understood, it appears that these offices were also hereditary in certain lineages. Councils of war were held at the village, tribal, and confederacy levels. These headmen planned military strategy and led warriors in battle; only under unusual circumstances do they appear to have played a significant role in other spheres of Huron life.

All of the internal affairs of a clan segment were managed by its civil headman, in consultation with the heads of the various households and lineages that made up the group. The murder of one member of a clan segment by another was a strictly internal matter, and any attempt by outsiders to interfere in the settlement of such a case would have been deeply resented. If a dispute between clan segments living in the same village became too severe, one of the segments might split off and found a separate village of its own, just as, contrariwise, if a suitable opportunity arose, friendly segments might join together to establish a single large village. The physical capacity to opt out of larger units allowed each clan segment to retain a maximum amount of autonomy.

The village, whether made up of one or more segments, constituted a second important unit of Huron society (Fenton 1951). The daily face-to-face interaction of villagers generated a concern for one another that did not exist at higher levels of Huron political organization. Villagers aided one another to build houses, helped those in distress, participated in many feasts and collective rituals, and shared in the common defence of the village. In large villages, intermarriage between clan segments helped to forge strong bonds of community solidarity.

The headmen for each village were the civil leaders of the clan segments. Because they represented clan segments, they could not be removed from office except by their own clansmen, nor could they be compelled against their will to accept any decision arrived at by other headmen. Though all were equal in this sense, one of the headmen appears to have been recognized as spokesman for the entire village. It is uncertain whether the clan segments were ranked in order of importance, so that the head of the senior clan automatically became the principal headman of the village, or if the prestige of individual headmen tended to fluctuate according to the personalities involved.

The village council appears to have met daily in the house of the principal headman, which was larger than the rest so that it could serve various community functions. The civil headmen of each of the clan segments, as well as the "Old Men" of the village, attended these meetings. While the title of the latter suggests that they consisted of all the older men in the village, it was probably conferred only on those who, in their mature years, had acquired sufficient reputation that their advice was considered to be of value. These men appear to have had considerable influence in village councils.

Often these councils had no specific business to discuss and the meeting was more like that of a social club. Nevertheless, decisions were made that influenced many aspects of village life. The council arranged public feasts, dances, and lacrosse matches, and decided for whom special curing rites requiring village participation would be performed. The council also undertook to see that no one was in need and coordinated communal projects, such as constructing palisades and relocating the village. All legal disputes arising between members of the different clan segments that lived in the village were adjudicated by the council. Any public announcements resulting from its deliberations were made by the principal headman or his deputy, who was a close relative and who frequently accompanied him and made announcements in his name. The political organization of both the clan segments and the village councils shows clearly that, while no Huron had the legal power to coerce another, individuals and lineages were far from equal in social prestige. The dichotomy between egalitarian ideals and the tendencies towards accumulating power and prestige that were part of Huron society was perennially a source of concern to the Huron.

The councils that governed each of the four Huron tribes appear to have been made up of all the civil headmen from each of the tribal villages; although in the case of the Tahontaenrat, who had only one village, village and tribal government were probably identical. Each tribe recognized one of the members of this council as its principal headman and treaties were made in his name. It was apparently his permission that foreign groups had to obtain if they wished to cross tribal territory. The name of the principal headman of the Arendarhonon was Atironta. Endahiaconc, the Attigneenongnahac leader, was also the leading headman of their main village, Teanaostaiaé. Anenkhiondic, who lived at Ossossané, was said to be head of the Attignawantan, but among the part of the tribe that lived in the Penetanguishene Peninsula a man named Auoindaon, and later Aenons, appears to have claimed similar honours.[35] There seems to have been a political cleavage between the northern and southern Attignawantan, of which the rival claims of these two chiefs were probably a reflection.

In spite of the importance that the French and the Algonkians attached to the Huron tribal headmen, their position was not analogous to that of a European head of state. The members of a tribe shared a common territory and common traditions, and were even willing to accept that because of the size of the tribal unit or for historical reasons, the leader of one of their clan segments should have the right to represent all of them on ceremonial occasions. This did not, however, give any headman the right to interfere in the internal business of any clan segment but his own. The powers of the tribal head were further limited because other members of the council had hereditary responsibilities that were complementary, rather than subordinate, to his own. For example, one of the Attignawantan headmen was responsible for dealing with the tribes the Huron visited by water along the shores of Lake Huron, and messages to these tribes were sent in his name. Presumably, these duties were imagined to have been entrusted to particular headmen when the tribal government was first established.[36]

It appears that any headman could call a meeting about a matter falling within his sphere of concern. Most meetings, however, were called by the tribal headman and met in his village which, in this sense only, was a tribal capital. Meetings were held at any time of the year. If the matter was particularly important, old men were sent as messengers to summon the headmen, as their word carried more weight than did that of younger men. One of the duties of the tribal councils must have been to help settle disputes between people living in different villages, particularly if their clan segments or village councils were unable to resolve them. The tribal councils also discussed matters of interest to the confederacy as a whole, with the aim of formulating proposals that would best serve their respective interests. For various reasons, including their differing geographical location, the views of the four tribes on matters of foreign policy often differed radically from one another.

Very little is known about the composition of the confederacy council, but its membership appears to have consisted of most, if not all, of the civil headmen who sat on the various tribal councils. The confederacy leaders thus represented most of the clan segments in the Huron country. If a similar system prevailed in modern Canadian politics, a single man would simultaneously serve as mayor of Toronto, prime minister of Ontario, and a senior ranking member of the federal cabinet.

The structure of the confederacy council must have been altered by the addition of the Arendarhonon tribe about 1590 and the Tahontaenrat as late as 1610. The Attignawantan and Attigneenongnahac were accorded senior status for being the founding members of the confederacy, and the Attignawantan, because of their size, occupied half the seats on the council. It is possible that the Tahontaenrat were not officially seated on the council even in the late 1630s, although they may have been allowed to attend meetings.[37] The admission of the Arendarhonon shows, however, that the Huron were not as inflexible as the Iroquois were later, when they refused to disrupt the traditional roster of council chiefs in order fully to integrate the Tuscarora into their confederacy (Hale 1963:79).

While special meetings were called in times of emergency, the main meeting of the confederacy council appears to have been each spring and to have lasted several weeks. On this occasion, new headmen were installed, there was much singing and dancing, and war feasts were held prior to raids being launched against enemy tribes. The main function of these meetings seems to have been to strengthen the confederacy by bringing together the headmen from all the Huron villages and giving them an opportunity to reaffirm old friendships and discuss topics of mutual interest. The main problems confronting the confederacy as a whole were to prevent disputes between members of different tribes from disrupting its unity, to maintain friendly relations with tribes with whom the Huron traded, and, where possible, to try to coordinate dealings with enemy tribes, in particular the Iroquois.

At meetings of the confederacy council the Attignawantan sat on one side of the longhouse, the remaining tribes on the other. The headman who presided over these meetings was an Attignawantan. Meetings began with speeches of welcome and thanksgiving and, after the reason for the meeting was formally announced, the headmen from each tribe and village were asked their opinions in turn. After consulting with his advisors and headmen from the same tribe, each would state his opinion slowly and distinctly, speaking in a special ceremonial style that was full of metaphors, circumlocutions, and other rhetorical devices that were uncommon in everyday speech. Every one listened attentively, politeness and good humour being considered essential. Violent outbursts were rare and, to the surprise of European visitors, were strongly disapproved of, even if the issue was a hotly debated one. Discussion often continued late into the night, until a satisfactory consensus had been reached.

The confederacy, tribal, and village councils all had public funds, which they used to carry on diplomacy, reward friends in other tribes, and make reparations payments. In part, these funds were maintained from gifts the councils received through diplomatic channels or in return for favours they had granted. When more was required, it was a matter of pride for Huron families to donate what was needed.

LAW

The Huron recognized four major categories of crime: murder and its lesser equivalents wounding and injury, theft, witchcraft, and treason.[38] In theory, murder placed an absolute obligation upon the kinsmen of the dead man to seek revenge by clamouring for the slaying of either the murderer or someone closely related to him. The obligation to do this fell particularly upon the clansmen of a murdered person, that is, upon his sisters, mother's brothers, and sisters' sons. The responsibility of a clan segment to defend its members did not cease when a member was married and living elsewhere. It was also the duty of clansmen to protect a man against death and injury, even when this was in retribution for his own deeds. Depending on the degree of relationship between the murderer and the murdered man, a killing might give rise to a prolonged blood feud between the clan segments, villages, tribes, or even confederacies to which they belonged. Thus, blood feuds varied in scale from family quarrels to major wars. The Huron were well aware that no tribal organization and no confederacy could survive if internal blood feuds went unchecked. One of the basic functions of the confederacy was to eliminate such feuds among its members; indeed, between Huron, they were regarded as a more reprehensible crime than murder itself.

In so doing, however, no effort was made to interfere with the right of a murderer's clansmen to defend him. To have done so would have constituted unwarranted interference with the affairs of the clan segments that made up the confederacy. Instead, it was agreed that within the confederacy, blood feuds would be settled by the payment of reparations from the social group to which the murderer belonged to that of his victim. Both the payment of these reparations and the presents received were shared, to some degree, by all the members of the groups involved. Only if after prolonged discussion, the clansmen of the murderer refused to pay compensation did the relatives of the murdered man have the right to take up arms against them.

The amount of compensation varied according to the rank and sex of the murdered person. If a chief or "Old Man" was slain, the compensation was greater than for someone of lesser importance, and the compensation for a woman was greater than that for a man. The average compensation for a man was about thirty presents and for a woman forty; each present having the approximate value of a beaver robe. After the amount of compensation was determined, a bundle of sticks, indicating the number of presents that were required, was divided among the murderer's tribe, village, or clan segment. It does not appear that his immediate family was asked to provide more presents than were other members; clansmen and fellow villagers often vied with one another to show their public spiritedness in helping the murderer's family. These gifts were presented to the victim's relatives in a formal ceremony with great expressions of condolence. At the end of the ceremony, the relatives of the dead man gave some small presents to the murderer's kinsmen to indicate that they were forgiven and the matter was closed.

The personal treatment that a murderer received was a matter for his clan segment and lineage to decide. Normally, it took the form of verbal rebukes, rather than physical punishment. Nevertheless, since all members of a group stood to lose through the misbehaviour of any one member, it was in their interest to bring pressure to bear upon a murderer to make sure that he did not kill again. The guilty person knew, moreover, that if he misbehaved repeatedly, he would gradually alienate his clansmen and lose their support. By making tribes, villages, and especially clan segments responsible for the behaviour of their members, the Huron were able to secure order without resorting to capital punishment or interfering with the traditional rights of the various groups that made up their confederacy.

Wounding was a less serious offence than murder and was compensated by presents that varied according to the seriousness of the injury and the status of the person who had been attacked.

The French were frequently critical of the Huron for the lenient attitude they took towards thieves. The simplicity and relative impermanence of Huron possessions, and the sharing of goods and housing among extended families, probably made ownership intrinsically a matter of less concern to them than it was to Europeans (Herman 1956; Stites 1905). More importantly, however, because of the semi-public nature of Huron dwellings and the lack of any formal policing in their villages, there was little that could be done to protect movable possessions against theft. The main concern of the Huron was therefore to minimize the disruptive consequences of quarrels that might arise from such actions.

This was done by defining theft very narrowly, as the taking of goods forcibly from an individual or from inside a longhouse without permission. In theory, a person was entitled to carry off anything he found lying about unattended. In order to protect their valuables, both from fire and thieves, the Huron either carried them around with them or hid them in caches dug into the soil beneath their houses. The Huron did not fine or penalize a thief, nor did they permit a man from whom goods had been stolen to reclaim them without first inquiring how someone else had come to possess them. A refusal to answer constituted an admission of guilt. If a man could prove who had robbed him, he and his relatives were socially sanctioned to go to the thief's longhouse and carry off everything on which they could lay their hands. Hence, relatives of a person who had stolen very little might find themselves bruised and despoiled. Again, pressure was put on kin groups to enforce good behaviour among their members.

TRADE

So far, we have been examining Huron efforts to curb violence and maintain amicable relations within their own society. Basic to such activities was a concern for a general sort of reciprocity, in which a willingness to redistribute possessions played an important role. A rough kind of reciprocity can also be seen in the hurly-burly of dealing with theft, and even a serious crime, such as murder, could be atoned for with gifts, if they were given in a spirit of contrition and with an evident desire for reconciliation. A murderer might kill in a fit of jealousy or anger, but his crime was not seen as alienating him from his society.

Relations of friendship and material reciprocity were extended beyond the Huron confederacy in the form of trading arrangements. In the historic period, trade was a source not only of luxury goods but of meat and skins which were vital to a population that had outstripped the resources of its nearby hunting territory. Important as these goods were, however, foreign trade was not merely an economic activity. It was embedded in a network of social relations that were, fundamentally, extensions of the friendly relationships that existed within the Huron confederacy.

The Huron traded with both the other Iroquoian tribes of southern Ontario and the Algonkian-speaking peoples who lived to the north of them; however, the nature of the trade was completely different. Almost all of the goods imported from the south were luxury items. One of the most important imports was tobacco, which grew better in the warmer territories of the Tionnontaté and Neutral than it did in the Huron country. From the Neutral country came tobacco and black squirrel skins, which the Huron made into cloaks that were highly prized by themselves and the Algonkians to the north. From the same area originated the so-called "Erie stones," which Gendron (1868:8) informs us the Neutral traded with other tribes. Gendron was later to take some of these stones, which were probably a naturally occurring form of calcium carbonate, back to France, to become the basis of his famous cancer cure (Jury and Jury 1954:106–7). In addition to its own products, the Neutral country was a source of goods from farther south. These included racoon skin robes, which came from the Erie country,[39] wampum beads, which seem to have originated among the Susquehannock, and conch and other shells, which ultimately came from the Gulf of Mexico and the eastern seaboard of the United States.[40] Gourds, which were used to store oil, also appear to have come from a considerable distance to the south.[41] Occasionally, Huron warriors would visit the Susquehannock in order to consolidate plans to wage war against the Iroquois and to trade with them directly.

A small amount of what the Huron obtained from the north could also be classified as luxury goods. These included charms, clothing, camping equipment, buffalo robes, which came from the west by way of Sault Sainte Marie, and native copper,[42] which was found around the shores of Lake Superior. In return, the Algonkians received tobacco and a few exotic luxuries, such as wampum. The bulk of the trade, however, was in more essential items. The northern hunters were anxious to obtain nets and rope, but, above all, the Huron country was a source of cornmeal, which helped to sustain them over the hard winters. Groups of Nipissing and Petite Nation Algonkin passed each winter in the Huron country, in encampments close to the Huron villages. In the middle of autumn, these groups began to move south, bringing with them the furs they had trapped or purchased from other tribes and catching and drying fish along the way. Both commodities were used to buy corn, tobacco, and nets from the Huron. The Petite Nation appears to have been on particularly good terms with the Arendarhonon and came each winter to live near the village of Cahiagué. The Nipissing wintered in the Wye Valley, among the Ataronchronon or Attignawantan. Each summer, groups of Huron men travelled north to trade for furs. These journeys may have taken some of them as far afield as Lakes Michigan and Superior, and into the central part of Quebec.[43] In winter, the Huron crossed the ice of Georgian Bay to trade cornmeal and nets for dried fish among the neighbouring bands.

In order to sustain this trade, Huron women planted considerably more corn than was required to feed their own families. The trade was highly advantageous to the Huron because it provided them with additional protein, in the form of dried fish, and with skins, which were badly needed for clothing. Because of the size of the Huron population, game in nearby areas was sorely depleted. It therefore seems unlikely that, without this trade, as large a population could have lived in the Huron country for any length of time as was found there in the early historic period (Trigger 1962*a*; 1963*b*).

Because the Huron valued their trade and did not wish it to be disrupted, they were careful to cultivate good relations with their northern trading partners. In so doing, they were conforming to well-established conventions that were tacitly understood and accepted by all the tribes in the region.

Trade was embedded in a network of social relations and the exchange of goods was carried out largely in the form of reciprocal gift-giving. Such reciprocity was considered an integral part of any friendly interaction, and ties between individual trading partners were modelled on those between relatives. Visits to foreign tribes for purposes of trade were seen as hazardous adventures that had to be hedged about with many formal courtesies. Before entering a village, all the members of an expedition would paint themselves and put on their best ornaments. Feasts, speech-making, and formal exchanges of gifts between headmen normally went on for several days, both before and after the more commercial trading.

The French could not understand why, although the Huron were clearly skilful in collecting furs, they scorned to haggle over the price of individual items and became annoyed when Europeans tried to do so. The Huron understood the operation of a market economy in the sense that they were aware of the relationship between the scarcity of an item and the price that could be obtained for it; nevertheless, they refused to express a profit motive openly. To haggle about the price of goods was interpreted as a lack of friendship. The success of the Huron as traders depended largely on their skill in maintaining good relations with other tribes, particularly with the northern peoples, who had cultures different from their own. All trading partners were expected to conform to the hospitality, gift-giving, and careful observation of various formalities that made up the conventions of this trade.

Many Huron appear to have had trading partners among each of the tribes they visited (Trigger 1960:23). These were the persons with whom they stayed and exchanged goods. They often referred to these partners as their kinsmen and were probably linked to them through formal bonds of adoption. Some partners seem to have exchanged children as evidence of trust and goodwill and also to provide hostages. Occasionally, Algonkians who came to the Huron country as exchanges married Huron and remained there.

There was always the danger that if a Huron and someone from a group with whom the Huron traded got into a fight and one of them were killed, the demand for blood revenge would lead to war. Because of the disastrous effect this would have on trade, the Huron were anxious to settle such disputes as quickly as possible. They were willing to pay much more to compensate for a murder of this sort than for the murder of one Huron by another. The chief factor which made the settlement of this sort of murder more difficult than the settlement of ones within the confederacy was the problem of finding a mediator who was acceptable to both sides.

Among the Huron themselves, trade was governed by elaborate rules. The rights to a particular route were said to belong to the family of the man who had discovered it. No other Huron was supposed to trade along such a route without first receiving permission from the head of the family that had legal title to it, and such permission was normally granted only in return for valuable presents. If a man engaged in trade illegally, the master of the route and his followers had the right to seize him and despoil him of his goods as he returned home. In keeping with the desire to minimize the effects of theft, however, once such a man had returned safely to his village, all they could do was to complain about his behaviour.

Although most trading seems to have been done by ordinary men in the prime of life, all of the major trade routes were under the control of leading headmen. Such control must have provided these headmen with an important means of acquiring wealth, which in turn could be used to validate their high status within their tribes. It appears that whoever discovered a new trade route, effective control of it soon passed into the hands of the headman of his clan segment or of an even more influential chief within his tribe. Further control was exercised over this trade by the headmen limiting the number of young men from each village who went out each year to trade.

Finally, in spite of the friendly relations that the Huron strove to maintain with the Algonkians, it is clear that their attitude towards these northern hunters was ambivalent. The uncertainty of their way of life was clearly recognized and they were treated in a condescending manner. When they attended Algonkian feasts, the Huron brought their own food with them and, while Huron men married Algonkian women who came to live in the Huron country, no Huron woman would consent to go and live among the Algonkians.[44] Moreover, in keeping with the key role they played in the trading networks of the region, the Huron did not bother to learn the languages of the northern tribes, but rather expected these peoples to learn theirs (Wrong 1939:86). Foreigners who experienced difficulty in learning to speak Huron were regarded as lacking in intelligence. In the historic period, Huron served as a *lingua franca*, not only in the trade that went on around the shores of Lake Huron, but in trade as far east as the Ottawa Valley and possibly as far west as the Winnebago, a Siouan-speaking group who lived on the shores of Green Bay, Wisconsin.

Enemies

We have already seen that among themselves and in their dealings with their allies, friendliness and reciprocity were important elements of Huron life. It is not to be imagined, however, that the opposite of these qualities was not important also. Although the Huron appeared to be open and friendly in their daily life, they were scarcely less afraid of treachery amongst their own people than they were of foreign enemies. Both kinds of hostile forces were seen as negations of the cooperative reciprocity which alone constituted the basis of trust and confidence among them.

WITCHCRAFT AND TREASON

The most dangerous of the enemies that the Huron believed existed within their own society were witches. Witches were individuals of either sex who used magic to bring death and sickness to people they disliked. Unlike ordinary homicide, witchcraft was an indication that a man or woman was a public enemy in much the same way that groups such as the Iroquois were. Such behaviour was held to be so disgusting and immoral that it put the witch beyond any claim of protection, even from his closest relatives. In theory, anyone had the right to slay a proven witch and the witch's relatives were not permitted to seek compensation or blood revenge for such killings.

Witches were believed to harm people by supernaturally causing charms to enter their bodies. These charms could be any foreign object, such as a tuft of hair, nail parings, an animal's claw, a piece of leather, a feather, or grains of sand. In order to make the object enter a body, it had to be rubbed with the flesh of an *angont*, or mythical serpent that lived under the ground or in the water and which was familiar to witches.

The principal motivation for practising witchcraft was believed to be jealousy. Thus, if anyone had been outstandingly successful in hunting or trading, or if a family's harvest had been particularly abundant, they were careful to share their good fortune with others in order to avoid trouble. Yet, since the slightest offence might arouse a witch's resentment, even the most generous person was in danger.

The Huron had shamans called *aretsan* who specialized in treating diseases caused by witchcraft. These specialists were consulted if any illness did not immediately show signs of responding to natural treatment. Proof of witchcraft could be obtained if the *aretsan* was able to remove one or more charms, by giving the patient an emetic, sucking the charm from his body, or extracting it with the point of a knife without leaving an incision. Yet, a sick man's dream, a rumour, or merely being seen alone in the woods without reason was enough to incite accusations of witchcraft against certain people. Especially in times of crisis, when tensions ran high or epidemics threatened the village, the fear of witchcraft reached dangerous levels. At such times, whole families who felt threatened by witches might move from one village to another. Those who were suspected of witchcraft were in danger of falling victims to mob violence.

It is clear that almost all accusations of witchcraft resulted from violations of Huron norms concerning cooperation and reciprocity. Overtly antisocial behaviour, such as speaking harshly to people, refusing to give feasts or to be generous with one's neighbours, or simply having an unusual desire for privacy, were enough to arouse suspicion. Likewise, repeated irresponsible actions left individuals open to charges of witchcraft. For the most part, these suspicions led only to veiled threats and accusations, meant to frighten the suspected witch and make him conform to social norms.

On the other hand, no one, even a man who believed that his relative had been killed by witchcraft, would dare to slay a suspected witch unless he was certain that public opinion would sanction his action and compel the kinsmen of the murdered man to accept the verdict. Most, if not all, of the cold-blooded slayings of witches appear to have been sanctioned by headmen or war chiefs, who often judged the victims at secret council meetings before appointing an executioner to slay them without warning. Sometimes, an accused witch was arraigned before such a meeting and tortured, in the hope that names of accomplices would be revealed. On rare occasions, those found guilty were slain in public as a prisoner of war might be.

The second crime that the Huron considered worthy of death was treason. Traitors were men who sought to betray the whole country to its enemies, either in the hope of material reward or out of generalized hostility. It is doubtful that the Huron regarded the latter as different from witchcraft. Fear of information being passed to the enemy was prevalent among the Huron and helped to strengthen everyone's loyalty in the face of potential danger. Those suspected of having dealings with the enemy were watched closely and, if a man was believed to be endangering the security of the confederacy, the headmen would give orders for him to be slain. Such killings were made to look like the work of enemy raiders. The headmen investigated all cases of violent deaths, hence were able to declare that no further inquiry into the nature of a particular case was necessary.

Since headmen could legitimize all slayings of witches and traitors, they were in a position to coerce individuals whose behaviour was socially disruptive, or who too greatly challenged their authority. They could even eliminate these people, if necessary. Because such action required the consent of the head of the clan segment to which their intended victim belonged, these headmen were likely to act only if they were convinced that the safety of village or tribe required it. Yet the fact that headmen were able to perceive such common interests, indicates that, at least to a limited degree, they saw themselves as a ruling group whose interests transcended more basic loyalties to their kinship groupings (Trigger 1963a).

Thus witchcraft and fear of treason were more than strong forces promoting a sense of community responsibility and assuring the realization of the communal ideals of Huron society. They also served as the basis of a *de facto* authority that was needed to manage Huron society, but which the emphasis on the dignity and rights of individuals and kin groups made overtly unacceptable to all concerned.

WAR

Foreign tribes with whom the Huron did not have bonds of trade and reciprocity were automatically not to be trusted. This mistrust generated hostility which frequently led to open conflict. Similar attitudes prevailed among the other northern Iroquoian tribes, who were all deeply influenced by the warfare that prevailed among them (Witthoft 1959; Trigger 1967; 1969a:42–53).

The French who visited the Huron country were accustomed to wars that were fought for territorial gain or commercial advantage, or because of religious differences. To their surprise, none of these motives played an important role in traditional Iroquoian warfare. The major reason that the Huron gave for waging war was to avenge the injuries that warriors from other tribes had inflicted upon them (Du Creux 1951–52:102–3; Thwaites 1896–1901, 17:65). Thus, if a Huron were slain, or was believed to have been slain, by Iroquois raiders, or was killed in battle against the Iroquois, his relatives clamoured for revenge. This was obtained only when the Huron had killed one or more Iroquois in retaliation. Since neither side regarded such killings as anything but fresh injuries, the result was a self-perpetuating cycle of violence that was broken only at irregular intervals so that exchanges of prisoners might be arranged.

War was also the principal means by which young men acquired the personal prestige that assured them the respect of their elders and an influential voice in the affairs of their village in later life. A reputation for skill and bravery in war gave even a candidate for a civil chieftainship a better chance of obtaining this office. Because of this, young men clamoured for war, and often committed acts of violence which disturbed the fragile peace treaties that the tribal headmen had concluded with their traditional enemies. Only within confederacies, and where strong trading alliances existed, could public opinion hold the young men in check and prevent hostilities from arising in response to an emotional cry for blood revenge.

Among the Huron, every man was a warrior and the virtues of man and warrior were identical. Boys were trained in the use of weapons from an early age and were encouraged to be brave, self-reliant, and stoical. Men sought every opportunity to test their courage; when no danger was present, some would hold burning sticks against their bodies until flesh was burned. In this way they reassured themselves that they still retained the courage necessary to fight the enemy.

The Huron and their neighbours did not normally wage war against each other from late autumn through early spring, when leaves were off the trees and it was hard to find cover. During the rest of the year the Huron were on the alert for enemy raiders and rumours about enemy plans circulated from village to village. The larger villages, especially those located on the exposed southern and eastern flanks of the Huron country, were protected by palisades and the Huron headmen endeavored to keep enough warriors at home during the summer to defend these villages. The Huron headmen also sought to cultivate friends among other tribes, who would provide them with advanced warning of an attack. These informers might be resident foreigners or headmen who had a personal interest in friendly relations with the Huron. Dealings with such men made the Huron fearful of similar traitors in their own midst. War chiefs were circumspect about their plans and visitors who were not trusted had to live in specially assigned houses and were not allowed to travel about unattended.

Military campaigns were organized by war chiefs in response to requests from families who had lost members to the enemy. These chiefs went from village to village explaining their plans, distributing presents to gain support for their expedition, and inciting the young men to join them. When support was won at the village level, a general council was held to confirm the plan. This was followed by a war feast, at the end of which, amidst much singing and dancing, the various war parties left to invade enemy territory.

Every warrior wore a kind of armour made of pieces of wood laced together with cords (plate 6). This armour covered his back, legs, and other parts of his body and was proof against stone-tipped arrows. Warriors also carried shields, some of which were made of cedar bark and covered the whole body, as well as clubs, and a bow and arrows. The same weapons were used in war as were used for hunting. In addition, Huron warriors wore red circlets of moosehair around their foreheads, as well as their finest shell necklaces and other ornaments. This finery emphasized the ritual nature of war. For food, each warrior carried a bag of roasted cornmeal that could be eaten without bothering to cook it or even to soak it in water. This concentrated food would last a man from six to eight weeks, after which he had to forage.

The Huron waged various kinds of campaigns. Occasionally, in retaliation for some serious injury, a band of several hundred warriors would lay siege to an enemy village. Fires were lighted against the palisade, in order to compel the enemy warriors to come out and defend the settlement. When they emerged, both sides lined up and fought a pitched battle, which nevertheless ended when a few deaths or injuries were suffered on either side. After a few of the enemy had been killed or taken prisoner, the Huron would retreat before enemy reinforcements arrived from neighbouring villages.

Usually, however, Huron war parties split into groups of five or six men each, who hid in the fields or along paths in the forest in hopes of surprising a few Iroquois. Sometimes, daring individuals stole into enemy houses at night and tried to kill some of the sleeping inhabitants before making their escape. Such acts won Huron warriors the respect of their comrades.

Nothing, however, was as desirable as to be credited with the capture of an enemy warrior. Women and children who were captured were usually tortured and killed on the spot and their heads or scalps kept as trophies. The scalps were tanned and, in time of war, were fastened onto poles and set upon the walls of villages to frighten attackers. The same fate might befall able-bodied men, if too many were captured or their presence otherwise endangered their captors' security. Usually, however, captured warriors became the victims of a sadistic game, in which hopes of escape or reprieve were balanced off against physical pain and the greater likelihood of a savage, if glorious death. In their treatment of such prisoners the Huron revealed a sinister aspect of the psychological finesse which was an important facet of their culture.

As soon as the Huron had an enemy in their power they tore out his fingernails, cut or bit off his fingers, and slit his neck and shoulders with a

PLATE 6. *Huron warrior wearing slat armour. From Champlain's*
Voyages *of 1619. While the slat armour accords with Champlain's text,
the solar ornament on the man's helmet is a European touch frequently
applied to representations of Latin American Indians. For a later,
stylistically different engraving of this picture, see Johan de Laet,*
L'histoire du Nouveau Monde, *1640, reproduced in W. P. Cumming, et al.,*
The Discovery of North America *(London, 1971), p. 272. Courtesy
McGill University Libraries.*

knife. These injuries made it difficult for him to escape from the leather thong with which his arms were then bound. At the same time, the Huron reminded him of the cruelties he and his people had practised on them, saying that he must now be prepared to suffer likewise. They also made him sing his personal chant, which prisoners often continued to sing all the way to the Huron country.

The capture of an enemy enhanced the reputation of a Huron warrior, but did not give him control over the fate of his prisoner. This was decided by the war chief who had organized the expedition. When a number of prisoners were captured, they were usually divided among the tribes whose warriors had participated in the expedition. As these prisoners passed through each village, they were stripped, bound hand and foot, and slowly led between two lines of Huron, who tortured them with clubs, thorns, knives, and firebrands, but were careful not to kill them. Afterwards, the tribal council assigned them to individual families who had lost members to the enemy. In this way, the lost relative was ostensibly replaced and the tears of those who had been bereaved were publicly dried. Since the number of prisoners who were taken was usually smaller than the number of Huron slain by the enemy, only the most important families were presented with such captives.

Every prisoner was adopted by the family to whom he had been given. Almost invariably, enemy women and children were integrated into these families and lived the rest of their lives with them, unless an exchange of prisoners was arranged as part of a peace treaty. If the appearance, personality, or skills of an adult male were pleasing to his adoptive family, they might decide to spare his life. So long as he behaved well, he would be treated kindly and might be given the rank and titles of the dead man he replaced. Like the women and children, he would gradually become a loyal member of his new family and in time he might go to war against his own people. This transformation was psychologically motivated by the captive's knowledge that the majority of male prisoners were condemned by their adoptive parents to death by torture. This was the most satisfying revenge that a family could take for the loss of one of its own members.

Even when an adoptive family condemned a prisoner to die, they continued to treat him with courtesy and an outward show of affection, and for a time provided him with every physical comfort. By treating the prisoner as the incarnation of their murdered relative, the family was able to work up greater enthusiasm to avenge the latter's death. Before his final torment, a farewell feast was given, similar to that celebrated by a Huron who knew himself to be on the point of death. Everyone was welcome to attend this feast and the prisoner was expected to show his courage by inviting those present to amuse themselves killing him. It was also his duty to sing and dance with the Huron at this time. Now, and throughout the gruesome ordeal that followed a prisoner was expected to display the primary virtues of a warrior: courage and the ability to suffer without complaining. If the Huron could not make a prisoner weep and plead for mercy, this was believed to indicate misfortune for them in future wars.

PRISONER SACRIFICE

The torturing of a prisoner took place inside the longhouse of the village's principal war chief.[45] It began in the evening and, while it might last one or several days, it was necessary for the prisoner to die in the open air at sunrise, since the sun was the special witness of the fate of warriors. In addition to being an act of blood revenge, the prisoner's death was viewed as a sacrifice to the sun. The sacred nature of what was about to happen was emphasized by the orders of the headmen that no one in the village should engage in sexual intercourse that night and that, while torturing the prisoner, everyone should behave in an orderly and restrained fashion and should burn only his legs at the beginning. It was also announced to what headmen the main parts of his body would be given after he was dead.

At this point, the prisoner was stripped of whatever clothes he still wore and his hands were bound together. He was then compelled to make his way from one end of the longhouse to the other, while the crowd thrust flaming sticks at him. To increase his torment, the Huron also tried to force him to run through the hearths that were ablaze down the centre of the building. At the ends of the cabin he was made to rest on beds of hot ashes, while the bones of his hands were broken, burning sticks were stuck through his ears, and his wrists were burned or cut through by wrapping cords around them and pulling these cords back and forth as fast as possible. Later, fire was applied to the prisoner's genitals and, while the sources are reticent on this point, it appears that some of the torture had strongly sexual connotations (Thwaites 1896–1901, 13:77; 17:65; Du Creux 1951–52:258). Occasionally, while making his way through the longhouse, a prisoner was able to scatter hot ashes from a hearth and set fire to the building. In the resulting confusion, he had a very slim chance of escaping; the dim hope of which must have sustained him up to this point. As the prisoner's strength failed him, however, it became necessary to carry him through the longhouse. At this point, the headmen ordered the people to stop torturing him, so that he would not die before sunrise. The prisoner was then placed on a mat and allowed to rest, while many people left for a breath of fresh air.

When the prisoner began to revive, he was forced to sing again and his torture was resumed. Hitherto, the aim had been to make him suffer, but not to endanger his life. To that end, punishment had been restricted to the extremities of his body. Now, when he could no longer run about, his tormentors, who were mainly young people, attacked the rest of his body. They made deep cuts into his arms, legs, thighs, and other fleshy parts and quenched the flow of blood by thrusting glowing brands into the wounds. To the horror and disgust of the French, women as well as men eagerly participated in these actions. Each tormentor patiently waited his turn, and showed no sign of anger or lack of self-control while he had the prisoner in his power. Frequently, they addressed him with mock benevolence. One youth would say he was caulking a canoe as a present for the prisoner, while in reality he was pouring burning pitch over the man's body. Others would assert that the prisoner was cold and proceed to warm him by roasting his flesh. From time to time, the Huron gave him something to eat or poured a little water into his mouth so he would last until morning. At the same time, they redoubled their efforts to make him cry out as much as possible.

On the morning the prisoner was to die, fires were lighted around a scaffold six or seven feet high that had been erected in a field outside the village.[46] The prisoner was made to mount the scaffold and was loosely tied to the branch of a tree that passed overhead. In this way, the crowd could watch his contortions. Once the prisoner was in position, the Huron continued to burn his body, but also began to attack his vital organs. He was made to eat pieces of his own flesh and brands were thrust into his throat, eyes, and rectum. Later, he was scalped and burning pitch was poured over his head. When it was clear he was about to die, his head was either cut off or smashed open, while, at the same time, the Huron cut out his heart and chopped off his hands and feet. They eviscerated his corpse and gave the children of the village bits of his intestines to hang on the ends of sticks and carry through the village as symbols of victory.

If the prisoner had been a brave man, his heart was cooked and eaten by the young warriors, who believed that they would acquire his courage in this manner. Others made cuts in their necks and let the prisoner's blood run into them to avoid being surprised by the enemy. Afterwards, the prisoner's body was cut up to be cooked and eaten. Some Huron ate it with horror, while others relished the taste of human flesh, but to all it was an act of religious significance. After sunset on the day the prisoner was killed, everyone made loud noises to drive his spirit from the village.

The Individual and Society

RELIGION

The Europeans who sought to convert the Huron found themselves combating a religion whose structure was completely different from their own. One indication of this was the absence in the indigenous culture of any office corresponding to that of priest. Like the other native peoples of Ontario and the northeastern United States, the Huron lacked specialists who performed regular religious ceremonies on behalf of the whole community. Moreover, they did not construct special buildings, shrines, or altars for religious purposes. This does not mean that religion was unimportant to the Huron; it merely indicates that instead of having its own institutionally delimited sphere, as it had in European culture, religion was indissolubly a part of all the things the Huron believed and did. The Huron did not perceive religion as being a well-defined set of beliefs that an individual could either accept, or substitute with another, at will. To them, their religion and way of life were one and the same. Many of the most important aspects of Huron religion were embraced by the term *onderha*, which meant the "prop" or "foundation" of a country. This term was used to denote the dances, customs, and ceremonies that bound a people together and promoted friendship, solidarity, and goodwill amongst them.

Collective activities were based upon beliefs that transcended clan and tribal affiliations and also served to bridge the gap between the male and female spheres of Huron life. Specialized knowledge of Huron beliefs and traditions was the property of certain old men, who at feasts were called upon to recite their stories. In this way, the traditions of the past were made known to the younger generation and the solidarity of Huron society, past and present, was reaffirmed.

The Huron lived in a world in which everything that existed, including man-made things, possessed souls and were immortal. Souls that had the power to influence human beings were called *oki*. These included the spirits that resided in the forests, lakes, rivers, and elsewhere in nature and which could bring good or bad fortune to people in such diverse activities as travel, war, and making love. The term was also extended to human beings who exhibited unusual qualities. These included shamans, witches, valiant warriors, outstandingly successful traders, and even lunatics. Such people were believed either to possess supernatural powers in their own right or to have a companion spirit whose power they could call upon.

Although the Huron had no well-organized pantheon of deities, their most important spirit was the sky, who controlled the weather and assisted human beings in times of need. The sky was invoked whenever an important bargain or treaty was concluded and it was believed that if oaths sworn in his name were broken, he would punish the offender. It was also believed dangerous to mock the sky. Lesser spirits were associated with particular islands or large rocks that the Huron encountered in their travels, and with natural features within the familiar landscape of the Huron country. Some of the spirits associated with these landmarks were friendly by nature, but others sought to hurt or kill human beings and some were ravenous to feed upon human corpses. To propitiate these spirits and secure their aid, offerings of tobacco were thrown into campfires or left in clefts in the rock whenever the Huron passed by their abode.

Observances of a religious nature were associated with every type of Huron activity. In particular, hunting and fishing were structured with many rituals. When Huron men engaged in these activities, they were careful not to permit the fat from their catch to fall into the fire or the bones to be burned or thrown to the dogs. If this were to happen, the souls of the dead animals would be angered and, in retaliation, living animals would no longer permit themselves to be caught. The Huron also believed that fish dreaded contact with the dead. Hence they were careful to keep human corpses out of sight of their fishing nets (which also had souls) and would not go fishing when one of their friends had died. To ensure good catches, some Huron villages married two girls, who had not yet reached puberty, to the spirit of a fishing net. This ceremony is reported to have originated amongst the Algonkians, when the spirit of a net appeared to a man in a dream and asked for a wife to replace the one he had lost. The ritual marriage apparently lasted for one year, during which the families of the two girls received a special share of the catch. These rituals illustrate very clearly the difference between the Huron's view of himself as a part of nature and the traditional European concept of man as having dominion over his environment.

In hunting and war, the Huron paid special attention to their dreams, which, as we shall see, they held in very special regard. Such dreams might give promises of success, or warnings of danger which an individual could then take action to avoid. Huron men are said to have often paid more attention to their dreams than to the advice of their leaders. This would be in keeping with the emphasis on masculine self-reliance that was so important to the Huron. Often a man's guardian spirit, who became associated with him at puberty, would render him advice and assistance in the form of dreams.

CREATION MYTH

Perhaps because of the absence of specific cults and a professional priest-hood, most Huron spirits seem to have been only very meagrely personified. Among the most important and best delineated of which we have knowl-edge, were Iouskeha and Aataentsic, who were identified with the sun and moon respectively. Both played an important role in the Huron myth of creation.[47]

The Huron believed that Aataentsic, the mother of mankind, had originally dwelt in the sky, where spirits live much as men do on earth. One day, when either chasing a bear or cutting down a tree to obtain medicine for her husband, Aataentsic slipped through a hole in the sky and began to fall. When the great tortoise, who swam in the primeval ocean below, saw this, he ordered the other aquatic animals to dive to the bottom of the ocean and dredge up soil to pile on his back. They did so, and in this way the earth was formed and Aataentsic landed gently upon it.

When Aataentsic fell, she was pregnant. She became the mother, or maternal grandmother, of two boys: Tawiscaron and Iouskeha. It was Iouskeha who created the lakes and rivers, made corn to grow, provided good weather, released the animals from a great cave in which they had been concealed, and made it possible for men to hunt them. He also learned the secret of making fire from the great tortoise and passed this knowledge on to mankind. Iouskeha grew old as men did, but never died, since he was able to rejuvenate himself in old age and become once more like a man twenty-five or thirty years of age. Aataentsic had an evil nature and spent her time trying to undo Iouskeha's good works. It was she who had charge of the souls of the dead, caused men to die, and bred epidemics. While she was by nature an old woman, she possessed the power to turn herself into a beautiful young girl, when it suited her to do so. Tawiscaron appears to have shared many of Aataentsic's evil qualities.

When they grew up, Iouskeha fought with Tawiscaron. In this fight, Iouskeha struck his brother and injured him. As Tawiscaron fled, drops of his blood fell on the ground and were turned into flint (*tawiscara*), which the Indians used to make their stone tools. After this, Iouskeha and Aataentsic continued to live together; the one seeking to help, the other to harm, mankind. They had a bark cabin surrounded by cornfields in a place far from the Huron country, apparently associated with the villages of the dead. Occasionally, they would visit the Huron and join in their festivals disguised as mortals. If Iouskeha was seen in the Huron cornfields carrying a well-developed stalk of corn, this vision signalled a good harvest, if he was seen gnawing on human flesh, it signified a bad one. It was also he who, as the sun, protected warriors.

It is tempting to see in these myths a fascinating commentary on Huron social structure (Trigger 1969a:92–93). The idea that Aataentsic was the mother of the human race and the unimportance attached to paternity are straightforward reflections of the matrilineal bias of Huron culture, but the roles assigned to Iouskeha and Aataentsic are in many ways the opposite of those that were assigned to men and women in everyday life. Among the Huron, men committed most of the real and symbolic acts of violence: chopping down the forests, killing animals, and hunting one another. Women were associated with life-giving pursuits: bearing children, growing crops, and caring for the home. Yet, in Huron myths, it is Iouskeha who makes the crops to grow and protects mankind, while his grandmother seeks to harm human beings whenever she can. It is possible that by conferring certain human characteristics on mythical figures of the opposite sex, these myths aimed at compensating both sexes for the psychological limitations of the roles assigned to them in real life. Women were flattered by being mythically endowed with dangerous and aggressive qualities, while men had their real role as destroyers of life complemented by a symbolic one as sustainers of it. The ambivalence men felt about their aggressive role may be symbolized by Iouskeha's attack upon his twin brother, who seems to have shared Aataentsic's aggressive and destructive nature. It is probably no accident that Tawiscaron's blood turned to flint, the stone used to make instruments of violence. Finally, the fact that Aataentsic and Iouskeha, though so different in nature, were made to live together, stressed the essential complementarity of their roles and, in this way, ultimately served to justify the sexual division of roles in Huron society.

CHARMS

Huron men relied on charms to bring them luck in activities such as hunting, fishing, fighting, gambling, and love. A charm was an object that had associated with it an *oki*, or spirit capable of helping the person who possessed it. Some charms could confer many types of benefits on their owners; others were useful for only one purpose. Those of proven worth were highly valued and were inherited from one generation to the next. New charms were revealed in dreams or might be found in the entrails of an animal that had been particularly hard to kill. Others were merely stones of curious shapes that had been found in the woods, where it was believed some spirit had made and lost them. Some were purchased at great price from the northern Algonkians who, because of their reputation as hunters and fishermen, were believed to possess very powerful charms. Men carried their charms in their pouches and, from time to time, would speak to the spirits associated with them and offer these spirits beads, or pieces of tobacco, as presents. They also gave feasts that were designed to reinforce the power of their charms.

SHAMANS

From time to time, either individually or as groups, the Huron sought the help of those among them who claimed to control supernatural powers. Most of these *arendiwane*, or shamans, were men and women who had obtained their special potency through visions or dreams in which a powerful spirit had revealed itself to them. Such visions normally required prolonged fasting and the avoidance of sexual intercourse for a period of time. As already noted in connection with the sacrifice of prisoners, sexual abstinence was important for the accomplishment of many activities of a sacred character; however, not even the most powerful shamans ever practised sexual continence for life, or even for long periods, and the Huron had no equivalent of the European concept of religious celibacy.

Some shamans went so far as to claim that they themselves were supernatural spirits who had become incarnate as human fetuses. These appear to have been mainly dwarfs, or people who were afflicted with other physical deformities. Such claims were based on the Huron belief that various mythical beings had such deformities; however, no matter what was the origin of his power, a shaman had to validate his claims by producing satisfactory results. Occasional failures could be attributed to sorcery or other malign influences, but, if a shaman had a notable series of failures, people generally lost faith in him. Hence, we may assume that most men who claimed supernatural powers had relatively short careers.

The powers claimed by shamans varied. Some men and women announced that they were able to control the weather and, in return for gifts, would offer to prevent frosts, produce rain, or eliminate diseases that were threatening the crops. Often, they would suggest public ceremonies which, if carried out properly, would avert the danger. Still others promised to bring luck in fishing or hunting, predicted the outcome of military ventures, determined by ritual means what was happening to warriors many hundreds of miles away, or undertook to recover objects that had been lost or stolen. All of this was done in return for presents, which were normally paid in advance.

The most important shamans were those who undertook to heal the sick, an activity that was performed by male shamans only. These were of two sorts: the *ocata*, who diagnosed and recommended treatment for all sorts of illnesses, and the *aretsan*, who specialized in extracting spells cast by witches. Both kinds of medicine men were highly esteemed and were well-paid for their services.

CURING SOCIETIES

In addition to these medical shamans, there were curing societies, whose work in healing the sick was considered to be extremely important. Each society had a leader, his office apparently being hereditary. Often these leaders were important headmen, whose ritual position complemented and strengthened their secular authority. Membership in these societies was generally open to those who had been cured by them and thereafter remained hereditary in such an individual's family.

Little is known about individual curing societies, although it appears that each specialized in treating certain types of illness. One of the most important and most general societies was the *Awataerohi*, whose members were held in awe for their ability to handle fire. Some chewed hot charcoal and either showered it over the patient or, after blowing it on their hands to warm them, rubbed the affected parts of his body. Others held glowing coals in their mouths and growled into the patient's ear, while still others danced around him holding red hot stones in their mouths. The power to handle such material, or to plunge their arms into boiling kettles, was said to be acquired supernaturally.

The *Atirenda* was another curing society which, in the 1630s, had about eighty members, including six women. This society was famous for treating ruptures. In their principal dance, the *otakrendoiae*, members of this society pretended to kill one another with charms, whose effects were then overcome. As they fell under one another's spells, they bit their cheeks so that blood poured from their mouths, or simulated it with red powder. The performance of dances by individuals who were disguised as hunchbacks and who carried sticks and wore wooden masks, suggests the existence of a curing society similar to the Iroquois False Faces. Still other men and women imitated animals or performed with sacks over their faces and straw stuffed around their waists. The sick person's family rewarded the performers of such rituals with food and other gifts.

The prominent role played by shamans and curing societies in Huron life indicates that combating illness was an important focus of Huron religious activity. Its importance is even greater when it is realized that the Huron did not limit the concept of health to physical well-being, but extended it to include anything that affected a person's happiness and sense of personal fulfilment. The latter included what we would call his good or bad luck.

PSYCHOTHERAPY

The Huron recognized three types of illness and mental disequilibrium. The first were those that had natural causes. These were diseases that could be treated successfully by means of herbs, drugs, incisions, poultices, and by profuse sweating. If such treatment did not succeed, the Huron concluded that the disease had a different origin.

The second type were those caused by witchcraft. Such diseases could be cured only if the shaman was able to discover and remove all of the spells that had been injected into a sick man's body. The third type of illness was caused by the presence in a person's soul of unfulfilled desires, of which even the patient himself might not be conscious. To cure illness of this sort, these desires had, in some manner, to be ascertained and fulfilled.[48]

The Huron attached great importance to dreams of all sorts and deliberately sought the answers to many of life's problems in them. It was believed that dreams were the language of the soul and that sometimes hidden desires were revealed to the patient through them. In the case of young children, such desires might be communicated to their parents in this form. Otherwise, it was necessary for the *ocata* to penetrate into the depths of his patients' souls to perceive what these desires were. This might be done by gazing steadily into fire or water, working himself into a frenzy, or sweating for a prolonged period, either alone or in the company of other men. Even when desires were revealed in the form of dreams, the *ocata*'s advice was required, as dreams sometimes were false and attempts to fulfil them could harm an individual.

Dreams gave promises of success or warnings of danger that could be averted only if certain desires of the soul were fulfilled. Sometimes these desires were for a specific object, such as a dog or a canoe. Among older people, they were not infrequently for socially unsanctioned forms of sexual gratification. Still other individuals believed that their souls commanded them to humiliate or even kill someone else. All of these commands ran directly counter to the Huron norms of generosity, sexual modesty, overt friendliness, and self-control. Still other desires arose from the promise of guardian spirits to confer special powers on an individual in return for ceremonies or presents which required the assistance of other people.

It was believed that failure to satisfy the desires of an individual's soul could result in that person's death. Because of this, the Huron felt obliged, as far as possible, to help to satisfy these wishes. Some desires, however, could not be fulfilled in the form in which they were asked, either because what had been requested could not be obtained or because the desire was destructive to the asker or to other people. In these cases, the *ocata* might suggest a symbolic equivalent that would be just as effective.

When specific objects were desired, villagers vied with one another to oblige the sick person. This was simply another example of the generosity in which the Huron took pride. Such gifts were given without expectation of anything in exchange; rather it was a matter of being able to help those in need. If demands were unreasonable, however, they were scaled down, again with the advice of the *ocata*. When a certain mother asked for one hundred cakes of tobacco to cure her son, ten were given instead (Thwaites 1896–1901, 10:173). In this way, individuals were prevented from making unreasonable demands on the community.

Acts which were self-destructive were also fulfilled symbolically. If a warrior dreamed that the enemy were burning him at the stake, he would seek to avoid this happening in reality by having his fellow villagers go through the preliminaries of torturing him, but a dog would be killed in his place.

A common desire of the soul was for curing rituals to be performed. Often these rituals were on a small scale, but, if the sick person was wealthy or a close relative of a headman, the entire community might participate in them. When the village council pronounced that a person's recovery was a matter of urgent public concern, everyone would join in performing the ceremony exactly as the sick person wished.

Often these ceremonies had sexual overtones. Occasionally, young people were asked to dance without wearing breechclouts, and on one occasion a woman is reported to have asked that during a dance a young man should urinate into her mouth (Wrong 1939:118). At other times, people were requested to eat vast quantities of food, even though they might have to vomit up part of what they had eaten in order to finish the meal; or they might be asked to eat biscuits which swelled their stomachs, although they believed that if they broke wind under such circumstances they would die.

The most sensational of all the curing rituals was the *andacwander*.[49] To perform this ceremony, the unmarried people of the village assembled in the sick person's house and spent the night having sexual intercourse with the partner of their choice, while the patient watched and two shamans shook their tortoise shell rattles and sang. Sometimes a sick man might request a young girl to have intercourse with him. Although this ceremony so shocked the Jesuits that they were hesitant even to mention it, it appears to have been a common one. This indicates the degree to which the Huron's concern for the welfare of members of their own society led them, in well-defined and short-lived contexts, to transgress even the most restrictive norms of their society.

The main Huron winter festival, the *Ononharoia*, belongs to the general category of soul-curing rituals. It was celebrated at least once a year in every large village. The main reason was either that many people in the village felt ill or depressed, or that some important individual was unwell. This boisterous celebration, which lasted three days, began with people breaking into houses, where they proceeded to upset furniture, break pots, and toss firebrands about. Following this, people who felt ill dreamed of objects, then went about the village propounding riddles and seeking to find someone who could guess what these objects were and give them to them. During this period, they were showered with many presents in the hope that one of them would fulfil their dream. If they were finally given what they were looking for, it was a sign that all their troubles were over. After the festival, all presents were returned, except those that were answers to dreams.

Through the medium of soul desires, individuals were able to treat personal frustrations and illicit desires as forces that were neither part of their overt personality, nor subject to conscious control. In a society where there were strong pressures for social conformity and personal restraint, this device provided a necessary outlet for personal feelings. Through their soul desires, individuals who felt neglected, abused, or insecure could indirectly make claims upon the community for psychological support. This support was given in a manner that in no way compromised the recipient's independence or sense of personal freedom, and which conformed to the general Huron principle of expressing friendship through generosity. From time to time, it also permitted people to relax the norms of their society and gratify themselves by doing, in public, things that normally were impermissible.

GAMES

The three most common Huron games were lacrosse, the dish game, and *aescara*. The dish game was played with five or eight dice made of fruit stones, painted black on one side and white on the other, while *aescara* required several hundred rushes, each about a foot long. Because teams from different villages frequently played against one another, these games provided an opportunity for various groups of Huron to come together in friendly rivalry and to indulge their inveterate passion for gambling. Betting was often for very high stakes, and individuals who had gambled away everything they owned are reported to have wagered their hair or even their fingers on the outcome of a game. Losers were expected to bear their losses graciously, although occasionally men who had gambled away a great deal of their household's property committed suicide, so great was their sense of dishonour.

Games that were played publicly had a strong religious element. Some were played in hope of curing a sick person, others to avert an epidemic, influence the weather, or honour the memory of a dead player. Once a game was decided on, the players from each village fasted, abstained from sexual intercourse, sought dreams that would bring them victory, and exhorted their personal charms to help them win. Lacrosse was played in an open field, but the other games were played inside a longhouse. The spectators supporting both teams seated themselves on either side of the main aisle of the longhouse and sought, by shouting, to attract luck to their side. Each side kept careful score of all points won and lost, and any player who suffered successive losses was replaced. Games might last for several days, with food and hospitality being extended to all present.

FEASTS

The Huron celebrated many events of both a public and private nature. The largest feasts were those that accompanied the annual meeting of the confederacy council and the investiture of new chiefs. Lesser ones were to celebrate personal good fortune or victories over the enemy, to solemnize life crises, such as marriage and death, and for the curing of the sick.

Invitations to attend feasts were sent out well in advance; sometimes people were invited individually, at other times whole villages were made welcome. It was regarded as an insult for anyone invited to attend a feast to refuse to do so without good reason. Each person who came was expected to wear his finest ornaments and to bring his own spoon and bowl with him. The guests assembled inside the longhouse of their host, the men seating themselves at one end, the women at the other. Once they had arrived the doors were closed, after which no one was supposed to enter. Failure to observe this rule was believed to disrupt the purpose for which the feast was given. Dancing was important to any such occasion. It was led by two older men, who shook rattles and sang, while the rest of the guests danced round them in an oval formation and joined in the refrain. Dancers did not hold hands, but each was expected to move vigorously and to make appropriate facial expressions (plate 7).

If the feast lasted all day, food was served both morning and afternoon. The man who gave the feast announced the contents of each kettle, which were then distributed by servers who went from row to row taking each person's bowl and filling it. Strangers, and those who had come from other villages, were given the best portions of what was available, while the heads of animals were reserved for the highest ranking headmen. Guests were expected to eat heartily, but the hosts ate little and spent most of their time seeing that everyone was entertained. In addition to singing and dancing, feasts were enlivened by various contests and games.

THE FEAST OF THE DEAD

By far the most important of all Huron ceremonies was the Feast of the Dead, which the Huron generally referred to as "the Kettle." At this feast, the bodies of all those who had not died violent deaths were removed from the temporary raised tombs in the village cemeteries and buried with great pomp in a common ossuary. A Feast of the Dead appears to have been held whenever a large village shifted location, the reason for this being that once the village was abandoned it was no longer possible to protect and care for the bodies buried in the adjacent cemetery. This created the regrettable necessity for the living and the dead, who had remained near to one another as long as the village lasted, to part company. The dead from nearby

PLATE 7. *Huron dance. This scene seemingly errs in showing the dance being held out of doors. Dances were normally performed in association with rituals held inside longhouses. The hairstyles are also not Huron. It is possible that the tortoise rattle is accurately represented, although recent Iroquois ones consist of a shell only. Courtesy McGill University Libraries.*

satellite villages were included in this final burial, along with deceased natives from the area who had gone to live elsewhere, and members of other Huron villages who wished to be interred close to a special friend. The significance of the mingling of the bones of the dead from many parts of the Huron country in a single grave cannot be overstressed. The Huron said that because their dead relatives were united in this way, it was necessary for the living to cooperate and be friends with one another. Friendly tribes from outside the confederacy were invited to attend the ceremony as an expression of goodwill, but only very close allies appear to have been asked to mingle the bones of their dead with those of the Huron.[50]

This final burial was believed to release the souls of the dead, who up to then had lived in the village cemetery, and allow them to travel westward to the land where Iouskeha and Aataentsic lived. In that land was a village of souls corresponding to each of the tribes, or major villages, of the Huron. Whether identified with the Milky Way or the trail running along the south shore of Georgian Bay, the journey to the land of the dead was an arduous one. At one point the terrestial route led past a tall standing rock called Ecaregniondi,[51] said to be daubed with the paint spirits used on their faces. Beyond this, a spirit called Oscotarach drew the brains out of the heads of the dead and, still farther along, was a deep ravine into which unlucky souls might fall and be drowned. Because of these difficulties, the souls of very young children and of the very old remained in the Huron country, where they planted their corn in the fields that the living had abandoned. Because the souls of those who had died violent deaths were believed dangerous, they were excluded from the villages of the dead. These included suicides and warriors who had died in battle, the latter forming a band by themselves in the hereafter. Those who reached the villages of the dead continued forever to hunt, fish, till the soil, and attend feasts and dances, much as they had on earth.

A Feast of the Dead was held in each major village once every ten to fifteen years.[52] Arrangements were made well in advance and invitations to attend were sent out through the whole country. The feast lasted ten days, eight of which were spent preparing the bodies for reburial and assembling the participants. In each village where there were bodies to be reburied, the latter were removed from their raised tombs. Then, unless they had died recently, the female relatives of the dead stripped them of any remaining flesh which, along with the mats and robes in which they had been wrapped, was reverently burned. This work is reported to have been done without overt repugnance, although the corpses were often putrid and swarming with worms. After the bones had been cleaned, they were

wrapped in a beaver skin bag, which was decorated with beads and sometimes fashioned to look like a man sitting in a crouching position. The
bodies of those who had died recently were merely wrapped in new skins
and carried on litters. A feast was then given in memory of the dead, at
which the vast array of presents collected in their honour was displayed.
Afterwards, both the bodies and the presents were carried to the village
where the feast was to be celebrated. Here, every visitor was assigned a
host, in whose house he placed the bones of the dead and the gifts that
accompanied them. In general, hosts and visitors appear to have belonged
to clan segments that were named after the same animal.

While continual feasting and dancing went on in the village, and prizes
were offered to the winners of various games, a pit about ten feet deep and
fifteen feet or more in diameter was dug in an open field near the village.
Around the pit, a scaffold was erected, about fifty feet across and ten feet
high, with crude ladders rising up to it on all sides. Numerous cross-poles
were erected on top of the platform (plate 8). On the seventh day, the
undecomposed bodies were brought to the edge of the pit and placed
beneath the scaffold on slabs of bark fastened to stakes several feet high.

The following day, the bundles containing the bones of the dead were
opened and mourned over for the last time. Then they were taken to the
field where the ossuary had been dug. There all the mourners arranged
themselves in groups according to villages and clan segments. The presents
that each group had brought to honour its dead were hung on poles and
remained on show for several hours. This display gave each clan segment
an opportunity to proclaim its affluence and piety towards its dead members, and also served to impress foreigners with the wealth of the country.
Afterwards, all of the packages of bones were taken and hung on the cross-
poles that had been erected on top of the platform, again arranged according
to clan segments. The headmen stood on the platform and announced the
recipients of many of the presents collected in the name of the deceased.
These recipients included his friends, those who had helped to bury him,
and those who were acting as hosts at the Feast of the Dead. In this manner,
a very significant redistribution of property was accomplished.

Towards evening, about fifty beaver robes, possibly one given by each of
the clan segments of the Huron confederacy,[53] were used to line the burial
pit. Then some old kettles were put into the pit for the use of the dead and
the undecomposed bodies were lowered into it. Fires were lighted, meals
cooked, and the mourners spent the night camped around the ossuary.

At sunrise, a signal was given and the crowd mounted the platform and
began emptying the bones of the dead into the pit, retaining, however, the

PLATE 8. *The Feast of the Dead. From Lafitau's* Moeurs des sauvages
amériquains*(1724). This is an eighteenth-century artist's attempt to
depict Brébeuf's description of the 1636 ritual at Ossossané. The dangling
articulated skeletons and unwrapped corpses draped over the mourners'
shoulders are the artist's macabre fantasies. Courtesy McGill University
Libraries.*

packages in which they were wrapped. At the same time, a great cry of lamentation was raised. A number of men were stationed in the pit, whose duty it was to see that the bones were packed in properly. The effect was to mingle the bones of different individuals together. When all the bones had been deposited, the robes bordering the edges of the pit were turned back and the space in the centre was covered over with mats and bark. Logs, probably scavenged from the platform, were then piled over the mouth of the pit, to prevent animals from burrowing into it, and the sand which had been dug out was used to erect a small mound on top of it. Dishfuls of corn were sprinkled over this mound to provide food for the souls of the dead. During the rest of the morning, further presents were distributed. Most of the fur bundles in which the dead had been wrapped were sliced apart and thrown to the crowd, who scrambled to get hold of them. Other presents were given to reward those in charge of the feast and to thank the headmen who had come from a considerable distance. Still other items that had been displayed were retained by the families who had used them to honour the dead.

Finally, wooden stakes were driven into the ground around the burial pit and a roof was erected on top of them. Similar huts appear to have been erected over the graves of those who had died violent deaths and may have been the sign of a final burial. No attempt was made to rebuild these huts after the original had rotted away. When the hut was finished, the participants feasted once again. Everyone was joyous at this time and returned home pleased that dead friends and relatives had received a fitting burial and been honoured with so many presents.

Important as the economic aspects of this feast may have been, the most important element remained the great affection that each Huron had for the remains of his dead relatives. By joining in a common tribute to the dead, whose memory each family loved and honoured, the Huron were exercising a powerful force for promoting goodwill among the disparate segments of each village, each tribe, and of the confederacy as a whole. The importance of this most sacred of Huron rituals made it, in effect, a microcosm of the structures and values upon which Huron society as a whole was based.

The Iroquoian Cultural Pattern

The Huron way of life was not unique, but was part of a cultural pattern shared by all the Iroquoian-speaking peoples who lived in the general vicinity of the lower Great Lakes. Although the northern Iroquoians frequently dwelt in settlements that had over 1000 inhabitants, the overall population density of this region was not particularly high. In historic times, the villages making up tribes, and sometimes confederacies, were drawn together in clusters of settlement, each of which was surrounded by vast tracts of hunting and fishing territory. Most of these clusters formed a loose ring around Lake Ontario, while others extended into the St. Lawrence and Susquehanna Valleys, and probably into the Ohio River watershed as well (map 2). Although sharing a common style of life, the inhabitants of each of these clusters generally spoke a distinctive Iroquoian language or dialect, while their customs and the things they made differed from one another in many details.[54]

The entire area occupied by the northern Iroquoians was one of hardwood forests, with increasing coniferous admixture in the north. It was also an area that abounded in fish, particularly whitefish and sturgeon, and in some districts in eels, and where nonmigratory animals were plentiful. The principal game was deer. These animals assembled in large numbers in the late fall and early spring in areas where oak and chestnut mast were abundant. Beaver, which also made good eating, reached densities of between ten and fifty per square mile in suitable country, but, both in numbers and quality of fur, they were inferior to the beaver that inhabited the lakes and rivers of the Canadian Shield.

NEIGHBOURING TRIBES

The nearest neighbours of the Huron were the Tionnontaté, who lived south of the great swamps of the Nottawasaga drainage basin. From Ossossané, a well-marked trail followed the curve of Nottawasaga Bay southward for some thirty miles before reaching their villages. Archaeological evidence indicates that these extended from Mulmer township in Dufferin County into Collingwood township in Grey, below the rugged portion of the Niagara Escarpment now called the Blue Mountain (Garrad 1970:238). It was from their location that the name Tionnontaté, roughly signifying Mountain People, was derived.[55] Their population is uncertain, but it likely numbered no more than a few thousand.[56] Although they are reported to have had nine villages, all but two appear to have been small hamlets, and two more may have been wholly or partly inhabited by the Algonkian-speaking peoples who lived farther to the west (Thwaites 1896–1901, 20:43; 21:125).

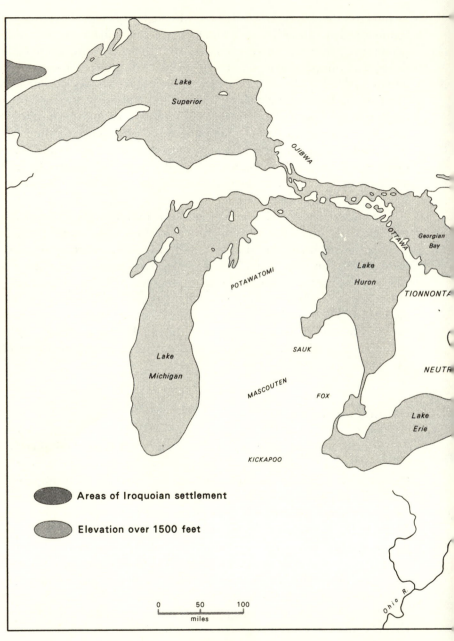

MAP 2. *Distribution of Iroquoian and other tribes in the lower Great Lakes area, c. 1630.*

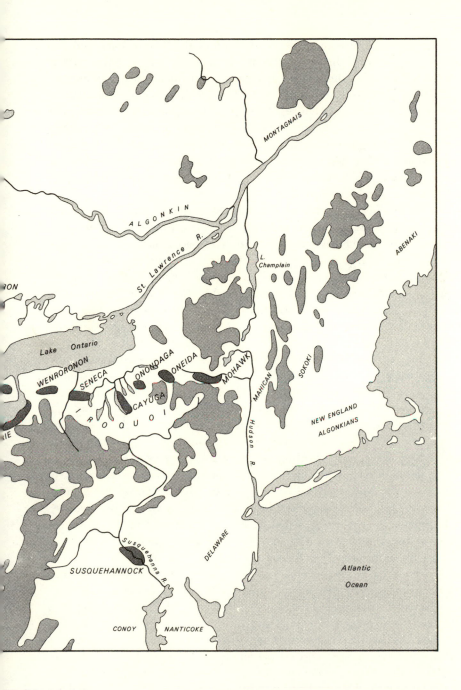

Frequent mention is made of the division of the Tionnontaté into two groups: the Nation of the Wolves and the Nation of the Deer. Some writers have suggested that these were two tribes who made up a Tionnontaté confederacy analogous to that of the Huron, but they seem more likely to have been the names of clan segments that were dominant in particular villages.[57] The Jesuits noted no linguistic differences between the Tionnontaté and the Attignawantan (ibid. 20:43), nor any cultural differences, except that the Tionnontaté were more given to tattooing than were the Huron (38:251). The Huron and the Tionnontaté were differentiated politically, rather than culturally.

The lake plain in the area of Tionnontaté settlement has a longer and more reliable growing season than the Huron country, or many areas farther south. In the seventeenth century, tobacco seems to have been grown there in large quantities. For this reason, the French called the Tionnontaté the Petun, or Tobacco Nation (ibid. 20:43; Biggar 1922–36, 6:248). Much of the better quality flint used by the Huron also may have come from this region (Heidenreich 1971:228). In spite of having these resources, the Tionnontaté did not attempt to go north to trade, since this would have required them to pass by or through Huron territory (Thwaites 1896–1901, 21:177). On the other hand, the Tionnontaté cultivated good relations with the Ottawa bands who lived to the west of them. The latter groups travelled freely and maintained close contacts with other Algonkian groups who lived along the eastern and northern shores of Lake Huron.

From the Tionnontaté villages, a trail led south across the high-lying interior of southwestern Ontario. This region had no permanent inhabitants and served as hunting territory for tribes whose homes were nearer to the Great Lakes. Between the lower part of the Grand River Valley and the Niagara River lived the tribes that made up the Neutral confederacy.[58] This sobriquet was applied to them by the French because, in historical times, they were not at war with either the Huron or the Iroquois, nor did they permit members of these groups to fight within their villages (Biggar 1922–36, 3:99–100; Thwaites 1896–1901, 21:193). The Neutral were not more peaceful, however, than were the other Iroquoian tribes. Instead, they carried on blood feuds with sedentary Algonkian peoples who lived to the west of them, probably in what is now the state of Michigan (Wrong 1939:157–58; Thwaites 1896–1901, 21:195; 27:25–27). In 1641, the Jesuit missionaries who visited the Neutral noted that they had about forty villages and estimated the total population of the confederacy to be about 12,000 people (Thwaites 1896–1901, 20:95, 105; 21:189–91, 223). This estimate was made, however, after a particularly serious epidemic. It is possible that, at the turn of the century, they had a population as large as that of the Huron.

We do not know for certain the number or names of the tribes that made up the Neutral confederacy. Although they remain to be confirmed archaeologically, French maps from the late seventeenth century seem to record the names and locations of three of them. These are the Attiragen-rega, due west of Lake Ontario near Hamilton, the Antouaronon in the lower Grand Valley, and the Niagagarega, just west of the river that still bears their name.[59] These maps suggest that the Neutral villages were not gathered together in one region, as were those of the Huron confederacy, nor were they dispersed evenly through the Neutral territory. Instead, they were probably gathered in tribal clusters like those of the Iroquois. Most of the Neutral appear, however, to have lived at the west end of Lake Ontario. The Jesuits report that four villages were located east of the Niagara River, but Marian White (1961:25–37) believes this was a temporary occupation between 1630 and 1645.

It is possible that the Neutral subsistence pattern differed in important ways from that of the Huron. They lived in the warmest part of southern Ontario, where the forest cover consisted almost entirely of deciduous hard-woods capable of supporting large numbers of wild animals. Thus it is not surprising that the reports which describe the Neutral attach great im-portance to hunting and indicate that, by contrast with the Huron, meat was available throughout the year. Skins were among their principal items of trade and Frank Ridley (1961 : 56) reports that bone refuse is much more common on historic Neutral sites that he has examined than on other sites of similar age in southern Ontario. This suggests that the Neutral may have been more dependent on hunting as a means of subsistence than were either the Huron or the Seneca. Related to this may also be the smaller size of Neutral villages, which the French figures suggest, on an average, were only half the size of Huron ones;[60] however, some villages archaeologists have examined appear to have been of considerable size.

The Huron and Neutral called each other "Attiwandaronk," which means "people who speak a slightly different language" (Thwaites 1896–1901, 21:193). While clearly different, their languages appear to have been more similar to each other than either was to the Iroquois ones. Both may have been derived from a common Ontario Iroquoian proto-language.

The Jesuits reported that the Neutral tortured female, as well as male, prisoners and that they were more inclined to extravagant ceremonialism than were their northern neighbours (21:195, 199–201). These may, how-ever, have been ill-formed impressions, reflecting the rather unsatisfactory relations that the Jesuits had with the Neutral. Like the Tionnontaté, the Neutral were given to extensive tattooing of the body and, like the Ottawa, men often dispensed with a loincloth in summer (21:197). The Jesuits also report that Neutral burial customs differed from those of the Huron. In particular, they appear to have kept corpses in their houses for as long as possible, prior to giving them temporary scaffold burials (21:199). Neutral ossuaries are considerably smaller than Huron ones and display unusual features, such as clay linings and upper and lower sections divided by layers of clay (Ridley 1961:56). The French also noted that the Neutral were not skilled in the use of canoes and did not travel great distances by water, as the Huron did (Sagard 1866:807). Like other Iroquoian tribes living south of Lake Huron, the Neutral lacked the canoe birch with which the Huron and the northern Algonkians constructed their light and easily manoeuvrable craft; instead they had to make do with coverings of elm or hickory bark.[61]

Even less well known are the Erie, a tribe or confederacy living at the southeastern end of Lake Erie. The Sanson map of 1650 suggests that the territory of this tribe extended from the east end of Lake Erie along the south shore as far as Cattaraugus Creek, or halfway to Lake Chautauqua (White 1961:40–51). This is partially supported by archaeological evidence, which indicates that between approximately 1535 and 1640, two contemporary communities, about eight to ten miles apart, were gradually moving southward through the eastern part of this region (White 1971a:25–27). After that time, the Erie are reported to have moved inland under pressure from their enemies (Thwaites 1896–1901, 33:63). It is unknown how many villages constituted the Erie cluster.

The Huron name for this group, Erieehronon, was construed by the French to mean *Nation du Chat*. They were so-named, it was stated, for the great numbers of wildcats in their country (Wrong 1939:224). It is likely, however, that the Huron word the French translated as "cat" (*tiron*) actually meant racoon (see n. 39, supra). Nothing specific is known about the Erie language. Archaeologically, they appear to share much in common with the Neutral (Wright 1966:83–84; 87–90). Unlike the other northern Iroquoian tribes, they are alleged to have used poisoned arrows (Thwaites 1896–1901, 41:83).

The Wenroronon were a small, probably tribal, group who lived east of the Neutral and "beyond the Erie."[62] They are said to have been allied in some way with the Neutral confederacy prior to their dispersal in 1638, after being decimated by war and disease.[63] No archaeological sites have been positively identified as being Wenroronon, although Hewitt

(1910c:932) suggested that their name, which he interpreted to mean "People of the Floating Scum," indicates that they might have lived close to the oil spring near Cuba, in Allegheny County, New York State. No historic sites have been found in that area and Marian White (personal communication 1973) suggests that they may have lived in the vicinity of Oak Orchard Swamp. Among the Huron, Wenroronon shamans were renowned for their skill in drawing arrows from wounds (Thwaites 1896–1901, 17:213).

South of the Iroquois lived the Susquehannock, or Andaste, about whom again all too little is known. The principal historic sites of these people have been found in Lancaster and York Counties, Pennsylvania, whither, it has been suggested, they had been drawn from the upper parts of the Susquehanna Valley in order to be able to trade more easily with Europeans, who were active in the Chesapeake Bay area at an early date (W. Hunter 1959:13). Susquehannock pottery has its closest stylistic affinities with Cayuga and Seneca (Witthoft 1959:36–42), but too little vocabulary has been preserved to establish the linguistic relationship between Susquehannock and the other northern Iroquoian languages with any degree of certainty.[64] In historic times, the Susquehannock were allies of the Huron against the Iroquois and, like the Huron, they appear to have been energetic traders. Some Susquehannock were reported to be living in the Huron country as late as 1647 (Thwaites 1896–1901, 30:253). They were the last northern Iroquoian people who remained unconquered by the Iroquois.

The *Jesuit Relations* mentions another group, the Scahentarronon, whose name suggests they lived on the Great Flats or Wyoming Plain along the north branch of the Susquehanna in the vicinity of Wilkes-Barre, Pennsylvania (8:115). Hewitt has identified this tribe with the Massawomecke, mentioned by Captain John Smith, in 1608, as being enemies of the Andaste.[65] If Hewitt is correct, the Scahentarronon were probably a tribe consisting of three villages of some importance. The alternative name that is given for this group, Akhrakvaeronon, has been identified as that of a people destroyed by the Iroquois in 1652.[66] It is possible that early writers may have subsumed two different groups, the Andaste and the Scahentarronon, under the general name Susquehannock, or that the two groups federated or became allies after 1608. Because of a lack of archaeological evidence and the ambiguities of our sources, the Scahentarronon remain a shadowy and uncertain entity.

Much more is known about the five tribes that made up the Iroquois confederacy. Unlike the Huron tribes, the Iroquois ones did not live

adjacent to one another, but were dispersed in tribal clusters in a line
stretching across upper New York State. The westernmost tribe was the
Seneca, who originally lived in two large villages, and several hamlets, in
the Genesee Valley. To the east of them, the Cayuga inhabited three
villages around Cayuga Lake. The Onondaga had one large and one small
settlement southeast of modern Syracuse, while the Oneida had a single
village in either the Oneida or Oriskany Valley. The tribe best known to
Europeans in the early historic period were the Mohawk, who had three
towns and five hamlets located in the central part of the Mohawk Valley
(Fenton 1940:200–31).

The five Iroquois tribes were culturally heterogeneous as well as geographically separated. Although the Mohawk and Oneida tongues were
very similar, and both were closely related to Onondaga, greater differences
separated these three languages, Seneca, and Cayuga.[67] The Seneca, which
was the most numerous tribe, may also have been the most dependent on
agriculture (Fenton 1940:230). The long separate development of the
people making up these tribes is reflected not only in distinctive languages
and pottery types but also in significant variations in their clan organization
and use of kinship terms. The Mohawk and Oneida used only three clan
names, whereas the other tribes resembled the Huron in having eight.

In spite of the difficulties inherent in estimating aboriginal populations,
it is frequently stated that, early in the seventeenth century, the Iroquois
confederacy had only half the population of the Huron one (Kroeber
1939:133). Some archaeologists have indulged in far-reaching speculations
about how this difference might have arisen (Noble 1969:22). Such
estimates are based, however, on Iroquois figures that are valid only for
the latter half of the seventeenth century, if at all. When we consider the
small size of the majority of Huron settlements, the ten large ones the
Iroquois are reported to have occupied prior to 1650 do not suggest a
population notably smaller than that of the Huron; indeed, it might be
argued that the Iroquois were more numerous. The Iroquois, like the
Huron, were stricken by serious epidemics beginning in the 1630s, and it
can be estimated that prior to that time their population numbered about
20,000. As a result of these epidemics, both confederacies appear to have
lost about half their population. Further losses from war and disease may
explain the failure of the Iroquois to increase in numbers in spite of the
many captives they incorporated into their tribes after 1640.

In the early seventeenth century, the Iroquois confederacy did not have
a common policy for dealing with their neighbours. Its main aim appears to
have been to suppress blood feuds among its members. Each of the tribes

had an unequal, but fixed, number of headmen on the confederacy council, who, as we surmise among the Huron, may originally have represented the various clan segments of which each tribe was made up. The traditional number of these sachems, or council chiefs, was fifty. The regular meeting of the confederacy council took place each autumn in the principal town of the Onondaga tribe, whose headman, Atotarho, enjoyed ritual precedence on such occasions. Since decisions could only be binding by mutual consent, neither unequal representation nor ritual precedence led to loss of autonomy for any of the member groups. In this respect, and in many details of their political organization, the Huron and Iroquois confederacies appear to have been very similar. Using the metaphor of the longhouse, the Onondaga regarded themselves as the keepers of the hearth for the confederacy, while the Seneca and the Mohawk were styled as its doorkeepers (Fenton 1971:138–39).

In the sixteenth century, a number of groups of Iroquoian-speaking peoples had been living in the St. Lawrence Valley, as far downstream as the Ile aux Coudres. All of these groups grew corn, but those living around Quebec City seem to have been particularly dependent on fishing and to have lacked the large, fortified settlements noted farther inland. The identity and disappearance of these groups will be discussed in detail in chapter 4.

While these groups exhaust the list of Iroquoian peoples known to have been living in the Great Lakes region in early historic times, it is possible that other groups lived to the south and west of the area we have examined. If so, they were dispersed by disease and warfare before they could be identified by European explorers. Seventeenth-century maps record many Iroquoian tribal names in these areas, but since all names, including those of well-known Algonkian tribes, are given in Iroquoian on these maps, it is far from certain that any of them were Iroquoian-speaking. It seems certain that these tribes had no direct influence on the Huron in the historic period and probably little or none at an earlier time.

CULTURAL SIMILARITIES

It is important not to over-emphasize similarities among the northern Iroquoian-speaking peoples. Many presumed similarities may be an illusion resulting from inadequate sources and undue extrapolation. Nevertheless, even granting the existence of important economic, stylistic, and behavioural differences between one Iroquoian tribe and another, it is possible to

define certain general characteristics that form a cultural pattern. These
are:

1. A primary dependence on horticulture as a means of subsistence, with
fishing ranking next in importance as a source of nutrition. The only
groups who may have been an exception to this rule are the St. Lawrence
Iroquoians in the Quebec City area, for whom fishing may have been more
important than horticulture, although this is far from certain. Among
groups such as the Huron confederacy and the Seneca tribe, horticulture
may have accounted for as much as eighty percent of the food eaten. All of
the northern Iroquoians practised a similar form of slash and burn agriculture, although their farming methods were skilfully adapted to local
variations in the environment (White 1963). Also, the same food crops
were grown throughout the whole area—corn, beans, squash, and sunflowers. All of these crops are ultimately of Mesoamerican origin, with the
possible exception of the sunflower, which seems to have been domesticated
in the southeastern United States (Yarnell 1964:118). Corn constituted the
bulk of the food that was produced and eaten.

2. All groups had a similar division of labour. Men cleared the land,
hunted, fished, built houses, carried on long-distance trade, and defended
their communities, while women grew and harvested crops, tended
children, and, in general, cared for their families.

3. The northern Iroquoians all lived in villages that were fortified, if
large or exposed to attack, and in bark-covered longhouses that sheltered a
number of individual families. These families were arranged on either side
of a row of hearths that ran down the centre of the dwelling. The preferred
material for constructing these longhouses seems to have been elm bark
among the Iroquois and cedar bark among the Huron. In historic times,
Iroquois houses had a rectangular floor plan, while Huron ones had
rounded ends. It is also likely that Iroquois longhouses had vertical walls
with an arching roof, while Huron ones were constructed by anchoring
poles in the ground and lashing them together overhead, in the form of an
arbour (plate 9). In spite of these minor differences, Iroquoians from one
population cluster would have had little difficulty understanding the living
arrangements of another.

4. The northern Iroquoian system of kinship varied in only a few details
from one group to another. Membership in clan segments and extended
families was based on matrilineal principles, which also governed the
inheritance of office. Residence appears to have been preferably matrilocal,
although, as we have suggested with respect to the Huron, it is likely that
a boy who was potentially heir to an hereditary position took up permanent

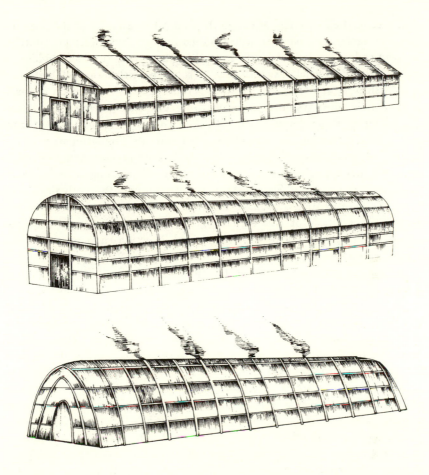

PLATE 9. *Alternative reconstructions of Iroquois (top and centre) and Huron (bottom) longhouses. The top reconstruction is based on an illustration from L. H. Morgan's* Houses and Houselife of the American Aborigines. *The centre one is based on John Bartram's diagram of an Onondaga longhouse of 1743 and is similar to ones depicted farther south along the eastern seaboard of the United States from the late sixteenth century. Below, a tentative reconstruction of a Huron longhouse following J. Lalemant and Antoine Laumet (Cadillac). The rounded ends of Huron longhouses were, in fact, more pronounced than this drawing suggests. From Trigger 1969a, Courtesy Holt, Rinehart and Winston.*

residence in the household of his mother's brother. In spite of these matrilineal preferences, Iroquoian kinship terminology and incest prohibitions
seem to reflect a bilateral ideal of social organization. It was forbidden to
marry either maternal or paternal blood relatives within several degrees of
relationship. Eggan (1952:43; 1966:104) has pointed out that, in general,
Iroquoian kinship systems resemble those of neighbouring, patrilineal,
Algonkian-speaking groups more than they do the "lineage" systems that
were prevalent in the southeastern United States.[68] The latter were of the
Crow type, which sharply distinguishes the kinsmen who belong to a man's
mother's matrilineal descent line from those who belong to his father's
matrilineal descent line. Such systems are associated with highly developed
matrilineal institutions. Looked at from an historical perspective, the
absence of features of this sort suggests that the northern Iroquoian
societies were less evolved in a matrilineal direction than were societies
found farther south.

5. Another feature of northern Iroquoian society was the recognition of
a bond of affinity between members of clan segments that had the same
name or symbol. This relationship was strong enough to prevent intermarriage between members of such groups. The Huron and the three
western Iroquois tribes had eight clan names. Six of them (Turtle, Wolf,
Bear, Beaver, Deer, and Hawk) referred to the same animals among both
the Huron and the Iroquois, but the Iroquois had Snipe and Heron clans
in place of the Huron's Porcupine and Snake (Tooker 1970b:94). The
extension of kin-type relations to all those whose clan segments were
named after the same animal made it possible for travellers to find
"relatives" in unfamiliar communities, and constituted a cross-cutting
bond that helped to hold tribes and confederacies together. Their unity was
further reinforced by the grouping of clans to form three phratries that
may also have been exogamous, and whose members had ritual obligations
towards one another for burial and other ceremonies.

6. Huron and Iroquois political organization had many common features
and these were probably shared by the other, less well-known tribes and
confederacies. Each clan segment had its own leaders for civil and military
matters. Each of the former was responsible for the internal affairs of his
segment and for peaceful dealings with other groups; each of the latter led
his fellow warriors. Tribal and confederacy organizations were made to
work by having the civil headmen of the various clan segments discuss
issues and try to coordinate action. The implementation of the decisions of
such councils required securing the consent of all those involved, since no
Iroquoian had the right to commit another to a course of action against his

will. In spite of their apparent precariousness, governments of this sort could successfully suppress blood feuds within confederacies having as many as 20,000 members and, up to the tribal level at least, could coordinate their policies when it came to dealing with outsiders.

7. The warfare practised by the Iroquoians in the early historic period conformed to a common pattern. Their aim was not to acquire land or basic foodstuffs. Instead, warfare was the means by which young men could gain prestige, by taking heads or scalps as trophies and capturing prisoners who could be sacrificed in a torture ritual. War was rationalized as blood revenge; warriors of a tribe or confederacy carried out raids to avenge previous killings, presumed to have been committed by members of some neighbouring group. As a side effect, warfare may have served to conserve game animals, since it reduced the amount of hunting in the no man's lands between the groups involved.[69] War was also a minor source of booty, in the form of the clothing and personal ornaments worn by prisoners. In particular, for the Huron, prisoners were a source of wampum, or shell beads, which originated on the coast and were scarce and valued items in the interior.

8. The Huron and Iroquois also shared many of the same religious beliefs and practices. Their creation myths were almost identical and many of the deities they worshipped were the same. So were most of the games they played, their feasts, and their celebrations. In addition, they shared with many of the northern Algonkian peoples a deep interest in healing rituals. Some of these were performed by shamans, but among the Huron and Iroquois others were enacted by healing societies, whose membership cut across the various kinship units. While it has been suggested that these societies developed as a response to epidemic diseases that were introduced by Europeans (Brasser 1971:263), linguistic studies indicate that shamanistic practices are of considerable antiquity in Iroquoian culture. More striking is the lack of evidence at this period for the celebration of calendrical feasts such as Seed Planting, Corn Sprouting, Green Corn, or, except as a healing ritual, Midwinter. Until recently, it was generally believed that the rituals which were associated with the ideal of renewal and which served to mark the annual crises in maize cultivation or natural vegetation were among the oldest and most basic features of Iroquoian culture. While it is possible that these rituals were overlooked by the first Europeans who visited these tribes, Elisabeth Tooker (1960) and W. L. Chafe (1964) have suggested that since the seventeenth century the principal emphasis in northern Iroquoian ceremonialism has shifted away from shamanistic practices and curing ceremonies to calendric rituals. The most important

changes seem to have come about late in the eighteenth century, with the development of the "New Religion" of the Seneca prophet Handsome Lake. The main forces encouraging these developments seem to have been a growing emphasis on plough agriculture and the more sedentary life resulting from acculturation. The similarities to rituals celebrated by tribes in the southeastern United States may result from contacts that the Iroquois had with that area during the eighteenth century.

9. Finally, the northern Iroquoians shared many of the same values and attitudes, which, if difficult to define, nevertheless were, and remain, important features of their way of life. The material culture of the northern Iroquoians was not impressive and for the most part their artistic productions were limited, both in quantity and in quality. Instead, the genius of Iroquoian culture is to be found in their psychological finesse, and the attention they lavished on social relations generally. A fundamental premise of Iroquoian life was a respect for individual dignity and a sense of self-reliance, which resulted in individuals rarely quarrelling openly with one another. Displays of violent emotions were publicly disapproved of and hostility tended to express itself in accusations of witchcraft, neurotic illness, and, more violently, in suicide. More easily definable aspects of Iroquoian behaviour were their love of speeches, their politeness and hospitality to fellow villagers and to strangers, and the kindness and respect they showed towards children.

Chapter 3 ⚜ The Birth of the Huron

It was long believed that the various northern Iroquoian tribes came into existence when a single people moved apart and became culturally and linguistically differentiated.[1] Earlier in this century, it was speculated that the original Iroquoian culture might have developed in the southeastern United States, where the Iroquoian-speaking Cherokee and Tuscarora were living in historic times (Lloyd 1904; Parker 1916). More recently, archaeological evidence has indicated that following a shift to horticultural production around the lower Great Lakes sometime after A.D. 500, the northern Iroquoian cultures began to evolve from hunting and gathering patterns that had been indigenous to that area (MacNeish 1952). Many of the most characteristic features of Iroquoian culture are now recognized as being the result of shared development in relatively recent times rather than cultural residue from an earlier period.

Glottochronological evidence indicates that the northern Iroquoian languages separated from Cherokee 3500 to 3800 years ago and from Tuscarora 1900 to 2400 years ago (Lounsbury 1961), thus making these linguistic relationships irrelevant for understanding the origins of northern Iroquoian culture. Neither sufficient physical anthropological nor archaeological information is available to reveal when Iroquoian-speakers first appeared in the vicinity of the Great Lakes, nor do we know whether the Iroquoian languages spread from south to north or north to south. All that can be said for certain is that the Iroquoian way of life, like those of their neighbours, was the product of a lengthy, indigenous cultural evolution. For this reason, it seems best to set aside the question of Iroquoian ethnic origins while surveying the developments that gave rise to the northern Iroquoian cultural pattern. It must be stressed that at present it is impossible to correlate any archaeological culture with even a broad linguistic grouping prior to about A.D. 500.

Ontario Prehistory

BEFORE AGRICULTURE

Southern Ontario is located close to the northern limits of the deciduous forests that cover most of eastern North America. Much of the southern part of the province lies in a transitional zone of increasing coniferous admixture, which gives way to boreal forest north of Lake Superior. Although southern Ontario is a rich biotic zone by comparison with the thinly soiled Precambrian Shield to the north, it suffers from long, cold winters. It is also remote from the Mesoamerican heartland, whose cultigens and burgeoning societies exerted a strong, if poorly understood, influence upon the cultural development of the eastern portion of North America. Because of the marginal location of southern Ontario, it is not surprising that hunting and gathering persisted until a late period and that only a few cultigens managed to penetrate that far north.

The earliest evidence of human presence in Ontario does not pre-date the retreat of the Wisconsin glaciation, which began uncovering land in the southwestern portion of the province about 13,000 years ago. The ice retreated in a slow and irregular fashion, which was interrupted by at least one major glacial advance and accompanied by numerous fluctuations in the water levels of the Great Lakes. The whole area south and west of the Ottawa Valley and Lake Nipissing was not irrevocably free of ice much before 6000 B.C. (Quimby 1960:19–26; Griffin 1965:656–58; Hurley and Kenyon 1970:105–8).

There is little evidence of human occupation from this early period. About fifty fluted spear points of the so-called Clovis type have been found across southern Ontario, from Elgin County in the west to Lanark County in the east. Most of these occur just north of Lake Erie (Garrad 1971). Both on the Prairies and in the northeastern United States, these points have been dated between 11,000 and 8000 B.C.,[2] and shown to be associated with a pattern of elephant (i.e., mammoth and mastodon) hunting that was widespread at that time. Quimby (1960:31) argues that no type of stone projectile point was as well suited for hunting these animals as were these large fluted ones.

With the decline of elephant hunting, fluted points gave way to simple lanceolate forms that are associated with the loosely defined Plano tradition. Griffin (1965:660) classifies this tradition among the earliest of the Archaic, or locally adapted hunting and gathering cultures.[3] The principal game animals in southern Ontario at this time are assumed to have been deer, moose, and barren ground caribou. Although evidence of Plano occupation is found considerably beyond the northern limits of the earliest fluted point traditions, sites are few in number and prior to 3000 B.C., the population seems to have been extremely low (Hurley and Kenyon 1970:107–8). This is not surprising; the boreal forest that was established in southern Ontario at that time seems to have had no greater carrying capacity than modern ones and away from now submerged lake shores probably supported only about one person for every 200 to 300 square miles (Fitting 1968). It is not unlikely that, at least in general principle, the social organization of these early hunters resembled that of Naskapi bands studied in the far north of Quebec early in this century. These bands were made up of thirty to fifty people each. By living off herds of caribou, their members were able to stay together throughout the year. The extremely low population density cut interaction between bands to a minimum and, because of this, individuals tended to marry cross-cousins within their own band. The structure of these bands was therefore neither matrilineal nor patrilineal, but bilateral.[4]

Between 6000 and 3000 B.C., the climate grew warmer and drier. In southern Ontario, pines, which had begun to increase about 7000 B.C., replaced spruce and fir as the dominant forest cover. These, in turn, gave way before hardwoods, which eventually spread northwards onto the southern flanks of the Canadian Shield. From 6000 to 3000 B.C., the Great Lakes stood at very low levels, only to rise again as the isostatic rebound of land recently freed of ice raised their outlets. As essentially present-day conditions came into being over large areas of southern Ontario and New York State, a new pattern of cultural adaptation developed. This pattern, known as the Laurentian Archaic, was appropriate to an area of hardwood forests in which fruit and nuts, as well as heavy concentrations of deer and other non-migratory game, could be found and where fresh-water fish were abundant. The Laurentian Archaic can be differentiated from the contemporary Maritime Archaic pattern, found along the east coast, where caribou, sea mammals, birds, and salt-water fish were major items in the diet, and from the Shield Archaic pattern, found in the boreal forests to the north. The Shield Archaic has been defined in terms of certain rather generalized tool types (bifacial and uniface blades, lanceolate and side-notched projectile points, many kinds of scrapers, and crude chopping and scraping-cutting tools) and by the absence of the more sophisticated artifacts found in Archaic traditions farther south. The Shield Archaic seems to be the continuation of an early Archaic pattern of adaptation to a boreal environment. In some areas it may have persisted into the historic period (Wright 1968:57).

The Laurentian cultures had a wide range of tools that were useful for coping with a hardwood environment. Woodworking tools, such as axes, adzes, and gouges, were pecked and ground out of hard igneous rocks. Such implements appear to have been unnecessary for working softer woods and are absent in earlier cultures. Other diagnostic traits of the Laurentian tradition are ground slate projectile points and knives, including the semi-circular knife known as the *ulu*, simple forms of banner stones, a variety of side-notched and corner-notched projectile points, and barbed bone points (Ritchie 1965:79–80). Banner stones were used as weights on throwing sticks or *atl-atls*, which hunters used to hurl darts prior to the introduction of the bow and arrow.

The earliest date ascertained for a Laurentian Archaic site in New York State is 4610 B.C.; for Ontario, it is 3290 B.C. (Hurley and Kenyon 1970:108). The latter comes from the "Allumette Island I" site on the Ottawa River. While these dates may indicate the later development of a Laurentian Archaic pattern in Ontario, fewer sites of this period have been excavated in Ontario than in the United States; hence information is bound to be more fragmentary and provisional. A distributional study by James V. Wright (1962) of surface finds of Archaic ground stone tools in southern Ontario reveals a greater number of bannerstones and ground axes in the west than in the east, and a greater number of slate points, *ulus*, and gouges in the east than in the west.[5] This division between the eastern and western parts of southern Ontario is of interest, because it crops up repeatedly in later times.

Many copper artifacts have been found in Archaic sites in southern Ontario. These were made from metal that occurs in a pure, or native, state in the rocks of the Lake Superior basin. Thousands of prehistoric mining pits have been located along the Canadian shore of Lake Superior, in the Keweenaw Peninsula, and on Isle Royale. Once the pure copper was extracted from the rock, it was worked into shape by cold-hammering, grinding, and annealing it (Quimby 1960:52–53; Griffin 1961). The copper artifacts found in Ontario and New York State appear to have been obtained by trade from the Old Copper culture, a variant of Laurentian that flourished in the upper Great Lakes region around 2000 B.C. (Ritchie 1965:82). The majority of artifacts were tools, some of which were equipped with socketed attachments. For the most part, these tools are replicas of stone gouges, adzes, and ground slate spear points. In spite of their utilitarian shapes, it seems likely that these copper tools were acquired mainly as prestige items. The presence of conch shell ornaments in Archaic sites in New York State, and of copper artifacts far to the south, indicates that exotic materials were traded over vast distances during this period (Winters 1968).

The many artifacts found in southern Ontario indicate that the population of this region was considerably larger than it had been previously. Although little is known about patterns of subsistence or settlement at this time, it has been suggested that the Archaic sites in the Ottawa Valley were base camps where groups, who spent the winter hunting in the interior, gathered each summer to fish (Hurley and Kenyon 1970:112–13). This pattern, which enabled maximum exploitation of the dispersed plant and animal resources of the area, was followed by the Montagnais, Ojibwa, and other nonagricultural peoples of Ontario and southern Quebec into the historic period.[6] In view of basic similarities in environment and subsistence patterns in the Archaic period and among these groups in early historic times, it appears that a broader analogy may be drawn.

It may be inferred that in the late Archaic period the population of southern Ontario was divided into hunting bands, each composed of several hundred members. Since the area now lacked herd animals, the members of these bands had to break up each autumn into small groups, that scattered in search of game in different parts of the band territory. Because if a lone hunter were injured or became seriously ill in the course of the winter, his wife and children would starve, these hunting parties were usually made up of two or more brothers, or a father and sons, together with their families. These relatives shared the dangers of the winter together, without expectation of any outside support. In summer, the various segments of the band would gather under the leadership of a recognized headman. Supported by abundant catches of fish, the members of these bands found time to enjoy each other's company, to arrange marriages, and to celebrate rituals, one of the most important of which, by the end of the Archaic period, was the burial of their dead (Ritchie 1965:178). These larger groupings functioned as political units insofar as members cooperated in the defence of a common territory. They were also necessary to regulate the economic exploitation of these areas and to provide long-term support for their constituent family groupings, whose very existence could be threatened by the loss of a single adult member.

Population densities may have approached the one person per twenty-five square miles found in historic times among groups such as the Ojibwa. The territories occupied by individual bands would have been much smaller than they had been previously, and this would have broken down the isolation between neighbouring, and probably multiplying and fissioning, bands. Under these conditions, band endogamy declined in favour of intermarriage between adjacent groups. In societies largely dependent on hunting, men who grow up together generally prefer to remain a team, hence women leave the band into which they are born to live with their husbands. As a result of such marriages, bilateral bands would have been transformed into clan groups, whose male members tended to claim descent from a real or a fictitious common ancestor. Like the clan segments of the Iroquoians, the vast majority of Algonkian patrilineal groups bore the name of some animal, although most were fish and birds rather than mammals. The word totem, now used by anthropologists to designate a patron animal spirit, is an Algonkian word meaning a local group of consanguines (Hickerson 1970:44). Because of the importance attached to the kinship relation between the male members of these clans, marriage within the group came to be viewed as incest and was forbidden. Cross-cousin marriage continued to play an important role in regulating marriage but cross-cousins were now normally born into different bands rather than into the same one, as they had been previously.[7]

Such marriage patterns forged informal, but nevertheless effective alliances between neighbouring groups. Allied bands frequently shared a common language or dialect, and constituted what have loosely been called tribes. Historic groupings, such as the Algonkin or the Ottawa, seem to have been alliances of this sort, although their members probably had less sense of common identity than European explorers ascribed to them. We have no way of knowing whether any of the tribes in the Archaic period had phratries, or a dual arrangement of patrilineal clans, that formed the basis for rivalry in games and ceremonial activities on the rare occasions when a number of bands might assemble in one place. Alignments of this sort served to strengthen and extend the clan system and are a feature of more densely populated areas (Eggan 1966:83).

Around 1500 B.C., in New York State, the Laurentian Archaic pattern began to pass through a transitional stage which, by about 1000 B.C., had given rise to a new cultural pattern known as Early Woodland. Typical Early Woodland artifacts include tubular smoking pipes, various types of gorgets, birdstones, boatstones, and bar amulets (all three made of polished stone and of uncertain function, although probably ornamental), and, for the first time, copper ornaments, as opposed to copper tools. The latter were mostly beads (Ritchie 1965:178–79). The most distinctive feature of the Early Woodland pattern is the appearance of pottery, which from this time on, is ubiquitous in the archaeological record. The earliest pottery is called Vinette I. These are thick-walled vessels, made with a coiling technique, and decorated with cord markings. Vinette I is far from being the earliest pottery in eastern North America; a simple, but distinctive, fibre-tempered variety being manufactured in the southeastern United States as early as 2000 B.C. Vinette I pottery is associated principally with the Meadowood culture, found in New York State and the St. Lawrence Valley (ibid. 192–93).

In Ontario, the Early Woodland phase is very poorly understood. While Early Woodland artifacts are widely distributed in surface collections and have been found mixed with later material in a number of sites, no purely Early Woodland assemblages have as yet been identified. Where radio-carbon determinations are available, Vinette I seems to date about 500 years later in southern Ontario than it does in New York State (Hurley and Kenyon 1970:114–15). Moreover, at the East Sugar Island site on Rice Lake, typical Laurentian material was found apparently associated with Middle Woodland pottery types (Ritchie 1965:209). This, and other considerations, have led various archaeologists to propose that the Vinette I ceramics found in Ontario are a late intrusion northwards and that there may not have been a separate Early Woodland period in the province (Wright 1967:131–32). This suggests that a basically Archaic (pre-ceramic) culture survived later in Ontario than it did to the south and east, but was influenced by the stone tool types of the Meadowood culture from about 1000 B.C. on.

Burials resembling those of the Glacial Kame culture have been found in southern Ontario. This culture is dated roughly between 1600 and 1000 B.C. and thus falls into the transitional period between late Archaic and Early Woodland (Ritchie 1965:131–34). The Glacial Kame culture is centred in the midwestern United States, and appears to be derived in some manner from the Old Copper culture. The many parallels between the Glacial Kame and Meadowood cultures include tubular pipes, copper celts and adzes, bar-shaped birdstones, rectangular gorgets, shell disk beads, red ochre in burials, and the practice of cremation (ibid. 198–200). Although both cultures appear to be contemporary, Glacial Kame lacked pottery, as the cultures of southern Ontario seem to have done. The presence of both Glacial Kame and Meadowood traits in southern Ontario may indicate that this area was an important avenue by which ideas, as well as raw materials, were being transmitted at this time. The elaboration of burial rituals in late Archaic and Early Woodland times marks the beginning of a pre-occupation with the honouring of the dead that was to persist, with fluctuations, in the lower Great Lakes area and culminate for the last time in the Huron Feast of the Dead.

The Middle Woodland stage in Ontario dates from some time before

500 B.C. to perhaps as late as A.D. 500. Its pottery is characterized by a much greater range of decoration than existed previously, but nevertheless consists only of sub-conoidal cooking pots made by the coiling method. The principal decorations that appear on Middle Woodland pottery are dentate stamp, pseudo-scallop shell, rocker stamp (dentate and plain), cord-marking, and dragged stamp (ibid. 179). At least three roughly contemporary Middle Woodland cultures have been delineated in Ontario: Laurel in northern Ontario and adjacent parts of Manitoba, Michigan, and Minnesota; Saugeen in southwestern Ontario; and Ontario Point Peninsula in the eastern part of southern Ontario (Wright 1967:95–125). It is possible, however, that as more sites are excavated, the pottery types associated with these three cultures will be shown to intergrade with one another, and with the Point Peninsula culture of New York State, to form a broad continuum of stylistic variation.

In general, pottery types appear to be much more homogeneously distributed throughout this region than are stone tool types and copper artifacts, which often vary considerably within the same "culture." While it was once believed that the Middle Woodland cultural pattern was introduced by a migration of people coming from the northwest, Brose (1970:67–68) has suggested that the pottery complex may have developed locally, possibly in the Illinois area, and from there spread throughout the Great Lakes region. If patrilineal bands were engaging in exogamic marriages, the diffusion of female potters would result in the widespread distribution of similar elements of ceramic design. At the same time, these marriage patterns would encourage artifacts manufactured by men to develop along local lines. Pottery would diffuse very rapidly in this manner and might give the impression of a sweeping occupation of the region by newcomers, when in fact no change of population had taken place.

There is good evidence that the centrally based wandering pattern, which we postulated began in the Archaic stage, was being followed at this period. Yet, it appears that the population was larger than before and that a greater range of food resources was being exploited. While still important, hunting probably accounted for a smaller part of the total diet than it had previously. The members of patrilineal bands seem to have lived together during the warmer months of each year when fishing was productive, catching sturgeon in the spring and whitefish in the autumn. Shellfish were collected in large numbers, and concentrations of sites in areas where wild rice was common suggest that it too was intensively harvested and eaten (Ritchie 1965:207–11). Wild rice may also have played an important role in helping people to survive the winter, although families still appear to have spent the leanest months hunting in small parties, mainly away from the major lakes and rivers. The artifactual evidence from Middle Woodland sites indicates that men and women lived together throughout the year. There is nothing to suggest that men left their families in order to hunt and fish for long periods elsewhere, as was the case with the Huron and neighbouring horticultural, or semi-horticultural, peoples in early historical times. The ecological adaptation of the people of southern Ontario in the Middle Woodland period appears to have been essentially the same as that of the Ojibwa and related nonagricultural peoples, who lived north of this area into the historical period.

To date, relatively little is known about the settlement patterns of the Middle Woodland period. At the Donaldson site, located near the mouth of the Saugeen River in southwestern Ontario and dated about 500 B.C., James V. Wright (and Anderson 1963) has identified the post mold patterns of at least two roughly rectangular structures measuring twenty-three by fourteen feet and seventeen by eleven feet respectively (plate 10). The larger structure is believed to have had a gabled roof and to have been open at the south end. Near the centre of this cabin was a large circular hearth. Traces of a fireplace were found near the wall of the smaller, and somewhat more elliptical, structure. Nearby were twelve burials, in which beads of copper and marginella shell were found, as well as perforated bear teeth and various stone tools. This site has been interpreted as a fishing station that was occupied in the spring and early summer.

From the other end of the Middle Woodland time span is the Kipp Island No. 4 site in eastern New York State. Dense concentrations of post molds bear witness to the prolonged recurrent occupation of this site. The most clearly defined house outline was a round one, eighteen to twenty feet in diameter, with a doorway facing south. Because of the intensive occupation of the site, no hearths or storage pits could be attributed with any certainty to this particular dwelling. Another, less satisfactorily defined structure was rectangular with rounded corners and measured about nineteen by ten feet. A final structure, only partially outlined, may have been an oblong building over forty feet in length, possibly a prototype of the later Owasco (early Iroquoian) longhouse (Ritchie 1965:247).

Some of the most informative data concerning the nature of Middle Woodland societies come from the Summer Island site in Lake Michigan. There was found a summer fishing camp that had been occupied, at most for a few seasons, sometime in the second or third centuries A.D. The outlines of four cabins, together with their fish and meat drying platforms, were located and two of them were excavated very carefully so that

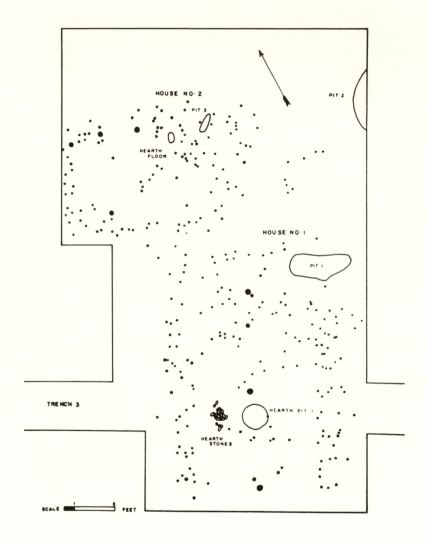

PLATE 10.   *Floor plan of house structures 1 and 2 from the Donaldson site near Southampton, Ontario (c. 500 B.C.). The post molds suggest two roughly rectangular structures. House 1 is believed to have had a gabled roof and been open at the south end. The Donaldson site was probably a fishing station occupied in the spring and early summer. Courtesy National Museum of Man, National Museums of Canada.*

distributions of artifacts in and around them could be analysed in detail. While three of the four structures appear to have been circular, and at least two of them had a single central hearth, the largest was an elliptical structure twenty-nine by twelve feet, with two hearths along its main axis. The distribution of artifacts within this structure indicated that it had been inhabited by two nuclear families. The careful manner in which sections of the cabin had been allotted to each of its adult inhabitants permitted Brose (1970:53–59) to infer that it had been lived in by two men with one wife each, two sub-adults, and an unknown number of children. A detailed examination of variations in pottery types, within and between houses, strongly rules out the possibility of matrilocal residence and suggests a patrilocal or bilateral pattern with probable cross-cousin marriage.

This clear-cut example of an extended family dwelling from about the beginning of the Christian era underscores what has long been known to Algonkianists, but has been ignored by Iroquoian specialists: that the hunting and gathering peoples of Ontario and Quebec, who have been interpreted as providing a model of what Iroquoian social organization was like prior to the introduction of horticulture, did not necessarily, or even in major part, live in single-family dwellings. It is clear from Le Jeune's description of life among the Montagnais in the seventeenth century that winter hunting parties consisted of two or more brothers and their families, who lived together in large conical tents constructed of poles and covered with portable bark mats (Thwaites 1896–1901, 7:107). The existence of patrilocal extended families among these hunting peoples indicates the shortcomings inherent in explanations that seek to account for the development of Iroquoian extended families out of a primordial nuclear family organization, and which see this development mirrored in a presumed transition from single family dwellings to multifamily longhouses (Noble 1969:18). Everything that is known about the mixed forest region of eastern North America indicates that extended families, and probably exogamic clans, existed there long before the development of a horticultural economy. As we shall see, the major problem concerning the development of Iroquoian social structure is not how these institutions came into being, but how, and under what circumstances, institutions based primarily on patrilineal descent were reshaped to become matrilineal.

The incipient longhouse from the Summer Island site also suggests that this type of dwelling was not necessarily an Iroquoian invention. As long as the number of nuclear families that live together is small and the house that must be supported on a framework of poles does not cover a large area, a variety of shapes is possible. The Montagnais lived in round cabins with a single fire in the middle and, even at Summer Island, there were round houses that were only fractionally smaller than the "longhouse" we have been discussing. Thus a longhouse is not the only structure suitable to house an extended family. Yet, as the number of families who live together increases, the difficulty of erecting a structure that is more than twenty-five feet across requires that houses be increased in length to provide additional living space. The architectural principles used to build bark-covered cabins were widely known in Middle Woodland times and it is possible that the longhouse is merely an application of these principles to meet the problem of placing more families under a single roof.[8]

In the early historic period, the longhouse was not restricted to the Iroquoian culture area. The normal housetype among the Algonkian speakers living in the vicinity of Georgian Bay was an elliptical structure equipped with two fireplaces and sheltering several families (Wrong 1939:185). This was also the style of cabin that Huron men constructed when they went north on their annual fishing expeditions. The Jesuits state that the Nipissing erected sizable longhouses for ritual purposes (Thwaites 1896–1901, 23:217) and medicine lodges were still being built in this style by the Ojibwa of northern Ontario as recently as the 1930s (Ritchie 1965:283, plate 95). Farther afield, Champlain's description of a fortified Montagnais summer camp at Tadoussac reveals that these Indians were living in longhouses in 1603 (Biggar 1922–36, 1:98–99), while a summer camp containing one longhouse, which was also used for holding village feasts, was observed among the Indians of New Brunswick in 1607 (Lescarbot 1907–14, 2:356).

The proto-longhouse from the Summer Island site indicates that multifamily dwellings, resembling the small early Iroquoian longhouse, may have developed among the northern Algonkians long before the end of the Middle Woodland period. A single dwelling approximately twenty-two feet wide and eighty feet long and dated circa A.D. 1300 has been excavated at the Juntunen site, a stratified fishing station on Bois Blanc Island in the Straits of Mackinac. The pottery from this site shows considerable Ontario Iroquoian influence and the excavator has suggested that the longhouse may be further evidence of contact with that area (McPherron 1967:103). Alternatively it may provide a link between the incipient longhouse of the Summer Island site and the longhouses reported among the historic Nipissing, Ojibwa, and other northern groups. Until strong evidence to the contrary is forthcoming, it seems preferable to view the longhouse as an extension of the smaller multifamily dwellings that were prevalent among the hunting tribes of this area and that only now are being recognized in the archaeological record. The longhouse may not have been the invention of any one group, but the result of a trend that manifested itself whenever larger houses were required. The greater frequency of longhouses on Iroquoian sites, and their exceptional size, may simply reflect the ability of larger numbers of related families to live together throughout the year once a horticultural economy was introduced.

Ontario and New York State remained relatively unaffected by developments that took place in the central Mississippi, Ohio, and Illinois River valleys between 300 B.C. and A.D. 250. Between these dates, the Hopewell tradition, which drew some of its inspiration from the earlier Adena culture of the Ohio Valley, evolved and flourished in this region. The beginning of Hopewell was marked by significant increases in population and in the size of local aggregations, by the development of a ceremonial and mortuary complex with strong evidence of status differences, and by increased interaction between groups over a wide area of the eastern United States. One feature of this interaction was the extensive trading of exotic raw materials, such as copper, silver, mica, gelena, obsidian, large marine shells, and fresh water pearls; another was the widespread sharing of selected artifact styles (Struever 1968:288). The luxury goods produced in this period, such as stone pipes with bowls in the form of birds and animals, personal ornaments made of copper and mica, and elaborate pottery figurines, marked a high point in the artistic expression of the northeastern United States. Cloth was manufactured by a finger weaving technique and decorated with batik patterns, or with designs worked in copper, pearls, and shell. Pottery also attained an artistic level, both in shape and decoration, that was not to be equalled thereafter in the region. Another spectacular product of Hopewell industry was large numbers of burial mounds and vast geometrical earthworks that seem to have been cult centres. These were usually located on cliffs and other eminences overlooking rivers.

In spite of a high level of cultural development, Hopewell sites are generally confined to the broad bottoms of flat river valleys that lie within the deciduous forest area of the American Midwest. Deer were more common in the broken forests of this region than they were in New York State and Ontario. Vast numbers of birds migrated along the river valleys, and the permanent lakes that dotted the valley bottoms abounded in fish. Hopewell culture was able to develop and flourish, at least in the Illinois area, largely because of an economic pattern based on the intensive collection of certain selected natural plant foods and, probably secondarily, upon floodplain agriculture. The main plant foods that were available were acorns, hickory nuts, and seed-bearing plants such as marsh-elder (*Iva*), smartweed (*Polygonom*), and lamb's-quarter (*Chenopodium*). All of these plants grew naturally in this area in sufficiently large concentrations that they could be harvested with a small labour input. The local seed plants may also have been grown on the floodplain, along with southern imports, such as gourds, pumpkins, sunflowers, beans, and maize. There is no evidence, however, that these imports, or indeed agriculture as a whole, bulked as large in the Hopewell cultural pattern as they did in the Iroquoian one (Struever and Vickery 1973).

Although Hopewell sites are found as far north as Grand Rapids, Michigan, none are known in southern Ontario. The main evidence of Hopewell influence in Ontario comes from the Middle Woodland burial mounds located in the Trent Valley region, and particularly along the north shore of Rice Lake. These mounds, which date roughly between 100 B.C. and A.D. 300, occur in an area rich in wild rice and which seems to have been one of the major centres of population in Ontario in the Middle Woodland period. Some of the burial mounds, such as the Le Vesconte Mound on the Trent River and the Cameron's Point one on Rice Lake, have yielded grave goods of Hopewellian type, including copper and conch shell pendants, cut mica, perforated sharks' teeth, and panpipe sheaths made out of silver and copper (Johnston 1968*a*). The majority of mounds, however, show few, if any, clear-cut traces of Hopewell connection. The burial mounds, as a whole, may be explained as products of a weak Hopewellian influence on the local Point Peninsula culture of southeastern Ontario. These influences may have arrived in Ontario from New York State, by way of the Squawkie Hill culture, which is itself a local Point Peninsula manifestation influenced by Hopewellian ideas and elements of material culture, many of which appear to be of a religious nature (Ritchie 1965:213–14). The Ontario sites thus occur on the outer fringes of the Hopewellian sphere, and were probably modelled after what were already "attenuated examples of Hopewellian practice" (Johnston 1968*a*:29). It is perhaps no accident that the mounds showing the clearest evidence of Hopewell influence seem to be the earliest in the region. This would indicate the very short-lived and tenuous influence that cultural ideas of southern origin exerted on southern Ontario at this time.

In spite of this, the widespread evidence of native copper artifacts and exotic shells indicates that Ontario was far from isolated during the Middle Woodland period. While these contacts were less extensive geographically than were those of the Hopewell culture, they maintained all of the links with the upper Great Lakes and the southeastern United States that have been noted in the preceding Archaic period. Although the bulk of copper found in any one site was generally smaller than found in earlier sites, this may reflect the marked increase in the population that was now drawing upon the copper supplies of the Lake Superior region. The rising demand for copper may, in part, explain why it was used increasingly for ornamentation rather than for manufacturing bulky prestige tools (Ritchie 1965:178).

THE EARLY IROQUOIAN PERIOD

Early in the Christian era, cultural change began to quicken its pace both in southern Ontario and New York State. In spite of the presence of some type of horticulture in the Hopewellian tradition, there is no proof, either direct or indirect, that crops were grown farther to the north much before A.D. 500. It has been suggested that tropical flint corn, which was the ancestor of most of the corn grown in the northeastern United States in later times, had not yet been adapted for areas where there were fewer than 150 frost-free days.[9] The flint corn which eventually would be cultivated by the northern Iroquoian-speaking peoples had a growing period of only 100 days, while the less popular flour corn matured in 130 days. These hardier varieties were eventually to grow as far north as Lake Nipissing and the south shore of Lake Superior. Despite the apparent lack of cultigens, pottery vessels generally became larger in the Middle and Late Point Peninsula cultures, possibly indicating a more sedentary way of life (Ritchie 1965:232). Pipes, which were already common in the Kipp Island culture in New York State, grew considerably more so in the succeeding Hunter's Home culture. This suggests that smoking was becoming more popular, but it has not yet been determined whether Indian tobacco (*Nicotiana rustica*) was among the substances being smoked. Ritchie (1965:232) is of the opinion that Hunter's Home marks the point at which *Nicotiana rustica* was introduced into upper New York State as a domesticate, rather than merely as an item of trade from the south, and that corn was probably being grown by this time also. In spite of these changes, the centrally based wandering pattern of Middle Woodland times does not appear to have given way to more sedentary village life anywhere around the lower Great Lakes prior to A.D. 500 (Fitting 1970:143).

In central New York, Hunter's Home evolved into the Owasco culture, which Ritchie (1965:271–72) divides into three phases: Early (or Carpenter Brook), Middle (Canandaigua), and Late (Castle Creek). The last of these phases persisted until about A.D. 1300 and is ancestral to the historic

Iroquois cultures. Throughout the Owasco period, there is evidence of growing dependence on food crops. It has been suggested that, in part, this may have been made possible by a relatively mild climatic phase, the so-called Neo-Atlantic Optimum, which lasted from approximately A.D. 900 to 1200 (Martijn 1969:96–97). Of at least equal importance may have been a crucial but as yet little understood breakthrough in acclimatizing crops to a shorter growing season. Corn, beans, and squash are evidenced in New York State in Early Owasco times (Ritchie and Funk 1973:186).

The introduction of horticulture is commonly believed to have resulted in a marked increase in population during the Owasco period (Ritchie 1965:280; Whallon 1968:236). In New York State many horticultural sites have been found on the second terraces of large streams, above the flood plain where the crops were planted, although others are located a considerable distance from any waterway (Ritchie 1965:273, 280). It has been argued that, in at least some areas, the northern Iroquoians were already inhabiting such sites on a year-round basis, as they did in historic times. Studies of faunal evidence from large sites in western New York suggest, however, that these were occupied only during the warmer months of the year, as fishing camps had been previously (White 1963:8–10). It is therefore possible that a sedentary village pattern developed more slowly than is generally believed, and remained incomplete throughout early Iroquoian times.

Whether or not this is the case, it is clear that these horticultural villages were not the only unit of settlement in Owasco times, any more than in the historic period. Fishing camps along lakes and rivers, hunting camps on the glaciated Allegheny Plateau and, finally, traces of habitation on the floodplains, which contain mostly pottery and probably were summer houses inhabited by women working in the fields, are all evidence of a variety of sites, which some or all of the inhabitants of these larger villages must have lived in at different times of the year (Ritchie 1965:279–80).

With the Owasco culture, the coiled pottery of earlier times gave way to an improved form of seamless pottery that was shaped out of a ball of tempered clay, using a small wooden paddle. Early Owasco vessels had flat lips; later, they were often sharply splayed out. Vessels gradually became less elongate and more globular and, in the Castle Creek phase, many were collared and had well-marked castellated rims. Pots were up to twelve gallons in capacity, suggesting that food was sometimes cooked for more than a nuclear family (ibid. 289–93). The exterior of these vessels was check-stamped, or cord or fabric impressed. Other decorations were confined to the upper portions of the vessel and were executed with a cord-wrapped stick or paddle edge.

The largest village of the Early Owasco period excavated so far is the Maxon-Derby site, near Syracuse. This site, which is dated about A.D. 1100, covers two acres and does not appear to have been fortified. Within the excavated portion of the site, post molds belonging to seven houses have been uncovered. These houses had parallel sides with rounded ends, and varied in size from twenty by twenty-three feet to sixty by twenty-seven feet. They appear to have been arbour-shaped structures covered with sheets of bark supported on a framework of poles. The latter were from two and a half to three inches in diameter and were spaced six to ten inches apart. The four principal houses show signs of having been repaired and enlarged several times and one of them may have had a vestibule by the doorway for storing provisions and gear. Contrary to late Iroquoian practice, fireplaces were arranged along one or both of the long sides of these houses. The total village is estimated to have contained at least ten houses and to have had a population of 200 to 250 people (ibid. 281–84).

These longhouses were not the only house-types in New York State during the early phase of Iroquoian cultural development. At the Sackett site, farther east in what would later be Cayuga territory, a series of circular houses, twelve to fourteen feet across and with a single hearth in the middle, has been uncovered. This site, which is assigned to the Middle Owasco period and dated about A.D. 1140, covers about three acres and was surrounded by a simple palisade. Its large size and estimated population of some 350 people make it highly unlikely that it was a seasonal hunting or fishing camp (ibid. 286).

The Chamberlin site, located only three miles from Maxon-Derby, but about two centuries later in time (circa A.D. 1290), shows a gradual development in the direction of the historic Iroquoian settlement pattern. Although the hearths remain near the walls of the houses, the houses themselves are now over eighty feet long. Like the Sackett site, Chamberlin was surrounded by a low ridge of earth, which probably once supported the base of a palisade that was set on, but not into, the ground (Tuck 1971:23–34). The fortifications that begin to appear at this site and others may indicate increasing warfare during the Middle and Late Owasco periods. At least some palisades consist of a single line of posts, about three inches in diameter and set three to eighteen inches apart. To be an effective barrier, such posts would have had to be interwoven with vines and smaller sticks (Ritchie 1965:284). Small trees were used to construct houses and palisades, in part because of the difficulty involved in felling large numbers of big trees with stone axes.

Although there is only slender evidence of areal stylistic variation within the Owasco culture, strings of village sites have been discovered that can be shown to have been inhabited in succession by a single community from Owasco times into the historic period. These studies reveal that the ancestors of the Mohawk, Onondaga, Seneca, and presumably the other Iroquois tribes, were located in their historic tribal territories from at least Owasco times onward, and that no theories of migrations are needed to account for their development (Tuck 1971).

On the whole, villages appear to have been smaller, more numerous, and more evenly spaced in Owasco times than they were later. There is no evidence that the individual tribes known in historic times existed as political entities this early. Nevertheless, such continuity of occupation, in circumscribed areas over long periods of time, provides some clue to the social reality that underlies the longstanding linguistic divisions between most of the tribes of the Five Nations. Since the Iroquois found themselves surrounded by other agricultural peoples, individual groups strove to defend their territories in the face of growing competition, probably over hunting and fishing grounds rather than agricultural land. The effect of such behaviour was not to make one group dominant over another, but to maintain a balanced distribution of groups, each holding on to its own territory. It is possible that, even during the early Iroquoian period, alliances may have embraced more than a single village, although this is far from certain.

The earliest horticultural economy yet known in southern Ontario belongs to the recently defined Princess Point culture or complex, which may have begun before A.D. 500 (map 3a). This culture has been interpreted as an extension of the Early Owasco culture into the southern part of southwestern Ontario, an area generally lying within the same deciduous forest belt as the Owasco sites in New York State. The pottery, pipes, and lithic material from Princess Point sites are said to be very similar to those from Early Owasco ones, although certain attributes, such as the high percentage of exterior punctates on the rims of pottery vessels, suggest affinities with the Black Duck culture in northern Ontario and Minnesota. All of the sites studied so far are located on river flats, small sheltered inlets, or streams close to rivers. The Porteous site, which dates near the end of this culture, has yielded traces of a longhouse, thirty-six feet long and twenty-two feet wide, with a central distribution of hearths inside it (plate 11). Carbonized corn has been found on even the earliest Princess

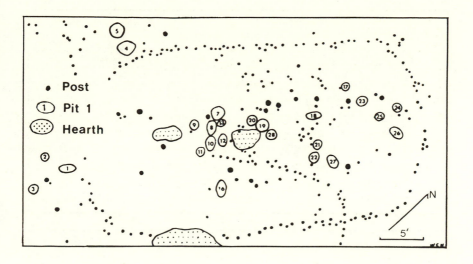

PLATE 11. *Plan of a small longhouse from the Porteous site, near
Brantford, Ontario (late Princess Point or early Glyn Meyer culture,
c. A.D. 700). This longhouse belongs to an early stage in the development of
a horticultural economy in southern Ontario. Two hearths are centrally
aligned 5½ feet apart. The structure resembles in many ways the "incipient
longhouse" from the much earlier Summer Island site. Courtesy
W. C. Noble.*

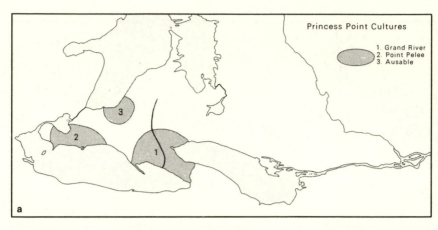

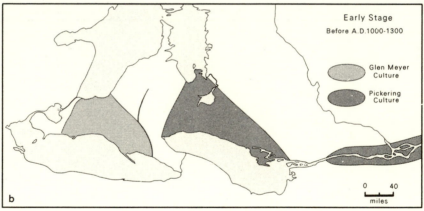

MAP 3. *Current synthesis of the Iroquoian developmental sequence in Ontario (based largely on Wright 1961 and 1972 and Stothers 1974).*

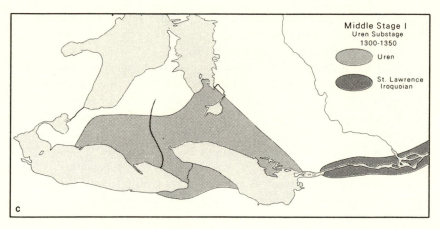

Middle Stage I
Uren Substage
1300-1350

Uren

St. Lawrence
Iroquoian

c

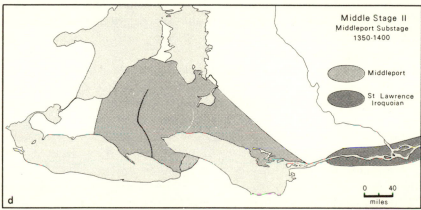

Middle Stage II
Middleport Substage
1350-1400

Middleport

St Lawrence
Iroquoian

0   40
miles

d

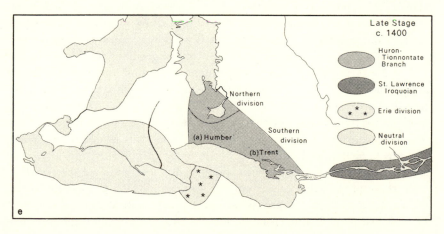

Late Stage
c. 1400

Huron-
Tionnontate
Branch

St. Lawrence
Iroquoian

Erie division

Neutral
division

Northern
division

Southern
division

(a) Humber

(b) Trent

e

Point sites. One carbonized bean has been tentatively associated with this culture, although beans are not attested elsewhere in Ontario until much later (Stothers 1970; Noble and Kenyon 1972).

The Princess Point culture appears to have evolved into what archaeologists call the Glen Meyer culture, which lasted until approximately A.D. 1300. The Glen Meyer culture was confined to southwestern Ontario. Most sites found so far are between Port Rowan, on Lake Erie, and Ipperwash, on Lake Huron; an area containing large tracts of sandy, easily worked soil (map *3b*). Because of lack of excavation, little can be said with certainty about the settlement pattern associated with this culture. Villages tended to be located between small ravines or on hilltops, in a manner that indicates a concern for defence. Such sites appear large by Iroquoian standards, many covering five to ten acres. They also occur in clusters, although it is unclear how many sites in any one cluster are contemporary. The size and clustering of village sites and an apparent absence of hunting camps has been claimed as evidence of heavy reliance on horticulture (Wright 1966:22–40; 52–53).

The Glen Meyer culture is distinguished from the contemporary, but possibly later-starting, Pickering culture, which occupied the region lying between Lake Ontario and the Canadian Shield and possibly extended down the St. Lawrence Valley and into New York State (ibid. 40–53; Trigger 1968*a*:436). Although the general character of the archaeological remains associated with the Pickering (plate 12) and Glen Meyer cultures is the same, they can clearly be differentiated from one another. While many ceramic attributes, including vessel form, paddle and anvil manufacturing, distribution of decoration, and bossing are held in common, the body of the pot was characteristically covered with ribbed paddle or checked stamp impressions in the Pickering culture and the technique of scarification was largely limited to the Glen Meyer culture. Also, pottery gaming discs and cup-and-pin game deer phalanges have so far been found only in Pickering sites, while slate pendants are found only in Glen Meyer ones. Pipes are scarce in both cultures, and are much cruder than those from Owasco sites in New York State (Wright 1966:51, 53; cf. plate 10, 6–16 and Ritchie 1965, plate 100). While it is generally assumed that tobacco was grown in Ontario at this time, its status as a domestic plant remains to be demonstrated. Corn was grown by the Pickering people, but their villages appear to have been smaller and more widely dispersed than were those of the Glen Meyer culture and, in addition to moderate-sized horticultural villages, there were numerous small campsites, usually located near good fishing spots. Because of this, it has been suggested that

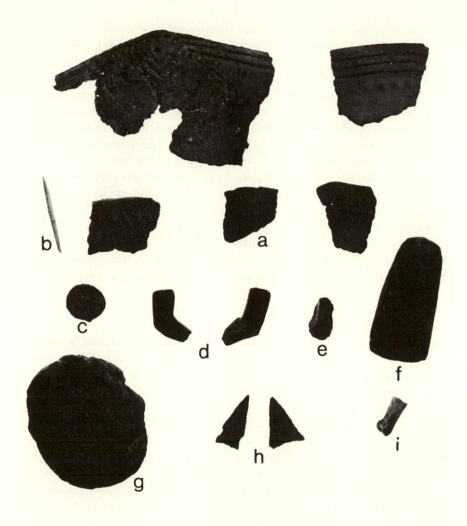

PLATE 12. *Typical early Iroquoian artifacts from Ontario (Pickering culture): (a) broken pottery; (b) bone awl; (c) pottery gaming disc; (d) pottery pipes; (e) stone scraper; (f) adze; (g) anvil stone; (h) arrowheads; (i) deer toe bone altered for unknown purpose. Courtesy National Museum of Man, National Museums of Canada.*

the Pickering culture may have been less dependent on horticulture than was its western counterpart (Wright 1966:22). In general, the larger Pickering villages were located inland, on naturally defensible sites.

Fortunately, two of these habitation sites have been excavated in sufficient detail to yield considerable information about their settlement patterns. The earlier of the two is the Miller site, east of Toronto. This site has been radiocarbon dated about A.D. 1125, and is thus roughly contemporary with the Maxon-Derby site. It covers approximately one acre and was surrounded by a palisade consisting of a single line of small poles, which were no doubt woven together in the same manner as Owasco palisades. Inside the village were five houses, each with parallel side walls and rounded ends (plate 13). These houses varied in size from thirty-eight by twenty to sixty by twenty-eight feet, and the largest of them had five hearths down the centre. This central alignment of hearths occurs in the Middle Woodland Summer Island site, but not in early Iroquoian sites in New York State. The houses were not arranged in any special relationship to one another and there is no evidence of internal structures, such as sleeping platforms running along the walls (although these seem present at the earlier Porteous site). The framework was constructed entirely of small trees, which could be cut and bent easily. As far as could be determined, each house had only a single door, located at one end of the structure (Kenyon 1968).

The partially excavated Bennett site is located about thirteen miles northwest of Hamilton and is dated circa A.D. 1260, near the end of the early Iroquoian stage of development. The village is located on a small knoll, about one mile from the nearest stream, and covers two and a half to three acres. It was surrounded by a palisade which, over much of its length, consisted of two rows of posts, running two to three feet from each other. The individual posts were about two and a half inches in diameter and six inches to one foot apart. The one house that was fully excavated measured fifty-five by twenty-two and a half feet, while other houses, which were not fully excavated, were approximately the same width and even longer (plate 14). Hearths were arranged along the main axes of these houses, as they were at the Miller site, and post molds six inches or more in diameter were found aligned parallel to the walls of the houses but about four feet, eight inches in from the walls. These posts appear to have supported two rows of sleeping platforms. One house had an extension at one end about fifteen feet long, but the absence of hearths or sleeping platforms in this section suggests that it was probably used for storage. Traces were also found of sheds built against the outside walls of these

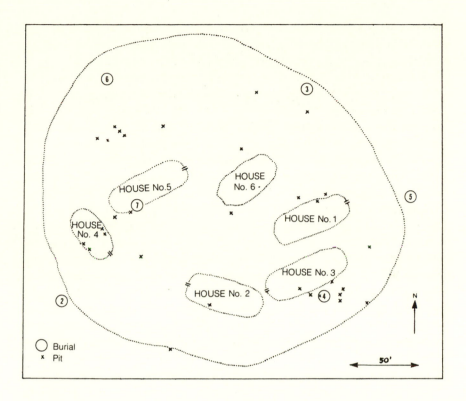

Burial ◯

Pit ×

HOUSE No.5

HOUSE No. 6

HOUSE No. 1

HOUSE No. 4

HOUSE No. 2

HOUSE No. 3

N

50'

PLATE 13. *Plan of the Miller site showing palisade and outlines of houses*
(c. A.D. 1125). This site is assigned to the Pickering culture. The palisade
is formed of a single line of poles; houses are from 38 feet to 60 feet long.
The largest had five hearths down the centre. Courtesy W. A. Kenyon and
Royal Ontario Museum, Toronto.

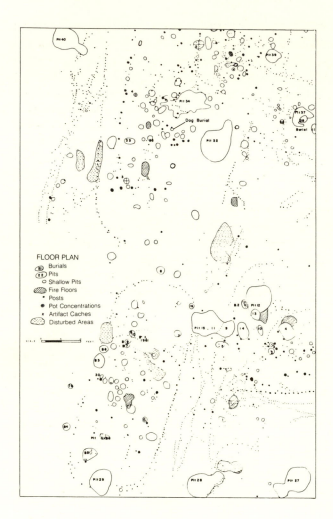

PLATE 14. *House patterns in a portion of the Bennett site* (C. A.D. *1260).
This site is also assigned to the Pickering culture. The palisade consisted,
in parts, of two rows of posts 2 to 3 feet apart. A few large posts inside each
house supported sleeping platforms and sheds were built against the outside
walls of the houses, probably to store firewood. The extension to house 1
lacked hearths and appears to have been a storage area. Courtesy National
Museum of Man, National Museums of Canada.*

houses. They may have been used to store wood. There seem to have been doors at either end of the one house that was completely excavated, but the evidence is not clear on this point (Wright and Anderson 1969).

On the basis of present evidence, numerous similarities can be observed in the development of settlement patterns in the Owasco and Pickering cultures. In both, villages were small and, throughout the early Iroquoian period, there appears to have been an increasing emphasis on their defence. The longhouse had a similar shape in both Ontario and New York State, and appears to have been increasing in length. In Ontario, however, the absence of circular houses and the central alignment of hearths suggest a more rapid development of the house-type of the historic period than is found in New York State.[10] The use of larger timbers to support sleeping platforms also may be a "progressive" feature which first makes its appearance in Ontario. This suggests that at least some features of the Iroquoian longhouse may have originated in the north and did not diffuse into the southern part of the northern Iroquoian culture area until considerably later. The many innovations observed in settlement patterns during the duration of the Pickering culture are in keeping with rapid changes noted in other aspects of this culture (Wright 1966:53).

The Owasco, Princess Point, and Pickering cultures provide evidence of what appears to have been a widespread, and fairly rapid, shift towards a horticultural subsistence pattern and a more sedentary village life amongst the Iroquoian-speaking peoples of the region, beginning before A.D. 500. This was a transition in which the Algonkian-speaking peoples of New England and the midwestern United States also seem to have participated. While, because of an uncertain growing season and limited amounts of soil, horticulture never became a dominant mode of subsistence on the southern fringe of the Canadian Shield, a significant amount of corn appears to have been grown at least as far north as the Straits of Mackinac by A.D. 1200 (McPherron 1967:103).

What caused the widespread adoption of horticulture at this time? The usual explanation has been that horticulture diffused among the hunting and gathering peoples of New England and the lower Great Lakes as soon as cultigens became available that were adapted to the shorter growing season of these regions. Such an explanation assumes that hunting and gathering peoples will inevitably perceive an agricultural economy to be superior to their own and will plant crops as soon as they become available. Today, this is not a position that all anthropologists are willing to accept. Some would argue, correctly I believe, that any explanation of the spread of agriculture must take account, not only of how suitable crops came to be present, but also of those factors in the recipient cultures that predisposed their members to accept them. It is possible to turn the argument around and to claim that a pre-existing need for new sources of food might have produced a situation in which experimentation took place and which, in turn, led to the development of corn with a shorter growing season.

One hypothesis holds that population pressure was the principal factor leading to the adoption of a horticultural economy. An increasing population in the late Middle Woodland period might have generated a need for new sources of food and created the conditions under which horticulture initially was adopted. The greater sustaining power of food crops led to a rapid increase in population during the Owasco period, which reinforced reliance on domesticated foods. At the same time, increasing competition over natural resources produced greater conflict, which forced scattered groups to band together for defence and, by concentrating the population, increased still further their reliance on horticulture (P. Smith 1972:418).

As yet we know very little about population trends immediately prior to the early Iroquoian period. While the evidence from New York State is generally interpreted as indicating a rapid growth in population during the Owasco period, it is unclear how much this evidence reflects real growth and how much it results from the greater ease with which archaeologists can detect larger and more sedentary sites. Nor is it clear whether increasing village size resulted wholly from a growing population or was the result of hitherto separate groups coming together to form larger communities. Until much more evidence is available than has been published to date, any speculations about population trends during this period are bound to be hazardous.

Moreover, even in the historic period, the overall population density of the northern Iroquoian culture area was probably no more than three persons per square mile.[11] The amount of land under cultivation was a minuscule portion of the total of easily workable soil that was available. It has been estimated that even the exceptionally dense population of the Huron country could have increased significantly before any kind of cyclical fallowing system would have been required as a response to pressure on the land (Heidenreich 1971:198). More plausible factors keeping overall population densities low might have been the inability of the Iroquoians to increase the amount of fish and meat that could be collected and, more importantly, the limited number of deer and other animals that were available to provide skins for clothing. Deer occur in greatest concentrations in areas where openings border on the edge of forests (ibid. 206). While such clearings would have increased significantly with the advent of slash and burn horticulture, the deer population was probably kept down by overhunting. Pressures on natural resources could have led to conflict between neighbouring groups, yet it is noteworthy that in historic times the majority of closely neighbouring tribes not only were at peace with one another but, in some cases, even shared their hunting territories. Population control was effected by the lengthy nursing of the young, which resulted in small families, and to a lesser degree by war and by inadequate care of women in childbirth. Thus, whatever demographic trends were like prior to the early Iroquoian period, the adoption of horticulture appears to have created as many, if not more, problems than it solved. Population increase is unlikely to have been exerting strong pressure on fish and game resources prior to the adoption of horticulture and, if it were, the adoption of food crops would have done nothing to remedy a resultant shortage of skins for clothing. The fact that even the historic Iroquoian populations were well supplied with such necessities suggests that natural resources were more abundant in relation to the population at an earlier time than any theory of cultural change resulting from population pressure would require.

My alternative explanation postulates that the seasonal cycle of the hunting and gathering peoples of this area pre-adapted them for horticulture. In modern times it has been noted that, among northern Algonkian peoples, the large summer gatherings at fishing sites are highly valued, as they provide an opportunity for social interaction that extends beyond a small segment of a patrilineage. Thus, when government subsidies or the profits of the fur trade increase the economic resources of a band, there is a strong tendency for its members to continue living together in one place throughout the year.[12] Where European traders or government officials are not present, leadership is provided for such groups by the traditional headman of the band, who formerly maintained order during the summer. Thus, even from a political point of view, these bands appear to have had the basic structures necessary to transform themselves into permanent communities. There is no reason why the Iroquoian-speaking tribes living south of the Canadian Shield should not have been similarly inclined and structured in prehistoric times.

Corn may originally have been experimented with as a substitute for wild rice. It had the advantage that it could be grown more widely and in proximity to a broader range of desirable locations; moreover, the danger of losing a crop was considerably less.[13] As soon as varieties of corn even marginally capable of growing in the north came to hand they would have been recognized as a valuable source of food and the amount grown would have been increased as a means of extending the length of time that a band could remain together annually. As corn was produced that was still better adapted to a shorter growing season, it gave rise to an economy capable of supporting a sedentary group, which does not appear to have been possible relying only on wild rice. An example of a transitional economy is provided by the Ottawa bands, who, in early historic times, lived along the western border between southern Ontario and the Canadian Shield. Each band had a main village where crops were grown and which was inhabited throughout most of the year by the women, children, and old men. During the summer, parties of both sexes wandered one hundred miles or more from the village to hunt, fish, and dry blueberries, while, in the winter, groups each made up of eight to ten men went on lengthy hunting expeditions, eventually transporting meat back to their villages in a processed form (Fitting and Cleland 1969:295–96).

This explanation suggests that the nuclei of the earliest sedentary villages in this area may have been the hunting bands of an earlier period. The patrilineal bands associated with a hunting and gathering economy ranged in size from about thirty members up to several hundred, the size depending largely on the resources that were available and the efficiency with which they were exploited (Service 1962:70). It is reasonable to assume that the bands living in the lower Great Lakes area in late Middle Woodland times would have been near the upper limits of this range and it may be more than a coincidence that the earliest sedentary villages appear to have had two or three hundred inhabitants. The small size of the early Iroquoian settlements suggests that, while a number of extended families lived at least part of the year in a single village, as previously they had lived together during the summer, separate bands had not yet begun to join together to form larger communities. It also suggests that, unless a rapid fissioning of groups was going on, the increase in population during this period was less than has been assumed. It is reasonable to suppose that these early Iroquoian bands were in some way the basis of the clan segments that made up the larger Iroquoian villages of later times. From the Huron data presented in chapter 2, it is clear that, while clan segments were joined together within larger political structures and larger units of settlement, they retained much of the political and jural autonomy that hunting bands had enjoyed prior to becoming sedentary.

At some point the basis of group membership must have shifted from being patrilineal to being matrilineal, although it is difficult to determine when this happened.[14] Iroquoian archaeologists generally have argued that the development of the matrilineal extended family can be traced in the development of the Iroquoian longhouse. As we have seen, however, extended families can be based on either matrilineal or patrilineal descent systems, and the mere presence of a longhouse cannot, by itself, determine which method of descent was being followed. Deetz (1965) has predicted that where women make pottery there will be a greater tendency for particular design attributes to cluster on the pottery produced in a matri-local community than in one with any other rules of residence. This is because women who are matrilineally related to one another will tend to live together and hence pass on particular styles to their daughters, where-as, in a patrilocal household, women from various families will be brought together; hence the girls they train will inherit a more heterogeneous repertoire of designs. In a preliminary study of Iroquoian pottery from New York State, Whallon (1968) has found that the stylistic homogeneity of pottery within villages and the clustering of attributes tend to increase during Owasco times and later, but are already high in the Early Owasco period. This suggests that matrilocal residence was widely practised by then, at least in New York State, even though it may have become more prevalent later on.

Various explanations have been offered for this presumed shift from patrilocal to matrilocal residence. It has been noted that some communities that are heavily dependent on fishing (such as were found among the tribes along the coast of British Columbia) have matrilineal kinship systems and matrilocal, or avunculocal, residence patterns. On this basis it has been suggested that heavy reliance on fishing might have led to a shift from patrilineal to matrilineal descent in the lower Great Lakes region in the later Middle Woodland period. Ritchie (1965:296) and Whallon (1968: 236) have argued, however, that the development of female work groups engaged in horticulture was the chief factor leading to the adoption of matrilocal residence patterns. A general theory of matrilocal residence postulates that it develops when women assume a dominant role in food production, or when horticulture becomes the main source of nutrition and hence women's work becomes more valuable than men's work (Schneider and Gough 1961:660–61; 667). The application of this theory to Iroquoian society assumes that the team that was of the greatest economic importance was a woman and her daughters cooperating to grow crops.

This argument ignores the economic importance of male activities, such as fishing, forest clearance, house building, trade, and defence, all of which are known to have required a considerable degree of teamwork and may have been at least as important in the Huron's estimation as were the planting, tending, and harvesting of crops. Moreover, while the women of a household may have shared their produce, there is little evidence that they worked together to produce it. The main work team in the fields appears to have been a woman and her young children, the boys being employed to chase away birds and wild animals. The important work teams in Iroquoian society seem to have been principally male ones.[15]

The development of larger extended family households and of their matrilineal bias may best be studied separately. The greater economic security that resulted from the sharing of all kinds of resources within these extended households must have played an important role in their development. Moreover, if feuding has as great an antiquity in Iroquoian culture as it appears to have, growing need for protection, as evidenced by palisades being constructed around villages, may have played an important role in inducing greater numbers of nuclear families to live together in a single house. Such an arrangement would have made a surprise attack more difficult. It is also likely that by this time a new division of labour in Iroquoian society was keeping men away from their villages and in scattered groups for much of the year, while the women remained at home, in daily face-to-face contact with one another. This situation was very different from the older hunting and gathering pattern, in which husbands and wives moved about together throughout the year. This new relationship between the sexes, combined with a higher mortality rate among young men than women because of war and accidents, may have encouraged the formation of matrilocal households as the most stable form of extended family.[16]

Because matrilineal descent generally develops as a response to matrilocal residence, rather than the reverse (Schneider and Gough 1961:551–54; 659–60), matrilineal clans and matrilineal inheritance of office could have arisen in response to a growing pattern of matrilocal residence. Yet, as already noted, even in the historical period the Iroquoian kinship system had not evolved a strongly matrilineal pattern. Bilateral tendencies were evident in kinship terminology and in marriage prohibitions, which extended to both the paternal and maternal side of the family. The Huron-Wyandot use of the term "father's sister" (*ahrä'hoc*)[17] to refer to "mother's brother's wife" and the reciprocal use of "mother's brother" (*häwäteno'rä*) for "father's sister's husband" suggests that, at some time in the past, the Huron and their neighbours may have practised cross-cousin marriage. This was something that Fred Eggan (1952:43; 1966:104) suspected about the Iroquoians in general long ago on the basis of other evidence, and which he points out, if true, would link the origins of the northern Iroquoian kinship systems much more closely to those of neighbouring Algonkian peoples, such as the Cree, Ojibwa, and Ottawa. The survival of this usage in Wyandot, but not in the Iroquois languages, suggests greater conservatism in kinship terminology in the northern part of the Iroquoian culture area than farther south. Yet, even among the Huron, cross-cousin marriage, if it ever existed, was suppressed in favour of bilateral marriage prohibitions, possibly in order to diversify marital alliances once multi-clan communities had developed.

More archaeological studies of the sort Whallon attempted are needed, both in Ontario and New York State, as well as the combined efforts of ethnologists and historical linguists, if further work is to be accomplished on the reconstruction and interpretation of early and proto-Iroquoian kinship systems. Until diverse knowledge of this sort is forthcoming, much will remain unknown about changes in Iroquoian social structure and we will be uncertain whether there was a significant time lag in the evolution of new kinship systems from one region to another. It is perhaps significant that while there is evidence for corn, beans, and squash in New York State at the beginning of the Owasco period, corn is the only domestic plant so far demonstrated to be present in either the Glen Meyer or Pickering cultures. The absence of beans would have seriously limited the Ontario Iroquoian subsistence economy. Corn, while rich in carbohydrates and varying in the total amount of protein, is always deficient in the vital amino acids lysine and tryptophane, which are abundant in *Phaseolus* species (Kaplan 1967:202–3). Any diet in which corn and beans are both present has a nutritional value adequate for all but the most protein sensitive members of the population, such as lactating mothers and newly weaned babies. While we know little about the Glen Meyer culture, it is possible that the small and dispersed nature of Pickering villages, and the large number of hunting and fishing camps in that culture, reflect the nutritional limitations of the horticultural complex that was available to them, as compared to the Owasco culture. Until more studies have been made of the ecology of Pickering sites, it can be questioned whether the agricultural villages were occupied throughout the year and whether they had yet become the foci of Iroquoian life that they were in historic times.

Some light may be shed on the role that these villages played by the burial customs of the period. Two well-separated Owasco cemeteries were found at the Sackett site, but most graves of that culture are randomly dispersed throughout the villages. The vast majority of interments are flexed primary burials, that were made soon enough after death that the body had not yet begun to decompose (Ritchie 1965:295–96). At the Miller and Bennett sites, bodies were found buried inside and around houses, and sometimes even outside the palisades, in pits containing from one to thirteen bodies. While some of these bodies were flexed primary interments, a significant number, particularly where multiple burials were involved, consisted either of bodies that had been dismembered, or of completely decayed ones whose bones had been wrapped in a bundle prior to being buried (Wright and Anderson 1969:11–13; Kenyon 1968:21–23). It is perhaps significant that at the earlier Miller site, only one body out of a total of thirty-two was a primary burial.

The multiple burials, and the varying condition in which bodies were interred, raise important questions. It is possible that during the warmer months individuals were buried soon after death. The disarticulated bodies could have been those who died far from their villages and had been brought back for burial or who had died over the winter and could not be buried until the ground thawed out in the spring. In a village of 250 people, six to nine persons might be expected to die of old age and disease in a normal year, most of them during the winter.

While it is possible that each extended family buried its dead separately, each multiple burial may also represent the dead of a whole village who were available for burial in the spring, possibly after bodies had been brought in from outlying campsites. The burial with thirteen bodies found at the Miller site suggests an unusually high mortality rate (from disease?), but there is no reason to interpret this single occurrence, or multiple burials in village sites generally, as necessarily being an incipient form of ossuary interment. The basic elements of the latter ritual, namely, the temporary interment of all, or most, of the community's dead and their reburial in a common grave when the village was abandoned, seem to be conspicuously missing from the Pickering sites that have been excavated so far. As yet, no rules have been formulated that can explain satisfactorily the pattern in which burials were distributed in relationship to houses and to the village as a whole.

Considerable light has been cast on Pickering burial customs by the discovery at the Serpent Mounds site, on Rice Lake, of three early Iroquoian burial pits, each containing a minimum of fifteen to twenty-nine secondary burials (Johnston 1968*b*:48–50; Anderson 1968:12–14). These pits were located near an important burial site of the Middle Woodland period, of which perhaps some traditions had survived into early Iroquoian times. There was, however, no evidence of an Iroquoian village site in the vicinity, and only slender evidence of an Iroquoian fishing camp. Here, it would seem, bodies that had decayed over the winter, or possibly over the course of several years, were buried in a site unattached to any permanent habitation. Such behaviour, which may prefigure the ossuary burial of later times, would nevertheless be distinctly unusual in the historic period, when efforts were made to save the bones of warriors killed in enemy territory, so that these could be brought back to their village for burial. The importance attached to the Serpent Mounds site suggests that, at least in the Pickering culture, villages may have been less of a ritual focus than they were in later times.

Other notable features of burials, in both Ontario and New York State, are the absence of grave goods, except for an occasional clay pipe or pottery vessel, and the apparent simplicity of the burial ritual. Ritchie (1965:179) notes that the mortuary ceremonialism which had played such a conspicuous role in late Archaic and early Middle Woodland times had waned throughout the late Middle Woodland period. It is also pointed out that there is little indication of long distance trade in Owasco sites and the impression is one of a "provincial, self-sufficient and locally orientated people" (ibid. 293). While this would seem to apply, in general, to the Ontario Iroquoians as well, a limited number of beads made of native copper and marine shell are reported from early Iroquoian sites in the province (e.g., Wright and Anderson 1969:74; Wright 1966:39). This indicates that, at least to a limited degree, contacts with the south and the northwest were providing the same exotic materials that are present in Ontario sites from the Archaic period onwards.

THE MIDDLE IROQUOIAN PERIOD

By about A.D. 1300, the evolving Glen Meyer and Pickering cultures had coalesced to give rise to a single middle Iroquoian culture that was present throughout most of southern Ontario west of Kingston and extended into the extreme northwestern part of New York State, close to the Niagara Frontier (Wright 1966:54–65). Whatever cultural connections may have formerly existed between the rest of southern Ontario and the St. Lawrence Valley were severed at this time. Henceforth, the cultures lying east and west of the Frontenac Axis (the rocky part of the Canadian Shield that extends across the St. Lawrence Valley between Kingston and Brockville) were to develop independently of one another. The middle Iroquoian culture of southern Ontario is divided into two substages: Uren, lasting from about A.D. 1300 to 1350 (map 3*c*), and Middleport, from 1350 to 1400 (map 3*d*).

James V. Wright (1966:53; Wright and Anderson 1969:62–77) attributes the emergence of a single culture in southern Ontario at the beginning of this period, to a conquest of the Glen Meyer people by warriors from the Pickering culture. He argues that some of the Glen Meyer people may have fled westward into Michigan, but, for the most part, the conquest led to the partial assimilation of the Glen Meyer culture by the Pickering one; the result being Uren. Uren pottery, which is best known from sites in southwestern Ontario, combines many of the diagnostic features of the earlier Pickering and Glen Meyer ceramics. To the scarified body treatment, formerly present in the region, ribbed paddle impressing and checked stamping, both characteristic of the Pickering culture, are added as important attributes. Other ceramic traits that appear to be derived from the late Pickering culture are castellations decorated with a chevron motif and pottery gaming discs, which begin to appear in southwestern Ontario at this time (Wright 1966:58; Wright and Anderson 1969:64–71, 74). In general, male-manufactured items of culture (stone and bone tools) show a greater similarity to Pickering antecedents than to Glen Meyer ones, although, since the majority of these items were common to both cultures, these similarities are of a minor statistical nature. The one unique Glen Meyer lithic item to carry over into Uren is the pebble pendant. The Glen Meyer end scraper also remains more popular in western Uren sites than it is in the east and lanceolate, stemmed, and corner-notched arrows continue as minor varieties, although they are not found in late Pickering sites such as Bennett, where the small triangular arrowheads characteristic of later times predominate (Wright and Anderson 1969:71–74).

If the development of a more or less uniform Uren culture throughout southern Ontario had been brought about by the rapid diffusion of only male- or female-manufactured items of culture, it might be explained as a result of the practice of exogamy by communities organized on a matrilocal or patrilocal basis, much as Brose has proposed to explain the rapid diffusion of early Middle Woodland pottery styles. Such an explanation is ruled out, however, by the all-embracing nature of the change that is observed in the archaeological record. In spite of this, no direct evidence of conquest has been produced (White 1971*b*). Such evidence might take the form of destroyed villages or settlement patterns which indicated that victors and vanquished were living side by side after the conquest took place. It is significant that in Wright's judgement the cultural homogeneity of Ontario was greater in the later Middleport substage than it had been in Uren, an odd situation if the fusion resulted from military conquest at the beginning of the Uren period. It is, therefore, necessary to consider alternative explanations for the cultural blending that Wright has observed. For example, the evolution of Ontario social structure might have reached a saddlepoint between a declining patrilocal residence pattern and an increasing matrilocal one. Unless exceptional hostilities interfered, there might have been a short period during which both male and female cultural items diffused rapidly from one part of southern Ontario to another, breaking down old cultural divisions. Such a process would have been speeded up if there had been an expanding population.

It is also worth noting that in spite of the general uniformity of material culture in southern Ontario during the one hundred years that the middle Iroquoian stage lasted, at the end of this period a new east-west split developed, which produced the Neutral-Erie and Huron-Tionnontaté cultures respectively. Although we have no certain knowledge of the degree of difference between the Huron and Neutral languages, Brébeuf's statement that Neutral was "not a little" different from Huron, and the trouble that the Jesuits took to draw up a lexicon and grammar comparing the two languages, suggest that the split between them was probably older than two hundred years (Thwaites 1896–1901, 20:105; 21:229–31). This, in turn, suggests that the split between the Glen Meyer and Pickering cultures, at least in part, may also have been a split between the Neutral and Huron languages. If this is true, the events which produced the cultural uniformity of middle Iroquoian times in Ontario did not disrupt ethnic patterns in the region.

Between A.D. 1300 and 1400, Iroquoian pottery in Ontario grew progressively more globular, and collars and castellated rims became more pronounced. The more elaborate decorations on the bodies of pots gave way to a plainer ribbed-paddle treatment and incised decoration around the rim gradually replaced decoration impressed with a cord-wrapped stick (Wright 1966:57–61). These developments paralleled, in a general way, ones in New York State, where Owasco was developing into the Oak Hill culture and giving rise to the cultural traditions that led to the historic Iroquois (Ritchie 1965:302–303). In spite of similar developmental trends, the pottery sequences of Ontario and eastern New York were clearly distinguished from one another (plate 15).

Pipes, some made of stone but most of them ceramic, became important in Ontario in the Middleport substage. Hitherto, pipes had been few in number and crude in execution, but from this time onwards they were abundant and occur in a variety of sophisticated shapes. Although some earlier forms persisted, the new types appear suddenly and apparently have no stylistic relationship to earlier local types. It has been suggested that the novel types were borrowed from the Oak Hill culture of New York State,

PLATE 15. *Typical middle Iroquoian artifacts from Ontario
(c. A.D. 1300–1400): (a) broken pottery; (b) stone and pottery pipes;
(c–h) bone objects: hair piece or comb, awls, netting needle, flute, antler
flaking tool; (i) stone adze; (j) gaming disc; (k) arrowhead; (l) juvenile
model pottery; (m) perforated bear canine; (n) stone scraper.
Courtesy National Museum of Man, National Museums of Canada.*

where prototypes appear to have evolved from the already more advanced pipe complex of the Owasco culture (Wright 1966:62–63). Henceforth, although pipes are less elaborate in Ontario than in New York State, there is a steady increase in their variety and complexity. The introduction of the Middleport pipe complex may mark the time when *Nicotiana rustica* began to be grown with any regularity. Although it is suggested that specific pipe designs may have been the property of particular clan segments, there is no convincing evidence to support this claim. Men may have purchased pipes that pleased them and designs, as such, may have had no social connotations.

Throughout the middle Iroquoian period, the population of southern Ontario appears to have lived in a relatively small number of large villages, but made extensive use of numerous, widely scattered hunting and fishing camps (Wright 1966:64). The largest sites cover more than five acres and longhouses began to be purposely aligned parallel to one another within these villages (Noble 1969:19). Such alignments permitted more structures to be located inside a palisade, and the planning involved was a significant response to larger village populations. It is uncertain, from the archaeological evidence, whether more than a single clan segment inhabited a village at this time, but the size of the villages makes it likely that sometimes they did. This would have required the development of town councils, as distinct from the traditional government of clan segments by a headman in consultation with the adult males of his group.

Houses probably continued to increase in length during this period, although the evidence is far from conclusive. Also, storage cubicles seem to have become more common at the ends of houses (Noble 1969:18). The most curious house plans are from the Webb site in Simcoe County, which dates from the Middleport substage. At this site, located on the edge of a marsh about a half mile from Georgian Bay, traces of a series of round cabins, each approximately ten feet in diameter and with a central fireplace, were discovered (Harper 1952). While the excavator thought that these might be single family dwellings which preceded the development of the longhouse, the subsequent discovery of earlier longhouses only a short distance away rules out this interpretation. It is just possible that we are dealing with an Iroquoian hunting or fishing camp, similar to the ones described for the seventeenth century by Gabriel Sagard (Wrong 1939:185).

Although relatively few sites are known for the Uren period, there is a marked rise in the number of villages and camp sites in the following Middleport substage. This suggests an increase in population at this time.

The palisades around villages evidence a continuing concern for defence, but this concern is only minimally expressed in the location of villages. The latter, for the most part, are built on dry ground bordering on streams or rivers (Wright 1966:56–61, 64). There is no proof that squash and beans were being grown, although the charred remains of sunflower seeds from the Uren site, in Oxford County, indicate the presence of one hitherto unattested cultigen (Kidd 1952:75).

Violence, particularly in the form of blood revenge, was undoubtedly a feature of life in the northern Iroquoian culture area from very early times. However, prior to the development of sedentary villages, raiding and blood feuds took place in the context of small, unfortified encampments and the evidence for such behaviour is very limited and often ambiguous. Bodies found riddled with arrows indicate violence, but do not inform us whether the individuals were slain as the result of an in-group quarrel or a premeditated act of blood revenge. Occasionally, headless bodies and extra skulls are found in graves of early times and many of these are perhaps best interpreted as evidence that heads were already being sought as trophies (Ritchie 1965:123).

The care taken to build palisades around early Iroquoian villages in Ontario and New York State provides additional evidence of violence for that period, although it is unclear whether violence was increasing or a more sedentary life was encouraging groups to undertake additional efforts to protect themselves. The cause of warfare at this time is also uncertain. Blood feuds were almost certainly a continuing reason and, as in earlier times, they may have served to rationalize other motives.

In the Uren culture there is evidence of a dramatic new dimension to warfare, in the form of cannibalism. The earliest witness of this practice is a small quantity of fragmented human bone recovered from the middens at the Uren site (Wright 1966:56–57). This site also yielded a number of perforated gorgets manufactured out of sections of human skulls. More fragments of human bones were found in the refuse of the Middleport site, and thereafter such remains become increasingly common in Iroquoian sites throughout Ontario (ibid. 60, 64). Some of these bones bear signs of cutting, cooking, and having been split open to extract the marrow (Kidd 1952:74). The small number of males between the ages of sixteen and twenty-five in the early Tabor Hill ossuaries, as compared with men of other ages, suggests that, at this time, many men were being lost through warfare, which would have been the main form of accident from which the body was unlikely to be recovered (Churcher and Kenyon 1960:256–57). Evidence of cannibalism has also been forthcoming in New York State.

In historic times cannibalism was not a simple gastronomic pleasure, but an integral part of a cult in which male prisoners of war were tortured to death as a sacrifice to the god of war or to the sun. While there were many differences between the sacrificial cult as it was practised in the south-eastern United States and among the northern Iroquoians, certain elements, including the use of prisoners, the removal of the heart, the killing of the victim on an elevated platform and in view of the sun, and finally the cooking and eating of all or parts of his body, connect the northern Iroquoian ritual with those practised in the southeastern United States and in Mesoamerica. The differences indicate that this cult did not diffuse in its entirety from one region to another, but rather that certain key ideas diffused, probably from south to north like the horticultural complex, and were used by the northern Iroquoians to develop a sacrificial complex of their own.

But if religious ideas, which diffused into the Iroquoian area from elsewhere, account for specific features of prisoner sacrifice, it is apparent that the northern Iroquoians placed less emphasis on the theological justification for what they did than on the much older custom of blood revenge. War was waged, at least in theory, to avenge the killing of a member of one's own confederacy, tribe, and probably originally of one's community, by an alien. In order to retaliate for such an injury, it was necessary to seize a member of the group that was held responsible so that he or she could be adopted as a replacement for the victim or, failing this, to slay an enemy and keep his head or scalp as a trophy. Women and children who were brought home were permitted to live, since they could be more easily enculturated; male prisoners were more dangerous and more likely to run away, hence were frequently slain. In the case of prisoner sacrifice, adoption and revenge were combined, since the prisoner was adopted by the murdered man's family before being killed. Blood revenge was considered a sacred duty and its serious disruptive effects were realistically taken account of by the Iroquoians.

It seems unlikely, however, that blood revenge would have generated the prolonged conflicts that were witnessed in early historic times, had other factors not been operative as well. The main influences promoting conflicts do not appear to have been economic. War was not waged to obtain agricultural land and we have already noted that pressure on hunting territories does not seem to have pitted groups against one another. The chief spur to conflict was that warfare was the principal means by which a young man acquired prestige. Prowess in war was not the only avenue to success, but it was the most general, and this made most young men ready and willing to fight whenever an opportunity arose.

The three themes that motivated Iroquoian warfare—blood revenge, individual prestige, and prisoner sacrifice—were woven together in such a way that each of them complemented and reinforced the other. The acts of daring that warriors performed in enemy territory not only avenged wrongs committed against their society, but provided a supply of captives to replenish its ranks, as well as for sacrifice. The method of sacrifice gave the Huron an opportunity to vent their hatred of the enemy on a particular victim and gave the victim, who was a warrior, a final and glorious opportunity to display his courage.

John Witthoft (1959:32–36) has argued that as corn growing replaced hunting as the dominant mode of subsistence, the resulting decline in the male role as food producers led them to seek to enhance their prestige as warriors. At the same time, women projected their resentment at the lack of male participation in routine tasks, such as planting and harvesting corn, by transforming themselves from being butchers of game into being butchers of male captives. As it stands, this theory has two weaknesses. First, it ignores the importance of fishing to the Iroquoian economy and also the important and arduous work that men performed in clearing new fields. Secondly, men, as well as women, played an important and active role in torturing prisoners.

In spite of these shortcomings, significant insights can be gained from Witthoft's analysis. In early times, when hunting was a major element of subsistence, it probably served as an important test of a man's courage and of his ability to use weapons. Even in historic times, deer hunting remained one of the Huron male's favourite activities. Fishing and clearing fields required energy and dedication, but such activities do not seem to have provided Iroquoian men with a satisfactory means of measuring themselves against one another. Moreover, these were the activities by which they were judged by their wives' matrilineages. It is reasonable to assume that, as hunting grew less important to subsistence, warfare became the principal means by which men acquired personal prestige and established a role for themselves in the life of their communities. The need for this prestige necessitated having an enemy and stimulated the spiralling pattern of bloodshed that was an integral part of the Iroquoian way of life. Under these circumstances, elaborations, such as prisoner sacrifice, were no doubt welcomed as additional excuses for waging war. It was probably as warfare became increasingly important that clan segments acquired war chiefs, in addition to the civil ones, whose office seems to have been a continuation of the traditional leader of a hunting band. While the growing importance of war alone might have led to the creation of such an office, it is worth noting that the distinction between war chiefs and civil leaders was wide-spread among the Indians in the southeastern United States in early historic times, and is also a trait of Mesoamerican culture (Driver 1961: 340). Here again, we appear to be dealing with a feature of nuclear American culture that penetrated almost to the northern limits of corn horticulture.

It is also in the middle Iroquoian period that we see in Ontario, at least west of the Trent Valley, the development of an interest in elaborate burial rites which, instead of being of external origin, appears to be the local expression of a repeated focus of interest among the Indians of the north-eastern Woodlands.[18] The ossuaries, or bone pits, that began to appear in the late Pickering culture, mark the first periodic interment of large numbers of bodies in a common grave. Beginning in middle Iroquoian times, the Feast of the Dead developed as a community ritual that was celebrated whenever a sizable village shifted to a new location. This communal reburial of the dead differs from the burial in individual graves that was practised by the Iroquois, Susquehannock, and Iroquoians of the St. Lawrence Valley, and possibly by the proto-Huron of the Trent Valley. The presence of multiple cemeteries in the vicinity of many Five Nations villages suggests that, even in death, their moieties, or clan segments, preferred to remain separate from one another (Noble 1969:23; Wray and Schoff 1953:55).

While most middle Iroquoian ossuaries appear to have been somewhat smaller, the one that has been best studied by a physical anthropologist was found to contain over 500 bodies. This is the Fairty ossuary which was located near the Robb site on the outskirts of Toronto and seems to date from about the end of the Middleport substage. Assuming a mortality rate in keeping with the ages of the skeletons and an average interval of ten years between ossuary burials (Anderson 1964:30–37), a regional population of between 1500 and 2500 people has been suggested. While this figure seems large for an individual community of this period, the interval of ten years is the probable life span of a large village. Smaller villages exhausted nearby fields and sources of firewood more slowly and probably were inhabited for a longer period. If we double the duration of the village, we derive a smaller population figure that seems appropriate for the medium-sized settlements typical of this period. It is perhaps indicative of the still isolated condition of the Iroquoian peoples of Ontario that few offerings were placed in these ossuaries prior to the historic period. Only a stone scraper and one shell bead were found in the Fairty ossuary (Wright 1966:61).

THE LATE IROQUOIAN PERIOD

The late Iroquoian cultures in Ontario evolved directly from the Middle-port one (ibid. 66). New styles of pottery decoration became fashionable during this period, but the principal innovations were modifications based on established conventions. Throughout the remaining years of the Ontario Iroquoian sequence, the only kind of pottery vessel continued to be the large globular pot that served as a soup kettle. Pipes became increasingly varied and, particularly after A.D. 1500, clay ones decorated with human figures grew common (ibid. 71; Noble 1969:24). Soon after A.D. 1400, beans and squash are attested for the first time in the archaeological record in Ontario (Wright 1966:98). This suggests either the late arrival of these two cultigens in Ontario or a long pause before they became popular. In addition to the eight and ten row corn known in Ontario since the early Iroquoian period, four, six, and twelve row corn appears (Noble 1969:21). There is also slight evidence that a greater number of animal species, particularly small animals, were being eaten at this time. This may reflect the growing pressure that increasingly dense population clusters were exerting upon the local fauna (ibid. 21, cited from Emerson 1961a).

From the beginning of the late Iroquoian period, there was a tendency for communities to cluster in restricted areas of southern Ontario and for these areas to be separated from one another by wider tracts of uninhabited forest. As parts of Ontario that had hitherto been occupied were abandoned, the most significant cleavage to develop was between the communities living north of Lake Erie and those living north of Lake Ontario (map 3e). Clear-cut differences between these two regions can be observed in pottery types and ossuaries (Wright 1966:66–68). Such differences distinguish sequences of development leading to the historic Neutral and Erie peoples on the one hand and to the historic Huron and Tionnontaté on the other (plate 16). Although relatively little is known about the development of the Neutral tribes, they appear to have gradually shifted, or contracted, eastward until, by the historic period, they were living between the Grand River Valley and the Niagara frontier (ibid. 84–87). The generally smaller size of Neutral ossuaries and the discovery of as many as eleven of them around a single site (ibid. 85), suggest that ossuary burial may not have served the same integrative functions among the Neutral that it did among most of the proto-Huron. On the whole, the split between the proto-Neutral and proto-Huron cultures appears to have reopened the division between Pickering and Glen Meyer.

The proto-Huron sites are located in a triangle between the Canadian

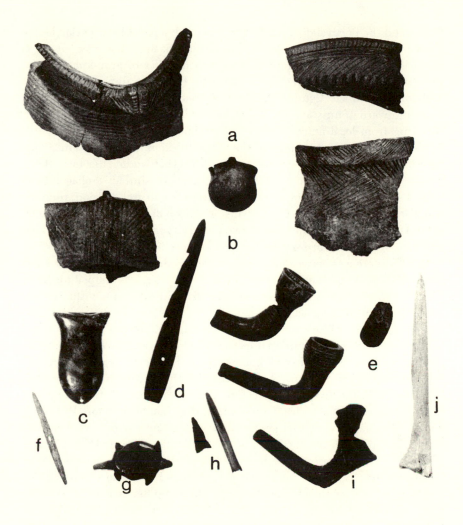

PLATE 16. *Typical Huron–Tionnontaté artifacts: (a–b) broken pottery vessels; (c) stone pipe; (d) antler harpoon; (e) stone scraper; (f) netting needle; (g) tortoise-shaped amulet; (h) stone and bone arrowheads; (i) pottery pipes; (j) dagger made of human ulna. Courtesy National Museum of Man, National Museums of Canada.*

Shield and the north shore of Lake Ontario, with a possible extension along the south shore of Georgian Bay. Even within this area, however, sites are not evenly distributed. Instead they form a number of groupings which, unfortunately, are still very poorly defined. The most important of these seem to be in Simcoe County, the Toronto area, and another farther east in Prince Edward County and the Trent Valley. The sites in each area appear to spring from local antecedents of the middle Iroquoian period, and the clusters themselves may represent the tribal divisions that were to make up the Huron confederacy, or groupings of villages that would later form these tribes. All of these groupings have a generally similar archaeological culture; however, in recent years, a "northern" cultural division, roughly congruent with the Simcoe County sites, has been distinguished from other proto-Huron groups on the basis of two pottery types: Lalonde High Collar and Sidey Notched. Future work may reveal specific, although perhaps less striking, differences between the sites in the Toronto area and those of the Trent Valley. At present, the sites in these two areas are lumped together as parts of a tentatively defined "southern division" culture, within which sites are only distinguished geographically.[19]

During the late Iroquoian period the average house was about twenty-seven feet wide and one hundred feet long. There was, however, considerable individual variation, and houses up to 190 feet long are reported (Heidenreich 1971:115–16). Architecturally, the Huron were more conservative than the Iroquois. Even into the historic period, the designs of their houses remained basically the same as they had been in late Pickering times. The majority tapered gently towards the ends, which were invariably rounded. With the exception of the posts that supported the sleeping platforms, these houses were constructed of slender poles covered with sheets of bark. Likewise, while village palisades had up to seven rows of stakes, most of these stakes were thin and placed up to a foot apart. By contrast, as early as A.D. 1350, in the Chance culture, which is ancestral to the historic cultures of the eastern tribes of the Iroquois confederacy, the round-ended longhouse had been replaced by the square-ended type characteristic of the Iroquois in the historic period. Although most of the poles used to construct the walls of these houses were about three inches in diameter, larger post molds, up to ten inches across, are encountered at regular intervals (Ritchie 1965:314–15; Hayes 1967). The palisade around the Garoga site, a late prehistoric Mohawk settlement, was constructed of two rows of stakes larger than any observed on earlier Iroquois sites, or on historic Huron ones. The individual post molds, placed about a foot apart, were fifteen to twenty inches in diameter and had been sunk approximately three feet into the ground (Ritchie 1965:318). This provides archaeological confirmation for Champlain's observation that Iroquois fortifications were far stronger than Huron ones (Biggar 1922–36, 3:70) and for Bogaert's description of an Oneida town with three wooden images over one of its gates; which is unparalleled for Huron villages (Jameson 1909:148).

There is more evidence of variation in Huron housetypes in the prehistoric archaeological record than from historic accounts. Four houses were uncovered at the Copeland site in Simcoe County, which dates about A.D. 1500 (Channen and Clarke 1965:5–10). One of these was a conventional longhouse eighty-eight feet long. Another, wider structure measured forty-two feet by thirty feet. While the doors at either end and the traces of sleeping platforms along the walls conformed to the normal longhouse pattern, the seven hearths inside this building were randomly scattered, rather than arranged down the centre. The same was true for the house next to it, which was forty-five feet long, but tapered from thirty feet at one end to twenty feet at the other. In this house, there was only one sleeping platform, which ran along the west wall. The most unusual building on the site was ninety by fifty-eight feet (plate 17). The side walls consisted of two or more rows of poles running parallel to one another, while a row of larger posts, eight to ten inches in diameter, ran down the centre of the building, presumably to support the roof. Twenty-three hearths were discovered inside this structure. These were arranged in no particular order, although most of them were located south of the centre posts.

This structure, which gives every appearance of having been a dwelling, seems to be similar to the central building excavated by Wilfrid Jury at the so-called site of "St. Ignace II," along the Sturgeon River (W. S. Fox 1949). Although the latter building was interpreted as a Jesuit church and mission centre, serious doubts have since been cast on the proposed date and identification of the village (Heidenreich 1966:125). Many of the longhouses at the "St. Ignace II" site are reported to have had a row of poles down the middle, presumably to support a wider roof span. Jury interpreted this as evidence of French influence, but it may be an architectural tradition indigenous to this region, the history of which remains to be unravelled. Similarly, no evidence of sidewall sleeping platforms has been found at the Sopher and Warminster sites (Noble 1969:20). These are both historic sites, apparently belonging to the Arendarhonon tribe. Considerably more work will have to be done on prehistoric sites before we know for certain whether all Arendarhonon houses lacked such platforms. It is

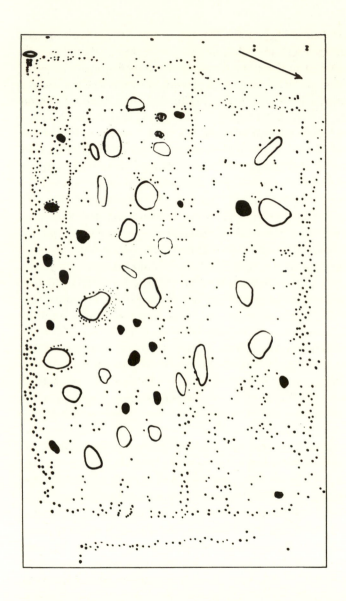

PLATE 17. *House 1 from the Copeland site, Simcoe County* (C. A.D. *1500).*
This prehistoric site contains a number of structures that depart from the
ideal longhouse style. House 1 is 90 feet by 58 feet and had a row of posts
running down the centre to support the roof. Courtesy E. R. Channen and
National Museum of Man, National Museums of Canada.

possible that additional work may reveal significant variations in Huron house styles corresponding to ethnic divisions.

In the late Iroquoian period, villages generally tended to grow larger and to be located in defensive positions remote from navigable waters. Some of them also began to cluster close to one another (Wright 1966:91). The increasing size of villages may be the result of population growth, but alternatively it may have resulted from smaller communities, each consisting of a single clan segment, agreeing to live together. The suggestion that the several clans that inhabited each of the large communities in the historic period might have resulted from the growth and fissioning of a single clan segment does not explain why the clan segments in any one town had such a heterogeneous assortment of names. When clans split they usually modified their names only slightly, such as Turtle becoming Mud Turtle and Little Turtle (Tooker 1970*b*:93). It also does not account for the political independence of clan segments in historic times.

The development of tribal clusters has only begun to be unravelled in Ontario, in part because the shifting of certain tribes in the late Iroquoian period makes it difficult to trace such developments from the archaeological record. The evidence for this process is much clearer in New York State, where the groups that made up each of the five Iroquois tribes remained within their tribal territories from at least Owasco times. Archaeological work indicates that originally at least three small communities existed in the later Onondaga territory. These were located some distance from one another, and each community shifted its location at regular intervals within a distinct area; hence it is reasonable to assume that each had its own hunting territory. After A.D. 1400, the three villages were reduced to two, but one of the new villages was now much larger than the other, suggesting that it arose through the fusion of two earlier villages. Sometime between A.D. 1450 and 1475, the two remaining villages relocated within two miles of each other. Although both of these villages were well defended, their greater proximity seems to indicate a friendly relationship. Tuck (1971:214–16) interprets this coming together as the result of a non-aggression pact, which prevented clashes that would have been disastrous for the smaller village, if not for the larger one. He goes on to suggest that this event marks the founding of the Onondaga tribe, although similarities in language and culture may have provided the basis of an Onondaga cultural, if not political, identity in earlier times.

While the actual events leading to the formation of the historic Onondaga tribe may have involved more village sequences than archaeologists have detected, we have here an example of how settlements, originally consisting of individual clan segments, could be drawn together into larger village units and then into tribal clusters. For the most part, the drawing together of the communities to form tribes led to the abandonment of many formerly settled areas, and produced larger, but more widely separated, clusters of habitation. This created ideal conditions in which homogeneous tribal cultures could develop. In addition, the considerable distances that now separated each tribal grouping favoured the development of distinctive cultures in each tribal area.

The development of tribal organizations required new institutions to maintain their solidarity. One of these may have been the linking together of clan segments named after the same animal to form exogamous clan structures that extended across tribes and later across whole confederacies. As a result of this development, the idea of clan membership became modified. Instead of being restricted to a local unit of kinship organization, it came to be also applied to a larger grouping of ritual affinity that was not geographically restricted. The resulting interdigitation of loyalties to clan and tribe, and to clan and village, constituted the warp and woof which helped to hold expanding Iroquoian societies together. The additional grouping of clans to form phratries, which regulated many aspects of Iroquoian ceremonial life, including burial rituals, further strengthened these ties.

Whether or not they existed earlier, medicine societies also must have played an important role in the integration of Iroquoian society at this time (Tuck 1971:213). Membership in these societies, which was an important aspect of Iroquoian ritualism, was open to those who had been healed by them and was inherited, no doubt matrilineally, upon a member's death. In this way, these societies acquired a membership that cut across lineage, clan, village, and even tribal divisions, thus linking together a wider assortment of people than did the clan organizations.

Games were another source of pleasurable interaction within and between villages. Lacrosse was a rough and dangerous sport, played by young men. It no doubt served to channel some of their aggressiveness and prestige-seeking along peaceful lines. Other activities, such as the dish game, brought the inhabitants of different villages together in friendly rivalry when their teams played against one another. Games of all kinds were accompanied by feasting and revelry. They periodically brought clan segments and the inhabitants of different villages together and reinforced their unity by providing a friendly setting within which aggression and rivalry might be discharged.

Clearly the prehistoric Iroquoian cultures were not static; nor were they totally integrated and harmonious within themselves. Instead, they must be seen as entities in a process of rapid transition from a subsistence economy based on hunting and gathering to an alternative one based on horticulture. In making this change, the Iroquoians generally showed themselves to be good handymen, capable of using whatever ideas were at hand in order to adapt their way of life to changing conditions. The important role played by shamanistic healing rituals provides one example of the manner in which elements of an older way of life found new roles for themselves in a changing social order; the importance of hunting magic in historic times provides another. While the latter practices were accorded an importance that was out of all proportion to their economic significance, they served to reinforce the prestige of traditional male activities in a way that was important to the harmonious operation of the society as a whole. On the other hand, borrowings, not the least of which was the horticultural complex itself, also came to play an important role in Iroquoian society. These borrowings, which seem to have included prisoner sacrifice and the distinction between war chiefs and civil headmen, were made, however, in a piecemeal fashion and adapted to the special requirements of Iroquoian society. Thus they emerged as distinctive features of the Iroquoian way of life. Evidence can also be found of compromises between old ways and new ones. The tenacity with which clan segments clung to traditional rights reveals the skill with which the Iroquoians managed to preserve older attitudes and institutions, and to use these as foundations for new and more complex structures. This is evidence not so much of conservatism as of a healthy and constructive attitude towards change.

Nevertheless, some of the complications that resulted from the social and economic transformation their society had undergone remained as unresolved tensions in historic Iroquoian culture. As the Iroquoians became more dependent on agriculture, men spent more time away from their villages hunting, fishing, trading, and fighting. Women, on the other hand, tended to remain in their villages throughout the year and became more closely identified with them than the men were. The male's position within his own society was further challenged by the declining economic importance of hunting, which was an activity he much valued and a source of prestige to skilful individuals. We have already argued that this decline may have led to an increase in warfare, as a compensatory avenue of male achievement. The resulting ambivalence that men had about their relationship with their community may also have produced the uneasy relations between men and women that are noted as a distinctive feature of Iroquoian culture. These tendencies were undoubtedly carried much further among the Five Nations Iroquois in historic times, as the growing demand for furs kept traders and warriors away from their villages for even longer periods. Under these conditions, women probably came to play a far more important role in domestic politics than they had done previously. Later, as the Iroquois fell under European domination, the importance of the male declined with the decreasing emphasis on trade and warfare and they were compelled to adapt, not too successfully, to European methods of agriculture. While the final collapse of male prestige may have led Iroquois women to idealize and exaggerate the power they had exercised in the past, it appears that in prehistoric times, no less than in our own, a changing economy generated social tensions as it altered the traditional roles between the sexes.

The Huron Confederacy

The archaeological record indicates that the region where the Huron were found living in historical times was occupied continuously by horticulturalists from the early Iroquoian period onwards. In the 1640s, the Attignawantan who lived in the extreme west of the Huron country claimed that they could point out the sites their ancestors had inhabited for over two centuries (Thwaites 1896–1901, 16:227–29). There is, therefore, little reason to doubt that this tribe developed in the area between Georgian Bay and Lake Simcoe and that at least some of the many prehistoric sites found there are those of their ancestors.

The Arendarhonon appear to have joined the Huron confederacy late in the sixteenth century.[20] The interest they had in the Trent Valley region, and the presence of many late prehistoric and protohistoric sites east of Lake Simcoe, suggest that they were among the original inhabitants of that area. The oldest sites seem to be near the east end of Lake Ontario and in Prince Edward County. This may indicate a gradual movement up the Trent Valley, beginning about A.D. 1500 (Pendergast 1964:13).

The origins of the two remaining Huron tribes are more ambiguous. Wright has suggested that the Attigneenongnahac may have evolved in the northern part of Simcoe County, no doubt east of the Attignawantan, while the Tahontaenrat developed in the Humber and adjacent valleys in the Toronto area, where numerous late Iroquoian prehistoric sites have been discovered (Wright 1966:78). This might account for the large number of prehistoric sites in the Oro township area of Simcoe County (Heidenreich 1969:23) and accords with the Jesuits' statement that it was both the

Attignawantan and Attigneenongnahac who could point out sites going back two centuries; however, the latter claim seems based on Attignawantan sources, and may not apply in its entirety to the Attigneenongnahac.[21] Moreover, the Tahontaenrat, who were a small group in historic times, may not have been sufficiently numerous to account for the many sites in the Toronto area. They are also stated not to have joined the Huron confederacy before about 1610, while the fusion of northern and southern division traits, that gave rise to the historic Huron culture, appears to have been underway in Simcoe County by about the middle of the sixteenth century (Wright 1966:66). In spite of a preference for matrilocal residence, this blending of ceramic traditions no doubt came about as a result of increasing intermarriage, as hitherto distinct tribes began to live in closer proximity to one another.[22] An alternative theory would have the Attigneenongnahac moving north from the Toronto area, by about 1550, and settling in the eastern part of the Huron country, before shifting to their historic tribal area. Over fifty years later, the Tahontaenrat would have entered the region from either the south or the east. It is possible that the cluster of protohistoric sites reported for Innisfil township in the southern part of Simcoe County (Popham 1950) may have belonged to the Tahontaenrat prior to their final migration northward.

The origins of the Tionnontaté are as obscure as those of the Attigneenongnahac or the Tahontaenrat. Their pottery types, for the historic period, are similar to those of the Huron and have only recently been differentiated on the basis of a few characteristic decorative motifs (Wright 1966:76). Little evidence has been found of prehistoric sites in their historic tribal area, hence it has been suggested that they must have originated elsewhere. Wright (1966:79–80) has proposed that they might represent a breakaway group from the original inhabitants of northern Simcoe County, but his theory is argued on the basis of an inaccurate interpretation of Huron social structure.[23] Garrad and Heidenreich tentatively derive them, along with the Tahontaenrat, from the Innisfil sites (Heidenreich 1971:map 22). Alternatively, future research may reveal them to have evolved from the Iroquoian groups who inhabited Huron and Grey Counties during the Middleport substage. These people disappeared from the shores of Lake Huron in the late Iroquoian period (Wright 1966:66) and may have clustered farther east to become the Tionnontaté.

What was the driving force behind the development of larger settlements and the emergence of tribal coalitions that are observed in the late Iroquoian period? The larger villages are frequently explained as being the result of a growing population, but this explanation is inadequate. When not confronted by other difficulties, Iroquoian farmers preferred to live in small villages. These exhausted nearby soil and supplies of firewood more slowly than did large villages and therefore they had to be relocated less often. Large villages, on the other hand, quickly consumed their adjacent hinterland and, because of this, women were forced to travel longer distances to and from their fields, which also became ever more fragmented. The increasing inefficiency of such arrangements compelled villages to be relocated more frequently as they grew larger. Relocation was, however, an arduous task for the men of the village and does not seem to have been practical more than about once every decade. These opposing considerations resulted in the largest stable communities having populations of about 1500 people. Even towns of this size seem to have been stretching the regulatory mechanisms of Iroquoian society, and factionalism was rife between clan segments (Heidenreich 1971:129–34). The fact that larger populations settled close to one another in big, adjacent communities indicates that other factors must account for the development of both large villages and tribal alliances.

One of these factors was almost certainly war. Warfare was a feature of Iroquoian culture from earliest times. In the late Iroquoian period, not only were towns surrounded by palisades, but many of the larger ones were located on hilltops or high ground where two streams came together. Evidence of such fortification is noted both in Simcoe County and among the sites from the early part of the late Iroquoian sequence in the Humber Valley. From the middens there are also indications of increasing cannibalism, which Wright (1966:91) estimates reached a peak before A.D. 1550. It is also possible that by promoting the growth of larger communities and settlement clusters, warfare created a situation in which hunting became less productive and thereby produced increasing dependence on horticulture.

The growing destructiveness of such warfare may have compelled friendly neighbouring groups to cooperate for mutual defence. Likewise, the desire of communities to protect themselves may have led them to suppress neighbouring settlements, if these were inveterately hostile. This may have involved incorporating defeated groups into the victorious community, an art at which the Iroquoians excelled in historic times. Any successful coalition left neighbouring communities at a disadvantage, unless they too managed to consolidate themselves into larger groupings. Thus, in one way or another, the need for defence produced larger settlements, until these reached the limits at which Iroquoian slash-and-burn horticulture could operate efficiently. Once these limits had been reached, these same forces led to the development of defensive alliances in which friendly villages settled in close proximity. The development of such alliances would have eliminated local blood feuds, which may have been most destructive in terms of people's lives and possessions. While putting an end to local battles, these alliances did not prevent warriors from acquiring personal prestige; but they compelled them to carry their quarrels farther afield.

Data concerning who was fighting whom in prehistoric times are scarce and largely ambiguous. It seems highly likely that proto-Huron villages carried on blood feuds with one another, but we do not know to what degree the individual Huron tribes fought with one another after they had come into existence. It is possible that much of the homogeneity in pottery types that was maintained during this period resulted from the movement from village to village of women who were taken captive in such raids.

There are few references to prehistoric warfare in Ontario in the historical records. The Huron spoke of struggles they had waged against the Tionnontaté not long before the arrival of the first Europeans and, even in the early historic period, war chiefs were attempting to organize raids against the Neutral confederacy (Thwaites 1896–1901, 20:43; Wrong 1939:151). It therefore appears that even in late prehistoric times the tribes of the Huron confederacy waged war against other Iroquoian tribes in Ontario. In the historic period, the Huron's chief adversaries were the Seneca, against whom they appear to have been fighting well before the start of the seventeenth century. They were also at war with the other tribes of the Five Nations, although engagements were more sporadic (map 4).

The most important clue to warfare patterns in prehistoric times seems to be provided by the foreign pottery which is found in many Iroquoian sites. Pottery vessels were frequently carried a considerable distance by canoe, but travel between Iroquoian groups was mostly overland. It is unlikely that on these trips the Iroquoians had any reason to carry such cumbersome and fragile vessels with them; hence, when pottery of a foreign type occurs in an Iroquoian site, it is likely to have been produced by foreign women who were living there. Such women could have arrived as peacefully acquired brides, as refugees, or as prisoners of war. While examples of all three events are found in the historical literature, it seems unlikely that the first of these, intermarriage, was frequent between groups living one hundred miles or more apart, or that, when it did occur, it was normally the woman who moved. When refugees are involved, their

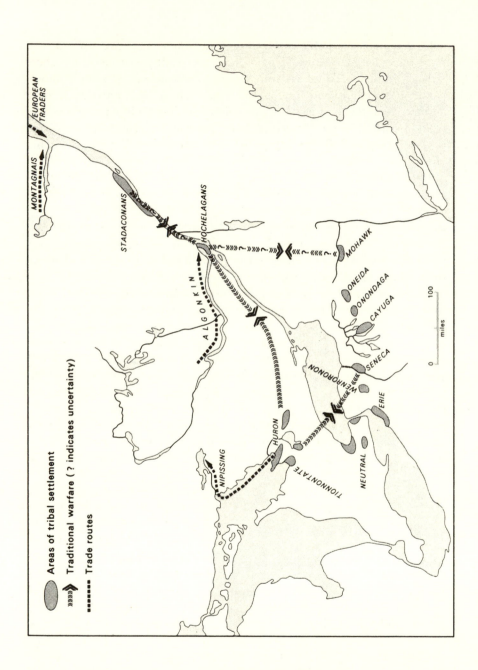

MAP 4.   *Intertribal relations, mid-sixteenth century.*

pottery is found in the sites to which they fled, while their host's pottery is unlikely to be found in the villages from which they came. The same kind of asymmetrical distribution is produced by the forced resettlement of a defeated group in the villages of their conquerors. When dealing with the more normal give-and-take of blood feuds, we can expect to find small to moderate amounts of each adversary's pottery in the sites on either side.

This index of female movement cannot be applied among the various proto-Huron groups, because their material culture was extremely similar to begin with. Moreover, the relative proximity of these groups would make it difficult to decide whether movement was a sign of friendship or hostility. It is also impractical to apply this measurement before the late Iroquoian period, since cultural patterns tended to be very widespread prior to then.

In the published data for proto-Huron sites, the amount of "Neutral-Erie" pottery is always small, and declines from about A.D. 1450 onwards. In part, this may reflect decreasing contact with the Neutral, as the proto-Huron villages located in the Toronto area gradually moved northward. "Cayuga" sherds occur from A.D. 1450 on, but "Seneca" and "Cayuga" ones become increasingly common only after 1550 and reach their maximum in sites of the historic period. Few Huron sherds are reported from Seneca or Cayuga sites much prior to the historic period. A different distribution can be plotted for eastern Iroquoian pottery, which occurs occasionally on proto-Huron sites before A.D. 1500, but increases in frequency after that time, then declines sharply not long before 1600.[24] The majority of eastern Iroquoian pottery types that have been identified could have come either from the Iroquoian tribes who lived in the St. Lawrence Valley or from the three eastern tribes of the Iroquois confederacy. Since Huron sherds occur with some frequency in sixteenth century sites of the St. Lawrence Valley, but rarely on Onondaga, Oneida, or Mohawk sites prior to the next century, it seems more likely that mutual raiding was going on between the tribes who lived west of Kingston and those in the St. Lawrence Valley. The end of this conflict appears to coincide with the disappearance of the St. Lawrence Iroquoians discussed in the next chapter. Until this time, the St. Lawrence Iroquoians seem to have been the main enemies of the Huron, although from 1550 on, "Seneca" and "Cayuga" sherds increase in frequency dramatically, suggesting an important shift in warfare. The archaeological evidence indicates that the brunt of warfare with the St. Lawrence Iroquoians was sustained by the Huron groups who lived in the Trent Valley and the Toronto area, rather than by those in Simcoe County (Wright 1966:74). An increase in "Seneca" and

"Cayuga" sherds in Simcoe County after 1550 seems to result from the shifting of tribal groups north and westward at this time, bringing the hitherto sheltered population of this region into more direct contact with the Iroquois.

On the other hand, it has also been noted that evidence of cannibalism appears to decline in Ontario after 1550 (ibid. 91). This possibly reflects the growth of new friendships and alliances among the proto-Huron. It may also reflect the disappearance of a major foe in the St. Lawrence Valley and the growing distance between the Huron tribes, who were generally moving northward, and the Iroquois, who became their main enemy. The expansion of alliances that seems to have been occurring at this time would have reduced fratricidal struggles among neighbouring groups and initiated a generally more peaceful time in Ontario. It probably also led the Ontario Iroquoians to look for new enemies farther afield against whom their young men could test themselves, when "just causes" gave them a reason for doing so.

So far, we have been discussing only the development of tribal groupings. Sometime, however, before the end of the sixteenth century, both in Ontario and New York State, neighbouring tribes came to be linked together in loose associations aimed at curbing intertribal aggression. The principal feature common to all Iroquoian confederacies appears to have been an agreement among member tribes not to resort to bloodshed to settle grievances among themselves. The suppression of blood feuds was supervised by a confederacy council made up of civil headmen from the member tribes, which gathered periodically for feasts and consultations, judged disputes, and arranged for reparations payments as the need arose. There is no evidence that the member tribes of a confederacy were bound to help one another in case of attack or to aid each other in their wars; often the foreign policies of the member tribes were very different from one another. Nevertheless, the confederacies did serve to restrain violence among neighbouring tribes and to this degree promoted greater security for all their members.

Unfortunately, very little is known about the origin of confederacies and speculation on this subject has been affected by disagreements concerning the influence that European contact had on indigenous institutions. Some anthropologists argue that the Iroquois confederacy was established as early as the middle of the fifteenth century, and even this is seen as the culmination of a series of local alliances between two or more Iroquois tribes (Tooker 1964:3–4 n. 1). It has been proposed that Dekanahwideh's blotting out of the sun, an event that is part of the traditional account of the founding of the Iroquois league, refers to a solar eclipse visible in upper New York State in A.D. 1451 (P. Wallace 1966:255). It may be noted that Tuck does not date the founding of the Onondaga tribe much earlier than this time.

Other scholars have accepted Iroquois claims that their confederacy was founded a lifetime before the Europeans came to trade as evidence that the league was established sometime between 1559 and 1570 (Hewitt 1894). This and later dates support an alternative line of thought which attributes the origins of all Indian confederacies to European influence. Confederacies are interpreted as tribal groupings formed to be better able to resist European intrusion. Alternatively, it is suggested that tribes living in the interior made alliances in order to break restrictive trading covenants between coastal tribes and the Europeans and to be able to participate in this trade themselves. Once formed, these confederacies were strengthened by the demands of the fur trade, and became mechanisms for dealing with European colonists (Tooker 1964:4 n. 1).

Yet, even if the Iroquois confederacy was strengthened in response to European intrusion, this appears to have happened with considerable ease. Unlike some later, short-lived confederacies that attempted to bring culturally heterogeneous groups together in opposition to European expansion, the Iroquoian confederacies embraced groups of people who were culturally and linguistically related, and who already shared similar political institutions. In many ways, the formation of such confederacies can be viewed as an extension of the same forces that had already created tribal, in place of band, structures. For this reason, it seems doctrinaire and unwarranted to reject the Huron claim that their confederacy began around A.D. 1440, with the Attignawantan and the Attigneenongnahac as its founding members. If both tribes were already living in Simcoe County, the alliance between them would have been little more than an extension of the process of tribal formation that was probably going on at that time. If, however, the Attigneenongnahac were living farther south, this early alliance may have closely resembled those between the tribes of the Iroquois confederacy in later times. For a long while, however, the Huron confederacy seems to have embraced only two of the four Huron tribes.

The Historic Location of the Huron

While the Huron and Iroquois confederacies appear to have had a similar council structure and were established to promote friendship among member tribes, the two groups differed from one another in certain critical aspects. Even after their confederacy was formed, the Iroquois tribes remained separate from one another, each living in the middle of its ancestral territories. Among the Huron, at least in later times, as tribes joined the confederacy, they moved from their separate territories into the northern part of Simcoe County to form a single population cluster. Each tribe may have retained its old hunting grounds, but this cannot be documented with certainty. The Attignawantan obviously gave up part of their hunting lands, and possibly part of the area where they had lived, as village land for incoming tribes and must have been compensated with rights to hunt elsewhere. The result was a concentration of population in the north of Simcoe County which far exceeded that of any other part of the northern Iroquoian culture area.

This raises two questions: Why did the Huron choose to settle near the shores of Georgian Bay; and why did they, unlike the Iroquois, locate all the settlements of their confederacy so near to one another?

The traditional explanation has been that the Huron retreated into northern Simcoe County because of Iroquois attacks. They were imagined to be cowering on the shores of Georgian Bay, making a last stand against the enemy, when the French arrived. The Huron were obviously concerned about Iroquois raids and carefully fortified their communities that were exposed to attack. Yet theorizing such as this is based on an incorrect evaluation of the military capabilities of the Huron by comparison with those of the Iroquois before 1640. Prior to that date, the Huron were not at the mercy of the Iroquois. Year after year, Huron raiding parties set off for the Iroquois country and usually returned with prisoners for their sacrificial killings. Moreover, the Huron were not at war with the tribes who lived to the north of them, whereas the Iroquois appear to have been at war not only with the Huron, but also with the Susquehannock, who lived to the south, and with various Algonkian tribes to the east and northeast. Yet, in spite of having more enemies than the Huron, no greater numbers, and little, if any, military superiority, the Iroquois tribes were not compelled to settle close to one another for protection. At most, the greater danger to which they were exposed seems to have expressed itself in the stronger defences of their villages. Given the secure nature of their northern frontier, it may be that concern about Iroquois attacks was one of the factors that induced some of the smaller Huron groups to shift northward. This does not explain, however, why a substantial number of Huron had lived in Simcoe County from the earliest stages of Iroquoian development, nor does it explain why the four Huron tribes ultimately elected to locate their villages close to one another near Georgian Bay.[25]

From an Iroquoian point of view, the historic Huron country had many natural advantages. Light soil, that the Iroquoians were able to cultivate, occurred there more abundantly than anywhere else in the eastern half of southern Ontario (Chapman and Putnam 1966:Summary Map). The region was also surrounded on three sides by lakes and rivers abounding in fish at every season of the year. This proximity of fish and good soil supplied the key elements in the Iroquoian subsistence economy and no doubt explains why Huron had lived there in considerable numbers from an early period.

On the other hand, climatic conditions in northern Simcoe County were less favourable than along the north shores of Lakes Erie and Ontario. Winters were colder, the average snowfall was about 40 inches more, and the growing season was somewhat shorter. While the latter did not seriously affect the cultivation of corn, it compelled the Huron to secure most of their tobacco from farther south. Corn, and all other crops, were also endangered by a low rainfall. While the Huron country had many natural advantages, it was less than ideal from a subsistence point of view. In order to explain why the population of southeastern Ontario chose to live in this area, it is necessary to consider other reasons than war or local subsistence resources.

One of the chief attractions of the historic Huron country seems to have been its location, which had great potential for trade and commerce. A rich agricultural area, capable of supporting a large population and producing food surpluses in most years, this region was located on the margin of the Canadian Shield. Corn could be grown as far north as Lake Nipissing, but a shorter growing season and, what is more important, a scarcity of good soil meant that a sedentary way of life had developed nowhere north of the Huron (Heidenreich 1970). The people of the north were dependent on hunting and gathering, their population density was low, and, in winter, food shortages were common. The Huron country was thus located on the border of two very different ecological zones, whose inhabitants had economies that were complementary to one another. Even among so-called primitive peoples, such a border between two different ways of life is more likely to be a zone of interaction than a barrier to contact.

Moreover, the northern part of Simcoe County was ideally placed for easy contact between the agricultural peoples of southern Ontario and the hunters of the north. By way of Lake Simcoe, the Severn River, and the smaller streams entering Matchedash Bay, people living throughout the Huron country could quickly reach Georgian Bay. While the Huron were

no less skilful in using canoes than were the northern Algonkians, neither
liked to travel by water out of sight of land (Biggar 1922–36, 3:45). This
was because their bark canoes were fragile, and tended to leak and be
damaged easily. Under these conditions, the safest and most direct water
route to the north followed the eastern shore of Georgian Bay (map 5).
Along this route a traveller would have encountered the Ouasouarini
(Fish), Outchougai (Heron?), Atchiligouan (Heron?), and a number of
other patrilineal bands, who may have been either Ottawa or Ojibwa. At
the mouth of the Nipissing River, a canoe could turn east, passing into the
tribal territory of the Nipissing. From there the Mattawa River led eastward to the Ottawa, along which one could travel either northward into
the boreal forest, with its maze of interconnecting lakes and rivers, or
south through the territory of the Algonkin. Alternatively, turning westward along the shore of Lake Huron, travellers would pass more Algonkian-
speaking bands, the Amikou (Beaver), Nikikouek (Otter), Oumisagai
(Mississague or Eagle), and the Outaouan, who inhabited Manitoulin
Island, until they came to the Baouichtigouian, who spent the summers
at Sault Sainte Marie.[26] The latter were certainly among those later known
as Ojibwa. From there, further water routes ran north into Lake Superior
and hence up various rivers to the north, or south along the shores of Lake
Michigan.

Thus it was possible to travel with relative ease from the Huron country
over a vast area of the north. In spite of the extensive boundary along
which the rich agricultural land of southern Ontario abutted the Canadian
Shield, the only comparable artery of travel between these two regions was
the Ottawa River, and it was made more difficult by frequent portages.
Any group established in the Huron country was also well-situated to deny
passage northward to groups who lived farther south and to prevent the
northern hunters from making contact with such groups. So long as they
were numerically superior, the people living in the Huron country could,
if they wished, monopolize much of the trade between southern Ontario
and the north.

We have already noted that in historic times the Huron took every
advantage of their country's location, trading their own products, as well
as acting as middlemen in the exchange of goods between the regions to
the south and north. By far the greatest amount of trade was between
themselves and the northern Algonkians. So important was Huron corn
among the northern hunters that the French referred to the Huron
country as the granary of the Algonkians (Thwaites 1896–1901, 8:115).
For the northern hunting peoples, corn, and the opportunity to pass the

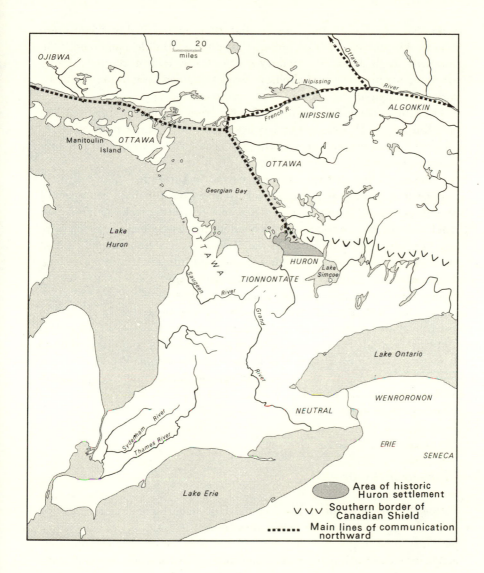

MAP 5. *Major lines of communication onto the Canadian Shield.*

winter among the Huron, meant that their chances of survival were considerably enhanced. This probably resulted in the development of an unusually high population density north of the Huron country. Being supported by imports would also have made these northern hunters increasingly dependent on the Huron.

The Huron depended on furs and meat from the north. Good soil was plentiful in the Huron country; hence, while it required more effort to grow additional crops, corn was the one elastic factor in the Huron subsistence economy. Fishing was highly productive among the Huron, so that the dried fish that the Huron received in barter for their corn may have been something of a luxury. Even so, however, the dried fish received in trade permitted Huron men to divert energy to other tasks. On the other hand, in spite of the tendency for deer to increase wherever there were clearings, the large population of the Huron country had virtually exterminated the deer population near at hand, and hunters had to travel long distances to find game. Difficulties in transportation made meat a luxury among the Huron and skins for making clothing were probably in short supply also. Yet, through trade, it was possible to secure furs and also some meat in return for agricultural products. It is extremely doubtful that without trade the population of the Huron country could have become as densely concentrated as it was in the historic period. Whether or not trade with the Algonkians was an important factor inducing people to settle in the Huron country, it was almost certainly a precondition for their high population density.

Prehistoric Trade

Before the role of trade in shaping the Huron settlement pattern can be assessed, enquiries must be made concerning the antiquity of the trading patterns noted in the historic period. There is no doubt that Huron interaction with the north was greatly intensified by the fur trade. Some scholars, however, view the fur trade as being added onto existing networks of trade, while others are of the opinion that these networks were much smaller in extent and carried only a small volume of trade in prehistoric times (Heidenreich 1971:227–32). Some of the latter would deny that prehistoric trade had any adaptational significance, at least as far as the Huron were concerned. There is also considerable difference of opinion concerning the antiquity of many Huron trading practices, such as recognizing trading routes as being the possession of individual lineages. Some interpret these as aboriginal institutions; others view them, like hunting territories among the northern Algonkians, as by-products of the European fur trade (Brasser 1971:261–62).

The view that trading was a recent development seems to find archaeological support in the very small quantities of exotic material that occur in Iroquoian sites prior to protohistoric times. There is some questionable evidence of local trade prior to the historic period. Flint from the Niagara Escarpment appears to have been reaching northern Simcoe County; likewise, there seems to have been a trade in the igneous rock used to make stone axes. On the other hand, the material originating outside the region found on prehistoric Iroquoian sites in Ontario usually amounts to only a few beads made from marine shell or from native copper (Wright 1966:99). This suggests that the trade links with the southeast and the upper Great Lakes region remained open, but that trade was limited in volume and possibly indirect. In sheer bulk, the exotic material found in Iroquoian sites is far less than from many sites of the Middle Woodland or Archaic periods. Ossuary burials are also largely devoid of offerings in prehistoric times. The contrast between the abundance of exotic material, both in village sites and ossuaries, during the historic period and the dearth of such material prior to that time supports the view that Iroquoian societies were self-sufficient and tended to be locally orientated prior to the development of the fur trade.

On the other hand, even in historic times, the bulk of trade appears to have been in perishable goods, such as corn, fish, and skins. These items either vanish completely, or are difficult to identify as trade goods, in the archaeological record. Yet, it is possible that the contacts involved in such exchanges have left indirect evidence in the archaeological record. The main evidence of contact between southern Ontario and the north is the pottery of Ontario Iroquoian type, or influence, that is found scattered over a wide area of northern Ontario (Wintemberg 1942; Martijn 1969). So far, this pottery has been studied very inadequately. In many cases, it remains uncertain whether it is of Iroquoian manufacture, or an Algonkian copy of Iroquoian originals (Martijn 1969:90). This problem is particularly severe in the case of a number of sites, as far north as Lake Nipissing, which contain assemblages of pottery that seem to be purely Iroquoian and have been labelled as such, on occasion, by Iroquoian archaeologists (Ritchie 1961:32).

The classic example is the Frank Bay site on Lake Nipissing. In this richly stratified site, Frank Ridley (1954) found Middle Woodland levels overlain by an unbroken record of occupation from Pickering times into the seventeenth century. The pottery from each level is essentially identical to coeval pottery found north of Lake Ontario. Thus, no matter how the site is interpreted, it provides clear evidence of Ontario Iroquoian influence in the north, beginning in early Iroquoian times. The interpretation of this site is, however, a matter of some controversy. It may have been a campsite visited annually by Iroquoians who were travelling, and possibly trading, this far north. Alternatively, it may have been a summer camp belonging to the Nipissing, who lived in this area in historic times. In support of the latter interpretation, Ridley has noted that the site is located close to the Nipissing village marked on the Gallinée map of 1670. The dog burials, the variety of abandoned European material in the historic stratum, and the presence of an ossuary nearby also suggest that it was a habitation site rather than a way station.[27] Since the Nipissing celebrated their own Feast of the Dead, it is not improbable that the site belonged to them and their ancestors. Small differences in the frequencies of pottery types, and the possible presence of linear stamped pottery from northern Michigan, also provide vague hints of possible non-Iroquoian ethnicity.[28]

If Frank Bay is Nipissing, it suggests that the close contact between this group and the Huron can be traced back into early Iroquoian times. Though the economy of the Nipissing remained dramatically different from that of the Iroquoians, close contact, which historically involved large numbers of Nipissing spending the winter among the Attignawantan or Ataronchronon, might have resulted in the Nipissing either acquiring Iroquoian-style pottery through trade, or learning to make it themselves. It appears that here, as elsewhere where cultural contact cuts across ethnic boundaries, pottery types cease to be reliable indicators of ethnicity.

Other prehistoric sites containing Iroquoian-style pottery have been found in Algonquin Park. These date from early Iroquoian times onward, but the majority of finds seem to be late Iroquoian. The nature of these sites indicates that the area was being exploited during the summer months by hunting and fishing parties who had home bases elsewhere (Hurley and Kenyon 1970:122–25). Some of the hunters may have been Huron, or proto-Huron, from southern Ontario, but it is equally probable that they were Algonkians using Iroquoian-style pottery. The latter may have come from the Lake Nipissing region or the eastern shores of Georgian Bay, but, since pottery resembling that produced by the St. Lawrence Iroquoians is also present, it is possible that some of the intruders may have been Algonkin from the Ottawa Valley.

North of Georgian Bay, Ontario Iroquoian pottery occurs alone only in small quantities. Such sherds may provide evidence of the passage of Iroquoian travellers, but unfortunately most of the occurrences have not been reported in sufficient detail that they can be interpreted with any confidence. Nor, in most cases, can such sites be distinguished from ones in which Iroquoian sherds occur alongside pottery of non-Iroquoian type and with stone tools that conform to a homogeneous pattern that has been identified as northern Algonkian. Sites of both types extend at least as far west as the Rainy River and as far north as Lake Abitibi (Wright 1965). The eastern extent of prehistoric Ontario Iroquoian pottery is more diffi-cult to determine. Many prehistoric sites in northern Quebec have yielded small quantities of Iroquoian-style pottery (Martijn 1969:76, 85), but most of these occurrences have been shown to represent a transmission of St. Lawrence Iroquoian pottery northward or, when studied more thoroughly, may be expected to do so. One of the most intriguing sites found to date is Matabachouwan on Lake St. John (Simard 1970). This site has produced, along with some St. Lawrence Valley pottery, a few sherds of what appear to be Ontario Iroquoian types that reached maximum popularity in pre-historic times. All but one of these sherds were found in areas of the site that do not appear to have contained trade goods. The absence of the pottery types that were most common among the Huron in the historic period (Huron Incised, Sidey Notched, and Warminster Crossed) suggests that this pottery may be prehistoric and that either proto-Huron or neighbouring Algonkian groups may have travelled as far east as Lake St. John sometime after A.D. 1400[29]. In the sixteenth century, copper from Lake Superior was being traded eastward to the Saguenay region, pro-viding further evidence for such contacts. It is possible, however, that the Nipissing were the main participants in such trade rather than the Huron.

Much of the Ontario Iroquoian-style pottery found in the upper Great Lakes region dates from an early period. At the Juntunen site, after A.D. 1200, the strongest ceramic affinities are with the Pickering culture of southern Ontario. Further evidence of Iroquoian influence at Juntunen, between A.D. 1200 and 1400, is an ossuary containing thirty-four bodies; some fully articulated, others completely disarticulated. This provides an unexpectedly early date for the possible diffusion of the Feast of the Dead among the northern Algonkians. A longhouse was also found at the Juntunen site, but, while its eighty-foot length may suggest Iroquoian influence, we have already noted the antiquity of this housetype in the north. It is of interest that over 770 pieces of native copper were found in the most recent levels of the site (A.D. 1200 to 1400). These ranged from unworked nuggets to completed awls, beads, and other implements. McPherron (1967:106) concludes that the inhabitants of the site were a marginally agricultural Algonkian group, who played an important role in the copper trade of the upper Great Lakes.

Farther west, at the Pic River site, on the north shore of Lake Superior, over ten percent of the pottery in level III, radiocarbon dated around A.D. 960, has been identified as being Pickering in type (Wright 1965: 203–5). A single Pickering sherd has also been found in the McCluskey site, at the mouth of the Rainy River (ibid. 194). These finds indicate some kind of contact, either direct or indirect, between the Iroquoian peoples of southeastern Ontario and the Algonkians of the Lake Superior region by early Iroquoian times.

These contacts continued throughout the prehistoric period. At the Michipicoten site, on Lake Superior, fifteen percent of the pottery in level III (dated A.D. 1472 ± 75) has been identified as Huron or Tionnontaté, while in level II, which is somewhat earlier, pottery of this type constitutes forty-three percent of the total (Wright 1965:203–5; 1969:49–50). Iroquoian pottery, tentatively dated between A.D. 1500 and 1600, has been reported from Isle Royale in Lake Superior (Griffin 1961:11). These finds provide evidence of extensive and persistent contacts between southeastern Ontario and the southern portions of the Canadian Shield, beginning in early Iroquoian times. There is little reason to doubt that they are indicative of some kind of trade going back to the beginnings of a horticultural economy in southern Ontario. The question that remains to be answered is who was involved in these contacts. Various interpretations have been suggested, which may apply in different cases.

Some of this pottery could have been made by the Huron and carried onto the Shield by Huron hunters and traders. It is known that Iroquoian travellers in the north carried pottery vessels with them on their canoe trips. They used them for cooking and (so Sagard noted) to urinate in when they were far from shore (Wrong 1939:59–60). Bark vessels would have been more convenient to carry, but seem to have had a short lifespan when used as cooking vessels (Martijn 1969:86 n. 5); hence the Huron must have concluded that the greater durability of clay vessels made their transport worthwhile. Some of the Iroquoian potsherds found in remote campsites probably betoken the breaking, or abandonment, of pots of this sort. Yet, even if specific pots were made by Huron women, it is often impossible to determine whether they were carried abroad by Huron or by their Algonkian trading partners. Martijn (1969:91) has suggested that the ownership of pots made by Iroquoian women may have been a status symbol among the Algonkians. He cites as an example of this a typical Iroquoian pot deposited in an Algonkian grave at Michipicoten.

It also has been proposed that many pots of Iroquoian design, particularly those found alongside other types of pottery, may have been made by Huron women who married Algonkian men. It is argued that, since the Algonkian bands were patrilineal and exogamous, once knowledge of making such pottery had been introduced into the north, it would have spread quickly from one group to another (McPherron 1967:106). While it is impossible to say what kind of relations existed between the Iroquoians and northern Algonkians in early times, in historic times no Huron woman would have consented to live among the Algonkians.

It is possible, however, that Algonkian women acquired pottery-making skills among the Huron and then, through intermarriage, transmitted these skills to groups living farther north. Such knowledge may have been acquired during the winter, when Algonkian bands resided near Huron villages. It is also possible that Algonkian girls may have lived with Huron families as part of a ritual exchange of children between trading partners. These girls would have learned to make pottery from their foster mothers and when they returned to their own people, would have carried these skills with them. Relations of this sort were probably most frequent with the Algonkian-speaking groups who lived closest to the Huron and may, in part, explain the almost identical nature of the pottery of the Nipissing and Ontario Iroquoians, beginning in early Iroquoian times. Unfortunately, the similarity of this pottery creates the possibility that the far-flung Iroquoian traits evident in the pottery of the upper Great Lakes, do not, in fact, indicate direct contact between the inhabitants of that area and those of southern Ontario. Instead, such pottery may have diffused through intermediary Algonkian groups, such as the Nipissing and Ottawa.

The archaeological record thus leaves unresolved the extent of the Huron trading network in prehistoric times. The small amount of copper in prehistoric Ontario Iroquoian sites might be interpreted as evidence that trade with the Lake Superior region was in the hands of Nipissing and Ottawa middlemen, who were diverting only a small part of it southward. Alternatively, it might be argued that as much, or even more, copper was reaching Ontario than had done so previously, but that an expanding population resulted in a thinner overall distribution. This, of course, does not answer the question of whether trade with Lake Superior was direct or indirect.

While the extent of Iroquoian contacts with the north in prehistoric times remains in doubt, by the early Iroquoian period extensive direct contacts clearly existed between some of the Iroquoian-speaking peoples of southern Ontario and the Algonkian groups who lived around the shores of Georgian Bay and Lake Nipissing. There is little reason to doubt that these relations centred around a reciprocal exchange of corn, nets, and tobacco for skins, dried fish, and meat. Even in earliest times, the northern part of Simcoe County was the agricultural area best suited for contacts with the north and hence had the greatest potential to sustain a large population through a symbiotic relationship. Even in the short run, the inhabitants of this region stood to benefit from limited trade. The degree to which they might wish, or were able, to enforce a monopoly over such trade would depend on their strength relative to neighbouring Iroquoian groups and on the nature of their relationships with these groups.

Unfortunately, we know all too little about the relationships among the various Huron tribes prior to the historic period. Culturally and linguistically, these tribes were more similar to one another than the five Iroquois tribes were; for example, only the Tahontaenrat are said to have spoken a significantly divergent dialect. On the other hand, cultural and linguistic similarities never secured membership in the Huron confederacy for the Tionnontaté, and the Huron never allowed them to share in their trade with the north. Relations between the Attignawantan and the Attigneenongnahac appear to have been friendly for a long time prior to A.D. 1600, but we do not know whether or not this friendship and sharing of trade preceded the arrival of the Attigneenongnahac in north Simcoe County.

Warfare with St. Lawrence Iroquoians and the Iroquois of New York State may have compounded the advantages of moving away from the shores of Lake Ontario, although by itself, it does not appear to have been sufficient to compel such a move. Had conditions to the north not been so favourable, the tribes who arrived latterly in the Huron country might not have been tempted to move and, had they been encircled by a solid ring of agricultural tribes, as the Iroquois were, they would not have been able to do so. The very ability of these tribes to move seems to have been the result of a frontier situation which also promoted peaceful and profitable relations with the north.

The Arendarhonon, Tahontaenrat, and possibly, still earlier, the Attigneenongnahac, seem to have been attracted towards the southeastern corner of Georgian Bay by the trading potential of that region. Once near Lake Simcoe, they were in a position to travel north without difficulty and to trade there, whether the Attignawantan wished them to or not. The Attignawantan and the Attigneenongnahac may have welcomed the gradual approach of the two other tribes, as offering them greater security against attack from the south and east. If the volume of trade was increasing, the admission of these other tribes may have involved little loss of profit for the original participants.

Moreover, since the Attignawantan had engaged in this trade the longest and were the most skilful at it, they would have been well able to cope with competition. On the other hand, the Attignawantan's inveterate refusal to permit the Tionnontaté, who were less advantageously placed to defy them, to participate in this trade suggests that they resented having to share their commerce with other groups. It may be that in respect of the Arendarhonon and Tahontaenrat the Attignawantan and Attigneenongnahac felt themselves insufficiently strong, and not well enough situated, to prevent this from happening. If the other tribes were growing increasingly anxious to participate in this trade, the Attignawantan may have concluded that it was in their own best interests not to oppose them, except in the case of the Tionnontaté. Hence, the final stages in the growth of the confederacy may have taken place without overt conflict.

As will be made clear in the next chapter, the admission of the Arendarhonon and Tahontaenrat to the confederacy and their resettlement in northern Simcoe County did not take place until European trade goods had begun arriving in Ontario. This makes it highly likely that both events were related to the early development of the fur trade. The evidence suggests, however, that long before this period, native commerce had been playing an important role in drawing the Huron tribes not already living in the north nearer to Lake Simcoe. At the same time, the union of the Attignawantan and the Attigneenongnahac had laid the foundations of the Huron confederacy. Therefore, in both the economic and political spheres, processes that had been influencing the Iroquoian peoples living north of Lake Ontario for many centuries had, by the latter half of the sixteenth century, reached the point where only the elaboration of native trading patterns resulting from the beginnings of the European fur trade was needed to bring about the expansion of the confederacy and the nucleation of population that was observed by the first Europeans who visited the region. The introduction of European goods did not alter the pattern of Huron development so much as it intensified it. The final coming together of the Huron population in northern Simcoe County would have been far more difficult, or even impossible, had trading relations with the north not existed in earlier times and if all the Huron tribes had not already been aware, at least to some degree, of the potential benefits to be derived from a symbiotic relationship with the northern hunting peoples. Many other peoples had their ways of life totally disrupted and transformed by their early commercial encounters with Europeans or with Indians who had been influenced by Europeans. In the case of the Huron, it seems that several hundred years of development on the edge of the Canadian Shield had prepared them for their historic role as the principal trading partners with the French in this part of North America. In this respect, the Huron though similar to the Iroquois in many other ways, were totally different from them.

Chapter 4   Alien Shadows

Before their earliest recorded encounter with the French in 1609, the Huron had already been heavily influenced by contacts between their eastern neighbours and European traders on the St. Lawrence River. Any discussion of these influences is bound to be highly conjectural and subject to revision as additional archaeological data becomes available. It is, however, a topic that cannot be avoided, if we are to understand Huron society in the seventeenth century. The aim of this chapter is to survey what is known about how the arrival of the Europeans influenced the Indians of eastern Canada prior to 1609 and to examine the responses of the Huron to these influences.[1]

Cartier and Roberval on the St. Lawrence

CARTIER'S FIRST VOYAGE

The first recorded meeting between Iroquoians and a group of Europeans took place in 1534. That year, Jacques Cartier, a master mariner from St. Malo, who had previously visited Brazil and Newfoundland, was commissioned by Francis I to discover new lands in America. Leaving France with two ships on 20 April, he crossed the Atlantic and sailed into the Strait of Belle Isle and along the south coast of Labrador as far as Bonne Esperance Harbour. There, he turned south to chart the unrecorded west coast of Newfoundland, then crossed the Gulf of St. Lawrence and skirted Brion Island, the Magdalens, and Prince Edward Island. From the latter, he sailed north along the coast of New Brunswick and entered Chaleur Bay, which for a time he hoped might be the long sought-for passage leading to the Pacific Ocean and the riches of the Orient. At the north entrance to the bay, a French longboat encountered two groups of Micmac in some forty to fifty canoes. Upon landing, these Indians made a loud noise and held up furs on the ends of sticks to indicate that they wished to trade. The French were alarmed by so many Indians and motioned them to move away.

When the Indians continued to pursue them on the water, the French fired two cannons and scattered fire-lances in their midst to frighten them off (Biggar 1924:48–51).

The Micmac were more experienced traders than Cartier's men seem to have been. The next day, nine canoes appeared near the French ships, obviously wary, but again making signs that they wished to trade. This time the French reciprocated, both parties landed, and a profitable trade ensued. The next day, as the French sailed along the north shore of Chaleur Bay, they spotted signal fires[2] at Tracadigash Point and a boatload of Indians came out and offered them cooked seal meat. As soon as two Frenchmen went ashore bearing trade goods, more than three hundred men, women, and children appeared. These Indians warmly greeted the French and bartered all of their furs for iron kettles, knives, and other wares (Biggar 1924:52–57). The behaviour of the Micmac indicates that they were already used to dealing with Europeans. They had evidently collected furs over the winter and brought them to the coast in the hope that Europeans would turn up with whom they might trade.

Several days later, Cartier was compelled by foul weather to take refuge in Gaspé Harbour, where he remained 16–25 July. There he encountered a party of about three hundred men, women, and children. They wore only loin cloths and a few old skins over their shoulders, had no furs to trade, and possessed nothing of value, except their canoes and fishing nets. In Cartier's estimation these Indians were "the sorriest people in the world" (Biggar 1924:60). One of the distinctive features of this group was that the men shaved their heads, except for a long tuft on top, which they tied into a knot with leather thongs. A word list was compiled which remains the oldest recorded Iroquoian vocabulary (ibid. 80–81; B. Hoffman 1961:157).

These Indians had come from the vicinity of Quebec City and were part of what, for lack of a more distinctive name, are called the St. Lawrence Iroquoians (map 6). On the basis of sixteenth-century accounts, the latter can be subdivided into two groups, who are denominated, after their principal settlements, Stadaconans and Hochelagans (Trigger 1968a:430–31; Pendergast and Trigger 1972:43–45). The Hochelagans, who lived in the upper part of the St. Lawrence Valley, occupied at least one large town surrounded by a triple palisade and extensive cornfields. They were a sedentary, horticultural people and resembled in detail the Iroquoian groups who lived farther inland at this time and in the seventeenth century. Other Hochelagan-type groups had formerly lived farther up the

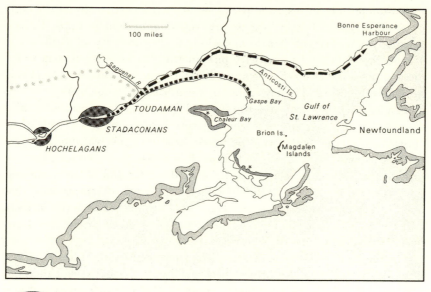

Coastline known to Europeans in 1534 (after Hoffman 1961)

Coastline inferred to be known to European traders by 1634

Location of Iroquoian settlement (by ethnic divisions)

Copper route from Lake Superior

Stadaconan summer fishing expeditions

Inferred Stadaconan summer expeditions

MAP 6. *The lower St. Lawrence, c. 1533.*

St. Lawrence Valley, although no archaeological sites with trade goods have been found there.

The Stadaconans were quite different. They inhabited about a dozen small, unfortified communities between the Ile aux Coudres and Portneuf, thirty-two miles up-river from Quebec City. They planted corn, but seem to have relied more heavily on fishing and eeling than did the other northern Iroquoian-speaking peoples. Moreover, their villages appear to have been mainly winter camps and places to grow corn. Every summer, groups, each consisting of several hundred men, women, and children, would travel down the St. Lawrence, to fish for mackerel on the Gaspé

Peninsula or to hunt seals and porpoises along the north shore of the Gulf of St. Lawrence (Trigger 1963*b*:94; 1968*a*:430; Bailey 1933; Fenton 1940:167–69; Trigger 1962*b*:242). While the majority of Stadaconan villages were on good terms with one another, there is no evidence of a general tribal structure. In keeping with the economic conservatism of this group, each village may have remained politically autonomous.

The relationship between the Hochelagans and Stadaconans is also obscure. Cartier says the Stadaconans were subjects of the Hochelagans (Biggar 1924:161), but there is no reason to believe this was the case. The distance separating them suggests that they constituted distinct tribes, or groups of villages. The relations that the Stadaconans and Hochelagans had with the Indians living farther inland were quite different from one another (Trigger 1968*a*:431). It seems likely that, just as between most tribes who were not members of the same confederacy, there may have been rivalry, or even hostility between the two groups.

The identity of the St. Lawrence Iroquoians constitutes a longstanding ethnological problem. Anthropologists and historians have seen in these two groups the ancestors of one or more of the Iroquoian tribes of the seventeenth century. Schemes have been proposed which would have these tribes moving inland, late in the sixteenth century, to become the Tionnontaté, one or more of the Huron tribes, the Seneca, Onondaga, Oneida, Mohawk, or even the Tuscarora (Pendergast and Trigger 1972:63). They have also been viewed by archaeologists as a branch of the Onondaga or Oneida, who allegedly spread out in the St. Lawrence Valley about A.D. 1100, and retreated into New York State after 1542.[3]

All of these interpretations do violence to current knowledge of these groups. Linguists, who have studied the vocabularies that record the language of Hochelaga and Stadacona are agreed that this language, or group of dialects, is closer to Huron than it is to any of the languages of the Five Nations Iroquois.[4] Hence it is impossible that these people are, to any substantial degree, the ancestors of one or more of the Iroquois tribes. Since the Huron tribes were already present in southern Ontario prior to the disappearance of the St. Lawrence Iroquoians and the material culture of the latter, as revealed by archaeology, is different from the Ontario Iroquoian tradition, it is unlikely that these people are the ancestors of any of the Huron tribes. Finally, James F. Pendergast's archaeological studies reveal the development of a distinctive Iroquoian culture in the St. Lawrence Valley, beginning as early as the Pickering culture to the west.[5] The similarities between the later phases of this development and those of the eastern Iroquois cultures in New York State appear to result from cultural contact between these two regions. The simultaneous discovery that the eastern Iroquois tribes developed *in situ* in their historic tribal territories supports the linguistic evidence and virtually rules out the possibility of any of the Iroquois tribes being descendants of the St. Lawrence Iroquoians.

Prior to the discovery of the antiquity of Iroquoian culture in the St. Lawrence Valley, the Stadaconans were viewed as a typical Iroquoian group who had taken corn agriculture as far north as Quebec, but, finding themselves in an environment that was less favourable to agriculture, had adopted something resembling an Algonkian type of hunting and fishing economy (Fenton 1940:172). Now, the Stadaconans can alternatively be viewed as an Iroquoian group that had not accepted the more complex patterns of intensive agriculture that mark their neighbours to the south-west. If we accept the implications of the *in situ* theory, it is no more surprising to find Iroquoian-speaking peoples who did not participate in all features of the Iroquoian cultural pattern than it is to find Algonkian-speakers who did share many of these features.

The fishing party that Cartier encountered had not come to the Gaspé with the intention of trading with Europeans. They had no surplus skins and, at first, were reluctant to have any dealings with the French. This suggests that, unlike the Micmac, they had little direct experience of Europeans. After the French mingled with them for a while on shore, they began to come in their canoes to the sides of the French vessels, where they were given knives, glass beads, combs, and other inexpensive trinkets (Biggar 1924:60). On 22 July the French again visited the Iroquoians' encampment and were greeted by the men with customary singing and dancing. All but a few of the young women, however, had retired into the woods. When Cartier gave a comb and tin bell to each woman who remained, the men ordered the twenty or so women who were hiding to return, which they did, rubbing Cartier's face and arms in a traditional Iroquoian greeting. Cartier gave each of them a tin ring, after which there was much singing and dancing (61–63). The account of this visit observes that the Indians stole what they could from the French (63). While the Iroquoians did not regard the acquisition of goods that were left unattended as theft, it is likely that these Indians, like many others who lacked the means to trade, took considerable risks to acquire the exotic possessions of Europeans. Elsewhere, this hunger for European goods often resulted in quarrels, followed by violence and bloodshed.

While the Stadaconans who came to the Gaspé were inexperienced in trading with Europeans, this does not mean that they did not know anything about them. Some Stadaconans travelled along the north shore of the

St. Lawrence to hunt seals and porpoises, perhaps occasionally reaching the south coast of Labrador. Some of these may already have met or traded with Europeans. Prior experience of this sort would explain the speed with which the Stadaconans became interested in establishing a trading relationship with the French. It would also explain an otherwise cryptic observation in the account of Cartier's second voyage. There it is stated that the Hochelagans "make their living by horticulture and fishing and the goods of this world mean nothing to them for they do not have knowledge of them and are not nomads like the Stadaconans" (160–61). If we assume that "goods of this world" mean European trade goods, this could be interpreted to signify that the annual visit of the Stadaconans to the north shore of the Gulf of St. Lawrence had already resulted in them having limited dealings with Europeans.

At the end of his stay in Gaspé Harbour, Cartier had a large cross erected, bearing the arms of Francis I. Seeing the religious ceremony that accompanied the erection of the cross, Donnacona, who was the leader of this fishing party, became angry that the French were presuming to use land that belonged to his people without first acquiring the right to do so. He set out in a canoe for Cartier's ship, accompanied by his brother and three of his sons (or nephews). Keeping well away from the French ships, Donnacona pointed at the cross and delivered a harangue, accompanied by many gestures, which made it clear that this region was his and the French had no right to erect anything without his permission. Cartier had an axe held up, pretending that the French wished to barter for the bear skin Donnacona was wearing and thus suggesting to Donnacona that he was willing to pay for the use of the land. As Donnacona warily approached the ship to collect the axe, he was seized by a group of French sailors, who made everyone in the canoe board the French vessel.

Cartier gave the Indians food and drink and attempted to tell Donnacona, again by means of gestures, that the cross was a land-mark and that the French would soon return, bringing him iron ware and other goods. Cartier also stated that he wished to take two of Donnacona's sons to France for the winter. As an expression of goodwill, he had Taignoagny and Domagaya dressed in shirts, ribbons, and red caps and gave each of them a brass chain. Donnacona appears to have understood that Cartier meant to keep the boys, but, rather than becoming angry, he accepted with a show of pleasure the hatchets and knives that were given to him and the two Indians who accompanied him, prior to their being released. Later, six boatloads of Indians came to say goodbye to the prisoners and to bring them a supply of fish. The following day, Cartier set sail (64–67). He circled the east end of Anticosti Island and returned to France by way of the Strait of Belle Isle.

During his stay in Gaspé Harbour, Cartier probably had learned that the Stadaconans were only visiting the coast and lived farther inland. His aim in kidnapping Taignoagny and Domagaya seems to have been to obtain Indians who could learn French and would later guide him to their villages. It is frequently asked why Donnacona did not try to secure the release of his sons. Some historians have suggested that his decision to cooperate with the French was motivated solely by political or economic considerations (Morison 1971:375). The previous year, two hundred Stadaconans, who were on their way to the Gaspé, had been massacred near the mouth of the Saguenay River by a people called the Toudaman (Biggar 1924:177–78). These were a group living to the south, probably the Micmac (B. Hoffman 1961:203–4). They and the Stadaconans appear to have been fighting for control of the Gaspé Peninsula, and Donnacona may have hoped to win the French as his allies in this struggle. Donnacona also may have wanted to establish trading relations with the French, to have as ready access to European trade goods as did the Micmac and other tribes who were living near the coast.

Alternatively, like the Huron and other Iroquoian tribes in the next century, the Stadaconans may have been in the habit of exchanging children with their trading partners as pledges of good faith. High-handed and unreciprocal as Cartier's actions were, Donnacona could have interpreted them in the light of such a custom and believed that, if he remained friendly, he would see his sons again and acquire a valuable trading partner. On the other hand, an attempt to rescue his sons might have resulted in them being killed or carried off, never to return. In later times, military alliances, trade, and personal goodwill were indissoluble elements of any alliance. Paternal affection, as well as practical political and economic considerations probably motivated Donnacona's restrained behaviour. Finally, Iroquoian politeness and tenacity in suppressing spontaneous emotions were able to add to Donnacona's actions a deceptive appearance of satisfaction and goodwill.

SECOND VOYAGE

In spite of Donnacona's composure, an anxious winter must have followed, which was followed by a still more anxious summer. Not until early September 1535 was Donnacona to learn that his sons had reappeared aboard three French ships that were sailing towards Stadacona. In October of the previous year, Cartier had been commissioned to sail once more and explore the lands beyond Newfoundland. In addition to searching for a route to the Indies, the stories that Taignoagny and Domagaya had told about the native copper trade had aroused Cartier's hopes of finding jewels and precious metals in the New World (Biggar 1924:105–6). These boys had also promised to lead him to the large settlement of Hochelaga, which lay up the St. Lawrence in the direction of these riches.

Leaving France in May 1535, Cartier reached Blanc Sablon in mid-July and then spent almost eight weeks exploring the St. Lawrence. Directed by his two prisoners, who by now had acquired a working knowledge of French, he slowly made his way up-river, crossing from one side to the other in order to see as much as possible. He may also have been delaying his arrival at Stadacona until Donnacona had returned from his annual trip to the Gaspé Peninsula. Off Tadoussac, Cartier encountered four canoes whose crews had come from the Quebec City area to fish and hunt for seals. These Indians were so frightened by the sight of the French ships that only one vessel came near enough for Donnacona's sons to hail them and invite them to draw alongside (114–15). On 7 September, the French anchored near the western extremity of the Ile d'Orléans, where many Indians were fishing. Seeing that Taignoagny and Domagaya had returned, these people welcomed the French with traditional singing and dancing, and some chief men came out to Cartier's ships bringing him a present of eels, fish, maize, and several large squash. This was followed by numerous deputations of both sexes, to whom Cartier gave small presents in order to ingratiate himself (119–21).

The next day, accompanied by twelve canoes filled with his men, Donnacona came abreast of Cartier's flagship. After sending ten of these canoes a safe distance away, he approached Cartier's ships with the other two. Seeing his sons were safe, he embraced Cartier in an affectionate manner, after which Cartier stepped into his canoe and ordered bread and wine to be brought to the Indians (121–23). Following this reception, Donnacona departed, apparently taking his two sons with him. Cartier travelled up-river in his longboats, in order to search for a good harbour for his ships. As he did so, he began to understand the geography of the Quebec City region (map 7). The Stadaconan settlements were all located along the north shore of the river. Cartier passed the villages of Ajoaste, Starnatam, Tailla, and Sitadin, before catching sight of Stadacona on the flank of Cape Diamond.[6] Just north of Stadacona, where the Lairet flows into the St. Charles River, Cartier found a safe anchorage for his ships.

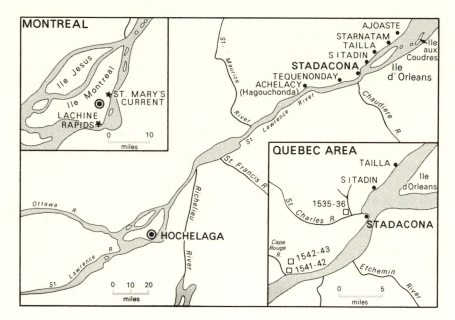

● Fortified settlement

• Village

★ Fishing camp

□ French settlements

MAP 7. *Approximate location of Iroquoian villages mentioned in the texts of Cartier's voyages.*

The site had the added advantage that the St. Charles River flowed between the proposed encampment and Stadacona, providing the French with additional protection against the Indians. As he left the river, the people of Stadacona thronged to greet him. A headman made a speech of welcome, women danced and, once again, Cartier distributed knives and glass beads (123–25). On 13 September Cartier brought all three of his ships up-river from the Ile d'Orléans, preceded by Donnacona and twenty-five canoes filled with Indians, who came up-river from the east. Once again, the Indians swarmed about the ships to welcome the French (127).

Many historians have noted that the days that preceded Cartier's docking on the St. Charles River marked the highpoint in his relations with the Amerindians. The Stadaconans were delighted that Donnacona's sons had been returned to them and Donnacona must have believed that he had acquired a powerful ally and trading partner. When, however, Donnacona came to greet Cartier on the way to Stadacona, Cartier noted that Taigno-agny and Domagaya, who had hitherto shown themselves to be friendly, were now reluctant to associate with the French and refused to board his ship, even when pointedly asked to do so (127–28). Although they assured Cartier that they intended to keep their promise to travel with him to Hochelaga, it is often assumed that Taignoagny and Domagaya began to avoid the French when they learned that their father did not wish Cartier to travel up-river (Morison 1971:406–7). This explanation seems inadequate, however, since Donnacona was still going to great lengths to manifest his goodwill towards Cartier. If Donnacona was willing to dissemble his feelings about the projected journey, there is no reason why his sons should not have done the same.

Taignoagny and Domagaya had personal reasons for behaving as they did. They had been kidnapped, made to endure an ocean voyage to an unknown destination, and to learn, by trial and error, a language the structure of which was totally alien to them. In addition, they had been compelled to eat strange food and, in France, were exposed to a wholly unfamiliar way of life and many customs that must have frightened and disgusted them. There is no reason to doubt that Cartier wished to treat them well; since both young men were endowed with Iroquoian self-reliance, they probably accepted most of what happened to them as an adventure and a challenge. They even acquired a taste for European clothes, which they continued to wear after their return home, and for some varieties of European food.[7]

They had, however, been brought up in a society in which young people enjoyed great freedom and were never physically punished or forcibly restrained by their elders. In the opinion of sixteenth and seventeenth century Europeans, physical coercion was essential for dealing with young people and Cartier probably did not hesitate to chastise them when he judged their behaviour merited it. Moreover, while we do not know their ages, Iroquoian attitudes towards sexual behaviour may have got them into situations that resulted in even more severe disciplinary action. Indian youths who had been to Europe rarely expressed the desire to return there. We may therefore assume that, even if Cartier believed that he treated Taignoagny and Domagaya fairly, his behaviour often must have seemed cruel and arbitrary. The Stadaconans were, no doubt, surprised by Taignoagny's and Domagaya's stories about their experiences in France, but tended at first to view them as the complaints of young people and not as a serious impediment to an alliance.

The following day, when Cartier was marking the place to dock his ships he noticed that, while many Indians were swarming about, Donnacona, his sons, and those who were with them (their clansmen?) kept apart. Seeing this, Cartier ordered a number of Frenchmen to go with him to find out what was the matter. Taignoagny informed Cartier that Donnacona was angry because the French were carrying their weapons while the Indians did not do so. Although vexed at being challenged, Cartier replied that it was the custom for Frenchmen always to bear arms, as Taignoagny knew well. Following this, Cartier and Donnacona again greeted one another warmly and the Indians who were present gave three loud shouts of approval (Biggar 1924:128–30).

This incident provides an example of the subtle and indirect way in which Iroquoian diplomacy was conducted. The complaint about the French carrying arms was undoubtedly a rebuke to behaviour that Donnacona interpreted as signifying a lack of trust in his people, but it also expressed displeasure over two other matters. Firstly, Cartier was beaching his ships, and thus again he was using land without obtaining permission to do so from its owners. Secondly, by now Donnacona had learned from Taignoagny and Domagaya that Cartier was planning within a few days to travel up-river to visit the Hochelagans. It has been suggested that Donnacona was opposed to the French travelling up-river because he wished to protect the Hochelagans, but nothing about his behaviour suggests that this is so (Fenton 1940:171).

On the contrary, it seems clear that Donnacona wanted to keep the commercial and political advantages of an alliance with the French to himself and did not wish Cartier to travel inland to make a separate alliance with potential competitors. Lacking a formal treaty with the French, Donnacona may have feared that Cartier sought to conclude such an alliance with the Hochelagans, to the detriment of the Stadaconans. Also, by travelling up-river without obtaining his permission, Cartier was infringing still further on Donnacona's territorial rights. Looked at in Iroquoian terms, Donnacona's opposition to Cartier's visit to Hochelaga seems to have been motivated by a reasonable mixture of fear, pride, and self-interest. It is unwarranted to dissect social, economic, and political motives among the Indians of eastern North America at this period, not because the Indians did not have such motives, but because the activities associated with them were so clearly interrelated that such motives cannot be compartmentalized as easily as they can be for Europeans. Nevertheless, interpreted strictly from an economic point of view, Donnacona's objection provides the first example of an Indian group in eastern North America attempting to establish a middleman position in the trading of European goods with the interior. Tribes that could secure and hold onto such a position were able to profit by exchanging furs they did not trap for European goods they did not have to manufacture. As a result, the role of middleman was to become a highly coveted one among some tribes.[8] The idea of informing himself about native customs occurred to Cartier no more than it did to most other early navigators. He had no idea what his actions signified to the Indians and failed to appreciate the reasons for Donnacona's complaint. He also began to fear that Taignoagny and Domagaya were plotting against him for no good reason. In the latter, we see further evidence of the deep-seated mistrust of the Indians that had led Cartier to fire on the peaceful Micmac a year earlier.

The next day, Cartier beached his two large ships, leaving his pinnace anchored in the St. Lawrence ready for his trip up-river. Donnacona and his sons appeared, accompanied by more than five hundred men, women, and children—most likely the entire population of Stadacona. A delegation of about a dozen leading Indians were entertained by Cartier on board ship and presents were given to them. This time, Taignoagny, as interpreter, informed Cartier that Donnacona was angry about his plan to visit Hochelaga and that he would not let his sons accompany the French. He added that the river was dangerous above Quebec. Cartier replied that he would press on, with or without Taignoagny and his brother, since he had to obey the orders of his king. He offered Taignoagny a rich present if he would go along, which the latter refused. At this point, the Indians withdrew to their settlement (Biggar 1924:131–32).

The next day, Donnacona sought again to persuade Cartier not to visit Hochelaga, or, if that were impossible, at least to conclude a formal alliance with the Stadaconans before doing so. Arriving at Cartier's ships, Donnacona gave the French leader a lavish present of fish and eels, after which the Indians sang and danced to express their goodwill. Then Donnacona invited the principal French and Indians to sit in a circle on the beach and made a long speech in the course of which he offered to "give" Cartier a girl about ten years old and two younger boys. Taignoagny explained as best his knowledge of French allowed that these prestations were to dissuade Cartier from going to Hochelaga. Donnacona's actions cannot be interpreted as the permanent surrender of these children. One of the boys was his own son, while the girl was his sister's daughter, who, as a clanswoman, stood in an especially close relationship to him. It is clear, from what happened next, that by offering to let these children live with the French, Donnacona was seeking to conclude a formal alliance with the newcomers.

When Cartier said he would not accept the children if, in return, he had to promise not to go up-river, Domagaya assured him that they were offered as tokens of goodwill and that he was prepared to accompany Cartier. By this, Domagaya appears to have meant that, if Cartier was determined to go up-river, Donnacona would be content if only Cartier would first formally assure him that a special relationship existed between them. At this point, Taignoagny and Domagaya exchanged some harsh words and Cartier was convinced that Taignoagny was rebuking his brother for offering to help the French. While Domagaya seems to have been a pliant individual, who was anxious to curry favour with the French and consequently often revealed things he should not have, there is no reason to believe that he liked the French any better than his brother did. What Cartier failed to perceive was that Taignoagny's and Domagaya's offers represented two stages in Donnacona's negotiations with him. Already suspicious of his two former victims, Cartier now suspected that each in his own way was trying to deceive him further. In return for the children, whom Cartier retained as hostages, Donnacona was presented with two swords and two brass wash basins. A salute of twelve guns was also fired from the ship, which much astonished the Indians. A rumour spread that two Indians had been killed by a similar volley from the pinnace that was anchored near Stadacona, whereupon all of the Indians fled. Cartier suspected Taignoagny of starting this rumour (132–35).

Donnacona was obviously not content with the response he had received from Cartier, and must have grown increasingly mistrustful of him as a result of this meeting. Nevertheless, he did not cease to try to dissuade Cartier from travelling up-river. The next day he sent three shamans, with blackened faces and wearing dogskin pelts and long horns, to paddle around Cartier's flag-ship, while one of them delivered a long speech. The shamans landed and were carried into the woods by Donnacona and his men, where they continued their harangue. About half an hour later, Taignoagny and Domagaya appeared, their caps under their arms and their hands folded in imitation of French acts of devotion they had witnessed. They said that one of their deities had informed these shamans that, if the French proceeded to Hochelaga, they would all perish from ice and snow. When Cartier laughed and said his priests revealed the contrary, Taignoagny and Domagaya returned to the woods and soon the other

Indians appeared before the ships expressing pleasure at the good news (136–40). Here we see another aspect of Iroquoian behaviour that was often to puzzle the French in the next century: the assumption that it is improper to question the beliefs of other people.⁹ Although the French laughed at the Stadaconan shamans' not unreasonable warning, the Stadaconans felt obliged to respect and show pleasure about the French shamans' pretended divination.

In a final effort to establish a proper alliance, Donnacona offered that Taignoagny or Domagaya might go to Hochelaga with the French, if, in return, Cartier would agree to send a Frenchman to live with him. Cartier was convinced that the two youths were rogues and announced that he would give no hostage and that he was going up-river even though he had neither a guide nor an interpreter (140). Not understanding the nature of Iroquoian diplomacy, Cartier had unwittingly spurned the alliance that Donnacona was hoping to establish with the French. He also appeared to be threatening to form an alliance with Donnacona's rivals. Whether, if Cartier had understood what was going on, he would have behaved any differently remains an open question.

On 19 September Cartier began moving up-river. Passing the village of Tequenonday, which was perched atop a hill, he arrived at Achelacy, which lay at the foot of the Richelieu Rapids, near the modern community of Portneuf. The headman of this village, who was apparently delighted to see Cartier by-passing Stadacona, presented him with a girl eight or nine years old and a boy who was less than three. In so doing, he was no doubt hoping to emulate Donnacona and to seal an alliance with the French. Cartier accepted the girl, but returned the boy because he was too young (142–44). Slowly, because of the shoals and dangerous currents, Cartier made his way up the St. Lawrence. Along the banks of the river, he noted the cabins of many Indians who had come there to fish. At the west end of Lake St. Peter, he traded some knives and beads for a pile of muskrat skins (147). It was there that he decided to leave his pinnace and make his way up-river in two longboats. Being shown the correct channel by friendly Indians, Cartier arrived off the south shore of Montreal Island on 2 October (13 October, New Style).¹⁰

Cartier's visit to Hochelaga the following day is too well known to require repetition here (plate 18). The Frenchman's arrival at the palisaded town, his reading of the gospel to the Indians, who brought their sick to him to be healed, and his afternoon climb to the summit of Mount Royal, from which he accurately surveyed the view on every hand, have become part of Canadian folklore. Less frequently commented on is the

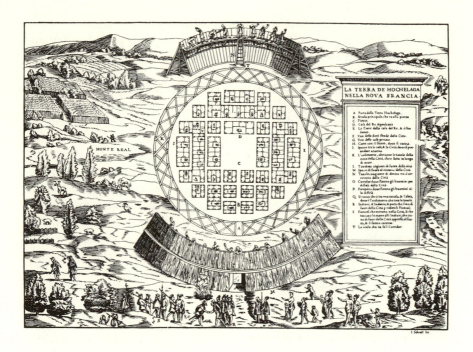

PLATE 18. *Ramusio's Plan of Hochelaga. This engraving that
accompanied Giovanni Ramusio's 1556 Italian translation of the Cartier
voyages frequently has been accepted as an eye-witness drawing.
W. D. Lighthall ("The False Plan of Hochelaga," Transactions of the
Royal Society of Canada, 3rd series, vol. 26 [1932], sec. 2, pp. 181 ff.)
convincingly refutes this belief. In particular, the groundplan of the houses
can be shown to be based on a misleading description of these houses in the
Cartier relation. Ramusio's plan thus becomes the first in a long list of
illustrations of early Canada that are of little or no ethnographic value.
Courtesy McGill University Libraries.*

brevity of Cartier's visit and the rapidity with which the sighting of the Lachine Rapids caused him to abandon his attempt to push farther up-river. Throughout the day, Cartier was apprehensive about his longboats and anxious to return to them by nightfall. He was also worried about the pinnace, which he had left with a small crew down-river (172). The speed with which he visited the town of Hochelaga and his obvious relief when the visit was over can only have communicated a sense of his mistrust to his hosts. Likewise, because the French did not like the taste of food cooked without salt, they refused to join in a magnificent feast that the women of Hochelaga had prepared for them (167). In spite of the knives, hatchets, beads, and tin trinkets that Cartier gave to the people of Hoche-laga, his behaviour must have seemed inexplicable and discourteous to them. While Cartier left amidst every sign of goodwill, he had failed to achieve anything that would contribute towards future good relations with the Hochelagans, or make this area a useful base for the exploration of the interior. Cartier not only lacked knowledge of how to deal with the Indians (which is understandable) but, convinced of his own superiority, he did not perceive the need for such knowledge. Nor can it be argued that his apprehensiveness on this occasion resulted mainly from the lack of an interpreter. Given his attitude, the lack of an interpreter probably neither helped nor adversely influenced his relations with the Hochelagans. It did, however, reduce the amount of cartographical information that he was able to collect.

While Cartier was away, the sailors who had been left on the St. Charles River built a small fort in front of the two ships and mounted artillery on the ramparts in order to cover the approaches (Biggar 1924:174). This was a still greater infringement on land belonging to the people of Stada-cona, and indicated that the French were intending to remain for the winter, if not to establish a permanent base there. Donnacona was happy to learn that Cartier had returned from Hochelaga and may have had his mind further set at ease by advance reports of what had transpired there. Soon after Cartier returned, Donnacona and some of the other headmen visited the French settlement to welcome him back. Cartier entertained them, although his chronicler observed sourly that the Indians were insincere and did not deserve such good treatment (175).

The next day, Cartier, the gentlemen of his crew, and some fifty sailors made their first formal visit to Stadacona, a mile or so away. They were greeted, as they had been at Hochelaga, outside the village. After speeches of welcome had been delivered and the French had distributed knives, tin rings, and other gifts (again stressed to be of little value), they entered the village and visited the houses in which Donnacona and Taignoagny lived, which they found to be well provisioned for the winter (175–78).

In the relatively friendly, but very brief, period that followed, the people of Stadacona came to the French fort to trade fish and eels for knives, awls, beads, and other ornaments. At this time, the French had an opportunity to observe how the Stadaconans hunted and fished, to experiment with tobacco, and to gather some curious information about Stadaconan sexual behaviour (179–87). Some of the French harangued the Indians concerning the supposed follies of their religious beliefs. The Indians listened politely, almost certainly understanding little of what was being said. Unable to conceive of an exclusive religion, the inhabitants of Stadacona decided to benefit from whatever rituals the French could teach them and came *en masse* to ask for baptism. Cartier was able to turn aside this request by saying that he lacked holy chrism, which he falsely assured them was necessary to perform this sacrament (180–81).

Soon, however, Cartier was annoyed to discover that Taignoagny and Domagaya were telling their people that the French were cheating them by exchanging for food goods that were worthless or of little value in their own country. The Stadaconans were not disinterested in such information. All the evidence from the next century indicates that the Indians of this region were experienced traders, who understood how to make the rules of supply and demand work to their own advantage and who could fully utilize knowledge of this sort (Biggar 1924:187–88; 1922–36, 2:171).

Cartier's fear of Donnacona and his two sons was nurtured by the headman of Achelacy,[11] who was jealous of Donnacona's proximity to the French. It was also sustained by Stadaconan individuals or lineages who seem to have been currying favour with the French (Biggar 1924:188). Cartier became especially alarmed when Donnacona's niece escaped to her own people, apparently after she had been beaten by a French youth. Fearing that Donnacona was planning to attack the French settlement, Cartier added wide ditches and extra scaffolding to his fort and strengthened the night-watch. Donnacona and his sons came several times to the bank of the river opposite the fort, but Cartier refused even to speak with them. Finally he accused them of numerous acts of bad faith, including having carried off the girl they had given him. Donnacona's people protested that the girl had run away of her own volition and a few days later they persuaded her to return to the French (188–92). For a time, this served to relieve the tension between Cartier and the Stadaconans, and the Indians again came freely to the French fort.

The *Bref récit* of Cartier's second voyage implies that the brittle truce between the supporters of Donnacona and the French lasted throughout the winter. For part of the winter, however, Cartier ordered the Iroquoians to stay away from his ships, because of a severe illness that had broken out among the Indians (204). When contact resumed, these Indians put Taignoagny's and Domagaya's advice to good use. Knowing that French provisions had run short, they demanded larger amounts of European goods in return for fish and venison. If the French refused to pay, they carried their food home, stating that they could easily use it themselves (217). A grimmer picture of relations between the French and the Indians is supplied by André Thevet (1878:422), who claimed to have interviewed Donnacona. He reports that, over the winter, the French amused themselves by robbing the Indians and cutting their flesh to test the sharpness of their swords. The truth probably lies somewhere in between. Among Cartier's crew, there were undoubtedly frightened or malicious individuals, who were ready to attack the Indians at the least provocation; men such as these were to cause trouble enough at Quebec in the early part of the seventeenth century. Likewise, the Indians' habit of carrying off things that were left lying about unattended, in the belief that the French no longer wanted them, was inevitably viewed as theft by the Europeans, and this occasionally led to violence. Finally, Taignoagny and Domagaya appear to have been only too willing to exacerbate whatever grievances arose against the French. A variety of unrecorded incidents must have kept both Cartier and the Indians on guard, whenever they met throughout the winter.

In the month of December, Stadacona was stricken by an illness which killed over fifty people (Biggar 1924:204). The French believed it to be scurvy, although this seems unlikely, since the Stadaconans are reported to have had a highly effective cure for that disease. Later, however, no doubt from a lack of fresh meat, almost all of the French contracted scurvy and twenty-five of them died from it. Fear of Indian attack led Cartier to take elaborate precautions to disguise the desperate condition of his men. In March, Cartier noted that Domagaya had recovered from what seemed to have been an attack of scurvy. When he told Domagaya that his servant was ill from the same disease, Domagaya did not hesitate to send two women to gather the fronds of the common white cedar (*Thuja occidentalis*) and to show the French how to brew a curative drink from it. According to Cartier, all of his crew recovered within a week of taking this cure. Some who were suffering from syphilis found that it relieved that ailment as well.[12]

In February, Donnacona, Taignoagny, and many others went hunting and were gone for about two months. In the seventeenth century, the Iroquoians hunted in the late autumn and the early spring, rather than in midwinter; however, among less horticultural groups, such as the Ottawa, men left their villages for extended winter hunts, and it is not unlikely that the Stadaconans followed this pattern. Cartier feared that the Stadaconans were collecting a force to attack him and became alarmed when Donnacona returned on 21 April, accompanied by many unfamiliar faces. Domagaya visited Cartier to inform him that his father had brought back a lot of venison, but even this visit aroused Cartier's suspicions because Domagaya refused to cross the river. Cartier believed that this was because Domagaya found the fort too well guarded (216–19). Cartier sent his servant, Charles Guyot, who was better liked by the Stadaconans than anyone else, to see what was happening there. He found Donnacona apparently ill and the house of Taignoagny full of strangers, but was not allowed to visit the other houses. It appeared that a political struggle was going on in Stadacona, since Taignoagny sent word to Cartier that, if he wished to please him, he should seize a man named Agona and take him back to France with him (219–20).

Cartier, and most modern historians, have interpreted this as a power struggle between Donnacona and Agona as to which man, or clan segment, should control Stadacona (Trudel 1963:110–11; Morison 1971:420); however, from what we know about Iroquoian political organization, a personal struggle of this sort seems highly unlikely. Among the Iroquoians, a headman could exercise power only by gaining the support of his followers for each decision that he made. No headman could force anyone to obey him against that man's will, nor would a headman retain the respect of his clan segment, if he were to betray one of its members to strangers. Headmen were elected to manage the affairs of their clan segment and could not, in their own right, control what went on in other clans or communities. Under these conditions, no additional personal power was to be gained by eliminating one of the protagonists. More likely, a dispute had broken out in the village, whether within or between clan segments makes little difference, about what policy should be pursued with respect to the French. The strangers that Guyot observed in the village were probably men who had come from neighbouring communities to join in the debate.

There were individuals in Stadacona who had reported Donnacona's hostility to Cartier (or so Cartier, with his defective understanding of the language, believed) (Biggar 1924:188). These men may have been urging a more conciliatory policy for dealing with the French than the one Donnacona and his sons wished to see followed. Divisions of this sort were the rule rather than the exception in Iroquoian politics, especially when it came to dealing with an enemy. If Agona were the leader of the conciliatory faction, Taignoagny's message to Cartier may have been more than the inexperienced scheming of a Machiavellian youth. Taignoagny (or his father) may have guessed that Cartier was planning to kidnap more Indians before he returned to France and hoped that, if he could incite him to try to seize Agona or even were able to spread a convincing rumour that Cartier was planning to do this, he could convince Agona of the need to oppose the French. Such a plan seems more in keeping with what we know about Iroquoian political behaviour than does the conventional interpretation of this request.

During the winter, Cartier had been fascinated by reports of a "Kingdom of the Saguenay," which he was told lay somewhere in the interior of the continent. Donnacona claimed to have visited this place and he described it, through his interpreters, as a land rich in gold, rubies, and other precious things and inhabited by white men who dressed in woollen clothing (200–202; 221). Some historians have speculated that this story may reflect knowledge of Spanish settlements far to the south, and it has been suggested that Indians from the St. Lawrence might even have visited these settlements (Trudel 1963:109). Yet Donnacona also claimed to have visited lands where men had only one leg or where they lacked anuses and ate no solid food (Biggar 1924: 221–22). This has led other historians to dismiss the Kingdom of the Saguenay as yet another of these imaginary lands. Viewed in terms of archaeological data, however, the bulk of the information about this so-called Kingdom of the Saguenay makes sense. The only metal that the Indians were familiar with, prior to the arrival of the Europeans, was native copper. Hence, one may conclude that it was either the greedy imagination of the French or the romanticizing translations of Taignoagny and Domagaya that led Cartier to believe that the Indians were talking about gold.

It is evident from Cartier's account that the Stadaconans were participating in a trade that had begun in the Archaic period. From the vicinity of Lake Superior, copper nuggets and artifacts diffused from tribe to tribe over much of eastern North America. Some of this copper was clearly reaching the Stadaconans. For example, when Donnacona left for France his people presented him with a large knife made of red copper (233).

Historians have been puzzled by seemingly contradictory accounts of how this copper was reaching the St. Lawrence. The Hochelagans indicated that one route lay along the Ottawa River, but that this route was blocked by *agojuda*, or "evil men," who were armed to the teeth, wore slat armour, and waged continual war (170–71). Some commentators have identified these people as the Iroquois, although this is geographically improbable, unless the story refers to Iroquois attacks on groups living in the Ottawa Valley. Others have suggested that they were the Ottawa Valley Algonkin (Lighthall 1899:204; B. Hoffman 1961:204; Fenton 1940:172). The latter were somewhat acculturated to Iroquoian ways, at least in the seventeenth century, and may have worn slat armour. They were, however, only a marginally horticultural people and, because of this, they and the Hochelagans should have been on good terms and had a symbiotic trading relationship, resembling that between the Huron and the Algonkian peoples who lived around the shores of Georgian Bay. This leaves the Huron. In the last chapter we presented archaeological evidence which suggests that, in prehistoric times, there may have been prolonged conflict between the Huron and the St. Lawrence Iroquoians. It is also noteworthy that Huron influence seems particularly strong in late sites on the upper St. Lawrence, suggesting a considerable amount of warfare between the two groups at this time (Pendergast and Trigger 1972:284). This warfare may have prevented the Hochelagans from travelling northward to trade with the Algonkians of the upper Great Lakes.

On the other hand, both the Hochelagans and Stadaconans agreed that the normal route by which copper was reaching the St. Lawrence Valley was down the Saguenay River (Biggar 1924:106, 171). This suggests that the copper was moving along the major auxiliary trade route of the historic period, which ran from Georgian Bay, across Lake Nipissing and the upper Ottawa Valley, into the network of lakes and rivers in central Quebec, finally reaching Lake St. John and the Saguenay Valley. This explains how the name Saguenay came to be applied both to the river and to the sources of copper much farther inland. It also provides the source for Cartier's description of the Saguenay and Ottawa Rivers coming together to form an island (201–2). It is even possible that Donnacona's description of a civilized people living in the interior was a vague reference to the Huron, who, although they may not have engaged directly in the copper trade with Quebec, would have been sufficiently different from the Algonkian-speaking peoples of the north to be noteworthy. The finds at Matabachouwan, described in the last chapter, may bear witness to this roundabout trade between the St. Lawrence Valley and the upper Great Lakes. The importance that the Indians attached to this trade was out of all proportion to its utilitarian value and this may have aroused undue expectations of wealth in the minds of the Frenchmen who listened to Donnacona.

From Donnacona, Cartier also learned that the Richelieu River led south to lands where there was neither ice nor snow, and whose inhabitants waged continual war against one another (202–3). These stories were embroidered by Taignoagny and Domagaya with references to oranges and other tropical produce, but seem based on a knowledge of New England. The Stadaconans and Hochelagans had considerable quantities of shell beads, with which they used to make "collars." Although Cartier tells a curious story about how these beads were drawn from the river after they had formed on the mutilated bodies of prisoners or criminals (158–60), it seems likely that they were obtained from the south, either through trade or as booty. Beads made from marine shells appear in prehistoric Iroquoian sites in Canada, but only in small quantities, and the development of the wampum trade is generally believed to post-date the introduction of metal tools, which permitted the Indians of Long Island and adjacent regions to manufacture large numbers of these beads. The reference to shell collars suggests that the wampum trade, or at least a trade in beads closely resembling wampum, may have begun earlier and that shell beads were more common by the early sixteenth century than the archaeological data suggest (Beauchamp 1898:3–4; 1901:329, 342, 354).

The stories that Donnacona told, together with Cartier's belief that Agona should be made the ruler of Stadacona to strengthen the position of the French in the St. Lawrence Valley, led the French leader to make a ruthless decision: he would not return to France without taking with him Donnacona, his sons, and his principal supporters (Biggar 1924:220–21). In this way, he believed, Agona would be free to rule in the Quebec City area and Donnacona could be made to tell his stories to the king, in order to enlist the latter's support for future voyages. Cartier also may have hoped that, once Donnacona had learned to speak French, more information could be obtained from him concerning what he had seen in the interior (Carleill, cited in Hakluyt 1589:723). Donnacona would be promised that, if he cooperated, he could return to Canada, but, in fact, Cartier feared his ill will and was planning never to allow him to return (Trudel 1963:113, 142; based on Biggar 1924:231).

To lure his intended victims, Cartier hinted that, if Taignoagny conducted Donnacona and Agona to the ships, the latter would be kidnapped; however, none of the Indians trusted Cartier and for two days not a single person from Stadacona came near the ships (Biggar 1924:222–23). This suggests that signs of Cartier's impending departure had given rise to speculation about more kidnappings. It also suggests that the divisions in policy among the Stadaconans were not as great as Cartier had hoped. The

Stadaconans were lured to the French fort, when news spread that Cartier had abandoned one of his ships and was permitting the people of Sitadin to remove the iron nails from it (223). Donnacona and his sons accompanied the rest of their people, but Donnacona refused to cross the river, while Taignoagny and Domagaya hesitated for over an hour before doing so. Cartier reassured Taignoagny that he only intended to take a few children to France but, as a favour, said he would seize Agona and maroon him on some island. Taignoagny promised to lead Donnacona and all the people of Stadacona to visit the French ships (223–24).

The next day, 3 May, the French erected a large cross by the river. In the afternoon, Donnacona and his two sons arrived, accompanied by a large number of men and women. Significantly, there is no mention of Agona being part of this group, which suggests that Donnacona had warned him to keep away from the French. Donnacona and his sons were uneasy and refused to enter the French camp. Instead, they lit a council fire outside it. After unsuccessfully urging Donnacona to enter the fort, Cartier instructed his men to be prepared to seize him, his sons, and two other headmen, and to drive the other Indians away. Seeing mischief afoot, Taignoagny ordered the women to flee, but, while he was doing so, his father and brother were lured into the fort. Taignoagny rushed after them to make them come out, but at this point the French seized the men Cartier had designated and took them on board their ships. Frightened and uncertain of French intentions, the other Indians sought the protection of the forest (225–27).

That night, the Stadaconans recovered from their shock and assembled on the bank of the river, shouting war cries and demanding to see their headman. In the meanwhile, Cartier promised Donnacona that if he cooperated and went to see the king of France, he would be given a fine present and returned to his people the following year. By noon the next day, a vast number of Indians had gathered, apparently from Stadacona and the surrounding villages, but most of them were hiding in the forest. Perceiving no alternative, Donnacona showed himself to these people and assured them that all was well and that he would return the next year. He added many other things that the French could not understand. A number of headmen presented Cartier with twenty-four shell bead collars to urge him to treat Donnacona well and said they would bring Donnacona food for the impending voyage. Cartier gave Donnacona two brass kettles, eight hatchets, and some knives and beads, which the headman sent to the women and children of his family (228–30).

At dawn the next day, four women came in a canoe to bring Donnacona large quantities of corn, meat, and fish. Cartier and Donnacona reassured these women that they would be returning the next year, after which each of the women gave Cartier another shell bead collar. Meanwhile, all of the people of Stadacona gathered by the river to say farewell to Donnacona and the other prisoners. As Cartier's ship made its way down the St. Lawrence several boatloads of Indians came up to the ship to present Donnacona with three bundles of beaver and seal skins and a copper knife. The bundles of skins suggest that these Indians were already aware of European interest in the fur trade. They also offered Cartier shell collars for Donnacona's safe return (231–33). These formalities must have hidden the deep anxiety and bitterness which the Indians, both aboard Cartier's ship and along the river, felt about what had happened. Taignoagny does not seem to have been allowed to speak publicly after he was captured, which suggests that he was being kept under physical restraint (229, 231, 233).

Cartier left twenty-five members of his crew dead in the New World and had aboard his ship ten Indians. These were Donnacona and his two sons, once more fated to return to France against their will; his niece ten to twelve years old; two younger boys, one of whom was a close relative of Donnacona; a younger girl from Achelacy; and three other Indians, two of whom were headmen (249). None of these Indians was ever to return to Canada. When Cartier reached France, he found the country at war with Spain. The war lasted until 1538, and was followed by three years of preparations and diplomatic difficulties before a new expedition could be launched. By the end of this period, all but one of the Indians had died from European diseases against which they had little or no immunity. The survivor was a young girl.

Not much is known about the lives of these Indians in France. By the time they landed, they appear to have been pacified by Cartier's promises that they would soon be returning to Canada with much wealth (Kerrigan 1951:20). It seems that most lived in St. Malo and in 1538 Cartier was reimbursed by Francis I for providing them with board and lodging (Biggar 1930:69–70). On 25 March 1539, three males were baptized (ibid. 82), apparently *in articulo mortis*. Donnacona eagerly performed his role of raconteur, obviously hoping that arousing the greed of the French would increase his chances of returning home. He appears to have learned French and studied the mentality of his captors carefully. When he was interviewed by the king, he spoke of mines rich in gold and silver and of lands where there was an abundance of spices. Donnacona promised that he and his people would help the French to reach these lands and embellished his stories with fashionable marvels, including men who had wings on their arms and flew like bats. He seems to have completely won Francis I's confidence, for, when the Portuguese ambassador questioned the veracity of these tales, the king replied that Donnacona's stories never varied and that even under pain of death he swore they were true (ibid. 77–80). Donnacona was interviewed by other important individuals, including the historian André Thevet (1878:407). Unfortunately, his cunning availed him nothing, since he died a Christian, so we are told, after being in France for four years (Hakluyt 1589:723). The fact that the Indians were not baptized for several years after they were brought to France suggests that they were under little pressure to conform to French ways and were regarded mainly as political prisoners or potential interpreters.

CARTIER AND ROBERVAL

Cartier's third voyage was to be one of colonization as well as exploration (plate 19). A French sailor stated that one of its goals was to subjugate the lands of the Indians (Biggar 1930:461). While the potential profit from this colony was seen to lie mainly in its mineral wealth, Francis I was also hoping for considerable profit from the fur trade (Lanctot 1963:79). In 1540, Cartier was made captain-general of a proposed expedition and was licensed to recruit fifty prisoners from the jails of northern and western France for his colony. The following January, however, there was a change in plans and Jean-François de La Rocque, sieur de Roberval was placed over Cartier and granted vice-regal powers in the New World. In Roberval's commission, much emphasis was placed on the conversion of the heathen, but this was to placate Pope Paul III and to counteract Spanish and Portuguese protests that the French were ignoring the decree of Pope Alexander VI, which had divided the New World between their two countries. In the spring of 1541, Roberval was having financial difficulties and decided to spend the following year raising money by practising piracy in the English Channel. Cartier was dispatched to Canada with five ships loaded with various domestic animals and a substantial number of male and female colonists. The colonists included some alleged members of the nobility, as well as condemned felons (Trudel 1963:119–43).

Cartier departed from St. Malo on 23 May, but his fleet had a rough passage and he did not arrive at Quebec for three months. Surprised that the French had returned after such a long interval, the inhabitants of

PLATE 19. *Canada in the Harleian map of* c. *1542. The delineation of the St. Lawrence is based largely on data collected during the Cartier voyage of 1535–36. That Hochelaga is located north of the St. Lawrence River indicates that Cartier was not aware of the existence of the Rivière des Prairies north of Montreal Island. The landscape painted south of the St. Lawrence seems to portray the region between Mount Royal and the Monteregian hills to the east. The Europeans and European settlement making up part of this scene probably reflected plans for French colonization along the St. Lawrence* c. *1642. Courtesy Public Archives of Canada.*

Stadacona rushed to the banks of the St. Charles River, expressing their joy and hoping to welcome back Donnacona and his compatriots. Cartier had no interpreter with him. He had decided not to bring the only surviving Indian for fear she would reveal that the others were dead. Hence he could communicate only by gestures and with the limited Iroquoian vocabulary that he and the other sailors had acquired on their previous visit or from their captives.

Agona enquired of Cartier what had become of Donnacona and the others and was informed that Donnacona was dead, but the rest had married and were living in France as great lords, for which reason they did not wish to return to Canada. Cartier imagined that Agona was pleased, because Donnacona's death confirmed his own position as "lord and chief of the country" (Biggar 1924:251–52). Yet, with so many Frenchmen about and his own people unaware of what had happened, it is unlikely that Agona would have quarrelled with Cartier on the spot and risked being carried off by him. His later actions make it clear that he neither believed the whole of Cartier's story nor was pleased to learn of Donnacona's death. Nevertheless, he placed the beaded headband he was wearing on Cartier's head, gave him two shell-bead bracelets, and embraced him. Cartier distributed presents to Agona and the women who were with him and the two men parted on what seemed good terms.

Although Agona and his people were outraged by Cartier's failure to honour his promise to return Donnacona and the other Indians, Cartier was soon to provide them with even more cause to hate him. Cartier no longer wished to live near Stadacona, but wanted a base farther inland, from which he would be free to explore up-river.[13] For this purpose, he selected a site near Cape Rouge, nine miles upstream from Stadacona, and had all five of his ships brought there. He unloaded cattle and supplies, planted crops, and set his men to work building a colony, which he named Charlesbourg-Royal. This consisted of a fortified habitation by the river, and for additional protection a fort on top of the steep cliff behind it. In Cartier's view, no better place for a settlement could be found. The soil appeared fertile, the forests abounded in useful trees and vines, a rich source of iron was at hand, at the base of the cliff there was a thick vein of rock containing "gold" and "silver," while on top of the cliff he found "diamonds." Two ships were dispatched to France with specimens of the mineral wealth of the new colony (254–55).

Cartier's behaviour was a serious provocation to the Indians. Without asking their permission, or acquiring use of the land from them, he had brought in settlers, erected buildings, and planted crops. He had also come with women as well as men, and with greater numbers than before, so that it was clear he intended to settle the land he occupied. Such behaviour constituted a challenge to all the Indians in the district. Furthermore, Cartier had denied the Stadaconans' right to control traffic along the river by locating his colony farther inland, thus reviving all the fears that Donnacona had experienced about an alliance between the Hochelagans and the French. Even if Agona had not resented the failure of the French to honour their promises to return his tribesmen, such behaviour would have left him with no alternative but to view Cartier as his enemy.

On 7 September Cartier left most of his people at work on Charlesbourg-Royal and went with a small party to explore the Lachine Rapids, prior to a major exploration into the interior the following spring. On his way up-river, Cartier visited the headman of Achelacy, whose daughter was among the Indians he had taken to France. Remembering this headman's former antagonism to Donnacona, Cartier presented him with a fancy red cloak, two bronze basins, knives, and hatchets, and persuaded him (again without benefit of an interpreter) to take two French boys into his household to learn his language (256–57). Cartier's experience with Taignoagny and Domagaya had obviously convinced him that Indian youths who were taken to France did not make trustworthy interpreters. Sending French boys to learn Indian languages was an action that the French were to repeat many times, and with much success, in the next century. The natives of Achelacy may have regarded the boys as an exchange for the girl who had not come back, but whom they hoped would be returned at a later date. This made Cartier's action appear to them to be one of courtesy and trust. The people of Achelacy may also have been pleased to see that Cartier was ignoring the Stadaconans. In spite of this, their headman must have been perplexed and grieved not to see his daughter and he may have been alarmed by news of the kind of settlement that the French were erecting not far from his village.

Arriving at Montreal Island, Cartier failed to navigate through the St. Mary's Current and spent the day following an Indian trail as far as the foot of the Lachine Rapids. Along the way, he passed through two fishing villages, but did not bother to visit Hochelaga.[14] Having learned a little more about the geography of the rapids from the Indian fishermen he encountered, he returned to his boats, where some four hundred Indians had gathered. They greeted him in a friendly manner and Cartier, in return, gave axes and sickles to the headmen and combs, tin and copper brooches, and similar ornaments to the rest. As on his previous visit, however, he did not trust the Hochelagans and, rather than staying to explore the Lachine Rapids properly, he set off down-river the same day (257–59). Curiously enough, though he had passed through two Indian settlements, he gave as one of his reasons for returning to his boats that he had spent the day without food and drink (258). His refusal to eat Indian food was evidently not limited to his first visit to Hochelaga.

On the way back to his settlement, Cartier revisited Achelacy, but found that the headman and his warriors were absent from the village. The headman's son told Cartier that his father had gone to Maisouna, which appears to have been a settlement or region south of the St. Lawrence.[15] When Cartier reached Charlesbourg-Royal, he was informed that the Indians were no longer visiting the settlement to barter their fish and game, but were prowling about in a suspicious manner. It also appeared that the headman of Achelacy had gone to Stadacona to confer with Agona, and that, in spite of his apparent friendship, he too was conspiring against the French (259). We have no information about what happened to the boys who were staying with the Indians at Achelacy, but circumstantial evidence would suggest they were withdrawn soon after Cartier's return from Hochelaga.

Very little information has been preserved about what happened thereafter. The Indians appear to have concluded that Charlesbourg-Royal was too strong to be attacked directly and had decided on a war of attrition. They invested the settlement, first killing some Frenchmen who had gone to cut wood and then others who ventured outside the fort. In the course of the winter, thirty-five Europeans are reported to have been killed by the Indians.[16] In 1542, news of these hostilities reached Europe, by way of Spanish fishermen who claimed to have obtained their information not only from French sailors but also from Indians who had come down the St. Lawrence from Canada to trade deer and wolf skins for axes, knives, and other items (Biggar 1930:462–63). Although the latter story has been dismissed as improbable, it is possible that some of the Iroquoian-speaking peoples from the Quebec City area were already in the habit of trading with European fishermen as far east as the Strait of Belle Isle, in conjunction with their annual hunt for porpoises (B. Hoffman 1961:204–9). These Indians were evidently on good terms with the Spaniards and, knowing them to be a dependable source of European goods, may have felt all the more confident in attempting to expel the French intruders, who were trying to seize possession of their land.

It is uncertain how widespread this dissatisfaction with the French had become. The village of Achelacy may have feared Cartier's intrusion on its land and seems to have joined in the attack. At some point, the Hochelagans also seem to have turned against the French (Biggar 1924:259). It has been suggested that the latter turn-about indicates that Cartier explored up-river the following spring, but, in view of the hostility of the Stadaconans, such a venture seems unlikely. By June 1542, Roberval had not arrived and Cartier judged that his small band was unable to resist the Indians, who were harassing the colony daily (264–65). Thus he set sail with his cargo of supposed gold and diamonds. In St. John's Harbour, Newfoundland, Cartier encountered Roberval, who was headed for the St. Lawrence with three ships. Roberval ordered him to return to Canada. Cartier, however, believed his ships to be laden with riches and had crews on board that might well have mutinied rather than spend another winter on the St. Lawrence. Hence he stole off in the night, setting a direct course for St. Malo. There, his diamonds became a byword for falseness and Cartier was never again entrusted with the command of an important expedition.

Yet, if the Stadaconans were rid of Jacques Cartier, their troubles with the French were not over. In July, they saw Roberval's three ships sail past Quebec without stopping and come to anchor off Cape Rouge. No mention is made of Cartier's settlement, which may have been dismantled either by Cartier or by the Indians after he had left. Whatever had happened to Charlesbourg-Royal, Roberval had to build, or rebuild, a settlement for the approximately one hundred and fifty people who were with him (Morison 1971:448). He named the new settlement France-Roy. Much more is known about Roberval's settlement than about the earlier one. The main habitation was built on the hill, probably where Cartier's lookout had been. It was surrounded by a palisade and equipped with barracks, mess halls, bedrooms, a mill for grinding corn, and an outdoor oven. At the base of the hill was another lodging, with a tower two stories high, used mainly for storage (Biggar 1924:266).

In the winter, rations ran short and, because Roberval lacked Cartier's knowledge of how to control scurvy, more than fifty people died. The Indians do not appear to have attacked the habitation and in the meagre references that survive there is no mention of hostility. In the spring, the Indians brought large quantities of shad, which they traded with the French (267). This change of attitude has been attributed to the stronger military forces and defence works with which Roberval had equipped his colony. It is possible, however, that much of the Iroquoian resentment was directed against Cartier and his companions personally. Although Roberval, no less than Cartier, was intruding on Indian land, the new leader enforced strict discipline among his settlers (268), and this may have led to better relations with the Indians. Even so, however, while the few accounts connected with this voyage describe the Indians as gentle people, their failure to mention any individual suggests that the latter may have kept their distance (268; 295–96).

By the spring of 1543 Roberval had decided that his colony would return to France. Before departing, he made an effort to reach the fabled Saguenay by way of the Ottawa River. He travelled up the St. Lawrence with sixty-nine people, apparently reaching Montreal Island.[17] There is no evidence that Roberval attempted to establish a colony on the island, as Beaugrand-Champagne (1948) has suggested, and the only statement that might suggest conflict with the Indians is the one hundred and twenty pounds of grain he is reported to have sent down-river to his settlement (Biggar 1924:270). This might have been stolen from the Indians of the upper St. Lawrence, as René de Laudonnière later stole Indian corn for his hard-pressed colony in northern Florida and as Champlain was planning to plunder it from the Iroquois in 1628–29 (Biggar 1922–36, 5: 304–5). It is equally possible, however, that Roberval purchased this corn from the Hochelagans. One boat was lost, causing the death of eight men, but there is no proof that this happened while Roberval was shooting the Lachine Rapids (Trudel 1963:162 n. 70). It would seem to have been on the way to Canada that Roberval's pilot, Jean Alfonse, had explored the lower part of the Saguenay River, without, however, reaching the falls at Chicoutimi.[18]

A hostile climate, bad relations with the Indians, the failure to find gold, and the inability of a nascent fur trade to support a colony were to give the St. Lawrence Valley a respite from colonization that was to last until 1600. We have no means of knowing what memories of these earliest attempts to transplant Europeans and a European way of life to this region survived among the Indians, or how far inland tales of these events spread. It is unlikely, however, that the Huron failed to learn something about what was happening and to become aware, for the first time, of the unsettling, alien forces that were eventually to engulf their society.

French efforts at colonization continued, but, between 1555 and 1560, they were directed towards Brazil and, between 1562 and 1565, to the southeastern seaboard of the United States. These colonies, even more ill-fated than those of Cartier and Roberval, were destroyed by the Portuguese and Spanish (Trudel 1963:177–212). Throughout this period, the Indians of eastern Canada must have continued to hear rumours about the activities of Europeans along the east coast of North America, about Hernando De Soto's savage expedition through the southeastern United States (1538–43), and about the epidemics that were decimating the Indian populations to the south. Whether or not these reports had sufficient clarity or immediacy to be of more than passing interest to the Huron is unknown. They must, however, have served as continuing portents of a changing world.

Trade on the St. Lawrence 1543–1600

The failure of French efforts at colonization by 1543 did not mean that European interest in the St. Lawrence had come to an end. After 1550, growing English competition in Newfoundland caused many French fishermen to frequent the shores of Nova Scotia and the Gulf of St. Lawrence. Moreover, the decline in Spanish fishing during that country's wars with England in the latter half of the century opened up for the French a new export market that preferred dry rather than wet processed cod, and this too encouraged the movement into the Gulf (Innis 1940:46). There, French sailors began to interact with increasing regularity with the Micmac of Nova Scotia and New Brunswick and the Montagnais of southern Labrador. These were peoples who were willing and able to trade large numbers of furs for European goods. By returning to the same place each year, French fishermen established a lasting trading relationship with particular bands of Indians.

Gradually, this trade brought about a major shift in the subsistence patterns of the Indians of the Maritimes. Previously, they had passed most of the year exploiting the abundant food resources of the coast, while only the winters were spent hunting in the interior. The desire for more trade goods led them to spend a longer period each year hunting in the forests. Because of this, they had to supplement their diet with biscuits, dried peas, and other preserved foods purchased from the French. While such food helped to compensate for the declining utilization of coastal resources, it made these Indians increasingly dependent on their European trading partners.[19] There is also evidence that, at least by the beginning of the seventeenth century, the Indians of the Maritimes were exchanging European goods for agricultural produce, and possibly for deer skins, with the Indians of Massachusetts (Biggar 1922–36, 1:395–96). The latter region was visited by Europeans only occasionally and, since a horticultural economy was well-established there, the tribes of that region were willing to supply part of the growing demand for additional food supplies among the non- or semi-agricultural Indians of the Maritimes in return for

European trade goods. It has been argued that, prior to British settlement in Virginia, the Indians from that far south were exchanging deer skins northward, in return for European goods from the Maritimes (McIlwain 1915:xxxii).

As the demand for furs increased in Europe, the relative profits to be derived from the fur trade, as compared with fishing, increased. Eventually this resulted in expeditions being sent to Canada whose primary goal was to trade for furs (Biggar 1901:32). At first, furs of all kinds were in demand: deer, marten, bear, otter, seal. In the latter part of the century, however, an old process for making hats out of felted beaver fur began to revive. The pelts best suited for this process had been taken in winter and worn by the Indians, with the fur next to the body, for some fifteen to eighteen months. The latter caused the long guard hair to drop out leaving on the pelt only fine, but barbed, underhair, about an inch long. This odoriferous product took time to produce and, as the fashion of wearing beaver hats grew more popular in Europe, fishermen and traders extended their operations farther into the Gulf of St. Lawrence to keep abreast of the demand (Innis 1956:12–14).

Sealing, walrus hunting, and whaling also attracted growing numbers of Europeans to the St. Lawrence. The Basques, who were already whaling off Newfoundland by 1527, gradually pushed their hunts into the St. Lawrence and established stations for rendering oil from their catch in harbours as far west as Tadoussac, at the mouth of the Saguenay River. Les Escoumins, which was not far away, was said to have been the centre of the whale fisheries. By 1578, twenty to thirty vessels seem to have been engaged in whale hunting in the St. Lawrence, and it may have been some of these whalers who, by 1550, had begun trading for furs with the Indians at Tadoussac.[20]

Traders and fishermen do not appear to have travelled beyond Tadoussac before 1580. According to a report of Captain C. Carleill, the kidnapping of Donnacona, and the bad manner in which Cartier had treated the Stadaconans, had caused the Indians of the Quebec City area to so dislike the French that they refused to have any dealings with them before 1580, when trade on the upper St. Lawrence was resumed (Hakluyt 1589:723). Carleill, however, had his information at second hand; hence his story is open to a number of different interpretations. It seems unlikely that, even if the Iroquoians were hostile to French, or European, intrusion into their territory and had been sufficiently powerful to compel whalers and fishermen to remain down-river, they would have refused to trade with them at a convenient and neutral place such as Tadoussac. A. G. Bailey (1933:

103) has suggested that the resumption of trade on the upper St. Lawrence did not result from a new attitude among the Stadaconans, but from their annihilation by the Algonkians, who inhabited the St. Lawrence Valley in the following century. In a period for which there is so little documentation, it is tempting to try to read a maximum amount of significance into the few data we have.

There is no doubt that European travel up the St. Lawrence resumed around 1580. About 1585, Cartier's nephew, Jacques Noël, ventured as far as Montreal Island and climbed Mount Royal in order to study the view to the west (Trudel 1963:222). Further trips are known to have been made that were involved with trade. In 1599, François Gravé Du Pont went as far as Three Rivers, possibly contributing the place names that replace those of Cartier on the Levasseur Map of 1601 (ibid. 249–52; plate 20). Basque whalers anxious for extra profits may also have been making their way up-river before 1600, but no record has been preserved of these voyages.

Until 1608, however, the main trading centre in the St. Lawrence Valley remained at Tadoussac, which became a port of call for professional fur traders, as well as for fishermen and whalers. The professionals did not succeed in their attempts to drive the part-time traders out of business. The latter were still active along the lower St. Lawrence River in the 1620s, in defiance of monopolies that had been granted to the professional traders by the French government.

Little is known about the early development of the professional fur trade on the St. Lawrence River. It appears to have started when a small French ship was sent to the St. Lawrence in 1581. This voyage was sufficiently profitable that the next year a larger ship was sent, followed by three ships in 1583 (Biggar 1901:32). That year Richard Hakluyt saw in Paris a depot containing furs estimated to be worth 5000 crowns that had come from the St. Lawrence (ibid. 33). In 1584, the merchants of St. Malo sent five ships to the St. Lawrence and were planning to send twice the number the year after. By 1587, rival traders were battling on the river.

In 1585, Jacques Noël and Etienne Chaton de La Jannaye managed to obtain a twelve-year trading monopoly embracing the St. Lawrence and adjacent regions, in return for undertaking to establish a colony there. This monopoly was relinquished almost immediately, after the other merchants of St. Malo secured cancellation of the monopolists' exclusive right to control the lucrative fur trade on the St. Lawrence (Trudel 1963: 221–26). This was clearly the only resource from which there was a hope of deriving substantial profits.

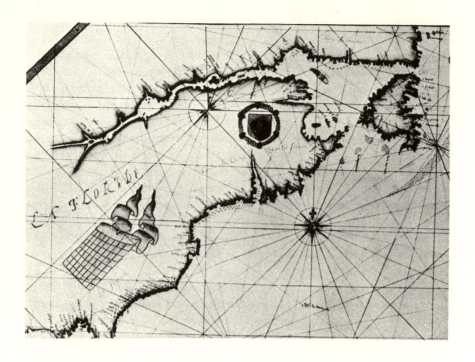

PLATE 20. *Part of the Levasseur map of 1601. On this map the toponymy of Cartier and Roberval is replaced for the first time by names such as Gaspé, Québec, Trois-Rivières, which have endured to the present day. These changes reflect a new era of French interest in the exploitation and colonization of the St. Lawrence Valley. Courtesy Public Archives of Canada.*

This short-lived monopoly is significant because it marked a revival of French interest in colonization in this part of the New World. In 1598 and 1599, Troilus de La Roche de Mesgouez and Pierre Chauvin were granted similar monopolies in New France and La Roche established a short-lived colony on Sable Island.[21] Thus began a long struggle between the proponents of free trade and those who sought authority to monopolize the fur trade of the St. Lawrence and the Maritimes in return for establishing colonies there.[22] Although most historians are sympathetic towards the colonizing point of view, both policies were riddled with inconsistencies and neither offered much hope for the long-term survival of French interests in Canada. The fur trade required only a small resident population for its effective management, as the Hudson's Bay Company was later to demonstrate. Yet, as the most eloquent advocate of colonization, Samuel de Champlain, pointed out, without strong colonies (and, he might have added, sufficient naval power) to enforce their hold on this part of North America, the French were unlikely to hold their trading posts against foreign competition (Biggar 1922–36, 6:361–74). On the other hand, monopoly holders correctly argued that the profits of trade were not enough to support colonization on the scale that was required. Lucrative as the fur trade was, by itself it was insufficient to support a thriving European colony on the edge of the Canadian Shield.[23] For such a colony to develop, either a more diversified economic base was needed or else massive support from the mother country. As Champlain and his successors were to learn, any scheme to build a colony solely on the resources of the fur trade was doomed to failure.

By 1584, the merchants of St. Malo appear to have been on good terms with the Indians who traded at Tadoussac. About that time a number of Indians were brought to France as visitors, at least one of whom came from the St. Lawrence Valley.[24] We are informed that these Indians spent the winter in France to increase the friendship between the French and the Indians (Trudel 1963:215, 223). It is unknown whether those from the St. Lawrence were Iroquoian or Algonkian-speakers, although circumstantial evidence suggests they were Algonkian. They travelled to France under very different circumstances from the Indians whom Cartier had seized several decades earlier. Like many Indians who were taken to France in the seventeenth century, they were probably the sons of headmen who already were on good terms with the French and could be confident that their sons would be returned to them the following summer. The traders from St. Malo hoped that these Indians would learn to speak French, so they might serve as interpreters when it came to discussing matters of policy. Already, however, a *lingua franca* was developing along the lower St. Lawrence that was made up partly of European and partly of Algonkian words, and was used for trading and elementary communication (Biggar 1930:453–54; Lescarbot 1907–14, 2:24).

The pre-eminent role that Tadoussac played in the fur trade into the early part of the seventeenth century was no accident. As we have already seen, even in prehistoric times, the Saguenay River was the terminus of a trade route stretching across central Quebec and westward to Lake Superior. Although the St. Lawrence Iroquoians travelled down-river beyond Tadoussac, they did not claim this region as their own territory. Its original inhabitants were probably Montagnais, an Algonkian-speaking, hunting and gathering people.

In 1603, Champlain observed that Tadoussac was a focal point for various groups who gathered there in the summer to trade. These included the Etchemin or Malecite, a Maritime group that was on good terms with the local Montagnais. By then the Etchemin were already hard-pressed by the Micmac who were expanding their hunting territories westward as their dependence on the fur trade was increased (Biggar 1922–36, 1:295–96). Since the Micmac had steadier access to iron hatchets, they were generally successful in their wars. By the 1620s, many Etchemin were forced to settle north of the St. Lawrence on a permanent basis (Sagard 1866:149–50). Once European traders began to visit Tadoussac, the hope of obtaining hatchets must have attracted these Indians northward, first to trade and later as settlers. It is also possible that in the early days the Stadaconans came there to trade, but this is purely hypothetical.

Of greatest importance, however, was the trade that passed through the hands of the Montagnais who lived in the Saguenay Valley. Unlike the Micmac and Malecite, these bands did not sacrifice their freedom to exploit the abundant food resources of the St. Lawrence Valley in order to devote more time to hunting in the northern forests.[25] Instead, they used their position astride the Saguenay River to obtain furs from Indians who already lived in the interior. The latter were not permitted to travel down the Saguenay to trade with the Europeans and, as competition became more intense, some were killed for attempting to do so (Thwaites 1896– 1901, 8:41). The Indians from the interior were encouraged to visit the Montagnais of the Saguenay region and to barter their beaver skins for goods the Montagnais had purchased from the French. Thus the Montagnais established for themselves an important role as middlemen who profited by exchanging trade goods supplied by the French for furs they did not have to trap. The extent of this trade in the late sixteenth century is revealed by geographical information that Champlain was able to collect on his first visit to this area. By means of intermediaries, European trade goods were reaching Hudson Bay and furs were coming south from there (Biggar 1922–36, 1:123–24). It also seems likely that this trade had extended westward along the old copper route to the headwaters of the St. Maurice and Ottawa Rivers.[26] The key location in this trading system was Lake St. John, which was the hub of a far-flung network of inter-connected lakes and rivers.

Advantageous as the position of middleman was for the Montagnais of Tadoussac, it should not be imagined as an *ad hoc* development. The rules underlying this trade appear to have been as old as trade in eastern Canada. Of fundamental importance was a general agreement that one tribe did not have the right to travel, without permission, across the territory of another. Groups who lacked experience trading with Europeans often preferred to allow dealings with these strangers to remain in the hands of Indians who already had an alliance with them. By spreading rumours about how dangerous the Europeans were, and, at the same time, preventing the Europeans and the Indians from the interior from meeting one another, the Montagnais both retained the friendship of these tribes and profited by giving them fewer European goods for their furs than they in turn received from the French for them.

The Disappearance of the St. Lawrence Iroquoians

Sometime between 1542 and 1603, not only the Stadaconans but all the Iroquoian-speaking inhabitants of the St. Lawrence Valley vanished. It is uncertain when this happened, and how it came about has been the subject of much tenuous and often misleading speculation. Many hypotheses have been based on assumptions about the ethnic identity of these people that now are either abandoned or rendered very doubtful. One thing is certain: in the seventeenth century no tribe, or portion of a tribe, was explicitly identified as being descended from these peoples.

No eye witness accounts of the St. Lawrence Iroquoians are available after Roberval ceased his efforts to colonize the St. Lawrence Valley. Marc Lescarbot, in his *History of New France*, attributed the disappearance of the Hochelagans to an Iroquois invasion around 1600.[27] Denis Jamet, a Recollet writing from Quebec in 1615, gave a similar explanation for the disappearance of the St. Lawrence Iroquoians, but dated the event nearer the time of Cartier's visit. He also claimed to know of an aged Huron who remembered seeing their villages prior to their destruction.[28] Later tales interpreted as accounting for the fate of the St. Lawrence Iroquoians have, however, received more attention from historians and anthropologists. Nicolas Perrot (1911:42–47), writing between 1680 and 1718, stated that the Iroquois were the original inhabitants of the St. Lawrence Valley and had been driven out by the Algonkians.[29] Perrot does not give the source for this story, which may be based on Mohawk or Algonkian oral traditions concerning the struggle for control of the St. Lawrence Valley that was going on between these groups early in the seventeenth century. The Iroquois were not, however, living in the St. Lawrence Valley at that time or, as the archaeological evidence shows, at any earlier period; hence they cannot be identified with the St. Lawrence Iroquoians. Thus, the claim must be rejected that Perrot's story, or a similar suggestion by Charles Aubert de La Chesnaye (cited by Bailey 1933:106), has any connection with the fate of the St. Lawrence Iroquoians. Similarly, a Jesuit record that certain Algonkin who were living in the lower Ottawa Valley in the first half of the seventeenth century claimed to have been driven from Montreal Island by the Huron has been interpreted as proof that the St. Lawrence Iroquoians were dispersed by the Huron (Thwaites 1896–1901, 22:215–17; 29:173).

There are serious doubts concerning the accuracy with which both the Perrot and Jesuit traditions were recorded. It has been suggested that Perrot confused the terms Iroquois and Iroquet and that his story is merely another version of Charlevoix's tale about how the Algonkin group known as the Petite Nation, or Nation of Iroquet, was driven into the lower Ottawa Valley by other Algonkian-speaking peoples. It has also been suggested that, in their story, the Jesuits inadvertently wrote Huron when they meant Iroquois (Pendergast and Trigger 1972:79, 80). Elsewhere, I have presented an extended critique of all the material from the seventeenth and eighteenth centuries that has a bearing on the fate of the St. Lawrence Iroquoians and have argued that none of it provides a reliable basis for reconstructing the history of the St. Lawrence Iroquoians in the late sixteenth century (ibid. 71–92). Instead, any study of this period must be based on an attempt to determine the general processes that were at work in the St. Lawrence Valley between the visits of Cartier and Champlain. This requires a detailed consideration of the effects that the growth of the fur trade, and of European influence generally, may have had on intertribal relations in this area.

In 1930, Harold Innis (1956:12–15) proposed that the Iroquoians were

expelled from the St. Lawrence Valley by the Montagnais and neighbouring Algonkian tribes. He argued that, because of their geographical position
and easy access to furs, the Algonkians were the first to receive iron axes
and thus they were able to wage war against the agricultural tribes living
up-river. Innis suggested that they attacked the Iroquoians in order to
control the St. Lawrence River as a trade route. Although this updating
of Perrot's theory won the support of Bailey (1933), Fenton (1940:174–75),
and others, it has serious weaknesses. It overlooks the fact that relations
between adjacent horticultural and hunting peoples in eastern North
America were generally friendly, since such groups were able to exchange
surplus corn for skins and dried meat. As the Algonkians living in the
interior spent more time hunting in order to participate in the fur trade,
they would have become more dependent on the Iroquoians for agricultural
produce and in this way the Iroquoians would have been able to secure
more furs to trade with the French. Thus, with the development of the fur
trade, relations between these two groups should have become friendlier,
rather than more hostile. Under these circumstances, it seems unlikely that
the St. Lawrence Iroquoians would have prevented the Algonkians from
using the river.

In the sixteenth century, large numbers of Stadaconans used to travel
to the Gaspé and the north shore of the Gulf of St. Lawrence, where they
were able to secure European goods. It is possible that easier access to iron
weapons enabled the Micmac to expel the Stadaconans from their fishing
grounds in the Gaspé Peninsula, but, at best, only vague memories of the
struggle for control of this region may be preserved in Micmac legends
concerning their wars with the Kwedech, a hostile tribe that used to live
along the St. Lawrence (Fenton 1940:174–75). The Montagnais around
Tadoussac could have been drawn into the wars that the Micmac may have
waged against the Stadaconans late in the sixteenth century. On the other
hand, these wars seem to have had a very specific objective: control over
hunting and fishing rights in the Gaspé Peninsula. There is therefore no
reason to believe that such a struggle would have culminated in the
destruction of the Stadaconans.

More recently, Bernard Hoffman (1961:202–14) has attempted to
explain the disappearance of the St. Lawrence Iroquoians in terms of
economic developments similar to those that were at work in the Maritimes.
He noted that the Stadaconan subsistence economy was heavily based on
the resources of the St. Lawrence, but ignored the horticultural orientation of the Hochelagans. Because of this, he erroneously assumed that
his analysis of the Stadaconans would apply to the whole of the St. Lawrence

Valley. Hoffman argued that, as the fur trade spread up the St. Lawrence Valley, the Indians grew increasingly dependent on hunting. Thus, when fur-bearing mammals became depleted near the river, they were forced to move inland in search of game. This led to a still further decline in time spent fishing, and hunting became the basis of their subsistence economy, as well as a source of furs. Because hunting was less productive than fishing, this change resulted in "social disorganization," which, in turn, made these Indians fall easy prey to the Iroquois who invaded the St. Lawrence Valley around 1600.

Hoffman's theory has several major weaknesses. It does not take account of the historical fact that the fur trade developed in the Saguenay Valley and then spread westward across central Quebec some time before the St. Lawrence became a major artery of trade. It does not explain why the Iroquois attacked the Indians in the St. Lawrence Valley or why the Stada-conans and Hochelagans disappeared as groups, as opposed to being forced from their tribal territories. The process of social disorganization is neither defined nor explained and, finally, Hoffman's reconstruction of events in the St. Lawrence Valley does not correspond with what is known about conditions there early in the seventeenth century. While it is true that, up-river from Tadoussac, the valley was largely deserted, this was not because its inhabitants had moved inland to hunt for fur-bearing mam-mals. As the fur trade grew, groups who lived along the St. Lawrence tended to become middlemen rather than hunters. The latter process has already been documented for the Tadoussac area and is later attested along the St. Maurice and Ottawa Rivers. There is thus no reason to believe that trade alone would have been sufficient to cause the Indians living near the St. Lawrence to abandon their prosperous riverine economy. On the con-trary, it would have encouraged them to remain close to the St. Lawrence.

Other hypotheses have been proposed to help explain the disappearance of the St. Lawrence Iroquoians. It has been noted that the St. Lawrence Valley lies close to the northern limits for growing corn and many writers have suggested that a series of bad harvests might have prompted these tribes to move farther south (Lloyd 1904:189; Fenton 1940:175; Barbeau 1949:228–29; Martijn 1969:96–101). There is evidence of a period of colder climates in North America beginning around A.D. 1550, but it is unclear whether the fluctuation was of sufficient amplitude to have affected the Stadaconans, who, in any case, were less dependent on horticulture than were their neighbours to the south. There is also no evidence that Iroquoian cultural development in the St. Lawrence Valley was adversely affected in any way by the cooler weather postulated between A.D. 1200

and 1450 (Martijn 1969:97). Finally, the theory of climatic deterioration
does not explain why the St. Lawrence Iroquoians disappeared, as opposed
merely to moving elsewhere as identifiable groups.

Fenton (1940:175) has suggested that the Indians in this region may
have been decimated by European diseases in the latter half of the sixteenth
century. While there is no direct evidence to support this suggestion, it is
not impossible that European diseases were a factor contributing to their
disappearance. In the next century, Father Pierre Biard attributed many
deaths and illnesses to the European food and drink that the Indians con-
consumed while gathering at the ships to trade (Thwaites 1896–1901,
3:105–7). Fenton (ibid.) has also speculated that, in order to trade more
easily, the Stadaconans may have abandoned their hilltop forts and settled
nearer the river, thus exposing themselves more to the attacks of their
enemies. While each of these suggestions is worth considering, more
aggressive hypotheses are required to bring the period we are discussing
into line with the historical realities of the better documented period that
follows.

It is clear from the writings of Samuel de Champlain that early in the
seventeenth century no tribe was living in the St. Lawrence Valley above
Tadoussac. Algonkian fishing parties visited the river for short periods, but
the Algonkians stood in mortal terror of the Iroquois, who dominated the
region. Champlain is emphatic that they were unable to travel along the
St. Lawrence for fear of the Iroquois war parties that were infesting
the banks of the river (Biggar 1922–36, 1:137). These reports add weight to
those of Lescarbot and Jamet and suggest that the depopulation of the
region was the result of warfare, which, by the beginning of the seventeenth century, had given the Iroquois, or more specifically the Mohawk,
control of the upper St. Lawrence Valley. They also suggest that the St.
Lawrence Iroquoians were either annihilated or dispersed in these wars, as
the early traditions maintain was the case.

The course of events leading to the destruction of the St. Lawrence
Iroquoians and to the Mohawk domination of the valley is more difficult to
reconstruct. At present, we can no more than suggest a number of alternative hypotheses. It is possible that the Stadaconans and Hochelagans were
destroyed at the same time by the same enemy, but it is also possible that
they met separate ends. The Stadaconans may have been destroyed by their
traditional enemies, the Toudaman, but, as already noted, the arguments
in favour of this theory are not entirely convincing. If we assume that the
Stadaconans were eliminated separately, the most attractive hypothesis is
that they were destroyed by the Hochelagans. Rivalry over trade was

already evident between these two groups in 1535, and it may have been the Stadaconans' desire to control trade with the interior, more than their hatred of the French, that led them to oppose Europeans travelling beyond Tadoussac after 1542. As the Hochelagans came to want more European goods, they may have grown increasingly hostile to Stadaconan claims. Unable to bribe the partly horticultural Stadaconans with their surplus corn, it is possible that the Hochelagans attacked and dispersed them around 1580, thus making it possible for Europeans again to travel up-river. If so, this event provides one of the earliest examples of the difficulties encountered by small tribes when they attempted to maintain an exclusive position as middlemen between European traders and more powerful tribes living farther inland.

The fate of the Hochelagans is equally problematical. Conceivably, they might have been attacked by the Algonkian-speaking peoples of central Quebec and the Ottawa Valley who desired more direct access to French traders below Quebec. Yet, the northern Algonkians are unlikely to have destroyed a horticultural group living adjacent to them. The Huron are another possibility and some antiquarians have interpreted the Ottawa Valley Algonkin tradition of a Huron attack on Montreal Island as having significance for the disappearance of Hochelaga (Lighthall 1899). Of still greater importance is the archaeological evidence that suggests a long tradition of warfare between the proto-Huron and the Iroquoians of the upper St. Lawrence Valley. This warfare came to an end late in the sixteenth century. The Huron may have conquered the Hochelagans, with the victorious tribes incorporating some of the vanquished into their own ranks.

Yet, even if the proto-Huron and the St. Lawrence Iroquoians had been enemies for a long time, what reason did they have for expanding their traditional warfare to the point of annihilation? The Hochelagans may have sought to control trade with the interior and this may have prompted the Huron to attack them. The use of iron weapons could also have given the Hochelagans an advantage, which caused the numerically superior Huron to unite and eliminate them as an act of self-defence. While the latter argument must be given some weight, neither of these explanations is particularly convincing. By themselves, the Hochelagans could not deprive the Huron of European goods, since such material came from the Saguenay along the old copper route. Moreover, the archaeological and early historical evidence does not suggest that the Huron were deeply involved in trading for European goods much before 1600, or that they were seeking to make direct contact with European traders prior to 1609.

Under these conditions, it is highly unlikely that the Huron were sufficiently motivated, either by an unsatisfied desire for trade goods or by fear of the Hochelagans, to attempt to eliminate the latter as middlemen. Because they lived so far inland, the Huron were relatively protected from the challenges that were transforming the lives of their neighbours nearer the coast.

In the late sixteenth century, the Mohawk found themselves in very different circumstances. In the north, their most productive hunting territories were directly adjacent to those of the tribes that lived in the St. Lawrence Valley. Because they were more dependent on hunting than were the entreprenurial Huron of Simcoe County, the Mohawk were seriously threatened by any change in the balance of power between themselves and their northern neighbours. Moreover, by comparison with these tribes, the Mohawk were very poorly located for trade with Europeans. The most direct water route to the St. Lawrence ran north through Lake Champlain and along the Richelieu River, but this was a route that could be barred by the St. Lawrence Iroquoians whenever they wished to do so. The Mohawk were also at a disadvantage by comparison with the coastal tribes of New England, who could obtain goods from occasional European ships or, on a more regular basis, from the Micmac and Malecite. Farther south, European ships appeared less frequently off the coast, but, even there, three short-lived European colonies were founded north of Florida between 1526 and 1590 (Trudel 1963:277). These colonies and irregular coastal trade seem to have aroused the interest of the Susquehannock in acquiring European goods, well before the beginning of the seventeenth century.[30] Verrazzano had viewed the mouth of the Hudson River in 1524, but no Europeans are known to have sailed up the river prior to 1609. Moreover, the Mohawk did not have direct access even to this potential artery of trade, since Mahican territory intervened. Instead of the tribes who lived nearest the sources of European goods being the friends of the Mohawk, they mostly seem to have been peoples with whom the Mohawk had been at war for a long time.

In spite of this, European goods appear in Iroquois sites as far west as the Seneca by the late sixteenth century. Most of the early material is found as offerings in individual graves. In the earliest sites, a few iron axes and large iron knives have been found, and occasionally some round or oval glass beads. Brass kettles and beads made from fragments of such kettles are also reported. The influx of European goods increased rapidly and soon such goods begin to appear in village refuse. Charles F. Wray and Harry L. Schoff (1953:54–55, 62–63) date the earliest European goods between

A.D. 1550 and 1575 and are convinced that, before 1590, stone axes and flint knives had given way to European equivalents as far west as the Seneca tribe. Yet, their dates for these sites, which are based on the estimated periodicity of the removal of villages to new sites, may be twenty-five to fifty years too early (W. Noble, personal communication 1970). Even so, the likelihood that small quantities of European goods were reaching the Seneca prior to 1600 suggests that all the Iroquois tribes must have been obtaining such goods.

Some of this material may have been obtained through trade, although items that were useful in war, such as iron axes, would probably not have been exchanged willingly by rival groups living nearer the St. Lawrence. When Champlain was accompanying his Algonkian allies in 1609, he encountered a party of Mohawk warriors at the southern tip of Lake Champlain. When they saw the enemy, the Mohawk are said to have erected a barricade with poor axes which they sometimes acquired in war or with ones made of stone (Biggar 1922–36; 2:96). The poor axes are clearly cheap iron ones, manufactured for trade with the Indians. Champlain's statement indicates that, as late as 1609, the main way the Mohawk acquired European axes was by capturing them in war. It also suggests that the earliest "trade goods" found among the four western tribes either were gifts from the Mohawk or were captured by warriors from these tribes fighting alongside the Mohawk against the Indians who lived in the St. Lawrence Valley. Once the Ottawa Valley Algonkin started to obtain European goods, the Oneida and Onondaga probably emulated the Mohawk and raided these groups in their home territory. By crossing Lake Ontario and following the Rideau River northward, it would have been easier for these tribes to attack the Algonkin than to wage war on the St. Lawrence.

The Iroquois may have been forced to fight to obtain trade goods, because the Hochelagans sought to treat them in the same manner as the Stadaconans had treated the Hochelagans. Possibly, the Mohawk and Hochelagans were traditional enemies. If so, the latter may not have wanted European goods to reach the Iroquois, or at least attempted to prevent them from getting knives and hatchets, which would have been useful in war. Such a situation would have put the Mohawk at a serious disadvantage and made obtaining European knives and hatchets seem a matter of life and death to them. The desire for unrestricted access to trading stations on the St. Lawrence, or to secure iron tools in war, may have led to an all-out attack on the Hochelagans resulting in their destruction not long before A.D. 1600, the date suggested by Lescarbot (map 8).

Yet, by invading the St. Lawrence Valley as far down-river as Tadoussac,

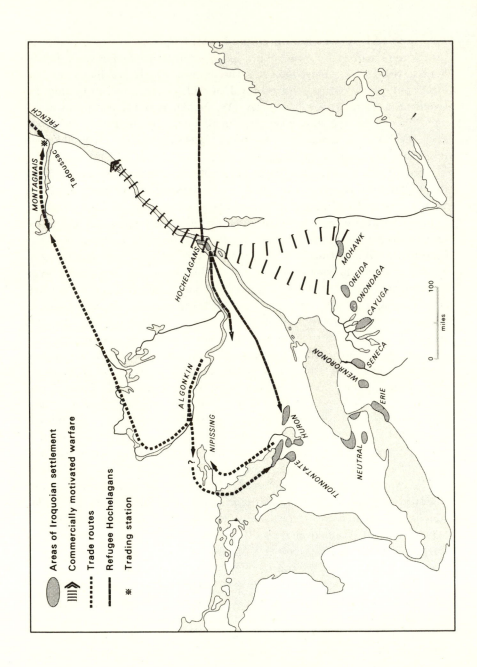

MAP 8. *Intertribal relations, late sixteenth century.*

the Mohawk seem to have encountered more difficulties than they had anticipated. Whether the Stadaconans were dispersed by the Iroquois, or had disappeared earlier, the Iroquois' attack on the lower parts of the St. Lawrence brought them into conflict with the Montagnais, who had always lived around Tadoussac and who were now laying claim to the Quebec City area. This generated a conflict, the first phase of which lasted until about 1610.

The climax of Iroquois power on the St. Lawrence seems to have been about 1600. Sagard reported that in 1625 the remains of an Iroquois fortification were visible at Quebec, which they had built after they had seized the spot from the Montagnais (Sagard 1866:271–72). The "Montagnais" mentioned in this story could be the St. Lawrence Iroquoians, especially since Sagard states that they had worked the soil prior to being driven away and forced to wander in the forests. It must be remembered, however, that, even in the seventeenth century, the Algonkians who lived in the St. Lawrence Valley planted limited amounts of corn, when conditions were peaceful enough to suggest a reasonable return for their effort.[31] The fortification that Sagard refers to was probably a temporary war camp, such as the Mohawk erected elsewhere in the valley, and it is not unlikely that the people they attacked were the Montagnais, who had settled at Quebec after it was abandoned by the Stadaconans. The fort does not indicate Iroquois settlement in the valley, but it does suggest that war parties had penetrated at least as far downstream as Quebec City. Significantly, however, Sagard states that the Iroquois were not able to hold onto this position and therefore ceased to frequent the region.

If our interpretation of these events is correct, we have in these early conflicts on the St. Lawrence the first evidence of the Iroquois becoming involved in wars that were not of a traditional type. The motive for this conflict was clearly economic and was connected with the fur trade. Instead of seeking to take individual prisoners, the Mohawk sought to annihilate or disperse whole populations whose activities were felt to be a threat to their well-being. In traditional warfare, the aim was to preserve one's enemies as a group in order to be able to go on fighting with them indefinitely. Wars may have been fought in prehistoric times to eliminate an enemy completely, but all known wars of this sort are in some way connected with trade with Europeans.

This war turned the St. Lawrence Valley above Tadoussac into a no-man's land, traversed by Iroquois raiding parties and generally avoided by the Montagnais and Algonkin, even though this meant losing some of their best fishing stations. At the same time, by having attacked the Montagnais and failed to secure control of the river as far as Tadoussac, the Mohawk had lost an important objective. Their principal short-term benefit was probably to secure European goods from groups they had either defeated or frightened into abandoning their settlements. Champlain was able to travel up-river as far as Montreal Island in the summer of 1603, but he wrote that a French settlement at Three Rivers would be a great boon for the freedom of tribes who dared not come that way for fear of the Iroquois. At the very least, such a settlement would permit the Algonkian-speaking tribes to trade in peace (Biggar 1922–36, 1:137). He added that it might also make friends of the Iroquois, no doubt because they would then have a place to trade.

I have already stated that it is unclear when, and under what circumstances, the Iroquois confederacy developed. Although it reveals nothing about relations among the five Iroquois tribes at an earlier date, the distribution of the earliest European goods among all five tribes may indicate a considerable degree of friendship in the latter part of the sixteenth century. It is possible that a common desire for such goods led to growing cooperation, which greatly strengthened the Iroquois confederacy, if it did not bring it into existence (Tooker 1964:3–4 n. 1). It is also possible that warriors from all five tribes participated in the initial attacks on the St. Lawrence.

The Iroquois confederacy does not appear, however, to have been designed as an offensive coalition; instead, it functioned to suppress blood feuds and to promote friendship among member tribes. Moreover, for several decades, it was the Mohawk who were to undertake aggressive action to secure trading privileges with Europeans, while the four other tribes were to play a more passive role in such endeavours. The main motives underlying the formation of the confederacy, or its development, may have been the desire of the four western tribes to secure trade goods and the reciprocal wish among the Mohawk for peace with their western neighbours in order to be able to pursue their warlike policies on the St. Lawrence more effectively. Moreover, as trade spread inland, peace among the Iroquois permitted the western members of the confederacy to campaign against the northern Algonkians and ultimately against the Huron, and, by plundering these groups, to secure increasing amounts of European goods. The simultaneous development of an enlarged Huron confederacy and the increasing amounts of trade goods becoming available to the Susquehannock and other tribes to the south must have served to maintain and reinforce the Iroquois alliance during the decades that followed.

Survivors

Even if the St. Lawrence Iroquoians were dispersed in one of the ways out-lined above, their ultimate fate remains uncertain. Lescarbot, apparently one of our more knowledgeable sources, speaks summarily of extermination, while Jamet states that they were dislodged by their fierce wars and retreated one after the other farther inland. Conceivably, some were taken prisoner by the Iroquois and absorbed into one or more of their tribes. Yet no historical, archaeological, or linguistic evidence affirms this. Some ethnologists have speculated that the St. Lawrence Iroquoians fled inland to join the Huron confederacy and are the ancestors of the Arendar-honon, Tahontaenrat, or both (Tooker 1964:3 n. 1). Archaeologically, this does not seem to be possible. Two other suggestions deserve more care-ful consideration.

The first is that remnants of the Hochelagan population survived among the Algonkin who lived in the lower part of the Ottawa Valley in the seventeenth century and that it was their presence which led these Algon-kin to claim they had once lived on Montreal Island (Lighthall 1899). The main arguments in support of this theory concern the identity of a group known as the Onontchataronon. It is generally believed that Onontcha-taronon was merely the Huron name for the Weskarini, or Petite Nation, an Algonkin group that lived in the vicinity of the Rouge, Petite Nation, and Lièvre Rivers. The two names are equated on the Sanson Map of 1656 and Sagard states that Onontchataronon (which he transcribes *Quieunon-tateronon* and is the same name he gives to the Tionnontaté) was the Huron name for the Petite Nation.[32] It is also significant that while one of the principal headmen of the Onontchataronon was called only by the Iroquoian name of Tawiscaron, the Jesuits regarded their mission to this tribe as one that required an Algonkian-speaking priest (Thwaites 1896–1901, 27:37). The Huron gave Iroquoian names to all the tribes and im-portant headmen with whom they had dealings; hence it can be argued that it is nothing more than coincidence that Iroquoian names were applied so often to this group and to its leaders.

On the other hand, the Petite Nation and the Onontchataronon are no-where explicitly identified as being the same people in Jesuit documents from the first half of the seventeenth century. Only the Onontchataronon are said to have lived on the Island of Montreal and, on a number of occasions, when lists of tribes are given, the Onontchataronon and Petite Nation are enumerated separately (18:229; 21:117; 24:269; 29:145).

While all of the sources agree that the Petite Nation lived east of the Ottawa Valley, the *Jesuit Relation* for 1640 suggests that the Onontchataronon lived to the west of the river (18:229). Finally, Percy J. Robinson (1942) has argued that the name of the group contains the Iroquoian root *onnonta*, signifying hill or mountain. He has also attempted to demonstrate that Onontchataronon and Hochelaga are the same name, but less convincingly in my opinion. Nevertheless, it is at least possible that the Onontchataronon were an independent tribe, or a branch of the Weskarini that contained considerable numbers of Hochelagan refugees. If the group was either wholly or partly of Iroquoian origin, all of its members must have been heavily Algonkianized by the early seventeenth century, since the Algonkian language seems to have been used alongside, or in place of, Iroquoian as its working language. It must be remembered, however, that any hypothesis concerning this group is highly speculative and that even a small number of refugees might have given rise to the claim that there was an historical connection between the Onontchataronon and the former inhabitants of Montreal Island. It may also be noted in passing that, if there is any truth to the Onontchataronon claim to include Hochelagan refugees, there may also be some truth to their claim that other Hochelagan refugees moved south to join the Abenaki (Thwaites 1896–1901, 22:215).

The second suggestion is that some of the St. Lawrence Iroquoians may have found refuge among the Huron, not as a single tribe, but as remnants who became members of already existing tribes. Until recently, however, the evidence to support this theory has been highly circumstantial. For example, Jamet's claim that in 1615 a Huron reported having seen a village along the St. Lawrence many years before has been interpreted as proof that this man and his people had migrated from there to the Huron country (Le Blant and Baudry 1967:350 n. 3). In view of the propensity of Iroquoian men to travel, this interpretation is at best hazardous.

In recent years, however, archaeological evidence has indicated that, sometime in the late sixteenth century, large amounts of St. Lawrence Iroquoian pottery began appearing among the Tionnontaté (at the Sidey-Mackay site) (Wintemberg 1946) as well as in Huron sites along the Trent waterway. In particular, this appears to be so at the Trent site, which has been partially excavated as of 1971. Peter Pratt (personal communication 1971) is of the opinion that the evidence from the Trent Valley indicates the absorption of groups of refugees from the St. Lawrence. Like the Wenroronon refugees of 1638, these people were adopted into several Huron villages to avoid economic hardship and the political complications that would ensue had they founded their own village or villages in Huron territory. If we are correct in believing that it was the Arendarhonon who were living in the Trent Valley prior to A.D. 1600, they may have absorbed most of the people who fled westward from the St. Lawrence.

While it may be objected that the St. Lawrence Iroquoians were unlikely to seek refuge among their traditional enemies, this objection is not insuperable. In later times, a whole Huron tribe was to settle among the Seneca, after the Iroquois had inflicted far more serious injuries on the Huron than would have resulted from the traditional warfare between the Huron and the St. Lawrence Iroquoians. Having been decimated by a Mohawk attack that went far beyond the limits of traditional warfare, the St. Lawrence Iroquoians may have been happy to seek refuge among former foes. With the Iroquois becoming more aggressive, the Arendarhonon and the other Huron may have been equally pleased to see their own ranks reinforced by newcomers.

If this reconstruction is accurate, it explains a number of isolated, but nevertheless significant, pieces of information that can be gleaned from the early records. First, it accounts for the Arendarhonon's special interest in the St. Lawrence Valley and the close relationship they had with the Onontchataronon and, possibly through them, with the Algonkin of the Ottawa Valley generally. Throughout the first half of the seventeenth century, large numbers of Onontchataronon were in the habit of spending each winter in Arendarhonon territory. This would be more easily explained if remnants of the St. Lawrence Iroquoians had become attached to both groups and were working to promote contacts between them.

It would also explain Champlain's belief that, at some time in the past, the Iroquois had driven the Ottawa Valley Algonkin out of the St. Lawrence Valley (Biggar 1922–36, 2:280–81) and had caused the Huron living in the Trent Valley to abandon their tribal territory and seek refuge in Simcoe County (3:59). While Champlain interpreted this information, gathered through inexperienced interpreters, as evidence of a massive Iroquois offensive sometime in the sixteenth century, it seems more likely that these traditions refer to the dispersal of Iroquoian refugees from the St. Lawrence Valley about twenty years before. Champlain also recorded an ambiguous claim to the effect that in the past either the Entouhonoron (a term which appears to mean the four western Iroquois tribes) were forced to flee some forty or fifty leagues, or that they had forced the Huron to remove that distance.[33] This has been interpreted as support for the now discredited theory that the St. Lawrence Iroquoians were the ancestors of one or more of the historic Iroquois tribes. More likely, it refers either to yet other St. Lawrence Iroquoians moving south to join their conquerors or to the Iroquois forcing such groups to flee westward to join the Huron and Tionnontaté.

The interpretation of events in the late sixteenth century outlined above has the advantage of explaining many hitherto enigmatic and apparently contradictory statements in a more satisfactory manner than so far has been achieved. Many other examples can be found of events which have happened to only a small number of people being expanded by oral traditions, to embrace much larger groupings to which these people belonged or became attached. It would appear that Sauk and Fox legends about origins on the east coast of the United States and a later flight inland, in fact refer to these groups accepting Sokoki and Mahican refugees from the Atlantic seaboard in the historic period (Brasser 1971 :263).

The Birth of the French-Algonkian Alliance

The Mohawk attacks on the Montagnais living around Tadoussac and Quebec were to have an important and lasting influence on the history of the St. Lawrence Valley, because they occurred at the same time that French merchants were hoping to expand the fur trade. The conflict that ensued was to provide these merchants with the means by which they could extend their trading network along the St. Lawrence and the major tributaries flowing into it.

In the autumn of 1599, Pierre de Chauvin de Tonnetuit, a wealthy merchant of Honfleur, obtained a ten-year monopoly over the fur trade of New France, in return for a promise to settle 500 people there. The following spring, he set sail for Tadoussac with his partner, François Gravé Du Pont, and Pierre Du Gua de Monts, a native of Saintonge. Against the advice of these two men, who preferred a settlement up-river, Chauvin decided to establish a token colony at Tadoussac to serve as a trading post. He constructed a house twenty-five feet long and eighteen feet wide, which had a fireplace in the centre and was surrounded by a weak palisade and ditch. Throughout the summer, Chauvin carried on a brisk trade in beaver and other furs, before departing for France. He left behind sixteen men, who were to maintain his monopoly and begin trading as soon as possible the following spring. As a result of sickness, quarrelling, and lack of provisions, only five of these men lived through the winter. The survivors owed their lives to the Indians, who fed and cared for them. This disastrous experiment temporarily put an end to efforts at colonization along the St. Lawrence (Biggar 1901:42–44; Trudel 1963:235–42).

The following year, Chauvin apparently sent out only one ship and, in 1602, he sailed for the New World with two. In 1602, Chauvin's monopoly was altered to include certain other traders from St. Malo and Rouen. When he died early in 1603 the monopoly passed to Aymar de Chaste, who sent three ships to the St. Lawrence to trade and survey the region to find a more suitable location for settlement (Biggar 1901:44–50). An account of this voyage was published by Samuel de Champlain, who was an acquaintance of de Monts. Born at Brouage, in Saintonge, around 1570, Champlain had fought in the French wars of religion and afterwards claims to have travelled in the West Indies. His main qualification for accompanying this expedition seems to have been his skill as a painter and map-maker.[34]

The monopoly holders who were now spending the summers at Tadoussac were more anxious to establish a firm alliance with the Montagnais than the casual traders of an earlier period had been. They had to protect their monopoly against illegal competition, and particularly against the Basque whalers who continued to frequent the St. Lawrence. It was also in their interest to expand trade as rapidly as possible, which meant developing new ties, either directly or indirectly, with the northern hunting peoples. General outlines of a policy for dealing with the Indians had emerged as early as 1602.[35] This policy was based on three observations which embodied the considerable experience that had already been gained from trading with the Indians.

The first was the realization that it was more important to maintain good relations with the Indians living north of the St. Lawrence than with tribes living to the south. This was because the furs coming from the north were superior in quality to those coming from the south. Moreover, because of the extensive network of rivers in the north, furs could be accumulated and brought to the St. Lawrence in greater quantities from that direction.[36] This put the Iroquois at a serious disadvantage and guaranteed that in any quarrel in which it was believed necessary to choose between them and the northern Algonkians, the French would opt for an alliance with the Algonkians.

The second observation was that good trading relations depended upon broadly based alliances between the French and their Indian partners. The Montagnais of the Saguenay area were at war with the Mohawk and for some time appear to have been hard-pressed by them. Because of this, it was necessary to help them in their wars, both to free them to engage in trade and to maintain their goodwill. Although the French were primarily interested in increasing trade, nothing won the confidence of these Indians more than did an offer of military assistance. Chauvin therefore promised the Montagnais that the French would settle among them and either compel the Iroquois to make peace or destroy them (Biggar 1922–36, 1:100).

The settlement in 1600 may already have been explained to the Indians as the fulfilment of such a promise, although we know nothing specific about Chauvin's relations with the Montagnais at that time. In 1602, two Indians from Tadoussac were taken to France and, while there, were presented to Henri IV. These Indians returned to Tadoussac the following spring to assure their people that the French king supported Chauvin's promises. This prompted Anadabijou, the headman of the Tadoussac band, to say the French would be welcome to settle there in order to help the Montagnais wage war on their enemies (1:101). In practice, however, the aim of the fur traders appears to have been to assist the Montagnais by supplying them with knives, hatchets, and other weapons that would give them an advantage over the Iroqouis. While not engaging directly in an Indian war, the French thereby showed their concern for the welfare of their Indian trading partners and were establishing a basis for closer cooperation and eventual settlement with a finesse that was lacking in Cartier's day. Although these fur traders are frequently condemned by historians for their reluctance to advocate the colonization of New France, in general their behaviour was admirably realistic and demonstrated a desire to get along with the Indians that did not exist among other Europeans who came to the New World.

The third observation was the need to encourage contact with tribes who lived in the interior. Until this time, most of the trade with the west had been channelled along the old copper route and thus was controlled by the Montagnais who lived around Tadoussac. Only a limited number of French ships travelled farther up-river, and those that did found few of the more westerly peoples coming to the banks of the St. Lawrence. Under normal circumstances, the Montagnais would have preferred to have these arrangements remain as they were; however, the Iroquois threat also made them anxious for allies who would help them to drive the Iroquois from the St. Lawrence. By 1603, or possibly earlier, they had drawn into an alliance not only some Etchemin, but also the Indians who lived north of the St. Lawrence as far west as the Ottawa Valley (1:103). The bands who lived to the east of Three Rivers were Montagnais, while those who lived to the west into the Ottawa Valley, were Algonkin (Thwaites 1896–1901, 23: 303–5). Although both groupings were Algonkian-speaking, they were differentiated linguistically. The Algonkin also shared a number of cultural traits with the Algonkian and Iroquoian peoples who lived in the less rigorous environments to the south and west of them and they were marginally horticultural, while the Montagnais planted crops only very infrequently. In return for a military alliance against the Iroquois, these bands seem to have been free to come to Tadoussac and trade with the French (map 9).

The demand for European goods may have been expanding rapidly enough in the region north of Tadoussac to minimize the economic sacrifice that was involved for the Montagnais in granting such a privilege. Nevertheless, the trouble that Champlain had to go to a decade later to expand trade as far west as Lake Huron suggests that even at this early date the French may have been encouraging the development of an alliance that would open the St. Lawrence, both militarily and diplomatically, as an artery of trade for the Algonkian-speaking peoples of the interior. This goal appears to have been achieved harmoniously, because both the French and the Montagnais stood to gain from it, though in different ways. By introducing the more westerly Montagnais and the Algonkin to the French as their military allies, Anadabijou and his people not only made it easier for these Indians to establish contact with the French but also were enhancing their own prestige within the new alliance. Later, Anadabijou's grandson was to list as his ancestor's chief accomplishment that he had maintained the peace between these confederated Indian bands and the French (Biggar 1922–36, 5:64). Presumably this had become a traditional role in this family, beginning in his grandfather's day.

By 1603, the Algonkian alliance was beginning to hold its own against the Iroquois. When the French arrived at Tadoussac in May of that year, they found that over one thousand Montagnais, Algonkin, and Etchemin had gathered there. These Indians had erected a series of longhouses and were celebrating, with a scalp dance, a victory that they had probably gained over the Iroquois the year before (1:107–9). Among those who were present to meet the French was Tessouat, the headman of the Kichesipirini, or Islander Algonkin, whose summer camping ground was on Morrison Island, in the upper part of the Ottawa Valley.[37] In later years, because of their strategic location, Tessouat and his people were destined to exercise an important influence over the development of the fur trade. In order to reaffirm his friendship with the Algonkin and gain their support for a new foray against the Iroquois, Anadabijou presented them with French axes, swords, kettles, ornaments, and with food (1:109). Later, when he was travelling up the St. Lawrence River to Montreal Island,

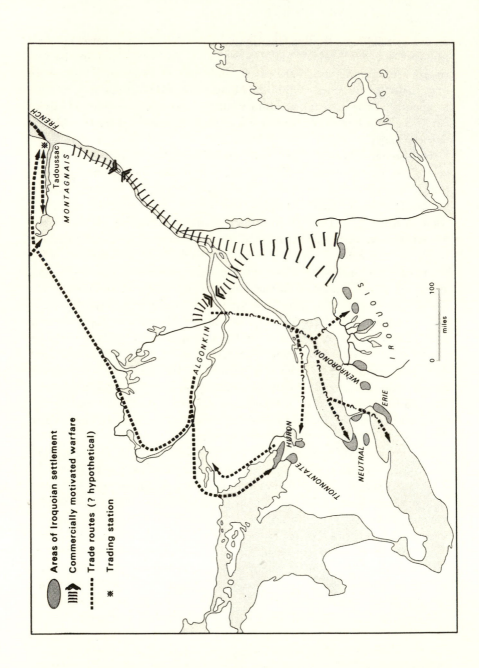

MAP 9. *Intertribal relations, 1603.*

Champlain encountered this confederated war party in a fortified camp at the mouth of the Richelieu River (1:141). They defeated three Iroquois canoes on Lake Champlain and returned to Tadoussac with the heads of the people they had killed. Before the French departed in mid-August, Begourat, the Montagnais leader of this party, entrusted his son to Gravé Du Pont, so that he might spend the winter in France. Begourat did this on the recommendation of Anadabijou, who was pleased by reports he had heard about the good treatment that the two Indians had received who had accompanied Gravé Du Pont to France the year before (1:188). Although the French do not appear to have reciprocated by leaving French youths to winter among the Montagnais, they had won the Indians' trust to the point that the latter were expressing their friendship in one of the most solemn ways known to them. They also expressed their sense of obligation for what they conceived of as being a military alliance with the French, by giving Gravé Du Pont an Iroquois woman captive to take back to France with him (1:188). Among the Iroquoians and Algonkians, the sharing of captives was the sign of a military alliance.

The trip which in 1603 took Champlain and Gravé Du Pont to within sight of the Lachine Rapids was for these men a valuable reconnaissance. From an ethnological point of view, it is of interest because it reveals that the St. Lawrence Valley was almost completely deserted for fear of the Iroquois, although it was a time of year when many people would normally have been using the river. Apart from the Algonkian war party already mentioned, only a few groups were encountered fishing, and most of these were below Quebec. Also of interest is the geographical information that Champlain collected from the Montagnais who accompanied him and from certain Algonkin he encountered on the way. Although Champlain misconstrued what he was told about Lake Huron to sustain his hopes of finding a short route to the Pacific Ocean, it is clear that these Indians had a good working knowledge of the lower Great Lakes and had travelled on them. They described the St. Lawrence River in detail, as well as Lakes Ontario, Erie, and parts of Lake Huron. All of Champlain's informants mentioned Niagara Falls and some were familiar with the Trent River flowing into Lake Ontario. The Montagnais had never been much farther than Lake Erie, but some of the Algonkin claimed to have travelled on Lake Huron, although none had been to the west end of the lake (1:153–161). It is not known whether such extensive travel was common among the Algonkin and Montagnais in prehistoric times, but it seems likely to have been stimulated, at least in part, by the fur trade. That the St. Lawrence Valley and the lower Great Lakes were open for travel at this time suggests that warfare between the four western Iroquois tribes, on the one hand, and the Huron and Algonkin, on the other, was not nearly so fierce as it was to become later.

In the course of his visit to the New World in 1603, Champlain became fascinated with the Maritime region of Canada. He saw it as a region with a milder climate than the St. Lawrence, potentially rich in mines, and possibly nearer an easier passage to the Far East than the St. Lawrence appeared to be. In 1603, Aymar de Chaste died and his monopoly passed to Pierre Du Gua de Monts. No doubt, Champlain's advice played an important part in de Monts's decision that while trading vessels would continue to be sent to the St. Lawrence, further efforts at colonization would be directed towards Acadia. A colony was established, first at the mouth of the Sainte Croix River in New Brunswick, and then at Port Royal in Nova Scotia. By 1607, however, it had become clear that it was impossible to enforce a monopoly along the winding and indented coasts of the Maritimes. Because of this, de Monts could not support a colony and compete on equal terms with those who were trading illegally. In 1607, the king, acting under pressure from the Paris hatters' corporation and from the merchants of St. Malo, who favoured free trade, had de Monts's privileges revoked, leaving him with a monopoly for only one more year. At this point, and again under Champlain's influence, de Monts began to turn his attention to the St. Lawrence, where furs were obtained at only a few critical points that could be policed more easily against rival traders. In the spring of 1608, Champlain was dispatched to the St. Lawrence to found a new settlement (Biggar 1901 : 51–68 ; 1922–36, 4 :27–30).

On 3 June Champlain arrived at Tadoussac which, because of navigational hazards farther up the St. Lawrence, was for many years to remain the head of navigation. There he must have renewed his acquaintance with Anadabijou and the other Indians he had met five years earlier. By reminding them of the benefits that they had agreed would flow from French settlement, he secured their consent to found a new colony up-river. Travelling beyond Tadoussac in a pinnace, he selected a site for the new trading post at the narrows of Quebec, a location that would allow the occupants to prevent illicit traders from passing up-river. A patch of forest was cleared and a storehouse and three buildings erected. This "Habitation" was surrounded by a palisade and a ditch fifteen feet wide. To test the soil, gardens were prepared and wheat, rye, and other European crops were sown.

Shortly after arriving at Quebec, Champlain barely escaped a plot, which he claimed was led by a locksmith named Jean Duval, to kill him and destroy the colony. Duval was said to be hoping for a reward from the Basque traders, whose commerce on the river was threatened by de Monts's monopoly (Biggar 1922–36, 2:25–34). By their action, he and his fellow conspirators also may have hoped to avoid a dangerous winter at Quebec. As a result of this conspiracy, the Indians were treated to what, to them, must have been the inexplicable sight of Duval's severed head being exposed by his own people from the most conspicuous point in their settlement.

During the summer of 1608, and the following disease-ridden winter, Champlain had ample opportunity to assess the situation on the St. Lawrence. In 1603, the Montagnais and their allies had been holding their own against the Iroquois and had been victorious in isolated skirmishes. Five years later, these Indians were still holding their own, but remained very much afraid of the Iroquois, who outnumbered them. The intervening period seems to have been largely one of inconclusive struggle. Although many Indians came to Quebec from mid-September to mid-October to fish for eels, they camped close to the French settlement and, on numerous occasions, their fear of the Iroquois was so great that they came to the habitation to spend the night. Champlain permitted the women and children to enter the habitation, but made the men stay outside, under French protection. These Indians expressed gratitude for the French presence and said that if the French remained at Quebec, they would learn to protect themselves (2:50–51). Later in the winter, the Indians left to hunt beaver and then elk. In February, they returned starving from the south shore of the river to beg food from the French, their supply of eels having run out long before (2:53–56). These Indians may have simply been enduring a hungry period in the early spring, or the weather that year may have produced a spell of bad hunting. More likely, however, Champlain was witnessing the disruption of a traditional subsistence pattern, resulting from fear of the Iroquois.

Since 1603, the Indians who lived in the valleys of the Batiscan, St. Maurice, and Ottawa Rivers had grown more accustomed to dealing with Europeans. An increasing number of Europeans may also have been travelling up the St. Lawrence to trade with them. In order to put an end to the Iroquois menace, so that these Indians could trade freely along the St. Lawrence, and to reinforce the prestige of de Monts's traders in the face of competition from freebooters, it was decided that a new policy was needed. Instead of merely supplying their Indian allies with weapons, henceforth armed Frenchmen would offer to travel with them on raids against the Iroquois, in an effort to defeat the enemy. We do not know

whether this idea originated with Champlain or Gravé Du Pont, who was
de Monts's deputy. Since de Monts's monopoly was about to expire, any
action that would strengthen his company's ties with the Indians of the
St. Lawrence must have seemed desirable. In addition, both Gravé Du
Pont and Champlain were keen to promote the exploration of the interior
and this would be achieved by Champlain accompanying his Indian allies
into regions that no European had yet visited. Early in 1608, Champlain
and Gravé Du Pont discussed plans for military aid to their Indian allies.
Later that year, Champlain seems to have agreed to accompany a Montagnais expedition up the Richelieu River the following summer (2:63–
64). In August, he conferred with the son of Iroquet, one of the most
important headmen of the Onontchataronon. Champlain declared that he
wished to help the Onontchataronon in their struggle against the Iroquois
and seems to have arranged a general rendezvous for the following year
(2:69). This meeting was to have important consequences, since the
Onontchataronon were in the habit of wintering among the Arendarhonon.

Whether or not Champlain had conceived of the idea, he was carrying
out a masterful piece of diplomacy. Up to this time, the French had sought
to maintain the goodwill of the Indians by arming them so they could better
fight their enemies, but they had only partly succeeded in their objective
of opening the St. Lawrence as a trading route. For a long time, the French
had hoped to arrange a peace between the Iroquois and Algonkians, so that
both groups would be free to trade with them (1:100, 137). Yet, the
French lacked the contacts, and their Indian allies the will, to bring this
about. By introducing themselves and their guns into the struggle, de
Monts's men hoped not only to drive the enemy from the St. Lawrence but
to confirm the goodwill of their allies. By this time, they must have
realized that among the Indians no better proof of goodwill could be
offered to trading partners than to join them in fighting their enemies.

The Huron and the Early French Fur Trade

Historical and archaeological evidence both indicate that the Huron were
obtaining European trade goods before they were in direct contact with the
French. It is more difficult, however, given the limited amount of archaeological evidence available, to determine when European goods began to
arrive in the Huron country. Sites containing small amounts of such goods
are found to the south and east of the area that the Huron occupied when

they were first described by Europeans in 1615. These sites extend into the southern part of Simcoe County and eastward into the Trent Valley system (map 10). Within the historic Huron country, a limited number of sites have been found that contain only small amounts of European goods. These contrast with a much larger number of historic sites, which occur only in this area and yield much larger quantities of European goods.

It is therefore clear that sometime prior to 1615, but after European goods had begun to reach this part of Ontario, Huron settlements extended over a considerably more extensive area than they did in the historic period. Either the population was larger or villages were less compactly clustered. While the possibility of population decline as a result of European diseases in the late sixteenth century cannot be ruled out, the scattered distribution of the villages containing small amounts of trade goods suggests that the population was, in fact, more dispersed.

Although the relative proportion of sites containing large quantities of European goods, as opposed to those containing small amounts, might be used to calculate when these goods began to arrive in the Huron country, this method is open to numerous objections and any conclusions derived from it must be treated with great caution. We do not know exactly when European goods began to reach the Huron in large quantities, although it was probably after direct contact was established with the French in 1615. While all of the sites outside the region known to have been inhabited in 1615 had been abandoned by this date, the distinction that is made between sites with large and small amounts of European goods within the area of historic settlement is based on very limited evidence (map 11). Finally, the areas outside the historic Huron country are less well surveyed, from an archaeological point of view, than are those inside it, and even certain parts of the historic region, particularly in the Penetanguishene Peninsula, have received more cursory treatment than the rest (Heidenreich, personal communication, 1970). Since we are dealing with shifting populations, this too may bias the results.

Nevertheless, approximately 117 sites containing large quantities of European goods are presently recorded within the area of Huron settlement in historic times.[38] If we assume that all these sites date after 1610 and that villages shifted on an average of once every ten years, this gives a total of twenty-nine sites per decade. This is more than the eighteen to twenty-five villages estimated to be in existence at any one time by the French,[39] although it is possible that this discrepancy reflects shortcomings in the historical data. Many small villages may have gone unrecorded, particularly in the eastern part of the Huron country, which was regularly visited by

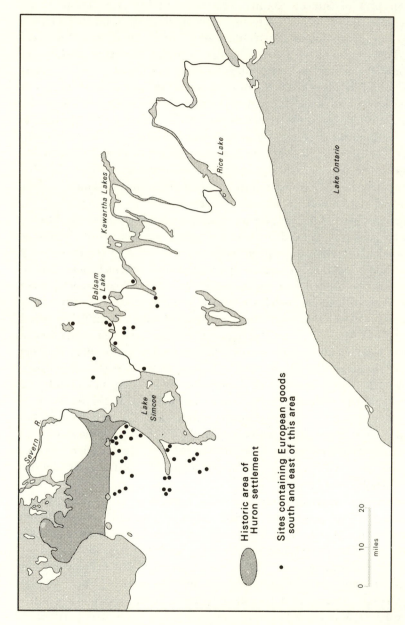

MAP 10. *Distribution of Huron sites containing small quantities of trade goods to the south and east of their area of settlement from 1615 onwards (after Heidenreich 1971: map 22).*

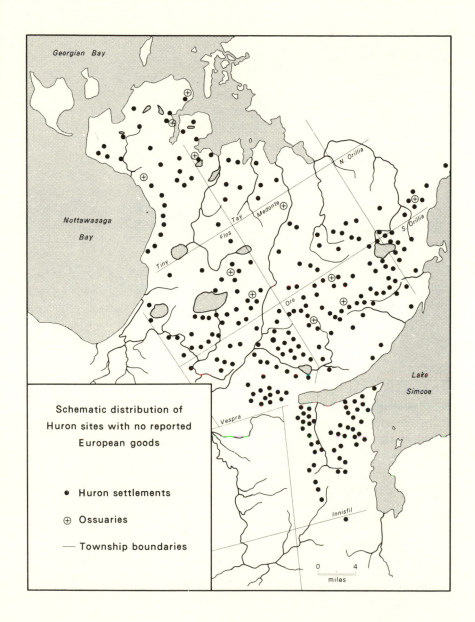

MAP 11. *Maps showing contraction of area of Huron settlement from prehistoric times into the historic period (sites dated in terms of quantities of European trade goods).*

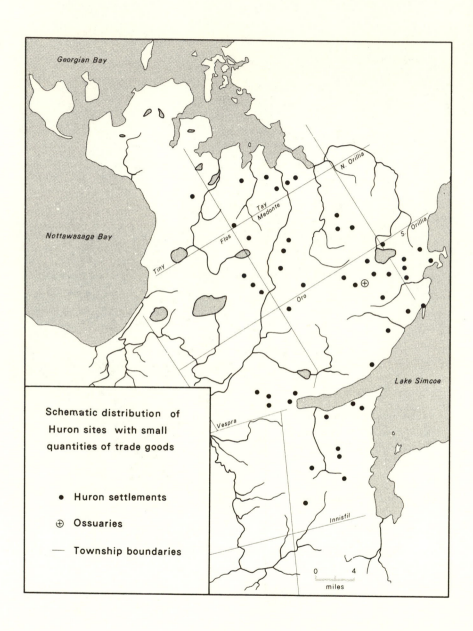

Georgian Bay

N. Orillia

Tay
Medonte

Nottawasaga Bay

Flos

Tiny

S. Orillia

⊕

Oro

Lake Simcoe

Schematic distribution of
Huron sites with small
quantities of trade goods

Vespra

● Huron settlements

⊕ Ossuaries

— Township boundaries

Innisfil

0   4

miles

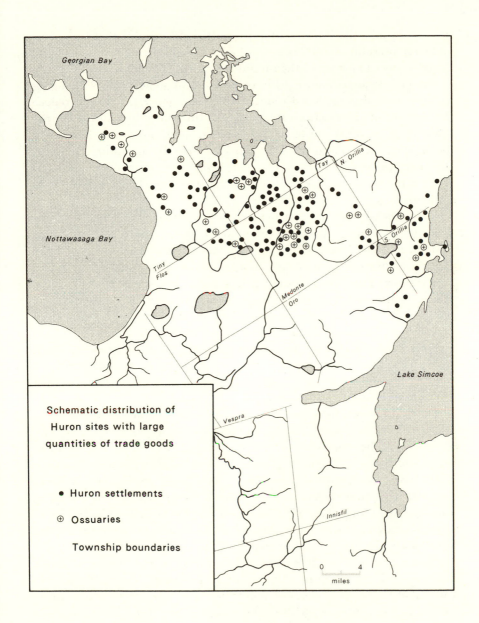

Georgian Bay

Nottawasaga Bay

Tay

N. Orillia

Tiny
Flos

S. Orillia

Medonte
Oro

Lake Simcoe

Vespra

Innisfil

Schematic distribution of
Huron sites with large
quantities of trade goods

● Huron settlements

⊕ Ossuaries

Township boundaries

0   4
miles

the French missionaries only after 1640. It is also possible that in earlier, and more peaceful, times this region had a more dispersed population, and hence produced more sites, than it did after 1640. The high mortality rate in the late 1630s is known to have resulted in some villages changing location twice during that decade; if this were general, it would reduce the number of villages in existence at one time to twenty-three. On the other hand, it is unrealistic to believe that all historic sites have been found, hence site counts are likely to go higher in the future. It must, therefore, be concluded that the archaeological enumeration includes out-lying hamlets and temporary stations that the French did not count as settlements.

Of the sixty-three sites that have been found to contain small amounts of European trade goods, thirty-six occur in the northern part of Simcoe County, fourteen in the south, and another thirteen to the east of Lake Simcoe. Estimating twenty-nine sites per decade, this would date the first appearance of European goods in the late 1580s or, using a lower site ratio, possibly a little earlier. While this argument is a highly circumstantial one, it is perhaps more than a coincidence that, on the basis of his study of an archaeological sequence of late Huron sites, William C. Noble (1971) has estimated that European goods did not appear in the Huron country much before 1580.[40] This suggests that the first appearance of such goods on a regular, though still limited basis, may correlate with the intensification of European trade on the St. Lawrence that began in 1580.

The earliest sites have yielded only very small quantities of European trade goods. The Sopher, Benson, and McKenzie sites each contained only a few items. These include one iron celt, an iron awl, a copper knife, sheet brass, and beads made out of rolled sheets of brass and copper. No glass beads have been reported from these sites. Metal beads were probably manufactured from broken kettles, which the Huron, or their trading partners, had cut up. The only trade item that has been described in detail so far is an iron celt that was associated with a bundle burial in the Sopher site ossuary. It was 113 millimetres long and was manufactured by the malleated fusion of two thin slabs of iron (Noble 1971). It had no socket and was evidently made in imitation of an Indian stone celt. It has been speculated that celts of this sort may have been hurriedly manufactured aboard ship in accordance with native specifications; however, it is equally probable that such tools already were being produced in Europe for barter with an Amerindian clientele. Slightly later but still probably dating around 1615, are the McMurchy, Graham-Rogers, and Warminster sites. These have produced a richer and more varied selection of trade goods, including brass rings, awls, and beads, iron hatchets, and glass beads. Numerous scraps of iron are also found on these sites. This indicates that, by the start of the historic period, increasing amounts of European material were reaching both the Huron and the Tionnontaté.

There is, however, no evidence that the Huron were trading directly with the French prior to 1609. In 1603, Champlain was informed that the Huron, who were called the "good Iroquois," were in the habit of bartering for French merchandise with the Algonkin. It was also from their Huron trading partners that Champlain's informants claimed to have heard about a copper mine to the north and from whom they had obtained some copper bracelets that they showed him (Biggar 1922–36, 1:164). One may assume that, by this time, the Huron had become interested in European goods, at least as novelties. Unlike the Iroquois, however, they had little trouble in obtaining what they wanted. The Algonkian traders were at best only marginally horticultural and were more than happy to exchange French goods for Huron corn, just as the Indians of the Maritimes exchanged European tools for corn with the Indians of Massachusetts. The Algonkians' role as middlemen in this trade became grafted onto an older exchange of meat and skins for Huron agricultural products. There is no direct evidence that the Nipissing and Ottawa engaged in trading European goods with the Huron much before 1615, although it is almost certain that they did. European goods must have been reaching these bands for some time, either up the Ottawa River or across central Quebec. Once they began receiving such goods, it would have been almost impossible not to share them with their Iroquoian trading partners in southern Ontario. The Nipissing and the Ottawa were probably the main suppliers for the Attignawantan, Attigneenongnahac, and possibly for the Tionnontaté. The Arendarhonon possibly got most of their trade goods from the Onontchataronon, who may have begun visiting them while they were still living in the Trent Valley. The arrival of St. Lawrence Iroquoian refugees who had been accustomed to receiving trade goods may have helped to stimulate the Arendarhonon's interest in such items. The interaction between the Arendarhonon and the Onontchataronon probably led to broader trading connections between the Huron and other Algonkian-speaking groups in the Ottawa Valley.

The quantity and type of European goods that were reaching the Huron do not appear significantly to have altered their daily life during the late prehistoric period. In particular, the technological impact of these goods must have been negligible. The most obvious change that can be observed in the archaeological record is the inclusion of trade goods and other valued items in ossuaries for the first time. This parallels the burial of European goods with the dead among the Iroquois and seems to indicate a growing interest in mortuary ceremonialism among both groups.

On the other hand, the influence of this early trade seems to have been considerably more far-reaching in its political consequences. It is not unreasonable to assume that a growing desire to trade with the northern Algonkians, by way of the long, but relatively easy Georgian Bay route, led the Arendarhonon and Tahontaenrat to settle in the northern part of Simcoe County as new members of the Huron confederacy, the former about 1590 and the latter about 1610 (Thwaites 1896–1901, 16:227–29). From about 1610 on, all the Huron tribes were living close to the shores of Georgian Bay and along minor waterways that allowed them to reach the bay easily. Whether the Tionnontaté were getting their European goods from the Huron or from their own northern Algonkian trading partners, their position was such that the Attignawantan were able to prevent them from travelling north. Moreover, with the formation of an expanded confederacy, the Attignawantan attained a political ascendancy that made it even easier for them to prevent the Tionnontaté from ever using this route (21:177).

The developments associated with the growth of the St. Lawrence fur trade broke down much of the localism that hitherto had been a feature of Iroquoian life. The disappearance of the St. Lawrence Iroquoians led to more intimate contacts between the Huron and Ottawa Valley Algonkin. As a result of these contacts, the Algonkin soon came to appreciate the value of Huron corn no less than did older trading partners, such as the Nipissing. The Iroquois also emerged as the main enemies of the Huron. Neither the Huron nor the Iroquois yet were as well-equipped with iron weapons as were the Algonkian allies of the French, nor did they have more than traditional motives for attacking one another. It is likely, however, that the new trade links between the Arendarhonon and the Onontchataronon caused Huron warriors to become involved in the hostilities of their allies; which resulted in growing conflict with the Onondaga, Oneida, and Mohawk. As more tribes joined the Huron and Iroquois confederacies and ceased to fight with one another, the young men of these confederacies would have found it necessary to direct their hostilities farther afield. Increasing warfare between these confederacies would have been an additional factor promoting their internal consolidation.

The development of trade in European goods also may have stimulated an expansion of trade generally. More interaction with the south is indicated by increasing amounts of marine shell in Huron sites. The first contacts between the Huron and the Susquehannock may date from this period, when the Susquehannock were also being stimulated to trade as a result of their own initial contacts with Europeans (W. Hunter 1959). The major changes, however, took place in southwestern Ontario. Huron control over goods coming from the north seems to have led to a cessation in their blood feuds with the Iroquoian tribes who lived to the south and west of them. The wars that the Huron had with the Tionnontaté in the late prehistoric period may reflect the latter's desire to share in this trade, but eventually such conflict seems to have given way to a mutually satisfactory trade, in which tobacco was exchanged for European goods (Thwaites 1896–1901, 20:43). The Neutral who were mainly suppliers of fancy furs and exotic goods from the south, were in a position to barter for European goods with both the Huron and the Iroquois and this may explain why they were friendly with both confederacies. The Neutral also seem to have been trading with the Algonkin at this period. Trading visits to the Neutral may have been one of the ways in which the Algonkin and Montagnais acquired their detailed knowledge of the lower Great Lakes.

It may be objected that I am exaggerating the influence of the still nascent fur trade. It must be remembered, however, that in the Indian history of this region, trading in exotic goods has often played a role that was out of all proportion to its utilitarian significance. It is therefore not surprising that, while the Huron were little affected technologically during this period of indirect trade, their political organization and foreign relations underwent extensive changes in response to it. What appears in the archaeological record as a few scraps of metal seems in fact to have been a sufficient catalyst to realize certain potentials for development that were inherent in prehistoric Huron society, but which otherwise might never have come to fruition.

Chapter 5   Forging an Alliance

The Huron on the St. Lawrence

THE FIRST ENCOUNTER

Although no detailed Huron account has been preserved concerning their first contact with the French, scraps of information recorded by the Jesuits in the 1640s reveal something about how the Huron remembered this event in later years. According to these accounts, the Huron first learned that European ships were coming to the St. Lawrence from neighbouring tribes, and, on the basis of this information, some Huron men decided to meet these newcomers for themselves (Thwaites 1896–1901, 39:49). The first who accomplished this were members of war parties, who, in the course of their excursions against the enemy, visited places where the French were trading with the Indians. Following these initial contacts, the Huron decided to secure a safe route to use to trade with the French every year (16:229). The first Huron to meet the French were members of the Arendarhonon tribe (20:19). Atironta, the principal headman of that tribe, was the first headman to go to Quebec to conclude an alliance with the French (20:35; 23:167).

It is tempting to assume that the war parties mentioned in these Huron traditions are the same ones that Champlain records as coming to the St. Lawrence in 1609 (Biggar 1922–36, 2:67–68). Nevertheless, two objections may be raised against the identification of these Huron stories with Champlain's account. First, the Huron dated their initial encounters with the French around A.D. 1600, rather than in 1609. Second, the first Huron headman to have dealings with Champlain was named Ochasteguin, not Atironta (ibid. 2:68).

The chronological objection is not a serious one. The Huron often referred to events taking place twenty, forty, or two hundred years into the past. These figures must be interpreted as signifying general periods of time, rather than a precise number of years; hence "forty years ago" may easily refer to an event that took place in 1609. The different names given for the Huron headman who first had dealings with the French are a greater difficulty. Names of individual Indians appear in a variety of forms, even in accounts by the same authors, and Champlain often confused the issue further, by failing to mention that Indian leaders with whom he had dealings were ones that he had written about earlier.[1] In spite of this, Ochasteguin and Atironta are both mentioned in the account of his voyage of 1615, so they cannot be merely variants of the same name. Ochasteguin does not appear in Champlain's accounts after 1615, whereas Atironta, the principal headman of the Arendarhonon, was a prominent figure throughout the whole segment of Huron history that we are considering.[2] It is possible that Ochasteguin was the name of an individual who later inherited the principal chieftainship of the Arendarhonon, in which case he would have been a close relative of the Atironta Champlain met in 1615. On the other hand, he may have been a less prominent Arendarhonon and eventually the Arendarhonon, for political or ritual reasons, may have chosen to pay less attention to his early encounters with the French. Atironta's visit to Quebec in 1616, which immediately followed Champlain's journey to the Huron country, seems to have been remembered by the Arendarhonon as marking the conclusion of a formal alliance between them and the French (Thwaites 1896–1901, 20:35; 23:167). On this basis, we may conclude that the first direct contact between the Huron and the French took place in 1609, while a formal alliance was concluded between them seven years later. This allows us to offer the following reconstruction of the events leading up to this alliance.

THE BATTLE OF LAKE CHAMPLAIN

In chapter 4, it was mentioned that in the summer of 1608 the son of Iroquet, one of the important headmen of the Onontchataronon, came to Quebec. There he was much impressed by the newly constructed French habitation and told Champlain about the conflict that his people were having with the Iroquois. Champlain said that he and Gravé Du Pont were anxious to help the Onontchataronon in their wars and invited them to join the French and the Montagnais on a military expedition up the Richelieu the following summer.

This novel French offer to fight alongside their Indian allies seems to have particularly interested the Onontchataronon, since the latter were anxious to avenge an act of treachery that the Iroquois had committed against them during a period of truce (Biggar 1922–36, 2:69). In the autumn, Iroquet and some of his people no doubt made their way up the

Ottawa River and travelled by way of Lake Nipissing and Georgian Bay to the territory of the Arendarhonon, where they camped for the winter near one of the large Arendarhonon villages, probably Cahiagué. While there, Iroquet seems to have invited some of his Arendarhonon trading partners to accompany him on the raid that was planned for the following summer. A small group of warriors, led by Ochasteguin, agreed to do this. They were anxious to meet the French and possibly to trade with them. Primarily, however, they seem to have been interested in winning renown by going to war alongside these strangers, who possessed a limitless supply of metal tools and powerful weapons that made a noise like thunder. In the company of the Onontchataronon, they would experience no difficulty travelling down the Ottawa River. Had they been alone, it might have been difficult to secure rights of passage, particularly if middlemen, such as the Kichesipirini, did not wish them to contact the French.

On the way down the Ottawa, this nucleus of Huron and Onontchataronon warriors was joined by many Algonkin men and women, who were interested only in trading with the French. By mid-June, this group, now swollen to some two to three hundred people, reached St. Eloi Island, near the mouth of the Batiscan River. There they heard rumours that the French did not intend to help them against the Iroquois, but were interested only in their furs (2:71). These rumours were probably started by the Montagnais, or possibly by Algonkin groups, who were angry that Iroquet was planning to introduce his Arendarhonon allies to the French.

Despite a cruel winter, during which most of his men had died from scurvy and dysentery, Champlain was enthusiastically awaiting the opportunity to explore the Richelieu River. On 5 June 1609, he learned that Gravé Du Pont had arrived at Tadoussac and, two days later, he set out to meet him there. The two men proposed that Champlain should embark on his proffered expedition, accompanied by twenty armed Frenchmen, while Gravé Du Pont would attend to the affairs of the settlement and supervise the trading at Tadoussac (2:63–64). Champlain returned to Quebec and had a shallop fitted out for his trip up-river. He left Quebec on 12 June in the company of his Montagnais allies, and a few days later reached St. Eloi Island, where he found the Algonkin and Arendarhonon waiting for him.

Two days were spent exchanging information and greetings. Iroquet explained that he and his men were there to fight the Mohawk and that he had solicited Indians who had never before seen a European to make an alliance with the French and join the federated Algonkian tribes in their war against the Iroquois. Iroquet and Ochasteguin both presented Champlain with gifts of furs and asked him to have guns fired for the benefit of those who had never encountered them before. Champlain did this and noted the astonishment of the newcomers when they heard them. The Indians also asked if they might visit Quebec before they set off for war, both to gratify their curiosity about the buildings that had been erected there and so that those who had brought furs might trade them. Champlain agreed, pointing out that he had brought no merchandise with him, since his sole aim was to help his Indian allies in their wars. He specifically repudiated the now familiar rumour that he was interested only in trade. The Algonkin and Arendarhonon, for their part, denied that they ever had heard such accusations made against him (2:71).

Champlain and the Indians returned to Quebec, where five or six days were spent eating, dancing, and trading. Gravé Du Pont was summoned from Tadoussac and arrived with two shallops full of French traders. To create additional goodwill, Champlain announced that Gravé Du Pont was sending some of these men to fight alongside his Indian allies and might come himself. On 28 June both men set off up the St. Lawrence but, by the time they had reached Point Platon, Gravé Du Pont seems to have decided that, since the trading was over, his time would be spent better elsewhere (2:73). Accordingly, Champlain was dispatched up-river, but with only nine Frenchmen to fight alongside him.

At the mouth of the Richelieu River, Champlain was surprised when most Algonkin men who, unknown to him, had never intended to accompany his expedition, continued up-river with their wives and the European merchandise they had obtained (2:76). This left sixty warriors who were prepared to do battle with the Iroquois. The war party was composed of Ochasteguin and Iroquet and their men, and some Montagnais (2:104, 105). It is doubtful that any Arendarhonon chose to return home at this time; from the beginning, Ochasteguin's followers had probably numbered no more than twenty.

On reaching the Chambly Rapids, Champlain found it impossible to move his shallop farther up-stream. He scolded the Indians for not warning him about this barrier, although it was no barrier to them. He was also acting unreasonably, since he had personally experienced difficulty when he had attempted to explore the Richelieu River in 1603 (1:141–42). He decided to send the shallop and most of his men back to Quebec and to continue south by canoe, in the company of the Indians and two French volunteers (2:80–81; map 12).

After the arduous portage around the Chambly Rapids, Champlain had an opportunity to begin observing the methods of waging war that were customary among the Indians of eastern North America. However much

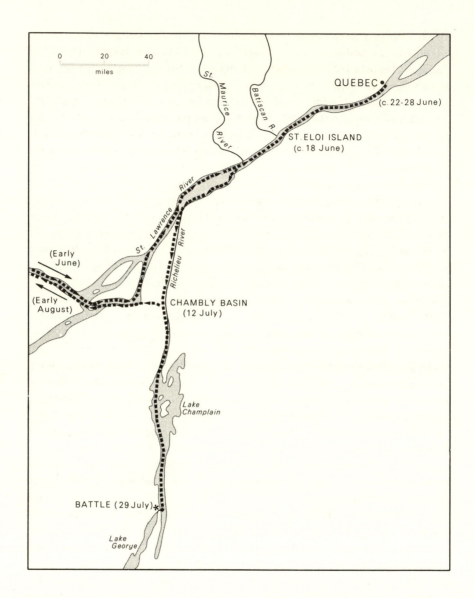

MAP 12. *Route followed by the Huron and Algonkin who accompanied the 1609 expedition against the Mohawk.*

the conflict between the Iroquois and the Algonkians had been heightened by Mohawk attacks on the St. Lawrence, techniques of warfare remained largely traditional on both sides. For seventeen days, the Indian war party travelled south along the Richelieu River and the west side of Lake Champlain. During the daylight hours, they split into three groups. Scouts went ahead to look for signs of the enemy, while the main body of warriors remained some distance behind, well-armed and prepared to give battle. The hunters, whose job was to provide game for the band, stayed in the rear (Biggar 1922–36, 2:85).

Every evening, the warriors hauled their canoes up along the shore, erected their temporary bark cabins, and felled trees to form a barricade around their camp on the landward side. This work took about two hours. Scouts were sent out, and, if they reported everything safe within several miles of the camp, the entire war party went to sleep for the night. Champlain criticized the lack of a night-watch, but was told by the Indians that they would be unable to work all day without a good night's sleep. He also observed shamans performing an Algonkian shaking tent ceremony each evening, in an effort to divine the movements of the enemy. Champlain states that he spared no effort to expose the folly of such practices and the general deceitfulness of shamans (2:86–88). No doubt, these harangues were almost incomprehensible to the Indians, which was fortunate, since, if they had been understood, they would almost certainly have offended his hosts. On the other hand, Champlain was impressed by the manner in which headmen discussed strategy and repeatedly drilled their men, so that no confusion would arise in battle (2:88–89). In a composite force of this kind, such drill was particularly necessary.

As the Indians moved south, Champlain collected a considerable amount of misinformation, which in part reflects the linguistic difficulties he was having. He was probably told that, because of the wars between the Mohawk and the Algonkin, the no man's land around Lake Champlain was no longer safe for hunting. He interpreted this to mean that, because of these wars, a formerly sedentary population had been driven from this area (2:90). He also believed that the Iroquois were living east as well as west of Lake Champlain at this period (2:93).[3]

Farther south, the Indians travelled only at night, and spent the days hidden in the forest. To escape detection by the enemy they did not light fires, and their main food was corn meal soaked in cold water to make a kind of porridge. As the chance of encountering the enemy increased, they became more attentive to dreams and other forms of divination, and eventually even Champlain began to report favourable dreams in order to encourage his companions (2:95).

Around ten o'clock on the evening of 29 July, Champlain's party spotted about two hundred Iroquois warriors. Both sides were intent on fighting, but, in accordance with their common traditions, neither wished to fight at night. This was a practice that the Iroquoians justified by saying that they desired the sun to witness their valour. The Iroquois landed and erected a strong barricade on the shore of the lake, near Point Ticonderoga, while the Algonkians and Arendarhonon spent the night on the lake, with their boats tied together so as not to become separated in the darkness. Throughout the night, the Iroquois danced and sang, and the protagonists on both sides boasted about their courage and shouted insults at their foes. Charges and countercharges were exchanged, suggesting that the leading warriors on both sides knew one another personally. The French remained under cover, so that their presence would come as a surprise to the enemy once the battle had begun. After preparing their arms, they separated, each going with a different canoeload of Montagnais, whom they recognized in this manner as being their oldest and most important allies (Biggar 1922–36, 2:97).

At dawn, the Algonkians and Arendarhonon landed and the Iroquois came out of their fort. Both sides lined up and prepared to do battle. Champlain regretted that his allies could not understand him, since he believed that if they had he could have led them in such a way as to exterminate the enemy (2:98). As it was, Champlain found himself participating in a traditional encounter, in which he could only hope to show his courage and goodwill. As soon as the Arendarhonon and Algonkians landed, they began to run toward the enemy, who remained near their fort. Nearer the Iroquois, they parted ranks in the centre and Champlain advanced some twenty paces ahead of the rest. They continued to move forward in this formation until Champlain was within fifty feet of the enemy. The Iroquois, astounded to see an armoured Frenchman, stood motionless for a time, gazing at him. Then, as they were preparing to fire a volley of arrows, Champlain raised his musket and aimed it towards the three headmen who were their leaders (plate 21). These men, each of whom wore wooden body armour, had been pointed out to Champlain by the Montagnais. When he fired, two of these headmen fell dead and another Mohawk was mortally wounded. This unexpected development caused great alarm among the Iroquois, which was intensified when another Frenchman fired at them from behind the trees. The Iroquois and the allied Indians began shooting arrows at each other, but the former quickly

PLATE 21. *Battle of Lake Champlain, 30 July 1609. From Champlain's Voyages of 1613. This engraving shows Champlain and two French musketeers assisting the Algonkians and the Huron in a skirmish with the Iroquois. On the right is shown the temporary camp in which the Iroquois had spent the night. The canoes look like French riverboats and the nudity of the Indians and their erroneous hairstyles undermine the credibility of the picture. The hammocks and palm trees are borrowed from scenes of Latin America. Under these circumstances it is difficult to accept S. E. Morison's (1972: 110–11) claim that Champlain drew this picture, quixotically borrowing the exotic elements from de Bry and other sources. Courtesy Public Archives of Canada.*

lost courage and fled into the woods, whither they were pursued by Champlain and his companions. Ten or twelve Iroquois were taken prisoner and perhaps fifty more were slain. By contrast, Champlain's Indians suffered only a few wounds. A large amount of Indian corn was plundered from the camp that the Iroquois had abandoned, as well as some suits of slat armour that the Iroquois had learned was not bullet proof (2:98–101).

After feasting and celebrating for several hours, the victors rapidly withdrew northward. That evening, they began torturing one of the prisoners. Eventually, his screams led Champlain to rebuke his allies for their cruelty and, since the prisoner was already almost dead, he offered to shoot him to put an end to his suffering. When the Indians refused to permit this, saying that they did not wish the Iroquois to have an easy death, Champlain walked away in anger. Seeing this, the Indians gave him permission to shoot the prisoner, which he did immediately (2:101–3). While one may wonder why Champlain waited so long before intervening, to his credit it must be noted that the ritual torture practised by the Indians did not disgust most seventeenth-century Europeans to the extent we imagine it should have done. Mutilations and prolonged and brutal forms of execution were part of the hangman's art in all parts of Europe at this time; so that Europeans who came to the New World were generally familiar with the sort of cruelties that the Indians practised. Champlain's anger was less an emotional revulsion against cruelty than the result of his conviction that his allies were acting unfairly in so treating a prisoner of war. It is doubtful that he would have objected to the torturing of someone who was guilty of treason, heresy, or sexual deviancy. Because he abhorred cannibalism, Champlain was also angered by efforts to compel the other Iroquois prisoners to eat the heart of the dead man.

When they reached the Chambly Rapids, the Algonkin and Arendarhonon departed for their own country. They travelled due west to the St. Lawrence River, thereby avoiding a long journey to the mouth of the Richelieu River and up the St. Lawrence to Montreal Island. No doubt, they took home with them their share of Iroquois prisoners and scalps, as evidence of their success. Before they left, Champlain promised that he would meet them the following summer at the mouth of the Richelieu River to assist them further in their wars. The Arendarhonon and the Algonkin, for their part, promised that as many as four hundred men would come with them and that, after their annual raid against the Iroquois, they would take Champlain inland and show him the Huron country, as well as some of the copper mines farther north (2:104–5; 119; 121–22). Such prospects for exploring the interior and establishing trading links between de Monts's company and tribes living north and west of the St. Lawrence must have greatly encouraged Champlain and justified the policy of personal involvement in Indian wars.

After the Arendarhonon and Algonkin had departed, Champlain travelled down the St. Lawrence River with the Montagnais. They stopped briefly at Quebec, where Champlain gave his companions bread and dried peas, as well as some beads they had requested to decorate the severed heads of their enemies. Then they continued down-river to Tadoussac, where the Montagnais were greeted by their relatives. Following local custom, the Montagnais women undressed themselves and swam out to the canoes to claim the heads of their enemies, which they later suspended around their necks for their dances. Numerous ceremonies followed, in the course of which the Montagnais promised that next year they would take Champlain up the St. Maurice River and show him the Northern Ocean (2:118–19). Thus, from the point of view of exploring, Champlain added another string to his bow. Several days later, a group of Algonkin from the upper Ottawa Valley arrived at Quebec, expressing regret that they had not been present at the recent victory and presenting Champlain with furs as a token of their appreciation for the help he had given to their friends (2:107). While gifts were expected in return as evidence of reciprocal goodwill, these presents were further proof that the new policy was successful as a means of gaining influence among the northern peoples and establishing trading alliances with them.

In September, Champlain and Gravé Du Pont returned to France leaving Pierre Chauvin, a Huguenot merchant and sea captain from Dieppe, in command at Quebec. Champlain reported on the success of his expedition to de Monts and described his voyage to the king, whom he presented with an Indian girdle made of porcupine quills (2:110). During the winter, Champlain must have watched with anxiety the increasing hopelessness of de Monts's efforts to secure a renewal of his monopoly over trade along the upper St. Lawrence. The hopes that both men had for maintaining the settlement at Quebec and exploring the interior depended, at the very least, on securing such a monopoly. Free trade won the day, however, and, until 1613, no new monopoly was granted. The old monopoly had already lapsed prior to the trading in 1609, but during that year there had been little competition for furs.

The threat of competition for the following year was, however, much greater and, faced with it, traders were unwilling to bear the additional costs involved in maintaining a permanent settlement at Quebec. De Monts was anxious to continue the settlement and, by hard persuasion, managed to form a company with some Rouen merchants, on condition that the settlement function as a warehouse for the fur trade. Yet, in the face of continuing free trade, even this arrangement had little hope of surviving for long (Biggar 1901:74).

THE BATTLE OF THE RICHELIEU

When Champlain arrived at Tadoussac on 26 May 1610, he found sixty Montagnais warriors awaiting his return. A few days later, when these Indians visited Quebec, Champlain was informed that some of the Basques and merchants from St. Malo, who had come to trade, were promising the Indians that they too would send men to fight alongside them. The Indians said that they regarded these promises as false ones that were designed to lure them into trading, and they ridiculed these traders as women who only wanted to make war on their beavers (Biggar 1922–36, 2:121). While the Montagnais were anxious to convince Champlain that their greatest friendship was reserved for him and Gravé Du Pont, their behaviour suggests that they were interested in obtaining good prices for their furs and would sell them, whenever possible, to the highest bidder. Their expressions of scorn for the other European merchants were intended mainly to curry favour with Champlain. Nevertheless, their desire for an alliance with Champlain probably gave de Monts's traders some advantage in their dealings with the Montagnais, especially when they were in a position to observe the latter having dealings with rival European traders.

While still at Tadoussac, Champlain was annoyed to learn that the Montagnais insisted on deferring their promise to show him the St. Maurice River until the following year (2:119). Already once, in 1608, these same Indians had been unwilling to let him, or any other Frenchman, accompany them up the Saguenay River beyond Tadoussac (2:19). The Montagnais obviously remained anxious to prevent the French from making direct contact with their trading partners in the interior of northern Quebec. Champlain still had hopes of travelling inland with the Arendarhonon; therefore, although he had been deceived by the Montagnais, he decided to ignore the slight.

Since speed was essential, if rival traders were not to carry off most of the furs from the upper St. Lawrence, Champlain left for Quebec two days after he arrived at Tadoussac. At Quebec, he found the French colony in good health and provided a feast for Batiscan, the headman of the Three Rivers area, who, in return, honoured him with another feast (2:120).

After the Montagnais arrived from Tadoussac, both groups of Indians decided to go up-river to await the arrival of the Onontchataronon and Arendarhonon at the mouth of the Richelieu River. Champlain promised to follow them and to send four shallops loaded with merchandise to trade with the Indians from the interior (2:121–22). He seems to have had two reasons for having arranged this rendezvous so far up the St. Lawrence River the previous year. First, it was to ensure that it would be within any new monopoly zone. Unfortunately, no monopoly had materialized, nor was Champlain able to prevent other traders from following de Monts's boats up-river to the appointed meeting place. Second, by establishing a trading centre on the upper St. Lawrence, Champlain hoped to develop more direct relations with the Algonkin and Arendarhonon who, although friends of the Montagnais, had to come as their guests when they traded at Tadoussac or Quebec. By establishing a trading station within Algonkin territory, Champlain hoped to forge a direct, rather than an indirect, bond between the Algonkin and the French. In this endeavour, he was completely successful. From this time on, trade took place separately at Tadoussac and on the upper St. Lawrence. Much as the Montagnais may have resented this arrangement, their fear of the Iroquois and need for an alliance in which they could rely on the support of the French and the Algonkin were sufficient to suppress overt opposition. Relations with the Arendarhonon remained indirect, inasmuch as they were still meeting the French as guests of the Onontchataronon, just as the Algonkin had previously traded with the French as allies of the Montagnais.

Champlain left Quebec to go up-river on 14 June. About twenty miles from Quebec, he encountered a canoe containing a Montagnais and an Algonkin, who were coming to tell him that in two days two hundred Arendarhonon and Algonkin would be arriving at the Richelieu River and that another party, led by Iroquet and Ochasteguin, would be arriving a little later. The Algonkin, who was a headman, presented Champlain with a piece of native copper a foot long, that he said he had obtained on the bank of a river where there were more pieces like it (2:123).

At the mouth of the St. Maurice River, Champlain found the Montagnais and the four shallops that had gone up-river waiting for him. The Montagnais entreated Champlain to recognize them as the oldest allies of the French by continuing to travel in their canoes when they went to war. Champlain promised to do this (2:124). The next day, the whole group travelled up Lake St. Peter and arrived at St. Ignace Island, directly opposite the mouth of the Richelieu River. There, the Montagnais began felling trees to clear a space for their camp, while they awaited the arrival of the

Huron and Algonkin, who were travelling to the rendezvous by way of Chambly. Soon, a canoe arrived at the Montagnais camp bringing word that the Huron and Algonkin had fallen in with a hundred Iroquois who had erected a fortified camp about four miles up the Richelieu River.

The Montagnais immediately decided to help their allies and asked Champlain to accompany them, which he agreed to do. He departed, taking with him four other Frenchmen who were under his command. The independent traders who were at the mouth of the Richelieu refused to join in this battle, except for Captains Thibaut and Des Prairies and their crews. The French and Indians made their way to the south shore of the St. Lawrence and proceeded across the narrow neck of land between the St. Lawrence and Richelieu Rivers to the Iroquois encampment. Marshes and dense woods hindered the French, who were wearing pike-men's armour and, because of this, the Montagnais reached the site of battle well ahead of them. There, the Montagnais and the Indians from the Ottawa Valley were repulsed in a premature assault on the fort, in the course of which several headmen were slain; however, the arrival of the French revived the spirits of the survivors. Both sides began firing swarms of arrows, one of which pierced Champlain's ear and entered his neck. The French fired on the Iroquois, but while, at first, the noise of the guns frightened them, they soon began to drop to the ground while the guns were being discharged, to avoid being struck by the shot.[4] Seeing that he was running out of ammunition, Champlain requested his Indian allies to take cover behind their shields and attach ropes to the logs that supported the barricade around the Iroquois fort (plate 22). The French covered the Indians with musket fire while they did this. Then, reinforced by Des Prairies's men, the French and their allies stormed the fort, swords in hand, and killed all but fifteen of its occupants. The rest were taken prisoner (2:125–34).

The only booty found inside the camp were some beaver skin robes and the blood-stained fur clothing worn by the dead. The Indians did not bother to plunder the latter and derided the French who did so. This shows that, while the Indians valued European goods, the desire or necessity of obtaining them had not yet eroded traditional values, which included scorn for an act of greed of this sort. The Indians scalped the dead or cut off their heads as trophies, and returned to St. Ignace Island, taking their prisoners with them. The next day was spent trading with the French and torturing several prisoners, whose flesh was fed to the dogs (2:135–37). The other prisoners remained in the possession of the Montagnais and Algonkin, who reserved a similar fate for them in their villages. Champlain claimed as his

PLATE 22. *Battle of the Richelieu River, 19 June 1610. From Champlain's Voyages of 1613. Although there are no hammocks or palm trees in this engraving, the depiction of the Indians suggests that it was produced in the same manner as the preceding illustration. Courtesy Public Archives of Canada.*

share of the booty an Iroquois prisoner, whom he hoped would be useful for promoting peace among the warring tribes of the region.

The battle of 1609 on Lake Champlain has been studied by historians more carefully than has this one. In particular, it has been debated whether or not Champlain should be censured for arousing the fury of the Iroquois, by attacking them without provocation at that time (Trudel 1966*a*:165–67). The battle of the Richelieu was a more important event, however, because it marks the last time that the Mohawk were to be a serious threat in the St. Lawrence Valley until 1634. Desrosiers (1947*a*:47) estimated that, in the major defeats the Mohawk had suffered on the St. Lawrence since A.D. 1600, they had lost 250 warriors and argued that it was these losses which compelled them to cease their attacks. While the figures on which Desrosiers's estimate is based are probably inflated, it cannot be doubted that these raids had been extremely costly for a tribe whose total population was probably no more than 5,000 and which, throughout much of this period, seems also to have been at war with the Susquehannock.[5] The loss of at least two of their headmen at Ticonderoga had been a serious blow to the Mohawk and this bloody defeat on the Richelieu, combined with knowledge that the Europeans were now actively and consistently aiding their Algonkian opponents, must have made them dread the prospect of further campaigns on the St. Lawrence. While the Iroquois quickly developed techniques to avoid being killed by French musketfire, guns continued to frighten them for a long time. Iroquois raiders continued to operate along the Ottawa River until the early 1620s, when they were frightened away by armed Frenchmen, who had begun to travel up that river in larger numbers (Wrong 1939:261).

Yet, serious as these losses may have been, they do not by themselves explain the Mohawk's decision to cease their attacks on the St. Lawrence Valley. For the preceding thirty years, that region had been the sole source of iron tools for the Mohawk. In 1609, Henry Hudson, an Englishman in the pay of the Dutch East India Company, ascended the Hudson River as far as the Albany area, thereby discovering the trading potential of that portion of the river. By a strange coincidence, this happened only about five weeks after Champlain had engaged the Iroquois at Ticonderoga, a mere eighty miles away. While the initial Dutch contacts were with the Mahican, who lived along both banks of the river, trade quickly developed with the Mohawk, whose territory lay to the west (O'Callaghan 1856–87, 1:14). Although intermittent conflicts with the Mahican may have disrupted these early contacts, the Mohawk eventually found peaceful trade with the Dutch a preferable alternative to their increasingly costly struggle

on the St. Lawrence. The opening up of an alternative source of European
trade goods is probably no less important than the defeats they suffered on
the St. Lawrence for explaining the Mohawk's decision to abandon their
attacks on that area.

The day after the first Mohawk prisoners were killed, Iroquet and
Ochasteguin arrived. Both of them regretted not being present for the
battle. They were accompanied by about eighty men, which brings the
total number of Huron and Algonkin who descended the Ottawa River that
year to about three hundred. About two hundred of these are said never to
have seen a European before. Since the tribes from the upper Ottawa
Valley had been visiting Tadoussac since at least 1600, this suggests that a
large portion of these Indians were from the Huron country. The Indians
remained on St. Ignace Island for three more days, engaging in trade
while their leaders continued to confer with the French (Biggar 1922–36,
2:138).

SAVIGNON AND BRÛLÉ

Champlain wished to have a young Frenchman who had already survived
two winters at Quebec learn the Algonkin language, and for this purpose
he proposed to have him spend the winter with Iroquet and his people. The
man he had in mind appears to have been Etienne Brûlé, who was then
about eighteen years old.[6] Brûlé had already expressed a desire to live with
the Indians and Champlain and Gravé Du Pont believed that, in addition
to learning to speak a native language, he could gather valuable information
concerning the geography and peoples of the interior.

Iroquet agreed to take Brûlé, but the other Algonkin headmen objected
to this arrangement. They argued that if an accident were to befall him
while he was in the care of the Indians, the French might seek blood
revenge. Champlain conferred with these headmen and informed them
that, by refusing to take this man, they were incurring his displeasure. He
said that to accept Brûlé would strengthen their ties with the French and
that if Brûlé perished from illness or enemy attack, the French would not
hold his hosts accountable. Eventually, the headmen accepted Champlain's
proposal, but insisted that Champlain reciprocate by taking a young Indian
to France for the winter so that he could report to his people what he had
seen there. Champlain agreed to the exchange and was given custody of
Savignon, who was the brother of a Huron headman named Tregouaroti
(Biggar 1922–36, 2:138–42, 186).

This is the first record of a Frenchman and an Indian being exchanged and sent to live for a time with each other's people. By conforming with a custom that Indian trading partners used to express goodwill and to guard against treachery, de Monts's traders took another step towards establishing an enduring relationship with the Indians of the interior. Such exchanges between French and Indian trading partners were to become the basis on which, in later years, many Frenchmen (who were all considered by the Indians to be tribesmen and therefore, in some sense, relatives of one another) were to live in security in the Huron country. Sending young Frenchmen to live with the Indians would also produce a proficient staff of interpreters and trading agents. By dwelling with the Indians, these men were to learn the customs of different tribes and become successful intermediaries in the dealings that these tribes had with the French.

The three-cornered exchange that was arranged between French, Huron, and Algonkin is understandable only if we assume that Iroquet was planning to spend the following winter among the Arendarhonon, as he and some of his people seem to have been doing regularly at this period. Officially, he and his followers would have provided the Arendarhonon with the required assurance for Savignon's return. In practice, however, the security was probably even more direct. Brûlé likely spent the winter living with a Huron, rather than an Algonkin, family, since, for the rest of his life, he worked as an interpreter among the Huron rather than among the Algonkin. Champlain did not explain, and probably never knew, how or why Iroquet and Ochasteguin arranged this complicated exchange. The Arendarhonon were probably anxious to have one of their young men live with the French, in the hope that this would establish closer ties between their peoples and eliminate the need to rely on Algonkian interpreters; however, since Iroquet had introduced these two groups, the Onont-chataronon were still officially viewed by the Huron as intermediaries between themselves and the French. The exchange was therefore arranged so as to recognize, at least in a nominal way, this prior relationship.

Champlain does not say why he did not attempt to travel up the Ottawa River, as he had originally planned to do. Certainly, he would have been a welcome visitor among the Huron. It is likely, however, that he was deterred by his wound and, even more so, by a desire to return to France quickly. Competition from the independent traders had been severe, both at the mouth of the Richelieu River and at Tadoussac, and Champlain must have been worried that de Monts's associates would again be threatening to withdraw their support. It is also possible that Algonkin groups such as the Kichesipirini, who wished to remain intermediaries in the trade with the Huron, were opposed to Champlain visiting the Huron country. Their opposition may have played a part in his decision not to attempt a journey into the interior at that time. Champlain promised the Arendarhonon and Algonkin that he would meet them the following year at the foot of the Lachine Rapids. He hoped that by again moving the trading station up-river, de Monts's traders might be able to outstrip their competitors.

Champlain returned to Quebec with Savignon and the Iroquois prisoner he had claimed as part of his spoils. While he was supervising the fortification of the French settlement, the prisoner escaped. Champlain states that he fled from fear of being tortured, in spite of the assurances given him by a woman of his tribe whom the French had living at Quebec (2:143). This woman was probably the Iroquois prisoner the Montagnais had given to Gravé Du Pont in 1603, and whom he had taken back to France with him. It is a sad commentary on the inadequacy of our sources concerning the Indians that we know nothing about what this woman was doing at Quebec in 1610, or what eventually became of her.

Jean de Godet Du Parc was left in command at Quebec when Champlain departed for France on 13 August. He was accompanied by Savignon, who became the first Huron to travel to Europe and to be presented at the French court. Because of Sagard and Lescarbot, we know more about his stay in France than we do about the Indians who were taken there in earlier times. Savignon seems to have been about the same age as Brûlé. He probably had participated in military expeditions and, while he lacked the political maturity and ritualistic knowledge of older men, he would have had an adult's knowledge of Huron customs and a corresponding pride in them. Sagard's comment that he was too old to learn well (1866:331) merely indicates that he was not as amenable to being taught French ways as the priests would have liked; which may explain why they do not seem to have baptized him. Lescarbot (1907–14, 3:22) saw Savignon in Paris, and described him as a tall, sturdy youth who enjoyed ridiculing Frenchmen whenever he saw them quarrelling without coming to blows. Huron men did not engage in verbal disputes and were not supposed to interrupt one another; hence to Savignon verbal quarrels appeared effeminate. When he returned to his people, Savignon praised the excellent treatment he had received in France, but never expressed any serious desire to return there (Sagard 1866:332). Like most Indians, he was appalled by the capital and corporal punishment that was a conspicuous feature of life in the French capital. He was also disturbed to see Europeans beating their children and physically restraining them. In later years, Savignon told his people that the French killed and hurt individuals without distinguishing the innocent from the guilty (ibid. 320). He said that if Huron children were allowed to go to France they were in danger of being beaten or killed there.

Someone unfamiliar with the Huron might dismiss such sentiments as the idealized reactions that a European author put into the mouth of an unsullied "noble savage," whom he wished to portray encountering the corruptions of civilized life. Knowledge of the Huron indicates, however, that these passages represent the authentic reactions of an Indian, reared in a tradition of personal liberty and blood feud, to European concepts of legal and parental authority. Sagard, who recorded these reactions, was fully convinced of the folly and immorality of Huron notions about child-rearing and dealing with crime.

As Savignon learned more French, he must have told Champlain and Gravé Du Pont a great deal about his people. A growing awareness of the size of the Huron confederacy and of the extent of their trading relations seems to have indicated to these men, for the first time, the important role that this confederacy could play in the development of the fur trade. As a result, a trading alliance with the Huron must have been recognized as a useful way to cope with the increasing competition for furs, now that the St. Lawrence had been thrown open to unrestricted trade.

TRADE AND TALK IN 1611

Champlain and Savignon set out for Canada on 1 March 1611 but, because wind and ice delayed their passage, they did not reach Tadoussac until 13 May. There were already several vessels in harbour when they arrived, but the Montagnais refused to trade for more than a few items that they required for their immediate needs. Instead, they were waiting for more boats to arrive, so that increased competition for furs would force the traders to exchange more goods for them (Biggar 1922–36, 2:171). By drawing increasing numbers of European traders to the St. Lawrence, free trade had terminated the artificial scarcity of European goods that a monopoly situation had created and which had made it possible for the French traders to demand a high price in furs in return for their stock. Champlain admired the sagacity with which the Montagnais were exploiting the European traders, but it was in his own interest to eliminate as quickly as possible a situation which played into the hands of the Indians.

Champlain continued on to Quebec, where he found that by eating fresh meat throughout the winter, the problem of scurvy had been overcome for a second season. He had planned to send two or three Frenchmen to explore the St. Maurice River, but once again Batiscan demurred and the expedition was put off for another year (2:173–74). Following this, Champlain and some of de Monts's employees travelled up the St. Lawrence to Montreal Island, which they reached 28 May. Finding that no Indians had arrived, Champlain went above the Lachine Rapids and explored the west end of the island. He then ordered a patch of forest to be cleared at Pointe à Callières (in the present harbour area) and planted crops to test the soil (plate 23). He also had an earth wall built on Market Gate Island, to see whether this site remained above water in the spring flood (2:175–79). Champlain contemplated establishing a settlement on Montreal Island, although it is doubtful that such a plan could have secured any backing in France, given the unfavourable conditions of trade at that time. On 1 June Gravé Du Pont arrived, followed by numerous other Frenchmen who hoped to share in the expected trade.

On 5 June Savignon and another Indian were sent up-river to try to hasten the arrival of their people, but they returned on the ninth, having sighted no one. They did, however, report seeing large numbers of herons on an island in the middle of the Lachine Rapids. Later Savignon, a Frenchman named Louis, and Outetoucos, a Montagnais headman, went hunting on the island. On the way back, their canoe capsized. Louis, who was hampered by his bulky clothing and who, like most Frenchmen of this period, did not know how to swim, panicked and was drowned. Outetoucos, a powerful man, abandoned the canoe and tried to swim to safety, but lost his life as he made his way towards the shore. Only Savignon managed to save himself by clinging to the canoe. He returned reluctantly to the French, fearing that they would blame him for Louis's death and avenge themselves by killing him (2:181–84). While he had strong opinions about French justice, Savignon had failed to observe that it did not operate on the principle of blood revenge.

Finally, on 13 June Iroquet and Ochasteguin arrived with two hundred companions, amongst whom was Savignon's brother, Tregouaroti. These Indians had with them Etienne Brûlé who had been entrusted to their care the year before. Champlain and Savignon went in a canoe to meet them, and speeches and shouts of approval from the Indians were met with a salute of gunfire by the French. The Indians then requested that there be no more firing since many who had come had never seen Europeans before and were frightened by the noise. Savignon and Brûlé both confirmed that they had been well-treated during the winter. The Huron were particularly glad to see Savignon, since the Montagnais had told them he was dead. They also told Champlain that several hundred more Indians

PLATE 23. *Champlain's map of a portion of Montreal Island. From
Champlain's* Voyages *of 1613.* L *indicates the Lachine Rapids;* D *the
St. Pierre River near the present Lachine Canal.* A *indicates land that
Champlain cleared in 1611 to test the fertility of the soil, and* E *an opening
in the forest where the Indians camped when they came to trade with the
French. Courtesy Public Archives of Canada.*

had planned to come down-river, but had decided not to when they heard that Champlain had secretly freed the Iroquois prisoner he had acquired the year before and had told him to encourage his people to exterminate the Algonkin (Biggar 1922–36, 2:189–90). It is possible that Champlain had discussed the likelihood of peace with his prisoner, since it had long been the desire of the French traders to reconcile the Iroquois and the Algonkian-speaking peoples. Champlain denied, however, that he had released the prisoner and the version of the story that reached the Algonkin and the Huron has all the earmarks of being a rumour spread by the Montagnais in order to sow distrust amongst the tribes of the interior. The aim of these rumours was to disrupt the developing relationship between these tribes and the French, without endangering the alliance that the Montagnais had with these tribes against the Iroquois.

The next day, the leading Huron and Algonkin consulted with Champlain about where they should locate their temporary encampment. They also had Brûlé, who could now speak Huron, inform him that they were concerned about the large number of Frenchmen who had come up-river and whom they knew would trade but would refuse to help them in their wars. Champlain assured the Indians that all the traders were subjects of the French king and that, even though each group was trading on its own, the Indians had nothing to fear from them (2:189). While these speeches may have been designed to flatter Champlain, it seems more likely that the tribes from the interior, particularly the Huron, were genuinely alarmed to see so many Europeans, especially when the latter were commercial rivals of one another. Hence, in seeking assurances for their own safety, the Huron may have been acting without ulterior motive. Champlain assured them that he had had no dealings with their enemies and, in return for one hundred beaver skins, he distributed trade goods among the Indian leaders who were present. Being reassured of his goodwill, the Indians told Champlain that in five or six days, another three hundred Indians would be coming to trade and to fight the Iroquois. These were presumably Algonkin, who had held back because they were afraid that Champlain had allied himself with their enemies. The next two days were spent trading, but the French traders quarrelled among themselves and various fights broke out among them. In the course of these quarrels, several Indians were attacked. Instead of using this situation to their own advantage, as the more experienced Montagnais would have done, the Huron and Algonkin were frightened and began fortifying their camp (2:192–93).

On the evening of the second day, Savignon was asked to come to the Indians' camp, and later Champlain and Gravé Du Pont were invited also.

There, they found the Huron headmen holding council. These headmen presented them with four strings of shell beads and fifty beaver skins, explaining that these presents had been sent by headmen who had not been able to come down-river, but who, like themselves, wished for an alliance with the French (Biggar 1922–36, 2:194–95). Presumably, the fifty beaver skins represented the major clan segments whose headmen sat on the confederacy council, while the four strings of beads represented the four Huron tribes. The Huron said they knew Champlain wanted to visit their country and that in the future they would take him there, even at the risk of their lives. They added that if other Frenchmen wished to winter with them as Brûlé had done, they would be made welcome. Champlain interpreted this as an invitation to join them in their wars and said that he would ask the French king for forty or fifty men and come the following year to meet their headmen and to help the Huron against their enemies. He also assured them that if their country proved suitable, Frenchmen would settle there. Champlain believed that the Huron approved of this, because they hoped the French would help them to fight the Iroquois and protect their settlements from attack. The Indians promised to provide Champlain and his men with provisions if he should visit their country, and the meeting came to an end at daybreak (2:195–96).

This meeting was attended only by Huron. Its purpose seems to have been to take the first steps towards a treaty of friendship between the Huron and the French that was no longer dependent on the Arendarhonon's special relationship with Iroquet and the Onontchataronon. The conclusion of such an alliance required that Champlain visit the Huron country, where he could meet the headmen who had been unable to travel down-river. Clearly, all fifty of the council chiefs could not leave home at the same time to go to the Lachine Rapids. Champlain's visit would also demonstrate that in the opinion of the French, the Algonkin were no longer intermediaries between themselves and the Huron, although the Algonkin would retain the right to levy tolls on the Huron for use of the Ottawa River. The impression that is gained from this meeting is that the question of an alliance with the French had rapidly become an important issue within the Huron confederacy.

On 17 June the Indians finished their trading and divided into small groups. They left Savignon and their camp under French protection and said they were going to hunt for more beaver. In fact, they established a new camp some distance above the Lachine Rapids, where the French shallops could not follow them. The next day, Iroquet and Tregouaroti returned to fetch Savignon and to invite Champlain and Brûlé to visit them. Savignon took leave of Champlain the following day, and the next day Champlain was conducted to their encampment. The journey involved a long trek across the island, probably to the shores of the Lake of Two Mountains. There, Champlain was invited to attend a feast at which, although he had already eaten, he ate again so as not to offend local custom. He then attended a meeting, where he was told that the Indians had abandoned their original camp because they had heard that the other French traders intended to kill them and they feared that Champlain would not be able to prevent this from happening (2:199–200). While Champlain's published emphasis on the Indians' distrust of the independent traders may have been partly to discredit these traders and partly a repetition of Indian blandishments designed to flatter him, it seems likely that, to some degree, the Huron and Algonkin were genuinely afraid of the French traders.

Nevertheless, they also informed Champlain that an independent trader named Bouyer was offering them valuable presents to allow a young Frenchman in his employ to spend the winter with them. The Indians said that they would not grant this request, unless it were acceptable to Champlain, since they were under special obligation to him for the help he had given them in their wars. Champlain replied that he did not object to them taking a boy who worked for a rival trader, but they must demand a large number of presents for doing so, and make sure that he remained in the care of Iroquet (2:201–3). This probably meant not only that he should not be allowed to live with a Huron family as Brûlé seems to have done, but that he was to remain in the lower part of the Ottawa Valley. Iroquet may have been planning not to winter in the Huron country, or alternatively Champlain may have been asking him to leave the young Frenchman among a branch of his people who remained in their tribal territory over the winter.

The Onontchataronon seem to have kept their promise; Marcel Trudel (1966a:178 n. 91) has identified Bouyer's young man as Thomas Godefroy de Normanville, who in later years worked as an interpreter, not among the Huron but among the Algonkin. It was also decided that Brûlé, whom Champlain refers to in an impersonal way as "my young man" should return to the Huron country with Tregouaroti (Biggar 1922–36, 2:205). After this was arranged, Champlain was requested to try to convince an Indian who had been captured three times by the Iroquois and cruelly tortured by them, that he should not set off with a small band to try to avenge his sufferings (2:203–4). Although Champlain was unsuccessful in this, the request that he intervene indicates the growing confidence that the Indians had in him. On his return to the French boats, Champlain shot the Lachine Rapids in a party of eight canoes, thus further enhancing his reputation among his Indian allies (Trudel 1966a:178). Since Champlain was unable to swim, this was an admirable act of courage, especially as Louis had drowned in these rapids only a short time before. Soon afterward, the Huron and Algonkin departed for the interior.

Following the departure of these Indians, the traders waited impatiently for the three hundred Algonkin who were still supposed to be coming down-river. Finally, on 5 July a canoe arrived bearing news that only twenty-four canoes would be arriving, since many Algonkin had died of a fever that had broken out amongst them, and others had already left to go to war. These Indians, who probably numbered about sixty, arrived on 12 July. Before trading, they gave a present to the son of Anadabijou, who was with the French, to express their regret concerning the recent death of his father.[7] They also offered ten beaver skins to the captains of each of the trading vessels to express their friendship and goodwill. Champlain assured them that the French traders would give them presents in return and that they would be allowed to barter in peace. This was followed by a successful trading session (Biggar 1922–36, 2:209).

The next day, these Indians brought Champlain a personal gift of forty beaver skins and expressed their pleasure at the reports they had received concerning his dealings with the first groups of Indians that had come down-river. They also stated that Champlain should found a settlement at the Lachine Rapids to protect this region from the Iroquois and to make trading with the French easier. The principal motive that the Algonkin had for approving this project was to have a permanent trading post that was in their own territory and therefore free from Montagnais influence. In this, and in other ways, the Algonkin were striving to free their trading relationship with the French from dependence upon their alliance with the Montagnais. Champlain gave them presents and assured them that he wished to found a settlement on the island. They then disinterred the body of Outetoucos and buried it with great ceremony on St. Helen's Island, where they felt it would be safe from Iroquois desecration (2:210–11).

On 15 July Tessouat, the powerful chief of the Kichesipirini, arrived with fourteen canoes. He too exchanged greetings with the French and the next day his people traded with them. Meanwhile, Tessouat gave Champlain a valuable present of thirty beaver skins. He spoke with him about possible travels in the north and said that, if any of Champlain's companions wished to go with him, they were welcome to come along. Champlain agreed to send a young man named Nicolas de Vignau with

the Kichesipirini and instructed him on what he was to observe. The Kichesipirini did not have many furs to barter, possibly because they were still
trading most of them eastward along the northern route to Lake St. John
and Tadoussac (2:211–12). On 18 July some of the Algonkin set off to raid
the Iroquois, while the rest returned up-river. It was decided that Champlain should return to France to report to de Monts.

THE NEW MONOPOLY

The continuation of free trade on the St. Lawrence had produced an
economic crisis for the European traders. De Monts's partners no longer
wished to support the settlement at Quebec and it was increasingly obvious
that Champlain's efforts to develop trading contacts in the upper part of
the St. Lawrence Valley were benefiting the free traders more than they
were his own employers. Without a monopoly, exploration would cease and
the chance would be lost to discover mineral wealth and the still anticipated
route to the Far East, both of which were expected greatly to benefit the
prosperity of New France. Without settlement, the St. Lawrence Valley
was without protection and the French claim to it remained ineffectual.

Champlain had long believed it necessary to plan the development of
New France in broad terms. Therefore, as de Monts's modest efforts
foundered, Champlain began to promote his own more grandiose proposals
for a colony on the St. Lawrence. The basis of Champlain's plan, as spelled
out in his two proposals written in 1618, was for a colony with a diversified
economy. Not only furs, but also fish, timber, gum, ashes, tar, dye roots,
hemp, silver, lead, clothing, gems, vines, and livestock were to constitute
the exports of the colony. In addition, it was hoped that revenue could be
derived from tolls charged for the use of a route to China that would
eventually run up the St. Lawrence. To ensure control of the St. Lawrence,
Champlain proposed to found a town in the valley of the St. Charles River
that would be as large as St. Denis in France, and would be named Ludo-
vica, after the new king, Louis XIII. Fifteen priests, three hundred families
of four persons each, and three hundred soldiers would be settled in the
colony, and forts would be built at Tadoussac, Cape Diamond, and on the
south shore of the St. Lawrence to protect it (Biggar 1922–36, 2:326–45).

Two features of Champlain's proposal deserve special notice. The first is
that furs would account for only a small fraction of the total revenue of the
colony, and the second is that one function of the colony, and a means by
which it would increase its population, was to convert Indians to the Chris-

tian faith and teach them to live like Frenchmen. Champlain believed that assimilation of this sort would not be difficult; once the Indians could speak French, they would quickly learn to think and feel like Frenchmen (3:6). He also argued, however, that European colonists were essential so that force could be brought to bear, when needed, to make the Indians abandon their "filthy habits, loose morals, and uncivilized ways" (4:320–21). None of these ideas was new for Champlain. As early as 1603, he had argued that it was essential, for their own good, that the Indians be compelled to adopt French ways, and that colonization was the best way of bringing this about (1:117).

The practical key to the realization of Champlain's dreams of empire continued, however, to reside in the despised and intractable fur trade. In the summer of 1611, he told the Huron that the next time he returned to the St. Lawrence he would be accompanied only by his friends (2:200). His aim was to have the fur-trade monopoly re-established on a more secure basis by grouping the more respectable traders, who annually visited the area, into one large company and by protecting the monopoly that would be granted to these partners by having a powerful nobleman offer the company his patronage, in return for an annual salary. In order to be permitted to join the company, the merchants would have to agree to support Champlain's plans for colonization and exploration (Biggar 1901:85–86).

At some cost to himself, de Monts secured a temporary respite for the settlement at Quebec. When, in the autumn of 1611, his partners refused to continue to support it, de Monts bought them out and agreed to maintain the settlement on an interim basis at his own expense. Meanwhile, Champlain won the patronage of Charles de Bourbon, Comte de Soissons. The count had himself appointed Lieutenant-General in New France and secured a twelve-year monopoly over the fur trade from Quebec westward. He, in turn, appointed Champlain to be his lieutenant in the New World. This empowered Champlain to administer justice, conclude treaties with the Indians, wage war, restrain illegal traders, and continue searching for mines and for a route to the Indies. When de Soissons died, his monopoly was transferred to his nephew, Henri de Bourbon, Prince de Condé. Condé also acquired the more exalted title of Viceroy of New France. On 22 November 1612, he confirmed Champlain in his new office, which made him governor of New France in fact, but not in title. Because of the delay caused by the death of the Comte de Soissons, there was not enough time to organize a new company before trading began in 1613. It was, therefore, announced that Condé would grant a limited number of passports that would entitle their bearers, and them alone, to send their vessels up-river past Quebec. All traders, whether operating above or below Quebec, were forbidden to pilot foreign vessels into the St. Lawrence or to sell firearms to the Indians (Biggar 1901:88).

Because Champlain was occupied throughout most of 1612 with his efforts to re-establish a monopoly for the fur trade, he was unable to visit Canada that summer. He did not send either the soldiers he promised would aid the Indians or anyone qualified to deal with the Indians in his place. As had happened the year before, many independent traders travelled up-river to Lachine. These were, for the most part, men in whom the Indians had little confidence and who seem to have lacked even the most rudimentary working knowledge of the intricacies of Indian trading relations. Growing competition generated conflicts among them that must have made trading difficult for the Indians. One account states that, in 1612, two hundred Indians turned up at the Lachine Rapids, another gives the number as 2000 (Biggar 1922–36, 2:217, 285). The latter figure is likely a misprint, although two hundred seems unusually low, considering the numbers that had come to trade the previous year.

The Indians were angry that Champlain failed to keep his promise to aid them in their wars. Even more importantly, however, they were alarmed that the principal European whom they trusted, and with whom their leaders had an alliance, was not there. They must have been further confused when some of the independent traders assured them that Champlain was dead, while de Monts's traders stoutly maintained the contrary (2:217–18). None of the French seemed willing, or able, to take Champlain's place and none was prepared to accompany them to war. In the absence of a leader who could represent the French traders and negotiate with the Indians, quarrels broke out, and some of the Indians seem to have been robbed. Because of this, the Indians announced that they would no longer come to the Lachine Rapids to trade. While Champlain may have exaggerated the unpleasant side of these events, his description of what happened illustrates the important role that traditional forms and personal relationships continued to play in the fur trade, at least among the Huron and Algonkin. Neither group was sufficiently dependent on European goods that they could not afford to break off trading with the French for one or two years. In any case, both groups could have continued to obtain such goods by trading with the Montagnais. The latter, as we have already noted, were seeking in subtle ways to undermine the confidence that these tribes had in the French, in hopes of recovering control over the flow of trade goods between the French and the tribes that lived farther inland.

So far, we have been viewing Champlain mainly as an agent of de Monts's trading company. He was obviously brave and adventurous, and apparently well suited to win the support of Indian trading partners by accompanying them on expeditions against their enemies. His criticisms of their religious beliefs might have offended the Indians, but, as Lescarbot (1907–14, 2:179) pointed out, because of difficulties of translation, and particularly because of the absence of the equivalents of many Christian theological terms in Indian languages, much of what Champlain said on this topic must have been totally incomprehensible to his listeners. As a man of action, Champlain impressed the Indians far more than did any of the traders, who came only "to make war on their beavers." Because of this, it has generally been assumed that Champlain was a man who understood the Indians and got along with them. He has been praised for his desire to see the French and Indians intermarry and become one people, although such sentiments indicate merely a lack of racial, as opposed to cultural, prejudice. Trudel (1966c:197) rather extravagantly lauds him for treating the Indians with consideration and for making them laugh and forgiving their offences, and Morris Bishop (1948:113) has argued that, because Champlain was horrified by the enslavement of the Indians in the West Indies, he was opposed to using force to convert them in Quebec.

Yet, beginning in 1612, another side of Champlain's personality became apparent. With increasing emphasis, he presented himself as a colonizer and a vice-regal official, rather than as the agent of a trading company. As he did so, the Indians, with whom as a trader he had established a relationship of trust, became a small part of larger plans. His writings indicate that he came to regard the Indians, and even most Europeans with whom he had dealings, less as individuals than as means whereby he could advance his own career. It is not surprising that, at this stage, Champlain should have been concerned about his future. He was now in his early forties, not wealthy and, except for his work for de Monts, had little to show for his life. Under such circumstances, he must have felt that his own destiny had become inseparably linked with that of Quebec and been desperately anxious to advance the welfare of his unpromising colony. Whether the personal plight of this insecure and ambitious man can excuse the cynical use he made of those around him is, of course, another matter.

In general, Champlain appears to have been extremely ethnocentric and inflexible. Since neither of these characteristics would have been particularly helpful when it came to interacting with Indians, it is likely that Champlain's early successes were the result more of the situation than of the man. It also appears that he pursued the Indian policies that he or his employers had formulated with less understanding of their ways, and less sympathy, than the majority of historians have imagined. Many of Champlain's personal weaknesses become clear in the dealings that he had with the Huron and Algonkin after 1612.

THE VIGNAU AFFAIR

In 1612, Nicolas de Vignau, who had spent the previous winter living among the Kichesipirini, returned to Paris and reported to Champlain that he had travelled with a relative of Tessouat to the territory of the Nipissing and from there had journeyed northward with them to a body of salt water, where he had seen the wreckage of an English ship. He said that he had been shown the scalps of eighty seamen, who had been slain when they tried to steal corn and other necessities from the Indians. He also reported that these Indians were holding captive a young Englishman. Vignau stated that it was possible to travel from the Lachine Rapids to this northern ocean and return again, by way of the Ottawa River, in seventeen days (Biggar 1922–36, 2 : 255–57). Champlain had heard from the Indians about this Northern Ocean, and had guessed the existence of Hudson and James Bays, beginning with his first visit to Canada in 1603 (Crouse 1924 : 139–40). He therefore determined to make a journey to this ocean the primary objective of his trip to Canada in 1613 (for his knowledge of Canadian geography in 1612, see plate 24).

Champlain left Honfleur on 5 March and arrived at Tadoussac 29 April. There, the Montagnais were dying from hunger, since the winter had been mild and, because of the lack of snow, hunting had been poor (2 : 249). Champlain remained from 7 to 13 May at Quebec, where again there had been no scurvy; then he set out for the Lachine Rapids, arriving on 21 May. There the traders encountered only a few Algonkin. Some of these were returning from the south with two Iroquois prisoners; others had come down the Ottawa River to trade. The latter informed the French that, because of the bad treatment they had received the year before, many Indians had decided not to come down-river. Instead, 1200 of them had embarked on a campaign against the Iroquois (2 : 253–54). While we do not know the details of this campaign, it appears to have been directed against the tribes who were raiding the Ottawa Valley to obtain European goods. Because of the large number of warriors involved, it is likely that Huron, as well as the Algonkin, were taking part in it.

The news that most of their Indian trading partners had gone to war

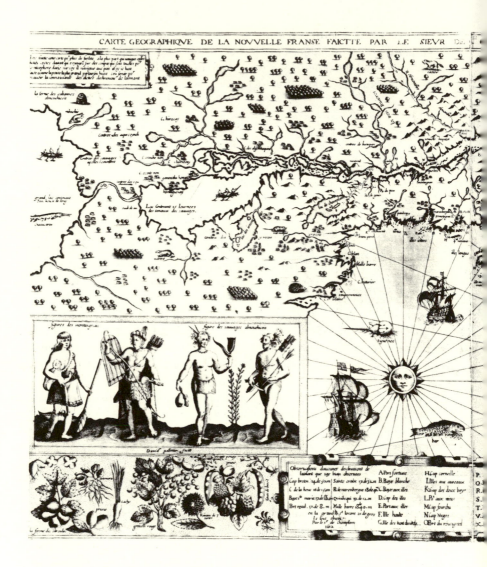

PLATE 24. *Champlain's* Carte géographique de la Nouvelle France, *dated 1612. From Champlain's* Voyages *of 1613. This map is remarkable for its detailed and accurate portrayal of the eastern half of Lake Ontario. The large islands at the head of the St. Lawrence are noted, as well as Prince Edward County, the Bay of Quinte, the Trent River flowing into the Bay of Quinte, and Lake Oneida* (lac des Irocois) *flowing through the Oswego River into Lake Ontario. This map appears to be based on a*

description of the interior collected by Champlain from an Indian informant in 1603 (Biggar 1922–36, 1: 159–61). Champlain apparently decided not to use this hearsay evidence on his small map of 1613. His representations of the east end of Lake Ontario on his maps of 1616 and 1632 are also far less accurate than on this one, although he personally visited the area in 1615. Courtesy Public Archives of Canada.

greatly discouraged the French who had been granted licences to trade. Since Champlain was once again responsible for relations with the Indians, he decided to travel up the Ottawa River to make a new alliance with the Algonkin and encourage them to trade. He left St. Helen's Island on 27 May, travelling with four Frenchmen and one Indian in two canoes. The French included Vignau and Thomas Godefroy, whom Captain Bouyer had formerly sent to live with the Onontchataronon. As far as the Chaudière Falls, each night was spent within barricades erected against the Iroquois warriors who were reported to be frequenting this region (2:260). Beyond the Long Sault Rapids, Champlain's party encountered fifteen canoes belonging to an Algonkin band known as the Quenongebin. These Indians had heard that Champlain was back and were travelling down-river to trade with the French. True to the Algonkin policy of seeking to retain control over trade passing along the Ottawa River, they attempted to dissuade Champlain from continuing his journey. Yet, after much persuasion, they agreed to provide him with an experienced canoeman to take charge of his second craft. In return, one of Champlain's French companions was ordered to accompany them down-river to protect them from the Iroquois (Biggar 1922–36, 2:264–65). Farther up the Ottawa, Champlain passed the mouth of the Petite Nation River, along which the Algonkin band called the Weskarini, or Little Nation, lived (map 13). He was informed that it was possible to travel across the interior of Quebec to the headwaters of the St. Maurice River by way of the Gatineau and that the Algonkin sometimes followed this route to avoid the Iroquois (2:266–67). Champlain also observed the offerings of tobacco that the Indians made to the spirit of the Chaudière Falls every time they portaged around it.

Farther upstream a long portage had to be made around the Rapides des Chats. This required the French to abandon some of their food and clothing in order to lighten their loads. Two more falls were passed before entering Lac des Chats, into which the Madawaska River was seen flowing from the south. The valley of this river was the territory of the Matouweskarini Algonkin, from which the name of the river has been derived. Above Lac des Chats, a dispute broke out between Vignau and the Indians, concerning whether it was preferable to follow the river to Morrison Island or to travel there over land. Champlain chose to follow the Indians' advice. The route, which was obstructed with fallen pine trees, took him past a series of small lakes until he reached Muskrat Lake, where a group of Algonkin, whose headman was named Nibachis, had its summer camp (2:275). These were probably the Keinouche (Pike) Algonkin, or Quenongebin. Circumstantial evidence indicates that Champlain lost his astrolabe near Green Lake. An

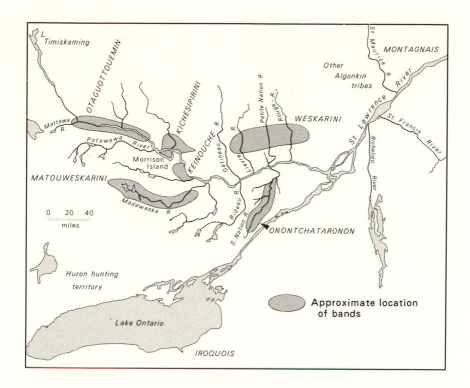

MAP 13. *Location of Algonkin bands definitely attested as living in the Ottawa Valley in the first half of the seventeenth century.*

astrolabe inscribed with the date 1603 was found near there in 1867. While it cannot be proved that this was Champlain's instrument, it seems almost certain that it was.[8]

Nibachis was surprised to see Europeans in his territory, but welcomed Champlain and offered to him and his companions tobacco and fish. He also showed Champlain the small fields where his people were growing corn. Champlain noted that the soil was poor and for that reason the Algonkin did not depend as heavily on agriculture as did the Huron. Nibachis had two canoes fitted out and, after seven leagues travel by water and an easy portage, Champlain arrived on the shores of the enlarged section of the Ottawa River that lies south of Allumette Island. There he was met by Tessouat, who had been forewarned of his coming. Tessouat conducted his guests across the river to Morrison Island, where the Kichesipirini had their summer camp. This small island, which was covered with oak, pine, and

elm trees, had rapids at either end. Champlain believed that the Kichesipirini lived there to avoid their enemies, but the real reason appears to be
that the island lay astride the main trade route along the Ottawa River.
Indians travelling in either direction had to land at this point, and thus
could be forced to pay for rights of passage (Wrong 1939:255). This island
gave the Kichesipirini control over the river such as no other Algonkin
tribe enjoyed and this explains, to a large degree, the special jealousy with
which they guarded their rights to tax and regulate trade in the upper part
of the Ottawa Valley. Sagard was later to describe the Kichesipirini as the
most arrogant and uncivil, but also the richest and best clothed, Indians he
had seen (ibid. 257–58).

Champlain examined the Kichesipirini village and visited their cemetery, where he found the graves to be covered with wooden structures and
adorned with carved representations of the deceased. He was informed that
the Kichesipirini buried with their dead all the things they had possessed
in life, in the belief that their spirits were able to use these objects. When
Champlain asked the Kichesipirini why they lived in this barren location,
they replied that, if Champlain kept his promise to establish a French
settlement at the Lachine Rapids, they would move south and join him
there (Biggar 1922–36, 2:280–81). It seems highly unlikely, however, that
the Kichesipirini would have abandoned Morrison Island, which would
have meant relinquishing their control over commerce along the Ottawa
River. I therefore interpret this reply as encouragement to the French to
found a trading settlement within Algonkin territory, similar to the one
they had founded in 1608 among the Montagnais. Later developments suggest that the Kichesipirini also may have thought of establishing a satellite
village on Montreal Island, both to develop closer relations with the French
and to be able to cultivate corn under more favourable conditions (Thwaites
1896–1901, 29:145–47). Champlain repeated his promise that he would
establish a colony there the following year.

The next day, Champlain was invited to attend a feast that was held in
the house of Tessouat, the headman of the Kichesipirini. All the men of the
settlement were present and the food consisted of corn soup, boiled fish, and
roasted meat. Champlain did not eat any of the soup, which he observed
was dirty, but asked for fish and meat to prepare in his own fashion. As was
the custom among the Huron, Tessouat did not eat, but spent his time
entertaining his guests (Biggar 1922–36, 2:282). Iroquoian influences can
be observed in this and in other details of the Algonkin cultural pattern.
When the feast was over, the young men withdrew and a half-hour was
spent smoking in silence in order to clear the brain. Champlain then assured

the Kichesipirini of his friendship and of his desire to help them in their wars. He explained that he had men for this purpose at the Lachine Rapids and had come to invite the various Algonkin bands to wage war. He also mentioned his desire to see the Northern Ocean. He then asked for four canoes to take him up-river, so that he might invite the Nipissing to accompany the French to war (2:283–84).

The Kichesipirini had no desire to make themselves the instruments by which Champlain would be able to contact the Nipissing and conclude an alliance with them. After conferring with his council, Tessouat replied that, as a result of the bad treatment the Algonkin had experienced at Lachine the previous year, their young men had already gone to war. It would therefore be better to postpone a French military expedition until the following year. He stated that Champlain could have four canoes, but warned him that the Nipissing were dangerous sorcerers and, for that reason, the Kichesipirini were not their friends. Tessouat added that the Nipissing were cowards and therefore of little value in any military campaign (2:284–86). He obviously hoped that Champlain would respect the Kichesipirini's disapproval of his plan to visit the Nipissing and would decline his offer of canoes. Champlain, however, was extremely anxious to visit the Northern Ocean and wished to contact the Nipissing, who travelled there. He therefore replied that he did not fear the dangers of the journey and thanked his hosts for their canoes (2:286–87).

A few hours later, while Champlain was examining the crops that the Kichesipirini had planted, Thomas Godefroy reported that Tessouat and his council had concluded that Champlain's expedition would have to be postponed until the following year. Enough Kichesipirini would then be available to ensure that the Nipissing did not harm him (2:287). This was all too clearly another case of Algonkians attempting to thwart Champlain's plans to travel north of the St. Lawrence. Champlain was angered by this news and told the Kichesipirini that if they failed to honour their promise to provide him with canoes, he would no longer regard them as his allies; but he added that if the journey were an inconvenience for them, he could make do with two canoes. He said that he was surprised that the Kichesipirini should object to him visiting the Nipissing, since they had already taken Vignau there and he had not found the route as difficult, nor the people as unfriendly, as they described them (2:288).

The Kichesipirini looked angrily at Vignau, and Tessouat asked him if he claimed to have been among the Nipissing. After some hesitation, Vignau replied that he had been there. Some Indians leapt upon the young man and Tessouat called him a liar. Tessouat added that he was not surprised that Champlain was importuning the Kichesipirini, after he had been told such fables. Champlain was also told that Vignau had passed the entire winter living with Tessouat. Champlain managed to rescue Vignau from his assailants, whereupon Vignau once again swore that it was true that he had been to the Northern Ocean (2:288–90).

At this point, Godefroy came to tell Champlain that the Kichesipirini had secretly sent, or were planning to send, a canoe to notify the Nipissing of his arrival. The aim of this expedition was, no doubt, to attract some Nipissing down-river so that Champlain would have no excuse for travelling to their country. Champlain returned to the council and announced to his hosts that it had been revealed to him in a dream that they planned to send a canoe to the Nipissing without telling him. He added that this angered him since he wished to go there in person. He also recounted to them Vignau's story of his trip north. When they had heard this story, the Kichesipirini demanded that Vignau prove he had been there, saying that if he could not do so, he should be killed. Vignau became very frightened, especially when Champlain threatened that if they should go farther and the story prove false, he would have him strangled. After some reflection, Vignau told Champlain that he had never been beyond Morrison Island and that all he had said concerning the Northern Ocean was untrue. Hearing this, Champlain became so angry that he could no longer tolerate having Vignau in his presence. Vignau told Godefroy that he had not thought Champlain would attempt the journey and had invented the story in hopes of a reward. To atone for what he had done, he offered to remain there and attempt to find the Northern Ocean. Champlain was determined, however, to take him back to Lachine, where he would compel him to face justice (Biggar 1922–36, 2:290–96).

Champlain now despaired of ever seeing the Northern Ocean and regretted that he had been wasting his time and had annoyed the Kichesipirini. He told Tessouat that he was convinced that Vignau was a liar. The Kichesipirini smugly admonished Champlain that he should have shown more confidence in their headmen, who were his friends and always spoke the truth, rather than in a mercurial young man like Vignau. They added that they were convinced that on the way up-river Vignau had tried to kill him, thus planting a further seed of suspicion, which quickly took root in Champlain's mind. The Indians said that if Champlain gave them leave to do so, they would kill Vignau; and they were about to lay hands on him when Champlain intervened, saying that he personally would see that he was punished.

Champlain informed the Kichesipirini that there were four French vessels at the Lachine Rapids and invited them to come there to trade. He also promised Tessouat that if he were able, next year he would return prepared to go to war with his Indian allies (2:298). On 10 June Champlain and Tessouat exchanged farewell presents and Champlain asked him to protect the wooden crosses he had erected to mark the stages of his journey up-river. Then, accompanied by forty Kichesipirini canoes loaded with furs, Champlain began to make his way down-river. As Champlain departed from Morrison Island, he was filled with trust and goodwill for the Kichesipirini, and especially for their "good old headman" Tessouat (2:298).

Champlain's plans to travel northward came to an embarrassing end, once he became convinced that Vignau was a liar. It is unclear, however, to what extent Vignau lied and whether or not his later confession was a true one. Trudel (1966a:200–1) believes that Vignau probably visited James Bay in 1612 and that it was only by threatening to kill him that the Indians frightened him into denying that his story was true. He points out that if Vignau had not believed what he said, he would not have offered to risk his life to search for the Northern Ocean. Trudel concludes that Champlain was the dupe of the Kichesipirini, and Vignau a victim of their machinations to control trade with the interior.

There is much to suggest that Vignau's original story contained at least an element of truth. When Tessouat first took Vignau to live with him, he spoke of a journey to the north and promised that Vignau would accompany him (Biggar 1922–36, 2:211–12). Champlain recorded this promise in the account of his voyage of 1611, but seems to have forgotten about it by 1613. The Nipissing were active traders and, in later years, one of their most important trade routes took some of them from Lake Nipissing to James Bay and back again once each year. That they offered to take Champlain north with them in 1616 (3:104) is evidence that this trade route was already established by that time, and it may have been a prehistoric trade route of some importance. Finally, Henry Hudson had spent the winter of 1610–11 on Hudson and James Bays and, the following June, he, his son, and six other men were forced into a shallop and cut adrift on James Bay by his mutinous crew (Neatby 1966:377).

There are, however, some serious objections to Vignau's story. It is possible, as Champlain feared, that Vignau had heard rumours about Hudson's misfortunes and had based his story on these rumours. The total of eighty men he reported were killed is an impossible figure; yet Trudel (1966a:200–201) has argued in Vignau's defence that eighty may be a misprint for eight, in which case the number would be almost correct. Also, the Cree who lived in the vicinity of James Bay did not grow corn, or any other crop; hence the statement that the English tried to rob them of their agricultural produce indicates a lack of personal knowledge of northern Ontario. Again, however, it could be argued that the corn Vignau refers to had been brought as trade goods from the south. It is not impossible that the Nipissing were carrying corn meal this far north, although the difficulties involved in transporting it would have meant that it was being traded in only very small quantities.

The most serious objection to Vignau's story is, however, his chronology. In 1641, Father Jérôme Lalemant reported that each spring a group of Nipissing went to trade with the tribes that gathered along the shores of James Bay. The journey northward, which probably followed the north shore of Lake Superior and down the Missinaibi River, lasted about thirty days, after which they travelled along the bay for about ten days. The journey home, by way of the Abitibi River and Lake Timiskaming, must have taken at least another month.[9] A statement that in the summer the whole tribe gathered on the shores of Lake Nipissing suggests that they returned from this journey sometime in early July, which would be possible if they had set out in late April (Thwaites 1896–1901, 21:239). Since the trade at Lachine was normally over by mid-July, Vignau and his Kichesipirini hosts would have had to follow a very tight schedule for Vignau to have been able to return to France in 1612. Yet it was not an impossible one. What gives the lie to Vignau's account is his claim that the journey took only seventeen days.[10] There is also the question of whether or not, even if the Nipissing and Kichesipirini were better friends than the latter wished Champlain to think they were, the Nipissing would have allowed the Kichesipirini and a French youth to explore one of their important trading routes, especially one that could be exploited from the Ottawa Valley.

There is no doubt that Vignau had some accurate information about the north. What is less certain is whether he had actually seen James Bay or merely had heard an account of the Nipissing's journey north in 1611. If they had stayed at James Bay long enough that year, they might have learned what happened to Hudson and his party after they had been abandoned by their shipmates. This explanation would account for Vignau's later offer to search for a route to Hudson Bay, which implies that he had not travelled such a route, although he was confident that it existed. It might also explain why Vignau, at no point, attempted to retract his confession of having lied; although his refusal to divulge more detailed information about his contacts with the Nipissing is a good indication that the Kichesipirini had frightened him into silence, as Trudel claims.

In any case, Vignau's confession cannot be accepted as a complete explanation for Champlain's hasty decision to cancel his journey northward. Champlain knew, from English reports, that there was a sea to the north and numerous Indians, from Tadoussac westward, had confirmed that it was possible to reach this sea from the St. Lawrence Valley. It was, therefore, illogical for him to conclude that, because of some geographical barrier, the people living in the Ottawa Valley had no knowledge of this sea (Biggar 1922–36, 2:293). Both the Montagnais and the Algonkin had already repeatedly thwarted his plans to travel northward. Therefore he ought to have been suspicious of further efforts to prevent his movement up-river. His credulousness towards the Kichesipirini suggests that he was intimidated as well as deceived by them; while the vehemence with which he turned on Vignau indicates that he was not the best judge of character, of either Indians or Europeans.[11] Considerable naiveté about the Indians is evident in Champlain's failure to take account of their policies, as is a patronizing attitude in his under-estimation of their ability to devise stratagems to deceive him.

After Champlain left Morrison Island, he travelled directly down the Ottawa River, thus having a chance to see the stretch of river that the portage by way of Muskrat Lake had enabled him to avoid. There were six or seven falls in this area, which made it more difficult to go up the river than to go down. Before they reached Lachine, the forty Kichesipirini canoes that accompanied Champlain were joined by nine large Weskarini ones, carrying forty men, and by twenty more Kichesipirini canoes that had set out ahead, each heavily laden with merchandise. Champlain arranged with the Indians that none of them should begin trading until he gave the word. In this way, he hoped to make sure that independent traders could not get a share of the trade (2:303).

Once Champlain returned to the Lachine Rapids, Vignau was made to confess his lies in the presence of both the French and his Kichesipirini accusers. He asked to be pardoned and promised that if he were allowed to stay in Canada, he would search for the Northern Ocean. When none of the Indians present would agree to take him, Champlain decided to abandon Vignau "to God's keeping" (2:307). This is the last that is heard of Vignau. If a French trader did not take pity on him and help him to return to France, it is likely that he was left at the mercy of the Kichesipirini who, seeing him abandoned by his people, probably killed him, as they had threatened to do, for revealing their secrets.

After trading was over, Champlain asked the Algonkin to let two young men stay with them for the winter. At first they objected, pointing out the trouble that Vignau had caused. Finally, however, when Champlain vouched for the behaviour of these men and insisted that the Indians take them as a pledge of friendship, they agreed to do so (2:307). Champlain left Montreal Island on 27 June, while the traders remained to await the return of the Indians from their wars. No Huron had arrived by this time and there is no evidence that any turned up later in the year. The Huron were not yet so dependent on European goods that they had to come annually to obtain them and, in view of the troubles they had experienced the year before, they may not have bothered. On the other hand, the many Algonkin who came to trade, in spite of a major military campaign, indicate the increasing organization of trade amongst the Indians of the Ottawa Valley.

CHAMPLAIN'S NEW COMPANY

In the course of the trading season of 1613, several boats belonging to privileged traders were waylaid and robbed on their way from Quebec to Tadoussac. This was apparently done by independent traders, who were still permitted to operate on the lower part of the St. Lawrence River. The attacks gave the Prince de Condé an excuse to ask for, and obtain, an extension of his monopoly as far as the Matane River in the Gaspé Peninsula. He was thus able to bring the lucrative trade at Tadoussac under his control and to enrich and enhance the prestige of his company (Le Blant and Baudry 1967:307–9). In the spring of 1614, the articles of the new *Compagnie du Canada* were agreed on. The shares of the company were to be divided into three portions; one held by traders from Rouen, the other two by those of St. Malo and La Rochelle; however, the merchants from La Rochelle refused to sign the contract and finally the shares were divided between the merchants from Rouen and St. Malo. These traders agreed to pay the Prince de Condé one thousand crowns annually and to take out six families each year as colonists. Champlain, as Condé's lieutenant, was to receive a substantial salary and to have at his disposal four men from every vessel that traded on the St. Lawrence. The settlement at Quebec became the property, and therefore the responsibility, of the new company (ibid. 310–21).

In 1614, the trade carried on by the *Compagnie du Canada* must have been considerable, since over 25,000 skins were exported from New France.[12] Champlain did not return to Canada that summer and his second failure to fulfil promises to build a trading post near Lachine and to help his Indian allies in their wars must have puzzled and annoyed them. If they had counted on Champlain joining them in a campaign that year, they were compelled to revise their plans.

It is unclear why Champlain did not visit Canada in the summer of 1614. It may have been partly for personal reasons. The previous autumn he had been having problems with his sixteen-year-old wife, whom he had married four years earlier, mainly for her dowry.[13] More importantly, however, he seems to have remained in France to promote the work of colonization. As yet, his governate was nothing more than a trading post, and previous experience had taught him not to trust the promises that traders made to promote settlement. Champlain was seeking allies who were as interested as he was in seeing French settlements established in Canada. One perhaps minor way he hoped these settlements could be made to grow was by encouraging Indians to adopt French ways and to settle down as French subjects. It therefore seemed worthwhile to encourage the clergy to undertake missionary work among them. Champlain lacked the resources to support such a project. Nevertheless, he persuaded Louis Houel, sieur de Petit Pré, to find three or four Recollet friars who were willing to go to Canada and to try to raise funds to support them. This man was a secretary of the King and Controller-General of the salt works in Champlain's home town of Brouage. Although Houel's initial efforts were not successful, at the meeting of the Estates-General that took place in the autumn of 1614, the cardinals and bishops approved Champlain's project and raised 1500 livres to sustain four missionaries. The following March, the associates of the *Compagnie du Canada* agreed to transport six missionaries to Canada without charge each year and to support them there (Trudel 1966a:210–12). Soon after, Champlain embarked for Quebec in the company of four Recollets: Fathers Denis Jamet, Jean Dolbeau, and Joseph Le Caron, and lay brother Pacifique Duplessis. Jamet was the superior of the mission, but it was Le Caron who chose to begin his mission work among the Huron. Le Caron, born about 1586 near Paris, had been chosen as chaplain and tutor to the Duc d'Orléans. When the Duke died, Le Caron joined the Recollets, making his profession in that order in 1611.

Sealing the Alliance

TRADE AND POLITICS IN THE HURON COUNTRY

The six years that had elapsed since the Arendarhonon first made contact with the French had brought about many changes within the Huron confederacy. The only Frenchman to witness these changes was the young

Etienne Brûlé, who seems to have been living among the Huron since
1610. Already in the spring of 1611 Brûlé was wearing Huron dress and
was well on his way to becoming a skilful interpreter and intermediary in
the fur trade. Unfortunately, he left no account of these years, or of his
life generally. His career is known only through the writings of Champlain
and various priests, all of whom hated and despised him.

Nevertheless, from what has been recorded it is possible to gain a general
idea of what happened among the Huron during these years. According to
the Jesuits, since the Arendarhonon was the first tribe to contact the
French, Huron law granted this tribe the sole right to carry on trade with
them. Yet, because of the importance of this trade, the Arendarhonon
decided that it was best to share it with the other tribes of the confederacy.
Of their previous right, they retained only the distinction of being the
oldest and closest allies of the French (Thwaites 1896–1901, 20:19).
Decades later, the Arendarhonon were willing to offer protection to
Frenchmen who were having difficulties with the other Huron tribes.

This sharing of trade among all the tribes of the confederacy took place
before 1615, since by then the Attignawantan were actively engaged in
both the diplomatic and economic activities that were associated with it.
In later years, it became clear that even if the Attignawantan were willing
to let the Arendarhonon claim the honour of being the oldest Huron allies
of the French, they were careful to monopolize important contacts, and
possibly the bulk of the trading between the Huron and the French. What
happened among the Huron was probably as follows.

In the winter of 1608–9, Ochasteguin had been invited to accompany
the Onontchataronon on an expedition against the Mohawk and to visit
the settlement that the French had recently established on the St. Lawrence. Ochasteguin accepted and, with a small band of Arendarhonon, he
became the first Huron to travel down the Ottawa River and meet the
French. According to Huron law, as a result of having opened up a new
trade route, Ochasteguin and the members of his clan segment became
the masters of that trade. This meant that they acquired full rights to
determine who would be allowed to participate in it. Since such permission
was normally granted only in return for gifts, or a share of the profits,
Ochasteguin was theoretically in a position to acquire immense wealth by
Huron standards, and, by redistributing it, to assume a dominant role in
Huron politics. Yet that control of this trade was assumed by Atironta
suggests that, because of its importance, the principal headman of the
tribe soon took charge of it, regardless of the clan segment to which the
actual discoverer of the route belonged.

While this usurpation may seem autocratic, it is in keeping with the political realities of a society lacking centralized control. There was no way to police trade routes; therefore, if the rest of the Arendarhonon were determined to trade with the French, Ochasteguin's clan segment would have been unable to enforce their theoretical monopoly. If conflict was to be avoided, the Arendarhonon had to agree how this trade was to be shared amongst the clan segments that made up the tribe and, at the same time, they had to stand together as a tribe to guard against claims by outsiders. This could not be accomplished if serious disputes were to break out between rival claimants. Hence, once it was decided that the trade was sufficiently important that all Arendarhonon should share in it, the principal headman of the tribe seems to have been recognized as its rightful master. By being empowered to collect the fees associated with this trade, Atironta would have been able to secure large quantities of European goods. The prestige that he derived from redistributing these goods among his own people not only protected his traditional authority, but permitted him to enhance his prestige.

Such an arrangement was particularly important for preserving the power of traditional headmen, once other traders began to acquire personal influence and renown from their enhanced ability to provide their fellow tribesmen with European goods. The ability of these headmen to acquire wealth from their formal control of the fur trade, without having to engage in trade themselves, probably explains the sobriquets *atiwarontas*, *atiwanens*, and *ondakhienhai* (big stones, elders, and stay-at-homes) which the Jesuits report were applied to them in later times (Thwaites 1896–1901, 10:231–33). Huron mechanisms for the control of trade seem to have been such that the opening of new trade routes enhanced the power of traditional office holders, rather than bringing about a major reorganization of the political structure.[14]

The same process was repeated at the level of the confederacy. Trade with the French could not help but be of vital interest to all Huron; hence the other Huron tribes were anxious to claim a share in it. While the Arendarhonon were the second largest tribe in the confederacy, the Attignawantan were more numerous. Moreover, the Attignawantan were the original inhabitants of north Simcoe County, and had received the Arendarhonon into their territory; hence they had the Arendarhonon at a psychological disadvantage. The great influence of the Attignawantan within the confederacy is reflected in the fact that their headmen occupied half of the seats on its council. They also referred to the Arendarhonon as cousins or offspring, rather than as sisters or equals. If the Arendarhonon had chosen to ignore the Attignawantan's wishes to trade with the French, conflict might have ensued which would have disrupted trade, exposed the Huron to the attacks of their enemies, and perhaps led to the break-up of the confederacy. Rather than risk these consequences, the Arendarhonon chose to share their trade with the other members of the confederacy. This seems to have meant granting the headmen of the other tribes permission to trade with the French without requiring them to pay the Arendarhonon for doing so. By appearing to do this willingly, the Arendarhonon were able to convert an act of political necessity into one from which they were able to derive honour and prestige. In this way, they also managed to obtain official recognition as being the special allies of the French.

The formal sharing of this trade, and a general discussion of future relations with the French, seems to have taken place at the annual meeting of the confederacy council held in the spring of 1611. No doubt, the redefinition of trading privileges that was worked out at this meeting made the Huron council chiefs anxious to conclude a treaty with the French, in which the latter would recognize these newly acquired rights. It is therefore likely that traders from tribes other than the Arendarhonon travelled down-river in 1611. I have already suggested that the fifty beaver skins and four strings of wampum that were presented to Champlain and Gravé Du Pont at that time appear to have been the first ritual exchange between the entire confederacy and the French.

The broader composition of the Huron trading expedition of 1611 also may explain why Champlain began to refer to the Huron as Charioquois, instead of Ochasteguin, and why both of these names appear on his small map of 1613 (plate 25). Champlain may have used Ochasteguin to refer specifically to the Arendarhonon, while by Charioquois he meant either the other Huron tribes, or the Huron in general. Although we do not know the origin of Charioquois, or many other names that Champlain used, its general significance is clear, since in the 1632 edition of his writings the more familiar term Huron is consistently substituted for it (Biggar 1922–36, 2:186 n. 2).

Hereafter, trading relations with the French appear to have been pursued most actively by the northern branch of the Attignawantan. Sagard reported that in the 1620s men from neighbouring villages came to Quieunonascaran to seek permission from the headman, Onorotandi, to trade along the lakes and rivers leading to the Saguenay and from his brother (i.e., fellow headman), Auoindaon, to go to Quebec (Wrong 1939:99). While neither was the principal headman of the Attignawantan (that was the prerogative of Anenkhiondic of Ossossané), the cleavage

CHAMPLAIN'S SMALL MAP OF 1613.

PLATE 25. *Champlain's small map of 1613. From Champlain's* Voyages *of 1613. Drawn late in 1613, this map is an improvement of another map by Champlain probably dating from the winter of 1612–13. The main difference is a more detailed portrayal of the Ottawa River resulting from his visit to that area in the summer of 1613. Both maps locate the Hochataigains (Ochasteguin's Huron) and the Charioquet (later called Huron) indeterminately north of the St. Lawrence and west of the Ottawa Rivers. This may reflect Champlain's growing awareness of a distinction between the Arendarhonon and the rest of the Huron after 1611. He later lost sight of this distinction. Courtesy Public Archives of Canada.*

between the northern and southern Attignawantan was such that this arrangement is not necessarily an objection to a general argument that control over major trade routes fell into the hands of the principal headmen in each tribe.

Unfortunately, we do not know enough about Brûlé to be certain where he was living during this critical period; however, by the 1620s, he was no longer with the Arendarhonon. Instead, he seems to have been domiciled at Toanché, which was the Attignawantan's chief point of departure for the St. Lawrence (Jurgens 1966:132). Brûlé may have been prized away from his original hosts by the Attignawantan, or he may have decided on his own to move to Toanché. In either case, his action is indicative of the degree to which trade with the French had fallen into the hands of the most powerful of the Huron tribes.

In terms of distance, it would have been easiest for the Huron to have traded with the French by way of the Trent Valley and the St. Lawrence River. This route was already known to the Algonkin, and presumably had been used by them in the preceding decade. For two reasons, however, it was not the route that the Huron chose to follow. First, it took them into Iroquois-controlled territory, which made it too dangerous for commercial purposes. Secondly, it went through an area that was uninhabited; hence the Huron would not have been able to acquire furs from traditional trading partners on their way to the St. Lawrence. While the route by way of Georgian Bay and the Ottawa Valley was a longer one which required making over fifty portages, it had definite advantages and, for all practical purposes, was the only one available to the Huron. This route gave the Attignawantan, and possibly the Attigneenongnahac, an advantage over the other Huron tribes, since it passed through the country of the Nipissing, who had long been their trading partners. On the other hand, the Arendarhonon were intimate with the Onontchataronon; hence, they had a compensating advantage when it came to travelling along the lower part of the Ottawa River.

CONFLICT ON THE OTTAWA RIVER

Increasing trade along the Ottawa River had attracted Iroquois raiders to that area. Their aim was to obtain trade goods, by robbing them from the Huron and Algonkin who were using the river. It is possible that some of these raiders were Mohawk, who stepped up their attacks along the

Ottawa once they decided that it was too dangerous to continue raiding on the St. Lawrence. Yet, the Mohawk were now also able to rob Indians nearer home, who were trading with the Dutch along the Hudson River. Such robberies may account for why the Mohawk were reported to have been fighting the Mahican in 1614 (Jameson 1909:47). The same year, the Dutch built a trading post called Fort Nassau, on Castle Island, near Albany, where they left ten or twelve men to trade with the Indians. This post remained in operation until 1618. It was probably during this period that the Mohawk began trading with Europeans. By as early as 1616, Dutch traders were being employed among both the Mohawk and the Mahican (O'Callaghan 1856–87, 1:14).

The tribes that had the most to gain from attacking the Ottawa Valley were the Oneida and Onondaga, who still lacked easy access to European trading posts. Such raids inevitably exacerbated any existing conflicts between them and the Huron and Algonkin. They also gave the latter peoples a common interest in freeing the Ottawa River, so that it could be used as a safe trading route, as they were now accustomed to use the St. Lawrence River. By 1612, conflict between these rival blocs had grown to the point where over one thousand warriors set out to attack the offending Iroquois. As a result of these raids, the Huron were drawn into a conflict with the Onondaga and Oneida that had probably not existed, or at least had been much less serious, prior to the development of the fur trade. The initial stages of this conflict continued until at least 1615.

Yet, if economic motivations were expanding the scale of warfare, they do not seem to have influenced its conceptualization. These expeditions remained primarily matters of blood revenge. Their aim was to discourage the Iroquois from attacking Indians in the Ottawa Valley, rather than to annihilate them as a people. In this respect, the warfare in the Ottawa Valley was more traditional than were the assaults that the Mohawk had launched against the former inhabitants of the St. Lawrence Valley several decades earlier. This warfare did, however, make it possible for the Huron to secure trading rights in the Ottawa Valley. Without the need for allies, it is unlikely that the Algonkin would have been willing to permit the Huron to travel down-river to trade with the French. The Algonkin now found themselves in the same situation that the Montagnais had been in earlier. To secure allies to fight the Iroquois, it was necessary for them to grant the right to visit the French to their former clientele to the west. By so doing, they risked losing their ability to maintain a middle-man position in respect to trade with the interior (map 14).

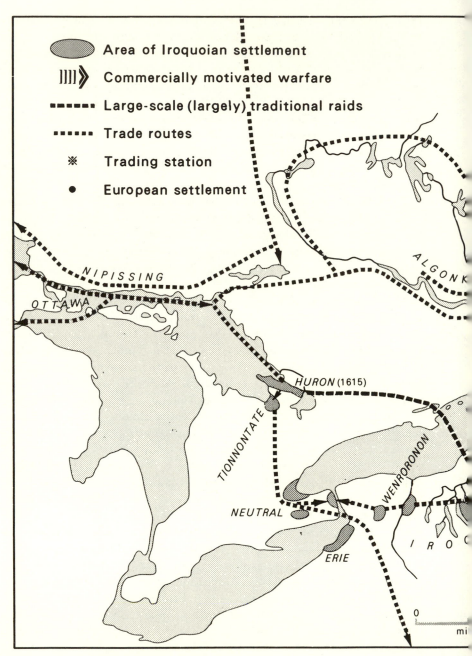

MAP 14. *Intertribal relations, c. 1615.*

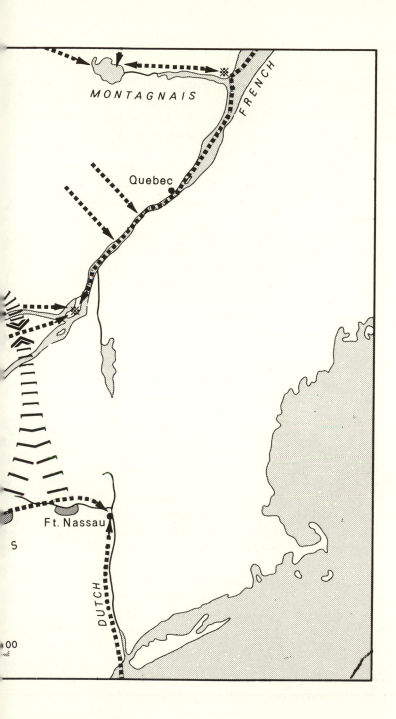

LE CARON AND CHAMPLAIN JOURNEY TO THE HURON COUNTRY

Champlain and the Recollets arrived at Tadoussac on 25 May 1615. As soon as the shallops were ready, Le Caron went up-river to meet the Indians who had come to trade. That year, the Huron and Algonkin gathered at the Lachine Rapids, but were also frequenting the mouth of the Rivière des Prairies, which flows north of Montreal Island.[15] The latter river provided an easier passage from the Ottawa River to the St. Lawrence since none of its rapids was so difficult to negotiate as were those at Lachine. It was also more sheltered from Iroquois attack than was the St. Lawrence.

After he had met the Indians, Father Le Caron decided to spend the winter in the Huron country. He hoped to study the Huron language and way of life and to see what hope there was of converting these Indians to Christianity (Biggar 1922–36, 3:26). The Huron do not seem to have had any objection to taking him and no doubt believed that by having an older, and therefore more responsible, Frenchman living amongst them, their alliance with the French would be strengthened. On 20 June Le Caron returned to Quebec to obtain provisions for the winter. On the way, he met Champlain, who was travelling up-river to meet the Indians. Champlain advised Le Caron not to visit the Huron that year, but to spend the winter at Quebec and go there the following spring. He argued that at Quebec Le Caron would have the companionship of his fellow priests and other Frenchmen, while little satisfaction could be hoped for if he dwelt among the Indians (3:28–31). At this time, Champlain had no intention of wintering among the Huron himself; hence his advice may partly have been motivated by jealousy that someone else would gain ascendancy over them. In any case, he regarded living with the Indians as something fit only for wild young men such as Brûlé. Le Caron believed that he could adapt to life among the Huron and silenced Champlain's objections by announcing that he was prepared to suffer hardship to accomplish his mission.

When Champlain arrived at the Rivière des Prairies, the Indians greeted him enthusiastically. The Huron requested that he honour his promise to return with them to their country with a number of armed Frenchmen, so that he could help them against their "old enemies," the Iroquois. They also reminded Champlain of his failure to fulfil his former promises to assist them in their wars (3:31). The Algonkin did not object to this visit and were themselves sending warriors to the Huron country to join a military expedition against the Iroquois. It would thus appear that by inviting the Algonkin to join in yet another major raid against their common enemy the Huron had manoeuvred them into dropping their overt opposition to letting Champlain travel inland to meet the Huron headmen and conclude an alliance with them.

Gravé Du Pont concluded that even though Champlain had not planned to accompany the Huron, it was necessary that he do so at this time in order to assure their continued goodwill. The two men also felt that this voyage would provide Champlain with an opportunity to explore the interior, since, if he were travelling with the Huron, the Kichesipirini could not oppose him ascending the Ottawa River (3:31–32). When Champlain agreed to help the Huron in their wars, they promised that 2500 men would accompany him on an expedition into the heart of the Iroquois country and that, before the end of the autumn, they would return him to Quebec. Champlain then explained to them the strategy by which he hoped to defeat the Iroquois. Finally, he returned to Quebec for four or five days to make arrangements for the journey. On the way down-river, his route again crossed that of Father Le Caron, who was returning to the Rivière des Prairies (3:32–33).

Champlain was absent for ten days. As he was headed back to the Rivière des Prairies, he met Gravé Du Pont and Father Jamet, who were returning to Quebec. They told him that because of his long absence, the Indians had decided that he was not returning and had set off for home with Father Le Caron and twelve other Frenchmen whom Gravé Du Pont had sent to spend the winter with them (3:34–35). A rumour had spread that Champlain had been killed by the Iroquois, but the speed with which the Huron departed seems more likely a measure of their lack of trust in his promises. No doubt, the Huron hoped that the four or five Frenchmen who were acquainted with handling firearms would help them in their wars.

Instead of blaming himself for his delay, Champlain expressed annoyance that he was unable to arrange his expedition properly and that so few armed men were available to accompany him. Nevertheless, on 9 July he set out to follow the Huron. He was accompanied by his servant, an interpreter, and ten Indians, all travelling in two large canoes of the sort the Huron used for long journeys on relatively smooth bodies of water. The Indians were probably Huron who had remained behind to see if Champlain would return.

We know little about Le Caron's journey to the Huron country. Sagard and Le Clercq state that he had to help paddle his canoe and suffered greatly (Sagard 1866:41; Le Clercq 1691:72). Both sources, however, are fond of exaggerating the hardships that were endured by the Recollets, and this may be another instance of this type of hagiography. Frenchmen were sometimes asked to paddle if their Indian companions were ill, but with twelve other Frenchmen on route it is unlikely that Le Caron would have suffered abnormal hardships, unless his behaviour had seriously annoyed his Indian companions.

Le Caron was well-received among the Huron and was induced to settle, not amongst the Arendarhonon, but at the Attignawantan community of Carhagouha. This village, which Heidenreich (1966:120–21; 1968), following Bressani, locates near Midland Bay, was palisaded and seems to have been the principal town of the northern Attignawantan. It was the predecessor of Quieunonascaran, which was founded in 1623 and was the residence of Onorotandi and Auoindaon, who controlled the northern Attignawantan trade with the Saguenay and St. Lawrence Rivers. Prior to 1623, these headmen had probably lived in Carhagouha, which was therefore a community of key importance for trading with the French. Huron families tried to persuade Le Caron to live with them and to be adopted, with a view to strengthening their relationship with the French (Sagard 1866:41).

Le Caron's religious scruples led him to request permission to live in a separate cabin outside the village. We do not know whether he would have done this in any case, or if he was led to make this request by aspects of Huron life that were morally objectionable to him. The Huron built him a cabin, where he lived until the following May. He is not reported to have converted any Huron, although he learned something about the Huron language and way of life. He also began work on a Huron dictionary, which Le Clercq (1691:88, 327–28) reports survived to his own day. The bulk of this dictionary seems, however, to date from his second visit to the Huron in 1623, especially the sections dealing with rules and principles.

Champlain and his small band travelled up the Rivière des Prairies and ascended the Ottawa River past Morrison Island. Beyond this island, he found a large number of rapids in the river, while the terrain on both sides was rocky and hilly. The area was thinly inhabited by a group of Algonkin known as Otaguottouemin, who lived by hunting, fishing, and drying blueberries for the winter.[16] When Champlain's party reached the Mattawa River, they made their way westward to Lake Nipissing, which they reached on 26 July. Champlain spent two days in the principal village of the Nipissing, whose headman entertained him with banquets, and took him hunting and fishing. Champlain observed that the area was rich in fish and game and estimated that seven hundred to eight hundred people were spending the summer there (Biggar 1922–36, 3:40). The Nipissing headmen told Champlain that they would be willing to take him north with them the following spring on a journey that would last for forty days and require an equal amount of time to return (3:101–5). Although Champlain did not plan to spend the winter in the Huron country, this promise to take him to James Bay revived his hopes of being able to extend his knowledge of the geography of North America in that direction. No doubt, the Nipissing made this promise because they were anxious to establish trading relations with the French. Champlain must have had some second thoughts concerning his treatment of Nicolas de Vignau, but in his writings he remained silent about them.

Champlain proceeded down the French River and into Georgian Bay. Throughout this region, he found only a little corn being grown and the country impressed him as being particularly desolate. Near the mouth of the French River, Champlain met three hundred Indians, whom he called Cheveux Relevés, because they wore their hair very high and carefully arranged. These belonged to the group of northern Algonkian bands that were later known as the Ottawa. The men tattooed their bodies and, unlike the Huron, they did not bother to wear loincloths. Their faces were painted, their noses pierced for ornaments, and many wore earrings. Champlain was given to understand that the people he had met were visiting this area to dry blueberries and that their principal villages were located to the west of those of the Tionnontaté, along the south shore of Georgian Bay. In later years, the Ottawa were active traders, particularly in the Lake Michigan area. The men Champlain encountered carried shields made of dressed leather from an animal like the buffalo (*bufle*), which suggests that their trading connections may already have been well-established in that direction. European goods, however, were still rare and highly valued. When Champlain presented the leader of this band with an iron hatchet, he regarded it as a rich present (3:43–45).

From the mouth of the French River, Champlain followed the traditional Huron canoe route south along the eastern shore of Georgian Bay. While doing so, he had a chance to observe the Thirty Thousand Islands and the rocky, thinly wooded coastline of Muskoka. On 1 August, as he crossed the mouth of Matchedash Bay and passed Beausoleil Island, which the Huron called Skionechiara, he observed a great change in the landscape. To the south, he beheld the hills of the Huron country, with its rich forests, extensive clearings, and beautiful river valleys (Biggar

1922–36, 3:46). After a five-hundred-mile journey across the Canadian Shield, he was approaching a fertile and well-cultivated land, where a Frenchman might feel at home.

The Indians Champlain was travelling with brought him first to Otoüacha (Toanché), which appears to have been the main Attignawantan point of departure for their journeys to Quebec. This village was located near Thunder Bay, on the Penetanguishene Peninsula (Heidenreich 1966:118–20). He remained in Otoüacha for several days, and while there also visited the village of Carmaron, two miles away. The headman of Carmaron celebrated Champlain's visit with a feast and entreated him to stay there (3:47). Champlain was unable to do this, however, since he had to reach Cahiagué, the Arendarhonon town that was the rallying place for the expedition against the Iroquois. Champlain returned to Otoüacha, where he waited two more days while arrangements were made for him to visit all the Huron settlements and to meet the leading Huron headmen as he travelled to Cahiagué.

In Otoüacha, Champlain had his first personal encounter with Huron sexual mores. One evening, when he left the house in which he was staying to escape its fleas, a Huron girl offered to have intercourse with him. She apparently believed that this was what he wanted, since he was wandering about the village after dark for no other apparent reason. This girl was, no doubt, very surprised when Champlain not only refused, but gave visible signs of his disapproval before retreating to the company of his male companions (3:47).

From Otoüacha, Champlain proceeded to Touaguainchain, an otherwise unknown village located somewhere between Otoüacha and the next settlement that he visited, Tequenonquiaye. At both of these villages, Champlain was received with great courtesy and entertained with feasts. Tequenonquiaye was the predecessor of Ossossané, and was the largest and most important town of the Attignawantan. The community that Champlain visited seems to have been located slightly farther south than the Ossossanés of later times.[17] Having visited the main town of the southern Attignawantan, Champlain was free to meet the less prestigious leaders of the northern Attignawantan. To do this, he made a considerable detour northward, travelling along the high ground lying to the west of the Wye Valley, as far as Carhagouha, where Father Le Caron was already living. Here on 12 August Le Caron celebrated a mass and a wooden cross was erected near the small house that was being built for him (3:48–49).

Meanwhile, Champlain learned that because the Huron had believed that he was not coming to their country, they had abandoned their plans for a major raid against the Iroquois. Now they were attempting to assemble a large war party but this was proceeding slowly. Because of this, Champlain remained at Carhagouha until 14 August before spending three days travelling to Cahiagué. In the course of this journey, he visited four or five important palisaded towns.[18] While his itinerary is unknown, it probably took him to the main settlements of the Attigneenongnahac and the Tahontaenrat, and then into the territory of the Arendarhonon (map 15). Champlain states that this circuitous journey was his own idea, but the Huron probably wished that before he went to war, he should meet the major headmen of the confederacy who had sent him presents in 1611. Many years later, Le Clercq claimed that Champlain visited all the Huron settlements to raise the arms of the King of France in them, to conclude close alliances with their headmen, and to prepare their young men for war (Le Clercq 1691:78). There is no reference, in Champlain's account, to the erection of crosses bearing royal arms and it is unlikely that the Huron would have responded favourably to such action. On the other hand, Le Clercq seems to have grasped the political significance of what Champlain accomplished. By visiting each village, he concluded treaties of friendship with individual Huron headmen, in which he promised to help them in their wars, and they, in return, promised that they would trade with the French (Biggar 1922–36, 3:226–27). Henceforth, these agreements would constitute the basis for closer cooperation between the French and the Huron.

The effectiveness of Champlain's diplomacy depended largely, however, on the interpretation the Huron gave to what he did. Champlain viewed his tour of the Huron villages more as an accidental ramble than as a round of serious negotiations. Although he visited every part of the Huron country, his ignorance of their political organization remained astonishingly great. He recorded the names of only a few Huron headmen in his writings and there is no evidence that he understood what role they played. He also referred to all Huron as Attignawantan, thereby revealing that he remained unaware of the nature of Huron tribal organization. His description of the operations of government is extremely vague and attributes to them an ad hoc quality that again indicates gross lack of information. Champlain concluded that the Huron had no punishment except vengeance, and that by acting on the basis of passion rather than reason, they generated more quarrels than they suppressed. Moreover, the Huron did not have any god or believe in anything supernatural whatever and, for this reason, lived like brute beasts (3:143). Champlain was a good observer of Huron economy and daily life, but, as a soldier and an aspiring

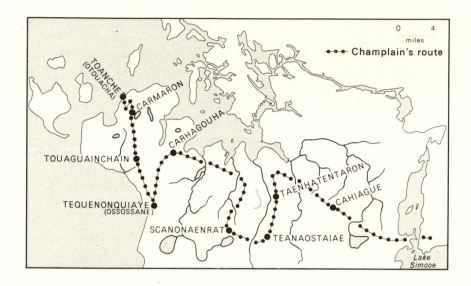

MAP 15. *Reconstruction of Champlain's route through the Huron country to Cahiagué, and beyond.*

vice-regal official, he was unwilling to see in their noncoercive social organization anything but chaos and barbarism.

Champlain arrived at Cahiagué on 17 August. This settlement was located three leagues from the Narrows of Lake Couchiching, in the general vicinity of Bass Lake (3:56). In recent years, it has been identified with the Warminster site, which is located on a long, gently sloping interfluve northwest of Bass Lake, in Medonte township.[19] The eastern and western borders of this site are protected by steep valleys containing running water. To the north it terminates at the edge of a post-glacial shore-line, beyond which lies a swampy tangle of cedar and alder, while on the south it extends nearly to the heads of the two boundary valleys. The cornfields of this village must have covered more than 1000 acres and appear to have been laid out south of the site, in a semicircular pattern (map 16). At Warminster, two Huron villages, covering nine and a half and five acres respectively, have been found within six hundred feet of one another. They appear to have been contemporary and to have constituted a single large double village. Each section of the village was surrounded by a massive palisade made up of three to seven rows of staggered posts. The two settlements are estimated to have contained a total of one hundred houses and

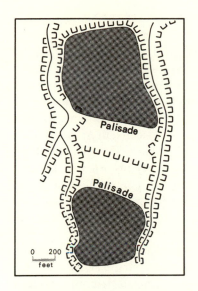

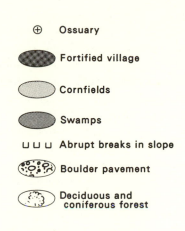

Ⓧ Ossuary

Fortified village

Cornfields

Swamps

ᴗ ᴗ ᴗ Abrupt breaks in slope

Boulder pavement

Deciduous and coniferous forest

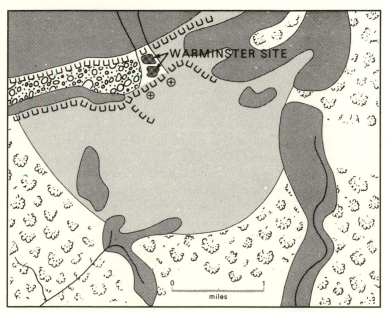

MAP 16. *Reconstruction of field pattern and natural setting of the Warminster site after ten years of occupation (Lot 10, Conc. XIV, Medonte Twp.). The expanded section shows outline of palisades in greater detail (both maps after C. E. Heidenreich).*

a population of about 3000 people (Cruickshank and Heidenreich 1969: 37–38).

Champlain described Cahiagué as being the principal Huron village, by which he probably meant that it was the largest. He also stated that it contained two hundred large cabins.[20] Champlain frequently over-estimated, but, even if he more than doubled the actual number of houses, there is no doubt that Cahiagué was a large settlement. The Warminster site is large by Huron standards; it is located in Arendarhonon territory; and, although the archaeological evidence has not yet been published in detail, it appears to date from the early historic period. Thus strong arguments can be presented in favour of identifying this site as Cahiagué. On the other hand, it is strange that Champlain would not have mentioned such an unusual feature as the village being divided into two separately palisaded units.

Sagard reports that when Cahiagué changed location, sometime before 1623, two new villages were founded in place of the single old one (Wrong 1939:92). This has generally been interpreted to mean that, as a result of quarrels between clan segments, the inhabitants of Cahiagué separated and founded new villages located some distance apart. It is possible, however, that Sagard is describing the formation of a double village and that the Warminster site is, in fact, the successor of Cahiagué, rather than the village Champlain visited. Until more details are published and the precise date of the Warminster site has been established, it will be impossible to decide which of these alternatives is correct. At present, we do not know the volume or nature of European goods that were reaching the Huron country in the decade that followed Champlain's visit, as opposed to what had been arriving in the preceding decade. If Cahiagué was abandoned soon after 1615, it will be especially difficult to determine whether the Warminster site was occupied shortly before or after that date.

Champlain remained at Cahiagué for two weeks, while the war party that was to proceed against the Iroquois was drawn together from all parts of the Huron confederacy. The number of warriors that finally assembled is not stated but, if it resembled the average large Huron war party, there may have been about five hundred. In addition to Huron warriors, Iroquet and his men joined the expedition as well as other Algonkian-speakers who were wintering among the Huron. Champlain, who viewed himself not as the Huron did (as an ally), but rather as the leader of this war party, chafed at the delay in assembling these warriors. As each group arrived, there was a succession of dances and feasting, in which the warriors vaunted their prowess and expressed their certainty of victory.

Then, the newcomers would go to live with the clan segment in Cahiagué that had the same name or which belonged to the same phratry as their own. Champlain imagined that these ceremonies were intended to welcome him alone, but they seem to have been the usual ones meant to confederate warriors from different tribes, villages, and clan segments for a campaign against a common enemy (Biggar 1922–36, 3:53, 56). Among those who were preparing to accompany the expedition was Atironta, the principal chief of the Arendarhonon and now the paramount Huron ally of the French. Champlain, as a new and powerful friend, was obviously an important part of the campaign, but he seems to have overestimated the military importance that the Huron attached to his participation. Mainly, it was interpreted as an expression of goodwill towards the Huron.

BRÛLÉ'S VISIT TO THE SUSQUEHANNOCK

While he was at Cahiagué, Champlain learned that the Susquehannock were interested in joining the proposed expedition against the Iroquois and were hoping that, by doing so, they would be able to meet him and form an alliance with the French. Champlain was also told that the Susquehannock had captured three Dutchmen, who had been helping their enemies to wage war on them; however, they alleged (probably untruthfully) that they had released these prisoners, thinking them to be French (3:54–55; for more about these prisoners, see chapter 6).

The Huron decided to dispatch a dozen warriors to carry the plans for their impending attack to the Susquehannock and to invite them to join the expedition. Brûlé asked Champlain for permission to accompany these warriors, which Champlain readily granted, since the journey would permit Brûlé to observe the country to the south (3:58). In so doing, however, Champlain deprived himself of the only interpreter who understood the Huron language well. Henceforth, he had to communicate with the Huron in a circuitous fashion, relying on Frenchmen to translate what he said into Algonkin and on Algonkin to translate it in turn into Huron. The route followed by Brûlé's companions is not described in detail and has been the subject of much controversy. The dotted line on Champlain's map of 1632 (plate 28) suggests that they travelled south to the Neutral country along the trail that ran westward through the Tionnontaté settlements and then south through the Beaver Valley and down the Grand River. Yet, the urgency of their mission, and Champlain's statement that the group started out, not from Cahiagué, but from the Narrows at Lake Couchiching, make it more probable that they travelled across Lake Simcoe to the Neutral country.[21] It is implausible that they travelled around the west end of Lake Ontario before pushing south between the Niagara and Genesee Rivers (cf. Cranston 1949:81–83; Jurgens 1966: 131). More likely they crossed southwestern Ontario to Lake Erie and made their way along its eastern shore, being careful to avoid the Iroquois. From there, they skirted south of the Iroquois settlements to the Susquehannock village of Carantouan. Throughout the latter part of their journey, the Huron travelled through bogs and thick forests to avoid Iroquois war parties (Biggar 1922–36, 3:214–15).

Nevertheless, the Huron encountered a small group of Iroquois who were returning to their village. They killed four of them and captured two others (3:215). These prisoners assured the Huron a particularly enthusiastic welcome in Carantouan, where the prisoners were probably tortured to death. A council was held and, after it was confirmed that Champlain was accompanying the Huron, the Susquehannock decided to send a war party north to join in the attack on the Iroquois village, which was only three days away (3:216). War was, however, an occasion for ritual among the Susquehannock, no less than among the Huron. Hence, while Brûlé fretted at the delay, the Susquehannock slowly made ready. They set out to join the Huron, but did not reach the appointed rendezvous until two days after the Huron had left for home. Learning that the Huron had departed, the Susquehannock returned to Carantouan, where Brûlé, lacking guides for his return to the Huron country, was obliged to spend the winter. It is not stated what happened to the Huron who accompanied him, but some of them may have slipped north to carry news of the Susquehannock's plans to their compatriots who were attacking the Iroquois (3:217).

During the winter, Brûlé visited the lower reaches of the Susquehanna River and the islands of Chesapeake Bay, possibly accompanying Susquehannock who went there to trade. In the spring, he set off with five or six Indians to return to the Huron country. It is uncertain whether these were Huron returning home or Susquehannock on their way to visit the Huron. On route, they were attacked by the Iroquois and in the ensuing fight Brûlé became lost in the forest. He grew very hungry and finally decided that it was better to surrender to the Iroquois than die of starvation. Brûlé followed a footpath until he encountered a Seneca or Cayuga fishing party returning to their village. He shouted at them and, after some initial hesitation, both sides laid down their arms and the Iroquois took Brûlé to their homes, where they offered him something to eat

(3:217–21). Some of Brûlé's companions who had escaped from the Iroquois reached Cahiagué by 22 April. In order to account for Brûlé not being with them, they euphemistically reported that they had left him on the trail when he had decided to return to Carantouan (3:168).

After he had eaten, the Iroquois took Brûlé to the longhouse of one of their principal headmen, who interrogated him. Brûlé denied that he was an *Adoresetoüy*, or man of iron, which was the Iroquois name for the French, but since he spoke Huron, they did not believe him. A dispute broke out about what should be done with him. The war chiefs and younger men regarded him as an enemy and began torturing him. They tore out his fingernails and part of his beard, burned him, and dragged him to the torture scaffold which the Iroquois erected in the middle of their villages. Brûlé attributed his salvation to divine intervention. Seeing himself in mortal danger, he recited a brief prayer; following which, as one of the Iroquois was seizing his *agnus dei* medal, a violent thunderstorm broke out. This so terrified the Iroquois that they desisted from torturing him further (3:221–24).

It has been suggested that Brûlé invented this pious story to please Champlain and the Recollets (Trudel 1966a:227–29). Whether or not there actually was a thunderstorm, it is clear that the Iroquois council chiefs, who generally exerted a moderating influence in intertribal relations, managed to rescue Brûlé from his tormentors. Hereafter, Brûlé was treated kindly by the Iroquois and invited to their feasts and celebrations. His knowledge of an Iroquoian language and his familiarity with Iroquoian customs seem to have quickly made him as popular among the Iroquois as he was among the Huron. The headmen, however, had a practical reason for befriending Brûlé. Neither the Seneca nor Cayuga were as well situated for trade with the Dutch, or for raiding the Ottawa Valley, as were their allies to the east. Hence the council chiefs were interested in exploring the possibility of establishing a trading relationship with the French. Brûlé knew what they wanted and saw an opportunity to expand existing trade networks. He promised his hosts that when he left them, he would do what he could to promote a three-way peace between them, the Huron, and the French and that he would return to them soon (3:224). After he had remained some time with the Iroquois, the latter conducted him to the borders of the Neutral country. He does not appear to have arrived in the Huron country in time to see Champlain, before the latter's departure on 20 May.[22] We do not know if Brûlé remained in contact with the Iroquois or if the promises he made to them were lies told to secure his release. There is, however, evidence that Brûlé had

dealings with the Seneca around 1630. This suggests that in the intervening years he maintained contact with the western Iroquois, possibly
in the course of his visits to the Neutral country.

THE EXPEDITION AGAINST THE IROQUOIS

On 1 September the Huron war party set out from Cahiagué and travelled
along the shore of Lake Couchiching to the Narrows. There, Champlain
saw the great weirs that the Huron had erected to catch fish as they moved
between Lakes Simcoe and Couchiching (3:56–57). The Huron remained
at the Narrows for about a week, while they waited for still more men to
arrive. From Lake Simcoe, they made their way eastward to the Kawartha
Lakes, portaging either to Balsam Lake or directly to Sturgeon Lake
(Needler 1949). After passing through these lakes, which lie along the
southern margin of the Canadian Shield, they followed the Otonabee
River to Rice Lake and went along the Trent River to the Bay of Quinte.
The journey through the Trent Valley was a slow one, with the Indians
stopping at frequent intervals to hunt and fish. They hunted deer com-
munally; driving them into the water where they killed them with arrows
and spears. Some spears, possibly belonging to Algonkin, were made by
fastening French sword blades onto the end of poles (Biggar 1922–36,
3:61; Sagard 1866:414). The French shot the deer with their muskets.
During one of these hunts, they wounded an Indian, who accidentally
wandered into their line of fire. The affair was quickly settled, however, in
the traditional Indian manner, by satisfying the wounded man with
presents (Biggar 1922–36, 3:61). The main purpose of this hunting and
fishing was to feed the army, although the deer skins were taken back to
the Huron country to be used for clothing. Champlain noted that in
former times the Trent Valley had been inhabited and that it had been
abandoned through fear of the enemy (3:59; 6:246). This provided him
with more grist for one of his favourite themes—the great war that he
imagined the Iroquois had waged in past times against the Huron and
Algonkin.

From the mouth of the Trent River, the Huron made their way down
the Bay of Quinte, then travelled among the islands at the east end of
Lake Ontario until they were south of the St. Lawrence. There they
landed on a sandy beach and hid their canoes in the forest. The precise
route that the Huron followed after they left the Bay of Quinte is uncertain.[23]

After carefully hiding their canoes, the Huron travelled on foot for some ten or twelve miles along a sandy beach. This was part of the nineteen miles of sand that stretches along the eastern shore of Lake Ontario from about a mile south of Little Stony Creek to two and a half miles south of the Little Salmon River. Peter Pratt (1964:31) identifies the three bodies of water that Champlain has drawn east of this section of his route on his 1632 map with North Pond, South Pond, and Little Sandy Lake. Somewhere along the beach, the Huron turned inland, travelled through the forest for four days, and crossed either the Oneida or Oswego Rivers, which flow from Lake Oneida into Lake Ontario (Biggar 1922–36, 3:64). On 9 October, when the Huron were about four leagues from their destination, they captured an Iroquois fishing party, consisting of three men, four women, and four young people. When Iroquet began to cut off a finger from one of the women, Champlain said that such behaviour was an act of cowardice and threatened that, if it continued, he would be unwilling to give his allies any further help in their wars (3:64–65). Iroquet replied that it was customary to torture prisoners, and at this point, one of the Kichesipirini accompanying the expedition seized an Iroquois child by its feet and broke its head against a rock or tree (Thwaites 1896–1901, 9:259–61). Champlain does not state what followed, but since the Onontchataronon had two female prisoners the following winter, it is possible that at least some of these women escaped their usual fate.

The next afternoon, the Huron and their allies came within sight of the community they were planning to attack. It was a large town, located near a pond or small lake and, if the drawing accompanying Champlain's account can be trusted, there was a stream on either side of it (plate 26). It was enclosed by a far stronger palisade than any Champlain had observed among the Huron. The wall was constructed of four rows of large stakes interlaced with each other and topped by galleries faced with large slabs of wood. Gutters ran between the posts, which allowed the defenders to extinguish any fires that might be lighted against the palisade (Biggar 1922–36, 3:70).

The location of this village has been hotly debated for over a century. From the information contained in Champlain's account, it could have been located near any large body of water in the central part of upper New York State. The three locations that have received the most support are the north end of Canandaigua Lake; Onondaga Lake in Onondaga County; and the Nichols Pond site in neighbouring Madison County (Pratt 1964: 35–41). In recent years, however, excavations at the Nichols Pond site

PLATE 26. *The Iroquois settlement under attack by Champlain and his allies in 1615. The schematic ground plans and distribution of houses, the geometrical plan of the fortifications and their curious construction, and the dress of the Indians leave no reason to trust the fidelity of this scene. Courtesy Public Archives of Canada.*

have shown it to be prehistoric, while no archaeological evidence of any sort has been forthcoming to support the other two locations (ibid. 41–50). A recent review of this problem has concluded that Champlain's account is not sufficiently detailed to permit the precise reconstruction of his travels in New York State and that the site of the town he attacked remains unknown (ibid. 50–51).

Nor is it any easier to ascertain the tribal identity of this town. Various authors have ascribed it to the Seneca, Cayuga, Onondaga, or Oneida, the latter two being the most popular candidates. Unfortunately, Champlain was no better informed about the tribal structure of the Iroquois confederacy than he was about the Huron one, and the term he uses to denote the enemy, Entouhonoron or Antouhonoron, cannot be identified as the name of any tribe known in historic times (ibid. 11). Biggar and his co-workers have led many readers astray by their unwarranted substitution of Onondaga for Entouhonoron in their translations of Champlain's writings.

Champlain seems to have been vaguely aware of the separate identity of the Seneca, whom he calls the Chouontouaronon (Biggar 1922–36, 3:55). This is a variant of Tsonnontouan, which was the standard French name for the Seneca. Yet, throughout this period, Champlain appears to have applied the term Iroquois only to the Mohawk, while by Entouhonoron he meant the four western tribes of the confederacy, including the Seneca. This corresponds to early Dutch usage, which distinguished between the Mohawk and the Sinnekin (the four western tribes), while the French made a similar distinction between the Lower Iroquois (Mohawk) and the Upper Iroquois (the other four tribes) throughout most of the seventeenth century (Hewitt 1910a:503–4). On his map of 1632, Champlain located the Entouhonoron west of the Iroquois and, in the index to this map, he stated that they lived in fifteen settlements, fought with the Iroquois against all other tribes, and denied passage along the St. Lawrence to all foreigners (Biggar 1922–36, 6:249–50). From his description of the route, Champlain and his allies might have attacked an Oneida, Onondaga, or Cayuga settlement. Since it seems to have been the Oneida and Onondaga who were harassing the Huron and Algonkin in the Ottawa Valley at this period, it was most likely one of these tribes that was being attacked. The Oneida normally had one settlement, the Onondaga two. The fact that the beleaguered town received no help suggests that there was no other community nearby. This in turn suggests that the town was Oneida rather than Onondaga.

THE BATTLE

As soon as the Indians who accompanied Champlain were near the Iroquois village, they constructed a fortified war camp, in which they were to live for the next ten days. Champlain did not wish his allies to let the presence of the French become known until the following day; however, the Huron and Algonkin were anxious to open fire on their enemies and, in their desire to secure prisoners, some of them pursued the Iroquois too near their village, where they themselves were in danger of being captured. To rescue these men, Champlain and several of his companions approached the enemy and opened fire on them. These Iroquois had never experienced gunfire before and speedily withdrew into their town, carrying their dead and wounded with them (Biggar 1922–36, 3:66).

Angered by what had happened, Champlain addressed harsh and angry words to his Indian allies. He stated that if everything were directed according to their wishes and the guidance of their council, the result was bound to be disastrous (3:67). We have no idea what the Huron and Algonkin headmen thought of Champlain's address, or how much of it they understood. Champlain believed that as a former soldier of France, he was infinitely better trained in the art of war than were the Indians, and that this alone gave him natural authority to command them and to censure any aspect of their conduct of which he did not approve. The Indians believed that Champlain had the right to express an opinion, like anyone else, but if he wished his advice to be followed, he had to convince them, either by his arguments or by his example, that it was good advice. The concepts of command and obedience, on which Champlain was to rely so heavily in the days that followed, were not ones that had meaning for the Huron or Algonkin.

Champlain did, however, persuade the Indians to construct a *cavalier*, or wooden platform with an enclosed area on top, which would hold four or five musketeers. This platform was to be positioned near the town and, from it, the French could fire over the palisades and prevent the Iroquois from using their galleries to defend themselves. Champlain also ordered a number of large wooden shields to be constructed, under cover of which the Huron could approach the palisades and prevent the Iroquois from extinguishing the fires that were to be lighted against them (3:67–69). Champlain was determined to breach the walls of the town and, having done so, to destroy it, as he had destroyed the Mohawk war camp in 1611. What he did not understand was that the principal aim of the Huron was to harass the village and, by threatening to set fire to its defences, to force the Iroquois warriors to come out and engage in hand to hand combat, as had happened during the battle on Lake Champlain.

The Huron hoped that Champlain's plans would draw the Iroquois from the town; therefore the next morning they set about cutting wood and building the platform and shields, as Champlain had directed. At the same time, the Iroquois strengthened their defences. The Huron and Algonkin were waiting for the Susquehannock to join them, but Champlain believed that they were strong enough to storm the town and that delay would be dangerous. He therefore urged an attack. Two hundred men carried the platform to within a few feet of the village walls and three Frenchmen began to fire from it. They soon forced the Iroquois to abandon the ramparts, from which they had been shooting arrows and hurling rocks at the Huron. Instead of carrying the shields forward, the Huron began shouting insults at the enemy and shooting arrows into the settlement. They also either set fires so that the wind would blow them away from the palisades or piled up so little wood that, when they set it ablaze, it did little damage. Champlain began to shout at the Indians that they were behaving badly and urged them to follow his orders (3:72–73). Given Champlain's inability to speak either Huron or Algonkin, it is unlikely that any of this advice, given in the heat of battle, was understood by the Indians. Champlain had regretted his linguistic deficiencies at the battle on Lake Champlain, but on this occasion he seems to have been totally oblivious of them. Eventually, he saw he could do nothing to control the situation, although with his own men he continued to fire on such of the Iroquois as he could see. The French on the firing platform are reported to have killed many of the enemy. The latter, however, returned to brave the French gunners. While some poured water through the palisades to extinguish the fires, the rest kept up a hail of arrows that wounded two Huron headmen, Ochasteguin and Orani, and hit Champlain in the knee and leg. Although only fifteen other men were injured after a three-hour battle, when the Huron saw that their headmen had been wounded they retreated in a disorderly manner into their fort (3:73–74).

When they had assembled within the fort, Champlain again upbraided them for their undisciplined behaviour. He noted, however, that his words had no effect on them and concluded that the Huron were no warriors; because headmen had no absolute authority over their men and there was no "concert of action" among them, all their undertakings were bound to come to a bad end. Champlain urged them to attack the Iroquois again, but they refused, explaining that many men had already been wounded and would have to be cared for on the way home. Therefore, they did not wish to risk more casualties. The Indians were willing to wait a few days longer, to see if the Susquehannock would arrive. They agreed that, if the latter came, they would launch another attack on the town and try to carry out Champlain's directions (3:75).

In spite of Champlain's persistent pleading that they set fire to the Iroquois fortifications, the Huron refused to do so. Instead, until 16 October they continued to skirmish with the enemy, who from time to time came out of the town to fight with them. If the Iroquois appeared to be gaining an advantage, Champlain's men would cover the withdrawal of their allies with their muskets. The Iroquois greatly feared these guns and retreated as soon as they saw them. The Iroquois protested that the French should not interfere in their conflict with the Huron and taunted the Huron for being cowards, since they required French assistance before they dared to attack them (3:76–77).

Finally, seeing that the Susquehannock had not arrived and that the weather had turned bad, the Huron and Algonkin decided to return home. They also must have feared that Iroquois reinforcements would arrive soon from nearby villages. They fashioned a number of baskets and bound the wounded in a crouching position so that they could be carried on the backs of other Indians. Champlain was impressed by the order with which the Indians withdrew. The older men and wounded were placed in the centre of the column, with well-armed warriors to the sides and in the rear. This order was maintained for three days, during which the Indians covered the twenty-five to thirty leagues back to the spot where their canoes were hidden. Because of his wounds, Champlain was among those who had to be carried on this march, an experience which caused him much agony. Everyone's discomfort was increased by a strong wind and a heavy fall of snow and sleet (3:77–79).

No doubt, Champlain's suffering added to his general feeling of disappointment. In his opinion, the campaign had been a disastrous failure. It also convinced him that his Indian allies had no natural ability as warriors and were unable to follow the most elementary instructions (3:72, 78–79). Because of this, he seems to have decided that he would never again accompany the Indians on such a campaign. Historians have generally agreed with Champlain. They describe this battle as the first triumph of the Iroquois over the French. Trudel (1966a:223) sees it as a turning point in the history of the Iroquois and the first of a series of victories that within forty years were to give them control of the lower Great Lakes.

Even if it were possible to speak collectively about the Iroquois at this period, such an assessment would be a serious misinterpretation of what happened. There is no evidence that any of the Iroquois were less frightened of the French after this battle than before. Many villagers had been killed by French gunfire and, as news of this spread, fear of the French must have increased rather than diminished. Nor is there evidence that any of the Indians who participated in this battle regarded it as a defeat for the Huron. The battle was not the equivalent of a European siege (Trudel 1966a:222). Its primary aim was not to capture an enemy town, but to challenge the enemy to fight, in the hope of killing or capturing some of them. We do not know how many prisoners the Huron captured, aside from the eleven that were taken at the start of the siege, but since a considerable number of the enemy were killed, it must have been a reasonably satisfactory campaign from the point of view of blood revenge. Moreover, the assistance of the French seems to have kept their allies' losses low, although their presence may also have been viewed as disadvantageous, since it deterred the Iroquois from engaging in as much hand-to-hand combat as the Huron and Algonkin might have liked. Champlain nowhere mentions that the Indians were dissatisfied with the campaign, and it seems likely that he alone regarded it as a disastrous defeat. The Huron probably viewed it as a major, but not an atypical, bout in a continuing blood feud with the Iroquois. They probably also hoped that by inflicting injuries on the latter, it might make them less able, or willing, to continue their attacks in the Ottawa Valley.

As a former soldier, Champlain was knowledgeable about European warfare. Yet, he made no effort to understand the nature of Indian warfare or even to determine why particular wars were being fought. He assumed that raids were made for the same general reasons that wars were fought in Europe and that any differences were a result of the technological inferiority and tactical ineptitude of the Indians. He also had no understanding of the important ritual implications of warfare in this region or of the Indians' treatment of their prisoners. For all these reasons, Champlain misjudged the aims of the expedition he accompanied. Because of this, he not only failed to understand the role that he was expected to play, but was unable to judge whether it had been a success or failure in the estimation of his Indian allies.

A WINTER AMONG THE INDIANS

When the Huron returned to where they had left their canoes, Champlain reminded them of their promise to take him down the St. Lawrence River to Quebec. Thereupon, he began to experience the usual vacillations with which the Indians were accustomed to turn down an unacceptable request made by a friend. At first, no one was willing to take him; then four volunteers were found; finally, no one would provide a canoe for the expedition (3:80). Champlain soon realized that the Indians had no intention of taking him home and that he would be forced to spend the winter in the Huron country. At first, he feared that the Huron might be planning to do him some injury, because the battle had not gone as they wished. Later, however, when he found himself well-treated, he decided that they were keeping him and his companions to protect them against Iroquois counter-attacks and so that he could participate in their councils and determine what they should do in the future to defend themselves against their enemies (Biggar 1922–36, 3:81). Much about Champlain is revealed by this immodest appraisal.

The Huron had different reasons for behaving as they did. The Iroquois frequented the St. Lawrence Valley above Montreal and to travel along that portion of the river was very dangerous. Because of this, one might question whether the Huron or Algonkin had been serious when they promised to return Champlain to Quebec along this route. To give them the benefit of the doubt, it is necessary to assume that they believed that if they were accompanied by musketeers, they would be relatively safe from attack.

Thus, while safety was a factor, the Huron had other important reasons for refusing Champlain's request. They and their allies probably mistrusted Champlain and feared that he wished to travel through Iroquois-controlled territory in order to make contact with their enemies. Only a few years before, rumours had circulated about Champlain having dealings with the Iroquois and the memory of these rumours could easily have given rise to such suspicions (Bishop 1948:240–41). His frequent criticism of his allies and his outbursts of rage during the campaign may have created additional doubts about his professed friendship for the Huron. Friendly contact between Champlain and the Iroquois was the last thing that either the Huron or the Algonkin wished to occur. Moreover, it would almost certainly have proved fatal for the Indians who accompanied him. For this reason, the most prudent course was for the Huron to refuse to take Champlain to Quebec by way of Iroquois-controlled territory. Had Champlain inspired more trust and striven to have better rapport with his allies, some of them might have been willing to risk their lives to take him to Quebec.

The return to the Huron country from the east end of Lake Ontario was even slower than the journey down the Trent Valley had been. On 28 October the war party split into small bands. Some headed for home, others remained north of Lake Ontario for the autumn hunt. It was decided that Champlain should go hunting with Atironta, either because by now the latter had replaced Ochasteguin as Champlain's official host or because Ochasteguin's wound made it impossible for him to go hunting. From the east end of Lake Ontario, Atironta and twenty-five of his men appear to have travelled up Cataraqui Creek and portaged the short distance to Loughborough Lake.[24] About twenty-five miles from there, they erected some bark cabins and constructed a large enclosure into which they drove and killed deer. In thirty-eight days, the Huron killed 120 deer, keeping the fat, skins, and a little of the meat to take home with them. While hunting with the Indians, Champlain became lost and was forced to wander in the forest for several days before he perceived the smoke of his host's camp. Hereafter, Atironta made certain that Champlain did not leave camp without an Indian companion. He said that if Champlain had not returned, the Huron should never again have dared to visit the French for fear the latter would hold them responsible for having killed him (Biggar 1922–36, 3:91).

In early December, Atironta's party set out for home. Each of the Huron had to transport one hundred pounds of skins and meat, while Champlain carried a burden of twenty pounds. As long as the ground remained frozen, most of these loads were transported on improvised sledges, but, as the weather turned warmer, it became necessary to travel on foot, sometimes through swamps of knee-deep water. At last, either on 20 or 23 December they returned to Cahiagué.[25] Champlain remained there for several weeks. He discovered that the Onontchataronon were wintering in an encampment near the village, where their wives and children probably had lived while the men had gone to war against the Iroquois. Iroquet was having his son treated by Huron shamans for injuries he had received while trying to kill a bear (3:94).

On 4 January Champlain left for Carhagouha, where he spent over a week living with Father Le Caron and discussing with him a proposed visit to the Tionnontaté. They set out together on 15 January and arrived in the first Tionnontaté village on the seventeenth, probably spending one night at Tequenonquiaye and another on the trail. The total length of this part of their journey was about thirty-five miles (Garrad 1970:237). Champlain and Le Caron visited seven Tionnontaté villages, two of which were in the process of being relocated. Champlain states that he and Le Caron were welcomed by the Tionnontaté and that at each village he contracted a treaty of friendship with its inhabitants and persuaded them to come to Quebec to trade (Biggar 1922–36, 3:95–96). Sagard, on the other hand, reports that Le Caron was not well received, possibly because he incurred the hostility of the Tionnontaté shamans, and that he was soon forced to return to the Huron country (1866:42). This story was repeated and slightly elaborated by Le Clercq (1691:87).

It is possible that Champlain and Le Caron were treated differently, although both of them returned to the Huron country at the same time. Champlain, however, has little concrete to say about the Tionnontaté. This suggests that, like later French visitors, Champlain and Le Caron incurred the wrath of the Huron by attempting to conclude a trading alliance with the Tionnontaté. This may have led to a Huron campaign of slander, in which the latter attempted to convince the Tionnontaté that the French were dangerous people with whom it was unsafe to have dealings. Such campaigns were frequently successful among both the Tionnontaté and the Neutral, and this one may have turned the Tionnontaté against Champlain. It is understandable that Champlain would not have wished to mention a humiliation of this sort. It is also noteworthy that, because of Huron opposition, Champlain's dream of trade between the Tionnontaté and the French was never realized. Charles Garrad (1970: 238), who has made a special study of Tionnontaté historic sites, suggests that the first village visited by Champlain was probably Ehwae, which was their principal, and most southerly, one. From there, he made his way north and west towards Craigleith, before entering the territory of the Cheveux Relevés.

Champlain devoted more space to describing his visit to the Cheveux Relevés. He was delighted by the warm reception they gave him and describes them as being the cleanest Indians he had yet encountered and the ones most given to celebrations and feasting (Biggar 1922–36, 3:98–99). Among his hosts were the Indians he had encountered at the mouth of the French River the previous summer and whom he had probably promised that he would visit some time in the future. He found that the main Cheveux Relevés settlements were located west of the Tionnontaté villages. It was there that they planted their crops and spent the winters; however, like the Stadaconans, they were more dependent on hunting and gathering than were their Iroquoian neighbours and both in summer and in winter they ranged extensively in search of food. In the summer, such travels were frequently combined with trade.

The Cheveux Relevés appear to have been on good terms with the Tionnontaté. Like the northern Algonkians among the Huron, some of them spent the winter living in, or on the outskirts of, Tionnontaté villages, engaging in trade with their inhabitants. They were also on good terms with the tribes of the Neutral confederacy. All these peoples were allies against the Assistaronon, which in this instance was probably a collective term for the Algonkian-speaking tribes of the Michigan Peninsula. It is uncertain how far westward the Cheveux Relevés settlements extended, but it is clear from Champlain's map of 1632 that he did not travel as far west as the Bruce Peninsula (Garrad 1970:238). It is possible that the Assistaronon dominated, if they did not inhabit, the southeastern shores of Lake Huron. The Bruce Peninsula and the region to the south may have been a no man's land between these two groups.

The Cheveux Relevés asked Champlain for military aid against the Assistaronon. Champlain replied that any assistance would have to wait until he made another trip to this region, since he currently lacked necessary supplies (Biggar 1922–36, 3:99). Knowing about the alliance between the Cheveux Relevés and the Neutral confederacy, he expressed a desire to visit the Neutral. The Cheveux Relevés declined to take him south into the Grand Valley, alleging that a Frenchman had accidentally killed a Neutral who was visiting the Iroquois village Champlain had attacked the previous autumn. Since this killing had not been atoned for with presents, the Neutral were likely to seek satisfaction by killing the first Frenchman who fell into their hands. Champlain realized that, once again, his plans were being thwarted by the reluctance of the Indians to promote contact between the French and the more remote tribes with whom these Indians traded. He must have been particularly aware of it in this instance, because some Cheveux Relevés, wishing to encourage his goodwill, assured him that no harm would befall him were he to visit the Neutral (3:100–101). Champlain had wished to use the Cheveux Relevés country as a point of departure for a trip south because of its geographical proximity to the Neutral, but also because his Huron hosts had already shown themselves reluctant to help him to establish contact with the Neutral. Unable to accomplish anything further in this region, Champlain and Le Caron retraced their steps towards Carhagouha, arriving there in mid-February.

DISCORD AT CAHIAGUÉ

When Champlain returned to the Huron country, he set off to visit the Nipissing, who habitually wintered in the lower part of the Wye Valley, not far from Carhagouha. His aim was to find out when they were planning to leave for James Bay so that he might travel with them. Before Champlain reached the Nipissing, however, he began to hear reports of a quarrel that had broken out between the inhabitants of Cahiagué and the Onontchataronon who were living near that village. According to Champlain, this quarrel had arisen over a male Iroquois (Entouhonoron) prisoner, whom the Huron had given to Iroquet in the expectation that he would torture him to death. The event Champlain refers to was probably a division of the prisoners that had been captured the previous autumn. In that case, as one of the participants in this raid, Iroquet would, by right, have received some of the prisoners as his share of the spoils. What angered the Huron was that, instead of killing the prisoner, Iroquet had found him to be an excellent hunter and had exercised his right to keep him alive as his adopted son. If Iroquet's injured son had died, he may have been anxious to find someone to replace him.

Either on general principles, or because this prisoner had injured one of their number, some of the inhabitants of Cahiagué felt aggrieved and determined to kill the prisoner themselves. One man was appointed to carry out this task. Coming upon the prisoner without his intention being suspected, the Arendarhonon slew him in the presence of the Onontchataronon headmen. The latter, indignant at such an act, and feeling obliged to avenge the murder of an adopted kinsman, slew the Arendarhonon on the spot. When the Arendarhonon learned what had happened, they armed themselves and fell upon the Onontchataronon. In the ensuing skirmish, Iroquet received two arrow wounds and some of the Onontchataronon cabins were pillaged. Unable to resist the Arendarhonon, the Onontchataronon offered them fifty wampum belts and a large number of shell beads, as well as various kettles, iron axes, and two female prisoners. The Arendarhonon remained hostile and the Onontchataronon feared that in spite of their efforts to restore goodwill, the Arendarhonon were planning to murder all of them (Biggar 1922–36, 3:101–3).

Champlain was soon met by two or three Indians from Cahiagué, who asked him to hurry back to their village to effect a reconciliation between them and the Onontchataronon. They declared that otherwise a general war would break out between the Huron and Algonkin. If this happened, the Huron, who still regarded the Algonkin as being closer allies of the French than they were themselves, would no longer be willing, or able, to come down-river to trade with the French (3:103). Threatened by the loss of lucrative trade, Champlain hurried to Cahiagué to use his influence to stop this quarrel. On the way, he visited the Nipissing to discuss with them their plans for their journey northward. They informed him that this journey had been broken off. Champlain was told that Iroquet had visited the Nipissing searching for him. In the course of this visit, he had given the Nipissing wampum and requested them to abandon their plans, so that they could come to Quebec in the spring and help to reconcile the Huron and the Algonkin (3:104). It is doubtful, however, that Iroquet's principal motive was to prevent the Nipissing from travelling north, or that the Nipissing would have abandoned the opportunity for some of their people to traverse their annual trade route to James Bay, which was an important source of furs for them. More likely, they gave Champlain the impression that they were not travelling north that year as a polite way of refusing to take him with them.

It would appear that the Algonkin and possibly the Huron had persuaded the Nipissing that it was not in their own interest to permit Champlain to make contact with their northern trading partners. The suggestion that some of the Nipissing should go to Quebec the following summer may have involved a promise that the Algonkin would help the Nipissing form a trading alliance with the French, in return for a Nipissing pledge not to assist the French to explore the interior. If so, this was a major shift in Algonkin policy, since, only two years before, the Kichesipirini had actively been opposed to Champlain making direct contact with the Nipissing. It is this opposition which originally may have induced the Nipissing to offer to take Champlain with them.

Champlain attempted, but was unable to persuade the Nipissing to change their mind. Although he was greatly disheartened by this news, he was now used to the Indians failing to keep their promises to introduce him to their trading partners. He consoled himself with the thought that, in the future, he might find the means of travelling north, as he had eventually found the means to visit the Huron. He concluded, however, that where there was no expectation of his help in warfare, the Indians tended to impede, rather than to facilitate, his exploration of their trading routes (3:31–32).

Champlain set out for Cahiagué with six of his men on 15 February. His arrival greatly pleased both the Huron and the Onontchataronon. Two days were spent hearing from both sides what had happened. It is indicative of the importance attached to Champlain's new alliance with the Huron that he stayed with Atironta, while one of his interpreters, possibly Godefroy, was sent to the Onontchataronon to gather their side of the story (3:106). On the third day, the headmen and other prominent men of Cahiagué went with the French to the Onontchataronon encampment, where the leaders from both sides gathered in a cabin. These leaders agreed that they wished to resolve their dispute peacefully and invited Champlain to act as an arbitrator (3:107).

We know from other sources that both the Huron and their Algonkin trading partners were especially concerned about disputes that arose as a result of murder or injury between different peoples. If not resolved, these disputes could transform a friendly trading relationship into bloody discord. Within a tribe or confederacy, there was always a headman or a council that had as one of its functions to mediate disputes of this sort when they arose within the group. The arbitration of disputes between the Huron and other groups was made more difficult because there was no statutory mediator of this sort. Hence, both the Arendarhonon and the Onontchataronon turned to a common ally for help in resolving their quarrel.

Nevertheless, Champlain's view of the role to be played by a mediator and that held by the Indians were significantly different. The Indians regarded mediation as they did any exercise of leadership, as a matter of persuasion; a mediator should listen to both sides and then make sure that they discussed their differences until a mutually satisfactory solution was reached. Champlain saw the position as conferring much greater authority on him. He claimed that by asking him to mediate their quarrel, the Indians had submitted themselves to his arbitration and he implied that they thereby recognized themselves as subjects of the French king. He asked them to promise in advance that they would follow his advice and to acknowledge that henceforth, as a vice-regal official, he might arrange their affairs as he thought best (3:107–8). While both sides verbally assented to this, they had no concept of authority that could confer such power on Champlain. It is therefore certain that they did not know what they were approving. Champlain interpreted their agreement as signifying that he was gradually acquiring the leadership over these tribes to which he believed his governorship of New France and his natural superiority as a Frenchman entitled him.

Champlain warned both the Huron and the Onontchataronon that, if their quarrel led to war, they would be greatly weakened when it came to resisting their common enemies. He also pointed out that if such warfare prevented one or both parties from coming to trade with the French, the French would be obliged to look for allies and trading partners elsewhere (3:109). This threat to conclude a trading alliance with the Iroquois was certain to intimidate the Huron and Algonkin, but, by exacerbating existing fears that Champlain was carrying on negotiations with the Iroquois behind their backs, it did little to cement the still-evolving relationship between the French and their Huron and Algonkin trading partners.

Champlain then proceeded to tell the contending parties that their blood feud was unworthy of reasoning men, and was characteristic, as he phrased it, of brute beasts. He took the opportunity to denounce again the individuality and lack of coordination in Indian warfare and to argue that greater cooperation was needed to oppose the common foe and to avoid a disastrous defeat at their hands. He argued that the Huron who had been slain had committed a serious crime in killing the Iroquois prisoner and that the Onontchataronon who had avenged the crime were a small minority who had been carried away by passion. He added that the Onontchataronon were not angry at the Huron as a whole, but only at the slain Huron for what he had done (3:109–11). In so arguing, Champlain remained totally oblivious of the principle of collective responsibility for kinsmen that was the basis of Huron and Algonkin justice. Champlain added that when the Iroquois had been attacked, he had retaliated by stabbing his assailant, prior to the latter being attacked by the Onontchataronon. Because of this, it was impossible to tell whether or not the Huron had been slain by the Onontchataronon (3:111–12). Whether this story was true or had been invented in self-defence by the Onontchataronon, it provided a far superior basis for reconciliation than did Champlain's other arguments. He also claimed that the Onontchataronon did not love the prisoner as much as the Huron believed and that after he was dead they had eaten him (3:112), presumably because they once more regarded him as an enemy for having wounded a Huron ally. This seems improbable and, in my opinion, the claim was likely invented, either by Champlain or by the Onontchataronon to assuage the Arendarhonon.

Champlain also argued that the Onontchataronon very much regretted what had happened and to prevent it gladly would have sacrificed their prisoner. He reminded the Arendarhonon of the large compensation they had received for their own tribesman who had been killed, even though he himself was guilty of murder. Champlain admonished both sides to forget what had happened and to live in friendship as before. If they did, the French would continue to trade with them and assist them in their wars. To assure that the summer's trading would not be interrupted, he advised them that if they were still not satisfied, all the groups involved should come to the St. Lawrence. There, in the presence of all the captains of the trading vessels, the French would renew their friendship with each of these tribes and plan new measures to protect them from their enemies

(3:113). By holding out this promise, Champlain hoped to assure not only that there would be trade the following summer, but that both sides would be reconciled within the broader framework of an alliance with the French that was based on military cooperation, trade, and ritual ties.

The Arendarhonon seemed pleased with Champlain's proposals and returned happily to their homes. The Onontchataronon, on the other hand, announced that because of this incident they would not come again to Cahiagué, although in future years they were still wintering among the Arendarhonon (3:114). Champlain returned to the longhouse of his host, Atironta, and continued to do all he could to cultivate his goodwill and encourage him to trade (3:114). By now, the French were well aware of the Huron's ability to amass furs in return for horticultural produce. They also realized how much their success in promoting trade depended on maintaining good relations with the Huron. Because of this, the relative importance of the Algonkin was rapidly declining.

While Champlain prided himself on the role he played in settling this dispute, it seems that, at least to a limited degree, he had again been tricked by Indian diplomacy. The Arendarhonon and Onontchataronon undoubtedly appreciated his assistance as a mediator, but because of the strong economic and political ties that linked them together, it is highly likely that, even without Champlain, they would have been able to resolve their differences. A major concern of both groups was to prevent Champlain from journeying northward with the Nipissing. The dispute that arose between them, while at first real enough, offered them an excellent opportunity to divert Champlain's attention, by convincing him that his services as a mediator were required if the alliance he had made with the Huron headmen was not to be disrupted. Champlain was clearly flattered by this request, as well as fearful that the Huron trade might be lost to the French. Thus, it was not difficult to convince him that he would have to abandon his plans to join the Nipissing, in order to accompany the Huron and Onontchataronon down-river and to see that both sides observed the peace and had free access to French traders. It seems most likely that, by the time Champlain returned to Cahiagué, the dispute between the Huron and Onontchataronon had become a charade that was being played out for his benefit (Trigger 1971*a*:93).

It is unclear where Champlain spent the rest of the winter. The Arendarhonon later claimed that he stayed most of the time with them (Thwaites 1896–1901, 20:19). This suggests that he remained with Atironta, although he visited Father Le Caron from time to time and met various other Huron headmen (Biggar 1922–36, 3:145). During the winter, Champlain was able to observe Huron customs and to formulate his own ideas about how relations between the French and the Huron should develop. In particular, he was convinced that priests alone would not be able to convert the Huron, unless French families were settled amongst them. These families would set an example for the Huron and also, by taking control of the country, would compel the Huron to behave properly (3:145).

The long-term policy that Champlain wished to see applied to the Huron was one that would make them not only Christian in religion, but French in language and culture (3:6). Although his appeal for French settlers to help in this project was phrased in terms of religion, it was clearly devised to promote his general plan for colonization in Canada. As a first step towards realizing this plan, Champlain and Le Caron discussed with the Huron headmen the possibility of French settlers coming to live among the Huron. Champlain was delighted by the ready agreement that the headmen gave to his proposals. They stated that while they did not understand many aspects of what he was talking about, they would be happy to have French families living in their country. They said that in return they would send some of their own children to live with the French (3:146).

The headmen seem to have interpreted Champlain's offer as an extension of the exchange of young men that had begun in 1609. Such an exchange would provide them with hostages to ensure the safety of the Huron who went to trade with the French. Since French, as well as Huron, would be endangered by enemy attacks on the Huron country, they would also ensure that the French would help to retaliate against such attacks. Finally the Huron hoped that if a limited number of French were to settle in their midst, they would be able to learn how to manufacture many items that they now had to purchase from Europeans. New plants and agricultural skills might also be acquired from them (3:146). This extremely practical attitude indicates that even at this early stage in French-Huron relations, the Huron were critically appraising European technology and believed themselves able to benefit by adopting selected items from it.

When, however, Champlain quoted the Huron as saying that their way of life was miserable by comparison with that of the French and, for this reason, it would be easy for them to abandon their old ways and learn to live like Frenchmen, he was either indulging in wishful thinking or quoting his own sentiments, which Huron headmen were echoing in an effort to be polite to him. The Huron had no intention of giving up their own way of life and probably had no idea that this was what Champlain expected them to do. Even when they expressed interest in adopting Christian religious practices, they no doubt had in mind rituals that they could adopt in addition to their own, as they regularly added rituals from neighbouring groups. The evidence that Champlain presents indicates overwhelmingly that the Huron were mainly interested in the material advantages to be derived from closer association with the French. Champlain's comment that "their words seemed to me to be good common sense, because they show the desire they have to gain a knowledge of God" (3:146) can only be interpreted as an invention to gratify readers who were interested in supporting mission work in New France.

ATIRONTA VISITS QUEBEC

In May 1616 the Huron began to make preparations for their annual trip down the Ottawa River to trade with the French. On 20 May Champlain and Le Caron set out from Otoüacha, or the vicinity of Carhagouha, in the company of Atironta (Biggar 1922–36, 3:168). It is uncertain whether all the French who had been in the Huron country returned to the St. Lawrence at this time, or whether some remained behind to help the Huron defend their settlements and to encourage them to trade the following year. It seems likely that this was Atironta's first trip down-river and that he had joined the expedition because he wished to demonstrate that among the Huron he, rather than Ochasteguin, was now the principal ally and trading partner of the French. His visit to Quebec was also intended to reciprocate Champlain's visit to the Huron country. The descent to Montreal Island took forty days and appears to have been an exceptionally pleasant one. A large number of fish and game were caught on the way and these added to the abundance and variety of the provisions that the Huron had brought with them.

On arriving at the Lachine Rapids, Champlain found Gravé Du Pont in a state of despair, having heard that Champlain was dead (3:169). While such a rumour may have been based on a report that Champlain had been wounded, the Montagnais or Kichesipirini had exaggerated this report in an effort to undermine, even briefly, the confidence that the French traders had in the Huron. Trading took place in 1616, as in previous years, on Montreal Island; however, once official greetings had been exchanged Champlain set out for Quebec on 8 July, taking Atironta with him. Before leaving, Champlain promised the Huron and Algonkin that he would continue to assist them in the future as he had done in the past.

He urged them to remember their promise to remain reconciled and assured them that if they kept this promise, he would bring them valuable presents in future years (3:170).

Champlain reached Quebec 11 July and Atironta remained with him for four or five days, examining the French settlement and observing how the French lived. Atironta expressed admiration for what he saw and repeated his earlier wish to have Frenchmen live among the Huron and for Huron youths to be sent to live among the French. He also requested that Champlain honour his proposal to establish a settlement on Montreal Island, in order to secure that part of the river against Iroquois attack. He stated that if Champlain did this, Huron would come and live there. No doubt, by making this promise, Atironta was hoping to develop even closer relations with the French. In view of Champlain's program to promote settlement on the St. Lawrence and to expand these settlements through the assimilation of Indians, it was a very welcome request. Before Atironta left to rejoin his companions, Champlain gave him valuable presents and asked him to return again to visit Quebec (3:171–72). Atironta must have interpreted his visit to Quebec as an indication that the French recognized his function as their principal ally among the Huron. The presents that Champlain gave him would likewise have been interpreted as a response to those that the Huron headmen had sent down-river in 1611.

Conclusion

The years 1609 to 1615 saw the development of a Huron trading relationship with the French, which gradually became free of the ties that either of them had with the Algonkin. By 1611, the Huron headmen seem to have agreed that all the tribes of the Huron confederacy had a right to engage in this trade. They also agreed that control of trade should be vested in the hands of the traditional council chiefs, with Atironta, the principal headman of the Arendarhonon, being recognized as the special ally of the French. These arrangements, which protected the Huron confederacy against internal discord and which also reinforced its traditional political organization, were to remain in effect until the dissolution of the confederacy in 1649.

Despite Algonkin opposition, the French and Huron succeeded in establishing direct contact with each other. At first, the Huron travelled down-river only in the company of their Onontchataronon allies, but by

1611 they had secretly sent presents to Champlain which expressed their desire for a separate alliance with the French. Yet, although the Algonkin were growing increasingly dependent on the Huron both for corn, which they could exchange for furs among the northern hunters, and for military assistance against the Iroquois, the Huron were anxious not to offend them by overtly challenging their rights as middlemen. Moreover, since the headmen who controlled trade could not all leave their country at one time, the conclusion of a formal treaty depended on Champlain travelling inland to meet these leaders in person and to confer with them.

Champlain's visit to the Huron country and Atironta's return visit to Quebec fulfilled Huron expectations concerning the manner in which a trading alliance should be concluded. Champlain visited all the major Huron villages and assured their headmen of his friendship and of the desire that the French had to trade with them. In addition, by accompanying a Huron war party, Champlain was able to impress his hosts with the general concern he had for their well-being. The Jesuits were to report, many years later, that the memory of Champlain's visit was still cherished by the Arendarhonon, who recalled his many good qualities and commented on his continence with regard to women (Thwaites 1896–1901, 20:19).

In spite of his success, Champlain was not aware of many Huron customs nor did he understand the significance that many of his actions had for them. He had, of course, little experience in dealing with the Arendarhonon prior to his visit to their country and Brûlé, who had lived amongst them for a number of years, was almost certainly regarded and treated by the Huron as a young man. Because of this, Champlain could have acquired little knowledge of the inner workings of Huron politics. In particular, Champlain seems to have placed undue emphasis on the role of war in making an alliance with the Huron. Such an alliance, in his opinion, consisted of a sworn friendship, in which an Indian tribe agreed to trade with the French in return for him agreeing to help them in their wars (Biggar 1922–36, 3:226–27). No doubt, the Huron were pleased that Champlain wished to accompany them on a raid, as they were pleased that he should hunt with them, but they were not particularly hard-pressed by their enemies. Military alliances were not a necessary part of their trading relations with the Algonkian-speaking peoples and long periods were to pass during which they received no military assistance from the French, yet continued to trade with them. What the Huron headmen did want was an assurance that their people would be well treated if they came to trade with the French on their own, rather than in the company of Algonkin. This assurance, amongst others, they received from Champlain.

On the other hand, Champlain's repeated criticism of Huron customs and his interference with their torturing of prisoners must have annoyed and troubled them. One can only imagine that such translations as the Indians had of what he said softened his remarks and made them more acceptable. More serious were Champlain's threats to abandon the Huron and Algonkin and to seek his allies elsewhere if things did not go as he wanted. The Huron tended to be suspicious of groups they did not know well and such threats must have served to heighten their fears that the rumours they heard about Champlain's dealings with the Iroquois were true.

Champlain's success in concluding a treaty with the Huron seems to have been achieved in spite of the broad gulf of mutual misunderstanding that separated him from the Arendarhonon. Each assumed the other's behaviour to be more like their own than in fact it was and each therefore interpreted the other's actions in terms of their own code. That such misunderstanding did not lead to serious difficulties must be attributed to the nature of the situation. Champlain's actions in the Huron country in the winter of 1615–16 do not reveal him as a man who understood the Indians and knew how to deal with them, as many historians have claimed. Instead, they show him to be a man who not only understood very little about Indian ways but was too inflexible in his opinions to learn about them. That a treaty was concluded at all seems to have been largely the result of Champlain accommodating himself, haphazardly and unwittingly, to the Huron conventions that had to be observed if such a treaty were to be made. It is therefore more accurate to speak of the Huron headmen concluding a treaty with Champlain than of Champlain concluding a treaty with them.

Once formulated, however, this treaty was the basis of all future relations between the Huron and the French. Hereafter, in spite of Algonkin and Montagnais intrigues, the Huron felt confident to undertake the journey to the St. Lawrence and to trade with the French on their own account. Frenchmen were now free to live among the Huron as allies, and henceforth the Huron would feel more secure in sending their people to live with the French. Aid in warfare and the activities of the French missionaries would be seen, not as the basis of the French-Huron alliance, but as an extension of the friendship and goodwill that was ritually established at the time of Champlain's visit and was renewed thereafter by repeated exchanges of gifts and formal expressions of good faith between the two groups.

Significantly, the only casualty of Champlain's visit to the Huron country appears to have been Champlain himself. He had not intended to spend the winter among the Huron and their refusal to return him to Quebec had frightened and angered him. The very thought of spending a winter among the Huron had been distasteful to him before his visit and there is no reason to believe that the actual experience changed his mind. In later years, Champlain was to find one excuse after another not to accompany the Huron, or any other Indian group, on their military excursions against the Iroquois and diplomatic missions to the Indians were entrusted to priests or trading agents. Perhaps Champlain now felt too old for such travel; more likely, however, he was determined never again to subject himself to Indian control. The winter that Champlain was compelled to spend among the Huron seems to have enlarged a basic fear and mistrust of the Indians, which hitherto had been concealed by a sense of superiority and of his ability to control them (Trigger 1971a:87–93).

Chapter 6 The Quiet Years

Introduction

The years 1616 to 1629 constitute a well-defined period of Huron history.
It is indicative of the important role that trading relations with Europeans
had come to have for the Huron that this period began with the conclusion
of a trading alliance between the Huron and the French and ended with
the latter's first expulsion from Quebec. Unfortunately, the documentation for this period is neither as abundant nor as varied as the historian
might wish. One very obvious gap is the lack of material dealing with the
Huron in Champlain's writings after 1618. Champlain never returned to
the Huron country and his later writings are preoccupied with the administration of the tiny and ill-supported colony at Quebec, on whose success
he saw his own future now depending. Even his interest in exploring the
interior, and possibly discovering a route to the Pacific Ocean, appears to
have declined in the face of this overriding concern. For example, the
delineation of the Great Lakes region in his map of 1632 shows no advance
over what was recorded by him in a map drawn up immediately after his
return to France in 1616 (Wroth 1954) (plates 27 and 28). Gross inaccuracies in the representation of parts of the interior explored by Brûlé and
others suggest little effective consultation with these men.

The only Indians with whom Champlain was in regular contact after his
return from the Huron country were the Montagnais who lived around
Quebec. Other tribes are referred to only in so far as Champlain found it
necessary to confer with their headmen. Regular trading with the Indians
was carried on by representatives of whatever company held the monopoly
at Quebec. It is perhaps indicative of the smooth course of French-Huron
relations during these years that none of the available documents suggests
that Champlain had personal dealings of any consequence with the Huron
after 1618.

A still more serious shortcoming is the failure of any other layman to
record his experiences in the Huron country between 1616 and 1629.
Everything that we know about such men who visited the Huron country
at this time was recorded either by Champlain or by the clergy, both of

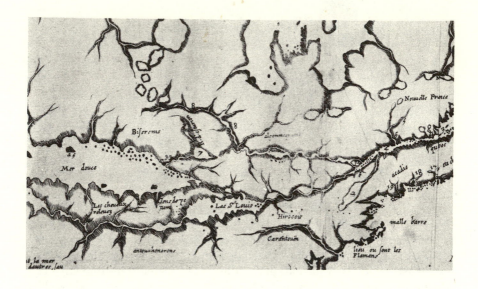

PLATE 27. *Detail of Champlain's map of New France, 1616. This map, probably a proof from an unfinished plate, embodies the cartographic knowledge that Champlain acquired from his visit to the Huron country in 1615–16. The St. Lawrence Valley and Georgian Bay are now brought into reasonable alignment though the geography of the lower Great Lakes remains poorly understood. The existence of Lake Erie is unsuspected and most of southwestern Ontario is eliminated. This map is valuable mainly because a comparison with Champlain's* Carte de la Nouvelle France *of 1632 indicates that his knowledge of the interior was unaffected by the important explorations of Brûlé, Daillon, and others in the intervening sixteen years. This may indicate that after 1616 Champlain lost his burning zeal to unravel the geography of the interior. Courtesy John Carter Brown Library.*

whom violently disapproved of the lives that many of these men led there. Yet these laymen often lived among the Huron for extended periods, helped to defend their villages, learned their language, and in some cases became members of Huron families. Even an illiterate description of their adventures would have provided more information about daily life among the Huron than do the writings of priests who refused to live in Huron villages. They might also have provided information about activities such as trade, war, and intertribal politics, about which the missionaries evinced only marginal interest.

The major sources of information concerning the Huron at this time are the writings of the Recollet missionaries who worked among them from 1623 to 1628. Contemporary Jesuit documents are few in number and the little that is known about Jean de Brébeuf's three-year stay among the Huron has been gleaned largely from his later writings. The most important Recollet sources are the two books written by Gabriel Sagard, a Recollet lay brother and former secretary to the provincial of the Recollets of Saint-Denis. These are *Le grand voyage au pays des Hurons*, published in 1632, and his longer *Histoire du Canada*, published in 1636. In the first of these books, Sagard described his stay in the Huron country during the winter of 1623–24. This book contains the best general account of Huron life by a single author and recounts miscellaneous incidents that happened while he was there. Sagard was anxious to enhance his own reputation by playing down the role of Father Joseph Le Caron, who was in charge of the Recollet mission to the Huron; indeed throughout his book, the humble but vain lay brother liked to give the impression that he was the *de facto* leader of the expedition. An annotated version of the *Grand Voyage* was reproduced in Sagard's *Histoire*, and to it was added an introductory part describing the activities of the Recollets in Canada from 1615 to 1625, and a final section covering the period from the arrival of the Jesuits in 1625 to the abandonment of Quebec by the French in 1629.

The *Histoire* was a semi-official piece of propaganda, protesting Cardinal Richelieu's refusal to allow the Recollets to return to Canada in 1632. While it was by no means an extravagant polemic, it was disapproved of by the Jesuits. It is not surprising therefore that the eighteenth-century Jesuit missionary and historian, Pierre Charlevoix (1866–72, 1:78), attacked Sagard's work on the grounds that he neither understood the Huron language nor took the trouble to verify what he reported. Charlevoix's comments have misled some later historians into believing that Sagard was an untutored and credulous person, whose work is not to be taken seriously. On the contrary, allowing for his self-importance and a

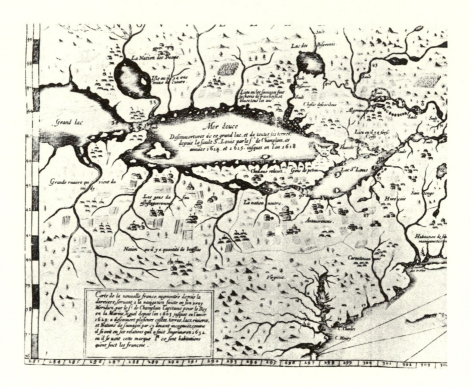

PLATE 28. *Detail of Champlain's* Carte de la Nouvelle France, *1632.*
From Champlain's Voyages of 1632. *The geography of southwestern*
Ontario remains poorly understood and the Neutral are shown living south
of the Great Lakes between the Assistaronon and the Iroquois (whose western
tribes are called Antouoronon). Lake Simcoe (unnamed) and the Huron
country are more accurately outlined than on the map of 1616. Dotted lines
indicate the routes Brûlé followed to the Susquehannock (Carantouanais)
and of Champlain's expedition against the Iroquois. The Lac des Biserenis
is Lake Nipissing. Courtesy Public Archives of Canada.

tendency (not uncommon for that period) to embellish his narrative with stories surreptitiously borrowed from other sources, Sagard's *Histoire* constitutes a valuable record of French-Huron relations.

Also of value is Chrestien Le Clercq's *Premier établissement de la foy dans la Nouvelle-France*, published in 1691. This was yet another piece of propaganda, but unlike Sagard's relatively even-tempered book, it attempted explicitly to discredit all of the work that the Society of Jesus had done in Canada. Although Le Clercq's facts are often inaccurate, the book reproduces in whole, or in part, numerous manuscripts dealing with the Recollet mission that have since been lost. These include parts of a relation written by Le Caron, Father Daillon's account of his visit to the Neutral country in 1626–27, and records of meetings at which missionary policy was discussed. For all of its shortcomings, Le Clercq's narrative provides a more balanced picture of Recollet activities in Canada than does Sagard and allows us to correct some of the distortions that Sagard's personal vanity introduced into his writings. Le Clercq's generalizations also help to clarify certain aspects of Recollet policy.

Archaeological work carried out in the Huron country, particularly in recent years, has begun to yield evidence which, in the future, will contribute to a more complete understanding of changes in Huron life at this period.[1] While the results obtained so far are interesting, the evidence remains too fragmentary to permit general conclusions. It appears, however, that further work will amplify and confirm, rather than revise, the general outline of Huron cultural development as it has been derived from written sources and is presented in this chapter.

Given the nature of the sources, it is impossible to discuss this period in simple chronological order. In the first part of this chapter, I will examine various facets of Huron external relations chronologically. In the second part, I will examine the evidence for changes in Huron life at this time, which cannot be treated chronologically. Many of the trends undoubtedly began prior to this period and became intensified later. This section is thus a general discussion of the effects of European contact, in the absence of deliberate efforts by the French to bring about change.

Trade with the French

VOLUME

The most striking feature of this period was the trade that was carried on between the Huron and the French. Every year after the Huron had concluded their alliance with Champlain, Huron traders came to the St. Lawrence to exchange their furs for European goods. Before long, the Huron, though not irreversibly dependent on these goods, were accustomed to obtaining them on a regular basis. In order to win a clear idea of the impact that this trade had on the Huron, it is necessary to determine the type and amount of goods that were being exchanged between the Huron and the French. Because detailed records of this trade are not available, this is not something that can be done in precise detail. Nevertheless, from the evidence that is available, it is possible to make some useful, if rough, estimates.

During this period, the French continued to trade for a variety of fancy furs such as moose, lynx, fox, otter, marten, badger, and muskrat (Thwaites 1896–1901, 4:207). As a sideline, they also purchased beaver glands, which they sold in France for medicinal purposes.[2] As already indicated, however, even before the turn of the century, beaver skins had become the main item of trade between the Indians and the French. Lescarbot states that in 1558 a beaver skin sold in France for only fifty sous ($2\frac{1}{2}$ livres). By 1611, the growing demand for skins had raised the price to eight and a half livres, and, by 1618, ten livres, a price that remained roughly constant for many decades (2:127; 4:207; 15:159; 28:235).[3] Most of the pelts that the Huron brought to Quebec were beaver skins.

The number of skins that came from the Huron country is less certain. Charles Lalemant, writing in 1626, said that 12,000 to 15,000 skins were exported through Tadoussac each year; however, on one occasion, as many as 22,000 skins had been exported (4:207). Even more skins may have left New France in 1627, which was described as the best year for the fur trade in a long time (Biggar 1922–36, 5:232). In 1630, 30,000 skins were exported, but this was probably because, during the two previous years, the French had lacked supplies of trade goods and hence had been unable to trade with the Indians.[4] A much smaller number of skins were exported from New Netherland at this time: 4700 in 1624 and 7685 in 1628 (Trelease 1960:43).

There is no direct evidence concerning how many of these furs were obtained from the Huron, rather than from the Algonkin or Montagnais. Champlain states that, in 1623, sixty Huron and Algonkin canoes came down the Ottawa River (Biggar 1922–36, 5:100–101), of which the majority appear to have been Huron. Le Clercq (1691:258) affirms that the following year sixty Huron canoes followed Le Caron down-river. Estimates of this sort are likely to be somewhat low, however, since at this period the Huron were coming in small groups to trade. Their canoes held from two to six people and, in general, larger ones were preferred for travelling on the Ottawa River (Wrong 1939:56, 246). In spite of the scarcity of data, Heidenreich's (1971:280) estimate of sixty Huron canoes each year, in all carrying about 200 traders, seems accurate. Sagard states that each canoe could carry about a hogshead of cargo (Wrong 1939:101), which appears to be equivalent to 200 skins weighing about a pound each.[5] This suggests that the Huron supplied the French with about 10,000 beaver skins annually, which was a high percentage of the total number of furs that they obtained. It may be noted, however, that the Huron traded corn for furs with the Algonkin on their way down the Ottawa River. Thus, by the time they reached the French trading stations, they had in their possession many furs collected by the Ottawa Valley tribes. The other principal suppliers of the French were the Montagnais at Tadoussac, but while the latter's trade network stretched as far north as Hudson Bay, because of the low population density in central Quebec, considerably fewer furs were collected by them than by the Huron. Also, by this time, intensive hunting had probably reduced the number of beaver in the Saguenay region. It seems likely, therefore, that the Huron supplied about two-thirds of all the furs that were traded along the St. Lawrence at that time. In particularly good years, or when the Huron had been unable to trade with the French the year before, the number of furs they brought probably exceeded 10,000. Considering the importance of the Huron trade, it is not difficult to understand why the clerks who traded with the Indians had to be as skilled in the Huron language as they were in Montagnais or Algonkin (Biggar 1922–36, 6:62–63).

TRADE ON THE ST. LAWRENCE

In the early days, expeditions in which Champlain fought alongside the Huron and Algonkin had proved a potent means of attracting Huron traders to the St. Lawrence. These expeditions had also blunted the power of the Mohawk and made the St. Lawrence River an important artery of communication. Moreover, by having Champlain accompany an expedition that was launched against the Iroquois from the Huron country, the Huron headmen had been able to circumvent Algonkin opposition and conclude a treaty with the French. Once the Mohawk were driven from the St. Lawrence and the French-Huron alliance was firmly established, expeditions of this sort became less important for encouraging the Huron to visit the St. Lawrence.

Champlain stated that in 1617 he had planned to assist the Huron and Algonkin, but had been prevented from doing so by the small number of warriors who turned up that year.[6] It seems that few Huron visited the St. Lawrence Valley that year because they anticipated Oneida reprisals, once the latter learned that Champlain and most of his musketeers had left the Huron country. Having obtained sufficient trade goods to satisfy their needs when they had visited the St. Lawrence in 1616, many Huron probably decided to stay home and guard their villages the following year, rather than join a campaign south of the St. Lawrence.

In 1618, Huron traders attempted to persuade Champlain to return to the Huron country with them. They stated that they were being harassed by their enemies and wished his help to defend their villages. Champlain had been angered by the failure of the Indians to turn out in force the previous year, and also by the Montagnais' murder of two Frenchmen, whose bodies had been discovered in the spring of that year. Because of this, he declined to help the Huron. Instead, he pointed out that he had intended to assist them the previous year, but they had failed to turn up; now he lacked the men and supplies to do so. He promised that he would return in 1619 to give them the victory that they wanted over their enemies (Biggar 1922–36, 3:210–11). Champlain states that he made this promise in order to make certain that the Indians would return to trade the following year; however, his promise to Brûlé that he would return to reward him and to aid his Indian friends in their wars (3:226) seems to indicate that, at least for the moment, he may seriously have been considering another expedition.[7] He can scarcely have intended to take part in any prolonged campaign, since he was planning to return to Quebec in 1619 with many settlers and the materials to establish his long hoped-for colony (3:229). In order to avoid the expense involved in such an enterprise, over the following winter the partners in the trading company sought to strip Champlain of his command at Quebec. While they failed to do this, they prevented him from sailing for the New World until 1620.

The Huron do not appear to have been particularly troubled by Champlain's failure to return. Twice before, in 1612 and again in 1614, he had not turned up for a rendezvous, hence his not doing so again can scarcely have surprised them. By this time, the Huron were sufficiently anxious to trade with the French, and sufficiently confident of their relations with company officials, that Champlain's failure to keep his promise did not cause them to cease visiting the French. They would only have done that if Champlain had openly expressed hostility towards them, or if they were convinced that he was planning to harm them in some way. In time, it must have become apparent to the Huron headmen that Champlain was no longer willing to accompany his Indian allies. Yet, they seem to have accepted Champlain's excuses for his inactivity and ceased to expect his personal assistance in their wars. They may have realized that his enforced sojourn amongst them had made him reluctant to entrust himself to them for a second time. More likely, they interpreted his unwillingness to travel as an indication of advancing age and status. They may have concluded that, as with their own council chiefs, official duties kept him at home.

This did not mean that the Huron ceased to expect military assistance from the French. Henceforth, however, they were satisfied with the armed Frenchmen who came with the authorization of the fur traders to winter, or to stay longer, in their country. By living in, or near, the Huron villages, these men helped to guard these villages against Iroquois raiding parties. The fear that French musketeers continued to inspire in the Iroquois at this period is likely to have resulted in fewer Iroquois invading the Huron country. This permitted the Huron men who normally remained to guard their villages to engage in trading activities. While we have no record of Frenchmen joining Huron raiding parties after 1615, in 1624 a number of Frenchmen volunteered to fight alongside the Huron in a projected war against the Neutral (Wrong 1939:157). More important, the French who travelled to and from the Huron country were able to protect the Huron from Iroquois attack in the lower part of the Ottawa Valley. Sagard records that once the Iroquois learned that Frenchmen were travelling with the Huron, they ceased raiding the Ottawa Valley, just as they had formerly ceased attacking the St. Lawrence Valley (ibid. 261).[8]

This apparently voluntary cessation of raids by the eastern tribes of the Iroquois confederacy indicates how completely the Mohawk and their neighbours had been intimidated by the French. As trading opportunities opened up along the Hudson River, they appear to have abandoned any serious attempt to obtain either furs or European goods by stealing them from trading expeditions that were likely to be accompanied by Frenchmen. Not enough was to be gained to make it worthwhile to risk a possible encounter with the French. The western Iroquois tribes continued to raid the Huron country, despite the presence of some armed Frenchmen. This was probably in part because they had less easy access to European trade goods than did the Mohawk or Oneida and because the number of French who wintered among the Huron was limited. Thus the chance of obtaining such items in raids against their traditional enemies encouraged them to continue these raids in the face of new dangers.

INTERTRIBAL POLITICS IN THE OTTAWA VALLEY

Once the Ottawa Valley was safe from attack, the Huron no longer had to travel in large war parties, as they had done on their earliest trading expeditions. Instead, small groups of traders could journey to and from the Huron country independently of one another. Sagard's descriptions indicate that over much of the route only one or two canoes might stay together (Wrong 1939:56, 255), although in some cases six or more did so (247). Frenchmen who set out for the Huron country at the same time, but in different canoes, were likely to encounter one another only once or twice en route, and then only accidentally (56). While little is known about the composition of trading parties, each group was probably made up of men from a single village. In 1624, Brûlé is reported to have travelled down the Ottawa River with five or six canoes from Toanché (247). Sagard mentions that as a sign of their passing the members of a trading party often erected a piece of birch bark painted with the symbol of their village (251–52). Travelling companions from large villages were probably further subdivided according to clan.

A trip to or from the Huron country took three to four weeks. Although only one watershed was crossed, forty to one hundred stretches of rough water had to be negotiated. Many of these necessitated unloading the canoes and carrying them and their contents overland for considerable distances. Others required crews to get into the water and guide the loaded canoes through the rapids by hand (264). At its highest point, the canoe route rose 677 feet above sea level. By comparison, the Huron country was at an altitude of about 580 feet, and the French trading stations were almost at sea level. Both the greater climb and the direction of the current made the homeward journey more difficult than the trip to the St. Lawrence (Latourelle 1952–53, 1:59).

The aim of the Huron was to reach the St. Lawrence between mid-June and mid-July. This was when other tribes from the interior gathered to trade for goods that had arrived from France a few weeks earlier. The trip down-river was generally a hurried one, for fear the French would depart before their arrival. By contrast, the journey home was more leisurely, with time taken out to fish and visit other Indians along the way (Wrong 1939:60, 63). The Huron approached the trading stations by way of both the Lachine Rapids and the Rivière des Prairies north of Montreal Island. As the trading stations were moved down-river, the Lachine route became less popular, although some Indians continued to use it throughout the first half of the seventeenth century (264–65). At first, the Huron may have preferred to use the Rivière des Prairies because it was more sheltered from Iroquois attack. Later, however, they preferred it because none of its rapids was nearly so formidable as were those at Lachine.

The decline of the Iroquois threat in the Ottawa Valley also eliminated the urgent need for cooperation between the Huron and their Algonkian-speaking allies along the St. Lawrence and Ottawa Rivers. These Algonkians begrudged the loss of their role as middlemen between the French and the Huron; however, for numerical reasons, and because they wished to barter for Huron corn, neither the Kichesipirini, nor any other Algonkin group, was prepared to resort to violence to try to disrupt trade between the Huron and the French. The Huron acknowledged the Kichesipirini's right to collect tolls in return for allowing other Indians to pass along their section of the Ottawa River. The Kichesipirini collected these tolls by compelling the Huron to give them presents and to barter corn meal for furs at rates that were highly favourable to the Kichesipirini. Thus the question of a right of passage did not lead to open hostility.

In spite of this, the cessation of Iroquois raids resulted in increasing friction between the Algonkin and the Huron traders. When the various tribes assembled to trade with the French in 1623, the Huron complained that the Algonkin had maltreated them, by robbing them and levying heavy tolls on their goods (Biggar 1922–36, 5:103). Although the French attempted to restore friendly relations, the next year Sagard reported the continuing high-handed behaviour of the Kichesipirini. The latter did not allow Huron canoes to travel down the Ottawa River individually, but held them back until a considerable number had gathered, in order to obtain corn meal more cheaply (Wrong 1939:255). Sagard witnessed the crews of his own and other canoes being compelled to trade their corn on terms set by the Kichesipirini. The Huron dreaded these annual encounters but recognized themselves bound, both by prudence and by intertribal law, to treat the Algonkin with respect. While the Huron were anxious to avoid having to trade with the Kichesipirini, they assumed, no doubt correctly, that the Kichesipirini would cause serious trouble if the Huron attempted to ignore the latter's right to regulate the trade that passed through their territory.

The Kichesipirini were able to create the most difficulties for the Huron, because their summer camp lay astride the Ottawa River. Algonkin groups who lived down-stream located their summer camps along the larger tributaries of the Ottawa River, possibly originally to avoid Iroquois attacks. There is no evidence that any of these groups attempted to levy tolls on goods passing through their territories in the systematic way that the Kichesipirini did. Nevertheless, they too caused trouble for Huron traders. In 1624, the Petite Nation told the first Huron who came down-river that year that the French fleet had been lost at sea and that it was a waste of time for them to continue their journey. Although the ships had been late reaching Tadoussac, the French were no doubt correct when they assumed that this report was being spread in the hope that the Huron would resume trading with the Algonkin, rather than continuing on to trade with the French (262–64).

The same year, when the Huron passed a Montagnais encampment near Sillery, the latter attempted to compel them to surrender a portion of their corn meal in return for a right of passage (268). The Montagnais were prevented from doing this by the French, who refused to recognize the territorial claims of the Montagnais in such matters and sent an armed shallop to assist the Huron. This episode nevertheless indicates that the Montagnais, like the Kichesipirini, demanded rights of passage from interior tribes who were passing through their territory to trade with the French. No doubt these were partly claimed as compensation for the monopolies over trade with the interior that had been lost, in turn, by both of these groups.

The Algonkin and Montagnais used rumours to frighten the Huron as well as to discourage them. When Sagard and Brûlé attempted to persuade the Huron traders to continue down-river to Quebec in 1624, the Algonkin and Montagnais who had gathered at Cape Victory, near the mouth of the Richelieu River, told the Huron that the Mohawk had given them twenty wampum belts to inform them of the Huron's arrival, so that they might come and kill them. The fact that the French had been negotiating a peace treaty with the Mohawk, which was to be formally ratified only a few weeks later, lent an air of plausibility to the story; nevertheless it was a fabrication designed to frighten the Huron and prevent them from going to Quebec. Sagard also suggests that by reminding the Huron of their dependence on their allies' goodwill, the Algonkin and Montagnais hoped to get presents from them. In fact, the Huron offered a considerable quantity of tobacco, corn, and fishing nets to the Algonkin and Montagnais headmen, to counteract the presents that these headmen claimed the Mohawk had given them (265–66).

There is no evidence of trading between the Indians and the French at Lachine after 1616. Thereafter, trading took place at Three Rivers or near the mouth of the Richelieu River, either at St. Ignace Island or Cape Victory (otherwise Cape Massacre, or in Huron Kontrandeen [Anthrandéen]). The latter spot was so named after the victory that Champlain and his Indian allies had won near there in 1610. While the accounts suggest that each of these places was a major trading station in different years, trading may have gone on at all three locations in the course of a single season.

The French were responsible for the removal of the trading place down-river. The earlier shifts up the St. Lawrence, from Quebec to Saint Ignace Island and then to Montreal Island, had resulted from rivalry between de Monts's men and the independent traders to whom the fur trade had been thrown open in 1609. The monopoly granted to the *Compagnie du Canada* in 1614 ended the competition for furs on the upper St. Lawrence and, once regular trading relations had been established with the Huron, the French traders no longer wished to journey from Quebec to the Lachine Rapids. It was convenient for them to centralize all of their trading with the Indians at Quebec, in so far as this was possible. This eliminated many disadvantages, including the cost of transporting goods up-river and the dangers of passing through the Richelieu Rapids (Biggar 1922–36, 5:97). In 1623, Gravé Du Pont, who was the chief factor at Quebec, went up-river to urge the Indians to come to Quebec. He only managed, however, to persuade sixteen canoes to venture down-river and, once again, French traders were forced to travel to Cape Victory (5:100). The next year, when Brûlé and Sagard tried to coax the Huron to Quebec, the latter were persuaded not to go by the Montagnais and Algonkin. The Algonkin realized that if no Indians went down-river, the French would have to come to Cape Victory to trade. This would spare them having to travel with their wives and children to Quebec, where, in any case, there was no food for them (Sagard 1866:753).

The Algonkian-speaking peoples who brought their families with them to trade were as anxious to avoid the long journey to Quebec as the French were to avoid having to transport their goods up-river. The French preferred to trade at Quebec; the Algonkin preferred Montreal. The stations at either end of Lake St. Peter, where the trading actually took place, were compromises between these conflicting interests. They were compromises that also pleased the Algonkians who lived in the Batiscan and St. Maurice Valleys. Not having women and children with them, the Huron traders were less burdened than were their Algonkian-speaking allies, and, because of this, they were probably less opposed to going to Quebec than the Algonkin were. Nevertheless, the farther downstream they travelled, the more intertribal difficulties they encountered. Hence, like the Algonkin, they probably preferred to trade at Montreal rather than at Three Rivers, and at Three Rivers rather than at Quebec.

A small number of Huron went to Quebec from time to time. Mostly, they visited the French settlement on business. They came in 1628 because, as a result of the French trading vessels not arriving in Canada that summer, the traders at Quebec did not bother to meet the Indians at the accustomed trading stations (ibid. 853). In the case of Sagard, the obligation to return a visiting friar to the Recollet house seems to have been the sole reason that his Indian companions agreed to travel down-river (Wrong 1939:267).

Curiosity about the French settlement probably also caused some Huron traders to visit Quebec, as Ochasteguin and Atironta had done earlier. These would have been headmen, who wielded enough influence to persuade their companions to accompany them. Such visitors returned home to report the wonders they had seen at Quebec. These included the tides in the river, a phenomenon that the Huron had never seen before. Sagard reports that, because of these tides, the Huron believed the St. Lawrence River to be controlled by a more powerful water spirit than any in their own country (Sagard 1866:470–71).

Unfortunately, little is known about the Huron who wintered at Quebec in 1625 (Le Clercq 1691:343). They may have been the Attignawantan families whom Le Caron is alleged to have persuaded to "settle" at Quebec, when he visited the Huron country in 1623–24 (ibid. 257). Yet, these Indians remained at Quebec only for a single winter, and it is unlikely they saw themselves as potential settlers there. Atironta, the principal headman of the Arendarhonon, and the successor of the first Atironta who had visited Quebec, spent the winter of 1645–46 living there with his relatives (Thwaites 1896–1901, 27:103). As the principal Huron ally of the French, Atironta no doubt felt he had the right to stay at Quebec at the expense of his allies, in the same manner that Huron extended hospitality to the French who visited their country. It is therefore probable that the Huron who visited Quebec in 1625 did so to satisfy the curiosity of their headman and to promote better relations between the Huron and the French. Since Father Daillon travelled to the Huron country in the company of these Huron in 1625 and was taken to Toanché rather than Cahiagué, it is likely that the leader of this group was a headman of the northern Attignawantan, who by this period seem to have replaced the Arendarhonon as the principal trading partners of the French.

PEACE WITH THE MOHAWK

The use of the St. Lawrence River was made even easier by the peace treaty that was concluded, in 1624, between the French and their Algonkian allies on the one hand and the Mohawk on the other.[9] The French first became aware of the possibility of peace in June 1622, when two Mohawk appeared at Three Rivers and proposed to put an end to the war that had gone on for fifty years between their people and the Montagnais (Biggar 1922–36, 5:73–80). They stressed that they were there unofficially and that their aim was to visit and eventually to recover relatives and friends who had been taken prisoner by the Montagnais; however, they also revealed to the French that tentative peace talks had been going on between the Mohawk and Montagnais for some time. Champlain was in favour of such a peace, since he believed that the French would derive many benefits from it. It would guarantee to everyone the free use of the St. Lawrence River and open up new opportunities for trade in the interior. It would also make it possible for both the Algonkians and the Iroquois to hunt in the vast no man's land that lay between the St. Lawrence River and the Iroquois country. This area, which embraced Lake Champlain and the Adirondacks, was particularly rich in game, since for a long time the conflict between the Iroquois and the Algonkin had permitted only sporadic hunting there. Finally, a peace treaty with the Mohawk might allow the French to persuade the entire Iroquois confederacy to trade with them (5:74).

Peace between the Mohawk and Montagnais had been a goal of French policy as early as 1603. Now for the first time, there seemed to be an opportunity to conclude such a treaty. Seizing the opportunity, Champlain invited these two Mohawk to visit Quebec, where they were entertained with feasts and dances. The Montagnais were also persuaded to have their spokesmen accompany the Mohawk when the latter returned to their country. These envoys invited the Mohawk headmen to come to Quebec and discuss a formal peace treaty. To indicate the goodwill of the French, Champlain sent a valuable present of beaver skins to the Mohawk headmen (5:80).

The Mohawk had reasons that were unknown to the French for wanting peace at this time. Since these reasons are important for understanding the whole structure of relations between Indians and Europeans in eastern Canada and the northeastern United States at this period, a brief explanation of them is required. We have already noted that, prior to 1609, the Iroquois had been forced to obtain European goods from the St. Lawrence Valley and that competition for these goods had generated a series of conflicts into which the French were drawn, and which ultimately proved very costly for the Mohawk. Because of this, the Mohawk welcomed the arrival of Dutch traders on the Hudson as an opportunity to disengage themselves from a losing struggle on the St. Lawrence.

The Dutch soon were trading with the Mohawk as well as the Mahican. The Mohawk appear to have been free, at least most of the time, to travel through Mahican territory to the Dutch trading post at Fort Nassau and later at Fort Orange. Their landlocked position put them at a disadvantage, however, in comparison with their eastern neighbours, whose tribal lands stretched along both banks of the Hudson River. In the first years of the fur trade, when the Dutch were anxious to promote good relations wherever possible, they were attentive to the Mohawk. This helped to offset the Mohawk's geographical disadvantage. We even learn that, in 1615, three Dutch traders, led by a man named Kleynties, accompanied a Mohawk raid against the Susquehannock. This suggests that the Dutch were willing to provide their trading partners with the same sort of military assistance that the French were extending to theirs. Unlike Champlain's expeditions, however, this one ended in total disaster; the three Dutch were captured by the Susquehannock, who tortured but did not kill them. The following year they were ransomed from their captors by Cornelis Hendricksen who was exploring and trading on the Delaware River.[10] No doubt, this early misadventure was, in part, responsible for the later reluctance of the Dutch to become directly involved in the wars of their Indian allies.

As the Dutch began to develop a more far-sighted trading policy, the landlocked Mohawk were of only marginal interest to them. The Dutch knew that in the northern hinterland of the St. Lawrence and Ottawa Valleys, the French had tapped a source of furs which, in both quantity and quality, exceeded what could be hoped for from the Indians of New York State. Henceforth, the principal ambition of the Dutch was to find a way to divert this trade from the French trading stations into their own hands (Van Laer 1924:55, 104). The most promising lead in such a venture initially seemed to be the friendship that existed between the Mahican and the Algonkian-speaking peoples to the north. The latter were accustomed to trade for wampum with the Mahican and, at various times in the past, both groups seem to have been allies against the Mohawk. The wampum beads, which the northern Algonkians valued very highly, were produced in the Long Island region so that the Dutch now controlled the supply of them (Van Laer 1924:223–24; Trelease 1960:48; J. Murray 1938:368–69). The French had no wampum to trade with their allies at this time, so it seemed possible that the Dutch could use this advantage to lure some of the northern Indians to their posts.

In spite of having free access to the Dutch traders, the Mohawk must have viewed with alarm the latter's efforts to court friendship with their powerful enemies to the north. There was always the danger that if hostilities broke out and the Dutch had to choose between the Mohawk and the northern Algonkians, the Mohawk would once again find themselves cut off from a regular supply of European goods. Under these circumstances, the Mohawk appear to have decided that rather than risk finding themselves in the same position they had been in prior to 1610, it was in their best interest to drive the Mahican from the vicinity of Fort Orange. By taking control of the river, they could compel the Dutch traders, who were few in number, to make an alliance with them on their own terms. In this way, the Mohawk could ensure that their own trade with the Dutch would not be interrupted and, at the same time, they could prevent the Dutch from making alliances with potential enemies to the north.

Casting their diplomatic net widely, as they did whenever relations with the Dutch or the English became strained in later years, the Mohawk moved to transform the detente they had with the French and the northern Algonkians into a genuine, if short-lived, peace. Their aims were to cover their northern flank while they attacked the Mahican and also to have an emergency source of European goods, lest either their war with the Mahican or Dutch sympathy for the latter were to result in their usual supply being cut off. It was no accident that the Mohawk ratified a formal treaty with the French and their Algonkian allies at Three Rivers in July 1624, the same year that war broke out between them and the Mahican (map 17). Six Mohawk headmen were present for this ceremony, which Le Clercq (1691:260) says was a solemn ritual, attended by representatives of all the Indian trading partners of the French, including the Huron. Trudel (1966a:370) argues that because Champlain does not describe such a ceremony, the treaty-making must have lacked the speeches, feasts, and dancing that normally characterized such events. The total absence of ceremony is highly unlikely, however, since without it the treaty would have had no meaning to the Indians. Even though Champlain played a major role in the negotiations that led up to the treaty, he may have been prevented by illness or some other reason from attending the ceremony, and, if Gravé Du Pont represented the French, Champlain may have overlooked the ceremony when he came to write his memoirs. Le Clercq reports that the Mohawk who concluded this treaty were accompanied by twenty-five canoes loaded with furs. The French must now have regarded the Mohawk as normal trading partners.

The role of the Huron in these negotiations is uncertain. Le Clercq (1691:260) implies that Huron traders participated in the ratification of this treaty. These traders would have had the authority to do this only if the issue had been discussed by the Huron the previous winter and the

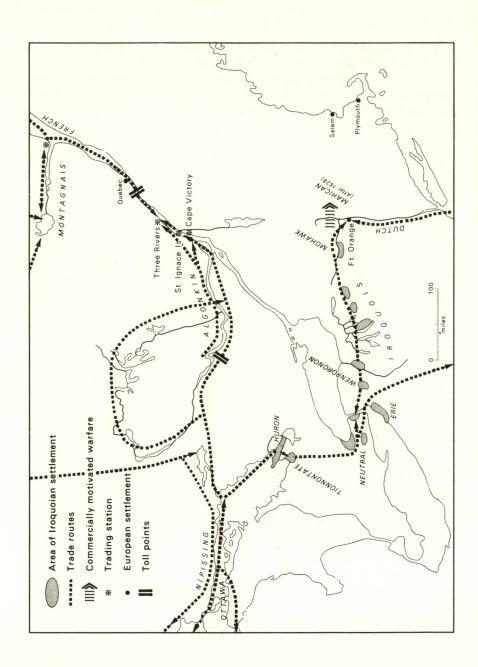

MAP 17. *Intertribal relations, c. 1625.*

headmen who were coming to trade had been empowered to make peace in the name of the whole confederacy. There is, however, no evidence that the Huron were more than passive beneficiaries of a peace in whose making they had little part. Whether or not they made peace with the Mohawk, the Huron continued to wage war against the Seneca and the three other western tribes of the Iroquois confederacy.

The new Mohawk policy towards the French and their allies seems merely to have confirmed the peaceful use of the St. Lawrence River that the French had already established by force of arms. There are, however, two pieces of evidence which suggest that prior to these negotiations the Mohawk may have been challenging the hegemony of the French. Le Clercq states that the missionary Guillaume Poulain and some companions were captured by the Iroquois on their way to the Nipissing country in 1621; however, the Iroquois agreed to exchange these prisoners for some of their own men who had been captured by the French (207, 219). Le Clercq also reports that, in 1622, about thirty Iroquois canoes appeared at Quebec, whose crews proceeded to attack the habitation and the Recollet house. Seven or eight Iroquois are said to have been killed and, in revenge, the Iroquois tortured and killed two Huron, whom they had taken prisoner (208–11). Both of these stories rest on insecure foundations. Le Clercq based his account of the attack on Quebec on information imparted to him by Guillemette Couillard, who was then about seventy years old and was recalling what had happened at Quebec in her youth. Trudel (1966a:369) doubts the accuracy of both stories and suggests that the silence of contemporary documents is more convincing than Le Clercq's evidence.

While it is certain that Couillard's story is much exaggerated, there is, however, a small amount of evidence which suggests that it might contain a kernel of truth. In 1624, Huron headmen extracted a promise from Sagard that he would ask the French to build a house below the Lachine Rapids, in order to protect them against their enemies (Sagard 1866:760). This request recalled a promise Champlain had made years before, but the fact that the Huron raised the issue again at this time perhaps indicates that renewed Mohawk attacks along the St. Lawrence were causing them some anxiety. If a couple of Huron had been killed in 1622, this might also explain why relations with the French were strained the following year. Given the independent behaviour of individual Iroquoians, renewed attacks do not indicate that all, or even most, of the Mohawk were spoiling for a fight. If there had been renewed attacks in the early 1620s, it would, however, have made the peace that followed seem all the more attractive to the French.

SOURCES OF HURON FURS

What made the Huron such valuable allies of the French was their ability to accumulate vast quantities of beaver pelts and transport them to the trading stations each year. During the period we are discussing some of these pelts were undoubtedly taken by Huron hunters; yet it is clear that hunting was never as important among the Huron as fishing. Moreover, the Huron hunting territories were not as rich in beaver as were certain other parts of southern Ontario. Their most productive beaver grounds were probably in the Holland Marsh near the south end of Lake Simcoe, although the Huron may have shared the southern part of this area with the Neutral. While beaver were no doubt plentiful in the Trent Valley, the Tionnontaté and the Neutral shared still richer areas in the swamps at the headwaters of the Grand River, while the Neutral and the tribes of southeastern Michigan vied for control of the swampy areas around Lake St. Clair and along the Thames and Sydenham Rivers (Heidenreich 1971:208). All of these areas were limited in extent and capable of rapid depletion, if heavily exploited by the relatively dense Iroquoian populations of southern Ontario. The unusually large number of beaver bones found in the Sidey-Mackay site, which is probably Tionnontaté, has been interpreted as evidence for the more intensive hunting of beaver by the Ontario Iroquoians as a result of the early fur trade (Wintemberg 1946: 155). Unfortunately, faunal remains from very few relevant sites are available for comparison with these data. It may be significant, however, that thirteen percent of the identified bone elements from the Maurice site, which is in the Penetanguishene Peninsula and approximately coeval with Sidey-Mackay, turned out to be beaver, as opposed to seven percent from the later Robitaille site (Savage 1971*a*:167; 1971*b*:176). This suggests an increase in local beaver hunting in the early contact period, followed by a decline, as beaver supplies became depleted. Beaver were still plentiful in the Neutral country as late as 1626, when Iroquet and a band of twenty men trapped 500 of them (Sagard 1866:803). It is of interest that the Neutral were prepared to let the Onontchataronon hunt their beaver. Probably Iroquet paid for this privilege by presenting European goods to Neutral headmen.

By around 1630, however, beaver seem to have become extinct within the Huron hunting territories. In his *Histoire du Canada*, Sagard (1866: 585) recorded that the Huron had overhunted the beaver within their country and were now finding none there. In 1635, Paul Le Jeune noted that the Huron had exterminated their own beaver and had to obtain from other Indians all the skins they traded with the French (Thwaites 1896–1901, 8:57). The latter statement makes it clear that depletion was not limited to the immediate vicinity of the Huron settlements. Some beaver hunting continued; for example, a Huron named Tsondihwané and his son left Ossossané to hunt beaver in the autumn of 1642 (26:249–51). Such hunting was probably done on the Canadian Shield and use of this territory would have required permission from the Algonkians. Continued hunting in this area may explain Gendron's (1868:13) otherwise anomalous comment that the Huron country was still rich in beaver in the 1640s.

There is no reason to believe that the Huron, even in the earliest days of the fur trade, trapped a large percentage of the furs that they traded with the French. Yet, as the fur trade grew in volume, they must have acquired increasing numbers of furs from trading partners. It probably came as little surprise to the Huron and created few problems for them when their own beavers became extinct. The Huron were already on good terms with Algonkian hunting groups who inhabited a vast area rich in beaver and laced with rivers that made the collection of pelts relatively easy. By tapping this source more intensively, the Huron were able to assure themselves of an almost inexhaustible supply of furs to trade with the French. Moreover, since the Algonkians would have used most of these pelts for clothing prior to trading them, either for corn or for European goods, this mode of acquisition saved the Huron the trouble of wearing these furs until the guard hairs had fallen out and they were of prime quality to trade with the French.

From the writings of Gabriel Sagard it is possible to gain a fairly clear picture of the extent and nature of Huron trade in the 1620s, although it is impossible to determine how many furs were coming from any one source (map 18). A number of the Huron's furs were obtained from the Ottawa Valley Algonkin and the Montagnais, who also traded with the French on a regular basis. Each year, when the Huron travelled downriver, they carried corn, cornmeal, tobacco, fishing nets, and black squirrel skins, the latter being an exotic luxury much prized among the Montagnais. The Huron's exchange with the Kichesipirini was, as we have seen, of a quasi-compulsory nature, with low prices being paid in furs for Huron corn, but among other groups the trading appears to have been more profitable. None of these groups had to trade with the Huron for European goods, but they were interested in obtaining corn, which only the Huron could supply to them in bulk.

The Huron's control of the fur trade, both in the Lake Huron region and to a lesser extent in the Ottawa Valley, depended on their ability to produce

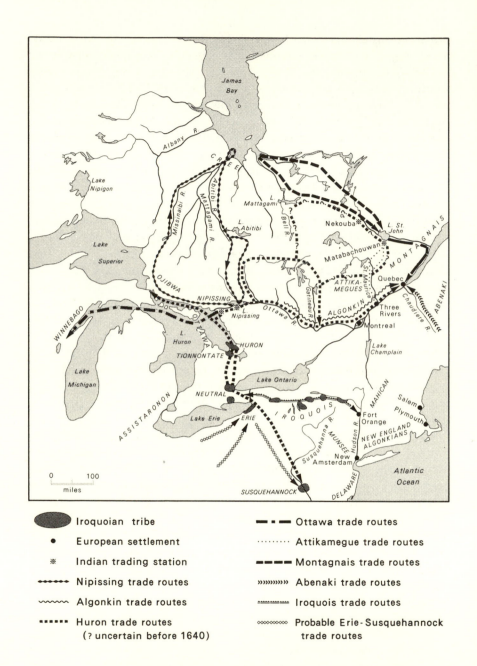

Iroquoian tribe

● European settlement

✳ Indian trading station

•••••••► Nipissing trade routes

〜〜〜 Algonkin trade routes

▬ ▬ ▬ Huron trade routes
(?uncertain before 1640)

▬ · ▬ Ottawa trade routes

············ Attikamegue trade routes

▬▬▬ Montagnais trade routes

»»»»»»» Abenaki trade routes

••••••••• Iroquois trade routes

∞∞∞∞∞ Probable Erie-Susquehannock
trade routes

MAP 18. *Major trade routes in the first half of the seventeenth century.*

large surpluses of corn on a regular basis. Some groups of northern Algonkians appear to have already been dependent on Huron corn in pre-historic times. With the development of the fur trade, however, the northern hunting peoples were compelled to spend more time either trading or trapping beavers, in order to obtain sufficient quantities of European goods to satisfy their wants. Because of this, the amount of time spent fishing and hunting for subsistence declined and these groups became increasingly dependent on agricultural produce to make up the deficit. The Montagnais purchased much of their food from the French, but for the more westerly tribes the Huron were a more reliable and less expensive source.

The influence exerted by this growing demand for corn on the development of trading networks is clearly illustrated by the trade that the Huron carried on with the Nipissing and Ottawa. By the 1620s, some Nipissing were travelling down the Ottawa River to trade with the French (Biggar 1922–36, 5:129), although this was a fairly recent development and the Nipissing did not trade with the French either as extensively or as regularly as did their Algonkin neighbours. In spite of this, every summer when the Huron traders returned from the St. Lawrence, the Nipissing met them as they passed through Nipissing tribal territory and exchanged furs for European goods. So vital was corn to the Nipissing economy that they preferred to focus most of their trading cycle on the Huron, rather than seek an extensive separate relationship with the French.[11]

Even more specialized were the Huron's relations with the Ottawa (Cheveux Relevés) bands, who lived around the shores of Georgian Bay, and with the Nation de Bois, which was probably a branch of the Ojibwa. The Ottawa controlled extensive trade networks which ran westward along the shores of Lakes Superior and Michigan. They were also famous, in Sagard's time and later, for their acumen as traders (Sagard 1866:192). Although French trade goods played as important a part in their trade with the west as they did in the Nipissing's trade with the north, there is no evidence that the Ottawa traded directly with the French prior to 1653. Instead, each summer they met the Huron traders returning from the St. Lawrence near the mouth of the French River. There, they exchanged furs, shell beads, pigments, and possibly native copper which they had obtained farther west, for the European goods that the Huron had brought back from the St. Lawrence. Sagard reports that trading sessions lasted over several days, while the Ottawa and Huron bargained over the terms of trade (Wrong 1939:66–67; Sagard 1866:192).

The furs that the Huron obtained by barter with other tribes on their way to and from the St. Lawrence each year accounted for only part of their total intake. More furs were obtained from northern Algonkians who wintered in the Huron country. During the winter, the Attignawantan and Ataronchronon bartered corn with the Nipissing, which the latter either consumed on the spot or kept for trade the following summer. In this way, the Huron were able to secure most of the furs that the Nipissing trapped themselves and which they collected on their annual trading expeditions to the shores of James Bay. Although they traded with the French more extensively than did the Nipissing, the Onontchataronon were also an important source of furs for their Arendarhonon hosts. While it is unlikely that the Onontchataronon brought many pelts from their beaver grounds in the lower Ottawa Valley, the 500 beavers that Iroquet trapped in the Neutral country were probably intended for trade with the Arendarhonon.

There is no record of Ottawa wintering among the Huron. Many had their villages to the west of the Tionnontaté and obtained their corn from them. Yet, if the Ottawa were less dependent on the Huron for corn than were the Nipissing and Algonkin, they were more dependent on them for European goods. By limiting themselves to receiving such goods from other Indians, the Ottawa were able to concentrate on trading with groups that had less access to these goods than they had and among whom relatively small amounts of trade goods were valued more highly than they were farther east.

The hazards of the latter form of trade are exemplified, however, by the difficulties that the Ottawa experienced with the Winnebago, a populous and sedentary Siouan-speaking people who lived in the vicinity of Green Bay, Wisconsin. The Winnebago are reported to have slain some Ottawa who may have been attempting to initiate trade with them. They perhaps did this to steal the Ottawa's trade goods and because they did not appreciate the military superiority that access to iron weapons had conferred on the Ottawa, whom they scorned as a weak and nomadic people, just as the Huron did. Whatever the reason, it is clear that the Winnebago did not yet appreciate the desirability of securing a regular supply of European goods. When war broke out as a result of these killings, the Ottawa and their allies, who were better armed with iron weapons, gained the upper hand. This led to a division of opinion between those Winnebago who wished to continue the war and those who argued that trade goods were useful and the killing of the Ottawa envoys had been a mistake. Bacqueville de La Potherie (1911–12, 1:293–95) reports that the Winnebago were forced in self-defence to found a single large village, where epidemics and other disasters carried off thousands of people and reduced the tribe to a few hundred individuals (Lurie 1960:797–803). While the chronology for these events is not entirely certain, the epidemics were probably the ones that began in the upper Great Lakes area in 1634, which suggests that the war between the Winnebago and the Ottawa had begun in the previous decade. The main problem bedevilling the Winnebago was the difficulty that a people primarily dependent on agriculture and who were unused to trading with hunting peoples had in adjusting to the requirements of the fur trade. These were problems that the Huron were able to avoid by building on pre-existing trading networks. By intensifying longstanding relations with the Nipissing and Ottawa, the Huron could tap trade routes leading north to the salt waters of the Arctic and deep into the watersheds of Lakes Superior and Michigan.

The Huron traders did not leave the centre of this vast network, however, only to transport their goods to the French trading stations. Every spring and autumn, Huron traders carried European goods to the Tionnontaté and Neutral villages. There they visited their trading partners and exchanged these goods for furs, tobacco, wampum, and other luxury items of southern origin. While few details of this trade have been recorded, the journeying of Huron traders to Tionnontaté and Neutral villages, and of Tionnontaté and Neutral traders to Huron villages, must have been an important activity at this period.

Huron traders were also active on Georgian Bay, visiting the various Algonkian-speaking bands that inhabited its eastern and northern shores. The statement that the Huron travelled in winter across the ice of Georgian Bay to trade corn for fish with neighbouring Algonkian groups shows that the origins of this trade were not entirely forgotten as the fur trade grew more important (Thwaites 1896–1901, 13:249). Summer expeditions took the Huron at least as far west as Sault Sainte Marie and possibly into the Lake Superior region. There is no evidence that the Huron journeyed into northern Ontario along the routes of their Nipissing trading partners, although they may have travelled westward along Ottawa trade routes. In 1639, François Du Peron listed the Winnebago as one of the tribes with whom the Huron traded (ibid. 15:155), and even earlier, Sagard had affirmed that Huron was a lingua franca that was used to trade with this tribe (Wrong 1939:9). It has also been suggested that seven Huron accompanied Jean Nicollet to the Winnebago country in 1634 (Hamelin 1966*b*:517).

In general, however, Sagard implies that it was the Ottawa, rather than the Huron, who traded with the Winnebago (cf. Wrong 1939:67; Sagard 1866:194). Moreover, while Nicollet is said to have left the Huron when he began his journey to Lake Michigan, his companions are identified only as Indians, and not specifically as Huron (Thwaites 1896–1901, 23:277). Evidence of trade and contact between the Huron and the Winnebago is therefore tenuous. Barthélemy Vimont states specifically that Nicollet's aim was to make peace between the Winnebago and the Huron (ibid.) and Bacqueville de La Potherie (1911–12, 1:293) affirms that in their war with the Winnebago, the Ottawa were aided by other tribes as well as by the French weapons they received. Vimont may, however, have been using the term Huron loosely to refer to any tribe served by the Huron mission (Lurie 1960:794). It is also possible that while the Huron did not regularly trade this far west, some of their warriors may have accompanied the Ottawa when they waged war against the Winnebago.

Although it has been suggested that the Huron did not begin to trade in the interior of Quebec before about 1640 (Heidenreich 1971:277, 279), it is clear that this is not so. According to Sagard, control of trade with the Saguenay was a carefully guarded prerogative of certain Huron headmen (Wrong 1939:99), and elsewhere he explained that this trade was one of the most profitable for both the Montagnais and the Huron (87). It is certain that the term Saguenay refers to the interior of Quebec and that Huron were following the old copper route eastward in order to trade with the hunting bands of that region. This is confirmed by Sagard's eyewitness observation that a party of Huron who were on their way to the Saguenay turned north along the Ottawa River instead of south, after they had reached the mouth of the Mattawa River (249, 253–54). From there, they may have made their way into the interior of Quebec by way of Lake Timiskaming and the Belle River, possibly as far as Lake Mattagami. Since there is no evidence that Huron ever came to Tadoussac, they then may have made their way eastward along the Ashuapmuchuan River to the headwaters of the St. Maurice, although they did not travel down this river either. Alternatively, their travels may have taken them no farther than the Cabonga region, whence they made their way back to the Ottawa Valley along the Gatineau River. Unfortunately, given the present state of the evidence, it cannot be determined whether or not, or to what degree, the Huron traded in that region in prehistoric times. If they did not trade into Quebec in prehistoric times, their routes may have developed from the relatively short Gatineau trip to much longer ones that by 1642 were taking them as far as Matabachouwan ("Maouatchi-hitonnam") in the Lake St. John region (Thwaites 1896–1901, 24:155).

If the Huron did trade along the copper route in prehistoric times, this developmental scheme may be totally invalid.

It seems inevitable that once trading had begun between the Huron and the French, the Europeans' growing demand for beaver pelts would have led to a considerable and rapid increase in the volume of Huron trade. If 200 to 300 Huron were carrying furs to the St. Lawrence each year, an even larger number must have been involved in collecting the pelts, and in Indian trade generally, in southwestern Ontario, around the shores of Georgian Bay, and eastward into central Quebec. While many of the same individuals may have been trading with other tribes and with the French, it is possible that 300 to 400 Huron were engaged in intertribal trade, in addition to those who did business with the French. As we have seen in chapter 4, archaeological evidence indicates that in prehistoric times the Huron traded at least with the Nipissing and with the Algonkian bands who lived around the shores of Georgian Bay. It may be that as the fur trade developed, the Huron gradually expanded their trading network. Alternatively, this network may already have existed in prehistoric times and the Huron may simply have intensified their contacts with these more remote areas after 1600. Whichever happened, it is clear that the Huron were experienced traders prior to their initial contacts with the French. It also may be that the historic trade routes that belonged to the Ottawa and Nipissing are intensifications of earlier trading systems. If regional trade was largely built upon pre-existing relationships, this would help to explain the rapidity and apparent ease with which the Huron were able to expand the volume of this trade to meet the demands of the French fur traders.

By the early 1620s, the fur trade appears to have penetrated as far north and west as it was to reach until after the dispersal of the Huron. Even in the late 1650s, the Sioux who lived at the west end of Lake Superior lacked iron weapons and, for this reason, were regarded as easy prey by the displaced tribes who crowded into their territory from the east (Perrot 1911:159–63). About the same time, when the Iroquois began raiding the lower part of the Ohio Valley, they encountered Algonkian-speaking groups who still used only stone hatchets and knives "and the other things that the Indians used before they began to trade with the French" (Thwaites 1896–1901, 44:49). As late as the 1670s, the tribes living south and west of the Illinois had no access to European trade goods, either from the east or from the Spanish settlements to the south (59:127). The limited capacity of the Huron and their trading partners to convey European goods into the interior hampered the spread of these goods until the Europeans established their own trading posts in the upper Great

Lakes region in the 1690s. The Huron may have reached the limit of their carrying capacity in the 1620s, although this seems doubtful. More likely, however, they increased their intake of furs after this period by more intensive collecting within the areas where they already traded. Such a procedure had the advantage of increasing trade without requiring the expansion of trade routes or the pioneering of trading relations with wholly unfamiliar peoples.

While changes were undoubtedly brought about by an increasing emphasis on trade, trading activities probably had less impact on Huron daily life than is generally imagined. If we assume that 250 men spent three months each year travelling to and from Quebec and another 350 spent two months each year trading with other Indians, this would mean that only about one adult male in six was engaged in external trade. This is about the same number that Sagard reports went each year to wage war on the Iroquois. Heidenreich (1971:153) has estimated that it took the Huron about three months to build and fortify a settlement for 1000 inhabitants. If a town was relocated every 12 years, this would have required an average of 1500 man days of work per year (although all the labour would have been concentrated in a much shorter period). Considerably more time had to be spent clearing fields. Using the figures worked out above, the men from Heidenreich's village would have spent only 2416 days each year trading. A large percentage of the furs collected by the Huron may have been brought to the Huron country by others, and one cannot necessarily equate the importance of trade and the time that was spent on it. Nevertheless, between 1615 and 1629 the male Huron still spent far more time waging war and performing domestic tasks than he did trading.

FRENCH IMPORTS

It is impossible to determine accurately the amount of French trade goods that the Huron were importing into southwestern Ontario at this period. De Caën, who held the trading monopoly, sent two ships to Tadoussac each year loaded with freight valued at 4800 livres (Thwaites 1896–1901, 4:207; Trudel 1966a:431). Charles Lalemant enumerates the cargo of these vessels as made up of cloaks, blankets, night caps, shirts, sheets, hatchets, iron arrowheads, large needles, swords, ice picks, knives, kettles, prunes, Indian corn, peas, crackers, sea biscuits, and tobacco (Thwaites 1896–1901, 4:207). Most of the food, tobacco, and clothing seems to have been destined for trade with the Montagnais and the Indians from the Maritimes (3:75–77; 5:25). The Huron had no need for more corn, and even nonindigenous specialities, such as prunes and biscuits, which the French took to the Huron country for their own use, seem to have been purchased by the Huron in limited quantities, if at all. These foods remained rare in the Huron country because of the difficulty involved in transporting them there, rather than because the Huron did not enjoy them. Sagard reports that when he set off for the Huron country he took along a small box of sea biscuits, hoping that it would last him until he reached his destination. When the Huron with whom he was travelling found out that he had these biscuits, they compelled him to share them with the whole group in accordance with their traditional norms of generosity. Thereafter, Sagard had to accustom himself to eating corn soup, for which his hosts encouraged him to overcome his initial distaste (Wrong 1939:56–58).

Although Louis Hébert arrived at Quebec in 1617, and began farming there under a contract that obliged him to sell his surplus produce to the trading company, the total amount of food available to the French for trade was insufficient to undercut the Huron. Throughout this period the Algonkin, although better located for trade with the French than with the Huron, continued to rely on the latter for supplies of corn. The cost of transporting goods to the New World ensured that French trading in agricultural produce was only with hunting groups, like the Micmac and Montagnais, who lived too far away to make the large scale transport of corn from the horticultural tribes living in the interior a practical proposition. The Huron country remained the granary for the Ottawa Valley Algonkin, as well as for the semi or nonagricultural peoples of the upper Great Lakes and central Quebec (Thwaites 1896–1901, 8:115).

The Huron do not appear to have bartered for large quantities of cloth or clothing, although they did not fail to appreciate these items. Blankets, capes, and shirts are listed among the things that they sought (5:265; 12:249), and these items were given as presents to leading Huron traders (Sagard 1866:797; Thwaites 1896–1901, 8:75). The Huron also requested stockings and shoes as presents from the French who visited their villages (Wrong 1939:245) and Sagard reports that women asked to borrow his cassock for travelling in the rain (ibid. 146). The general impression, however, is that European clothing remained relatively unimportant among the Huron. The Montagnais, on the other hand, began wearing French clothes at an early period, and it is likely that at least some of the Algonkin did also (Thwaites 1896–1901, 5:25; 7:9–11). It may have been their traditional style of dress, more than anything else, that won the Huron their French name, which implies that the French regarded them as rustics or hillbillies.

Huron traders were primarily interested in obtaining metal ware. This preoccupation is reflected in the Huron name for the French, which was Agnonha, meaning "Iron People" (Wrong 1939:79). The most common iron objects found in Huron sites are the blades of table, butcher, and jack-knives (Garrad 1969:3; Latta 1971:127). Often iron knives outnumber the combined total of all other metal objects. Awls, either round or square in cross-section, are also common, as are trade axes. So many axe heads are reported to have been ploughed up when Simcoe County was cleared for settlement in the last century, that scrap dealers found it profitable to travel from farm to farm collecting them (Hunter 1902:67; Jury and Jury 1954:53). These three implements were popular because their cutting edge was superior to that of stone or bone tools.

The metal arrowheads that were manufactured from iron, copper, and brass for trade with the Indians could pierce Iroquois slat armour. The stemmed metal points found at some sites appear to be specimens of such trade goods (Latta 1971:127). Kettles made out of thin sheets of brass or copper bent around iron hoops were also favourite trade items and, when worn out, the Huron cut them up to make arrowheads, as well as pendants and other decorations. These decorations were often pierced and appear to have been sewn on to clothing.

In addition to these common items, the ossuary at Ossossané, which dates from 1636 (only slightly later than the period we are considering), contained scissors, iron bracelets, metal rings, a key, and a burning glass (Kidd 1953:367–69). The Huron may have carried the key off from some sailor's chest; Sagard states that they hung such keys as ornaments around their children's necks (Sagard 1866:380). In addition, Huron sites of this period contain numerous red, blue, white, and polychrome glass beads. These beads occur in a variety of shapes, such as round, tubular, and twisted, and while some are in solid colours, others are striped or have cores that are a different colour from the exterior (Kidd and Kidd 1970). Kidd (1953:367–69) suggests that one type imitates native beads of red slate that were much prized by the Huron. The glass is a dull red that can be differentiated from slate only on a fractured surface. Moreover, the shapes of these beads imitate tubular, square, and triangular native beads. Kidd's suggestion that the French produced these beads especially for the Indians is perhaps supported by the marketing skill embodied in

Sagard's observation that every tribe, except the Nipissing, made more of red beads than of any other kind (Wrong 1939:250).

The fragmentary archaeological evidence suggests a marked increase in the amount of European goods reaching the Huron country by the second decade of the seventeenth century. The annual trade seems to have been somewhat larger after 1634 than it was from 1616 to 1629 and the per capita annual inflow of European goods was certainly greater after the population decline of 1634 to 1640. On the other hand, trade does not appear to have been disrupted any year prior to 1628, although it was frequently disrupted after that date; therefore, the total increase in goods reaching the Huron was probably not as great after 1634 as might be inferred from trade figures referring to individual years. At no period did the flow of European goods into the Huron country keep pace with the demand for these items. The Huron frequently objected that they were short of things they needed (ibid. 245), and besieged Frenchmen who were visiting the trading posts with personal requests to return with beads, awls, and other items.

The Huron were also notorious for their thieving when they visited Three Rivers and Quebec. Sagard (1866:379) states that the French traders were unable to avoid loss, even when they watched the Huron carefully. This accusation was made at a time when complaints about the Indians living nearer to Quebec seem to have been diminishing. The French also complained that the Huron stole from Frenchmen living in the Huron country, if the latter had not entered into a kinship relation with them (Wrong 1939:81). It must have been obvious to the Huron that taking goods in this manner angered the French, even though much of what they did was probably not wrong by Huron standards. It must therefore be concluded that trade alone was unable to satisfy the Huron's craving for European goods and that they were willing to annoy the French and to risk injury in order to obtain more.

The Huron's desire for European goods did not mean, however, that they had become totally dependent on these items. The economic relationship between the Huron and the French can best be brought into focus by a comparison with coastal peoples, such as the Micmac and Montagnais. The culture of these groups had undergone extensive modification as a result of the fur trade and their reliance on their European trading partners was much greater than that of the Huron. By 1623, the Montagnais who lived around Tadoussac and Quebec were spending so much time trapping and trading that they were unable to manage without supplies of peas, corn, and sea biscuits. By contrast, the Huron were not dependent on the French, or any other Indian group, for their subsistence (Biggar 1922–36, 5:251, 267).

The Montagnais were also no longer cooking in birchbark baskets (Wrong 1939:108; Thwaites 1896–1901, 5:97)[12] and were so committed to the use of copper kettles that the French were uncertain whether or not they had formerly made clay pots (Sagard 1866:271). They had also ceased to make, or use, stone axes (ibid. 271). The Huron continued to manufacture and use pottery, birchbark vessels, and stone axes (Wrong 1939:61). The Montagnais had also been able to obtain guns, not from the official traders at Quebec, but from others who were operating illegally below Tadoussac (Biggar 1922–36, 5:3; Le Clercq 1691:194–95). It is suggested that these traders hoped that by arming the Montagnais and encouraging their resentment over the high prices that the official traders were charging for their goods, they could incite the Montagnais to attack Quebec. The sale of guns to the Indians was illegal at this time and their obtaining them was a source of anxiety to the French at Quebec, because the Indians were opposed to the monopoly that the officials there were attempting to enforce. Since the Huron lacked any contact with traders other than those at Quebec, they were unable to obtain firearms. It is also reported that while the Montagnais continued to build canoes, they bought longboats from the French so that they could travel more safely along the lower St. Lawrence River (Sagard 1866:251).

The gradual loss of major items from Montagnais traditional culture, and their replacement by European goods that the Montagnais did not know how to manufacture, resulted in a degree of dependence on European traders that was as yet unknown among the Huron. The Huron's larger population and greater remoteness from the French trading stations were sufficient to ensure that not enough European goods could be transported to the Huron country to satisfy the demand for them. These limitations in supply compelled the Huron to rely more heavily on their own products.

The Huron not only were less dependent on trade with the French than were the Montagnais, but also were less sophisticated about it. Below Tadoussac, monopolies were difficult to defend and the Montagnais were accustomed to doing business with rival European traders. In spite of efforts to enforce a monopoly, clandestine trade continued. Early in the 1620s, Protestant merchants from La Rochelle erected a stockade to protect themselves while bartering with the Indians (Biggar 1922–36, 5:50–51). They are also reported to have directed a stream of anti-Roman Catholic propaganda at the Montagnais, in an effort to make the French at Quebec seem more odious to them (5:4). The experience that the Montagnais gained encouraged them to drive hard bargains with Europeans. Where rival traders were known to be operating, the Montagnais would refuse to trade until a number of rivals were present, to enhance their own bargaining position. When the Montagnais headman, Erouachy, was offered too small a present by the captain of one of the company ships that arrived at Tadoussac in 1623, he threw the present into the river and ordered his men to board the ship and carry off whatever they needed, leaving only what they wished in exchange. Rather than risk a blood feud, the French stood by as the Montagnais plundered their ship. They considered themselves fortunate when the Montagnais returned that evening and sought to restore normal relations (Wrong 1939:45–46). According to Sagard, the French were considerably more frightened of offending the Montagnais than the Montagnais were of offending them (ibid. 46).

The Montagnais were extremely angry when the enforcement of the trading monopolies at Tadoussac and Quebec led to a rise in the price of trade goods at these key centres after 1614. Although they had welcomed French settlement at Quebec as protection against the Iroquois and a year-round source of food, the adverse effects of the monopoly soon produced mixed feelings. Collective resentment against the official traders resulted in personal quarrels between French and Indians, leading to the killing of two Frenchmen in 1617 and two more in 1627. Evidence from elsewhere indicates that if the Montagnais and the traders at Quebec had been on generally good terms, these murders would not have occurred. Moreover, the heavy-handed, but vacillating manner in which the French reacted to these murders produced further resentment among the Montagnais (Trigger 1971a:94–100). By 1624, Champlain's worst suspicions about the Montagnais seemed justified when he learned that they were boasting that if they were to kill all the French at Quebec, other vessels would come and they would get their goods more cheaply (Biggar 1922–36, 5:124–25).

The Huron, by contrast, had known free trade only between 1610 and 1612 and, being inexperienced in dealing with Europeans, had been frightened by the competition for their furs. The effective exclusion of rival traders from the upper St. Lawrence after 1613 allowed Champlain to establish a trading relationship with the Huron which, in the latter's eyes, closely approximated the kind of intertribal trading relationship to which they were accustomed. Each year when they came to the St. Lawrence, several days were devoted to speeches, feasts, and the exchange of valuable presents, both before and after the bartering took place. These c   es reaffirmed the treaty of friendship between the Huron and tı.   ɩch, without which the Huron would have felt uneasy about returning to the St. Lawrence the following year. So long as their treaty was reaffirmed, the Huron traders remained confident that they would be well-received and expected the French to have the same trust in them. Not having close contact with the Montagnais, and sometimes being on bad terms with them, the Huron probably remained unaware of events down-river and accepted the prices charged by the company for its goods as fair.

In addition to their general treaty, the Huron were anxious to establish relations of real or fictional kinship with individual Frenchmen who visited their country. In this and in other ways, they hoped to elicit the support of these individuals as intermediaries when they traded with the French. Huron traders were anxious to have Le Caron accompany them to the St. Lawrence in 1624 (Le Clercq 1691:258) and Sagard reports that before he left, the people of Quieunonascaran asked him to keep the French traders well disposed towards the Huron and to do all he could to see that Huron traders got what they wanted from the French at a reason-able price. In return, the Attignawantan promised to provide the French traders with furs of the best quality (Wrong 1939:244). The Huron traded with the French, as with other tribes, in the Huron language. They did not bother to learn the jargon that was spoken at Quebec, which Le Jeune describes as an amalgam of French and Indian words that the French believed was Indian and the Indians believed was French (Thwaites 1896–1901, 5:113–15). This jargon appears to have employed words derived from French and from various Algonkian dialects.

All of this shows that the Huron were still able to view their trade with the French in terms of a traditional system of intertribal friendship and alliance. The Huron wished to receive as many European goods as possible for their furs, but, instead of haggling over individual pelts, a request for more trade goods was phrased as an appeal for further proof of friendship. The Huron regarded generosity to friends and allies as an obligation; there-fore, if the French traders really were their friends, they would treat the Huron who came to Quebec generously. This embedding of marketing within a framework of political and social relations puzzled the French traders. The Huron, like the Montagnais, knew how to bargain, but instead of trying to negotiate directly, or to play different traders off against one another, they insisted on bargaining within the framework of a political alliance. The Huron expected the French to share the same values that they did and were appalled when merchants haggled over the price of individual skins (Wrong 1939:140). Unfortunately, few details have been recorded about this encounter between tribal and bourgeois values.

The evidence suggests that in spite of the important role that the Huron played in the fur trade, their contacts with the French were essentially of a traditional type. In part, this reflects the low frequency and specialized nature of these contacts. It also indicates, however, that although the Huron were highly successful as fur traders, their economy was still largely independent of that of the French and they remained a tribal people. The role they played in the fur trade was an extension of prehistoric trading relations that provided the Huron with a model for their dealings with the French.

The French in the Huron Country

Direct contact with the French was limited in one direction to the brief visits of 200 to 250 Huron men who went annually to the St. Lawrence Valley to trade. Between 1615 and 1629, only one woman is reported to have made this journey. In the other direction, it was limited to a small number of priests, traders, and other Frenchmen who went to live among the Huron and were welcomed by them as tangible evidence of French goodwill. The Huron regarded it as an essential condition of their alliance with the French that they treat these guests well, and individual Huron traders were anxious to establish special personal relations with them. In particular, they hoped to adopt or conclude matrimonial alliances with these visitors, either of which meant that the French entered into kinship with a particular Huron family (Wrong 1939:70–71). Sagard reports that when he was taken into the home of Oonchiarey, the Huron who had brought him to the Huron country, he was treated as a member of the family and called son, brother, cousin, and nephew by different members (71). Efforts to persuade priests to marry Huron women caused the former considerable embarrassment and resulted in the Recollets drawing the erroneous conclusion that Huron men were anxious to debauch and prostitute their women (133–34). Like many tribal peoples, the Huron viewed all social relations as an extension of kinship; hence they were behaving quite normally in attempting to establish such relations with the French, not only symbolically but also in the most literal way possible.

Although the Huron knew and frequently used (albeit in a phonetically altered fashion) the Christian names of the French who lived in their midst, sometimes they gave these people specifically Huron names (Thwaites 1896–1901, 16:239–41). Some of these became hereditary titles of respect. Achiendassé, Father Jérôme Lalemant's name, was later used to designate all the superiors of the Jesuits at Quebec, in the same way that Huron council names were passed from one office-holder to the next. In a more personal way, Pierre Chaumonot, who seems to have been called Aronhiatiri ("Heaven-Bearer") at the time of the Huron mission (Jones 1908:371–74), later was given the name Echon (Jean ?), which had been Brébeuf's Huron name. Other names appear to have been more in the nature of sobriquets; Sagard reports that a French boy who lived with the Recollets in the Huron country was called Auhaitsique, after a small fish, while another Frenchman was called Houaonton, "a quarreller." There was probably an element of irony in the name Garihouanne, "Big Chief," which Sagard says the Huron gave him either because of his bravery or because of the respect that the officials of the trading company had shown him when he embarked for the Huron country. More likely, it was invented to make fun of his self-importance.

Because of the Huron's remoteness from Quebec, Champlain did not attempt to assert his authority as a vice-regal official over them. Although he appears to have employed priests as his emissaries to the Huron, his aim was to retain the friendship of the confederacy rather than to try to regulate its activities. This contrasts with his treatment of the Montagnais, whom he regarded as an integral part of his colony and wished to subject to his authority. In particular, he tried to bring pressure to bear on the Montagnais to force them to settle down as horticulturalists and to recognize themselves as French subjects. Champlain was, however, unable to control the Montagnais, in large part because neither the headmen nor their followers had any understanding of the European concept of authority, which was a first requirement if Champlain's schemes were to work. He also lacked the physical power to force the Indians to obey him, and his aim to have the Montagnais become sedentary was directly opposed by the fur traders, who had more influence among the Indians than he had. Because of this, Champlain grew increasingly frustrated and callous in his dealings with the Montagnais; to the point where his behaviour, which at first must have seemed merely incomprehensible and erratic, greatly angered them. Eventually, Champlain was to call the Montagnais his worst enemies (Trigger 1971a:102–4).

TRADERS

The most influential Frenchmen who lived in the Huron country between 1616 and 1629 were sent there by the trading company. Of greatest importance were the highly salaried individuals known as *truchements* or interpreters. Brûlé may have been the only Frenchman who properly held this title among the Huron (Trudel 1966a:390). His duties were to encourage Huron to trade with the French and, if necessary, to travel with them when they came to trade so that he might act as an intermediary. Other men were paid smaller salaries and allowed to trade for furs in return for living among the Huron and helping to guard their villages and annual journeys to the St. Lawrence. Most of these men bore muskets. By sending them to live among the Huron, the French traders retained the Huron's goodwill and encouraged the Huron to trade with them.

Although individual Frenchmen reacted to the Huron differently, the majority of these traders appear to have adapted fairly easily to the circumstances in which they found themselves. While some lived in their own cabins on the outskirts of Huron villages, others followed Brûlé's example and went to live with Huron families. Sagard (1866:166) was among the first to record how much more easily the average European could adapt to Indian ways than Indians could adapt to European ways. From this he concluded that it was dangerous to encourage Europeans to live among the Indians. These early coureurs de bois wore Huron items of clothing; indeed, the young Brûlé was dressed entirely in Indian fashion when he first returned from the Huron country in 1611 (Biggar 1922–36, 2:188). They also hunted with Indian men and joined them in their ritual steam baths without embarrassment or religious scruples (Sagard 1866:611). Like secular Europeans in similar situations elsewhere, most of them were delighted by the frankness of native sexual relations and enjoyed seducing Huron women and being seduced by them. In spite of their reservations about the physical appearance of the French, Huron girls appear to have made themselves available to these visitors, whom they no doubt found interesting because of their novelty, as well as because they were able to give them European goods as presents. It appears that some Frenchmen persuaded Huron girls to live with them as *asqua* or companions, thus giving rise to Sagard's charge that the French had established "brothels" in various parts of the Huron country (Wrong 1939:134). The popularity of the French did not elicit expressions of jealousy from Huron men, since promiscuity was characteristic of youth and the Huron frowned on the public expression of jealousy and on men trying to restrict the sexual freedom of unmarried women. Promiscuous behaviour was therefore not incompatible with good relations between the French traders and the younger men with whom they lived and worked in the Huron country.

A more serious consequence of such behaviour was the tension that it created between traders and missionaries. The Recollets accused all but a few traders of subverting, by their actions, the moral teachings that the missionaries were trying to impart among the Huron. At first, the traders must have viewed the exhortations of the missionaries with some amusement, but this gave way to hostility when the priests accused them of deliberately seeking to undermine their missionary work for fear that it might put an end to their carnal pleasures. The traders were specifically accused of informing the Indians that French women were not chaste, as the priests claimed (Sagard 1866:327), and of telling them other unspecified lewd tales (Wrong 1939:137). This clash between Christian ideals and normal European behaviour amused the Huron but embarrassed the Recollets because it undermined their credibility. It also needled the Recollets because it revealed that they lacked sufficient influence either among the Huron or with the traders to put a stop to such behaviour. The trading company protested that it was unable to control employees who were stationed hundreds of miles from its nearest trading post, and in any case its representatives at Quebec were hostile to the Recollets. Since the Huron subjected the Recollets to the same temptations, it is little wonder that these celibates viewed Brûlé and his associates as the devil incarnate.

The priests, who are our only source of information for this period, never admitted the validity of native marriages between French men and Huron women. In spite of this, it is certain that such marriages took place. In 1637, when the Jesuits attempted to discuss the terms by which their lay employees might contract Christian marriages with native women, the Attignawantan headmen expressed surprise and said that the French who formerly had married Huron women had done so without discussions in a general council (Thwaites 1896–1901, 14:17–19). Some men who remained in the Huron country for long periods probably developed genuine attachments for particular Huron women and lived with them and their families on a more or less permanent basis. If marriages were contracted with women from influential families, they would have enhanced the prestige of individual French traders. When it became necessary for a Frenchman to leave the Huron country, the break-up of a marriage would not necessarily cause ill-will, provided that he gave appropriate presents as compensation to his wife and to her family. It would appear, however, that not all traders did this (ibid. 14:19–21).

These permanent and temporary alliances with Huron women served to bind French traders and their Huron hosts together in ways that were readily understandable to the Huron. By accepting Huron hospitality in all its forms, the French came to understand the Huron better, and gradually found themselves ensnared in a web of obligations and kinship which made it difficult to refuse to aid them. These traders were strengthening the secular relationship established by Champlain in 1615 by living with the Huron on a more long-term and often more intimate basis than Champlain would have countenanced.

The earliest and most important of these traders was Etienne Brûlé. As already noted, he appears to have arrived in the Huron country in 1610. The following winter, Brûlé made good progress in learning the Huron language and adapting to Huron ways. Because he was liked by the Huron, Champlain decided that he should return to the Huron country for another year. As he grew older, he seems to have demonstrated effective qualities of leadership and, as these became apparent to his Huron hosts, he won their respect as an intermediary with the French. Eventually, he was hired by the trading company to live and work among the Huron as their agent. The French traders were especially anxious that he should prevent the Dutch from contacting the Huron to persuade them to trade at Fort Orange. So important was Brûlé's work judged to be that he was paid over 100 pistoles a year, which was many times the wage of an ordinary employee of the company, and almost equal to Champlain's official salary (Biggar 1922–36, 5:132; Thwaites 1896–1901, 4:209).[13] In addition to encouraging the Huron to trade, Brûlé was expected to inform Champlain and the trading company as he learned about the geography and peoples of the interior (plate 29).

Brûlé normally travelled to the St. Lawrence in the company of Huron traders from the village of Toanché where he lived, but once there he acted as an interpreter and intermediary for all the Huron who traded with the French. Brûlé had begun to live with the Huron while he was young and spent most of his adult life among them. It was therefore not difficult for the French to view him as being half Indian. Sagard states that he was as credulous as any Huron when it came to believing the lies that the Algonkin told to prevent the Huron from going to trade (Wrong 1939:266). This has suggested to some commentators that because he had lived so long among the Huron he had come to think like them. Brûlé understood and approved of many Huron customs and, as the years passed, his personal

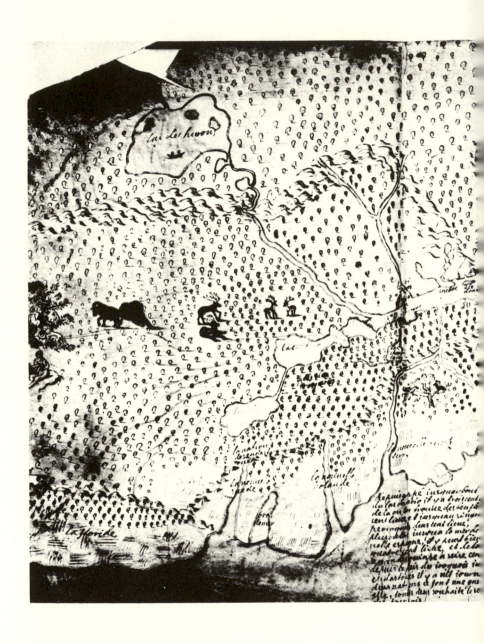

PLATE 29. *Early manuscript map of the Great Lakes. The reference to New Sweden indicates that it is no earlier than 1638; on the portfolio page on which it is mounted 1665 is pencilled in a modern hand. The authorship of the map is uncertain. Its representation of the Great Lakes differs considerably from Champlain's maps of 1616 and 1632 and is based on better knowledge of parts of southwestern Ontario than Champlain possessed. Yet it reveals less knowledge of the Great Lakes than the Jesuits acquired soon after their return to the Huron in 1634. The references to the Susquehannock, Lake Superior, and to copper deposits are noteworthy. The prototype may have been based on information supplied by Brûlé. Brûlé's exploration of the upper Great Lakes and to the Susquehanna Valley may have led him to visualize Lakes Ontario and Erie on the one hand and Huron and Superior on the other as two diverging systems. Map 4040B of de la Roncière 1907 (Album 66, Bibliothèque Historique de la Marine), no. 1. Another copy is numbered 4044B (= Album 67), no. 2.*

relations with the Huron probably seemed more real to him than did the memories of his youth among his own people. Even in a situation of extreme danger, the only Christian prayer he could remember was the ordinary grace said before meals. It is also likely that once he was adopted by a Huron family and began to live like them, the Huron came to regard Brûlé as one of themselves (Jurgens 1966:131). It will become clear, however, that although Brûlé lived for many years in the Huron country, he viewed his role as a trading agent separately from his friendship for the Huron and was willing to sacrifice Huron interests to benefit his employers, whoever they might be. Like many others in his situation, Brûlé seems to have felt little genuine attachment to his identity either as a Frenchman or as a Huron, but was capable of sacrificing either in order to accomplish whatever duties he was hired to perform.

It is uncertain how many Frenchmen were resident in the Huron country throughout most of this period. Fifteen had accompanied Champlain there in 1615, but most of these returned to Quebec the following year. Five or six Europeans are said to have been living among the Huron when the French who were sent there in 1623 arrived (Le Clercq 1691: 248). Du Vernay, who was reputed to have been of noble birth and who had formerly been in Brazil, arrived in Quebec by 1621 (Biggar 1922–36, 5:364) and is known to have spent the winter of 1622–23 in the Huron country (5:101). It has been assumed that a man named Grenole was resident there before 1623, since he travelled with Brûlé to Sault Sainte Marie before Sagard returned to France in 1624. Butterfield (1898:99–108) has dated this trip between 1621 and 1623, but Trudel (1966a:229) more prudently puts it "around 1623," thus leaving open the possibility that Grenole did not arrive in the Huron country prior to that summer.

In 1623, eleven French laymen were dispatched to the Huron country. They were to spend the winter there to help defend Huron villages and ensure that Huron traders would come to the St. Lawrence the following spring. In addition to Brûlé and Du Vernay, who had been in the Huron country the previous winter, other members of this group were Guillaume Chaudron and La Criette, both of whom appear to have been servants of Champlain;[14] Grenole, already mentioned; La Montagne, who was almost drowned on his way back to Quebec the following year (Sagard 1866:744); and La Vallée. There also seems to have been at least one Frenchman who had arrived in the Huron country previously and had not come down-river in 1623 (Biggar 1922–36, 5:129).

The majority of Frenchmen who went to the Huron country in 1623 were also there during the winter of 1624–25 (ibid. 5:129). One of these was Auhaitsique, who was drowned on his way back to Quebec in 1625. When Father Nicolas Viel returned to Quebec that year, he is reported to have left his books with some French who were remaining in the Huron country (Jones 1908:282–83), and Charles Lalemant is explicit that there were traders among the Huron in the winter of 1625–26 (Thwaites 1896–1901, 4:197). Grenole and La Vallée are known to have been among the Huron in 1626–27 (Sagard 1866:800). Some laymen were in the Huron country the following winter, since a number of them accompanied Father Daillon to the trading station in 1628 (Jones 1908:294). Among these may have been a young man named La Marche, whom Le Jeune states had visited the Huron before 1629 and had nearly been abandoned by them on the way back to Quebec (Thwaites 1896–1901, 8:85). Finally, in 1628, twenty Frenchmen were sent to the Huron country when no supplies of food or trade goods came from France. Since they bore arms, they were undoubtedly welcomed by the Huron as previous lay visitors had been (Biggar 1922–36: 6:41).

The evidence indicates that, throughout this period, a number of traders lived among the Huron, not all of whom travelled down-river to Quebec each year. In addition to the salaries they were paid, men who were sent to the Huron country were given the right to trade with the Indians for a limited number of skins each year (Thwaites 1896–1901, 4:209), which they were obliged to sell to the company at a fixed price. Sagard (1866:902) states that some of the French who returned from the Huron country in 1629 had 700 to 800 livres worth of furs with them.[15] Undoubtedly, the opportunity to trade was a powerful incentive for men to seek permission to live among the Indians (Le Clercq 1691:329). Anyone arriving in the Huron country with trade goods was certain to be welcomed and, after living with the Huron for even a short time, it was no doubt possible to acquire a vocabulary sufficient for trading purposes. More influential relations must have depended, however, on the acquisition of linguistic skills and the building up of personal relations, such as only Brûlé and a few other Frenchmen were able to accomplish.

We know regrettably little about the specific activities of these traders. In 1623, some of them were residing with Huron families in Ossossané (Sagard 1866:602). At the same time, Le Caron discovered that other Frenchmen were using his old cabin near Carhagouha (Le Clercq 1691: 249), and later that year Du Vernay, who was one of the few traders of whom the Recollets approved, appears to have lived with them at Quieu-nonascaran (Wrong 1939:193). It may be that we only have records of traders living among the Attignawantan because the priests who came to the Huron country lived only with that tribe. On the other hand, Brûlé's apparently early move from Cahiagué to Toanché suggests that the Attignawantan may have used their influence to make certain that not only the priests, but also most or all of the French traders came to live with them. We know, however, that these men travelled considerably, so that even if their formal ties were with Attignawantan families, they probably visited all parts of the Huron confederacy.

Even making allowances for the extreme bias of Recollet accounts, it is clear that relations between individual traders and the Huron were not always without incident. Given the cultural differences between the Huron and the French, it is inconceivable that they would have been. In 1623–24, a Frenchman stole a quantity of wampum beads from the village of Toanché but became frightened and fled to the Recollet cabin at Quieunonascaran when he learned that a shaman had been hired to detect the thief. The Recollets learned what had happened only after they had accepted him as their guest (141). In the estimation of the Huron, a more disgusting example of European behaviour was exhibited by a number of Frenchmen on their way to trade with the Neutral. As they were passing through the Tionnontaté country, a servant of Champlain named Guillaume Chaudron became seriously ill. Rather than stop to take care of him, his companions left him among the Tionnontaté, stating that if he died the Indian who was looking after him was to bury him, but could keep his clothes in payment for his services.[16] The Tionnontaté were shocked by the callous way in which the young man had been abandoned by his companions. News was sent to Chaudron's Indian host who lived in Ossossané. He hastened to the young man and, with the help of the Tionnontaté who was taking care of him, carried Chaudron back to his longhouse, where he died after being confessed by Father Le Caron (194–95). It is clear that the Huron were horrified by the manner in which the French traders had put gain ahead of responsibility to one of their own people. Stories of this sort do not mean, however, that the Huron did not welcome these traders; on the contrary, they much preferred them to the priests. This was largely because they were able to carry firearms, but also because their behaviour generally accorded more closely with the Huron's own standards than did that of the priests.

The confidence that the Huron had in these traders is evidenced by their letting them travel with them or even alone to visit many of the tribes with whom the Huron carried on trade, in spite of their suspicions that the French wished to conclude separate trading treaties with these groups. The first known of these journeys occurred when Brûlé was allowed to accompany the Huron envoys to the Susquehannock country. Brûlé's description of the Neutral country, which was influential in persuading Father Daillon to go there in 1626 (Sagard 1866:800), may date from this time, although his biographers speculate that he made another visit around 1625 (Butterfield 1898:110–12). He may well have visited the Neutral several times after 1615, since Frenchmen who lived among the Huron often went there to trade. One example was the journey discussed in the preceding paragraph, which took place in 1623, and Grenole and La Vallée are reported to have visited them in the autumn of 1626 (Sagard 1866:800). It is interesting that two or more traders set out on both of these trips and that they travelled south through the Tionnontaté country, as Champlain had hoped to do in 1616. This means that they set out from Ossossané, rather than from Teanaostaiaé, which was their departure point later, and may be another indication of the control that the Attignawantan were exerting over the activities of the French at this time. Evidently, French traders were permitted to visit both the Neutral and the Tionnontaté and did so freely.

Around 1623, Brûlé and Grenole were also permitted to travel northward. It is uncertain, however, whether they accompanied Huron or Ottawa who were going to trade. As a result of this trip, Brûlé reported the existence of the rapids at Sault Sainte Marie, which were named the Sault de Gaston in honour of Louis XIII's brother (589). He was also able to show the Recollets a bar of native copper that he had obtained from Indians who lived about eighty or one hundred leagues from the Huron (212–13). These Indians were probably the same group that Grenole said obtained copper from a mine, and among whom he had seen women who had the tips of their noses cut off as punishment for promiscuous behaviour (328). This punishment was later reported among the Miami and some other tribes living in the upper Great Lakes region (Kinietz 1940:184–85). It is possible that Brûlé and Grenole went no farther than Sault Sainte Marie and that their knowledge of Lake Superior was based on hearsay. The fact that Brûlé gave a slightly different estimate for the size of Lake Superior from the one he claimed was given by the Indians has been interpreted as evidence that he travelled as far west as where the cities of Duluth and Superior now stand (Butterfield 1898:108). This, however, is highly speculative.

The French who visited the Huron were thus permitted to trade with neighbouring tribes in the same way that individual Huron were. Perhaps they could do this even more easily, since it is nowhere mentioned that they had to buy the right to carry on such trade from the headmen who controlled the trade routes, as ordinary Huron had to do. No doubt, however, they gave various presents to their hosts and to prominent headmen, so that even in this respect they may have appeared more like ordinary Huron traders than the records suggest. The French traders were subject, however, to a number of special restrictions. Sagard reports that they were not allowed to travel along the "Saguenay" routes (Wrong 1939:87), obviously because the Huron feared that the French would attempt to exploit the trade of that region from Three Rivers, once they made contact with the Indians who lived there. It is also stated that Frenchmen were not allowed to winter among any of the tribes with whom the Huron traded, for fear they would encourage them to trade with the French (Sagard 1866:809–10). The Huron believed that while there was little danger in a short visit, in the course of a winter it might be possible for a Frenchman to win the confidence of a tribe and organize them to visit the St. Lawrence. Thus, while it is a measure of their confidence in these men that the Huron permitted the French to visit their trading partners, their restrictions are a measure of their prudence and the degree to which they valued their monopoly control over the trading networks of the interior. It may also be an indication of the mutual respect that existed between the Huron and the French traders that the one attempt that was made to undermine the Huron monopoly during this period was the work not of a French trader, but of a priest.

RECOLLET POLICY

Although the Recollets had judged the Huron country to be their most promising mission field after Father Le Caron returned to Quebec in 1616, the Recollets did not resume work among the Huron until 1623. Father Guillaume Poulain wintered among the Nipissing in 1621–22, but the handful of priests who were resident at Quebec at any one time devoted almost all their efforts to converting the nearby Montagnais (Trudel 1966a:330–33). Although the Recollets blamed this cutback on the poverty of their order and lack of support by the trading company (Sagard 1866:783), it is clear that they had additional reasons for not continuing Father Le Caron's work. Until they had the manpower and financial support to launch a major effort, they preferred to work among smaller groups, especially since these groups lived near to Quebec and their behaviour was of crucial importance to the French settlement.

Nevertheless, in the intervening years, the Recollets worked hard to establish at Quebec a base that was adequate for their projected operations. In 1619, aided by their old benefactor, Louis Houel, as well as by the Archbishop of Rouen and others, they secured a dozen workers and began building a residence on the south bank of the St. Charles River. There they constructed a small stone house equipped with a chapel, kitchen, and lodgings for workmen on the ground floor, and rooms for the missionaries and that could be used for the care of the sick on the floor above. Underneath was a cellar seven feet deep. The residence was fortified with wooden bastions, and a palisade and ditch surrounded the courtyard. The ditch may, however, have been intended more to keep the cellar dry than for protection. The chapel was later moved into a stone tower that guarded the entrance to the establishment. The Recollets had a barn stocked with pigs, poultry, and a pair of donkeys they had brought from France. By 1622, they were growing enough grain that, supplemented by hunting and fishing, their farm was able to support twelve people without receiving any provisions from France. In 1623, the Recollets received letters patent conferring on them the ownership of 200 arpents of land around this establishment (Trudel 1966a:318–23). The rapid progress made on this project and the wonders associated with it, not least of which were the donkeys, must have been a source of intense interest to Huron and other Indians who visited Quebec.

During this period, the Recollets had an opportunity to elaborate a general policy for carrying out their mission work. The outlines of this policy had been adumbrated at a meeting held at Quebec in July 1616, following Le Caron's return from the Huron country (Le Clercq 1691: 91–100). This meeting was attended not only by the Recollets but also by Champlain and six other "well-intentioned" people. The Recollets' policy closely resembles the missionary program that Champlain had been advocating since 1603. Le Caron may have been influenced by discussions that he had with Champlain the previous winter (Biggar 1922–36, 3:145) but, in general, the approach that the Recollets advocated for New France was similar to that adopted by Franciscan orders in other parts of the world (Stanley 1949); thus it seems more likely that Champlain enlisted Recollet support because he knew their policies to be in keeping with his own aims. Since the program laid down by the Recollets was to influence over two decades of missionary work among the Huron, and was to become one side of a prolonged controversy over Indian policy in New France, it is necessary to examine it in some detail.

On the basis of their missionary experiences elsewhere, the Recollets were convinced that in Canada they faced special difficulties. It was generally agreed that civilized non-Christians such as Hindus or Buddhists were easier to convert than were Amerindians. The former already understood the nature of religious dogma and of an organized religious hierarchy; therefore, conversion consisted largely of substituting one set of religious beliefs for another. The Indians, on the other hand, had no more idea of religious authority, as opposed to personal beliefs, than they had of a coercive political hierarchy. The individual freedom that was fundamental to Indian culture ruled out both the idea of heresy and of subordinating one's will to priestly guidance. That a priest alone might have the authority to perform certain rituals was understandable, since Indian shamans claimed such privileges, and even ordinary people had exclusive rights to sing certain songs or to perform specific rituals in healing societies. Nevertheless, the idea that an individual might, in the name of such beliefs, claim the right to judge another man's actions, or tell him what he had the moral right to say and do, was something that no Indian who was encountering Europeans for the first time could have imagined possible. The concept of authority and the respect for it that was inculcated into all civilized peoples provided the missionary and the civilized non-Christian with a common basis of understanding that was totally lacking between the missionary and the Indians of eastern Canada (Le Clercq 1691:515). The fundamental problem that the Recollets saw impeding their work was that the Indians were too "primitive" to be converted. From this they drew the devastatingly simple conclusion that if they were to convert the Indians they had first to find ways of "civilizing" them.

As early as 1616, the Recollets had assumed that it would be a simpler task to convert sedentary peoples than nonsedentary ones. Thus the Huron were assumed to be easier to convert than the Indians of the Maritimes or those who lived along the shores of the St. Lawrence (ibid. 91; Sagard 1866:793). In the name of religion, these latter groups had to be compelled to become sedentary. Even those individual nonsedentary Indians who had lived with the French for a considerable period and had been instructed by them, tended to lose their Christianity when they went back to their own people (Sagard 1866:166).

The Recollets did not believe that even sedentary Indians could be converted satisfactorily, unless they were first made to adopt standards of behaviour that were more in keeping with Christian practice. Specifically, this meant learning to live like Frenchmen. In the eyes of the Recollets, the Indian way of life was synonymous with the total absence of discipline, law, and government. One could therefore not hope to convert an Indian before he had been changed, as they put it, from a "savage" into a "human being" (Le Clercq 1691:96, 143). Le Caron believed that the latter task would be harder to accomplish than conversion (ibid. 264).

To teach a sedentary group how to live like Frenchmen, it was envisaged that French colonists would have to be settled in their midst who could instruct them and, at the same time, provide the coercion that the Recollets, like Champlain, believed would be necessary to make them give up their old ways. Farmers and artisans were especially desired and, since the settlers were to be a model of religious devotion as well as of secular habits, Protestants were to be rigorously excluded from any such enterprise (Sagard 1866:167; Le Clercq 1691:96–99). The Recollets viewed nothing short of the total replacement of Huron culture by the French way of life as a necessary prerequisite for the conversion of the Huron. Among other things, this involved the ultimate suppression of the Huron language and its replacement by French. It is curious to find Sagard (1866:340), who responded so sensitively to many aspects of Huron life, digressing in his *Histoire du Canada* to advise authorities that they should do all in their power to eliminate native languages and force the Indians to speak French, since priests should not have to waste their time learning difficult languages spoken by only small numbers of people. These were probably expressions of general Recollet policy that Sagard was instructed to insert into his book and it is not certain to what degree Sagard personally espoused this policy. It is perhaps significant that Sagard left the order a few months after his *Histoire* was published.

While the Recollets wished to convert Indians, they were firmly opposed to early or easy baptism. They realized that Indians asked to be baptized without understanding the significance that this rite had for the French. They did so to obtain presents, or because baptism appeared to cure ailments, or to establish a ritual relationship between themselves and the French. After consulting with theologians at the Sorbonne, it was decided that only converts who were dying should be baptized immediately. Others were to be baptized only after prolonged instruction and careful trial of their faith, or if they agreed to live like Frenchmen (Le Clercq 1691:147). As a result of this ruling, few Indians were baptized, except those who on their deathbed had recourse to baptism as yet another healing ritual.

Since the Recollets lacked the resources to undertake a massive program of assimilation among either the Montagnais or the Huron, they laid considerable emphasis on having Indian boys live with them, in the hope that these boys could be indoctrinated with French culture and Christian beliefs and later would be helpful for mission work among their own people (ibid. 99). In 1621, they sought royal subventions to found a residential school for fifty boys at Quebec, but efforts to finance an institution of this size received their final setback when their chief supporter, the bishop of Rouen, died. At no time did the Recollets have more than one or two pupils living with them and only six boys were ever sent to France for further study (Trudel 1966*a*:323–30). Another ambition that was never realized was to train some of these boys for the priesthood. The Recollets hoped that Christianity would appear more attractive to the Indians if they could see their own people serving as priests (Le Clercq 1691:225).

The view that the Recollets had of conversion made them zealous guardians of French culture in the New World. If the Indians were to be persuaded to become French in culture and Roman Catholic in religion, it was necessary that nothing other Frenchmen did should be allowed to compromise the authority of French institutions or Christian beliefs. For this reason, the Recollets were violently opposed to accepting reparations payments from the Montagnais for the two Frenchmen who were killed near Cape Tourmente in 1617 (or 1616). To do so, they argued, would be to sell the lives of Christians for skins and to authorize murder (Sagard 1866:56–57).

Such policies inevitably made the Recollets bitter foes of the trading company. Their desire to promote French colonization as an integral part of their mission work was in accord with Champlain's wish to increase the settled population of New France and to diversify its economic base. This policy was squarely opposed by the traders, both because of the expense involved and because they feared that European settlers would eventually seek to control the fur trade. The company was also opposed to the suggestion that Indian trappers should be encouraged to become sedentary. When the Recollets sought to persuade a number of Montagnais families to settle near Quebec and grow corn, they were warned that if they persisted, the traders would drive these Indians away (ibid. 165).

The Recollets' firm stand about punishing offences committed by the Indians and their desire to compel them forcibly to adopt French ways were also in keeping with Champlain's desire to gain control over the Montagnais. The company, on the other hand, was interested in furs and therefore was satisfied with the Indians remaining as they were. Realistically appraising the situation, the traders preferred good relations with the Indians to having control over them. Finally, Champlain and the Recollets had a common interest in seeking peace with the Iroquois, since such an arrangement would promote exploration and further mission work. It appears that from the beginning, the traders foresaw the dangers to trade that were inherent in such plans and either opposed them or approached them more cautiously than Champlain and the Recollets did.

The Recollets soon began to assume responsibility for promoting Champlain's plans to develop New France. In 1616, Joseph Le Caron and Denis Jamet accompanied him back to France to lodge complaints with the directors of the *Compagnie des Marchands de Rouen et de St. Malo* about the behaviour of their agents, whom they accused of hindering mission work. Le Caron returned to France again in 1625, where he published two tracts attacking the *Compagnie des Marchands*, hoping thereby to influence the king's council. Meanwhile, in 1620, another Recollet, Father Georges Le Baillif, had been sent to Quebec to investigate conditions there. On his return to France, he submitted to the king a list of the needs of the colony, which summarized all the demands hitherto made by Champlain and by the Recollet order. These included building fortifications, forbidding Protestant religious observances in the colony, founding a residential school for Indian children, harsher punishments for wrong-doers, and an increase in Champlain's salary and authority (Dumas 1966). Both priests were well-connected, Le Caron having been tutor to the Duc d'Orléans and Le Baillif a member of a noble French family. They were particularly hostile to Guillaume de Caën, the Protestant ship owner who held the trading monopoly in New France from 1621 to 1627—accusing him of neglecting the colonization of New France and being openly hostile to Roman Catholicism. While it is true that like all traders in New France, he neglected his promises to develop the colony, there is no evidence that de Caën was ever hostile to the Recollets. Sagard described him as a "polite, liberal, and understanding man" and there are frequent references to the good services he provided for the missionaries (Trudel 1966*b*: 160). In spite of this, the Recollets' activities resulted in de Caën being forbidden to travel to New France in 1626 and his monopoly being cancelled the following year in favour of a new program of intensive and exclusively Roman Catholic colonization. While the anti-Protestant fanaticism of Le Caron and Le Baillif may have been their own, their efforts to secure support for the program of colonization and mission work that they and Champlain had devised together, made these two men Champlain's most valuable allies. Through these activities, the Recollet missionaries became important agents and champions of New France.

LE CARON'S MISSION TO THE HURON

In 1623, the Recollets had an opportunity to expand their diplomatic activities and mission work. That spring, the French at Quebec became worried about their alliance with the Huron. Le Clercq states that they feared that the Huron were about to make an alliance with the latter's enemies (1691:246–47). The French knew that the Dutch were attempting to expand trade and believed that any peace between the Huron and the Iroquois would soon lead to trade between the Huron and the Dutch (Sagard 1866:811). To reinforce their ties with the Huron, Champlain decided to send a large party of French to visit them that year, including a number of Recollets.

This decision indicates the importance that the French attributed to their trade with the Huron and their nervousness about the state of the French-Huron alliance at that time. What precipitated this particular crisis? Historians have mostly treated the fears of the French as if they were justified (Trudel 1966a:364–66), although they have almost certainly erred in doing so. The French may have been alarmed by rumours concerning one of the periodic peace treaties that Huron and Iroquois tribes negotiated in the hope that families on both sides would be able to recover kinsmen who had been taken prisoner but not yet killed. Yet, in spite of fulsome protestations of good faith, such truces usually lasted no longer than was needed to repatriate these relatives. Moreover, if there was talk of peace between the Huron and the Seneca, fighting had resumed by the time the missionaries arrived in the Huron country; another possible truce between the Huron and the Iroquois, to be discussed below, seems to have been a later response to a Huron victory in the autumn of 1623. The French miscalculated if they believed that any treaty of this sort would last, let alone lead to a diversion of trade southward.

The Dutch were undeniably attempting to divert trade from the St. Lawrence Valley to their own posts. They were doing this, however, by seeking closer ties with the Montagnais and the Algonkin. Their traders appear to have had only very limited knowledge about the interior of North America, to the extent that the structure of the Iroquois confederacy was still unknown to them. It is likely that they knew about the Huron from Champlain's published accounts, but this does not mean that they knew precisely where the Huron lived or how they might contact them. Furthermore, it is inconceivable that the Mohawk, or any other Iroquois tribe, would have permitted the Huron or the Dutch to travel through their territory to trade with one another. The Mohawk were already fearful that an alliance between the Dutch and the northern Algonkians would disrupt their supply of trade goods if intertribal wars were to break out again. The Huron could supply more and better quality furs than could the Mohawk; hence there was the added danger that if trade developed the Dutch would favour the Huron rather than them in any future conflict. The only terms on which the Mohawk might have accepted a trading arrangement centred on Fort Orange would have been if they retained the exclusive right to act as intermediaries. It is impossible to imagine, however, that at that time the Huron would have considered breaking off trade with the French only to make themselves totally dependent on their traditional enemies for supplies of European goods.

Finally, while some historians have stressed French fears that the Huron were geographically closer to Fort Orange than they were to Quebec and therefore would naturally be inclined to trade with the Dutch, this argument does not survive closer scrutiny. Irksome as the long journey down the Ottawa River may have been, it was a water route. The alternative route, down the Trent Valley, across Lake Ontario, up the Oswego Valley to Lake Oneida, and then down the Mohawk Valley, was far more difficult to traverse, even if no political complications had beset its use. For all these reasons, it is unlikely that there was any danger of Huron trade being diverted to New Netherland or that either the Huron or the Iroquois had yet considered the possibility of such a thing happening.

The French undoubtedly had other reasons for wanting to renew their ties with the Huron at this time. The Huron were annoyed about the ill-treatment that they were receiving from the Kichesipirini, who were older allies of the French than they were. Also, if two Huron were killed at Quebec in 1622, their compatriots may have blamed the French for letting this happen. More importantly, however, the French were in the process of arranging a peace between themselves, their Algonkian-speaking allies, and the Mohawk. Not long before, the Mohawk had been attacking Huron traders in the Ottawa Valley and, in any case, they were members of the Iroquois confederacy and therefore enemies of the Huron. This put the French in a very difficult position. On the one hand, they did not wish a tactical arrangement with the Iroquois to undermine relations with their most important trading partners—who probably mistrusted their motives far more than did the Algonkians who were helping to negotiate the treaty. On the other hand, the French did not want the treaty to promote good relations between the Huron and the Mohawk, lest this should serve Dutch interests. Apprehension over the consequences of their own actions may have made the French uncertain of their relations with the Huron, and hence anxious to strengthen their alliance with them. There is no contemporary evidence to support the suggestion that the priests who were sent to the Huron country had specific instructions to disrupt whatever treaties the Huron might be negotiating with the Iroquois (cf. Le Clercq 1691:258; Charlevoix 1866–72, 1:34–35).

The Recollet party, which was made up of Fathers Joseph Le Caron and Nicolas Viel, Gabriel Sagard, and possibly two secular assistants who had come to serve the Recollets in New France in 1619, set off with the eleven armed Frenchmen who were being sent to defend the Huron villages (Jones 1908:276). One of the two Recollet assistants was probably the young man known only by his Huron name, Auhaitsique. It is uncertain whether the Recollets merely accompanied the laymen as a way of getting to the Huron country, or whether Le Caron travelled there as Champlain's personal representative, as Le Clercq later maintained (1691:246). Considering the similar policies of Champlain and the Recollets, Champlain could have relied on Le Caron much more than on any trader to pursue objectives that were in keeping with his own plans for the development of New France. It is also certain that Le Caron would have been willing to act, at least informally, as Champlain's emissary. Even if he did not receive a specific commission from Champlain, Le Caron may well have regarded himself not only as a missionary but also as a servant of the French government.

The request that the Huron traders take three members of a French religious order home with them must have come as a surprise. Although Le Caron had lived among the Huron seven years before, the traders at first refused to accept the missionaries. They said that they wanted men who could bear firearms and help them to fight their enemies. They were, however, mollified when they were informed that the priests had supernatural powers that would be useful to them in their wars. Three canoes were finally made available, after Guillaume de Caën generously donated a quantity of axes, knives, beads, and other trade goods that were given to the Huron to encourage them to accept the missionaries. These presents, supplemented by additional gifts of fish and meat that the missionaries obtained by barter from passing Algonkin, assured them the goodwill of the Indians and eventually they arrived safely in the Huron country (Sagard 1866:170–96).

Because each missionary travelled with a different group of Huron, they did not all arrive at the same time or in the same place. Le Caron was taken back to Carhagouha, where he had lived previously, while Viel probably landed at Toanché. Sagard travelled with Huron from Ossossané who were led by a man named Oonchiarey. They landed along the shores of Matchedash Bay and travelled overland to their village. Sagard lived for a time with Oonchiarey's family, who treated him kindly and gave him a compartment of his own within their longhouse. He describes Ossossané as a well-fortified town, containing thirty or forty longhouses and 200 to 300 families. Sagard called this town Quieuindahian or Tequeunonkiaye, the latter being similar to the name Champlain used (Wrong 1939:70). The new name may indicate that the location of the community was changed between 1623 and 1634. Other evidence suggests that Sagard visited the Ossossané that was abandoned in 1636. The latter has been identified with a high degree of probability with an archaeological site on lot 16, Concession 7 in Tiny township (map 19). The site is located on a well-defined promontory bounded on the west by an abrupt escarpment and on the south by a somewhat less precipitous streambed. Below the promontory, one and a half miles of swampy dunes lie between the site and Nottawasaga Bay. The cornfields of the village must have been located above the promontory and surrounded the village to the east in a large semicircle (Ridley 1947; Heidenreich 1971:fig. 11). Both Viel and Sagard followed Le Caron's example in naming the village they were first associated with after their patron saint. Thus Carhagouha, and later Quieunonascaran, became St. Joseph, while Ossossané became St. Gabriel, and Toanché was St. Nicolas (Sagard 1866:296).

If Heidenreich (1966:120) is correct, Le Caron must have returned to Carhagouha while that village was being relocated. Shortly afterwards, he was living in the relocated village, which was called Quieunonascaran. After a time, Father Viel and a number of other Frenchmen arrived in Ossossané and Sagard was ordered to accompany Viel to Quieunonascaran. To ease his departure, Sagard informed his hosts that he had possessions belonging to Le Caron that he had to take to him (Wrong 1939:76). Out of necessity, the three missionaries lived for a time at Quieunonascaran with one of the principal headmen, but Le Caron requested the village council to build a separate cabin for them outside Quieunonascaran to replace the abandoned missionary residence at Carhagouha. The council tried to persuade the Recollets that they should live with one or more families in the village. Le Caron replied that it was "not possible to receive enough enlightenment from heaven to instruct them in the bustle of their lodges," and that the Recollets did not want to show more preference for one family than for another (ibid. 77–78). Because they already attributed shamanistic powers to the Recollets, the Huron must have concluded that they wished to live alone in order to exercise these powers.

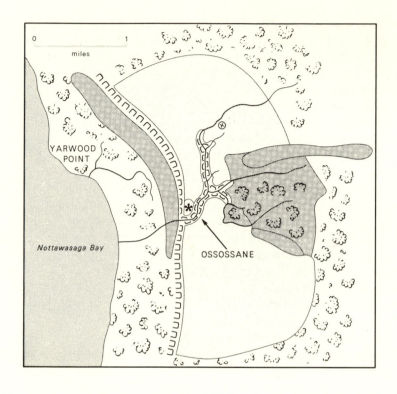

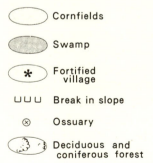

Cornfields

Swamp

* Fortified
  village

⊔⊔⊔ Break in slope

⊗ Ossuary

Deciduous and
coniferous forest

MAP 19. *Reconstruction of the field pattern and natural setting of Ossossané prior to 1634 (Lot 16, Conc. VII, Tiny Twp.) (after C. E. Heidenreich).*

Seeing that Le Caron could not be persuaded to change his mind, the council agreed to build a cabin for the priests. A site was chosen in a ravine only a few hundred feet from the town. There the men of Quieunonascaran erected a lodging about twenty feet long and covered it with tree bark; but because the bark had not been gathered in the spring it soon split, letting in rain and cold. The Recollets had their workmen divide the interior of the building in two, in order to separate their chapel from a general living area. Between these two rooms was an enclosed space used to store their vestments and other valuable possessions (ibid. 81; Sagard 1866:214). Around the cabin the Recollets planted a small herb garden, which they fenced off in order to keep out children. The garden did poorly, allegedly because the soil was poor, but more likely because it was planted too late.

Le Caron's decision not to live with the Huron was based mainly on his conviction, formulated as early as 1615, that the so-called "lewd" habits of the Huron were incompatible with the spiritual requirements of a priest. The clergy could at most venture into such an environment in an attempt to change it; they could never agree to live in it (Sagard 1866: 41–42). By isolating themselves in this way, the Recollets were, in effect, rejecting the hospitality that the Huron wished to extend to them. As adopted members of the community they continued to enjoy the same rights as every other household. A communal work force helped to construct their house and they were given a share of *auhaitsique*, small fish that were collectively harvested in seines by the villagers (ibid. 694). On the other hand, because they lived by themselves, they were compelled to barter with the Huron for food, whereas, if they had lived with Huron families, they would have been fed without charge (Thwaites 1896–1901, 4:197; Wrong 1939:71–72). The Recollets did not understand why the Huron charged them for food and complained that the latter gave nothing to strangers without demanding payment for it (79). They also protested that Huron who came to visit them frequently stole things. These included not only items that were left outside their house but also objects from their living room (84). By contrast, Sagard states that his hosts at Ossossané took special care to guard his possessions and warned him to beware of thieves, particularly among the Tionnontaté who came as visitors to the town (71). This clearly indicates that the thieving at Quieunonascaran resulted from the lack of integration of the Recollets into that community. This lack of solidarity was also reflected in the complaint of a Huron youth who was helping to build the Recollets' cabin to the effect that such work was unnecessary since the priests were not relatives (78). Relations with the inhabitants of Quieunonascaran were made more difficult by the frequent refusal of the priests to attend feasts to which they were invited. In part, they did this for religious reasons, but Sagard states that they also did it because they lacked the resources to reciprocate (84). This refusal of the priests to join in communal activities must have puzzled the Huron and hampered the effectiveness of the Recollets' work.

The Huron had much difficulty when it came to categorizing the Recollets. Unlike other Frenchmen, they did not carry arms and insisted on living apart from the Huron. They refused to participate in friendly activities, such as attending feasts or joining Indian men in sweat baths (198). In addition, they refused to consider marrying Huron women or to respond to their sexual advances (125–26), and they reproved women for proposing sexual liaisons either with them or with other Frenchmen (134). That the Recollets were some variety of shaman had been confirmed by the assurances that the French had given the Huron traders to the effect that their supernatural power would help the Huron to defeat their enemies. Fasting and sexual abstinence were necessary to become a shaman and teams of Indian men acquired supernatural power in these ways before engaging in intervillage athletic contests and games of chance. Priestly celibacy must have been interpreted as evidence that the Recollets sought, or possessed, supernatural powers of extreme potency. Such powers could, of course, be used for good or evil, but the secretiveness and unsociable behaviour of the Recollets must have made the Huron fear that they were engaging in some form of witchcraft that was designed to harm them.

The Recollets were willing to try to perform many of the same tasks that the traditional shamans did in the hope of supplanting them. They did not doubt that God would be willing to grant their prayers to help promote their missionary work. When the Quieunonascarans agreed to build a cabin for the Recollets in 1623, they asked the priests to stop the rain, which was excessive at that time. Sagard notes with satisfaction that after they had spent the night praying, the rain stopped and fine weather prevailed until the cabin was finished, after which it began to fall again. The Huron are reported to have regarded this as a proof of supernatural power and to have proclaimed everywhere the greatness of the spirit whom the Recollets invoked (78).

The priests who lived in the Huron country had remarkably good luck in such endeavours if we are to believe their accounts. Sagard reports that the rains were very heavy in April and May 1624. After trying all of their own rituals in vain, the headmen of Quieunonascaran held a council, where it was decided that they would offer the Recollets a cask of corn if they would produce fair weather. Sagard was sent to the council where, after pointing out that God did not always answer men's prayers, he agreed that the Recollets would intercede for the people of Quieunonascaran. The Recollets had no sooner started to pray and to march around their cabin reciting the litany than the rain ceased, after which the skies remained clear for about three weeks (178–81). Sagard believed that such activities greatly strengthened the influence of the Recollets in Quieunonascaran; for example, the village council is reported to have resolved that henceforth they would call the priests their "spiritual fathers." The Recollets' apparent success in controlling the weather was also given as one of the reasons why, following a drought in the summer of 1626, the Huron were anxious to have the priests return after a year's absence (Thwaites 1896–1901, 4:223). Such activities did not, however, advance an understanding of Christianity; they merely enhanced the Recollets' reputation as shamans.

Because of their religious scruples, the Recollets were not always so obliging. One day, after Sagard had been making shadow pictures with his fingers, his Huron companions caught an especially large number of fish. Although they implored him to perform more of this magic, Sagard refused so that he would not encourage "such superstition" (Wrong 1939:187–88). Baptisms, although rarely performed, appear to have been viewed by the Huron primarily as healing rituals. In Quieunonascaran, the wife of Ongyata, a headman of some importance (Sagard 1866:395), was baptized as she was about to die. To everyone's surprise, she rallied and remained in good health for some time. In spite of the pious Christian sentiments that are attributed to this woman, it would appear that both she and her husband continued to regard baptism as a curing ritual. Her request to be rebaptized shortly before her death indicates her hope that another baptism would restore her health (Wrong 1939:175–76).

The supernatural powers that the Recollets either claimed or had attributed to them further heightened the Huron's awe of them and of the clerical equipment they had brought with them. The Huron and the Algonkin attributed magical powers to their scarlet damask chasuble and believed that if they could carry it into battle, or hang it from their battlements, they would overcome their enemies (Sagard 1866:411). The Kichesipirini were sufficiently convinced of this that they offered the Recollets eighty beaver skins in exchange for it (Wrong 1939:155). The mass chalice, which the Huron called a kettle (*anoo*), is also reported to have been an object of fear (Sagard 1866:476), although it is unknown whether the Huron already interpreted the doctrine of transubstantiation as implying that the Roman Catholic mass was similar to their own rites involving cannibalism. Many Huron believed that the carved wooden skull that Sagard carried on his rosary had been the skull of a living child (Wrong 1939:146). A woman is reported to have stolen a priest's garment from the Recollets, but whether she valued it as an item of clothing or for its presumed magical properties is unknown. She returned it to the Recollets, claiming that a Tionnontaté had stolen it (Sagard 1866:476).

The Recollet missionaries interfered in Huron affairs whenever they felt that their own interests, or those of the French generally, were being threatened. Sagard recounts their strong opposition to a war with the Neutral that certain Huron headmen were advocating. He reports that after considerable effort the Recollets managed to dissuade the Huron from attacking the Neutral. Although the Recollets claimed that they were opposed to the war because they believed the odds were against the Huron winning, their real concerns seem to have been that the war would be a barrier to their projected conversion of the Neutral and would interfere with the fur trade (Wrong 1939:157). On the other hand, Sagard abandoned his idea of trying to promote peace between the Huron and the Iroquois. He had thought that such a peace would help to spread the gospel to the Iroquois and would promote commerce. The French traders warned him, however, that it was more likely to lead the Huron to trade with the Dutch, which would be a theological as well as an economic disaster (Sagard 1866:811).

During the winter of 1623–24, the Recollets frequently met the Nipissing, who were living about three leagues from Quieunonascaran, and persuaded them to allow Father Viel to go to James Bay with them the following spring. Sagard boasted that this was something the Nipissing had never agreed to before, since they feared to reveal the sources of their furs to Europeans (Wrong 1939:86–87, 269). In fact, a similar promise had been made to Champlain. Arrangements were also made for Sagard to travel some 200 or 300 leagues beyond the Huron country in a southerly direction, possibly to visit the Susquehannock (ibid. 269). According to Sagard, both journeys had to be called off when he and Le Caron were unable to return to the Huron in 1624. On the basis of earlier experiences, it seems doubtful that the Indians would have kept their promises with respect to either of these journeys.

There was an unpleasant encounter between the Recollets and the Huron headmen at Ossossané concerning the burial of Guillaume Chaudron. The Recollets insisted on an inhumation burial in a special, presumably consecrated, location away from the Ossossané cemetery. The Huron joined in the funeral and the women of the village did their traditional mourning on orders from their headmen. In spite of this, the French did not distribute any presents to honour the bones of the deceased and to express their gratitude to the mourners. This annoyed the Huron, who said that, because of this, the dead man would have to share the goods that the Huron gave to the spirits of their dead relatives. A shaman who attended this funeral was ordered to leave by the French, on the orders of the priests. He had previously been refused permission to try to cure Chaudron, although he had asked to be allowed to do so (ibid. 195; Sagard 1866:603).

Arrogant behaviour of this sort may explain an incident that happened in the Recollets' cabin at Quieunonascaran in the winter of 1623–24. Many Huron were in the cabin and one of them, who did not have a place to sit, tried to push aside a Frenchman who already had one. We are not told why the Huron acted as he did, but a legitimate principle of rank or seniority likely was involved. When Le Caron told the Huron to be quiet, the latter became angry and struck at the priest with a stick. The French who were present prevented the priest from being hit, but, as a result, a brawl broke out between the French and the Huron youths (Wrong 1939: 164; Sagard 1866:394). Sagard ran to the village to secure the intervention of the principal headman, Auoindaon, as well as other prominent people (Onorotandi, Yocaisse, Ongyata, and Onnenianetani). A general council was held the next day, at which the French were asked to forget what had happened and were presented with some bags of corn and invited to a general feast (Wrong 1939:165–66). This incident reveals some of the tensions that were generated by the inability of the Recollets either to understand Huron culture or to accept it on equal terms with their own. Because of this, the Recollets were more feared than loved by the Huron, although not sufficiently feared to be fully protected from the supreme insult of being attacked in public.

The Huron who courted the friendship of the Recollets were men who traded with the French. Foremost among these was the aged headman, Auoindaon, who, at least among the northern Attignawantan, claimed to control the trade route leading to Quebec. Auoindaon is reported to have visited the Recollets often and to have shown great solicitude for them. If he found them at prayer, he would get on his knees and imitate their gestures until they had finished. When Sagard was left alone in the Recollets' cabin, Auoindaon offered to spend the night with him to protect him from the Iroquois or against evil spirits that might trouble him (ibid. 174–75). He also asked for baptism, no doubt hoping that this might lead to a closer alliance with the French (Sagard 1866:478). Many Huron who

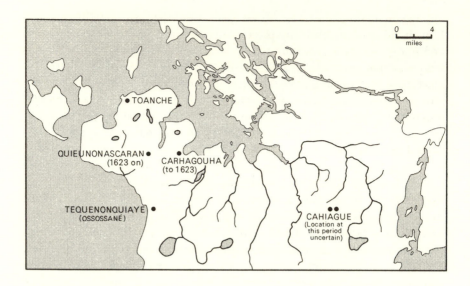

MAP 20. *Huron settlements mentioned by name for the period 1623–29.*

associated with the priests did so in the hope of receiving small presents in
return either for services or for expressions of interest in their teachings.
The headmen and traders were, however, clearly interested in promoting
closer relations with the French in hopes of improving their trading
relations with them. Specifically, this meant persuading the Recollets to
report the good treatment they had received and to intercede with French
traders so that the Huron could get their goods from these traders at a
reasonable price (Wrong 1939:244). The desire of the Huron traders to
preserve and strengthen their alliance with the French guaranteed that
all Frenchmen who were living in the Huron country would be well
treated, so long as the Huron traders who had dealings with the French
were treated in the same way.

The Recollets often went out from Quieunonascaran to visit other groups
(Le Clercq 1691:250). Undoubtedly they visited most, if not all, of the
northern Attignawantan villages, none of which was far from their headquarters (map 20). Le Caron was in Ossossané for Chaudron's funeral, and,
at some point during his stay in the Huron country, Father Viel struck up
an important friendship with Soranhes, a prominent trader from Teanaostaiaé (Sagard 1866:795). We do not know, however, whether the
Recollets travelled in the eastern part of the Huron confederacy. Sagard

was able to report that the town of Cahiagué had been relocated and split into two parts since Champlain's visit (Wrong 1939:92), but it is unclear whether the Recollets had visited the new town or had merely been told what had happened. There is also no evidence of any missionaries visiting either the Tionnontaté or the Neutral settlements at this time. An otherwise cryptic reference to the slight work they had started among the Neutral (Sagard 1866:408) suggests that possibly one or more of their lay workers may have visited these people disguised as traders.

One of the Recollets' principal aims was to continue the study of the Huron language that Father Le Caron had begun in 1615. They realized that unless they could speak the Huron language fluently any effort to inculcate a satisfactory knowledge of Christian teaching was bound to be unsuccessful. Le Caron continued to work on his dictionary and added to it various notes on Huron grammar. He was assisted in this work by Father Viel, who continued to send him material after Le Caron had returned to Quebec. Le Caron's dictionary appears to have been finished by 1625, when Father Georges Le Baillif presented a copy of it to the king (Le Clercq 1691:327–28). Another product of the linguistic studies of this period was Sagard's list of Huron words and phrases which he called *Dictionnaire de la Langue Huronne* and published as an appendix to his *Grand Voyage*. This is the only one of the Recollets' linguistic studies that is known to have survived to the present.

Sagard noted that one of the more serious obstacles to the eventual explanation of Christian beliefs to the Huron was the absence in their language of many necessary theological terms. The Huron had no single words by which it was possible to express concepts such as sacrament, kingdom of heaven, trinity, holy spirit, angels, resurrection, or hell. Even apparently more universal concepts, such as temptation, faith, and charity, seemed to have no precise equivalents in Huron. The explanation of the simplest religious texts thus required elaborate periphrasis (Wrong 1939: 73–74), and there was no way of being certain that the intended meaning had been adequately conveyed.

The problem of communication was, in fact, more serious than Sagard, or any of the Recollets, realized. All of the basic teachings of Christianity had, from the earliest days, been tailored for a complex society in which ideas of authority, hierarchy, and punitive justice were taken for granted. To express Christian doctrines in a way that was compatible with the beliefs of people whose whole way of life was founded on exactly the opposite principles required more than linguistic skills which could translate the Christian message. It required the remoulding of Christian teachings to fit a different social code. This was something that the Recollets were incapable of perceiving and would have been opposed on principle to doing.

On the contrary, their second major objective was to try by precepts and teaching to begin to Europeanize Huron attitudes as a necessary first step towards eventual conversion. The low priority accorded to conversion at this time was given as the reason why the lay brother Sagard was added to the party rather than a third priest (Le Clercq 1691 : 246). Because the Recollets had already determined that Indians should be baptized only after a severe trial of their faith, they tended to assess all protestations of interest in Christianity with scepticism. They recognized that the Indians often showed an interest in their instructions in hopes of specific material gain (ibid. 280). What they did not realize was that other Huron sought their friendship for fear of falling victim to the Recollets' witchcraft.

Many Huron came to visit the Recollets in order to exchange corn, squash, beans, and smoked fish for awls, iron arrow heads, or a few glass beads (Wrong 1939:84); in brief, they treated the Recollets as petty traders. When families gave feasts but did not have enough metal kettles of their own, they asked to borrow the Recollets' kettles but never returned them without food in them (84). Huron men visited the Recollets in order to obtain enough tobacco for a smoke. Much of the tobacco that was consumed by the Huron was imported from the south, hence was a valuable commodity. Because of this, Huron men accepted it from the French as evidence of their hospitality (85).

It was also realized that the Huron's desire not to contradict anyone resulted in their appearing to agree with what the missionaries were saying, when in fact they did not understand or agree with them. This made it difficult for the missionaries to determine whether or not individual Huron were sincerely interested in their teachings. Knowledge of this practice did not, however, prevent the Recollets from criticizing Huron religion. Huron beliefs and customs were consistently mocked and abused, and the refusal of the Huron to defend their views aggressively was misinterpreted by the triumphant priests as indicating a lack of religious conviction. Women were rebuked for their personal behaviour for reasons that must have been totally incomprehensible to them. Although these reproofs appeared to be accepted in a lighthearted manner (Sagard 1866:327), it is clear that the Huron were often annoyed by such behaviour and, in very trying circumstances, their anger sometimes showed through. For example, on their return to Quebec, Sagard's companions were unable to convince him that a rocky hill they were passing was the home of an important guardian spirit. Because of this they remained sullen for a long time.

Only three conversions are reported for the period 1623–24: Ongyata's wife and a man and his daughter (Le Clercq 1691:257). In keeping with Recollet policy, efforts were made to persuade families that seemed inclined to be converted to move to Quebec, where they were told they could settle on the Recollet estate (ibid. 257). The Recollets mainly sought, however, to persuade a number of Huron familes to allow boys to be taken to Quebec, or to France, where they might receive instruction. In order to prepare for this, Le Caron ordered Sagard to teach some elementary reading and writing to a group of Huron children, but his efforts came to naught because the children lacked sufficient discipline (Sagard 1866: 330). Many adults came to observe these classes and asked Sagard to teach them some French words. Sagard also attempted to explain such things as the European view of the relationship between the sun and the earth (462). Although Sagard persisted with his efforts to prepare five or six boys to accompany the Recollets to France, their families refused to let them go. These families might have been expected to act differently on the grounds that they were thereby sealing a closer trading alliance with the French; however, Savignon, by recounting his own experiences, convinced them that the French were too cruel and unjust to be trusted with Huron children (320).

FATHER VIEL'S "MURDER"

In 1624, both Le Caron and Sagard returned to Quebec. Sagard shared a canoe with a war chief named Angoiraste and two of his companions, Andatayon and Conchionet (Wrong 1939:244). Le Caron remained at Quebec, but Sagard, who had expected to return with supplies for the Huron mission, received a letter from the Provincial, Father Polycarpe Du Fay, ordering him to return to Paris. This left Nicolas Viel as the sole missionary among the Huron during the winter of 1624–25. We know little about his life there, except that he continued to study the Huron language and expressed the wish that he might be allowed to continue working among the Huron for the rest of his life. In the spring of 1625, he decided to come down-river to make a brief spiritual retreat. As he was passing through the Sault-au-Récollet, in the Rivière des Prairies, his canoe overturned and he was drowned. His body was recovered from the water a few days later and was buried at Quebec.

The generally accepted version of Viel's death maintains that for some unknown reason he was murdered by his Huron companions who in order to hide their crime also murdered a Huron boy named Auhaitsique, who had become his disciple and was travelling to Quebec with him. This story was widely believed in the latter part of the seventeenth century and was recorded by Le Clercq, who presented Viel and Auhaitsique to his readers as "the first two martyrs of Canada" (Le Clercq 1691:322). In recent years, however, Archange Godbout (1942) and Marcel Trudel (1966a:340–42) have shown this story to be a tendentious fabrication. Auhaitsique was not a Huron, but the nickname the Huron had given to a young Frenchman who was probably a servant of the Recollets. Likewise, none of the contemporary accounts of Viel's death describe it as anything but a simple accident (Sagard 1866:789, 794; Thwaites 1896–1901, 4:171). It was only in 1634 that Paul Le Jeune claimed that Viel had died as a result of foul play (7:233). Two years later, Brébeuf wrote that the Kichesipirini had informed him that the Huron had murdered not only Etienne Brûlé but also Viel and his companion (10:79). He had been told this story, however, in an effort to persuade the Jesuits to stop living among the Attignawantan. Although Sagard popularized this claim of martyrdom in his *Histoire du Canada*, the desire of the Kichesipirini to undermine the renewed friendship between the Attignawantan and the French seems reason enough for them to have invented the claim that Viel had been murdered. When travelling down-river, Huron traders not infrequently preferred to shoot rapids, rather than to make an excessive number of portages. Canoes sometimes overturned in these rapids, and it is not surprising that in such an accident the Indians might swim to safety, while the French, who wore bulky clothes and mostly did not know how to swim, drowned. Sagard reports that when he came down-river in 1624, the Huron let him remain in their canoe while they got into the water and guided it through the Lachine Rapids. Under such circumstances, an accidental drowning is not improbable, and the absence of any suspicion of foul play for nine years after Viel's death makes later charges seem unlikely.[17]

Because of Father Viel's death, two missionaries who had planned to return to the Huron country with him had to postpone their journey. One of these was a Recollet: Father Joseph de La Roche Daillon, the son of a nobleman from Anjou. The other, Jean de Brébeuf, was a Jesuit. The scion of petty Norman aristocracy, Brébeuf had entered the Jesuit novitiate at Rouen at the age of twenty-four. He taught for several years at the College at Rouen and at the age of thirty-two the Jesuit Provincial, Pierre Coton, had chosen him to go to New France, where he arrived in April 1625.[18] Charles Lalemant stated that the journey to the Huron country was called off because, with Viel dead, there was no cleric there who knew the Huron language or who could help the newly arrived missionaries to establish themselves (Sagard 1866:789). Considering the general lack of goodwill between missionaries and French traders at this time, the lack of direct contacts with the Huron may have been reason enough to call off the journey. The Huron traders were undoubtedly frightened by Viel's death, since, according to the terms of their alliance with the French, they were charged with responsibility for his safety and well-being. Therefore, in the absence of strong pressure from the French traders, the Huron may have wanted to consult with other headmen, or even with the confederacy council, before agreeing to take any more priests home with them. The clerks of the trading company no doubt understood the Huron's anxiety and helped to dissuade the priests. There is no need to invoke suspicion of foul play in order to explain the behaviour of either the French or the Huron at this time.

The most important accomplishment of Father Viel's two years in the Huron country was gaining Soranhes's permission that his fifteen-year-old son Amantacha might be educated in France. Soranhes lived in Teanaostaiaé and was therefore an Attigneenongnahac (Trigger 1966*a*). He was also an early and active participant in the fur trade. Throughout his life, his dealings with missionaries seem to have been motivated largely by a desire to court favour at Quebec. There is, therefore, little reason to doubt that, however much Soranhes may have liked and trusted Father Viel, this unusual promise was prompted by his wish to establish a special relationship with the French. Even so, Soranhes appears to have hesitated. He had promised Father Viel that he would send Amantacha to Quebec in the spring of 1625, but neither Soranhes nor his son travelled down-river that year.

Nevertheless, after Viel's death Soranhes kept his promise and, in 1626, he came to Quebec, where he is said to have entrusted Amantacha specifically to the care of Father Le Caron. To the latter's delight, Amantacha was a handsome and intelligent youth, who, from the start, got on well with the French (Le Clercq 1691:367). Soranhes was, however, an ambitious trader who was anxious to contract many alliances with the French, and who probably believed that by doing so he was helping to ensure Amantacha's welfare. He therefore accepted friendship presents not only from the Recollets but also from the Jesuits and from Emery de Caën, who was in command at Quebec in Champlain's absence (Sagard 1866:796–97). A three-cornered dispute about the boy's guardianship

broke out, in which de Caën appears to have discreetly supported the
Jesuits (Le Clercq 1691:372; Sagard 1866:796). It was finally decided
that Amantacha should travel to France on Emery de Caën's ship and that
his education should be entrusted to the Jesuits. He travelled in the care
of the Jesuit priest, Philibert Noyrot, and was accompanied by Etienne
Brûlé, who was returning to France that year and whom Amantacha is
said to have loved like a father.[19]

Amantacha went first to Rouen, where he lived with Emery de Caën
and his uncle, Ezéchiel. He was then taken to meet the Jesuits of Paris
who, along with the new Viceroy of New France, the pious Henri de
Lévis, Duc de Ventadour, undertook to pay for his education. Amantacha's
schooling proceeded slowly, however, because Brûlé was the only man in
France who knew how to speak Huron and the Jesuits found him too
coarse and uneducated to assist them adequately (Thwaites 1896–1901:
4:213–15). It was probably for this reason that the Jesuits decided not to
keep their promise to return Amantacha to his father in 1627, in spite of
an agreement that if Soranhes were satisfied with the treatment his son
had received in France, he would let him return there for several more
years (4:225).

During his stay in France, Amantacha learned to speak and write
French (5:245) and was sufficiently well instructed in the principles of
Roman Catholicism that the Jesuits decided to baptize him publicly in
December 1627. To draw attention to their achievement, a special stage
was erected in the Cathedral of Rouen for the benefit of onlookers (Du
Creux 1951–52:34) The service was conducted by the Archbishop, François de Harlay, while two members of the nobility stood as Amantacha's
godparents (Trudel 1966a:329). Amantacha was given the Christian name
Louis de Sainte-Foi. A rumour, spread by the sailors, that Amantacha
was the son of the King of Canada caused numerous townspeople to flock
to the ceremony (Sagard 1866:798). Du Creux (1951–52:34) reports that
in spite of the cold weather there was a flash of lightning during the
ceremony and a flame seemed to play about the stage that had been
erected for it. It was not until the spring of 1628 that it was decided to
send Amantacha back to his people.

DAILLON'S NEUTRAL FIASCO

During the winter of 1625–26, Father Daillon studied the Huron language
at Quebec with the aid of Le Caron's dictionary and the Huron who were

spending the winter there (Le Clercq 1691:344–45). In order to gain the latter's goodwill and to persuade them to take him to the Huron country, Daillon supplied them with food (ibid. 343). Thus, when the Huron came to trade the following summer, Daillon had no trouble securing a place in one of their canoes. He probably travelled with the people he had befriended over the winter. This may also explain why Daillon settled at Toanché rather than at Quieunonascaran, where the Recollets formerly had their headquarters (Jones 1908:292).

The effect this change had on relations between Quieunonascaran and Toanché is not known. After Viel had drowned, the people of Quieunonascaran may not have wanted to be responsible for another priest. Alternatively, Quieunonascaran is known to have declined in importance between 1623 and 1637 and it is possible that some of the clan segments from that village moved to Toanché. If so, the change may simply reflect the differing fortunes of these two villages. Since the people of Toanché had brought Viel to the Huron country, it may be that by securing another priest they felt they were regaining what had doubly been lost to them, first by Viel moving to Quieunonascaran and then by his death. Daillon was accompanied to the Huron country by Brébeuf and Father Anne de Nouë, both of whom were Jesuits.

More than any other missionary who visited the Huron confederacy, Daillon felt charged with a political as well as a religious mission. This feeling was increased when, before setting out for the Huron country, he received a letter from Le Caron ordering him to visit the Neutral. On 18 October, Daillon left the Huron country with the traders Grenole and La Vallée, who were going to trade with the Neutral. Passing through the Tionnontaté villages, they were on the road for five days before they reached the first Neutral village (Map 21). They then visited four more settlements before they reached Ounontisastan, where lived Souharissen, the principal headman of the Neutral. Through an interpreter, Daillon announced that he wished to conclude a treaty of friendship between the Neutral and the French and to make the two peoples trading partners. He also offered presents to Souharissen as a pledge of his sincerity. In return, Souharissen granted Daillon his protection and agreed that he could remain among the Neutral over the winter. At this point, Grenole and La Vallée returned to the Huron (Sagard 1866:800–802).

Daillon's actions not only were aimed at weakening the Huron's role as middlemen but also violated their rule that Frenchmen living in the Huron country should not winter among the tribes with whom they traded. It is not known whether Daillon was acting on his own in seeking

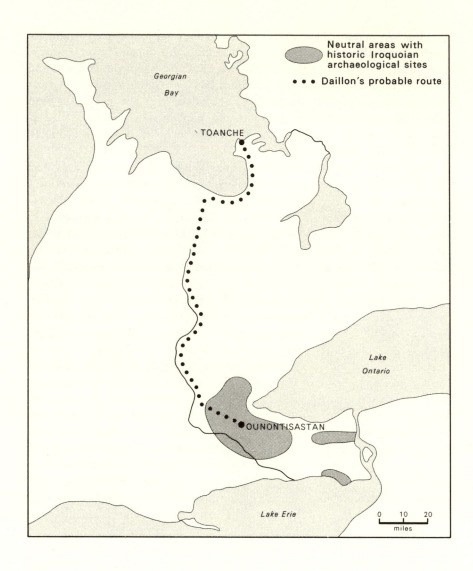

MAP 21. *Daillon's route to Ounontisastan (partly based on information supplied by W. Noble and M. E. White).*

an alliance with the Neutral, or whether the Recollets were cooperating with either Champlain or the French traders in an effort to undermine the Huron monopoly. No doubt, the traders would have been pleased to pit the Huron and Neutral against one another in order to get furs more cheaply. Nevertheless, this was a sufficiently dangerous game that the French traders who were living among the Huron did not wish to play it themselves. It is possible that a scheme of this sort might have been worked out between the higher echelons of the Recollet order and the trading company in France. The Recollets may have been hoping to prove to the company that they could be more useful in Indian diplomacy than were the hated interpreters.

Eventually, Daillon persuaded the Neutral to promise that they would send four canoes to trade with the French. The Neutral were evasive, however, and pleaded that because they did not travel extensively by canoe, they did not know the route from their country to the St. Lawrence. Daillon knew that this route led along the north shore of Lake Ontario, and from the Huron and Algonkin he had learned that by following it a person could reach the French trading stations in about ten days. When Daillon tried to learn the details of the route from Iroquet, who was in the Neutral country hunting beaver, the latter refused to tell him anything (803). It is likely that Iroquet soon headed north to inform his Huron allies what Daillon was doing.

The Huron did not delay in counteracting Daillon's influence. They began spreading rumours that Daillon was an evil sorcerer and that the French were monsters who ate thunder and lived on serpents. Because the Neutral knew little about the French, these rumours soon produced the intended effect. Individual Neutral who fell ill accused Daillon of bewitching them and he was beaten and had his baggage pillaged. As long as Daillon remained under the personal protection of Souharissen he was, however, relatively safe. To circumvent this, Huron agents appear to have persuaded, or bribed, some men fron Ouarorono (either a Neutral village near the Niagara River or the Wenroronon tribe) to slay him. These men invited Daillon to Ouarorono but, when he would not come, they waited until Souharissen and his men had gone hunting, then came to Ounontisastan with the intention of killing him. When their first hatchet blow failed to hit him, fear of Daillon's supernatural powers overcame them and they contented themselves with pillaging his possessions. Later, perhaps under pressure from Souharissen, they agreed to return some of these. By this time, however, rumours were reaching the Huron country that Daillon had been murdered. Fathers Brébeuf and de Noüe persuaded

Grenole to go to Ounontisastan and retrieve Daillon, if he were still alive. In spite of the humiliating circumstances from which he was rescued, Daillon continued to maintain that Frenchmen should be sent to live among the Neutral (807).

Daillon's mission ended in failure and served to confirm the Huron's fears that the missionaries were living in their midst for no good purpose. Daillon's attempts to undermine their trade, while ably counteracted by the Huron, were probably interpreted as further evidence of the malevolent sorcery that they feared lay behind the professed goodwill of the missionaries. This, even more than the apparent confirmation that the missionaries were commercial rivals, must have troubled the Huron in the years to come.

Yet, it is unlikely that Daillon's mission ever had any chance of success. The Neutral were reluctant to trade directly with the French and their claim not to know the route to the St. Lawrence was probably a polite way of rejecting Daillon's proposal. No doubt they feared that any attempt to develop their own trade would lead to war with the Huron. Since they were also receiving European goods from the Iroquois, the latter probably would not have allowed them to use the St. Lawrence River. Indeed, to protect their trade and to prevent the Neutral from receiving French military assistance, the Seneca might have gone to war with them more readily than the Huron would have done. Faced with the threat of war on two or more fronts, the Neutral probably concluded that an independent trading alliance with the French was not worthwhile.[20]

In spite of the anger he had created among the Huron, Daillon remained in the Huron country for another year. He returned to Quebec in the summer of 1628 and lived there over the following winter. In 1629, he left for France with the other priests who were in the colony. Daillon was the last Recollet to visit the Huron.

THE JESUITS RETURN TO NEW FRANCE

Daillon's departure from the Huron country foretold the general waning of the Recollets' fortunes in New France. After 1625, they were no longer the only missionaries in Canada. While they later claimed that they had invited the Jesuits to join them because they lacked the resources to exploit their mission field adequately (Le Clercq 1691:297), it is doubtful that they would have been able to resist the designs of the politically astute and ambitious Society of Jesus for long, even if they had been inclined to try.

Instead of seeking an alliance with Champlain, as the Recollets had done, the Jesuits undertook to control the highest echelons of the colonial administration in France itself, in order to ensure that no traders, officials, or other religious orders in New France could oppose them. This operation was carried out with great discretion and required both tact and a willingness to come to terms with vital trading interests. Bitter experience had taught the Jesuits the need for compromise on this score.

The Society of Jesus had been involved in mission work in Canada before the Recollets arrived at Quebec in 1615. In 1610, through the influence of Pierre Coton, who was Henri IV's confessor, and other prominent people, the Jesuits secured a royal command that their order should accompany Jean de Biencourt de Poutrincourt to his colony at Port Royal, in Nova Scotia. Prior to making this choice, they had turned down Champlain's proposal that they come to Quebec and share in the fur trade there, in return for an investment of 3600 livres (Bishop 1948:155). Poutrincourt objected to having the Jesuits and it was only the following year that Fathers Pierre Biard and Enemond Massé arrived in Nova Scotia. Their subsequent bitter quarrels with Poutrincourt and Samuel Argall's destruction of the colony that the Jesuits attempted to establish on Mount Desert Island off the coast of Maine brought an end, in 1613, to their first round of activity in New France. The supporters of Poutrincourt denounced Biard as a traitor for having accompanied Argall to Port Royal, and hereafter nearly everyone concerned with trade and colonization agreed that the Jesuits should be kept out of New France. Champlain turned to the Recollets, when he again sought missionaries for his colony at Quebec. In spite of these inauspicious beginnings, the Jesuits did not lose interest in New France. Father Massé, in particular, hoped to return to New France and, as a teacher in the Jesuit college at La Flèche, he inspired many of his students with a wish to go there (Trudel 1966a:94–149).

Following his release from prison in 1619, the Duc de Condé yielded his rights as Viceroy of New France to his brother-in-law, Henri II, Duc de Montmorency, in return for 30,000 livres. Montmorency confirmed Champlain as his lieutenant and, like his predecessors, committed himself to a policy of developing the colony. He withdrew the fur trading monopoly from the associates of St. Malo and Rouen and granted a fifteen-year contract to a new company directed by Guillaume de Caën and his uncle Ezéchiel. The *Compagnie de Caën*, headed by both Protestant and Roman Catholic members of an important shipowning family of Rouen, was formally obliged, among other things, to settle six families each year at Quebec and to construct five houses. After a bitter struggle with the old company, the shareholders in the latter were given permission to join the *Compagnie de Caën* as individual members. Although criticized for failing to promote settlement, Montmorency accomplished much during the five years that he was viceroy of New France. The habitation was rebuilt, the first fort was built on Cape Diamond, and the Recollets' mission house was constructed. Louis Hébert was formally possessed of the land on which his house and farm were located, and Guillaume de Caën was granted a seigniory at Cape Tourmente, where he built a habitation and began to pasture some cattle (ibid. 297).

In 1625, Montmorency seems to have been compelled by Cardinal Richelieu to relinquish some of the many offices he had acquired. His impending resignation led the Jesuits to persuade his young nephew, Henri de Lévis, Duc de Ventadour, to acquire his uncle's rights in New France in return for 100,000 livres. Both the Duc de Ventadour and his wife were extremely zealous Roman Catholics. In 1630, the Duke was to found the Compagnie du Saint-Sacrement and, in 1643, following the death of his wife, he became a priest. From 1624 onwards, his confessor was the Jesuit Philibert Noyrot, who seems to have persuaded his patron to purchase the office of viceroy (Du Creux 1951–52:26–27).

In the spring of 1625, Ventadour arranged, at his own expense, to send three Jesuits to Quebec: Charles Lalemant, Enemond Massé, who had formerly been in Nova Scotia, and Jean de Brébeuf. Neither Louis Hébert nor the traders at Quebec were happy to see the Jesuits, since they feared that with Ventadour's backing, they would soon be interfering in the affairs of the colony. The Jesuits therefore encountered open hostility and efforts were made to persuade them to return to France. Champlain and the Recollets were probably equally worried about Jesuit interference in their own activities; however, being aware of the powerful backing that the Jesuits had acquired, the Recollets received them with a show of friendliness. When the Jesuits were refused permission to stay at the habitation, the Recollets offered them accommodation in their own house on the banks of the St. Charles River.

It soon became clear that the Jesuits had not come to New France simply as missionaries. Instead, they were armed with special powers to curb the interpreters, whom the Recollets had long complained were interfering with their mission work, but whom they had been helpless to do anything about. The Jesuits had the authority to send these interpreters back to France, where they might be broken of their independent and seemingly immoral ways. Almost immediately, Brûlé and the Montagnais interpreter, Nicolas Marsolet, were ordered to return to France, although this decision was bitterly opposed by Emery de Caën. Marsolet won a reprieve by expressing contrition and promising to teach the Jesuits the Montagnais language if he were allowed to remain. He is reported to have kept his promise faithfully, although for ten years he and the other interpreters had refused to teach the Recollets anything (Thwaites 1896–1901, 4:209–13; 5:113). Brûlé seems to have been more recalcitrant and, in spite of de Caën's efforts to prevent it, he was ordered to sail for France. Before the ships left, however, he conveniently became ill and was forced to spend the winter of 1625–26 in the care of the Jesuits. He too was persuaded, in due course, to teach the Jesuits to speak Huron (4:213–15).

However successfully the Jesuits may have asserted their control over these men, once they had extracted the desired linguistic information from them, they ordered both of them to return to France in 1626. Brûlé was sent, in part, to accompany Amantacha and to provide linguistic assistance to his tutors (4:225). The reason for Marsolet's exile in spite of his apparent reform, is unknown. Marsolet was back in New France in July 1627, when he helped a Recollet lay brother to baptize the dying Algonkin shaman Napagabiscou (Sagard 1866:522); Brûlé may have returned the same year, but it is not clear if he was allowed to resume living among the Huron. The bitterness that these two men felt towards the Jesuits is evident in their behaviour after the capitulation of Quebec, when both were in the employ of the English.

In 1626, with the help of some workers from the habitation and a carpenter borrowed from the Recollets, the Jesuits erected a four-room house, to which an outbuilding containing a hand-mill was added. The same year additional missionaries arrived, bringing twenty workmen and confirmation of a concession of land stretching northward from the mouth of the St. Charles River. These workmen seem to have been lodged in the original house the Jesuits had built, and although they were able to stay in Canada for only one year, they cleared land and built a new residence called Notre-Dame-des-Anges at the confluence of the Lairet and St. Charles Rivers.[21]

In 1625, Father Brébeuf was prevented from setting out for the Huron country by the death of Father Viel. His missionary zeal led him, however, to spend the winter living with a band of Montagnais. While this allowed him to experience Indian life, it prevented him from studying the Huron language as intensively as Father Daillon did and also from winning the confidence of the Huron who were wintering at Quebec. He did, however, manage to pick up some knowledge of the Huron language (Thwaites 1896–1901, 4:221). In the summer of 1626, Brébeuf and Father Anne de

Noüe, who had just arrived from France, were ordered to accompany Daillon to the Huron country. Daillon quickly obtained passage with the Huron, although they were reluctant to accept the Jesuits (Le Clercq 1691:344). In general, this probably reflected the Huron's lack of enthusiasm to embark any white man who did not bear arms; however, the Jesuits' heavy boots and wide-brimmed hats made them more dangerous to have in canoes than were the grey-robed and sandalled Recollets, and Talbot (1956:56) suggests that their unfamiliar black robes also may have caused the Huron to be wary of them. It was only after many presents were offered to compensate the Huron for extra paddling and loss of cargo that two crews agreed to provide space for them.

Brébeuf, de Noüe, and Daillon settled in Toanché, where they had a cabin erected on the outskirts of the village, as the Recollets formerly had done at Carhagouha and Quieunonascaran. The Jesuits remained there, while Daillon made his infamous journey to the Neutral country. They appear to have had no distinctive missionary program, but attempted to follow that of the Recollets, which meant applying themselves to the study of the Huron language and not baptizing anyone for fear it would prove premature. Brébeuf baptized only one person during the three years that he remained in the Huron country. This was a baby who appeared to be dying, but who recovered and was alive in 1635 (Thwaites 1896–1901, 8:135–37). Like the Recollets, he and de Noüe exhorted the Huron to live in conformity with Christian standards and attempted to exemplify these standards in their daily life. They also came to share the Recollets' distaste for the traders and, in particular, their hatred for Etienne Brûlé.

By early 1627, it was clear that Father de Noüe was unable to learn the Huron language and it was decided that he should return to Quebec. No missionaries came to the Huron country that year, so that Brébeuf and the discredited Daillon were alone in Toanché. Alarmed by Daillon's flirtation with the Neutral, the Huron brought an unusually large number of furs to the French trading stations (Biggar 1922–36, 5:232). A highly successful trade, accompanied by a suitable reaffirmation of the French-Huron alliance, may have helped to repair the damage that Daillon had done, and this, in turn, may have made it possible for Daillon to trust his life to the Huron and return to Quebec the following year. In any case, Daillon left the Huron in 1628 and Brébeuf became the sole missionary among them.

1628 was a year of drought in the Huron country, and Toanché was among the places hardest hit. When Tehorenhaegnon, who was one of the most famous shamans in the region, failed to make rain, he announced that this was because the red painted cross that had been erected in front of Brébeuf's cabin was frightening the thunderbird and causing the rain clouds to divide as they approached the village. This charge has been interpreted as evidence that, even at this time, the shamans felt hostile towards the priests for encroaching on their traditional domain. More likely, however, Tehorenhaegnon was genuinely concerned about the effect that this fiery symbol had on the behaviour of the thunderbird, and his jealousy was merely the professional rivalry one shaman felt towards another, without involving any specific malice towards Brébeuf as a foreign interloper. The seriousness of Tehorenhaegnon's charge lay in the belief already prevalent among the Huron that the French priests might be practising witchcraft, of which causing famine was one possible manifestation (Thwaites 1896–1901, 10:43–49).

When the headmen of Toanché sent for Brébeuf and asked him to take down his cross or to hide it for a time in his cabin or in the lake, Brébeuf refused. He threatened the Huron with supernatural punishment if they removed the cross themselves and, at the same time, decried their ignorance in believing that the thunder was a spirit. In order to turn the argument to his own advantage, Brébeuf agreed to paint the cross white, but stated that if it did not rain immediately thereafter, Tehorenhaegnon would be exposed as an impostor. When several days passed and it did not rain, Brébeuf went to the village council and demanded that its members paint the cross red again and, to restore its honour and ensure a harvest, that they each bring a dish of corn as an offering, which he would then redistribute among the "needy families" of the village. Anxious to try whatever shamanistic rite Brébeuf was proposing, they did what was asked and followed Brébeuf's example by kneeling down and kissing the cross. In Brébeuf's words "they did so well that the same day God gave them rain and in the end a plentiful harvest" (10:49). This victory over Tehorenhaegnon emphasized the superiority of Brébeuf's magical powers and also demonstrated his goodwill towards the people of Toanché. It conformed, however, to traditional Huron religious beliefs and, while enhancing Brébeuf's authority, did not contribute to a better understanding of Christian teaching.

The goodwill of the Attignawantan was especially valuable that summer since the French trading vessels did not get through to Tadoussac that year. Because of this, the French had little to trade. The Huron had to pay higher prices for what there was and, even so, returned home with many skins unbartered. In addition, Amantacha had not been returned to his father. Huron annoyance was partly offset by twenty Frenchmen being sent to live with them for the winter. This was the largest contingent of armed Frenchmen that had ever arrived in the Huron country. Although they were sent mainly because there was not enough food for them at Quebec, they served to retain the goodwill of the Huron at a difficult juncture.

During the three years Brébeuf was in the Huron country, in the Huron's estimation he gained a better working knowledge of their language than anyone who had been there before (Biggar 1922–36, 6:46). By the end of this period, he was able to recite Bible stories, to explain simple theological matters (Thwaites 1896–1901, 5:191), and had translated Father Ledesma's catechism into Huron. The latter was appended to the 1632 edition of Champlain's *Voyages* (Latourelle 1952–53:18–19).

With the situation at Quebec becoming increasingly uncertain, all Frenchmen living in the Huron country were ordered to return to the St. Lawrence in 1629. This included a command from Father Massé that Brébeuf should return. Thus, in the spring of 1629, Brébeuf took his leave of the Huron. He was present at the surrender of Quebec in July and subsequently had to return to France with the other missionaries.

Huron Life

The main problems that the Huron faced were adjusting to European goods rather than to the Europeans themselves. Trade goods had become available to the Huron in moderate quantities, but, as we have seen, contacts with white men were still limited and nondisruptive. During this period no more than twenty to thirty Europeans lived among the Huron at any one time and often there were less than ten. Most of these men were traders who had no desire to challenge the Huron way of life, and in many ways were assimilated with it. No French officials lived among the Huron, and the priests who were there after 1623 had neither the skills nor the coercive power to challenge the Huron way of life or to interfere in their affairs to any significant degree.

An initial period during which political and cultural initiatives remain in the hands of indigenous groups has been a feature of contact between Europeans and tribal peoples in many parts of the world. The introduction of iron tools frequently reduces the time required to perform certain important routine tasks and permits energies to be directed elsewhere. The result is not a disruption of the indigenous culture or a breakdown in existing social relationships, such as may occur when direct European intervention is involved. Instead, this period witnesses the realization of potentials that existed in the native culture. Particularly, one finds the elaboration of social status, increasing emphasis on ceremonialism (especially involving conspicuous consumption), greater artistic endeavours, and heightened competition to control scarce resources (Averkieva 1971; Salisbury 1962).

TECHNOLOGICAL CHANGE

The data on trade already presented indicate that the Huron were primarily interested in obtaining iron tools with sharp cutting edges and copper and brass kettles. While stone artifacts are not particularly abundant on prehistoric sites (Emerson 1967:137), preliminary reports of research carried out in the Penetanguishene Peninsula suggest a rapid decline in these artifacts in the historic period. In respect of the Robitaille site, it is claimed that "lithics seem to have been almost abandoned" (Latta 1971: 130). As the Huron acquired iron knives and axes in considerable numbers, these replaced their traditional stone adzes and cutting tools. Indeed, Sagard's observation that the Huron fashioned arrow shafts with a knife or, when they had no knife, with sharp-edged stones (Wrong 1939:98) suggests that, already by 1623, iron tools may have been used more commonly than stone ones for this purpose. Sagard's comment refers to the Attignawantan, from whose territory most of the published archaeological evidence has been recovered. Only more research can determine whether the other Huron tribes were as well supplied with iron tools at this time.

Iron awls are common in Huron sites of the historic period. At least some of them were probably used to punch holes in scraps of brass and copper (Latta 1971:127), but it seems likely that metal awls were used mainly as drills and for working wood and bone. As such, they fall into the general category of Huron cutting tools. The popularity of iron knives and axes is not difficult to explain. The knives had an edge that was superior to that of stone scrapers or other Huron cutting tools. They were, moreover, fairly lightweight objects; hence large numbers of them could be transported with little difficulty. Iron axe heads were considerably heavier and more difficult to transport. As we shall see, however, they were more effective for felling trees than were their stone counterparts. It also probably required less effort to carry an iron axe from the St. Lawrence Valley to the Huron country than to chip and grind a stone one out of a block of chlorite schist.

It is equally certain, however, that in spite of the popularity of iron cutting tools, the knowledge of how to make stone ones was not about to be lost. The Robitaille site has yielded numerous examples of triangular stone projectile points, that are reported to be extremely well made, as well as a number of stone adzes (Latta 1971:129). A major factor keeping a knowledge of stone-working alive was, no doubt, the inability of traders to satisfy the demand for European goods. While this is not surprising in view of the size of the Huron population and its distance from the trading stations, the situation contrasts sharply with the apparent abandonment of a lithic industry among the Montagnais at this time.

Considerable numbers of bone artifacts are found in historic Huron sites. Projectile and harpoon points are fairly common; awls and netting needles abundant (Kidd 1952:73). The relative commonness of bone tools suggests that the advantages of metal implements over their bone counterparts were not great enough to stimulate a strong demand for the former, so long as iron cutting tools remained in short supply. Faced with the need to choose what was most essential, iron axes, knives, and awls were preferred, especially since these tools made it easier to manufacture the traditional bone ones.

It has been suggested that women's tools remained largely unchanged, either because of greater conservatism on their part or because male traders habitually chose items that were useful to themselves rather than to their womenfolk (Latta 1971:130–31). It must be remembered, however, that bone tools were produced by men, hence they would have been interested in replacing them with metal ones if they had been especially difficult or time-consuming to manufacture. Bone netting needles and bone or stone arrowheads were made and used by men and are more common than metal imports. This reinforces the argument that, given the difficulties involved in obtaining and transporting goods to the Huron country, European items that replaced ones which were difficult to manufacture, or which performed markedly better than their Huron counterparts, were preferred to those that replaced ones that could be manufactured relatively easily. It may also be noted that in spite of the importation of glass beads, native beads were still manufactured in considerable quantities out of bone and marine shell. The Huron's red slate beads may have been imported from elsewhere, since unworked fragments of this material are missing from Huron sites (Latta 1971:128–29; Kidd 1952:73).

The glass beads at the Robitaille site are generally in poor condition, probably indicating that they were kept until wear or breakage made it impossible to string them (Latta 1971:128).

Although the Huron purchased large numbers of copper and brass kettles, there is no evidence of a decline in pottery-making. Broken pottery vessels occur in even the latest Huron sites in quantities that suggest little curtailment in manufacture as a result of trade with the French (Kidd 1950). There is no evidence that pottery was "definitely on the way out" as has been claimed was happening among the Seneca at this time (Wray and Schoff 1953:56–57). Once again, it is clear that the number of metal kettles that could be imported by the Huron was insufficient to supply their needs and this ensured the survival of the native product.

Another factor preventing the accumulation of large numbers of metal kettles by the Huron was the ease with which they wore out. Like the axes that were supplied to the Indians, poor quality kettles were foisted by the Europeans on their inexperienced and goods-hungry trading partners. We have noted that the Huron in Quieunonascaran were in the habit of borrowing kettles from Europeans when they had feasts (Wrong 1939:84).

Aside from their prestige value and supernatural powers, one of the practical advantages of metal kettles was for travelling by canoe, since they were lighter and broke less easily than the clay pots that the Huron normally carried with them. The Huron were also interested in these kettles because they provided them with a supply of scrap metal. There is extensive evidence that worn out kettles were cut into pieces, which were used to make arrowheads, beads, plaques, and pendants. The arrowheads that the Huron made were triangular in outline, like their stone ones, while tanged arrowheads appear to have been obtained ready-made (Latta 1971: 127). The copper and brass pendants normally had holes bored through them that would have served either for suspension or for sewing them onto clothes. A sheet of brass recovered at the Robitaille site had been cut into the outline of an animal standing on its tail (ibid. 128).

The Huron also reworked iron artifacts. Notches were filed into knife blades to turn them into harpoon points, knives having handle and blade made of a single piece of metal being preferred for this purpose (Garrad 1969). The reworking of all types of metal was done by filing, grinding, and hammering—techniques that for millennia had been used by the Indians of this region to work native copper. There is no evidence that the Huron acquired any additional metal-working skills at this time. They did not know how to mend items that were broken or worn through, and repeatedly asked Sagard and other Frenchmen to perform such services for them. The Huron must have viewed scrap metal as the equivalent of native copper. Its abundance resulted in the florescence of an old, but hitherto restricted, technology.

It has been assumed that the introduction of iron knives and axes reduced the amount of time that men had to spend performing essential tasks, such as clearing fields and manufacturing other tools. Technologically, this argument appears to be sound, although the amount of time saved by using iron tools remains problematical. The iron knife must have speeded up the working of bone and wood, and fewer stone axes would have had to be manufactured than formerly. Yet, considering the many hours that were spent cutting trees, both to clear fields and to erect houses and fortifications, it seems likely that the greatest saving was made through the use of iron axes. Experiments carried out using flint axes mounted in the traditional European fashion, in ashwood handles through a rectangular hole in the haft, have demonstrated that an oak tree over a foot in diameter can be felled in less than half an hour (Iversen 1956), while a conifer seven inches in diameter can be cut through in five to seven minutes (Clark 1945). To employ such axes effectively, however, the user must chip at the tree with short, quick strokes, using mainly the wrist and elbow. In New Guinea, experiments and observations have shown that a stone adze fitted into an elbow haft is about one-third to one-quarter as efficient for forest clearance as a European steel axe. A man who is experienced in using both types of implement can chop down a tree (species unstated) just under thirteen inches in diameter in twenty-four minutes with a stone adze, while a tree of the same species fifteen inches in diameter can be cut down in eight minutes using a steel one (Salisbury 1962:219–20; Townsend 1969; Cranstone 1971).

In spite of the close agreement of these figures from Europe and New Guinea, they cannot be applied automatically to the Huron data. The iron axes that the French supplied were manufactured specially for the fur trade and were made of metal that was much inferior to the steel ones that are in use today. They also lacked the large, heavy head above the socket which accounts to no small degree for the efficiency of modern axes (Kidd 1949a:115). The Huron probably used them in the same way that they used stone axes, that is, cutting with short, quick strokes. Even if a trade axe used in this manner was not as inefficient as it looks, it was probably less time saving than a modern one. Yet, if such axes speeded up forest clearance by only a factor of two, instead of three or four, they would have resulted in a considerable saving of energy.

The acquisition of iron axes also made it easier for the Huron to cut down larger trees than they had been accustomed to previously. The novel manner in which such logs were used to construct walls and supports for sleeping platforms in houses of the historic period can be illustrated by a comparison of the plan of a house from the Robitaille site with another from the earlier Maurice site, both of which are similar in size and shape (Tyyska 1969:76; plate 30). It must be noted, however, that, even in prehistoric times, the Iroquois frequently used large posts to construct their houses and palisades. It therefore appears to have been technologically feasible for the Huron to have handled larger logs at an earlier period, had they been convinced that the investment of energy was worthwhile. Iron axes simply made it possible to use larger logs without expending additional energy to cut them down.

In spite of this, it is questionable whether Huron men spent less time clearing forests than they had done previously. Expanding trade with the northern hunting peoples must have markedly increased the demand for Huron corn, which, in turn, necessitated increased production. In the first of what has become a succession of bizarre and overblown theories about the effects of the fur trade on Huron life, Hunt (1940:59) suggested that as the Huron grew increasingly preoccupied with trade, they ceased to produce food of their own and imported all they required for their own needs and for trade from the Neutral and Tionnontaté. This suggestion is without foundation. There are frequent references to Huron being engaged in horticultural activities up to, and including, 1649 and 1650. Moreover, it is ludicrous to imagine that the numerically much smaller Tionnontaté population could have produced enough food to supply Huron requirements, or that it would have been economically feasible to transport large amounts of corn northward from the Neutral country. Carrying this corn overland would have consumed too much time and energy to make it worthwhile.

It seems likely that much of the time saved by greater efficiency in forest clearance was lost through the need for increased production. Part of the demand for more corn may have been met by the annual export of surpluses that formerly were reserved to offset years of drought or crop pestilence. This would explain the apparent vulnerability of the Huron to crop failures in the later historic period, even though they were still reported to be producing surpluses to protect themselves against such failures. In addition, however, larger crops must have been grown. Since women's tasks were not influenced by the new technology, the amount of time they spent tending crops must have increased sharply. Thus one of the results of the fur trade seems to have been the very opposite of what Hunt believed. Trade did not become a substitute for food production; on the

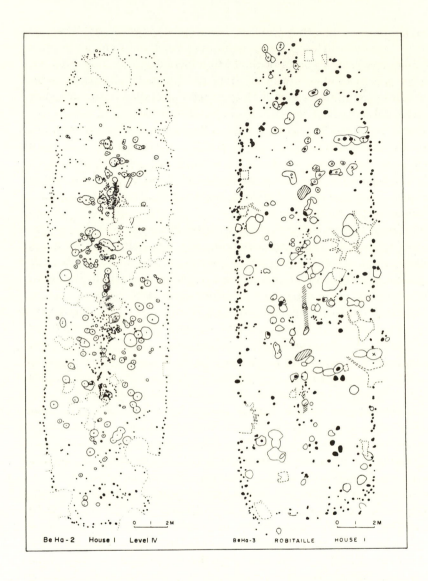

Be Ha - 2   House I   Level IV   BeHa-3   ROBITAILLE   HOUSE I

PLATE 30. *Plans of longhouses from the Maurice (BeHa-2) and Robitaille (BeHa-3) sites. Both sites are in the Penetanguishene Peninsula. The first is dated* A.D. *1570–1620, the second is later. The large post molds in the house from the Robitaille site indicate that bigger trees were being felled in later times to construct houses. Courtesy C. E. Heidenreich and W. M. Hurley.*

contrary, increasing food production became the basis of expanding Huron trade.

The Recollets who lived among the Attignawantan in 1623 planted a small kitchen garden with peas, herbs, and "other trifles" (Wrong 1939: 81). In spite of this, contacts with Europeans do not seem to have influenced Huron methods of cultivation or their choice of crops. Sagard reports that a Huron trader from Toanché planted a few peas and that these produced seeds twice as big as Sagard had seen growing in France or at Quebec (ibid. 91). In view of the dominant role conventionally ascribed to Iroquoian women as horticulturalists, it is interesting that in this case it was a man who was experimenting with new crops. This is scarcely surprising, however, since men also grew the Huron's one speciality crop, tobacco. We may be seeing here an example of how, in prehistoric times, geographically mobile warriors and traders played an important role in diffusing crops throughout the Iroquoian culture area. The balanced repertoire of crops already being grown by the Huron may explain their failure to adopt new crops at this time, or it simply may be that not enough time was available for European crops to become established prior to the destruction of the Huron confederacy.

It has been suggested that hunting declined in importance as trade developed. As evidence, it is pointed out that stone artifacts are scarce in historic Huron sites, while few of the metal tools are suitable for hunting (Latta 1971:130). It is also argued that, at least in the late northern Attignawantan sites, considerable amounts of dog bone (*Canis* sp.) are found, but few bones of deer or other wild animals. This, it is claimed, indicates that, by historic times, the Huron obtained little meat by hunting or trading, but were dependent on horticulture and fishing, supplemented by dog meat (Savage 1971a:148).

It must be noted, however, that none of the northern Iroquoian cultures has left distinctive hunting kits in the prehistoric archaeological record and that hunting was probably never as important as fishing from at least Owasco times onward. Moreover, as the population in northern Simcoe County increased in late prehistoric times, many types of game must rapidly have become depleted, particularly in areas such as the Penetanguishene Peninsula. The apparently high percentage of wolf, as opposed to domestic dog, bones at the Maurice site (c. 1570–1620) (Savage 1971b) may represent a continuing shift in local hunting patterns that began with the depletion of local stocks of deer, followed by that of other wild animals. This does not mean, however, that the Huron did not range farther afield for their hunting. The meat from such hunts was fleshed from the bone and would leave no trace in Huron middens. It is known that the traditional spring hunts continued as late as the winter of 1647–48 (Thwaites 1896–1901, 33:83–85) and that Huron men were skilled hunters at a much later date. The relatively minor role of hunting in prehistoric times and the decline in local supplies of game as the Huron population became more concentrated suggest that the diminution of wild animal bones that can be observed in village middens may not have resulted from more time being spent trading. Indeed, since the fur trade led the Huron to exhaust the beaver within the entire range of their hunting territories by 1630, it may be argued that, for a time, the fur trade produced more intensive hunting, which continued into the period we are discussing.

A notable feature of all Huron settlements at this time is their location either near the shores of Georgian Bay, or close to rivers that flow directly into it. By crowding nearer the lake, these villages came to occupy an even smaller total area than they had previously. Their distribution, which differs from the more inland one of earlier times, no doubt reflects a continuing adjustment of population to the geographical requirements of the fur trade, as well as the growing effectiveness of the confederacy council in promoting unity among the member tribes.

On the other hand, the largest settlements continued to be stoutly defended and were constructed in naturally fortified locations. The reason for this was continuing hostilities with the Iroquois, and particularly with the Seneca. As we have already noted, the traditional prestige system of the Huron and Iroquois made endemic warfare, at least on a limited scale, essential for both groups. Sagard reports that in the early 1620s, about 500 men set out each year to raid the Iroquois. This must have been at least as many as at any other time in Huron history (Wrong 1939:152). It seems that as the growth of trade made peaceful relations with neighbouring tribes more desirable, the Huron directed their raids against their remaining enemies, the Iroquois. Also, the Iroquois may still have hoped to capture European goods from the Huron, just as the Huron captured shell beads from them.

Iroquois raiders were reported to be active in the Huron country in the summer and autumn of 1623 (ibid. 175). The same year, a raiding party led by a young man from Quieunonascaran won a signal victory over the Iroquois south of Lake Ontario. In a single engagement, they captured about sixty Iroquois, slaying most of them on the spot. The others were brought back to the Huron country to be tortured to death. These prisoners were divided among a number of villages, including Ossossané and Toanché, whose warriors had taken part in the raid (ibid. 152; Sagard

1866:423–24). This was a major victory by Iroquoian standards and demonstrates that at this time the Huron were more than holding their own against the Iroquois. Perrot (1911:148), although scarcely a reliable source for this period, reports that there was a truce between the Huron and the Iroquois in 1624, but it is not known which Iroquois tribes were involved. Conceivably, however, the truce was related to the Huron victory of 1623.

In general, relations between the Huron and the other Iroquoian tribes of Ontario were peaceful. The Huron and Tionnontaté seem to have been on particularly good terms and only the continuing refusal of Huron headmen to let the Tionnontaté trade with the French seems to have prevented them from becoming part of the confederacy. Relations with the Neutral were more strained, no doubt because the Neutral also traded with the Iroquois and were less dependent on the Huron for European goods. In 1623, a dispute seems almost to have led to war between the two groups. Fear of a Neutral attack-in-strength prompted even the northern Attignawantan to dismantle isolated houses and move into Quieunonascaran, which they heavily fortified (Sagard 1866:416). At the same time, weapons were made ready, provisions stockpiled, and warriors held councils to coordinate their plans for defence (Wrong 1939:156–57). An alliance was planned with the Assistaronon, who were sworn enemies of the Neutral. As soon as some Neutral had been captured, three or four Huron were to daub themselves with their blood and visit the Assistaronon (Wrong 1939:157–58). Although the Assistaronon were enemies of the Tionnontaté and the Ottawa as well as of the Neutral, the Huron evidently did not regard an alliance with them as out of the question. In spite of these preparations and the eagerness of certain war chiefs, peace prevailed. This seems to indicate that already by this time considerations of trade weighed more heavily in relations between the Neutral and the Huron than did those of blood revenge.

Between 1616 and 1629, new offensive capabilities seem to have been altering the pattern of Iroquoian warfare, although the nature and reason for these changes have been misunderstood in previous studies.[22] It was at this time that the Huron and Iroquois were beginning to obtain and to manufacture arrowheads of iron, copper, and brass (Wray and Schoff 1953:56–57). The strongest of these arrowheads were able to pierce the wooden Iroquoian body armour that had hitherto protected warriors. This seems to have discouraged the traditional form of encounter, in which both sides lined up in the open and shot arrows at each other until one side gave way. Sagard's description of Iroquoian warfare suggests that, by 1623, both the

Huron and the Iroquois preferred to maraud each other in small groups. Warriors would remain hidden until they could rush upon the enemy and engage them in hand to hand combat prior to any arrows being discharged. Armour continued to be worn because it helped to protect the body against blows sustained in close combat and because it afforded protection against stone and bone-tipped arrows, which continued to be used.

Throughout this period, the Huron probably enjoyed a slight advantage over the Iroquois. This may have been, in part, because they were able to obtain more metal arrowheads than could the Seneca. The armed French who lived in some of the Huron villages were also an asset that the Seneca did not have. While the French did not prevent the Seneca from raiding Huron territory, they compelled them to be more wary of approaching Huron villages than they would have been otherwise. Yet, while the traditional modes of warfare were altered, it is clear that the concepts that animated Iroquoian warfare in the past remained alive and that the balance of power between the Huron and Iroquois that had emerged several decades before was basically unaltered.

Another change that the introduction of European goods brought about was the supplementing of traditional forms of torture with techniques that involved the use of metal implements. These included searing and piercing the flesh with red hot iron objects and placing glowing hatchets strung on willow swathes around the necks of prisoners.

SOCIAL CHANGE

In recent years there has been much speculation about changes in Huron society between 1615 and 1629. Wallis M. Smith (1970) claims that this was a period of rapid social change which was a reaction to a crisis situation. He argues that a growing emphasis on trade strengthened the role that men played in Huron society, effectively undermined the matrilineal kinship system, and led married women to live with their husbands' families. While this "social disruption" was incomplete, even by 1629 it had "radically alter[ed] Huron social organization."

Smith's analysis is based primarily on data presented by Cara Richards (1967) which attempt to demonstrate that in the majority of Huron and Iroquois households that were described in detail in the seventeenth century, women were living with their husbands' relatives. Smith differs significantly from Richards in interpreting her case studies as evidence for the partial breakdown of a prehistoric pattern of matrilocal (uxorilocal) residence, rather than for a prehistoric pattern that was itself other than strictly matrilocal. He overlooks published critiques of Richards's paper in which it has been pointed out that a goodly number of the situations she interprets as evidence of non-matrilocal residence may be nothing more than Frenchmen treating Huron kinship terms as if they were being used in the same way that French ones were (Abler 1970:28–29; Trigger 1969a:55–56). Occasionally there is clear evidence of sons and nephews being confused, and it seems likely that the French misunderstood many of the relationships that were described to them by the Huron. That the seventeenth century Jesuit writers never understood what a lineage or clan segment was, must dispel any illusion that we can find in the writings of this period a knowledgeable description of Huron social organization.

I have also suggested that young men who were eligible to inherit clan offices may have gone to live permanently with their mothers' brothers, since in a traditional matrilineal system this is one way in which a headman can continue to reside with his own clan segment (Trigger 1969a:56). If the Huron followed this custom, it would explain much of Richards's evidence, since it was precisely these important families with whom the Jesuits had the most to do. Chiefly families were probably also the ones that intermarried most frequently with women from other villages, tribes, and ethnic groups, which would also explain why such women feature so prominently in Richards's analysis.

In view of all of these possibilities for a contrary interpretation of the evidence, the small number of case studies that Richards has assembled do not bulk very large against some important evidence that both she and Smith have overlooked. Pierre Boucher (1664:103) stated explicitly that among the Huron, men went to live with their wives. Boucher worked in the Huron country for four years and may have had a better opportunity to experience Huron family life firsthand than did the Jesuits. Du Creux (1951–52:98) also seems to have been referring to the Huron when he wrote in his *History of Canada* that among the Indians a man generally moved into his wife's lodgings. Because of Boucher's explicitness, it seems rash to postulate a shift away from matrilocal residence patterns at this time on the basis of evidence that is at best equivocal.

Moreover, it can be shown that the theoretical basis for such a position is inadequate and possibly completely erroneous. Smith has accepted the conventional argument that matrilocal residence existed among the Huron in prehistoric times because of the important role played by women in food production. He argues that as trade became more important, male influence increased and this tended to undermine traditional residence patterns.

In chapter 3, I cast serious doubt on the theory that Huron matrilocal residence can be explained as resulting from the role played by women in horticultural activities. I argued that, on the contrary, it resulted from men being absent from their villages and scattered in small groups for much of the year, whereas women remained in the villages in permanent face-to-face association. This made it more practical for extended families to be structured on a matrilineal than on a patrilineal basis. Since I first published this interpretation, Mary Helms (1970) has shown that matrilocal residence was reinforced among a number of Amerindian peoples as a result of men being drawn away from their communities with increasing frequency in early historic times. Helms suggests that long-term male absence from a sedentary community may be a general factor promoting the development of matrilocal residence among basically bilateral groups, of which the Huron would count as one example. Whether this theory will supplant Schneider and Gough's explanation, based on the relative economic importance of male and female work teams, or whether it will become merely an additional explanation remains uncertain.

Alternatively, it can be argued that if matrilocal residence among the Huron were a reflection of the important role women played in food production, the development of the fur trade should have strengthened, rather than weakened, this pattern. This is because the basis of expanded trade was increased corn production, which could come about only as a result of increased labour by Huron women. If men had formerly been dependent on women for most of the food they ate, they were now also dependent on them for their key item of trade. Far from being subordinated to men, the power of women should have increased under such conditions. Either explanation of the origins of matrilocal residence suggests that such patterns should have been strengthened among the Huron as a result of the fur trade. In view of these theoretical considerations and the flimsy nature of the evidence, I find it impossible to accept the argument that a breakdown in matrilocal residence patterns was taking place among the Huron at any time prior to 1650. If alternative forms of residence were prevalent at this period, these are likely an indication of the incompleteness of the shift away from the earlier patrilocal forms of residence that were associated with the organization of hunting bands.

Smith also has argued that, with the enhancement of the male role, the traditional powers of descent groups were eroded and matrilineal succession to office became less important than it had been previously. The basis for this argument is Brébeuf's statement, in 1636, suggesting that at that time the Huron were no longer paying as much attention to the selection of their headmen as they had done previously and thus they no longer called them *Enondecha*, "as if a good headman and the country were one and the same" (Thwaites 1896–1901, 10:231). This is admittedly a difficult passage, but it may be yet another example of a concept of progressive moral degeneration that often guided the Jesuits' interpretation of history. It is noteworthy, for example, that Brébeuf said precisely the same thing about the *arendiwane* or shamans (10:199). The major arguments that Smith advances to demonstrate a decline in the corporate strength of descent groups are based on the untenable view that the Huron confederacy was a single tribe and the Huron tribes were clans; hence these arguments do not prove what Smith intends. All they demonstrate is that the Huron tribes were not clans or descent groups. There is no evidence that clan segments were losing their corporate function at this time or that the matrilineal principles which governed the inheritance of offices were being weakened; indeed, a careful reading of the *Jesuit Relations* indicates the contrary (e.g., 26:297).

It has also been suggested that the reduction in the overall length of houses that has been observed at the Warminster site and other sites of the historic period provides additional evidence of the breakdown of matrilineal extended families as a result of the influence of the fur trade. Such influences are also allegedly evident in a greater variety of house types and the breakdown of traditional patterns of arranging pits and hearths inside of houses (Tyyska and Hurley 1969). Tuck (1971:221), however, has demonstrated that a similar reduction in the length of Onondaga houses began long before the earliest evidence of European trade goods and thus must be related to indigenous changes in Iroquoian social structure. In chapter 3 I suggested that larger longhouses may have evolved as one means of defence during the early Iroquoian period. It is therefore possible that a decline in the size of longhouses, and an accompanying decrease in the size of extended families, may reflect either the greater security of the late Iroquoian period or the transformation of protection from being both a lineage and a village concern into being a purely village one. The evidence from New York State demonstrates the danger of indiscriminately attributing every change in the archaeological record to the impact that contact with Europeans was having upon Indian life.

This does not mean, of course, that the fur trade did not bring about important changes in Huron social organization. I have already suggested that it probably enhanced the power and prestige of the council chiefs, who were able to profit from their control of trading networks and use these profits to play a more important role in the traditional redistributive system. Such activities would have heightened the distinctions between head-men and other members of Huron society, while the control of major trade routes, such as the one leading to Quebec, by tribal leaders must have pro-duced greater inequalities not only between lineages within clans, but also between clan segments belonging to the same tribe. Such developments would explain how Bressani came to speak of Huron society as being made up of nobles and plebeians (Thwaites 1896–1901, 38:247). They may also account for allegedly new epithets, such as "big stones" or "stay-at-homes," that were being applied to Huron headmen in the 1630s (10: 231–33). A desire to obtain goods in order to enhance their individual prestige could also explain the alleged corruption of the "Old Men and notables of the country" who are reported to have "secretly taken possession" of a considerable number of fur robes at the Feast of the Dead held at Ossossané in 1636 (10:303). There is, however, no confirmation that in doing this, these headmen were behaving contrary to traditional norms. Brébeuf's claim that in such ceremonies the poor lost all they had, while the rich lost little or nothing (10:303–5) may be a condemnation of a non-Christian religious custom that is without foundation.

Privileged individuals were given the best portions of food at feasts and they and their families had access to communal healing ceremonies that were not performed for persons of lesser importance. While this hierarchy of prestige accorded with a hierarchy of wealth, it would be wrong to assume that position was derived from wealth. It seems more likely that the opposite was true: that a man's ability to derive wealth from the fur trade largely depended on his traditional position in the Huron political structure. Tensions may have developed between the numerous Huron who engaged in trade and the headmen who controlled the trade routes. There is, however, no evidence, even in later and more troubled times, of *nouveau riche* traders attempting to challenge the power of traditional head-men through the conspicuous distribution of European goods, as is reported among the West Coast Indians. This potential conflict was probably muted, in part, because the headmen and the traders under them often belonged to the same, still-functioning clan segments and therefore shared a com-mon interest in enhancing the prestige of their group. The remoteness of the trading stations also helped to inhibit individual initiative. It would be unwise to imagine that inequalities did not exist in Huron society before the start of the fur trade, especially since we know that at least some of the Huron tribes engaged in trade, as well as farming, long before European goods had begun to arrive in their midst. The changes that the fur trade brought about in social stratification were therefore changes in degree, rather than a revolution in Huron political organization.

Archaeological evidence from the Warminster site provides additional information about the distribution of goods in Huron society at this period. While Huron items appear to be fairly evenly distributed, the amount of European goods found in the pits in different houses at the site varied considerably. Two of the nine houses that were excavated contained by far the most goods, and one house contained none at all. It was also noted that in the two "richest" houses, the cluster of pits around one hearth was rich in European goods at the expense of other clusters. This suggests marked discrepancies not only between extended families but also between individual nuclear families (Tyyska 1968). Considerable caution is needed, however, in interpreting such data. House pits were used for storage and, except when a village was destroyed, contain only items that became lost or were not thought worth carrying off when the settlement was abandoned. It may be questioned therefore whether the material recovered from these pits provides an adequate indication of their owners' wealth. While it seems likely that most wealth would remain in the hands of the head man and woman of a longhouse, the varying distribution of European artifacts between houses raises certain problems. Men vied to accumulate material possessions, but their aim was ultimately to gain prestige by redistributing such goods to other members of the community. There may have been a growing tendency for traders to try to retain possession of European goods, particularly if these were useful for production, and it could be this sort of accumulation that is represented in the varying amounts of goods found in the different houses at the Warminster site. On the other hand, the distribution of goods in a village after a major redistributive ritual such as the Ononharoia, was almost certainly different from what it was immediately before such an event, when particular individuals were seeking to accumulate as many items as they could. It is therefore possible that the Warminster data represent the accumulative phase of a redistributive cycle, rather than permanent differentials in individual access to scarce commodities.

For a redistributive economy to withstand changes of the sort we have been describing it must be able to reinforce its norms which encourage and require redistribution against the growing desire of successful entrepreneurs to retain a larger share of the wealth that pours into their hands. Among the Huron, traders must have been especially tempted to hang on to productive tools that were useful and in short supply. If a way could have been found to validate retaining possession of such goods, the result would have been the erosion of the Huron ethic of redistribution and its replacement by an ethic that rationalized acquisitiveness and conspicuous display.

A redistributive ethic seems clearly to have prevailed in Huron society. Even in succeeding decades, when reparations had to be paid, everyone vied in making contributions so that they might appear solicitous for public welfare (Thwaites 1896–1901, 28:51). The Ononharoia continued to be celebrated in the traditional manner, and Sagard tells of a headman giving up a domestic cat that Le Caron had given him, when a sick woman dreamed that she would be cured if the cat were presented to her. To underline the extent of this sacrifice, Sagard adds that the headman's daughter loved this cat so much that she died of grief when it was taken from her, in spite of her desire to help her neighbour (Wrong 1939:118–19).

An indirect, but nevertheless effective, measure of the strains that the fur trade was posing for the traditional redistributive system may be found in the pattern of Huron witchcraft accusations after 1615. As is the case in many societies where the majority of human relations are close personal ones, witchcraft accusations tend to mirror the changes that occur as traditional obligations become modified. Many instances of witchcraft, especially those recorded after 1634, reflect breakdowns in traditional relationships resulting from culture change. Though the evidence is not susceptible to statistical treatment, the frequency of such accusations also seems higher than it had been earlier. Many of the cases that have been recorded reflect the effects that conversion to Christianity had on the obligations particular Huron owed to their society. Others seem to have had primarily economic causes. One instance is reported of a "rich" Christian convert being accused of witchcraft and then threatened with death, presumably because he was no longer willing to participate in the redistributive activities that were associated with the Huron religion (Thwaites 1896–1901, 30:19–21). Another Huron expressed relief, after he had been converted, at no longer having to bear the expense of participating in such rituals (23:129). These examples show that by the 1640s some prominent Huron who had access to trade goods were happy to escape from these obligations. In spite of this, the use of accusations of witchcraft to force such men to live up to their traditional obligations tells us something about the operation of Huron society at this time.

Witchcraft accusations can function in one of two ways. On the one hand, they can be directed by the beneficiaries of traditional obligations against those who fail to discharge their duties towards them. Alternatively, they can be made against the traditional recipients of such obligations by those who are anxious to avoid them, but who feel guilty about neglecting kinsmen or fellow villagers. In the latter case, the guilt is projected on to the very persons who are being wronged: at once intimidating them and soothing the conscience of the defaulter for his break with tradition (Macfarlane 1970; Douglas 1970). The former response is characteristic of traditional societies, while the latter seems to be associated with ones in which the traditional social order is breaking down and change has become the norm. It seems highly significant that no witchcraft accusations of the latter sort are recorded, or even hinted at, for the Huron. This indicates that the basic pattern of Huron economic and social relations remained essentially the same as it had been in late prehistoric times. While the control of particular lines of trade, most probably by traditional headmen, served to intensify status differences already existing among the Huron, this did not result in a crisis in Huron society or a breakdown in traditional structures or values.

CULTURAL FLORESCENCE

The fur trade also stimulated the elaboration of certain Huron crafts and other forms of artistic expression. We have already discussed the florescence of metal working at this time. It needs only to be stressed that the aim of much of this metal working was to produce plaques and more elaborate effigy ornaments that could be sewn on to clothing or worn in other ways. Ornamental bone carving also appears to have become more common and elaborate among the Huron, although this is a craft that still requires careful study. It is generally asserted that combs with decorated handles, human face plaques, and small bone figurines are considerably more common in historic sites than in prehistoric ones (Kidd 1952:73). These figurines may have had a religious function, like the so-called "bone dolls" of the Seneca and Cayuga, which were meant to avert witchcraft or to warn their owners of approaching danger (Carpenter 1942:111).

Both stone and clay pipes became more numerous and varied in the historic period. While ring bowl pipes remained the most common type, mortice and coronet, as well as effigy pipes grew increasingly popular. Among the human effigy pipes is the so-called blowing face type, on which a face with pursed lips and often an entire crouching body is depicted. Some of these bodies are represented in a skeletalized fashion. At one site, bodies but no heads were found in the middens, suggesting that the breaking of these pipes had ritual significance (Latta 1971:125–26). Other clay effigy pipes had bowls depicting the heads of human beings, wolves, ducks, owls, and other animals. Stone pipes were most frequently whittled out of limestone and then polished. It has been suggested that the elaboration of pipes among the Huron may reflect the acquisition of new wealth, which permitted the purchase of more or better tobacco from the Neutral and Tionnontaté (ibid. 130).

Two observations can be made about the elaboration of metal working, bone working, and pipe manufacture. The first is that this elaboration was not confined to the Huron, but can be observed among the Iroquois and other Iroquoian tribes between 1600 and 1650 (Wray and Schoff 1953: 56–57). This suggests that new tools and materials, and possibly greater wealth generally, were stimulating a higher level of artistic expression. Specific explanations for developments among the Huron therefore bear little weight unless they also explain similar developments elsewhere. Equally important, however, is that each of these developments represents the elaboration of skills that had been a part of the Iroquoian cultural pattern for a long time. In particular, the steady increase in the variety and elaborateness of Huron pipe types throughout late Iroquoian times and the appearance of most of the new effigy types by the early contact period (Emerson 1967:189) indicate that what happened in historic times was the florescence of an already dynamic tradition, rather than any radical departure from it. Similar antecedents can be demonstrated for bone carving and metal working had been limited in earlier times mainly by the scarcity of raw material.

In spite of this, the material manifestations of Huron culture remained unspectacular. The most remarkable impact of the wealth produced by the fur trade was on ceremonialism, and particularly on those rituals that involved the redistribution of goods. These developments can be traced most clearly in connection with the Feast of the Dead. While originally a community ritual, by historic times the Feast of the Dead had become one of immense importance for promoting unity within the expanded Huron confederacy, and between the Huron and many of the Algonkian peoples with whom they traded (Hickerson 1960). Whenever such a feast was celebrated, the representatives of all these peoples were invited to attend and they both contributed and received gifts at various stages in the ceremony. Brébeuf states that over 1200 presents, which were either to be buried with the dead or redistributed to honour their memory, were exhibited at the Feast of the Dead held at Ossossané in 1636. At the end of the ceremony, twenty beaver skin robes (in all containing 200 skins) were reserved by the Master of the Feast to thank the headmen of the other tribes for attending (Thwaites 1896–1901, 10:303).

A striking characteristic of historic ossuaries is the numerous offerings they contain by comparison with prehistoric ones. Forty-eight robes, of ten beaver skins each, were used to line the Ossossané ossuary, and each undecomposed body that was interred in it was wrapped in one or more such robes. The artifacts which occurred throughout this ossuary were mostly items intended for the personal use or adornment of the dead. Objects of North American origin included marine shell beads, projectile points, pigments, textile fabrics, and pipes. One complete conch shell, no doubt intended as raw material for manufacturing beads in the afterlife, was found near the bottom of the pit. Nevertheless, European goods made up a large portion of the offerings. In addition to glass beads, iron knives, rings, and similar items, two or three badly decomposed copper kettles were found (plate 31). These last seem to have been intended for the collective use of the dead (Kidd 1953:364). Nor was this the most splendid of Huron interments. As many as twenty-six French kettles have been discovered in a single ossuary, as well as up to sixteen conch shells and miscellaneous iron axes, copper bracelets, glass beads, metal arrowheads, and iron cups (Bawtree 1848; Hammond 1924). While many of the kettles appear to have been damaged and incomplete prior to burial, the loss of scrap metal, as well as of many other valuable items, through interment would periodically have removed a moderate amount of European goods from circulation. This would have increased the Huron's demand for such goods, which was already high because of intense use and a rapid rate of attrition (Innis 1956:17).

The elaboration of the Feast of the Dead gave ritual expression to the expanding network of relationships on which the Huron had come to depend. It was also a practical means for promoting social interaction and reinforcing goodwill among the peoples who made up this trade network. The Feast of the Dead not only was an old ritual among most of the Huron tribes but also was their key ritual for expressing solidarity. This aspect of the ritual appears to have been unique among the Huron, rather than a feature shared by all Iroquoians. It was noted in chapter 3 how an increase in the size of ossuaries appears to have paralleled the development of Huron social and political integration in prehistoric times. The final elaboration of this ritual, under the influence of the fur trade, was therefore the florescence of a traditional feature of Huron culture rather than a radical departure from it.

PLATE 31. *Copper kettle* in situ *in the Ossossané ossuary of 1636.*
Because K. E. Kidd has convincingly correlated this ossuary with the
Feast of the Dead that Brébeuf described for the spring of 1636, the
material it contains constitutes a valuable base line for determining the
variety of European goods in circulation among the Huron at this time.
Courtesy K. E. Kidd and Royal Ontario Museum, Toronto.

It is significant that the Huron chose to elaborate a ritual that depended so heavily on redistribution and making offerings to the dead. This provides further evidence that they did not view either their beaver skins or the wealth that was derived from the fur trade solely as items of commerce. Instead, they viewed them as a means of realizing the traditional values of their society. The continuing importance of these values is indicated by the fact that the Huron should have chosen to make a ritual that was already a microcosm of these values an anchor point to which their developing trade, and the new relations associated with it, might be tied.

The Huron View of the French

No detailed information has been preserved concerning what the Huron thought about the French or how they perceived the specific items of culture they adopted from them. What has been transmitted to us is seen through the distorting optic of French culture. In spite of this, it is possible to delineate some general ways in which the Huron reacted to the French.

The Huron admired the trade goods that the French sold to them and were aware of the technological superiority of certain French tools over their indigenous counterparts. Because Savignon had seen craftsmen at work in France, the Huron knew that these tools were made in Europe, rather than obtained elsewhere. Since the Huron lacked any division of labour, except by sex and age, it was difficult for them to understand that not every Frenchman was capable of making or repairing everything that the French sold to the Huron. The Huron frequently asked French visitors to mend broken kettles and to provide other services for them (Wrong 1939:183) and did not understand why their requests usually went unanswered.

The Huron were also not equipped to understand the hierarchical structure of French society or a lack of correlation between authority and technical skills, that was so different from their own ways. They believed that only the oldest and most experienced French headmen were capable of making things as complicated as iron knives and kettles and that the king made the largest kettles. For this reason, they asked only seemingly important Frenchmen to do the more complicated jobs of mending and altering European goods (183). It may also be, although there is no direct proof of this, that the Huron attributed much of the technological skill of the French to magic. Thus the ability of the French would have seemed connected less to technological superiority than to the luck they had in acquiring magical arts. Since supernatural powers were believed to be inherent in nature, the possession by the French of a particular kind of magic was no indication of their intrinsic cultural superiority. There is little evidence that the Huron regarded the French as superior to themselves, while there is much evidence that they regarded them as inferior.

The Huron were curious about many things they saw the French doing or using, but which they were not motivated to try themselves. Huron are said to have taught Sagard their language in order to watch him writing down what they said; the expression that they used for writing was "marking it with a snowshoe," a neat phrase likening the marks a pen leaves on paper to the imprint of a snowshoe (73). The Huron also understood that writing could be used to make a person's meaning understood at a distance, which must have been interpreted as a supernatural quality (173). Yet, in spite of the Recollets' efforts to teach Huron children how to write, it was not a skill that any Huron had the initiative to try to acquire.

The Huron were also fascinated by the missionaries' books. Some were said to spend whole days counting their pages and admiring the letters and the pictures they contained (ibid.; Sagard 1866:330). The magical power of these books was suggested by the missionaries and by the illustrations they contained. European pictures and images were far more detailed and realistic than any representations the Huron had ever produced or seen. Because of this, the Huron seem to have believed that some, if not all, of these representations were alive. Le Jeune reports that they called certain saints' statues at Quebec *ondaqui* (sing. *oki*) or spirits and believed them to be living things. The Huron asked if the tabernacle was their house and if they dressed themselves in the ornaments seen around the altar (Thwaites 1896–1901, 5:257). Similarly, Sagard's wooden death's head was considered to be the head of a real child.

The Huron accepted on trust many things that the French told them and which they could not check for themselves. They were, for example, informed that French women had beards the same as men and, according to Sagard, only learned differently when they met Hélène de Champlain, who came to Quebec in 1620 (Wrong 1939:137). If true, this story provides further evidence that the Huron visited Quebec only infrequently prior to 1620, since Louis Hébert's wife had been there since 1617.

In the process of trying to understand the French, the Huron not unnaturally tended to overestimate, as well as to underestimate, the newcomer's abilities. They wanted to know whether the French ate thunderbirds and requested, on occasion, that the French use their guns to shoot a thunderbird in order to divert a storm (183). Likewise, seeing that the dogs at Quebec had ears which hung down, unlike their own that had pointed ears, the Huron asked the Recollets to cause their dogs' ears to bend in a similar manner. Once they knew that the French could not perform specific miracles, they revised their estimates of their abilities in a realistic fashion. On the other hand, when the Recollets demonstrated that they were at least as able to heal the sick and to control the weather as Huron shamans were, the Huron continued to make use of, and further test, their abilities. In this respect, the Huron treated the French priests just as they treated any person who claimed shamanistic powers (173).

Individual Huron also expressed a faddish interest in isolated facets of French culture. Almost everyone wanted to try on the clogs worn by the Recollets, and many attempted to persuade the Recollets to make such shoes for them (146). The Huron were also interested in sampling French food, lemon rind being one of the delicacies that particularly pleased them (Thwaites 1896–1901, 5:257). On the other hand, they invariably refused to eat corn soup if the French had added salt, spices, or wild herbs to flavour it. This, they said, made it smell bad (Wrong 1939:82). One young man of foppish temperament is reported by Sagard to have refused to go hunting and to have amused himself cooking in the French manner (124). Unfortunately, this story is so similar to one Marc Lescarbot (1907–14, 2:247–48) told about a young Micmac that it seems likely that Sagard stole the story from him. French fashions did, however, produce cultural innovations. After the Recollets arrived in 1623, several women gave their children clerical haircuts (Sagard 1866:363).

The Huron showed great interest in domestic cats, which they believed were possessed of reason since they came when called. This they interpreted as evidence that they were controlled by a powerful spirit. The chief source of these cats was the Recollet house at Quebec, and giving them as presents was a potent method of cultivating good relations with Huron headmen. There was already at least one cat in the Huron country by 1623, which was a gift from Father Le Caron to an important headman (Wrong 1939: 118). Another was given to the war chief, Angoiraste, after he had brought Sagard back to Quebec (ibid. 270; Sagard 1866:761). The Huron were used to keeping tame animals as pets; thus the novelty of these cats was the species, rather than tame animals as such.

While the Huron admired selected items of European culture, they were far from uncritical of the French. Some of this criticism reflected the opposing cultural ideals of the two groups. The Huron were offended by Frenchmen gesticulating with their arms, talking all at once, and interrupting one another, and for this reason they jokingly called them women (Wrong 1939:140). The Huron likewise despised French merchants for haggling over the prices of individual pelts, which they felt was contrary to the spirit of the alliance that existed between them (ibid.).

Other criticisms of the French seem to reflect the high opinion that the Huron had of themselves and the general condescension with which they treated their Algonkian neighbours. They regarded the difficulties that the French had in learning to speak Huron as evidence of their stupidity, and thus explained all difficulties the French had in acquiring skills that the Huron held to be commonplace (138). The Huron also ridiculed beards as unnatural and disfiguring, and Huron men feigned amazement that women would look favourably on a man who had one. They claimed that beards were the cause of the intellectual deficiencies of the French (137). The Huron fancied themselves as being superior to the French, not only because they were taller but also because they were glabrous and therefore more intelligent.

Specific events served to discourage respect for the French. Because of Recollet opposition, the French had been unable to accept reparations payments for the two Frenchmen who had been slain by the Montagnais in 1616 or 1617; however, the growing hostility of the Montagnais forced the French to pardon the killer officially when the Indians gathered to trade at Three Rivers in 1623. As testimony of this pardon, the French threw a sword into the river and distributed presents among the assembled tribes (Trigger 1971a:95–98). The Huron, who had come to trade, watched this ceremony in silence, but the following winter they joked among themselves that it cost little to kill a Frenchman (Sagard 1866:226). They were also shocked by the callous manner in which the French traders treated one another, and were horrified when they were told that in France the poor had to beg for food (Wrong 1939:89).

Individual personality traits played a major role in determining how well any particular Frenchman got on with the Huron. The most important test that he faced was how well he behaved on his journey to the Huron country. The reputation that he gained at that time spread rapidly and strongly influenced other Huron's opinions of him (74). A traveller was expected to be generous and to share what food he had with his travelling companions (57). He was also expected to bear hardships without complaint and to maintain a cheerful disposition, so as to encourage the rest of his party (58). Once in the Huron country, a willingness to participate in Huron activities was a decided advantage.

There is no reference to the Huron drinking, or attempting to obtain alcoholic beverages, at this time. While they may have consumed a small amount of alcohol when they visited the trading places along the St. Lawrence, they evidently did not think it worth the trouble to carry wine or spirits home with them. Indeed, the only wine that is known to have been transported to the Huron country at this time was taken there by the Recollets to celebrate communion and entertain occasional French visitors.

The Huron's lack of interest in alcohol correlates with their unbroken self-esteem. In their relations with the French, the Huron were still their own masters. Their role in the fur trade was built on earlier trade relations and the cultural florescence which this trade made possible was a realization of tendencies that had been inherent in their traditional culture, rather than a disrupting or degrading process. All of these developments contributed to a sense of achievement and well-being. The Huron had no reason to resent the French or to feel inferior to them. On the contrary, they seem to have felt more justified than ever in regarding other peoples as being inferior to themselves. Sagard summed up the general feeling of the Huron when he wrote that Auoindaon, the principal headman of the northern Attignawantan, asked to be spoken of as the brother or cousin of the French king and expressed his equality with the king by pressing the two forefingers of his hands together (149). While this may be another colourful story stolen from Lescarbot (1907–14, 2:355), it faithfully represents Huron sentiment at this time. The most distinctive feature of this period was its freedom from the negative aspects of European contact that were to become so prominent in the grim decades that followed.

Notes

CHAPTER ONE

1. Among recent books dealing with Amerindian history and Indian-White relations, the following are of major importance: Fenton 1957; Fiedler 1968; J. Forbes (ed.) 1964; Hagan 1961; Leacock and Lurie (eds.) 1971; Spicer 1969; Washburn (ed.) 1964.

2. For a critique of the role of this theory in Canadian historiography, see A. Smith 1970.

3. A partial exception are the Beothuk of Newfoundland, who were denied access to their coastal hunting and fishing grounds by Europeans. In the middle of the eighteenth century, exasperated by their petty thieving, the French offered a bounty for Beothuk heads (Jenness 1960:266–67).

4. See also Bailey 1938.

5. For other recent publications that suggest a growing interest in Canadian Indian history, see Walker 1971; Baker 1972; Morton 1972.

6. "Anthropologists have customarily conducted studies of cultural change as if change did not exist until Europeans appeared on the scene" (Gamst 1969:6).

7. For an analysis of the view that efforts to civilize the Indians would destroy them, see Pearce 1965. For a typical statement of the view that the Indian was doomed as a result of European contact, see C. Lavollée, cited in Harper 1971:41.

8. For general summaries of North American prehistory, see J. Jennings 1968; Willey 1966; Willey and Phillips 1958; Caldwell 1958; Griffin 1952.

9. For a critique of these stereotypes, see Hunt 1940:3–12.

10. Robertson 1812. For an appreciation of his work, see Hoebel 1960.

11. For summaries of the development of anthropology in Canada, see McIlwraith 1930, 1949, and Cole 1973.

12. For notable examples of the use of written documents by anthropologists, see Kroeber 1952; Hallowell 1955; Eggan 1966; Fenton 1940. Recent work on Indian land claims in the United States has also resulted in more anthropologists using primary documents (Hickerson 1970:2).

13. For discussions of the scope of ethnohistory, see Sturtevant 1966; Hudson 1966; Fenton 1966; Hickerson 1970:5–7.

14. For a comparison of what is known about Huron culture prior to 1650 with what is known about Wyandot and Iroquois culture more recently, see Tooker 1964.

15. For basic traits, see Driver 1961. Claude Lévi-Strauss (1968, 1971) has drawn attention to pan-Indian traits in Indian mythology. These, he believes, suggest the existence of pan-Indian themes at a "deep-structural" level. Anthropologists working with American Indians are profoundly aware of widespread similarities in values and attitudes. It is unclear, however, to what degree these are an aboriginal heritage or a more recent reaction to similar acculturative pressures.

16. For discussions of historical method, see Carr 1967; Elton 1969; Fischer 1971. A more extensive bibliography is in Hickerson 1970:3–4.

17. For more detailed comments, see Trigger 1970:13–14.

18. For Canadian efforts to write biographies of this sort, see Girard 1948 and Pouliot 1958.

CHAPTER TWO

1. The main primary sources on which this description of the Huron is based are the writings of Samuel de Champlain (Biggar 1922–36); Gabriel Sagard (1866; Wrong 1939); and the annual relations and other documents of the Jesuits published in Thwaites 1896–1901. For corrections and additions to the latter, dealing mainly with details of Roman Catholic theology, ritual, and organization, see Donnelly 1967. For ethnological information Grant's (1952; originally published 1907) partial translation of Champlain is in some respects preferable; for maps and illustrations many prefer Laverdière 1870. For a discussion of the works of Sagard, see Warwick 1972. For a critical study of the *Jesuit Relations*, see Pouliot 1940; also Spalding 1929; McGuire 1901.

Minor primary sources that have been consulted include Boucher 1664; Chaumonot 1869; Gendron 1868; and original documents reproduced in Le Clercq 1691. An English translation of the latter work, not cited because it does not include the French text, is Shea 1881.

Later sources consulted include: Charlevoix 1866–72 and 1923; Du Creux 1951–52; and Lafitau 1724.

Detailed and comprehensive studies of Huron culture have been published by Kinietz 1940:1–160; Tooker 1964; Trigger 1969a; and Heidenreich 1972. In Tooker's publication, all the material concerning the Huron in the main primary sources has been collated and paraphrased. Footnotes correlate these data with what is known about the related Wyandot and Iroquois cultures. Because Tooker's work has been designed to serve as a guide to the ethnographic data concerning the Huron, I am able to omit a plethora of references documenting my description of Huron life. The main use of notes in this chapter is to draw the reader's attention to more detailed studies of various facets of Huron life and to indicate, where necessary, on what basis controversial interpretations are offered.

2. The earliest reference to this etymology occurs in Jérôme Lalemant's account of the Huron mission for the year 1638–39 (Thwaites 1896–1901, 16:229–31). Lalemant expresses reservations about the authenticity of the story. Godefroy (1938, 4:532) states that in Old French Huron was a "*qualificatif méprisant, désignant un personnage grossier.*" Grandsaignes d'Hautrive (1947:357) lists "*rustre*" and "*vilain*" among its original meanings. For a more detailed discussion of this term, see Hewitt (1907:584). For comments relevant to understanding differences in the degree of acculturation of the coastal peoples and the Huron, see Sagard 1866:251, 271.

3. Hewitt (1907:584) has accepted this etymology. Alternative interpretations have Wendat meaning "speakers of a common language" (Jones 1908:419–20) or the "Villagers" or "One Village" (Heidenreich 1971:300–301). French translations of Huron speeches referring to their country as an island (Thwaites 1896–1901, 15:21; 33:237–39) and the Jesuit gloss "quia in insula habitabant"

that is given to the entry Huron in one of their dictionaries (Jones 1908:419) provide strong support for the general accuracy of Hewitt's interpretation. The suggestion that Wendat evolved as a generic name for the Huron confederacy in the late 1630s (Thwaites 1896–1901, 5:278 n. 17) is vitiated by the inclusion of this name (*Hoüandate*) in Sagard's dictionary (1866), which presents word lists collected in 1623–24 (Sagard's dictionary is not paginated, but see under the heading *Nations, de quelle nation*).

4. The term Bear Nation was consistently applied to the Attignawantan by the French and appears to be a literal translation of the name. In his dictionary, Sagard (1866) lists *agnouoin* as one of the Huron names for bear (see under *Animaux, bestes à quatre pieds*). See also Heidenreich 1971:301.

5. These etymologies have been suggested by Hewitt (1907:584), Jones (1908:72, 178–79, 181) and Heidenreich (1971:301–2). Hewitt's translation of Tahontaenrat as "Deer People" is preferred on non-linguistic grounds by Wright (1966:79–80), but see below chapter 3 *n.* 23. In the *Relation* of 1656–57, the Jesuits referred to the Attignawantan, Attigneenongnahac, and Arendarhonon as the Nations of the Bear, Cord, and Rock, although not specifying which was which (Thwaites 1896–1901, 43:191). It is generally agreed that Cord is a nonsensical gloss; however, "Corde" could have been a typesetter's misreading of manuscript "Cerf." In that case the Attigneenongnahac would be the Deer people. Until a competent linguist takes the Huron language in hand further speculation seems unwarranted.

6. Fenton 1940:181. Jones (1908:314) suggests "People who dwell beyond the fens, morass, or silted lake." The nature of this grouping is obscure. Heidenreich

(1971:84–85) accepts them as a fifth tribe of the confederacy, while Jones (1908:447) surmises they were not a tribe but a collection of people who had settled for protection near the Jesuit mission of Sainte-Marie. The latter suggestion is unlikely for chronological reasons. The failure of the Jesuits to mention the Ataronchronon in their description of the Huron confederacy (Thwaites 1896–1901, 16:227–29) suggests that they did not constitute a formal part of the Huron tribal system.

7. For references, see Heidenreich et al. 1969:114–17 and, for a detailed study of the geography of the Huron country, Heidenreich 1971:54–74. For a briefer discussion of the physiography of this region in the context of southern Ontario, Chapman and Putnam 1966: 299–312. For soil types, Hoffman et al. 1962.

8. Trigger 1969a:11–13. Champlain estimated the Huron population to be 30,000 (Biggar 1922–36, 3:122) and Sagard 30,000 to 40,000 (Wrong 1939:92). The Jesuits consistently followed Champlain's estimate, which seems to have been the generally accepted one at that time (Thwaites 1896–1901, 7:225; 8:115; 10:313). Mooney and Kroeber (see Kroeber 1939:140) have estimated the combined population of the Huron and Tionnontaté to have been 18,000, but their figures generally seem too low. Heidenreich (1971:96–103), in a detailed study employing several methods of calculation not used by me, has estimated an aboriginal population of 21,000. The median of his estimates was 16,000 to 22,500.

9. This description of the settlement pattern of these three tribes is based on the information recorded by the Jesuits who spent their early years in the Huron country among the Attignawantan and

did not work extensively among the other tribes until after 1640. It is not in complete agreement with the archaeological data. For a discussion of this problem, see chapter 4, final section.

10. Driver 1961, map 6. For the northeastern United States and the Great Lakes areas this map is more accurate than Kroeber 1939, map 18.

11. Heidenreich (1971:162–64) estimates the Huron diet as follows: 65 per cent corn, 15 per cent other cultivated vegetables, 9 per cent fish, 5 per cent meat, 5 per cent wild vegetables. Popham (1950:88) has estimated that 75 per cent of their diet was corn, although he probably meant all cultivated foods. While there are not sufficient data to render any estimates more than informed guesses, corn clearly played a dominant role in Huron subsistence. Corn is one hundred times more common than are other vegetable remains in Huron sites (Heidenreich 1971:160).

12. The French designated all cucurbits as *citrouille*. Both squash and pumpkin are claimed to have been identified in Huron sites. Heidenreich (1971:173) identifies the Huron cucurbit as *Cucurbita polymorpha* (summer squash).

13. Yarnell (1964:107) classifies both flour and flint corn in this area as part of his Eastern Complex. This corn characteristically has eight rows or more, with strong pairing of rows. Most sites with cultigens in eastern North America are in areas with more than 130 frost-free days, although some approach the 120-day limit (ibid. 137, 150).

14. Traces of Huron corn hills are reported to have been common in the last century. The hills were about four feet across, four feet apart, and irregularly spaced (i.e. not in rows) (Heidenreich 1971:176–78). Heidenreich estimates

2500 to 4700 hills per acre, the average, with reductions for tree trunks, being 2500. On the utility of this method of growing corn see ibid. 184–86.

15. For the effects of Huron agriculture on soil profiles, see Cruickshank and Heidenreich 1969.

16. Trigger 1969a: 28. This acreage was calculated for a population of 20,000 using an average yield of 30 bushels of shelled corn per acre and a need for a minimum of 10 bushels per person (15 is safer) to carry an Indian family over the winter. These figures were supplied by William N. Fenton on the basis of ethnographic fieldwork on Iroquois reserves (Pendergast and Trigger 1972:8 n. 6). More recently, on the basis of very detailed calculations of nutritional requirements and crop productivity, Heidenreich (1971:197) has estimated that a population of 21,000 would have required 6500 acres under crop. In view of the nature of the data, these two calculations are very close indeed. They cast doubt on Popham's (1950:88–89) earlier estimate that 23,300 acres would have had to be under cultivation to feed a population of 30,000 (15,500 acres for 20,000).

17. For major discussions of Huron pottery, see MacNeish 1952; Emerson 1968; and Wright 1966. Jury and Jury (1954:101) suggest that the Huron did not place their pots over the fire but cooked by dropping hot stones into them, in the same manner that the northern Algonkian peoples cooked using vessels made of bark. Sagard (Wrong 1939:109), who is the only one of our early sources to describe the manufacture and use of Huron pots, is explicit that they were set over fires, the stones being used to support them.

18. Boucher (1664:101) says that among the Huron "C'est aussi eux (les

hommes) qui font les champs de tabac."
The Jesuits observed that one Huron had
a small plot of tobacco near his cabin
(Thwaites 1896–1901, 15:79).

19. For a description of a communal
deer hunt, see Biggar 1922–36, 3:82–85.
The Huron failure to bring large amounts
of meat home contrasts with descriptions
of more than 40 to 50 dried and quartered
deer hanging in each longhouse in a
Mohawk village (Jameson 1909:156).
In part, this difference may reflect the
greater proximity of the Mohawk and the
other Iroquois to their hunting territories.

20. Trigger 1969a:60. According to
Kenyon (1968:18) experiments have
shown that deciduous trees can be bent
overhead to enclose a space up to at least
24 feet across.

21. Archaeological evidence suggests
that storage porches were often located at
only one end of a house (Heidenreich
1971:118–19). Noble (1969:16–28) notes
the absence of sidewall sleeping platforms
at the Sopher and Warminster sites, in the
eastern part of the Huron country. He
suggests that these platforms may have
been characteristic of Attignawantan and
Attigneenongnahac houses, but not of
Arendarhonon ones. Further
documentation is needed to confirm this
hypothesis. It appears that there is much
variation in Huron housetypes that
remains to be documented and explained.

22. Heidenreich (1971:141) notes that
in an unpublished report dated 1965
J. N. Emerson and W. S. Russell have
argued that Huron palisades consisted
only of upright poles, without additional
covering. Heidenreich shows that this
sort of palisade could not have protected a
village and is contrary to contemporary
descriptions of those structures.

23. For a reconstruction of such a gate,
based on archaeological evidence, see
Heidenreich 1971:141–42. This

reconstruction agrees with French
descriptions of such gates (Wrong
1939:92), although the gate could not be
reconstructed from the written description
alone.

24. Very little attention has been paid
to these minor works of art. For
descriptions and illustrations, see Kidd
1952:73 and his figure 27. It is generally
assumed that true catlinite is present in
historic times, but Kidd (personal
communication 1970) states that to his
knowledge this contention has not been
sustained by petrological analysis.
Boucher (1664:101) says that men made
pipes, but does not specify whether he
meant of stone or clay, or both. The stone
pipes were almost certainly made by men.
They were carved from a "greenstone
like serpentine or steatite, as well as from
slate, limestone and even harder
materials" (Kidd 1952:73). Bowls are
often vasiform (sometimes conoidal,
rectangular, or wedge-shaped) and were
used with a detachable wood or reed stem.

25. For a discussion of the quality and
manufacture of clay pipes, see Kidd
1952:73. For a preliminary classification
of Iroquoian pipe types from Ontario,
see Emerson 1967:181–90; 237–40.
Noble (1969:24–25) has suggested that
effigy, and possibly non-effigy, pipes
represent lineage totems and that a study
of their distribution patterns should
provide information about kinship and
marriage. By lineages, Noble appears to
mean clan segments, although the 22 pipe
types he recognizes would represent less
than half the estimated number of Huron
clan segments. More detailed evidence and
a more sophisticated analysis are needed
before Noble's claim can be accepted.

26. These figures are based on the
Jesuit "census" of 1639–40 which,
although reported only in summary, was
the only serious effort to determine the

Huron population (Thwaites 1896–1901, 19:127). The Huron and Tionnontaté are reported to have had 700 longhouses and 2000 hearths. Calculating 2 families per hearth, this indicates an average of 5.7 (i.e. 6) families per longhouse. Figures reported for individual longhouses are as low as one family and as high as 24.

27. The terms cited here are derived from Sagard's dictionary. Under the heading "Paréntage et consanguinité," Sagard gives only one term *ayein*, meaning "my son/my daughter" and another *ataquen*, "brother/sister." The Wyandot terms for son and daughter are *aneah'* and *eneah'* respectively, while *haye'uh* and *aye'uh* are used for older brother and older sister and *hayea'hä* and *yayeah'hä* for younger brother and younger sister. This suggests that Sagard missed an analogous (to him) small difference in these Huron words. The Wyandot terms and their meanings are derived from Morgan 1871:291–382.

28. Only the skeletal remains from Tabor Hill (*c.* A.D. 1200) have been studied in detail. The high female mortality between ages 16 and 25 years probably resulted largely from problems of childbirth. 66 per cent of all females over the age of 16 died in this range (Churcher and Kenyon 1960).

29. When a Huron headman asked people not to engage in sexual activities while a ritual was being performed, he is reported to have said that "they were not to go and amuse themselves in the woods" (Thwaites 1896–1901, 13:61).

30. We assume that the statements that those who died violent deaths were buried and not removed from the grave at the Feast of the Dead (Thwaites 1896–1901, 39:31; 10:163–65) and that some bodies were buried in the ground and a hut or shrine was erected over them (Biggar 1922–36, 3:160–61; Wrong

1939:208) refer to the same burials. Noble (1968) has suggested that numerous inhumation burials at Sopher and other sites indicate that this may have been the original form of burial among the Arendarhonon and that the differences in burial customs described by the French may be ethnic ones. This conclusion is premature in view of the explicit ritual reasons that are given for these differences. Large numbers of inhumation burials at specific historic Huron sites may reflect wars or local catastrophes.

31. For the original definition of a clan segment, see Trigger 1969*a*:54–57. On the overall organization of the Huron clan system, see Connelly 1900 and Tooker 1970*b*. Many Canadian anthropologists have insisted on viewing the Huron as a single tribe and the four tribes as clans. This error, which has caused much needless confusion and greatly complicated Iroquoian studies, arose as a result of Biggar arbitrarily translating the French *nation* as clan rather than tribe (1922–36, 3:42 n. 2; 96 n. 1; 112 n. 1; 121 n. 2). Tooker's paper exposes the erroneous nature of this interpretation, which has never been entertained by scholars properly familiar with both Huron and Iroquois institutions.

32. For a discussion of these phratries, see Tooker 1970*b*:93; Connelly 1900:106; and Barbeau 1917.

33. See Heidenreich 1971:130 for the Warminster site. The description of the Attignawantan village of Khinonascarant as split into three small villages close to one another (Thwaites 1896–1901, 13:125) suggests an analogous situation.

34. See Tooker 1964:127; Richards 1967; Trigger 1969*a*:56.

35. The relationship between Auoindaon and Aenons is discussed in chapter 7. Talbot (1956:148) is almost certainly wrong when he suggests that

Anenkhiondic was the title conferred on a headman when he was charged with conducting the Feast of the Dead. Anenkhiondic is described as "captain-general of the whole country" (Thwaites 1896–1901, 10:289) and his name appears in contexts that have nothing to do with the Feast of the Dead (e.g. Thwaites 1896–1901, 13:169, 185).

36. This is suggested by analogy with the sachems, or council chiefs, of the Iroquois confederacy.

37. This is based on the Jesuits' description of a council meeting held in August 1637 (Thwaites 1896–1901, 15:39).

38. This analysis of Huron law was first presented in Trigger 1963a and 1969a:78–82. Tooker (1964:52 n. 78) gives more emphasis to the formal role played by clans in settling disputes. In reply, see Trigger 1969a:79.

39. Sagard noted robes made from skins of *chats sauvages*, which appear to have come from the Erie people, whom the Huron called the "People of the Cat" (Rhiierrhonon, Erieehronon). Thwaites (1896–1901, 21:315 n. 11) cites J. G. Henderson that the animal Sagard called the *chat sauvage* was not the common American wild cat (*Lynx rufus*) or the Canadian lynx (*Lynx canadensis*), both of which the French call *loup cervier*, but the common racoon. The Huron word that Sagard translates *chat sauvage* is *tiron*, the Iroquois cognate of which means racoon. The racoon is still called *chat sauvage* in French Canada.

40. Conch shells (*Busycon contrarium*), both whole and worked, are common in Huron sites, while *Olivella* and *Marginella* occur usually in the form of beads. "Wampum beads" (*Fulgor perversa*) are also noted. Ritchie (1965:248) notes that two species of *Busycon* are present along the eastern seaboard of the United States

from Cape Cod south, while *Marginella* and *Olivella* occur from the Carolinas to Florida. In historic times, the Huron traded with the Susquehannock for marine shells (Thwaites 1896–1901, 33:185–87).

41. Wrong 1939:186. The reference is to bottles made of the rind of a fruit that comes from a distant country. The nearest archaeological evidence for the occurrence of gourds is from the Ohio Valley (Yarnell 1964:118–19).

42. Native copper is very rare, if it occurs, in historic Huron sites. Historical references make it clear, however, that the Huron were interested in this metal and the trade in it.

43. The extent of Huron trading relations will be discussed in detail in chapter 6.

44. On Huron attitudes towards Algonkians, see Wrong 1939:110–11; Thwaites 1896–1901, 10:145. Under those circumstances, it is unlikely that Huron women would have gone to live among the Algonkians (cf. McPherron 1967:106). In times of crisis, however, whole Huron families might seek refuge among the Algonkians (Thwaites 1896–1901, 30:87). For references to an Algonkian man raised from infancy among the Huron, see ibid. 13:139.

45. For comparative studies of Iroquoian torture, see Knowles 1940 and Rands and Riley 1958. This description is based mainly on a particularly detailed account of one instance of torture contained in Le Mercier's Huron *Relation* of 1637 (13:37–83). Obvious idiosyncrasies have been omitted and comparisons with other, briefer accounts of torture suggest that the description given here is fairly representative of this ritual.

46. In descriptions of Iroquois torture, the platform for killing prisoners was erected in the centre of the village.

47. For comparison with a similar but better recorded Iroquois creation myth, see Tooker 1964:151–55.

48. For a comparative discussion of Huron and Iroquois psychotherapy, see A. Wallace 1958.

49. The only detailed description of this ceremony is that of Sagard, who watched it through a chink in the walls of a Huron longhouse (Wrong 1939:120). Jesuit references suggest that it was not uncommon (Thwaites 1896–1901, 17:179).

50. For a discussion of a modified form of this ritual among the northern Algonkian tribes who traded with the Huron, see Hickerson 1960.

51. For attempts to identify this rock, see Jones 1908:241–48; Lawrence 1916.

52. This description is based largely on Brébeuf's detailed account of the Feast of the Dead held at Ossossané in 1636 (Thwaites 1896–1901, 10:279–305). This ossuary has been convincingly identified as the one excavated by Kidd (1953) in 1946. Archaeological data from elsewhere suggest variations in the details of the ritual.

53. The account states that 48 robes were used. The Iroquois confederacy has positions for 50 sachems, or council chiefs, although the position named for the legendary founder of the league went unfilled. If the organization of the Iroquois confederacy was similar to what we propose for the Huron, both may have had approximately 50 clan segments, although small segments may not have been represented and some larger ones may have had two council chiefs to reach a number that had ritual significance. While such close parallels in the governments of the two confederacies would suggest that the number of council chiefs was an essentially artificial one, this need not, at least originally, have

been the case. The *Jesuit Relations* indicate that there were several clan segment heads in each large Huron village. If "several" is taken to mean four and the average population of a large village was 1500 to 1600, this gives each clan segment a population of 400, which coincides with Heidenreich's estimate of 300 as the population of small, presumably single-segment, villages. An average of 400 per clan segment would allow 45 to 50 segments in a population of 18,000 to 20,000. While the precontact Iroquois are often stated to be fewer in number than the Huron, the available data suggest that both had about the same population (Trigger 1969a:19). Hence a roughly equal number of clan segments may have been present in both and it may have been the number of these that, at the founding of the confederacies, determined, at least in a general way, the number of seats on the confederacy council.

54. For the best general survey of Iroquoian culture, see Fenton 1940. This study was written prior to the general acceptance of the notion that Iroquoian culture had developed *in situ* in the Northeast.

55. Tionnontaté does not mean Tobacco Nation, but contains the root *onnonta*, meaning "mountain." Petun is a Brazilian word meaning tobacco, introduced into France along with the herb by André Thevet (Morison 1971:428).

56. For a discussion of the indirect evidence of population size, see Trigger 1969a:13. From the Jesuit census of 1639–40, there would appear to be a post-epidemic population of 2000, suggesting an aboriginal population of 4000 to 5000. Even if all but one or two of the Tionnontaté villages were tiny hamlets, these nine villages, as compared with about twenty Huron ones, suggest

either that this population estimate is too low or that the Tionnontaté settlement pattern was even more dispersed than that of the Attignawantan.

57. Tooker 1964:12 n. 11. Note that among the Mohawk, each major village was ascribed to whichever of the three clans or moieties was dominant in it.

58. On maps prior to 1950, Neutral villages are shown extending all the way from the Niagara to the Detroit Rivers, as they do on French maps produced in the latter half of the seventeenth century (e.g. N. Sanson, *Le Canada*, 1656; Du Creux, *Tabula Novae Franciae*, 1660; but not Bressani, *Novae Franciae Accurata Delineatio*, 1657). Lee's (1959:91) archaeological survey has shown that historic Iroquoian sites generally lie east of the Grand River, although since then at least one historic site has been located a short distance west of the Grand River (MacDonald n.d.). A popular theory advanced at the end of the nineteenth century attempted to account for the neutrality of the Neutral by claiming that both the Iroquois and the Huron were dependent on them for supplies of flint, which came from the east end of Lake Erie. "As the Neutrals controlled the chert beds, neither nation could afford to make the Neutrals its enemy" (Harris 1896, cited in Thwaites 1896–1901, 8:297 n. 34). Unfortunately for this theory, supplies of flint were available and utilized at many points along the Niagara Escarpment.

59. See in particular the map of *c.* 1680 attributed to Bernou (Service historique de la Marine, Recueil 67, map no. 51; reproduced here as plate 50). The Kakouagaga, who appear east of the Niagara River, were probably Erie, although the Kahkwa of Seneca tradition have been identified as being either Erie or Neutral (Thwaites 1896–1901,

21:313–15 n. 11). For a recent discussion of historic Neutral geography, see White 1972. Current archaeological research is rapidly amplifying our knowledge of the historic Neutral (W. C. Noble, "Neutral Settlement Patterns," paper presented at Canadian Archaeological Association, 1972 Conference, St. John's, Newfoundland; I. T. Kenyon, "Neutral Villages in the Hamilton Region," ibid.).

60. If we estimate the Huron and Neutral populations to have been about equal before as well as after the epidemics of 1634–40, the forty Neutral villages, as opposed to the twenty Huron ones, make the average size of a Neutral village half the average of the Huron ones.

61. On this topic, see Beauchamp 1905:139–46; Fenton and Dodge 1949; Morgan 1852.

62. Thwaites 1896–1901, 17:25; 21:233. The Wenrononon appear to have been favourably located for trading with either the Dutch or the Swedes (ibid. 39:141).

63. Concerning this alliance, see Thwaites 1896–1901, 16:253. Yet the Jesuit failure to recognize the true limits of the Neutral confederacy until some years later (ibid. 21:191–93), makes it unlikely that the Wenrononon were a Neutral tribe.

64. Witthoft (1959:20) identifies the Susquehannock as most closely allied to the Cayuga and Seneca. B. Hoffman (1959) sees close linguistic affinities to the Iroquois languages and St. Lawrence Iroquoian. The data appear too limited, however, to sustain these speculations.

65. Hewitt 1910b:657–58. According to Hewitt, they are also the Carantouanais of Champlain's 1632 map.

66. Cf. Thwaites 1896–1901, 18:233–35 and Atrakwaeronnon (ibid. 37:105, 111).

67. See Hickerson, Turner, Hickerson 1952.

68. In support of Eggan's contention that the Iroquoians once may have practised cross-cousin marriage, see Trigger 1969*a*:59 n. 8.

69. For an application of this theory in an area where game animals played a critical role, see Hickerson 1970:106–19.

CHAPTER THREE

1. For a detailed survey of shifting theories of Iroquoian origins and a critical assessment of these theories, see Trigger 1970.

2. Authorities differ as to the precise dates for Clovis points. Those given here are intended only as approximations.

3. Many archaeologists refer to Griffin's *Early Archaic* as *Lithic* or *Palaeo Indian*, reserving the term *Archaic* for his *Late Archaic*.

4. Eggan 1966:87–88. Eggan notes that restrictions against marriage within the nuclear family are generally extended to the children of two brothers or two sisters. Yet marriage has to take place with someone and in small, isolated groups cross-cousin marriage permits social life to proceed with little disruption. For an alternative interpretation of PalaeoIndian social organization, see Ritchie and Funk 1973:333–37.

5. Hurley and Kenyon (1970:110) report that their findings correspond well with Wright's eastern pattern.

6. Fitting and Cleland (1969:293–94) have termed this settlement and subsistence pattern the Chippewa type.

7. Eggan 1966:82–91; Hickerson 1970:28–29. This does not mean, of course, that all marriages followed or were able to follow the ideal pattern.

8. This is especially the case if our reconstruction of Huron building methods presented in chapter two is correct. Huron longhouses would be typologically intermediate between northern Algonkian and Iroquois ones.

9. For a summary of evidence for corn in the eastern United States prior to A.D. 500, see Yarnell 1964:101–6. White (1963:2) finds the evidence for corn in the northeastern United States insufficient prior to late Middle Woodland times; a conclusion not altered by more recent finds.

10. Noble (1969:19) claims a central alignment for the hearths from the single longhouse at the Bates site. This is not confirmed by the published plan of the longhouse (Ritchie 1965:285).

11. Kroeber (1939:140) estimated a population density of 7.49 persons per square kilometre for the Iroquois and 12.90 for the Huron-Tionnontaté; however, these estimates are based on populations of 5500 and 18,000 respectively. Assuming that both groups had a population of 23,000, a rough estimate of their hunting territories produces a density closer to Kroeber's Huron-Tionnontaté than to his Iroquois one.

12. Eggan 1966:94–95. For an excellent study of an isolated Berens River band, see Dunning 1959. The shift towards endogamy observed among this group probably reflects the isolation of this community and would not apply to the less isolated groups we are discussing.

13. Among the Huron there was the danger of a serious crop failure about once every 10 years. Hickerson (1970:106) reports that among the Ojibwa, because of flood, wind, drought, or hail, the wild rice harvest was successful only one year in three.

14. Murdock (1949:190) has argued that a direct transition from patrilineal to matrilineal descent is impossible. His

reasoning (pp. 217–18) is, however, highly particularistic. In a subsequent statement (1959:140–41) his opposition to this shift is softened and two examples of it (one he considers doubtful) are discussed. Although Murdock's arguments formerly led me to reject the idea of a direct (or rapid) transition from patrilineal to matrilineal descent in Iroquoian society (Trigger 1967:156), I now believe that it is perhaps Murdock's theory that should be reconsidered. Alternatively, recent work suggests that many patrilineal groups were more bilateral than was believed formerly.

15. This view is clearly contrary to the idealized one that agricultural activities were carried out under the leadership of "clan mothers" on clan-owned land. The latter does not accord with descriptions of seventeenth century Huron practice, but may reflect the more hierarchical organization of Iroquois society after 1650, when many thousands of captive women had been incorporated into it.

16. Trigger 1969a:56. See also Helms's (1970) discussion of male absence as a factor in promoting matrilocality among the Meskito, Mbaya, and some Apache. This paper is discussed in more detail in chapter 6.

17. That a proto-Iroquoian root (*-rahak-) can be reconstructed for this term hints that a Hawaiian type bilateral kinship terminology is unlikely to have intervened prior to the historic one (Lounsbury 1961:15–16).

18. Wright 1966:64. On the rarity of ossuaries east of the historic Huron country, see Heidenreich 1971:151.

19. Wright 1966:68–74. For the distinction between the Toronto (Humber) and Trent groups, see Pendergast 1964. For the Toronto (southern)—Simcoe County (northern) division, see Wright

1966:68–80. The last three pages survey a long and bitter controversy about the relationship between these sites and offer what appears to me to be a sound re-interpretation of the data. For literature related to this controversy, see Ridley 1952a; 1952b; Emerson and Popham 1952; Ridley 1958; Emerson 1959; 1961b; Ridley 1963; Pendergast 1965.

20. Thwaites 1896–1901, 16:227. Speaking of the Arendarhonon and Tahontaenrat in 1639, Lalemant says the one came fifty years ago, the other thirty. This seems to mean that the Arendarhonon came about 1590, although this figure might refer to the Tahontaenrat.

21. Prior to 1639, when this information was recorded, the Jesuits had been living and working mainly among the Attignawantan. It seems most likely that their knowledge of the Huron was based on Attignawantan sources.

22. This is not necessarily an argument against matrilocal residence being the preferred or even the prescribed type. It does suggest that, as among other groups, the preferred type was not necessarily realized in many cases. It also suggests that proposals that matrilocal residence was more common in prehistoric times (e.g. W. Smith 1970) may be in error.

23. Wright (1966:79–80) interprets the Huron as a tribe and the four Huron tribes as clan-units. He suggests that the Wolf and Deer (Petun) clans may have left the Huron country when the Bear (Attignawantan) and Cord (Attigneenongnahac) clans, with whom they had been living until then, decided to accept the Rock (Arendarhonon) and One White Lodge (Tahontaenrat) clans into their country. Wright's arguments are based on a view of Huron clan structure that is rejected by Tooker 1970b.

24. On the basis of Wright (1966), the

following table showing the maximum and minimum percentages of aberrant sherds of different geographical origin occurring in Huron-Tionnontaté sites of different periods has been compiled:

Approximate Date	ORIGIN Neutral-Erie
1600	1%*–0
1550–1600	1–0
1500–1550	0–0
1450–1500	1–trace
	Max.–Min.

Approximate Date	ORIGIN Seneca-Cayuga
1600	21%**–2
1550–1600	6–3
1500–1550	5+–1
1450–1500	2–trace
	Max.–Min.

Approximate Date	ORIGIN Eastern Iroquoian†
1600	0%–0
1550–1600	8–3
1500–1550	10–3
1450–1500	3–0
	Max.–Min.

* Percentage is of total number of rim sherds analysed.

** Ridley (1973) presents cogent arguments that many of these may be Wenroronon.

† Eastern Iroquoian means Onondaga, Oneida, Mohawk, or St. Lawrence.

25. Subsequent to the original paper in which my views on the reasons for Huron settlement in northern Simcoe County were outlined (Trigger 1962a), Heidenreich (1967:16) attempted to uphold the traditional view that warfare was a major factor, by arguing that a nomadic people would more likely move towards an agricultural one than the reverse. This argument overlooks the location of the Huron country on the edge of the Canadian Shield and at the head of a water-route to the north.

26. For lists of these bands, see Thwaites 1896–1901, 18:229–31; 33:149–51. For suggested meanings of names, see Hickerson 1970:44.

27. A single dog burial has, however, since been reported from the early Iroquoian Bennett site (Wright and Anderson 1969:13).

28. Wright (1965) uses the term Ojibwa in a general sense to refer to all the peoples living north of Lakes Huron and Superior.

29. James F. Pendergast (personal communication 1971) tentatively identifies one sherd of Lawson Opposed (from a possible historic context), one each of Black Necked and Sidey Crossed (from possibly a pre-contact context) and one of Lawson Opposed (from an uncertain context). Because all of these types occur in low frequencies on historic Huron sites, it cannot be demonstrated that they result from contacts with the west in prehistoric times.

CHAPTER FOUR

1. For general background concerning the discovery and early exploration of the east coast of Canada by Europeans, see Biggar 1901; B. Hoffman 1961; Ganong 1964; Morison 1971; and Trudel 1963 (translated and abridged as the first part of Trudel 1973). For collections of original documents concerning this early period: Biggar (ed.) 1911 and 1930. For specialized studies: Innis 1940 and 1956; La Morandière 1962–66. For a

comprehensive examination of the impact of European discovery upon the Indians of eastern Canada: Bailey 1937.

2. On the use of smoke to signal the arrival of European traders in this area, see Denys 1908:82.

3. For typical views, see MacNeish 1952:57, 84; Witthoft 1951:316–17; Wright 1966:4. For a critique of these views, see Trigger 1968a and Pendergast and Trigger 1972:47–71.

4. Robinson 1948; B. Hoffman 1959; Lounsbury 1961. Barbeau (1961) concludes that most of the words in the Cartier vocabularies are Huron, but a small number are Mohawk. This, he argues, is evidence that members of both groups were living in the St. Lawrence Valley. Barbeau assumes (possibly wrongly) that general resemblances between words in Cartier's vocabularies and either Mohawk or Huron are proof that individual words came from one or the other of these languages.

5. For a summary of Pendergast's findings as of 1968, and full bibliographic references, see Trigger 1968a:436–37.

6. Biggar 1924:196. The exact location of Stadacona is not known. Wintemberg (1936) and Bailey (1972:18) have both speculated where on Cape Diamond the village might have been located, but as yet no archaeological evidence has been forthcoming to resolve the problem.

7. Biggar 1924:138, 191. Note that hats were not items of native Iroquoian dress.

8. Hunt 1940:17. Lescarbot (1907–14, 2:105) was the first to suggest that the Stadaconans were enemies of the Hochelagans.

9. There was also a religious sanction for such behaviour. Contradiction of a dream or prophecy of good fortune could be interpreted as a desire to thwart the outcome of the dream, which was itself a form of witchcraft.

10. For a refutation of the arguments that Cartier travelled up the Rivière des Prairies rather than along the north shore of the St. Lawrence see Lanctot 1930 and Pendergast and Trigger 1972:25–30. For details concerning the location of Hochelaga and Cartier's visit there, see ibid. 3–41.

11. The headman is said to have come from Hagouchonda, but it is clear that he is the same person formerly called the headman of Achelacy.

12. Biggar 1924:204–15; for the identification of the tree used, see Rousseau 1954–55.

13. Plans to locate the new colony up-river had been made already *c.* 1539 (Biggar 1930:77).

14. Hochelaga is not mentioned by name but appears to be the same community that is called Tutonaguy (Pendergast and Trigger 1972:39–41).

15. Maisouna may be the same as Mocosa (Moscosa) located south of the St. Lawrence and east of the Richelieu on the second map of Ortelius (1572) (Du Creux 1951–52:131 n. 2).

16. Spanish examination of Newfoundland sailors regarding Cartier: Biggar 1930:456–57; 462–63. Lanctot (1963:70–71) has cast doubt on this claim, but has been adequately refuted by Trudel 1963:152 n. 17.

17. Biggar 1924:269–70; see also the inscription on Descelier's map of 1550, "jusques icy a esté mons^r. de roberval."

18. Trudel 1963:157. Morison (1971:451) suggests that Alfonse explored the Saguenay at the same time Roberval went to Hochelaga.

19. Bailey 1937. A valuable primary source is Denys 1908.

20. In 1610, Champlain (Biggar 1922–36, 2:117) refers to the early arrival of ships at Tadoussac as being a 60-year record, according to old seamen.

21. In 1577 and 1578 La Roche had obtained commissions to trade and colonize in New France, but his efforts to exploit these commissions had come to nothing. At first, Chauvin and La Roche held overlapping commissions, but in 1600 Chauvin was made a lieutenant of La Roche with fishing rights from the Gulf of St. Lawrence to Tadoussac. On the Sable Island colony, see Trudel 1963:231–35.

22. This theme is developed in Trudel 1963 and 1966a.

23. Trudel (1966a:431–32) has estimated that between 1615 and 1629 the average yearly gross profit on furs was about 150,000 livres of which after expenses 76,000 livres net profit remained. While this profit seems large, it would have been sufficient to maintain less than 400 more men in New France even if no investment in buildings, etc. had been necessary.

24. Trudel 1963:223. It has been claimed that three Indians brought to France in the reign of Charles IX were Iroquoians (Beaugrand-Champagne 1936:195–97) but the evidence is far from convincing.

25. This theme was developed in opposition to B. Hoffman (1961:202–14) in Trigger 1962b.

26. Innis 1956:15; see geographical knowledge displayed in Biggar 1922–36, 1:136.

27. Lescarbot 1907–14, 3:267–68. A variation in the Erondelle translation (1609) gives a date of c. 1600 for the invasion (B. Hoffman 1961:203).

28. LeBlant and Baudry 1967:350. The expression "80 years" was frequently used by Indians in eastern Canada to mean "long ago." Champlain (Biggar 1922–36, 3:263) appears to follow Jamet in stating that wars forced Cartier's Indians to withdraw into the interior.

29. Perrot's story is repeated by Charlevoix (1923, 1:288–93) and Bacqueville de La Potherie (1753, 1:288–94).

30. W. Hunter 1959; however, the Susquehannock told Captain John Smith that they obtained their European goods overland, which suggests that they were still coming from the Maritimes early in the seventeenth century.

31. See e.g. Sagard 1866:846. For the Montagnais practising horticulture: Biggar 1922–36, 5:61–62. Although they were encouraged to do this by the French, the basic techniques of swidden agriculture seem to have been familiar to them.

32. Sagard, *dictionnaire*, under heading " *Nations, de quelle nation.*"

33. Cf. the translations offered in Biggar 1922–36, 3:125 and Grant 1952:314.

34. For biographies of Champlain, see Dionne 1891–1906; Bishop 1948; Trudel 1966c. For documents concerning his life and times: Le Blant and Baudry 1967; for his Indian policy, Trigger 1971a; on his claims to have travelled in the West Indies, Vigneras 1953; Flores Salinas 1964.

35. Biggar 1922–36, 1:99–101. This policy had received the approval of the French government the previous winter.

36. Innis 1956:3. Innis's point is valid although the text cited in support of it seems not to be the one the author intended.

37. The name is given as Besouat, but it is clearly the same name (Biggar 1922–36, 1:108).

38. These figures are based on Heidenreich 1971, map 18, which in turn is largely a summary of A. Hunter 1899; 1900; 1902; 1903; 1904; 1907.

39. Maximum estimate 25 (for 1624) (Wrong 1939:91–92); minimum, 18 (for 1615) (Biggar 1922–36, 3:122).

The Jesuit estimates are about 20 (Thwaites 1896–1901, 8:115; 10:313; 11:7).

40. Professor Noble has kindly informed me that since this chapter was written he has obtained a radiocarbon date of A.D. 1505 ± 85 (I–6846) on burned bark that formed part of the lining of the Sopher ossuary. The Cleveland Neutral site, which has yielded an iron celt and four rolled brass beads, has produced a date of 1540 ± 90 (I–6514) (personal communication 1972). While it is possible that a trickle of European goods was reaching Ontario from 1535 on, work done by Stuiver and Suess (1966) indicates that dates in the 400 years b.p. range (i.e. 400 years before 1950) generally have a true age in the fifteenth century, which is hopelessly early for these sites. On the other hand, specimens from the sixteenth century have radiocarbon dates from 250 to 330 b.p. (i.e. A.D. 1620 to 1700). Because of fluctuations in C_{14} formation around this time, radiocarbon dates appear to be of little use for determining precise calendrical age.

CHAPTER FIVE

1. See, e.g. Champlain's treatment of Tecouehata (i.e. Tessouat) (Biggar 1922–36, 2:211), whom he had met as early as 1603 (Besouat, ibid. 1:108).

2. See E. Jury's (1966b, c, d) biographies of the three Atironta who flourished from c. 1615 to 1672. The spelling of Atironta's name used by Sagard and Champlain is D'Arontal (Danontal, Durantal). Atironta, the form used by the Jesuits, is here employed in preference to these early ones.

3. On these problems, see Day 1971.

4. Lescarbot (1907–14, 1:112) notes

that the Indians of the southeastern United States also quickly learned to avoid bullets.

5. Desrosiers 1947a:74; based on Thwaites 1896–1901, 45:205. While correct about many points prior to 1609, A. Forbes (1970) is wrong in arguing that the Iroquois were powerful and able to intimidate their neighbours at all periods thereafter.

6. For biographies of Brûlé, see Butterfield 1898; Sulte 1907; Cranston 1949; and Jurgens 1966. Because so little is known for certain about Brûlé, there has been much speculation about his life.

7. Biggar 1922–36, 2:208. E. Jury (1966a) incorrectly identifies the Anadabijou of 1603 as the father, rather than the grandfather, of Miristou.

8. For the weakness of the view that this astrolabe belonged to Champlain, see Trudel 1966a:196 n. 51. On the other hand, the date on the astrolabe, 1603, corresponds with Champlain's first visit to Canada, which suggests that he may have bought it or had it made at that time.

9. Thwaites 1896–1901, 21:239. Champlain (Biggar 1922–36, 2:293) said that the journey from the Huron country to James Bay took 35 to 40 days; Sagard gave the duration of the journey to James Bay as one and a half months (Wrong 1939:86). Hunt (1940:58) has the Nipissing traders return from the north in the autumn, but no evidence is cited in support of this assertion.

10. Biggar 1922–36, 2:256. In the *Jesuit Relation* of 1657–58, Father G. Druillettes reported that the Nipissing reached the Northern Sea from Lake Nipissing in only 15 days (44:243). This differs from earlier accounts (see n. 9) and Druillettes was reporting from hearsay after the Nipissing had been driven from their tribal territory and were no longer using this route.

11. One wonders if a similar lack of

judgement influenced his treatment of Jean Duval, whom he had executed for treason in 1608 (see chapter 4).

12. Trudel 1966a: 207. About this time beaver skins sold for 10 livres each (Lescarbot 1907–14, 2:192).

13. Le Blant and Baudry 1967:330–33. It seems less likely that concern about the Prince de Condé's political intrigues kept him in France, since Condé's arrest did not prevent Champlain from visiting Canada in 1617.

14. In further support of this claim, one may also note the general stability of the roster of sachems among the Iroquois in spite of far more extensive changes in their way of life. The main challenge to the council chiefs was not a threat to their individual offices, but a general challenge to their authority by the war chiefs in times of crisis.

15. Jamet has been read to imply that the trading took place at the mouth of the Richelieu River in 1615 (Le Blant and Baudry 1967:350 n. 3); but compare Biggar 1922–36, 3:25–36.

16. Biggar 1922–36, 3:38. They have been identified, but very insecurely, with the Outaoukotwemiwek, of whom it is stated that they hardly ever visited the French and that their language was a mixture of Algonkin and Montagnais (Thwaites 1896–1901, 35:239).

17. Tequenonquiaye used to be thought to be located between Spratt Point and Cranberry Lake. Heidenreich (personal communication 1972) proposes this new, more northerly location on the basis of work done in the area by Frank Ridley.

18. Biggar 1922–36, 3:49. Champlain states that he visited five villages, but it is not clear if Cahiagué was included in the count.

19. See McIlwraith 1946; 1947; Emerson 1961a; and Cruickshank and Heidenreich 1969.

20. Biggar 1922–36, 3:49. It has been suggested that because of the number of houses at Cahiagué, they may have been nuclear family dwellings. This would make Cahiagué different not only from other Huron but also from other Arendarhonon sites. Moreover, Champlain speaks of fairly large houses.

21. It has been suggested that they followed the same route as the main expedition, which would mean that they moved east through the Trent Valley and then cut south between the Oneida and Onondaga villages, but this proposal has won no support (see Cranston 1949:83 n.).

22. There seems to be no proof for Trudel's (1966a:229) statement that Brûlé returned to the Huron country while Champlain was still at Carhagouha. The general scepticism that Trudel expresses about the veracity of Brûlé's report seems unwarranted. The most curious claim Brûlé made was that the Indians of Chesapeake Bay preferred the French to the Dutch; Brûlé may have been reporting a hyperbolical expression of friendship. If the Dutch were helping the Mohawk to wage war on the Susquehannock, the Susquehannock had good reason to dislike the Dutch.

23. One interpretation has them departing opposite Traverse Point and moving along the False Ducks, Main Duck, Great and Little Galloo, Calf, and Stony Islands, until they reached Henderson Bay or the mouth of Stony Creek (Biggar 1922–36, 3:62 nn. 4, 5). Another has them crossing farther down the St. Lawrence (L. Murray 1931: frontispiece; French 1949:7).

24. Biggar 1922–36, 3:82. Grant (1952:297) suggests this geography. Biggar suggests they travelled up the Napanee or Salmon River.

25. Biggar 1922–36, 3:94. The edition of 1632 gives 23 December.

CHAPTER SIX

1. Archaeological work on historic sites in the Huron country before 1948 is summarized in Kidd 1952: 72–73. Surveys of historic sites began in the last century as part of A. F. Hunter's detailed site surveys, reported in successive issues of the *Annual Archaeological Report for Ontario* from 1899 to 1907 (for references, see chapter 4, n. 38; also Hunter 1889). Hunter's work was taken account of by Jones (1908) in his effort to identify Jesuit missions. Little more was done on historic Huron sites until after World War II when Ridley (1947) and Kidd (1949*b*) continued this survey work. The early postwar period also saw excavations carried out at the Ossossané ossuary (Kidd 1953), the Orr Lake site (Kidd 1950), St. Louis (Jury and Jury 1955), and the beginning of work at the Warminster site (McIlwraith 1946; 1947). Recent work, such as the study of the Penetanguishene Peninsula reported in Hurley and Heidenreich 1969 and 1971, shows growing interest in problems of an historical and anthropological nature. While much important work remains incomplete or unpublished at this time, some of the more important studies will be reviewed in this chapter.

2. The Gendron letters describe this trade as follows: "...our French obtain...even the testicles which our medical doctors in France use for the curing of several ailments that befall women. On this subject I might say...that one usually delivers to the apothecaries, in place of the true testicles of beavers, only certain glands that these aquatic animals have near their testicles. This is because most hunters tear off and throw away the real testicles as soon as they catch the animal to avoid the bad odour that corrupts the flesh and skin. I have often observed this when I have been hunting with them and have compared the said glands, which are filled with an oily liquid somewhat black in colour, with the true testicles, which, on the contrary, are filled with a whitish liquid accumulated in small lumps, much more stinking than is that of the glands that these Indians carry to the French" (Gendron 1868: 13–15). The glands that Gendron says were being sold to the French were the castor or scent glands, which produce castoreum, a reddish-brown oil used in medicine and perfumery, as well as for making lures. Between 1858 and 1884, 25,000 pounds of castoreum were sold by the Hudson Bay Company. In recent years properly dried glands sell for six to seven dollars a pound or one to one and a half dollars for a pair of mature beaver glands (Longley and Moyle 1963: 15).

3. On the basis of French commercial records, Le Blant (1972) suggests marked fluctuations in prices for furs in France after 1642. There is no similar evidence for fluctuations in the prices paid in Canada during the period of the Huron mission.

4. Champlain gives only the total value of the furs: 300,000 livres (Biggar 1922–36, 6: 183). Fur prices were higher than usual in France at this time because of the loss of Quebec (Le Blant 1972: 62). If Champlain is stating the current value of the furs rather than their normal value, the number of skins may have been less than 30,000.

5. Le Blant (1972: 65), on the basis of French commercial data, estimates that each beaver skin weighed an average of 1.5 pounds. At a later period, nine beaver skins were said to weigh 17 pounds (Thwaites 1896–1901, 69: 261); however, in the first half of the seventeenth century

the price of a beaver skin and of a pound of skins is the same (Thwaites 1896–1901, 28:235), suggesting that for conventional purposes the two were treated as equivalent.

6. Biggar 1922–36, 3:209–10. While doubt has been expressed about the authenticity of Champlain's voyage of 1617, these data suggest that he did visit New France that year, even if he was back in Europe by 22 July (Trudel 1966c:193).

7. That Champlain made this commitment to Brûlé indicates that this aid was promised to the Huron, although this is not specified elsewhere in Champlain's narrative.

8. In his biographical sketch of Nicollet written in 1643, Vimont implies that the Algonkin made peace with the Iroquois between 1618 and 1622 (Thwaites 1896–1901, 23:277). The lack of any contemporary reference to this event suggests that Vimont may have erred in his chronology (which only accounts for 10 or 11 years of Nicollet's life from his arrival in New France in 1618 to his appointment as clerk at Three Rivers in 1633). The peace referred to may be that of 1624.

9. Most of the following section is based on Trigger 1971c. That paper should be consulted for more complete documentation.

10. For opinions concerning this confused episode, see Trelease 1960:33–34 and J. Murray 1938. For original documents, see Biggar 1922–36, 3:54 and O'Callaghan 1856–87, 1:33.

11. Sometimes the Nipissing may have obtained trade goods from the Cree, who are said to have had axes, leggings, and other items from European traders operating on Hudson Bay (Wrong 1939:86–87). This is probably a reference to English visits to the bay.

12. Le Jeune was told that in an emergency the Montagnais still made and cooked in bark kettles. Their rarity is attested by the fact that Le Jeune does not appear ever to have seen such a kettle (Thwaites 1896–1901, 5:97).

13. Champlain's salary was 1200 livres (Trudel 1966a:431). One pistole = 10 livres (Thwaites 1896–1901, 4:269 n. 42).

14. La Criette is specifically described as a servant of Champlain (Sagard 1866:208). Chaudron was said by the Jesuits to have died at Ossossané (Thwaites 1896–1901, 10:305–9); he must therefore be the anonymous youth who died there in 1623–24 (Sagard 1866:602) and who, in turn, can be identified as the servant of Champlain who died the same year (Biggar 1922–36, 5:129). This identification is certain, since only two Frenchmen (Brûlé and Chaudron) died in the Huron country prior to 1648 (Thwaites 1896–1901, 10:305).

15. In ordinary speech, a livre and a franc signified the same value (Thwaites 1896–1901, 4:269 n. 42).

16. This suggestion was not as heartless as it appears to modern readers or as it did to the Huron. The French of this period did not normally bury clothes with the dead.

17. As Trudel (1966a:342) points out, Charlevoix writing over a century later expressed some reservations about the theory of foul play.

18. For biographies of Brébeuf, see Talbot 1956; Martin 1898; Latourelle 1966. All of these works are written primarily from a religious point of view. For a study of his writings, see Latourelle 1952–53.

19. Thwaites 1896–1901, 4:225. It is generally assumed that it was Marsolet who returned to France with Amantacha (Trudel 1966a:329). The interpreter that Charles Lalemant stated received a salary

of 100 pistoles (Thwaites 1896–1901, 4:209), who worked among the Huron, and whom Amantacha loved like he did his father (ibid. 4:225) can only have been Brûlé. There is, however, also good evidence that Marsolet returned to France at the same time (Archives nationales, Paris Zld, liasse 103). I have discussed these conclusions with Professor Trudel and he concurs with the interpretation given here in personal communications dated 1971 and 1972.

20. For a different estimate of the Neutral's attitude towards this trade, see Trudel 1966a:367–68.

21. Trudel 1966a:347, 426–28. Kenneth E. Kidd (personal communication 1974) believes he uncovered fragments of this house in 1959.

22. Otterbein (1964) attributes the break-up of Iroquoian formation fighting to the introduction of guns rather than metal arrows.

Chapter 7 The Interregnum and the New Alliance

New France in Eclipse

Relations between the Huron and the French were disrupted by the brief war that began between France and England in 1627. In the course of the war, Quebec was captured by the English, thus upsetting the precarious balance of relations that had existed in eastern Canada since 1615. The years 1628 to 1634 were a period of great uncertainty for the Huron, not only in their trading relations with Europeans, but also because of the intrigues of the Algonkin, who were anxious to exploit a confused situation to regain their former role as middlemen.

The war also wrecked important plans for the development of New France that the French Jesuits had played a major role in helping to formulate. In 1626 the Duc de Ventadour's confessor, Philibert Noyrot, returned to France after a brief sojourn in Quebec, in order to seek official support to have the monopoly of the Compagnie de Caën revoked and for the development of New France as a Roman Catholic colony. The plans that the Jesuits proposed were similar to those being advocated by Joseph Le Caron, but they pursued their objectives with much greater vigour and perspicacity. Soon after he returned to France Noyrot had an audience with Cardinal Richelieu, who was seeking to strengthen French naval power and to encourage commercial adventures abroad. Later, through the intervention of the Duc de Ventadour, he persuaded Richelieu that Protestants should be forbidden to settle in New France. It is also believed to have been on Noyrot's advice that the Duc de Ventadour resigned his vice-regal office and the Marquise de Guercheville gave up her rights in Acadia (Monet 1966a). These initiatives significantly aided Richelieu's efforts to improve the management of New France by founding a merchant company on the model of ones already being operated by the English and the Dutch. Ventadour's resignation allowed the cardinal to assume direct control of New France and to dissolve the Compagnie de Caën. The latter was replaced by a new company, called the Compagnie des Cent-Associés and later the Compagnie de la Nouvelle France. This company was granted a fifteen-year monopoly over all trade with North America and a perpetual monopoly of the fur trade. In return it had to agree to establish 4000 settlers in New France by 1643, to subsidize mission work, and to provide adequate defences for the colony. To prevent these obligations from being ignored by profit-hungry traders, Richelieu arranged for courtiers and officials to be enrolled as shareholders; it was stipulated that noblemen and churchmen could engage in this trade without incurring a loss of status. It was also decreed that Indians who were baptized should enjoy the same rights of citizenship as did settlers from France (Lanctot 1963:131).

To honour its obligations, in spring 1628 the company set about establishing an unprecedented 400 settlers in New France at a cost of 400,000 livres. Although the French and English were already at war, these vessels sailed unescorted from Dieppe under the command of Claude Roquemont de Brison. Roquemont's vessels were accompanied by a Jesuit supply ship that had been chartered by Father Noyrot and by a number of fishing boats that sought the protection of the larger vessels for the Atlantic crossing.

With the outbreak of war, Gervase Kirke, an English merchant who had lived in France and who may have had business connections with Guillaume de Caën (Morton 1963:33), formed a company that secured a commission from Charles I authorizing it to seize Canada from the French. In 1628 his sons sailed up the St. Lawrence with Jacques Michel, who had formerly worked for Champlain as pilot. The Kirkes seized Tadoussac, where they were welcomed by the Montagnais as independent traders. The Montagnais concealed the arrival of the English from the French at Quebec and informed the English that the latter were on the point of starvation (Biggar 1922–36, 5:275, 307). The English pillaged the farm at Cape Tourmente (5:274–75) and demanded the surrender of Quebec. Champlain, however, was still expecting the arrival of Emery de Caën's ships and therefore refused this demand. David Kirke decided against attacking the settlement, but on the way home he intercepted and captured the fleet belonging to the Compagnie des Cent-Associés, near Gaspé. The loss of these ships was a financial disaster for the company and meant that in 1628 no supplies or trade goods got through to the already hard-pressed trading post at Quebec.

One of the passengers aboard the captured French vessels was Amantacha, who was returning home after his two years in France. When the Kirkes were told that he was the son of a native "king," they thought he might be useful to them; thus, when they returned to England they kept him in their custody, although the other prisoners were allowed to return to France. Amantacha appears to have spent the winter of 1628–29 in London, where he was treated as a person of some importance and presented with several new suits of clothing. By that time, American Indians were no strangers in England. The first had arrived as early as 1502 and since then a number, including Pocahontas, had become celebrities. Amantacha was, however, the first person born in Ontario to set foot in the British Isles. The failure of the French to return him to his father for the second consecutive year must have greatly troubled the Huron and may explain why no Huron youth was ever again permitted to travel to France.

Champlain continued to weaken his desperate position by his foolish and high-handed treatment of the Montagnais, who were already angry about the high prices that the traders at Quebec charged for their goods. He refused to release an Indian whom he had imprisoned because he suspected him of the murder of two Frenchmen in 1627. The Montagnais regarded this as an unwarranted form of punishment and, as the prisoner's health deteriorated as a result of his confinement, they became increasingly angry. Had he died while being held captive by the French, the Montagnais would surely have sought blood revenge. When the autumn fishing was over, the Montagnais agreed among themselves that until the prisoner was released, they would sell the French only a small number of eels at the exorbitant price of one beaver skin for every ten eels (5:298). In this way, the Montagnais forced the French to part with 120 skins, which the Indians no doubt intended to trade with the English the following summer. When Champlain still refused to release the prisoner, another council was held and it was decided to sell no food to the French until he was freed. Only the alcoholic and obsequious Chomina and his family broke this agreement.

When the spring came and once again no ships arrived from France, the inhabitants of Quebec were forced to go into the forests to dig for edible roots. To ensure the safety of his men, Champlain decided that he had best release the prisoner, who was now so ill he could not walk. Even so, he demanded that in return the Montagnais headmen should agree to supply him with food and to obey his orders. In spite of their apparent acceptance of these demands, Champlain rightly concluded that they had no intention of fulfilling the promise he had extracted from them. Champlain made matters worse by also demanding in return for the prisoner's freedom that a council of headmen be formed, which would henceforth regulate relations between the French and their Algonkian-speaking allies. The despised Chomina was to be recognized as the head of this council, while influential headmen, such as Erouachy from Tadoussac, Batiscan from Three Rivers, and Tessouat from the Ottawa Valley, were to be only subordinate members (6:7–22). Chomina and his equally alcoholic brother, Negabamat, were the only Indians who had rushed to Quebec to help defend the settlement the previous year and Champlain's aim in so conspicuously rewarding this loyalty was to encourage other Indians to emulate it.

All Champlain accomplished was to insult respected headmen who, while maintaining friendly relations with the French, put their own people's interests first. Matters were made worse by Champlain's refusal to return to their families two Montagnais girls whom he had obtained under duress early in 1628, and whom he was planning to take to France and enrol in a convent school. These personal abuses, combined with longstanding Montagnais resentment over the trading monopoly, led most of the Indians to wish for the expulsion of the French from Quebec. It was therefore not surprising that as the summer of 1629 began to pass and no French ships appeared, only Chomina and his relatives remained at Quebec. The rest of the Montagnais were at Tadoussac awaiting the return of the English.

Since the French had no trade goods and were expecting the return of the English, they did not go up the St. Lawrence to meet their Indian trading partners in 1629. Some Montagnais made the journey in the hope of obtaining some much-needed corn from the Huron. Having become dependent on agricultural produce, they were almost as near to starvation as the French traders were as a result of no ships having come from France. On 17 July some Huron arrived at Quebec, accompanied by all the French who had been living in the Huron country. Champlain reports there were twelve canoes (6:45); Sagard says there were twenty (Sagard 1866:847). Both figures seem low, since a minimum of twenty-one French had wintered among the Huron in 1628–29, and it is unlikely that more than one Frenchman would have travelled in each canoe. It is possible, however, that some Huron had been content to trade with the Montagnais and Algonkin on the upper St. Lawrence and a number of French had travelled the rest of the way to Quebec with the Montagnais. In any case, because they feared there might be no trade goods, fewer Huron seem to have come to the St. Lawrence than in normal years.

The amount of corn that the residents of Quebec were able to acquire was disappointingly small. Most of the French who returned from the Huron country preferred to transport furs for their own profit rather than corn to succour their hungry comrades. Some had 700 to 800 livres worth of furs with them, which, depending on whether the value cited was that of the furs in France or Quebec, could mean from seventy skins to many times that number (902). Brébeuf brought four or five sacks of corn meal, weighing fifty pounds each, for the use of the Jesuits (Biggar 1922–36, 6:47), and the Recollets managed to purchase two more sacks from the Huron (Sagard 1866:895). Olivier, an assistant agent at the trading post, secured another sack on behalf of Gravé Du Pont (Biggar 1922–36, 6:47; Sagard 1866:895). Champlain had hoped to obtain some corn for himself by giving Chomina knives to barter at Three Rivers, but Chomina brought nothing back (Biggar 1922–36, 6:42); whatever extra corn the Huron brought with them was sold to the Montagnais and Algonkin. Champlain complained bitterly about the unwillingness of the French who were living at Quebec to share what they had with one another and, in particular, about their lack of concern for him, although he was their commander (6:48). These complaints indicate not only Champlain's weakness, but the disarray resulting from the competing factions that had developed at Quebec during the previous two decades.

Two days after the Huron arrived at Quebec, the settlement surrendered to the English on the best terms that Champlain was able to negotiate. The relief ships he had counted on to save the colony were blown off course and when Emery de Caën finally arrived, he was defeated by the Kirkes. The latter refused to accept de Caën's word that the war had ended in April, since to have done so would have been to admit the illegality of their retaining possession of Quebec. Some of the priests thought of going to live with the Algonkin in order to pursue their mission work and to maintain French influence among them until Quebec was restored to the French (Sagard 1866:844). It was finally agreed, however, that they, along with Champlain and most of the French who lived at Quebec, should be re-patriated. While the Recollets were treated with some courtesy by the English, the Jesuits were handled more roughly. David Kirke accused the Jesuits of seeking to control the fur trade that had formerly belonged to Guillaume de Caën and Jacques Michel said they were more interested in beavers than in saving souls (Biggar 1922–36, 6:137).

The Huron and the English

While most of the French returned home, some decided to remain and work for the English. A few men had entered the service of the Kirkes even before they set sail for Quebec. One of these was Jacques Michel, the French shipmaster who piloted the English fleet up the St. Lawrence in 1628 and 1629 (Biggar 1922–36, 6:81). Another was Le Baillif from Amiens who had formerly worked as a trading agent for de Caën (5:88). Many of the interpreters also entered the service of the English. These included Brûlé, the Huron interpreter, Marsolet, the Montagnais one, and an Algonkin interpreter nicknamed Gros-Jean, who was probably Jean Richer.[1] These men had been intermediaries for their respective tribes for so long that the company or nationality employing them was probably of little importance. Whatever they thought of the English, they must have welcomed the chance to throw off the yoke that the Jesuits had fastened onto them. It was probably, in part, on the basis of their complaints that the English accused the Jesuits of having meddled in the fur trade. Either by accident or by design, Jean Nicollet, the Nipissing interpreter, continued to live with his people, probably spending the winters with them in the Huron country. He seems to have made no public profession of loyalty to the English and later it was claimed that he had tried to discourage the Nipissing from trading with the English (Hamelin 1966*b*: 517); however, Nicollet became a friend of the Jesuits who may be representing his behaviour at this time in as favourable a light as possible. Thomas Godefroy was another interpreter who lived among the Indians between 1629 and 1632 (Vachon 1966). The Couillard family, who inhabited the Hébert farm, also chose to remain at Quebec. The English let them trade their surplus produce for furs and agreed to pay them four livres for every beaver skin. Under French rule, trade of this sort had been forbidden to settlers (Biggar 1922–36, 6:70–71).

The man most pleased by the arrival of the English must have been Soranhes. He had travelled to Quebec for a third summer only to find that the French had not brought back his son. When the English arrived, Amantacha appeared dressed in an expensive suit of English clothes. Sagard recounted with some glee that when Thomas Kirke learned that Amantacha's father was not a king, but a "hungry, naked Indian," he wanted to take back all the clothing that the English had given Amantacha. He was persuaded, however, perhaps by Brûlé, that it was unwise to anger the Huron by doing this. Amantacha was, therefore, allowed to keep the clothes he was wearing and was told that if he led many Huron to trade the following year, he would be allowed to take away all the clothes that the English had given him (Sagard 1866: 835–37). Amantacha returned to the Huron country with Brûlé and his father, and there had a chance to describe in detail what he had seen in France and England (Biggar 1922–36, 6:101–102).

Because of his natural abilities, and also because he was old enough to have mastered the basic skills needed to operate in his own culture, Amantacha was not fatally damaged by his stay in France, as the young Montagnais child Pastedechouan had been. The Recollets had taken Pastedechouan to France in 1620 and had kept him there for six years, teaching him to read and write both French and Latin. Pastedechouan never had an opportunity to learn how to hunt or get along in the forest; hence when he returned to Canada he found himself reduced to a parasitic existence, which led him to be dependent on, and ultimately to loathe, both his own people and the French. As a result of his inability to adapt to either culture, he became increasingly addicted to alcohol and in 1636 he starved to death in the forest (Grassmann 1966a).

By contrast, Amantacha seems to have resumed life among his people where he had left off, and soon was an active hunter and young warrior. Because of his long sojourn in Europe and his ability to speak and write French, he was able to inform his people about his experiences with greater accuracy and understanding than Savignon had done. He was also a successful intermediary between the Huron and the Europeans. In 1629, the French observed that he had already accommodated himself to the "freer ways" of the English (Biggar 1922–36, 6:101), and later Jesuit accounts written in the Huron country were to note that there he was living after the fashion of his own people and "not as he ought to be" (Thwaites 1896–1901, 8:149). In spite of this, when he visited the Jesuits at Quebec, he always managed to convince them of the sincerity of his Roman Catholicism. While his efforts to insinuate himself with both the French and the English might suggest that he, like many of the interpreters, had developed the psychological characteristics of a "marginal man" who is deeply committed to neither of the cultures with which he has dealings, Amantacha's behaviour amongst his own people makes it clear that he was first and foremost a Huron.

Although Quebec had been seized in peacetime, Charles I was reluctant to restore it to France until the French court agreed to pay the remaining portion of his wife's dowry. Negotiations over the dowry and the ownership of the furs that the Kirkes had seized at Quebec proceeded slowly. Meanwhile, the Company of Adventurers continued to use Quebec as a trading post until the treaty of Saint-Germain-en-Laye was signed in 1632. During these three years Thomas Kirke was in charge at Quebec, with ninety men under his command during the winter months (Biggar 1922–36, 6:183). These were more men than had ever been there during the French period. Altogether, over 200 men were maintained in Canada by the Company of Adventurers (Moir 1966:405). Although the land that had been cleared by the Recollets and Jesuits was cultivated by company employees, because of the uncertain future, the Kirkes did not proceed with their plans to expand the fur trade and to exploit more of the colony's natural resources (Biggar 1922–36, 6:103–04). A major accomplishment of this period was that large ships were taken up-river to Quebec for the first time in the seventeenth century (6:182). Hitherto, the channel above Tadoussac had been judged too dangerous for regular navigation. This development would ultimately terminate Tadoussac's importance as the head of trans-Atlantic navigation.

The trade carried on at Quebec in 1630 appears to have been a record up to that time; perhaps 30,000 skins were purchased from the Indians (6: 183).[2] Many Huron must have come down-river that year, bringing with them the furs they had collected but had been unable to barter with the French over the two previous years. The Huron must have been running short of European goods and were therefore anxious to benefit from the arrival of the English in order to replenish their supplies. Their confidence in the English was strengthened by the return of Amantacha and the favourable reports that he and Brûlé provided.

In spite of this, it seems that the Huron encountered problems in their dealings with the English. These problems may have resulted from the sale of alcohol by the English (Thwaites 1896–1901, 5:49). Wine and liquors had been made freely available to the Indians by the independent traders who had long been operating along the lower St. Lawrence (6:251); hence they were well known to the Montagnais. The latter viewed these beverages as magical substances that enabled a person to become possessed by powerful supernatural forces. Champlain, however, had vigorously opposed the sale of alcohol to the Indians in areas under his control (6:253); thus the Huron may have been unfamiliar with and terrified by the riotous conduct that resulted from excessive drinking. Such an experience could have persuaded many Huron not to return to Quebec the following year and made the rest more susceptible to the rumour-mongering of the Algonkin, who were always looking for ways to discourage Huron journeys to the St. Lawrence in order to regain their former role as middlemen.

Whatever the reason, trade plummeted in 1631. Guillaume de Caën secured a license to operate in New France that year and the English agreed to share the trade with him. When, however, the English saw how few Indians were coming to Quebec, they forbade his cousin, Emery de Caën, to have any dealings with the Indians. De Caën was only permitted to unload his goods and leave a clerk at Quebec with permission to barter with the Montagnais over the winter (Biggar 1922–36, 6:214–16). That the Huron did not have an exceptionally large number of furs to trade in 1632 suggests that they may have traded some of their 1631 supply to the Algonkin in return for European goods.

The Return of the Mohawk

As the position of the French at Quebec grew more untenable, the established pattern of relationships on which trade in eastern Canada had depended for over a decade began to be disrupted by a resurgence of Iroquois militancy in the St. Lawrence Valley. To understand what was happening, it is necessary to examine briefly what occurred among the Mohawk after they made peace with the French and the Algonkin in 1624 and had begun to wage war on the Mahican. The ensuing conflict was not an easy one and for a time it appears to have gone against the Mohawk, whose easternmost settlement was destroyed about 1626 (Jameson 1909: 157). The Dutch traders at Fort Orange knew that the Mohawk wished to gain control of the territory around their settlement to prevent the Dutch from developing trading relations with the Algonkin and Montagnais. It is therefore not surprising that as the war began to turn against the Mahican, these traders abandoned their official policy of neutrality and commissioned the commandant at Fort Orange, Daniel Van Krieckenbeeck, and a small party of musketeers to help these Indians. This expedition was soundly defeated and some of its members were consigned to the flames by the victorious Mohawk. When the Dutch traders realized the danger in which they had placed themselves, they hastened to dispatch an itinerant trader, Pieter Barentsen, to visit the Mohawk and re-establish good relations with them (ibid. 84–85).

This defeat did not, however, prevent Isaack de Rasiere, the provincial secretary of New Netherland, from revealing his own wishes and those of the traders at Fort Orange when he wrote later in 1626 that if the Mohawk were unwilling to grant the northern Algonkians a perpetual right-of way to visit the Hudson Valley, the Dutch should go to war to compel them to do so (Van Laer 1924:212–15). American historians have erroneously assumed that because the Amsterdam directors opposed this policy, de Rasiere's proposal was only an idle threat. It is clear from Champlain's writings that this was not so. By the following year, the Dutch had distributed presents among the northern Algonkians who visited Fort Orange to persuade them to break their truce with the Mohawk (Biggar 1922–36, 5:214–15). The men who did this were probably associates of the late Van Krieckenbeeck, the man whom Kiliaen Van Rensselaer, a settler and therefore no friend of the company traders at Fort Orange, was later to accuse of having led the Mahican into the war in the first place (Van Laer 1908:306). Van Krieckenbeeck did not arrive at Fort Orange, however, until after the war had begun; hence, in making this accusation, Van Rensselaer must have been thinking of Van Krieckenbeeck's efforts to expand trade northwards. These efforts were part of a general policy that had angered the Mohawk.

The Algonkian-speaking headmen who accepted presents at Fort Orange returned to the St. Lawrence Valley and began to urge their followers to join the Dutch and Mahican in an attack on the Mohawk villages (Biggar 1922–36, 5:215). When Champlain learned about this, he was very angry and threatened to aid the Iroquois if war broke out (5:217). Many of the Algonkian headmen were also opposed to a renewal of warfare at this time, and they and the French were well on their way to preserving the peace, when a party of young warriors treacherously captured two Mohawk who had gone fishing and began to torture them. Even then, Champlain persuaded the Algonkians to release these prisoners and to try to renew their treaty with the Mohawk. A party that included a Frenchman, Pierre Magnan, and the Montagnais headman, Cherououny, set out to escort the prisoners home. These men were slain when they reached the first Mohawk village, allegedly because a Kichesipirini, who disliked Cherououny, had informed the Mohawk that his main reason for coming was to spy on them (5:308–12).[3] There was, however, a more important reason for these killings: Mohawk anger and resentment had been fanned by news of the negotiations going on between the northern Algonkians and the Dutch. It is quite likely that either the Dutch or the Mahican informed the Mohawk about these negotiations, hoping thereby that the peace between the Mohawk and the northern Algonkians would collapse.

Early in 1628, the Mahican suffered a decisive defeat. Those living near Fort Orange who were not taken prisoner were forced to abandon their band territories and flee eastward to the Connecticut Valley, where they settled down and began to cultivate the land (Jameson 1909:89, 131). While the Mahican sold the legal title to their abandoned land to Van Rensselaer in 1630 and 1631 (Van Laer 1908:166–69, 181–83, 306), the victory of 1628 gave the Mohawk control to the very doorstep of the Dutch trading post. This made it possible for them to enforce their policy of not permitting the Algonkians, or any other northern people, to trade with the Dutch. If more furs were to be obtained from the north in the near future, it would have to be with the Mohawk as intermediaries. While Dutch traders and officials were anxious to circumvent this boycott, their military weakness, combined with rising trade figures, reconciled them to the new political situation, at least until more settlers should arrive and the Dutch were strong enough to control the Mohawk (ibid. 248). The French traders benefited from the Mohawk victory, because it temporarily elimi-nated the possibility of northern Algonkians being able to play French and Dutch traders off against one another to lower the value of European trade goods. This more than offset their loss of trade with the Iroquois and the disruption of hunting patterns that renewed warfare brought about among the Algonkian bands with whom the French traded.

Those who emerged most disadvantaged by these events were the northern Algonkians. They were again at war with the Mohawk, who no longer had the Mahican to deal with and whose supplies of European goods were more secure than ever. There is, however, no evidence that the Mo-hawk sought to press their advantage immediately after their defeat of the Mahican. Both the Algonkin and the Mohawk sent raiding parties against each other, but some of the prisoners taken on both sides were released to explore the possibility of a renewed peace (Biggar 1922–36, 6:3). The Montagnais similarly expressed an interest in ending hostilities. The northern Algonkians wanted peace because they dreaded the Iroquois and were afraid that the French would no longer be able to protect them. The Mohawk wanted to maintain good relations with the French so that they could continue driving down the price of European goods by playing French and Dutch traders off against one another. The main problems were that the French could not agree to a treaty from which their Indian allies were excluded, while neither they nor the Mohawk could afford a peace that would allow these same allies to trade with the Dutch. To get around the first of these difficulties, the Mohawk were evidently seeking peace with the northern Algonkians in order to trade with the French. In so doing, however, they left unresolved the long-term problem of how to prevent these Algonkians from trading with the Dutch once a general peace had been arranged. The French traders, no less than the Mohawk, seem to have clung to the hope of profiting from a series of short-term solutions to this problem.

Champlain, however, had made up his mind that no further accommo-dation with the Iroquois was possible. Even if they showed signs of wishing to be friendly, to him they were allies of a colonial power that threatened the existence of New France, as well as an impediment to exploration and the development of trade routes in the upper part of the St. Lawrence Valley. After 1627 Champlain consistently advocated that the Iroquois should either be exterminated or have French laws and customs imposed on them. In the winter of 1628–29 he fancied that if no help arrived from France the following spring, he and his men might seize an Iroquois village and live there on the corn they had captured until they were relieved

(5:304–05). Likewise, when he returned to Quebec in 1633, he had plans to form an army of 120 French soldiers and several thousand Indians, equip it with explosives, and use this army to conquer the Iroquois (Bishop 1948:330–31). The ineffectiveness of such expeditions, even when New France was far more populous than it was in 1633, shows that although Champlain's analysis of the basic problem may have been accurate, his proposed solution was unrealistic.

During 1628 and 1629 mutual hopes for peace helped to keep warfare between the Mohawk and Algonkians at a low key. The collapse of French power on the St. Lawrence meant, however, the disappearance of the major factor that for many years had maintained a balance of power in the region. Blood feuds slowly began to spiral into a major war, once the Iroquois realized that they could again attack the upper St. Lawrence Valley with impunity. Sometime after the summer of 1629, Iroquois raids led to the abandonment of a settlement that the Montagnais and Algonkin had built at Three Rivers prior to 1623 (Sagard 1866:846; Thwaites 1896–1901, 6:151). Le Jeune reports that this village, which he saw after it had been "burned by the Iroquois," had been surrounded by a strong palisade and by several acres of corn fields (Thwaites 1896–1901, 8:27–29).

Not all of the victories were on one side. In October 1632 a number of Algonkians were defeated in battle by the Iroquois (5:93); on the other hand, not long before, the Montagnais had returned from a foray with nine male Iroquois captives, six of whom were claimed by the Montagnais from Quebec and three by the Montagnais from Tadoussac (5:27–29; 45–49). While the Montagnais spoke of using these prisoners to negotiate for peace, all but one of them were killed during a bout of general drunkenness. The remaining youth was spared only after Emery de Caën had offered the Montagnais valuable presents not to kill him. He remained a prisoner among the Montagnais and apparently died a few years later (7:171). In spite of such successes, the Montagnais were so terrified of the Iroquois that once again they feared to disperse for their winter hunts and ran to the Europeans for protection whenever they thought that the Iroquois were near Quebec (5:107). Thus, by the early 1630s the political situation in the St. Lawrence Valley resembled that of 1608, when Champlain arrived at Quebec.

One of the reasons for the return of political chaos to the St. Lawrence Valley was the refusal of the English to police the river, or to provide military aid to their Algonkian-speaking trading partners. When the Indian headmen pressed them for support, they were told that it was necessary to keep all of the English at Quebec to guard it against recapture by the French (5:195). The English were willing to sell muskets to the Indians, and a few Montagnais learned to use these weapons proficiently (6:309). Yet, these few guns did not provide the crucial psychological advantage over the Iroquois that an English presence on the upper St. Lawrence would have done. Because of this, it is likely that all the tribes who formerly had alliances with the French came to mistrust what seemed like cowardice and neutrality on the part of the English. War and mistrust as well as Huron grievances account for the falling-off of trade at Quebec in 1631.

Quebec: A Jesuit Mission Colony

When Quebec was restored to France in 1632, Guillaume de Caën was granted permission to trade there for one more year to compensate him for the termination of his monopoly by the charter given to the Compagnie des Cent-Associés. Emery de Caën was named commandant for the year, with Charles Du Plessis-Bochart, the head clerk of the Compagnie des Cent-Associés, as his lieutenant. At the same time, the Jesuits pressed for exclusive missionary rights in Canada so that they might work without interference from other orders. Richelieu's adviser, the Capuchin Father Joseph, disliked the Recollets and persuaded the Cardinal to assign the mission field to his own order. The Jesuits mounted an intensive, though discreet, opposition to this appointment and their supporter, Jean de Lauson, director of the Cent-Associés, finally persuaded the Capuchins to work in Acadia and to help him convince Richelieu to grant the rest of New France to the Jesuits. In 1632 Richelieu issued letters patent ordering the Jesuits to resume their duties at Quebec. For the next three years, Lauson countered, by fair and foul means, all of the Recollets' efforts to return to Quebec (Lanctot 1963:148–49). The Recollets were angered by this and accused the Jesuits of having intrigued to get rid of them. Thus began a series of polemics and a struggle for the religious control of New France that was to outlast the century.

Whatever intrigues were involved in gaining control of the Canadian mission, the Jesuits' success in defending this monopoly for several decades must be attributed to the nature of their mission program, as it then began to unfold. Although they returned to Quebec with far greater powers than any missionaries had possessed previously, the Jesuits were anxious to avoid the antagonisms that had formerly pitted Recollets and traders against one another. The Jesuits clearly recognized that trading alliances with the Indians made their mission work possible, and that much of the money for the support and expansion of missions was derived from the profits of this trade (Du Creux 1951–52:92). Thus, while the Jesuits strove to control the manner in which the fur trade was conducted, they agreed that the prosperity of New France and of their missions depended on the successful operation of this trade. They were therefore prepared to consider the needs of the company and to fashion policies that were in harmony with these needs, in a way that the more narrow-sighted Recollets had never been willing to do.[4]

Jesuit policy was diametrically opposed to that of the Recollets in a number of ways. Whereas the Recollets believed it necessary to settle a large number of French families among the Huron in order to convert them, the Jesuits preferred to isolate them as much as possible from Europeans. Far from believing, as the Recollets did, that these settlers would provide a model of Christian life that the Huron might emulate, the Jesuits feared that they would acquaint the Huron with the vices of France which were no less repellent to these missionaries than was a non-Christian religion. As an extension of the policy, the Jesuits rejected the Recollets' idea that to be Christian the Indians had to become French in language and culture. On the contrary, the Jesuits had to master the language and beliefs of the Huron so that they could use this knowledge to persuade the Huron to become Christians. The Jesuits' aim was to eliminate, or replace, only those customs that did not accord with Christian teachings and morality. At first, they did not anticipate any need for a major refashioning of Huron life.

The Jesuits applied the same policy of keeping the Indians separate from the French and teaching them in their own language to the Montagnais, abandoning it only very unwillingly and temporarily when forced to do so by the French government in the 1660s (Lanctot 1964:63). A similar policy was applied successfully by Spanish-speaking Jesuits among the Guarani Indians of South America (Métraux 1948; Mörner 1953) and the reports of this work were well known to the Jesuits when they renewed their Canadian mission (Thwaites 1896–1901, 5:33). This approach was therefore not adopted as a matter of convenience, but reflected the attitude of the order to the whole question of conversion.

Another aim of the Canadian Jesuits that differed from those of the Recollets was to convert whole communities as quickly as possible. If the Huron were to become practising Christians, a framework of social sanctions was required that only a Christian community could provide. Whereas the Recollets tried to persuade Huron converts to move to Quebec, the Jesuits hoped to use these converts to start a chain reaction that would lead to a whole village becoming Christian. That community would then become the framework within which they could expand and refine their converts' understanding of Christianity. Le Jeune, writing in 1633, was of the opinion that the conversion of the Indians would be a simple matter since being "removed from all luxury, they are not given to many sins" (5:35). Earlier, however, the more realistic Charles Lalemant had expressed the opinion that six to twelve years would be required before there were many converts (4:223).

All of the Jesuits who came to the Huron country had received an education that was rigorous and exacting by the standards of the age. Part of their training involved the inculcation of new standards of observation and experimentation. The result is evident in their reports, in which they were careful to distinguish between their conclusions and the evidence on which these were based, and to record and evaluate their sources of information (Tooker 1964:7). Their linguistic studies were methodologically far in advance of those of the Recollets (Hanzeli 1969), while their geographical training enabled them to produce the first tolerably accurate maps of the interior of eastern Canada and to use eclipses to investigate the longitude of French and Huron settlements (Crouse 1924).

The intellectual approach of these seventeenth-century Jesuits to the task of conversion and their careful reporting of strange customs strikes a sympathetic chord in modern scholars who, for this reason, are tempted to regard the Jesuits as entertaining more modern views than, in fact, they held. Sharing experiences that their missionaries had gained working in India, China, Japan, South America, and elsewhere had made the Jesuits keenly aware of the diversity of human behaviour and the degree to which customs and values varied from one culture to another. Le Jeune summarized this view in 1633: "Oh, how weak are the judgments of men! Some see beauty where others see nothing but ugliness. In France, the most beautiful teeth are the whitest; in the Maldive Islands white teeth are considered a deformity, so they paint them red to be beautiful, and in Cochin China, if I remember correctly, they paint them black. Who is right?" (Thwaites 1896–1901, 5:107).

This statement, and others like it, have led certain scholars to conclude that by the seventeenth century the Jesuits had adopted a concept of cultural relativism similar to that held by most anthropologists (Kennedy 1950; Duignan 1958). This would mean that the Jesuits had abandoned any universal criteria for judging human behaviour and were attempting to evaluate all beliefs and practices in terms of the meaning assigned to them within each particular culture. The belief that the Jesuits in this or any other way transcended their own time to anticipate modern secular concepts is totally unwarranted. While the Jesuits may have been able to treat cultural variations in what they regarded as relatively trivial or morally neutral matters with equanimity or even intellectual curiosity, they were wholly unprepared to extend the same toleration to the sphere of religious beliefs or morality. Like the vast majority of Europeans, they were convinced that their own beliefs about such matters were correct and that all other beliefs were wrong. It was therefore their ambition, whenever possible and by whatever means, to win converts to Roman Catholicism and to stamp out other religions.

We have already noted that in 1625 the Jesuits had taken action to curb what they regarded as the immoral behaviour of the French interpreters who were living among the Indians by gaining control over them. As the Jesuits developed their plans for renewing their mission work, they decided that their plan to convert the Huron would succeed only if there were no Europeans living among the Indians who by word or deed might work at cross purposes to them. This made it necessary to broaden their earlier campaign against the interpreters and seek to prevent all independent traders from living among the Indians. The Jesuits had sufficient influence to gain their way in this matter, and men such as Jean Nicollet, Thomas Godefroy, and Nicolas Marsolet were compelled to settle down in new jobs at Quebec or Three Rivers. No new interpreters were sent to replace these men among the Algonkin and Nipissing even though no Jesuits went to live with these groups. Presumably this was because the Jesuits feared that such interpreters might spend the winters in the Huron country. In return the Jesuits agreed to have a number of laymen attached to the Huron mission, who could discharge the most vital functions that the traders and interpreters had performed hitherto. These included encouraging the Indians to trade and travelling with them to and from the St. Lawrence each year to protect them against Iroquois attacks and Algonkin intimidation.

Thus, the *coureurs de bois* of former days were replaced by men who were employed by the Jesuits and controlled by them. The Jesuits were reimbursed by the trading company for the wages and maintenance of these men, whom Le Jeune stated explicitly "we keep with us so they may not become debauched among the Indians and offer a bad example, as did those who were here formerly" (Thwaites 1896–1901, 6:83). In the early days of the renewed Huron mission, these tasks were carried out by hired men, who also performed domestic chores for the Jesuits. Seculars were preferred to lay brothers, as the latter were forbidden to carry guns, which were essential for hunting and to reassure the Huron that the French desired to protect them (21 : 293).

The Jesuits' obvious involvement in the Huron fur trade added apparent substance to widespread charges that the order as a whole was profiting from this trade. These rumours were sufficiently damaging that the Jesuits found it necessary to deny them publicly in the *Relation* of 1642–43. They also appended to that relation a letter from the directors and associates of the Compagnie des Cent-Associés stating that they were in no way involved in the administration of the company or in the trafficking that was carried on by it (25 : 75–79). There is no evidence that the Jesuits were exporting furs from New France or making money at the expense of the company. Instead, they were unobtrusively selling their furs to the trading company, either directly or indirectly, at the fixed price that was set for the purchase of all furs.

There is, however, no doubt that within Canada the Jesuits, like other colonists, derived some profit from trading in furs, which were the principal medium of exchange. The concern that the Jesuits expressed in 1645 about a declaration to the effect that henceforth no one was to be allowed to trade for furs with the Indians (27 : 99) suggests that this internal trade was of considerable financial importance to them (Jaenen 1970). Some of the furs the Jesuits sold to the company were given to them as gifts by converts. Others were purchased from the Indians at lower rates than the company would have paid; yet, if such sales saved the Indians the trouble of carrying these furs to the St. Lawrence, they probably did not view them as a bad bargain. It is known that the Jesuits shipped wampum beads, elk skins, and other items to the Huron country in order to exchange them for things they needed (Thwaites 1896–1901, 9 : 175). This trade may have been extended to include the purchase of beaver pelts.

The Jesuits pointed out that they were compelled to give the Indians considerable quantities of trade goods as presents and in return for favours, while the profits that they made no more than compensated them for the twenty-five percent markup on goods imported from France (9 : 173). Whatever profits they made, even when combined with the subsidies they received from the trading company, were insufficient to support the Jesuit missions in Canada without substantial donations from well-wishers in France. In 1672 Frontenac was to repeat Jacques Michel's accusation that the Jesuits were more interested in beavers than saving souls, and through him this remark has passed into history (Delanglez 1939). More recently the Jesuits have been described as clerks of the fur trade and agents of French imperialism, thereby implying that such activities were their primary aims (Hunt 1940:70–71). Francis Parkman (1927:466) was undoubtedly much closer to the truth when he concluded that "to impute mercenary motives [to the Canadian Jesuits] is manifestly idle." The Jesuits undoubtedly managed their finances in a resourceful way and saw the success of their mission as related to the general prosperity of New France, but economic and political considerations remained for them means to ends rather than ends in themselves. The driving ambition of the Jesuits during the first half of the seventeenth century was to use rational and worldly means to achieve other-worldly ends. The behaviour of the Jesuits in New France makes sense only if viewed in terms of counter-reformationary zeal.

Three Jesuits were sent to Quebec in 1632 to lay the foundations for future work in the colony. Their leader was Father Paul Le Jeune, who was to remain the Jesuit superior at Quebec until 1639. A youthful convert to Roman Catholicism, Le Jeune was one of many young Jesuits who had been exposed to Father Massé's enthusiasm for the Canadian missions while studying at the Jesuit college at La Flèche. In addition to formulating clear policies for the Jesuit mission in New France, Le Jeune's first report, dispatched to the French Provincial of the Society of Jesus in August 1632, became the prototype for the annual *Jesuit Relations*, which continued to be published until 1673, and upon which so much of our knowledge of the history of this period is based. The aim of these duodecimal volumes was to disseminate knowledge of Jesuit mission work in Canada among well-to-do Frenchmen and to encourage temporal and spiritual aid for this work. While this influenced the selection of material that appeared in the *Jesuit Relations*, it does not prevent them from being used as reliable, though partial, sources of information about this period. Le Jeune was accompanied by Father de Noüe, who was to serve at Quebec and Three Rivers until his death in 1646, and by lay brother Gilbert Burel, who had first come to Canada in 1625.

The Huron, who probably had learned the previous year that the French were likely to return to Canada in 1632, came to Quebec that year in fifty canoes (Thwaites 1896–1901, 5:71). Le Jeune's statement that they made a fine sight upon the river suggests that unlike their usual custom, these Huron travelled together. They probably did this to defend themselves against the Mohawk and so they might better confront unexpected developments at Quebec. Although the Huron do not appear to have brought an unusual number of furs with them, they were no doubt anxious to obtain trade goods to make up for the small trade the year before. While Aman-tacha travelled with the Huron and impressed the Jesuits with his intelligence and knowledge of Roman Catholicism, no mention is made of Brûlé. No doubt, as a self-proclaimed traitor whom Champlain had already threatened with exemplary punishment, he was afraid to put in an appearance. There is no mention of any formal ceremony to reaffirm the French-Huron alliance and it appears that the Huron were more anxious to sound out the French than to conclude new treaties with them. Referring to their negotiations, Le Jeune said that it was impossible to describe "how cunning this nation is" (5:73).

Brûlé's Murder

In the spring of 1633 Brûlé was murdered at Toanché. Sagard, writing in France, stated that he was condemned to death and eaten by the Huron (Sagard 1866:431). This has given rise to much lurid speculation about how and why a man who had known the Huron for twenty-three years suddenly should have been killed by them. The most popular suggestion is that he was tortured to death because of some sexual indiscretion;[5] though, given the nature of Huron attitudes towards sex, it is difficult to imagine a less likely reason. Moreover, the fact that Brûlé was given a proper burial indicates that he was not tortured or eaten, as Sagard imagined. While the burial of his body in the earth and away from the regular cemetery may have been done in imitation of the burial the Huron had seen the French give Guillaume Chaudron a decade earlier (Thwaites 1896–1901, 10:305), interment was the traditional form of burial for anyone who had died a violent death. Brébeuf spoke of Brûlé being barbarously and treacherously murdered (8:93), but not as having been eaten by the Huron.

The reason for Brûlé's murder was not made clear until 1641. When Fathers Brébeuf and Chaumonot visited the Neutral confederacy, the Huron grew concerned about their trading monopoly and a rumour began to spread that the missionaries had gone south to make an alliance with the Seneca in order to harm the Huron. The Jesuits report that "some [Huron] warned us privately to beware of this undertaking as there had been no other cause for the murder of one of our Frenchmen that occurred here some years ago, than just such journeys which made the country uneasy and fearful of a transference of trade" (21:211). Since Brûlé was the only Frenchman whom the Huron had killed, it seems certain that this account refers to him (Talbot 1956:227), and this, in turn, makes it clear that his murder was not a crime of passion or a senseless butchery, but a political assassination. Brûlé was killed because certain Huron knew or believed him to be dealing with the Seneca, or some other tribe whose rivalry the Huron feared. In 1616 he had lived among the Seneca for several months and, on leaving, had promised that he would make peace between them, the Huron, and the French. Thus the Huron's fears may have been far from groundless.

What is less certain is what Brûlé was planning to do. He may have been trying to persuade the Seneca to trade with the French, hoping that if he succeeded, Champlain would pardon him for his dealings with the English. This policy would almost certainly have earned him the undying hatred of the Huron headmen, who did not want their worst enemies to become rival trading partners with the French. The Huron would have been as determined to prevent the conclusion of an alliance between the Seneca and the French as the Mohawk had been to prevent one between the Dutch and the northern Algonkians. Alternatively, Brûlé may have surmised that Champlain was implacable and, knowing that the Jesuits were determined to get rid of him, he may have decided to defect to the Iroquois and work for the Dutch. Such a switch in political allegiance was not unknown among the *coureurs de bois* of later decades.

The individual who was believed to be chiefly responsible for Brûlé's murder was an important northern Attignawantan headman who bore the hereditary name Aenons. Unfortunately, a certain amount of mystery surrounds the identity of this man. At the time of Brûlé's death, Aenons appears to have been living in Toanché; later he resided in Wenrio, one of the two villages into which Toanché divided. His influence, however, extended beyond Toanché. In 1636 he presided over the torture of an Iroquois prisoner at Arenté (Thwaites 1896–1901, 13:61). The same year he played a leading role in the preparations for the Feast of the Dead that the Attignawantan were about to celebrate (10:305) and in the negotiations for reuniting certain northern Attignawantan villages (10:235–43). He claimed that it was he who had brought Etienne Brûlé to the country (10:309). Even if this only means that it was he who arranged that Brûlé should live among the Attignawantan rather than the Arendarhonon, it suggests that Aenons was connected with the fur trade at an early period.

Aenons's position as a council chief among the northern Attignawantan and his connections with the fur trade help to account for the leading role he appears to have played in Brûlé's murder. Indeed, given the grave implications of an assassination of this sort, it appears unlikely that any northern Attignawantan would have dared to do it if he had not been sanctioned by a leading headman who was credited with a special understanding of Huron relations with the French. All of this suggests that Aenons was the principal headman of the northern Attignawantan, which would make him the same person as, or the successor of, Auoindaon, who was the principal headman of this grouping at the time of Sagard's visit. Although the two names seem quite different, it is significant that there is no mention of Auoindaon after 1630, while Aenons is not mentioned before that time.

This identification is, however, beset by problems. Throughout his long sojourn among the Attignawantan, Brûlé was associated with the village of Toanché, where Aenons was living at the time of Brûlé's murder. If Aenons had brought Brûlé to the Attignawantan country after 1615, it seems likely that he would have taken him to his own village. On the other hand, in 1623 Auoindaon was living, not in Toanché, but in Quieunonascaran (Wrong 1939:174). As we have seen, however, sometime after 1623 Quieunonascaran split apart and became three hamlets, although these were still located near to one another (Thwaites 1896–1901, 13:125). It is significant that when the Jesuits were planning to return to the Huron country in 1633, Toanché and Ossossané were rivals to receive them, while Quieunonascaran, although it had been the first Huron village to have a resident priest, made no such effort. This suggests that Quieunonascaran not only had split apart but had declined in political importance. It may be that as Quieunonascaran declined, Aenons and his clan segment moved to Toanché, which, in any case, was more favourably located for trading with the French than was Quieunonascaran.[6]

Another problem is Aouandoïé, who in 1634 was living in Ihonatiria, the other of the two villages into which Toanché had split (8:93–97). He is described as having been one of the wealthiest Huron. Although he does not appear to have been a headman of any significance, it has been suggested that he, rather than Aenons, was the descendant or namesake of Auoindaon (E. Jury 1966e). While one would still have to account for why he moved from Quieunonascaran to Toanché, it is possible that sometime between 1623 and 1633 the leadership of the northern Attignawantan shifted from one leader to another. If Aenons was not Auoindaon's legitimate successor, he had managed to supplant him as the leader of the northern Attignawantan. By 1633 Aenons was clearly recognized by all the Huron as the spokesman for this group.

Not all of the Huron, or even all of the people of Toanché, approved of Brûlé's murder. We are informed that the dissensions it aroused led to the abandonment of Toanché and the founding of Wenrio and Ihonatiria (Thwaites 1896–1901, 5:255). This split was probably between clan segments that supported the murder and those that were anxious to disclaim responsibility for it. It is unlikely, however, that a headman of Aenons's standing would have permitted Brûlé to be slain unless he had been certain that the French were unlikely to demand satisfaction for his death. No doubt, one of the things that Amantacha and the other Huron who visited Quebec in 1632 sought to determine was whether Brûlé was still regarded as a traitor. From what they were told, Aenons may have concluded that Brûlé was no longer protected by the French-Huron alliance and thus felt free to kill him because of his dealings with the Iroquois. Other Huron may not have felt so certain and, in spite of repeated French assertions that Brûlé's death meant nothing to them, these latter continued to express anxiety about it for a long time to come. In spite of the murder, a very large number of Huron decided to travel to Quebec in 1633, where their headmen could conclude a new alliance with Champlain, who was expected to return from France that year. Their aim was to repeat the formal initiation of an alliance as this had been done on Montreal Island in 1611. The one headman who absented himself from this journey, on the plea that he had business elsewhere, was Aenons (10:237–39). Even he saw no point in taking chances.

The New Alliance

The Compagnie des Cent-Associés never recovered from the many losses it suffered, beginning with the disaster of 1628. To reduce their obligations, in 1632 the associates agreed to lease their trading rights for the next five years to a private association that had Jean de Lauson as its director. Thus, once again, merchants were in control of the company and its obligations to settle New France were to go unfulfilled (Lanctot 1963:151). The Jesuits were less concerned about this than the Recollets would have been, since colonization was not of such direct importance to their missionary program as it had been to that of the Recollets. While the Jesuits did what they could to establish schools, hospitals, and even an Indian reserve at Quebec, their program assisted, rather than sought to undermine, that of the company. In 1633 three English vessels continued to trade at Tadoussac, suggesting to the Montagnais that free trade had been restored on the St. Lawrence. This was, however, the last year that such vessels would visit

New France. On 22 May 1633 Champlain returned to Quebec having been appointed not Governor, as he had wished, but Commander of New France in the absence of Cardinal Richelieu.

After Ventadour became Viceroy of New France, Champlain had gradually shifted his allegiance from the Recollets to the Jesuits, though he must have found the latter's mission program far less congenial to his own aspirations. In 1626 he invited Charles Lalemant to become his confessor (Thwaites 1896–1901, 4:227), and it has been suggested that he allowed the last edition of his *Voyages* to be revised and put through the press by a Jesuit editor.[7] Great prominence is given in this publication to the Jesuits, while there is no longer such lavish praise for the early missionary work done by the Recollets. After his return to New France Champlain attempted to run the habitation along quasi-religious lines, having the lives of the saints read at supper, presiding over public self-examination and prayers each evening, and ordering the angelus to be sounded according to church custom (6:103). On his deathbed in 1635, he was to forget his wife and make the Virgin Mary his heiress.

Yet, in spite of the control that the Jesuits exercised over him in the last years of his life, they do not seem to have regarded him as an indispensable ally. Champlain was to die not knowing that Charles Huault de Montmagny had already been appointed Governor of New France, and was to arrive in Quebec the following spring with orders to relieve him of his command. Montmagny was a knight of the Order of Malta, had been educated by the Jesuits, and was very well disposed towards them. From the Jesuits' point of view, no better appointment could have been made. Under Montmagny's administration, the closest possible coordination of Jesuit policy and that of the vice-regal administration was to be achieved.

Two days after he had returned to Quebec in 1633, Champlain met a group of Montagnais from Three Rivers, who were accompanying their headman, Capitanal, down-river to Tadoussac (8:55). Champlain pleased these Montagnais by promising to defend them against the Iroquois and telling them that the French planned to establish a settlement at Three Rivers which would protect the Indians in that area. The Montagnais' enthusiasm cooled, however, when Champlain let them know that he would be very displeased if any of them were to attempt to trade with the English at Tadoussac. Capitanal replied that he would tell his people that they should not go there, but that it was difficult to restrain young men and there was no guarantee that he would be obeyed (5:209). While stressing his friendship for the French, Capitanal warned Champlain that if the French attempted to re-introduce their trading monopoly, this would anger the Indians and might lead to acts of violence, as it had done on two previous occasions (5:211).

In the following weeks, the French were heartened to see that in spite of the danger of Iroquois attacks, Algonkians, among them a group of Nipissing accompanied by Jean Nicollet, were coming down the St. Lawrence River to trade. Not long before, the French had experienced the Iroquois menace on the upper St. Lawrence firsthand. A party travelling up the St. Lawrence to meet Indian traders had been ambushed by thirty to forty Iroquois who scalped two Frenchmen and discharged a hail of arrows at the rest. The Iroquois were only prevented from boarding the shallop that the dead men had been towing when they were fired on and when they saw that a larger vessel was closing in on them (5:213–15). This attack demonstrated that the Mohawk were once again active in the St. Lawrence Valley and that their fear of Europeans had diminished. Greater familiarity with firearms, as well as their victory over Van Krieckenbeeck, may have contributed to this confidence.

The determination of the French to reinforce their trading monopoly soon had its familiar consequences. The Montagnais at Tadoussac were displeased by the resurgent power of the French traders (7:61) and on 2 July a Frenchman who was washing his clothes at Quebec was attacked and killed by a Weskarini Algonkin. The assailant had allegedly been planning to kill a certain Iroquois when he went to war, but, being in a drunken condition, he had attacked and killed a Frenchman instead (5:223–25). The Indians claimed that this was an unfortunate accident for which the alcohol of the French was responsible. The fact, however, that it followed so closely a warning that violence might occur if the French attempted to interfere with free trade, indicated that the resentment and hostility that had been felt towards the French monopolists prior to 1629 were still very strong. Even allowing for the drunken condition of the Indian, it is unlikely that this murder would have occurred had the Algonkians been generally well disposed towards the French. To make matters worse, two Montagnais informed the French who the murderer was and Champlain had the accused arrested and imprisoned him in the fort. Champlain's refusal to accept a reparations payment as a settlement for the killing or to release the man greatly angered the Algonkin, as similar action had done among the Montagnais in 1628–29.

The same day this murder was committed Amantacha arrived at Quebec. Although he was accompanied only by a few Huron (5:225), his arrival pleased the French who feared that the threat of Iroquois attacks might have dissuaded the Huron from travelling down-river that year (5:191–93,

219). In the course of his stay, Amantacha carefully sounded out the French before telling them that Brûlé had been murdered and that a great number of Huron had come down-river but that they were reluctant to appear at Quebec unless they knew that Champlain would not punish them for Brûlé's murder. Champlain informed him that Brûlé was no longer regarded as French because he had gone over to the service of the English (5:241). He asked Amantacha to return to the other traders, who were in the Ottawa Valley, and persuade them to continue their journey to Quebec.

When Amantacha reached these traders they already knew about the murder that had been committed at Quebec. The Algonkin were warning them that if they attempted to trade with the French, Champlain would condemn one or more of them to death to avenge Brûlé, just as he was planning to kill the Weskarini he had arrested (5:239–41). The Huron leaders knew that the Algonkin were anxious to purchase Huron furs at a low rate of exchange so that they themselves could carry them to the French and English (5:241). They were therefore not inclined to believe the Algonkin; nevertheless they wanted assurance that it was safe for them to go to Quebec. Amantacha's reassurances were such that all but a few Huron who had lost their furs gambling decided to continue on their journey (5:241). In spite of the crisis that had arisen, the Algonkin were unable to regain their role as middlemen. Soon groups of seven to twelve Huron canoes began to arrive at Quebec and, finally, on 28 July an immense fleet of 140 canoes appeared, carrying an estimated 500 to 700 Huron (5:239). While the reports of these figures may be inflated, they suggest that this was the largest number of Huron ever to travel to the St. Lawrence in a single year. The reason was not only the danger of Mohawk attack but also because sixty or more headmen and elders accompanied this expedition. The safety of so many leading men must have been of exceptional concern to the Huron; hence they were accompanied by many warriors.

Four more Jesuits arrived at Quebec in 1633. These were Fathers Brébeuf and Massé, who sailed from Dieppe with Champlain, and Antoine Daniel and Ambroise Davost, who had spent the previous winter on Cape Breton Island. The wish of the Jesuits was that Brébeuf, Daniel, and Davost should proceed to the Huron country as soon as possible, accompanied by three hired labourers. Antoine Daniel had been born in 1601 and had studied law before he entered the Jesuit novitiate at Rouen in 1621. Between 1623 and 1627, he had taught junior classes at Rouen and it is possible that Amantacha was one of his pupils. Thereafter he studied theology at Clermont, and taught and was minister in the College at Eu before leaving for the New World. Ambroise Davost had been born in 1586, became a Jesuit in 1611, and had studied principally at Bourges.

Brébeuf and Le Jeune asked Amantacha to help them gain approval from the Huron to renew their mission work among his people. Being a young man, Amantacha lacked the authority to discuss such matters, but he assured the Jesuits that many Huron were anxious for Brébeuf to return and promised to transport one of them in his own canoe. He also asked for an illustrated religious book to show to his countrymen and wrote letters of respect to the Jesuit provincial in France and to various other Frenchmen (5:245). The training that he had received in France was not yet lost on him.

The day after the Huron arrived in strength at Quebec, their headmen and elders held a general council with the French. Those from each tribe and village sat near one another on the ground (5:247), while the younger men, who did not have a voice in the proceedings, stood about looking on. Champlain attended as the chief representative of the French and the Jesuits were accorded a prominent place in the assembly. The meeting began with the chief spokesman for the Huron announcing that his people regarded the French as their friends and brothers and that the purpose of the assembly was to strengthen the alliance between them. As proof of his sincerity, he presented Champlain with several packages of beaver skins amidst general expressions of approval (5:249). While the Huron sought to renew their alliance, they expressed no regret about the killing of Brûlé, nor did they offer any condolences or reparations presents. No doubt, they accepted Champlain's denunciation of Brûlé as a traitor as indicating that the French did not claim the right to expect such observances.

Through an interpreter Champlain reassured the Huron that he had always loved them and that his king had ordered him to do all he could to protect them. This was the reason he had sent the vessels up the St. Lawrence River that had been attacked by the Iroquois. He also admonished the Huron not to listen to rumours that were being spread by tribes who were trying to make them fear the French and break off trading with them. Champlain described to the Huron in what high esteem the Jesuits were held by the French and how their aim, in wanting to live with the Huron, was not to promote trade with other tribes but to instruct them, as Amantacha could verify. Champlain stated that if the Huron loved the French, they would allow the Jesuits to live with them. He thereby implied that the Huron's acceptance of the Jesuits, and their continued good treatment of them, were necessary conditions for the renewal of the French-Huron alliance.

The Huron had always been pleased to have Frenchmen living in their country to protect their villages and vouch for the good treatment of Huron who went to the St. Lawrence to trade. This, however, was the first time that the French had implied that the acceptance of specific individuals was a necessary condition of this alliance. The Huron did not reply specifically to this proposal, the novelty of which made it something that would have to be discussed by the confederacy council before a formal reply could be given. Instead, two headmen reaffirmed their respect for Champlain and their goodwill towards the Jesuits. The council ended with Brébeuf delivering a speech in the Huron language, in which he stated that the Jesuits wanted to spend the rest of their lives in the Huron country and become a part of the Huron people. He assured the Huron that the Jesuits were equally well disposed towards all of them, but pointed out that because the missionaries were still few in number, they could not live everywhere. He promised that the time was not far off when one priest would be stationed in each village (5:253). This promise, which was meant to prevent undue envy among the Huron villages, was met with general approval.

Even if the Huron were not particularly anxious to have the missionaries return with them at this time, once it became clear that Champlain was insisting that they be embarked, competition arose concerning where they would settle. The Huron from Toanché offered to provide transport for the Jesuits if they would agree to live with them. They pointed out that this would demonstrate that the French had truly forgiven these people for the death of Brûlé and might put an end to the schism that had led to the establishment of two separate villages. The traders asked if the Jesuits wished to live with the Indians or in a separate house and, when they were informed that the Jesuits preferred the latter, they promised to erect such a house for them, around which they might reassemble their village (5:255).

Anenkhiondic, the headman of Ossossané, talked with Father Brébeuf in private and tried to persuade him to settle in that town. He pointed out the importance of Ossossané, which was the principal town of the Attignawantan, who, in turn, were the largest and most important tribe in the Huron confederacy (5:259). He also offered to transport as many French to the Huron country as Brébeuf wished to send there. Brébeuf discussed this offer with Le Jeune and they concluded that since Ossossané was the place where most meetings of the confederacy council took place, mission work should begin there (5:261).

In order not to offend other communities, Brébeuf persuaded Champlain to announce that it was his desire that all the French going to the Huron country should settle in Ossossané under Brébeuf's direction and control. This proclamation satisfied everybody except the people of Toanché, whose headman protested vigorously. In an attempt to soothe his feelings, Brébeuf asked the leading Huron to gather once more in council. The men from Toanché refused to attend and reproached Anenkhiondic with having been the cause of the French not agreeing to go to their village. As a result of this attack, Anenkhiondic withdrew his offer to furnish passage to any of the Jesuits, giving as an excuse that his canoe was manned only by inexperienced young men. It was decided that as a compromise, canoes from other villages should help to carry the Jesuits and their secular assistants up-river. Since the French gave presents to Huron who provided passage in their canoes, this arrangement meant that these presents would be distributed more evenly among the tribes and villages that made up the confederacy (5:259–63).

After several days were spent trading, Champlain provided a great feast for the Huron on 3 August. Corn soup flavoured with peas, bread crumbs, and prunes was served to the guests, who showed their appreciation with much singing and dancing (5:267). The following day, which was the one before the Huron were to leave for home, another council was held at which Champlain distributed presents corresponding in trade value to the furs that the Huron had given him a week earlier (6:7). At this council Champlain attempted to settle the final details concerning the departure of the Jesuits for the Huron country. The Huron asked that as a favour to them, the Algonkin prisoner should be released. Champlain explained that according to French law, this was not a proper thing to do. When it became apparent that he would not change his mind, the Huron did not press the matter. They spoke of their alliance with the French and said that if having the Jesuits come to live in their country would strengthen the alliance, they would be happy to take them. Those who were to embark the Jesuits were given their presents in advance and the baggage that was to accompany the Jesuits was entrusted to them (6:7).

Prior to this council, a meeting had been held at which the Algonkin and Montagnais headmen had asked the Huron to secure the release of the Algonkin whom Champlain was holding prisoner. Although the Huron were reluctant to become involved in this affair, had they refused this request they would have endangered seriously their relations with their eastern neighbours. They therefore asked the French for his release, though they made the request in a rather half-hearted manner. The night after this request had been rejected, Tessouat visited the Huron camp and warned them not to embark any Frenchmen in their canoes because the relatives of the prisoner were watching along the Ottawa River and planned to kill any French they could in retaliation for what Champlain had done (6:7–9). This resulted in feverish consultation between the Huron and their Indian allies.

The next morning, the Huron delayed their departure and Champlain met all the Indians who were at Quebec. Tessouat pointed out that if any Huron were killed while attempting to defend the French who were travelling with them, it would lead to a blood feud between the Huron on the one hand and the Weskarini and their Algonkin allies on the other. This implied that either Champlain had to release his prisoner or the Huron must not be allowed to take any Frenchmen home with them. If the French had agreed to the first option, the Algonkin, under Tessouat's leadership, would have won a significant victory; if they did not the French-Huron alliance, at least in Algonkin eyes, would have been that much weaker. The Huron, for their part, said they would be pleased to have the Jesuits in their country, but the Ottawa River did not belong to them and the feelings of the Algonkin had to be respected if they were to travel safely through their territory (6:11). Champlain threatened that he would punish the Algonkin if they did not behave better, but he was mockingly reminded that under French law the Indians who were at Quebec could not be held responsible for the behaviour of the prisoner's kinsmen.

In a final effort to persuade the Algonkin to relent, Le Jeune publicly requested that Champlain pardon the prisoner. This was done, however, by pre-arrangement. Champlain replied that he could not do this, but agreed to suspend the execution of the sentence until he could learn the king's pleasure in this matter. Le Jeune then addressed the Huron and Algonkin, pointing out that the Jesuits did not desire the man's death and, for this reason, his kinsmen should let them travel up the Ottawa River. Tessouat was in no way deceived by these amateur dramatics and informed the Jesuits that they could not travel to the Huron country until the prisoner was released. Champlain became furious and said he would not give in to blackmail of this sort; until the Algonkin learned to behave "properly," he gave his men permission to fire on any of them seen bearing arms (6:15). This outburst effectively put an end to any hope that the Jesuits would reach the Huron country in 1633. Champlain and Le Jeune agreed that nothing should be done that might lead to further conflict between the Huron and Algonkin, since such conflict would seriously damage the fur trade and the prosperity of New France (6:17). The Jesuits and the Huron parted on good terms, with both sides expressing the hope that the Jesuits would be able to travel to the Huron country the following year.

It is impossible to unravel the full web of intrigue that lies behind these events. No doubt, the Algonkin would have liked to put an end to all direct trade between the French and the Huron, provided that they did not consequently expose themselves to attack by the Iroquois. The simplest way of halting this trade would have been for the Algonkin to have provoked a war with the Huron. Such a war was impossible, however, for two reasons. Firstly, the Huron greatly outnumbered the Algonkin and they probably could have counted on the French for support. Secondly, if the Algonkin were at war with the Huron, they could not have profited from being middlemen between the Huron and the French.

It is reasonable to conclude that a wily politician like Tessouat did not aim to cut off all trade between the French and the Huron. He probably hoped, however, that by preventing the French from travelling to and from the Huron country, he could exact higher tolls from the Huron and prevent the re-establishment of the close relationship that had formerly existed between these trading partners. This would make it easier to sow distrust and anxiety among Huron traders and to dissuade some of them from travelling to the St. Lawrence, thus allowing the Algonkin to regain control of at least part of the fur trade that was currently in the hands of the Huron.

The intentions of the Huron headmen are more difficult to fathom. Did they prefer to have French seculars living with them, but decide that if Champlain insisted that they take priests they would do so? Or did they fear that if they had Frenchmen living with them and a young Huron were to injure these guests, they would be compelled either to surrender this man to the French (which, by their own laws and customs, they could not do) or to break off relations with them? Some may have feared that Brûlé's murder had set a precedent that irresponsible persons might be tempted to imitate. Or was it that the Huron did not want the priests and found the crisis that had developed a good excuse for not having them?

Brébeuf seems to have been popular with the people of Toanché and they may have been pleased that he wished to return to their country. On the other hand, the clear preference that the Huron had for men who could bear arms had not diminished (7:217). Moreover, for all the respect the Huron had for the priests' shamanistic powers, many probably still suspected them of being sorcerers and were annoyed by their persistent refusal to live with Huron families. Le Jeune believed that the desire expressed by the Huron to have the Jesuits in their country was largely feigned because Champlain insisted that the renewal of the alliance required the Huron to allow the Jesuits to live among them (6:19–21). The Huron may have hoped that by the following year Champlain would have reconsidered the matter, and men more to their liking would be sent to them.

It is unreasonable to assume that all of the Huron headmen shared the same opinions. Given the unsettled conditions that followed Brûlé's murder, the Huron may have found the turmoil at Quebec a convenient excuse for delay and for avoiding still more argument and division concerning with whom the Jesuits should live. Whatever they thought of the Jesuits, most Huron probably felt that such an exchange was premature until the new alliance had been ratified by the confederacy council and confirmed by another round of visits.

The Defeat of the Algonkin

The resumption of French patrols on the St. Lawrence combined with other factors to produce a reorientation of Mohawk foreign policy that was decidedly to the advantage of the French. For some time the Mohawk and Oneida had been annoyed by the high prices that the Dutch were charging for trade goods. Their anger reached the boiling point, however, when Hans Jorissen Hontom was appointed the new commissary at Fort Orange. Hontom was a trader who appears to have kidnapped a Mohawk council chief and murdered him by castration (Trelease 1960:51; Grassmann 1969:44). In October 1633 the Mohawk attacked the Dutch settlement, burned the trading company's yacht, and killed most of the cattle at Rensselaerswyck. The Dutch realized the weakness of their position and immediately acted to improve their relations with the Iroquois tribes (Van Laer 1908:302–4, 330). In spite of this, the eastern tribes remained fearful of Dutch reprisals and, being determined to reduce the price of trade goods through competition, were anxious to re-establish an alternative trading relationship with the French. The first step in doing this was for the Mohawk and Oneida to make peace with the Algonkin and Montagnais.

By a curious conjunction of circumstances, the turmoil at Quebec provided the Algonkin with pressing reasons for wanting to diversify their trading relations at this time. Tessouat, in particular, believed that a treaty which made it possible for his people to secure European goods either from the Mohawk or the Dutch would greatly strengthen his position when it came to bargaining with Champlain. A formal treaty was concluded with the Mohawk in the autumn of 1634, after the Montagnais released an Iroquois prisoner they had captured recently (8:23–25; map 22). News of this treaty caused great anxiety among the French as well as the Dutch. Both began to distrust the loyalty of their Indian trading partners, and feared what the other stood to gain from it. The Dutch knew that the Mohawk were making peace with the Algonkin in hopes of being able to trade with the French (Jameson 1909:139), and, while Le Jeune attributed the desire of the Algonkin for peace to weariness of war (Thwaites 1896–1901, 8:25), the French traders feared that the Algonkin were once again being seduced by the wampum traders at Fort Orange. Any arrangement that made it possible for the Algonkin to obtain trade goods from the Hudson Valley, whether from the Dutch or from the Iroquois, was seen as making the Algonkin that much more difficult to control.

It is clear, however, that this treaty, unlike the one negotiated in 1624, involved neither the French nor the Dutch and therefore gave neither Indian group the right to trade with the other's European partner. No doubt the Algonkin and Mohawk hoped that this peace would eventually permit them to trade with the Dutch and the French respectively, but, while both sides wanted this privilege for themselves, neither was willing to see it extended to the other. The main advantage of this treaty was that, given the difficulties that the Algonkin and Mohawk were having with their respective trading partners, it allowed them to obtain European goods from each other. Unsatisfactory as this arrangement might have been in the long run, for the moment it lessened both groups' dependence on their European trading partners and gave them additional bargaining power in their dealings with them.

The Mohawk, however, enjoyed one advantage that the Algonkin did not. The Dutch accepted that in their present state they were not strong enough to risk a confrontation with the Mohawk. Therefore, however much they wished to develop trade with the Algonkian-speaking peoples to the north, they knew that this was impossible so long as the Mohawk were opposed to it (Van Laer 1908:248). The French traders, on the other hand, were seeking not only to regain but also to expand their former trading network. One manifestation of this was the dispatch of Jean Nicollet on his famous voyage to the shores of Green Bay, Wisconsin in July 1634. Historians have speculated that the purpose of this trip was to prevent a trading alliance between the Winnebago and the Dutch, to find a route to China (since he took with him a robe of Chinese damask), or to take possession of copper mines around the upper Great Lakes.[8] None of these

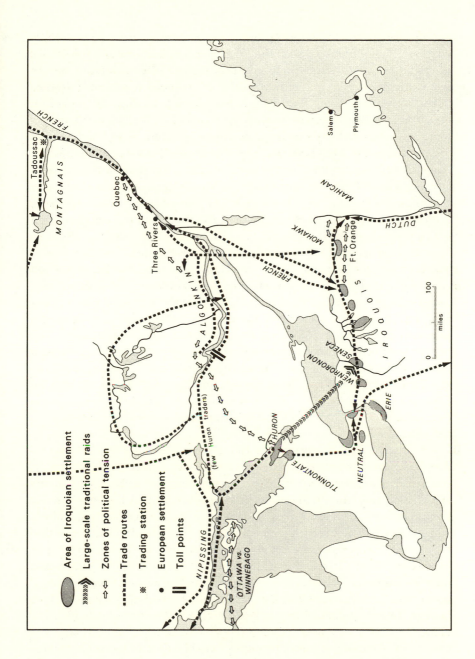

MAP 22. *Intertribal relations, 1634.*

explanations is at all convincing, however. The stated aim of his journey was to negotiate peace between the Winnebago and the Ottawa,[9] no doubt so the latter could resume trading in this region. It is uncertain whether this particular conflict was only with the Winnebago or extended to other tribes; however, in 1632 Le Jeune reports having baptized at Quebec an "Assistaronon" child whose parents had been captured in war and tortured to death by the Algonkin (Thwaites 1896–1901, 5:73). Even if the term Assistaronon were here being applied to the Winnebago, this passage suggests that the conflict had wider ramifications than are commonly attributed to it. It appears that the truce Nicollet arranged came to an end sometime before June 1636. It was then that the headman of the Amiskou, or Beaver band of the Ottawa, requested the French to provide protection for his people; two of whom had been eaten by the Winnebago (10:83).

In the summer of 1634 six French traders visited the Oneida and possibly the Onondaga and offered them high prices for their furs (Jameson 1909:148–54). It is not known whether these traders reached the Oneida by travelling overland or up the St. Lawrence River to Lake Ontario and then inland by way of the Oswego River to Lake Oneida (Crouse 1924:16). Interestingly enough, this remarkable journey is nowhere reported in the French sources and it took place only a year after Champlain had been formulating plans to subjugate or destroy the Mohawk. This suggests that the traders at Quebec were pursuing policies that ran counter to those of Champlain and that, for strategic reasons, they deemed it best to keep secret. Brûlé could have been involved in plans to extend these trading links to the Seneca.

When the Dutch learned about the activities of these French traders, they became alarmed and dispatched a surgeon named Harmen Meyndertsen van den Bogaert to investigate the situation. He visited the Mohawk and Oneida and found that both of these groups wanted higher prices for their furs, similar to those they said were being received by the Indians who traded with the French (Jameson 1909:139). He also discovered that they wanted peace so they could hunt safely in the Adirondacks. The Oneida praised the generosity of the French, but informed the Dutch that if they gave them better value for their furs and promised that the types of goods the Iroquois wanted would be on hand when they came to Fort Orange, they would be willing to trade exclusively with them (ibid. 151). Some Onondaga who were visiting the Oneida also promised that if the Dutch were willing to pay more, they would bring many skins to Fort Orange. They likewise promised to show the Dutch where the French came to trade each year on the St. Lawrence (ibid. 154), which suggests that at least some of them had visited this area along with the Oneida and the Mohawk. The Iroquois might have made these expressions of goodwill toward the Dutch simply as a matter of diplomacy. More likely, however, they regarded the truce with the Algonkin as temporary and were anxious to derive what benefits they could from it before the Dutch were once again their only trading partners.

In the spring of 1634 over 500 Huron went to attack a Seneca village, apparently in the style of their raid against the "Entouhonoron" in 1615. It is possible that this raid was undertaken to retaliate for the dealings that the Seneca had, or were suspected of having, with Brûlé. Unfortunately for the Huron, the Seneca learned of their plans and assembled a large force of warriors, which surprised the Huron as they were travelling south. In the ensuing conflict, over 200 Huron were killed and another hundred taken prisoner. Amantacha was among the latter, while Soranhes fled the battle and, although crippled by illness, eventually made his way home by way of the Neutral country. Amantacha managed to free himself, but only after the Iroquois had cut off one of his fingers (Thwaites 1896–1901, 7:213–15; 8:69, 139, 149, 151).

Rather than following up their victory by an attack on the Huron, the Seneca decided to entreat for peace. They spared the lives of their most important prisoners, and dispatched some of their headmen to discuss a treaty with the Huron (7:215). The Huron accepted their proposals and, in 1635, an embassy was sent to the Seneca to confirm the peace. The four other tribes of the Iroquois confederacy also expressed an interest in making peace with the Huron (8:115–17). This suggests that in spite of their remarkable victory, the Seneca did not feel free to treat the Huron with contempt. Conceivably, Seneca and other Iroquois had been taken prisoner by the Huron in recent years and their relatives hoped to recover them by means of a truce. In spite of this isolated defeat of the Huron, the peace that followed is evidence that a balance of power continued to exist between the Huron and the Iroquois.

After his return to Quebec, Champlain set about fortifying the colony and extending French control farther up the St. Lawrence River. A fort was built on Sainte Croix Island to guard the Richelieu Rapids and, in 1634, a settlement was established at Three Rivers, which hereafter was the main trading post for Indians who came from the interior. The same year, six more Jesuits arrived in New France, including Father Charles Lalemant. It was decided to try again to send Brébeuf, Daniel, and Davost to the Huron country. They were to be accompanied by four hired men, François Petit-Pré, Simon Baron, Robert Le Coq, and Dominique, and by two youths, Pierre and Martin. The latter were no doubt sent to learn the Huron language so that they might serve as interpreters and trading agents under Jesuit supervision.[10]

Unfortunately, because of the defeat they had suffered and their fear of further attacks by the Seneca, few Huron came to trade with the French in 1634 (7:215). Those who did ventured down-river in small parties after they had learned about the truce between the Iroquois and the Algonkin. While these traders had no doubt been given permission to come to Quebec by the headmen who controlled these routes, they do not seem to have included many influential Huron, or any men who were empowered to negotiate with the French or to make treaties with them. By 5 July only a small number of canoes had arrived at Three Rivers, some manned by Attigneenongnahac, others by Arendarhonon. These were insufficient to transport both the men the Jesuits wanted to send to the Huron country and the European goods that the Huron had come to purchase (8:71). In spite of this, the Jesuits persevered with their efforts to get to the Huron country. Father Brébeuf spoke to the Huron in private and persuaded them to take at least some Frenchmen home with them. When, however, an influential Kichesipirini called the Partridge heard about these promises, he publicly warned the Huron not to embark any Frenchmen. The clear implication was that the Weskarini were still prepared to kill any Frenchmen they found passing through their territory.

This threat frightened the Huron into withdrawing their offer. Du Plessis-Bochart, the chief clerk of the company and the general of its fleet, held a meeting with the Algonkin and tried to persuade them to drop their opposition to letting the Jesuits travel with the Huron. In spite of strong objections from the Partridge, the Algonkin eventually seemed won over by the presents that were offered to them (7:215–17; 8:71). The next morning, however, when the plan was discussed jointly by all the parties concerned, the Huron traders continued to demur, apparently because although the Algonkin now appeared to be well-disposed towards the French, they were secretly continuing to intimidate the Huron traders. Thus, while the Huron might have been willing to take armed Frenchmen with them, they were frightened to embark unarmed priests who might be killed on route, and whose deaths could involve the Huron in a blood feud with both the French and the Algonkin (7:217). Because of this, the Huron were unwilling to agree publicly to embark any Frenchmen for a journey into the interior.

After the meeting was over, however, one of the Attigneenongnahac invited Brébeuf to his cabin and announced that he was willing to risk taking three Frenchmen up-river, if the French would agree to trade his load of tobacco at a more favourable rate than usual (7:217). When Du Plessis-Bochart agreed to do this, the Arendarhonon became enthusiastic for a similar arrangement, and they too agreed to take three French (8:71). Presents were lavished on these Huron by the French and a feast was provided for them. Before they left, however, several Indians became ill and fear of sickness was used as an argument to reduce the number of French from six to three. The Huron's insistence that these should be two hired men and one priest shows that they were still frightened of the Algonkin and were having second thoughts about the offer they had made. Under great pressure from the French, the Huron were persuaded to take two priests and one hired man, although the priests had to promise to help paddle the canoes in which they were travelling. Thus, on 7 July Fathers Brébeuf and Daniel and the hired man Baron embarked for the Huron country, leaving behind instructions that if the others could make their way there, they should all gather at Ihonatiria, one of the successors of Toanché, the town Brébeuf knew best (7:219; 8:75, 99).

Additional small groups of Huron traders came to Three Rivers after the first ones had departed. Among these were one or more groups of Attigna-wantan, including Aenons, who was now willing to trust his life to the French. He is reported to have been well treated and returned home convinced that the part he had played in Brûlé's death was not held against him. He is the only headman of note who is mentioned as visiting the St. Lawrence in 1634, and it may be that his visit was an exception prompted by his failure to come the year before. The other Attignawantan who is mentioned by name as being among those who visited Three Rivers was Oukhahitoüa from the village of Onnentisati (8:139). When these late-comers learned about the presents that had been lavished on the Attignee-nongnahac and the Arendarhonon for agreeing to take Frenchmen home with them, they were anxious to emulate their example. On 15 July Father Davost and two others embarked in three Huron canoes and eight days later the rest were able to leave Three Rivers with yet another party (7:221; 8:75).

The transportation to the Huron country that the Jesuits had secured by bribery, rather than with the approval of the confederacy council or in most cases even of individual headmen, turned out to be far from satisfactory. Because many of the Huron became ill, the Jesuits had to help paddle the canoes (7:225–27). Brébeuf, who was an experienced traveller, had a fairly uneventful passage; however, his Attigneenongnahac travel-ling companions complained about the weight of the equipment that he carried with him in order to celebrate the mass. He was also told that, at one point, the owner of his canoe had spoken of abandoning him, although he was treated with such affection that he doubted the truth of this story (8:83–85).

The other Frenchmen, who were unknown to the Huron and did not speak their language, had a much harder time. Father Daniel's companions decided to visit a settlement that was located away from the Ottawa River and, failing to find it, they were all on the verge of starvation (7:227). Later, his companions, many of whom were ill, proposed to leave him among the Kichesipirini, and were persuaded only with great difficulty to take him any farther. Finally, he encountered Anenkhiondic travelling in a canoe paddled by six men. This powerful headman rescued Daniel and took him to Ossossané (8:85).

Father Davost was well treated during the early stages of his journey (7:227), but later was robbed by his companions and left among the Kichesipirini. He was also compelled to throw away a little steel mill, many of the books, and most of the paper and linen he was carrying with him (8:81). The young men, Pierre and Martin, were abandoned on route, although the latter was left among the Nipissing, who travelled to the Huron country in September (8:81). The Huron also talked about abandoning Baron among the Kichesipirini (8:85) and, on the day that they arrived in the Huron country, his companions were prevented only by force of arms from robbing him of everything he had with him (8:81). In general, those who suffered least were the four hired men who were armed and thus were able to command the respect, if not the affection, of their travelling companions.

These difficulties must be viewed in a broader context. The year before, many Huron headmen had travelled to the St. Lawrence to renew their alliance with the French, but had decided that the situation was not propitious for the Jesuits to visit their country. The next year, only a few traders came down-river and although they had no sanction from their headmen to bring the Jesuits and their staff home with them, they were bribed by the French to accept them as passengers. Given the additional burden of widespread illness, it is not surprising that these Huron fulfilled their promises badly. The abandonment or threatened abandonment of individual Frenchmen among different Algonkin groups, particularly among the Kichesipirini, must have stemmed from their lack of confidence in dealing with these formidable people, who were both allies and competitors of the Huron. This weakness was compounded by the Huron traders' realization that they were not committed in advance to answer for the safety of the French to their own people. This attitude inadvertently had been encouraged by Du Plessis-Bochart's statement that he would not hold the Algonkin responsible for what happened to the Jesuits while they were living among the Huron (7:215–17). From this the Huron traders inferred that if they abandoned the Jesuits among the Algonkin, the latter, rather than themselves, would be held accountable for them by the French.

The French were unwise to commit themselves to Huron who lacked an understanding of intertribal relations or sufficient authority to assure the safety of the French who were travelling with them. It was also unwise for newly arrived Jesuits to travel with members of Huron tribes who knew that the Jesuits had no intention of coming to live with them. In this respect, it was significant that Anenkhiondic, who was the principal head-man of the Attignawantan, took Father Daniel into his canoe with such a warm display of friendship. If the last group of Frenchmen to travel up-river did so under Aenons's protection, this may explain why no particular difficulties are reported for at least three Frenchmen. In the final analysis, it appears that the difficulties that were experienced by the Jesuits at this time resulted from their impatience to reach the Huron country and their consequent circumvention of the alliance that assured their safety and good treatment.

Brébeuf arrived in the Huron country on 5 August and was left alone at the embarkation place for the village of Toanché, while his companions headed south to their homes in Attigneenongnahac territory. Finding the landing place deserted, and knowing that the people of Toanché had moved, Brébeuf had asked these Huron either to accompany him to the new village or to sleep on the beach and guard his belongings until he had made his presence known. Instead, they left Brébeuf with the assurance that someone was certain to find him (8:89–91). Brébeuf hid his packages in the woods and, taking with him what was most valuable, set out to find the people of Toanché. He passed the former village which, except for one longhouse, was in ruins and following a well-beaten trail he came to the new village of Ihonatiria.[11] There he was welcomed by many old friends and a band of young people helped him to fetch his baggage (8:93). That evening and the whole of the next day were spent receiving greetings, visits, and salutations from the people of the village (8:97).

On the following days, old acquaintances came to greet Brébeuf and to each of them he gave a small present as an expression of goodwill. These visitors complained of bad harvests during Brébeuf's absence and expressed the hope that his shamanistic powers would once again produce better ones. The traders of Ihonatiria interpreted Brébeuf's arrival as evidence that the

French bore them no ill will. They told him that the Algonkin and the inhabitants of other Huron villages had been telling them that if they went to trade with the French, the French would kill them in order to avenge Brûlé, but now that Brébeuf had returned, they would be able to trade without fear (8:99).

While waiting for all of the Frenchmen to arrive in the Huron country, Brebeuf decided to live in the house of Aouandoïé, who was one of the richest and most hospitable men in the village. Twice, when Toanché had caught fire, Aouandoïé's longhouse had been saved. In order to avoid any suspicion of witchcraft, he had distributed over 100 bushels of corn among his fellow villagers (8:95). Brébeuf was on good terms with this man and judged that his household would be the least inconvenienced by visitors who required food and shelter until they had their own cabin (8:93).

Brébeuf spent two weeks visiting other villages and assembling the French, who were arriving in different parts of the Huron country (8:99). These travels took Brébeuf at least as far as Ossossané, where Father Daniel had arrived on 9 August. Davost did not appear until 24 August and was in such a state of fatigue and dejection that it was feared he would not recover. For over a month and a half Brébeuf, the two other priests, and another Frenchman continued to live with Aouandoïé, while the rest were billeted with another household (8:97).

Once all the French had arrived in the Huron country, Brébeuf decided to make Ihonatiria their headquarters, at least for the near future. Although Ossossané had been the Jesuits' choice the year before, that community was planning to relocate the following spring; hence any decision to settle there immediately would have involved extra work for both the French and the Huron (8:101). Brébeuf was convinced that other advantages were to be gained by remaining in Ihonatiria. Its inhabitants were accustomed to priests, while those of Ossossané were not. Moreover, the close ties that Brébeuf had with them would make it easier for the French to work in Ihonatiria and gradually acquire a knowledge of the Huron language. Brébeuf feared that in Ossossané the young people would harass the newcomers and thus make it more difficult for them to become accustomed to working among the Huron (8:103). He also hoped that since the people of Ihonatiria had been exposed to Christian teachings longer than other Huron, more conversions might be expected there (8:101). Finally, if the Jesuits left Ihonatiria, this would be interpreted as evidence of French ill will and might frighten the villagers into abandoning their trade with the French (8:103).

Although it was the wrong time of year for building bark houses, presents were offered to the councils of Ihonatiria and Wenrio to encourage them to work together to erect on the outskirts of Ihonatiria a Huron-style longhouse in which the Jesuits and their workmen could live. The workers from Wenrio proceeded very slowly, since their headmen still hoped to persuade the Jesuits to live in their village. Their bad example discouraged the volunteers from Ihonatiria so greatly that the cabin was not finished until October. Its interior, which was about thirty-six feet long and eighteen to twenty feet wide, was divided into three compartments by the French. The first served as a storeroom, while the second was a general living room, work room, and bedroom. In the latter, the Jesuits set up a carpentry shop and their mill for grinding flour, though they soon discovered that they preferred maize that had been pounded, Huron-style, in a wooden mortar (8:111). The third room was a chapel. The carpentry of this house, and the furnishings that the Jesuits brought with them, greatly interested the Huron. In particular, they were impressed by the European-style doors that were placed at the entrance to the cabin and between the first and second rooms, by the mill, and by the clock (8:109). Visitors took turns working the mill and believed that because the clock made a noise, it was alive. For this reason, they called it the Headman of the Day and enquired about the kind of food it ate and what it was saying. The Jesuits found that by telling the Huron that when it sounded four times it was telling them to leave, they could assure themselves of being left alone after four o'clock (8:113).

While these novelties had been brought to the Huron country for their utilitarian value, the Jesuits had transported other items hither especially to interest the Huron. These included a lodestone, a glass that reflected a single object eleven times, and a phial in which a flea looked as big as a beetle. All of these things enhanced the reputation of the Jesuits as possessors of supernatural power, so that they came to be called ondaki. While the Jesuits were pleased to think that this increased the respect that the Huron had for their Christian teachings (8:109), such a reputation was two-edged, because the Huron believed that these powers could be used for evil purposes no less than for good ones.

By the autumn of 1634, it was clear that even if the Jesuits had not come to the Huron country with the consent of the Huron headmen, their arrival was welcomed as a pledge of French goodwill. The Jesuits' role as guests of the Huron was officially confirmed on 22 July 1635 at a council that was held between the Huron and the French at Quebec. The Huron travelled down-river rather than trading at Three Rivers, thereby showing that they attached much the same importance to this meeting as they had to the bigger one in 1633. Champlain again stressed the love that the French had for the Jesuits and other Frenchmen who were living among the Huron, and made it clear that if the Huron wished to maintain their trading alliance, they had to treat these men with respect. At Le Jeune's request, Champlain also told the Huron that in order to preserve and strengthen their friendship with the French, they must agree to become Christians and, the following year, they must bring many little boys to Quebec, whom the Jesuits would care for and instruct in a residential school they were planning to establish there. Champlain assured the Huron that if they became Christians, God would make them victorious over their enemies. He also promised that many French men would come to live in their country who would marry their daughters and teach the Huron how to make iron hatchets, knives, and other useful items (8:49).

Because the Huron believed Christianity to be only one more ritual society, the advantages they might derive from such an arrangement must have seemed very enticing. Moreover, the French traders assured the Huron that it was not necessary for them to become Christians at once; it was enough if they did so in four years (17:171). Thus by postponing the least comprehensible aspect of Champlain's proposal, these traders softened the demands that the Jesuits had persuaded them to make. Champlain asked the Huron to call a general council when they returned home at which Brébeuf could read a message that Champlain was addressing to their headmen. At this council Brébeuf would also present a goodwill present that the Jesuits in Quebec were sending to the council chiefs of the Huron confederacy. The Huron traders agreed to convey this message, but complained that while all the Huron cherished their friendship with the French, the Jesuits had decided to settle in only one village (8:49–51). They also agreed to take two more Jesuits, François-Joseph Le Mercier and Pierre Pijart, home with them. Although many Huron volunteered to take these priests, they travelled with individuals whom Brébeuf had designated in a letter as being particularly reliable.

The Algonkin did not cease their efforts to prevent the renewal of a close relationship between the French and the Huron. To undermine confidence in the Huron, the Kichesipirini began to accuse them of Father Viel's murder. This story was reported by Le Jeune as early as August 1634 (7:233) and may have been told to the French at Three Rivers when the Partridge was trying to dissuade the Jesuits from embarking for the Huron country. As Brébeuf was travelling to the Huron country, the Algonkin told him that the Huron would kill the Jesuits as they had killed Brûlé. They urged the Jesuits to break off the journey and remain with them, promising them that if they did they would be well treated (8:83). When Tessouat visited the Huron country in the spring of 1636, he again urged the Jesuits to leave the Huron, or at least to stop living with the Attignawantan, whom he regarded as his worst enemies. He charged that the Attignawantan had murdered Viel and Brûlé, as they had murdered eight of his own people. Tessouat argued that it was foolish for a man of Brébeuf's importance to risk his life among the Attignawantan; as soon as he perfected his knowledge of the Huron language, he should return to Quebec and conduct his business with the Huron from there (10:79). At the same time, Tessouat was telling the Huron that Champlain did not wish to have the Jesuits remain in their country and that he was determined to avenge the death of Brûlé by cutting off four Huron heads (8:103). By playing on the fears of the Huron and the French, Tessouat was hoping to undermine their good relations.

To terrify the Huron traders a Kichesipirini headman, who bore the hereditary name Oumasasikweie and was known to the French as La Grenouille (The Frog), spread a rumour that the Iroquois were inciting the Algonkin of the Ottawa Valley to wage war on the Huron (8:59). The French believed that this story was true and that the Dutch had instigated the Iroquois to do this in order to prevent the Huron from coming to trade on the St. Lawrence (8:61). The Algonkin were clearly anxious to elimi- nate trade between the Huron and the French, but, as we have already stated, it was not in their own interest to attack the Huron. Therefore, it is reasonable to conclude that unless the Mohawk had miscalculated, it was the Algonkin who invented this rumour. No doubt they hoped that the Huron would become even more uncertain and circumspect in their annual trips to the St. Lawrence if they believed that the Iroquois might be urging the Algonkin to attack them.

In 1635 the Kichesipirini overreached themselves. Once a peace had been arranged with the Mohawk, their next hope was to be able to trade with the Dutch as well as with the French. This not only would have permitted them to bargain for better prices, but would have compelled the French, who tended to slight the Kichesipirini in favour of the Huron, to pay more attention to them. When Oumasasikweie, who had played a leading role in arranging the peace treaty with the Mohawk, tried to slip through the Mohawk country on his way to Fort Orange, he and twenty-two of his companions were slain by the Mohawk (9:95–97). Desrosiers (1947a: 149) suggested that the Dutch had encouraged Oumasasikweie's mission, because they knew that it would force the Mohawk to slay these allies of the French and thus would put an end to friendly relations between the

French and the Mohawk. The Kichesipirini accused two Montagnais of receiving presents from the Iroquois and of having played a role in persuading them to kill Oumasasikweie. These accusations brought the Algonkin and the Montagnais to the brink of war, which was averted only when Du Plessis-Bochart convinced the Kichesipirini of the Montagnais' innocence (Thwaites 1896–1901, 9:245). It seems evident that given the interests of both the Mohawk and the Kichesipirini, external intrigues need not be invoked in order to explain what happened. While it was in the interest of every group of Indians to trade with more than one group of Europeans, no group was sufficiently self-confident that it was prepared to allow enemies, or even potential enemies, to trade with the same European power with which it had an alliance.

Oumasasikweie's death brought an end to the truce between the Mohawk and the Algonkin. In August 1635 it was reported that the Iroquois had attacked the Weskarini (8:59), and in March 1636 the Kichesipirini tried to enlist the support of the Algonkin, Nipissing, and Huron for a war of revenge against the Iroquois. The Nipissing refused to participate, however, because of the extortion that had been practised against them by the Kichesipirini. Help was also not forthcoming from the Huron, in part because the Kichesipirini refused to have dealings with the Attignawantan, whom they accused of having killed some of their men. Mainly, however, the Huron seem to have been angry with the Kichesipirini because of their interference with trade.

Tessouat threatened that he would permit neither the Huron nor the Nipissing to visit the French trading places in future. He further boasted that he was the master of the French and could make them recross the sea, if he so wished (10:75–77). The Huron were not intimidated by these threats and, faced with renewed hostility by the Iroquois, the Kichesipirini and their Algonkin allies eventually were forced to mend their diplomatic fences with the French and the Huron. Though the Huron feared they would not be allowed to use the Ottawa River in 1636, an advance party found that the Algonkin made no attempt to stop them. Thus, after a period of considerable disruption, the patterns of trade and warfare in eastern Canada began to re-acquire the same general pattern they had prior to 1629. The schemes of the Kichesipirini had been decisively crushed and a good working relationship had been restored between the French and the Huron. Except for the influence that the Jesuits now exercised over the government of New France, everything was moving forward as if the British interregnum had never happened.

Chapter 8   The Deadly Harvest

The New Beginning

By an unlucky coincidence, the return of the Jesuits to the Huron country coincided with the beginning of a series of virulent epidemics that were to reduce the Huron population by approximately fifty percent within six years. These same diseases infected all the tribes who had dealings with the French and penetrated along the trade routes into areas no European had yet visited.

Prior to the arrival of the Europeans, the American Indians had never been exposed to many infectious diseases common in the Old World and had little natural immunity against them; hence when these diseases were transmitted to the Indians, they died in great numbers. The most dangerous killer was smallpox although various respiratory illnesses accounted for many deaths. Even childhood diseases that had a low mortality rate in Europe, such as measles, chickenpox, and whooping cough, killed many people of all ages when they broke out in Indian communities. As these diseases gradually spread westward across North America, aboriginal populations were cut drastically. Entire peoples lost their identity through depopulation (Dobyns 1966:410–12; Stearn and Stearn 1945).

Epidemics of this sort may explain the marked decline that took place in the population of the southeastern United States and in the level of cultural development in that area in the sixteenth century (Sauer 1971: 302–3). It has also been suggested though without evidence that epidemics played an important role in the dispersal of the St. Lawrence Iroquoians (Fenton 1940:175). In the summer of 1611 numerous Algonkin died of a fever (Biggar 1922–36, 2:207) and in the winter of 1623–24 many Weskarini perished of disease and hunger in the Ottawa Valley (Wrong 1939:263). It is impossible because of inadequate reports to determine whether or not these were epidemics of European diseases. Although there were such epidemics along the east coast of the United States prior to 1620, there is no evidence of a major epidemic in eastern Canada prior to 1634. Nor is there evidence that the Huron had been affected by European diseases prior to that time. The reason for the swift succession of epidemics beginning in 1634 is unknown, but it may be connected with the rapid increase of European settlement along the eastern seaboard of North America.

While the Indians of eastern Canada died by the thousands between 1634 and 1640, the French rarely became ill and, when they did, they almost always recovered. When the Indians failed to arrest these epidemics with their inadequate pharmacopoeia and rituals that were meant to appease malevolent spirits, they became convinced that they were victims of a powerful witchcraft. Since the French had the power to remain well, or to cure themselves, it seemed inexplicable that they did not use this power to assist the Indians unless they wished to see them die. A remorseless logic, innocent of any knowledge of the varying susceptibility of different populations to the same infection, led the Indians to conclude that the French were using witchcraft to destroy them. Many reasons were suggested why the French should do this and the Indians disagreed whether the French should be appeased or slain as sorcerers. The most fatalistic were the Montagnais around Quebec City, whose hunting territories were becoming depleted and who were increasingly poverty stricken and dependent on the French (Thwaites 1896–1901, 16:93). They were convinced that the French had determined to exterminate them so they could take possession of their land.

THE EPIDEMIC OF 1634

In the summer of 1634 an epidemic, possibly introduced by the ships that had arrived from France in June, began to sweep the St. Lawrence Valley. The oft-repeated claim that the disease was influenza (Talbot 1956:131) is only a layman's guess. Le Jeune described it as "a sort of measles and an oppression of the stomach" (Thwaites 1896–1901, 7:221). Brébeuf stated that among the Indians the disease began with a high fever, followed by a rash and, in some cases, by blindness or impaired vision that lasted for several days and was terminated by diarrhoea. The rash was described as "a sort of measles or smallpox, but different from that common in France" (8:89). The ailment was not smallpox which was recognized immediately when it broke out among the Indians in 1639. Some French became ill, but the symptoms were much milder than among the Indians and all recovered after a few days (7:221). Brébeuf was not even certain that the French and the Indians had suffered from the same disease.

When the Huron arrived at Three Rivers in July 1634, the Montagnais and Algonkin were dying there in large numbers (6:61; 8:87). Before they started for home the disease had spread up the Ottawa Valley, infecting many more Algonkin (7:221). At Three Rivers many of the Huron became ill, which in part explains their reluctance to embark Frenchmen as passengers in their canoes (7:217). Few of the Huron who returned home from Quebec escaped being ill and the epidemic spread through all the Huron villages during the late summer and autumn. So many were sick that fishing and harvesting of crops were seriously impaired and much food was left rotting in the fields. Many who had been ill remained debilitated throughout the winter (8:87–89).

There can be no doubt that many Huron were stricken by this epidemic. Brébeuf stated that he personally did not know anyone who had escaped it and that a large number had died (8:87–89). In spite of this the Jesuits baptized only a few people who they judged were about to die, and the Huron do not seem to have regarded the epidemic as being of unprecedented severity.[1] It is unclear whether the French also overestimated the death rate among the Algonkin and Montagnais or whether, because of their nomadic existence, the latter were physically less fit to withstand this particular epidemic. What does seem certain is that this was the least lethal of the epidemics that were to afflict the Huron in the course of the next six years.

JESUIT POLICY AMONG THE HURON

Brébeuf was a man of courage and physical endurance who combined a humble sense of duty with a mystical temperament and a burning zeal to convert the Indians. Although able to learn languages easily and to express himself well, Brébeuf's most valued qualities were not intellectual ones but those of the heart and will (Latourelle 1966:126). He was neither a politician interested in promoting the welfare of his mission among the powerful in France nor a theoretician anxious to devise the intellectually perfect strategy to convert the Huron. His approach was empirical and based on a belief that sincere effort and personal sacrifice, accompanied by divine favour, would suffice to accomplish the task. On numerous occasions, his reliance on such favour, combined with overzealousness, led him to do tactless things and to expose himself and his co-workers to great danger in their efforts to save souls. Brébeuf's natural conservatism and his former association with Father Daillon probably explain why the Jesuits who went to the Huron country in 1634 carried on their day-to-day work of conversion much as the Recollets had done, in spite of the fundamental differences between the general philosophy of missionary work of the two orders. The implementation of the distinctive features of a Jesuit approach remained to be worked out in the critical years that followed.

Like the Recollets, the Jesuits under Brébeuf's leadership were anxious to usurp the role of shamans by using masses and prayers to stop droughts or otherwise protect crops. They also believed that the best way to convert the Huron was to establish their influence among the young; hence much of their early mission work was concerned with the instruction of children. Like the Recollets, they were convinced that it was necessary for them to live apart from the Huron, although Brébeuf knew that doing so increased the danger of being accused of witchcraft and made it necessary for the Jesuits to buy food and other necessities from the Huron, which otherwise would have been supplied free of charge. While Brébeuf echoed Le Caron's arguments that for missionaries to live permanently with particular households would incite the jealousy of others, he was also aware that a better understanding could flow from this close association with the Huron. Some Jesuits were appalled by the physical discomfort of living with a traditional Huron family, but the discipline of the order was such that these discomforts alone would not have deterred them from such a life if they had believed it necessary to achieve their goals.

What made a prolonged stay in a traditional Huron longhouse an intolerable proposition was not its physical discomfort, but its psychological dangers. On the way to the Huron country, the Huron noted with surprise that the Jesuits were too ashamed to undress in order to wash although only men were present. Nor could the Jesuits endure to see Huron men do so (Thwaites 1896–1901, 13:51). The naked children, the scantily clad women, the bustle of domestic life, and the religious rituals of the Huron were all abhorrent to the priests, who feared their influence and needed a cloister to which they could retire for work and meditation. Even before their departure for the Huron country, Charles Lalemant had ruled out living with Huron families on the simple ground that "religious eyes could not endure the sight of so much lewdness" (4:197).

The Jesuits' own austere life also involved many voluntary forms of self-mortification which would have been difficult to explain to the Huron, even though Huron men were used to vigils, fasting, and testing their courage by means of various ordeals. In spite of such customs, the wearing of belts equipped with iron points next to the skin or self-flagellation once or more a day using a whip with iron points (39:261; 40:23) would have seemed monstrous to them. These were activities that the Jesuits realized it was prudent to perform in seclusion.

In spite of their intellectual accomplishments, the Jesuits believed themselves to be serving a god who could intervene in human affairs at any moment. War, disease, and drought were among the means he employed to advance or hinder human designs. Moreover, while the Jesuits did not believe in magic in the strict sense of thinking that Roman Catholic rituals gave them the power to control nature automatically, they were convinced that their god would answer prayers for rain or good harvests, if this would convince the Indians of his glory and help the priests to undermine the Indians' respect for their own shamans. In their fasts, vigils, and the course of their daily activities God and the saints appeared to these missionaries in visions of compelling realism to offer them advice and encouragement.

In addition to believing in the power of their god, the Jesuits ardently believed in the power of Satan and his attendant devils. The latter were identified with the deities the Huron worshipped and the work of converting the Indians was conceived of as a valiant struggle to liberate them from thraldom to these supernatural enemies. Some Jesuits, including Brébeuf and Jérôme Lalemant, believed that these devils personally opposed their work among the Huron. Sometimes they became incarnate before the eyes of the priests, only to vanish before the sign of the cross. Other Jesuits were more sceptical and tended to explain most of the Huron's behaviour in terms of their "foolishness" or "ignorance of the truth" (33:197). None of them, however, doubted the existence of Satan or the importance of the spiritual war that they were waging against him.

The climacteric event in this struggle was the ritual of baptism. All of the Jesuits who worked among the Huron were convinced that any human being who remained unbaptized was doomed after death to suffer in the fires of hell. Curiously enough, this folk belief had never been affirmed by the church as dogma, and Thomas Aquinas had taught that the unbaptized might put themselves in a state of grace, either by personally choosing good rather than evil or by a sincere act of charity (Robinson, in Du Creux 1951–52:199 n. 2; Thomas Aquinas 1852–73; 13:107, 752). The wretched fate that they believed was facing the unbaptized embued the disciples of Ignatius Loyola with a special sense of militancy as they marched into battle against the devil. An infant who died after being baptized was assured a place in heaven, while for an adult convert there was every hope of salvation, so long as he did not lapse into heretical belief or sinful conduct (Thwaites 1896–1901, 8:169). Thus to baptize the Huron and lead them to heaven was an act of charity for which the Jesuits were willing to court martyrdom (8:175). Martyrdom was viewed as a sacrifice that supernaturally would further their efforts to convert the Huron and might well be vital to achieve that end.

In terms of their beliefs about the supernatural forces that were at work in the world, Jesuit and Huron shared considerably more in common with each other than either does with twentieth-century man, whose values have been moulded in a tradition of rationalism and evolutionary thought. It is precisely because we can now view this clash between the religious ideas of the Huron and the Jesuits dispassionately, that its real nature has become apparent (LeBlanc 1968).

FIRST FRUITS

The Jesuit priests spent the autumn and winter of 1634–35 in Ihonatiria. Although the Huron knew that the epidemics that raged in the autumn had come from Quebec, the Jesuits encountered no hostility, nor did the Huron attempt to avoid contact with them. Much of the time was spent learning the Huron language. Brébeuf could already speak Huron and, prior to leaving Quebec, Davost and Daniel had studied the manuscript material that was available there (Thwaites 1896–1901, 6:37). Throughout the winter of 1634–35, the two newcomers compiled lists of Huron words and, under Brébeuf's direction, practised putting them together to form sentences. The grammatical complexities of Huron and its unfamiliar structure were formidable obstacles to learning the language, but by the spring Brébeuf reported that Davost and Daniel knew as many words as he did, although they could only put a limited number of sentences together in a halting manner (8:131–33).

In October 1634 Brébeuf briefly visited the Tionnontaté, passing through Ossossané and other Huron villages along the way. Likely he accompanied some of the Jesuits' hired men who were also working for the trading company. The aim of their visit was to renew relations between French and Tionnontaté traders and to encourage the latter to come to the Huron country. In the course of his journey, Brébeuf baptized three small dying children (8:135). In mid-January Brébeuf set out from Ihonatiria to visit Amantacha and his father, who had returned to Teanaostaiaé from their disastrous expedition against the Seneca. He was welcomed by Soranhes and Amantacha, but was disappointed to learn that, among his own people, Amantacha was not living according to the Christian principles that he professed whenever he came to Quebec (8:149). As Brébeuf was passing through Onnentisati, he found that Oukhahitoüa, who had brought one of the Jesuits' party to the Huron country the previous summer, was very ill and managed to baptize him shortly before he died (8:139).

In the autumn and winter of 1634–35 the Jesuits baptized ten more Huron. Nine baptisms were in Ihonatiria, the other was in nearby Wenrio. None of the Indians who permitted themselves or their children to be baptized understood the Christian significance of this rite. The Jesuits continued to observe the regulation that only Indians who were obviously dying should be baptized without prolonged instruction and trial of their faith, but the epidemic led the Jesuits to try to save as many souls as possible during it. To elicit the goodwill of the people of Ihonatiria and nearby villages, they distributed their supply of prunes and raisins to the sick and sent their hired men hunting so that they could carry portions of game to the sick (8:149). The good health of the French and the reputation that the priests had already acquired as shamans convinced many Huron that they possessed the power to cure the current illness. Baptism was thus interpreted as a healing rite, similar in nature to those performed by the Atirenda or Awataerohi, and becoming a Christian was viewed as analogous to a sick person joining one of these societies. The only clue that it was different lay in the fact that the Jesuits gave each person they baptized a Christian name. While they did this strictly in accordance with their own beliefs, it was an action that the Huron might have been expected to interpret as symbolizing the assumption of new duties and a new role in society.

The first four people who were baptized lived in the same longhouse as did the child Brébeuf had baptized prior to his departure from the Huron country in 1629. This child had been expected to die, but after being baptized had recovered and was still alive in 1635 (8:135–37). His recovery must have suggested to his relatives that baptism was an effective curing ritual. It is, therefore, not surprising that soon after their return to the Huron country the Jesuits were able to baptize two very young sick girls who were members of this family. Both died soon after, but since shamans were not always successful with their cures this did not seriously impair the Jesuits' reputation (8:133). On 26 October they baptized another resident of the same longhouse, Oquiaendis, who was a grandmother of one of the girls and the mother of Sangwati (10:11), the headman of the village (8:133–35). She recovered soon afterwards, which her family attributed to the shamanistic skills of the Jesuits. After 20 October Joutaya, the father of the boy Brébeuf baptized in 1629, also was baptized. Although near death, he lingered for a considerable time and the prolongation of his life was seen as yet another manifestation of the Jesuits' life-giving powers

(8:135). These results led many other Huron, including ones who were only slightly ill, to clamour for baptism (8:141–43).

On 21 October the Jesuits baptized Sondaarouhané, a man forty to fifty years old, who survived for about a month, and Tsindacaiendoua, who was said to be about eighty and who died the next day (8:137). Another old man, Tsicok, was baptized 27 November and died in mid-December (8: 139). Following this, either because the epidemic had run its course in Ihonatiria or because the Huron had lost faith in the efficacy of the ritual, there were no more baptisms until late March when Oatij, a young man who had been ill since the autumn, was baptized. He died a few weeks later (8:139). This was followed by the baptism of Tsindacaiendoua's daughter who was living in Wenrio (8:141) and of his grandnephew in Ihonatiria (8:155). The latter recovered, to the joy of the missionaries, who hoped that this would refute the growing opinion that no one could hope to recover from an illness after being baptized.

The latter opinion was encouraged by the emphasis that the Jesuits placed on the after-life in the instructions that preceded baptism. This suggested to the Huron that baptism might not be a curing ritual but one designed to send the soul of the sick person to the realms of the dead. The degree to which one or the other interpretation was believed depended largely on the experiences of friends and relatives, but the Jesuit policy of baptizing only those who were gravely ill seemed to support the more sinister interpretation.

The Huron were also troubled when the Jesuits told them that the souls of the baptized would go to heaven rather than to the traditional Huron villages of the dead. The idea of alternative destinations for human souls was not unfamiliar to the Huron, who believed that some souls, such as those of the very young, the very old, and of people who had died violent deaths, lived apart from the majority of the Huron dead. Such differences had no ethical significance, however, and the Huron no doubt interpreted the notion of Christians' souls going to heaven in this ethically neutral sense also. It is significant in this regard that while most Huron did not question the Jesuits' claims about heaven, few appear to have taken seriously their claim that non-Christian Huron would go, not to the villages of the dead, but to a fiery hell.[2] The Jesuits further emphasized the dichotomy between the after-lives of traditional Huron and Christians when they gained permission to bury Tsindacaiendoua and Joutaya with Christian rites and in a place removed from the village cemetery of Ihonatiria.

The emphasis that the Jesuits placed on the separation of Christians and non-Christians after death influenced individual Huron in opposed ways. Many were loath to be baptized if they believed that this would cut them off from friends and relatives who had already died without being baptized; for example, after Joutaya had been baptized, he dreamt that one of his dead brothers was reproaching him for having chosen not to live with him after death (8:137–39). On the other hand, once baptized Huron had died, some relatives were motivated to seek baptism so as not to be separated from them after death. The desire of Tsindacaiendoua's daughter to follow him played an important role in her "conversion" (8:141) and similar considerations may have influenced his family to allow the Jesuits to baptize his grandnephew.

Thus differing opinions as to whether baptism was a curative ritual or showed people the way to heaven and the desire to join particular kinsmen after death led some Huron to seek baptism and others to oppose it. These opinions tended to run in families and to reflect their particular experiences. Only a small number of Huron were compelled to make such decisions and, as the winter wore on, most sick people seem to have avoided contact with the Jesuits until they could ascertain better what was going on. There is no evidence of personal animosity being expressed, either individually or collectively, towards the Jesuits at this time. Not enough Huron were yet involved nor had the epidemic been serious enough to make this a vital public issue.

A PUBLIC WITNESS

In early December, after the people of Ihonatiria had settled down for the winter, Brébeuf began preaching to them. Periodically, men, women, and children were invited to the Jesuits' cabin, either by a public announcement or by the ringing of a hand-bell. Male attendance was encouraged in traditional Huron fashion by the liberal dispensation of tobacco (Thwaites 1896–1901, 13:141, 219), which, moreover, was a scarce commodity at that time (10:301). When an audience had gathered, the Jesuits chanted the Lord's Prayer in Huron and the children were invited to participate in a catechism at which a good performance was rewarded with highly valued glass and wampum beads. The Huron were happy to see their children win such prizes and encouraged them to learn the correct answers; indeed, some adults learned the answers themselves so they could teach them to their children (10:25). To set an example for the Huron, the two French boys who had been sent to learn the Huron language were made to participate in these catechisms. The principal message that the Jesuits sought to convey at this time was the choice that each person had of going to heaven or hell after death. By speaking so much about death, the Jesuits manifested a preoccupation with a topic that adult Huron found worrisome and repugnant (8:143–45).

The Jesuits concluded their sessions by soliciting the reactions of the headmen and old men of the village. They were exasperated by the way in which these men would approve of their teachings, and sometimes even ask for more instruction, but then refuse to renounce their old ways (10:17–19, 25). Some Huron attempted to harmonize their traditional beliefs with the teachings of Christianity, such as a man who stated that he had learned in a dream that all the Huron souls had left the villages of the dead and gone to heaven (8:147). The older men, who were most knowledgeable about Huron beliefs, explained them to the Jesuits, and must have been offended when Brébeuf repeatedly used such occasions to censure and ridicule what they were saying. The Huron reminded the Jesuits that they had different customs and should respect each other's beliefs (8:147). Every Huron, when pressed by the Jesuits to explain why he believed something, replied that it was the custom of his country and soon the Huron began to complain that the Jesuits were seeking to overturn the Huron way of life (10:27). The Jesuits did not realize that the Huron approved of what they said from a sense of politeness which they expected the French to reciprocate. Instead, they concluded that the Huron were so attached to their old ways that they were content to recognize the truthfulness of the Christian religion without embracing it.

As the Jesuits acquired more linguistic skills they began to visit the houses in Ihonatiria daily to instruct the women and children. They attempted to teach the children to cross themselves and to recite a few simple prayers, which were no doubt memorized because they were believed to be shamanistic spells. Religious services were held for the children every Sunday morning and in the afternoon they were taught the Ledesma catechism. Many children attended these sessions, obviously drawn there by material rewards and by their curiosity to observe the behaviour of the strange newcomers (10:19–25).

The Jesuits attempted to provide separate instruction for older men, whom they were anxious to convert since they managed the public affairs of the village (10:15). At first these men listened to them more attentively than the women and children did; but, as the winter progressed, they became so engrossed in their own councils and in the traditional round of feasts, dances, and games that it became increasingly difficult to draw them together to discuss religion. Moreover, while these men continued to listen politely to what the Jesuits had to say, it was impossible to persuade them to become Christians (10:15–19).

The open hostility of the Jesuits towards Huron religious beliefs eventually began to create serious difficulties with the people of Ihonatiria. In January 1636 a man named Ihongwaha became psychologically disturbed after he public-spiritedly had broken a fast designed to make him a master shaman in order to perform an Awataerohi curing ceremony for a sick person in the village. When three or four public curing ceremonies failed to alleviate Ihongwaha's difficulties, many Huron said that the Jesuits were to blame because they had condemned these rituals and thereby rendered them ineffective (10:199–201). The wrongdoing that the Huron were objecting to was not religious intolerance, which had no meaning for them, but rather opposition to helping a member of one's own community regain his health. To the Huron, such behaviour was little different from witchcraft.

In the spring of 1635 the Jesuits offered presents to the headmen of Ihonatiria and Wenrio urging them to settle their differences and re-establish a single village (8:105). Aenons, in particular, wished the two villages to unite and the Jesuits approved the scheme because it would permit them to minister to a larger number of people more easily and eliminate the rivalry between the headmen of these villages as to where the Jesuits should live. Moreover, Brûlé's murder had been the cause of Toanché splitting apart and the Jesuits wanted the Huron to forget that this event had ever happened. Yet, while the reunification of these villages was discussed at intervals over the next several years, nothing came of it. Having just erected new houses and cleared new land, few Huron were prepared to relocate until a longer interval had passed.

About this time, Brébeuf was invited to join a delegation made up of representatives of all the Huron tribes that was on its way to the Seneca country to reaffirm the recent peace treaty between them (8:117). Since the French were allied with the Huron it was appropriate that Brébeuf should have been invited to participate in this mission. Brébeuf refused to go, however, to avoid giving the Huron cause to suspect the Jesuits of being other than missionaries. No doubt remembering Daillon's difficulties, Brébeuf was anxious not to suggest that he might wish to have dealings with the Seneca.

The winter of 1634–35 was short and mild (8:155) and was followed by scarcely any rain from the end of March until the middle of June (10:35). According to Heidenreich (et al. 1969:121), this was the worst drought on record in the first half of the seventeenth century. Because of the extreme dryness, houses caught fire easily. Two Huron villages were totally consumed by flames within ten days and the large town of Teanaostaiaé was partly destroyed (Thwaites 1896–1901, 8:105). The Jesuits' own cabin caught on fire, although the blaze was quickly put out.

Because of the drought, crops were failing and the whole Huron confederacy feared a famine over the coming winter. Villages and tribes sought help from reputable shamans. Brébeuf's former rival, Tehorenhaegnon, promised to produce rain if he were given a present worth ten iron axes and the appropriate ceremonies were performed. As in 1628, these ceremonies failed to produce rain and Tehorenhaegnon blamed his failure on the cross that the Jesuits had erected in front of their cabin. He also accused the Jesuits of being sorcerers whose sole purpose in coming to the Huron country was to make the Huron die. This charge was also pressed by Huron not living in Ihonatiria, who reported that the Algonkin were attributing the epidemic of the previous autumn to a spell that the French had cast on the Huron. Certain Huron told the Jesuits that they should take down their cross and threatened that if the crops did not mature they would be slain as sorcerers. There were also rumours that certain Huron planned to tear down the cross themselves (10:35–39).

Within Ihonatiria, however, there was considerable support for the Jesuits and the people of the village asked the Jesuits to make rain for them, as Brébeuf had done in the past. Brébeuf told them that if they resolved to abandon their traditional behaviour and to serve God as he would instruct them, the Jesuits would offer a novena of masses and organize a procession to implore divine assistance. Nine days later, as the procession was making its way through the village, rain began to fall and showers continued for about a month. There was a further drought in the latter half of July, but after another novena was begun this drought was also broken and there was a plentiful harvest (10:39–43). These apparently successful ventures in rainmaking silenced the rumours that had been circulating against the Jesuits and greatly enhanced their reputation as shamans. They also belittled the power of the native arendiwane who had failed to produce rain.

THE SUMMER PROGRAM

Efforts to proselytize the Huron were suspended temporarily in the summer of 1635, when the Huron men left the villages to trade and wage war and the women went with their children to tend their fields. As they were to do each year thereafter, the Jesuits withdrew to their cabin to perform their spiritual exercises and consolidate their knowledge of the Huron language. The latter involved drafting dictionaries and grammars, based on what each Jesuit had learned from the Huron (Thwaites 1896–1901, 10:55), rather than on the manuscript studies of the Recollets, which were now judged to be inadequate. These works served as a record of what had been accomplished and made it easier for newcomers to learn the language. Nor were the latter long in arriving. In August 1635 Fathers François-Joseph Le Mercier and Pierre Pijart joined the mission. Responsible headmen had taken charge of these men at Three Rivers and consequently they were well-treated on their journey to the Huron country (10:57). They too began to study the Huron language. The Jesuits viewed the ability to express themselves as an essential weapon in their battle against Satan. Language learning was therefore an endeavour in which individual priests expected and claimed to experience supernatural aid (19:129).

Throughout the year the Jesuits spent much time listening to native conversations in the hope of catching new words and phrases. Often they had to interrupt such conversations to ask for explanations. They did this with such enthusiasm that in 1637 Brébeuf had to warn missionaries travelling to the Huron country not to trouble their Indian travelling companions by asking them too many questions (12:119). Like modern linguists, the Jesuits also worked with selected native informants, recording and analysing their answers to questions and reading material back to them. Whole narratives were taken down from these informants so that the style of the language, as well as formal points of grammar, might be investigated (21:225). In later years, these informants were often converts.

The study and preparation of manuscript grammars and dictionaries continued to be an essential first step for each Jesuit in learning the Huron language. This was followed by the translation into Huron of liturgical texts, songs, prayers, and catechisms, and later by the translation of important Biblical passages, homilies, and rites. In order to produce accurate translations, these works were read to native informants before being used and were revised by a succession of priests, each of whom attempted to improve the work of his predecessor (Hanzeli 1969:53).

In the course of translating Roman Catholic dogma into the Huron language, numerous problems were encountered. For example, the obligatory use of person markers in Huron made impossible a literal translation of the expression "Father, Son, and Holy Spirit." After a painstaking review of church teaching, the Jesuits suggested that the phrase might be translated "our Father, his Son, and their Holy Spirit" (10:119); however, the implementation of this proposal required approval from ecclesiastical officials in Europe. Huron linguistic etiquette also had to be learned and respected. This included not referring to God as Father in the presence of a Huron whose own father was dead, since under this circumstance even inadvertent references to a father constituted a serious affront (10:121).

Individual Jesuits had varying linguistic ability. Brébeuf, Chaumonot, and Daniel displayed outstanding talent, while Chabanel and de Nouë had exceptional difficulties. Even a man endowed with linguistic skills, such as Daniel, required more than six months to acquire a rudimentary working knowledge of Huron, while, after living among the Huron for three and a half years, Brébeuf's knowledge was far from perfect. In 1723 Father Sébastien Rasles was to express the opinion that even with the initial aid of a good grammar, a missionary was fortunate if he could speak eloquently after ten years of study (67:147).

During the summer, the Jesuits also had a chance to review their impressions of Huron life and to decide what changes were necessary if the Huron were to become Christians. Although the Jesuits totally disapproved of Huron religious beliefs, as yet they had no awareness of the degree to which these beliefs penetrated every sphere of Huron life. Instead, they confined themselves to approving, or seeing the need to abolish, specific customs. They were pleased to find that the Huron practised monogamy and avoided marrying blood relatives in direct or collateral lines (8:119). They also believed that the Huron's sexual modesty, their stoicism, and their generosity to one another and to strangers offered hope of producing Christians whose behaviour was in certain respects superior to that of Europeans (8:127–31). On the other hand, the Jesuits disapproved of what they felt was laziness and a lack of respect for private property (8:127) and were determined that divorce (8:119–21), blood feuds, and torture (10: 227) be abolished. While some of the changes that the Jesuits believed were necessary, such as the abolition of divorce, might have been effected solely through religious conversion and a change in values, others, such as the abolition of blood feud, would have required a far-reaching remodelling of Huron society along European lines. Thus, while the Jesuits laid far less emphasis on the assimilation of French culture than the Recollets had, their tacit identification of European and Christian values often led them to view Europeanizing (or "civilizing") the Indians as part of their general work of conversion (10:27). Even at this early period, the Jesuits' concept of conversion was implicitly committing them to a far more extensive program of trying to alter Huron life than they themselves foresaw.

BEING USEFUL

Although the Huron now had a truce with the Seneca, who were traditionally their principal enemies, peace did not materialize with the other four
Iroquois tribes. There was fear of raids even in Ihonatiria, although it lay
far from the frontier of the Huron country. One alarm lasted through June
1635 and seems to have been caused by a few Iroquois raiders. Another
alarm, the following winter, turned out to be without foundation (Thwaites
1896–1901, 10:49–53). The inhabitants of Ihonatiria were, on both
occasions, ready to disperse in the forest or to take refuge in the nearest
fortified village. These threats were regarded as sufficiently serious that
in February 1636 the young men of Ihonatiria were expected to help
construct a palisade around Angoutenc (10:203). This village, located not
far from Ossossané (Heidenreich 1966:121), appears to have supplanted
Quieunonascaran and Toanché as the principal village of the northern
Attignawantan.

The Jesuits won the approval of the Attignawantan by supplying them
with iron arrowheads and promising that if the Iroquois attacked, their
hired men would defend the threatened village with their muskets
(Thwaites 1896–1901, 10:53). In this way the Jesuits not only honoured
Champlain's promises to help the Huron, but appropriated the credit for
doing so. Their ability to command armed men gave substance to the
stories that French traders told about the power of the priests to defeat the
Huron's enemies.

Brébeuf also urged the Huron to erect square palisades around their
towns. In this way, a few Frenchmen armed with muskets could defend
even a large settlement from towers erected at the four corners. The Huron
are reported to have applied this advice when Ossossané was relocated
about a quarter of a league north of its previous position in the spring of
1635 (10:53; 8:101; Heidenreich, personal communication 1972). The
fortifications of the new Ossossané were apparently under construction in
1637, when Charles Garnier wrote that two towers, made of about thirty
poles each, were being built at the corners of the ramparts, so that each
would command two sides of the enclosure (Jones 1908:306; plate 32).
While this was a modification of Brébeuf's original plan, it was a strategi-
cally sound one that would have permitted two or more gunmen to defend
the perimeter of the town. We are also informed that the palisade around
the new Ossossané was of stakes ten or twelve feet high and about six
inches thick. The use of larger posts appears to be yet another change

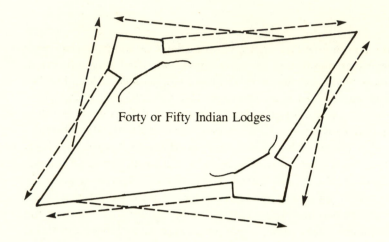

Forty or Fifty Indian Lodges

PLATE 32. *A. E. Jones's reconstruction of the fortifications erected under Jesuit guidance at Ossossané c. 1637. Jones bases this reconstruction on letters by Charles Garnier. From* Wendake Ehen, *p. 306. Courtesy Archives of Ontario.*

brought about by European technology. It is unclear how widespread quadrilateral palisade construction became, but it seems likely that other communities would have copied what was done at Ossossané, in the hope that the French would protect them too. Jury (and Jury 1954:28; 1955) claims to see evidence of French influence in the fortifications and layout of houses at the site he has identified as the small village of St. Louis, burned in 1649. At the same period, Taenhatentaron was regarded as impregnable because of the defences the French had constructed there (Thwaites 1896–1901, 39:247). This suggests, although it does not prove, that the Jesuits may have initiated considerable changes in military architecture throughout the Huron country after 1635.

The Huron particularly appreciated the renewed French protection of their villages because of some small defeats they had suffered in the spring of 1636. Twelve warriors who were members of a group that was on its way to attack the Iroquois were killed in the night on the southern borders of the Huron country (10:83). After Easter, Amantacha and his uncle joined a raid against the Iroquois, in the course of which Amantacha was again taken prisoner (10:81). While some of his relatives maintained that he had been killed, others believed that he was still alive and had been adopted by a Mohawk family (14:45–47). No more was heard of him, and it may be assumed that he was killed by torture. His death was a serious loss for the Attigneenongnahac and for the Huron as a whole, since it meant that their council chiefs and traders no longer had the advice of a man who, although young, had a far more detailed knowledge of European ways than any other Huron was to acquire prior to their dispersal.

The Jesuits deeply regretted Amantacha's death. In the autumn of 1635 he had expressed the desire to lead a more Christian life and, to prove his sincerity, he said that he wished to spend the winter living with the Jesuits at Quebec. He apparently did this because his father was anxious to forge closer ties with the French to allow him to ask for more European goods in return for his furs. Although Amantacha found an excuse not to go to Quebec, he spent part of the winter living with the Jesuits at Ihonatiria (10:31). There he assisted them by translating some catechisms into Huron and by acting as their interpreter (14:11). He also began to pray, confess, and attend mass regularly. Finally, he spent Holy Week with the Jesuits, prior to setting out for the Iroquois country (10:81). Such behaviour convinced the Jesuits that he was once more a sincere Christian and that his death represented the loss of considerable support for their mission.

Huron fear of the Iroquois was intensified in August 1636, when an eclipse of the moon that appeared in the southeast was interpreted as the omen of a grievous defeat for them (10:59). The shaman Tehorenhaegnon organized a great feast in an effort to turn aside the unluckiness of the eclipse.

RELIGION AND POLITICS

Although Brébeuf visited Teanaostaiaé and Scanonaenrat in the autumn of 1635 (Thwaites 1896–1901, 10:11), the Jesuits spent their second year in the Huron country, as they had their first, in Ihonatiria. At first they continued to baptize a few children and adults who appeared to be dying. Among those who did die was Sangwati, the headman of Ihonatiria (10:11–13).

In spite of the occasional baptism, the Jesuits feared that their mission work would be jeopardized when they realized that most of the people of Ihonatiria and Wenrio had become convinced that baptism would shorten their lives. To counteract this fear, the Jesuits decided to baptize some young children who either were ill but seemed likely to recover or had shown a special interest in their catechisms. The recovery of a pregnant woman who was extremely ill, after she had agreed to be baptized, marked another turning point in the northern Attignawantan's attitude towards baptism (10:67). On 8 December 1635, three young girls were baptized, and, before the end of the month, twenty-seven more people had been (10:69). Of the eighty-six Huron who were baptized between the summers of 1635 and 1636, ten or fewer died, four being adults. This makes it possible that as many as eighty baptisms were of children (10:11).

The Huron began to believe that baptism was a ritual that protected children against sickness and misfortune (10:13, 73) and children were brought to the Jesuits from distant parts of the country. While the Jesuits knew that the parents interpreted baptism as a physical healing ritual, they saw in their work the saving of many souls, particularly if the children should die young. They also hoped that by reminding the Huron, at a later date, that the souls of baptized children would be separated forever from those of non-Christians, they might persuade the parents of these children to want to become Christians (10:31). In order to increase the respect that the Huron had for baptism, the Jesuits made it a rule to baptize healthy children only at solemn ceremonies in their own chapel (10:83). Because of this new policy and a healthy winter, the Jesuits soon found themselves cleared of all former suspicions and their rituals again popular as good shamanistic practices.

As a result of their growing popularity, in the spring of 1636 the Jesuits received numerous invitations to live elsewhere than in Ihonatiria. These came from the Arendarhonon and from important towns such as Teanaostaiaé and Ossossané (10:235); however, the most persistent invitation was from Aenons who won the Jesuits' support for a plan to have the five small villages in the northern part of the Penetanguishene Peninsula, including Wenrio and Ihonatiria, join together to form a single town that could be fortified against the Iroquois (8:105; 10:245). Aenons hoped that if he could persuade the Jesuits to move to Wenrio that village would become the nucleus of the new town and his claim to be its principal headman would be assured. He pointed out that since Sangwati's death, there was no experienced headman in Ihonatiria who could protect the Jesuits and ensure they were treated properly; on the other hand, in the new town, Aenons promised to see that they were provided with all the food they needed and with transportation to and from Quebec (10:241–43).

To convert the Huron, Brébeuf was prepared to follow the example of early Christian missionaries and, where it seemed appropriate, to treat the matter as a political issue. He announced that the Jesuits did not look with disfavour on the plan to found a new village, but they were unwilling to commit themselves to live in that community unless the headmen of the five villages would pledge that they and their "subjects" would become Christians (10:245). Brébeuf still misunderstood the nature of Huron society and believed that headmen had the power to treat clansmen as subjects and commit them to a predetermined course of action. The Jesuits were not present at the council that met to discuss the move, but later were informed that the headmen had agreed to their proposal and were coming to transport the Jesuits to the site of the new town (10:245–47). Yet in spite of this conference, the planned merger of the villages did not take place and soon Aenons was asking the Jesuits to move to Wenrio and settle in his longhouse (10:247). Most of the people the Jesuits had baptized were living in Ihonatiria and the various disputes that were troubling the northern Attignawantan made any move a delicate matter. The Jesuits therefore decided to remain at Ihonatiria for another year (10:247). This pleased the inhabitants of the village so much that they enlarged and repaired the Jesuits' now dilapidated cabin, while accepting only a portion of the presents that the Jesuits offered them. All the men of the village, young and old, joined in this work and completed it within three days (10:247–49).

The transferring of Ossossané to a new location in the spring of 1635 was the occasion for the celebration of a Feast of the Dead among the Attignawantan. During the winter, meetings were held to make arrangements for this feast and at one of them Aenons was commissioned to ask the Jesuits if the bodies of Guillaume Chaudron and Etienne Brûlé might be disinterred and reburied with the Attignawantan. Among the Huron, the burial of their dead in a common grave constituted the most solemn expression of friendship between two groups of people. If the Jesuits would agree, the Attignawantan and the French would be united by the most sacred of alliances (10:305).

To their surprise, Brébeuf did not accept this proposal. He explained to Aenons that church regulations forbade that Christians and non-Christians be buried together and that it was not a Christian custom to raise the bodies of the dead (10:305). Seeming to meet the Huron halfway, Brébeuf offered to rebury Chaudron and Brûlé near the Ossossané ossuary, but only provided that all the Huron who had died after being baptized could be buried in the same separate grave with them. Brébeuf hoped that in future such a precedent would make it easier to persuade converts to have their bodies interred separately from those of non-Christians and in cemeteries specifically consecrated for that purpose. He also believed that by reburying these bodies within the context of the Feast of the Dead, he could claim official sanction for the public performance of other Roman Catholic rituals and that by erecting a cross over the grave, the Huron would be compelled to honour it publicly. In this way, the Huron might be dissuaded from abusing or desecrating other crosses that the Jesuits might erect (10:305–7). What Brébeuf did not reveal to Aenons was that he had serious moral reservations about moving Brûlé's body, since this would require giving the renegade a Christian burial (10:309–11). Aenons and the other Attignawantan headmen agreed to Brébeuf's proposal. Nevertheless, since the Huron regarded the mingling of bodies as a symbol of unity and friendship, it is highly unlikely that Brébeuf's emphasis on the ritual separation of Christians and non-Christians either pleased or reassured them.

Towards spring a quarrel broke out between the headmen of the five northernmost Attignawantan villages and those of the rest of the tribe. According to Brébeuf, the northern headmen complained that they were being excluded from secret councils and were not receiving a fair share of the reparations payments and other gifts that were made to the tribe as a whole (10:281). Because of this quarrel, the five northern villages decided to hold their own Feast of the Dead (10:307). It is not certain, however, that the Feast of the Dead was necessarily a tribal ritual and the

celebration of separate feasts by the major Attignawantan villages may
have been more common than Brébeuf surmised. The proposal that Brébeuf
mentions for a single feast embracing all the Attignawantan villages may
have been an innovation reflecting a growing sense of tribal unity as a
result of the fur trade. Alternatively, it is possible that the argument
between Aenons and Anenkhiondic, who were apparently the headmen in
charge of the Feast of the Dead in their respective areas, was never about
whether there should be two feasts or one, but about the role that each
division of the Attignawantan should play in the other's feast. Aenons
seems to have nurtured a personal grievance about the southern Attignawantan spoiling an earlier feast he had arranged.

In April, Brébeuf was invited to be present when the principal Attignawantan met to discuss the Feast of the Dead one more time. Brébeuf took
advantage of this opportunity to draw attention to Champlain's exhortations of 1635 that all Huron should become Christians if they wished to
seal their alliance with the French, and that they should send some Huron
children to Quebec the following summer to be instructed by the Jesuits.
After preaching a sermon, Brébeuf presented the council with a collar[3] of
1200 wampum beads that he said was to smooth the way to heaven for the
Huron (10:27–29). Although one headman replied that no Huron was
enough of a coward to fear torture in the Jesuits' hell (10:29–30), the
acceptance of this collar, and the nominal approval of what Brébeuf had
said, convinced the Jesuits that these headmen had no strong objections to
Brébeuf's teachings or to his proposals. Presumably the Huron respected
the right of their French trading partners to ask for Huron children in
return for the Jesuits; however, aside from their desire to preserve and
strengthen their alliance with the French and to be polite, these headmen
manifested no positive enthusiasm for Brébeuf's proposals.

At this same meeting, Brébeuf was asked about a matter that had evidently become a subject of controversy among Attignawantan: did the
French wish to rebury their dead at Ossossané or at the Feast of the Dead
that the five northern villages were planning to celebrate? Brébeuf tactfully left the solution of this problem to the Attignawantan headmen, who
eventually decided that Chaudron's body should be buried at Ossossané
where he had died, while Brûlé should remain in the north. In the course
of the discussion, one of the southern Attignawantan was heard to remark
that it was appropriate that Aenons should honour Brûlé's bones since it
was he who had murdered him. Although the meeting proceeded in an
orderly fashion, once it was over a bitter quarrel broke out between Aenons
and Anenkhiondic. In his anxiety not to reopen the dispute about who had

killed Brûlé, Aenons ceased to lay claim to his body. Anenkhiondic and the Jesuits jointly decided that under the circumstances, neither Brûlé nor Chaudron ought to be buried at Ossossané, and the whole question of a separate Christian burial was dropped (10:307–9).

Brébeuf states that the five northern Attignawantan villages celebrated their own Feast of the Dead in 1636. Yet he does not describe the northern ceremony and it is uncertain that the French attended it. After the quarrel between Aenons and Anenkhiondic, Brébeuf and Anenkhiondic were on good terms (10:309), but some Huron were furious that no Frenchmen were reinterred, since this prevented them from claiming to be kinsmen of the French and foreign tribes would say that there was no real friendship between the Huron and the French (10:311). These sound like the sentiments of Aenons and his people, who remained in disrepute about the murder of Brûlé. Still, the Jesuits mention attending only one Feast of the Dead in the fifteen years they lived in the Huron country; hence their failure to mention attending this northern Attignawantan one may be simply an oversight.

They did attend, and describe in detail, the ceremony at Ossossané (10:279–305). That bodies were taken from Ihonatiria to Ossossané for burial does not contradict the assertion that Ihonatiria and neighbouring villages had their own ossuary; the bodies were probably of people who had been born in the eight or nine southern villages, but had gone to live in the north after marriage. Although given temporary burials in the cemeteries of the villages in which they died, most people were probably interred in the ossuary of the community into which they had been born. Having failed to secure a separate ossuary for the Huron they had baptized, the Jesuits were to witness fifteen or twenty such bodies buried without Christian rites in the Ossossané pit.

During the ceremony, Anenkhiondic offered the Jesuits a beaver robe in return for the collar Brébeuf had given to the Attignawantan; however, Brébeuf refused the gift and told Anenkhiondic that the only thing the Jesuits wished in return was for the Huron to become Christians. Even if Christianity were perceived by the Huron merely as a healing ritual or as the expression of an alliance with the French, the Jesuits had already made their intentions plain enough that such a remark could only be interpreted as further evidence of their desire to undermine Huron traditions.

Early in the summer of 1636 there was so much talk of war with the Iroquois as well as concern about Algonkin hostility that the Jesuits feared the Huron might not go to trade with the French that year (13:7). Yet, as noted in chapter 7, Aenons succeeded in restoring a working relationship with the Kichesipirini, and he and six other Huron continued on to Three Rivers. Aenons and a Huron named Kionché agreed to transport Fathers Pierre Chastellain and Charles Garnier to the Huron country (9:251). Like Pijart and Le Mercier the year before, these missionaries were well-treated on the journey. They were allowed to wear shoes, although the Huron usually made Frenchmen travel bare-footed, so as not to injure their canoes (9:277). As a matter of course, the French now provided each canoe in which a priest was travelling with a sheet that could be used as a sail. This was done to compensate for the priests not paddling.

While Aenons and his companions headed down the Ottawa River from Morrison Island, two Huron returned to Georgian Bay to inform the other traders that the Ottawa River was open again (9:247). By late July, many Huron and a large quantity of furs were ready to depart for the St. Lawrence. Fathers Daniel and Davost and several hired men accompanied the crews as they set out in small groups (9:273–75; 13:9). On route, they were joined by some Nipissing traders. When the first Huron reached Morrison Island, they learned that Tessouat had died and the Kichesipirini once again were not allowing the inland tribes to use the river. These Huron remained where they were until Father Daniel arrived; he negotiated with the Kichesipirini and secured the latter's agreement that they might continue down-river, presumably without having to present the immoderate condolence presents that the Kichesipirini were demanding (9:275–77). In a letter that he wrote while supervising the passage of the Huron past Morrison Island, Father Daniel noted that the role the French played in this sort of difficulty helped to convince the Huron that it was important for the Jesuits to remain in their country (9:273). Father Daniel and the vanguard of the Huron traders arrived at Three Rivers on 19 August.

In spite of this, Huron traders continued to straggle down-river until well into September. Since a permanent French settlement had been established at Three Rivers, they knew that they would be able to trade there no matter how late in the year they arrived. Father Davost did not reach Three Rivers until late August and it is possible that he had become involved in the rituals for installing the new Tessouat (12:125). Although none of the Huron visited Quebec on official business that year, their headmen began their councils with the French at Three Rivers by presenting gifts to Du Plessis–Bochart to condole the French for the death of Champlain and to renew the friendship they had made with him many

years before (9:281–83). The new governor, Charles Huault de Montmagny, was not at Three Rivers, but it may have been on this occasion that
he was given the name Onontio or "Great Mountain," a literal translation
of Montmagny (20:221). The name is not attested, however, before 1640.
One wonders if it was because of Jesuit influence that his name, rather than
Champlain's, was the one that the Huron, and later the Iroquois, were to
apply to all the governors of New France.

When the commercial trading was over, a second set of councils was
convened, at which it was the custom for the French to present their
counter-gifts and discuss their business with the Huron. The usual presents
were given to encourage the good treatment of the Jesuit missionaries and
to ensure that the Huron would return to Three Rivers the following
summer. As usual, the traders from Ossossané demanded to know why no
Frenchmen had come to live with them. To try to satisfy them, they were
given the lucrative task of transporting Father Isaac Jogues to the Huron
country.

THE JESUITS AS SCHOOLMASTERS

Since at least 1635, one of the Jesuits' main goals had been to gain custody
of a number of Huron children whom they could instruct for one or more
years. The Jesuits already knew that the Huron respected old people more
than young ones and that all important matters of public concern were
regulated by mature males (Thwaites 1896–1901, 10:15). Brébeuf had also
learned from experience that it was easier to discuss theological questions
with men than with women and children (10:19). In spite of this, the
Jesuits clung to the Recollets' belief that the long-term hope for converting
the Huron lay in influencing the children, who were as yet uncorrupted by
traditional beliefs (10:21). In spite of their equivocal experience with
Amantacha, they were determined to secure more Huron children to train
as a corps of missionary assistants (8:181).

To ensure necessary isolation from their families, Le Jeune argued that
Montagnais children should be sent to France for two years of training
(6:85–89), while Huron should be brought to Quebec (6:153–55). The
resulting separation from their families would give the Jesuits a free hand
to instruct these children in the French language and customs, since their
relatives would be unable to carry them off whenever they wished. Le
Jeune feared that the Indians would object to their children being scolded
and physically punished, which he regarded as essential to their education.

He also argued that the children would experience fewer distractions if they were removed from their own people and that the Huron children would serve as hostages to ensure that the Jesuits and their assistants were well-treated. No doubt, the Jesuits wished to send some Huron children to France for additional training, but after the delays in returning Amantacha to his family, such a request would likely have been turned down by the Huron.

In 1635 Etienne Binet, the French Provincial of the Society of Jesus, authorized Le Jeune to open a school for Indian children at Quebec, since donations were now available to support such an enterprise.[4] The Jesuits judged this project to be of such great importance that it was decided that Fathers Daniel and Davost should return to Quebec to instruct these children, although they were the missionaries who, next to Brébeuf, had been in the Huron country the longest and who best knew the Huron language (13:9). The Jesuits began to give special instruction to twelve young boys from Ihonatiria whom they wished to take with them (9:283; 12:39). No girls were chosen, because there were as yet no nuns at Quebec. The Huron were also probably unwilling to allow girls to be taken to Quebec, since this involved exposing them to a dangerous canoe voyage and to life among a strange, and therefore potentially hostile, people. Dangers of this sort were appropriate adventures for young men, but not for young women.

Only one youth seemed anxious to go with the Jesuits. This was Satouta, the grandson of the council chief Tsondechaouanouan, who was entrusted with all matters pertaining to foreign peoples whom the Huron visited by water, and in whose name the Huron sent formal messages to other tribes and confederacies (12:53–55). Satouta was nearly an adult and was in line to inherit his grandfather's office, which would require him to have many dealings with the French. It is therefore not surprising that in his desire to secure the Jesuits' goodwill, he said he was willing even to go to France, if they should wish it (12:41).

When the time came to depart, the women of the households that these twelve boys came from raised so many objections that only three of the twelve boys were permitted to embark with their fathers or uncles (9:283; 12:41). The departure of these boys was a matter of vital concern to their extended families, and in family matters Huron women had a strong voice. The key role ascribed to the grandmothers, or head women, of these households, clearly indicates that matrilineal and matrilocal principles remained important among the Huron. When the trading at Three Rivers was over, Satouta was the only boy whose male relatives were willing to let him stay with the French. To honour Satouta and encourage other Huron to leave their children with them, the French, in defiance of Huron custom, gave him seating precedence ahead of Huron headmen at formal meetings. In spite of this, the relatives of the two other children made excuses for taking them home with them (9:285). Du Plessis-Bochart rebuked such behaviour for showing a lack of trust in the French. He promised that if the Huron allowed up to twenty children to come to Quebec, he would send an equal number of armed Frenchmen to defend the Huron villages (9:287). Since only three children were present, it is difficult to know whether or not this promise was made in good faith.

Father Daniel warned the Huron headmen that by refusing to leave these children with the French, they were breaking pledges they had made to the Jesuits both individually and in council. To maintain the alliance the Huron must send some of their own people to live with the French, in return for the French who were sent to live with them. This appeal to Huron traditions, accompanied by much individual persuasion, finally resulted in the two other youths being left with the Jesuits. News of this decision encouraged a spirit of emulation among the Huron and a group of traders who came to Three Rivers later left three more children with the French. These too were taken to Quebec. It is unclear whether these included some of the twelve children that the Jesuits had selected in the Huron country. Not all were, however, since at least one boy had never heard Christian teaching prior to coming to Quebec and some were not Attignawantan. Still more youths were offered by traders who arrived early in September, but these could not be accepted because all the Huron interpreters, who were necessary for holding a formal council, had returned to Quebec. Before returning home, Endahiaconc came to Quebec to see how his nephew was faring and was persuaded to take home with him one of the Huron boys (not his nephew) who could not get along with the others (12:45–47; 13:125). Endahiaconc was also accompanied up the Ottawa River by Simon Baron.

Who were the five youths who remained at Quebec and why had their male kinsmen given in to French demands, in spite of the opposition of their female relatives? Satouta, as we have seen already, was the grandson and heir of an important Attignawantan headman who had relatives in both Ihonatiria and Ossossané (9:273; 13:119–23). Tsiko was a nephew of Endahiaconc, the principal headman of the Attigneenongnahac,[5] and Tewatirhon was the nephew of a council chief named Taratouan who seems to have lived near Teanaostaiaé (12:97) and of an unnamed war chief (12:95). After his return to the Huron country, and possibly after he had married, Tewatirhon lived in Taenhatentaron, which may have been his home village (21:173). About the other two boys, Andehoua (Ariethoua) and Aiandace (Aiacidace), we know only that the former came from Scanonaenrat.[6] All of these boys appear to have been matrilineal kinsmen (nephews or grandsons) of important headmen who profited from controlling their clan segments' trade with the French. These men were therefore the Huron who had most reason for wanting to establish close ties with the French. The exchange of children or adults traditionally constituted a bond of friendship between trading partners. Thus Taratouan and other headmen could now boast that they were kinsmen of the French and, in that capacity, lay claim to be counted among the "masters of the St. Lawrence River" (13:125).

The Huron boys experienced various difficulties adjusting to life among the French. They had to accustom themselves to wearing French clothes and eating French food. Their habit of caressing people as a sign of friendship was also wrongly interpreted. Satouta and Tsiko both became ill and died not long after they had fights with Frenchmen. Although they appear to have succumbed to infectious diseases, the Jesuits attributed their illnesses to overeating, resulting from their unfamiliarity with the solid nature of French food. To prevent a recurrence of this tragedy the surviving boys were fed partly, after the Huron fashion, on corn soup (12:53). The deaths of Satouta and Tsiko were witnessed by an Algonkin who knew Satouta's family and the Jesuits feared that he might report they had died from fighting or witchcraft, for which the French would be held accountable (12:51). If their relatives believed such charges, it was feared they might retaliate by trying to kill some of the Jesuits in the Huron country.

The surviving boys followed a well-defined daily routine at Quebec: following prayers, attendance at mass, and breakfast, they were taught reading, writing, and catechism. After the noonday meal, there were more prayers, followed by instruction and a free period during which the older boys often made weapons and hunted and fished near the Jesuit house. After supper, there was an examination of conscience, prayers, and early bed (12:63–65). In their free-time activities the younger boys followed the example of the older ones (12:67). During the winter, the latter cleared a patch of ground which, since there were no women present, they themselves sowed with corn in the spring. They also built a cabin near the field, in which the harvest could be stored (12:77). They urged the Jesuits to baptize them (12:67–69), so they might conclude a closer alliance with the French, and announced that if they could obtain their families' permission, they would persuade some Huron girls to marry them and return to found a Huron colony at Quebec (12:79). No doubt, they were attracted in part by the food, clothing, and tools that the French were giving them (12:79), but they also may have believed that such a colony would benefit Huron traders.

During their first two years in the Huron country, the Jesuits had made progress in learning to use the Huron language and had begun preaching to the Attignawantan. They had also established themselves as the sole representatives of French officials and fur traders among the Huron and had persuaded the Huron to send some young people to Quebec to be indoctrinated and to serve as hostages for the safety of the missionaries. These successes were based on the Huron accepting the Jesuits in their country as a necessary condition of their trading alliance with the French. Instead of tactfully working to transform this relationship into an even more solid one based on personal trust and confidence, Brébeuf proceeded to exploit the French–Huron alliance and to offend cherished Huron beliefs in the hope of bringing about mass conversions. By so doing, he accomplished little that was positive and did many things that were to harm the Jesuits in the critical years ahead. Already, his behaviour had created widespread resentment, which was still fairly well controlled on the political level, but was giving rise to many rumours that the Jesuits were practising witchcraft.

The Black Years

THE EPIDEMICS OF 1636 AND 1637

The autumn of 1636 saw the beginning of a far more prolonged and deadly series of epidemics than had afflicted the Huron in 1634. A disease that appears to have been influenza began to spread from the St. Lawrence Valley in mid-August and reached the Huron country before mid-September. It also diffused through northern Ontario and during the winter it caused many deaths, both directly and from subsequent starvation, among the hunting peoples of that area (Thwaites 1896–1901, 11:197). The northward spread of the epidemic was attributed to trade goods that the Nipissing had carried there (11:199), thus indicating that the Indians had pinpointed the source of the epidemic. Of the six priests and four hired men at Ihonatiria, only Brébeuf and Petit-Pré escaped the infection. For about two weeks, the French were confined to their beds with cramps and fever. For a time, one of the domestics was believed to be dying (11:13; 13:87–111). Nevertheless, although not all of the Jesuits and their assistants were out of danger until 15 October, all of them did recover.

The Huron were less fortunate. Already in early September, some people were ill at Ossossané, Ihonatiria, and elsewhere, but the disease grew more common as the Huron settled into their villages for the winter. In Ihonatiria, it began to spread rapidly after 29 September (13:115). By mid-October, thirteen or fourteen out of a population that could not have exceeded 300 were ill at one time (13:131) and the epidemic did not reach its peak there until after 10 November (13:145). About a week later, the number of people who were falling ill declined sharply and those who survived began to recover (13:149); however, it was not until spring that the malady ceased completely (13:165; 14:85).

In other villages the epidemic followed a similar course, although the timing was different. There were few, if any, sick in Onnentisati prior to mid-October, but many inhabitants were stricken afterwards (13:131–33). At Ossossané, the epidemic did not reach its peak before December (13:165), but the outbreak was especially severe there and remained critical into January (13:235). Fifty were sick by 4 December (13:165) and, shortly after, Simon Baron bled over 200 who were ill (13:181). The winter of 1636–37 was a particularly long one (13:249) and the cold weather seems to have dampened the spread of the disease. In the early spring, however, it flared up again, particularly in such villages as Andiataé and Onnentisati (14:7–15). Probably because food was running low, the disease had a higher incidence of fatality at this season than it had earlier (14:53).

It is clear that many, if not all, of the Attignawantan settlements were visited by this epidemic. Unfortunately, we have no information concerning the three other tribes of the Huron confederacy, although it seems unlikely that they could have escaped it. Nevertheless, Le Mercier's comment that the disease assailed only some villages (15:13), and a statement that the Attigneenongnahac village of Ekhiondastsaan escaped the epidemic (14:29), suggest that the eastern parts of the Huron country may not have been as badly affected as Ossossané and the Penetanguishene Peninsula. In the description of Brébeuf's visit to Teanaostaiaé and Scanonaenrat in the spring of 1637, for instance, there is no mention of these places having suffered a high mortality (14:25–29).

The number of Huron who died in this epidemic is especially difficult to estimate. The statement that many were ill in Onnentisati, "several (plusieurs) of whom died" (13:133) does not suggest a high mortality. It is clear, however, that many people died in other Attignawantan villages. Ihonatiria was devastated by the epidemic (13:165), with numerous deaths reported in most longhouses (13:163). By January, over fifty people had died in Ossossané (13:213). The Nipissing, who were wintering in the Huron country, carried away seventy bodies when they left for the north the following spring (14:37). Since Champlain had estimated the entire Nipissing population to be between 700 and 800 (Biggar 1922–36, 3:40), this suggests a mortality rate of about ten per cent. If a similar ratio were applied only to the Attignawantan, it would indicate that nearly 1000 Huron died. Yet, allowing for the better diet and housing of the Huron, this may be too high an estimate. Doubling the partial estimate for Ossossané suggests about 500 deaths among the Attignawantan. What is imponderable, however, is how many died among the other tribes.

Soon after the Huron had departed to trade at Three Rivers in the summer of 1637, there was a new outbreak of disease that affected the entire Huron confederacy (Thwaites 1896–1901, 15:13). Unlike the previous epidemic, many who became ill died within two days (15:69). The Huron who went to Three Rivers to trade were also stricken, either on their way down the Ottawa River or while they were trading, and many died on route (12:231). Unlike the previous year no Frenchmen became ill, either at Three Rivers or in the Huron country (12:261; 14:229). Thus, while it is possible that this epidemic was yet another outbreak of the former one, it is more likely to have been a European childhood ailment against which most Frenchmen had already acquired immunity. Although the epidemic reached the Huron country before the beginning of the trading season, this does not rule out the possibility that it was carried inland from the St. Lawrence. Alternatively, and in my opinion more likely, the epidemic spread northward from the Susquehannock, who in February 1637 suffered from an unidentified malady (14:9). The new ailment, which seems to have killed many more people than did the last one, persisted into the autumn of 1637.

Except for Guillaume Chaudron in 1623, the Huron had probably not seen a Frenchman seriously ill before the autumn of 1636. The people from Ihonatiria flocked to visit the ailing French and offer them advice. They were surprised by Brébeuf's efforts to keep his cabin quiet and to prevent those who were sick from being disturbed (13:99–101). The Huron regarded this treatment, which was so different from their own, as further evidence of the deviant, hence sinister, practices of the Jesuits. Much as he would have liked to, Brébeuf found himself unable to prevent these visits.

Tsiouendaentaha, who prided himself on his friendship for the Jesuits, requested that they allow a famous shaman to visit them. This was Tonneraouanont, a small hunchback from Onnentisati who claimed to be the incarnation of a powerful spirit that had penetrated into a woman's womb (13:105–7). No doubt, in making this claim, Tonneraouanont was trading on his deformity, since the Huron visualized a number of important mythological figures as dwarfs. Tonneraouanont offered to heal the French in return for a payment of ten glass beads and an extra bead for each patient (13:103). Since this shaman valued his services highly, his fee indicates how highly such trade goods were still valued and esteemed. When the Jesuits refused to have anything to do with his healing rites, Tonneraouanont pointed out several roots that he believed were helpful for alleviating fevers and instructed the Jesuits how to use them; yet the missionaries ignored even this advice in order to scorn all assistance from someone they believed to be in league with the devil (13:105). This incident demonstrates the considerable extent to which the later hostility between priests and shamans was of the Jesuits' own making.

When the Jesuits recovered from their own illnesses, they began extending practical help to the Huron. Meat and broth were given to those who were ill and prunes, raisins, sugar, lemon peel, senna, and similar items were distributed for whatever medicinal value they had (13:113–15, 147). At the same time, Simon Baron was kept busy bleeding those who were ill (13:115). Although well aware of the limitations of their pharmacopoeia, the Jesuits hoped that by doing the work of physicians, they might be able to undermine or discredit the shamans (15:69). Such work also brought them into contact with the dying, thus increasing their chances of being able to baptize them.

As the original epidemic of 1636 grew worse, the Huron turned to their shamans and curing societies in hope of finding an individual or group who possessed the knowledge to control the disease. It was regarded as a moral duty for anyone who had such skills to put them at the service of their community. When the Jesuits began to recover from their own bouts of influenza, and thereby demonstrated their power over it, the people of Ihonatiria turned to them for help. The Jesuits were anxious to use the epidemic as a means of advancing their mission work and for this purpose were willing to rely on their own idea of supernatural aid. Brébeuf informed the Huron that the only certain way to overcome the epidemic was to believe in the Christian deity and vow to keep his commandments. He recommended that the people of Ihonatiria should make a public vow that if it would please God to end the contagion, they would agree to serve him and in the following spring would erect a cabin in his honour. On 29 November, the headmen of Ihonatiria visited the Jesuits and promised to do whatever they said was necessary to combat the disease. The Jesuits were annoyed, however, that various men, including Taretandé, the new headman of the village (13:215), left before any Christian ceremony began (13:161).

The next day, while still professing to be Christians and saying they were ready to be baptized, Ihonatirians who were members of healing societies donned their masks and performed traditional rituals (13:175). At the same time, they enquired when they should assemble to pray. This led the Jesuits to denounce their hypocrisy. What the Jesuits did not understand was that the Huron regarded Christianity as another curing society and membership in one society did not rule out membership in another. Far from the Huron being hypocrites, the Jesuits had failed to convey to them their own understanding of baptism.

Early in December 1636, the headmen of Wenrio invited Brébeuf to attend a village council in order to discuss what curing rituals the Jesuits might perform for the village. Disappointed about what had happened at Ihonatiria, Brébeuf stated that the people of Wenrio would have to agree that marriages would be binding for life and that they would give up their belief in dreams. They would also have to stop eating human flesh, attending eat-all feasts, and participating in andacwander and Awataerohi rituals. Aenons and Onaconchiaronk, who were the principal headmen present, said that it was impossible to accept Brébeuf's proposals, as to do so would destroy the Huron way of life. They asked Brébeuf to recognize that French ways were not suited to the Huron and to respect that they served different gods. Brébeuf openly rejected this suggestion and the council broke up with no more being said (13:169–75). The epidemic had grown so serious, however, that the next day it was decided that it was better to agree to Brébeuf's conditions than to go on dying. The men of Wenrio therefore agreed to accept Brébeuf's proposals and promised to build a chapel in the spring if the epidemic was brought to an end. As at Ihonatiria, however, villagers soon turned to other cures when those offered by the Jesuits proved ineffective (13:175). On 12 December the council of Ossossané agreed to the same terms that Wenrio had and Okhiarenta, an important shaman, was sent through the town stating what must be done if the Jesuits were to stop the epidemic (13:187). The epidemic continued, however, and, as happened elsewhere, the people of Ossossané soon looked elsewhere for an effective cure.

As illness increased, the Jesuits regarded it as their duty to try to baptize as many of the dying as possible. Throughout the fall and early winter, and again in the spring of 1637, small parties of Jesuits visited most of the Attignawantan villages searching for children to baptize and dying adults whom they might attempt to instruct. Although Ihonatiria remained the base for their operations, many visits were to Ossossané, the largest and most important of the Attignawantan settlements. Other communities they visited were Wenrio, Anonatea, Onnentisati, Arenté, Andiataé, the three hamlets of Khinonascarant (Quieunonascaran), and Iahenhouton. Their renewed emphasis on baptizing the sick reopened the question of whether baptism healed or killed the sick. In Ossossané, where the Jesuits had arrived fairly recently, many people seem to have still regarded it as a healing rite, but in and around Ihonatiria, where Jesuit teachings were better known, increasing numbers of people rejected this explanation. The Jesuits described baptism as showing the way to heaven, a claim that linked baptism with death in the minds of these Huron. The Jesuits reinforced this interpretation by stressing to potential converts that baptism was a medicine not for the body but for the soul (13:189).

In spite of such beliefs, a certain number of Huron still wanted baptism, either for themselves or for their children. Some were people who no longer believed that it restored health, but who were anxious, after death, to join relatives who had already been baptized (13:29, 127–29, 149). To counteract this, the Jesuits began to refuse baptism to those who did not explicitly acknowledge some other reason for requesting it. Others, who had seen relatives recover after being baptized or who knew of people who had, still seem to have been convinced that baptism was a healing rite, in spite of what the Jesuits said about it. Some people apparently agreed to be baptized in order to be left in peace or so as not to offend the Jesuits. Their state of mind is made credible by a Huron named Joachim Annieouton who, around 1671, confessed that although he had been considered a good Christian for more than twenty-five years, he had been one in appearance only. He had given this impression in order to gratify the Jesuits and so they would stop trying to convert him. He explained that while he had originally said "Yes, I will be converted," the Huron had two ways of saying the word *aaao*; a clipped form meaning "yes" and a more drawn-out one that they used when they wished only to appear to yield to a request (55:297). The latter was the form that Annieouton had used. That this could be found out in 1670 is some indication of the gap in understanding that must have separated the Jesuits from those they baptized in 1636. Huron who recovered after baptism ignored the admonitions of the Jesuits and continued to live as before (13:133). Such behaviour does not indicate perversity or ingratitude but simply that on an individual as well as a collective level, the Huron were unaware of the significance that the French attached to baptism.

In general, however, resistance to baptism stiffened during 1636, especially in and around Ihonatiria. Even at Ossossané, baptisms plummeted as the death rate soared. Many households refused to permit further baptisms after the deaths of baptized members (13:183). Individuals refused baptism because they did not want their souls to be separated from close relatives and friends who had died without it (13:135, 151). When Arakhié, who was one of the boys the Jesuits wished to take to Quebec, fell ill, his family partitioned off the section of the cabin in which he lay and kept watch so that the Jesuits could not get near to baptize him (13:117–25). They did this because a kinsman named Akhioca had died without baptism at Ossossané only a short time before (13:123). Some people expressed the fear that heaven would be full of Frenchmen, who would be unwilling to share their food with Indians (13:127). Others gave more idiosyncratic reasons, such as a woman who refused to promise that she would never divorce her husband since this was an unacceptable constraint on her liberty (13:141). Still others began to manifest open contempt for the teachings of the Jesuits and to ridicule them (13:141–43); however, an old man named Anerraté requested baptism when his daughter Khiongnona died after she had refused it (13:133–41).

The growing reluctance of Huron to permit their children to be baptized led the Jesuits to attempt to baptize ailing children without their families' knowledge. This was done by the pretext of giving the children raisins or sugar water (13:167; 14:41), by pretending to feel their pulse or wipe their brow (14:67–69), or straightforwardly when no one else was looking (14:7–9). In each instance, a handkerchief dipped in water was used. The Huron were no doubt aware of these baptisms and the clandestine behaviour of the Jesuits must have aroused additional fears.

Between the summers of 1636 and 1637, the Jesuits baptized about 250 people (14:107). Most were in the autumn of 1636 and the early part of the following winter; about fifty were in the spring of 1637 (cf. 13:35; 14:53, 107). These baptisms were performed in various Attignawantan villages, but many were in Ossossané. Both children and adults were baptized and almost all were believed to be in danger of dying (13:35). The following year, few people were baptized, except in Ossossané, where the figure reached 100 (15:69). At least forty-four of these died, including twenty-two children still on cradleboards. In addition, there were eleven baptisms in Ihonatiria (15:129).

The spread of illness also encouraged a general upsurge in Huron healing practices. The curing societies performed their rituals in every village, and shamans sought to enhance their reputations by divining the cause of the epidemics and recommending effective cures. Tsondacouané, who was in much repute around his home town of Onnentisati, entered into communion with various spirits who inhabited features of the landscape and on their recommendation prescribed the Awataerohi and the erection of straw masks above the doors of houses and human figures on the roofs (13:227–33). Later, he advised that the dead should be buried in the ground for a time before being placed in bark tombs in the village cemetery (13:259). Another cure was revealed to Tehorenhaegnon after a twelve-day fast on the shores of Nottawasaga Bay. In January 1637 he shared his new power with three other shamans, Saossarinon, Khioutenstia, and Iandatassa (13:241), who were deputized to practise his cure. At the climax of this ritual those who were sick were sprinkled from a kettle filled with a mysterious water, while the shamans followed the kettle fanning them with a turkey wing that had been supplied by Tehorenhaegnon (13:237–43).

The sprinkling of the sick may have been imitated from the ritual of baptism. Alternatively, the claim that the ritual was revealed by a lake suggests a possible resemblance to those performed by the Iroquois Otter Society, who also sprinkle the sick with water (Tooker 1964:103 n. 96). It is possible that an indigenous pattern for this ritual already existed in Huron culture. It is also possible that Tehorenhaegnon's rite was a syncretistic one, at least in terms of its symbolism. Its popularity may have been derived from the fact that it equated the powerful magic of the Jesuits with practices that were familiar to the Huron and were recognized by them as being unambiguously beneficent. The novel features of this ritual may explain why Tehorenhaegnon and his assistants showed a professional interest in measuring its efficacy (13:243). While the Jesuits condemned the ritual as a failure and claimed that its practitioners were soon discredited, the same rite was performed at Ossossané in 1639 (19:243) and a similar one, in which those who were ill drank from a kettle, was performed the same year among the Arendarhonon (20:29). If this rite originated in 1636, it appears to have enjoyed approval and diffused rapidly among the Huron tribes.

Harold Blau (1966:577–79; Thwaites 1896–1901, 13:243, 263) has also suggested that a ceremony first reported in February 1637, in which the participants appeared as hunchbacks, wore masks, and carried sticks, was an invention of this period and was first performed in honour of Tonneraouanont who had died two weeks earlier, after he was injured in an accident. Blau suggests that the purpose of this ceremony organized by Tsondacouané was to gain the power credited to Tonneraouanont or to trick the disease-causing spirits into believing he was still alive. Yet, the placing of masks at the entrances to the houses, which took place at the end of this ceremony, resembles the ritual performed some time before Tonneraouanont's death, also on the orders of Tsondacouané. Inasmuch as dwarfs or hunchbacks seem to have had considerable religious significance among the Huron (10:183), both Tonneraouanont's claims of power and these rituals may be traced to a common theme in Huron culture, rather than being historically related to each other in the way Blau has proposed.

THE SEARCH FOR A CAUSE

Measured by any standards familiar to the Huron, the epidemics of 1636 and 1637 were extraordinarily severe. To stop these illnesses, the Huron attempted to determine their cause. They believed that uncontrollable illnesses were likely to be brought about by especially powerful witchcraft. The problem thus was to find and counteract those who were practising it. The Nipissing blamed the epidemics on the Kichesipirini and claimed that the latter had afflicted surrounding nations with pestilence because these groups had refused to help the Kichesipirini wage war against the Iroquois (Thwaites 1896–1901, 13:211); however, almost all of the Huron who believed that witchcraft was the cause of the epidemics blamed them on the French, and more specifically on the Jesuits. The Jesuits recognized that the most intelligent Huron were driven to this conclusion by their inability to understand why the Jesuits wanted to live in their country and why the French traders insisted that the Huron let them do so (17:125). Traders and warriors had legitimate reasons for visiting remote tribes and men and women might intermarry with foreign groups, but what reason could these bizarre, celibate shamans have for wishing to dwell among them? The Huron saw the Jesuits as protecting themselves and other Frenchmen from disease and, like other Indians, they concluded that the Jesuits were not ordinary men, but possessed of powerful spirits (13:165).

Questions that were not so easily answered were why the Jesuits did not use their power to help their Indian allies; and what the significance of baptism was. The Jesuits' behaviour suggested extremely sinister motives. Death was a source of great anxiety for the Huron, who did not think it right that the Jesuits should ask a sick man if he wished to go to heaven or to hell; instead, they should wish for his recovery (13:127). The Huron perceived a seemingly ungenerous spirit (which was the hallmark of witchcraft) in other aspects of Jesuit behaviour. The frequently closed door of their cabin and their refusal to admit Huron visitors except at specified times of the day strongly suggested that sorcery was being practised within (15:33). Likewise, their adamant refusal to give presents to satisfy the desires of people's souls was proof that they wished to see individual Huron suffer and die (15:179–81). The same lack of desire to help was also apparent in the Jesuits' condemnation of curing rituals, such as the Ononharoia and the andacwander (17:171–89). It even appeared to manifest itself in the stinginess that the Huron believed led the Jesuits to skim the grease from the broth they gave to the sick. This led the Huron to accuse them of making the broth merely to accumulate grease for their own use (13:147).

The Huron also saw evidence of witchcraft in the Jesuits' public utterances. It was claimed that when Brébeuf had returned in 1634, he had said he would remain with the Huron for only five years. This was interpreted as evidence that the Jesuits believed they could annihilate the Huron within that space of time (15:59). The wampum collar that Brébeuf had presented to the Attignawantan in 1636 in order to show them the way to heaven was an even clearer statement that he intended to kill them (13:209). It was reported that in 1636 Father Daniel had warned a Huron youth who was planning to return to the Huron country that he should remain at Quebec, since pestilence was about to devastate his country (15:25). It was over a year before the Huron headmen were to proclaim Daniel innocent of this charge (15:139). Among those who were most active in spreading these rumours was the shaman Tonneraouanont, whose skill and goodwill the Jesuits had scorned and rejected (13:213). When Tonneraouanont was injured and dying, he refused a Jesuit offer of ointments to treat himself, just as they had refused his cures (13:225).

As the Huron became convinced that the Jesuits were responsible for their illnesses, supernatural evidence began to accumulate against them. It was claimed, for example, that a Tionnontaté who was stricken by the epidemic had vomited up a lead pellet, which proved that the French had bewitched him (15:21). It was also widely rumoured that an Arendarhonon had returned from the dead to report that in the other world he had met two women who came from England. These women said that the Jesuits were evil men who would not return home until they had killed all the Huron (15:51). Another story that was current in the autumn of 1637 was that four English pinnaces had ascended the St. Lawrence River as far as the Rivière des Prairies and that their commanders had said that the Jesuits were the cause of all the sickness (15:31). It is uncertain whether or not this story incorporates knowledge of anti-Jesuit propaganda that was current at Quebec after 1629. Both stories, however, seem to reflect a romantic memory of the English as trading partners who did not foist their shamans on the Indians.

The Huron believed that until the Jesuits' methods were known, they would be unable to combat their witchcraft. Most speculation saw the Jesuits acting, not on their own initiative, but as agents of the French officials at Quebec. Much credence was given to an Algonkin report that shortly before his death Champlain had told a Montagnais headman that if he died, he would carry off the Huron with him. This story, which was undoubtedly spread by the Algonkin to undermine the Huron's confidence in the French, was believable because Indian headmen who thought themselves bewitched sometimes requested that if they died, their relatives should exact blood revenge from those whom they held to be responsible for their condition (12:85–87; 13:147).

This story was similar to the still more popular one that the Jesuits had been sent to the Huron country to avenge the murder of Etienne Brûlé (12:87). Many Huron suspected that the disowning of Brûlé by the French was a ruse to cover their intended revenge. Rumours, fashioned in the idiom of a matrilineal society, claimed that either Brûlé's sister (14:53) or his uncle (14:17) was seeking to annihilate the Huron. One Algonkin reported seeing a French woman infecting the whole country with her breath (14:53), although this supernatural agent by no means absolved the Jesuits of responsibility for what was happening. When the epidemic afflicted a group whom Le Mercier identifies as Cheveux Relevés, but who were probably the Nipissing,[7] they concluded that it was because some of them had once robbed Brûlé of a collar containing 2400 wampum beads. They therefore offered to return a like number of beads to the Jesuits if they would withdraw their scourge. The Jesuits refused to accept these beads because they feared that if they did, the Huron would assume that they were concluding some agreement with the Nipissing that was detrimental to the Huron (14:101–3).

Even more varied were the means by which the Huron imagined that the Jesuits were practising their witchcraft. The sugar that the Jesuits gave to the sick was an obvious means of injecting charms into victims; therefore Tsondacouané and other shamans warned the Huron not to allow themselves to be fed this "French snow" (14:51). Such warnings were extended to all the food and drugs that the Jesuits distributed in their efforts to counteract the influence of the shamans. Because the Huron practised cannibalism, the Jesuits tried to keep their belief that the communion wafers were the body of Christ secret from all except those whose faith in Christianity had been well tested. In 1637 a rumour began to spread that the Jesuits had brought a corpse from France which they kept in the tabernacle in their chapel and that it was this corpse that was causing the Huron to die (12:237–39; 15:33). It was also said that the Jesuits had caused a great many children to die by taking a child, or a picture of a child, into the forest and stabbing it with a large needle (15:33; 12:237). The Huron regarded as spirits the anthropomorphic beings that were portrayed in the colourful paintings of religious themes that the Jesuits were importing as objects of instruction. Rumours circulated about the dangerous influences that emanated from the images that the Jesuits kept in their chapel and which reputedly penetrated into the bodies of Indians who looked at them (14:53, 97). When life-sized paintings of Christ and the Virgin Mary were exhibited in the chapel at Ossossané in 1637, these were said to cause illness. Illustrations of hell were interpreted as representations of the fevers and other torments that afflicted the Huron (14:103; 15:35). During the epidemic of 1637–38, certain Tionnontaté who had seen the Jesuits' chapel offered them a beaver robe if they would prevent illness from issuing therefrom (15:57). Finally, there was a rumour that the French had bewitched a cloak and buried it near Three Rivers, but in such a way that the Huron were bound to steal it (12:87; 13:147). This, or a cloth that the Jesuits kept hidden in their cabin, was said to cause the epidemic (15:45). It is possible that clothing stolen at Three Rivers was in fact one of the means by which European illnesses were communicated to the Huron.

Disasters always gave rise to charges of witchcraft among the Huron themselves and the epidemics of the 1630s were no exception. In November 1636, a man named Oaca accused a Huron living in Ihonatiria of causing his illness. Others took up the charge and it was said that the accused had been seen roaming about at night casting flames out of his mouth (13:155–57). Although he was only threatened with death, in the hope that this would make him stop practising witchcraft, within a year two other suspected witches were slain among the Attignawantan (15:53). These may or may not have included a woman who was tortured in order to force her to name her accomplices before being killed in Ossossané in April 1637 (14:37–39). All of these killings were sanctioned by headmen or war chiefs in the hope that such action would frighten other witches. For any Huron who had many enemies or whose behaviour was regarded as deviant, it was a dangerous time.

As the circumstantial evidence against the Jesuits increased daily, there was talk of either killing them or forcing them to go back to Quebec (11:15); however, during the autumn of 1636 and the following winter, such talk was confined principally to Ihonatiria and the four other villages that were at odds with the rest of the Attignawantan. As the headmen of these villages pondered what the Jesuits had said and done since their return, their distaste for the Jesuits' teachings grew. They began to argue that mankind could not have come from the Garden of Eden, as the Jesuits claimed, since the Indians could not have crossed the ocean in their frail canoes; moreover, if they had done so, they would have known how to make the same things that the French did (13:219). Some expressed the opinion that nothing the French said was true. By clearly defining their own beliefs in opposition to those of the Jesuits, these headmen began to dissipate some of the aura of mystery that had formerly surrounded the Jesuits' teachings.

In December Taretandé, the new headman of Ihonatiria (probably the brother of the dead Sangwati), and his brother Sononkhiaconc met the headmen of neighbouring villages in order to discuss what should be done with the Jesuits. Taretandé said that if anyone in his family died, he would murder the first Frenchman he encountered, while Achioantaeté, who otherwise claimed to be a friend of the Jesuits, said that if he were the principal headman of the Attignawantan, he would order the Jesuits to be killed. The council seems to have decided that the most prudent policy for dealing with the Jesuits was the normal one of accusing them of witchcraft, in the hope that this would frighten them into desisting from the practice. Taretandé visited the Jesuits and denounced them as sorcerers. He said that the best they could hope for was to be sent back to Quebec in the spring (13:215–17). The children of Ihonatiria teased the Jesuits that they would soon have their heads split; and the Jesuits began to fear from these taunts that the headmen had already given orders for this to be done (11:15). From December onwards, the Jesuits found it necessary to stop visiting Ihonatiria to preach and instruct the children. Any mention of death aroused the instant hostility of the villagers (13:221).

THE MOVE TO OSSOSSANÉ

By late spring 1637 the epidemics had come to an end in most places and with it the hostility to the Jesuits had ceased. Ihonatiria, however, had suffered many deaths and was a ruined village (Thwaites 1896–1901,

13:165). Already in the spring of 1636, when evidence was uncovered that seemed to indicate that witchcraft was being practised in the village, one of its wealthiest inhabitants, possibly Aouandoïe, moved with his household to Arenté (10:285).[8] In January 1637 Taretandé, Sononkhiaconc, their mother, and other members of the village headman's family died (13:217–23). The mother was Oquiaendis, who had been baptized in 1634, but was now as opposed to the Jesuits as her sons were. These losses, together with a generally high rate of mortality, made it likely that in the near future those who were still alive in Ihonatiria would transfer to other villages. Under these circumstances, the Jesuits began to consider moving to a larger and friendlier community.

On 17 March Brébeuf and Le Mercier met with the headmen of the five northernmost Attignawantan villages. At this meeting they posed two questions: Were the northern Attignawantan now prepared to believe what the Jesuits taught? Would it be possible for some of the Jesuits' hired men to marry Huron women (14:15–17)? In the Jesuits' minds, these two questions were closely linked. Champlain had been anxious to see French men and Huron women intermarry to produce a single people and Brébeuf believed that under the right circumstances such marriages could help to promote the spread of Christianity. It would appear, however, that the main reason that the Jesuits wanted to see their hired men married was to prevent a resurgence of the promiscuous relationships with Huron women that had existed prior to 1629.

The Attignawantan were not inclined to show much enthusiasm for the Jesuits' teachings, even though they stressed that they no longer bore them any personal ill-will. The headmen stated that Frenchmen were free to marry Huron women and noted that, in the past, they had done so without asking the permission of headmen. This reference to Brûlé and his companions led Brébeuf to explain that whereas those Frenchmen had been content to live like Indians, his desire was to turn the Huron into Christians. Therefore, any further marriages would have to follow French custom and be indissoluble. A few days later, the head of the council came to enquire into certain practical aspects of the proposal: the kind of betrothal presents a man would give his wife; whether or not a husband would take his wife to France with him if he left the Huron country; and if there were a divorce, what property a woman would have the right to keep (14:19–21). The inability of the headmen to view the problem of marriage as a religious issue convinced the Jesuits that it was best to drop the subject. This left unsolved the problem of controlling their hired help.

Since any relocation of their mission would entail fewer difficulties if the

Attignawantan were again on good terms, Brébeuf was anxious to smooth over as many difficulties within the tribe as possible. He therefore enquired on 17 March if the northern villages wished to be reconciled with the rest of the Attignawantan. Being informed that they did, he made several journeys to and fro in the hope of persuading the Attignawantan to convene a general council for this purpose. He also offered to present 1200 wampum beads to the two parties to help forge a new bond between them. The headmen of Ossossané and the other southern villages agreed to meet at Andiataé to effect a reconciliation but because of Aenons's reluctance to attend, the meeting had to be called off (14:15–23). These negotiations nevertheless provided the Jesuits with an opportunity to establish still closer relations with the headmen of Ossossané (14:33).

On 29 March the Jesuits met with the leaders of Ihonatiria to learn whether they would remain where they were for another winter or were planning to unite with the people of Wenrio. They replied that they intended to remain in the village for one more year, but might rejoin the people of Wenrio the following spring. Pressed to state whether they believed what the Jesuits taught, the men of Ihonatiria replied that some believed but the rest could not be answered for (14:23–25).

In the spring, it was once again safe to travel and Father Garnier accompanied Brébeuf on a visit to Teanaostaiaé, where Brébeuf offered condolence presents to Amantacha's family. Both Scanonaenrat and Ekhiondastsaan were visited in the course of this journey. Brébeuf hoped that in the near future the Jesuits would be able to establish a residence at Teanaostaiaé (11:17). Later, Father Garnier accompanied the Jesuits' hired men on a trading expedition to the Tionnontaté. The Jesuits had heard that many people were sick there, although the peak of the epidemic was past before Garnier arrived. He managed to baptize only ten children and two old women (14:35).

After further inconclusive negotiations designed to reunite Ihonatiria and Wenrio and to promote goodwill among the Attignawantan, on 17 May the Jesuits informed Anenkhiondic of their desire to establish a residence at Ossossané. This was approved by the Ossossané council who agreed to provide a cabin twelve yards long for the Jesuits to live in. The people of Ossossané were so anxious to have the Jesuits living in their village that when the council was over, each member took his hatchet and they and a large crowd began to prepare the building site (14:57). On 21 May Father Pijart and two French workmen left for Ossossané to supervise the building of the cabin, which was finished by 7 June (14:75). On 9 June forty or fifty men and women came from Ossossané to Ihonatiria in order to carry the Jesuits' corn and furniture to their new home. Headmen supervised this operation and the people of Ossossané worked without asking for presents in return (14:105). All of the large towns along the southern border of the Huron country expressed pleasure that the Jesuits were moving nearer to them. Brébeuf, Le Mercier, and Garnier were to spend the following winter at Ossossané with Father Paul Ragueneau who had arrived in the Huron country in the summer of 1637 while, for the time being, Pijart, Chastellain, and Jogues remained at Ihonatiria.

HURON HOSTILITY BECOMES GENERAL

When the second epidemic broke out in all the Huron villages in the summer of 1637, the fear and hatred of the Jesuits that formerly had been confined to the northern villages of the Penetanguishene Peninsula became general throughout the Huron confederacy. The previous autumn, Frenchmen as well as Huron had been ill and this had tended to alleviate the hostility that was felt towards the French (Thwaites 1896–1901, 13: 111). This time, however, the Jesuits remained in good health and fears that formerly had been confined to the north began to spread. Within a few days it was generally agreed that the Jesuits were responsible for what was happening. Only the Jesuits' new hosts in Ossossané remained more favourably disposed towards them.

In Angoutenc, where the epidemic was particularly severe, people were reluctant to speak to the Jesuits and would not let them enter their houses, fearing they would fall victims to their witchcraft. Several visits were made there to minister to the dying, but without effect (15:23). When one war chief saw some Jesuits about to enter his longhouse, he threatened to split their heads if they advanced any farther. As the epidemic grew worse the war chiefs, who were responsible for the elimination of witches, began to clamour for action against the Jesuits and to challenge the power of the more conservative headmen.

Early in June Ondesson, one of the most celebrated Huron war chiefs, and another headman invited the Jesuits in Ossossané to attend a council in Angoutenc to clear themselves of the accusations that were being made against them. At the same time one of the Ossossané headmen warned the French that the people of Onnentisati were convinced that the Jesuits were sorcerers (15:25–27). It was clear that the Jesuits were being summoned to Angoutenc to stand trial for witchcraft. In spite of the danger to which they were exposing themselves, the Jesuits decided to go to Angoutenc.

The village headmen received them courteously and invited them to explain to the people of the village what had brought them to the Huron country. The Jesuits explained that they had come out of goodwill. They consoled the Huron for their dead and stated that it was their aim to live and die themselves among the Huron. Two headmen recapitulated what the Jesuits said and warned the young men of the village not to strike a blow that the whole country would regret (15:29). This and accompanying expressions of goodwill convinced the Jesuits that they had been found innocent. Notwithstanding, the Jesuits continued to be treated with so much hostility that they decided to discontinue their visits to Angoutenc (15:31). Later, rumours had it that after the Jesuits had left, the council had reassembled and resolved to kill the first Frenchman who fell into their hands (15:25–31), thereby terminating the French–Huron alliance.

Throughout the summer the public clamour against the Jesuits increased, even in Ossossané. On 4 August the headmen of the Huron confederacy met in Ossossané to coordinate their foreign policy and to deal with the Jesuits. The majority of those who were present were council chiefs; however, some war chiefs attended in place of council chiefs who had died in the epidemic but whose successors had not yet been named (15:43). The presence of these war chiefs was another indication of their growing influence during this episode of crisis.

At the first session of this council, which discussed peace and war, the Jesuits presented several hundred wampum beads as evidence of their concern for the general welfare of the Huron. The second meeting was held on the evening of the same day. It was presided over by Ontitarac, an elderly, blind man, who lived in Ossossané but whose name is otherwise not recorded (15:39). He admonished those who were present not to conceal anything they knew about the cause of the epidemic or how it might be halted. Anenkhiondic more pointedly suggested that the Jesuits were among those who had knowledge of what was happening. Ostensibly so that he might follow the proceedings more easily but, in fact, in order to sway the council more easily, Brébeuf asked for and was granted permission to sit among the principal headmen in the centre of the longhouse. The headmen who were present then lamented the suffering of the country and each enumerated the sick and dead among his own clansmen. They blamed the Jesuits for what was happening and demanded that they be punished. No one defended the Jesuits and as the meeting progressed the headmen began to urge Brébeuf to produce a piece of bewitched cloth that was said to be the source of the illness. The Jesuits were promised that their lives would be spared if only they would admit that they had caused the epidemic and would reveal how they had done it. The Huron believed that such a confession automatically would strip the Jesuits of the power to do evil.

When Brébeuf found the headmen unwilling to believe his denials, he offered to let them search the Jesuits' cabin and to destroy all the cloth they found there. Ontitarac replied that this was the way sorcerers and guilty people always talked (15:45). Brébeuf then attempted to deliver a sermon explaining the nature of the Christian God and the rewards and punishments he inflicted on mankind. Contrary to normal Huron practice, this speech was interrupted repeatedly, especially by Ontitarac. Even Anenkhiondic, who had so far remained silent, accused the Jesuits of always repeating the same thing and only talking about the oki or spirit they worshipped (15:49). Many headmen walked out in the middle of Brébeuf's speech and one announced that if someone were to kill the Jesuits, the Huron leaders would have no objection. Many Huron expected that the confederacy council would order the Jesuits to be slain and the fact that the council was taking the charges against them seriously greatly enhanced fears and mistrust of them among the general population (15: 53). The headmen decided to postpone any final decision about what would be done with the Jesuits until the traders had returned from Three Rivers, so that if they were killed, as many Huron as possible would be safe from French reprisals (15:47).

In the following weeks, the Jesuits were told that the headmen were losing control over the young men, who were anxious to purge the country of sorcerers (15:53). An uncle of Amantacha suggested that the priests should help several stricken headmen to recover, since the war chiefs would be without restraint if they died. The Jesuits were warned that their cabin at Ossossané would be burned when they least expected it and when a fire broke out on 3 October, they believed this to be an attempt on their lives (15:53).

Soon after the traders had returned from Three Rivers in mid-October, the headmen of Teanaostaiaé are said to have exhorted the young men of their village to kill the Jesuits while the people of Ossossané were away fishing (17:59). When the Jesuits learned of this, their hired men prepared to die fighting and Le Mercier went to summon Brébeuf from Ihonatiria (15:57–59). Soon the Jesuits learned that their would-be assailants had been persuaded not to take unilateral action, but that a meeting was being held in Ossossané at which new plans were being formulated to kill them. It was reported that when the Jesuits entered this meeting, it had already been decided that if their faces betrayed any sign of fear or guilt, they were to be slain on the spot. The only headman who remained well disposed towards them had been persuaded to leave town so that any decision to massacre the Jesuits might be unanimous. When Brébeuf arrived that evening and went to greet the principal headmen, they bowed their heads, indicating that the Jesuits were condemned men. Faced with the likelihood of death, Brébeuf drew up a spiritual testament that he entrusted to one of the few Huron who were still well inclined towards the French. He also gave orders that the French who survived any massacre should shelter among Huron who were their personal friends and that special efforts be made to convey the manuscript of their principal Huron dictionary to Quebec (15:61–65).

At the same time, in order to show that he did not fear death as a sorcerer might, Brébeuf gave an athataion, or death feast, to which he invited the people of Ossossané. He addressed them, as he had a right to do on such an occasion, concerning the interest that the Jesuits had in the welfare of the Huron and explained to them the nature of Christian beliefs about life after death. Many Huron attended this feast and listened to Brébeuf without interrupting him. Several days passed and, to the astonishment of both the Jesuits and the people of Ossossané, the headmen ceased to threaten the missionaries (15:67). By 6 November the epidemic had run its course and the missionaries were left in peace.

THE JESUITS' PROTECTION

How did it happen that when native sorcerers were being slain and the Jesuits were almost universally believed to be responsible for the epidemics, they too did not perish? In their *Relations*, the Jesuits expressed wonder at this and piously ascribed their survival to God's providence (Thwaites 1896–1901, 20:75); however, the Jesuits' real protection was the fur trade. Since the French officials emphasized that the continuation of this trade required the Huron to accept the Jesuits in their country and treat them well, the Huron believed that any action that endangered the Jesuits also endangered trade. That the Jesuits were not slain or even asked to return to Quebec at this time, despite the extreme hostility that many families must have felt towards them, is evidence of the degree to which the Huron now felt themselves to be dependent on French trade goods.

As might be expected, the most vocal supporters of the Jesuits were the headmen most deeply involved in trading with the French. One of these was Aenons. When during the winter of 1636–37 the headmen from the

Ihonatiria region debated whether the Jesuits ought to be killed or at least deported, Aenons argued that such action would be very dangerous and might lead to the destruction of the country. He said that if the Huron were unable to trade with the French for only two successive years, they would be reduced to such extremities that they would consider themselves lucky if they could beg assistance from the Algonkin (13:215–17). He persuaded the other headmen to come with him to ask the Jesuits not to send reports of their ill treatment to Quebec, lest the French retaliate against Huron traders who went to the St. Lawrence (12:89; 13:233). Later that same winter, Aenons was one of the principal exponents of the theory that the Mohawk had transmitted the current illness from the Susquehannock to the St. Lawrence (14:9). He was seeking to protect the Jesuits by shifting responsibility from them to the Huron's chief enemies. Another outspoken defender of the Jesuits was the headman Taratouan, whose nephew was living in the school at Quebec and who therefore claimed to be a relative of the French. He offered his fellow headmen a rich present of wampum beads in return for a promise not to harm the Jesuits (12:89).

Although the major epidemic in 1637 broke out prior to the trading season, the trade that year was not interrupted. While some Huron feared that everything that came from France was bewitched and therefore capable of transmitting disease, only one village (not identified by name) decided to abandon the use of European goods and break off all relations with the French (15:21). When it was most feared that the Huron might kill the Jesuits, Huron who were on good terms with them asked for written testimonials so that they might visit Three Rivers and Quebec safely, to trade as well as carry news of what had happened (15:13–15).

When the Huron gathered at Three Rivers to trade in September 1637, Achille de Bréhaut Delisle, who was Montmagny's lieutenant, formally denied that Champlain had ever wished to harm the Huron people and he rebuked Oumasasikweie, the namesake and successor of the Kichesipirini headman who had been killed by the Iroquois in 1635, for spreading this rumour. No Huron could be found who would substantiate the other accusations that were being levelled against the Jesuits; instead traders from one village said they had first heard them from another (12:245–47). Bréhaut Delisle praised the steadfast friendship that bound the French and Huron together and repeated some of the same religious sentiments that Brébeuf had expressed in the Huron country. He gave the Huron traders hatchets, iron arrowheads, and a large quantity of dried peas to wish them a safe journey home. He also presented a fine kettle and still more hatchets and arrowheads to the inhabitants of Ossossané for having accepted the Jesuits and built a cabin for them (12:257). He reminded the Huron of the love that the French felt towards the Jesuits and warned them that they must continue to treat the Jesuits well if they wished to remain on good terms with the French (12:259). Le Jeune commented that it was generous of the French officials to ascribe to religious motives what in any case had to be given to the Indians in order to retain their friendship (12:257).

Bréhaut Delisle's speeches and presents and the friendly treatment that the Huron traders had received at Three Rivers caused them to return home in a good mood. Since they had observed nothing that was sinister or suspicious at Three Rivers, they no longer believed that the Jesuits were the cause of the epidemic (15:55). While this did not prevent a final outburst of hostility against the Jesuits in late October, the Jesuits attributed their survival during this dangerous period to the goodwill of the traders (15:55–57).

It is ironic to note, however, that while the safety of the Jesuits depended almost entirely on the Huron's reluctance to break the terms of their trading alliance with the French, the French officials at Quebec were worried about having committed themselves too firmly to a policy of stopping trade if the French who were living in the Huron country were mistreated. It seems to have been agreed that if the Jesuits were killed as a result of a general conspiracy, the only course of action would be to stop trading with the Huron. If, however, their murder was the work of individuals, the French were anxious to assure those Huron who were innocent of their continued friendship (14:245). Had the Huron known or guessed that the fur trade was as important to the French as it was to them, the fate of the Jesuits might have been very different.

BECOMING FRENCH

The vast majority of adult Huron who were baptized in the early years of the Jesuit mission viewed it as a curing ritual or a means of joining friends and relatives who had died and were believed to be living in heaven. Almost all of those who recovered from their illnesses showed no further interest in Christianity and were regarded by the Jesuits as apostates. Such experiences made the Jesuits unwilling to baptize healthy adults (13:121). In spite of this, a small number of able-bodied Huron actively sought baptism. These were traders who saw baptism as a means of becoming kinsmen of the French, just as headmen sending their sons or nephews to live with the French was another. The first traders who actively sought baptism were not headmen and it may be that ordinary traders saw baptism as a more expedient means of establishing a personal alliance with the French. Such men were willing to risk the dangers that seemed inherent in baptism in order to enjoy the advantages that accrued from a ritual kinship with their trading partners.

This attitude was encouraged by the trading company, which offered substantial benefits to Indian traders who were Christians that they did not extend to those who were not. Since Christian Indians were theoretically French citizens, they had the right to receive the same set prices for their furs that Frenchmen did, which were considerably higher than were those paid to Indians. Moreover, money was set aside so that additional presents could be given to Christian Indians who came to trade, as evidence of the love that the French had for those who shared their religion (16:33; 12:257). It was also general policy to give converts places of honour in all the councils that were held at Three Rivers and Quebec (9:287; 12:243).

The Jesuits knew why these traders sought baptism. Yet, they were convinced that if they held out the hope of eventual baptism, this would be an effective way of motivating these men to acquire greater knowledge of Christianity, and that eventually they would believe in it. The Jesuits were especially anxious to convert older and more influential men. Thus a contest developed between Huron traders, who wished to convince the Jesuits of their sincerity, and the Jesuits, who wished to exploit the traders' desire for baptism as a means of genuinely converting them.

The first trader to request baptism was Amantacha's father, Soranhes. He attributed his escape from the Iroquois to the intervention of the Jesuits' god and, the following winter, declared that he and his entire household were anxious to be baptized and to see Teanaostaiaé become Christian. Brébeuf regarded both him and Amantacha as "crafty spirits" and refused to grant his wish (8:149–51). In September 1635, Soranhes again requested that his family be baptized and about the same time Amantacha began to express a renewed interest in Christianity. In November, Brébeuf and Pijart returned to Teanaostaiaé and, with Amantacha as their interpreter, they instructed his family in basic Christian beliefs. These teachings were received with apparent interest and approval. Soranhes stated that he would encounter little trouble in learning the necessary prayers, but had difficulty learning to cross himself. While the Jesuits were present, the family also observed Friday and Saturday as fast days, as was the custom in Catholic Europe at that time (10:61–67; 13:23–25). Soranhes came to stay with the Jesuits from time to time during the following winter, but, although he repeatedly asked to be baptized, the

Jesuits detected his continuing attachment to worldly interests. They were confirmed in these doubts by Amantacha's report that his father was expecting to benefit from baptism in his trading relations with the French. To ingratiate himself with the Jesuits, Amantacha explained that he had offered his father all of his wampum necklaces if he would desist from such thoughts of worldly profit (9:281).

In the spring of 1636 Soranhes revealed these interests even more clearly when he asked for letters of recommendation to take with him when he went to trade. He also said that he wished to be baptized when the ships arrived at Quebec. Brébeuf informed him that the place of his baptism was of no importance, but invited him to stay with the Jesuits for a few days before he left for Quebec, in order to consider whether or not he was ready to be baptized. Soranhes promised to do this but sensing that Brébeuf was unwilling to permit his baptism, he left to trade immediately after-wards (13:25–27). On his return from Three Rivers, he travelled as far as the Nipissing country with one of the Jesuit priests, but there he changed into another canoe and returned directly to Teanaostaiaé (13:27). He died unbaptized in August of that year. Although his relatives would not confirm the report, Soranhes was said to have committed suicide over the loss of his son (13:23, 27).

The first adult Huron to be baptized in good health was Tsiouendaentaha (14:77–95).[9] A resident of Ihonatiria, he was about fifty years old and although apparently not a headman the Jesuits described him as an influential person with good connections. Like Soranhes, he had expressed a wish to be baptized, but the Jesuits had put him off, fearing the Huron tendency to dissemble and believing that he was motivated by self-interest and a desire for presents. Moreover, while he made a point of listening to the Jesuits and approving of what they said, when he fell ill he had traditional Huron rituals performed for his recovery. In spite of this, his attachment for the Jesuits increased, particularly when his family came through the epidemic of 1636 without loss. As spring approached, he became more anxious for baptism and during Lent he came to receive instruction almost every day. He also won the confidence of the Jesuits by praising their teachings to other Huron. Moreover, Tsiouendaentaha no longer pressed for baptism; on the contrary, he argued that he had not been able to remember enough of what he had been taught to qualify for it. This persuaded the Jesuits of his sincerity.

Finally, the Jesuits began to press Tsiouendaentaha to be baptized. When he promised to give up all Huron customs that were incompatible with Christianity, it was agreed that he should be baptized prior to his departure for Three Rivers. With the Jesuits' approval, Tsiouendaentaha celebrated this event by providing a great feast for the people of Ihonatiria. The Jesuits hoped that if he made a public declaration of what he intended to do, his own people would give him more liberty to live as the French did. In reciprocity, the Jesuits gave their own feast to express their rejoicing at his conversion; however, when Tsiouendaentaha began to speculate about what kind of presents he would be given when he went to Three Rivers, the Jesuits had to console themselves with the hope that someday he would understand Christianity better (14:91).

Tsiouendaentaha's conversion did not go unrewarded at Three Rivers. Bréhaut Delisle took him aside and gave him a fine present as evidence of the affection that the French now felt for him (12:257) and he was publicly entrusted to carry to the Huron country the picture of Christ that was to hang in the chapel at Ossossané (12:251). These honours encouraged Tsiouendaentaha to remain a Christian although his wife and a niece died in the summer of 1637 and, shortly after he returned from trading, one of his daughters and a brother-in-law were carried off by disease (15:19). Many Huron pointed out that his family had not been stricken until after he had become a Christian.

A different attitude towards baptism was exhibited by the headman Aenons. To win and retain the goodwill of the French, he consistently urged his people not to harm the Jesuits, listened to the priests, and approved of what they said. Nevertheless, he declined to express any wish to be baptized in the near future, saying that he doubted he could live as the Jesuits wished him to (11:135). He became ill on his way to Quebec in 1637 and arrived there in a weakened condition in early August. Knowing he was about to die, he offered a present to the French governor and urged him to treat well the Huron who were coming to trade. Likewise, he told his own people that he did not hold the French at Three Rivers responsible for his death and that they should not attempt to avenge him by doing any harm to the French who were living in the Huron country (12:199; 11:135). Asked whether he wished to become a Christian, he stated that since he had been invited to visit the French, it was well that he should die firmly allied to them (12:199). He was baptized on 6 August and died soon after. Because he had become a Frenchman, his Huron companions permitted him to be buried in the French cemetery at Three Rivers, rather than burning his body and taking his bones home with them. No doubt the French gave him a fine funeral procession as they had another Huron who had been baptized when already almost unconscious on 18 July. This procession had greatly pleased the Huron (11:127–31) and news of it may have stimulated Aenons to covet a similar honour for himself. Aenons's baptism led to those of two more traders, Tsondaké and Arachiokouan, who also were stricken with illness when they arrived at Three Rivers (11:135).

CHIHWATENHA'S CONVERSION

A different kind of conversion was that of Chihwatenha, an inhabitant of Ossossané. He was about thirty-five years old and although not a wealthy or prominent man, was a nephew of Anenkhiondic. While occasionally he may have visited Three Rivers prior to his conversion, he had trading partners among the Tionnontaté and his main trading activities seem to have been in that direction. The *Jesuit Relations* report that he had married only once and never in his life had smoked, gambled, given curing feasts, or relied on charms (Thwaites 1896–1901, 15:79). These claims are hagiographic and almost certainly exaggerated. If only partly true, however, they suggest that his personality was an abnormal one by Huron standards. As soon as the Jesuits began to visit Ossossané, Chihwatenha showed himself anxious to please them and after they settled there he spent much time talking with them and helping to baptize young children (15:81). In the summer of 1637, he was stricken by the epidemic then raging in Ossossané and immediately went to the Jesuits in hopes of being cured. Although the Jesuits believed that he accepted their offer of baptism in the spirit of a true Christian, more likely he sought it as a curing ritual. He attributed his recovery to his baptism and at a feast of rejoicing that he gave to celebrate his cure he publicly announced his desire to live as a Christian (15:81–85).

Unlike most baptized Huron, Chihwatenha continued to manifest friendship for the Jesuits and a desire to live according to the rules they prescribed. At first, he may have been motivated to do this by gratitude for his recovery and by the belief that he could become a member of the Jesuits' curing society, thereby continuing to protect his own health. Gradually, however, he also seems to have been attracted by the prestige, or at least the notoriety, that accrued from being the Jesuits' favoured disciple and closest Huron associate. Eventually he was to boast that in this capacity he would be remembered forever among the Huron (19:155).

As an expression of his adherence to the Jesuits, Chihwatenha spent considerable amounts of time praying and receiving instruction. He refused to participate in Huron rituals, was assiduous about confession, and took pleasure in repeating the Jesuits' teachings to fellow Huron (15:95–97).

When his own longhouse was stricken by the epidemic less than a month after he had recovered, he refused to let any shaman enter it. His son, sister-in-law, a nephew, and three nieces were all baptized, although the son and one niece died soon after (15:89–91). Many of the people of Ossossané, including his relatives, rebuked him for preventing those who were sick from seeking traditional forms of aid and, in derision, the people of his longhouse were called "the family of Christians" (15:89, 99). Chihwatenha's wife, Aonetta, was for some time unwilling to give up her traditional beliefs, but soon after the death of her son she agreed to be baptized.

To celebrate his wife's baptism, Chihwatenha provided a great feast for his relatives and friends, who included some of the most important men in Ossossané. A large crowd flocked to the Jesuits' cabin where the rite was performed. Following Aonetta's baptism, she and Chihwatenha were re-married according to the rites of the Roman Catholic Church and, after the crowd had dispersed, they and their nephew were allowed to participate in a mass. The other members of the family, who had been baptized in illness but had not yet proved themselves as Christians, were not allowed to receive this sacrament (15:101–5; 16:59). While this was going on, Chihwatenha's sister-in-law fell ill and died. She had already been baptized and her sudden death led bolder Huron to ask the Jesuits' hired men what reparations the Jesuits planned to give Chihwatenha's family for having murdered her (15:105). Chihwatenha and his family continued to follow the precepts of the Jesuits although for about ten months they were the only Christian family in Ossossané (17:41). The Jesuits hoped that their example would demonstrate to other Huron that it was possible for Indians to live as Christians.

During the winter of 1637–38 Chihwatenha asked the Jesuits to teach him to write. They accepted the task and he was able to compose letters by the spring. It was, however, much harder for him to learn to read. His professed aim in learning how to write was to record not only religious matters but also the affairs of the country. This, no doubt, would have been a great source of prestige for him. In return, he helped the Jesuits to analyse Huron grammar and compose religious homilies (15:111–13).

A DEFEAT ON THE ST. LAWRENCE

The truce that the Huron had arranged with the Seneca appears to have been observed by both sides until 1638. Blood feuds continued with the four other Iroquois tribes and thus the Huron country was never completely free from the threat of raiders. In September 1637 a band made up of Attignawantan, Attigneenongnahac, and Arendarhonon warriors surprised twenty-five or thirty Iroquois who were fishing along the shore of Lake Ontario. Eight Iroquois were taken prisoner; one was killed on the spot and the seven others were brought home to be tortured (Thwaites 1896– 1901, 13:37). One of these was a Seneca about fifty years of age. He had refused to accept the peace treaty that his tribesmen had concluded with the Huron and had married among the Onondaga so that he might continue fighting (13:45). In April 1637 an Indian who had recently come from the Seneca country was said to have warned the Huron that the other Iroquois tribes were planning to attack either the Huron traders on their way to the St. Lawrence or the Huron country while these traders were away. The Jesuits doubted the truth of this story, since similar ones were circulated by the Huron headmen every year in order to make sure that enough armed men remained at home to protect their villages (14:39). Prior to April, however, the Huron had been discussing plans to wage war on the Iroquois to ensure that their fields were safe for the women to work in the following summer (13:265).

The main clash between the Huron and the Iroquois during the summer of 1637 occurred, not in Ontario, but along the St. Lawrence. After the murder of Oumasasikweie, both the Algonkin and the Montagnais were again at war with the Mohawk and they therefore decided to forget the differences that for a time had divided them (9:245). In 1636 it was reported that as many as 300 Iroquois warriors had penetrated the Riche- lieu Valley. Some stragglers belonging to this group were slain and later a Montagnais war party lay in ambush near one of the Mohawk villages, where they killed twenty-eight of the enemy and took five prisoners (9:251–55). In contrast, a joint force of Montagnais and Algonkin that attempted to invade the Mohawk country in the spring of 1637 was soundly defeated. Both of their leaders were killed and those who escaped returned home in disarray (12:153–61). In June, a group of Onontchataronon warriors defeated their Iroquois opponents in a battle fought on a lake or river and captured thirteen prisoners, one of whom was sent to Three Rivers to be slain. This victory was attributed to the birchbark canoes of the Onontchataronon, which were lighter and swifter than the elm bark ones used by the Iroquois (12:181).

During this period the Algonkin and Montagnais were unsuccessful in securing support from either the French or the Huron. The French refused to accompany their war parties because they regarded Algonkin warriors as undependable and feared their lack of discipline. They also claimed that the refusal of these Indians to offer their children to the Jesuits for instruction relieved the French of any obligation to fight alongside them (9:219). The Huron had been angered by the Kichesipirini's efforts to sever their trade with the French and thus saw little reason to help the Algonkin. Moreover, up to and including 1636 their traders had not seriously been attacked by the Iroquois while they were on their way to or from the St. Lawrence.

In August 1637 a force of Iroquois estimated at 500 men established a camp on the north shore of the St. Lawrence at the head of Lake St. Peter. Their aim was to watch the river and intercept Indians as they came downriver to trade with the French (12:207). The French first learned about the presence of the Iroquois when the latter attacked some Huron who were returning up-river. One of the two canoes that were attacked escaped and its crew returned to Three Rivers (12:199–201). The seriousness of the Iroquois menace was only fully realized, however, when an Iroquois canoe appeared at Three Rivers and challenged the French and their allies to come out and fight (12:201). A pinnace that was sent to drive away this canoe, reported that Lake St. Peter was thick with Iroquois, both on the water and along the shore. Later that day, a single Huron canoe arrived at Three Rivers and reported that nine other canoes making up the party of the Huron headman, Taratouan, had been attacked on their way to Three Rivers. The attack had taken place in the narrow north channel of the St. Lawrence River at the west end of Lake St. Peter (12:99–105; 207–09). Twenty-nine Huron, including Taratouan, had been captured, and one prisoner had been killed immediately. Taratouan was seen being tortured by the Mohawk, but presumably he was kept alive until they returned to their villages (12:215). On 11 August two armed pinnaces made their way up-river, only to find that the Iroquois had withdrawn the day before. This retreat permitted the main body of about 150 Huron traders to arrive at Three Rivers without mishap in late August (12:235).

The need to avenge Taratouan and his companions was the final factor compelling the Huron to reactivate their military alliance with the Algonkin. The general council of the Huron confederacy that met to discuss a question of war on 4 August 1637 was convened too early to be a response to this incident, especially since the issues being debated had already been discussed by each village council. Nevertheless, rumours of an impending Iroquois attack on the St. Lawrence had been circulating since the spring and these may have prompted the Huron headmen to consider possible courses of action. If this was the reason for this council, the Huron were well prepared for the decisive response they were to make the following spring.

THE JESUIT SCHOOL CLOSES

In the spring of 1637 Father Pierre Pijart attempted to recruit more Huron children for the school at Quebec. It was feared that this would be more difficult than the year before since meanwhile accusations of sorcery had been levelled against the Jesuits (Thwaites 1896–1901, 12:91) and a rumour had been current among the Huron since the winter that two of the boys who had gone to Quebec the previous summer were dead. In spite of this, various families expressed an apparent willingness to send their sons to live with the French (14:45). These offers came from Ossossané, Teanaostaiaé, Ekhiondastsaan, and five or six other villages, and were more numerous than the French were able to accept (12:113–15). Although the Jesuits feared that Tsiko's and Satouta's relatives would be angered by their deaths and might seek blood revenge, neither family appeared to blame the French when the news was confirmed. Both agreed that the boys had been well looked after and stated that since so many people had died in the Huron country, their deaths were not unexpected (12:93). It is impossible to know whether this attitude reflected greater trust in the French among Huron leaders or it was the politic dissimulation of traders who did not wish to undermine their relationship with the French.

At the beginning of the summer the three boys who had survived the winter at Quebec were sent to Three Rivers to await their relatives. On his way down to Three Rivers Tewatirhon's uncle, who was a war chief, heard what under the circumstances was a highly plausible rumour: that two Frenchmen had been killed in the Huron country. Fearing that when the French heard this rumour they would exact blood revenge, Tewatirhon's uncle asked to take the boy home with him. When the French learned why he wanted to remove his nephew they attempted to detain the uncle and finally arrested him when he tried to steal away secretly with Tewatirhon and another boy (12:95). Even after the rumour was revealed to be false, Tewatirhon said that he wished to return home to visit his relatives, especially his mother. This was agreed to, and Tewatirhon and Father Paul Ragueneau left for the Huron country in the same canoe. As they were travelling up the Ottawa River they met Tewatirhon's other uncle, Taratouan, who was on his way to Three Rivers. Taratouan chided Tewatirhon for leaving the French when they had treated him so well, and made him return to Three Rivers with him (12:97). Tewatirhon was thus with his uncle when the latter was captured by the Iroquois. During the attack, Tewatirhon made his way to shore and after hiding for a day managed to steal an Iroquois canoe and reach Three Rivers (12:101–3, 211). Tewatirhon returned to Quebec where, in obedience to Taratouan's wishes, he remained over the following winter. In the spring of 1638 he wished to join the Montagnais in a raid against the Iroquois, but the Jesuits would not give him permission to do so (12:105). Andehoua, the second of the Huron scholars, had apparently become accustomed to the relative ease and luxury of Quebec and he and his relatives were willing for him to stay with the Jesuits until 1638 (12:105–9). By contrast, the youngest of the boys wished to go home for a year and he embarked with Father Pijart (12:109). It appears that he died the next year, after becoming ill on his way back to Quebec (15:137).

Two of the youths from Teanaostaiaé who were supposed to remain at Quebec were captured by the Iroquois, but a third escaped and agreed to spend the winter with Tewatirhon (12:109–13). Two other boys offered to stay with the Jesuits, but when Tewatirhon informed the Jesuits that one of them suffered from melancholy, that boy was sent home. Of the many youths who had been promised by the Huron, four were accepted by the Jesuits, although one of these was soon enticed away by his relatives (14:231). The new students are reported to have given themselves up to gluttony, gambling, idleness, and other irregularities. They responded in a hostile manner to the Jesuits' efforts to discipline them and mocked Tewatirhon and Andehoua for obeying the priests. Finally, they stole enough provisions for the trip home and set off one night, carrying with them as many other things as they could manage (14:233). Thus the youths returned home with what they had stolen, while their families kept the presents that they had been given for them.

The two boys who remained showed the same favourable disposition as they had the year before. Both were baptized during the winter and Andehoua was persuaded to mortify his body by holding his hands in ice water and standing up to his waist in it (14:235). Although self-testing was part of the Huron cultural pattern, under Jesuit tutelage Andehoua developed an aversion to sexuality that was alien to traditional Huron behaviour (14:237). When Andehoua was travelling home the following year, he risked his life to save a portable mass kit that he was transporting in his canoe (14:245–47). Tewatirhon, who was older, showed less enthusiasm for Jesuit teachings and was therefore judged to be the duller of the two, as Savignon had once been judged duller than Amantacha (14:239).

One disappointment for the Jesuits was their failure to promote the idea of a Huron colony at Quebec (12:255). When 150 Huron traders arrived at Three Rivers in September 1637, Bréhaut Delisle exhorted them to bring some families to live near the French. He assured them that these settlers would be given food and helped to clear land and build houses. In reply the Huron said that their women would not undertake so long a journey or go to live among foreigners (12:255). The central role played by Huron women as guardians of village life was clearly manifested.

Throughout the winter of 1637–38 the reports that were received in Quebec led officials to fear that there might be a general massacre of the Jesuits and their assistants in the Huron country (14:243). In the spring, Montmagny was anxious to send some Frenchmen to the Huron country to learn what was happening there. Tewatirhon and Andehoua argued that these Frenchmen might be murdered if the Huron had already declared war and that it would be safer if they performed this task (14:243). They may have hoped by doing this to extricate themselves from possible French reprisals. Their offer was accepted and they, together with Father Daniel and a young French workman, were dispatched with some Algonkin in June 1638 (12:243–45). Daniel's orders were to return to Quebec immediately if the Jesuits had been killed on the orders of the Huron confederacy council, but if the murders turned out to be the work of individuals, he should remain and assure the rest of the Huron of the continued friendship of the French (14:245). Thus a fine line was drawn between business-as-usual and protecting the Jesuits who went to work among the Huron.

When Daniel reached Morrison Island, he encountered some of Andehoua's relatives and learned that the Jesuits had not been in any danger since the previous autumn. In spite of this, he decided to continue inland with a group of Huron who were on their way home. Two days later they met some friends of Tewatirhon who were going to trade; deeming it advisable that Tewatirhon should pass one more winter at Quebec in order to strengthen him in the Christian faith, Daniel persuaded him to return to Three Rivers. When they reached the Huron country, Daniel joined the Ossossané mission while Andehoua returned to his natal village to become a native preacher (14:251–53). He was obviously proud of his connections with the French and the zealousness with which he discharged his job of preaching led the Jesuits to request that Tewatirhon be sent home as soon as possible to assist him (14:255). They also requested that the Jesuits at Three Rivers should attempt to enrol as many Huron youths as possible in their school; after the troubles of the preceding year, it was impossible for the Jesuits in the Huron country to persuade parents to send their children to Quebec. Yet, likewise, Huron who came to Quebec were reluctant to leave any young men behind. They feared that more trouble might arise with the Jesuits in the Huron country and were therefore reluctant to leave any of their people as hostages at Quebec.

The difficulties of keeping Huron boys at Quebec had already become evident there in the autumn of 1637, but at that time the troubles had been compensated for by the devotion of Andehoua and Tewatirhon. After the latter were back in the Huron country for a while, the problems involved in using young men as native preachers began to reveal themselves. Andehoua settled in Scanonaenrat and was later described as living a morally pure life and professing to be a Christian. In 1641 he accompanied a war party on a raid against the Iroquois and his prayers were credited with saving their canoes from shipwreck when they were caught in a storm on Lake Ontario (23:173–77). There is, however, no evidence of him serving as a preacher after 1638. No doubt because of his youth, the Huron paid little attention to what he had to say (16:171).

Tewatirhon quickly returned to traditional ways, particularly in his sexual behaviour. He continued, however, to profess a belief in the Jesuits' teachings and after he had been badly burned in a fire about 1641, the Jesuits were convinced that he died a good Christian (21:173–75). A member of Atironta's family who had spent a winter at Quebec appears to have hated the time he spent there and after he returned home he persistently mocked the Jesuits and their teachings. He too, however, asked the Jesuits to pardon and baptize him shortly before he died about 1641 (21:171–73).

By 1639 experience had convinced the Jesuits who were working in the Huron country that their original plan of trying to convert the Huron by first instructing their children was in error. It was very difficult to instruct most of the children or to make them behave contrary to their will. Moreover, even if one did succeed in instructing a young man, this had no effect upon his elders since the latter did not take young people seriously. This attitude would, in turn, discourage Huron youths from trying to proselytize. It was also agreed that if young men returning from school did not marry quickly, most would be drawn into promiscuous behaviour and, thereby, into resuming their old ways generally (16:251). Yet Christian marriages were impossible until girls were available who understood and accepted the Christian faith and there had been no suitable converts (15:125). If a Christian man were to marry a non-Christian woman and she were to leave him, by Roman Catholic law remarriage was impossible for him. Such considerations threw strong impediments in the way of any plans to instruct large numbers of young men.

This led the Jesuits to reject completely the policy that they and the Recollets had followed since their arrival in the Huron country. The Jesuits concluded that far from being able to convert the Huron by instructing their children, the instruction of children was impossible without the prior conversion of their parents (16:251). It was decided that the primary aim of the Jesuits should be to convert older men and especially the heads of stable families (17:33). Their experience with Chihwatenha suggested that when the male head of a household had been converted, other members tended to follow his example (15:109). Henceforth, only the children of Christians and adults who wished to receive more intensive instruction were to be allowed to live with the Jesuits at Quebec.

We do not know how many Huron boys spent the winter of 1638–39 at Quebec under Father Pijart's direction. None of them had been there before and the decision taken the following year to stop having Huron youths stay at Quebec (24:103) suggests that these ones must have been as difficult and unpromising as those of the previous year. The most curious scholar that winter was an elderly Huron named Ateiachias who had resolved to spend the winter at Quebec after Tewatirhon told him how well he had been treated (16:169–79). The Jesuits could not dissuade him and probably agreed with his argument that it was more profitable to instruct an old man than a young one. They decided, therefore, to let him stay. Like Andehoua, he showed great enthusiasm to learn whatever the Jesuits wished and to imitate their behaviour. Possibly he hoped that by so doing he would acquire their shamanistic powers.

Some fifteen or sixteen Huron who had come with Ateiachias to Quebec and found themselves stranded there over the winter lived for a time near the Jesuits' residence. These men censured Ateiachias for deserting the ways of his own people and no longer wanting to be a Huron (16:175). Ateiachias paid no attention to them, however, and by the spring he was ready to be baptized. When he was preparing to return home in order to select new recruits for the school, his canoe overturned and, wearing bulky and absorbent French clothes, he drowned (16:177–79). Following this accident, Father Pijart returned to the Huron country and for several years no attempt was made to recruit new students for the school.

Interlude

AVENGING TARATOUAN

In the spring of 1638 the Huron went to war against the eastern tribes of the Iroquois confederacy to avenge the killing of Taratouan and his companions. As in the raid of 1615 they were accompanied by Algonkin allies and altogether made up a force of about 300 men (Thwaites 1896–1901, 17:71). It is not known whether the expedition set out from the Huron country and travelled down the Trent Valley or moved south from the Ottawa Valley. Nor is it known where the Huron had their principal encounter with the enemy. Eventually, however, they made contact with about 100 Iroquois, who in Du Creux's (1951–52:257) words had come to rob rather than to fight. This suggests that the Iroquois were on their way to the Ottawa or St. Lawrence Valleys to plunder Indians who were bringing their furs to Three Rivers. The Iroquois were first discovered by a Huron scouting party. One Huron was captured and told the Iroquois that the Huron were few in number and could easily be overpowered. Because of this, the Iroquois decided not to withdraw with their prisoner, but to build a fort and await the enemy. They were therefore taken by surprise when 300 Huron and Algonkin surrounded their fort. In retaliation for his deception, the Huron captive was immediately torn to pieces (Thwaites 1896–1901, 17:71–73).

Seeing that they were surrounded, the majority of Iroquois were in favour of making a run for their lives. This was opposed by the headman, Ononkwaia. He argued that such cowardice was possible only if it were night-time or if the sky were overcast, but that since the spirit of the sun could see what was happening, it was necessary for each man to fight as bravely as he could. In the ensuing combat, seventeen or eighteen Iroquois were killed and only four or five managed to escape. About eighty prisoners were shared by the victors. Most of them were taken back to the Huron country, where they were distributed among different villages and finally tortured to death (17:73). Over twenty more Iroquois were taken prisoner in other engagements that year, bringing the total number of prisoners to well over a hundred (17:63).

It is certain that Ononkwaia was an Oneida (17:65) and that at least one Mohawk was captured. The latter individual had gone to visit another (unidentified) tribe, intending to trade wampum for beaver skins, but when he lost his wampum gambling he decided to join this expedition rather than return home (17:77). This story makes it likely that the Iroquois war party was made up largely of Oneida. If so, this battle may account for the particular hatred that the Oneida felt towards the Huron a few years later, as well as their claim that the Huron and Algonkin had slain most of the men of their tribe in a battle. Because of their losses, the Oneida women are said to have been compelled to ask for Mohawk men to marry so that their tribe might not become extinct (27:297; 28:281). In later decades, the Oneida are estimated to have had about 140 men capable of bearing arms (49:257). If this figure applies even approximately to the 1630s, the Oneida may indeed have lost the majority of their warriors at this time.

The prompt action that the French had taken against the Mohawk in 1637 and this disastrous defeat of the Oneida less than a year later seem temporarily to have restored the St. Lawrence Valley as a peaceful artery of trade. This may explain why in the summer of 1638 the Huron felt safe to travel to Three Rivers in small, straggling groups (14:255). Nevertheless, there is evidence of at least some Iroquois marauding that year (16:213). Chaumonot noted in 1640 that each year a number of Huron were killed on the way to or from Three Rivers (18:33). These killings probably took place along the Ottawa River, where French control had always been least effective.

This great victory over the Oneida also seems to have encouraged certain Huron youths to murder a member of the Seneca tribe. Following this, the Huron decided to resume war with the Seneca rather than pay reparations to preserve the peace (17:111). Although some headmen probably opposed the resumption of war, most Huron were sufficiently confident that they were willing to encourage the young men of their tribes to win more honours by fighting the enemy on a broader front. The reason generally given for attacking the Seneca was that some Huron families could no longer control their desire to avenge losses that the Seneca had inflicted on them prior to 1634. By the spring of 1639 the first raid had been launched against the Seneca, and by the end of May twelve prisoners had been brought back to the Huron country (17:111).

THE JESUITS BECOME RESPECTABLE

As soon as the epidemic of 1637 was over, the Huron ceased to live in dread of the Jesuits and the latter were no longer in danger of losing their lives. While many Huron continued to regard the Jesuits as potentially dangerous they began to elicit their goodwill either in hopes of receiving better treatment when trading with the French or because they hoped that the Jesuits could be persuaded to use their magical powers to confer long life and other benefits on them. The summer of 1638 was another dry one, although less so in the Huron country than farther south where many Neutral had to enter into special trading relationships with other tribes in order to avoid starvation (Thwaites 1896–1901, 15:157). As the fields of Ossossané became parched, the Jesuits were asked to produce rain, and, once again, were greatly admired when three days of it followed the first mass that was said for this purpose (17:135–37). This exhibition of concern for the Huron's welfare led many of them to apologize for their former animosity towards the Jesuits (17:115).

As early as December 1637 the Jesuits were free to renew their mission work at Ossossané. They began by inviting about 150 headmen and heads of households to a feast at which they announced their intention to resume public instruction. In return, Anenkhiondic invited the Jesuits to a feast in Ossossané on 9 January. At this assembly, Brébeuf was given an opportunity to reiterate the reasons why the Jesuits had come to the Huron country and to answer those who still asked why no Frenchmen had died during the epidemics (15:113–17). Once again the Jesuits were being listened to with respect by men who were anxious to live up to the terms of the French-Huron alliance (17:117–19). After this meeting, several weeks were devoted to performing an Ononharoia ceremony for one of the wealthiest men in Ossossané.

When it was over, Brébeuf persuaded an influential man to sponsor yet another feast so that he could address the Huron on the subject of hell. This feast was held on 1 February and was attended by more people than the first two. When it was over, the headmen who were present announced that henceforth they would recognize Brébeuf as a fellow headman. This gave him the right to announce and hold public meetings in his cabin any time he chose. It was also the first time that the Jesuits had been accepted as a fully enfranchised segment of a Huron community (15:117–19). Thus, with the official sanction of their headmen, many of the people of Ossossané began to satisfy their curiosity to see the Jesuits' images and hear their songs by attending prayers on Sundays and Feast Days. The prayers were followed by a catechism and a discussion period in the fashion of the early services at Ihonatiria. At Ossossané, however, Chihwatenha played an important role, explaining the Jesuits' ideas to fellow Huron and engaging in debate with men who were older and of higher status than himself (15:121–23).

In 1638 the Jesuits undertook to erect the first European-style building in the Huron country. This was a timber chapel thirty feet long, sixteen feet wide, and twenty-four feet high (15:139, 175). Like the missionary cabin, it appears to have stood on the outskirts of Ossossané. The chapel was built by the Jesuits' hired men, who were now twelve in number (15:157–59), and was described as a handsome edifice. It was meant to serve as yet another indication to the Huron of the technological superiority of the French.

During the summer of 1638 the Jesuits were also kept busy by the arrival of several hundred refugees. These were a portion of the Wenroronon tribe who, when they found themselves constrained to abandon their homeland in western New York State, decided to join the Huron. Accordingly, they sent some of their headmen to ask the Huron to accept them. The proposal was debated in each Huron village and was approved by the confederacy. A considerable number of Huron then set out to defend the Wenroronon refugees and to help them carry their possessions northward. In spite of this help, the hardships of the journey were such that a large number of Wenroronon became ill, either along the way or soon after they arrived in the Huron country, and many who became ill died (17:25–27). Chihwatenha was among those who journeyed the entire way with the Wenroronon, following which he suffered from a fever for forty days (17:49–51).

Ossossané was the first Huron settlement that the Wenroronon reached and although some eventually went to live in other Huron villages, the majority were to remain there.[10] They were given temporary lodgings with Huron families and in spite of the fear of a bad harvest, chests of corn were put at their disposal. The Jesuits bled those who were ill and provided them with other forms of medical assistance. They also risked their reputations by trying to baptize all those who were in danger of dying. For two months, the Jesuits at Ossossané were so busy attending to the Wenroronon that they had to abandon their routine mission work in the village (17:25–31; 15:159–61). According to Bressani, the Wenroronon had been in contact with Protestant traders along the east coast of the United States prior to their arrival in the Huron country and soon after their arrival they repeated many harmful stories about the Jesuits that they had heard from these traders (39:141).

When the Jesuits returned to their regular routine in November 1638, they discovered that a number of Huron individuals, and even whole families, were anxious to follow Chihwatenha's advice and become Christians (17:31). During the winter, twelve families and a total of fifty persons were solemnly baptized (15:169–85, 189; 17:33). Husbands and wives celebrated Roman Catholic remarriages and were presented with wedding rings by the Jesuits (15:173–75). Unfortunately, we know little about these early converts except that the Jesuits tended to delay the baptism of young men and to favour the baptism of older men and the heads of families (15:125, 193). Among those who were baptized in good health were a few visitors to the Huron country, possibly Susquehannock, who were about to return home (17:37). Many of the sixty people who professed to be Christians in Ossossané in the summer of 1639 were Wenroronon who had been baptized in ill health. During the previous year, the Jesuits had baptized over 120 sick people in Ossossané, perhaps including Iroquois captives who were about to be slain (15:189). Fifty-two of those who were ill were children and of these twenty-seven died, while seventy-four were adults, of whom twenty-two died (17:25). Many baptized in the extremity of their illness showed no further interest in Christianity after they had recovered (17:37).

THE MISSIONS EXPAND

The Jesuits remained in Ihonatiria until the summer of 1638, baptizing eleven more people there and in neighbouring villages. Atsan, a leading war chief from Arenté (Thwaites 1896–1901, 13:57–59), expressed an interest in being baptized (15:131). By the spring of 1638, however, Ihonatiria was generally abandoned, the survivors of its epidemics having moved away to join more flourishing communities. The Jesuits interpreted the disappearance of the village as divine punishment for the contempt that its inhabitants had shown for Christianity (17:11). Many Huron feared that the destruction of the village presaged what would happen to any Huron settlement in which the Jesuits were allowed to establish themselves (17:115).

The Jesuits decided to transfer their oldest mission from Ihonatiria to Teanaostaiaé. Even if the latter community had been extremely hostile to them in 1637, the Jesuits probably had more personal contacts there than elsewhere. Moreover, with its eighty houses and an estimated 2000 inhabitants it was now the largest Huron settlement and, therefore, of considerable importance to Jesuit strategy. Brébeuf visited Teanaostaiaé and spoke with the village council. The latter, no doubt with an eye on French trade, agreed to accept missionaries and to provide them with an empty cabin that probably had been abandoned as a result of the epidemic. By 25 June the Jesuits were established in the principal town of the Attigneenongnahac (17:61).

Events in Teanaostaiaé followed much the same course as at Ossossané. During the following year, forty-nine sick children were baptized and forty-four adults who may include twelve or thirteen Iroquois prisoners (17:63); of these, eighteen children and twenty-six adults died (17:61). The first convert in good health was not baptized until December 1638. This was Aochiati, a man about seventy years old and the master of the Dance of the Naked Ones (17:79–81). In order to be baptized he had to agree to give up his membership in the curing society. Two of his grand-daughters were baptized with him and, soon after, eleven other people. As the inhabitants of Teanaostaiaé came to believe that baptism did not automatically cause people to die, more presented themselves as candidates. Of the fifty people who either in sickness or in health received reasonable instruction before being baptized (15:189), about thirty continued to call themselves Christians (17:83). As elsewhere, many who sought healing through baptism had no further interest in the Jesuits' teachings once they recovered.

The Jesuits' success in Teanaostaiaé encouraged them to visit other Huron settlements to lay the foundations for the eventual establishment of still more residences. Their immediate objective was to establish themselves in Scanonaenrat, which was located between their two existing missions. The inhabitants of this town were famous for their shamanism and healing rites (17:89). It was also a town that Brébeuf had visited a number of times on his way to Teanaostaiaé and the home of Jean-Armand Andehoua. The first mission to Scanonaenrat began in November 1638 and lasted over the winter (15:169). The two priests assigned to this mission found lodging in a cabin that was occupied by a single family. They then met with the ten or twelve headmen who made up the village council and informed them that they had come to preach to the people of Scanonaenrat, as they had done at Teanaostaiaé. Here too, with an eye to establishing closer trading relations with the French, the priests were made welcome (17:91–93).

By this time, experience had taught the Jesuits that it was best to commence their missionary activities with a number of general meetings to which all the villagers were invited. The relative novelty of the Jesuits ensured that these first meetings were well attended and they could be used to determine those who were inclined to be friendly towards them (17:93). After that, the Jesuits encouraged the headmen and elders of the village to attend more select gatherings with generous distributions of tobacco. Chihwatenha addressed some of these meetings and the Jesuits were also helped to some extent by their former pupils (17:95; 15:171). After a month of hard work in Scanonaenrat, four heads of families were baptized. These included the Jesuits' host and two headmen. Their wives and children were not baptized, however, since in this community, unlike in Ossossané and Teanaostaiaé, the fear that baptism caused death was still too great. In all, only twenty people in good health and a few who were ill were baptized that year (15:171; 17:97). It is noteworthy that in this community where the Jesuits as yet had few personal contacts, it was men, and especially prominent men, who sought baptism, while the women feared it. This is an indication of the degree to which the Huron still viewed Christianity as a ritual of alliance with the French and of the important role that trade must have played in encouraging requests for baptism. The manpower required in Ossossané, Teanaostaiaé, and Scanonaenrat prevented the Jesuits from establishing other missions. They did, however, make a brief visit to Taenhatentaron in November 1638 (17:99), and the following spring two groups of priests were sent out to visit all the Huron villages (15:185; 17:103–5). These tours provided an opportunity to baptize the dying but mainly were intended to accustom all Huron to receiving visits from the Jesuits in the hope that this would make the establishment of future missions easier (17:105). This was the first time that the Jesuits visited the eastern villages of the Huron confederacy (map 23).

MODUS VIVENDI

Even though less than a year earlier, the vast majority of Huron had regarded the Jesuits as malevolent sorcerers, by the summer of 1639 the Jesuits counted almost 100 professing Christians among them (Thwaites 1896–1901, 17:53) and another 200 people had been baptized (15:187). The Jesuits tended to regard their success as an intellectual triumph. According to them, the Huron were greatly impressed not only by the logic and authority with which they expounded Christian doctrines, but also by the strict conformity of these doctrines as they were explained both at Three Rivers and in the Huron country (10:19; 15:121). The Jesuits also attributed their success to the confidence that the Huron had learned to place in written messages as opposed to oral traditions, and to the impact that the courage of the Jesuits, as well as their generosity and moral self-control, had upon the Huron (15:121).

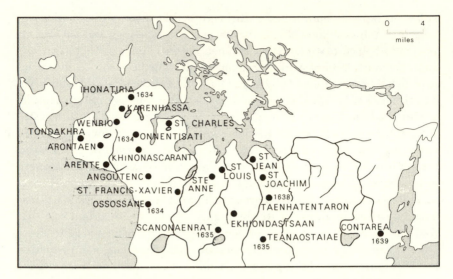

MAP 23. *Dates at which certain Huron villages were first visited by the Jesuits after 1634.*

There can be no doubt that the Huron regarded the Jesuits as shamans or sorcerers who controlled immense power and, therefore, had to be treated with great circumspection. Evidence of this power was perceived in their ability to transmit messages on pieces of paper, to control the weather, and to avoid or easily recover from illnesses that proved fatal to the Indians. The Jesuits further enhanced their reputation by predicting the lunar eclipses of 1637 (15:139) and 1638 (15:175), which made many Huron believe they had caused these events to happen (17:119). The Jesuits also acquired prestige as the representatives of a people of recognized technological superiority. This allowed them to argue that if the Huron regarded French tools as superior to their own, they should regard the Jesuits' teachings in the same manner. Whether or not the Jesuits suggested the idea to him, Chihwatenha was to argue publicly that if the Huron valued French kettles and axes more than they did their own, it was wrong for them to deny that the Jesuits' teachings were superior to their traditional religion (17:49).

To the majority of Huron, such an argument was unconvincing. In the past they had tended to regard the French as intellectually inferior to themselves and to attribute European technology to the possession of magical powers that essentially were no different from their own. Moreover, if the Jesuits were sorcerers, all of their teachings might be lies that would lead the Huron to destruction. There was nothing in the Huron cultural tradition that would incline them to be interested in theological disputations for their own sake. Most of their religious beliefs were part of a tradition that no one ever questioned, and new rites, charms, and songs were judged empirically by their effectiveness. In their dealings with the Jesuits, the aim of the Huron was to determine the kind of powers the priests possessed and to put themselves into a position where these powers could be acquired and benefited from if the Jesuits were willing, or neutralized if the Jesuits proved hostile. Beyond this, the Jesuits' teachings were only of passing interest. When the Huron visited Three Rivers, it was reported that all talk of religion had to precede the distribution of presents to the Indians, since otherwise most of the Indians would leave as soon as the priests began to speak (12:249).

Father Jérôme Lalemant observed that in 1638 and 1639 the Huron's principal aims in seeking baptism were to secure long life and prosperity for themselves and for their children (17:133; 18:19). This does not mean that all converts believed that the Jesuits were not responsible for the epidemics; on the contrary, many of them probably hoped that by gaining the Jesuits' goodwill they would be spared in any future epidemic. The majority of these so-called converts probably wished to continue practising their traditional beliefs and were only prevented from doing so by their fear that if the Jesuits found out about it, they would inflict supernatural punishments on them. A few Huron, like Ateiachias and Chihwatenha, seem to have believed that by identifying themselves with the Jesuits they could acquire their magical powers, and to accomplish this they were willing to incur the enmity of their own people.

Additional problems were posed for Huron who traded with the French. The Jesuits had been accepted as guests as one of the conditions that the French had laid down for renewing the French-Huron alliance. The French extended special privileges to Christian traders and furthermore had stated that the realization of a perfect alliance would require all Huron to become Christians. Under these circumstances, traders must have felt impelled not only to avoid the anger of the Jesuits but also to realize the practical advantages of a closer alliance with the French by being baptized. Many temporized, however, by being friendly with the Jesuits and holding out the promise that eventually they would become Christians.

Still other Huron resented the efforts of the French to intimidate them and began to realize the threat that Jesuit activities posed for their traditional way of life. These people accused the Jesuits of wanting to ruin the Huron country and to destroy the Huron way of life through the prohibition of many Huron customs (17:115). Many, whose relatives had died after being baptized, continued to hold the Jesuits responsible for these deaths and to nourish resentment against them. The Jesuits were also accused of harming individual Huron by their refusal to satisfy the desires of their souls. According to Huron thinking, this made the Jesuits responsible for the prolonged sickness and eventual death of individuals whose relatives were entitled to reparations or blood revenge (15:181; 17:173). Still more Huron were offended by the Jesuits' mockery of their customs (17:173, 201).

This resentment resulted not only in individual criticism of the Jesuits but in headmen denouncing them in general meetings. The most hostile headmen warned people not to attend Jesuit meetings, as their purpose was to harm the Huron; instead ways should be found of getting rid of them (17:117). Other leaders attended Jesuit meetings in order to oppose what they had to say (17:117). The opposition of such men encouraged children and ordinary people to harass the Jesuits by breaking down the doors of their cabins and throwing snowballs, sticks, and other rubbish over their heads or into their dwellings (15:165; 17:117). The most gruesome event of this sort occurred in December 1638. After the Jesuits had baptized an Iroquois captive whom the Huron were torturing, the Huron burned holes through his hands and feet with a red hot iron in mockery of the crucifixion, and after they had killed him they threw one of his hands into the Jesuits' cabin, as if giving them their share of the feast (17:73–77). Baptized Huron were mocked and were told that by having dealings with the Jesuits, they were bound, sooner or later, to bring misfortune and death upon themselves (17:85, 129). These rumours were reinforced when some Susquehannock visited the Huron in 1638. They reported that their English trading partners had informed them that the Jesuits wanted to destroy the whole world and that whenever the English discovered a Jesuit they promptly put him to death (17:121–23). In spite of this, a Susquehannock named Arenhouta was baptized. Eight years later, he was reported to be living in his own country and still calling himself a Roman Catholic (30:85–87).

Despite this hostility, none of the French who were living in the Huron country were killed, nor were any of them attacked except a young boy whom some Huron were said to have tried to strangle in the spring of 1638 (15:51). There were rumours that some hot-headed young men planned to harm the Jesuits, but none of their threats materialized. Such people were restrained by public opinion and this, in turn, was influenced by headmen and elders who believed that the best interests of the confederacy made it essential that the Jesuits not be harmed, since the Huron's trading alliance with the French depended on it. This argument had been strong enough to protect the Jesuits during the epidemic of 1637, so it is not surprising that it was effective in better times. Some of these same men also tried to persuade the Jesuits that being so critical of Huron ways only made enemies for themselves (17:171). Rarely has well-meaning advice fallen on deafer ears. The headmen were most effective in restraining their clansmen during the trading season. When, however, the traders returned and the Jesuits renewed their "batteries of sermons and instructions," many Huron could no longer be restrained from harassing them, even if everyone agreed that no serious harm should befall them (17:115).

In their eagerness to be successful, the Jesuits acted overhastily and planted the seeds of future difficulties for themselves. It formerly had been their policy not to baptize healthy adults before they had made prolonged trial of their sincerity and understanding. Now, in their eagerness to see the beginnings of a Christian church, the Jesuits relaxed these standards. Although Easter and Pentecost were the traditional dates for baptizing converts it was felt that this was too long to make many of them wait (17:31). Baptism was extended to all who requested it and had received sufficient instruction, leaving the "perfecting" of these converts until later. To make life easier for converts, certain observances were also relaxed. For example, the Jesuits did not insist on converts kneeling, since this was an unfamiliar and painful position for a Huron. Moreover, since spring was one of the few times of the year when deer meat was relatively plentiful, converts were not obliged to abstain from eating it during Lent (15:183). Some did, however, give up eating meat in order to imitate the Jesuits.

By contrast, the Jesuits were very inflexible when it came to liturgical matters for which they themselves were reponsible. Wheat and wine for celebrating the mass were imported from Quebec until the Huron mission began to grow its own grain and to press wild grapes, probably in 1637 (15:137–39, 159). They would have regarded Lescarbot's (1907–14, 1:187–88) suggestion that communion be celebrated using the standard bread and drink of each country as utterly impious. If they ate beaver, muskrat, and otter on fast days, this was only because these aquatic animals had long been regarded as fish by the clergy, and therefore were appropriate for such occasions (Denys 1908:361).

The Jesuits also insisted that their converts had to abandon all the traditional rituals that had been proscribed in the vows they had administered at Wenrio and Ossossané in 1636. They also began a minute examination of Huron beliefs and practices in order to provide converts with more precise spiritual guidance (Thwaites 1896–1901, 17:145). These prohibitions proved far more trying than the Jesuits had anticipated. Because converts were forbidden to attend any feasts, they were deprived of the best food that was available and of the main source of entertainment during the winter (17:129, 163). Their inability to participate in these feasts resulted in a breakdown in reciprocity and of good relations with their neighbours (17:163–65). At the same time, the converts' sense of security was undermined by demands that they abandon the charms and rituals they relied on to preserve their health and to bring them luck in war and hunting (17:121, 129–31).

To some degree, Christian medals and prayers replaced traditional charms and rituals, but on the whole they seem to have been regarded as less effective, perhaps because the Jesuits did not explicitly attempt a one-to-one replacement. Members of curing societies had to leave them and Christian headmen were forbidden to perform many of the traditional functions of their office. It is, therefore, not surprising that those who persevered as practising Christians usually did not hold the highest positions in Huron society. The latter either refused to become Christians or quickly abandoned their affiliation. Others claimed to be Christian but continued to discharge their traditional duties; if the Jesuits learned about such behaviour, they expelled such individuals from any further meetings of Christians (17:139). When Ondihorrea, one of the principal headmen, became ill and found that the usual Huron ceremonies did not cure him, he asked to be instructed and baptized. As he had done more than anyone else to make it possible for the Jesuits to settle in Teanaostaiaé, they were happy to grant his wish. After he recovered, however, he attended mass only once. When he learned that he would have to give up many of his chiefly duties and his membership in a curing society, he was no longer interested in remaining a Christian (17:137–39).

BAPTIZING THE IROQUOIS

One of the most extraordinary aspects of mission work during this period was the large number of Iroquois prisoners that the Jesuits managed to instruct and baptize before and while these prisoners were being tortured to death. The Jesuits regarded it as their duty to try to save the souls of these men and when they were successful they consoled themselves with the thought that God had caused these Iroquois to be captured and slain so that he might confer the gift of eternal life upon them (Thwaites 1896–

1901, 13:81–83). The first such prisoner was baptized in Arenté in the autumn of 1636 (13:37–83). In 1638 the Jesuits baptized twenty-one of the many prisoners that were captured that year (15:173). Three were baptized at Scanonaenrat and thirteen or fourteen at or near Teanaostaiaé (17:63). One of the latter was the Oneida headman Ononkwaia, who defied his Huron tormentors to his last breath (17:65–71). Still another prisoner was baptized at Taenhatentaron (17:101–3). All the prisoners who were assigned that year to settlements where the Jesuits had missions or to villages in their vicinity appear to have been baptized (17:63–65). The Jesuits baptized eleven Seneca prisoners tortured to death in May 1639 (15:185; 17:105); the twelfth refused baptism. These prisoners seem to have been brought first to Ossossané, where they underwent preliminary torture and where nine of them were killed. When the other three were taken elsewhere, they were accompanied by Jesuits who managed to baptize two of them (15:185–89).

It is uncertain why these prisoners agreed to be baptized. They were probably aware that the Jesuits were French; in any case, it was clear to them that the Jesuits were friendly with the Huron. The Jesuits believed that the Iroquois were moved by their kindness and disinterested compassion (13:43), but one cannot be sure that the Iroquois were able to distinguish such sentiments from the mock kindness with which they were treated by the Huron. Jesuit offers to save them from the fires of hell may have led these prisoners to hope for rescue from torture if they were baptized, although this does not explain why many of them continued to repeat phrases that they had been taught by the Jesuits throughout their torture. Nor is such constancy likely if their acceptance of baptism was a mock response to what they conceived of as a taunting offer. Probably they too viewed the Jesuits as sorcerers and saw in baptism a charm that would give them more courage to face their final hours. The repetition of phrases such as *Jesus taïtenr* ("Jesus, have pity on me") may have been regarded as analogous to a death song. Others set Jesuit teaching into song and used these songs to brave their tormentors (17:65).

The Huron did not understand why the Jesuits wished to baptize Iroquois prisoners. Many Huron drew an analogy between Jesuit descriptions of hell and their own ritual torture and were angry that the Jesuits were seeking to save the souls of their enemies from eternal torment (13:73). In 1636 a young Huron was willing to assist the Jesuits by acting as an interpreter for them on such an occasion (13:43–45). Later, when the people of Ihonatiria wished to decline further Jesuit exhortations to become Christians, they said that it was a pity that the Jesuits had baptized an Iroquois prisoner since his soul would try to drive them away from heaven if any of them wished to go there (13:177–79). The Huron also suggested that the Jesuits had shown kindness to this prisoner out of fear, hoping that if they were captured by the Iroquois they would be treated better for it. They warned the Jesuits that this was a vain hope and gently berated their cowardice (13:73).

Some Huron related the Jesuits' general objections to Huron torture to their efforts to baptize prisoners and this led them to suspect that the Jesuits were seeking to be friends with the Iroquois. In an effort to find out if this were the case, the Jesuits were asked if the French did not kill anyone. They replied that men indeed were executed, but not with such cruelty. Then, perhaps guided by stories that Savignon or Amantacha had told them about France, the Huron asked if the French never burned anyone. To this the Jesuits replied that the French did, but only for enormous crimes, and that those who were condemned often were strangled first (13:75). In fact, the habits of seventeenth-century Europeans were not so far removed from those of the Huron in this respect as the Jesuits wished to imply. Later, exceptional fortitude was shown by some of the Iroquois who had been baptized. Since failure to make a prisoner scream and plead for mercy was believed to bring misfortune on his executioners, the Huron blamed the Jesuits for this, and many resolved to let no more Iroquois be baptized (17:65). Thus, in the spring of 1639 the Jesuits found themselves having to struggle hard to gain access to prisoners and to obtain permission from their adoptive kinsmen for their baptism (17:105).

The New Order

JÉRÔME LALEMANT

In August 1638 Brébeuf was replaced as superior of the Huron mission by Father Jérôme Lalemant who had arrived in Canada for that purpose the same summer. Jérôme was a younger brother of Charles Lalemant who returned to Paris the same year to become the first procurator of the mission of New France. The new superior of the Huron mission was highly esteemed for his administrative abilities, which he had demonstrated at Clermont College and as rector of the Jesuit College in Blois. Two other priests arrived in the Huron country in 1638: François Du Peron and

Simon Le Moyne. There were now twelve hired men working for the Jesuits in the Huron country (Thwaites 1896–1901, 15:157)—a doubling of both clerical and lay staff since 1634. This increase, combined with a growing conviction that the success of the Huron mission was vital for the long-term security of New France, had convinced Jesuit officials in France that it was necessary to have a trained administrator take charge of this mission. Lalemant knew nothing about the Huron language and was inexperienced as a missionary, but these officials did not regard this as an impediment to his appointment. The missionaries who were already working among the Huron regretted that the new superior lacked local experience and remained critical of him throughout his four-year tenure of office (30:149; 32:61–63).

In spite of the doubts of his co-workers, Lalemant's arrival in the Huron country marked the continuation of a successful career both in Canada and in France. In 1644 he returned to Quebec to become the superior of all the Jesuits in New France, a post which he held until 1650 and again after 1659 when he played a leading role in revitalizing mission work in Canada. In the intervening years he served for a time as rector of the *Collège royal de La Flèche* in northern France. Not the least of Lalemant's talents was his sense of discretion, which allowed him to retain the confidence of the rival factions whose quarrels dominated the administration of New France in his later years.

Yet, in spite of his undoubted administrative talent, Jérôme Lalemant now seems a curious choice to be superior of the Huron mission. He was deeply interested in complicated problems of international diplomacy as these affected the Jesuit missions in New France, but was unable to convince even his own brother of the wisdom of what he advocated.[11] By contrast, his entries in the *Journal des Jésuites*, which he kept from 1645 to 1650, reveal a preoccupation with trivial details of rubrics as they were observed or not observed in the churches at Quebec, and with recording petty animosities among the local religious orders. These entries seem to be those of a parish priest rather than of a trained administrator. This aspect of his character was evident to Marie de l'Incarnation, who wrote approvingly that "he seems to have been brought up in all the ceremonies, which is not usual for a Jesuit" (Pouliot 1966:414). Moreover, even measured by the standards of the time, the literal manner in which he perceived himself doing battle against the devil suggests considerable naïveté.

It is evident, in retrospect, that the positions that Jérôme Lalemant held in the Jesuit colleges of France were not the best preparation for running the Huron mission. Lalemant was determined to enforce punctiliousness and careful observance of routine and was unwilling to adapt these routines to the habits of the Huron or of his fellow missionaries, who had already gained considerable experience working among them.[12] Throughout his stay in the Huron country the Huron's houses appeared to his fastidious mind to be "a miniature picture of hell" filled with "fire and smoke, on every side naked bodies ... mingling pellmell, with dogs sharing the beds, plates, and food of their masters." In his opinion, merely to visit a longhouse was to befoul oneself with soot, filth, and dirt (17:13–15), while to have to live and work amongst the Huron was to be a martyr without being killed (17:13). He was also appalled that at the time of his arrival the food and lodging of the missionaries differed hardly at all from those of the Indians. Lalemant's aversion to Indian life had been strengthened during his journey up the Ottawa River, when he was attacked by a Kichesipirini whose child had died after being bled by a Frenchman a few days before (15:151).

DISCIPLINE

Lalemant's ideas about how the Huron mission should be run were to alter drastically the relationship between the Huron and the Jesuits. This is ironic, since the common motive for all of his innovations was the desire to ensure greater discipline and punctiliousness among the Jesuits and their workmen. His reforms were directed against the relatively informal spirit of cooperation that had hitherto prevailed among the Jesuits. Either through lack of familiarity with the situation or because of the ingrained habits of a schoolmaster, Lalemant was willing to sacrifice the close relations that the missionaries had been building up with the Huron in order to achieve this goal. Yet, while some of his ideas proved wrong and ultimately had to be abandoned, his policies were valuable in one respect; the administrative machinery that he constructed ensured that the vastly expanded mission that was soon to develop under his leadership would function adequately.

Lalemant was determined that in spite of their mission work, the Jesuits' routine would be as well ordered as it was in the colleges of France. Periods were assigned in the morning and afternoon when the priests might visit the Indians and special days of the week were set aside for teaching children, the leading people of the village, and converts only (Thwaites 1896–1901, 16:241–49; 15:165–67). Lalemant required the doors of the missionaries' cabins to be closed by four in the afternoon and that no one was to go out after that hour. To preserve the quiet of these residences, he also decreed that, henceforth, only Indians who came on proper business might be admitted. Lalemant soon discovered, however, that it was not a simple matter to refuse to admit the Indians (17:15), especially since the latter were used to visiting the Jesuits whenever they pleased (16:241). Ossossané and Teanaostaiaé were divided into as many districts as there were priests who spoke enough Huron to make daily rounds. Unfortunately, we do not know to what degree this primordial parish system corresponded with the divisions of these towns into clan districts (16:243; 17:29–31).

DONNÉS

The second problem that Lalemant tackled was ensuring discipline among the lay workmen attached to the Jesuit mission. By 1639 there were fourteen of them. The previous year Le Mercier had praised, perhaps too hopefully, the chastity and good behaviour of these men (Thwaites 1896–1901, 15:137). In 1637, however, the Jesuits had been anxious to guard against sexual laxity by arranging Christian marriages between some of their hired men and Huron women. This plan had not worked out and Montmagny and the trading company were charged by the Jesuits with ensuring the irreproachable conduct of these men (17:47). This suggests that the labourers were threatened with disciplinary action, should the Jesuits report they were not behaving properly. Yet, control based on negative sanctions had obvious drawbacks as far as the missionaries were concerned.

Even before he arrived in Canada, Lalemant planned to introduce to the Huron mission a new category of lay assistant known as a donné. The use of such men had been experimented with in the province of Champagne and been approved by the French provincial, Father Binet (Côte 1956–57; 1961–62). The Canadian donné was to bind himself by civil contract to abjure all personal possessions, to work for the Jesuits without pay, to obey the Jesuit superior, and to be chaste. The Jesuits, for their part, guaranteed to provide the donné with clothes, food, lodging, and other necessities, and to care for him in sickness and old age. This plan won the whole-hearted approval of Brébeuf and Le Jeune, who were convinced that devout laymen would do more for the mission than ordinary hired men could do. The Canadian Jesuits pressed for the maximum incorporation of these men into the order, including taking of vows and wearing a religious

costume. The latter proposals were disapproved of by the Jesuit provincial
in France and by the general of the order, Mutius Vitelleschi, and were
therefore abandoned by Lalemant in 1643 (Rochemonteix 1895–96, 1:
390). The French provincial also disapproved of the agreements to care for
the donnés being made binding on the whole order, rather than on the
Huron mission. As a compromise, it was agreed that the Jesuit mission to
New France, rather than the Huron mission, would guarantee these
obligations (Thwaites 1896–1901, 21:297).

In spite of the restrictions, the donnés soon became an important part
of the Huron mission (21:293–301). The first to enrol was the hired man
Robert Le Coq, who signed his contract 23 December 1639 (21:305).
Since his arrival in 1634 he appears to have served as the *negotiator*, or
business manager, of the mission and in this capacity he travelled between
the Huron country and Quebec each year (Jones 1908:302). The three
other men who had been working for the Jesuits since 1634, Petit-Pré,
Dominique, and Baron, ceased to do so about this time. Since hired men as
well as donnés later joined the mission, it is possible that they were dismissed by the Jesuits. By the summer of 1640, Lalemant had recruited six
donnés, some of whom may have been present among the fourteen seculars
who were working for the Jesuits in the autumn of 1639. Nine years later,
more than twenty donnés were working for the Huron mission, as compared with eleven hired men and six boys (ibid. 384–85).

A NEW MISSION SYSTEM

The most significant change that Lalemant proposed to carry out was to
abandon the individual residences that the Jesuits had sought to establish
in each of the major Huron towns and to construct in their place a single
mission headquarters that would be independent of any particular Huron
settlement. Lalemant argued that by doing this the missionaries would
not have to move their residences every decade when the Huron relocated
their villages (Thwaites 1896–1901, 19:133); hence they could erect
French-style buildings of stone and timber in which they could live much
as they did in a Jesuit residence in France. Such a headquarters would also
eliminate a duplication of services in different Huron villages and permit
the Jesuits, who were increasing in numbers, to grow their own food,
rather than having to buy corn from the Indians. This, it was reasoned,
would reduce the long-term cost of the mission. Although Lalemant did not
explicitly state so in his public writings, his arguments imply that the

European-style chapel that Brébeuf had erected at Ossossané was a waste of effort, since the settlement would soon be abandoned. Lalemant planned for all the Huron settlements to be served by itinerant priests, who, rather than having permanent accommodation in each town and being supported there by a staff of domestics, would return to headquarters at regular intervals for prolonged periods of study and devotion. The implementation of Lalemant's plan was a setback for Brébeuf's efforts to have individual priests become identified with particular communities and develop a prolonged and intimate relationship with their inhabitants. Instead, his plan stressed the role of the Jesuits as representatives of a foreign although allied people living among but apart from the Huron (Talbot 1956:209).

In proposing to found a mission centre, Lalemant was specifically influenced by the reports of Jesuit mission work in Paraguay. The missions to the Guarani had begun in 1587, and in 1609 the Jesuits had founded the first of their reductions or mission centres in which the Indians were encouraged to settle down as Christians. In return the Jesuits offered them protection against enslavement. By 1631 the Jesuits were compelled to resettle farther down the Alto Paraná River, where a new series of reductions was founded. These flourished until the Jesuits were expelled in 1767. Under Jesuit supervision over 100,000 Indians observed Christian discipline and were taught to produce large surpluses of cotton and linen cloth, tobacco, wood products, hides, and maté for export to Europe. Some were also trained as armourers, silversmiths, painters, musicians, and printers. The ideal Paraguayan reduction was located on slightly elevated land, along the bank of a river, and was surrounded by fields cut out of the forest. In the centre of the village were a church, a priests' house, a school, a hospital, and a cemetery, while the houses of the Indians were arranged in rows along a series of shaded streets (Rochemonteix 1895–96, 1:385–86).

The idea of the Paraguayan reduction had already helped to inspire the Indian settlement founded at Sillery, near Quebec, in 1638 (Thwaites 1896–1901, 12:221). The beaver in that area had been overhunted and, as the Indians grew poorer, they became a charge on the trading company. To alleviate this situation, the Jesuits proposed to found a settlement in which the Montagnais would be encouraged to settle down and become farmers (8:57–59). As an inducement, houses, food, and clothing were provided for these Indians from funds the Jesuits collected. Only Indians who agreed to become Christians were allowed to enjoy these benefits and they had to submit to close supervision by the Jesuits who ran the settlement. Because it was now a practical economic proposition, this first

Indian reserve in Canada received the enthusiastic support of the French traders, although only a few years before these same traders had violently opposed the Recollets' plans to settle the Montagnais.

The apparent success of the Sillery scheme must have encouraged Lalemant to hope that individual Huron converts might be persuaded to leave their villages and settle around a Jesuit headquarters on the Paraguayan model. Eventually, this headquarters, or a number of them, would become a new Christian society, replacing the traditional Huron settlements. This scheme was radically different from the earlier Jesuit plan to convert one entire Huron village, and then more, until all the Huron had become Christians. Lalemant, like the Recollets, assumed that the best course of action was to convert individuals and families, and use these to build new Christian communities.

In the spring of 1639, Lalemant sent out the Jesuit missionaries in groups of two to visit all the Huron settlements (17:103–5). This was followed by another round of visits the following summer, when a saint's name was given to every Huron village (19:125). It was probably at this time that Lalemant began his "census" of the houses and families in each Huron and Tionnontaté village (19:125–27), the purpose of which was to allow him to organize mission work more systematically. Although the detailed findings of this survey have not been preserved, the figures in the *Jesuit Relations* suggest that it was neither as thorough nor as detailed as Lalemant implies. The reconnaissance of the villages was apparently not completed before the winter of 1639–40. The unnaturally low average of three persons per family and the fact that the combined population of 12,000 for the Huron and the Tionnontaté continued to be accepted as accurate for the next decade suggest that the published figures were adjusted to take account of the substantial loss of population that occurred in the autumn of 1639 and over the following winter.

Another result of Lalemant's surveys seems to have been the preparation of a map of the Huron country. This was almost certainly the prototype of the large-scale *Corographie du Pays des Hurons* (plate 33), a manuscript map showing the location of Huron villages between 1642 and 1648. Heidenreich (1966:111–13) has studied this map and on the basis of the handwriting has tentatively suggested that the surviving copy may have been drawn by Jérôme Lalemant. There is also no doubt that a map of this type was the basis of the detailed representation of the Huron country that Du Creux published in 1664 in his *Historiae Canadensis* (plate 34). These maps represent what might be called the official Jesuit cartography of the Huron country.

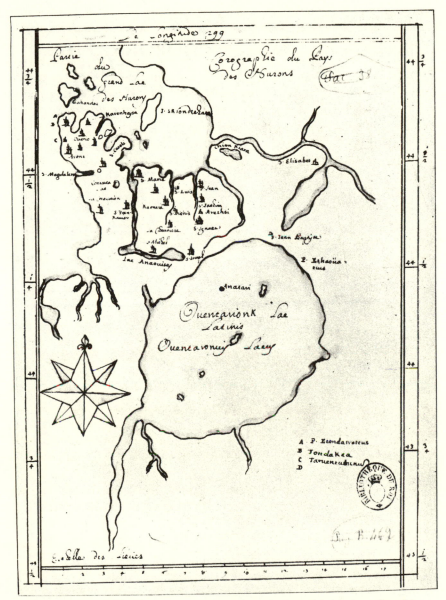

PLATE 33. Corographie du Pays des Hurons. *Heidenreich describes this manuscript map as the best large-scale one of the Huron country. It shows the area between 1639 and 1648 and may have been drawn by Jérôme Lalemant. Courtesy Public Archives of Canada.*

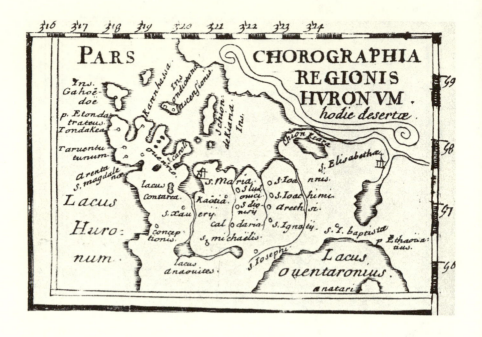

PLATE 34. Chorographia Regionis Huronum, hodie desertae. *This large-scale inset map is taken from the* Tabula Novae Franciae, *published in François Du Creux's* Historiae Canadensis. *Long believed to be the only large-scale map showing the Huron country in the middle of the seventeenth century, it now appears to be based on the* Corographie du Pays des Hurons, *with minor differences resulting from faulty copying.* Courtesy Public Archives of Canada.

An alternative tradition is represented by a manuscript map titled *Description du Pais des Hurons* (plate 35), bearing the date 1631, later amended to 1651, and by the engraved inset entitled *Huronum Explicata Tabula* (plate 36), which is part of a map of New France published in 1657 (plate 37) and probably drawn by Father Bressani. Although the place names on these two maps differ, the outlines are very similar; therefore Heidenreich (1966:115) suggests that Bressani copied the outlines of the older map and placed on it the distribution of Huron villages as he remembered them. Heidenreich (ibid. 114) also suggests that the earlier map may be the work of Father Brébeuf. It depicts the locations of settlements between 1639 and 1648, except for an *x* which marks the site of Sainte-Marie II built in 1649. Thus, despite its date, it is essentially contemporary with the *Corographie*. While more of Georgian Bay appears on this map than on the *Corographie*, the delineation of the Huron country is of inferior quality. It is possible that this map was found among Brébeuf's papers in 1649 and that he may have begun to work on it soon after he returned to France in 1629.

Around 1639 the Jesuits also prepared a general map of the lower Great Lakes region, noting on it the Huron names of many of the sedentary peoples of Ontario, New York State, Ohio, and Michigan. Although this map has been lost, the names Father Vimont copied from a duplicate that Father Ragueneau sent him, indicate that it served as the prototype for the Sanson map of 1656 (plate 38) and others (plate 39). It is uncertain how the Jesuits collected so much accurate information about the outlines of lakes and rivers, but much of it must have come from Indian informants. Other data may have been collected by the Jesuits' assistants, in the course of trading voyages. Detailed knowledge of the area is reflected in the *Novae Franciae Accurata Delineatio* which, as we have already noted, was probably the work of Father Bressani who lived in the Huron country from 1645 to 1649. The accuracy and scale of this map are better than on any other maps of the lower Great Lakes prior to Dollier and Gallinée's map of 1670 (ibid. 105–9).

On the basis of his preliminary survey, Lalemant was able to select the ideal location for his headquarters and planned reduction. The site was along the east bank of the Wye River, midway between Mud Lake and Georgian Bay. There, a low rise of well-drained land provided space to erect buildings and plant crops, while the river on one side and the marsh on the other offered the settlement a considerable degree of protection. From this location it was possible to travel down the Wye River to Georgian Bay, less than a mile away. The site also stood equidistant between the

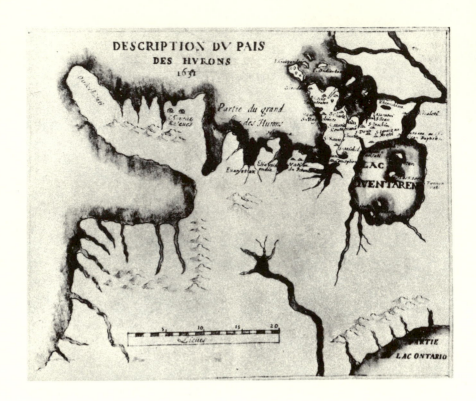

PLATE 35. Description du Pais des Hurons. *This manuscript map is dated 1631 but was changed to 1651, probably when an x was added to indicate the location of Sainte-Marie II on Gahoendoe. Heidenreich suggests that the map may have been drawn by Jean de Brébeuf. Courtesy Public Archives of Canada.*

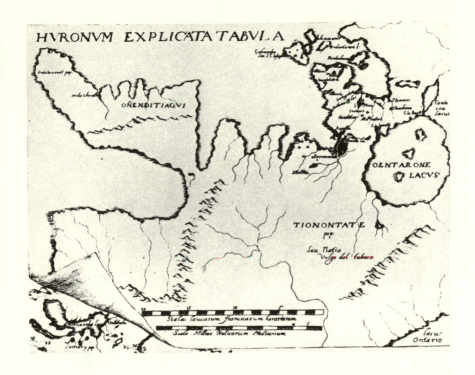

PLATE 36. Huronum Explicata Tabula. *This inset map is from the* Novae
Franciae Accurata Delineatio, *1657. The map was engraved by Giovanni
Federico Pesca and was probably the work of François-Joseph Bressani.
St. Ignace and St. Xavier are both misplaced and St. Jean and St. Joachim
are along the wrong river. Courtesy Public Archives of Canada.*

PLATE 37. *Part of the* Novae Franciae Accurata Delineatio, *1657. This map was probably drawn by Bressani, who had access to Jesuit maps already in existence by 1640. Heidenreich describes it as the most accurate map made of the Great Lakes prior to Dollier and Gallinée's map of 1670 and as one of the most beautiful maps of eastern Canada ever drawn. Courtesy Public Archives of Canada.*

PLATE 38. Le Canada, ou Nouvelle France, *published by N. Sanson*
d'Abbeville, 1656. Already in 1650, Sanson had published his map
Amérique septentrionale *on which the whole of the Great Lakes system*
except the west end of Lake Superior and the south end of Lake Michigan
is accurately portrayed. The 1656 map is more detailed and is
ethnographically interesting for the many tribal names that it bears.
It is not known from where Sanson obtained his information but presumably
he had access to manuscript maps made by the Jesuits in the preceding
decade. While Bressani had access to one or both of Sanson's maps, he also
had access to additional information when he produced his Novae Franciae.
Courtesy Public Archives of Canada.

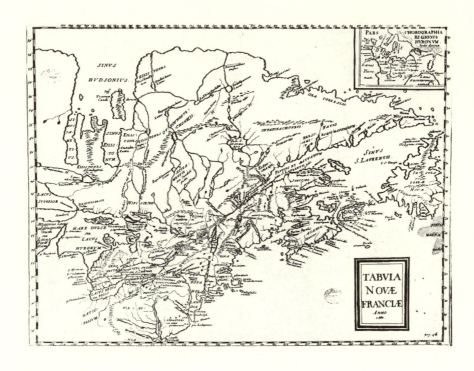

PLATE 39. *François Du Creux's* Tabula Novae Franciae, *1660. This map was published in 1664 in Du Creux's* Historiae Canadensis. *It is not a simple copy of Sanson's maps, although both appear to be derived from similar sources. Courtesy Public Archives of Canada.*

most easterly and westerly of the Huron villages. The location was well suited for communicating with Quebec and for carrying out mission work.

The land that Lalemant wanted belonged to the Ataronchronon and their permission was required before the Jesuits could begin to build there. Lalemant had reason to fear that they might not agree to his proposal and he later commented that if the affair had been delayed for even two hours, the Jesuits might not have succeeded in getting what they wanted (Thwaites 1896–1901, 19:135). It may be that some of the Ataronchronon feared to have the Jesuits living nearby, although such feelings had not prevented other communities from welcoming the Jesuits. More likely, if the people of Ossossané or Teanaostaiaé had learned that the Jesuits were planning to withdraw from their midst, they would have exerted pressure to make sure that neither the Ataronchronon nor anyone else allowed them to build elsewhere.

In the summer of 1639, Lalemant had his lay assistants begin work on the new residence of Sainte-Marie. The first year, only a single building seems to have been erected, without an adjoining palisade. Wilfrid Jury has identified this building with the remains of a Huron-style house, some forty feet long and twenty feet wide that he found beneath later French constructions at the site (Jury and Jury 1954:21–23). He claims that this house differs from Huron ones in having uniform-sized post molds and walls that ran in straight lines, while inside the house he noted traces of a partition. Finally, he states that there was evidence that the building had been chopped down to make way for a later Jesuit construction that covered its southern end. Jury's claim gains support from Father Chaumonot's statement that when he arrived in the Huron country in 1639, the Jesuits were living in three residences constructed of bark, like the houses of the Indians (Thwaites 1896–1901, 18:17).

Unfortunately, it is extremely difficult to evaluate Jury's claims since no detailed report of his findings at Sainte-Marie has so far been published. While it is true that Lalemant complained about the lack of tools and workmen at this time, a European-style chapel had already been erected at Ossossané, with no more tools and even fewer French labourers. More-over, when describing a vision that he had in February 1640, Brébeuf mentions a gable on the house at Sainte-Marie (Ragueneau 1925:73), which suggests that the original building was not precisely like a Huron long-house. It is possible that Jury uncovered some hybrid structure that was soon demolished; however, until more evidence is published, it is also possible that he found a small Huron longhouse that predated the arrival of the Jesuits.

In the autumn of 1639 the Jesuits abandoned their residence at Ossos-sané, leaving the town with no resident priests. The chapel was placed in the care of Joseph Chihwatenha. The residence at Teanaostaiaé was not abandoned, possibly because it was feared that it would offend the inhabitants of the village to do so so soon after settling there. Lalemant divided the Huron country into four mission areas, assigning to each a central community from which the priests could make their rounds during the winter. Four villages, now named Ste Anne, St. Louis, St. Denys, and St. Jean were served from the new Jesuit headquarters. This mission was called Sainte-Marie to the Ataronchronon. The mission of St. Joseph to the Attigneenongnahac operated out of Teanaostaiaé (which the Jesuits called St. Joseph) and embraced Scanonaenrat, Taenhatentaron, and other nearby villages; while La Conception to the Attignawantan had its headquarters in Ossossané and served twelve other Attignawantan villages. The mission of St. Jean-Baptiste to the Arendarhonon was to Contarea, St. Joachim, and an Algonkin encampment called Ste Elizabeth. A fifth mission was to the Tionnontaté. While these missions roughly corresponded with tribal divisions, they did not do so precisely. The mission to the Attigneenongna-hac also served the Tahontaenrat, while the one to the Arendarhonon served at least one Algonkin winter camp (Thwaites 1896–1901, 19:125). The return of Father Pierre Pijart in 1639, following the closing of the Huron school at Quebec, and the arrival of Fathers Joseph-Antoine Poncet de La Rivière and Pierre-Joseph-Marie Chaumonot brought the total number of priests in the Huron country to thirteen. The new mission system came into operation 1 November 1639.

The Great Illness

SMALLPOX

In the summer of 1639 smallpox spread through the St. Lawrence Valley, killing many Indians who came to trade at Quebec and Three Rivers (Thwaites 1896–1901, 15:237; 16:53). This epidemic appears to have started in New England and was carried to the St. Lawrence by a group of Kichesipirini returning from a visit to the Abenaki (16:101). Soon the Algonkin were dying in such numbers that the living were unable to bury the dead, whose bodies were eaten by hungry dogs (16:155, 217–19). The epidemic reached the Huron country when the Huron traders returned from Quebec. The first Huron who suffered from smallpox landed near Sainte-Marie and was carried to his home in the Ataronchronon village of Ste Anne (19:89). The epidemic lingered throughout the winter (21:131), striking an extraordinarily large number of Huron. The Jesuits baptized more than 1000 people who were in danger of death; of these, 360 children under the age of seven died, as well as 100 more children under the age of seven who had been baptized in previous years. In addition, many older children and adults died (19:77–79, 123). These figures suggest a total mortality of several thousand. By the time the epidemic had run its course, the Huron population was reduced to about 9000 people, or only about one-half of what it was before 1634. Of the three cycles of epidemics that had attacked the Huron since that date, the smallpox epidemic accounted for by far the greatest loss of life.

RENEWED FEARS

This new illness coming from the St. Lawrence resulted in fresh outbursts of hostility against the Jesuits. When Robert Le Coq was returning from Quebec, he became ill and was so covered with pustules that his Huron travelling companions judged him as good as dead and abandoned him on the shores of Georgian Bay. When these Huron returned home, the story began to circulate that before he died, Le Coq had told these men that the Jesuits caused disease by nourishing in their cabin an *angont*, or supernatural serpent used to perform witchcraft. Others reported him saying that the disease was caused by a spirit that the Jesuits concealed in the barrel of a gun, which they fired off to send it anywhere in the country. Soon, every Huron man, woman, and child had heard these stories which were widely believed because they were said to have come from the mouth of a dying man who wished to help the Huron (Thwaites 1896–1901, 19:95–97).

For a long time Le Coq lay on the shores of Georgian Bay. He was avoided by many Huron who were too frightened of his illness to help him, although one group did not scruple to rob him. He was finally rescued by a Huron whom he had helped the year before. This man and a companion transported Le Coq back to Sainte-Marie, where he was nursed to health by the Jesuits (19:97–113). Le Coq's public denial that he had ever made any accusations against the Jesuits made little impression on the Huron. A new rumour began to circulate that his illness was a ruse to deceive the Huron, and his recovery was interpreted as evidence of the control that the Jesuits exercised over the epidemic (19:115).

If the Jesuits were seen kneeling by a fire to recite their office, this constituted evidence of witchcraft. So was asking people's names so they might record them in their register of baptisms (19:129). It was widely believed that the Jesuits later tore these names out of their books in order to cause the death of the persons concerned. Their efforts to reach the dying by visiting as many villages and houses as possible were viewed as further evidence of witchcraft, particularly since none of the French except Le Coq became ill (19:93). The suspicions of the Huron were exacerbated by the special efforts that the Jesuits made to baptize dying children even against opposition from their families (19:93).

By moving about as much as they did, the Jesuits may unwittingly have helped to spread the epidemic. Thus there may have been a factual basis to the Huron claim that the most people died in places where the Jesuits were the most welcome and where they had baptized the largest number of people (19:93). Within a short time the majority of the Jesuits' converts had publicly renounced Christianity and taken up the old healing cults (19:81). They did this either because deaths in their families convinced them of the inability or unwillingness of the Jesuits to cure them in spite of their being Christians (19:233), or because they feared that if they remained Christians they would be included in any general massacre of the Jesuits and their supporters.

The missions that began in November were the most difficult and dangerous that the Jesuits were ever to undertake in the Huron country. The single-minded zeal with which they pursued their objective of instructing and baptizing those who were ill testifies to the sincerity of these missionaries. As soon as it became clear to the inhabitants of Ste Anne that baptism did not restore health, the Jesuits were accused of sorcery and many longhouses were closed to them (19:167). As the smallpox spread, the other villages of the Ataronchronon mission became similarly hostile. For at least part of the winter, the Jesuits were forbidden to visit one or more of these villages (19:169). When Le Mercier encountered Oscouenrout, a principal headman of the Attignawantan, in St. Louis, the latter fell into a frenzy and told the priest that he would never leave the village alive, since its inhabitants had resolved to burn him to death as a sorcerer (19:175). While this threat was not carried out, it undoubtedly reflected the continuing debate that went on within most Huron villages concerning how the Jesuits ought to be dealt with.

The Ataronchronon's hatred of the Jesuits appears to have been less intense than was encountered among the missions to the Attignawantan and Attigneenongnahac, where the Jesuits had been active for a longer period. In Ossossané only a few converts remained faithful. These included Chihwatenha and his family and a man named Tsondihwané, who was the head of one of the most important families in the community. Yet, Tsondihwané's family, especially his wife, were violently opposed to his behaviour and, after many had died in his longhouse, they persuaded him to have a curing ceremony performed for his daughter when she fell ill (19:239–45). An old woman who bore the Christian name Anne refused to renounce Christianity, even when the death of two daughters and a niece left her with three ailing children to care for (19:233–39).

These were exceptions, however. The Attignawantan knew more about the Jesuits' teachings than other Huron did and they became more vociferously hostile than any of the other tribes as the mortality rate soared. The Jesuits accused them of circulating the worst rumours about them and of calling the most loudly for their deaths. The Jesuits believed that the Attignawantan hoped that someone from one of the other tribes would kill them. In this way, the Attignawantan would be rid of the Jesuits without being directly responsible for their murder (19:209–11). The Huron groups adopted this strategy on other occasions and since many would have been happy to be rid of the Jesuits, there is no reason to doubt that the Attignawantan were encouraging others to murder the Jesuits. They were doubtlessly not the only Huron tribe to do this.

The widespread mortality among baptized families led many of them to abandon Christianity and to refuse to let the Jesuits enter their longhouses. This happened not only in Ossossané but in all the Attignawantan villages (19:213). If the Jesuits entered a house without permission, the Huron refused to listen to them and either drove them out or left themselves. When Father Ragueneau tried to enter the village of Ste Térèse, a young man seized him by the throat and was about to strike him with a hatchet. A woman stopped him from doing this and the young man finally contented himself with carrying off Ragueneau's crucifix. When Ragueneau asked the village council to restore the crucifix, the young man agreed to do so, but only if the Jesuits promised that smallpox would no longer ravage the village (19:213–15). One Huron, said to be among the most intelligent men in Ossossané, stated that he did not believe the Jesuits were practising witchcraft; rather their god was punishing the Huron for having listened to the Jesuits without following their teachings. To the Jesuits' surprise, he suggested that the solution was for the Huron to stop listening to them (19:217).

In Teanaostaiaé, the Jesuits were staying with a headman named Tsondakwa (23:241). A few Huron who lived in this community asked for baptism apparently during the early stages of the epidemic. One of these was Torichés, a headman who had fallen ill and was hoping for a cure (19:191). Another was a man who had formerly listened to the Jesuits but who had become terrified when he thought that a picture of Christ looked at him in such a way as to threaten him with death (19:203–7). Yet another was a young man who wished to go to heaven because the word the Jesuits used to translate heaven was part of his name (19:191). On the whole, however, the inhabitants of Teanaostaiaé were more violently opposed to the Jesuits than were those of Ossossané. As public resentment grew, most Christians, including Saouenhati, who was the head of a notable family, abjured their conversions in order to avoid rising public anger (23:139). Leading headmen talked of having the Jesuits killed. Young people harassed the Jesuits by throwing sticks at them, hitting them, knocking down their crosses, and threatening to set fire to their cabin.

Brébeuf was singled out as the most dangerous sorcerer (19:195; 34:185–87). A young man whom Brébeuf had told that he was taking the path to hell dreamt that his life could be saved only if he killed the missionary. He became so violent that the more responsible headmen warned the French not to venture outside their houses. To appease the man's dream, the village council presented him with the recently taken head of an enemy, thus satisfying his soul wish and diverting his anger from the Jesuits.

Finally a riot broke out. Brébeuf and Chaumonot were attacked and beaten, their domestic, Pierre Boucher, was wounded in the arm, and their house seems to have been set on fire. After this, the Jesuits were ordered to leave Teanaostaiaé and return to Sainte-Marie (18:25; 19:195; 34:185–87). The councils of Scanonaenrat and Taenhatentaron also forbade the Jesuits to visit these towns. The reason that the headmen of these towns gave was their desire to protect the Jesuits against plans that some young men had made on their lives. In fact, they were trying to prevent the Jesuits from visiting these towns to stop them from practising their witchcraft in them. The Jesuits were unable to work in these settlements until the epidemic was almost over (19:207).

Although the Arendarhonon were the oldest Huron allies of the French, 1639 was the first year that the French attempted any serious mission work among them. Arendarhonon territory extended as far west as the Sturgeon River, but their prinicipal town, which at this period was called Contarea, was located near the Narrows of Lake Couchiching, considerably to the east of its predecessor, Cahiagué (Heidenreich 1966:114, 123–24). The very isolation of this eastern "bulwark" of the Huron country probably helped to delay the arrival of the smallpox, which became generally prevalent only after Fathers Daniel and Le Moyne had come there. The Jesuits' arrival in Contarea was greeted with great joy, as their arrivals in Ossossané and Teanaostaiaé had been. After the priests took up residence in the longhouse of Atironta and had erected a small chapel there (Thwaites 1896–1901, 20:25), the village council granted them permission to address the community, individual households invited the Jesuits to visit them, and everyone spoke of becoming a Christian.

Rumours about the dangers of baptism that were common among the three western tribes do not seem to have penetrated this far east, or if they had the Arendarhonon had paid little attention to them. Baptism was sought for both young and old who were ill (20:23) and the Jesuits' raisins and sugar were in demand for their presumed curative powers (20:21). The Jesuits' reputation as healers was enhanced when a number of Arendarhonon recovered after receiving their aid. Ononrouten, a young man noted for his ability as a hunter and warrior, had been stricken with smallpox in September but survived after he was baptized. When Daniel and Le Moyne arrived in Contarea in November they found him blinded by an inflammation, but when they applied holy water to his eyes he recovered his vision (20:23–25). A young girl was likewise cured of a dangerous ulcer and a woman named Atatasé recovered from colic after she was shown a picture of Christ and had been baptized (20:25–27). As smallpox became more prevalent and people who were baptized began to die, most of the people of Contarea grew hostile towards the Jesuits. They began to repeat the same accusations against them that the rest of the Huron were making and the Jesuits were forced to remain inside Atironta's longhouse. Even there, however, everyone except Atironta began to harass them in an effort to drive them away. The leader of this persecution was the eldest female in the house (20:31–33).

The Arendarhonon's dislike of the Jesuits was reinforced by dreams that people in Contarea reported having. In one, the Jesuits were seen outside the village palisade or on the shore of a lake, unfolding books from which sparks of fire spread everywhere, carrying the smallpox with them (20:31–33). Another man reported that when he was fishing, Iouskeha appeared to him in a vision and informed him that he was the spirit that the Jesuits called Jesus, but about whom the French knew very little. Iouskeha stated that it was the Jesuits travelling in pairs throughout the Huron country who were causing disease and that they would not stop until all the Huron were dead. Iouskeha advised that if the people of Contarea wished to save themselves, they should drive away the Jesuits and perform a ritual that

Iouskeha proceeded to describe in detail. The man reported his vision to the village council, which gave orders that the ritual should be performed. It began in Atironta's longhouse and, in addition to dream-guessing, involved carrying a great kettle of ritually treated water through the village, from which the sick were encouraged to drink (20:27–31). This vision is of special interest because it is the first recorded attempt by a Huron group to reassert traditional beliefs and to denigrate those being advocated by the Jesuits. The vision marks the beginning of a series of minor nativistic movements in which Huron visionaries attempted to organize some sort of ideological resistance to Christianity by reinforcing the basic tenets of the Huron oral tradition. As a result of the upsurge in native ritualism in Contarea and growing doubts about the efficacy of baptism, the Arendarhonon whom the Jesuits had baptized soon rejected their teachings.

In spite of this, Atironta, as the successor of the first Arendarhonon headman who had concluded an alliance with the French, continued to take seriously his role as protector of the Jesuits. It was he who called a meeting at which the Jesuits were invited to defend their innocence. Chihwatenha addressed this meeting for over two hours, explaining the Jesuits' teachings. No one expressed any desire to be baptized, but the persecution of the Jesuits soon ceased and once again they were able to visit the majority of households. Thus they baptized more than 140 people, most of whom died soon after (20:37). A war chief refused to be baptized, saying that he had no fear of death or hell and even in Atironta's household the Jesuits were not allowed to baptize at least one child (20:37–39). The Jesuits also visited neighbouring Arendarhonon and Algonkin settlements but their mission work made no significant progress there.

By far the most dangerous mission was the one to the Tionnontaté. No Huron would accompany Fathers Garnier and Jogues on their journey there. As they travelled from one Tionnontaté village to another, children cried out that disease and death were coming and women fled and hid their infants. In most villages it was impossible to find a house in which to sleep and nowhere were the Jesuits allowed to say mass. At Ehwae the principal headman at first protected the Jesuits and allowed them to stay in his longhouse; however, when he saw them praying, he accused them of sorcery and drove them out (20:43–51). The Huron who came to trade with the Tionnontaté accused the Jesuits of even worse crimes, no doubt hoping that they might persuade the Tionnontaté to kill the missionaries. Soon the Jesuits were warned that if they set foot in certain villages they would be slain (20:51–53). During this period the Jesuits were joined by

Chihwatenha who attempted to use his influence with his trading partners ("relatives") to secure better treatment for the missionaries. While he succeeded in winning a single night's lodging for the priests in several villages, as soon as they were discovered trying to baptize the dying, they were forced to leave and Chihwatenha was denounced for associating with sorcerers. When the Jesuits returned to Ehwae, they found that community more hostile than before and were forced to leave before nightfall. The principal headman of the village gave a feast at which he exhorted some young men to slay the Jesuits, but they were unable to overtake them before they reached the next village. The next day this same headman visited the Jesuits and apologized. He was denounced by Chihwatenha for abandoning the hospitality and good manners that were customary among the Huron and Tionnontaté (20:55–65). It is unclear how much longer the Jesuits remained among the Tionnontaté or how many of the dying they managed to baptize. Some of the latter were Neutral Indians who had been forced to seek refuge among the Tionnontaté, apparently by a second consecutive year of famine in their own country (20:49–51).

LIVES IN THE BALANCE

Since the Huron and Tionnontaté both agreed that the Jesuits were using sorcery to cause yet another epidemic, it is surprising that the Jesuits managed to survive the winter. Most Huron, including many council chiefs appear to have wished and called for their death and specific plans were formulated to accomplish this. None of these plans came to anything, however, and when individual Jesuits were attacked, other Huron came to their aid. To a large degree, the Jesuits were protected by the segmentary nature of Huron society, which made not the confederacy but the tribes, villages, clan segments, and even individual lineages responsible for the actions of their members. Each group wanted closer trading relations with the French and was convinced that if it took the initiative in killing or even harming the Jesuits, other groups would profit at its expense. The internal quarrels that had arisen following Brûlé's assassination were too flagrant an example of the disintegrative effects of such behaviour to encourage any group to take responsibility for murdering the Jesuits. Huron headmen spent their time trying to persuade other Huron and non-Huron to kill the Jesuits while refusing to be persuaded themselves. Even the Tionnontaté, who did not trade directly with the French and therefore had less to lose, understood what was going on and refused to become cat's-paws for their

Attignawantan neighbours. The Huron discussed refusing to sell the Jesuits any more corn in an effort to force them to stop practising witchcraft, but even this relatively innocuous plan foundered on the self-interest of the groups involved (Thwaites 1896–1901, 17:229). None of them was willing to forego the supplies of European goods that were received in payment for the corn.

In March 1640 a general council met at St. Louis to discuss what the Huron confederacy as a whole should do about the Jesuits. An entire night was spent debating this issue and the majority of headmen who were present said they were in favour of killing them as soon as possible. One tribe, however, opposed this action arguing that it would ruin the country (19:177). It is not stated which tribe this was, although it may have been the Arendarhonon, playing their traditional role as allies of the French. This led to further argument about which tribe would bear responsibility if the Jesuits were killed, and finally the project was abandoned. It was decided that since it was likely that native sorcerers were also at work, these should be hunted down and slain before further action was taken against the Jesuits (19:179). There is no evidence that the Huron attempted to revive the old plan of compelling the Jesuits to return to Quebec the following spring.

The fundamental reason that the Jesuits survived was that the Huron dared not kill them or force them to leave the country. When they were angry, Huron might prevent the Jesuits from preaching, or they might insult or even strike a priest. In spite of this the Huron believed that the French governor gave the Jesuit mission his complete backing. Because of this, they were convinced that the survival of the French-Huron alliance depended on the Jesuits remaining in their midst and being well treated by them. That this knowledge could be converted into sufficient psychological pressure to protect the Jesuits' lives, in spite of the hostility that their behaviour generated, is a measure of the degree to which the Huron·were now dependent on the French.

In the beginning, French trade goods had appealed to the Huron as novelties, but over the years these goods had become increasingly vital to the Huron economy. At first the Huron could reduce or suspend trade for a year or more if it was in their own interest to do so; however, by 1636 Aenons said that the Attignawantan (and presumably the rest of the confederacy) could not afford to let more than two years go by without trading with the French. Yet, so long as the Huron did not perceive themselves as dependent on the French, they were able to deal with the latter as equals. The relatively small amount of political or cultural pressure that the French exerted on the Huron prior to 1629 did not challenge this feeling of independence.

In 1634 the Huron headmen found their trading and military alliance with the French transformed into a mechanism for compelling them to allow missionaries to live in their midst whose behaviour was incomprehensible to them and who wished to overturn the traditional Huron way of life. The Huron headmen were convinced that these priests had the backing of the French traders and officials and could only be expelled at the cost of giving up the French alliance. To make things worse, there was no alternative to trading with the French. European goods could no longer be done without and the Iroquois, who were the principal enemies of the Huron, lay between them and the Dutch. The Huron could therefore perceive no opportunity in the foreseeable future of switching their trade from the St. Lawrence to the Hudson Valley. Knowledge that there was no alternative and that they were dependent on the French inculcated a sense of frustration and resignation among a number of Huron headmen. Yet, while a realization of the need for good relations with French traders seems to have been widespread enough to ensure the protection of the Jesuits, its more crippling effects were not generally realized until some time later. The period between 1634 and 1640 was not the time when most Huron first became aware of their loss of independence.

Lalemant records that when the Huron went to trade in 1640, Montmagny punished them for the acts of violence they had committed against the Jesuits during the previous winter (21:143). Nothing is recorded concerning the precise nature of this punishment, although it was probably directed against the traders who had been most active in opposing the Jesuits rather than against the Huron as a whole. Punishments meted out to the Montagnais suggest that some traders may have been seized, imprisoned for a few days, and made to pay fines. Alternatively, they may have been denied the right to trade until they promised to behave differently in future. Montmagny warned the Huron of severe penalties that he would inflict on any Huron who in future attempted to harm the Jesuits.

However much the Huron resented such coercion, they were intimidated by Montmagny's threats and did not attempt to defend their honour by making any sort of counter-threats against the French. When the traders returned home, several Huron tribes offered reparations to the Jesuits to atone for the behaviour of those who had sought to injure them. From this time on, however hostile certain individuals may have felt towards the

Jesuits, the Huron headmen treated them with circumspection. Lalemant rejoiced at the success of Montmagny's action, which he described as a pious employment of secular power.

This event, though inadequately reported, was clearly a turning point in French-Huron relations. Not long before, the French had feared the loss of the fur trade and were making contingency plans to try to come to terms with the Huron even if the Jesuits were slain. Now that half of the Huron population had died, the French became convinced that the Huron were economically and politically dependent on them, and this encouraged Montmagny to assert his power. As the Jesuits in the Huron country observed the success of this new policy, Montmagny was encouraged to press home his advantage.

SULLEN AFTERMATH

By the spring of 1640 the smallpox epidemic had come to an end. With its termination, Huron hostility towards the Jesuits subsided. Once again, it became possible for them to visit all of the Huron settlements. Of Christian converts of former years, only three or four heads of families and a few old women continued to profess their adherence (Thwaites 1896–1901, 17: 229). The rest had publicly renounced Christianity or their faith had been swept away in the upsurge of healing cults that had taken place during the winter. Bitter feelings against the Jesuits persisted and reflected themselves in a number of different ways. In May 1640 a shaman in St. Jean predicted the death of Brébeuf, who was once again working in Teanaostaiaé. The same day Brébeuf suffered from a high fever and pains in the stomach, which lasted for more than twenty-four hours. The Huron regarded Brébeuf as the leader of the Jesuits, and the Jesuits suspected that one or more shamans had attempted to poison him (19:179–81).

A more certain victim of Huron resentment was Joseph Chihwatenha, who was killed on 2 August while he was cutting down some trees in a field near Ossossané. His death was not witnessed by anyone, but the Huron headmen who investigated the slaying reported that it had been committed by two Seneca who had rushed at Chihwatenha from the woods, wounded him with a spear, finished him off with two hatchet blows, and carried off his scalp as a trophy. His body was not discovered until evening when his failure to return home caused others to look for him (20:79). While the Jesuits accepted the claim that he had been slain by the Seneca (20:95; 21:161–63, 211), there are strong reasons for believing that he was murdered by his own people and that the headmen in Ossossané had either ordered his murder or at least approved of it in advance.[13] Killings of this sort were among the ways that Huron headmen dealt with those who were believed guilty of sorcery and treason. The killing occurred only a few days before Chihwatenha was planning to leave for the St. Lawrence (20:79).

In the summer of 1639 Chihwatenha had visited Quebec, where he met Marie Guyart and two Ursuline nuns, who had arrived from France that year planning to found a nunnery and a school for French and Indian girls (19:161). Following this visit, and at considerable inconvenience to himself, he had transported some relics and other religious equipment from Quebec to the Huron country (19:251). Far from faltering in his support for the Jesuits during the smallpox epidemic, Chihwatenha went to great lengths to aid them and identify himself with them, not only in Ossossané, but throughout the Huron country and among the Tionnontaté (19:259). These activities strengthened Huron suspicions that he was in league with the Jesuits to kill his own people. On several occasions Chihwatenha replied to these accusations by stating that he was willing to be slain as a sorcerer rather than cease helping the Jesuits (19:247–49). In 1640 Chihwatenha was persuaded to spend eight days performing spiritual exercises at Sainte-Marie to help him cope with the stresses of the period (19:137). In the course of these exercises Chihwatenha persuaded one of a group of Huron, who had come to Sainte-Marie to denounce the Jesuits, to be baptized. This convert, named Louis, was described as one of the noblest spirits in the country (19:151).

After these exercises Chihwatenha visited a village near Sainte-Marie, where he attempted to persuade a brother, or maternal cousin, to become a Christian. He informed this relative that, because he intended to do more to help the Jesuits in the future than he had done in the past, he anticipated that the charges of sorcery that were being levelled against him would increase. Chihwatenha told this kinsman not to be surprised if he heard that he was condemned and slain as a sorcerer (19:153). Chihwatenha denied being a sorcerer. He also told his kinsman that he would continue to regard him as a brother only if he became a Christian (19:159). The relative confirmed to Chihwatenha that there was talk of killing both him and the French and warned him that his death might be imminent (19:157). When Chihwatenha attempted to convert other people in the village, he was told that this was a matter for the headmen to decide which implied that it was an affair in which a young and unimportant individual like himself should not be meddling (19:163).

The idea that Chihwatenha was in league with the Jesuits to destroy his own people had been entertained at Ossossané as early as 1637 (15:99). With his increasing involvement in mission work, this opinion became more widely accepted. It is indicative, however, of the manner in which the Huron dealt with matters related to the French, that they waited until most of the traders had left for Quebec before they took steps to eliminate him.

Chihwatenha appears to have had some knowledge of the immediate danger he was in on 2 August. Around noon, he ordered his three nieces who had accompanied him to the fields to gather some squashes and return home as quickly as possible (20:81). Had he suspected that the Iroquois were lurking nearby, he would have accompanied his nieces to safety and raised a war party to track the enemy. His actions are logical, however, if he knew that his own people were determined to kill him and make it look like the work of Iroquois raiders; by sending his nieces home, he prevented them from being killed as witnesses. It appears that his whole family knew why and by whom he had been killed, but in the face of general hostility they dared not complain or question the findings of the village council. When one of Chihwatenha's nieces heard that he had been slain, her only comment was that even if "they" massacred the whole family, she would never cease to believe in the Christian god (23:195). This statement suggests that she believed that her uncle was killed by his own people.

Such knowledge may also explain the decision that Chihwatenha's elder brother Teondechoren made, only three days after the killing, to become a Christian and carry on his brother's work (21:149–51). For many years Teondechoren had been a prominent member of the Awataerohi society and although he and Chihwatenha lived in the same village and probably in the same longhouse, he had rejected all of Chihwatenha's proposals that he should become a Christian. Teondechoren's sudden change of mind may be interpreted as a tacit protest against the killing of his brother. He remained a faithful convert and, as an outward symbol of his desire to continue his brother's work, the Jesuits followed Huron custom and allowed him to "revive" his brother's Christian name.

Enough information is presented in the *Jesuit Relations* to permit present-day scholars (including Jesuit ones) to infer that Chihwatenha was killed by his own people (Talbot 1956:221–22). It therefore seems highly unlikely that the Jesuits working in the Huron country also did not suspect this. Why then did they remain silent, preventing Chihwatenha from being recognized as the first martyr of the Huron mission? It may be that they lacked proof and therefore felt obliged to accept the Huron's explanation of what happened. Or they may have felt, as they did after Father Chabanel's murder, that it was more prudent "to let suspicions sleep which might have been a ground for animosities and nothing more" (Du Creux 1951–52:553). This would have been an even more honourable policy had the Jesuits known that Chihwatenha was slain for political reasons such as helping the Jesuits among the Tionnontaté, rather than because his affirmation of Christianity had convinced the Huron that he was a sorcerer. It must be noted, however, that as a result of the Jesuits' missionary work among the Huron, Le Caron's opinion that it was impossible to be a martyr among the Indians was no longer valid (Le Clercq 1691:283). The Jesuits had built up an image of Chihwatenha as a model convert in successive instalments of their *Relations*; they may therefore have feared that if they publicly attributed his death to the Huron, they would lose the sympathy of their readers for the continuation of the Huron mission. What is more surprising is that scarcely any references are made to Chihwatenha in later volumes of the *Jesuit Relations*.

Conclusion

If the great political and psychological development of the period 1634–40 was the Huron's gradual realization of the degree to which their reliance on French trade goods was curtailing their freedom of action, an equally serious tragedy was the loss of approximately half their population. A large number of those who died were children and old people. The loss of the former must have meant that towards the end of the following decade, when the attacks of the Iroquois increased sharply, the Huron had fewer young men to defend their villages than their total numbers would suggest. The high mortality rate among older people was even more serious because of their key role among the Huron. They included many of the most skilful artisans, both male and female, as well as headmen and village elders who were knowledgeable about local and foreign affairs and had the most experience in dealing with the Jesuits. Traditional religious lore was also largely a prerogative of the elderly (Thwaites 1896–1901, 8:145–47). In the epidemics many must have died before they could transmit this knowledge to their heirs. The loss of such a broad spectrum of experience made the Huron economically still more dependent on the French and less equipped to resist the theological inroads of the Jesuits. The Jesuits, of course, could not resist seeing the hand of God at work in the death of the native religious specialists. This was interpreted as evidence that the Almighty was intervening to win the Huron to Roman Catholicism.

The remnants of the Huron found themselves living in villages that were too large for them. Many longhouses were empty or almost empty, since up to half of their inhabitants were dead. In the summer of 1640 this resulted in a decision to relocate the town of Ossossané, although the existing settlement was only five years old (21:159). The extra labour involved in founding a new, albeit smaller, town so soon after the last move must have been a heavy burden to the people of Ossossané. It may be assumed that similar, premature moves were made in other parts of the Huron country.

It has often been assumed that this decimation of the Huron people put them numerically at a disadvantage by comparison with other tribes and, in particular, with the Iroquois. This conclusion is based on the erroneous assumption that the Huron were decimated while other Iroquoian peoples were not. When Bogaert visited the Mohawk in the winter of 1634–35 the principal headman of Onekagoncka, their most easterly fortified village, was living about a quarter of a mile away because so many people had died of smallpox (Jameson 1909:141). The Susquehannock were stricken by an epidemic in 1636 or early 1637 (Thwaites 1896–1901, 14:9) and the Wenroronon's decision to move to the Huron country in 1638 is said to have been made, in part, as a result of large numbers having perished from disease (15:159). The Neutral suffered to an unusual degree from wars, famine, and disease prior to 1641. Even if Neutral villages were smaller than Huron ones, the estimate of only 300 people per village in 1641 hints at population losses that may have been of a similar magnitude to those experienced by the Huron. Finally, in the winter of 1640–41 a serious epidemic, probably smallpox, was reported to be raging among the Seneca (21:211). During the following decade, particularly in 1646 and 1647, the Iroquois were afflicted with contagious diseases that do not appear to have reached the Huron (30:229, 273; 31:121). These random reports, combined with what we know about the ravages of disease among the Indians of the St. Lawrence and Ottawa Valleys, complete a picture of general population decline throughout the region. It therefore seems reasonable to conclude that the Huron and Iroquois had been roughly equal in numbers before the epidemics began and that both had lost approximately one half of their population by 1640. In strictly demographic terms this gave neither side an advantage over the other.

Chapter 9  The Storm

The Huron and the French

GROWING DEPENDENCE ON TRADE

By 1640 not only the Huron but most of the Indians in eastern Canada and adjacent parts of the United States had become dependent on the fur trade. Novel economic pressures were transforming their lives and inter-relationships at an accelerating rate. In particular, increasing demands for European goods began to generate new kinds of conflicts as tribes were driven to compete for the limited supplies of beaver skins that were available. Exacerbated by the competitiveness of rival European traders, these conflicts were to shatter the established tribal patterns of this area within scarcely more than a decade. Unlike some earlier conflicts, the new ones were not over access to European traders or trade goods, but over obtaining the furs with which European goods could be purchased.

Serious readjustments in the economic life of the entire region were necessitated by the sharp drop in human population between 1636 and 1640. Since both the Huron and the northern hunting peoples probably declined by about half, it would be reasonable to expect a proportional decrease in the number of furs that were traded after this time. Yet the figures for the decade between 1640 and 1650 suggest that the annual volume of furs supplied to the French did not drop. In 1645 an estimated 30,000 pounds of beaver skins were exported from New France (Thwaites 1896–1901, 27:85). The following year the figure was 32,000 pounds (28:235), and in 1648 it was 22,400 pounds (32:103). While a beaver pelt weighs approximately one and a half British pounds, Jérôme Lalemant's statement that furs were selling in France for ten livres per pound in-conclusively suggests that at this period a pound generally signified an individual skin (28:235). This would make possible a direct comparison with earlier documents in which statistics are given in terms of skins rather than weights. Yet even if the pounds referred to are actual weights, these figures indicate an increase in the annual volume of trade over the average 12,000 to 15,000 skins that were exported before 1627 (4:207). It thus appears that after 1635 the number of skins obtained by the French rose as the Indian population declined. In part, this may be explained by an increase in the extent of French trading networks along the St. Lawrence. Closer relations with the Abenaki, who lived in Maine and adjacent parts of New England, brought some furs to Quebec. Yet this increase could not have offset losses proportional to the probable decline in the Indian population of Ontario and Quebec.

It may also be argued that these high figures are for the few years in the 1640s when trade was successful and include furs that the Huron and other tribes had accumulated over several preceding years, when they were unable to trade with the French. There are, however, major rebuttals to such an argument. In most years when the Huron and other tribes failed to trade with the French in large numbers, they made an effort to do so, often losing most of their furs to the Iroquois. The years when the Iroquois were most active were also those when it was least possible for the Algonkin and Montagnais to hunt or trade with other tribes, hence the returns carried forward to the following year were unlikely to be of considerable volume. For both of these reasons, it is reasonable to accept the figures for such peaceful years as 1645 and 1646 as indicating the volume of furs that the Indians who were allied to the French were capable of supplying them in any single year.

There are no direct figures concerning the number of furs that the Huron supplied in any one year, but there is information about the number of Huron who came to trade with the French. Like the data for earlier times, these figures mainly take account of traders who arrived in sizable groups; hence they probably fall short of the totals for most years. We know, for example, that in June 1643 a single group of about 120 Huron came to Quebec to trade and were attacked by the Iroquois on their way home a few weeks later (24:121; 26:235–37). We also know that at least two bands of Huron were attacked that year on their way to or from Quebec (28:45), so the total number of traders must have considerably exceeded 120. The following year, sixty Huron came to Three Rivers, proclaiming that their aim was to fight the Iroquois rather than to trade. They returned home, however, laden with presents and no doubt with trade goods, and were accompanied by an escort of French soldiers (26:53–73). The same year three other bands of Huron traders were attacked by the Iroquois (28:45). Even if these were bands of no more than forty men each, the minimum number of Huron attempting to trade on the St. Lawrence that year would have been 180.

In 1645 no Huron came to the St. Lawrence before September, when sixty canoes arrived at Three Rivers (27:89, 277). Although approximately thirty Frenchmen were travelling with them, it is reasonable to assume that there were about 200 Huron in this group. At least some of them visited Quebec and their safe return home filled the Huron country with joy, since they brought with them an abundant supply of French goods which had become scarce during the previous five or six years as a result of Iroquois attacks on traders travelling to and from the St. Lawrence (29:247). In late August of the following year, over eighty Huron canoes came in a single group to trade (28:141, 231). These canoes carried about 300 Indians (29:233), in addition to some thirty warriors who had come down-river earlier (29:229). At least two canoeloads of Huron were still at Quebec a month later (28:235). So many skins were brought down-river that year that the Huron had to take twelve bundles home with them for lack of French merchandise (28:231). In 1648, 250 Huron came to trade in about sixty canoes (32:179, 185). While none of these figures is as high as the 140 to 150 canoes that were reported to have come down-river in 1633, the annual totals are as large, or larger, than the average of sixty canoes and 200 traders per year that has been estimated for the period 1615 to 1629. The figures for 1646 are also the second highest on record. This suggests that not only the total amount of trade with the French, but also the number of Huron who were participating in it, were no less after the epidemics than they had been prior to 1629. As before, the Huron probably provided close to half of the total number of furs exported from Quebec each year, which probably meant 12,000 to 16,000 skins.[1] Lalemant reports that the twenty-two French soldiers who were sent to the Huron country in 1644 returned the following year with 3000 to 4000 furs (27:89). The dispute that arose concerning who had the right to purchase these skins clearly indicates that they were ones these soldiers had obtained by barter, rather than the total Huron consignment for that year.

Even though the mortality of 1639 to 1640 had fallen most heavily on the young and old, the number of Huron and Algonkians who died in the prime of life must have been very great. For a population that had been halved to maintain its former level of trade with the French required very considerable changes in organization. These changes must have represented an even more severe drain on manpower because of the large numbers of traders who were killed or taken prisoner by the Iroquois, particularly between 1641 and 1644. Unfortunately, we have no clear evidence to explain how the Huron managed to maintain the volume of their trade at its former level. It is theoretically possible that they extended their trading networks geographically, although the only evidence that there is of this (which I will discuss later) is of the Huron taking over markets that were abandoned by their trading partners. There is no evidence that the Huron tapped new sources of furs to the north or west, which alone would have augmented the numbers of furs reaching Quebec by way of the Huron country. More intensive exploitation of the fringes of the existing Huron trading network may have netted more furs than before, without requiring greater effort on the part of individual Algonkian hunters, but this is unlikely to have maintained the intake of beaver pelts at its former level. The conclusion therefore seems inescapable that throughout much of this trading area, individual Algonkians were encouraged to trap considerably more beaver than they had done previously.

While the deaths of many hunters may have allowed those who survived to increase the number of beaver that they caught with less than a proportional increase in effort, it is unlikely that the numbers of animals being trapped could have been doubled without considerably more time being devoted to this task. This was probably accomplished as it had been among the hunting peoples of the Maritimes, by using time that tradition-ally had been spent fishing and hunting larger game animals. The resulting weakening of the subsistence base was compensated for by relying more heavily on corn and beans, which the northern Algonkians obtained from their Huron trading partners. It is possible that the Algonkians were more than happy to do this, since this arrangement seemed to offer them more security against starvation during the winter than did their traditional subsistence pattern. All that may have been needed to stimulate more trapping at the expense of hunting and fishing was an increase in the volume of corn that the Huron made available to their northern trading partners. It is also likely that as a result of the epidemics, the Algonkians, like the Huron, had lost many of their most skilful artisans and were more anxious for European goods than they had been previously. Thus, growing dependence on both the Huron and the French drew the Algonkians more deeply into a network of interrelationships that made them increasingly dependent on what was happening among their southern neighbours.

If an equal proportion of the Huron and their northern trading partners died between 1634 and 1640 and the economic relations between them had not changed, the surviving Huron would have had to spend no more or no less time producing corn than they had done previously. Growing reliance on Huron foodstuffs by the Algonkians must, however, have increased the amount of time that Huron women had to spend tending their crops and that Huron men had to spend clearing new fields. Moreover, in relationship to the population, approximately twice as many Huron men must have been involved in trading with the Algonkians and the French as had been before. This increase is well documented in terms of the number of Huron who came to the St. Lawrence to trade each year, which remained roughly constant in spite of the dramatic decline in population. It is also likely that because of increasing production and consumption, as many men as before were required to transport corn and skins between the Huron country and the north in spite of the decreased population.

The greater input of labour into the fur trade meant that less time was available for other activities. In particular, the amount of time available for traditional warfare, which, like trading, was a warm weather activity, must have been sharply reduced. Whenever French trade goods could be substituted for traditional Huron products that took long to manufacture, the increasing time taken up by the fur trade must have encouraged the Huron to substitute these items for their own. Thus, the demand for French goods, which had already been intensified by depopulation and the loss of old skills, was further increased as a result of the fur trade. It is also possible that the need to grind more corn and manufacture more nets for the northern trade may have reduced the time that was available during the winter for traditional ritual activities. A decline in such activities would have left the Huron more vulnerable to the ideological assaults of the missionaries.

With their growing dependence on the fur trade, the geographical position of the Huron rendered them far more vulnerable to attack than were the Iroquois. The Mohawk had to travel only forty to fifty miles down the Mohawk Valley to trade at Fort Orange; hence individuals and small groups were able to move easily and at any time of the year between their own villages and the Dutch settlements. While the western Iroquois tribes had to walk overland for much longer distances, their route was through territory belonging to the other tribes of the Iroquois confederacy. Huron or Susquehannock raiders might ambush these traders, but at this period such ambushes seem to have been uncommon. Finally, for all of the Iroquois tribes, protecting their tribal territory and their trade routes were one and the same operation, while for the Huron, they were not. The Huron had to defend their villages and tribal territory against Iroquois raiders, who mostly came from the western part of the Iroquois confederacy. In addition, whenever Huron traders travelled along the Ottawa and St. Lawrence rivers, they were in danger of being attacked by Mohawk and Oneida. Since small bands of Iroquois were able to hide along the banks of these rivers and wait the best opportunity to fall upon their victims, these attacks were much easier for the Iroquois to launch than for the Huron to guard against. One response was for the Huron to travel in large groups, which they began to do as early as 1643. Prior to 1648, however, these bands had a tendency to split up if no danger appeared to be threatening and this resulted in unexpected attacks. Huron also came to the Ottawa and St. Lawrence valleys to fight the Iroquois, but as attacks on the Huron homeland grew more severe a strong element of risk was involved in diverting large numbers of men to fight there.

Thus, as the Huron grew more dependent on European goods and their manpower was increasingly tied up in trading activities, their inland location that had formerly sheltered them from so many of the disrupting effects of European contact became a liability. Because of this, the balance of power that had formerly existed between the Huron and the Iroquois began to tip in the latter's favour. The Huron found themselves not only economically, but also militarily, more dependent on the French than they had been before. To many, the goodwill of the French must have seemed essential to their survival. The desire that most Huron seem to have had for closer relations with the French encouraged Montmagny and his Jesuit advisers to design new strategies to promote at least an external acceptance of Christianity.

TAKING OVER ALGONKIAN TRADE ROUTES

During and after the epidemics, the Huron enjoyed a number of advantages which made it easier for them to collect furs to trade with the French. As I have already noted, when the Jesuits returned to New France in 1632, they made certain that no employees of the trading company were allowed to live among the Nipissing or Algonkin. Nicollet, who had resided for a long time among the Nipissing, settled as a clerk of the Compagnie des Cent-Associés at Three Rivers in 1633 and, thereafter, since the Jesuits did not establish a mission among the Nipissing, there were no Frenchmen living with them. It is therefore not difficult to understand why, when the Nipissing incurred Tessouat's wrath in 1636 for refusing to help him wage war on the Iroquois, they no longer dared to travel down the Ottawa River to trade with the French. It was not until the summer of 1640 that they ventured to send a few canoes to Three Rivers (Thwaites 1896–1901, 21:241). To encourage the Nipissing to trade, the Jesuits decided to establish a mission amongst them and Fathers Claude Pijart and Charles Raymbaut were sent to the Huron country for this purpose. In the winter of 1640–41 these missionaries made contact with 250 survivors of the tribe who were wintering in the Wye Valley, and in the spring of 1641 they travelled with the Nipissing to their tribal territory (21:239–49). In 1642 the Jesuits again travelled north with the Nipissing and participated in an Algonkian version of the Feast of the Dead that was held along the eastern shore of Georgian Bay. This ceremony was attended by all the trading partners of the Nipissing, who were given presents at two separate assemblies: one held for the Huron and the other for the Algonkian-speaking tribes. At this gathering, the Jesuits had a chance to meet the various bands who lived along the eastern and northern shores of Lake Huron.

At this Feast of the Dead, the Baouichtigouian or Ojibwa Indians from Sault Sainte Marie, who had already entertained Brûlé and other Frenchmen, invited the Jesuits to visit their country. Thus, in September Fathers Raymbaut and Jogues accompanied a party of Huron to Sault Sainte Marie, but returned to the Huron country in the late autumn (23:225–27). This marked the beginning of a series of Algonkian-speaking missions to the Indians at the Sault, to the Ottawa bands living west of the Tionnontaté and along the northern and eastern shores of Georgian Bay, and to the Algonkin who came to winter or find refuge among the Arendarhonon. The most important of these missions was that of St. Esprit to the Nipissing. It is uncertain to what degree the Huron-based missionaries were able to encourage the Nipissing to resume their trade with the French. No priests were available to travel with them to Three Rivers and, while there are occasional references to the Nipissing coming to Three Rivers to trade, there is nothing to indicate that this trade was carried on even to the limited degree that it had been before 1636. The chief beneficiaries of this Nipissing reluctance to trade must have been the Huron who until 1640 and probably afterwards obtained more furs from the Nipissing than they had done for many years previously.

The Huron may also have gained direct access to more furs as a result of growing disorder among the Algonkin. Starting apparently in the late 1630s, the Iroquois began to supplement their summer attacks on fur shipments along the Ottawa and St. Lawrence River with winter raiding parties. The aim of these raids was to penetrate Algonkin and Montagnais hunting grounds and to rob these Indians of their catch while they were dispersed in small family groups and therefore unable to come together to defend themselves (27:37). The Iroquois also hunted in these territories. Because of these raids, many Algonkin and Montagnais were too frightened to hunt and began to seek the protection of the French at Sillery, Three Rivers, Fort Richelieu, and the new French settlement at Montreal. Still others sought temporary refuge in the upper part of the Ottawa Valley (14:225) or in the Huron country (24:267).

When Tessouat wintered along the St. Lawrence in 1640–41, he was still self-confident enough to persuade the Montagnais at Sillery to defy the Jesuits by resuming traditional religious practices. In the winter of 1642–43, however, even the Kichesipirini were refugees from the Iroquois and the following spring both Tessouat and Oumasasikweie embraced Christianity and expressed a desire to settle under French protection at Montreal (24:237–45). That the headmen of the Kichesipirini, who prided themselves on their independence of the French both before and after this period, should have become so submissive can be accounted for only by their fear of the Iroquois. The same year, the Onontchataronon, who traditionally wintered among the Arendarhonon, were joined there by Algonkin from all parts of the Ottawa Valley, who were seeking refuge from the Iroquois (24:267–69; 27:37). These refugees were reported to be hoping that once the Montreal area became more secure, they could establish a permanent village there under French protection, no doubt much like the Indian village at Three Rivers.[2] Although the Algonkin had long discussed the advantages of having a refuge on Montreal Island, the fact that large numbers of them were now willing to abandon their tribal territories is an indication of the danger that existed at this time. For the Kichesipirini to consider having their summer headquarters there was a particularly desperate move, since it meant foregoing the lucrative tolls they collected on Morrison Island.

Many Algonkin, particularly from bands in the lower part of the Ottawa Valley, began to frequent the French settlement of Ville Marie and to plant crops there (29:145–47), while the Onontchataronon asserted traditional claims to Montreal Island as being their ancestral home (Pendergast and Trigger 1972:77–80). Henceforth, the majority of Algonkin hedged their bets by maintaining their connections with the major centres of French population, whatever the political situation was like and wherever they spent most of their time. It is not surprising, however, that as soon as a shaky peace was arranged with the Mohawk, Tessouat and his people returned to Morrison Island (Thwaites 1896–1901, 29:149).

HURON TRADE IN CENTRAL QUEBEC

The general disruption of Algonkin life at this time may have stimulated the Huron to intensify their trade with the Indians of central Quebec.

We know from Sagard that the Huron were trading into that area by the 1620s, while archaeological evidence hints that even in prehistoric times some of them may have travelled as far east as Lake St. John. In the 1640s, however, the references to Huron trade in central Quebec become more abundant. The Huron were reported to come each year to "Maouatchihitonnam" to trade with the Kakouchakhi and other hunting groups of central Quebec (Thwaites 1896–1901, 24:155). It is tempting to identify this trading place as Matabachouwan on Lake St. John, which may have been the eastern terminus of the prehistoric copper route leading from Ontario. Such a location was ideal for trade with the bands of the upper Saguenay and was probably where the Attikamegue, or White Fish people, who lived in the upper part of the St. Maurice Valley, came to trade with the Huron. In 1647 when the Huron were unable to come down the St. Lawrence, the Jesuits at Three Rivers asked the Attikamegue to carry letters destined for the Huron country to Huron with whom they traded in the interior of Quebec. They not only delivered these letters, but returned bearing others that the Jesuits in the Huron country had asked the Huron to send to Quebec by way of the Attikamegue (31:219). From these letters we know that some fifty Huron traders came to Maouatchihitonnam, bringing with them corn, corn meal, nets, and other small wares (probably including tobacco), which they exchanged for animal skins (31:209, 219).

The goods that the Huron brought with them also demonstrate that they came directly from the Huron country. Moreover, the fact that none of these Huron is described as coming to Three Rivers or Tadoussac and, more specifically, their failure to deliver the letters from the Huron country to the French in person suggest that after their trading they returned to the Huron country or at least to the Ottawa Valley, where they exchanged their furs with Huron who were authorized to trade with the French (32:289).[3] It is uncertain by what route they made their way eastward and westward across the network of lakes and rivers of central Quebec. Those who went by way of Lake Timiskaming may have travelled as far north as Lake Matagami before turning southeastward to Lake St. John. This route would have taken them through Nekouba which, when it was first visited by the French a few years later, was described as the location of an annual market, similar to Maouatchihitonnam (46:275). Indeed, Father Ragueneau may have been referring to Nekouba when he mentioned a group of Huron who in the summer of 1641 left their country on a trading expedition to Ondoutawaka (22:75). Two years later, Jérôme Lalemant explained that the Huron went every year to trade with the Andatouha people who lived "about a hundred leagues above the Saguenay towards the north" (27:27). These people were reported to have acquired a smattering of Christian knowledge on their visits to Tadoussac and Three Rivers.

There clearly were opportunities for the Huron to expand trade in this region and, as the fur trade became more important to them, they must have taken advantage of such opportunities, particularly as the Algonkin's control of the trade of this region became less effective. Yet these references to Huron activity in central Quebec do not prove that their trade in this area was a new thing; they may simply reflect a growing awareness on the part of the French of what was going on north of the St. Lawrence. Huron traders had been active in Quebec for at least two decades and possibly longer. Whatever expansion of Huron trade took place in the 1640s was based on established patterns.

HURON VISITORS TO THE ST. LAWRENCE

Another feature of this period was the growing number of Huron men who wintered in the St. Lawrence Valley, either among the French or in the Indian settlements at Sillery and Three Rivers. It has been suggested that they may have initiated the Huron trade in the Lake St. John region (Heidenreich 1971:259, 261, 264). I have not, however, been able to discover any satisfactory evidence that these men engaged in trade with the north and, as we have already seen, the logistics of this trade necessitated that it be a separate operation conducted from the Huron country. In the 1620s a few Huron had wintered at Quebec, apparently mainly from bravado or curiosity, and such motives should not be under-rated even in the 1640s; however, five additional motives explain why individual Huron wintered in the St. Lawrence Valley in the 1640s. Three reflect the growing menace of the Mohawk in the Ottawa and St. Lawrence valleys, while the other two indicate a growing sense of dependence on the French.

Some Huron came to avenge Mohawk attacks on Huron traders. By wintering in the St. Lawrence Valley, they could join the Montagnais in their spring raids. In April 1647 a number of Huron who had wintered at Sillery and Three Rivers set out on such a raid, although Montmagny tried to persuade them not to, in the hope that a short-lived peace with the Mohawk still might be preserved. One of the leaders of this band was Andehoua, the most loyal of the Jesuits' former pupils (Thwaites 1896–1901, 30:165–67).

Other Huron who wintered in the St. Lawrence Valley had been captured by the Mohawk and escaped from them, but were too late or too ill to return home before winter. Montreal, in particular, gained a reputation for being the nearest refuge for these escaped prisoners. Thirdly, because of their fear of the Iroquois, still other Huron delayed their return home past the season when travel was possible and these too took advantage of French or Montagnais hospitality to pass the winter. The extension of such hospitality was an accepted part of intertribal trading relations, but the Huron appear to have made more use of this privilege as Iroquois attacks increasingly disrupted their trading schedules.

The Compagnie des Cent-Associés had for some time supplied European goods to Christian Indians more cheaply than they supplied them to non-Christians. After 1640 discrimination in favour of Christians was intensified to put more pressure on traders to convert. At the same time, however, the Jesuits became more insistent on subjecting potential converts to a strict probation before baptizing them. This led to enterprising attempts by young men to convince the Jesuits of their religious sincerity.

When Brébeuf returned to Quebec in 1641, it was decided that it would be useful to re-open the Huron school, but this time to use it to instruct adults and confirm them in the Christian faith. An attempt was made to persuade a few Huron to stay at Quebec, but no suitable volunteers could be found. Soon after, two Huron from Scanonaenrat, Atondo and Okhukwandoron (Aotiokwandoron, 26:295), returned to Quebec stating that they preferred hunting with the Montagnais to facing the dangers involved in travelling home at the beginning of winter. They were brought to Sillery, where Brébeuf took charge of them and found them receptive to instruction. This seemed surprising since prior to 1640 Atondo, who was a headman of some importance, had shown considerable aversion to the Jesuits.

Atondo and Okhukwandoron remained at Sillery for the winter. They listened attentively to Brébeuf, prayed often, and observed fast days. They were well cared for by the French and the Christian Montagnais and received much special attention both from Montmagny and from the Ursuline and Hospital nuns who were now established at Quebec. Finally, the two men asked to be baptized. This was done with Paul de Chomedey de Maisonneuve and Jeanne Mance as godparents. The latter were spending the winter at Quebec before proceeding to found a colony on Montreal Island. When spring came and Atondo and Okhukwandoron prepared to leave for home, the Montagnais presented them with two parcels of smoked moose meat to feed them on the journey. The Huron promised that when they got home they would host a feast at which they would make a public profession of their new faith and that, hereafter, they would urge their relatives and tribesmen to become Christians (22:135–53).

The success of this new effort to instruct Huron in Christian beliefs led the Jesuits to repeat the experiment under Brébeuf's direction the following winter. Andehoua, who had received the baptismal name of Jean-Armand, and who was now known among his own people as Andeouarahen (23:175), retained the belief in, or fear of, Christianity that he had acquired when he had been a pupil at the first school the Jesuits had established at Quebec. In 1642 he was caught in a dangerous storm on Lake Ontario and vowed that if he escaped, he would again live as the Jesuits had directed. When he returned to the Huron country, he told the Jesuits of his vow and accepted their advice that he and another young Huron named Saouaretchi who had expressed the desire to become a Christian should spend the following winter at Sillery. Other Huron who came to Quebec no doubt had heard from Atondo and his companion how well they had been treated by the Jesuits during the previous winter; therefore a number of other young men volunteered to spend the winter there. The Jesuits were unable to support them, however, since they lacked room and board. The others were persuaded either to return home or to join the Kichesipirini at Fort Richelieu, in order to hunt and go to war with them.

In the middle of January one of these men, who was nephew of a headman from Arenté, came to Sillery and asked to be instructed in the faith. He was fed and lodged by the Hospital nuns. About a month later, room was found for two other men from Arenté, Atarohiat and Atokouchi-ouani, who were allowed to live with the Jesuits' workmen. These young men all behaved to Brébeuf's satisfaction and were baptized during the winter. In mid-June, they left Sillery to join the Huron who had come to trade at Three Rivers and to return to the Huron country with them. Brébeuf was now convinced that by having a number of young men spend a single winter each living amongst the French and the Indians of Sillery, the Jesuits would be able to instruct a corps of Christians who could assist them to convert their own people, as Chihwatenha had done. These men would be especially effective if they came from chiefly lineages and were in line to inherit important offices. Such men were anxious to establish a close relationship with the French for political and economic reasons (24:103–21).

Some Huron men stayed at Sillery during the winter of 1643–44 and received lessons from the Ursuline nuns, who, in turn, were attempting to learn their language (25:243). Brébeuf spent this winter at Three Rivers where, as procurator, he was concerned with the pressing problems of forwarding supplies to the Huron mission. There, a new school was opened in the Jesuit residence and six Huron received instruction. Four had come from the Huron country specifically for this purpose, while the other two were young men who had escaped from the Mohawk. Within two months of their arrival, all six had been baptized. Although they were troubled by dreams throughout the winter, they claimed not to obey these dreams and scrupulously observed Roman Catholic rituals. In late April these Huron set out for home in three canoes, taking with them Father François-Joseph Bressani, an Italian Jesuit who had arrived in New France in 1642 and had spent the following winter helping to instruct these Huron. They were also accompanied by a French boy twelve or thirteen years old. Although some of the Huron carried guns, they were depending mainly on the early date of their departure to save them from Iroquois attack. Seven or eight miles from Fort Richelieu, their canoes were attacked by a Mohawk war party, which included some of their Mahican allies and six former Huron who had been taken prisoner and were now naturalized Iroquois (26:37). In the ensuing conflict, one of the Huron, Sotrioskon, was killed and later eaten by the Iroquois. Seeing that escape was impossible, Bressani ordered the men in his canoe to surrender and finally all of the other Huron were captured by the Iroquois. None of the prisoners was subjected to preliminary torture except Henry Stontrats and Michel Atiokwendoron (not to be confused with Jean Baptiste Okhukwandoron), each of whom had one finger cut off (26:37). They were all carried off to the Mohawk country except Stontrats, who escaped and made his way back to the St. Lawrence (26:19–35).

The fate of the other Huron prisoners is unclear. One appears to have escaped torture by proclaiming his enmity towards the French (39:67, 73), but at least two others were killed (39:95). Bressani was taken from one Mohawk village to another and cruelly tortured for over a month before he was adopted by a Mohawk woman whose grandfather had been killed by the Huron (39:55–97). Rather than ordering his death, she gave the Mohawk presents not to kill him and then sold him to the Dutch for about 200 livres worth of trade goods (39:266 n. 8). After he was ransomed, Bressani returned to France, but by July 1645 he was back in Canada.

Although there is no explicit mention of Huron being instructed at Three Rivers or Quebec after Brébeuf's return to the Huron country in 1644, a Huron named Arenhouton was baptized at Quebec in May 1646 (28:191), perhaps after receiving instruction over the preceding winter. He may have been one of several Huron who spent the winter at Sillery and who were accused of stealing salt pork from Pierre Godois and beating him in retaliation for his having stolen some furs from them (27:91). While it would be unwarranted to deny these Huron some element of religious belief, most of them appear to have viewed a winter living with the Jesuits at Quebec or Three Rivers as an efficacious way to conclude a firm alliance with the French and to secure substantial material benefits from them. As such, it was a role that was especially popular among potential headmen and men who were anxious to trade on the St. Lawrence.

This period also saw a Huron girl brought to Quebec to be educated by the Ursulines. This was Chihwatenha's eleven or twelve-year-old niece Oionhaton.[4] Chihwatenha had met Marie de l'Incarnation and the Ursuline nuns at Quebec in 1639 and when he returned home had expressed the wish that his niece should go to live with the Ursulines for a time. In 1640, Teondechoren carried out his dead brother's wishes and took Oionhaton to Quebec, where she remained until 1642. During this period, she learned to read and write and attempted to follow the religious practices of the nuns. Like other precocious Iroquoian children, she loved to display her newly acquired knowledge by lecturing visiting Huron on the subtleties of Christian doctrine (22:191–97). When Oionhaton was travelling home in 1642 with her uncle and a number of other famous warriors, they were attacked by the Mohawk and she was taken prisoner (22:197).

Another manifestation of the desire to achieve a closer relationship with the French was Atironta's decision to bring his wife to Three Rivers with him when he attended the peace conference in 1645, and to remain with her, his small son,[5] and another Huron, named Acharo, at Quebec over the following winter. Atironta wished to be on hand to await news of the treaty that Huron envoys had gone to conclude with the Mohawk; traditionally he was also the principal Huron ally of the French and in addition he was now a Christian. No doubt, he regarded it as fitting that on a visit to the French, he and his relatives should spend some time with them. The French, however, who had to provide them with flour and eels, complained that the accommodation they occupied in the hospital at Sillery could better have been used for sick people (27:91–93, 103). During the winter Atironta's wife and son were baptized and were allowed to sit in the governor's pew in church (27:113). Stopping at Montreal on his way home, Atironta was said to have been so impressed with the corn that he saw growing there that he proposed to come with his own and another household and settle on the island (29:181). While the Jesuits hoped that he might persuade other Huron to settle near Ville Marie and that these might form the nucleus of a settlement of Christian Huron, nothing came of this suggestion. That it was made at all is a reflection of Atironta's conviction in his role as an ally of the French and therefore as having the right to consider himself one of them.

Trade and Warfare

THE IROQUOIS'S NEED FOR FURS

The 1630s witnessed a gradual resurgence of Mohawk attacks on the St. Lawrence Valley. These were encouraged at the beginning of the decade by the political instability at Quebec and were discouraged by the decisive steps that the French took to police the river in 1633 and 1637. In spite of this, increasing harassment of both Algonkin and Huron traders in the Ottawa Valley seems to indicate that the Mohawk and Oneida were more than taking advantage of an easy situation. Their attacks became more serious in the 1640s, while the western tribes of the Iroquois confederacy were becoming more aggressive towards their neighbours to the north and west. Many explanations have been offered for this increasing bellicosity, but none of them has gained general acceptance. It is therefore necessary to examine closely what was happening among the Iroquois at this time.

Unfortunately, the only Iroquois tribes for whom there is significant historical documentation prior to the 1650s are the Mohawk and Oneida. Most information concerns the Mohawk, who had the most intimate trading relations with the Dutch. The evidence suggests that their closer proximity to Europeans had resulted in their acquiring a wider range of European goods than is reported for the Huron. As early as 1634–35 Harmen van den Bogaert noted doors of hewn boards with iron hinges inside some Mohawk houses (Jameson 1909:141). Such doors would have had to be purchased ready-made or stolen from the Dutch and carried from the Hudson Valley inland to the Mohawk villages. Bogaert also reported seeing iron chains, harrows, hoops, and nails in their villages. By 1644 guns, swords, axes, and mallets were in common use among the Mohawk (ibid. 176), while, about the same time, Jogues and Bressani spoke of them possessing numerous iron rods and chains (Thwaites 1896–1901, 28:125; 39:71). By 1634–35 the mother of an Oneida headman had cloth to repair items of dress (Jameson 1909:153–54). It is perhaps significant that the Mohawk called the Dutch not only iron-workers (*charistooni*: a term analogous to the Huron's "men of iron"), but also cloth makers (*assirioni*) (ibid. 178). All of this suggests a dependence on European goods that much exceeded that of the Huron. The archaeological evidence indicates that by the 1630s even the Seneca had access to a considerable volume of European goods. Allowing for the difficulties of dating archaeological sites to within a few decades, glass beads, brass kettles, and iron goods appear to have been at least as abundant among the Seneca as they were among the Huron by this period (Wray and Schoff 1953:56–58). In the epidemics of the 1630s and 1640s the Iroquois must have lost many skilled craftsmen and like the Huron become more dependent on European goods.

The Dutch records indicate that prior to 1640 the number of beaver skins that were traded by the Iroquois was considerably less than the number traded by the Huron. In 1624 a total of 4700 beaver and otter skins reached the Netherlands, although this number rose to 7685 by 1628 and to 16,304 by 1635 (Trelease 1960:43). Only a portion of these skins came, however, from the upper part of the Hudson Valley and not all of the latter came from the Iroquois. Kiliaen van Rensselaer estimated that between 1625 and 1640, 5000 to 6000 skins were traded each year at Fort Orange (Van Laer 1908:483–84), and even in 1635 only 8000 furs came through that trading post.[6] These figures compare unfavourably with the 12,000 to 15,000 skins that the Huron appear to have supplied to the French each year. If, however, most of their furs were trapped by the Iroquois themselves rather than obtained from other tribes as the Huron's were, the profits that accrued to the Iroquois for each fur would have been considerably greater than those realized by the Huron. As long as the Iroquois were able to trap about 8000 beaver and otter per year, it is likely they could supply their wants at the level to which these had developed by the 1630s.

THE BEAVER SUPPLY

It is clear that beaver were still prevalent in the Iroquois country as late as 1635. Bogaert saw 120 beaver skins in a single Mohawk house and was shown streams where many beaver and otter were being trapped (Jameson 1909:142–47). Yet he found the Oneida anxious for peace with the Algonkin so they could hunt in safety in the Adirondacks and in the north generally (ibid. 150). This desire to expand hunting into the northern no man's land suggests either that the beaver supply in the Iroquois heartland was proving inadequate to meet the Iroquois's growing demand for trade goods or that it was diminishing as a result of beavers being over-hunted. The depletion of beaver was not an unusual phenomenon in eastern North America at this time. In the early 1640s, fear of their extinction in the St. Lawrence Valley led Le Jeune to advocate assigning specific hunting territories to each Montagnais family in order to encourage conservation (Thwaites 1896–1901, 8:57–59).

Unlike the Huron, the Iroquois were surrounded on all sides except the extreme northeast by peoples who, like themselves, were horticulturalists. For the most part, these groups traded with the French, the Dutch, or the Swedes. They were, therefore, competitors in the fur trade rather than potential suppliers of furs. The Seneca could trade European goods for furs with the landlocked Neutral, but even in this trade they had to compete with the Huron. It may be hypothesized that the increasing aggressiveness of the Iroquois was a response to a growing demand for furs that could not be satisfied either within their own heartland or by exploiting the no man's land that lay between them and their northern neighbours.

A proper evaluation of this proposal requires answers to two more specific questions: why did the Iroquois need to secure more furs? How was their warfare intended to achieve this end? In *The Wars of the Iroquois*, Hunt (1940:33–35) has offered what he believes are definitive answers to both of these questions. In his opinion, the Iroquois were driven to seek supplies of furs outside their tribal territories because by 1640 their local supply of beaver had been exhausted. He agreed with McIlwain (1915:xlii–xlv) that the aim of the Iroquois was to force the northern and western tribes, including the Huron, to trade with them rather than the French, thus establishing themselves as middlemen in a vast network of trade between the northern tribes and the Dutch.

Unfortunately, the evidence concerning the depletion of furs within traditional Iroquois hunting territories is highly unsatisfactory. There is no doubt that the Iroquois placed a high value on furs throughout the 1640s, as the Huron and Algonkin recognized when they exchanged furs for wampum at peace conferences (Thwaites 1896–1901, 27:295);[7] however, this does not prove that beavers were extinct in upper New York State. That the Mohawk were anxious to prevent the Dutch from developing trading relations with the northern Algonkians could be interpreted as evidence that they sought for themselves a middleman position in such trade. Alternatively, and in my opinion more probably, such behaviour can be interpreted as evidence that the Mohawk were still determined that their enemies, who had access to more and better furs than they did, should not have an opportunity to conclude treaties with the Dutch which in turn might be used to undermine the Mohawk's own security. The best evidence that Hunt could raise in support of his argument that beaver were exhausted by 1640 is a statement contained in a narrative of Governor de Courcelle's voyage to Lake Ontario (for 1671) that the Iroquois, and especially the four western tribes, had long ago exhausted the beaver on the south side of Lake Ontario and could now find scarcely a single one there (O'Callaghan 1856–87, 9:80). Hunt (1940:34–35) also construed a comment by Kiliaen van Rensselaer to the effect that the falling off in trade at Fort Orange in 1640 did not occur because the independent traders at Rensselaerswyck had siphoned off the available furs to mean that the Iroquois no longer had access even to the limited supplies of beaver skins that had been available to them in former years.

Hunt omitted, however, to consider a section of Van Rensselaer's letter which stated explicitly that the Mohawk did not lack furs. Van Rensselaer went on to suggest that the failure of the Dutch to obtain these furs resulted from a lack of trade goods, from the high prices they charged, and, most importantly, because the English in the Connecticut Valley were contacting the Mohawk and offering them more trade goods for each pelt in order to draw off their furs. Van Rensselaer suggests that the Mahican, who were now allies of the Mohawk, had played an important role in bringing the English and the Mohawk together (Van Laer 1908:483–84). This totally vitiates the arguments that Hunt based on this passage. Arent van Curler was to note a similar dearth of skins at the Fort Orange trading post in 1643, although "so great a trade was never driven" as that year. In 1643, however, the culprits were not the English, but the Dutch settlers, to whom freedom of trade had been granted in 1639 (Trelease 1960:118 n. 12).

Francis Jennings (1968:24) has attempted to demonstrate that beaver were not extinct in the Iroquois country using Adriaen van der Donck's (1841:209–10) statement that about 80,000 beaver a year had been killed in New Netherland and adjacent territories in the nine years since 1642. The figure he cites seems, however, to be the total number of skins traded in the French, English, Dutch, and Swedish colonies and cannot be cited as necessarily having a bearing on the condition of the fauna of upper New York State at this time.

There are strong reasons for believing that prior to 1640 the Iroquois were hunting beaver more intensively in their own territories in an effort to satisfy their growing demand for European goods. It is quite possible that this might have led to the exhaustion of beaver in that area, although there is no proof that this happened as early as 1640.[8] What is clear is that the Iroquois's demand for trade goods was increasing rapidly and that eventually, to satisfy these demands, it was necessary to obtain furs from beyond their tribal territories. A depletion of beaver may have intensified this trend, but in the long run it can account for only a small part of it. By the late 1630s a growing desire for trade goods seems to have pressed the annual fur budget of the Iroquois to the point where not only the Mohawk, but all of the Iroquois tribes, were looking for new sources of furs beyond their tribal territories.

STRATEGIES FOR OBTAINING FURS

In the late 1630s, three methods of obtaining furs were feasible for the Iroquois: they could attempt to bring about a realignment of trading patterns by persuading or compelling fur-rich peoples like the Huron to trade with them; they could expand their hunting territories by expelling or asserting their authority over adjacent peoples; or they could steal furs or trade goods from their neighbours. The first of these solutions, which is the one that McIlwain and Hunt suggest they attempted to put into practice, was probably the most effective long-term solution for their problems. Moreover, so long as the Mohawk were able to prevent the Dutch from concluding separate alliances with the Huron and the northern Algonkians (and now that the defeated Mahican were the Mohawk's allies, the chances of the Dutch doing this seemed more remote than ever), this solution must have seemed an attractive one to the Dutch traders since it would permanently have diverted the northern fur trade away from the St. Lawrence and destroyed the economic basis of New France. It is probable that the Dutch were urging their Mohawk partners to establish trading links with the north both in the hope of getting furs and that the Dutch might later establish direct trading links with these tribes in spite of Mohawk objections. Van Rensselaer may have had such plans in mind when he wrote in 1641 that he hoped within a few years to be able to divert much of the French trade to the Hudson Valley (Van Laer 1908:553).

It is certain, however, that formidable difficulties lay in the way of such an arrangement. Under normal circumstances the Huron would have been unwilling to abandon their alliance with the French or to become dependent for trade goods upon traditional enemies, with whom no peace treaty had ever proved to be more than a short-lived truce. Only if trade between the

Huron and the French had been made impossible, might the Huron have been bullied into accepting such an arrangement. If the Huron would not make peace, an alternative strategy was for the Iroquois to destroy them and to attempt to trade directly with the Huron's northern trading partners. Evidence of an attempt to coerce the Huron into a trading alliance has been read into the diplomatic activities of the Mohawk prior to 1646; however, the Mohawk's refusal to consider an offer to trade that the Huron made to the Iroquois the following year can hardly be attributed solely to their jealousy of the Onondaga or to pique over the failure of earlier efforts. Furthermore, the Iroquois's failure even to try to establish any kind of peaceful trading relations with the northern hunting peoples for several decades after the dispersal of the Huron suggests that they lacked either the skill or inclination to engage in such activities.

It is at this juncture that the major cultural difference between the Huron and the Iroquois noted in chapter 3 becomes important. The Iroquois traded with neighbouring tribes for flint, wampum, and other luxury goods, but had not acquired the subtlety and expertise that characterized the far more vital and extensive trade that the Huron had long been carrying on with the northern Algonkians. Even in their dealings with the Dutch, the Mohawk revealed a quarrelsomeness that was only offset by the willingness of the Dutch to tolerate robbery, personal abuse, and the destruction of their property in the interests of trade. To the Dutch, the Iroquois were a source of prosperity; therefore their other characteristics had to be endured (Trelease 1960:115). As late as 1664, Pierre Boucher (1664:101) observed that the Iroquois had shown no skill as traders. According to him, they did not trade with other Indians because they were hated by them; while, by contrast, the Huron traded everywhere. This difference was noted by Parkman and other nineteenth-century writers, although it was explained by them in terms of ethnic stereotypes and was forgotten when explanations of this genre became discredited.

I have already suggested that historical and geographical reasons explain this difference. The Huron lived in an area where a symbiotic trade in vital goods had grown up with hunting peoples long prior to European contact. The Iroquois, on the other hand, were surrounded by peoples who had economies similar to their own and who were competing for the same resources. Because of this, waging war and building political alliances were the main skills that the Iroquois had acquired for dealing with their neighbours, while trade was of relatively little importance. Given this background, the Iroquois were unpromising candidates to replace the Huron as large-scale middlemen.

TERRITORIAL EXPANSION

There is, however, ample evidence that the Mohawk were anxious, and able, to exploit more hunting territory. After the peace of 1645 they hunted throughout the no man's land between themselves and the Algonkin, exploiting areas that both sides had avoided for many years for fear of each other (Thwaites 1896–1901, 28:279). They are reported to have killed many animals in this area, although the Jesuits do not refer specifically to beaver, but to some 2000 deer that the Mohawk slaughtered during a single winter (28:287). It also appears that the Iroquois who invaded Algonkin and Montagnais territory each winter were active as hunters as well as warriors. Nevertheless, these examples do not provide evidence of the permanent annexation of such hunting territories, in a manner comparable to what had been going on for some time among the Indians of the Maritime provinces.

There is, however, some evidence that has been interpreted as an indirect indication that such annexation was going on. Marian White (1971a:32–36) has suggested that the Wenrononon were expelled from their tribal territories in western New York State by the Seneca, who were in need of more furs and hence anxious to expand their hunting territories at the expense of their neighbours. Other factors that may have contributed to the Wenrononon's inability to defend themselves were epidemics (which may have been critical for a small population) and the severing by their former allies, the Neutral, of an alliance that had existed between them (Thwaites 1896–1901, 17:25–27). Under these circumstances, the Wenrononon decided in 1638 to abandon their tribal territory, some seeking refuge among the Huron and others among the Neutral (21:231–33).

White's explanation of the dispersal of the Wenrononon makes sense in terms of the strategy of the fur trade. It is possible that in order to preserve their neutrality between their Huron and Seneca trading partners, the Neutral were willing to sacrifice an ally in the face of Seneca determination to expand their hunting territories. If the Wenrononon had closer trading connections with the Susquehannock than with the Iroquois (39:141), the Seneca would have had good reason to decimate them, rather than attempt to secure their furs through trade.

Unfortunately, the evidence in support of this interpretation is far from satisfactory. Only once is it definitely stated that the Wenroronon decided to disperse because of Iroquois attacks (15:159) while references to a disagreement between the Wenroronon and the Neutral might be construed as evidence that the latter were the cause of their dispersal (17:27). Although the Jesuits stated that the Wenroronon who were living in the Neutral village of Khioetoa were refugees (21:231–33), it is not impossible that they came there as captives. The Wenroronon may also have been attracted to Khioetoa by the hope of being reunited with relatives who had been captured by the Neutral. A final possibility that cannot be dismissed out-of-hand is that the Wenroronon were forced to disperse by the same enigmatic enemies "from the west" who compelled the Erie to move inland about the same time (33:63).[9]

Another possible example of the Seneca's efforts to expand their hunting territories is their destruction in 1647 of the principal town of the Aondironnon, who are described as the Neutral living nearest to the Huron.[10] The reason given for this attack was that a Seneca warrior, who had been raiding in the north the previous winter, had been pursued and slain by the Huron at the gates of this village. To punish the Neutral for their failure to provide this man with sanctuary, Seneca warriors visited the village under the guise of friendship and fell upon their hosts while they were being feasted (33:81–83). Hunt (1940:90–91) has interpreted this attack as part of an attempt to disrupt contact between the Huron and their Susquehannock allies. It is possible, however, that its real aim was to gain access to Neutral beaver grounds.

The Neutral provide the clearest example of a people who were waging expansive wars at this time. Early in the 1640s, the Neutral won a series of spectacular victories over the Assistaronon, which again was probably a generic term for all the Algonkian-speaking tribes living in southeastern Michigan.[11] In 1640 the Neutral are reported to have captured over 100 Assistaronon prisoners and an army of 2000 took 170 more the following year (Thwaites 1896–1901, 21:195). In 1643 an army of equal size laid siege to an Assistaronon village for ten days and brought back some 800 prisoners. They also tortured seventy of the best Assistaronon warriors to death before their return, and blinded and girdled the mouths of all the old men before abandoning them to die in the forest (27:25–27). Even allowing for gross exaggeration, these accounts suggest that the Neutral were taking advantage of easier access to iron weapons to inflict serious injuries on their traditional enemies. Their aim may have been to secure undisputed possession of the rich beaver hunting grounds around Lake

St. Clair. It is even possible that the Neutral sought to extend their hunting territories into southeastern Michigan and that by so doing it was they, rather than the Iroquois, who were responsible for the retreat to the north and west of some of the tribes who lived in this area. The central Algonkians probably did not distinguish between the Neutral and the Iroquois, but called them both Naudoway, meaning snakes or enemies; hence their later assertions that they had been driven from their original homeland by the Iroquois (55:183) may be interpreted as a memory of the wars that the Neutral had waged against them at this time (Hunt 1940:116 n. 28).

By 1642 some of the Potawatomi had abandoned their territory and sought refuge among the Ojibwa at Sault Sainte Marie (Thwaites 1896– 1901, 23:225). The same wars may account for the retreat of the more southerly Michigan tribes, including the Sauk and Fox, into Wisconsin prior to 1650 (H. Wilson 1956). These tribes lived in river valleys in a parkland environment, where they raised corn and hunted deer, while at certain times of the year they moved west into the grasslands to hunt buffalo. This cycle of activities may have rendered them more vulnerable to attack and hastened their decision to retreat west of Lake Michigan, where the power of the Winnebago had already been broken by a series of wars and epidemics. Eventually the Wisconsin area was to become the overcrowded refuge not only for these people but for other tribes from Ontario and Michigan who were fleeing the Iroquois. The major dispersals of tribes in the lower Great Lakes area do not seem to have begun with the militancy of the Iroquois, but as a result of the Neutral exploiting the advantages that accrued to them from their geographical position in relationship to contemporary trading networks.

It is clear that the Mohawk combined hunting with raiding in their excursions against the Algonkians. What is uncertain is whether any of the Iroquois tribes consciously pursued a policy of seizing the hunting territories of other tribes as a means of obtaining more furs prior to the 1650s. The evidence that they did is, at best, equivocal. Moreover, as an explanation of the eventual expulsion of the Huron from southwestern Ontario (Trelease 1960:120), this proposition has serious shortcomings. If the Huron had exhausted the beaver in their own hunting grounds by 1630, the Iroquois would have been unable to obtain any extra furs by annexing this territory. They may have known that if an area is not hunted for a decade or more, its beaver population will revive, but to suggest that they sought to annex this area in the hope that it would eventually regenerate is to attribute to the Iroquois long-range objectives that bore no relationship to their immediate requirements for furs. In 1701, when the Iroquois placed their beaver grounds in southern Ontario under the protection of the King of England they stated explicitly that they had conquered the region in order to hunt there (O'Callaghan 1857–87, 4:908). There is no doubt that as early as the 1670s the Iroquois and their allies were trapping large numbers of beaver in that region.[12] It is therefore understandable that by 1701 they had come to believe that the use they were then making of southern Ontario was their reason for attacking its original inhabitants half a century before. This was, however, an anachronism and there is no sound reason to believe that the Iroquois regarded the Huron hunting grounds as worth fighting for in the 1640s.

FUR PIRATES

The third way of obtaining European goods was by piracy. At least among the Mohawk, the robbing of such goods from other tribes dates as early as the latter half of the sixteenth century. The amount of goods that could be acquired in this way must not be underrated and the continuation into the 1640s of attacks upon Huron and Algonkin leaving Three Rivers with European goods indicates that the Iroquois still had not abandoned this technique. Gradually, however, stealing European goods appears to have declined in favour of stealing furs, which were more portable and allowed the Iroquois to purchase what they wanted from the Dutch. Piracy seems to have been an important aspect of Iroquois warfare from the late 1630s at least through the 1650s. Winter as well as summer raids into Algonkin territory, summertime attacks on Huron and Algonkin traders on their way to and from French settlements, and increasingly violent attacks on the Huron and their neighbours all seem to reflect the efforts of the Mohawk, and later of the western tribes of the Iroquois confederacy, to satisfy a growing demand for European goods and for the furs needed to barter for such goods. These attacks became so violent that in some areas they resulted in the destruction or dispersal of the very people whom the Iroquois were robbing and thus reduced the base on which the Iroquois were able to prey in later years. Such behaviour is no evidence of irrational behaviour on the part of the Iroquois, but indicates how hard pressed they were to obtain furs. Hunt erred in assuming that the Iroquois necessarily followed the course of action that represented their best long-term interests; on the contrary, confronted by a pressing need for European goods, their behaviour became geared to very short-term objectives. Like most European traders, they were interested in doing what on an annual basis would bring in the most satisfactory returns with the least losses and trouble.

The Iroquois were clearly capable of profiting from alternative strategies, such as establishing trading relations with the French or the Algonkin when the opportunity for such relationships arose. Yet, not only was robbery the Iroquois's established means of acquiring furs and trade goods, but also, because of their geographical location and historical background, it required less reorienting of their lives than an effort to emulate the Huron as traders would have done. Finally, the number of economic stratagems that were open to the Iroquois was limited by political considerations. The Mohawk had learned from bitter experience that it was necessary, at all cost, to avoid situations in which their European trading partners were tempted to sacrifice the interests of the Iroquois in order to establish trading links with the Indians who lived in the rich fur-bearing regions to the north. So long as robbery satisfied their needs on a yearly basis and not too many Iroquois warriors were being killed, the majority of Iroquois probably paid little heed to the long-term negative features of such a policy.

The Iroquois had a further motive for waging war on their neighbours that was not primarily economic. Unlike the Huron, they were surrounded by potential enemies and on this account must have been particularly distressed by loss of population in the epidemics of the 1630s and 1640s. This led them to try to recoup their numbers by incorporating prisoners and conquered peoples into their society. The Iroquois had faith in their ability to use a combination of rewards and punishments to integrate large numbers of former enemies and were anxious to capture as many enemies as possible. As warfare escalated, the mortality rate increased and warfare became a means of trying to compensate for its own losses. Yet, in spite of the large numbers of prisoners and refugees that the Iroquois managed to incorporate into their tribal structures, they succeeded only in maintaining their population at about half of its aboriginal level in the face of continuing attrition resulting from disease and warfare.

GUN POWER

The Iroquois's motivation to acquire the furs they needed by violence does not explain their marked success in achieving this goal, especially after 1640. Before that time the Huron and Iroquois appear to have been about equally powerful and, with the help of the French, the Huron and the northern Algonkians could control the St. Lawrence River. In 1633 and again in 1637 the French had been able to stop Iroquois raids there by merely showing the flag. The Mohawk's success after 1640 did not result from any deterioration of French power along the St. Lawrence, which was considerably strengthened during the following decade, though not fast enough to match the growing power of the Iroquois.

The French realized that as long as the Mohawk were powerful enough to prevent the Dutch from concluding trading alliances with the northern tribes, it was in the interest of the Dutch traders to encourage the Mohawk to pirate furs from among these tribes. As early as 1633 Champlain had proposed to terminate this threat by conquering the Iroquois and then driving the Dutch and English settlers out of the territories adjacent to New France (Bishop 1948:331). Hating the Dutch came easily to the Jesuits, whose order had suffered serious setbacks from Calvinist opposition in India, Japan, and the East Indies (Robinson in Du Creux 1951–52:xviii). It was therefore not difficult for the Jesuits to believe that the Dutch were seeking to injure them in Canada as well. In a letter to Cardinal Richelieu in March 1640, Jérôme Lalemant accused the English and Dutch of inciting the Iroquois to attack the tribes allied to the French. Lalemant worded his letter to imply that the drop in Huron population, which he said was from 30,000 to 10,000 people in less than ten years, was entirely to be blamed on Iroquois raids (Thwaites 1896–1901, 17:223).

Lalemant's fear that Iroquois attacks might ultimately sever the commercial link between the Huron and the French was well founded, but his flagrant misrepresentation was obviously designed to make credible his request that action be taken to stop this trouble at its source by driving the Dutch out of North America. All of the Jesuits in Canada agreed that the Dutch should be expelled from the Hudson Valley and this was the plan that Father Le Jeune presented to Cardinal Richelieu in 1641 when he visited France to plead for help against the Iroquois (21:269–73). While his proposal was given some consideration, the French government was embroiled in the Thirty Years War and unwilling to risk a conflict with the Dutch by attempting to seize one of their colonies. Charles Lalemant, who was now the procurator of the Canadian Jesuits in France, understood the diplomatic subtleties that stood in the way of realizing Le Jeune's scheme. He recorded with apparent agreement the technical reasons which rendered it impractical as state policy (21:269–71).

Richelieu's niece, Marie de Vignerot, Duchesse d'Aiguillon nevertheless succeeded in obtaining the cardinal's promise to help defend New France

(21:269). Ten thousand écus were provided to send soldiers to the colony and to establish Fort Richelieu at the mouth of the Richelieu River. The purpose of this fort was to hinder the incursions of the Iroquois into the St. Lawrence Valley. The same year the colony of Ville Marie was founded at Montreal, thus providing the French with a post farther up-river. If strong enough, this colony could guard the entrance to the Ottawa River.

Charles Lalemant, who espoused the possible rather than the impossible, played a leading role in the planning of the colony. It was through his personal intervention that Montreal Island was ceded to the Société de Montréal and it was he who introduced Paul de Chomedey de Maisonneuve, the future governor of the colony, to Jérôme Le Royer de La Dauversière, the moving spirit in the founding of Ville Marie. He also did much to persuade Jeanne Mance and Louis d'Ailleboust de Coulonge and his wife to join the colony (Adair 1944). In spite of its contributions to the defence of the St. Lawrence Valley, this small settlement with its semi-autonomous status was to play a major role in undermining the control that the Jesuits had acquired over New France and which allowed them to treat the French settlements along the St. Lawrence almost exclusively as a base for their missionary work.

How then did the Mohawk overcome these efforts by the French to strengthen their control of the St. Lawrence Valley? The answer seems to be that they were able to obtain guns in greater numbers than were the Indians who were allied to the French. That the possession and use of guns conferred a military advantage on tribes has never been doubted. Yet the practical advantage of a cumbersome musket over a metal-tipped arrow is doubtful. The real power of the gun in Indian warfare appears to have been psychological; its noise and mysterious operation added to the terrors of foes and to the confidence of those who used them. For this reason, if no other, guns were a source of strength to the Indians, apparently largely in proportion to the numbers that any group possessed. The Mohawk soon learned to use their guns to intimidate other Indians and to meet the French on equal terms. Hunt (1940:9–10; 165–75) did a great disservice to the understanding of this period of Canadian history by denying that the Iroquois enjoyed superiority in the number of guns they possessed after 1640. The major errors in his argument have been exposed only recently (Tooker 1963:117–18).

The sequence by which the Indians of the St. Lawrence Valley and the lower Great Lakes area acquired firearms now seems reasonably clear. Both the French and Dutch trading companies opposed the sale of guns to the Indians, lest this would endanger the security of their ill-defended trading posts. As early as 1620, however, Champlain records that two illegal vessels from La Rochelle had traded a large supply of firearms, gunpowder, and shot to the Montagnais (Biggar 1922–36, 5:3). Fears were expressed that once the Montagnais were armed, their resentment of the trading monopoly might encourage them to attack Quebec. Throughout this period no guns were traded to the Huron or Algonkin, who both depended solely on the official trade that was carried on from Quebec. During the English occupation more firearms were sold to the Montagnais (Thwaites 1896–1901, 6:309), possibly after the English realized that they had no hope of retaining Quebec and hence had no interest in guarding the security of the colony. Le Jeune, writing in 1634, describes some of these Montagnais as good marksmen. Once the French returned to Quebec, the sale of guns appears to have been halted and only small quantities of powder and shot were bartered to Indians who already had them (6:309). There is no evidence that these guns gave the Montagnais any significant military advantage. We must therefore conclude that they had bought only a small number of guns and that since the Indians had no knowledge of how to repair them, most were soon out of commission.

It is clear that the Iroquois did not get guns as early as the Montagnais. None were in evidence when Van Krieckenbeeck and his men were killed in 1626, nor was anything but curiosity shown about them when Bogaert visited the Mohawk in 1634–35 (Trelease 1960:95). By 1639, however, the fur trade in New Netherland was no longer a company monopoly. Henceforth, settlers were free to import trade goods, to barter with the Indians for any number of furs, and to export these furs to Europe on their own account (ibid. 61, 112–13). The same year it was noted that individual traders were disobeying the standing orders of the West India Company by selling guns and ammunition to the Indians, and the death penalty was prescribed for those found guilty of this offence (Van Laer 1908:426). It is uncertain whether this particular ordinance was directed against the Dutch living around New Amsterdam or in the upper part of the Hudson Valley; but by 1641 such trade was specifically forbidden in Rensselaerswyck, under pain of a 100 guilder fine and deportation (ibid. 565).

The Rensselaerswyck ordinance was framed to curb a burgeoning trade in arms between the Dutch settlers and the Mohawk. So long as the fur trade had remained a company monopoly, considerations of security and the necessity of obeying orders seem to have kept guns out of the hands of the Iroquois. Once trade was made free, thoughts of security were thrown to the winds by traders who were anxious both to profit from selling guns and to arm the Mohawk, so that they could more easily pirate furs from the Indians who were allied to the French. The Mohawk must have found it necessary to obtain more furs to pay the high prices that were being demanded for weapons and ammunition.

Another factor also accounts for Dutch willingness to sell guns to the Mohawk at this time. The Mohawk are said to have got their first guns from the English (Jameson 1909:274); indeed, this seems to have been what was making them ignore the Dutch and carry their furs to the English traders from Windsor and Hartford who were operating along the Connecticut River in 1640 (Van Laer 1908:483–84). Thus commercial rivalry with the English as well as with the French convinced the traders at Rensselaerswyck of the soundness of their illegal enterprise. French figures provide some measure of the extensive trade in guns that went on between 1641 and 1643 and explain why the private traders at Rensselaerswyck were so prosperous by the latter date (Trelease 1960:118 n. 12). In 1641 a war party of 350 Mohawk had only thirty-six guns (Thwaites 1896–1901, 21:35–37), but by June 1643 the Mohawk had nearly 300 guns (24:271, 295). The passing of so many arms into the hands of the Iroquois must have had much to do with the first informal treaty that Arent van Curler negotiated between the Dutch and the Mohawk in 1643, and which was followed by another agreement in 1645 (O'Callaghan 1856–87, 14:15). These treaties appear to have legitimized the sale of arms to the Mohawk, thus fulfilling promises that the Dutch had first made in 1641 to assist the Mohawk against their enemies (Thwaites 1896–1901, 22:251). In 1644 a board of accounts in Holland reported that the Mohawk had enough guns and ammunition to supply 400 men, although trafficking arms with other Indians was still forbidden (F. Jennings 1968:24 n. 29). Thus, an illicit trade, carried on first by the English and then by the Dutch settlers, gradually persuaded Dutch officials to abandon their policy of caution in trading arms to the Mohawk. This policy was replaced by a new one that was designed to give the Mohawk the power to seize the furs that the Mohawk would not let the Dutch obtain from other Indians by means of trade.

The Dutch gun trade expanded through the 1640s, although French protests resulted in the re-enactment of the earlier ban against it in 1645 and Governor Peter Stuyvesant actually brought charges against two traders at Fort Orange in 1648. Fears that the Indians might become dangerous if they were officially denied arms led the Amsterdam directors to advise company officials to sell moderate quantities of arms to all the Indians, rather than having these supplied by private traders (O'Callaghan 1856–87, 14:83). In spite of official misgivings both in Holland and in

New Amsterdam, throughout the 1640s guns and ammunition became available not only to the Mohawk but also in smaller numbers to the other tribes of the Iroquois confederacy.

The arming of the Mohawk soon resulted in the French supplying guns to their allies as well. Yet, it was decided, no doubt under Jesuit influence, that guns should be made available only to Indians who had become Christians. It was hoped that this would provide a strong inducement for young men to become Christians and, when combined with the rigorous standards of conduct that the Jesuits required before they would baptize anyone, would serve as an anvil on which the Jesuits could remould the character of these men.

Guns appear to have been made available to the Montagnais and Algonkin in moderate numbers. In 1643 the Sieur de Maisonneuve gave Tessouat a high-quality musket and accessories as a baptismal present (Thwaites 1896–1901, 24:235–37), while Madame de La Peltrie gave a similar present to Oumasasikweie (24:233). By 1642 bands of Algonkin invariably had a few members who were armed with muskets (24:289–91), and by the middle of the decade the Algonkin living on Montreal Island had enough guns that they were able to fire a neat salute on festive occasions (29:181). In spite of this, it is generally agreed that fewer of the Algonkian-speaking allies of the French were able to obtain guns than was the case for the Mohawk. These guns were also of inferior quality, being shorter and lighter than those supplied by the Dutch (32:21).

Most authorities attribute the relatively small number of guns reaching the Algonkin to the tighter controls exercised by French officials and to their vigilance in denying guns to non-Christians. Hunt (1940:174) has concluded, however, that high French prices, held up by a monopoly and by an excessive desire for profits, were responsible for this situation, rather than political or religious considerations. This conclusion is feebly supported and ignores a fundamental difference between the French and Dutch colonists. The Dutch were prepared to take risks with their Indian trading partners and to arm them in the hope of greater commercial gain, even though this might later mean having to suffer from their insults and intimidations. Naroll (1969) has reminded us that the officials and priests who governed New France at this period did not share this bourgeois attitude. Accustomed to an older European tradition, they were sensitive of their honour and anxious, whenever possible, to have their Indian allies under control. While the French were willing to protect these allies if it were in their own interests to do so, they were unwilling to augment their fighting capacity without good reason since they feared that on some occasion the Indians might use this power against them. These attitudes, more than commercial reasons, seem to account for the smaller number of guns that the French were willing to make available to their Indian allies.

The French were even more reluctant to arm the Huron than to arm the Algonkin. They were afraid that guns might fall into the hands of non-Christians or apostates and be used against the Jesuits and their assistants. Moreover, it was recognized that by providing reliable converts with guns, the desire of the Huron men to become Christians would be strengthened and the power of these converts amongst their own people would be enhanced. The first Huron to possess a gun was Anenkhiondic's son, Charles Tsondatsaa (Thwaites 1896–1901, 20:215). It was given to him by Governor Montmagny, following his baptism at Quebec in June 1641. Montmagny said that he gave this gun so that Tsondatsaa could use it to protect himself against the Iroquois. Montmagny also promised that henceforth he would protect all Huron who were willing to declare themselves Christians, thereby implying that a similar protection was no longer being extended to non-Christians (20:219–21). At the same ceremony the Montagnais from Sillery presented Tsondatsaa with powder for his gun. Tsondatsaa replied that his having a gun would be a wonder to his countrymen and would demonstrate the goodwill that the French showed towards those who embraced their religion.

This policy allowed only a few guns to reach the Huron. Until the last three chaotic years of the Huron mission, relatively few Huron were accepted for baptism. Moreover, for a Christian to obtain a gun it was necessary for him to travel to Quebec or Three Rivers as a fur trader. Yet, as late as 1648 the number of Christian traders did not exceed 120 (32:179). Since only one gun was given or sold to each convert and care was taken that they were not passed from hand to hand, this figure may represent the maximum number of Huron who were eligible to obtain guns. The only statement that is contrary to this interpretation occurs in a letter said to have been written by François Gendron in 1644 or 1645. He expressed the opinion there that the military strength of the Huron had declined because they were trusting too much in the arms that the French sold to them at Quebec (Gendron 1868:17). This could be a reference either to the gun trade or to the older trade in iron axes and metal arrowheads. Gendron is a difficult source to use because of problems concerning the origin of part of his text and because other statements he makes contradict reliable contemporary sources.[13]

War on the St. Lawrence

NEW STRATEGIES

The acquisition of guns by the Iroquois altered their military tactics. Nevertheless, until the late 1640s the overall strategy was maintained of the Mohawk and Oneida directing their attacks against the Ottawa and St. Lawrence valleys, while the western tribes attacked the Huron in their own country. While there were changes in the nature and intensity of warfare in both theatres, the Mohawk's rapid acquisition of firearms and their close relationship with the Dutch initially produced far more dramatic changes in the east than in the west.

Prior to 1640 the Mohawk had slain a small number of Huron and Algonkin traders in their efforts to rob them of furs or European goods (Thwaites 1896–1901, 21:21). After their incursions along the St. Lawrence were checked by the French, they continued to raid the Ottawa Valley. By the late 1630s, however, these attacks were not securing enough furs and the Mohawk began to formulate a new policy. They sought to penetrate Algonkin and Montagnais territory in order to plunder furs and hunt there. Their first objective was probably the Rideau Lakes area, lying between the Ottawa and the St. Lawrence valleys. It was an especially productive hunting ground adjacent to Iroquois tribal territory (Heidenreich 1971:208). Prior to acquiring guns, the Mohawk had found it dangerous to penetrate Algonkin territory, particularly when the latter were on good terms with the Huron and the French. To overcome this opposition, the Mohawk resorted to their traditional strategy of trying to make peace with most of their enemies so they might wage war more effectively against one of them at a time. To secure their eastern frontier the Mohawk made peace with their former enemies, the Mahican, and with the Sokoki of the Connecticut Valley. Both tribes had formerly maintained alliances with the Algonkin, but were now willing to fight with the Mohawk against their former allies (Thwaites 1896–1901, 28:275). Prior to 1628 the Montagnais and Algonkin had regularly come south to trade for wampum with the Mahican and the Dutch; we must therefore assume that these good relations had come to an end after the Mohawk had disrupted this trade.

In 1645 the Mohawk reminded the Huron of peace talks that had taken place between them five years earlier (27:263). While nothing more is known about these talks, the Mohawk may have tried to persuade the Huron not to aid the Algonkin when the latter came under attack. What the Mohawk could have promised in return was to let Huron traders use the Ottawa and St. Lawrence rivers in safety. The Huron had probably been unwilling to abandon their renewed alliance with the Algonkin because they were convinced that the Mohawk could not resist the temptation to rob the rich Huron convoys. They therefore rejected the negotiations.

The Mohawk next sought to make peace with the French. In the autumn of 1640 ninety Iroquois made their way north of the St. Lawrence River to rob the Algonkin who they knew would be hunting between Montreal Island and Three Rivers (21:23). In February these warriors captured two Frenchmen, Thomas Godefroy and François Marguerie, who were hunting near Three Rivers, and carried them off to their villages. They were not tortured and, after some discussion, the Mohawk decided to return them to Three Rivers the following spring and to offer to make peace with the French, apparently on behalf of all the Iroquois tribes. Some Mohawk who had formerly been held prisoner at Quebec and Three Rivers and who had been well treated by the French had interceded for the lives of these two Frenchmen, as did Iroquois from some of the other tribes (21:23–41).

In April 1641 about 500 Iroquois set out for the St. Lawrence Valley. Some broke off to pillage the Huron and Algonkin, but 350 of them continued on to Three Rivers (map 24). In early June they built two forts, one on the south shore of the St. Lawrence from which they could negotiate with the French, and the other hidden away in the woods to which they could retire if they were attacked (21:63). Then, they released their prisoners and proposed to make peace with the French. As inducements they promised that following such an agreement, all the Iroquois tribes would come to trade at Three Rivers (21:47) and the French would be invited to erect another trading post near their country (21:39). In return, they asked the French to give them thirty muskets to add to the thirty-six that they had already purchased from the English and the Dutch (21:37).

François Marguerie made it clear that the Iroquois were only interested in making peace with the French and that they were determined to continue fighting with the Huron and Algonkin (21:37). Montmagny realized that it was impossible to make peace on these terms, since to do so would endanger the trade of New France even more than did the attacks that the Iroquois were making on the Indian allies of the French. He also feared that if the French concluded a separate peace with the Iroquois, the Algonkin and Montagnais might turn on them and cause them more trouble than did the Iroquois (21:55–57). Montmagny, therefore,

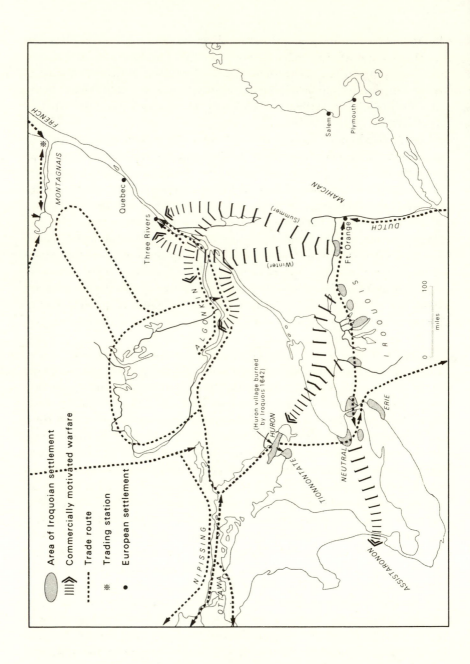

MAP 24. *Intertribal relations, 1641.*

informed the Mohawk that any peace would have to include the Huron and the Algonkians as well as the French. The Iroquois pretended to consider this request, but their attacks on isolated groups of Algonkin travelling to Three Rivers convinced the French that they were only trying to conclude a makeshift peace so they might attack the Huron and Algonkin without fear of immediate French reprisals (21:55). Matters came to a head when during the course of these negotiations, a French pinnace and longboats appeared and prevented the Iroquois from attacking seven Algonkin canoes loaded with beaver skins (21:59). The morning after this incident Montmagny approached the Iroquois fort to propose another meeting. The Iroquois jeered at him for not giving them guns and began shooting arrows and firing their guns at his boats. In retaliation the French opened fire on the Iroquois. Seeing that nothing further was to be gained at Three Rivers, the Iroquois stealthily retreated the next night (21:61–65).

While these events were taking place at Three Rivers, the remaining 150 Iroquois lurked along the banks of the St. Lawrence, hoping to plunder Huron and Algonkin traders on their way to the trading post. Father Brébeuf, who was travelling with four Frenchmen and six Huron, was spotted by the enemy, but reached Three Rivers unopposed on 20 June. A day or two later, five Huron canoes were attacked and plundered by the Iroquois. Some of the Huron escaped, but the rest were either killed or taken prisoner (21:65; 23:35). Some of those who escaped made their way to Three Rivers, while the rest went up the Ottawa River to warn other Huron of the danger. The St. Lawrence remained blockaded for some time, but eventually it was learned that the Iroquois had retired and the Huron traders were able to make their way down-river (21:75). No doubt on the basis of previous experience, the Iroquois were afraid that the French would send their gunboats up-river and had decided to retreat rather than to face them. As in former years, groups of traders were ambushed and robbed at various points along the Ottawa River (22:307).

The Mohawk were disappointed that they had failed to make peace with the French, and increased their attacks against the Algonkin. The following winter 200 Mohawk warriors came north and divided into two bands. One band roamed in the vicinity of Three Rivers hoping to capture some French, but withdrew when the death of one of their leaders was interpreted as a bad omen. Their arrival so terrified the Algonkin living at Three Rivers that most of them fled the area. Some went to Sillery, others joined the Kichesipirini in the upper part of the Ottawa Valley (22:93, 127, 249), a region that had hitherto been beyond the range of Iroquois attacks. Unfortunately, the rest of the Mohawk warriors were heading for precisely this area. They travelled over ice and snow as far as Morrison Island, where they surprised the few people living there (22:249). Following this, they spread out to attack Kichesipirini hunting parties dispersed in the forest and to seize their furs (22:253). Many Kichesipirini were killed and eaten on the spot, while others were carried off to the Mohawk villages. There the Mohawk avenged their failures of the previous year by torturing to death most of the men and older female captives. About thirty younger women were also tortured but their lives were spared so that they might be naturalized into Iroquois families. The following spring these women were used to carry provisions for the war parties that set out for the St. Lawrence (22:265–67).

Although the Mohawk talked of sending 700 men to raid the St. Lawrence Valley in 1642 (22:251), fewer raiders went north at any one time than the 500 who had set out the previous year. In the spring, 300 Mohawk attacked the Onontchataronon, killing some and carrying off a number of families (22:267–69). They next seem to have dispersed along the St. Lawrence to intercept traders on their way to Three Rivers. On 2 August two of these bands attacked twelve Huron canoes above Lake St. Peter. These Huron were returning home and had with them Father Isaac Jogues, Guillaume Couture, and René Goupil, a donné, who were carrying letters and supplies to the Huron mission. The Iroquois who launched this attack were well supplied with guns and the Huron became terrified and attempted to flee into the forest. All of the French and about twenty-five Huron were taken prisoner. The latter included Teondechoren, his brother or cousin Pierre Saoekbata, his niece Oionhaton, and Ahatsistari, a famous warrior from Teanaostaiaé. An old man named Ondouterraon was slain on the spot when he refused to try to keep up with the others (28:121; 39:183), but the rest of the prisoners were taken back to the Mohawk villages (22:269–71; 28:119–35). The French who were captured were not accorded the mild treatment that Godefroy and Marguerie had received. They and the Huron were tortured in the traditional manner immediately after they were captured and more severely in the Iroquois villages. Ahatsistari and his nephew Onnonhoaraton were killed in the villages of Tionontoguen and Ossernenon and a third Huron was slain at Gandagaron (26:195; 39:199; Grassmann 1969:610–37).

Although more Huron canoes were probably lost in this encounter than in any other, this was not the only serious loss that the Huron traders sustained that year. The same day that Jogues and his Huron companions were captured, a Huron trading party was attacked in the lower part of the Ottawa Valley and four Huron were taken prisoner. One of these was later tortured to death by the Mohawk (Thwaites 1896–1901, 26:195). It is unclear whether this was the same attack that the Mohawk made on a party of Huron traders who were hunting on an island in the Ottawa River, probably near the Chaudière Falls (26:35). There were eleven Huron canoes in this group, but the Iroquois only managed to carry off those individuals who had penetrated the island and were driving the game towards the water. Some of the survivors continued on to Three Rivers, while others returned up-river to warn other Huron of the danger (22:273).

In August 1642, 200 to 300 Mohawk set off for the St. Lawrence where they hoped to intercept the main Huron fur convoys going to Three Rivers (28:123). To their surprise, they found Montmagny and a party of workmen at the mouth of the Richelieu River, guarded by three pinnaces and engaged in constructing a fort there. Perceiving this threat to their easiest means of reaching the St. Lawrence Valley, the Mohawk abandoned their usual caution. They approached the fort from three sides and rushed upon the French in an effort to take them by surprise. The Mohawk fought bravely and some were able to fire into the fort through its gun holes. One Frenchman was killed and four wounded. Only after two Mohawk headmen and three ordinary warriors had been killed did the rest withdraw in good order. They first retired to a fort that they had constructed several miles up the Richelieu River and then set off for home. The repulse of this assault on Fort Richelieu prevented the Iroquois from carrying out their plan to harass the Huron and Algonkin who were on their way to Three Rivers (22:275–79).

Thus for two consecutive summers the Mohawk's efforts to lay siege to the St. Lawrence had ended unsatisfactorily for them. They had been able neither to secure the neutrality of the French nor to challenge their military superiority on the St. Lawrence. Moreover, with the building of Fort Richelieu and the new colony at Montreal, the French occupation of the St. Lawrence was more secure then ever before. While the Mohawk were soon to have 300 guns, these were more effective for intimidating the Algonkin and Huron than for winning any decisive victories over the French.

It became clear that the latter could be brought to terms only by depriving them of the furs on which they depended for their prosperity. The Mohawk therefore decided to abandon their large expeditions in favour of a new kind of warfare that would divert more of the furs destined for Three Rivers into their hands. Father Vimont noted that in former times the Iroquois had visited the St. Lawrence in large war parties for short periods in the summer. In 1643 the Iroquois separated into smaller bands that stationed themselves at points along the river and were organized so that when one band was ready to return home, another band replaced it (24:273) (map 25). The deployment of these war parties was probably the same in 1643 as it was the following year when there were said to be ten bands in action at any one time. Two of these were at the Chaudière Falls; one each at the foot of the Long Sault Rapids, above Montreal, on Montreal Island, and along the Rivière des Prairies; and three more between Montreal and Three Rivers. The tenth band went farther up the Ottawa Valley (26:35–37). The deployment of fighting men at so many strategic places from early spring until the following winter made it impossible for Huron or Algonkin traders to use the Ottawa or St. Lawrence rivers without being spotted. This cancelled out customary Huron efforts to avoid the Iroquois by coming to the St. Lawrence in the early spring or late autumn. Finally, the Iroquois avoided Fort Richelieu by blazing a trail across the narrow neck of land between the Richelieu and St. Lawrence rivers, about two leagues south of the fort (24:287–89).

This new strategy was to net a rich harvest of furs for the Mohawk. As early as 9 May Algonkin traders were attacked, and the robbing and killing of Algonkin persisted throughout the summer (24:275, 291). The Mohawk also continued to seek revenge for the five men who had been killed near Three Rivers the year before. Thirty Mohawk went marauding near Montreal; while twenty of them feigned an attack on the fort by firing over 100 gun shots, ten others managed to kill three Frenchmen who were working near the settlement and to carry off two others (24:277).

In August a considerable number of Iroquois were prowling in the vicinity of Fort Richelieu and indicating that they wished to discuss peace. A Huron who had travelled to Quebec in 1640 or 1641 and had been captured by the Iroquois was involved in this affair. This Huron, who had become an "Iroquois by affection," was deputized to carry a letter written by Father Jogues to the French and to discuss peace with them (24:291–93). The French suspected, however, that any talk of peace might be a ruse and believed that the Iroquois wished to ambush the fort.[14] Thus, when the Iroquois advanced towards the fort and refused to stop when ordered to do so, the French fired on them and drove them into the forest. A few days later under a similar pretext of wanting to discuss peace, about 100 Iroquois tried to lure some Onontchataronon into a trap, but although they fired on them, the latter escaped. This band of Mohawk came down to Fort Richelieu, but retreated when they perceived that the French were expecting them (24:293–95).

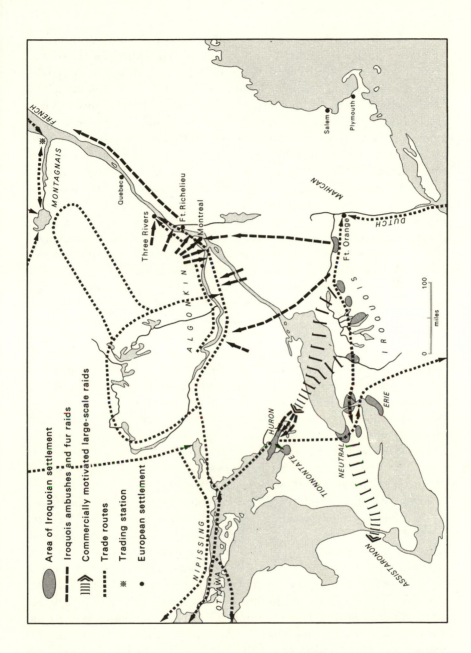

MAP 25. *Intertribal relations, 1643.*

It was the Huron, however, who suffered the most severely from the Mohawk's change in tactics. To avoid Iroquois ambushes the Huron had decided to descend to the St. Lawrence earlier than usual in 1643 with 120 traders travelling together in a single group (24:121). The size of this band seems to have intimidated the Mohawk and the Huron traders reached Three Rivers safely in early June. On 9 June, however, another band of sixty Huron on their way to Three Rivers in thirteen fur-laden canoes were attacked near Montreal by some forty Iroquois. One version states that the Huron were put to flight by gunfire. A variant account claims that they were attacked after the Iroquois had lured them into their fort under some friendly pretext. About twenty-three Huron were taken prisoner, while the rest escaped and made their way towards Montreal. Thirteen prisoners were beaten to death the next day and the rest were led off to the Mohawk country. So many furs were taken in this raid that the Mohawk were unable to carry all of them away with them (24:275–77).

Still greater misfortunes overtook the 120 Huron traders on their way home. They left Three Rivers in mid-June and somewhere near the Chaudière Falls about twenty of them were killed or taken prisoner. After they had passed this point, they continued up the Ottawa River and eventually believed themselves to be out of danger. The Mohawk, who had watched them come down, were unwilling to let them escape and, somewhere in the upper part of the Ottawa Valley, they attacked the Huron while they were making a dangerous portage. The attack was so swift that those who were not killed or captured abandoned most of their trade goods and fled (26:235–37). Lalemant was exaggerating only slightly when he described these traders as returning to the Huron country "naked or pierced with musket balls after having escaped seven or eight times from the hands and cruelties of those barbarians" (27:63).

These two attacks resulted in serious economic loss to the Huron and further depleted their dwindling reserves of manpower (28:45). The latter loss was partially compensated by the escape of a number of Huron who had been taken prisoner by the Mohawk the year before and who were made to accompany the Iroquois on their raids. Three prisoners escaped from a band that was prowling along the north shore of Lake St. Peter; two were Teondechoren and his brother or cousin Saoekbata (24:279–81, 285). Huron who had been captured in former years also escaped from Iroquois bands that visited Lake St. Peter later in the summer (24:287) and another Huron escaped from the Mohawk after he had been captured at Montreal (26:21). Teondechoren wished to return home and to do so he joined the 120 Huron traders who were travelling up-river. On his way the

Iroquois shot him through the shoulder with a musket ball, so that he bled almost to death (26:237). Teondechoren managed to make his way home, filled with enough tales of adventure to satisfy a lifetime (26:233).

A TURNING POINT

During the winter of 1643–44 the Mohawk continued to attack Algonkin and Montagnais hunting parties. They increased their attacks until it was unsafe for these Indians to hunt south of the St. Lawrence even opposite Tadoussac. By depriving the Montagnais of important winter hunting grounds, the Mohawk reduced many of them to the point of starvation and forced them to seek charity from the Jesuits at Sillery (Thwaites 1896–1901, 25:107–9). The Iroquois exploited these hunting territories and greatly increased the number of beaver that they trapped that winter.

Even before spring had come, the Iroquois were laying siege to the St. Lawrence River in the same way that they had done in 1643. Among the first Huron to fall into their hands were the six converts who were taking Father Bressani to the Huron country. They had set out from Three Rivers on 27 April believing that because there was still ice on the river, there was little danger of Iroquois attack (26:29–31). In the course of the summer two other groups of Huron were attacked, one near Montreal, the other 150 miles up the Ottawa River (28:45).

Conversely, a group of sixty young men who came down-river with the intention of fighting any Iroquois they encountered reached Three Rivers without challenge. One of the leaders of this group was Charles Tsondatsaa, whose baptism Montmagny had sponsored in 1641. After they had arrived at Three Rivers, news was received that Iroquois canoes had been sighted on Lake St. Peter and the Huron, accompanied by a number of Algonkin, pursued the enemy as far as Fort Richelieu. During the night, two Huron canoes made their way past some thirty Iroquois who were posted as sentinels along the river, but discovering that the Iroquois force was larger than they were, these Huron beat a hasty retreat. They took with them two Huron who had managed to escape from the Iroquois. During this excursion, the Huron learned that ten Iroquois were hunting for Frenchmen in the vicinity of Fort Richelieu. The Huron and Algonkin surrounded these men and managed to capture three of them. The Huron retained two of the prisoners as their share of the booty and one was claimed by the Algonkin. Then they and the Algonkin returned to Three Rivers to celebrate their victory (26:53–57).

Hearing that three Mohawk had been captured, Montmagny hastened to Three Rivers, hoping to secure these prisoners so that he might use them to negotiate with the Iroquois. The Algonkin were persuaded to stop torturing their prisoner and to hand him over to the French in return for many presents. The Huron warriors refused to give up their prisoners, alleging that this was too important a decision for young men to make. They took their prisoners home with them, but offered to transmit Montmagny's presents to their headmen, which were to attest his desire that the prisoners be used to negotiate peace with the Iroquois. Montmagny agreed to this and the Huron promised him that the prisoners would be brought back to Three Rivers the following year (26:59–71).

As a result of Iroquois attacks, some Huron were saying that the cost of trade with the French was too dear and were suggesting that this trade might be broken off, at least on an annual basis (28:57). To strengthen the alliance with the Huron and to protect and encourage Huron traders, Montmagny decided to send twenty-two French soldiers to winter in the Huron country (26:71). These soldiers travelled up-river with the sixty Huron warriors and were accompanied by Brébeuf and by two other priests, Léonard Garreau and Noël Chabanel, who were on their way to join the Huron mission (26:71–73). The soldiers were newly arrived from France and the Jesuits had serious misgivings about dispersing them to various Huron villages (26:71; 28:47). The Jesuits appear to have solved the problem of controlling the morals of these soldiers by keeping them at Sainte-Marie. That it had not been intended the soldiers should live there may explain why Lalemant later complained that the company did not reimburse the Jesuits adequately for the cost of their maintenance. This involved providing them with food and lodging, as well as repairing their arms and nursing those who were ill. The soldiers were not, however, so cut off from the Huron that they could not use their trading privileges to barter for between 3000 and 4000 beaver skins, which they brought down-river with them in September 1645 (27:89).

The Mohawk continued to harass the St. Lawrence Valley throughout the summer of 1644. In late September ten or twelve Huron were killed or captured on an island near Fort Richelieu. Among those who escaped was a Christian named Aonkerati who had been attacked by the Iroquois twice before that year (27:223). The Iroquois continued to besiege Fort Richelieu until July 1645 (27:223–27).

Throughout this period of warfare the Mohawk continued to hope that they might break the alliance that united the French, Huron, and Algonkin and especially that they might persuade the French to play a more neutral role in their dealings with the Indians. The French, for their part, hoped that some kind of peace treaty might be arranged with the Mohawk. The least known of the diplomatic manoeuvres of this period were the persistent efforts of the Mohawk to negotiate with the Huron. There were fresh talks in the summer of 1643 and these made such progress that the Huron who spent the following winter in the school at Three Rivers believed that a peace treaty had already been concluded. This was one of the reasons why they had been willing to venture on to the St. Lawrence in April 1644 (26:31).

Jogues reports that he had been a prisoner of the Mohawk for only a short time when a dispute broke out whether or not he and the other French prisoners should be returned to their countrymen (28:127). Although this talk of repatriating the French may have been intended only to please the Dutchman Arent van Curler, who wished to ransom Jogues (39:201), it seems more likely that two factions were already in existence among the Mohawk, or at least were in the process of forming. One of these factions favoured making peace with the French and possibly with the Huron as well, no doubt in the hope of thereby being able to exploit Algonkin hunting territory; the other faction believed that peace with the French was impossible and favoured waging war against them and all their allies. These factions were soon to be identified with the two moieties into which the Mohawk were divided. The peace party was associated with the moiety made up of the Tortoise and Wolf clans, who were identified with the villages of Ossernenon and Tionontoguen respectively; while the war party was associated with the moiety of the Bear clan, whose main town was Gandagaron, located between the other two (8:300 n. 34; Jameson 1909:178–79). These three main Mohawk villages were located not far from one another, on three hilltops that flanked the Mohawk Valley (map 26).

This well-attested factionalism among the Mohawk makes it impossible to describe a single, clear-cut foreign policy for them, let alone to explain this policy purely in economic terms. The tribes of the Iroquois confederacy generally held differing opinions concerning matters of war and peace and there was no more unanimity within the other tribes than there was among the Mohawk. Bacqueville de La Potherie (1911–12, 2:44) observed that when it came to foreign policy, Iroquoian peoples generally divided into two factions, especially when they were afraid of the enemy. He also noted that instead of weakening them, these alternative positions made their foreign policy more flexible and helped them to fend off humiliating defeats.

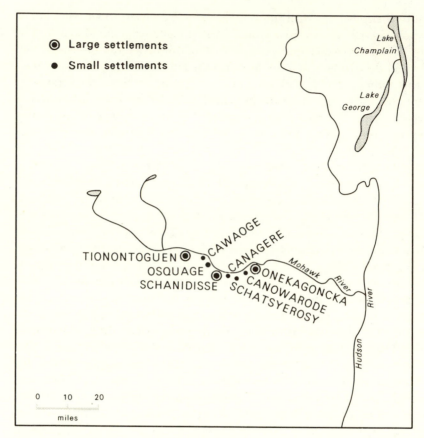

MAP 26. *Hypothetical placing of Mohawk settlements described by Van den Bogaert for 1634–35. The corresponding large settlements mentioned by Jogues for 1643 were Ossernenon, Gandagaron, and Tionontoguen. Megapolensis (1644) associated these settlements with the Tortoise, Bear, and Wolf clans respectively.*

After they had been tortured Jogues and his French companions were adopted into the Wolf clan. René Goupil was killed, not as a matter of public policy, but because an old man believed he was practising witchcraft when he saw him making the sign of the cross upon the body of a child (Thwaites 1896–1901, 28:133–35). At first, Jogues was treated badly by his adopters, but later he became the ward of a powerful old woman who protected him (39:213). In spite of this, he was again in serious danger when the Iroquois returned home to report that after they had delivered his letter to Fort Richelieu, they had been fired on by the French and five of their men had been killed (25:45–47). Even then, Jogues's adoptive relatives gave him permission to travel by himself. On the way back from their fishing camp he learned that the inhabitants of the town where he was living were planning to kill him, and accepted an offer from the Dutch to help him escape. Bressani was rescued from public torture and Guillaume Couture likewise had his life saved. While Mohawk families who had warriors slain by the French must have been anxious to see Frenchmen tortured to death in retaliation, the more moderate elements seem to have kept such passions in check to a remarkable degree.

THE PEACE OF 1645

The French were more anxious for peace than were the Mohawk. When in the autumn of 1642 a Sokoki who had been taken prisoner by the Algonkin was brought to Sillery, the French tended his wounds and persuaded their Indian allies to send him back to his own country (Thwaites 1896–1901, 24:183–85). Out of gratitude for being saved from his tormentors, this Sokoki arranged to have presents sent to the Iroquois allies requesting them to release at least one Frenchman. Jogues reports that contrary to normal practice the Iroquois kept the Sokoki presents but, for the time being, did not grant their request (25:53).

The opportunity that Montmagny had been waiting for came in the summer of 1644, when he obtained from the Algonkin at Three Rivers the Mohawk prisoner that they and the Huron had just captured. Although this man named Tokhrahenehiaron was half dead from torture, the French nursed him back to health. The next spring, a band of Algonkin armed with muskets defeated another group of Iroquois raiders and captured two more prisoners, whom they turned over to the French unharmed. One of these prisoners was Honatteniate, Jogues's adoptive cousin (27:265). Montmagny ordered Tokhrahenehiaron to be taken from Sillery to Three Rivers and there released to find his way home. He was instructed to tell his headmen that the French were willing to release the other two prisoners and that they wished to discuss a general peace with the Iroquois (27:229–45).

On 5 July Tokhrahenehiaron returned to Three Rivers, accompanied by two Mohawk headmen. Kiotsaeton, the leader of this deputation, arrived covered from head to foot with belts of wampum. He brought with him Guillaume Couture, whom the Iroquois released in exchange for

Tokhrahenehiaron. Montmagny hurried to Three Rivers and on 12 July a meeting was held between him and Kiotsaeton. This meeting took place in the courtyard of the French fort and was attended by Father Vimont, the superior of the Jesuit Mission, and by all the Indians who were at Three Rivers. Kiotsaeton presented five wampum belts to the French and two to the Huron at this meeting. Each belt was accompanied by an elaborate oration, which thanked the French for releasing Tokhrahene-hiaron, gave Couture his freedom, expressed a desire to bind the French, their allies, and the Iroquois together as allies, and invited the French to visit the Mohawk country. Kiotsaeton also affirmed that some of Montmagny's presents had been forwarded to the other Iroquois tribes to invite them to join in a general peace with the French and he urged the Huron to conclude a treaty of their own with the Iroquois (27:251–65). Significantly, no presents were given directly to the Algonkin.

When the public ceremony was over, Kiotsaeton asked to speak with Montmagny privately and offered him a rich present if he would come to a secret understanding with the Mohawk. The arrangement that he proposed was that the Mohawk would stop attacking the French and their Huron trading partners if, in return, the French would cease to protect the Algonkin. Montmagny rejected this proposal and, for a time, it seemed that there would be no peace treaty. Finally, Fathers Vimont and Le Jeune persuaded Montmagny to promise secretly that if the Iroquois refrained from attacking Christian Algonkin, the French would regard other Algonkin as a separate issue (28:149–51; for trans. of the Latin see ibid. 315 n. 16).

Hunt (1940:78–79) is vehement in his denunciation of this understanding, which he interprets to mean that the Jesuits were prepared to forsake all Algonkin. How, he asks, was an Iroquois warrior to distinguish a Christian Algonkin from a non-Christian one? Such an argument may, however, be misleading. The intertribal warfare of this region was far less anonymous than our own and one may assume that the leaders of Mohawk war parties were often familiar with the people they were attacking and knew that certain of them were Christians. Cynical as the Jesuits' attitude appears to have been, they may have rationalized their actions by believing that this was yet another way to encourage more Algonkin to convert to Christianity. Moreover, their fears for the survival of the Huron mission, should trade be broken off as a result of continued hostilities along the St. Lawrence, may have convinced them that the dishonour involved in breaking a longstanding treaty with the non-Christian Algonkin was by comparison of far less consequence.

There are, however, good reasons to believe that this agreement was only a temporary manoeuvre designed to save the negotiations. On 14 July Montmagny gave the Mohawk envoys presents of his own and it was provisionally agreed that the Mohawk should commit no act of hostility against the French or any of their allies before bilateral treaties had been negotiated among all these groups. Afterwards the Algonkin, both Christian and non-Christian, were left in peace by the Mohawk. This seems to indicate that after the Jesuits had intervened to prevent the negotiations from breaking down, the French had been able to persuade the Mohawk not to wage war against the Algonkin. This may also explain why Jérôme Lalemant later recorded in his journal that the story of this secret agreement as rumoured by the Mohawk, was false, "at least for the most part" (Thwaites 1896–1901, 28:155).

At the time, the Algonkin do not appear to have suspected any duplicity in these negotiations on the part of either the French or the Mohawk. Only the Huron traders were uneasy about what was going on and one of them unsuccessfully attempted to undermine Kiotsaeton's confidence in the sincerity of the French (27:269). The Huron feared that friendly relations between the French and any of the Iroquois tribes might undermine the willingness of the French to give them military aid. It would also allow the French to play the Huron and Iroquois off against one another as commercial rivals. On 15 July Kiotsaeton left Three Rivers for home, accompanied by Guillaume Couture and another young Frenchman. The French helped Kiotsaeton to transport his presents, but were also sent as an indication of French confidence in the Mohawk (27:271). It was agreed that later in the year the Mohawk should return to ratify a formal truce with the French and to discuss peace with the latter's allies.

Word of what had happened was soon carried to all the Indians who traded with the French and their headmen were invited to assemble at Three Rivers in the autumn. The Montagnais reached Three Rivers in late August and the headmen of the various Algonkin bands arrived somewhat later. On 10 September sixty Huron canoes arrived, escorted by the twenty-two French soldiers who, we are told, after a winter under Jesuit tutelage returned better supplied with "virtue and a knowledge of Christian truths" than when they had gone to the Huron country (27:277). In these canoes were some of the principal headmen of the Huron confederacy, who had come on behalf of the confederacy council to discuss peace with the Mohawk. They also brought back with them one of the two prisoners who had been captured the year before. They alleged that the other, who was an Oneida, had escaped along the way (29:297).

Finally, on 17 September the four Mohawk envoys arrived. In all, more than 400 Indians had gathered at Three Rivers.

During the next few days speeches were made and many presents were exchanged. The Mohawk assured the French that they wished to be their friends and would welcome them in their villages, but added that if the peace were to continue, the Huron and Algonkin would have to bring their own presents to the Mohawk country and confirm a peace with the Mohawk headmen as the French had already done. They also added that if these negotiations were successful, the Mohawk were prepared to release all the French, Huron, and Algonkians who were prisoners in their country. The Huron freed the Mohawk prisoner they were holding and told the Mohawk to make ready to receive the envoys they would soon be sending to their country. They also invited the Mohawk to send to the Huron country envoys who would bring presents to secure the release of other Iroquois prisoners who were being held there. The Algonkin likewise said that they were ready to visit the Mohawk country to discuss peace. As a result of this conference, the peace treaty between the French and the Mohawk was confirmed, while the separate negotiations between the Mohawk and the Huron and the Mohawk and the Algonkin were carried forward. Montmagny celebrated these developments by providing a feast for all the Indians who had gathered at Three Rivers.

After this feast the Mohawk envoys returned to their own country accompanied by two Frenchmen, two Algonkin, and two Huron. Three Mohawk were left as hostages for the safety of the French, while the French who accompanied this expedition were meant, in part, to assure the safety of its Huron and Algonkin members (27:279–303). Both the Huron and Algonkin had further discussions with the Mohawk headmen in New York State (28:279) and it is likely that Mohawk envoys visited the Huron country. While the result of these negotiations was a short-lived peace between the Mohawk and all the allies of the French, we have no detailed information about the treaties that were concluded among these groups. This has given rise to much speculation about the general significance of the treaties of 1645. Unfortunately, such speculations are based almost entirely on the record of the Three Rivers meeting which, for the Huron and Algonkin, was only a preliminary step towards such agreements.

The most influential interpretation of the treaties of 1645 is that of Hunt (1940:81–82). He regards all of the events leading up to this peace as being narrowly concerned with trading rights. The sole aim of the Mohawk, according to Hunt, was to force the Huron and Algonkin to trade at least some of the furs they normally took to Three Rivers with them.

At first, they tried to accomplish this through negotiations, but when these failed they waged war on the Huron and Algonkin traders so successfully that the French had to sue for peace. The Mohawk hoped that as a result of this peace, the allies of the French would trade equally with the latter and with them. The French, however, were totally opposed to this happening and when the Huron and Algonkin continued to barter all of their furs to the French, the Mohawk were compelled to go to war again.

Hunt himself was uneasy that he could cite only two minor pieces of evidence in support of his interpretation. During the preliminary negotiations in July, Kiotsaeton presented the Huron with a wampum belt to encourage them not to be bashful but to pass by the Algonkin and the French and go to the Iroquois country (Thwaites 1896–1901, 27:263). During the September conference, the Mohawk presented the Algonkians with a belt urging them to hunt so that the Iroquois could benefit from their skill (27:291). Hunt claims that these exhortations constituted a plain demand that henceforth the Huron and Algonkians were to trade with the Iroquois, and he regards these as the principal terms of this treaty. All of the rest, he says, were nothing more than the "vague promises of amicability which are included in all treaties and which mean so little" (p. 78).[15]

It would be gratifying if matters were so simple. Unfortunately, there is no proof that these particular requests, made along with so many others in a preliminary discussion of the peace, were the key elements of such a treaty. When he told them to by-pass the French and the Algonkin, Kiotsaeton was almost certainly inviting the Huron to visit the Mohawk not to trade but to discuss peace. This is evident, since the request was made immediately after a present had been given to the Huron to remind them of the peace treaty they had been invited to make five years before (Thwaites 1896–1901, 27:263). Likewise, his invitation to the Algonkians to hunt was made in the context of a description of the common no man's land that both groups had been avoiding for many years. The Mohawk were obviously looking forward to being able to hunt in this region without fear of encountering enemies. The Mohawk "benefiting from the Algonkians' skill" is an allusion to both sides respecting the peace, if they met in this zone. The Iroquois were saying that since the Algonkians were renowned hunters, they expected to be entertained to a roasted animal whenever hunters from both sides met in this area.

On the basis of the existing evidence, we cannot rule out the possibility that one of the reasons the Mohawk agreed to make peace was because they hoped to secure furs from the north. They probably obtained a goodly number in the course of their formal negotiations with the Huron and Algonkin. Yet, to suggest as Hunt does that any interpretation but his own is meaningless is to fly in the face of much solid evidence. If the conclusion of fur trading alliances with the Huron and Algonkin were the Mohawk's primary goal, it would hardly have been in the long-term interests of the French to undermine their own trade by encouraging friendly contact between their trading partners and the Mohawk. Fear of diverting trade to the Dutch and of rendering their own allies more independent and more "insolent" almost certainly would have offset the anticipated benefits of peace. Moreover, to suggest that if trade of this sort had been the Mohawk's sole aim, they would have been so negligent or credulous as to agree to a treaty that gave their enemies freedom to use the St. Lawrence River with no specific promises in return, is seriously to discredit their political acumen.

The evidence suggests that Hunt erred seriously when he attempted to view the peace of 1645 as a European-style treaty and therefore as essentially different from the truces that the tribes of this region were accustomed to negotiate. The principal aim of these truces was to regain relatives or tribesmen who had been captured by the enemy, but were still alive. All Iroquoian-speaking peoples saw warfare as a means by which individual men acquired prestige and, hence, could not remain in a condition of total peace for any extended period. The Mohawk had also for several generations used this traditional warfare to steal European trade goods and, later, furs from their northern neighbours. The recent neutrality of the Dutch in quarrels between different groups of Indians must have made the Mohawk hope for a similar neutrality from the French. Moreover, French neutrality would have allowed the Mohawk to play two groups of Europeans off against one another in order to get the best prices for their furs. Under the right terms, peaceful relations with the French were highly desirable. When Montmagny proposed to release prisoners, the Mohawk were therefore willing to discuss peace. It is doubtful, however, in spite of their solemn rhetoric, that the Mohawk regarded their agreements with other Indian tribes as more than traditional truces which would last for only a few years. Mohawk families whose members were held prisoner by the French or their allies must have been especially anxious for such a truce.

The most crucial issue that the Mohawk had to face was whether such a truce was economically feasible. To get back all their prisoners, the Mohawk had, at least temporarily, to stop attacking Huron traders, and, under pressure from the French, they were persuaded to extend the truce to cover all the allies of the French. Hunt is correct that such an agreement would have cut off a major source of furs from the Mohawk, but he is wrong in suggesting that this loss could have been made up only if the Huron and Algonkin promised to trade with them. During previous years the Mohawk had penetrated Algonkin and Montagnais hunting territory and in the course of their negotiations with the French, they expressed keen interest in the hunting territories that lay in the no man's land between them. During the period of the truce, the Mohawk were free to trap as many furs as they wished in this area (27:289–91). It also may be that the ritual kinship acquired through the truce gave the Mohawk the right to hunt in Algonkin territory.[16] In addition, the Mohawk, along with the Mahican and Sokoki, seem to have begun their attacks on the Abenaki about this time (31:195). Peace with the French and their allies might have facilitated these attacks, which the Mohawk hoped would net them many furs with less danger than was incurred in their attacks along the St. Lawrence. Whatever the precise arrangements may have been, it seems likely that the Mohawk counted on either hunting in the north or waging war elsewhere to provide them with enough furs to compensate them, at least for a few years, for the furs lost through the cessation of their raids against the Huron and Algonkin. Although it lacks dramatic appeal, this explanation conforms better with what is known about Iroquoian behaviour than does Hunt's and accounts more completely for the manner in which the treaty was made and ultimately disintegrated.

WAR RESUMES

During the winter of 1645–46 the Algonkin became uneasy when rumours began to circulate concerning the secret talks that had taken place between the French and the Mohawk the previous summer. The source of these rumours was a Huron named Tandihetsi who seems to have been a member of the Huron negotiating party that visited the Mohawk after the September conference. Tandihetsi claimed that the Mohawk had revealed to him that in mid-February 300 of them would be coming north to attack the Algonkin (Thwaites 1896–1901, 28:149). When he heard this report Tessouat withdrew from Montreal to Three Rivers, and more Algonkin followed when the Mohawk informed them that the Oneida and Onondaga had decided not to make peace and that some of them might attack Montreal (29:147). A meeting was held at Three Rivers, which was attended by Atironta. At this meeting it appears to have been demonstrated that Tandihetsi's claim of an imminent attack by the Mohawk was false (28:155) and probably that the Mohawk had been persuaded to include all the Algonkin in their truce. The Mohawk were true to their word and did not attack the Algonkin that winter. During that period, some Mohawk visited Montreal Island to see the French. One of them was probably no more than stating the blunt truth when he sang in the presence of Algonkin that he wished to slay some of them but that Montmagny had arrested his anger (29:151). The only grave incident was the slaying of a number of Montagnais by the Sokoki, which at first was blamed on the Mohawk (28:277).

On 22 February Kiotsaeton and six other Mohawk envoys appeared at Montreal in the company of Couture and the two Huron who had visited their country in September. These Mohawk hunted in the vicinity of Montreal until 7 May when they met Montmagny at Three Rivers. There they renewed their treaty with the French and protested their innocence of the murders committed by the Sokoki. They warned the Huron that the other Iroquois tribes had refused to make peace, but stated that Mohawk envoys would soon be visiting the Huron country to discuss this problem in greater detail (28:301). Tessouat also offered presents to reinforce his own tenuous peace with the Mohawk (28:297–301).

At the conclusion of this meeting Montmagny decided to send Isaac Jogues and Jean Bourdon, an engineer and mapmaker, to reaffirm his peace with the Mohawk (28:303). They left 16 May, accompanied by four Mohawk and two Algonkin who were bearing gifts from Tessouat to the Mohawk. These envoys travelled south by way of Lake Champlain to Fort Orange and thence were led by the Mohawk to their villages. There Jogues attended a general council, where he attempted to negotiate the release of Oionhaton and a young Frenchman, whom the Mohawk still held prisoner. The Frenchman was released, but the Mohawk seemed unwilling to consider Oionhaton. They said she was now married and living among the Onondaga, and gave only a sibylline assurance that she would be restored to the French once she had been returned to the Mohawk (29:55).

In addition, Jogues urged the Mohawk to prevent the other Iroquois tribes from crossing their territory if their aim was to attack the French. The Mohawk genially promised to do what they could, knowing that they were not in a position to stop these tribes even if they wished to do so (29:59). Jogues annoyed the Mohawk when he gave 2000 wampum beads to visiting Onondaga headmen to announce the desire that the French had to visit their country. He added that the French and Onondaga might visit one another by way of the St. Lawrence River and Lake Ontario, or by travelling across Huron territory, as well as through the Mohawk country. The Mohawk expressed surprise at this proposal, which challenged their established role as intermediaries between the French and the other Iroquois tribes. Their main fear seemed to be that if the Onondaga established separate trading relations with the French, it would be difficult for the Mohawk to control these relations. The Mohawk informed Jogues that the other roads were too dangerous and that if the French wished to maintain friendly relations with them, they would be wise to conduct their dealings with the other Iroquois tribes through them. In spite of this, Jogues persevered with his efforts to establish a separate relationship between the French and the Onondaga (29:57). This episode is of special interest because it reveals for the first time a latent rivalry among the Iroquois tribes over relations with Europeans. Both French and Huron were later to try to exploit this rivalry.

During the summer of 1646 the peace between the Mohawk and the allies of the French permitted a record number of furs to be exported from New France (28:235; map 27). The calm of that summer was marred only by a few acts of violence. Tessouat and a group of Kichesipirini were attacked above the Long Sault Rapids of the Ottawa River by a band of Oneida, among whom were said to be two or three Mohawk. In this attack an Algonkin man was killed and a woman taken prisoner. The woman was rescued, however, when these same Oneida were defeated by the Onontchataronon (28:225). A Huron trader by the name of Ondiwaharea was also captured by the Iroquois when he tried to return to the Huron country by way of Lake Ontario (28:231). This is the only recorded instance of a Huron attempting to travel this dangerous route.

In September Father Jogues was commissioned to return to the Mohawk country, where he was to continue to promote peace with the other Iroquois tribes (29:181–83). He was accompanied by Jean de La Lande, a young donné, and by a number of Huron who were going to visit their captive relatives. Jogues and his companions were fearful about the outcome of this journey (31:111) and scarcely had got beyond Three Rivers when all but one of the Huron turned back. When Jogues and La Lande arrived in the Mohawk country they were both stripped and beaten, but not threatened with public torture. The day after he reached Ossernenon, Jogues was killed with a hatchet as he was entering a longhouse. La Lande was slain in a similar fashion early the next day and their bodies were both thrown into the river (31:117–19). The Huron who accompanied Jogues was not slain and he returned to Three Rivers in June 1647 and informed

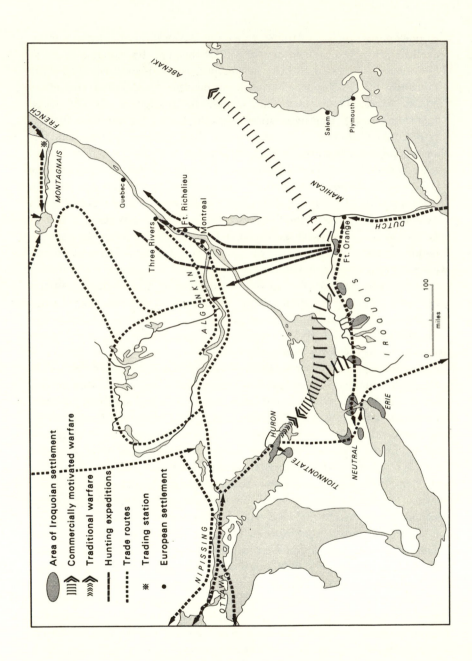

MAP 27. *Intertribal relations following the peace of 1645.*

the French what had happened. He is identified as the son of Ignace
Otouolti [*sic*] (30:175–77).

Jogues was not slain with the general consent of all the people of
Ossernenon, but by members of the Bear clan. The Tortoise and Wolf clans
did what they could to save him and his adoptive relatives were particularly
angered by his death. Moreover, the two other large Mohawk towns were
not consulted before the deed was committed (31:117; 32:25–27). The
previous summer had been a bad one for the Iroquois. An epidemic had
caused many deaths, and after Jogues had departed in the spring worms
had destroyed much of the Mohawk's corn crop (30:229, 273; 31:121).
The Iroquois interpreted these disasters as evidence of sorcery and many
people blamed them on a small chest of clothes that Jogues had left behind
(30:229; 31:115). Hunt (1940:85–86) rejects this explanation on the
grounds that if Jogues was really held to be guilty of sorcery, his death
would have been more popular. Hunt argues that Jogues's death was a
minor incident in the outbreak of a new war between the Iroquois and the
French and their allies. According to Hunt, this war occurred because the
French and Huron failed to live up to the terms of the commercial treaty
they had made with the Mohawk in 1645; for two years, not a single
Huron pelt had been traded to the Iroquois.

This explanation suffers from the general weaknesses of all Hunt's
arguments. Had the Mohawk really believed themselves betrayed by the
French, it is more likely that they would have been unanimous in their
condemnation of Jogues and tortured him to death in the style they
reserved for captive enemies. As it was, Jogues and La Lande were killed
in the fashion prescribed for witches. It is reported that at this period
Huron prisoners were telling the Mohawk that the Jesuits were demons
whose aim was to destroy the Indians (Thwaites 1896–1901, 30:227).
Among Iroquoians accusations of witchcraft tended to be controversial and
easily led to just such differences of opinion as appear to have surrounded
the slaying of these two Frenchmen. What happened to Jogues and
La Lande is what might have happened repeatedly to Jesuits in the Huron
country, had they not been protected by the trading alliance between the
French and the Huron.

In any case, there is little reason to believe that the truce between the
Mohawk and the northern Indian groups could have lasted long once it
became evident that no more prisoners were to be released. It is also likely
that hunting did not prove as prolific a source of furs as piracy, and that a
growing need for furs played a major role in driving the Mohawk into
battle once again. Even before Jogues's death, the Mohawk had sent

presents to the other Iroquois tribes urging them to attack the French (30:227). Soon after, the Mohawk warriors spread out in order to attack as many French, Algonkin, and Huron as they could. It became dangerous to wander outside the fortifications of the French settlement at Montreal and Algonkin were being robbed and murdered in their winter hunting grounds (30:161, 229–51). While furs were preferred as booty, the Iroquois continued to steal whatever they could lay their hands on. In March 1647 they stripped two French houses near Three Rivers of all clothing, blankets, ammunition, and other valuables while their owners were attending mass. It was estimated that fifteen men were required to carry off everything that was taken (30:253). After two prosperous years, the economy both of New France and of the Huron country was once again being threatened by the attacks of the Mohawk.

War in the Huron Country

NEW GOALS

The attacks of the western Iroquois tribes on the Huron homeland grew increasingly severe through the 1640s. It is difficult to determine how important a role muskets played in all but the final years of this conflict, and evidence for Mohawk participation in these raids is equivocal (Thwaites 1896–1901, 26:35–37) except after 1647. It may be that the growing strength of the western Iroquois evident at this time resulted to a large degree from the Iroquois allocating more manpower to their attacks on the Huron than the Huron with their far-flung trading commitments were able to muster in their own defence. The nature of the attacks also changed as the western Iroquois sought to steal furs and trade goods from the Huron. The murder of a few individuals working in their fields or while moving between villages or the siege of a settlement with its attendant challenges to fight did not yield the amount of booty that the Iroquois now required. It therefore became necessary to penetrate Huron villages in order to seize the furs and trade goods that were stored inside them. The *Jesuit Relations* do not provide a systematic account of warfare between the Huron and the Iroquois from 1640 to 1647; nevertheless, from what is recorded, some understanding can be gleaned about what was happening at this time.

The most enigmatic event was the attack made on Ehwae, the main

Tionnontaté village, in the spring of 1640. Most of the houses of the village were reported to have been burned in this attack and many people were slain or taken prisoner (21:181). This attack is often attributed to the Iroquois, although on the basis of no direct evidence, since the attackers are not named.[17] It is unclear whether the Tionnontaté were traditional enemies of the Iroquois as the Huron were, or if they were too remote to have been drawn into conflict with them. The earliest explicit reference to an Iroquois raid on the Tionnontaté dates no earlier than the winter of 1646–47 (33:83). On the other hand, the Tionnontaté were close friends of the Ottawa who, in turn, were allies of the Neutral against the Assistaronon. It is therefore worth considering the alternative possibility that Ehwae was attacked by the Assistaronon (Jones 1908:224). This may have been one of the early events in the war between the Neutral and the Assistaronon that was to result in many Algonkian-speaking groups being expelled from southern Michigan. If we are correct in believing that prior to this time the Assistaronon controlled the eastern shore of Lake Huron south of the Bruce Peninsula, an attack on Ehwae is not impossible.

If the Iroquois were not responsible for the destruction of Ehwae, there is no evidence of a basic change in the pattern of Iroquois warfare in Ontario prior to 1642 except perhaps for the growing scale of conflict. A prominent figure in the engagements of this period was Ahatsistari, a man from Teanaostaiaé, who is said to have been regarded as the greatest Huron warrior of his time. In the summer of 1640 he and a band of Huron raiders were crossing Lake Ontario when they encountered several large Iroquois canoes on their way north. Although most of the Huron were in favour of using their lighter and swifter vessels to beat a retreat, Ahatsistari leapt into one of the Iroquois canoes and upset it. He then swam about killing the Iroquois before he returned to his own canoe. The Huron pursued the rest of the Iroquois who, in the meantime, had begun to flee. They captured a large number and brought them home as prisoners (Thwaites 1896–1901, 23:25–27).

The following summer, Ahatsistari led a band of fifty Huron which claimed to have scattered a force of 300 Iroquois and captured some of them (23:25). These prisoners were divided among the Huron tribes so that those whose relatives had recently been slain by the Iroquois might avenge their deaths (23:33). Raids into Iroquois territory continued as usual throughout the summer of 1641 and a band of warriors from Scanonaenrat almost perished when they were caught in a violent storm on Lake Ontario on their way home (23:173–75). It was at this time that the Jesuit scholar Andehoua decided to renew his commitment to Christianity. Not all Huron raids were successful, however. In particular, an Arendarhonon group was defeated by the Iroquois and among those who were taken prisoner and later slain was the tribal headman Atironta. His brother Aëotahon escaped from the battle and became the new Atironta. The Jesuits derived some short-term satisfaction from this defeat because the Arendarhonon had performed a "shameless" ceremony before setting out, in the hope that they would thereby assure themselves of victory over the Iroquois (23:159). This ceremony may have been the andacwander, which involved public fornication.

A NEW STYLE OF WARFARE

Already by 1640 Lalemant was alarmed by the extent of Iroquois penetration of the Huron country. Small bands of raiders appeared to be lurking in the forests everywhere and remained throughout most of the year. Women and children were not safe, even within sight of their own villages and sometimes, in traditional fashion, the Iroquois would steal into the villages at night and kill a few people, then try to escape unharmed (Thwaites 1896–1901, 22:305). These attacks appear to have been most severe among the Arendarhonon, whose geographical isolation from the rest of the confederacy made them a vulnerable target (23:33).

In the winter of 1641–42 a rumour spread that an Iroquois army was on the point of overwhelming Contarea, the principal village of the Arendarhonon. While this rumour was later found to be false, it was believed throughout the confederacy and created panic as far away as Ossossané (23:105–7; 57). There may have been a sound basis for Huron fears since, in June of the following year, a band of Iroquois attacked and burned a Huron village and was so successful that only a score of people are said not to have been killed or taken prisoner (26:175). One may imagine that, as happened with the destruction of other Huron villages, the strongest of these prisoners were kept alive and driven south, burdened with furs and other spoils that the victorious Iroquois were carrying off with them (34:135). Although the village that was destroyed is not identified by name, it was long believed to have been Contarea, since both were described as frontier villages and as hostile to Christianity (Jones 1908:331). This identification could only be sustained, however, so long as Contarea and St. Jean-Baptiste (which was still in existence until 1647) were believed to be different villages, whereas it now seems certain that they were the Huron and Jesuit names for the same community (Heidenreich 1966:123–24). The community that was destroyed in 1642 appears to have been a smaller Arendarhonon village, the name of which was not recorded. It was probably located near Contarea and it is not surprising that it followed the same course as the larger community in its reactions to the Jesuits.

The destruction of this village marks an important turning point in relations between the Huron and the western tribes of the Iroquois confederacy. Hitherto, warfare between these groups had been largely a matter of blood feud with ritualistic overtones, robbery being of only secondary importance. For the Huron with their easy access to furs, there was no need to change. Among the Onondaga, Cayuga, and Seneca, however, a growing need for European goods encouraged the development of an economically oriented warfare, analogous to that practised by the Mohawk and the Oneida for some time. Instead of robbing trading convoys and hunting parties, the western Iroquois concentrated on plundering the Huron in their own homeland. This not only led to more violent and intensive warfare but also encouraged the Iroquois to attack Huron houses and villages in order to seize the furs and trade goods that were stored inside them. Thus, the traditional siege of a Huron village aimed at challenging its defenders to come out and fight gave way to surprise attacks at dawn, followed by pillaging, burning, and long trains of captives carrying away booty. The year 1642 seems to mark the beginning of this pattern, although the 300 Iroquois who were defeated the year before may have made up a raiding party of this sort. Major attacks were supplemented by traditional assaults on individuals or small groups. Even in these cases, however, the stealing of valuables, including the skins that the victims wore as clothing, may have become a more important motive than was blood revenge.

In order to avenge their dead, the Huron continued to invade the Iroquois country. Tsondatsaa left on such an expedition not long before the attack on the Arendarhonon village in 1642 (Thwaites 1896–1901, 23:195–97). The following year a Huron raiding party of about 100 men suffered a stunning defeat. Before these men were able to disperse, they were surrounded by several hundred Iroquois and after a fight that lasted through an entire night all of them were either killed or taken prisoner (28:45, 89–91).

1643 was a year of devastating Iroquois attacks on the Huron country. Hundreds of Huron are reported to have been taken prisoner and many women were killed while working in their fields (27:65). Forty people who left Teanaostaiaé to gather hemp were attacked by the Iroquois in the night. Although there were only twenty assailants, they managed to kill or capture most of these Huron, only a few being able to escape (26:203–5). Bands of warriors who attempted to hunt down these raiders were themselves ambushed and individuals who had escaped from the Iroquois with bodies half burned and fingers mutilated were a common sight (27:65). The Huron also were afflicted by famine in 1643. It is unclear whether this was because women were unable to work in their fields or because of natural conditions, although the statement that famine prevailed for 100 leagues around suggests that drought may have been at least partly responsible. Hunger compelled the Huron to gather nuts and wild roots, which further exposed them to attacks by the enemy (27:65).

While there is very little information for the year 1644, Iroquois attacks appear to have been as bad or worse than they had been the year before. In the winter of 1644–45, the Huron feared the approach of an Iroquois army which was reported to be coming to ravage their settlements; however, the arrival of the French soldiers who accompanied Brébeuf to the Huron country that autumn was credited with making the Iroquois change their plan (28:47). Whether or not the Iroquois entertained such a plan, these rumours illustrate the insecurity of the Huron.

The truce that was arranged with the Mohawk in 1645 did not free the Huron from attack by the four other Iroquois tribes. Yet, according to Ragueneau, the Huron had somewhat more success in dealing with their enemies that year than they had formerly (29:247). Some of their raids were successful and resulted in the capture of prisoners who were brought home and tortured to death (29:251). At one point a band of Iroquois who were prowling in the vicinity of Teanaostaiaé managed to kill two Huron sentinels who had fallen asleep while guarding a village watchtower. To avenge this killing three Huron went to Sonnontouan where they entered a longhouse in the dead of night, killed three Seneca, and carried their scalps home (29:253–5).

Encouraging as these minor victories may have been, they did not check the incursions of the enemy or offset the growing drain on Huron manpower in which these raids were resulting. In spring of 1645 a band of Iroquois concealed themselves in a forest near Contarea and seized a group of women as they went out to work in the fields. The Iroquois carried these women off so quickly to their canoes, beached along the shores of Lake Simcoe, that 200 armed Huron were unable to rescue any of them (29:249).

Later in the summer a band of Huron discovered a group of Iroquois warriors hiding in the forest. They encircled their fortified camp and had almost seized them when the Iroquois asked to parley. They laid down their muskets and offered a number of large wampum belts to the Huron headmen and elders, then invited these men to confer with them in their camp. Tobacco was distributed to entertain the younger Huron warriors who remained outside. While this conference was going on, an Iroquois who some years before had been a prisoner of the Huron talked to the younger warriors and frightened them into withdrawing. Once most of them had gone, the Iroquois fell on the Huron headmen and killed or made prisoners of all who could not escape (29:249–51). The Iroquois were reported to have had designs on Teanaostaiaé during this period (29:251), and nearly destroyed at least one other Huron village (29:149).

Did these raids have any more long-term purpose than to secure furs and European goods by stealing them? Hunt (1940:91) has suggested that the original aim of this harassment was to bring pressure to bear on the Huron to compel them to trade their furs with the Iroquois as well as with the French. He argues that when the Iroquois saw this was impossible, they decided to drive the Huron from their tribal territory so that they could seize their trade for themselves. Alternatively, it has been suggested that the Iroquois wished to disperse the Huron so they could seize their land as hunting territory (Trelease 1960:120). Others have viewed the Iroquois as being motivated simply by a desire to settle old scores once their foes were no longer able to maintain the balance of power. All of these arguments have sought support in a letter that Jogues wrote from Ossernenon on 30 June 1643 in which he stated that the Iroquois' plan was to capture all the Huron, kill their leaders, and compel the rest to live as Iroquois (Thwaites 1896–1901, 24:297).

Those who stress the deviousness and cunning of the Mohawk interpret this letter as evidence that the future policies of the Iroquois were formulated almost a decade before they came to fruition. From this it must follow that all evidence that the Iroquois were behaving differently is only an indication of their duplicity. It is possible that certain Mohawk were considering plans for the destruction of the Huron confederacy. These might have been individuals who were especially intent on seeking blood revenge or who had been inspired to think along these lines by Dutch traders wishing to sabotage French commerce. Yet there is very little evidence that the Mohawk were participating in attacks on the Huron country prior to 1647, and it is difficult to see what gain there was in such a plan for Indians whose principal aim was to rob Huron and Algonkin fur convoys. Nor is there any evidence that Jogues's letter indicates that the Onondaga and Seneca were deliberately seeking to expel the Huron from their tribal territories. It is more likely that the plan he was describing was for dealing with the Huron traders whom the Mohawk were harassing each year on the St. Lawrence.

We have already ruled out the likelihood that the Iroquois were seeking new hunting territories at the expense of the Huron. It may have been that the Iroquois hoped to reduce the Huron to client status and force them to trade their furs with them, but, if so, this policy was badly executed. More likely, in their dealings with the Huron as in their dealings with the French, the Iroquois were not pursuing any long-term policy. Instead, they were following a number of short-term ones. The only constant requirement was to obtain enough furs or booty each year to supply their growing need for trade goods. If this was the case, desultory looting may have remained the principal objective of the western Iroquois as well as of the Mohawk until a more lucrative alternative presented itself or became necessary.

Chapter 10   The Storm Within

The Jesuit Mission

The changes that took place in Huron society between 1640 and 1647 had no less fatal consequences for the Huron than did the growing menace of the Iroquois. In these changes, the Jesuits played the leading role, which makes it necessary to understand their specific aims and organization at this period. The key to such an understanding is the headquarters of Sainte-Marie, which Jérôme Lalemant had established in the expectation that it would fulfil a dual role as a European-style Jesuit residence and the nucleus of a village of converts. While Sainte-Marie did not develop as Lalemant originally had planned, the growth of this headquarters significantly altered the Jesuits' role in relationship to the Huron.

PERSONNEL

Before 1640 the Jesuits and their lay assistants were few and were dependent on the Huron for food and protection. After this time, the number of Frenchmen in the Huron country slowly increased from thirteen priests to eighteen, and from fourteen lay assistants, of various categories, to a high of about forty-six, which was reached during the winter of 1648–49.[1] During this same period, Sainte-Marie grew from a single hut into a substantial, well-fortified French settlement, which at certain times of the year sheltered almost as many Europeans as Quebec had in 1629 (Kidd 1949a; Jury and Jury 1954; Desjardins 1966; Rochemonteix 1895–96, 1:385–88).

Lalemant intended that the farm that was attached to this settlement should feed all the French who were working in the Huron country. This would eliminate the cost of buying food and assure the Jesuits of a supply, should the Huron refuse to sell them what they needed. Lalemant also sought to make the settlement strong enough to withstand attack either by the Iroquois or by the Huron themselves and to ensure that it was able to provide enough services so that the Jesuits could continue to live as

Frenchmen in the Huron country, even if the Mohawk severed their contacts with Quebec. The hostility of the Huron in 1639 and the growing menace of the Iroquois thereafter were persuasive arguments for developing such independence. Moreover, pending the formal establishment of a *reduction* for Huron converts, the mission was able to provide various services for these converts. These included caring for the sick and providing a retreat where religious activities of both a personal and public nature could be carried on without distractions from non-Christians.

The core of the mission was a group of priests who had lived in the Huron country long enough to have learned the Huron language well and who had made the kind of personal contacts among the Huron that allowed them to sway particular individuals and whole communities. Fathers Brébeuf, Ragueneau, Daniel, and Poncet de La Rivière[2] were sent on business from the Huron mission to the French settlements in Quebec for periods of one to several years, but each of them eventually returned to the Huron country to resume his duties there. Three others, Ambroise Davost, Charles Raymbaut, and Pierre Pijart, were forced to return to Quebec by extreme ill-health; the first two died soon after they did so. Jérôme Lalemant left the Huron country for good in 1645 to become Jesuit superior for the whole of New France. His rigidity and preoccupation with rubrics had not won him the affection of his fellow missionaries, hence they were delighted when he was succeeded by Father Paul Ragueneau, who already had eight years of experience working among the Huron (Thwaites 1896–1901, 25:83; 30:149). Finally, Isaac Jogues did not return to the Huron mission after he was captured by the Iroquois in 1642. Yet, nineteen of the twenty-four priests who came to the Huron country, beginning in 1634, either died there or remained until the mission ended in 1650—a remarkable stability in personnel. Ten of these men worked among the Huron for ten or more years,[3] and seven saw from twelve to eighteen years of service. On the basis of such experience, the following priests made up the core of the Huron mission: Jean de Brébeuf, Antoine Daniel, François Le Mercier, Pierre Chastellain, Charles Garnier, François Du Peron, Simon Le Moyne, Pierre Chaumonot, and Paul Ragueneau. The latter's calm judgment and general good sense, which were conspicuously displayed at this period, combined the best qualities of his two predecessors as superior of the Huron mission.

The priests were assisted by a corps of workmen who erected buildings, grew crops, and provided many personal services for them. Some of these men were also responsible for encouraging as many Huron as possible to trade each year, a duty inherited from the long-banished company traders.

In the winter of 1644–45, and again in 1648–49 and 1649–50, soldiers were sent to protect Sainte-Marie and the Huron villages, but normally the Jesuits' assistants were lay brothers, donnés, hired men, and boys. The latter came to learn the Huron language and to assist the workmen. In the initial years of the Huron mission, lay brothers had not been wanted because regulations did not allow them to carry arms. After 1640 a more specialized division of labour developed and jobs were found for up to four of them at a time. Dominique Scot worked as a tailor until he was forced to return to France because of illness; Louis Gaubert was a blacksmith; Pierre Masson was first a gardener, but replaced Scot as tailor in 1645; Ambroise Brouet was a cook; and Nicolas Noircler arrived late and his occupation is unknown. None of these lay brothers did work that took him beyond the mission headquarters at Sainte-Marie.

The most valued assistants were the donnés, who grew from two in 1641 to twenty-three in 1648. Some had already signed on in this capacity before they came to the Huron country, others were hired men, or youths, who had been attached to the mission before they decided to dedicate their lives to supporting the work of the Jesuits. Spiritual motives or a desire for a more prestigeful role in the mission must have motivated such decisions, since becoming a donné required foregoing wages and giving up the right to trade for one's own profit (21:305).

The majority of the donnés are not listed as having particular trades and many were probably handymen who performed a wide variety of tasks.[4] Robert Le Coq, the first donné, was the business manager of the mission, a post which required him to travel to Three Rivers and back each summer. The surgeons who were recruited for the mission were also donnés. The first, René Goupil, was captured by the Iroquois before he reached the Huron country, but François Gendron, who in later life became a priest and king's counsellor, worked there from 1643 to 1650. He was assisted by another donné, Joseph Molère, who was pharmacist and laundryman. Charles Boivin was the master builder who supervised the erection of buildings for the Jesuits throughout the Huron country. An important part of his work was designing the scale models of proposed buildings that were the blueprints of the period (Jury and Jury 1954:49–50). While many of the donnés must have worked on Boivin's projects, Jean Guiet, who arrived in 1646, is the only one listed as a carpenter by profession. Jacob Levrier and Christophe Regnault were shoemakers.

Skilled trades were not restricted to donnés and lay brothers. Pierre Tourmente,[5] a professional stonemason, was employed by the Huron mission from 1646 to 1648, and again in 1649–50 (Thwaites 1896–1901,

34:59). In 1649 Pierre Oliveau, who was "a miller, or sent from France as such," was dispatched to the Huron country (32:101; 34:59), although probably not in his professional capacity.[6] Hired men not only received wages, but were granted certain rights to profit from trading for furs with the Indians (27:91). The latter privileges must have encouraged many ordinary labourers to learn to speak a little Huron or Algonkian and to acquire valuable experience in dealing with the Indians. Charles Le Moyne, who was an indentured servant of the Jesuits, was later to become a prosperous fur trader and the father of Pierre Le Moyne d'Iberville, the noted soldier and explorer. Médard Chouart Des Groseilliers worked in the Huron country before 1646, during which time he must have acquired experience valuable for his later travels of discovery in North America.

Donnés, as well as workmen, became proficient in dealing with the Huron and some of them later put these skills to public as well as private use. Pierre Boucher became governor of Three Rivers and author of a valuable description of New France, while Guillaume Couture, who was captured by the Iroquois in 1642, was later an important Indian diplomat and explorer. Eustache Lambert, who became a donné by 1646 (Jones 1908:356), eventually settled at Pointe-Lévy and carried on extensive trade with the Indians.

SAINTE-MARIE-AUX-HURONS

The Jesuits' *Relations* and surviving letters yield little information about the construction of Sainte-Marie. In May 1640 Lalemant wrote that the French were working to establish an abode that was suitable for their needs (Thwaites 1896–1901, 19:135), which suggests that a European-style dwelling was being constructed or enlarged. In 1641 the Jesuits had a Huron longhouse erected to shelter Indians who came to Sainte-Marie to perform their devotions (21:141; 23:21) in a chapel that had also been built by this time. The services in this chapel were said to be more elaborate than the Huron had previously beheld, while the chapel, although poor by French standards, was regarded by the Huron as one of the wonders of the world. This splendour was judged to be useful because it enhanced the Indians' respect for Christian rituals (23:23). It is possible that this building incorporated material from the French-style chapel built near the old site of Ossossané. No effort had been made to keep this building in use after Ossossané was relocated. A chapel to serve the new Ossossané had been constructed within a Huron longhouse (21:159).

Prior to the autumn of 1642 the Jesuits erected a hospital at Sainte-Marie (26:203). This hospital was built away from the priests' quarters so that women as well as men might be cared for in it. At the same time, a church was established for public worship, which was separate from the Jesuits' private chapel and seems to have been intended mainly for use by the Indians. A cemetery was consecrated near the church and, in addition to the cabin for Christian visitors, a separate facility was established where non-Christian Indians might be admitted by day, provided with hospitality, and hear the word of God (26:201–3). A woman from Ossossané had herself brought to Sainte-Marie so that she might die there. She was pregnant and, after she miscarried in the course of her illness, she and the infant were buried in the same grave (26:209). The second burial was of Christine Tsorihia, an elderly woman from Teanaostaiaé. She died in the winter of 1642–43 and her body was transported to Sainte-Marie for burial in spite of the bad weather (26:211, 289–91). In the spring of 1642 Cardinal Richelieu provided funds for the construction of a strong fort in the Huron country (Robinson, in Du Creux 1951–52:xxiv). Sainte-Marie appears to have been fortified from an early date, although the only explicit reference to the building of fortifications dates from the spring of 1649 (Thwaites 1896–1901, 33:253–55). Twice, however, in 1642 and again in 1649, Sainte-Marie was referred to as a French fort in the Huron country (23:205; 33:255).

Considerably more information has been obtained about the layout and architectural history of Sainte-Marie as a result of the archaeological work carried out there between 1941 and 1943 by Kenneth E. Kidd (1949a), and between 1947 and 1951 by Wilfrid Jury (and Jury 1954). From this work, a general impression can be gained of a complex structure almost 800 feet long and over 200 feet wide at the north end. The western edge of the settlement curved gently to follow the bank of the Wye River, while it grew narrower towards the south to avoid the swampy area that sheltered the site to the east. Jury (and Jury 1954:90–107) has named the southern half of the site the "Indian Compound." It was separated from the "European Compound" to the north by a projecting V-shaped wooden palisade which was inside a ditchworks that remained visible into the last century (ibid. 78; Kidd 1949a:17–20). The Indian Compound was subdivided into an inner and outer court which were both surrounded by palisades. Inside the inner court a large number of post molds were noted, which included the outline of a longhouse (plate 40).

The prevalence of Indian artifacts suggested that this was the area that had been cleared for the erection of a house for Huron visitors in 1641, and

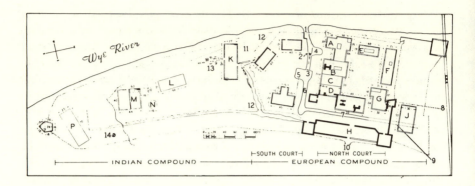

A—Dwelling   F—Dwelling   L—Huron longhouse
B—Chapel   G—Dwelling   M—Hospital
C—Carpenter-shop H—Barracks   N—Algonquin dwelling
D—Blacksmith-shop J—Barn   P—Huron longhouse
E—Cookhouse   K—Indian Church

1, 2, 3—Locks   7—North-south water 11—Escape tunnel
          channel
4—Loading basin   8—Drinking-water 12—Ditchworks for defence
          aqueduct
5—Landing basin   9—Aqueduct   13—Christian cemetery
6—East-West water channel 10—Gateway   14—Well

Timber construction ═══ Stone construction ____ Palisade line - - - - -

PLATE 40. *Wilfrid Jury's plan of Sainte-Marie I. Illustration by J. Griffith and P. Buchanan. Courtesy W. and E. Jury and Oxford University Press, Canadian Branch.*

which was subsequently used by the Christian Indians who came to visit the Jesuits. Traces of additional temporary Indian shelters were also noted in this area, as well as the plans of two large European buildings. The latter had walls constructed of two rows of horizontal two-inch planks, held in position by thick, upright posts and packed in between with clay and stones to provide insulation. This type of construction is known as *colombage pierroté* and was still common in France in the seventeenth century (Jury and Jury 1954:38–39). Jury has interpreted the more southerly of these buildings as the hospital, which the Jesuits said was kept separate from their own living quarters, while the other building is believed to be the church that was constructed for public worship. It was a structure seventy feet long and twenty-seven feet wide. Immediately to the south of this building was a cemetery, containing twenty Indian graves. Traces of coffins were found in these graves; of these, three were small and each may have held the remains of one or more children. The positions of the adult skeletons indicate that the bodies had been placed in their coffins either on their sides with the knees flexed or lying on their backs with their legs stretched out. Rosaries were buried with some bodies, but most graves contained more traditional offerings. One body was accompanied by a quantity of wampum beads, another by the teeth and jawbone of a dog.

A flexed male interment was accompanied, in the same coffin, by a native bundle burial. In the upper right-hand corner of this coffin was a small copper vessel, the bottom of which had been damaged. Alongside it was an iron knife-blade and a pewter pipe, fourteen inches long and beautifully decorated with a pattern that incorporated two fleurs-de-lis. This appears to have been the grave of an influential Huron whose wife had predeceased him and been buried in the traditional manner. Since non-Christians would not have been allowed to be buried in this cemetery, it must be assumed either that this woman had been baptized and given a traditional scaffold burial prior to her husband's death, or that she was a non-Christian whose bones were slipped into the coffin without the Jesuits knowing about it. Jury and Jury (1954:93) note that the grave offerings indicate that the Jesuits had not yet succeeded in suppressing the Huron custom of burying food and trinkets with the dead and they suggest that the pot may have been broken deliberately, to permit its spirit to escape. One of the Indians who was buried in this cemetery had died as the result of a gunshot wound in the head (ibid. 94).

The outer court was separated from the inner one by a palisade that was also flanked along the east side by a ditch. This outer court had a pentagonal blockhouse at the south end and, being itself surrounded by a palisade, it provided the inner court with a second line of defence. Post molds indicated that a seventy-foot longhouse had been erected in this court, which Jury has identified as the area to which non-Christians were admitted during the daytime only. The historical evidence suggests that this part of Sainte-Marie was completed by 1642, or 1643 at the latest.

In the layout of this section of the Jesuit settlement, we see various expressions of Lalemant's concern for authority and discipline. By forbidding entry into the inner court to non-Christians and not permitting the latter to sleep at Sainte-Marie, the privileged relationship that had already been accorded to Christian Indians was further emphasized. The building of the church also eliminated the need to admit Indians to the chapel that had been erected in what became the European section of the settlement. The public services that impressed Indian converts were transferred to the church, while the chapel was transformed into a setting for the Jesuits' own devotions. While privileged male converts may have been admitted to the Jesuits' living area, especially when they were performing retreats or spiritual devotions, the construction of the church made possible a total separation between the Jesuits' living area and the part of the settlement to which converts were admitted. The creation within the heart of this mission headquarters of an all-male, European section, completely separated from the world around it, gave physical embodiment to Lalemant's concern to maintain the detailed forms, as well as the spirit, of religious devotion among the Jesuit missionaries. In 1641 Brébeuf noted in a letter to Mutius Vitelleschi, the general of the Society of Jesus, that religious discipline was being enforced among the Jesuits in the Huron country exactly as in the great colleges of Europe and that the punctual observance of all the rules was being increased day by day (Thwaites 1896–1901, 20:103). Brébeuf's allusion to boarding schools was aimed at Lalemant and his comment may be construed as a veiled criticism of Lalemant's notorious emphasis on rituals and forms.

The northern half of Sainte-Marie, which Jury calls the "European Compound," contained many more buildings than did the Indian Compound and was more complicated in its layout. Immediately to the north of the Indian Compound was the "South Court," which was surrounded by a wooden palisade and separated from the living area to the north by a deep ditch. Inside the South Court were three European-style buildings. Two were built of earth-packed walls, while the third was of vertical cedar posts, flattened on the inside and plastered with mud both inside and out. None of these buildings had cellars, nor was anything noted inside them that would indicate that they had been used as living quarters or workshops. Jury and Jury (1954:78) have suggested that these buildings may have been storehouses. Supplies brought from Quebec could have been kept in this court, and, since it adjoins the Indian Compound, it is possible that it was from here that the Jesuits' assistants carried on their trade with the Huron. It was also in this area that Jury found traces of a three-foot-square set of timber molds that led to the riverbank. He has interpreted these as the remains of an escape tunnel (ibid. 78–81).

North of the main ditch, which bisects the site in an east-west direction, was a palisaded rectangle that appears to have been the main living area for Europeans. Jury has called this the "North Court" and interprets it as made up of an area facing east that was fortified with four stone bastions and which gave access to a large quadrangle flanked with wooden buildings, which extended almost to the bank of the river. Jury has interpreted these buildings, all of which had mud-packed walls, as serving a variety of functions: some as dwellings, others as a chapel, cookhouse, blacksmith shop, and carpentry shop. Two channels ran from north to south through this area. These carried water which flowed through underground wooden mains from springs located on the rising ground to the north. Both channels emptied into the main east-west ditch. At the extreme north end of the site was another quadrilateral courtyard, adjoining the North Court. It too was surrounded by a wooden palisade and in the northwestern corner was a large stone bastion. The remains of a large building that stood in this courtyard are interpreted as those of a barn and Jury and Jury have suggested that this area, as well as a row of what appear to have been stables along the west side of the North Court, constituted the farm buildings of the settlement.

CONTROVERSIES ABOUT SAINTE-MARIE

Unfortunately, there is still a good deal of uncertainty about the layout and history of the European Compound. Jury has not published a detailed account of his excavations at Sainte-Marie and the popular record of his work leaves many questions unanswered. In particular, difficulties arise when one tries to tie in Jury's findings with those made by Kenneth Kidd when he excavated the part of the North Court that lies inside the four stone bastions. Kidd's findings are described in detail in a report in which a very high standard of archaeological recording was achieved and which is one of the key publications of historic site archaeology in North America.

Jury's reconstruction of the layout of buildings in this area is based largely on grey-black soil stains, each about a foot wide, which indicate where earth-packed timber walls formerly stood. On the basis of these stains Jury delineated buildings which occupied three of the four sides of his proposed courtyard. The east side of the courtyard had, however, been excavated by Kidd. In this part of the site, and under and between the two eastern bastions, Kidd (1949a:87–88) recorded further soil stains of this kind, although the overall pattern was incomplete and what remained was highly confusing. What was clear was that throughout this part of the site these walls had been replaced by later ones constructed of stone or wood, although the floors and foundations of the wooden structures were preserved only where they had been charred (plate 41). Along what would have been the east side of Jury's quadrangle, Kidd (1949a:37–59) discovered the remains of two later buildings that had wooden floors and walls made of wooden stakes or upright timbers wedged into horizontal wooden sills. These sills were held in place and kept off the damp ground by iron clamps or wooden stakes. The buildings were better preserved on the west side than on the east, which suggests that they had burned when an east wind was blowing (plate 42). In his reconstruction of Sainte-Marie, Jury combined the smaller of the buildings that Kidd excavated with one of his own to make a single large building. In so doing, he seems not to have taken account that all four walls of Kidd's building were clearly defined, that his building was of earth-filled construction while Kidd's was of upright timbers, and, finally, that the more clearly defined of the two north-south trenches had run between these two structures.[7]

The condition of the stones in the fireplace of Kidd's (1949a:57–58) smaller building convinced him that this fireplace had been built late in the history of the settlement and was not used for long. The superimposition found throughout this part of the site suggests that extensive rebuilding went on in the later years of occupation. Older buildings, with walls filled with earth and stone, were replaced by new ones of timber construction. This rebuilding may have been limited to the eastern part of the North Court, where Kidd excavated. It is possible, however, that it was more extensive and that later structures were dug away without being noticed by Jury in the heavy deposits of ash, charcoal, and burned timbers that he says covered large areas of the site (Jury and Jury 1954:39). If there was a general replacement of earth-filled walls with wooden ones, this might indicate that the building nearest the river in the South Court was built somewhat later than its nearest neighbours (ibid. 77).

It is also likely that the stone bastions flanking the eastern entrance to Sainte-Marie were constructed late in the history of the settlement. The

A—Residence

B—Chapel

C—Storage pit

D—Southwest Bastion

E—Southeast Bastion

F—Northeast Bastion

G—Northwest Bastion

H—North Curtain

J—East Curtain

K—East Postern

L—Masonry Wall

M—Masonry Wall

N—Forge Flue Foundation

O—Masonry Foundation
  Wall

P—Double Hearth

Q—Refuse Pit

R—Central Hearth

S—Chapel Hearth

T—Well

V—Central Ditch

W—Main Moat

X—West Moat

Y—False Wall

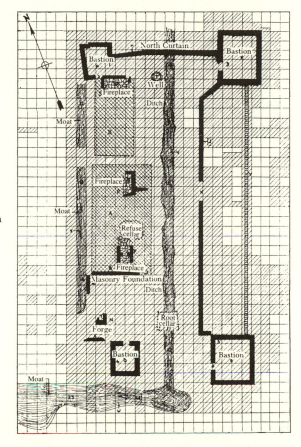

PLATE 41. *K. E. Kidd's plan of features revealed by the excavation of the central part of Sainte-Marie I. The arrangement of buildings should be compared with that proposed by Wilfrid Jury for the same part of the site. Courtesy K. E. Kidd and University of Toronto Press.*

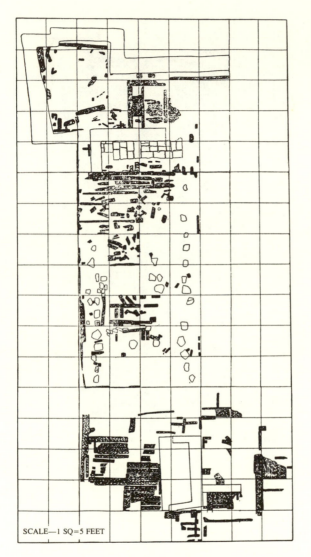

SCALE—1 SQ=5 FEET

PLATE 42. *Plan of a portion of Kidd's excavation, showing the remains of wooden flooring. This shows in its entirety the remains of the northernmost of the two buildings Kidd excavated within the area of the stone walls. The better preservation of the wood on the west side of the building results from greater charring and suggests that an east wind was blowing when the buildings were burned. Courtesy K. E. Kidd and University of Toronto Press.*

evidence for this is clearest for the northeast bastion, which covers the remains of a functionally similar structure built of *colombage pierroté* rather than stone (Kidd 1949*a*:55; plate 43). There also appear to be wooden prototypes for the stone walls joining these bastions. This indicates that stone fortifications replaced earlier wooden ones. There is some suggestion of haste in the later phases of the work and more than a little evidence that it was never finished. The northwest bastion is irregular in shape and far inferior in the quality of its construction to the others (Kidd 1949*a*:71). It may well have been altered in the course of its construction in order to hasten the progress of the work; however, the small south-west bastion seems to have been covered inside and out with a layer of hard white plaster (ibid. 65). Other bits of masonry have been interpreted as parts of a plan to join the four bastions with stone walls, in order to enclose a heavily fortified citadel within Sainte-Marie. If so, this work was abandoned before it was completed (ibid. 77–79).

Kidd and Jury also differ in their interpretation of the stone walls along the eastern perimeter of this part of the site. Jury (and Jury 1954:54) judges them to have been built of stone to a height of nine feet or more, whereas Kidd (1949*a*:36, 75) regards them as low curtain walls that were probably supplied with wooden superstructures. Jury (and Jury 1954:55) has used these walls to reconstruct a long, narrow building between the eastern bastions of Sainte-Marie, with the main entrance to the European Compound running through the centre of it and he has suggested that this building probably served as a barracks. Curiously, all but the northern portion of the east wall of this proposed building was of stone, while the latter, though an exposed outer wall, would have been built of timber (ibid. 55–56). Moreover, traces were found of a wooden palisade running between the north and south bastions, but farther east than either of these rows of stones. Kidd (1949*a*:77) has interpreted the east "wall" of this building as a mere line of stones that was intended to mark the line of a single stone wall that was later built twenty feet farther west. Since Kidd excavated this part of the site, his interpretation deserves more careful consideration than Jury and Jury have given it. It appears that much rebuilding was going on in this area about the time Sainte-Marie was abandoned. Half finished, half dismantled, and temporary constructions may be conflated in the archaeological record.

It is possible that the stone fortifications were begun in the spring of 1647, following the arrival of Pierre Tourmente late the previous year (Thwaites 1896–1901, 28:233). A growing concern with defence at this time is shown by the dispatch of a small cannon and a number of soldiers

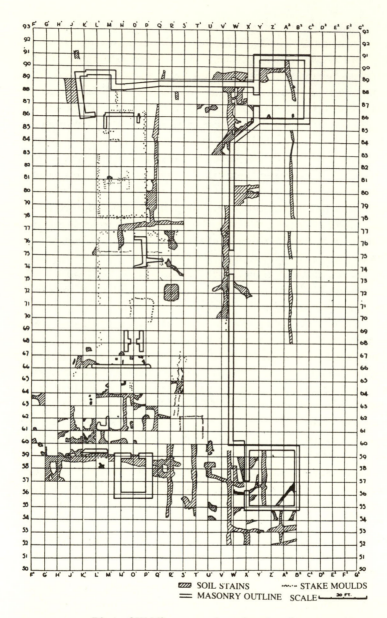

PLATE 43. *Plan of Kidd's excavations showing the arrangements of post molds and soil markings. The soil stains around the northeast stone bastion suggest that it replaced an earlier, similar structure of wood or colombage pierroté. Courtesy K. E. Kidd and University of Toronto Press.*

to the Huron country in August 1648 (32:99). The cannon is probably the same one that was later taken to Christian Island and was found there in the present century (Kidd 1949*a*:plate II*b*). A considerable amount of energy must have been expended on the erection of these stone fortifications. Much of the rock that was used came from granite boulders that were collected nearby, about half of which were cut and trimmed before being used (ibid. 64). Flat limestone rocks, probably brought on a barge from Flat Rock Point near Port McNicoll, were used for corners or for chinking as well as for building fireplaces in some of the houses. It is uncertain whether the stone-laying operations came to an end with Tourmente's departure in 1648, or whether they continued under someone else's direction until 1649 (Jones 1908:378; Thwaites 1896–1901, 33:253). The speed with which the stone work was erected at Sainte-Marie II, under very trying circumstances, suggests that the work at Sainte-Marie I could have been finished in a relatively short period of time. It is possible that the north bastion, which was also of stone, was built about this time (Jury and Jury 1954:25). It is unclear whether this bastion was to afford increased protection to the route north, or if it was part of a plan for the more extensive rebuilding of Sainte-Marie in stone.

A final major problem in the reconstruction of Sainte-Marie is posed by the ditches associated with the North Court. The most prominent of these were the deep east-west ditch on the south side of the court and the two shallower north-south trenches that joined it. Originally it was assumed that these ditches had been built for defensive purposes. While most of the main ditch was above present river level, if in former times the level of the river had been higher, this section of the system might have been a moat used to unload canoes or barges laden with stone. Enlargements along the moat were interpreted as unloading basins; however, the discovery that the original pilings lining this ditch were burned off only about a foot above the present river level demonstrates that the Wye River stood at about the same height in 1649 as it does at the present time (Russell 1965:14). An alleged drop of four and a half feet in the level of the river since 1820 cannot be extrapolated back to the seventeenth century.

Wilfrid Jury uncovered the remains of wooden mains that brought spring water into the two north-south ditches. Jury and Jury (1954:60–61) pay scant attention to the more westerly and prominent of these ditches, but interpret the eastern one as part of a system of locks that permitted boats to be raised from the level of the Wye River into the heart of the settlement. They argue that this channel facilitated the building of the fort and the unloading of canoes (Jury and Jury 1954:61–75). Although

Jury's theory of locks has been incorporated into the Ontario government's reconstruction of Sainte-Marie, it has been viewed with misgivings
by historians and archaeologists. Since no detailed account of what was
found has been made available, it is impossible to evaluate the validity of
the present reconstruction satisfactorily. In spite of this, serious objections
can be raised against Jury's interpretation. Even allowing for a greater
supply of water in the seventeenth century than at present, the operation
of the locks would have been a slow process. One can scarcely credit that
Frenchmen or Indians, who made over thirty-five portages on their way
from the St. Lawrence, would have considered a series of locks at Sainte-
Marie as worth the trouble that it took to build and operate them. The
twisting nature of the waterway also makes it unsuitable for transportation
and, as W. A. Russell (1965:14–15) has pointed out, the locks are too short
to accommodate the normal-sized canoes that would have been used on
Georgian Bay. At most, the canal might have been used to raise small
barges loaded with stone, but this is an unlikely reason for such an elaborate
construction. Recognition of these difficulties led Russell to suggest that
the system might have been used to drive an undershot waterwheel, which
turned a gristmill to produce the flour and meal required by the settlement; however, only circumstantial evidence can be advanced in support of
this theory.

Moreover, still other problems require answers. The "upper lock" in
the system was located along the eastern north-south channel, and was
excavated and described in detail by Kenneth Kidd (1949a:61–64), who
interpreted it as a storage pit that had been constructed by the French
after they had ceased to use this water channel in favour of the one to the
west. His detailed description of this feature appears to rule out any
possibility of it having been a lock. On the other hand, the fact that the
stone wall between the northeast and northwest bastions was built so as to
pass over this channel and leave it open suggests that it may have been in
operation late in the occupation of Sainte-Marie and this may indicate that
the large quantities of seeds found in this pit were thrown in about the
time the site was abandoned. The pit itself and the two other so-called
locks discovered by Jury in the east-west ditch may have been chambers
for storing water to make a reasonable supply available for fires and other
emergencies.[8]

In all early seventeenth-century French settlements in Canada, much
trouble was taken to ensure good drainage and this was required by the
many cellars under the main buildings at Sainte-Marie. The system of
ditches at Sainte-Marie may have been to provide such drainage and, at

the same time, a controlled supply of drinking water for the settlement. Much of the system may have been cribbed with stakes and covered over for greater safety, cleanliness, and convenience.

In the reconstruction of Sainte-Marie, the western north-south channel has been totally ignored and several buildings, including the blacksmith's shop, have been erected where it stood. This has been done in spite of Kidd (1949a:86–87) having published clear evidence that this trench was open in 1649, when fragments of charred timber from an adjacent building collapsed into it. This trench appears to have been an open ditch, which probably passed between, rather than underneath, buildings before entering the main ditch.

I have not drawn attention to some of the problems involved in interpreting the archaeological evidence from Sainte-Marie in order to disparage the efforts that Jury has made to interpret these remains. It is important, however, to dispel the notion that his reconstruction of Sainte-Marie (plates 44, 45) is necessarily a duplicate of the original buildings. Not only do the interpretations of the archaeological evidence differ on many crucial points, but additions and rebuilding appear to have been going on up to the time the settlement was abandoned. No single reconstruction could hope to reconcile all of the alternative interpretations of the evidence or to reflect adequately the many transitions through which this site passed. Finally, we know of at least some projects that were never realized. In 1646 funds were provided to found a college in the Huron country, where young Indians would have been able to receive a Christian education without having to expose themselves to the dangers involved in travelling to Three Rivers or Quebec (Robinson, in Du Creux 1951–52:xiv). No doubt, this college would have been built at Sainte-Marie if time had been available or the state of the Huron country had allowed it. There is, however, no evidence that such an institution was founded prior to the collapse of the mission.

THE JESUIT ECONOMY AND MISSION PROGRAM

During the decade of its existence the missionaries endowed their settlement with a thriving subsistence economy. Already by 1636 they had brought a hen and a rooster from Quebec (Thwaites 1896–1901, 13:93, 101). The following year the Jesuits sowed a small plot of wheat at Ossossané so that wafers could be prepared for the Eucharist (15:137–39). With the founding of Sainte-Marie these first efforts at food production were

PLATE 44. *A general view of the modern reconstruction of Sainte-Marie, looking south. The European Compound is in the foreground. Courtesy Ontario Ministry of Natural Resources.*

PLATE 45. *A general view of the modern reconstruction of Sainte-Marie from the Wye River. Courtesy Ontario Ministry of Natural Resources.*

expanded greatly. The site was chosen with an eye to clearing fields and the first crops were harvested there in the autumn of 1640. By 1643 the Jesuits had sufficient reserves of corn that they could dispense it to their converts during the famine of that year (27:65–67), and in the final years of the mission they boasted of their settlement's self-sufficiency (32:61). Large crops of maize were harvested in order to provide food for both Indian visitors and the French themselves (19:135). At the same time, the Jesuits continued to buy corn from the Huron in good years in order to build up their reserves against an emergency.[9]

While there is no direct evidence that barley, wheat, or oats were planted, these crops were grown at Quebec[10] and they may have been grown at Sainte-Marie as well (Jury and Jury 1954:33). In 1641 Charles Garnier requested his brother to send the seeds of various medicinal herbs from France so that these might be planted by the missionaries (Thwaites 1896–1901, 20:101). It has been argued that every European seed or root crop grown at Quebec must eventually have made its way to Sainte-Marie in order to add greater variety to the diet there (Jury and Jury 1954:34). It has also been suggested that an apple orchard was planted near Sainte-Marie, from which 200 years later the military garrison at Penetanguishene were able to obtain their trees. It is, however, difficult to estimate how much credence should be given to claims that this and other pioneer orchards in the area were started from trees in the "old Jesuit orchards" (ibid.). From 1637 on, the Jesuits manufactured their own wine, but did so from wild grapes (Thwaites 1896–1901, 15:137–39; 35:135).

It is also not certain where the Jesuits' crops were planted. Some vegetables were probably grown within the walls of Sainte-Marie, where they were tended by Brother Masson. The ash swamp to the southeast of the settlement prevented agriculture in that area, but fields might have been planted either on the rising ground to the north and northeast of the site, or more likely, as Jury and Jury (1954:34) suggest, on the fertile flats on the opposite bank of the river. The Jesuits had a boat that was used to ferry French and Indian visitors across the Wye River (Thwaites 1896–1901, 33:247) and this would have made it easy for workmen to farm on the opposite shore. Production was limited, however, since neither horses nor oxen were available for ploughing. Because of this the Jesuits' farming, like that of the Indians, was horticultural rather than agricultural. As the Jesuits learned to use maize flour in European ways, they may have come to prefer maize as an easier crop to grow in this fashion than was wheat.

While the Jesuits may never have sought to make European cereals more than a source of variety in a vegetable diet based mainly on Indian corn, they worked hard to acquire a more familiar European diet by introducing European farm animals. The first pigs may have arrived at Sainte-Marie about 1644, since it is claimed that the jaw of a boar estimated to be about five years of age has been found there (Jury and Jury 1954:33); the first pigs would no doubt have been dispatched from Quebec soon after they had been weaned. The Jesuits' workmen are reported to have taken calves to the Huron country in May and August 1646 (Thwaites 1896–1901, 28:187, 229–31) and a heifer was sent there in August 1648 (32:99). Conveying such animals to Sainte-Marie must have been a formidable task, even when the animals were young, and small barges may have been built to accompany the canoes. These animals multiplied in the Huron country and by 1649 pork, beef, and milk products were providing the French with a diet similar to what they were used to at Quebec or in France (33:255). At an earlier period, the absence of milk products made it difficult to recruit workers for the mission (Desjardins 1966:39–40). Likewise, while most clothes and luxury items such as glassware continued to be imported from Quebec, many of the necessities of the mission eventually were manufactured on the spot. These included most goods made of wood, leather, and iron. The blacksmith manufactured not only the iron nails, fitments, and ornaments needed at Sainte-Marie, but also a considerable number of axes and other iron objects that the Jesuits traded with the Indians (Jury and Jury 1954:52; plate 46). He also appears to have repaired guns (Thwaites 1896–1901, 27:89).

Kidd (1949a:12) suggests that the Jesuits attempted to use Sainte-Marie to introduce new customs to the Huron. He thinks that it was meant in part as a model farm where the Huron would learn to tend domestic animals and to cultivate new species of fruits and vegetables. Perhaps too, the Jesuits wished to teach the Huron to manufacture pottery in the European style.[11] Insofar as Lalemant was taking the Paraguayan reductions for his model, he could have had such a plan in mind. What is lacking, however, for the Huron missions is evidence that even the slightest attempt was made to implement such a policy. The primary reason for transplanting French material culture to the Huron country seems to have been to make the lives of the Frenchmen who were living there easier and more secure. Eventually, Sainte-Marie might have been used for acculturative purposes, but these long-term aims do not explain what happened in the 1640s.

Lalemant's plan to persuade Christian families to leave their villages and settle around Sainte-Marie was soon abandoned. He was still hoping in the spring of 1641 that a reduction might be developed (Thwaites 1896–1901,

PLATE 46. *Iron axes recovered in the course of Wilfrid Jury's excavations at Sainte-Marie I. Courtesy Ontario Ministry of Natural Resources.*

21:141), but hereafter this plan is no longer mentioned. Lalemant had failed to reckon on the strength of village ties among the Huron. Even Christians remained too attached to their villages and clan segments to abandon them and settle near the French. Moreover, while the Jesuits had abandoned their residences at Ossossané and Teanaostaiaé in 1639 and 1640, these and other large villages continued to be the centres of their missionary activity; it was in them that the Jesuits spent most of their time and won by far the largest number of converts. It is, therefore, not surprising that in 1643, even before Lalemant was replaced as superior of the mission, the decision was taken to establish or re-establish Jesuit residences in these communities. This change made little difference to Jesuit routine as the priests already usually lived with Christian families when they made prolonged visits to the larger villages. Yet, the wheel had come full circle and the emphasis was once again being placed on encouraging the development of Christianity within Huron settlements, rather than on seeking to persuade individual converts to move elsewhere.

In the principal Huron communities chapels were enlarged, crosses erected, old kettles hung on poles to serve as bells, and Christian cemeteries consecrated and funerals solemnized in them (27:67). These communities served as headquarters for the Jesuits' work in neighbouring villages and became the foci of Christian religious life in each area. By 1646 the Jesuits had constructed chapels in these towns (29:259). Most appear to have consisted of ends of longhouses which the Jesuits' workmen partitioned off. Eventually, however, proper churches, probably resembling the chapel that had been erected by Brébeuf in Ossossané, were built in settlements that had large Christian congregations, such as Ossossané and Teanaostaiaé (33:259). The establishment of Christian cemeteries for each major community no doubt explains why so few graves were found at Sainte-Marie. Hereafter, only Christians who died at Sainte-Marie or who for special reasons requested it were buried at the Jesuits' headquarters. One such burial was of a child from Scanonaenrat in 1648–49 (34:111–15).

With the restoration of residences to the mission centres, the system that had existed prior to 1639 was in effect reconstituted, except that the Huron mission as a whole could now count on the support of a flourishing central headquarters. A considerable number of priests tended to the needs of this headquarters and all of the missionaries gathered there three times a year to confer about their work and encourage one another (29:257–59). Ideally, each mission was supplied with two priests who lived most of the year in the principal community of their mission.

As the years passed, the number of converts in the larger towns increased and they required the services of a resident clergy. To accommodate these needs more missions were established. A new mission was established at Scanonaenrat (St. Michel) in 1642, and another at Taenhatentaron (St. Ignace) in 1644. After the abandonment of Contarea in 1647, a separate mission was founded for the Attignawantan villages in the Penetanguishene Peninsula. This mission had its headquarters at Sainte-Magdelaine (33:143), which is identified as Arenté on the *Chorographia Regionis Huronum* (1660) and as Wenrio on the *Description du Pais des Hurons* (1651). For lack of missionaries Teanaostaiaé and Contarea were treated as a single mission in 1640–41 (21:169) and Scanonaenrat may have been attended from Taenhatentaron in 1646–47 (Jones 1908:360). The communities assigned to particular missions also varied from year to year. In 1641 the village of St. Jean, which was located in the northern part of the Sturgeon River Valley, was dropped from the Sainte-Marie mission, while the Attignawantan village of St. Francis-Xavier was added to it (Thwaites 1896–1901, 23:39). By 1648 twelve or thirteen unnamed villages were said to belong to this mission (33:143). In 1639–40 Scanonaenrat belonged to the mission of Teanaostaiaé, while in 1641–42 it was tended from Contarea (21:283). Likewise, Taenhatentaron was originally part of the Teanaostaiaé mission, but from 1640 until it became a separate mission it was serviced from Contarea (27:29; map 28). The manner in which individual villages were assigned first to one mission and then to another shows that the requirements of the mission and the growth of Christian congregations, rather than any concern for Huron tribal organization, were the principal factors determining the development of the mission system.

Brébeuf and the Neutral

In 1639 Jérôme Lalemant established a mission to the Tionnontaté in addition to the four that he set up for the Huron country. The following year the ambition of the Jesuits to work even farther afield led them to entrust the missions of Teanaostaiaé and Contarea to a single pair of priests and to establish new missions to the Neutral and Algonkians. The Jesuits had long desired to work among the Neutral, but had been prevented from doing so by a lack of manpower and by explicit orders that they should not attempt to do mission work among more distant peoples until they had scored substantial successes among the Huron (Thwaites

1896–1901, 21:187). Although the cutbacks that were involved seem to indicate that this effort to expand the scale of Jesuit operations was premature, Lalemant argued that he was justified in establishing a mission to the Neutral and looked forward to the time when a mission headquarters similar to Sainte-Marie would be built in their country. Because it was necessary to study the Neutral language Fathers Brébeuf and Chaumonot, who were both highly regarded for their linguistic skills, were chosen for this mission (21:187–89). It was decided that both of them should spend the winter in the Neutral country. In reaching this decision the Jesuits ignored longstanding Huron policy. Brébeuf had been living in the Huron country when Father Daillon's attempt to spend a winter among the Neutral and conclude a treaty with them had violently angered the Huron and confirmed their worst fears about the intentions of the Recollet priests. This was a precedent from which the Jesuits, and particularly Brébeuf, ought to have learned a lesson.

Brébeuf and Chaumonot left Sainte-Marie on 2 November with two servants, who were sent along so that the party might appear to be a regular group of French traders. Lalemant says that this was done so that the arrival of the priests would not alarm the Neutral, but it may also have been meant to deceive the Huron into believing that only a brief visit was intended and that the priests would return with the traders. The Huron were suspicious of the journey from the start. When the French arrived at Teanaostaiaé those who had promised to guide them to the Neutral country refused to do so, and the Jesuits had to be content with a young man they recruited on the spot (21:205). Leaving Teanaostaiaé, the Jesuits slept for four nights in the woods and on the fifth day arrived at the Neutral settlement of Kandoucho. From there they pressed on through a number of other villages until they came to Teotongniaton where Souharissen, the principal headman of the confederacy, was living. In Daillon's time this community, which the Jesuits describe as being in the middle of the country, had been called Ounontisastan.

The Jesuits' arrival spread fear in the villages they passed through, since their reputation as sorcerers had preceded them. These fears were largely calmed, however, by the Jesuits' pretext of having come to trade, and pursuing this role they were able to reach Souharissen's settlement in safety. There they were informed that Souharissen was at war and would not return until the following spring. The Jesuits presented a collar of 2000 beads to the town council and explained that they wished to form a special alliance with the Neutral by persuading them to become Christians. The council claimed that it lacked the authority to accept this present but

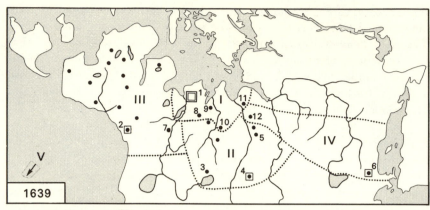

SAINTE-MARIE □

• Huron settlement   □ Mission centre   ..... Mission area, as far as known

NAMES OF VILLAGES

1. Sainte-Marie (Jesuit headquarters)
2. Ossossané
3. Scanonaenrat
4. Teanaostaiaé
5. Taenhatentaron
6. Contarea

7. St. Francis-Xavier
8. Ste Anne
9. St. Louis
10. St. Denis
11. St. Jean
12. St. Joachim

NAMES OF THE MISSIONS TO THE HURON
(numbered in order of foundation)

    I. Sainte-Marie to the Ataronchronon
   II. St. Joseph to the Attigneenong-
       nahac
  III. La Conception to the Attignawan-
       tan

   IV. St. Jean-Baptiste to the Arendar-
       honon
 VIII. St. Michel to the Tahontaenrat
    X. St. Ignace
   XI. Ste Magdelaine

MISSIONS TO OTHER TRIBES

    V. The Apostles to the Tionnontaté
       a. St. Jean at Etharita
       b. St. Mathias at Ekarenniondi
   VI. The Angels to the Neutral
  VII. The Holy Ghost to the Nipissing

   IX. Ste Elizabeth to the Onontchat-
       aronon
  XII. St. Pierre (Manitoulin Island)
 XIII. St. Charles (Algonkians)

N.B. Mission boundaries often unknown.

MAP 28. *Centres and boundaries (where known) of Jesuit missions to the Huron from 1639 to 1648.*

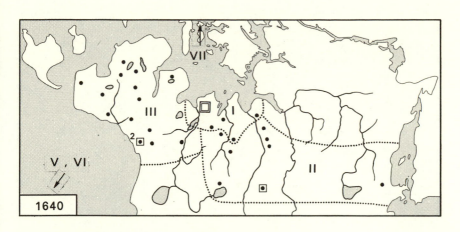

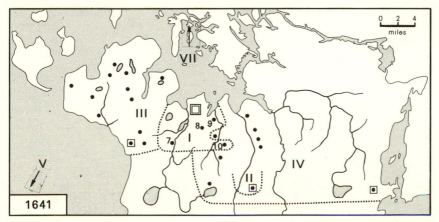

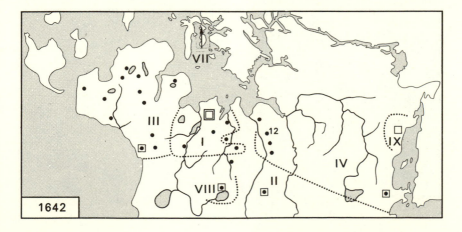

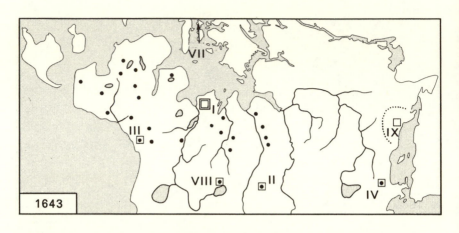

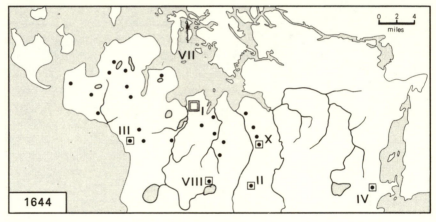

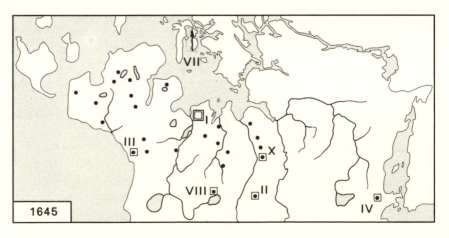

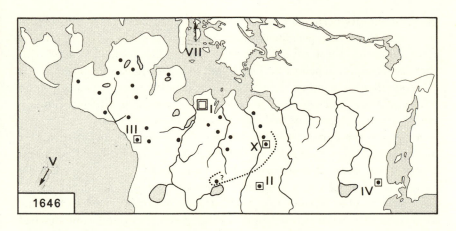

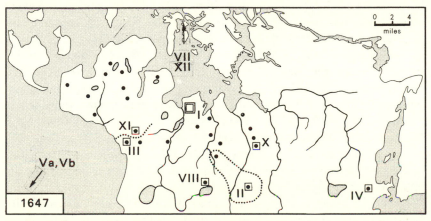

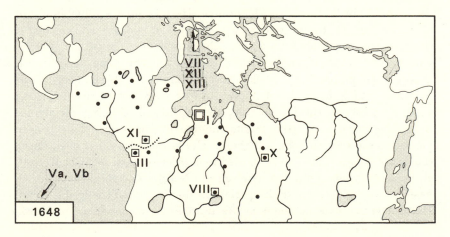

gave the Jesuits permission to remain in the country until Souharissen returned. Once this permission had been granted the French laymen returned to the Huron country with their skins. The Jesuits travelled with them as far as Kandoucho and then began to move systematically from one Neutral village to another, doing what they could to instruct people. In the course of their journey they passed through eighteen villages, possibly reaching Onguiaahra near the Niagara River (21:207–11).[12]

As soon as the Huron realized that the Jesuits were intending to winter among the Neutral, they sought to have the priests withdrawn. The Huron charged that Brébeuf had travelled south to make an alliance with the Seneca and that he was urging the Seneca to destroy those Huron whom the Jesuits had been unable to kill with their witchcraft. The Jesuits in the Huron country were warned that similar journeyings and rumours had been responsible for Brûlé's death eight years before. The Huron, however, aimed their most persuasive propaganda at the Neutral. They told the Neutral that the Jesuits had first plotted to destroy the Huron by witchcraft and were now plotting to kill them in a similar manner. As these stories spread through the Neutral country the Jesuits became ever greater objects of fear and hostility. It was also rumoured that Brébeuf had come south to bewitch the Seneca and cause them to die in retaliation for the Seneca having slain Chihwatenha (21:209–11). This story must have frightened the Neutral not only because of what it implied about Brébeuf's power, but also because if the Seneca blamed the epidemic that was raging in their country on the Jesuits, they might hold the Neutral responsible for letting the latter approach their borders.

Awenhokwi, the nephew of a Huron headman, visited many of the Neutral villages seeking to persuade their headmen that in self-defence they should kill Brébeuf and Chaumonot. He presented a valuable gift of nine iron hatchets to the confederacy council and told the Neutral that if they had not already slain the Jesuits, the Huron were prepared to do so as soon as they returned to the Huron country. At the same time he was making these proposals Awenhokwi befriended the Jesuits and urged them to travel with him, no doubt hoping to lead them into a trap (21:213; 34:173). Although the Huron were too frightened of losing their trade with the French to kill the Jesuits themselves, many would have been pleased to see someone else kill them. The Huron also must have hoped that if the Neutral could be persuaded to murder Brébeuf and Chaumonot, all hope of a trading alliance between the Neutral and the French would be eliminated. The same trading relations that protected the Jesuits in the Huron country exposed them to the murderous machinations of Huron politicians when they visited other tribes. Fortunately for the Jesuits the Neutral saw through these plots and were unwilling to oblige the Huron.

A Huron named Oëntara visited the Neutral settlements and repeated all of the accusations of sorcery that the Huron had made against the Jesuits in previous years. He denounced their religious observances and use of writing as proof of sorcery and stated that the Jesuits' aim was to kill all the Indians they could. Oëntara advised the Neutral that unless they wished to see themselves destroyed, they should close their longhouses against the priests and refuse to listen to them. He also confronted Brébeuf in a council and while Brébeuf believed he had cleared himself of the accusations that were made against him, many other Huron arrived at that time who reaffirmed Oëntara's charges. These accusations so frightened the Neutral headmen and elders that they held a meeting at which they decided that even in Souharissen's absence, the Jesuits' presents should be returned to them. In this way the headmen withdrew their sanction for the Jesuits to remain in their country. They also told Brébeuf that if the Jesuits had any consideration for preserving good relations between the Huron and the Neutral, they should leave immediately (21:213–17).

In spite of this warning Brébeuf and Chaumonot refused to leave. For a month and a half they continued to wander from one village to another. They were met with open hostility on every hand, often being forbidden to enter a single house. They were unable to write or even to wash their clothes without being accused of practising witchcraft and when they were given food their hosts were too frightened to eat from the same pots that they did. The Jesuits were forced to pay dearly in trade goods for any hospitality they received, while the Neutral would not accept freely given presents from them for fear they were bewitched (21:219–21).

The Neutral headmen kept warning the Jesuits that Seneca visitors might slay them and pointed out that since the last council meeting no one was under any obligation to protect them. Individual Neutral attempted to intimidate the priests and in their presence there was much banter about killing and eating them. In spite of such intimidation, which was no doubt meant to frighten the Jesuits into leaving, no real harm was done to them (21:221–23).

An exception to this ill treatment was found in the village of Khioetoa, which was inhabited by a considerable number of Wenroronon refugees. These people knew about the good treatment that the Jesuits had given to the Wenroronon when they had arrived in the Huron country, and for this reason they treated the Jesuits well and listened to them. Among them the Jesuits managed to baptize a few elderly persons and some sick children

(21:231–33). Eventually, however, as the hostility of most Neutral continued to grow, the Jesuits deemed it expedient to return to Kandoucho where they believed themselves to be the least unwelcome. They were halted by a snowstorm in Teotongniaton and there they were given shelter by an old woman who proved to be well disposed towards them. They stayed with her for almost a month, during which she helped them to draw up a dictionary and syntax comparing the Huron and Neutral languages (21:229–31). In spite of arguments and threats from the other villagers and even from people living in the same house, this woman refused to drive the Jesuits away. Because of this she and her father, who approved of her action, were accused of being sorcerers although nothing came of this (21:227). Nevertheless, she was unable to prevent other members of her household from attacking Chaumonot or other Neutral from robbing the two missionaries of their possessions (21:229). The individualism that was so highly prized by Iroquoians is exemplified by this woman's steadfast friendship for the Jesuits.

Throughout the winter the Jesuits in the Huron country received little news from Brébeuf or Chaumonot, since the Huron entrusted with their letters frequently threw them away either from malice or more often from fear of witchcraft. Rumours circulated, however, that they were in great danger and on the basis of these reports it was decided that a rescue party should be sent to fetch them home. Robert Le Coq, Teondechoren, another Huron from Ossossané, and an unidentified Frenchman made up this party which had the two Jesuits back to Sainte-Marie by 19 March 1641.

The Huron were furious that Brébeuf and Chaumonot had spent the winter among the Neutral. Many may have believed that Brébeuf had gone there in order to conspire with the Seneca; but the popularity of this rumour is best interpreted as a measure of the widespread resentment towards the Jesuits that remained from previous years. For the average Huron few actions could have been more threatening than the Jesuits having dealings with the Huron's most dangerous adversaries. Among Huron traders, however, a more immediate fear must have been that if the Jesuits succeeded in establishing a mission among the Neutral, the Jesuits would attempt to conclude a separate trading alliance with them that would undercut the Huron as middlemen.

The effect of this resentment was quickly felt by the Jesuits. Soon after Chaumonot returned he was assigned to assist Father Daniel. When they reached Scanonaenrat a Huron youth hit Chaumonot on the head with a rock and grabbed a hatchet to kill him (21:235–37). While Lalemant states that the Huron was prepared to attack either priest, the fact that he assaulted Chaumonot may be evidence of the resentment that some Huron felt against him for his part in the Neutral mission. Other Huron, however, helped to rescue Chaumonot.

The anger that was directed against Brébeuf was far stronger and can be documented more certainly. It was clearly because of this anger that Brébeuf returned to Quebec early in the summer of 1641 and remained there until 1644. For reasons of discretion, the real reason for Brébeuf's departure is nowhere stated in the *Jesuit Relations*; Lalemant merely notes that in the course of his affairs he was compelled to send Brébeuf to Quebec (23:35). Brébeuf had broken his left clavicle in a fall on the ice while crossing Lake Simcoe on his return from the Neutral country and some writers have attributed his departure to this injury (Latourelle 1966:123; Talbot 1956:241–42; Jones 1908:324). It is very difficult to believe, however, that a man with a disabled arm would have left the relative comfort of Sainte-Marie and undertaken an excruciating journey to Quebec to seek help for such an injury. More significantly, it was two years before he disclosed the nature of his injury to a surgeon there. When Lalemant writes of sending Brébeuf to Quebec it is within the context of Huron rumours about him being bribed by the Iroquois. Brébeuf travelled in a convoy of two canoes manned by four French and six Huron, all of whom were Christians or converts undergoing intensive instruction (Thwaites 1896–1901, 23:35). One of the latter was Charles Tsondatsaa. The composition of the convoy and the haste with which it travelled to Three Rivers ahead of the other Huron traders suggests a concern for Brébeuf's safety at the hands of the Huron.

That care was needed is evident from a rumour that arose on the way down the Ottawa River. Brébeuf's canoes reached Three Rivers safely but some others that followed them were attacked by the Iroquois. This caused the Huron traders to speculate that Brébeuf was not attacked because he had a secret agreement with the Iroquois. A Huron who had escaped from the Iroquois said that the Iroquois confirmed that Brébeuf had talked with the Seneca the previous winter. He also claimed that the Mohawk had recently met Brébeuf at night and that he had given them presents and told them where they might ambush the Huron who were following him (21:75–77; 23:35–37). According to this Huron Brébeuf aided the Iroquois because he wished to exterminate the Huron. This improbable rumour indicates how deeply the Huron hated and feared Brébeuf and explains why a series of excuses were found to keep him at Quebec and Three Rivers until Huron anger had cooled. Even after Brébeuf returned to the Huron country he was attached to the Sainte-Marie mission until his death, rather than working farther afield (34:169–71).

The miscalculation of the Neutral mission affected more than the lives of Brébeuf and Chaumonot. Although certain Neutral headmen invited the Jesuits to return to their country (23:183), the Jesuits feared Huron displeasure to the point where they felt obliged to abandon this mission (23:179–81). To help compensate for this, a number of Huron Christians visited the Neutral in 1642 and 1643 and instructed them. One of these native preachers was Etienne Totiri from Teanaostaiaé. He visited one of the northern Neutral villages in the company of his brother. Another was Barnabé Otsinonannhont from Scanonaenrat, who went to the heart of the country and made a longer stay there. His work was of particular importance as he was one of the leading headmen of his tribe and had numerous trading partners among the Neutral. All of these men probably did their preaching in the course of regular trading activities. Yet their influence among the Neutral was no doubt greater because of this, and in the spring of 1643 about 100 Neutral came to visit the Jesuits in the Huron country (27:21–25). In spite of this, the Jesuits' mission to the Neutral was never re-established and there is no evidence that these indirect mission efforts had any more substantial results.

It is even more indicative of the depth of Huron feeling that their resentment also brought an end, albeit a temporary one, to the Tionnontaté mission. In the winter of 1640–41 Fathers Garnier and Pierre Pijart spent several months among the Tionnontaté. They found themselves better treated than they had been the year before (20:97), although their presents were rejected by the Tionnontaté council as they had been by the Neutral one (21:179). Nevertheless, Huron accusations of sorcery continued to generate fear and resentment of the Jesuits (21:177). On one occasion, while they were travelling from one village to another they were knocked down and their assailants shouted that they were dead men, but in spite of this nothing happened to them. While some headmen were convinced that the Jesuits wished to destroy the Tionnontaté and one of them ordered the priests to leave the country, the missionaries generally found themselves favourably received in the villages and were able to baptize a few children (21:179–85).

Despite this substantial progress, in 1641 it was decided that the Tionnontaté mission would be abandoned. One reason that was given was that more attention needed to be paid to the Huron missions (21:283), but Huron opposition was probably the key consideration. In 1641–42 the work of the Jesuits among the Tionnontaté was confined to a few brief journeys, which did not arouse the antagonism of the Huron; hereafter the Tionnontaté were left alone until 1646. A few Tionnontaté Christians are reported to have left their country and settled near Sainte-Marie so as not to lose contact with the Jesuits and others visited the Jesuits from time to time (21:283; 23:179–81).

The Huron Church

THE JESUITS ADOPT A HARD LINE

Although the missions to the Neutral and Tionnontaté had suffered a severe setback, from 1640 onwards the Jesuits began to enjoy success in their efforts to convert the Huron. After most of their former converts had abandoned their profession of Christianity during the smallpox epidemic, the Jesuits acknowledged that in their haste to convert the Huron they had adopted too lax a standard for baptism. It was therefore decided that converts would have to be instructed and tested more thoroughly than they had been in recent years before they could be baptized (Thwaites 1896–1901, 26:213; 30:115). By this time the developing linguistic skills of the Jesuits made it possible for them not only to explain the details of their dogmas (28:65) but also to understand the intricacies of Huron religion as explained to them by their converts. This new knowledge convinced the Jesuits that they had erred in believing that there was little to native religious beliefs and that all that was required to convert the Huron was to convince them of the truth of Christian teachings. It was recognized for the first time that the Huron had a complex set of beliefs which had to be understood and counteracted before a genuine conversion was possible (23:151–53). To prevent backsliding and to encourage conversion the Jesuits continued to emphasize the torments that they believed would be inflicted on a non-Roman Catholic or an apostate after death. These threats were vividly impressed on the imagination of the Huron by explicitly drawing parallels between the sufferings of the damned and the torments that the Huron inflicted on prisoners of war.

Few Huron desires were so selfish or materialistic that the Jesuits disdained to make use of them in order to induce Huron to want to become Christians. Tangible rewards of many kinds were lavished on converts, which exploited their acquisitiveness or sense of need. One old man named Atiessa was accused by his fellow villagers of having converted only in order to obtain a blanket from the Jesuits (23:51). In times of famine and other difficulties the Christians were the first, and sometimes the only, Huron to receive charity from the Jesuits; indeed, the Jesuits described the food that was distributed in the famine of 1643 as a public testimonial to the close union that existed between them and the Huron Christians (27:65).

The advantages Christians enjoyed when they traded at Quebec and Three Rivers had long been an inducement for Huron traders to convert. More psychological pressure was brought to bear on these traders in 1641 when Montmagny gave his annual presents to the Huron. On this occasion he stated that these presents were given not solely on account of the French-Huron alliance, but also as a pledge of the truth of what the Jesuits were saying. This affirmation was widely discussed in Huron councils after the traders returned home. Many headmen believed that the French traders would soon insist on at least a nominal adherence to Christianity as a prerequisite for their continued friendship. As a result of this belief the Jesuits in the Huron country claimed to have considerably larger audiences when they preached to the Huron (22:311). There can be no doubt that trade played an important role in encouraging Huron men to become Christians at this time. By 1648 when less than fifteen per cent of the Huron population was Christian, over half of the 250 traders who came to Three Rivers either had been baptized or were receiving instruction (32:179).

The sale and distribution of muskets only to Christians became another strong inducement for young and middle-aged men to seek baptism after Charles Tsondatsaa became the first Huron to own a gun in 1641. By 1643 twenty-two men in a single war party were Christians and the Jesuits were informing their readers that God seemed to intend selling guns only to Christians to be a legitimate way to render Christianity acceptable among the Huron (25:27). It may be that it was specifically in order to be able to buy guns that young men were willing to spend a winter in the Jesuit school at Quebec or Three Rivers. This may also explain why men who were actively engaged in warfare began to express a desire for baptism and to learn about Christianity from their fellow warriors (23:199–203; 28:89–91). In dangerous situations Huron Christians sometimes granted preliminary baptisms to fellow warriors who might not live to return to the Huron country. Because of the abhorrence that the Huron felt about being separated from their kinsmen after death, the conversion of a warrior often led to the conversion of his whole family. In this way the Jesuits were able to start a snowballing process which they had good reason to believe would eventually lead to the conversion of whole villages and tribes (29:277–79).

Had the Jesuits been willing to baptize every Huron who expressed the desire to become a Christian, they might quickly have acquired a series of congregations made up of nominal Christians. The Jesuits were aware of this and were determined to use the materialistic desires of the Huron only as a means of bringing pressure to bear on potential converts to undergo prolonged instruction. By requiring such people to offer proof of their ability to live as Christians prior to baptizing them, the Jesuits were, in effect, compelling them to make radical changes in their behaviour and to acquire a working knowledge of basic Christian doctrines insofar as the Jesuits could make these intelligible. It was the Jesuits' hope that this would lead to understanding and eventually produce genuine Christians. Such methods would have seemed not unusual to most seventeenth-century Europeans, who viewed censorship, enforced church attendance, fines, public penances, brutal tortures, and public executions as efficacious means of promoting and safeguarding religious values. Except in cases of serious illness, probationary periods of one to two years were now required prior to baptism (30:115). Once an individual was deemed worthy of baptism he was sent to Sainte-Marie, where he was carefully examined before the ceremony was performed. Most baptisms were at Christmas, Easter, and Pentecost, when large numbers of Christians assembled at mission headquarters (23:21–23).

The new Jesuit policy was facilitated by the cessation of the epidemics and the abundant harvest that was collected in the autumn of 1640 (21:131). The return of prosperous conditions led to a reduction in overt hostility towards the Jesuits, although many Huron continued to fear them. Some became alarmed when they saw a Jesuit because they feared that he would bring sickness to their village; others demanded assurances of longevity before they would consent to have dealings with any of them. Many Huron professed to be interested in what the Jesuits said, no doubt hoping that in this way they could avoid becoming victims of sorcery without having to live as Christians (21:133–35). Gradually, however, baptism began to lose its odious connotations of sorcery and came again to be viewed as a means by which initiates were able to join relatives in heaven rather than in the traditional villages of the dead. These conditions provided a milieu in which the Jesuits, under the protection of the French-Huron trading alliance, were able to carry out an effective program of instruction.

In spite of the more than 1000 Huron who were baptized during the smallpox epidemic, by the spring of 1640 only a few Huron professed to be Christians. Between the summers of 1640 and 1641, 100 Huron were baptized (20:99), of whom about sixty survived illnesses and other misfortunes to become professing Christians (20:103). The following year 120 persons were baptized (23:23), and in 1642–43 about 100 more (23:267; 26:213). Many were baptized in 1643–44 (27:69); over 170 in 1644–45 (28:61); and 164 in 1645–46 (29:261). This suggests an average of about 100 baptisms a year until 1643, and over 150 a year thereafter. Some baptisms were undoubtedly of people who were dying and a considerable number of Christian warriors were probably killed in encounters with the Iroquois. The figures suggest, however, that by 1646 there were probably about 500 professing Huron Christians.

CONVERTS

The Jesuits had their greatest success in the larger towns. This happened, in part, because the Huron headmen and traders who had the closest ritual and economic ties with the French lived in these communities. They were also the settlements that the Jesuits had chosen as their mission centres and where they spent the most time. It is no accident that after 1640 the majority of conversions were made in Ossossané and Teanaostaiaé, where the Jesuits had lived prior to the founding of Sainte-Marie (Thwaites 1896–1901, 23:151; 25:85).

The most flourishing of the Christian missions was at Ossossané (23:43). By 1643 there were already so many professing Christians in this town that the Jesuits and their converts were looking forward to it becoming entirely Christian and the first indigenous centre of Christianity in the Huron country (26:255). When the Huron were fearing an Iroquois attack in the winter of 1641, they asked the Jesuits to baptize the whole community so that all of its inhabitants might go to heaven together (23:107).

The nucleus of this church was the family of Chihwatenha, whose members were model Christians. In particular, Chihwatenha's brother Teondechoren was zealous in his support of the Jesuits. The village headmen began to seek his assistance in matters in which his friendship with the Jesuits and the French was thought to be of value (21:147–57). After he escaped from the Iroquois in 1643 his stories of Jogues's fortitude and his attribution of his survival to his faith in Christianity did much to enhance the prestige of the missionaries (26:233–43). Neither Teondechoren nor Chihwatenha's widow, Aonetta, expressed any doubts about

Christianity, although both lost young daughters through illness and this was widely interpreted as the result of their being Christians and refusing to allow curing rituals to be performed for them (23:59–61). Devotion to Chihwatenha's memory was undoubtedly an important factor inspiring his relatives to remain, as well as to become, Christians.

The most influential single member of the Ossossané church, after Chihwatenha's death, was René Tsondihwané (21:159–65). Tsondihwané was about sixty years old and was the head of one of the most important families in the town (19:239). He appears to have been baptized early in 1639 and although eleven people in his longhouse died of smallpox in the months that followed (19:211), he continued to profess to be a Christian; although at one point he yielded to his wife's demands and permitted Huron curing rituals to be performed for one of his daughters, who subsequently died (19:243–45). By 1640 Tsondihwané was recognized as the leader of the Ossossané congregation. In the absence of the missionaries, he kept the key to their chapel and conducted the prayers that were said there (21:159). In the autumn of 1642 he went hunting with his eldest son and while they were away he persuaded him to become a Christian (26:249–51). Tsondihwané was noted for his zeal in visiting the sick, instructing Christians, preaching to non-Christians, and saying long private prayers (23:77–81; 29:287–91).

Another convert was Charles Tsondatsaa, a relative of Chihwatenha and the son of Anenkhiondic, the principal headman of the Attignawantan (20:215). Although he was the leader of an important curing society, before the smallpox epidemic he had expressed a desire to become a Christian and during the epidemic he had permitted his relatives and even his own children to be baptized (20:215). In the spring of 1641 Tsondatsaa burned his hunting charms and publicly renounced the customs of his ancestors, but the Jesuits preferred to test his faith further before baptizing him (20:215–17). When he accompanied Father Brébeuf to Quebec in 1641, Montmagny publicly interceded on his behalf (no doubt following prior arrangement with the Jesuits) and he was baptized at Sillery on 26 June (20:217–31). After returning home Tsondatsaa insisted that his wife should allow herself to be baptized (20:225) and by 1642 there were twelve Christians living in his longhouse (23:93). Tsondatsaa appears to have gone each year to trade with the French. In 1642 he was attacked by the Mohawk and lost not only all of his trade goods but also a brother and son who were travelling with him (26:219). It must have been to avenge them that Tsondatsaa joined the Huron war party that went to the St. Lawrence Valley in 1644 (26:65).

About 1643 an important headman named Hotiaouitaentonk became a Christian (30:75). He too appears to have been a fur trader. The conversion of some of the principal inhabitants of Ossossané disposed many Huron to follow their example and eventually a number of whole families were converted. One man who was ill persuaded first his daughter and then a son to be converted. This, in turn, induced their mother to be baptized. Soon after, an entire family requested to be baptized at one time (26:223–25). These examples indicate the strong role that family loyalty played in the spread of Christianity.

Prior to 1642 Christianity made little progress in Teanaostaiaé (21:175). One of the few Huron who had been baptized before or during the smallpox epidemic and who continued to profess to be a Christian was an old woman Marie Outenen (23:121–23). Of greater importance was the family of Etienne Totiri. In the winter of 1641–42 they invited the Jesuits to construct a chapel at one end of their longhouse even though this deprived the dwelling of much of its storage space (21:285; 23:135). Totiri was related to some of the most important families in Teanaostaiaé. His mother, Christine Tsorihia, had been baptized in 1639 (26:289), and the rest of the family before 1642. These included Totiri's wife, Madeleine, his daughter Catherine, and his younger brother Paul Okatakwan. Totiri became the guardian of the chapel in Teanaostaiaé and also a catechist and prayer leader (29:275). This encouraged both Totiri and his wife to be zealous proselytizers. As we have already noted, it was Totiri and his brother who carried Christian instruction to the Neutral in the spring or summer of 1643.

The previous summer Totiri had been travelling with Isaac Jogues when the latter was captured by the Iroquois. Totiri escaped, but lost all of his trade goods and did not return to the Huron country until the following spring (26:259–61). In September 1643 he visited the Jesuits before leaving to avenge the attack of the previous year (26:291). Saouenhati was another individual who prior to the smallpox epidemic had professed the desire to become a Christian; however, during the epidemic he renounced such interests in order to avoid persecution. By 1642 he began to live like a Christian and claimed that he had never lost his faith in Christianity (23:139). In 1642 Saouenhati spent about a month in the hospital at Sainte-Marie and soon after this he was slain by the Iroquois while gathering hemp with other people from Teanaostaiaé (26:203–5; 23:241).

In 1642 the Jesuits greatly strengthened their position in Teanaostaiaé by baptizing a number of important residents. The most important was the forty-year-old warrior Ahatsistari (23:25). Ahatsistari had requested baptism in the spring of 1639, but at that time he had refused to give up certain practices of which the Jesuits disapproved (23:27). It is possible that his greater willingness to meet Jesuit demands by 1642 was the result of his desire to obtain a gun. Whatever his motives, he convinced the Jesuits of his sincerity and was baptized at Sainte-Marie on the Saturday preceding Easter. After Easter, Ahatsistari went to war against the Iroquois; he then travelled to Quebec with Totiri, Teondechoren, Tsondatsaa, and a number of other companions. On the way home he was captured by the Mohawk and tortured to death.

Ahatsistari's brief career as a Christian was important for the development of the Huron mission. Because he was a famous warrior, many young men were encouraged to become Christians. His conversion thus accorded social respectability to a trend that was already nurtured by the desire of these men to obtain guns. After he was slain, many of his companions were inspired to convert so that they would not be separated from him after death. Among these was his close friend Tehoachiakwan, who also lived in Teanaostaiaé. He was a famous warrior and one of the principal headmen of the Wenroronon who were living among the Huron. Tehoachiakwan had promised Ahatsistari that eventually he would become a Christian and rather than turning against the Jesuits when Ahatsistari was killed, his desire to be reunited with his friend after death led him to seek baptism immediately (26:293). Tehoachiakwan's baptism encouraged many Wenroronon to follow his example.

Of no less importance were the conversions of an important headman named Tsondakwa and his sister Andiora.[13] Since 1639 the Jesuits had stayed in Tsondakwa's longhouse when they visited Teanaostaiaé; although they would have preferred to live with Etienne Totiri in order to be near their chapel, they believed Tsondakwa's support to be of such importance that they dared not reject his hospitality (23:241). Tsondakwa had always professed friendship for the French, but being a headman he had refused to give up the responsibility for directing the traditional rituals for which his office made him responsible. He also refused to become a Christian because he did not want to be cut off after death from friends and relatives who were not Christians (26:265–269). In the autumn of 1642 he was with Thomas Saouenhati when the latter was killed by the Iroquois. Tsondakwa's desire not to be separated from Saouenhati after death finally led him to become a Christian and adopt his dead friend's Christian name (26:203–5, 265–67). After his conversion, the Jesuits were able to leave his longhouse and go to live with Totiri (23:241).

A clear example of the moral dilemma that faced converts to Christianity can be seen in the case of Assiskwa, a young headman from Teanaostaiaé. Assiskwa had demonstrated his sincerity to the Jesuits and was invited to Sainte-Marie to be baptized at Easter 1642. As he was about to enter the church, he felt himself seized by a supernatural force. He cried out that a spirit had entered his body and had ordered him to kill all the French since they were ruining the Huron people. He set off for home, but as he travelled through the villages of St. Jean and Taenhatentaron he burst into long-houses and went about smashing their contents. Since he was possessed by a spirit no one attempted to restrain him. When he returned to Teanao-staiaé he struck people and, when seized and questioned about his soul desires, he demanded that all the French should be killed. This statement released a wave of anti-Jesuit feeling throughout the community. Assiskwa then began to attack the Huron Christians and tried to break into their chapel.

When the Jesuits returned to Teanaostaiaé from their Easter assembly, they found that he had gone for almost a week without food or rest. Seeing them Assiskwa became calm, but for several days he continued to abuse them. Following this he reverted to his old self. He announced that the spirit that had been controlling him had departed and visited the Jesuits at Sainte-Marie to ask their pardon and to request that they proceed with his baptism (23:141–49). This was done several months later and he remained an ardent Christian (23:243). Assiskwa's crisis was probably only a more dramatic and public display of the doubts and social and moral confusion typical of most conversions at this time. In spite of such doubts, the baptism of several leading men in Teanaostaiaé within a short time played an important role in persuading other people, there and in surrounding villages, to follow their example (26:275–77). In particular, the Jesuits valued the moral example set by their lives and actions, which seemed in every way to live up to the Jesuits' expectations.

The work of conversion went on more slowly in Scanonaenrat. There were no Christians in the community prior to 1642 except Andehoua, who claimed to believe the Jesuits' teachings but does not seem to have professed his faith publicly. The Jesuits visited Scanonaenrat in the winter of 1641–42, but although they were listened to, no one expressed willing-ness to become a Christian (23:169–71). The first converts were the head-man, Paul Atondo, and his friend Okhukwandoron who had spent the winter of 1641–42 at the Jesuit school at Quebec. Following their return home, Atondo made a public profession of his new faith at a feast that he gave in his capacity as a headman. At this feast he renounced his former claims that the Jesuits had practised sorcery against the Huron. He gave further proof of his unwavering loyalty to the Jesuits after his niece died of illness and his sister was slain by Iroquois raiders. It was through his efforts and those of Okhukwandoron that a chapel was erected at Scanonaenrat in the autumn of 1642 and the village was made the centre of a new mission (26:293–99). These activities rekindled Andehoua's interest in Christianity and led to the conversion of Barnabé Otsinonannhont, who was one of the principal headmen of the town (26:307–9).

The Jesuits' work tended to progress more slowly in the eastern part of the Huron confederacy (33:141). At first considerable attention was paid to Contarea, which was not only the principal town of the Arendarhonon, but also the residence of the senior Huron ally and trading partner of the French. No doubt because of this alliance, both Atironta and his brother Aëotahon had requested baptism as early as 1641, although the Jesuits said they were not yet ready for it. Soon after, Atironta was slain and his brother was baptized prior to being installed as the new tribal headman of the Arendarhonon. The new Atironta was the first adult of this mission to be baptized in good health (23:159–61). His conversion induced many other Arendarhonon to ask for baptism, although the Jesuits selected carefully in order to maintain their standards (23:169). They erred seriously, however, when they agreed to baptize a shaman who had been frightened by their teachings about hell and had publicly thrown his charms into the fire. Before he was baptized he changed his mind and soon became one of their most dangerous opponents (27:33–35). In spite of their early successes, in the long run the Jesuits made little progress in Contarea and later the town was notorious for its aversion to Christianity (42:73). On the basis of existing evidence, it would appear that converting Taenhatentaron got started even more slowly than at Contarea (27:29). Eventually, however, a chapel and residence were established in the longhouse of Ignace Onaconchiaronk who was one of the richest men in the village and whose family appears to have been largely Christian (33:167).

Most Huron seem to have become Christians in order to obtain guns, more favourable trading relations, or other tangible benefits from the French, or to be able to join dead relatives in heaven; some, however, had other motives. A few converted to be able to refuse to participate in traditional rituals which required them to redistribute their possessions. Many Huron noted that Christianity made fewer material demands on a convert than did their own religion (23:129, 173), but very few consciously became Christians in order to escape from such responsibilities. Converts who did not find ways to compensate their fellow villagers for withdrawing from their traditional obligations found themselves in serious trouble.

After Onakonchiaronk was baptized in 1645–46, he soon found that the whole village had turned against him. Opportunities were sought to attack him and he was accused of being a sorcerer whom anyone had the right to slay as a public enemy (30:19–21). While the origin of this hostility is not explained, it undoubtedly arose because Onakonchiaronk was violating Huron rules of generosity.

When the Huron learned about Jogues's conduct after he had been captured by the Iroquois, many of them admired his courage and began to treat the Jesuits with more respect. All of the Christians who escaped from the battle were loud in their praise of Jogues and attributed their own safety to the Christian god (26:259). Those who escaped from the Mohawk country related additional tales of Jogues's courage. In the midst of battle Jogues had baptized the pilot of his canoe. This man named Atieronhonk later escaped from the Mohawk and, when he reached home, reported his experiences to everyone (26:187–89). After Bressani returned to the Huron country in 1645, the Huron examined his hands with admiration, noting where the Iroquois had cut off his fingers. The sufferings of Jogues and Bressani proved to them that the Jesuits were willing to suffer in order to live with them and that the Iroquois were, indeed, their common enemy. This, as Ragueneau noted, was a more persuasive preacher than all the words the Jesuits had uttered (30:69).

Although the Jesuits remained convinced that the consistency of their doctrine and the supernatural powers the Huron attributed to writing played major roles in the acceptance of their teachings, considerations of self-interest and of an emotional sort were probably considerably more important. As the general concern about the epidemics subsided, it again became possible for the missionaries to contact and influence Huron on an individual basis. At least a few converts regarded learning prayers and catechisms as an intellectual challenge and, in some families, this became a group activity (23:103). No doubt, these converts equated the learning of catechisms with mastering the myths and rituals of their own healing societies. Some Huron were genuinely interested in the theological content of the Jesuits' teachings, although these were couched in a cultural idiom that made it very difficult for the Huron to comprehend them. The Jesuits noted that the most intelligent Huron were often the hardest to convince of the validity of Christian beliefs (23:129). They also observed that the greatest difficulty that the Huron had was in understanding the notions of judgement after death and of the resurrection of the body (30:73). Explaining the former had been a longstanding problem.

THE SOCIAL IMPACT OF CHRISTIANITY

By 1640–41 the Jesuits had launched an ambitious scheme to counteract instability in Huron marriages in which one or both partners were Christians. It was noted that one of the main causes of divorce was a man's inability to provide the things that his wife and her family expected of him. Therefore, readers of the *Jesuit Relations* were requested to donate money that could be used to provide assistance to such families (Thwaites 1896–1901, 21:135–39). In some cases, perpetual annuities of ten or twelve écus were established with the understanding that Huron who were supported by these stipends should be given the Christian names of their benefactors. Although it is unclear how this money was spent, it was probably used to provide the heads of selected families with the trade goods they required. It was hoped that this charity would give the Jesuits sufficient influence to regulate the lives of the recipients and their families much as they wished. While this technique must have been effective only for controlling less productive families, according to Lalemant it resulted in the conversion of a goodly number of Huron (23:187–89; 27:69–71). Although this may be a pious exaggeration, we have here an early example of a later world-wide technique for enticing converts: "rice Christians."

The decision to live as the Jesuits required of a Christian must have been a very difficult one for any Huron to make, especially since the rationale for most of the rules that converts were asked to observe was not understood by them. The Jesuits now appreciated the important role that the traditional religion played in everyday Huron life and observed that it was more difficult to keep a Huron Christian than it was to convert him in the first place (28:55). The Jesuits also realized that the Huron depended on religious practices to cure the sick, ripen crops, and bring almost every kind of activity to a successful conclusion. In spite of this, to become a Christian the Jesuits still required a man or woman to renounce all of the charms and rituals that had hitherto provided them with a sense of security (23:185–87; 28:53). On a more general level, the Jesuits observed that the Huron had no concept of hierarchical authority nor did their laws permit the personal punishment of those who had committed crimes. It was concluded that this spirit of liberty was contrary to that of Roman Catholicism, which required men to submit their will and judgement to a law that was "not of this earth and is entirely opposed to the laws and sentiments of corrupt nature" (28:49–51).

The Jesuit missionaries recognized the degree to which Christianity was the expression of a coercive, state-organized society. They were, however, unable to transcend this limitation and search for a way to adapt Christianity to the needs of a tribal organization. Instead, while admitting that Huron society functioned well enough, they justified their own beliefs by concluding that Huron society was institutionally, as well as theologically, primitive. In order to provide the church with the authority required to enforce its decrees and to establish the punitive justice that Christian morality required, the Jesuits now foresaw that the Huron must be made to evolve some rudimentary state institutions. The implementation of such a scheme was impossible, however, until the Christians were in a majority in at least one large community. Until then, the Jesuits could only hope to restrain traditional practices among their followers.

When it came to providing moral support for their converts, the Jesuits were also not very successful. They vigorously attacked any reliance on dreams as guides to action without providing any other guide except an ill-defined and amorphous recourse to prayer (21:161–63; 30:43–45), which was also advocated as a general substitute for all charms and shamanistic practices. Because they still did not replace these time-honoured sources of moral support with more specific and more easily recognizable Christian substitutes, the Jesuits continued to undermine their converts' self-confidence. The temptation to have recourse to traditional aids was consequently very strong, and even long-standing converts required careful supervision to prevent backsliding. The situation was made worse by the converts' uncertainty concerning which aspects of their traditional culture were contrary to Jesuit teachings and which were not. Christian families would rehearse their weekly confessions before going to the priest, in the hope of sorting out such problems ahead of time. Most Huron seem to have been totally unable to distinguish between major and minor offences or even between permissible and impermissible behaviour (23:107–15). The result was uncertainty about even the most trivial actions. It seems certain that few if any Huron understood what Christianity as a whole meant to the Jesuits. They were attempting to satisfy the Jesuits by doing in a piecemeal fashion what was required of them.

THE DEVELOPMENT OF A CHRISTIAN FACTION

In order to protect converts from traditional influences, the Jesuits encouraged them to avoid contact with non-Christians as much as possible. As more Huron were converted, Sainte-Marie became the centre where, at the main Christian festivals and once every fortnight during the summer, large numbers of converts gathered for religious observances. At these assemblies converts would encourage one another and, under Jesuit guidance, would hold meetings to plan for the advancement of Christianity and for the eventual elimination of what they were taught to view as the paganism of their fellow tribesmen (26:211). A strong sense of Christian identity was also built up by the prayer meetings and church services that were held with some frequency in the larger settlements. In the absence of the priests converts acted as native preachers, instructing potential converts and leading public prayers (27:67–69). These meetings developed a sense of common identity among Christians and distinguished them from non-Christians (30:43). In an effort to maintain the ritual purity that was demanded of them by the Jesuits, Huron Christians broke many of their links with the rest of Huron society.

An example of this can be given in terms of its effect on a particular relationship. A non-Christian woman of high status wished to contract a ritual friendship with a Christian woman. This was an accepted thing to do, and as the friendship was greatly to the advantage of the Christian the latter readily agreed to it. The non-Christian sent her a dog, a blanket, and a load of firewood as presents and gave a feast to proclaim their new relationship. Later, however, the Christian woman and her husband learned that the non-Christian woman had sought this friendship after a spirit had ordered her to do so in a dream. As soon as this was known the husband returned the presents and repudiated the friendship on behalf of his wife. The Jesuits rejoiced that there was "no bond of friendship that Faith will not sever rather than see a Christian separated from God" (23:125).

As early as 1642 while they were gathered at Sainte-Marie a group of Huron Christians resolved, probably under Jesuit direction, that they did not wish to be buried alongside non-Christians in their village cemeteries, nor did they wish their bodies reburied at the Feast of the Dead (23:31). This resolution formally realized a desire to provide separate burials for Christians that the Jesuits had first tried to implement in 1637. By refusing to participate in what was the most sacred of Huron rituals and the supreme expression of community solidarity, these Christians were striking at the heart of Huron unity. They were also severing ties with their families and with other Huron on which their own sense of identity depended. In addition, they resolved that when travelling they would lodge, whenever possible, with other Christians rather than with their clansmen as they had been accustomed to do. They agreed to reveal their problems and difficulties only to one another and not to non-Christians. In this way it was hoped that the bonds of friendship uniting Christians could be made to exceed in importance all other bonds (23:31).

As early as 1641 groups of Christians were tending to travel together to Quebec, often in the company of the Jesuits or their lay assistants. By 1643 the Huron who came to trade at Three Rivers were publicly separated into Christian and non-Christian (traditionalist) groups. As might be expected the Christians played a prominent role in dealing with the French, while the traditionalists were reported to be decreasing both in numbers and boldness (23:267). Because of the shamanistic divinations associated with traditional warfare, Christians were also refusing to fight alongside non-Christians. When in the summer of 1642 a shaman predicted that Iroquois warriors would be located and defeated to the south, the Christians decided on principle that they could not seek the enemy in that direction. They set off by themselves towards the west. The Huron who went south encountered the Iroquois, but, lacking sufficient manpower, were defeated (26:175–79).

The Jesuits continued to forbid Christians to participate in any traditional religious rituals, which were a part of almost every public gathering or celebration. This resulted in physical as well as psychological hardships, since it deprived converts of most opportunities to eat meat and other delicacies (23:65, 187). When the Ononharoia was celebrated at Ossossané during the winter of 1641–42, the Christians met separately, not to guess each other's dreams but to state desires of a religious nature, such as to go to heaven or to live better. As everyone celebrating the Ononharoia had to pass through their longhouse, this was believed to be an effective means of disseminating Christian propaganda (23:103–5). Similarly, at the installation of an important headman an old man who was responsible for reciting the Huron creation myth, but who had become a Christian, insisted on reciting the Christian one instead. When the headman who was in charge of the investiture heard this, he requested the old man to stop and began to recite the traditional myth himself. After listening for a while the old man told the headman to be silent and denounced the traditional myth as a lie (30:61–63). Such attacks on cherished beliefs, combined with a refusal to participate in celebrations and curing rituals, emphasized the growing rift between Huron Christians and those who remained faithful to Huron traditions.

The increasingly frequent conversions of high ranking Huron posed crucial political problems. The Jesuits observed that to be a headman and a Christian was a contradiction in terms, since the principal duties of a headman consisted of "obeying the Devil, presiding over hellish cere-monies, and exhorting young people to dances, feasts, and most infamous lewdness" (23:185). Most headmen who became Christians seem to have tried to avoid such duties (23:109), which must have made the manage-ment of the country more difficult; however, when Assiskwa became a Christian he insisted on resigning his public office so as to break all of his connections with curing rituals (23:243). Yet, from all appearances, he continued to wield considerable influence in his village. Another headman, who is described as being one of the highest rank in the whole country, also renounced his office rather than participate in a non-Christian ritual. This led to a political crisis which it was feared might split his community apart. Finally an agreement was worked out, whereby the Christian continued to be a headman and to administer public affairs, while a deputy was appointed to take charge of traditional religious matters (28:87–89). This must have seemed a great victory to the Jesuits, as it set a precedent for separating political power from traditional religious beliefs. For the still small Christian community it represented further isolation from the majority of their people, while to the Huron as a whole it signified the erosion of their traditional culture and increasing social disintegration.

Until 1645 the zeal of Christian converts had largely confined itself to the longhouses of Christians and to separate assemblies. The Jesuits had persuaded converts to wear rosaries around their necks as a sign of their faith (26:287), but, in general, the Christians had avoided antagonizing their neighbours by a too public display of their new beliefs and practices. By 1645, however, the Christians felt sufficiently numerous and influential to abandon this façade. Since the 1630s most Huron had opposed the baptism of Iroquois prisoners, either because they believed that their souls should not be allowed to go to heaven or because they objected to the Jesuits showing any friendship for the Iroquois. Hence the Jesuits often found themselves objects of public abuse when they persisted in such endeavours and the Huron expressed their resentment by torturing the prisoners more cruelly (21:169–71; 23:33–35; 26:179–81). Converts sometimes attempted to help the Jesuits, as Anne Outennen did when she secretly went to a family that had adopted a prisoner and offered them an iron axe if they would permit him to be baptized (29:269–71). In general, however, converts were frightened to aid the Jesuits publicly, lest they be thought traitors.

In 1645–46 Totiri broke with this attitude when he attended the torture of a prisoner at Taenhatentaron. After the prisoner had been tortured for some time, he began to proclaim publicly that here one could see a demonstration of the eternal fate of non-Christians and in spite of pushing and many insults, he succeeded in giving summary instruction to the prisoner and then baptized him. Many traditionalists who were present regarded Totiri's behaviour as evidence of madness or spirit possession and it was greatly admired by the other Christians (29:263–69). It is significant, however, that neither Totiri nor any of the other Christians dared to offend public opinion to the point of seeking to prevent a prisoner from being tortured; nor did the Jesuits regard this as a feasible goal.

The Christians also began to organize public processions, such as one held in Teanaostaiaé in which a large cross was carried from the chapel and erected in the Christian cemetery outside the town (29:275). Christians now began to make a point of praying aloud and in public in order to bear witness to their affiliations. They did this especially when they believed that it was likely to annoy non-Christians (30:53–57). While rationalized as a kind of martyrdom, the Jesuits must have hoped that such witness would help to undermine the self-confidence of the traditionalists. Christians also began to carve crosses on trees near the town (30:47) and to expiate their sins gave feasts to which traditionalists were invited. At these the penitent would testify to his belief in Christianity and announce that henceforth he would do nothing contrary to Jesuit teachings (30:77–79). The Christians simultaneously intensified their efforts to persuade their relatives to become Christians (29:277–79).

All of these activities strengthened a growing feeling among the Christians that they constituted a group set apart from other Huron. Seeing their numbers increase, many Christians became confident that the whole confederacy would eventually be converted and they no longer feared the ability of traditionalists to reverse this trend (26:255). Often they treated traditionalists who complained about the abandonment of the customs of their forefathers with contempt (27:69). Totiri summed up the factional spirit of many Christians when he stated that he was more attached to the Jesuits than to his country or to his relatives and vowed that he was willing to follow the Jesuits wherever they might go (23:137).

THE TRADITIONALIST REACTION

The majority of Huron were deeply troubled by the growing success of the Jesuits and the breakdown of their traditional way of life. They noted that since the arrival of the Jesuits, one disaster after another had befallen the confederacy, while the Iroquois who had no contact with the Jesuits and had not forsaken the ways of their ancestors were prospering (Thwaites 1896–1901, 25:35–37). In spite of this the traditionalists did not seriously consider killing the Jesuits or expelling them from the country. Individual Huron chased the Jesuits out of their houses (23:39), and in the winter of 1645–46 a priest in Teanaostaiaé was threatened with an axe during the celebration of the Ononharoia (30:101); however, the only priests who seem to have been in any real danger were Brébeuf and Chaumonot and this was because of their visit to the Neutral and their suspected dealings with the Iroquois. In the Huron country traditionalists, as well as Christians, took pains to protect the Jesuits from every possible danger. The reason for this was clearly their desire to continue trading with the French. This relationship had saved the Jesuits' lives during the epidemics, hence there was no question of it not being effective when conditions were easier and the Huron's dependence on the French was greater than before. However much the traditionalists may have resented what the Jesuits were doing, there seemed to be no practical way of getting rid of them. This allowed the Jesuits to undermine the traditional Huron way of life with little fear that the Huron would or could do anything to stop them.

If, however, the traditionalists were unable to express their strong disapproval of what the Jesuits were doing, the same was not true of their feelings towards their countrymen who had become Christians. The principal charge that was levelled against converts was that of witchcraft. This resulted from them refusing to perform various traditional functions that the Huron believed were necessary to assure the welfare of their community and of its individual members. We have already noted that wealthy converts were not only accused of sorcery but also threatened with death for refusing to participate in redistributive rituals (30:19–21). Christians were accused of endangering their communities by failing to join in rituals to avert the threat of crop failures. For example, in 1641 two women in Ossossané refused to obey a public order to burn tobacco in their fields and to stop gathering wild hemp in order to prevent a bad harvest. This resulted in a further proclamation by the town council stating that the Christians were causing a famine and in a general denunciation of these women (23:55–57). It was also said that rosaries and medals could be used to do evil, since they stole away the souls of those who looked at them as well as caused blood to pour forth (23:135).

The majority of witchcraft complaints were about the refusal of Christians to join in healing rites, including dream guessing. Frequently, these accusations arose within a convert's own household. A man from Ossossané, who is described as of no particular importance and the only remaining Christian in his household, was driven out by his relatives after the death of his niece who had also been baptized. These relatives urged him to renounce Christianity and when he refused they would not give him anything to eat. Lacking other relatives to whom he could turn, he was forced to beg for food and to do his own cooking, which made him an object of ridicule throughout the community. Men amused themselves picking quarrels with him and if he attended a feast, people would cry out that because he was a Christian he ought not to be there. He was said to bring misfortune wherever he went and people warned him that since he was a sorcerer, he must be prepared to die at any moment (23:67).

In Teanaostaiaé a husband and wife who had lived together in the wife's longhouse for fifteen or sixteen years and who had five children were both baptized. As soon as the wife's mother learned about this, she flew into a rage and persuaded her daughter to renounce her baptism. When the husband refused to follow his wife's example, the older woman ordered him out of the house and forced her daughter to divorce him. A young man who refused to renounce Christianity in spite of repeated promises and threats admonished his grandmother that even if he were burned, he would not give in to her. He clearly expected that his stubbornness would result in charges of witchcraft (23:127).

Shortly after Charles Tsondatsaa announced to his family that he had been baptized, one of his nephews fell ill, a niece became frenzied as a result of spirit possession, and another nephew was reported drowned. Some of his nearest relatives accused him of being responsible for these misfortunes and a quarrel broke out that nearly led to bloodshed. Tsondatsaa refused to renounce his conversion and, ultimately, all three relatives were found to be out of danger. Sometime later another niece fell ill, and her sickness was diagnosed as being curable by means of the dance of which Tsondatsaa had formerly been the leader; however, Tsondatsaa refused to perform this dance or to permit it to be performed for her. She too recovered (23:85–89). After Tsondatsaa refused to fulfil a dream wish for a friend, the friend invited him to join him and some other Huron in a steam bath. There, the traditionalists promised not to tell the Christians if Tsondatsaa would fulfil his friend's wish. At the same time they threatened to suffocate him if he did not. In spite of increasingly violent threats, Tsondatsaa refused to grant this man's request. Finally, he passed unconscious and the Indians who were with him rescued him from the steam bath (26:243–49).

Tsondatsaa was not the only prominent Huron who was persecuted by friends and relatives for becoming a Christian. When the new Atironta refused to allow shamans to attend his ailing son, his wife left him, took the boy with her, and soon remarried (23:165). This left Atironta unable to remarry according to the laws of the Roman Catholic church. We do not know whether this first wife died or returned to him, or whether some special dispensation allowed him to remarry, but when Atironta visited Quebec several years later he was accompanied by a wife and two-year old son (27:113). This quarrel demonstrates the bitterness that was generated by conversions even within the most important lineages of the confederacy.

Christians were also blamed for not taking part in healing rituals that were prescribed by their village councils. Sometimes the organizers of these rituals would tell Christians that the Jesuits had secretly agreed that they might join in them or would argue that by confessing afterwards, converts could obtain forgiveness for their participation. On other occasions, the traditionalists stated that the country was being ruined because the sick were no longer being cared for, and would plead with Christians to join in the ceremonies one more time. When such pleas were unsuccessful, the traditionalist headmen frequently became angry and denounced the Christians for conspiring to kill their fellow countrymen. Sometimes hatchets were wielded over the heads of Christians to frighten them into joining in traditional celebrations (23:43–53).

The leaders of the curing societies came to play an active role in persuading converts to renounce the new religion and sometimes were successful in doing so. Threats, promises, and bribes were all used for this purpose. The most strenuous efforts of these societies were directed towards recovering members who had become Christians. One of these was a woman named Andotraaon who lived in Taenhatentaron and was probably a member of the Awataerohi society. A headman who was one of the principal officers of this society informed her that at a secret meeting its leaders had resolved that if she did not rejoin their group, they would murder her the following summer. By scalping her while she was working in her fields, the killing would be made to look as if the Iroquois had done it (as Chihwatenha's had been done) (30:23). While the curing societies obviously had a special corporate interest in resisting the spread of Christianity, the members of this one were primarily objecting to Andotraaon's unwillingness to help her fellow Huron, which they interpreted as evidence of sorcery.

The shamans also had a vested interest in opposing the spread of Christianity, and were among the harshest critics of those who converted (23:117–19; 27:33). They were able to use their expert knowledge of

Huron religion to indicate how Christians were endangering people's lives by refusing to participate in the religious life of their communities. In this way they managed to stir up much hatred of the Christians (23:55). Sometimes, however, the Jesuits were able to undermine the resistance of these shamans by converting relatives, thus bringing pressure to bear on them to convert also (23:117–21).

The relationship between Christians and traditionalists was much affected by Jesuit demands that Christians should abstain from all forms of extra-marital sexual intercourse. The Jesuits strove to inculcate in their converts what in their opinion was an appropriate sense of shame about sex and although their teachings ran counter to Huron culture, they appear to have succeeded somewhat in this endeavour. As early as 1642 a fifteen or sixteen-year-old Christian girl rebuked her traditionalist companions for talking about sexual matters (23:99). The Jesuits believed that some Christian girls tried to appear melancholy in public in the hope that men would not be tempted to approach them (23:71–73). A Christian adolescent was approvingly reported to have gone into the forest and rolled unclad in the snow for a long time in order to stifle his sexual urges (30:39).

The refusal of young Christians to respond in what the Huron regarded as a normal way to sexual advances astonished other Huron. It was regarded as yet another example of antisocial behaviour with sinister connotations of sorcery. This was particularly so when young people met in the woods or in other remote places where their sexual intercourse would not become public knowledge and thus be brought to the Jesuits' attention. Christian men were reported to have fled from one village to another to make certain that they would not succumb to a woman's advances (23:63), while a girl told her traditionalist admirer that she would prefer to be slain rather than submit to him (26:229). Most traditionalists regarded such behaviour as folly and told the Christians that they were making a mistake to deny themselves the pleasures of youth through their fear of an imaginary hell. Those who were rejected sometimes became angry with the Jesuits because of it (26:229).

Sexual temptation was, however, clearly one of the weak points of converts, especially young ones. By 1645 the traditionalists were deliberately exploiting such weaknesses in order to undermine commitments to Christianity. Headmen publicly incited girls to seduce Christian men. The Jesuits viewed this as a serious threat and took comfort in the steadfastness of those who resisted such advances. They reported that one woman who had no success in seducing Christian men concluded that Christianity must indeed confer special powers on the believer and expressed the wish to become a Christian (30:33–37). Gradually, the prudery of converts seemed to undermine the traditional patterns by which young Huron met and came to know one another. One young Christian is reported to have asked his uncle to provide a wife for him, sight unseen (30:37–39).

The traditionalists collectively opposed the spread of Christianity in many ways. Christians were taunted and ridiculed as a group in an effort to persuade them to give up their religion. In Teanaostaiaé they were nicknamed Marians, because they were frequently heard invoking the Virgin Mary in their prayers (23:135). Children and adults were mocked that they had become Christians because they were cowards and were afraid of the fires of hell (23:97; 26:229). Among the children, such taunts sometimes led to fights and vigorous exchanges of insults between Christians and traditionalists.

Organized resistance to Christianity varied considerably from one community to another. In Ossossané, which was the oldest of the missions, there was little organized opposition. When the OnONharoia was celebrated in the winter of 1641–42, the leading men of the town approached every Christian separately and attempted to bribe or frighten them into joining in the celebration (23:43–55). When the Christians stood firm efforts at intimidation ceased. At the opposite extreme was Teanaostaiaé, where the communal persecution of Christians was violent and prolonged. The first outburst was in spring 1642, when French workmen arrived to construct a chapel in Etienne Totiri's longhouse. People began to say that the progress of Christianity would ruin the village and that converts should be made to renounce it or be expelled from the community. Even Totiri's kinsmen joined in the demand that he and his Christian relatives should leave Teanaostaiaé. One of the council chiefs warned Totiri's nephew that if they did not cease to practise Christianity, they would be torn out of the earth like a poisonous root; this was a stock expression that the Huron used to intimidate suspected sorcerers (23:133–35). Hostility against the Christians continued and rose to a fever pitch when Assiskwa returned from Sainte-Marie and demanded that all Frenchmen should be slain (23:145).

This hostility was renewed the following winter when the Christians, who were somewhat more numerous, again refused to join in Huron religious ceremonies. They were accused of practising witchcraft and thereby exposing their countrymen to dangers of war, starvation, and disease. The growing strength of the Iroquois was also attributed to the

Christians' public condemnation of the customs of their forefathers. Suggestions were made that a general council should be called that would require all Christians to renounce Christianity or to practise it secretly and without criticising Huron customs. If Christians would not do this, they should be expelled from the country; meanwhile, all contact should be broken off with them and they should not be allowed to attend any Huron feasts or councils. Public antagonism against the Christians became so fierce in Teanaostaiaé that the Christians were forced to consider ways of conciliating public opinion (26:279–81). When the Ononharoia was celebrated in 1645–46, a serious commotion broke out in the course of which several Christians were beaten and an old man named Laurent Tandoutsont was wounded with a blow from a hatchet. He had raced into the crowd, which was milling about the chapel, shouting "Today I shall go to heaven" (30:101–3). The same year the Christians were mocked when they formally erected a large cross in their cemetery. Later the children of Teanaostaiaé pelted the cross with rocks and filth (29:275).

The public opposition in other villages appears to have been less persistent and less well organized than it was in Teanaostaiaé. In 1643–44 a Kichesipirini headman named Agwachimagan wintered at Scanonaenrat and began to denounce the Jesuits and the French. At a secret meeting with the headmen of the village, he compared the teachings of the French with what he had seen at Quebec and Three Rivers. On this basis he found their teachings to be lies. Agwachimagan said that the real aim of the French was to destroy the Huron as they had already destroyed the Montagnais and the Algonkin. As proof he described a house at Quebec that was kept full of fleshless skeletons and lame, crippled, and blind people who had resolved to be Christians. This was his understanding of the hospital. He told the Huron that if they converted to Christianity, not one of them would be alive within three years. News of this warning spread terror through the town. Christianity was denounced and many who had requested baptism now decided to postpone it a while longer (26:301–7).

In Taenhatentaron the first persecutions of Christians are recorded for 1645–46, but they may have started earlier. Although they were as violent as elsewhere, they appear to have consisted mainly of individuals being threatened with death rather than of public expressions of opposition to Christianity. Headmen and leaders of curing societies played a prominent role in opposing Christianity (30:19–25). The late dissemination of

Christianity to this town, and possibly a lack of headmen among the converts, may explain the form that this opposition took. It may also explain why in autumn 1645, some of the Christians decided to offer a gift to the traditionalist headmen of the village, to induce them not to try to persuade Christians to join in customary Huron rites. When the Jesuits learned about this they reproved these converts, because they feared that this example might encourage traditionalists to attempt to extract similar presents elsewhere (29:271).

There can be no doubt that the development of Christian factions in various Huron villages gave rise to new tensions that cut across the segmentary structure of lineages, clan segments, and tribes. The traditional religion had helped to unite these disparate groupings and to assure the unity of the Huron confederacy. Moreover, until the coming of the Europeans, new rituals had supplemented rather than conflicted with existing ones. The exclusive nature of Christianity prevented it from fitting into this traditional pattern and its gradual spread created a rift in Huron society between Christians and traditionalists that threatened to cut across all existing social groupings. The unity of Huron society had never before been threatened in this manner and the traditionalists were faced for the first time with an organized threat to the Huron way of life.

Yet, in spite of these efforts to intimidate the Christians, there is no evidence that any Christian was killed or expelled from his village and very few of them were injured. One may conclude that the aim of these attacks was to coerce Christians into conforming with traditional norms of behaviour. What the traditionalists did not appreciate was that under Jesuit guidance the Christians were no longer sufficiently tied to the values of their society for coercion of this sort to be effective. Often the traditionalists found their own norms being used against them. For example, when the cross in the Christian cemetery at Teanaostaiaé was attacked, Totiri summoned a general meeting of all the people in the town and accused the traditionalists of one of the most heinous of all Huron crimes: violating a cemetery. This charge so troubled the traditionalist headmen that they ordered that hereafter the children should leave the cemetery alone (29:275–77).

While the majority of non-Christians remained attached to the old ways and believed that Christianity was responsible for most of the troubles that were afflicting them, the Jesuits noted, with considerable satisfaction, that a growing number of them seemed to feel that there was no longer any hope of resisting the spread of the new religion. The Jesuits believed that such a spirit of despondency and resignation would facilitate the dissemination of Christianity. A certain amount of evidence appeared to justify this opinion. Some headmen, when going through villages to invite people to join in curing ceremonies, publicly declared that Christians need not attend or even encouraged them to remain in their houses (26:255–57). In a similar vein a non-Christian woman, who became the guardian of a little girl after her parents died, refused to have traditional curing ceremonies performed for her. She argued that since the child's parents had been Christians, she must not be separated from them after death. When the child died she buried her body in a separate place away from the non-Christians (26:227).

By 1645 the headmen in one of the larger villages complained that the traditional rituals lacked the fervour of former years and attributed this to the growing number of conversions. Yet, instead of attacking the Christians, they went through the community asking that the converts cease to be Christians for twenty-four hours and join in the traditional rites so that they might be performed properly (29:273). One result of this growing lack of confidence was the tendency for some Huron to convert in order to emulate those who had already done so. An aged man at Teanaostaiaé sought to become Christian so as not to be excluded when his friends went to the chapel to pray (30:99–101). Another, named Saentarendi, was one of the greatest opponents of Christianity in Taenhatentaron. Nevertheless, when he was near death he inexplicably requested baptism and urged the traditionalists, who had come to drive the priests away, to recommend to everyone that they should become Christians (30:105–7).

NATIVIST MOVEMENTS

What the Jesuits paid less attention to, but which seem to have been important in the light of what happened later, were movements that aimed at organizing some sort of ideological resistance to Christianity. These appear to have begun to gather strength about 1645. Although little was recorded about them, their goal seems to have been to refute the teachings of the Jesuits and to reinforce the oral traditions of the Huron. One group of reports stated that Iouskeha had appeared to various people in the forest in the form of a giant holding ears of corn in one hand and fish in the other. He announced that it was he who had created the world and taught the Huron how to earn a living and promised that if the Huron honoured him he would bring them good fortune. He also said that to believe that anyone was destined to be burned and tortured after death was a false idea that the Jesuits had propagated in order to frighten people. He assured the souls of all Huron who were faithful to their traditions a happy life in the villages of the dead (30:27).

Two other stories attempted to counteract the Jesuits' teachings even more specifically. One stated that some Algonkin had recently returned from a distant journey, in the course of which they had come across the villages of the dead. There, they had learned that the stories the Jesuits told about heaven and hell were untrue; instead, after death all souls find new bodies and a more comfortable environment, but continue to live much as they did on earth (30:27). The second story was specifically anti-Jesuit. It claimed that a Huron woman who was buried at Sainte-Marie had returned from the dead to warn her people that the French were false friends whose aim was to capture and torture the souls of Indians. According to this story, as soon as this woman died her soul went to heaven, but when she arrived there she found that the French were waiting for her at the gate armed with firebrands and burning torches which they used to torture her. She learned that the souls of all Indians who converted to Christianity were treated in heaven as prisoners of war. After the woman had been severely tortured, she was tied down for the night, but someone who felt sorry for her had broken her bonds and shown her a deep valley through which she could descend to the earth. On her way she saw from afar the villages inhabited by the souls of Huron who were not Christians. There she heard singing and dancing in a true paradise from which all unpleasantness had been banished. Rather than go there, however, she felt obliged to return to the living to warn her people what the Jesuits were doing (30:29–31).

The Jesuits were unable to discover in what part of the Huron country this story had originated and it was unclear whether it was the report of someone's dream or a deliberate fabrication. It is easy to understand why the story became so popular, was believed in all parts of the Huron country, and was remembered years afterwards. It not only served to discredit the Jesuits and to justify a longstanding belief that they were hostile to the Huron but provided traditionalists with a highly plausible explanation of why the Jesuits had come to the Huron country. The story was also convincing, since the geographical proximity of the Christian heaven to the sun suggested to the Huron that it might be a place of fire (30:31–33). The Jesuits were thus compelled to face a popular rumour that equated them with enemy warriors lurking in the Huron country to snatch victims for their fires.

Conclusion

It is difficult to believe that the Jesuits did not perceive in these stories evidence of growing opposition to their work among what was still a majority of the Huron people. It must be assumed, therefore, that they felt sufficiently sure of their own safety (as guaranteed by the French-Huron alliance) and of the ultimate success of their plans to convert an increasing number of Huron that they no longer saw the need for caution in their dealings with non-Christians.

It is also difficult to believe that the Jesuits were unaware of the divisive effects that their mission was having on Huron society. Christians now observed Huron customs only when they did not conflict with their religion and this meant a growing rift between Christians and traditionalists about many vital issues. The mutual distrust of these two groups made political decisions more complicated and the refusal of Christians to fight alongside traditionalists lessened the military effectiveness of the confederacy at the same time that the growing hostility of the Iroquois made more fighting necessary. While the new factions that were developing among the Huron were not yet openly antagonistic, it must have been clear to the Jesuits that their work was not conducive to the well-being of the confederacy at such a critical period. They may have believed that their goal of converting the Huron was soon to be achieved and that a Christian people would once more be a united people; however, it seems unlikely that they could have believed that this process would outstrip the growing power of the Iroquois. The Jesuits must have known that their efforts to convert the Huron would multiply loyalties and viewpoints precisely when as much unity as possible was required. Their actions therefore make sense only if we assume that the Jesuits placed the conversion of the Huron ahead of all other considerations. The Jesuits may have known that it was impossible, under the circumstances, to be both a good Christian and a good Huron. Nevertheless, in accordance with their own values, they placed the salvation of souls ahead of preventing divisions in Huron society.

Chapter 11  The End of the Confederacy

The Growing Power of the Iroquois

NEW COOPERATION AMONG THE IROQUOIS

No later than the autumn of 1646 the Iroquois tribes began to coordinate a series of military campaigns that were soon to fulfil the Jesuits' earlier, and then unfounded, predictions that they would destroy the Huron. Prior to the death of Isaac Jogues, the Mohawk sent valuable presents to confirm their alliances with the other Iroquois tribes and to invite them to join in an attack on the French and their allies (Thwaites 1896–1901, 30:227). One of their aims was to harass, and if possible to destroy, the French settlements at Montreal and Three Rivers so that these might no longer hinder their raids against the Algonkin. They probably also hoped that by cutting off trade at these posts, they would cripple the economy of New France sufficiently to force the French to adopt a genuinely neutral policy in their dealings with the Indians (45:191). At the same time, the Mohawk, with help from the Oneida and Onondaga, intensified their raids against the Indians living to the north and east. Roving bands of Mohawk warriors took advantage of what they had learned about the distribution of Algonkin hunting bands during the two years of peace to attack and plunder these bands more effectively. There were numerous raids both north and south of the St. Lawrence River, one of which culminated in the capture of over 100 Algonkin south of Three Rivers in March 1647 (30:161, 227–53). Another successful raid was launched against the Algonkin, from the upper part of the St. Lawrence Valley, who had gathered on Morrison Island while waiting to travel down-river with the Huron. Forty prisoners, as well as a vast quantity of beaver pelts that had been collected for trading with the French, were taken in this raid (30:281–95). Hereafter, Mohawk predation in the north increased steadily in range and intensity for several decades. The Mohawk were also encouraged to attack the Susquehannock by the Dutch, who saw this as a way of harming their Swedish trade rivals (F. Jennings 1968:24–25).

By 1646 the western tribes of the Iroquois confederacy were better armed and more self-confident than they had been previously, although they probably still did not have nearly as many guns in relationship to their numbers as the Mohawk had. The Onondaga, who had formerly been the dominant tribe in the confederacy, became increasingly jealous of the growing power and arrogance of the Mohawk, but they, like the Seneca and Cayuga, were in need of furs. Thus they were willing to join in schemes that were likely to increase the volume of furs that were available to them. As has already been noted, the western tribes of the confederacy were surrounded by agricultural peoples. These other tribes engaged in the fur trade and therefore any attacks that were launched against them were likely to yield furs. Because of their sedentary way of life, however, such tribes were far more dangerous to attack than were the hunter-gatherers and semi-horticulturalists who were being attacked by the Mohawk. It was only to the north and west of the Huron country that the Seneca and their neighbours could hope to find hunters and hunting territories that they might prey upon as the Mohawk were preying upon the Algonkian-speaking peoples of Quebec and northern New England.

Possibly after discussions with the Mohawk in the summer of 1646, the Seneca adopted what seems to have been a radically new policy towards the Huron. Hitherto, they had been content to raid them for furs. These raids had steadily become more violent and had resulted in the destruction of a Huron village in 1642. They had, however, grown out of the blood feuds of an earlier period and, no doubt, had continued to be viewed as such by the Seneca. Now the Seneca decided to destroy the Huron confederacy and disperse the Huron people (map 29). Ordinary Seneca may have viewed the dispersal of the Huron as an act of blood revenge, but the scale and planning that went into it far exceeded any military efforts reported for earlier times among the four western tribes of the Iroquois confederacy. The success of this campaign depended on the Seneca securing the active assistance of the other Iroquois tribes and, in particular, of the Mohawk, who had the most muskets. Mutual self-interest therefore compelled the Mohawk and the Seneca to coordinate their activities against the Huron and the French.

It is not known precisely how the Seneca formulated this policy; however, their efforts to secure more furs resemble the methods that the Mohawk had adopted prior to 1609 to steal European goods. The annihilation or dispersal of groups that interfered with such activities was nothing new for the Mohawk. It is possible that by 1646 the Mohawk, in an effort to enlist more support from the rest of the Iroquois confederacy, drew on their own experience to suggest this policy to the Seneca. It is also possible that the Mohawk had been urged to do this by Dutch traders, who were anxious that the number of furs falling into the hands of the Iroquois should increase as rapidly as possible. It seems likely, however, that as the

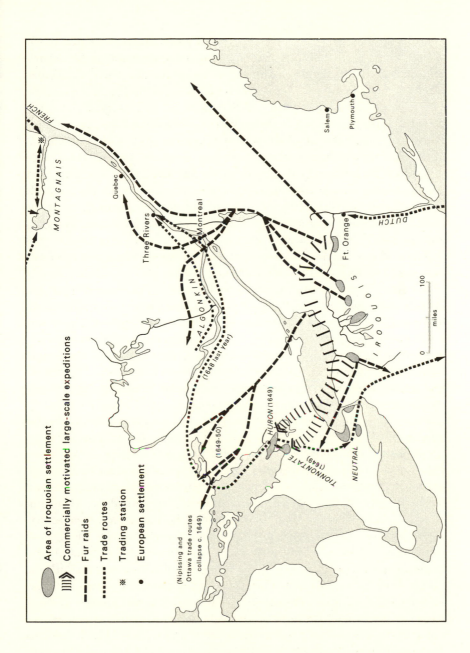

MAP 29. *Intertribal relations, 1648 to 1650.*

Seneca's need for furs increased, they would have sought these furs in the regions to the north and west of them. Therefore, any strategy for dealing more effectively with the inhabitants of those regions would have been carefully considered.

The crucial question is what the Seneca hoped to gain by dispersing or destroying the Huron. In keeping with his obsession with middlemen, Hunt (1940:91) has suggested that the Iroquois sought to divert the trade of the Huron into their own hands. As he put it, "It became evident that so long as the Hurons held the Georgian Bay–Lake Simcoe region they would control the northern fur trade. Repeated attempts to get the trade by treaty had failed, but there remained one way of obtaining it. If the Hurons were gone, nothing would stand in the path of Iroquois prosperity and ambition. The Hurons must go."

This explanation leaves vital questions unanswered.Why did the Iroquois believe it necessary to disperse the Huron, rather than try to force them to barter their furs with the Iroquois instead of with the French? Had the Iroquois been able to do the latter, they would have had at their disposal all of the Huron's entrepreneurial skills and been able to benefit from existing trading relations between the Huron and the northern Algonkians. Hunt claims that having already negotiated trading agreements that the Huron had failed to honour, the Seneca and Mohawk were unwilling to trust them any longer. This, he says, explains why these tribes refused to listen to any offers of trade that the Huron made after 1646.

This is not a plausible explanation, if we consider the broader context of what happened after 1649. It does not explain why the Iroquois attacked the Nipissing and Ottawa as soon as the Huron had been dispersed. These were the major trading partners of the Huron and if the Iroquois had been anxious to secure the Huron's trade for themselves, they should at least have tried to establish a stable trading relationship with them. Hunt implies that this is what the Iroquois intended to do, using force, if necessary, to compel these groups to cease having dealings with the French. They were foiled, however, when the Ottawa, encouraged by the French, began to play a role in the fur trade of the upper Great Lakes region similar to that played by the Huron. This does not explain, however, why the Iroquois dispersed the Nipissing and Ottawa without making any effort to negotiate with them or even to intimidate them. This dispersal destroyed the trading patterns of the Georgian Bay area, which Hunt saw the Iroquois attempting to control for their own benefit. Hunt implies that the Iroquois miscalculated.

But did they? None of the Iroquois tribes were located in an advantageous, or even a suitable, location to continue the Huron's trade with the north. Either the Algonkians or the Iroquois would have had to travel an additional 300 miles to trade with one another and this would have involved carrying heavy loads of furs and corn overland for half that distance. There is no evidence that the Iroquois planned to resettle in the Huron country; indeed, none lived anywhere in Ontario until some of the Cayuga settled along the north shore of Lake Ontario to escape the attacks of the Susquehannock in the late 1660s (Hunt 1940:140). This meant that if the Iroquois wished to trade, they had to have agents in Ontario who would barter with the north and re-sell the furs to them. Yet the Iroquois systematically eliminated not only the Huron but all the groups that might have played such a role.

The evidence thus supports the conclusion that the aim of the Iroquois was not to replace the Huron as middlemen in their trade with the north, but to intensify the warfare that they were waging against the Huron and their neighbours to the point of dispersing them. In the short run, both the Mohawk and the Seneca stood to gain by uniting their forces to attack the Huron and plunder their villages of all the furs and European trade goods that could be found inside them. In the long run, the Seneca stood to gain from the dispersal of the Huron, who hitherto had prevented their hunting and raiding parties from safely penetrating into the fur rich territories to the north (A. Saunders 1963:8–10). With the Huron out of the way, the Seneca could hunt in central Ontario and raid the Algonkian-speaking peoples around the shores of Lake Huron in the same manner that the Mohawk raided the Algonkin, Montagnais, and Abenaki. Because these northern hunting peoples were more dispersed than the Huron, they were easier to attack and thus seemed to be a stable prey that the Seneca could continue plundering for a long time. The violent attacks that the Iroquois launched against the northern hunting peoples, as soon as the Huron were dispersed, thus were not a mistake, but an integral part of Iroquois strategy. This strategy aimed to provide the Seneca and the other western Iroquois tribes with a northern hinterland in which they could hunt and rob furs, as the Mohawk were already accustomed to do farther east.

The substantial plunder that the Mohawk hoped to seize while helping to disperse the Huron no doubt was viewed by them as adequate compensation for helping the Seneca. To secure this plunder the Mohawk temporarily diverted their raiding away from the St. Lawrence Valley to the Huron country. In 1648 and 1649 the French enjoyed a respite from Iroquois attacks while the Mohawk mustered their forces to attack the Huron (Thwaites 1896–1901, 34:85).

The Iroquois's strategy was to concentrate their attack in its early stages against the Arendarhonon settlements, which lay on the eastern borders of the confederacy. Having destroyed these villages, they planned to press westward and attack the Attigneenongnahac and Tahontaenrat towns. Only after these had been destroyed were the Iroquois prepared to attack the Attignawantan, who remained the largest of the Huron tribes. In this way, they hoped to be able to devastate one or two Huron communities at a time while holding out promises of peace to the others, in the hope that the Huron tribes would not band together to oppose them (Perrot 1911:148). Even before the Mohawk joined in the attack, the deteriorating ability of the Huron to resist the Iroquois had produced a growing feeling of insecurity throughout the confederacy. By 1645 a number of Huron families had retreated to a remote place called Tangouaen, which was surrounded on all sides by lakes and rivers. There, on the Canadian Shield, they lived among the Algonkians hoping to be safe from Iroquois incursions (30:87).

NEGOTIATIONS WITH THE ONONDAGA

The Huron were anxious to find ways to counteract or turn aside the (to them) inexplicably growing menace of the Iroquois. Two events, which occurred early in 1647, gave the Huron some hope of doing this and led to a flurry of diplomatic activity that continued for over a year (Desrosiers 1948). The first event was the arrival in the Huron country of a delegation of Susquehannock who offered to help the Huron make peace with the western Iroquois tribes or, failing this, to help fight them (Thwaites 1896–1901, 30:253). The Susquehannock wanted to renew their alliance with the Huron because of the growing danger of war between themselves and the Mohawk. Just as the Mohawk and Seneca were coordinating their efforts for aggressive purposes, the Susquehannock were proposing to the Huron that they coordinate theirs in order to defend themselves better.

The second event was the capture by the Huron of an important Onondaga headman named Annenraes. He was one of a band of Onondaga raiders who were sighted on the frontiers of the Huron country early in 1647, and who were pursued and defeated by a Huron war party. The Iroquois who led this band was killed on the spot and the rest of the prisoners were tortured to death, but because of his importance Annenraes's life was spared. He continued to live among the Huron as their prisoner, probably in Taenhatentaron, which was either an Arendarhonon or an Attigneenongnahac town.

The arrival of the Susquehannock and the capture of Annenraes stimulated a fierce debate among the Huron concerning the policy to follow with
regard to the Iroquois. The Jesuits reported that the Attignawantan, who
had as yet suffered relatively little from Iroquois attacks, were strongly
opposed to making peace with them, while the Arendarhonon wanted
peace in the hope that their people who were being held prisoners by the
Iroquois might be released as a result of it (33:119–21). This difference in
the attitude of Huron tribes towards peace may also have been a difference
between Huron Christians and traditionalists. It is probably no accident
that the Attignawantan had the largest number of converts of any of the
Huron tribes, while the people of Contarea, the main Arendarhonon
village, were later described as having a strong aversion to Christianity
(42:73). The diplomacy that followed suggests that by 1647 a self-conscious
traditionalist faction had developed within the confederacy and that many
of its more active supporters had come to oppose not only the Jesuits and
their Huron followers, but also the trading alliance with the French from
which the Jesuits derived their protection and influence. The composition
of delegations and the political activities described by the Jesuits also testify
that the split between those who were for and against Christianity had
become the dominant factor in Huron politics by this time.

It is not unlikely that in their efforts to support the French-Huron
alliance, the Jesuits encouraged their converts to oppose any discussion of
peace with the Iroquois. On the other hand, the more active traditionalists
favoured such negotiations and also appear to have wished to discuss the
possibility of developing trading relations with the Iroquois. In this way,
they hoped to win the goodwill of the Iroquois. Moreover, so long as European goods could be obtained only from the French, the Huron Christians
enjoyed a great advantage and used this advantage to bolster their own
prestige and power within the confederacy. Trade was carried on only with
the French because the Huron, as a whole, feared the Iroquois and had
wanted an alliance with the French for military and economic reasons.
Now, a growing number of traditionalists came to view the Iroquois as less
of a threat to their way of life than were the French. The leaders of this
group sought to obtain European goods from the Iroquois in order to
eliminate the Huron's total dependence on the French and to counteract
the growing claims to power that were being made by the leaders of the
Christian faction.

In the spring of 1647 some Huron who were angry that Annenraes had
been allowed to live talked about killing him. Learning of this, Annenraes
had discussions with certain important council chiefs who decided to help

him return to his own country. These headmen secretly gave Annenraes a series of presents to convey to the Onondaga headmen and escorted him safely from their village in the dead of night (33:117–19).

Unfortunately, we are not told who these headmen were or what their motive was, except that they hoped that Annenraes might do them a good service. Council chiefs generally favoured peace and often acted in a circumspect manner when they believed public welfare to be involved, but did not wish to antagonize popular feeling. It is also possible that these headmen were traditionalists seeking to advance a factional cause. In any case, it is evident that afterwards Christians and traditionalists were still able to agree on a policy that was flexible enough that for a short period it offered both sides the hope of ultimately achieving their particular objectives.

The basis of this policy was a decision to begin, if possible, to negotiate a peace with the Onondaga, in the course of which the Huron would present gifts of furs to the Onondaga headmen and perhaps offer to trade with them. It would also be implied that if conditions were right the Huron were willing to extend this treaty to embrace the other tribes of the Iroquois confederacy. Those who wished for peace, to offset the growing power of the Jesuits, undoubtedly hoped for the success of these negotiations, while the Christians supported them in the hope that they might secure the neutrality of the Onondaga or at least their temporary withdrawal from the war. This compromise solution meant that it was unnecessary for the Huron to resolve among themselves the question of whether they wished for peace or merely to divide the enemy. The answer to this question could be postponed until the intentions of the Iroquois became clearer.

On 13 April the Huron dispatched their envoys to the Susquehannock. It is indicative of the power of the Christians that this mission was led by a devout Christian, Charles Ondaaiondiont, and that he was accompanied by four other Christians and four traditionalists. The Huron carried large numbers of presents with them and arrived at the Susquehannock town of Andastoé early in June. There, a number of meetings were held at which Ondaaiondiont outlined the problems that the Huron were facing. It was arranged that the Susquehannock should send envoys to the Iroquois who would urge them to conclude a peace treaty with the Huron that "would not hinder the trade of all these countries with one another" (33:131). The Onondaga were, however, the only tribe who were approached about this matter, the Susquehannock leaving their gifts with them prior to 20 August. While Ondaaiondiont was waiting for these envoys to return, he visited New Sweden, which was only three days' journey from Andastoé.

He was well treated by the colonists, but was surprised to learn that they were not Roman Catholics and were uninterested in missionary work. At the same time, he learned of the death of Isaac Jogues from a European vessel whose crew had recently visited New Amsterdam.

When the Susquehannock envoys had not returned from the Onondaga by 15 August, Ondaaiondiont decided to leave for home before the winter set in, so that he might tell the Huron what the Susquehannock were doing. He left one of his companions at Andastoé to bring later reports and with the remainder of his men reached the Huron country on 5 October, after making a long detour to avoid the Seneca. The latter had learned about his mission and were seeking to intercept him on his way home (33:129–37, 183–85). In addition to whatever official presents Ondaaiondiont carried from the Susquehannock to the headmen of the Huron confederacy, he brought 14,000 wampum beads that he had obtained in trade from either the Susquehannock or the Swedes. Thus for him it proved to be a very profitable journey. He decided, however, to give half of these beads to the Jesuits as a grateful offering for his safe return (33:185–87).

In the meanwhile, when the freed Annenraes reached the south shore of Lake Ontario, he met 300 Onondaga warriors who were making canoes in order to cross the lake and join a large number of Seneca and Cayuga to attack the Huron. The immediate purpose of the Onondaga was to avenge the death of Annenraes and his companions. Annenraes persuaded them not to embark on the raid, but to return with him to the main Onondaga town. There he conveyed the Huron's proposals to the Onondaga headmen and persuaded the tribal council to begin negotiating with them. The Onondaga agreed to do this because they were pleased that Annenraes's life had been spared and because they resented the growing power of the Mohawk and the dominant role that they were trying to play in the affairs of the confederacy. The Onondaga also saw a peace treaty with the Huron as a means of avoiding trouble with the Susquehannock and of assuring that if the latter went to war with the Mohawk, the Onondaga might keep clear of this struggle and force the Mohawk to defend themselves. In this way, the Onondaga had reason to hope that without destroying the confederacy, they might see the Mohawk cut down to size (33:123).

In June the Onondaga dispatched their envoys to negotiate with the Huron. They were led by a famous warrior named Soionés who was a Huron by birth, but had lived among the Onondaga for so long that he regarded himself as one of them and had led many raiding parties against his former homeland. The Onondaga brought with them three recently captured Huron and released them after they arrived at Taenhatentaron on 9 July (33:119). The Onondaga presented a number of wampum collars to the Huron headmen, signifying that they were interested in making peace. Their positive response gave rise to a new and more heated debate between those Huron tribes and religious factions who really wanted to make peace with the Onondaga and those who opposed it.

Ultimately, the opinion seems to have prevailed that it was best to make peace with the Onondaga, if only to divide the Iroquois confederacy. It was therefore decided to send envoys to the Onondaga. Under the leadership of Atironta, five Huron set out on 1 August, carrying valuable presents of furs in return for the wampum that Soionés had brought them. It was perhaps because of the reluctance of the Attignawantan to join in these discussions that the leader of the delegation was an Arendarhonon; nevertheless it seems indicative of the power of the Jesuits and of their Christian supporters that this man was their convert Atironta. Although Atironta was the principal headman of the Arendarhonon, his close ties with the French and the Jesuits made him a poor choice to represent the interests of the vast majority of his tribesmen who were not Christians. On the other hand, the Huron may have considered a Christian who was also an Arendarhonon to be an ideal choice to lead a delegation on a mission about which Huron opinion was so divided. Atironta may have been one of the few headmen acceptable to both the pro-French and pro-peace factions that were emerging among the Huron. Unfortunately, we are not informed who the four other members of Atironta's party were.

Atironta travelled to the Onondaga country in the company of Soionés and arrived there after a journey of twenty days. This was followed by a month of councils and celebrations, during which both sides proclaimed their desire for peace and the adjacent Iroquois tribes were sounded for their opinions. The Cayuga announced that they too were ready for peace and released a Huron captive with two wampum collars as evidence of their benevolent intentions. The Oneida also proclaimed their interest in making peace, in spite of strong opposition from the Mohawk and Seneca, who were bent on waging war. This division within the Iroquois confederacy suggests that in addition to rivalries over tribal rankings, the central tribes may have felt that in the long run they had less to gain from the expansion of hunting and raiding territories than did the Mohawk and Seneca. Under these circumstances, the prospect of getting Huron furs through trade or ritual exchange, even for a short time, may have seemed more promising to them than did joining at once in an attempt to annihilate the Huron.

After these meetings, the Onondaga decided to make peace with the Huron and resolved to send a second embassy to the Huron country with

Atironta. This delegation was led by an aged headman named Scandouati, and contained two other prominent Onondaga. To guarantee their safety, one of Atironta's companions agreed to remain with the Onondaga. The Onondaga took with them as gifts seven splendid wampum collars, each consisting of 3000 or 4000 beads, and fifteen Huron captives, whom they granted freedom. They also carried a promise that if the peace endured, 400 more Huron would be released. These envoys arrived at Taenhaten-taron on 23 October, having taken thirty days to cover the route because of bad weather. When the other envoys returned home, Scandouati and two other Onondaga remained with the Huron as a pledge of their people's good faith (33:117–25). From the point of view of all of the Huron, the main benefit derived from this round of negotiations was that the Onondaga had remained out of the war for the summer and there was hope that they and their neighbours would stay out of the conflict longer still.

In spite of these diplomatic gains, the Huron decided not to trade with the French in 1647. As a result of two years of successful commerce, the Huron had large quantities of French goods and were less inclined to expose themselves to danger than they had been in previous years. The Huron knew that the Mohawk had resumed their blockade of the Ottawa and Saint Lawrence Rivers and feared that if they attempted to visit Three Rivers, they would be attacked (30:221; 32:179; 33:69). This did not, however, prevent about fifty Huron from travelling through central Quebec to trade with the Attikamegue. This made it possible for letters to be conveyed between Quebec and Sainte-Marie by means of these inter-mediaries (30:189; 31:219).

The main reason that Huron men had decided to stay home was a rumour that the Iroquois were planning to launch a major attack against the Huron country that year (33:69). In the middle of the summer, a report that the Iroquois were only a short distance from Teanaostaiaé caused much dismay in that community before it was realized that it was a false alarm (33:99). A war party, reported to number over 1000 men, had, in fact, been raised among the Seneca, Cayuga, and Onondaga in the spring of 1647, but the expedition had been called off after the Onondaga and Cayuga withdrew their support. Later in the summer, the Seneca fell upon the Aondironnon Neutral. The Seneca stated that this was an act of blood revenge, although some additional motive seems necessary to explain the ferocity of this attack upon former friends. We have already discussed the possibility that it was an effort to secure much needed hunting territories, although Hunt (1940:90) and Desrosiers (1948:243–44) regarded it as a foolish act resulting from the Seneca's fear of isolation and encirclement.

Whatever the explanation for the timing of the attack, the Seneca probably viewed it as the first phase in a projected dispersal of the Neutral, which would give them free access to the rich beaver grounds around Lake St. Clair. When the massive raid against the Huron failed to materialize, the Seneca may have selected this single Neutral village as an easy prize, which would yield considerable quantities of furs and trade goods. That the Seneca decided so easily to rupture the longstanding peace between themselves and the Neutral suggests that rather than being terrified or desperate, they were supremely self-confident, as they well might be against a group that had neither muskets nor any direct source of European goods.

Events were to justify their confidence. The Huron hoped that the Neutral would go to war against the Seneca and for a time both sides were on the alert for fear of further attacks. War was not declared, however, and while the Huron continued to speculate that the Neutral were hoping to secure the release of some of their own people before they declared war, it is more likely that the Neutral feared to attack the Seneca (Thwaites 1896–1901, 33:81–83).

While the threat of a concerted Iroquois attack was averted for 1647, harassment of the Huron continued and seems to have been intensified. The effectiveness of Mohawk and Seneca raids increased as more Huron prisoners could be pressed into serving as guides for these expeditions. More Iroquois marauders began to be sighted around Sainte-Marie as the military situation in the eastern part of the confederacy continued to decline (33:75). In late summer 1647 a band of Iroquois attacked a Huron fishing cabin on an island in Lake Simcoe, killing four or five Huron on the spot and taking seven others prisoners. The latter included a Christian woman named Marthe Andionra. A man who escaped from this attack carried the news of it to Contarea. There, a rescue party was organized, which cut the Iroquois off some twenty to twenty-five miles to the south. In a swift encounter, the leader of the Iroquois war party was captured and all the Huron prisoners were rescued unharmed (33:91–93).

Minor victories of this sort were all too rare, however, and after the harvest was in, the Arendarhonon living near Lake Simcoe decided that their position was no longer tenable and abandoned their villages. Some seem to have sought refuge in Taenhatentaron, although the dispirited state of this town soon afterwards suggests that this community was also doubtful about its future. Antoine Daniel, who had been the resident missionary at Contarea prior to this time, was sent to replace Charles Garnier at Teanaostaiaé (Jones 1908:369); this suggests that the majority of people from Contarea and adjacent villages may have found refuge there.

Each family probably carried its own food reserves along with it and thus they did not constitute the same burden to their hosts that refugees from farther away would have done. Nevertheless, houses had to be built for them and it is unlikely that enough fields could have been cleared by spring to permit them to plant all of the crops they required. Since their hosts would be obliged by Huron custom to share their fields with them, this move must have threatened some Huron towns with food shortages in the coming year. As a result of the retreat of the Arendarhonon, the Huron gave up their control of the rich fishing resources of Lakes Simcoe and Couchiching and the Sturgeon Valley became *de facto* the eastern frontier of the Huron country.

THE GROWING POWER OF THE JESUITS

As the Huron grew increasingly uncertain about their ability to defend themselves, ever greater numbers turned to the Jesuits for aid and protection. When nearby villages were believed to be in danger, women and children often sought temporary refuge in the Indian Compound at Sainte-Marie (Thwaites 1896–1901, 33:101). Ragueneau estimated that between April 1647 and 1648, over 3000 people had sought protection and sustenance at Sainte-Marie, each being given an average of three meals (33:77). By March of the following year, an additional 6000 had done so (33:257; 34:199). Huron Christians naturally sought aid with more confidence than did non-Christians (33:77) and it is reasonable to assume that the Jesuits tried to convert any non-Christians who visited them. The growing danger also encouraged non-Christians who wanted to join Christian relatives after death to seek baptism. When Teanaostaiaé was thought about to be attacked in the summer of 1647, many Huron who had been indifferent to Christianity hastened to the village church and asked to become Christians (33:99). Under these circumstances, Father Daniel felt obliged to grant their requests. Yet, even though the report turned out to be a false alarm, the majority of those who had been baptized remained practising Christians.

   In 1647–48 the Jesuits relaxed many of their more stringent requirements for baptism and adopted a more tolerant attitude towards numerous traditional practices. Their aim in so doing was to increase the number of converts and to realize their goal of converting whole communities. Unlike their early laxity, however, this action was a measure of the Jesuits' success among the Huron. It also reflected an improved understanding of Huron thinking. The superior of the mission, Father Paul Ragueneau, played a leading role in the Jesuits' reassessment of Huron customs. Unlike his predecessors, he was sceptical that witchcraft was practised by the Huron. He stated that after careful examination, he found no reason to believe that those who were accused of practising witchcraft actually did so any more than shamans were able to extract charms from people's bodies (33:217–21). He likewise doubted that the devil used the Huron's beliefs in dreams to lead them astray. He regarded their dreams as a natural phenomenon whose truth or falsehood tended to be largely a matter of chance (33:197).

On the basis of such observations, Ragueneau concluded that the Jesuits had required exemplary behaviour from their early converts that went far beyond the limits of what was required of born Christians. They had forbidden, as contrary to Christianity, many practices that were "foolish" rather than diabolical and anti-Christian, thereby depriving their converts of many harmless amusements. This prevented these converts from having everyday contact with other Huron and bearing a full witness of their faith. Ragueneau stressed the need to re-examine Huron customs and not to confuse what was offensive to the Jesuits as Europeans with what was offensive to them as Christians. Many traditional customs could best be dealt with, not by forbidding them, but by slowly encouraging the Huron to see their folly and hence to abandon them of their own volition (33:145–47).

While Ragueneau did not doubt the superiority of French customs over Huron ones, his policy marked a significant step forward in the Jesuits' understanding of Huron ways and in their taking account of these ways in their work. Yet this new toleration of Huron customs did not evolve as an end in itself; it was adopted as a policy to hasten the conversion of the Huron, at a time when the Jesuits felt that the groundwork for such an accelerated program had been laid.[1] Having worked until then to segregate Christians from traditionalists in order to protect their converts' faith, the Jesuits now judged Christianity to be well-enough established that their converts could be trusted again to participate in community activities, and even to assume a leading role in them.

Unfortunately, the Huron *Relations* are preoccupied with describing the rapidly developing political crisis and lack the detailed descriptions of the behaviour of individual converts that formerly were an important part of these accounts. Therefore, little is known about how these policies affected the lives of individuals. It is clear, however, that the Jesuits now heartily approved of efforts to reinterpret traditional practices in keeping with Christian concepts. For example, Christians who were dying were encouraged to celebrate an athataion, or death feast, at which they publicly proclaimed their steadfast belief in Christianity. The changing attitude towards the athataion is evident in the performance of this rite for a young Christian boy in the Scanonaenrat mission. When he learned that his mother was preparing such a feast, he asked her to stop, because he understood the custom to be among those that were forbidden by the Jesuits. Finally the boy's mother, who was judged to be an excellent Christian, had the priest in charge of the mission explain to her son that in its revised form, this rite was no sin (34:113). The child was later carried to the hospital at Sainte-Marie, where he died and apparently was buried in the mission cemetery.

These new regulations and the growing sense of dependence on the Jesuits as the Iroquois became more menacing, resulted in many more conversions. We have estimated that by the spring of 1646, about 500 Huron considered themselves to be Christians. The following year over 500 were baptized (30:223) and in 1647–48, another 800.[2] There were approximately 1700 baptisms in 1648–49, not counting the many that took place during the destruction of Teanaostaiaé (33:257). From July 1648 to March 1649, about 1300 people were baptized.[3] These figures indicate the degree to which the Huron turned to the Jesuits for leadership in the final crisis that overwhelmed them. By the summer of 1648 about one Huron in five was a Christian and as the crisis deepened, this figure rose to almost one in two. By 1648 the number of Christians in Ossossané, Teanaostaiaé, Scanonaenrat, and Taenhatentaron had increased to the point where people had to stand outside the village chapels during Sunday services, even though successive masses were said (33:141).

Another indication of the growing influence of the Jesuits was that in 1646 they were able to renew their work among the Tionnontaté, which Huron opposition had forced them to abandon after 1641. The Jesuits claimed that the Tionnontaté urged them to return (33:143) and the latter may have done so to develop closer relations with the French. The Jesuits were undoubtedly eager to continue this mission, which suited their desire both to work farther afield and to extend French influence among other tribes, who might be useful trading partners for the French should the Huron be dispersed or break off their alliance.

To make a new beginning among the Tionnontaté, Fathers Charles Garnier and Léonard Garreau were dispatched to Ekarenniondi, the chief settlement of the Deer group, in October 1646 (Jones 1908:361). There they began the Mission of St. Mathias. The following year, Father Garreau remained at Ekarenniondi, while Garnier opened the Mission of St. Jean at

Etharita, which was the principal village of the Wolf group and also the largest of the Tionnontaté settlements (ibid. 370; Thwaites 1896–1901, 33:143; map 30). In February 1649 Noël Chabanel became a missionary to the Tionnontaté at Ekarenniondi (St. Matthieu) (Jones 1908:380). The work among the Tionnontaté was considered sufficiently important that in 1648 a member of the royal family was persuaded to become its patroness. This no doubt involved extending considerable financial support to these missions (Thwaites 1896–1901, 32:137).

THE END OF THE TRUCE

Early in January 1648 the Huron dispatched another embassy to the Onondaga to reaffirm the peace between them and to present beaver pelts to the Onondaga headmen to counteract gifts from the Mohawk and Seneca urging them to resume their attacks on the Huron. Six Huron were chosen to make this trip and they set out with one of the three Onondaga who had remained behind as hostages after the rest of the Onondaga had returned home the previous autumn. The other two hostages remained behind, one of whom was Scandouati, the chief ambassador. Not far from Taenhatentaron 100 Mohawk warriors killed all but two of the Huron envoys; those who escaped are reported to have continued on their way. They also spared the life of the Onondaga hostage, planning to return him to his own country (Thwaites 1896–1901, 33:125). It is likely that these Mohawk warriors had been sent to intercept the Huron envoys and thereby to break off communications between the Huron and Onondaga, just as the Seneca were trying to disrupt contact between the Huron and Susquehannock.

It is uncertain how quickly the Huron learned about the fate of their mission; however, Scandouati disappeared from Taenhatentaron about 1 April and it was generally believed that he had fled to save his life. A few days later, his corpse was found in the nearby forest and it was publicly stated that he had cut his own throat. His companion who remained with the Huron stated that Scandouati had killed himself because of the affront that the Mohawk and the Seneca were committing against his honour by continuing to attack the Huron. He told the Huron that Scandouati had instructed the Onondaga who returned home the previous autumn to remind their allies that he was an important man for whom they should cease their attacks so long as his life was in any danger. While the refusal of the Mohawk and Seneca to do this might have affronted Scandouati's

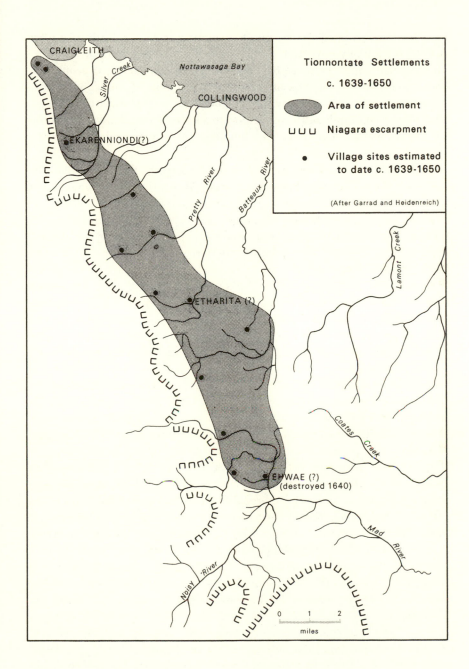

CRAIGLEITH

Silver Creek

Nottawasaga Bay

COLLINGWOOD

EKARENNIONDI(?)

Pretty River

Batteaux River

Lamont Creek

ETHARITA (?)

Coates Creek

EHWAE (?)
(destroyed 1640)

Mad River

Noisy River

Tionnontate Settlements
c. 1639-1650

Area of settlement

⊔⊔⊔ Niagara escarpment

• Village sites estimated
to date c. 1639-1650

(After Garrad and Heidenreich)

0   1   2
miles

MAP 30. *Tionnontaté settlements, c. 1639 to 1650.*

honour to the point of driving him to commit suicide, his death (if it were suicide) more likely resulted from his conviction that as a result of what the Mohawk had done, the truce between the Huron and his own people was bound to collapse. Yet, even after he was dead, some Huron continued to hope that their negotiations with the Onondaga might continue (33:127) and they asked Scandouati's companion to absolve them of any responsibility for his death. Soon after, the Onondaga were once again raiding the Huron.

Scandouati thus appears to have judged correctly the effect that the slaughter of the Huron embassy would have. When the Onondaga saw that their two most powerful allies were not interested in obtaining Huron furs through the ritual exchange associated with a peace treaty and were determined to have them join in an attack on the Huron, they must have decided that the best way to satisfy their requirements for furs was by joining these allies.

Towards the end of the winter of 1647–48, a band of Seneca attacked an isolated cabin of Huron men and women who were part of a larger group of some 300 Huron who were hunting deer two days south of Taenhatentaron. Seven Huron were killed on the spot and twenty-four more were taken prisoner. Most of the inhabitants of this cabin were Christians and among those who were killed was a young man named Ignace Saonaretsi whom the Jesuits regarded as a model convert. The Seneca also captured the Onondaga who had remained behind with Scandouati as a hostage. He had been invited to accompany the Huron on their hunting expedition. When the Seneca recognized him, they treated him as an ally, but compelled him to join them as a member of their band (33:83–89, 165–67).

A few days later the rest of the hunting party from Taenhatentaron visited the site of this cabin to collect the bodies of the dead and to retrieve the deer meat that remained there. Being convinced that the Seneca had retired with their booty, they returned home in small groups. They did not know that the Mohawk warriors who had attacked the Huron envoys in January were still roaming in the vicinity of Taenhatentaron in the hope of intercepting any further messages to the Onondaga. These Mohawk had been in contact with the Seneca and thus knew what had happened a few days before. They therefore lay in wait for the Huron as they retired to Taenhatentaron and killed, or took prisoner, some forty more of them (33:89). The most important of those who were taken prisoner was Nicolas Annenharisonk, the only son of Ignace Onaconchiaronk, in whose cabin the Jesuits lived. In addition, Onaconchiaronk lost five nephews and a niece in these raids (33:167). One woman was captured by the Onondaga hostage who had joined the Mohawk. As the Iroquois made ready to return to their own country, he announced that he could not follow them, as his honour constrained him to remain with the Huron and his own people would not forgive him if he were to return to them under the present circumstances. The Iroquois allowed him to return to Taenhatentaron and to take with him the Huron woman he had captured. It was from her that the Huron learned the details of what had happened.

These attacks convinced the inhabitants of Taenhatentaron that the Mohawk and Seneca were planning to launch a major assault on their town. Because of this they began to disperse. Many sought shelter in villages that were located closer to Sainte-Marie and the Jesuits dismantled the chapel that they had established in one of the longhouses (33:89, 167). By the middle of April, the village was nearly deserted. Felix Martin and later writers have assumed that following the advice of the Jesuits, the inhabitants of Taenhatentaron founded a new village located closer to Sainte-Marie, where the French could more easily come to their aid. Father Brébeuf is said to have helped the Huron to fortify this settlement in the French manner. The site of the new community has been hypothetically fixed on the west bank of the Sturgeon River, near where it enters Matchedash Bay (Jones 1908:366). According to this theory, the new town bore the same name, or at least the same Christian name, as had the previous one.

The major objection to this theory is that the Taenhatentaron (St. Ignace) that was attacked by the Iroquois in 1649 was no nearer to Sainte-Marie than the original village had been; both were about two leagues distant and appear to have been located on the east bank of the Sturgeon River.[4] Thus the strategic advantage of the proposed move seems highly problematical. Bressani states that St. Ignace was impregnable in 1649, both because of its natural location and because of the defences that the French had constructed there (Thwaites 1896–1901, 39:247). This suggests that after an initial panic, when the inhabitants of Taenhatentaron fled towards Sainte-Marie, they were persuaded to return to their settlement by the Jesuits, who agreed to protect them against the Iroquois.[5] Presumably the strengthening of the defences of the town did not involve rebuilding the sixteen-foot-high stockade of pine trunks that already surrounded it, but rather meant the addition of towers from which French musketeers could defend these stockades. It may even be that when Taenhatentaron was originally constructed, its walls were laid out with such defences in mind, as had happened considerably earlier at Ossossané. Whatever aid the French provided, it seems that at least some of the inhabitants of Taenhatentaron returned to their town and planted crops there; however, by the beginning of the winter of 1648–49, many of the inhabitants again grew fearful of Iroquois attack and withdrew to other villages, leaving only about 400 people to spend the winter there.

The Defeat of the Traditionalists

It might have been anticipated that as the Iroquois pressed their attack against the Huron, the more radical anti-Jesuit faction would have become discouraged and cease to fight for their cause. On the contrary, by the spring of 1648 the wrath of a goodly number of the more traditionally oriented Huron had increased to the point where they were prepared for the first time to act decisively to put an end to the influence of the Jesuits, even if this meant breaking off trading relations with the French. The Jesuits do not identify the leaders of this movement by name, but it is clear that important headmen from various parts of the Huron country were involved in it (Thwaites 1896–1901, 33:229–31) and that they counted on support from many Huron in an open confrontation with the Jesuits and their Christian supporters. It also appears that the refugees from Contarea, who were now dispersed in other Huron villages, were among those who most zealously supported this movement. They had formerly been the most vocal in support of the peace treaty with the Onondaga and their behaviour at this time may explain why the Jesuits later felt such an aversion to them (42:73). The Jesuits mention that one individual who was very hostile to Christianity lived in Scanonaenrat (34:115). Doubtlessly men of this sort could be found in most Huron communities.

These ardent traditionalists felt strongly enough to challenge the basic pillar of the French-Huron alliance: the French demand that the Jesuits be permitted to live and teach in the Huron country. That they were prepared to do this suggests they were convinced that an alternative to the alliance with the French existed. This meant that they believed they could find an alternative source of European goods. While the Jesuits, not unexpectedly, have little to say about the activities or motivations of these people, it seems clear that they thought that peace with the Iroquois was possible if the Huron agreed to stop trading with the French and diverted their surplus furs to them. They must have convinced themselves that the Mohawk and Seneca had refused to consider earlier peace proposals because they believed that the Christian Huron who were negotiating with the Onondaga were seeking to sow dissension among the Iroquois rather than to make peace. Even the Onondaga might have sensed this duplicity and consequently rejected Huron peace proposals. The logical outcome of this line of reasoning was a conviction that the Huron had to make a dramatic gesture of good faith before their proposal would become credible to the Iroquois and be accepted by them. The most dramatic gesture would be the renunciation by the Huron of their alliance with the French.

The termination of this alliance was, of course, fraught with danger. It would deepen the existing cleavages between Huron who were Christians and those who were not and the expulsion of the Jesuits from the Huron country might induce many Huron Christians to follow them, thus reducing the numerical strength of the confederacy. There was also no assurance that the Iroquois would not take advantage of any weakness that would result from the rupture of the French-Huron alliance and attack the Huron more violently than before. Finally, the traditionalists must have known that even if they succeeded in making peace with the Iroquois, they would henceforth be dependent on their former enemies for all types of European goods. This was tantamount to accepting a position of permanent subordination to the Iroquois.

Yet, in spite of the warfare that had gone on between the two groups for many generations, the Huron and Iroquois shared a common cultural pattern; therefore domination by the Iroquois posed no cultural threat to the traditionalists. Indeed, an alliance with the Iroquois could be expected to strengthen precisely those aspects of the Huron way of life that were being undermined by the Jesuits. It is a measure of how threatened those Huron who were committed to maintaining traditional ways had become that now, for the first time, a respectable body of opinion had emerged which viewed an alliance with longstanding enemies who shared similar beliefs to be preferable to one with European allies who were seeking to change the Huron way of life. To be rid of the Jesuits, many Huron were now willing to gamble their very survival in an effort to secure the goodwill of the Iroquois.

It is unknown whether the leaders of this emerging anti-Jesuit faction had any contact with the Iroquois. It is not unlikely, however, that such contacts did take place, possibly through the Onondaga hostage, who was living with the Huron as late as April 1648. It is possible that the Seneca and Mohawk sought to divide their intended victims by encouraging the more extreme Huron traditionalists to believe that peace was still possible.

In April 1648 six leading headmen from three different (unnamed) communities decided to precipitate a crisis by murdering a Frenchman and then demanding that the Jesuits be expelled from the Huron country. To appreciate the significance of this act, it must be remembered that only one Frenchman had ever before been slain by the Huron. That was Etienne Brûlé, who was killed because he was suspected of having dealings with the Iroquois and then only after it was clear that the French had disowned him. Even in the midst of epidemics, for which most Huron blamed the Jesuits, none of the Huron dared to carry out the threats that they had made against the Jesuits' lives.

The six headmen persuaded two brothers to go to Sainte-Marie and kill the first Frenchman whom they met alone there. The brothers left their village on the morning of 28 April and journeyed over twelve miles to Sainte-Marie. Towards evening they encountered a twenty-two-year-old donné named Jacques Douart who was wandering near the settlement. They killed him with a hatchet and left his body to be found by the French. He was almost certainly buried in the cemetery at Sainte-Marie and his grave plausibly has been identified as that containing a skeleton of European type found there by Wilfrid Jury. This skeleton was of a man five feet, two inches tall and around its neck was a brass religious medal and a rosary of blue porcelain beads (Jury and Jury 1954:94–95). Douart had come to Sainte-Marie as a boy helper in 1642 and had become a donné four years later.

As news of the murder spread, Christians came from neighbouring villages to warn the Jesuits that a conspiracy against them was afoot and to offer to help protect them. The French put Sainte-Marie on a defensive footing and took out of service the ferry that ran between their settlement and the west bank of the Wye River (Thwaites 1896–1901, 33:247). Meanwhile, the whole of the Huron country was reported to be in a state of great excitement and headmen were summoned to attend a general meeting of the confederacy council which lasted for two or three days. It is not recorded where this meeting was held and because the Jesuits were not invited to attend, little is known about what happened at it. It is known, however, that the headmen who had instigated Douart's murder demanded that the Jesuits be refused entry to all Huron villages and that they should be made to leave the Huron country as soon as possible. They further demanded that Huron who had become Christians should either agree to abandon their religion or be made to leave the country also. The *Jesuit Relations* do not reveal whether these headmen proposed that the Huron should break off trade with the French and henceforth ally themselves with the Iroquois. Yet it seems inconceivable that they could have proposed the expulsion of the Jesuits without also advocating a realignment of trade and a solution to the deteriorating military situation. The Christians accused these traditionalists of secretly receiving rewards from the Iroquois for betraying the Huron to the enemy.

The contest between the Christian headmen and those who had instigated this crisis, or who espoused their views, was also a personal contest for power. Hitherto, Christian headmen had derived additional prestige from the importance that the Huron attributed to maintaining good relations with the French. If Christianity were to flourish in the Huron country and the French were to continue to discriminate markedly in favour of Christian traders and headmen, it was inevitable that Huron leaders who chose not to become Christians would suffer a continuing loss of influence among their own people. An alliance with the Iroquois offered headmen who did not wish to become Christians an opportunity to regain their influence and to undercut that of the Christian headmen.

Unfortunately for these traditionalists, the very nature of Huron society, with its emphasis on individual freedom and lack of any concept of religious exclusiveness, made the development of an anti-Christian faction impossible until Christianity had become a force among a sizable portion of the population. In the late 1630s, when the Jesuits were widely believed to be sorcerers seeking to destroy the Huron, it might have been possible for a determined group of traditionalists to persuade the Huron to expel them, had they been able to propose an alternative trading arrangement. At that time, however, there was no clear awareness of the threat that the Jesuits posed to the Huron way of life and an alliance that made the Huron dependent on the Iroquois was inconceivable. By 1648 it was a feeling of total desperation that drove a minority of the traditionalists to propose such a relationship as being preferable to tolerating the continued presence of the Jesuits. As it turned out, a majority of the non-Christians still feared the Iroquois to the point that they were unwilling to break off their trade with the French, even though not doing so meant accepting the continued presence of the Jesuits and the growth of Christianity. Many of the moderate traditionalists probably resented the missionaries as much as did the more radical ones. For them, however, there was no alternative to the alliance with the French. In the end, these traditionalists sided with the Christians to oppose the termination of the alliance. It was therefore concluded that public reparations should be made to the Jesuits in the name of the whole confederacy (33:229–33).

Once this decision had been made, the Jesuits were invited to the council. A spokesman informed Ragueneau that the Huron regarded the alliance with the French as essential to their survival and condemned the murder of Douart as a heinous crime. Only the Iroquois, he said, could derive satisfaction from seeing their enemies fighting among themselves. The Jesuits were asked not to withdraw from the Huron country and thereby abandon it to its enemies, but rather to state what compensation they required to re-establish normal relations with the Huron.

The Jesuits understood the operation of the Huron legal system and realized that only by conforming with local practice was it possible for them to re-establish a good working relationship with the Huron and ensure their own safety. The Huron Christians advised them that in order to protect Christians generally they must demand a large amount of compensation. The Jesuits therefore asked for approximately 100 presents, each worth ten beaver skins. This was the largest reparations payment ever recorded among the Huron. The Jesuits presented a bundle of sticks to the council, indicating the number of presents that were required. These were divided among the representatives of the tribes and clan segments of the confederacy and the representatives returned to their villages to collect what was required. As usual, the Huron vied with one another in contributing to the public good (33:233–41).

Towards evening on 10 May, a large number of Huron gathered outside Sainte-Marie and four headmen (two Christians and two traditionalists) approached the settlement to speak with Father Ragueneau. At the entrance, they presented their first reparations that the gate might be opened and they might be permitted to enter. Three presents were then given to Ragueneau to placate his anger and nine more which were meant symbolically to erect a sepulchre for the deceased. Following this, eight headmen representing each of the Huron clans presented gifts that symbolized the bringing together of the principal bones in Douart's body. In accordance with Huron custom, Ragueneau reciprocated by offering them 3000 wampum beads to indicate that his anger was abating (33:241–43).

The following day the Jesuits erected a platform outside Sainte-Marie, on which fifty presents were exhibited. It is possible that each of these presents was given by one of the fifty clan segments that were represented on the Huron confederacy council, as the first round of presents had been given on behalf of the four Huron tribes and the second on behalf of the eight clans. The Jesuits had the right to examine these presents and to reject any that did not satisfy them. Finally, a series of presents were given that were meant symbolically to clothe the deceased, erase the memory of his murder, and restore normal relations between the French and the Huron. The latter presents included one asking that Sainte-Marie be re-opened to Huron visitors, who seem on principle to have been excluded from the settlement since the crisis began. The last three presents were given by the three principal Huron headmen, either the tribal chiefs of the Attignawantan, Attigneenongnahac, and Arendarhonon, or, more likely, the heads of three Huron phratries. These presents urged the Jesuits always to love the Huron.

In return, the Jesuits gave presents to the representatives of each of the eight Huron clans. These presents were designed to assure the Huron of the Jesuits' friendship and to refute the rumours that the Jesuits were responsible for all the wars, famines, and disease from which the Huron suffered. They also exhorted the Huron to remain united and assured them that the French at Montreal, Three Rivers, and Quebec would forget this murder and treat them kindly since they had made reparations for it (33:243–49).

The defeat of the anti-Jesuit faction put an end to organized resistance to the missionaries in the Huron country and averted any danger that the Huron would renounce their trading relationship with the French. In the short term, the Jesuits had every reason to be pleased with the outcome of this crisis. A well-organized attempt to expel them from the country had been unsuccessful and a majority of the Huron had once again been forced to acknowledge their dependence on the French, and now more specifically on the Jesuits. Any danger that the Huron confederacy would break their alliance with the French and conclude an alternative one with the Iroquois could now be ruled out.

Fears of such a treaty, which would have diverted the Huron fur trade from the St. Lawrence into the Hudson Valley, had haunted the French for a long time. Although such an alliance might have assured the survival of the Huron confederacy, it would almost certainly have undermined the prosperity of New France to the point where the survival of the colony, and of the French presence in North America, would have been very doubtful. While the destruction of the Huron confederacy was to be a serious set-back for the French, within a short time they were able to put together the rudiments of a new trading network in the upper Great Lakes area. Whether or not the Jesuits realized it at the time, the destruction of the confederacy was less of a threat to French interests than its survival as an economic satellite of the Iroquois and the Dutch would have been.

In spite of this, the Jesuits' victory was not achieved without cost to the Huron people, as the Jesuits themselves must have realized. They urged the Huron to remain united so that they might better resist their enemies. Yet, the factionalism that they deplored was mainly of their own creation and the bitterness of those Huron who resented the spread of Christianity was no less because most of them also believed that their trading alliance with the French was indispensable since it protected them against the Iroquois. The rejection of the proposal that they expel the Jesuits at the cost of breaking the alliance revealed to many Huron into what a weakened and dependent state they had fallen. The majority of Christians already looked to the Jesuits for leadership and had staked their future on the Jesuits providing them with the guidance and protection that they required for their survival. This, however, was leadership that still had to be put to the test.

Following the crisis, overt opposition to the Jesuits' teachings declined sharply and many Huron who had formerly been outspoken in their opposition ceased to speak against the Jesuits and even began to pay attention to them (34:101–3). While the Jesuits rejoiced that the progress of Roman Catholicism was surpassing their fondest hopes, it is possible to detect in this reaction a growing feeling of apathy and resignation among the traditionalists, who no longer felt able to control their own destiny. Far from being animated by a new faith, many Huron apparently ceased to try to influence events and looked towards the future with a sense of bitter resignation. Numerous Huron who had supported the expulsion of the Jesuits were probably as prepared to see an Iroquois victory as to see the creation of a Christian Huron nation. Those who had relatives living as captives among the Iroquois were lured by hopes of being reunited with these relatives and, by becoming Iroquois, to remain part of a traditional Iroquoian society.

As the Iroquois menace increased, the Huron traditionalists split internally between those who were willing to throw themselves on the mercy of the Iroquois, or to find refuge among some other traditional Iroquoian group, and those who sought the protection of the French. Later, when the Jesuits revealed their inability to offer adequate leadership or protection against the Iroquois, many who had relied on their protection also sought a home for themselves among the Iroquois. As the Jesuits outflanked the opposition to their activities amongst the Huron, they found themselves responsible for a situation in which a growing number of Huron lacked the will to provide leadership or to continue to assume responsibility for the destiny of their own society.

The Destruction of the Huron Confederacy

THE END OF THE ATTIGNEENONGNAHAC

Because of their fear of the Iroquois, the Huron did not go to trade with the French in 1647. This resulted in considerable financial loss for the French traders and made them uncertain about the future. Their fears were doubtlessly compounded by new ones for the safety of the Jesuits, since rumours about the Huron's negotiations with the Iroquois were reaching Quebec. Early in 1648 it was decided that an envoy should bear the French governor's voice to the Huron councils to acquaint the Huron with the state of affairs in Quebec and to encourage them to come to trade. Conditions were so uncertain, however, that the messenger was given further orders that when he arrived in the Huron country, he should obtain Father Ragueneau's permission before saying or doing anything. The man chosen for this job, a soldier surnamed Chastillon, left Three Rivers in the company of two Huron Christians, René Oheraenti and Michel, on 24 April. A pinnace escorted them as far as the Rivière des Prairies and they presumably arrived safely in the Huron country (Thwaites 1896–1901, 32:69, 85). While this gesture may have helped to reassure the Huron, the necessity of obtaining hatchets, gunpowder, and other French products that were in short supply had already convinced them that in spite of the dangers involved, they had to trade with the French that year (32:179). By the beginning of July, many Huron men had left their communities and were preparing to carry their furs to the St. Lawrence or to engage in trade elsewhere. Still others appear to have gone in search of the enemy, no doubt in the hope that they might give warning of any impending attack. Because of the need to trade, the Huron were compelled to abandon their careful defensive posture of the previous year.

It was just as these traders were preparing to leave that a force of several hundred Iroquois managed to penetrate the Huron country undetected and to destroy Teanaostaiaé, one of the largest and best-fortified Huron settlements. They also sacked a small neighbouring community, probably the one variously known as Ekhiondastsaan, Tiondatsae, or La Chaudière (Heidenreich 1971:44). Both communities were Attigneenongnahac and Teanaostaiaé had been singled out for possible attack because it was located in the upper part of the Sturgeon Valley, which was now the southeastern frontier of the Huron country. The destruction of Teanaostaiaé spread terror throughout the Huron confederacy.

The raiders, who were well-armed with muskets, approached Teanaostaiaé on the night of 3 July. From some prisoners they had captured, they learned that many young men were absent and on the basis of this information they resolved to attack the town. Teanaostaiaé was located above the fork of a steeply banked stream flowing into the Sturgeon River; the Iroquois were therefore only able to approach it from the north (39:239; map 31). At sunrise, the Christians of Teanaostaiaé had gathered in the local church to hear mass. Scarcely was the mass over, when the Iroquois burst into the town and began to loot, kill, and set fire to the longhouses. In spite of the confusion, many Huron took up arms and, for a time, they seem to have contained the enemy. Father Daniel encouraged this resistance and, by sprinkling water into the crowd, baptized large numbers of Huron who sought this additional form of supernatural protection as they hurled themselves into the battle. At the same time, many women and children took advantage of this respite to flee through the various gates of the town and to try to make their way to safety.

Eventually, however, the defenders began to disperse and it became evident that the Iroquois would soon control the town. At this point, Father Daniel went through the remaining longhouses to baptize certain sick and aged people he had been instructing and finally made his way back to the church, which was full of Christians who had gathered there to receive baptism and absolution. When the Iroquois learned that a large number of Huron had gathered in the church and that much booty could be obtained there, they hastened to attack it. Father Daniel advised the Christians to flee, but he himself advanced to the front door of the church to meet the enemy. His appearance surprised the Iroquois, who stared at him for a time before they killed him with arrows and gunfire. They stripped him of his robes in anger because they had not taken him alive, and began to hack up his body. After the flames from the longhouses had set fire to the church they tossed his body into the burning building (33:259–65; 34:87–93; 39:239–43).

This diversion gave the Huron more time to escape. Although the Iroquois later searched for these refugees in the nearby forests, many managed to reach other villages and no small number made their way to Sainte-Marie, where the Jesuits provided them with food and clothing. On their way home, the Iroquois compelled their captives to carry the furs and trade goods that they had pillaged from the two communities and killed those who were unable to keep up with them. Of a normal population of about 2000, which was doubtlessly swollen by Arendarhonon refugees, 700 people are estimated to have been killed or taken prisoner by the Iroquois. Most of these were women and children (34:99). While more Huron

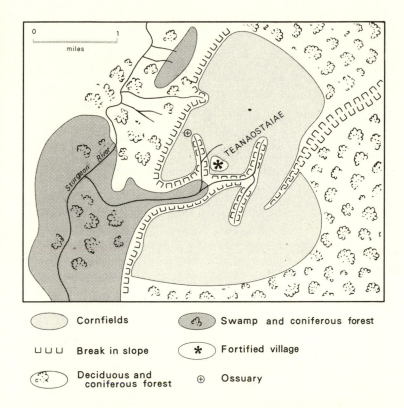

Cornfields		Swamp and coniferous forest	
⊔⊔⊔ Break in slope		✳ Fortified village	
Deciduous and coniferous forest		⊕ Ossuary	

MAP 31. *Reconstruction of the field pattern and natural setting of Teanaostaiaé c. 1648 (Lot 12, Conc. IV, Medonte Twp.) (after C. E. Heidenreich).*

escaped from Teanaostaiaé than were lost there, the destruction of this one community cost the Huron about one-tenth of their remaining population. It was thus a very serious blow to the confederacy. Moreover, while Father Daniel's death again demonstrated that the Jesuits were willing not only to live with the Huron but also to die alongside them (39:243), it did little to reassure the Huron that the French were able to protect them.

After this attack, Teanaostaiaé remained abandoned. The dislocation of over 1000 Huron in mid-summer, when it was impossible to clear and plant new fields, combined with the general panic that seems to have seized the Huron elsewhere, probably accounts for the famine of the following winter. Since the Jesuits had no problem with their crops (33:259), drought or natural crop damage had little to do with this famine. The likely destruction of the crops at Teanaostaiaé and the fear that women had of going to work in their fields elsewhere would have used up the surpluses and cut into the essential supplies of the remaining Huron villages. Hunt (1940:94) has correctly noted the important role that starvation played at this time in weakening the Huron, but he was wrong about the reason for it. He argued that in the years prior to their destruction, the Huron had engaged so exclusively in trade that they neglected farming and obtained most of their corn from the Neutral and Tionnontaté. According to Hunt, the Iroquois raids of this period were sufficient to destroy the finely spun trading networks on which the Huron were totally dependent for their subsistence. The inadequacies of Hunt's theories about the decline of Huron agriculture have been discussed in chapter 6 and they do not explain the famine at this time.

THE TRADE OF 1648

In spite of the disaster at Teanaostaiaé, about 250 Huron accompanied by Father Bressani and two other Frenchmen journeyed to Three Rivers in order to trade with the French. They departed under the leadership of five headmen and, unlike most years, kept their canoes close together over the entire route in order to be able to defend themselves better. No Iroquois were encountered along the Ottawa River, no doubt because the Mohawk and Oneida bands who habitually waited to attack the traders as they came down-river were inadequate to challenge so many Huron at one time.

When the Huron came within sight of Three Rivers, they anchored their canoes in the reeds along the north shore of the St. Lawrence to paint their faces and grease their hair so as to be suitably attired to meet the French. Some Huron who were acting as scouts were sighted by Iroquois lurking on the opposite bank of the St. Lawrence. The latter crossed the river in force to attack the Huron. The Huron's forward guard observed what was happening and before the Iroquois arrived, the Huron had time to seize their weapons and form a semi-circle in the woods around the spot where the Iroquois were landing. The Iroquois charged the Huron line, firing their muskets. The Huron escaped injury by dropping to the ground; then, as the Iroquois charged, the Huron rose and fired their guns at them. The Iroquois broke up in confusion, some fighting their way through the Huron line. The more agile Huron pursued these refugees, killing and scalping some and taking others prisoners (Thwaites 1896–1901, 32:179–83). The desire to reach Three Rivers prevented the Huron from pursuing the

Iroquois as relentlessly as they might have done, but the extent of their victory is indicated by the fact that in addition to the ten or fifteen Iroquois who were killed (32:97), eighteen to twenty more were taken prisoner (32:179). One Iroquois was so frightened that he made his way to Montreal, where he voluntarily surrendered himself to a French woman in the courtyard of the hospital (32:183). Another, however, when he saw his brother taken prisoner, made his way to Three Rivers and surrendered to the Huron. He did this because he had promised never to abandon this brother (33:43–45).

After the battle was over, the Huron took their prisoners into their canoes and ordered them to sing as they approached Three Rivers. When they landed, the Christians, who made up about half of the expedition, forced the prisoners to kneel with them before a cross that had been erected at the gate of the fort. This was done to make them apologize for having broken down a cross that the French had set up near the mouth of the Richelieu River (33:45). The prisoners were then made to ascend a scaffold and one of them was given to the Algonkin, who killed him, but without torture, so as not to anger the French. A Huron who had become naturalized among the Iroquois was tortured to death; to mollify the French, it was pointed out that he was a heretic who had been baptized but had abandoned the Christian religion after he had been adopted by the Iroquois (32:185). The other prisoners apparently were kept by the Huron and eventually were taken home with them.

The Huron reached Three Rivers between 17 and 22 July (32:97, 173–75), and, soon after, Montmagny arrived to attend the annual reaffirmation of the French-Huron alliance. The Huron offered their traditional presents to salute him and request that the price of trade goods be reduced. Then, two extra presents were given to thank the Jesuits for exposing themselves to so many dangers to carry out their mission work and to urge them to persevere in the propagation of Christianity among the Huron (32:185–87). While these presents undoubtedly reflect the growing influence of the Christian faction, they were also an elliptical request for protection against the Iroquois. So long as the Jesuits continued to live among the Huron, the latter felt assured that the French would do all in their power to protect the Huron. Montmagny gave the Huron presents to assure them that the French at Quebec no longer sought revenge for the murder of Douart, since the Huron had atoned for this murder according to the laws of their country (32:187). For the Huron, these presents marked the formal end of the Douart affair. Montmagny also required the Huron to keep their promise to listen to the Jesuits. The Huron traders were given an escort of eight soldiers, who were to remain at Sainte-Marie over the winter. They were to defend the settlement and possibly to help with the fortifications that were being constructed there. The soldiers were to return to Quebec the following summer with the Huron traders (33:253).

The French also dispatched to the Huron country four missionaries newly arrived from France, Gabriel Lalemant (nephew of Jérôme), Jacques Bonin, Adrien Greslon, and Adrien Daran; one lay brother, Nicolas Noircler; nine workmen; and three boys (32:99). Four more soldiers were to be picked up at Montreal, although these do not appear to have reached the Huron country (33:253). The French also took with them large quantities of supplies to replenish Sainte-Marie. These included a heifer and a small cannon. They left Three Rivers on 6 August. After reaching Montreal Island, some proceeded up the Rivière des Prairies, while others visited Ville-Marie seeking the four soldiers that had been promised them. The French feared that this splitting of the Huron convoy would expose them to attack by the Iroquois (32:189–91), but all of the Huron reached their homes safely in early September (34:101). They were jubilant about their victory over the Iroquois and their successful trade.

NEW TROUBLE ON THE ST. LAWRENCE

What must have pleased the returning Huron far less was their discovery that the French had again been discussing peace with the Mohawk. These discussions had begun on 18 May, when two Iroquois canoes arrived at Montreal. Their occupants had reiterated the longstanding Mohawk offer to make peace with the French, provided the latter would let them wage war on the Algonkians, whom they described as their sole enemies. Their main aim seems to have been to secure the release of a Mohawk who had been taken prisoner by the French the previous autumn. This man, who was believed to have slain Jogues, had remained behind to aid his wounded brother. What the Mohawk did not know was that this prisoner had been taken to Sillery, where Montmagny had turned him over to the resident Indians. The latter had slain him shortly after he was baptized in October 1647 (Thwaites 1896–1901, 32:19–27).

The French were anxious to recover two of their own men, but finally they had to admit that their Mohawk prisoner was dead. The Mohawk claimed not to be upset by this news and announced that soon some of the oldest and most prominent of their headmen would be coming to Montreal to confer with the French. Yet, at the same time a Frenchman who had gone hunting near Montreal was attacked by an Iroquois and the nets that the French had set in the river near the fort were carried off by the departing "peace mission" (32:143–49).

On 30 May a Mohawk and a Huron who had been adopted by the Mohawk voluntarily surrendered to a party of Frenchmen who were fishing opposite Three Rivers. The three other Iroquois who accompanied these men feared to approach the French when they saw that the latter were accompanied by their Huron and Algonkin allies. They tried to flee, but one was overtaken by an Algonkin, who killed him and tore off his scalp. The Iroquois who had turned himself over to the French announced that he was one of the prisoners whose lives Montmagny had saved in 1644. He claimed to have been wounded trying to save Father Jogues and that his intention was to promote better relations between his people and the French. The French did not trust either him or his companion and put both of them in iron leg-fetters.

On 20 June twenty-nine Iroquois entrenched themselves on the south shore of the St. Lawrence and began to communicate with Three Rivers. At first they claimed to number about 400 and to have with them headmen who wished to discuss peace, but later they admitted that these claims were untrue. After conferring with the Iroquois who was held prisoner, two more Iroquois agreed to remain as hostages with the French. In return, the French temporarily released their prisoner and sent him and the younger of the hostages back to their own people to urge them to negotiate in good faith (32:149–57). They returned soon after.

On 3 July the Huron who had surrendered to the French was given permission to go to Montreal in order to collect some beaver skins that he claimed to have left there. His aim, however, was to meet a band of over eighty Mohawk, who he knew would be lurking in the vicinity of Lake St. Peter. He told these Iroquois that the Mohawk who were held prisoner at Three Rivers were being treated badly by the French and were certain to be killed by them. This report incited the Mohawk to conduct a raid near Three Rivers, in the course of which a number of French and Huron were killed and taken prisoner. Not long after, the French learned that 100 Mohawk commanded both sides of the St. Lawrence near Three Rivers. They also learned that these warriors were confused by the conflicting stories they had heard from the envoys who were seeking peace and the former Huron who was spreading rumours that the French were ill-treating their prisoners.

The French therefore gave the oldest of the prisoners permission to visit his people, after which he returned to the French. The Mohawk warriors asked for food at this time, claiming to be hard pressed, although eighty sacks of corn were later found in their fort. While the Mohawk were negotiating an exchange of prisoners, they continued to harass the Indians around Three Rivers. Further negotiations were cut short, however, when the Iroquois, as mentioned above, were defeated and scattered by the Huron traders who were coming to Three Rivers (32:157–85). The Iroquois who had originally surrendered to the French was sent to France, where he remained in the care of the Jesuits. In 1650 he died of a lung infection in Paris (36:21–45).

The motive for these tortuous negotiations is far from certain. Possibly, the Mohawk were interested in trying once more to persuade the French to abandon their allies and assume a more neutral role in their dealings with the various Indian tribes. By now, however, the Mohawk must have been fully aware of the unlikelihood of this happening. The prisoners had likely been seeking to reconnoitre the defences at Three Rivers prior to an attack and were surprised when the French kept them in such close confinement that their intended escape became impossible. This compelled the Mohawk to negotiate for their release before an attack could be launched. Rumours had reached the Huron country prior to the departure of the Huron traders that the Mohawk were intent on attacking Three Rivers and were directing their war songs against both the French and the Algonkin (32:169). A Huron captive, who was part of the Mohawk band in the vicinity of Three Rivers, also warned a Huron who was living with the French that the Iroquois would soon invite the French to a conference where they planned to kill the lot of them (32:175). Not long afterwards, about a dozen Iroquois ambushed some Frenchmen who were working near Montreal and killed one of them (32:169).

The Huron did not comment on the negotiations between the French and the Mohawk while they were at Three Rivers. They must, however, have viewed the actions of the Mohawk as an attempt to separate the French from their Algonkin and Huron allies so that they might attack each of the latter more easily. The Huron had always been mistrustful of negotiations between French and Mohawk, for fear they would undermine their own relationship with the French. It was undoubtedly from Huron who had returned from Quebec that the Tionnontaté heard that in order to prevent an Iroquois attack on the French settlements, Montmagny had sent presents to the Iroquois urging them to attack the Huron instead. According to these rumours, which were probably spread by Huron traditionalists,

Montmagny had ordered the French to aid their Huron and Algonkin allies in appearance only, but to load their guns with powder but no shot so they would do no harm to the Iroquois (35:165).

A POSSIBLE REPRIEVE FOR THE TRADITIONALISTS

After 1645 important changes took place in the organization of trade in New France. It is unlikely, however, that the Huron were sufficiently aware of the nature of these changes to be able to assess the impact they would have on the ability of the Jesuits to impose their will upon them. In March 1645 the French government approved an arrangement whereby the Compagnie des Cent-Associés granted an absolute monopoly of the fur trade to a new association made up of French settlers who were resident in the colony. This Communauté des Habitants undertook to meet the colony's public expenses and to promote settlement as previous monopoly holders had done.

The decree announcing these changes was posted at Quebec in August 1645. Soon after, the new directors reversed the former policy of the Compagnie des Cent-Associés by forbidding anyone to have individual dealings with the Indians in beaver or other furs, under penalty of fines and confiscation. The Jesuits who had helped to promote the new trading association were, however, secretly excluded from this order, provided that they conducted their business discreetly (Lanctot 1963:183–87; Thwaites 1896–1901, 27:99). In 1647 a new regulation granted settlers in New France the right to purchase furs directly from the Indians, but only in exchange for produce originating in New France. The settlers were required to sell all such furs to the community stores at prices set by a council that was established to manage the affairs of the colony (Lanctot 1963:190). This regulation gave the Jesuits considerably more bargaining power, since they could threaten to allow private trade at Sillery. This would divert skins from direct exchange at the official warehouse at Quebec and reduce the profit made by the community (Thwaites 1896–1901, 30:187).

After the death of Cardinal Richelieu, the Jesuit missionaries lost the support of the Duchesse d'Aiguillon at the French court (Lanctot 1963:183) and in the later half of the decade the influence of the Société de Notre-Dame de Montréal increased rapidly. In 1648 the Jesuits suffered a further setback when their protégé Montmagny was replaced as governor of New France, after he had held that office for twelve years. He was succeeded by the thirty-six-year-old Louis d'Ailleboust, who had settled in Canada in 1643 and had served as Maisonneuve's lieutenant at Montreal. As soon as he returned from France, d'Ailleboust published a new decree authorizing the settlers to import their own trade goods and granting them the legal right to barter furs among the Indian tribes of the interior (ibid. 192–94). While primarily designed to stimulate the dwindling and imperilled fur trade of New France, the right of laymen to visit distant tribes on their own initiative eliminated the de facto control over contact between French and Huron on which the Jesuit mission program had been based. If large numbers of traders began to frequent the Huron country, the Huron would soon realize that being a Christian was no longer a vital part of their trading relationship with the French and an indifferent attitude towards Christianity might reassert itself. The Jesuits also must have feared that these traders would undermine the high moral standards they had striven to set for their converts. Commercial interests were threatening the Jesuits' monopoly of souls in the Huron country.

While the last regulation was announced too late to allow French settlers to visit the Huron country in 1648, the soldiers who went there for the winter took advantage of their new rights to trade with the Indians without restriction. When two of these soldiers, the brothers Desfosses, returned to the St. Lawrence in 1649, they brought with them 747 pounds of beaver skins that they had obtained from the Huron (Thwaites 1896–1901, 34:59–61). While it is safe to assume that these soldiers lived under Jesuit supervision, the furs indicated what enterprising traders might hope to achieve there. Privately financed expeditions, whose members were independent of Jesuit control, were now only a matter of time.

CHRISTIAN SUPREMACY IN OSSOSSANÉ

The famine and dislocation resulting from the dispersal of the Attigneenongnahac led increasing numbers of Huron to turn to the Jesuits for relief and protection. Throughout the summer of 1648 and the following winter, thousands of Huron visited Sainte-Marie for varying periods in search of food and shelter. Thus, for a while, the influence of the Jesuits increased still more as the Huron looked to them for leadership. One result of this was particularly evident in Ossossané, which was the oldest of the surviving Jesuit missions. As late as the summer of 1648, the traditionalists were a majority there, although three of the principal headmen of the town were Christians and they were able to enforce respect for Christianity (Thwaites 1896–1901, 33:141).

By the beginning of the winter, however, the Christians had become a majority. At that point, they assembled and conferred about their future course of action. It is not clear that any Jesuits were present at this meeting, but it is likely that beforehand the Jesuits had coached their leading converts what to say so that their policy would appear to be the Indians' own ideas. At this council it was decided that the priest who had charge of the Ossossané mission would henceforth be regarded as the principal headman of the community. He was also empowered to forbid any public practice that was contrary to Roman Catholic teaching and, more generally, to reform the ritual and moral life of the community.

Throughout the winter the Christian headmen conferred with Father Chaumonot and carried out his orders. Because the Christians occupied a majority of seats on the village council, they were able to prevent public approval from being given for the performance of all non-Christian rituals, thus effectively putting a stop to them. No public assistance was extended to anyone to help him to fulfil dream wishes. A traditionalist of some renown attempted to challenge the hold that the Christians had acquired over life in Ossossané. When the villagers assembled to perform a war dance, he announced that a dream had ordered him to break open the door of the church and to cut down the pole from which the Jesuits' bell was suspended. Normally, he could have relied on public opinion to support him in fulfilling his wishes, in either a literal or symbolic fashion. As he advanced towards the church, an old Christian, probably René Tsondihwané, announced that this man would have to kill him before he could attack these symbols of Christianity. Seeing that the majority of those who were present supported the old man, rather than himself, the traditionalist stopped singing and desisted from further action (34:105–9).

The traditionalists now found themselves in an unanticipated, and hitherto inconceivable, situation. It would never have occurred to a Huron to refuse to lend assistance to anyone to perform the ceremonies that he believed were necessary for his health and well-being, although the extent of this support would have varied according to the status of the individual and of his lineage. Refusal to perform such rites would have been regarded as evidence of public enmity bordering on witchcraft. Now, however, under Jesuit supervision, such behaviour had become the public policy of Ossossané, which embodied the moral requirements of the new religion.

In March the traditionalist minority decided to appeal for support to neighbouring villages. A sick man requested that a traditional dance be performed to cure him and that this be followed by an andacwander. The latter ritual, involving public sexual intercourse, was, of all Huron practices, the one most certain to anger the Jesuits. When the Christians learned about this request, they opposed it so strongly that no local headman dared to announce the ceremony. A shaman from a neighbouring village was invited to Ossossané to perform the ceremony and with him came some headmen who had promised to support the traditionalists; however, these visitors were compelled to leave the town when they found themselves unable to influence the local council (34:107, 217). Traditionalists now had the option of either conforming with Christian rules and regulations or moving elsewhere. Ossossané was called "the village of Christians" by the rest of the confederacy (34:217).

It may have been in Ossossané that a number of incidents took place about this time that reflect the growing influence of Christianity over the daily lives of the Huron. Husbands and wives are described as resorting to prayer to settle domestic quarrels, which they were taught were caused by the devil (33:163). A "very good Christian woman" is also reported to have beaten her four-year-old son (33:177–79), an action which the Huron regarded as unnatural and reprehensible. The Jesuits considered the traditional Huron attitude to be scandalously indulgent and as nurturing low moral standards; hence they viewed this innovation with great satisfaction.

ST. IGNACE AND ST. LOUIS

In the autumn of 1648 the Iroquois assembled an army of over 1000 men, mainly Seneca and Mohawk, who were well supplied with firearms and ammunition. These men spent the winter in the forests north of Lake Ontario so that they might surprise the Huron early in the spring. The dispersal of the Arendarhonon and Attigneenongnahac seems effectively to have deterred the Huron from attempting to use their hunting territories east of Lake Simcoe that winter and, as a result, this large Iroquois war party was able to advance as far as the Sturgeon Valley without being detected (Thwaites 1896–1901, 34:123–25).

On the night of 16 March the Iroquois reconnoitred Taenhatentaron, which, like Teanaostaiaé, was protected on three sides by ravines. In spite of the fortifications having been strengthened by the French to the point where they were believed to be impregnable, the Iroquois soon learned that the Huron had largely abandoned the town the previous autumn. More-over, none of its remaining inhabitants was expecting the Iroquois so early in the year; hence the watchtowers were unguarded. During the night, the Iroquois made a breach in the palisade and quietly entered the town while the Huron were still asleep. Some Huron were killed on the spot; the others were taken captive. The settlement was not burned, but its palisades and houses, along with their provisions, were turned into an armed camp by the Iroquois. Of the 400 people who remained in Taen-hatentaron, only three men are reported to have escaped. Ten Iroquois lost their lives in this operation.

Still before dawn, part of the Iroquois force set out to attack the fortified village of St. Louis, which was located midway between Taenhatentaron and Sainte-Marie. Before they reached the village, however, the refugees from Taenhatentaron warned what was happening. The headmen ordered the women and children to flee and more than 500 of the inhabitants of St. Louis departed for Sainte-Marie, carrying their more valuable possessions with them. Eighty warriors remained to fight the Iroquois and with them stayed Father Jean de Brébeuf and the newly arrived Father Gabriel Lalemant. These priests had charge of the five villages making up the Mission of St. Ignace. The Huron repulsed the first two assaults of the Iroquois, killing about thirty and wounding others. Finally, however, the Iroquois were able to break down the palisades in several places and entered the village. They killed the sick and aged, who had been unable to flee, and either slew or took captive all but two of the warriors, both Christians. The latter, in spite of serious wounds, carried news of the battle to Sainte-Marie. Brébeuf and Lalemant had been urged to escape at the first alarm, but had stayed behind to baptize those who wished it and to give absolution to the Christians, who appear to have made up the larger part of the defenders. When the situation appeared desperate, one of the traditionalists advised making a run for it, but he was overruled by Etienne Annaotaha, a famous Christian warrior who refused to abandon the Jesuits. The Jesuits, as well as the warriors who had been taken prisoner, were led back to Taen-hatentaron, while the houses at St. Louis were plundered and set on fire (34:25–27, 125–31; 39:247–51). This fire was visible from Sainte-Marie about nine o'clock in the morning.

As soon as Brébeuf and Lalemant were captured, they were stripped and some of their fingernails were torn out. On entering Taenhatentaron, they were made to walk between rows of Iroquois warriors and were beaten by them. The Iroquois then proceeded to torture them and the other prisoners in the usual manner (plate 47). Because of his stoicism, Brébeuf became the object of intensive torture and died the same afternoon, whereas Lalemant suffered more lingering torments until the following morning (34:139–49). Many Huron were present who in the past had been taken prisoner by the Iroquois and been adopted by them. These Huron played a leading role in torturing the Jesuits, whom they regarded as sorcerers responsible for the ruin of their homeland. Their animosity against Brébeuf was particularly evident in their taunting of him. In addition to the usual torments, the Huron amused themselves by repeatedly pouring boiling water over the priests in mockery of baptism (34:27–29, 145). Their attitude probably was typical of the Huron who had been captured by the Iroquois up to that time. These prisoners all must have had relatives still living in the Huron country, whom they were anxious to rescue as the Huron confederacy collapsed. Their hatred of the Jesuits was probably shared by most traditionalists still living in the Huron country. Those who tortured Brébeuf were nevertheless impressed by his fortitude and, once he was dead, they roasted and ate his heart and drank his blood in order to acquire his courage (34:31).

On the evening of 16 March the Iroquois sent scouts to reconnoitre Sainte-Marie and, on their return, a war council was held and it was decided to attack the Jesuit settlement the next morning. The destruction of Sainte-Marie not only would eliminate the strongest defensive position in the Huron country, but would provide the Iroquois with many furs and the Mohawk with valuable prisoners to use in their bargaining with the French. At the same time, after learning of the destruction of Taenhatentaron and St. Louis, about 300 Attignawantan armed themselves and gathered near Sainte-Marie to oppose any further advances by the Iroquois. Most of these warriors were Christians and the majority of them came from Ossossané, although more northerly villages were also represented.

The next morning, the Iroquois left a small force behind to garrison Taenhatentaron, while their main body of men moved westward across the snow-covered hills to attack Sainte-Marie. An advance party of about 200 encountered some of the Huron warriors and forced them to retreat to within sight of the French settlement. Many Huron were killed, but, finally, the Huron mustered their strength and drove this advance party inside the palisade at St. Louis, which, unlike the cabins, had not been destroyed by the fire. About 150 Huron assaulted and took possession of the village, capturing some thirty Iroquois (34:131–33).

Soon, however, the main body of the Iroquois arrived. Rather than proceeding to Sainte-Marie, they tried to regain St. Louis. The Huron who

PLATE 47. *The martyrdom of Brébeuf and Lalemant from the* Novae
Franciae Accurata Delineatio, *1657. This engraving is probably the earliest
on this theme in existence and if Bressani was the author of the map it is
based on first-hand information about Iroquois torture. As in the vignette
on the left half of the map (see plate 37) captives are shown bound facing a
stake rather than as modern artists show them with their backs to it. Huron
captives played an active and willing role in killing these two Jesuits.
Courtesy Public Archives of Canada.*

were occupying the village fought long and hard against the Iroquois, re-pelling numerous attacks. An important Iroquois headman was seriously wounded and nearly 100 of their men were slain in the course of the battle. St. Louis was not recaptured until late in the night and, by the time the Iroquois had entered the village, not more than twenty Huron remained alive and most of these had been wounded. The ferocity of this contest is indicated by the fact that contrary to custom, it continued after sunset (34:133–35). Among those killed were a large number of leading Christians from Ossossané. According to reports emanating from the battlefield, these included René Tsondihwané's son-in-law Tsoendiai, while Charles Ondaaiondiont, who had been the Huron envoy to the Susquehannock, and René Tsondihwané's son, Ihanneusa, were taken prisoner (34:217–19). It is clear, however, from later reports that the Iroquois released at least some of their prisoners probably hoping that they would persuade friends and kinsmen to join the Iroquois.

Their losses at St. Louis discouraged the Iroquois from attacking Sainte-Marie. After they had re-captured St. Louis, the Iroquois withdrew to Taenhatentaron, where they spent the following day recuperating. By 19 March the Iroquois were reported to be frightened and some were with-drawing from the Huron country on their own initiative. To prevent the premature breakup of their army, its leaders ordered a retreat. Those prisoners who were unable to follow the Iroquois were tied down inside various tinder-dry longhouses, which the Iroquois set on fire as they left the village. The rest were loaded, often beyond their strength, with vast quantities of spoils and made to march south. Those who could not keep up were hatcheted or burned along the way. An old woman who escaped from Taenhatentaron carried news of the Iroquois retreat to Scanonaenrat. Several hundred warriors from that town pursued the Iroquois for two days, but, because they had few guns, they were careful not to confront the enemy. Finally, lacking provisions, they returned home (34:135–37).

On 25 April 1649 Charles Garnier (1930:40) wrote that the Iroquois had destroyed four Huron villages at the end of the previous winter in addition to the two villages they had burned in 1648. None of the more detailed accounts of the Iroquois attack in the spring of 1649 mentions the destruc-tion of villages other than Taenhatentaron and St. Louis, hence the "four" in Garnier's letter may be a scribal error or his own confusion. On the other hand, it is possible that while the Iroquois were bivouaced in the ruins of Taenhatentaron they destroyed the neighbouring hamlets of St. Jean and St. Joachim, as well as St. Louis. This would have eliminated the last Huron settlements in the Sturgeon Valley (cf. Heidenreich 1971:53).

The Winter at Gahoendoe

THE DIASPORA

Although the Huron, particularly those who were Christians and had guns, had put up a creditable resistance to the Iroquois, the confederacy had lost at least another 700 people and everyone had been thrown into a state of terror. The Huron were already gripped by famine and the presence of the Iroquois so early in the season indicated that women would be unable to tend their crops in peace in 1649, any more than they had been able to do the year before. The remaining Huron, whether Christians or traditionalists, quickly became convinced that their position was untenable. Within less than two weeks, all of the Huron villages had been deserted and burned by their inhabitants, lest they should be used by the Iroquois as Taenhatentaron had been (Thwaites 1896–1901, 34:197) (map 32). Thus the Huron abandoned not only their houses and villages but also their fields, on which they had formerly depended for their subsistence (35:79). Because of the dislocation of the previous year, these refugees had little in the way of food reserves to take with them and it was probably the prospect of prolonged famine that led them to divide into smaller groups, once they had abandoned their villages. The exception were the people of Scanonaen-rat, who had been the last tribal grouping to join the confederacy and seemingly the least integrated members of it. They stayed together both as a tribe and as a community. Accompanied by some Arendarhonon refugees who had adhered to them in 1647, the Tahontaenrat moved south and joined the Neutral (36:119).

Ossossané was one of the first towns to be abandoned. News of the defeat of its war party did not reach there until the night of 19 March. When it did, the cry went up that the Iroquois were about to attack. The old men, women, and children made their way through the snow along the trail that led to the Tionnontaté country, where many of them remained for several months. They were followed in their flight by Father Chaumonot (Jones 1908:382). Like Ossossané, the other Huron villages split up and clan segments, lineages, and individual families scattered in search of new homes. Many Huron sought refuge among the Tionnontaté. Some probably went to live with their trading partners, on whom, as adoptive relatives, they had the right to call for support (Thwaites 1896–1901, 34:223, 203; 35:79–81). This influx of refugees, combined with a drought in the summer of 1649, led to a shortage of food among the Tionnontaté, which, by the following winter, had become a serious famine (35:147, 127). Other

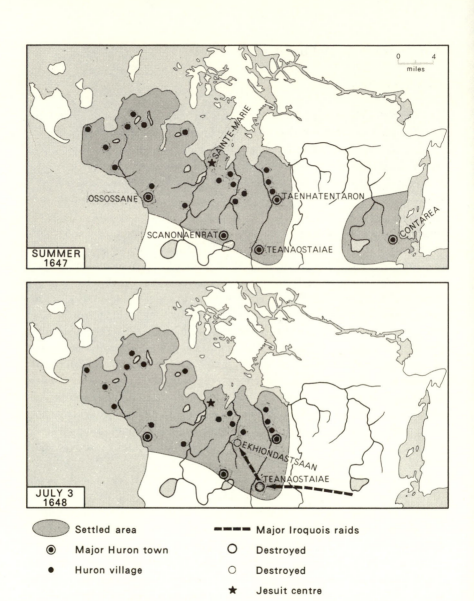

MAP 32. *Disintegration of the Huron confederacy, 1647 to 1650.*

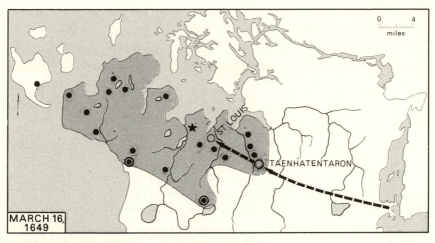

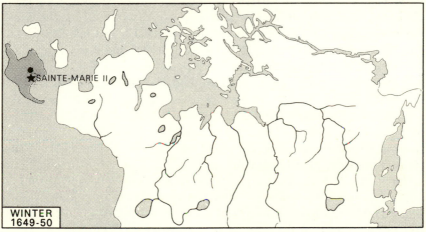

Huron besides the Tahontaenrat sought refuge with the Neutral (35:79), among whom many of them probably had trading partners. There is no warrant for Hunt's (1940:94) claim that the Neutral fell upon these refugees, killing some and enslaving the rest, since his only source attributes this behaviour to the Iroquois rather than to the Neutral.[6] Many other Huron fled north, seeking refuge either on the small islands in the northern part of Georgian Bay or along the shores of remote lakes and rivers (Thwaites 1896–1901, 35:79, 173). There they hoped to open small clearings and plant crops and if these failed, to live off the fish and wild vegetable foods that could be collected in the adjacent forests.

Other Huron remained in their own country for a time, but sought refuge by moving closer to Sainte-Marie. Some of these Huron proposed to move to Quebec and sent a headman there to find out if the French governor would approve this plan and be prepared to assist them (34:223). It may have been this Huron who arrived at Quebec on 20 July and first informed the colony of the dispersal of the Huron and of the deaths of Brébeuf and Lalemant (34:57). Other Huron fled to Gahoendoe, or Christian Island, which lies within sight of the Ontario mainland off the western tip of the Penetanguishene Peninsula. Some Huron had settled on this island a year or more before, since Ragueneau states that Jesuit missionaries had begun to visit the island in 1648 (34:203). Father Chaumonot and some of the refugees from Ossossané arrived on Gahoendoe by 1 May 1649. Most of his followers were reduced to eating acorns and wild roots, and the work of clearing new fields and erecting cabins was impeded by the lack of adult males in his party, which was made up mainly of the widows and children of men who had fought the Iroquois at St. Louis (34:215–17). It is questionable, however, whether Chaumonot's widows and children were significantly worse off than most Huron who were attempting to live on their own by the summer of 1649 (34:197).

THE MOVE TO GAHOENDOE

In spite of the dispersal of the Huron, Ragueneau continued the Tionnontaté missions and sent missionaries to visit different parts of Georgian Bay in order to instruct the Algonkians and Huron refugees who were living there (Thwaites 1896–1901, 35:81). As no Huron dared to continue living in their homeland, it became clear that Sainte-Marie was no longer either a suitable mission centre or a safe place to reside. It was exposed to Iroquois attack and the Jesuits feared that without Huron villages to draw their fire, the next time the Iroquois returned they would focus their whole attack against this settlement. Even if they were unable to capture Sainte-Marie, they could destroy the Jesuits' crops and cut off movement to and from the settlement. The Jesuits therefore decided to abandon Sainte-Marie and establish a new mission centre elsewhere, where they hoped to draw some of the Huron refugees together and ensure that trade with the French and their own mission work would continue (34:203). At first the Jesuits thought of moving to Manitoulin Island, where they had begun an Algonkian-speaking mission the previous autumn. The island was more remote from the Iroquois and was convenient for maintaining contact with the Neutral and Tionnontaté, as well as with Indians living to the west. The Jesuits had noted that the island was fertile and the fishing good. They anticipated that once the Huron were settled there, they would recover and soon be able to resume the fur trade (34:203–9).

This idea did not appeal to the Huron with whom the Jesuits remained in contact, and for good reason. In spite of its many natural advantages, Manitoulin Island had a shorter frost-free season than the Huron country and was very close to the line beyond which it was impractical to depend upon maize for subsistence (Yarnell 1964:129). If the Huron had moved to Manitoulin Island, they might have continued to plant corn, but they could not have depended on it for their own subsistence, let alone for trade.

On 12 May twelve headmen held a formal council with the Jesuits. They presented the missionaries with ten large wampum collars and told them that many Huron intended to settle on Gahoendoe Island. They invited the Jesuits to join the Huron there in order to minister to them and to protect them from the Iroquois. To attract the Jesuits they stated that even the traditionalists who planned to settle on Gahoendoe had resolved to become Christians and that the presence of the missionaries would make Gahoendoe an island of Christians. The headmen spoke for over three hours and after they had finished, the Jesuits agreed to abandon their plan to move to Manitoulin Island and to follow this remnant of the Huron people to Gahoendoe (Thwaites 1896–1901, 34:209–11). Many historians have criticized the Jesuits' decision to do this on the grounds that the new mission was almost as exposed to attack as the old one had been; however, so long as the Huron were unwilling to change their mode of life, the Jesuits had no alternative but to act as they did.

The Jesuits stripped Sainte-Marie and built a large raft. On 14 May their workmen loaded the raft with their livestock, food supply, and all the portable objects from their settlement, including the cannon. Sainte-Marie was then put to the torch to prevent it from falling into the hands of the

Iroquois or the Dutch, who might use it as a trading post. The Jesuits then journeyed about thirty miles to a site on the northern side of the great bay that indents the southeastern shore of Gahoendoe where the Huron refugees were founding a new settlement, named Sainte-Marie by the Jesuits. As the Jesuits travelled along the shores of the Penetanguishene Peninsula, bands of Iroquois were roaming the countryside, capturing and slaying Huron stragglers (34:223–25; 35:81–83).

When the Jesuits arrived on Gahoendoe, they found that approximately 300 families had taken refuge there (34:223). Most of them were Christians who were continuing to count on the Jesuits for leadership. Some fields had been cleared but the crops that had been planted were threatened by a serious drought (35:85). The Huron had been able to clear too little land to supply their needs and in spite of a temporary improvement in the weather, 1649 was a year of desperately poor crops. As soon as they arrived the Jesuits set their men to work cutting trees, so that they and the Huron might at least hope to harvest enough corn the following year (34:225). Because so many Huron families lacked adult male members, the French had to help them clear their fields (35:27).

Shortly after they arrived, the Jesuits began to build fortifications both for themselves and for the Huron. The main unit was a fort about 120 feet square with bastions at the four corners. It was located over 100 feet from the lake shore. To prevent the Iroquois from setting fire to this fort, or undermining it, both the bastions and the curtain walls were solidly built of stone and the rules of military architecture were carefully observed (35:85). Ragueneau contrasted the stone wall surrounding this fort with the wooden palisades that had surrounded much of the European compound at Sainte-Marie on the Wye up to the time the latter was abandoned (35:27). In the centre of the fort was a stone-lined cistern, about nine feet square, to provide water for the defenders (Jones 1908:6–8; plates 48 and 49). While the interior arrangements of this building are unknown, it evidently enclosed the Jesuits' living quarters. The masonry was finished by the end of the summer (Thwaites 1896–1901, 40:47).

The Jesuits also fortified the Huron village which was adjacent to their residence. Palisades were erected and strengthened with bastions guarding the approaches, which armed Frenchmen were to man (35:85). During the summer the population of the Huron village grew, as various groups of refugees learned of its existence and flocked there in search of protection and succour. Eventually there were said to be over 100 cabins in the village. Although Ragueneau's statement that its population rose to between 6000 and 8000 people must be an exaggeration (35:87), even a few thousand

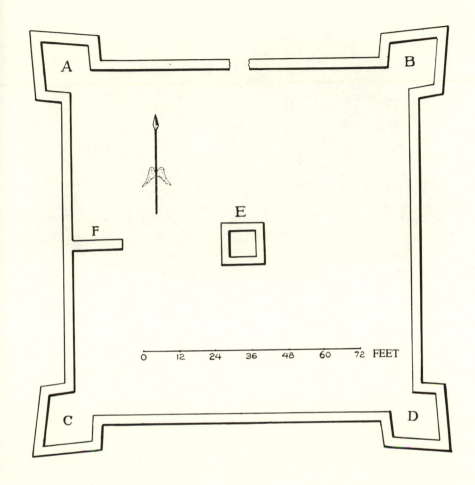

PLATE 48. *Plan of the remains of Sainte-Marie II on Christian Island.
Prepared by Félix Martin in 1855. Courtesy Archives of Ontario.*

PLATE 49. *Sketch of the ruins of Sainte-Marie II. By Félix Martin, 1855. Courtesy Archives of Ontario and Archives de la Compagnie de Jésus, Province du Canada-français.*

would have created unprecedented difficulties. Most of these people were dependent on fish, wild fruit, and vegetables and, large as Gahoendoe was, it was unable to supply the needs of so large a population from natural resources. The Huron were thus forced to visit the mainland to search for food, even though roving bands of Iroquois made these visits extremely dangerous. To attend to the spiritual needs of their converts, priests sometimes accompanied the Huron on these expeditions, although none were attacked by the Iroquois while doing so (34:225–27).

When the Jesuits arrived at Gahoendoe, they brought with them the surplus corn that they had accumulated at Sainte-Marie. Enough remained to feed themselves and their workmen for over a year, as well as 400 bags that were earmarked for the Huron (40:49); however, the latter were kept in reserve for the difficult winter ahead. In the autumn, the Jesuits dispatched canoes to buy food from the Algonkian peoples who lived around the shores of Georgian Bay. This netted 500 to 600 bushels of acorns, as well as a supply of dried fish (35:99–101).

TRADE IN 1649

On 6 June 1649 thirty-four Frenchmen and two Huron left the St. Lawrence Valley for the Huron country (34:53). The French in Quebec did not yet know about the dispersal of the Huron and the purpose of this expedition is not stated. In a letter that he wrote in September 1649, Jérôme Lalemant implies that d'Ailleboust had sent this "expedition" to the Huron country to carry ammunition there and to help to resist the Iroquois (34:83). He also stated, however, that the expedition was to return in the autumn. Possibly the French feared that the Huron would not come to Three Rivers in 1649, as they had not come in 1647; hence some traders may have decided to take advantage of their right to visit the interior to trade for furs. On 7 August about twenty Huron arrived at Three Rivers and five days later a number of French soldiers and domestics left for the Huron country to spend the winter there (34:59, 83). Lalemant states that altogether about sixty Frenchmen travelled to the Huron country in 1649 (34:83). In mid-August Father Bressani was ordered to journey from Gahoendoe to Quebec. It is unclear how many Huron accompanied him on what, in normal years, would have been the annual journey to Three Rivers. Indirect evidence suggests, however, that his expedition was made up largely of Frenchmen who either like the brothers Desfosses had spent the winter in the Huron country, or had gone into the interior in June. One of the members of the expedition was Robert Le Coq, who spent the following winter at Sillery (34:65). Bressani left Gahoendoe 12 August and arrived at Quebec September 19. In spite of the disruptions of the previous year, the French brought 5000 pounds of beaver skins with them that they had obtained from the Huron (34:59–61). On 28 September Bressani started to return to the Huron country with four canoes, but after reaching the Rivière des Prairies, this group turned back and Bressani and his companions spent the winter on the St. Lawrence.

The ownership and disposition of the 5000 skins that were brought to Quebec is a mystery, which serves to reveal how little we know about the fur trade at this time and of the role that the Jesuits played in it. The following year Ragueneau stated that he planned to use 20,000 livres worth of furs that had been brought for the Huron from their own country in order to help cover the expenses incurred in caring for Huron refugees at Quebec (36:250). The value of these skins suggests that they amounted to most, if not all, of the 5000 brought to Quebec in 1649, which would have sold for four or five livres per pound. Elsewhere, however, it is implied that the profits from these furs belonged to individual Frenchmen (34:59–61). These two statements are not irreconcilable since if most of the French were donnés, their earnings would have belonged to the Jesuit order (*see also* Jaenen 1970:68).

THE DISPERSAL OF THE TIONNONTATÉ

Although the Jesuits were in control at Gahoendoe where the Huron were mainly Christians who acknowledged their leadership and looked to them for support, the situation elsewhere was different. Many Huron Christians had sought refuge among the Tionnontaté, but others who joined them were traditionalists who blamed the Jesuits for the destruction of their country and spread rumours about a secret understanding between the French and the Iroquois. These stories led a group of Tionnontaté headmen to hold a meeting in St. Matthieu (Ekarenniondi) to discuss how the spread of Christianity might be halted and the Tionnontaté might thereby escape the fate of the Huron. It was reported that a Huron who had recently escaped from the Mohawk had seen wampum belts that the French governor had sent to the Mohawk inviting them to attack the Huron rather than the French. Some of the headmen urged that the French missionaries ought to be killed and it was finally agreed that the Tionnontaté should murder the first Frenchman that they met, just as Douart had been slain. When the two resident priests returned to the village a few days later, they were treated as if they were prisoners of war. The headmen were, however, unable to agree who should kill them and they were soon allowed to continue their rounds (Thwaites 1896–1901, 35:165–67). In another village the chapel and bell pole that the Jesuits had erected were torn down and the furniture from the chapel carried about as if it were the spoils of war, while it was proclaimed that the Jesuits ought to be slain (35:169).

Throughout the summer small bands of Iroquois continued to harass the Huron country; however, towards the end of November two Huron Christians reported that they had escaped from a band of 300 Iroquois who were undecided whether to attack Gahoendoe or to proceed against the Tionnontaté (35:91, 107). Although there is no proof of serious hostility between the Iroquois and the Tionnontaté prior to the late 1640s, the Iroquois evidently feared the Tionnontaté, both as a nucleus around whom the Huron might attempt to stage a revival and as a group that could be drawn into a trading partnership with the French. Either development might strengthen them to the point where they could menace Iroquois raiders attempting to penetrate the north and thereby protect the northern hunters as the Huron had done. For these reasons it is likely that the Iroquois were intending to attack the Tionnontaté, but had designated Gahoendoe as an alternative objective in case such an attack proved impossible.

When the Jesuits learned that a large Iroquois force was advancing northward, they persuaded the Huron at Gahoendoe not to set out after them and sent news of their approach to the Tionnontaté. Far from dismaying the latter, this news delighted them, since they anticipated that they would be able to surprise and defeat the Iroquois. When the latter were slow in arriving, the warriors from Etharita grew impatient and decided to go and meet them. They set out 5 December and made their way along the route they expected the Iroquois to follow. The Iroquois advanced towards Etharita along another route and, learning that the men of the town were away, they entered and plundered it. Some of the inhabitants fled to nearby villages, but many were slain or taken prisoner. Among the dead was Charles Garnier, the resident missionary. When the men of Etharita returned on 9 December, they were stunned to find the town in ashes and spent a day sitting motionless in grief. The Iroquois, in the meanwhile, retreated southward with their prisoners and booty (35:107–19).

When Father Ragueneau warned the Tionnontaté that the Iroquois were approaching, he ordered Father Garnier's missionary companion, Noël Chabanel, to return to Gahoendoe. He did this because of the famine and because he thought it unwise to expose two missionaries to the enemy unnecessarily by having them remain in the same community. On 5 December Chabanel left Etharita in the company of seven or eight Huron Christians and travelled northward through Ekarenniondi. On the night of 7–8 December he and his companions slept in the forest. About midnight they heard the victorious Iroquois, who were journeying homeward with their prisoners. The Huron scattered in the dark and made their way to the nearest Tionnontaté village, inadvertently leaving Chabanel alone in the forest.

The next day Chabanel made his way towards Gahoendoe, but was robbed of his possessions and murdered soon after he had crossed the Nottawasaga River. At first it was thought that he might have been killed by the Iroquois. A Huron named Honareenhac, who had renounced Christianity, was in possession of his hat, blanket, and book bag but claimed that Chabanel had given these things to him after he had ferried him across the Nottawasaga River, in order to be less encumbered on his journey. The Jesuits soon learned, however, that among the Huron Honareenhac was boasting that he had killed Chabanel to avenge himself for the extraordinary misfortunes that had afflicted him and his family after they had been baptized. Honareenhac was living in Ekarenniondi, which suggests that there was substance to Ragueneau's claim that Chabanel's murder was related to the outbreak of .hostility against the Jesuits that had centred in this village only a short time before (35:147–51, 169; Jones 1908:394–96). Ragueneau was convinced that Honareenhac could be proved guilty of the murder, but felt that under the circumstances it was best for the Jesuits to close their eyes to what had happened (Thwaites 1896–1901, 35:151). A quarrel with Honareenhac's friends and kinsmen about whether or not he had killed Chabanel was more than the Jesuits wished to enter into at this time.

After Chabanel's death Fathers Léonard Garreau and Adrien Greslon, who were stationed at Ekarenniondi, were made responsible for the whole Tionnontaté mission. Because of illness Greslon had to be recalled to Sainte-Marie by January 1650 and Garreau was recalled the following spring. This ended the Tionnontaté mission.

THE HUNGRY WINTER

Evidence concerning the fate of some of the Huron who sought refuge by fleeing north is provided in the Jesuit account of the Mission of St. Charles.

In the summer of 1649 two Jesuits, who were visiting the shores of Georgian Bay to minister to indigenous Algonkians and Huron refugees, found a considerable number of Huron living in a single location and recommended that a priest spend the winter with them. One was dispatched on 1 October. He was received into the homes of some Christian Huron who encouraged him to erect a small chapel. Some other Huron, who were not Christians, came to receive instruction but still others, and in particular those who had the most provisions, refused to do so. The latter attributed the Huron's misfortunes entirely to abandoning their old ways. In the course of the winter provisions ran out and fishing through the ice proved unproductive. As the famine grew worse the traditionalists ceased to denounce the Jesuits and the whole village began to turn to the resident priest for suggestions. Towards spring the inhabitants of the village were forced to disperse in different directions in search of food. Some followed the priest on a six-day journey across the ice of Georgian Bay in the hope of finding relief on Gahoendoe. While the Jesuits claimed that these Huron were not courting the priest's favour for material gain, their behaviour seems to belie this conclusion (Thwaites 1896–1901, 35:173–77).

For many of the Huron who had fled north, the winter of 1649–50 was one of terror, as well as of hunger and starvation. No longer having to fear being cut off by the Huron, the Iroquois launched a series of raids into central Ontario, attacking and robbing the Indians and probably trapping beaver there as well (35:181). These raids were directed against the indigenous Algonkians as well as Huron refugees. The Nipissing, who were wintering around the shores of their lake, were attacked and dispersed. The following spring two Iroquois forts were found to have been erected to the east of that lake (35:201). At the same time, smaller bands of Iroquois roamed the shores of Georgian Bay, looting and killing (35:181, 199). These raids continued the following year (36:189), by which time most of the indigenous inhabitants of central Ontario had fled to the north and west. The area then became a hunting territory for the Iroquois.

As more Huron made their way to Gahoendoe in the autumn and winter of 1649, a situation that had been desperate gradually became hopeless. Only the Jesuits had any reserves of food but, in spite of their intrepid efforts to accumulate as many fish and sacks of acorns as possible, these were inadequate to support more than a few hundred people over the winter.[7] To make matters worse, fishing through the ice proved exceptionally unproductive on Georgian Bay that winter (35:175), thus limiting the Huron's capacity to provide for themselves. Moss, bark, and fungus were eaten, but these were totally inadequate to support the large numbers of people who crowded onto Gahoendoe. As the winter progressed, the death rate began to rise sharply as a result of malnutrition and illness and all of the Huron on Gahoendoe turned to the Jesuits for whatever help they could provide. The Jesuits, who were now called the "fathers of the Huron people" (35:25), spent their days tending, as best they could, to what they perceived as being the essential physical and spiritual needs of the Huron. They passed many hours each day visiting the Huron village in order to assist the hungry and the dying and to try to convert any remaining traditionalists to Christianity.

In order to regulate the distribution of food, the Jesuits made small copper tokens, which each missionary distributed, as he judged best, among the Indians who were in his charge. This was done once a day, usually in the morning. The Indians who received these tokens assembled at the door of the Jesuits' residence about noon and exchanged their tokens for acorns, smoked fish, or, in the case of the most favoured, corn meal boiled in water (35:99). While it was necessary to control the distribution of food, this particular system was susceptible to various abuses, although the Jesuits probably did not view them as such. It encouraged starving Huron to make a display of Christian piety in the hope of receiving preferential treatment. Inducements such as this, and the lack of anything else to do, may explain the displays of intense religious fanaticism that were a feature of life at Gahoendoe that winter. The church was filled to overflowing with Huron ten or twelve times each morning and again in the late afternoon. Those wishing to be baptized were assiduous in attending instruction, while confession was also popular.

The Jesuits spent the middle part of the day making their rounds of the Huron longhouses and, following the afternoon church services, they encouraged neophytes to give an account of what they had thought each day: how often they had remembered God, how they had served him; whether they had offered him their labour, their hunger, and their misery (35:101–105). The Jesuits perceived that material wants played an important role in encouraging these displays of piety, but instead of regarding them as insincere, they thanked God that by thus afflicting the Huron and giving the Jesuits the means of aiding some of them, he had made their hearts so tractable that they could now quickly be persuaded to become Christians (35:91, 97). Convinced that the Huron were near to extinction, the Jesuits viewed the inadequate supplies of food that they had to distribute less as a means of keeping them alive than of preparing them for heaven (35:97, 105). The Huron were said by the Jesuits to be greatly pleased by the charity that was extended to them (35:95–99); yet few would have dared to appear otherwise. It could not have gone unnoticed among the Huron that while they died by the hundreds, the Jesuits, who reserved a special allotment of supplies for their own use, neither became ill nor went hungry. The Jesuits were able to satisfy their own consciences by viewing such efforts to keep fit as essential so that they, as priests, could attend to the needs of the dying (35:27, 97).

In terms of baptisms, the Jesuits' program was a success. Between the middle of March 1649 and the following August, more than 1400 Huron were baptized (34:227), and between then and March 1650 about 1600 more (34:227; 35:23, 75). Some of these baptisms undoubtedly took place among the Tionnontaté and others at the old Jesuit settlement of Sainte-Marie prior to its abandonment. Yet, the vast majority of baptisms after 14 May took place on Gahoendoe and must have numbered more than 2000. The majority of Huron who went to Gahoendoe were either Christians or Huron who were inclined to accept Jesuit leadership. One may conclude, therefore, that many of the Indians who were baptized at Gahoendoe had indicated a willingness to become Christians prior to their decision to settle there. It is clear, however, that some others were traditionalists who had gone to Gahoendoe either because they were desperate for food or wished to live with Christian relatives.

As the winter progressed increasing numbers of Huron died from hunger and contagious diseases, which became more lethal as poor nutrition robbed progressively more people, particularly children, of their ability to resist infection (35:91). In a desperate effort to survive, Huron began to eat the excrement of men and animals and to disinter the bodies of the dead in order to devour them. The latter was done in secret since the Huron regarded eating kinsmen and fellow countrymen with even greater abhorrence than did the French. In spite of this, necessity was driving people to feed upon their deceased parents, siblings, and children (35:21, 89).

The mortality rate was made worse by a lack of clothing. Some Huron are reported to have sold the few items of fur that remained in their possession for a single meal of acorns (35:93). This might suggest that Huron who had food were using it to accumulate skins to trade with the French. Yet such behaviour was contrary to the customary rules of sharing that were observed by the Huron and would have done the small number who had extra food little good, since they too would have gone hungry unless at some point they had been able to trade the furs they were accumulating for still more food.

It seems likely that the Huron had been largely depleted of their furs during the summer when the French traders had visited them. Possibly at that time many Huron had been willing to exchange their furs for European trade goods, in the expectation that they could later exchange these goods for corn or fish with neighbouring tribes. By the winter the lack of furs became sufficiently serious that the living had begun robbing the dead of clothing in order to keep warm (35:95). That furs continued to be sold for acorns suggests that the soldiers or other laymen who were working for the Jesuits may have been carrying on a clandestine trade with the Indians. A few Huron may have been recruited to work as agents for these Frenchmen in return for enough food to trade and to survive the winter. While the priests probably knew little or nothing about such activities and almost certainly would have disapproved of them, the resulting perversion of Huron social values compounded the outrage to Huron consciences that was embodied in the Jesuits' well-meaning efforts to save the souls of what they saw to be a dying nation. The Huron grew so weak that towards spring they were unable to dispose of the bodies of their own dead. Some of the priests and French laymen then charged themselves with laying out and burying the corpses that were accumulating in the long-houses. They described this as an act of charity that they extended to fellow Christians "however barbarous and lowly they may have been" (35:95).

The Move to Quebec

SPRINGTIME AT GAHOENDOE

At the beginning of March a considerable number of Huron left Gahoendoe in bands of fifty or more, or even as single families. Their aim was to search for acorns in places where the snow was beginning to melt or to try their luck at favourite fishing spots. Before leaving, they confessed and received holy communion, since many of them did not expect to survive the journey. They hoped, however, that by splitting into small groups, at least some of them might avoid the Iroquois. The ice was still frozen between Gahoendoe and the mainland, but as they crossed it began to break up and many Huron, especially children and old people, were drowned or froze to death. It was hoped that the dispersal of so many from the island would relieve the pressure on those who remained behind. Unfortunately, on 25 March an Iroquois war party, whose aim was to ensure that the Huron did not resettle in their own country, reached the Penetanguishene Peninsula. Within two days they killed or captured every band of Huron that had returned to the mainland (35:183–89).

The Huron who remained on Gahoendoe were thoroughly terrified when they learned what had happened, but the Jesuits' supplies of food ran out and disease, starvation, and cannibalism grew worse than before. More Huron felt obliged to leave the village. On Easter day, 17 April, a general communion was celebrated and the following day another band departed for the mainland, leaving what possessions they had in the care of the Jesuits. Most of them publicly made the Jesuits their heirs, as they had no hope of surviving. A few days later a few members of this band returned to Gahoendoe to report that the rest had either been slain or taken prisoner by the Iroquois. Some of the latter, including women and children, had been burned on the spot. In spite of this, hunger overcame many Huron's fear of death or being taken prisoner by the Iroquois and within a week still more of them crossed to the mainland to meet a similar fate. It was then that the Huron learned that two more Iroquois armies were on their way northward to relieve, or reinforce, the one that was already at work. The aim of these expeditions was to see that no Huron resettled or planted crops on the sites of their former villages and to kill, or capture, any who attempted to do so (35:189–91).

LEAVING GAHOENDOE

Most Huron were now convinced that they had to abandon Gahoendoe and find permanent places of refuge elsewhere. The majority intended either to scatter in small groups in the forests of central Ontario or to seek refuge in the vicinity of Lakes Michigan and Superior. The former were probably not yet aware of the extent of Iroquois raids into central Ontario or of the latter's determination to use this area to obtain furs. Others spoke of making their way south to join the Susquehannock or of voluntarily joining the Iroquois. Many of the latter were in contact with relatives who had been taken prisoner and who were counselling them to leave Gahoendoe as soon as possible, rather than perish there (Thwaites 1896–1901, 35:193). It is unclear how these contacts were made, but messages may have been carried by Huron who "escaped" from the Iroquois, and Huron allied with the Iroquois may have visited Gahoendoe without the French knowing about it.

While the French not unexpectedly have little to report about Huron voluntarily joining the Iroquois at this time, many Huron clearly did this. It is likely that as soon as the Huron dispersed in 1649, many who had relatives already living among the Iroquois went to join them. This probably involved more Arendarhonon than other Huron, since more Arendarhonon were prisoners among the Iroquois than were members of any other tribe. Moreover, a larger percentage of Arendarhonon were traditionalists than were members of other tribes and integration with the Iroquois must have seemed more acceptable to them than it did to even nominal Christians. By 1650, however, even many Christians had come to believe that throwing themselves on the mercy of the Iroquois offered them the best chance of survival, particularly when this meant rejoining relatives.

In late May or early June the leaders of the various groups who remained on Gahoendoe held a council in the dead of night, without the French being present. They discussed plans to leave the island and scatter in various directions. The next day two headmen, representing some 600 people drawn from all the Huron tribes, approached Father Ragueneau. After informing him that the Huron had decided to abandon Gahoendoe, they asked the Jesuits to lead them to Quebec. The Huron argued that if the French would support them there until they could harvest their own crops in the summer of 1651, they would be able to stay together as a group and remain practising Christians. As it was, the Jesuits were too few in number to accompany all of the tiny bands into which the Christians of Gahoendoe were being forced to split up (35:191–95).

At first, the Jesuits were uncertain what course of action they should follow, but after numerous conferences and forty hours of prayer, they decided that neither Gahoendoe nor the Huron country was defensible. While the French felt unable to provide for large numbers of Huron at Quebec, the relatively few Christians who were seeking refuge seemed manageable. Allowing them to settle at Quebec would permit them to remain under Jesuit guidance and would also supply men who were experienced in guerilla warfare to help defend the colony.

To prevent the Iroquois from learning about their plans, the Jesuits decided to leave for Quebec as quickly as possible. About half of the 600 Huron chose to remain at Gahoendoe until the corn ripened, but promised that afterwards they would come to Quebec (36:179–81). These Huron took possession of the French fort as soon as the French left. On 10 June the remaining 300 set off with the Jesuits for Quebec. They followed the usual route past Lake Nipissing and down the Ottawa Valley. In order to defend themselves, the Huron and French travelled in a tight formation.

As far as Lake Nipissing they found evidence of successful Iroquois raids during the previous winter.

The Kichesipirini derived no little satisfaction from seeing the Jesuits in full retreat, since they held them responsible for encouraging the Huron to ignore the Algonkin's role as middlemen. When Ragueneau gave orders that the Huron should pass Morrison Island without paying their usual tolls, and justified this by claiming that the French exerted sovereignty over the Algonkin, Tessouat had him seized and suspended from a tree by his armpits (Perrot 1911:176–78). While the French deeply resented this indignity, they and the hungry Huron who accompanied them were no match for Tessouat's men and the tolls were paid.[8] This was probably the last occasion on which the hard-pressed Kichesipirini were able to humble the French and assert their claim to control the upper part of the Ottawa River.

News of the abandonment of the Huron country came as a great surprise to a mixed party of Frenchmen and Huron who had left Three Rivers on 7 June in order to visit the Huron country. The party was made up of Father Bressani, a lay brother, and three domestics, who were carrying supplies to the Jesuits on Gahoendoe, as well as of twenty-five to thirty French traders and an equal number of Huron who had spent the winter at Quebec (Thwaites 1896–1901, 35:45, 201–3). The traders must have been well aware of the disasters that had befallen the Huron the previous summer, although they did not know about the even worse winter that had followed on Gahoendoe. It is difficult to understand how they could have expected the Huron to have many furs to trade, but their cupidity probably led them to hope that either the Huron or some of their former trading partners would be able to provide them with skins. On the way up the Ottawa River, seven Huron belonging to this group were killed by the Iroquois. All of them were described as good Christians and one was Atironta, who had wintered at Quebec after he had accompanied Bressani there the previous autumn. It is of interest that the paramount headman of the Arendarhonon should have left the Christian remnant of his own tribe in a time of major crisis. It would seem that as a result of cultivating his roles as a Christian and as the principal ally of the French, Atironta had forfeited much of his traditional importance as a tribal leader.

When Bressani's group encountered that of Father Ragueneau, all of the French decided to return to Quebec; however, at least some of the Huron who were heading up the Ottawa River continued on their way, hoping to join the 300 others who were spending the summer on Gahoendoe. When they were on Georgian Bay, about thirty miles from Gahoendoe, they were attacked by 300 Iroquois who lay in wait as they passed (36:181). All of the members of this band, which included two Huron named Andotitak and Thawenda, were reported to have been taken prisoner (36:119).

A smaller group of Huron warriors, led by Ohenhen, returned to the Huron country in the autumn of 1650. Three of his men were slain when they were attacked by Iroquois, but Ohenhen withstood the attack and eventually he and the rest of his men forced the Iroquois to take flight (36:121). Ohenhen's mission was to carry two wampum collars from the French governor to either the Tahontaenrat or the Neutral, urging them to trade with the French and form an alliance with them against the Iroquois (36:133). A band of fifty Tionnontaté who attempted to travel to Quebec in order to trade or get guns were attacked and wiped out by the Iroquois who were lying in wait for anyone using the Lake Nipissing trade route.

Throughout the summer of 1650 the Iroquois continued to roam through the Georgian Bay area, killing many of the Huron who had sought refuge there (36:181). Late in the summer a Huron named Atendera and his six companions were captured on Beckwith or Hope Island, near Gahoendoe. One of the members of this party was Ondaaiondiont, who was reported to have been killed at St. Louis, but who seems to have escaped from that battle.[9] The following summer he was forced to accompany eleven Iroquois in a raid against Quebec, but he escaped from them and carried a warning of their plans to the French (36:119).

In the summer of 1650 some thirty Iroquois landed on Gahoendoe and built a fortified camp from which they sallied forth to kill and capture some of the Huron who remained on the island. An attempt was made by the Huron to drive these Iroquois away, but they defended themselves bravely and killed a leading Huron warrior. For a time, the Iroquois besieged the Huron, who remained inside the French fort (36:181). These attacks, which prevented the Huron women from tending their fields no doubt did more to ruin the harvest than did a late frost that was reported to have injured the crop. The famine continued and when the autumn came the Huron neither had enough food nor did they feel safe enough to undertake their intended journey to Quebec. Some corn appears to have matured, however, and a population of only 300 probably had a reasonable chance of surviving on Gahoendoe by foraging there and on the adjacent mainland.

In late autumn, Onondaga warriors erected a fort on the mainland, opposite Gahoendoe, in order to capture any Huron who were compelled to venture in that direction in search of food. Although over 100 Huron were reported to have been taken prisoner (36:123), the Onondaga's main objective appears to have been to persuade the rest of the Huron to live with them. When they captured the warrior Etienne Annaotaha, they sent him back to the Huron to tell them that the Onondaga had brought rich presents inviting them to join them and become a single people. Three Iroquois accompanied him to the island as envoys. Although Annaotaha and the Huron headmen mistrusted the Onondaga and had no intention of going with them, they pretended to accept their proposal. The Huron women were urged to be ready within three days to leave for the Onondaga country. When this was reported to the Onondaga, the latter were confident that the Huron would return home with them and many visits were exchanged on both sides until the Huron had attracted over thirty Iroquois into their fort. At this point, the Huron fell on these Onondaga and killed all but three of them in order to avenge former injuries. The three who escaped did so because Annaotaha warned them what was about to happen. He did this because these were the men who had released him and also because the Iroquois had spared his life when they had captured him at St. Louis, no doubt as part of a general policy to encourage the Huron to desert to them. When the rest of the Iroquois learned that so many of their comrades had been killed, they gave up the siege of Gahoendoe and returned home as quickly as possible (36:181–87).

Because the Huron were certain that the Onondaga would return to avenge those who had been slain, they hastened to abandon the island as early as possible in the spring of 1651. Some left before the ice had broken up on Georgian Bay, others as soon as it was possible to launch their canoes. The latter did not leave too soon, as a few families and some children and old people who had no one to care for them were slain by the Iroquois before they could get away. These Huron fled north to Manitoulin Island (36:187–89). Both Manitoulin Island and the Lake Nipissing area were found to be exposed to the Iroquois (37:111); therefore, after a short time, the Huron left Manitoulin and in some forty canoes made their way to Quebec, where they joined the Huron who had arrived there the year before. They brought no provisions with them. All of those who arrived at Quebec were said to be Christians (36:189–91).

After the summer of 1651 few Huron remained in the Huron country or anywhere in the vicinity of Georgian Bay or central Ontario. In the summer of 1652 it was learned in Quebec that the Onondaga had defeated a small group of Huron who visited Gahoendoe towards the end of the previous summer to gather Jerusalem artichokes (37:105). Prior to July 1651 fifty Iroquois attacked and defeated the people of Tangouaen, somewhere along the shores of Lake Nipissing (36:131). These included, if they did not consist entirely of, Huron who as early as 1646 had retreated north to elude the Iroquois. From this time onwards, the Huron country and much of the region to the north remained desolate and uninhabited, while the Huron were scattered in every direction.

Chapter 12  Betrayal and Salvation

Temporary Havens

The Huron confederacy ceased to exist in 1649 and only one of its tribes, the Tahontaenrat, outlived it as a coherent group. Individuals, families, and clan segments scattered in every direction in search of new homes. Many Huron joined other Iroquoian-speaking groups, hoping to be absorbed by them. Others banded together in various places, seeking to survive and to preserve their identity. This chapter is an account of the early years of this struggle for individual and collective survival by the remnants of the Huron confederacy.[1]

THE DISPERSAL OF THE NEUTRAL

The Huron who fled to the Tionnontaté, Neutral, and Erie found only temporary refuge among these groups. A famine that broke out among the Tionnontaté, partly as a result of the influx of so many Huron, soon forced many of the latter to move to Gahoendoe or to join other tribes. Many women and children were killed when Etharita was destroyed in December 1649. After Father Garreau was recalled to Gahoendoe in the spring of 1650, the Tionnontaté abandoned their tribal lands and retreated to the northwest. Some Huron travelled with them although we do not know how many. The number of Tionnontaté-Huron refugees who survived the decade was no more than 500.

As soon as the Tionnontaté had been coerced into leaving southern Ontario, the Iroquois mustered their forces to attack the Neutral. While in the long run this campaign was primarily of interest to the Seneca as the Huron one had been, the relative lull in Iroquois attacks on the St. Lawrence indicates that many Mohawk and Oneida participated in it (Thwaites 1896–1901, 36:177). Until 1647, the Neutral had been friendly with both the Huron and the Iroquois and probably had obtained European goods from both groups. Consequently, after the Huron had been dispersed, the Seneca might have maintained good relations with the Neutral and sought to become the sole suppliers of European goods to them. Yet, although the Neutral were reputed to lack skill in handling canoes, the Tahontaenrat who had taken refuge among them were no doubt seeking to continue their role as middlemen between the Neutral and the French. Furthermore, the French had attempted to conclude a trading alliance with the Neutral in 1626 and again perhaps in 1640; therefore they might try once more, now that the combined power of the Huron tribes did not stand in their way. As a result of this, the Neutral themselves might fill the commercial vacuum that had been created by the dispersal of the Huron. The Tahontaenrat may also have been encouraging the Neutral to seek alternative sources of European goods among the Erie and the Susquehannock in order to curtail the influence of the Seneca.

Such considerations persuaded the Seneca that it was necessary to attack and disperse the Neutral, rather than to nourish an insecure trading relationship with them. It was also recognized that by attacking the Neutral, all the Iroquois might secure other benefits that were important to them at this time. First, they could seize the beaver skins that must have been accumulating in many of the Neutral villages since the Huron trading network had collapsed. Secondly, they might open an alternative route by which Iroquois warriors could travel north through Michigan, as well as through Ontario, to raid the tribes of the upper Great Lakes. Thirdly, they could gain possession of the rich beaver grounds around Lake St. Clair and along the Thames and Sydenham Rivers, for control of which the Neutral themselves recently had been fighting. For geographical reasons, the latter objective was of more interest to the Seneca than to the other Iroquois tribes. The desire to secure these goals no doubt contributed to the growing enmity between the Iroquois and the Neutral in the late 1640s. Fear that the Neutral would seek revenge for the attack of 1647 must have encouraged the Seneca to seek their dispersal as quickly as possible.

The Iroquois seem to have resumed raiding the Neutral in the spring of 1650; by that summer a large-scale war was in progress. Six hundred Indians who were living in the Neutral country (very likely the Tahontaenrat) sent word to Quebec that the following summer they were coming to solicit arms and other support from the French (35:215). It was probably in reply to this message that Ohenhen was sent on his perilous mission to carry two wampum belts from the governor of New France to the Neutral country (36:133). Ohenhen accomplished this mission, in spite of his encounter with the Iroquois on Georgian Bay. There were also reports that the Neutral and Susquehannock had formed an alliance against the

Iroquois (37:97). If so, this was probably an alliance that Huron refugees had helped to promote.

The Iroquois struck too soon and too hard, however, for any of these new contacts to be of use to the Neutral. The Neutral had no guns, except for a few that were owned by Christian Tahontaenrat who were short of ammunition. In the autumn of 1650 an Iroquois force, variously estimated to be of between 600 (36:121) and 1500 (36:119) men, destroyed a major Neutral village. Later, however, the Neutral, led by the Tahontaenrat, fell upon this army, killing or capturing some 200 of the enemy (36:119). It may have been this victory that gave rise to the report told to the French eighteen months later by the Mohawk that, at one point in the war, the women of the principal Seneca town had been terrified by rumours of a Neutral victory and had fled to the Cayuga (37:97).

In the winter of 1650–51, 1200 Iroquois returned to the Neutral country to avenge the losses of the previous autumn (36:119). This force destroyed the principal town, Teotongniaton (36:141–43). Many prisoners were taken and this raid effectively spelled the end of the Neutral confederacy. The inhabitants of the remaining Neutral villages decided that they were unable to resist the Iroquois and abandoned their houses and fields to the enemy (36:177). Some 800 Neutral are reported to have spent the winter of 1652–53 at Skenchioe, which seventeenth-century maps locate on the large peninsula between Saginaw Bay and Lake Huron (38:181). Although these Neutral planned to join the Tionnontaté, there is no evidence that this happened and nothing more is known about this group.[2] The Sanson map of 1656 suggests that a sizable number of Neutral (Attiouandaron) may have found refuge in the Ohio Valley. Some Huron may have accompanied these and other Neutral groups. Wherever the Neutral went, however, they dispersed and lost their identity so that none were later recorded as an identifiable ethnic unit.

Other Huron who had been living with the Neutral sought refuge among the Erie and Susquehannock. On 27 May 1651 messengers arrived at Three Rivers to say that some of these Huron were coming to join the ones already at Quebec (36:179). There is, however, no record that these refugees ever arrived. When the resourceful Tahontaenrat saw what was happening, they and the Arendarhonon who had joined them proposed to go and live among the Seneca. The Seneca, as we shall see, had their own reasons for being lenient at this time and allowed them to establish a village on Seneca tribal territory, where they might retain their own customs and special usages. Hereafter, the Tahontaenrat and the Seneca lived side-by-side in the greatest amicability (36:179; 44:21; 45:243). By the autumn of 1651 rumours were reaching Quebec that the Tahontaenrat were encouraging the Seneca to make peace with the French and begin trading with them. It was also rumoured that four Tahontaenrat and two Seneca envoys were coming to confer with the French (36:141–43).

THE ERIE WAR

In the winter of 1651–52, with Dutch encouragement the Mohawk had attacked the Susquehannock, hoping to disperse them as the Iroquois had already dispersed the Huron, Tionnontaté, and Neutral. The Susquehannock were, however, well armed by their Swedish trading partners and the Mohawk seem to have suffered the worst of this engagement. It was not until after the Dutch had seized New Sweden in 1655 that they were able to coerce the Susquehannock into making peace with the Mohawk (F. Jennings 1968:23–26; Thwaites 1896–1901, 37:97). In spite of the later success of a combined force of Iroquois against the Scahentarronon (37:111), this failure to deal with the Susquehannock was complicated for the Mohawk by the growing hostility of the Mahican and Sokoki, who once again were allied with the Abenaki and the Canadian Algonkians. Both the Mahican and Sokoki had supported the Mohawk in the 1640s, but they resented the lack of respect that the Mohawk had shown for them, as well as the Mohawk's heavy demands for wampum as the price of continued friendship (36:103–5). Now, the Mohawk were forced to penetrate into increasingly remote areas in search of furs (map 33). In the early 1650s their raiding parties entered the territory of the Attikamegue for the first time and they also made their first appearance in the Lake St. John area (36:147; 37:67, 69). By the end of the decade, raids were taking the Mohawk as far east as Tadoussac and deep into the Hudson Bay watershed of Quebec (46:173, 205, 287, 289).

Under these increasingly difficult circumstances, it is not surprising that the Mohawk called upon the western Iroquois tribes to repay the assistance they had given them, by helping them to attack the French (38:61–63). The Mohawk hoped that by destroying Montreal and Three Rivers, their raiders would be able to penetrate into the northeast more easily and satisfy their need for furs. Even after the Neutral had been dispersed, however, the Seneca refused to help the Mohawk, claiming that they still had dangerous enemies on their borders whom they had to eliminate. These were the Erie, who appear to have been trading partners of the Susquehannock.

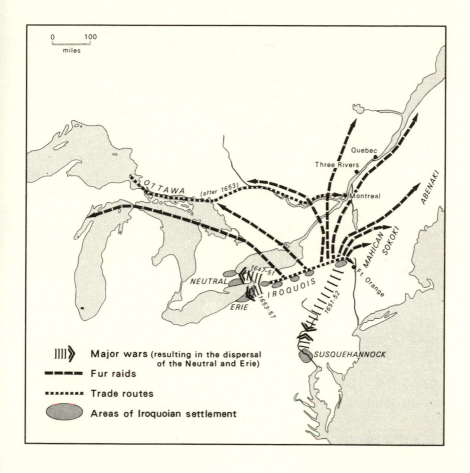

MAP 33. *Intertribal relations, 1650 to 1657.*

Just as the Huron had blocked Seneca raiding in the north and diverted the northern furs to the French, so the Erie prevented the Seneca from hunting and raiding in the Ohio Valley and carried the furs from this region to the Susquehannock and New Sweden. While this does not appear to have been as lucrative a trade as that of the Huron, the Ohio Valley was a worthwhile prize for Iroquois who sought to secure more furs by raiding and hunting. The Seneca and Onondaga had more important reasons, however, for refusing to repay the help that the Mohawk had given them. They resented the arrogance of the Mohawk, which resulted from their larger supply of guns and trade goods and also from their right to grant or withhold permission for the western tribes to travel across their territory to trade at Fort Orange.

Huron and Neutral refugees were encouraging anti-Iroquois feeling among the Erie and eventually provided the Seneca with an excuse to declare war on their hosts (41:83). When thirty Erie envoys visited the Seneca to reconfirm the peace between them, a Seneca was accidentally slain by an Erie. The Seneca were so angered by this killing that rather than accepting reparations, they slew all of the Erie envoys they could lay their hands on, thus challenging the Erie to fight. A band of Erie probably led by Huron refugees penetrated southern Ontario and cut to pieces the rear guard of a victorious force of Onondaga, who were on their way home from Georgian Bay. One of the men they captured was Annenraes, whose release by the Huron in 1647 had led to the final short-lived truce between the Huron and the Onondaga. Although the woman who adopted Annenraes was expected to release him, she demanded that he be slain and eventually the Erie gave in to her demands. His death by torture greatly angered the Onondaga and led the four western Iroquois tribes to join in the war against the Erie (41:81; 42:177–79). The Erie were reported to have attacked and set fire to a Seneca town, although this may have been a false rumour reflecting the current mood of crisis. The Seneca and Onondaga followed traditional Iroquois policy by offering to make peace with the French and their allies in order to fight the Erie more effectively (41:217).

The four western tribes began to negotiate with the French in the spring of 1653. Their aim was to conclude a peace treaty that would allow them to trade with the French. The Onondaga also wanted to persuade the French to settle in their midst to trade and to offer them military aid as they had formerly offered such help to the Huron. This would have involved repairing their guns and helping to defend their towns against enemy attack (44:151). The Mohawk were appalled by these negotiations since they threatened to divide the confederacy and to ally most of its members with the French, whom the Mohawk regarded as their most dangerous adversaries. Rather than risk such a split, the Mohawk decided to conclude a temporary peace with the French themselves (37:109–11).

Although the French were aware that the Mohawk had no intention of stopping their raids on the Algonkin and Montagnais, their military position was so precarious that they made no effort to dictate terms to the Mohawk envoys. The Jesuits strongly supported making peace. They no longer had the Huron mission to protect and therefore saw little reason to continue fighting the Iroquois. They also reasoned that peace would allow them to re-establish contact with many Huron who had been baptized and were now living among the Iroquois. It would additionally open up a new mission field to replace the one that they had lost among the Huron. Thus, by the autumn of 1653 the French were in fact, if not yet by treaty, at peace with all the Iroquois tribes.

In spite of this, the rift that became apparent between the Mohawk and the other Iroquois tribes was to last for a long time. In their efforts to end the friendship between the upper Iroquois and the French, the Mohawk appear to have murdered three important Seneca who visited Quebec over the winter of 1656–57 to have talks with the French. This led to an armed confrontation between the Seneca and the Mohawk (43:99–103; 44:149–151). Even after the peace with the French had collapsed, the Mohawk remained angry and showed little interest in helping their neighbours. They tended to remain aloof from the conflict that dragged on from 1659 to 1675 between the Susquehannock and the three western Iroquois tribes, and which resulted in frequent and serious setbacks for these tribes (map 34).

All of this, however, was some time in the future. In the summer of 1654 the western Iroquois tribes raised an army of 1200 to 1800 men, and attacked the Erie (31:83, 121; 42:179). The Erie did not possess firearms (41:83) and the few Huron refugees among them who did were short of ammunition (42:181). Two of the Iroquois who led the expedition dressed in French clothes in order to intimidate the Erie by making them believe that Europeans were fighting alongside the Iroquois (42:181). After the fall of important towns such as Gentaienton (61:195) and Rigué, the Erie rallied in a fortified location where they defended themselves bravely for a time with their poisoned arrows.[3] Among those who died in Rigué was René Tsondihwané, the elderly Huron from Ossossané who had been baptized as early as 1639. Tsondihwané had led his family to Rigué by unknown stages and had continued to pray and to maintain other Christian

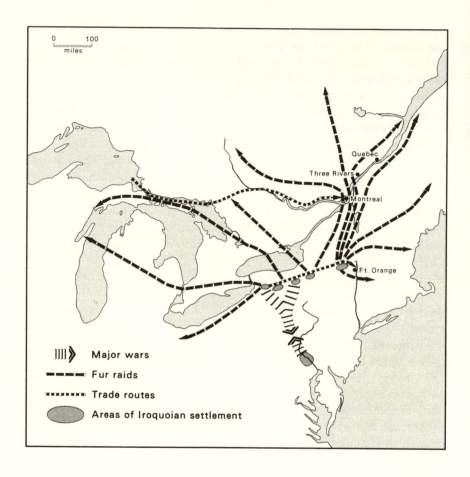

MAP 34.   *Intertribal relations, 1659 to 1663.*

observances. His daughter, Gohatio, was taken prisoner by the Iroquois but after seeing her twin children killed, she too was slain by her captor because of an ailment from which she suffered. Her son, Tehannonrakouan, was killed by the Susquehannock. It is unclear whether this happened before or after he was captured by the Iroquois (42:75, 187–89).

Desultory fighting continued until at least 1657, with Iroquois warriors returning home from time to time with small numbers of captives and loot from the Erie country (42:191–99; Adams 1961:63). Many Erie were taken prisoner, but others drifted southeastward and established themselves near Chesapeake Bay,[4] possibly under the protection of the Susquehannock (plate 50). About 1680 some 600 men, women, and children of this group surrendered themselves to the Iroquois, fearing that otherwise the Iroquois would attack them (Thwaites 1896–1901, 62:71). Others may have survived for a time as the "Black Minquas," but as a recognizable ethnic group the Erie, like the Neutral, disappeared. The Seneca and their neighbours were now free to raid into the Ohio Valley, where they are said to have encountered tribes that still had no knowledge of European goods (44:49). These raids eventually brought the Iroquois into conflict with the Shawnee, Illinois, and other tribes living to the south and west of them (47:145; Perrot 1911:154–57).

THE HURON ON THE ST. LAWRENCE: 1647–1650

During the three last years of the Huron confederacy, many Huron had spent considerable periods of time in the St. Lawrence Valley. As before, some were prisoners who had escaped from the Iroquois and made their way to the French settlements. One of these was Jean-Armand Andehoua, who was captured by the Iroquois in 1647 and severely tortured. The following year he was forced to accompany a Mohawk raiding party that was investing the St. Lawrence River near Three Rivers. Knowing he was near a French settlement, he managed to escape from the Iroquois and made his way there, where he was recognized and warmly welcomed (Thwaites 1896–1901, 32:161–63).

Other Huron had come either to trade or to help the Algonkin and Montagnais wage war on the Mohawk and were prevented, either by the winter or by Iroquois blockades, from returning home. Some spent the onset of winter living under Jesuit supervision at Sillery or joined the Montagnais in their winter hunts south of the St. Lawrence River. Others appear to have hunted by themselves in the same area (30:165). Still other

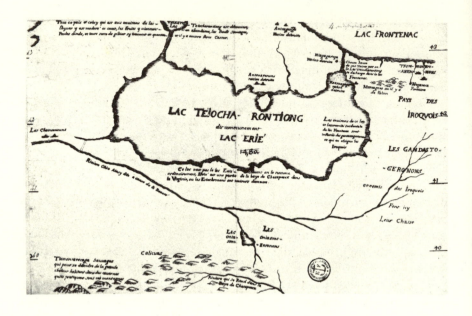

PLATE 50. *Anonymous map of Lake Erie, probably by Abbé Claude
Bernou, c. 1680. The inscriptions indicate that at this period the
Susquehannock were hunting in the upper part of the Ohio Valley.
The claim that the Erie had always lived around Chesapeake Bay refers
to Erie who sought refuge there after their defeat by the Iroquois.
Courtesy Public Archives of Canada.*

Huron wintered among the French at Quebec (34:63) or Montreal (30:229), or with the Algonkian-speaking Indians who lived under French protection at Three Rivers (30:173). In 1649 many Huron who came to the St. Lawrence on business were unable to return home before winter set in. Because of this, approximately twenty Huron spent the following winter at Three Rivers and twenty more at Quebec. Half of the latter were lodged at the hospital and, to maintain them over the winter, the Jesuits had to supply them with a cask of eels, a barrel of corn, six blankets, two pairs of snowshoes, and other goods (34:63).

In spite of the informal nature of these groups, they made decisions that formerly would have required ratification by tribal councils in the Huron country. When in the spring of 1650 a Huron named Skandahietsi was discovered to have surrendered to the Iroquois and to be acting as a spy for them, the Huron who were wintering at Quebec condemned him to death and executed him. One of these Huron, Outarahon, made a long speech justifying the execution. In it, he assured the French that the Huron head-men would approve what had been done (35:47–49, 217–23). While the Huron executed traitors, it is likely that the men who were wintering at Quebec, all of whom were Christians, were influenced to act on their own initiative by the French. Formerly such a decision would have been dis-cussed by Huron headmen very carefully, and in full council, before steps were taken to implement it.

In 1646–47 the various groups of Indians who were wintering at Three Rivers appointed the Algonkin headman, Simon Pieskaret, to be respon-sible for good relations between them and the French, and also between the Huron and Algonkin (31:287). The Huron who were wintering at Quebec and Three Rivers remained in close contact with one another and travelled back and forth between these two settlements at frequent intervals. These trips made it easier for the French to relay letters and verbal messages from one community to the other during the winter (32:69, 77, 107).

The mortality rate among these Huron was high, since many were killed or captured in encounters with the Iroquois. In the spring of 1647 some Indians from Sillery accompanied three French pinnaces up the St. Lawrence River, seeking to discover and flush out Iroquois raiders. On their return from Montreal a Huron canoe that was in the vanguard of this expedition was captured by the Iroquois on Lake St. Peter, while a Huron who was reconnoitring an Iroquois fort was shot and eaten by the enemy (31:171–75). Other Huron were captured by the Iroquois when they went into the forests to hunt (30:229–31). More than a dozen were killed or captured in 1647 alone. Another Huron was killed accidentally. This was

Aonchiarre, who came from the village of Caldaria (Tiondatsae or Ekhiondastsaan), near Teanaostaiaé. He was shot in the leg by a companion on the last day of December 1647, carried to the hospital at Quebec, and baptized the same day. His leg had to be amputated and he died from complications about two weeks later. At the request of his companions, he was interred in the cemetery at Quebec as an expression of solidarity between the Christian Huron and the French (32:71, 243).

The number of Huron requesting baptism at Quebec or Three Rivers appears to have been less than it had been previously and there is no evidence that young men were still coming to these places specifically to receive instruction. This suggests the greater ease with which baptism could now be obtained in the Huron country. Aside from Aonchiarre, only two Huron baptisms were recorded. One was that of Saondionrhens, who was from Ossossané. He was baptized on Easter evening 1648 (32:81).

In spite of this, examples of Huron piety were not lacking. In 1646 Michel Exouaendaen (Ekouaendaé) brought a young girl to Quebec to join the Ursulines in their nunnery. He was an Assistaronon, who had been taken prisoner as a child and adopted by a Huron family in Scanonaenrat. In his adolescence, he suffered from a lingering ailment that left him partially paralysed. It is reported that when his relatives ignored him, he turned to the Jesuits for help. Being told about the miraculous cures resulting from pilgrimages to Roman Catholic shrines in Europe, he decided to make a similar pilgrimage to Sainte-Marie. Although he had not attempted a long journey for a number of years, he covered the distance from Scanonaenrat to Sainte-Marie in fifteen hours and upon arriving there, was instantly cured (30:89–97). It appears to have been in return for this cure that he volunteered to transport this young girl to Quebec. She was the next Huron after Thérèse Oionhaton to be instructed by the Ursulines.

When Exouaendaen was ready to return to the Huron country, it was already too late in the year for him to do so safely. He therefore spent the winter living in the house of the Ursulines' chaplain and doing odd jobs for them. Although most of the Huron staying at Quebec were Christians, it is indicative of their more independent attitude that they ridiculed Exouaendaen for taking orders from women and performing tasks such as hauling water, which the Huron believed women should do for themselves. He was especially ridiculed when he refused to join an expedition against the Iroquois without permission from the Ursulines (31:175–79). Because of Iroquois raids, the girl that he brought with him was unable to return to the Huron country until 1648. When she left, the Ursulines gave her a complete set of French clothes and sent presents to her parents to express the joy they had experienced from having her live with them (32:215). Exouaendaen returned to Quebec after the dispersal of the Huron and died in the care of the Hospital nuns sometime prior to October 1651 (36:205).

Another indication of the growing involvement of some Huron in the mission work of the Jesuits was the entry into their service on 9 August 1648 of Pierre Onaatichiae. Since he turned over twenty-one pounds of beaver skins to the Jesuits, and they remained accountable to him for them if he should leave their service, it would appear that he became a donné (32:99). He had been baptized, apparently at Quebec, on 17 July (32:95).

What is unclear is whether any Huron families were settled in New France at this time. Etienne Girault de Villeneuve, writing in 1762, suggests that in the decade prior to 1650, a considerable number of Huron had settled at Sillery in order to live a peaceful life there (70:207). There are, however, no contemporary references to entire Huron families having settled at Sillery or elsewhere in the St. Lawrence Valley and it seems likely that Girault de Villeneuve misinterpreted references to individual Huron wintering at these places. To be sure, Ationta and his family spent the winter of 1645–46 at Sillery, but they do not count as settlers any more than do the various groups of warriors and traders.

The Huron Refugees at Quebec

THE SETTLEMENT ON THE ILE D'ORLEANS

Prior to the Jesuits moving to Gahoendoe in 1649, a Huron headman was sent to determine whether the French authorities would approve of Huron refugees settling at Quebec (Thwaites 1896–1901, 34:223). Caring for such refugees depended upon charity, which, according to the ideas of the day, was a concern of the religious orders and of interested individuals rather than of the government of New France. The Jesuits at Quebec discussed this problem at Easter 1650, so that Father Bressani could convey their answer to the Huron when he returned to Gahoendoe. At this meeting the Jesuits decided that it was their duty to permit Huron families to settle on their lands at Beauport, near Quebec, but that these families must be few in number and carefully selected for their Christian piety. The Jesuits estimated that initially they would have to spend 3000 livres a year in order to establish these Huron (35:39). Cold as this decision may seem, it was economically realistic. The few French settlers at Quebec did not produce enough food to support a large number of refugees, nor could the trading company have imported what was needed on short notice, even if its directors had been inclined to do so.

Father Ragueneau's decision to lead 300 Huron from Gahoendoe to Quebec was taken independently of discussions at Quebec and brought more Huron refugees to the St. Lawrence than the Jesuits at Quebec had planned to support. When Ragueneau's Huron arrived at Montreal, they rested for two days and were cared for by the French settlers. The latter tried to persuade some Huron to settle there, hoping that they would help to re-establish trade with the interior; however, the Huron were too frightened to remain in a place that was as exposed to attack as Montreal was and they soon hurried down-river. Some stayed at the Indian settlement at Three Rivers (37:181), while the rest continued on to Quebec, arriving there 28 July. Three or four leading Frenchmen at Quebec each agreed to care for one (extended?) Huron family. The Hospital nuns took charge of the sick and of several more families, while Madame de La Peltrie and the Ursulines undertook to feed and clothe the numerous family, or clan segment, of Pierre Ondakion, who was one of the leading headmen of Ossossané and an early convert to Christianity (35:209). They also enrolled a number of little girls in their school, including Ondakion's daughter, Geneviève-Agnès Skanudharoua, who, with the financial support of a god-mother in France, was able to remain with the Ursulines. She took her final vows as a nun shortly before she died in 1657 (44:259–75). The Ursulines also took in a twenty-three-year-old widow named Cecile Arenhatsi, who agreed to work for them as a servant (36:213). When the Ursulines' dwelling burned to the ground at the end of 1650, the Huron had their headman, Louis Taiaeronk, present two large wampum belts to the Ursulines as a token of their sympathy (36:215–21).

This charity left 200 other Huron in need of food, clothing, and shelter and caring for them became the responsibility of the Jesuits. Most Huron erected their longhouses in the Upper Town between the Ursulines' residence and the hospital, whose chapels served them as parish churches (35:211; 36:55, 59). There, the Huron were under the protection of near-by Fort St. Louis. The Jesuits and the nuns distributed corn and pea soup to the Huron, who came each day to their residences to collect it (35:211; 36:59–61). During the first year, it cost the Jesuits about 8000 livres to feed the Huron and additional funds had to be obtained in order to supply them with iron hatchets, kettles, clothing, and other necessities (36:203; 41:139). In the course of the winter, only three men and two women died, which indicates that the Huron were being well looked after (36:203–5).

Knowing that more Huron were on their way to Quebec, the Jesuits were anxious to secure a suitable location for permanent Huron settlement. On 19 March 1651, they obtained possession of some cleared land that belonged to Eléonore de Grandmaison. This land was located on the west end of the Ile d'Orléans, within sight of Quebec (36:117). Some thirty Huron families, who had wintered either at Quebec or among the Algonkians at Sillery, moved to the island in March 1651. Each family was assigned a plot of land, none of which was larger than half an arpent (36:117). Although these could not produce enough to feed the Huron over the following winter, crops were planted soon after they arrived and French workmen helped the Huron to clear more land. Wood from these clearings was used by the Huron to construct their longhouses. These were located under the shelter of a fort that the Jesuits constructed and which was said to be about the same size as the one on Gahoendoe. The Jesuits also constructed a chapel for the Huron and a house where Father Garreau, another priest, and four donnés were to live. Although the Huron had a good harvest in 1651, not enough land had been brought under cultivation to feed them; moreover, the population of the settlement was increased that autumn by the arrival of forty canoes bearing the starving and impoverished Huron who had made their way from Gahoendoe to Manitoulin Island (36:143, 189). By 1653 the two groups had cleared about 300 arpents and were able to feed themselves.

The Jesuits were anxious that the Huron who settled at Quebec should become fully self-supporting as soon as possible. Yet, until the Huron produced surplus corn, they were not in a position to resume trading for furs. The hard-pressed Montagnais of the Quebec City area, who had joined the Jesuits' settlement at Sillery as supplies of game declined in their hunting territories, had been encouraged by the Jesuits to trade European goods with Indian groups who lived farther down the St. Lawrence. By purchasing European goods at the cheaper prices available to Christians and reselling them at a higher price to Indians who were not converts, these Montagnais were able to make a small profit in furs, which covered the cost of food and other necessities that they needed to obtain from the French. By reselling French trade goods to non-Christians at just under the price that the latter were charged for them at Quebec, the Indians at Sillery were assured of a long-term source of income.

There is some evidence that the Jesuits encouraged the Huron to engage in an analogous form of trade. In November 1651, three Frenchmen who worked for the fur trader Robert Giffard de Moncel were drowned while crossing the St. Lawrence at night, in order to trade for beaver skins on the

Ile d'Orléans (36:147). On 6 June 1652, six Huron men and three children were drowned in a storm while returning from Tadoussac, where they had gone to trade cornmeal for skins in order to make robes "for their own use." All of these Huron were from Ossossané and the dead included Joseph Teondechoren (37:169). Since the Huron were not able to feed themselves at this time, the cornmeal that they were trading must have come either from the Jesuits or from French traders. Since the best quality furs were worn for some time before being traded with the French, the Huron's making robes "for their own use" does not rule out the likelihood that they later sold these furs to the French. Radisson states that the Huron on the Ile d'Orléans made robes of greased beaver skins from which the Jesuits derived a "profit" of 10,000 livres tournois annually (Adams 1961:50); possibly this figure represents the total value of the furs that the Huron supplied to the trading company. Since skins exchanged for from three to five livres each, this suggests that the Huron were supplying more than 2000 skins a year. While the volume of this trade is surprising, it is not unexpected that the Jesuits would encourage extensive commercial activities to reduce the expenses they incurred in running the Huron settlement. The development of trading along the lower St. Lawrence would also explain why, when Jean Bourdon made his journey around the coast of Labrador in the summer of 1657, he took two Huron guides with him (Thwaites 1896–1901, 44:189). Some time before he turned back, these Huron were killed by Indians or Eskimo, who also wounded one Frenchman.[5] In spite of the volume of this trade, it was only of marginal significance to the French traders, since it tapped fur resources that were already available to them.

IROQUOIS HARASSMENT CONTINUES

From 1650 to the summer of 1653 the Mohawk sent raiding parties into the St. Lawrence Valley with increasing frequency. During this period a minimum of forty Huron were killed or carried off by Iroquois, not counting those who were captured but later escaped. Although this was not a large number of individuals, it represented the loss of between five and ten percent of the Huron population along the St. Lawrence. Most of these Huron were taken in the vicinity of Montreal and Three Rivers. In the autumn of 1650 seven Huron, led by Hondakont, were captured close to Montreal even though there were ten canoes in their party, while the Mohawk had only three (Thwaites 1896–1901, 35:59). In the spring of

1651 Jacques Ondhwarak and his uncle Aontrati were captured while hunting, although the younger man later managed to escape (36:133). In July another group of Iroquois killed one Huron and captured another, who were gathering hay for the French opposite Three Rivers (36:133–35) and in the autumn of 1651 another Huron was captured at Montreal (36:149).

Early in 1652 three Huron were captured after they had set out from Montreal on a raid against the Mohawk (37:95–97). In March ten more Huron were captured, at least three of whom were killed. These Huron were accompanying a party of Algonkin men and women from Three Rivers to Montreal. Their leader, Toratati, was among those who were tortured to death (37:93; 38:49). A Huron named Ahoskwentak, who was taken prisoner, later managed to escape (37:101). On 15 May a Huron woman, her daughter, and the latter's four-year old son were seized near Montreal when they went to flesh a moose that had been shot nearby (37:101). In spite of their former avoidance of Montreal, at least a few Huron were now living or wintering there.

The rest of the incidents recorded for 1652 took place around Three Rivers. On 10 May Thomas Tsondoutannen, who was accompanying Father Jacques Buteux up the St. Maurice River, was captured by the Iroquois in an engagement in which the priest and his French companion were slain; however, Tsondoutannen soon managed to escape and returned to Three Rivers. On 8 June two Huron were killed while fishing opposite Three Rivers (37:105; 38:53). On 7 August one Huron of a group of eighty Huron and Algonkians who were returning from Montreal was slain (37:111) and ten days later Saouenhati and his wife were killed while working in their fields at Three Rivers (37:115). This Saouenhati was the namesake of an early Christian convert from Teanaostaiaé. In November another Huron woman was killed (37:117) and in December two more men were captured a few miles from Three Rivers (38:169). In the spring of 1653 four more Huron were seized while hunting or travelling between Three Rivers and Quebec (38:171). Another Huron was taken prisoner on 30 May but was later rescued (38:177). Two others, who were captured three weeks later, were not so fortunate (38:179).

The majority of Huron were killed or captured as a result of the general warfare that was going on between the Mohawk and the French; however, the emphasis that the Mohawk placed on capturing Huron prisoners reflected their long-term ambition to incorporate all of the Huron who had come to Quebec into their own society or, failing this, to kill them. This would rob the French of allies who were skilled in guerilla warfare and would neutralize the desire of Huron prisoners among the Iroquois to join relatives who were living with the French. It also provided a means by which the Mohawk, who were hard-pressed by spiralling losses from disease and warfare, could augment their numbers.

When the Mohawk harassed Three Rivers in July 1652, the French and Algonkin were displeased to note that sundry negotiations went on between the Huron and the Iroquois. The Huron were anxious for news about their relatives who were living among the Mohawk and who made up part of the Mohawk force, while the Mohawk were equally interested in persuading the Huron to desert the French (38:55). The French believed that it was only in order to encourage defections that the Mohawk headman, Aontarisati, pretended to wish to discuss peace with them. The French persuaded a number of Huron to seize him when he landed for these talks, and he and a companion were burned at Three Rivers the next day (37:107–111). The French hoped that this would rule out any further friendly relations between Huron and Iroquois.

Although the Mohawk swore to avenge the death of Aontarisati by henceforth killing every Huron they captured (40:97), their main resentment appears to have been directed against the French at Three Rivers. In August 1653 the Mohawk besieged the settlement, after failing to take it by surprise. As the siege was prolonged, it provided another opportunity for the Huron to renew their contacts with the Mohawk. Soon the meetings between these two groups became more important than the warfare that was going on. Some Huron who were fighting with the Mohawk joined their kinsmen who were living with the French, but another carried off his daughter who had been staying at Three Rivers (40:113–15).

THE RAPE OF THE QUEBEC HURON

When the Mohawk who were besieging Three Rivers learned that peace talks were progressing well between the Onondaga and the French and about the defeat of another Mohawk band on Montreal Island, the leaders of this war party decided that, rather than be left out, the time had come for them to negotiate for peace also. They delegated several Mohawk, led by the headman Andioura, to accompany the Onondaga to Quebec. Andioura met secretly with the Huron headmen from the Ile d'Orléans and offered them presents to induce their followers to leave the island and settle among the Mohawk. Later, Atsina, a Huron headman living at Three Rivers, gave the Mohawk three presents to signify that the Huron accepted this proposal (Thwaites 1896–1901, 41:19).

The Onondaga delegates also visited the Huron settlement on the Ile d'Orléans. Although they claimed that they had come only to make peace with the Huron (40:165–69), the Onondaga were as interested as were the Mohawk in persuading these Huron to live with them. It is therefore not surprising that the Huron also gave the Onondaga presents as tokens of their willingness to join them (41:21). These presents explain why, when the Montagnais denounced the idea of making peace with the Iroquois, the Huron remained unmoved, while their headmen unexpectedly announced that in the past the Montagnais and Algonkin had behaved as badly as the Iroquois (40:189).

The Huron at Quebec and Three Rivers doubted that the French could defend them against a concerted Iroquois attack and therefore were anxious to encourage at least the appearance of cordial relations with their formerly avowed enemies. It is clear, however, that these Huron had no desire to surrender themselves to the Iroquois. They rightly feared that the Onondaga would avenge former injuries should they get them in their power and that rivalry between the Mohawk and Onondaga would result in whichever tribe these Huron decided not to live with seeking to harm them (41:59).

Such fears are evident in the Huron's dealings with the four Onondaga who arrived at Montreal on their way to Quebec in January 1654. When the French learned that they came to have dealings with the Huron on the Ile d'Orléans, they were at first reluctant to let them continue on their journey. At a secret night session Tsiraenie, the leader of this group, informed the Huron that the following spring, 400 Onondaga men and 100 women were coming as far as the St. Francis River to help the Huron transport their possessions to the Onondaga country. He instructed the Huron headmen that they were to tell their people that since peace now prevailed, they were going to re-settle at Montreal; only the Huron headmen should know the actual destination of this move until they had contacted the Onondaga. Terrified by the implications of this suggestion, the Huron headmen replied that their promise of the previous year had been misunderstood; they had merely meant to assure the Onondaga that if war broke out again between the French and the Iroquois, the Huron and Onondaga would remain on sufficiently good terms that any Onondaga the Huron captured would not be slain (41:21).

Desperate for the safety of their own people, the Huron headmen decided to inform the Jesuits and French officials about their secret dealings with the Iroquois. The French temporarily suspected a conspiracy between the Huron and the Onondaga; then they feared that it would endanger the fragile truce between the Iroquois and the French if the Onondaga were to believe that there was no hope of the Huron at Quebec ever joining them voluntarily. The Jesuits and Governor d'Ailleboust told the Huron to inform Tsiraenie that the French knew about their discussions and that he would have to apply to the French for permission before the latter would allow the Huron to join the Onondaga. It was agreed that d'Ailleboust would delay approving such a move by saying that he would discuss it only once the peace between the French and the Onondaga was well established (41:21–23). The Huron were also instructed to tell the Onondaga that the Jesuits wished to found a settlement in their country and to imply that the Huron would only be allowed to go there after this had been accomplished (41:61–63). A desire to escape further pressure from the Mohawk may explain why most of the Huron who were at Three Rivers joined the settlement on the Ile d'Orléans in April 1654 (70:205–7).

While serving to placate the Onondaga and to advance certain French interests, the advice that the French gave to the Huron did little to make the latter feel secure about their future or about the long-term willingness of the French to protect them. Indeed, these negotiations indicated the increasing expendability of the Christian Huron at Quebec in the eyes of French officials and the Jesuit clergy. The peace of 1653 seemed miraculous to the French, who did not understand why the various Iroquois tribes needed to disengage themselves from fighting with them. While the French might be rueful about a peace that had been dictated by the Iroquois rather than imposed on the latter by force, they had a desperate interest in seeing that it continued.

Both the Mohawk (40:185) and the Onondaga (42:53) were anxious that the French should conclude an alliance with them that would involve having Frenchmen settle in their midst, as they had formerly done among the Huron. This would provide them with hostages to ensure that the French would not aid their enemies and a garrison for their protection, as well as facilitating trade. With a French settlement in their midst, the Mohawk could play French and Dutch traders off against one another and dominate the western Iroquois. Conversely, the Onondaga hoped for a French settlement so that they might have an alternative source of European goods and no longer be dependent on the goodwill of the Mohawk. They also hoped for French assistance against the Erie and other enemies (42:53).

The Jesuits were delighted at the prospect of undertaking mission work among one or more of the Iroquois tribes and believed that if the Quebec Huron were resettled among the Iroquois under Jesuit protection, the move would not harm the Huron and would help to promote the spread of Christianity. The hitherto inexplicable dispersal of the Huron was now seen by the Jesuits as an act of divine providence that was about to open promising new mission fields. The Jesuits' enthusiasm to placate the Iroquois and to exploit these mission fields supports Radisson's claim that it was mainly at their insistence that most of the Huron ultimately left Quebec to join the Iroquois (Adams 1961:50).

The Onondaga visited Quebec in September 1655 to reaffirm their treaty with the French and the latter's Indian allies. This was done in the name of all the Iroquois tribes except the Mohawk. While there, the Onondaga formally invited the French to live in their country as they had formerly lived among the Huron (42:53). The Jesuits enthusiastically accepted this invitation and Fathers Pierre Chaumonot and Claude Dablon were dispatched to the Onondaga as an advance guard of the seven priests and approximately fifty workmen who were to establish the Jesuit residence of Sainte-Marie-de-Ganentaa the following summer (42:57–59). The Onondaga interpreted the acceptance of their invitation as ensuring that the Huron at Quebec would join them rather than the Mohawk, and the Jesuits recognized the resettlement of the Huron as being one of the conditions for establishing a mission there.

The Huron correctly perceived that further dealings with the Onondaga would arouse the bitter enmity of the Mohawk. When the latter saw themselves being out-manoeuvred by the Onondaga, they became more determined than ever that they would compel the Huron to live with them. No course seemed open but to coerce the Huron, while at the same time offering to maintain peace with the French (42:49). On 25 April 1656 two Mohawk raiders killed one Huron and wounded another along the shore of the St. Lawrence below Quebec. The Huron set out in pursuit of the raiders and captured one of them some fifty miles up-river. The French urged the Huron to spare the prisoner's life so they might use him to turn away a large band of Mohawk who were reported to be on their way to harass the Huron settlement; however, the relatives of the murdered man were influential and they demanded that the prisoner be tortured to death, which was done after he was baptized (43:105–7).

The Mohawk warriors continued down the St. Lawrence River, camping at Three Rivers and cordially conferring with the Jesuits and French officials there. The French gave the Mohawk presents and attempted to dissuade them from attacking the Huron, but at no time did they threaten to use force to stop them for fear this would endanger the security they derived from their own tenuous peace treaty. When the Mohawk finally disbanded to go hunting and raiding in different directions, the French believed they had been successful (43:107–13). On 18 May, however, the Mohawk reassembled and two days later, without being sighted from Quebec, they landed on the Ile d'Orléans near the Huron village. In the morning, after mass had been said, the Huron set out to work in their fields and the Mohawk, who meanwhile had secreted themselves between the church and the fort, fell upon them. Some Huron found refuge in the Jesuits' fortified house but approximately seventy, including many young women, were killed or taken prisoner. All the while, the Mohawk were careful not to harm the French who were living on the island (43:115–19). They forced their prisoners to embark in forty canoes and travelled up-river past Quebec in broad daylight. As they passed the French settlement they compelled the prisoners to sing, in order to mock both the Huron and the French. When the Mohawk reached Three Rivers, one of the Jesuits visited their camp to console the Huron captives, but no attempt was made to rescue them (43:123).

Many French settlers were surprised that the governor accepted what had happened passively. It was later explained that nothing was done to save the Huron because the lives of the missionaries who were already working among the Iroquois would have been endangered if war broke out (Perrot 1911:192–93). In fact, the military and economic situation in the colony was so precarious that few traders or officials were willing to risk another war with the Iroquois in order to protect these refugees. Among the prisoners was Jacques Oachonk, who was judged to be the most fervent Christian in the settlement, and Joachim Ondakont, a famous warrior (43:119–23). Both men were tortured to death by the Mohawk, but many others were allowed to live. Perrot (1911:158, 193) later observed that none of the Huron, whether living among the Iroquois, at Quebec, or with the Tionnontaté, ever forgave this act of treachery by which the French abandoned so many of their people to the mercy of their enemies. The Huron who remained at Quebec realized that they could not count on the French to protect them so long as they lived on the Ile d'Orléans and on 4 June they returned uninvited to Quebec (70:207). Some of the French, appalled by what had happened, offered plots of land to these Huron to compensate them for the fields they had abandoned. One of the Huron who was offered the most land was the popular Ignace Tsaouenhohoui, who was later recognized as the principal headman of the Huron colony.[6] Although he was given this land for his own use, he distributed it, in Huron fashion, to the families who had the greatest need of it (53:121). Many Huron seem to have gone to live at Sillery, which was fortified and at that time was partially abandoned by its Algonkian inhabitants (43:35; 45:115).

In spite of moving to Quebec, the Huron could not feel secure until they had settled their differences with the Mohawk. An agreement was concluded the following autumn, but only after all of the remaining Huron had again promised to join their enemies. This agreement was formally ratified by three Huron who visited the Mohawk villages to confer with the Mohawk headmen. The latter stated that their people would come to fetch the remaining Huron in the spring of 1657 and warned the Huron not to attempt further delays or evasions (43:187). Four Mohawk returned to Quebec with these envoys, to remain with the Huron and observe their good behaviour (42:261). Both the Huron and the French knew that this promise conflicted with the Huron's previous undertaking to join the Onondaga. To complicate matters, in November 1656 the Oneida publicly offered presents to the Huron inviting them to resettle among them. This was apparently a proposal that the Oneida had made twice before (42:253–55). Father Ragueneau saved the Huron from having to reply to the Oneida by giving the latter to understand that further negotiations would have to be conducted through Father Le Mercier once the French and Huron were established among the Onondaga (42:257).

The Onondaga became extremely angry when they learned about the latest agreement between the Mohawk and the Huron. In April 1657 fifty of them arrived at Quebec publicly vowing to wage war on the Huron and Montagnais. The Onondaga had already wounded a Huron woman while crossing Lake St. Peter (43:35). At Quebec they killed another Huron, and the young men vented their anger against the French by killing their domestic animals. The French did nothing to hinder them and breathed a sigh of relief when it became evident that the aim of these warriors was to force the Huron to honour their earlier promise to join the Onondaga. While a protracted series of conferences during the month of May accomplished little, the Huron lost hope that the French would do anything to defend them and eventually the Arendarhonon at Quebec agreed to join the Onondaga. The large number of Arendarhonon already living among the Onondaga explains this choice. By contrast, the Attignawantan preferred to join the Mohawk rather than the western Iroquois tribes who were their traditional enemies. In spite of the small number of Huron who came to Quebec, tribal affiliation remained crucial in determining foreign policy (43:35–43, 199–207).

The Arendarhonon publicly agreed that they would join the Onondaga

when the French went to live there in the summer and several days later
the Onondaga departed, accompanied by three Huron envoys. Although the
Mohawk who had spent the winter at Quebec were present throughout
these negotiations and had joined in them in an apparent spirit of goodwill,
the Mohawk at Three Rivers and Montreal prevented the Huron envoys
from journeying any farther. These Mohawk included about 100 armed
men, who had come to transport the Huron to their villages (43:45–47,
187). Their main force bivouaced up-river, while twenty-five or thirty
Mohawk travelled to Quebec to summon the Huron to depart. They
arrived there 28 May (43:45, 187). The Huron did not want to leave
Quebec, but, with the French unwilling to defend their right to stay, they
believed they had to go or die at the hands of the Mohawk (43:191).

A whole night was spent in urgent consultation. The Attigneenongnahac
refused to leave Quebec, while the Arendarhonon reluctantly reaffirmed
their pledge to join the Onondaga. The Attignawantan promised to join the
Mohawk. The next morning Atsina, the headman of the Attignawantan,
announced his people's willingness to follow the Mohawk, regardless of the
consequences. Pathetically, he intimated that if the Attigneenongnahac
and the Arendarhonon saw that the Attignawantan were well treated by
the Mohawk, they might be willing to join them at a later date. The
Mohawk promised to treat the Attignawantan as relatives and, appreciating
the crucial role that the Jesuits had played in encouraging the Huron to
join the Iroquois, they formally invited the Jesuits to visit them so the
Attignawantan might remain Christians. Although the Mohawk asked the
French to provide pinnaces to transport the Huron up-river, the French
refused to do this. Thus, the Indians worked for several days to make extra
canoes and spent the nights giving farewell feasts. The most splendid of
these was given by Atsina to take leave of the French and of the Indians
who remained at Quebec (43:187–95); however, when the time came to
leave, all but fourteen women and children deferred their departure
(43:49). If those who remained behind hoped that rivalry between the
Mohawk and Onondaga over their custody would save them from having
to join either tribe, they were mistaken. In August 100 Mohawk returned
to Montreal, of whom twenty travelled down-river to Quebec. On 21
August some more Attignawantan left Quebec with these Mohawk, while
the final group, led by Father Le Moyne, followed them a few days later
(43:53–55; 44:189).

The fifty Arendarhonon who had opted to join the Onondaga left Quebec
on 16 June. The French conveyed them to Montreal in pinnaces and there
they awaited the arrival of a group of Seneca and Onondaga who were to

lead them to the Onondaga country (43:51, 207). On 26 July they and a group of Frenchmen under the direction of Father Ragueneau departed in the company of fifteen Seneca and thirty Onondaga. As they paddled up the St. Lawrence, some of Ragueneau's assistants were forced to return to Montreal when the Iroquois refused to transport a portion of the Jesuits' baggage any farther. Then, on 3 August some Iroquois killed one of the Huron with a hatchet. Seven or eight Huron men took up arms to defend themselves, but were assured by the Iroquois that no harm would befall them. As soon as the Huron were off guard, however, the Onondaga killed all of the Huron men except an aged headman, who was famous for once having saved the lives of a number of Iroquois who had been taken prisoner (Adams 1961:55). This Huron later escaped from the Onondaga and made his way to the Mohawk country, where he denounced the French, and particularly the Jesuits, for having betrayed his people. His denunciation helped to confirm the Mohawk's own suspicions of the French and was one more factor disposing them to renew fighting with them (ibid. 70). After they had killed the Huron men, the Onondaga despoiled the women and children of their possessions and treated them as prisoners of war (Thwaites 1896–1901, 44:73). Ragueneau ordered the French, who were outnumbered, not to interfere. Later, he attempted to secure better treatment for the survivors, but the Onondaga bluntly informed him that by abandoning the Huron, the French officials and Jesuits at Quebec had empowered the Onondaga to treat them as they wished (44:73–77). In spite of these ominous beginnings, the French proceeded to establish their mission centre among the Onondaga.

The reason for these killings was never clear to the French. Radisson suggested that the Onondaga were angry because several comrades had drowned on their way to Quebec (Adams 1961:51), while Ragueneau stated that it was because an Arendarhonon woman had rejected the sexual advances of an Iroquois headman (Thwaites 1896–1901, 44:73). It is more likely, however, that the Onondaga sought to avenge the massacre of their men on Gahoendoe in the winter of 1650–51. The Huron who were responsible for this had since come to Quebec and some of them may have been among this group.

Out of self-interest French government officials and Jesuits had delivered many of the Huron refugees who had sought their protection into the hands of the Iroquois. Thus the Huron joined the growing ranks of Indians who ceased to be treated with respect by Europeans once they ceased to be an economic asset. Compared with the political and commercial advantages that the French hoped to gain by expanding their influence among the

Iroquois, nothing these refugees could offer was of much importance. The Huron believed that bonds of religion and the economic and military alliances that had linked them with the French for over thirty-five years gave them a special claim on the latter's friendship and support. It was their misfortune that at the height of their adversity they had to learn otherwise.

It can be said in the Jesuits' favour that in order to realize their missionary goals, they exposed themselves to as much danger among the Iroquois as they did their Huron converts. They appear to have assumed that the conversion of these Huron implied a commitment to advance the Christian cause in whatever way the Jesuits saw fit. The self-sacrificing devotion of the Jesuits thus continued to be combined with the same paternalism that in the Huron country had repeatedly sacrificed the collective welfare of the Huron to the interests of spreading Roman Catholicism. At Quebec, however, the pitiable adversity of the Huron threw these policies into sharp relief and provided the Jesuits' enemies within the colony with substantial ammunition to use against them.

From a modern point of view, the least attractive aspect of the Jesuits' handling of this situation was their refusal to accept moral responsibility for the consequences of their own actions. In spite of the vast amount of human suffering that their actions produced, the Jesuits never exhibited the slightest misgivings about the high-handed way in which they had manipulated the destiny of this small remnant of Huron Christians. Instead, they argued that the Huron were to blame for what had happened to them; since it was they who had agreed to join the Iroquois in the first place, it was necessary for them to suffer the consequences of their own actions (43:191). While this attitude may reflect the intellectual arrogance of the Jesuit order, it also indicates the insecurity of the Jesuit missionaries in New France after 1650. As the Canadian Jesuits moved into a more complicated political situation, which they were progressively less able to control, their clear vision of earlier times gave way to a policy of political and moral compromise.[7] Later, as the enemies of New France grew stronger, even their primary goal of converting the Indians became subordinated to protecting the one bastion of Roman Catholicism in North America which constituted the base for their operations.

The Jesuits did not long enjoy the fruits of their political intrigues. With the Erie defeated and most of the Huron at Quebec now in Iroquois hands, the Onondaga and Seneca had fewer reasons to desire the friendship of the French. Moreover, the Mohawk were determined that the Onondaga should not enjoy the advantage of having a French colony in their midst. In

1657 the Mohawk headmen decided to attack and destroy this settlement and soon won support for this action, even among certain sections of the Onondaga tribe (44:149–53). Garakontie, the principal headman of the Onondaga, was a friend of the French and was later to become a Christian. Seeing that an attack on Sainte-Marie-de-Ganentaa could not be stopped, he informed the Jesuits what was being planned. This permitted the French to abandon the settlement on the night of 20 March 1658 and to reach Montreal safely. Meanwhile, d'Ailleboust, who was again in charge of New France, became convinced that it was necessary to replace the Jesuits' policy of appeasing the Iroquois by a new one of resistance (Lanctot 1963:228–29). A new round of guerilla warfare was about to begin between the French and the Iroquois.

In September 1657 the Onondaga had made a final effort to persuade the Huron who remained at Quebec to join them. The Huron had not yet learned what had happened to the Arendarhonon, but were determined not to accompany the Onondaga. Lacking the support of the French, they were compelled to rely on delaying tactics, but finally they persuaded the Onondaga to let them postpone their departure until the following year. On 6 October the French learned about the massacre of the Arendarhonon and that the Onondaga were plotting once more to attack the French. As a result of these revelations, d'Ailleboust decreed that hereafter the French must support their Huron and Algonkian allies and prevent the Iroquois from harassing them within sight of French settlements (Thwaites 1896–1901, 44:191–93).

THE LONG SAULT AND LATER

The Huron who had remained at Quebec now had less reason to fear being abandoned to the Iroquois, although they remained uneasy. Past experience gave them little cause to trust French promises. In 1660 the Jesuits decided to expel the Huron who had taken up residence at Sillery, but their aim in so doing seems to have been to compel the Huron to form a single settlement under Jesuit supervision.[8] Until 1668 the Huron continued to live in a fortified encampment that d'Ailleboust had built for them in the heart of the French settlement at Quebec (Thwaites 1896–1901, 45:245; 47:285). These Huron cultivated about forty-four arpents on the south shore of the St. Lawrence opposite Quebec (47:261). Although safe from Iroquois intimidation, the Huron, like the French, suffered from Iroquois raids in the years that followed. On 30 September 1662 a Huron man, his wife, and daughter were captured by the Iroquois on the Ile d'Orléans, where they apparently had gone to fish. A week later, Huron working in their fields opposite Quebec were attacked and a man and woman were carried off (47:291).

Although the French were unable to protect the Huron beyond the limits of their own settlements, French officials encouraged their Indian allies to attack the Iroquois even before it was clear that the French and the Iroquois were again at war (44:193). In August 1658 the new governor, Pierre de Voyer d'Argenson, distributed arms to his Indian allies. Guns, powder, and shot went to the Algonkin and Montagnais, while the Huron received swords, hatchets, and iron arrowheads (44:103–5). This is possibly an indication that the French still feared that the remaining Huron might desert to the Iroquois and were reluctant to provide them with guns. The same year twenty-three Huron set out from Quebec to avenge themselves by slaying or capturing some Iroquois warriors. Such militancy on the part of the small number of Huron who remained at Quebec suggests that so long as the French had sought to maintain peace with the Iroquois, they had to restrain the Huron from attacking the latter and possibly did this by depriving them of firearms. If so, the remaining Huron had yet another reason to resent the manner in which they had been treated by the French.

The renewal of the war between the French and the Iroquois resulted in another heavy loss for the Huron colony. In the spring of 1660 the Huron headman, Annaotaha, and forty of his men, "the flower of all those of importance at Quebec" (45:245), joined Adam Dollard des Ormeaux and a number of French and Algonkin who planned to plunder the Onondaga who were returning from their winter hunting and pillaging expeditions in the north. They also intended to meet the Indians who were coming from the upper Great Lakes to trade that year. Dollard's force was hopelessly outnumbered at the foot of the Long Sault Rapids of the Ottawa River by a war party made up largely of Mohawk and Oneida who had been summoned from the Richelieu area to support the Onondaga. Annaotaha proposed that they parley with the Iroquois. An Oneida who had been adopted by the Huron and two leading Huron were loaded with gifts and sent out of Dollard's fort to negotiate with the Iroquois. While they were doing this, some Huron who had been adopted by the Iroquois contacted the Huron who remained with Dollard and persuaded most of them to desert.

In the confusion that followed, the French fired on the Iroquois, who in response assaulted the French fort. Annaotaha was killed in the attack and, when the battle was over, only seven Frenchmen and four Huron who had stayed with them were still alive (45:245–61). After the battle, the Iroquois made all of the Huron who had either surrendered or been taken prisoner mount a scaffold and treated them as prisoners of war (45:257); however, when the Onondaga returned to their villages, only one of these prisoners was condemned to death to avenge an Onondaga who had been killed in the early phases of the battle (46:37). The latter may have been the head-man whose severed head the Huron had stuck on a pole above Dollard's palisade. Eventually, however, the family who had adopted this prisoner agreed that he too should be spared. Thus all the Huron who surrendered to the Iroquois were allowed to live (46:49). Three prisoners escaped (46:23–53) but, as far as is known, the rest continued to live among the Iroquois, renewing contacts with friends and relatives whom they had not seen for over a decade. The conduct of these Huron has long been regarded as extremely cowardly, although the outcome of the battle was scarcely open to question. Given the experience of repeated French betrayal that the Huron refugees had at Quebec, it is hardly surprising that most of them felt under no obligation to fight to the death, especially when other Huron offered them a plausible alternative. Their abandonment of Dollard was a response to many years of similar treatment by the French.

The loss of more than thirty-five men was a serious blow to the Huron community at Quebec. The women and children depended more than ever upon the Jesuits for support and so few men were left that, for a time, it seemed that the community might die out (46:61–63). It is likely that the marked piety that later characterized this group, and which was not evident in the preceding decade, dates from this time. The number of men in the settlement was slowly augmented by Huron who, for various reasons, came there from the Iroquois villages. The arrival of two such men, one named Tsanhohy and the other escaped from the Mohawk, are recorded for the autumn of 1660 (45:163–65). Other Huron returned to Quebec during various intervals of peace between the French and the Iroquois. One of these was Jeanne Assenragenhaon, in whose longhouse many Jesuits had been entertained when they had visited Ossossané. After being captured by the Iroquois, she converted her Iroquois husband and eventually persuaded him to move to Quebec so that she might practise her religion there (60:297–301).

In spite of their survival, the Huron who remained or settled at Quebec continued for a long time to be heavily dependent on the Jesuits. When Bishop François de Laval arrived at Quebec in 1659, the Huron who welcomed him lamented their fate at the hands of the Iroquois and asked him to avenge these wrongs by encouraging the French to burn the Iroquois villages (45:39–43). When Alexandre de Prouville de Tracy came in 1665 to wage war on the Mohawk, the Huron formally urged him to take steps to induce Huron and other Indians who had gone to live among the Iroquois to desert them. The Huron orator also spoke of their old homeland and expressed the hope that the Huron were about to be reborn as a people and might soon return there (49:227–35).

This was, however, the last time that the Huron at Quebec are recorded as expressing such a hope. In 1667 the French again made peace with the Iroquois and the following spring the Huron left Quebec and settled at Beauport (52:229). The next year they went to Côte St. Michel, where the mission of Notre-Dame-de-Foy was founded. From there they moved to (now) Ancienne Lorette in 1673 and Jeune Lorette in 1697 (70:207; map 35). While at Notre-Dame-de-Foy the Huron settlement was further augmented by the arrival of a number of Christian Mohawk (56:29; 58:171), as well as by the continuing influx of a few Huron Christians, either from the Iroquois or from the upper Great Lakes (57:37). In 1675 the population of Lorette was about 300 Huron and Iroquois (60:27), almost double what it had been a few years earlier (54:287).

Although Louis de Buade de Frontenac was to accuse the Jesuits of continuing their old policy of keeping the Huron separate from the French and teaching them in their own language, through their efforts to promote Christian behaviour, the Jesuits were influential in persuading the Huron of Lorette to adopt French ways. One missionary was of the opinion that had the Huron remained flourishing, the Jesuits would not have acquired so great an ascendancy over them in a century as they gained over these survivors in a few years (57:69). While the Jesuits continued to pay lip service to the policy of adapting traditional Indian customs to Christian usage, the few examples of this being done at Lorette were innovations suggested by Huron converts (55:271–73). On the other hand, the Jesuits took full credit for compelling the Huron to abandon the ritual painting of their faces (60:93).

The Europeanization of the Huron at Lorette took place more quickly in the spheres of religious behaviour and etiquette than in their subsistence pattern. Even after they had settled at Jeune Lorette, they continued to live in bark longhouses (58:147) and to practise slash and burn agriculture. European-style farming was adopted in the eighteenth century, but hunting and trapping remained important until the end of the nineteenth century. Various handicraft industries have played an important role in the Lorette economy since the beginning of the last century and the manufacture of snowshoes and canoes remains an important source of revenue.

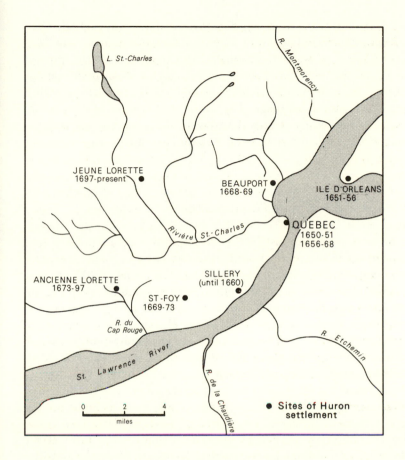

MAP 35. *Locations and dates for Huron settlements in the vicinity of Quebec City.*

By the end of the last century, the Huron of Lorette had so much identified with their new home that they were showing Indian visitors the place where their ancestors traditionally had come out of the ground (Trigger 1970:13). Memories of both their clan and tribal organizations persisted for a long time, but vanished in the last century along with a knowledge of the Huron language. The history of Lorette and the gradual evolution of Huron society within the context of French Canada is, how-ever, another story (Gérin 1900; Lindsay 1900; Morissonneau 1970).

The Huron of the Upper Great Lakes

The Huron who decided to cast in their lot with the Tionnontaté moved with them to Michilimackinac Island in the summer of 1650 (Thwaites 1896–1901, 56:115). This island was noted for its fisheries. Within a short time Iroquois incursions compelled them to retreat to another island at the mouth of Green Bay. Sometime about 1653, news that a large Iroquois war party was headed in that direction caused the Huron and Tionnontaté to retreat still farther. They lived for a time among the Potawatomi and other Algonkian-speaking groups along the shores of Green Bay[9] but, after attempting to poison a group of Iroquois who were besieging their settle-ment, the Tionnontaté and Huron made their way westward to the source of the Black River in Wisconsin (45:235). Their encroachment on the hunting territories of the Sioux soon involved them in warfare with the latter. By 1661 they had abandoned their settlement on the Black River and moved to Chequamegon, on the south shore of Lake Superior, settling near a village of Ottawa refugees who had already established themselves in that location (46:143–45). The Ottawa and the Tionnontaté-Huron fared badly in their struggle with the Sioux and in 1671 both groups left Chequamegon and returned to Lake Huron. While the Ottawa settled on Manitoulin Island, the Tionnontaté-Huron built a palisaded village at St. Ignace, on the mainland opposite Michilimackinac Island (56:115–17; map 36). The Tionnontaté-Huron remained there until 1701, when the French trader Antoine Laumet de Lamothe de Cadillac persuaded them to settle near the trading post of Ft. Pontchartrain on the Detroit River.

Although they had been driven westward by the Iroquois, it was necessary for the Tionnontaté-Huron and the Ottawa to secure European goods. In July 1653 three light canoes arrived at Three Rivers. These carried seven Indians, representing various refugee groups. They announced that men from these groups would be coming to the French trading posts the following year with many beaver skins that they hoped to trade for guns and ammunition in order to make themselves more formidable to their enemies (40:213–15). One of the members of this expedition was Aenons, the namesake of one of the principal headmen and traders of the Attignawantan (38:181). In June 1654 approximately 120 traders came down the Ottawa River. Some were Huron or Tionnontaté, the rest were Ottawa, whom the Huron were bringing to trade with the French for the first time (41:77). Médard Chouart des Groseilliers and another Frenchman accompanied these Indians when they returned to the upper Great Lakes to trade and explore that region.[10] Two years later they reappeared on the St. Lawrence, accompanied by 250 Indian traders, mostly Ottawa (42:219–21). For several decades, the latter were to dominate the trade with the upper Great Lakes, much as the Huron had done prior to 1650. Later most of the fur trade was conducted from French posts that were established at focal points in the interior, such as Sault Sainte Marie, Michilimackinac, and Detroit. These eliminated the need for the Ottawa, or any other Indian group, to travel to Montreal (Rich 1966:18–20).

Nicolas Perrot (1911:157) attributed the success of the Ottawa traders to their skill as canoemen. Nothing is known for certain about the Tionnontaté's nautical abilities prior to 1649. They did not engage in trade with the north and it may be that, like the Neutral, they were less expert with canoes than were the Huron and Ottawa. This would also imply that the number of Huron men who joined the Tionnontaté was small. So long as they were kept on the move and compelled to live in the north, the Tionnontaté-Huron were unable to produce agricultural surpluses that they could barter for furs; a situation that must have created very serious difficulties for the Huron's former trading partners. During the 1650s the Tionnontaté-Huron lived mainly by hunting and fishing and often were on the verge of starvation. Like their Algonkian-speaking neighbours, they were compelled to obtain their furs either by hunting or by exchanging European goods for them with other hunting bands. By the end of the seventeenth century, their subsistence pattern was little different from that of the other semi-horticultural tribes of the upper Great Lakes. As a result of this new adaptation, in many significant respects late seventeenth-century Tionnontaté-Huron band organization probably resembled that of the Iroquoians prior to the development of tribes and confederacies.

In 1653 the Huron had an important role to play in introducing their Tionnontaté hosts and the Ottawa to their French trading partners. Hereafter, the Tionnontaté-Huron are reported to have remained more

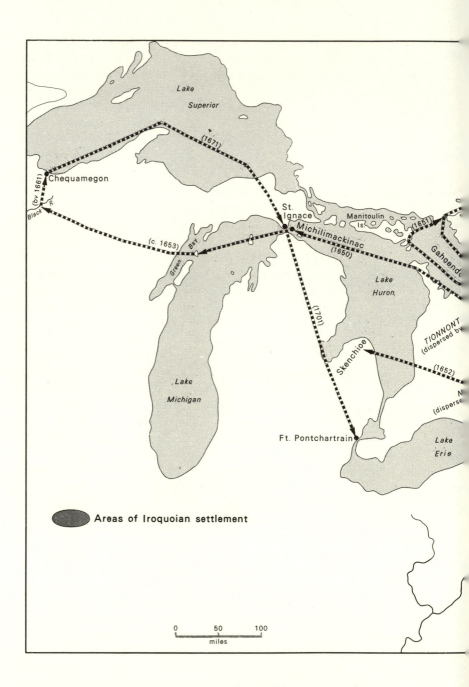

MAP 36. *Dispersal of Huron refugees after 1649.*

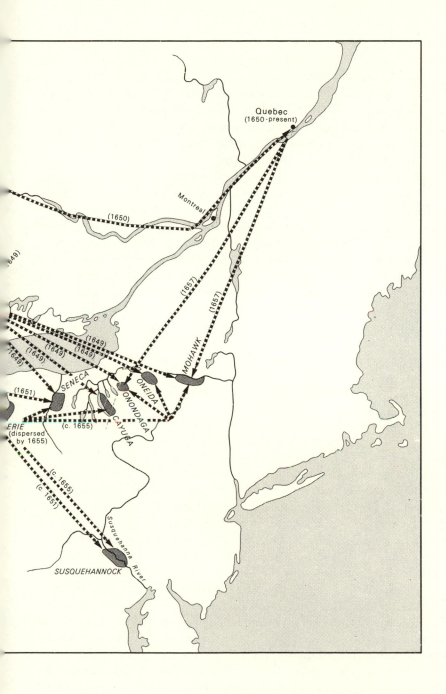

Quebec
(1650-present)

Montreal

(1650)

(1657)

(1657)

(1649)

(1649)

(1649)

(1649)

(1649)

(1651)

SENECA

ONEIDA

MOHAWK

ONONDAGA

(c. 1655)

CAYUGA

ERIE
(dispersed
by 1655)

(c. 1655)

(c. 1651)

Susquehanna River

SUSQUEHANNOCK

provident than the other tribes of the region and their trading customs and sophisticated political conduct set a standard for their less-experienced Ottawa and Ojibwa neighbours (Bacqueville de La Potherie 1911–12, 1:283). At least some of these skills were probably specifically of Huron rather than Tionnontaté origin. On the other hand, neither the Huron nor the Tionnontaté had an economic advantage when it came to competing with the Ottawa, who were more numerous than they and were operating in territory that was more familiar to them.

The renewal of trade with the French meant that limited contacts were maintained between the Huron who remained around the upper Great Lakes and those who lived at Quebec. A few individuals went to join relatives at Quebec and there were discussions in 1671 about whether the Tionnontaté-Huron might join the Huron colony at Quebec to avoid both the Iroquois and the Sioux. Although the Jesuits gave the Tionnontaté presents inviting them to relocate and become Christians, nothing came of these discussions and the Tionnontaté remained near Michilimackinac (Thwaites 1896–1901, 54:283–85).

The Tionnontaté did not trust the French. They knew what had happened to the Huron at Quebec when the French had sought good relations with the Iroquois, and they themselves had suffered from this policy. In 1656 the Tionnontaté agreed to take Father Léonard Garreau (who had been their missionary before 1650) home with them as an expression of their trading alliance, but when they were travelling up the Ottawa River they were attacked by the Mohawk and many of them were taken prisoner. Although Father Garreau was mortally wounded in this encounter (probably by a renegade Frenchman who had deserted to the Iroquois), the French made no effort to punish the Mohawk or to rescue the Tionnontaté. These prisoners were carried off by the Mohawk to their villages where, after preliminary tortures, their lives were spared (Perrot 1911:157–58). Two of these prisoners escaped from the Iroquois and accompanied Groseilliers on his return to Lake Superior, where they rejoined their relatives (Adams 1961:111). Although the Tionnontaté-Huron continued to seek friendly relations with the French and to discourage alliances between them and the Iroquois, they also cultivated their own good relations with the Iroquois. These developed particularly well when the Iroquois took advantage of the general peace they had been forced to conclude with the French in 1667, to send gifts to the Ottawa and Tionnontaté-Huron and to initiate trade with them (Thwaites 1896–1901, 57:23–25).

In time the separate ethnic identity of the individuals who composed the Huron-Tionnontaté was forgotten. Although, at first, they were called either Huron or Tionnontaté, they eventually became known as Wyandot, thus taking the name of the more prestigeful Huron. The similar language and institutions of the two groups made this a relatively easy process. Just as any memory of the dichotomy between the Huron and the Tionnontaté was forgotten, so was any memory of Huron tribal affiliations.

In their new circumstances, the Wyandot failed to retain any accurate conceptions of Tionnontaté-Huron history or of their political organization in the seventeenth century. When Peter Dooyentate Clarke published his *Traditional History of the Wyandotts* in 1870, he did not realize that his people had ever been more numerous or had lived differently before they were driven from the shores of Lake Huron than they did afterwards. Of the Jesuit martyrs, whose deeds later missionaries must have recounted, only the death of Antoine Daniel was remembered. For the Wyandot, who were struggling to survive after 1650, the complex social and political organization of the past no longer had any meaning; hence it was forgotten. On the other hand, the formal division into eight clans and three phratries survived into the last century because its ritual functions remained valid in spite of the collapse of tribal and confederacy organization. It is not known to what degree Huron and Tionnontaté clan and phratry structure were identical; however, the domination of the Tionnontaté by what appear to have been Wolf and Deer phratries does not suggest an obvious prototype for the organization of all but one of the Wyandot clans into two phratries with the Wolf clan constituting a third, mediating group (Connelly 1900:105–6). Some specifically Huron influences may be involved here, although the basic principles of this kind of organization were common enough to all Iroquoian groups that this is far from certain.

Throughout the eighteenth century, the Wyandot played an important role in the struggles between French and British, and later between British and Americans, for control of Michigan and the Ohio Valley. This was, however, a period of considerable dissension among the Wyandot themselves. In 1842 the Wyandot living in Ohio and Michigan sold their remaining tracts of land and moved first to Kansas and then farther south to Oklahoma, where a small reservation is still occupied by several hundred of their descendants. Early in this century, Marius Barbeau (1949; 1960) studied the native language of this group, shortly before it ceased to be spoken. A small group of Wyandot, known as the Anderdon band, continued to live near Sandwich, Ontario but had almost entirely disappeared by the beginning of the twentieth century (Tooker 1964:10 n. 3; Hewitt 1907:588–90).

The Huron among Their Enemies

THE HURON IN CAPTIVITY

While several hundred Huron found permanent shelter at Quebec and a smaller number joined the Tionnontaté, many more were taken prisoner by the Iroquois or joined them voluntarily, either immediately after the Huron confederacy disintegrated or after they had found temporary refuge elsewhere. Five hundred to 1000 Tahontaenrat joined the Seneca in 1651, and about 400 Huron later left Quebec to join the Mohawk and Onondaga. While no figures are available concerning the number of Huron who joined the Iroquois between 1648 and 1650, several thousand must eventually have been incorporated into Iroquois society in addition to the many hundreds who had been taken prisoner previously. It is difficult to estimate the accuracy of Jacques Bruyas's statement that in 1668 two-thirds of the Oneida were naturalized Huron or Algonkin (Thwaites 1896–1901, 51:123) or to assess the Jesuits' affirmation that a similar number of aliens lived in the principal Mohawk town of Gandagaron (51:187). There is, however, nothing intrinsically improbable in their estimate that over a thousand Huron who had been baptized in the Huron country were living among the Iroquois (41:133).

The Iroquois societies into which the defeated Huron were being absorbed were in the throes of a major crisis. The adoption of so many aliens was both a response to this crisis and a further aggravation of it. Since 1640 the Iroquois had grown increasingly dependent on raiding and hunting to obtain furs. Both methods compelled men to wander ever farther from their villages and brought them into conflict with more surrounding tribes. The result was an abnormally high male death rate. The Iroquois were also afflicted by European diseases just as the Huron had been. Smallpox was reported as early as 1634, and it and other epidemics revisited the Iroquois periodically thereafter. Over 1000 people are reported to have died in the smallpox epidemic of 1662 (50:63). Because the economy and defensive capability of the Iroquois depended on being able to pillage their neighbours, it was essential for them to maintain their population and fighting strength at as high a level as possible.

This was accomplished by adopting prisoners of war and defeated enemies on an unprecedented scale. Although the application of a traditional custom to a novel situation was in keeping with Iroquoian practice, the scale on which the Iroquois attempted to incorporate former enemies created many problems for them. Not the least of these was preventing insurrections or large scale defections by these prisoners, especially since Iroquois men stayed away from their villages for longer periods than had been usual in the past. Although there is little direct evidence concerning social conditions among the Iroquois at this period, it is likely that the responsibility must have fallen largely upon Iroquois women to supervise the acculturation of former enemies into their society and this must have substantially enhanced their power. While the principal matrilineal institutions of Iroquoian society antedate this period, the role of women in managing the affairs of their village and tribe seems partly to have resulted from the growing militarism of the Iroquois at this time. The celebrated right of Iroquois matrons to forbid men to wage war when they believed that to do so would be injurious to the interests of the community (Snyderman 1948) is one example of the sort of custom that may have developed under these circumstances. While the growing power of women was fundamentally a response to the demands of the fur trade, it was also the continuation of a process that had begun centuries earlier, when increasing reliance on horticulture led women to become more closely identified with their communities than men were.

The basic techniques that all Iroquoian peoples used to acculturate prisoners have been discussed in connection with the Huron in chapter 2. They involved a prolonged threat of torture and death if the prisoner should displease his adoptive relatives, which was counterbalanced by strong positive rewards for identifying with these relatives and their tribesmen. While a prisoner would first identify himself as an Iroquois in order to avoid torture, the prolonged rewarding of such behaviour eventually produced a genuine sense of kinship and identity. Prior to 1650 Huron and Iroquois who had remained long in captivity often proved to be among the most vigorous adversaries of their own people, both in warfare and diplomacy.

The incorporation of many Huron, Neutral, and Erie into the Iroquois confederacy after 1649 interfered with this process, especially since large numbers of prisoners from specific tribes were brought to live in the same Iroquois villages. This helped these prisoners to retain their language, customs, and a common sense of identity. When the Jesuits began their mission work among the Onondaga in 1656, they found it useful to establish separate congregations or prayer groups to serve the Huron, Neutral, and Onondaga (Thwaites 1896–1901, 44:41). Many Huron who were living among the Onondaga were Arendarhonon who had been captured before the destruction of Teanaostaiaé and Taenhatentaron (42:73). Others had come of their own accord after the dispersal of the Huron, in order to live with their relatives. Many of these refugees appear to have been bitterly opposed to the French. A large number of Arendarhonon who joined the Onondaga voluntarily had probably supported the anti-Christian faction. While not necessarily liking the Iroquois, they were convinced that living with them was preferable to the continuing domination of their lives by the Jesuits.

The largest number of Huron who were incorporated as a group were the Tahontaenrat. Many members of this tribe may have perished in the war between the Iroquois and the Neutral, but the Tahontaenrat managed to hold together in a way that no other Huron tribe or major village did. The town of Gandougarae, which they founded, was inhabited by Tahontaenrat and other refugee groups (map 37). The latter included Huron from other tribes, Neutral who had been allies of the Tahontaenrat, and another group known as the Onnontioga (54:81). The Tahontaenrat retained their identity for a long time and became as famous among the Iroquois for their curing rituals as they had been among the Huron (58:229; 17:89). Although the inhabitants of Gandougarae were granted no seats on the Iroquois confederacy council, this may have been of little concern to them, especially if they had not been directly represented on the Huron council previously. The Jesuits noted with astonishment the apparent friendship and good feeling that existed between the people of Gandougarae and the Seneca, in spite of their former hostility (44:21).

The arrangement whereby the Tahontaenrat were allowed to retain their own customs and live separately from the Seneca, but as their dependents, was more realistic than any attempt to force the total integration of so many aliens. In time, intermarriages probably forged links between the Seneca and the people of Gandougarae, and it may have been in this way that the Tahontaenrat eventually merged with the Seneca. While there is no historical record of Huron refugees being allowed to establish their own villages elsewhere among the Iroquois, archaeological evidence of another such village has been reported from Mohawk territory.[11] Gandougarae, therefore, may not be the only example of the Iroquois resorting to alliances rather than incorporation in an effort to deal with some of the larger groups of Huron who joined them.

Huron who joined the Iroquois voluntarily generally seem to have been well treated. Not infrequently, however, individuals and nuclear families who came from the same Huron village were scattered among various Iroquois communities and adopted into different Iroquois extended families to speed their acculturation. Men who were adopted by specific Iroquois families were eligible to fill any of the offices that belonged to their

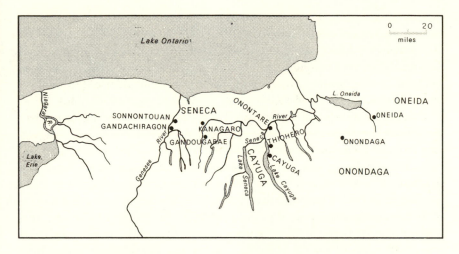

MAP 37. *Settlements of the four western Iroquois tribes, showing the location of Gandougarae.*

particular lineage. On the other hand, whole extended families who voluntarily joined the Iroquois seem to have been adopted by a clan segment,
rather than by families, and were allowed to live in separate longhouses.
The heads of such households were not granted any voice in public councils,
which conservatism and deliberate policy seem to have restricted to old
Iroquois families (43:293). In time, however, even these Huron families
became united with Iroquois ones through intermarriage, which no doubt
promoted cultural assimilation.

The distinction between Huron who joined the Iroquois voluntarily and
those who had been taken prisoner was not always a clear one or carefully
observed by the Iroquois. This is illustrated by the treatment of the Quebec
Huron who joined the Onondaga under duress and by the preliminary
torture of the Huron who surrendered at the Long Sault. An Iroquois who
felt especially obliged to avenge a dead kinsman, or who identified a
particular Huron as an enemy who had inflicted specific injuries on members of his family, might demand that this Huron be treated as a prisoner
of war, even if he had surrendered voluntarily. Prisoners of war almost
always were treated roughly. Men or women who were ill or seriously
injured and hence unable to keep up with a war party were killed immediately and almost all the men were tortured to some degree as soon as
they were captured. When the Iroquois returned home, families were
broken up and individual prisoners were assigned to different Iroquois long-

houses for adoption (42:75). These extended families had the right to kill such prisoners and often exercised this right if the prisoner was old or weak, or a member of their own family had been slain. One important headman is reported to have adopted some eighty prisoners and had them tortured to death to avenge his brother who had been killed in war (48:169). A prisoner who was allowed to live could be killed any time that his or her behaviour displeased their adoptive relatives (42:137), while other Iroquois, anxious to avenge old scores, might seek to kill or injure a Huron even though he had been formally adopted.

As the number of prisoners increased out of all proportion to what the Iroquois were accustomed to deal with, the Iroquois became insecure and more anxious to intimidate these prisoners. Prisoners were known to be slain if they became seriously ill (43:295, 303), if their behaviour displeased any of their adoptive kinsmen (49:107), or for quite capricious reasons. A warrior killed two female captives and their children rather than permit the village council to assign them for adoption. Likewise, the Iroquois did not question the propriety of children being slain if they hindered their mothers from working (Adams 1961:69). Prisoners were made to perform much of the hardest and least pleasant work, such as hauling food and trade goods over long distances (ibid. 28). Some headmen were now accompanied by a number of prisoners wherever they went (Thwaites 1896–1901, 48:171). The French called such prisoners slaves, in reference to the brutal manner in which they were treated. The term failed, however, to take account of the kinship basis of Iroquois society and of the fact that the ultimate aim of this brutality was the assimilation of these aliens as full members of Iroquois society.

Yet, in spite of the harsh treatment of prisoners, the Jesuits exaggerated the loss of life that resulted from it. Pierre Esprit Radisson, who lived as a prisoner among the Iroquois, describes Huron captives as generally living in a state of freedom. Many men may have been killed because particular Iroquois bore personal grudges against them or feared them. Yet, because of the similarity in their cultural patterns, Huron men had many skills which made them an asset to Iroquois society. Because of this, the Iroquois did not kill them on principle as they did Algonkian men (27:287). A male or female prisoner who was capable, and showed signs of wanting to please and identify with their adoptive parents, appears to have had a tolerably good chance of surviving. Some Huron men were forbidden to accompany war parties against their own people for a long time after they were captured for fear they would attempt to escape (Adams 1961:25–27); others were soon made to accompany such expeditions to test their reactions.

Forced involvement in wars was believed to strengthen a prisoner's loyalty to his adoptive relatives, since he was made to experience hardship and danger alongside them.

For those who survived the first few years of captivity, life appears to have become increasingly secure and normal by Iroquoian standards. At least one Huron headman who was taken prisoner became an Iroquois headman soon after he was adopted into a lineage that had a vacant office (Thwaites 1896–1901, 42:57). He participated, along with other Onondaga headmen in confirming the peace that was made at Quebec in September 1655. Iroquois men are reported to have preferred to marry Huron women because these marriages did not oblige them to serve their wives' kinsmen. Radisson's adoptive parents lived together for over forty years and his Huron mother was reported to be well-loved by her Mohawk husband (Adams 1961:26). In the 1680s the Jesuits drew attention to a leading headman of the Onondaga who, in their opinion, was much abused by two former prisoners whom he had adopted to replace his deceased sisters. Yet, because public opinion did not support him, he was unable to do anything to make them behave better (Thwaites 1896–1901, 62:61–63). These stories illustrate the fate of prisoners who survived the early years of assimilation, as well as later wars and epidemics, to become Iroquois. The large numbers of aliens who were successfully incorporated into the Iroquois tribes at this time and the thoroughness with which their natal allegiances were eliminated are evidence of the outstanding success of the emergency measures that the Iroquois were forced to adopt at this time.

THE HURON REFUGEES AND THE FRENCH

How did the Huron who joined the Iroquois feel about the French and the Jesuits and what were the feelings of the 1000 or more refugees who had been baptized in the Huron country? Because our data come almost entirely from French accounts, only partial answers can be given. In general, most Huron who were taken prisoner prior to 1649 and the traditionalists who joined the confederacy afterwards appear to have been vocal in their denunciation of the French. They accused the Jesuits of being sorcerers and warned that if they were permitted to visit the Iroquois, they would use their spells to ruin crops and slay the Iroquois, as they had done to the Huron (Thwaites 1896–1901, 31:121). They also repeated the more specific accusations against the Jesuits that had circulated in the Huron country. These included charges that the Jesuits bewitched the names they recorded in their baptismal records in order to make the bearers of these names die (42:135) and that they sought to convert Iroquois so they could torture their souls in heaven (42:151). Many Huron who had been baptized renounced their Christian affiliations and hastened to confirm the accusations of the traditionalists (43:291). Most of these were probably Huron who had favoured their own traditions, but had been led by opportunism or affection for relatives to become Christians.

When the Jesuits began to visit the Iroquois villages in the 1650s, many Huron traditionalists and former Christians became still more vocal in their opposition. They praised the Dutch for allowing the Iroquois to live in their own fashion and said that by doing this they had preserved the Iroquois, whereas the Jesuits had ruined the Huron by trying to convert them (43:291). They clearly perceived the difference between the secular approach of the Dutch traders and the intertwined economic and religious goals that had dominated the policies of New France since 1625. When the Jesuits first visited the Cayuga in 1656, they were received very coolly on account of the fears that the Huron had instilled (43:307). Over a decade later, when the Jesuits tried to baptize the daughter of a Huron convert, her father pointed out that in former times Brébeuf had made people die in just such a manner (52:187). Brébeuf's reputation as a malevolent sorcerer had outlived him among the Huron for over two decades. When the Jesuits were constructing boats to escape from the Onondaga in the spring of 1658, a Huron named "Jaluck" saw what was going on and reported that the Jesuits were planning to flood the world and had built an ark in which they hoped to survive (Adams 1961:71–72). Such accusations indicate the deep hatred that many Huron continued to feel towards the Jesuits. These feelings were reinforced as the Huron who had joined the Iroquois saw Huron forced to come from Quebec to the Iroquois villages, and as Huron and Tionnontaté traders were carried off in peacetime with the apparent acquiescence of the French. Accusations by these people that the French had betrayed them (ibid. 70) must have helped to convince many Huron captives that their only hope of survival lay in pleasing the Iroquois.

On the other hand, when the Jesuits visited the Iroquois, numerous Huron, including some who had once fulminated against the Jesuits, welcomed them as old friends and courted their favour. In particular, Huron women who had been baptized sought out the Jesuits so that they might perform their devotions. Some did this secretly, alleging to their Iroquois kinsmen that they were going to fish or trade (Thwaites 1896–1901, 47:197). Others presented their children for baptism, assembled in cabins to receive instruction to renew their faith, and, where the Jesuits were allowed to construct chapels, began regularly to attend services as they had formerly done in the Huron country (51:187, 191, 209–11). The Jesuits were told that before they had arrived among the Mohawk, Huron women gathered in the forests and in remote cabins to hold prayer meetings, even though by doing so they were laying themselves open to charges of witch-craft (47:57; 49:107; 50:115). Huron were reported to have professed their faith openly elsewhere among the Iroquois, in spite of similar dangers.

The Jesuits credited much of their influence among the Iroquois to help they received from Huron captives (52:163). As early as 1653, the Onon-daga were reported to have been well disposed to the French because of favourable statements that certain captive women had made concerning the missionaries (41:119). Even many Huron from Contarea, which had been notoriously hostile towards the Jesuits in the later years of the Huron mission, welcomed the Jesuits to the Onondaga country in 1656 and feigned to listen to their teachings (42:73). In 1670 the Jesuits reported that the vast majority of Christians were either of Huron descent or other aliens (54:41–43).

It cannot be doubted that some Huron who were living as prisoners or refugees were well disposed towards the French. Those who had been hosts to the Jesuits in the Huron country or who had been the recipients of special benefits or acts of kindness from them almost certainly felt such an attachment, which they expressed by being receptive to the Jesuits' teach-ings. Many of these Huron were among the "Iroquois" who later went to join the Huron at Quebec or to the other mission settlements along the St. Lawrence River (55:35; 57:75; 60:295). A far larger number of Huron, however, including traditionalists as well as professing Christians, seem to have resumed their old policy of being outwardly friendly to the French, whatever they personally felt about them. In dealing with the Jesuits, this took the form of listening politely and not contradicting them. The Jesuits often interpreted this more as approval of what they had to say than, in fact, it was. Real or imaginary former relationships were also appealed to, in an effort to forge bonds of friendship and reciprocity with the Jesuits. Nor was this practice limited to the Huron. A dying Cayuga whom the Jesuits encountered in 1656 claimed to have offered two wampum belts to the Mohawk in exchange for Fathers Brébeuf and Lalemant. He said that he had intended to return them to the French, but the Mohawk had later reclaimed and burned the two men (43:311–13). His motive for telling this story was obviously his hope that the Jesuits would cure him.

This policy no doubt seemed a prudent one to the Huron, most of whom continued to regard the Jesuits as possessing dangerous supernatural powers that could be turned against them; however, the traditionalists were also aware of the strong mistrust that the Iroquois had of the French and knew that so long as the Iroquois traded with the Dutch or the English, the Jesuits would never acquire the same influence among the Iroquois that they formerly had among the Huron. Thus they could relax and deal with the Jesuits with some of the same assurance they had prior to the development of Christian and traditionalist factions in the Huron country. When the various Iroquois tribes sought good relations with the French, the Huron were able to serve Iroquois interests as well as their own by befriending the French who visited their villages. Conversely, when the Iroquois ceased to be on good terms with the French, the Huron would compromise their own good relations with the Iroquois if they continued to be friendly with the French. At such times, all but the staunchly believing Christians seem to have become cool to the Jesuits, while anti-Jesuit feeling which was generally covert in peacetime was again expressed openly.

This pattern is clearly exemplified by the Jesuits' relations with the people of Gandougarae. When Father Chaumonot first visited them in 1656, he was received as an old friend. Christians asked for absolution for themselves and baptism for their children and many adult Huron who had formerly despised Christianity asked to be baptized (44:25). The Tahontaenrat also invited the Jesuits to establish a mission in their settlement (46:73). Although this was not accomplished until after the peace of 1667, the Jesuits entertained high hopes for Gandougarae and described it as already inhabited entirely by Christians (47:113) or at least by a goodly number (52:55). A chapel was erected there in September 1669. In addition to about forty adults whom the Jesuits judged to be practising Christians, there seemed to be a great eagerness for baptism among the rest of the Huron (54:81–83). A few years later, some converts discussed the possibility that they might join the Huron settlement at Quebec (56:67).

While a small number of the inhabitants of Gandougarae lived up to the Jesuits' expectations, the missionaries soon realized that their success was to be limited. Father Jacques Frémin found it necessary to live with one of the leading traditionalists in the town, so that this man might protect him against ill treatment by his enemies (54:121) and, with few exceptions, the villagers refused to give up any of their traditional rituals (58:229). When Gandougarae caught fire and burned to the ground, its inhabitants were persuaded that this might be supernatural retribution for their resistance to the Jesuits' teachings. Yet this is an indication of the degree to which fear rather than affection coloured their attitude towards the Jesuits. While they asked Father Julien Garnier to remain with them and promised to build a better chapel for him than the one that had been destroyed, the superior of the Canadian missions doubted their sincerity (55:79). In fact, for a year Father Garnier does not appear to have been missed when he did not bother to return to the town (57:191).

The Jesuits soon learned that the apparent desire of any Seneca community to be converted depended on temporal considerations and particularly on the Seneca's attitude towards peace with the French (56:59). As the Iroquois once again drifted towards conflict with the French in the 1670s, the Seneca's receptiveness to Christian teachings declined markedly (55:89–91). The Jesuits reluctantly concluded that the Seneca were particularly hard to convert because of their remoteness from the French and that the Tahontaenrat were no more promising than the rest (58:229, 237). The missionaries who remained among the Seneca were reduced to baptizing children without their parents' knowledge and received many rebuffs as they tried to instruct the sick (62:227). In later years, neither Gandougarae nor the other Seneca villages were to testify to anything but the failure of these missions.

The Huron who lived among the Cayuga showed a similar shift in sentiment as the Iroquois' policies towards the French changed. When the Jesuits first visited them, the Cayuga were reported to have shown them more goodwill than did any of the other Iroquois tribes and the missionaries were received with joy by the Huron who lived there (47:185–87). By 1671, however, the missionary to the Cayuga was experiencing difficulty as the result of an aversion to Christianity that was attributed to certain "renegade Huron" (56:51). A decade later, the Cayuga were ranked alongside the Seneca as being particularly unreceptive to Christianity (62:227).

The kinds of choices that were made, even by Huron favourably disposed towards the French, are exemplified by the fate of Chihwatenha's niece, Thérèse Oionhaton. The French had failed to secure her release in the peace negotiations of 1645, about which time she was given in marriage to an Onondaga. In 1655 she was still living among the Onondaga and came with a baby in arms to greet Fathers Chaumonot and Dablon when they visited that tribe. Although she was happy to see the Jesuits and stated that she had baptized her own child, there is no evidence that Oionhaton ever again visited Quebec or attempted to settle there. One of her sisters was living as a prisoner among the Onondaga (42:81) and it would appear that Oionhaton's loyalty to blood kin, her child (or children), and possibly to her husband were sufficient to fill her life. If this was so for a woman who had lived with the Ursulines and who had learned to speak and write French, it must have been even more so for the average Huron who found himself gradually becoming a respectable member of Iroquois society.

THE HURON AS IROQUOIS

It appears that the overwhelming majority of Huron prisoners and refugees, whatever their personal attitude towards the French may have been, were convinced that it was in their interest to behave in accordance with Iroquois policy. When the Iroquois were anxious to convince the French of their goodwill, the Huron were encouraged to emphasize their former friendship with the Jesuits, but when the French and the Iroquois were at odds, the Huron were free to express any hostility they felt towards the French for what the latter had done to them.

At first a considerable number of Huron may have been motivated to act in this way by their fear of the Iroquois; but to attribute all their behaviour to this motive is grossly misleading. The relatively small number of Huron who took advantage of opportunities to move to the special missions that the Jesuits established for their Iroquois converts indicates that the majority must eventually have found it rewarding to continue living among the Iroquois. This feeling was reinforced by intermarriage, as well as by daily contact, which forged personal bonds between former enemies. The development of such bonds eventually led the descendants of these refugees to forget that they were of non-Iroquois origin. The Huron language totally disappeared, and an ethnic identity emerged based on membership in the five Iroquois tribes that was as strong as it had been among the Iroquois prior to the incorporation of these other Iroquoian peoples.

It is almost impossible, on the basis of historical evidence, to trace the contributions that the Huron made to Iroquois culture in the course of becoming Iroquois. The high degree of similarity between the Huron and Iroquois ways of life precluded a wide range of influence at the same time that it facilitated the assimilation of the Huron. The popularity of Tahontaenrat curing rituals suggests that in this sphere, the incorporation of the Huron helped to diversify and enrich at least one aspect of Iroquois life. Harold Blau (1966:577–78) has also suggested that the False Face curing society was introduced by Huron refugees. Further evidence would be required to substantiate this.

In 1668 François Le Mercier distinguished the Seneca from the other Iroquois tribes by saying that they were more inclined to be farmers (*laboureurs*) and traders than warriors (Thwaites 1896–1901, 52:53). Assuming that there is some truth to this statement, it might be asked whether this distinction was an aboriginal one or reflects the influence of Huron who, because of the Tahontaenrat, probably joined the Seneca in larger numbers than they joined any other Iroquois tribe. Again, we are posing a question that it is impossible to answer. Differences in the natural resources of the tribal territories may account for minor variations in the subsistence patterns of the various Iroquois tribes. It may be no accident that the Seneca, who were the most numerous tribe, were apparently also the most dependent on horticulture (Fenton 1940:224, 230; Trigger 1963*b*:96).

What does seem fairly plain is that whatever talents as traders the Huron brought with them, were squandered by the Iroquois. It was not until 1659 that there is an explicit reference to the Mohawk inviting the Algonkin and Quebec Huron to come to their villages to trade (45:103) (plate 51). More than a decade was to pass before the Iroquois tribes began to develop trading relations with the Ottawa and Tionnontaté and even then they did this very tentatively. This appears to have been a development that would have taken place whether or not large numbers of Huron had been incorporated into Iroquois society.

It must be concluded that because of the geographical difficulties involved in trading with northern peoples and the success of Iroquois hunting and raiding expeditions at the time of the Huron's dispersal, the Iroquois were not interested in making use of their captives' special talents. Many of the leading traders may have been killed in battle or murdered by the Iroquois because they considered them to be dangerous and wished to deprive the Huron refugees of leadership. Other Huron men appear to have been quickly drafted into Iroquois raiding parties to satisfy a pressing need for manpower. By the time that the Iroquois war machine had begun to falter and an alternative means of acquiring furs was recognized as desirable, the special skills and, what is more important, the personal contacts that the Huron could have used to develop this trade were irretrievably lost. Whether certain basic skills were transmitted from one Huron generation to the next that would have been useful to the Iroquois in their later entrepreneurial ventures is another question.

The dispersal of the Huron thus presents a curious irony. The handful of Huron who survived their betrayal by the French and stayed at Quebec remained Huron in name, but were subject to continuing acculturative pressure by Europeans. Those who joined the Tionnontaté eventually gave their name to the larger group, but this group regressed because of its small

PLATE 51. *Anonymous map of southeastern Ontario, probably by Abbé Claude Bernou, c. 1680. The inscriptions identify central Ontario as a major beaver hunting area for the Iroquois and Mahican and also refer to*

trade relations between the Iroquois and the Ottawa. Courtesy Public
Archives of Canada.

size and a growing emphasis on trapping, until their economy and way of life resembled those of northern hunting peoples more than they did those of the historic Huron.

Many times the number of Huron who found refuge in these two groups ended up living with their traditional enemies, the Iroquois. Although their initial sufferings at the hands of the Iroquois should not be under-estimated, within a generation the descendants of these Huron had fully merged with the Iroquois and the two groups had assumed a common Iroquois identity. After a continuing struggle to avoid, and then to cope with, white domination, these Iroquois remain one of a small number of native peoples of eastern North America who continue to reside in the heartland of their ancestral territories and who have kept their sense of identity and many of their traditions alive to the present day.

As a result of the conflicts engendered by the fur trade, the Iroquois must have killed, either directly or indirectly, several thousand Huron, although not nearly so many as died of European diseases. Ironically, how-ever, they also provided homes and an acceptable life for more Huron than were to survive anywhere else. Having been pitted against one another in the earliest phases of European activity in eastern North America, the aboriginal Iroquois and these assimilated Huron were henceforth to con-front as one people the growing power of Europeans to direct their lives. Conquerors and conquered were to share a single destiny.

Chapter 13  Conclusions

The Huron were only one of hundreds of Indian groups that were dispersed or lost their independence as a result of European activities. It is appropriate, therefore, to conclude this study by summarizing certain aspects of the Huron experience that may be useful for interpreting the early phases of interaction between Europeans and other Indian groups, or between complex and small-scale societies generally.

Archaeological data demonstrate the fallacy of the notion that prior to European contact the northern Iroquoian-speaking peoples were in a state of cultural equilibrium. Changes went on in the Indian cultures of eastern North America at all periods, but beginning before A.D. 1000 the way of life of the Iroquoians started to change more rapidly as they adopted a horticultural subsistence economy. Large, multi-clan communities came into existence, whose social organization grew more complex as bonds of kinship were supplemented by increasingly important ties of reciprocity. Gift giving, curing societies, and ritualized forms of competition came to have growing regulatory importance in Iroquoian life. Village councils on which clan segments had representation provided a model for political integration that could be expanded to embrace tribes and ultimately whole confederacies.

Far from being unchanging in prehistoric times as many ethnologists formerly imagined, almost every facet of Iroquoian culture appears to have undergone significant change in the centuries preceding European contact. By expanding and altering existing institutions to meet the requirements of rapid change, the prehistoric Iroquoians show themselves to have been the very opposite of conservative. At the same time they appear to have forged a set of cultural values that have permitted the survival to the present day of a distinctively Iroquoian identity and style. While a similar degree of change cannot be attributed automatically to other Indian groups, archaeological work indicates that such changes were not unusual in late pre-Columbian times. If historians are to interpret correctly the impact that Europeans had on other groups, it is necessary that they pay adequate attention to archaeological and other types of evidence that bears on the nature of change among these groups prior to the time of contact.

It can also be ascertained from the archaeological record that both the Huron and the Iroquois had been obtaining European goods from Indians living nearer the coast for some time prior to any direct encounter with Europeans. These goods were prized for their novelty from the beginning and the superiority of iron tools and weapons was quickly recognized. As rival groups began to obtain iron tools on a regular basis, the economic and military advantage that this conferred on them made it essential for tribes living farther from the trading places to find ways of obtaining these goods in larger quantities.

The manner in which different Indian groups went about this strongly supports Nancy Lurie's (1959:37) observation that Indians made their first adjustments to the problems posed by Europeans in terms of existing institutions. Among the Iroquoians, the early years of the fur trade were a period of broadening alliances and increasing warfare with more remote groups. For the Huron at least, major changes were brought about even at the stage when trade goods were regarded principally as a novelty. Both the Huron and the Iroquois confederacies appear to have expanded to include more tribes, if they did not come into being at this time. While the forging and maintaining of these confederacies are evidence of great political skill, the confederacies themselves were extensions of political institutions already existing at the tribal level and did not require the formulation of new principles of political organization. These developments encouraged more emphasis on ritualism to promote political and social integration. This can be seen in the elaboration of the Huron Feast of the Dead and in the increasing emphasis that was placed on grave goods among the Iroquois.

It is also apparent that pre-existing differences between Iroquoian societies helped to mold the different responses that these societies made to the challenge of securing European goods. The Iroquois, who in the sixteenth century were surrounded on all sides by groups that had a horticultural subsistence economy similar to their own, first attempted to secure European goods by waging war against the inhabitants of the St. Lawrence Valley who had easier access to these items. For many decades the Iroquois were to rely almost exclusively on warfare as a means of obtaining the pelts and additional hunting territory that they required if they were to continue bartering with their Dutch and English trading partners.

By contrast, archaeological and ethnographic evidence indicates that, for at least several centuries, the Huron who lived in Simcoe County had systematically traded with the semi-horticultural hunting and fishing bands living to the north of them. When confronted first by the desire and then by the need to obtain more European goods, the Huron expanded their trade with these northern groups and, in this manner, secured the furs that they needed to trade with the French. The Huron likewise became suppliers of trade goods to the other Iroquoian tribes of southern Ontario and seem to have begun trading with the Susquehannock at this time. These developments, which reflect the Huron's skill as traders, probably were responsible for the suppression of blood feuds among all the tribes of southern Ontario.

The contrasting responses of the Huron and the Iroquois reflect not only their different geographical locations, but also longstanding cultural differences that had arisen as a result of cultural adaptation to these locations. The persistence of these respective responses throughout the first half of the seventeenth century suggests grave limitations to Hunt's (1940:5) thesis that "old institutions and economies had profoundly altered or disappeared completely at the electrifying touch of the white man's trade, which. . .wrought social revolution a thousand miles beyond the white man's habitations, and years before he himself appeared on the scene."

While the overall impact of European contact upon Iroquoians can scarcely be minimized, it can be demonstrated that the response that each Iroquoian group made to the challenge of the fur trade was determined by that group's interpretation of what was happening and by their experience in dealing with analogous situations. There was no single overriding "logic of the fur trade" that existed independently of prevailing customs and intertribal relationships and which could supplant these relationships instantaneously. Instead, the fur trade developed largely in terms of responses by Indians who were guided by their former experiences and who extrapolated from these experiences to adapt to novel and ever-changing situations. This does not mean that, in due course, Iroquoian and other tribes did not find themselves being used against their will as instruments of policy by rival fur traders or colonial administrations. Nor does it mean that even in the early period Indian history can be understood independently of European colonial history, any more than the latter can be understood without the Indians. It does mean, however, that in dealing with the early historic period, the specific cultures of the Indian groups involved, as distinguished from their general mode of adaptation, must be taken into account, as well as the history of intertribal relations preceding the rise of the fur trade.

Although the officials who came to New France in the early days lacked power to coerce the Indians, they considered it their natural right to do so. Unlike the Dutch, the French did not bother to purchase land from the

Indians prior to settlement nor did they recognize them as sovereign peoples. Instead they sought to have the Indians formally pledge their allegiance to the representatives of the French crown. Most of these officials resented having to deal with Indians from other than a position of strength and in terms of other than their own conceptions about law and government.

The Huron, however, lived too far from the areas of French settlement to be affected by these ambitions. The kind of alliance that was concluded between the French and the Huron and the rules that governed their trade conformed wholly to the traditional practices by which the Huron regulated their relations with other tribes. French merchants quickly discovered that conforming with such practices was the most effective way to promote trade with the Indians. Until 1634 almost all of the French who visited the Huron were sent there by trading companies to maintain the friendship of the Huron and to encourage them to come to the St. Lawrence Valley to trade. These agents were few and because their aim was to win the trust and friendship of the Huron, they did not criticize or openly challenge the latter's ways of doing things. On the contrary, traders such as Brûlé were happy to adopt many outward trappings of Huron behaviour. Their attempts to change Huron culture were limited to encouraging the Huron to want more trade goods.

Because of their lack of basic language skills, the Recollet and Jesuit missionaries who visited the Huron country prior to 1634 were unable to work there effectively. The principal changes that occurred at this time came about as a result of the Huron responding to an influx of trade goods into their villages, rather than to the presence of the French. The influx of European goods tended to emphasize existing status differences but there is no evidence that this did more than magnify properties that were inherent in Iroquoian society. Trade appears to have been controlled by the traditional headmen, who enhanced their status by distributing the European goods they acquired as they previously had distributed other wealth. There is nothing to indicate that these developments were compromising the tribal basis of Iroquoian society, or that social classes were emerging that were based on the retention rather than the redistribution of wealth. The increasing involvement of men in warfare, trade, hunting, and other activities that kept them away from their villages for longer periods seems to have reinforced the matrilineal tendencies in Iroquoian society. These developments were pushing Iroquoian social organization along the same trajectory that it had been following in prehistoric times.

There is no evidence that any fundamental restructuring of Iroquoian society was about to take place.

The period from 1610 to 1634 can thus be classified as one of "non-directed contact" between the Huron and the French (Spicer 1961:521). This implies that the French who traded with the Huron neither were able to bring regular sanctions to bear against the Huron nor were they interested in doing so in order to effect changes in their behaviour. The French and Huron had to treat one another as equals, since each alone was able to supply what the other wanted. It was also characteristic of this period that both sides remained convinced of their cultural superiority. Because of their greater numbers, and because it was they who visited the French settlements to trade and who determined what Frenchmen might live in their midst, the Huron viewed the French as they did their other northern trading partners. While they interpreted the trade goods supplied by the French as evidence of superior achievements in the technological sphere, they regarded the difficulties that the French experienced in learning to speak Huron and to live and travel with the Indians as proof of innate physical and intellectual inferiority.

From 1634 onwards, relations between the French and the Huron were controlled by the Jesuits. By that time the Jesuits had acquired sufficient influence, both at the French court and over the Company of New France, that they were able to exclude from the Huron country all Frenchmen who were not subject to their authority. Armed with this power, they began a determined campaign to convert the Huron to Roman Catholicism. Unlike the Recollets, who believed that it was impossible to convert the Huron or any other group of Indians before they had first Europeanized them, the Jesuits sought to convert the Huron while changing their way of life as little as possible. They did not believe that converts needed to learn to speak French; on the contrary, they were convinced that by preventing them from having verbal as well as physical contact with other Frenchmen, they were protecting them from corrupting influences. Although it has been suggested that the Jesuits wished to introduce European methods of farming among the Huron, there is no good evidence that they contemplated doing so, or altering any other aspect of Huron culture that was not in conflict with Christian beliefs and moral practice. On the contrary, when they arrived in the Huron country, the Jesuits were convinced that by eliminating a small number of Huron customs and catechizing them, the Huron could be converted to Christianity.

There can be no question that in undertaking this work, the Jesuit missionaries were acting altruistically. While the Jesuits were well aware that the Huron mission was dependent on the prosperity of the fur trade in New France and therefore were anxious to support this trade, suggestions that they went among the Huron primarily to trade with them or to promote French colonial interests cannot be substantiated. Their work was dominated by their conviction that every Huron they converted was a soul saved from certain damnation and eternal suffering. To save these souls most, if not all, of the Jesuits were willing to risk their own lives. Their fanaticism also meant that the Jesuits did not feel obliged to restrict themselves to reasoning with the Huron in their efforts to convert them. On the contrary, the Jesuits found it all too easy to believe that their religious ends justified the means they used to pursue them. They did not hesitate to use their influence over the Company of New France to have its traders insist that the Huron allow missionaries to live in their country as part of the French-Huron trading alliance, or even to force the Huron headmen to let them remain there when most of the Huron wanted them to leave. By ensuring that Christians could buy French trade goods more cheaply than non-Christians could, and that only Christians were permitted to obtain guns, the Jesuits created strong incentives for many Huron men to become at least nominally Christian. This, in turn, permitted them to exploit the Huron's dread of being separated from friends and kinsmen after death in order to convert still more Huron.

While the French colonists in Quebec remained few in number, under the guidance of the Jesuits their officials began to bring pressure to bear that was designed to compel the Huron to change their behaviour along lines that the Jesuits, rather than they themselves, judged to be desirable. Because of this, relations between the Huron and the French entered into a phase of what anthropologists have termed "directed contact" (Spicer 1961), but which might better be called "coercive contact." This is because the Jesuits erred when they believed that they were able to bring about the changes they desired while leaving most facets of Huron life unaffected. They lacked sufficient understanding of the Huron way of life to predict what impact their activities would have upon it. While the Jesuits had the power to coerce the Huron to change, they lacked the skills to refashion Huron society along predetermined lines.

The problems involved in the attempt by persons reared in a seventeenth-century European monarchy and an Amerindian tribal society to interact understandingly with one another are illustrated by the difficulties that the Huron and the French experienced when they attempted to communicate on the subject of religion. Because the Jesuits were accustomed to think about religion in terms of formal institutions, at first they believed that the Huron had few religious beliefs and concluded that it would be easy to fill this void with their own teachings. Later, when they realized the extent of Huron beliefs and practices, they interpreted these as the means by which satanic powers were corrupting and misleading the Huron. Hence, they dramatically visualized their missionary work as a struggle with the devil, who was using the Huron as his pawns.

The Jesuits were even slower to recognize the degree to which Huron religious beliefs permeated every facet of their lives. They were misled by the European view that religious beliefs and practices could be clearly defined and treated separately from other aspects of a person's life. The Jesuits regarded this particular feature of Roman Catholicism and of other international religions as being a characteristic of all religions. Yet, while the Huron had no explicitly formulated creed or corpus of ritual that could be renounced in favour of any other, they possessed a network of beliefs and practices that embued them with confidence in all of their everyday activities, provided the occasions for their most important public celebrations, and armed the individual with potent powers to deal with social pressures and psychic disturbances. This far-reaching interpenetration of religion and everyday life meant that whether the Jesuits wished it or not, if the conversion of the Huron was to be effective, it required major alterations in aspects of their culture that the Jesuits, on the basis of previous experience, had no reason to suspect had anything to do with religion.

In his own doctrinaire way, Jérôme Lalemant may have had in mind a major restructuring of Huron life when he advocated withdrawing Christian Huron from their villages and having them found a new settlement, or *reduction*, at Sainte-Marie. The Huron attachment to their kin, as well as the Jesuits' desire to exploit this attachment to promote the conversion of whole villages, meant that this policy was not carried out. Instead, the Jesuits attempted to eradicate non-Christian practices among their converts without offering them effective substitutes. The result was to undermine their converts' supernatural sources of self-confidence and peace of mind at the same time they cut them off from normal social contact with other Huron. This systematic effort to destroy many of the most cherished and significant features of Huron life eventually forced a considerable number of Huron to oppose the Jesuits openly, thus fragmenting Huron society into factions based on varying degrees of sentiment for and against both the French and the Jesuits. The multiplication of social cleavages, at the same time that many individuals were disorientated either by the Jesuits' teachings or by the erosion of important landmarks in Huron culture, was a serious handicap to a people already threatened by increasingly powerful enemies. These problems were undoubtedly made worse by the death of many knowledgeable Huron leaders and ritualists during the epidemics of 1634 to 1640.

The Huron were unable to muster an effective resistance to the Jesuits' efforts to convert them because at first they were unable to understand the nature of the demands that the Jesuits were making on them. Nothing in Huron religious experience prepared them to cope with the requirements of an exclusive and intolerant religion, the very concept of which was alien to them. The Huron readily borrowed rituals of all kinds from each other and from neighbouring peoples and incorporated these rituals into their society alongside existing ones. Drawing on their own experience, they initially viewed Christianity as a ritual society and the Jesuits as its adepts. Although they were puzzled by the lifelong celibacy of the Jesuits, even this could be interpreted as an extension of their own practice of seeking supernatural power through sexual abstinence. This view of Christianity accounts for the initial willingness of many Huron to become Christians, which elated the Jesuits, and for their apparent apostasy soon after. Even after it was apparent to the Huron that the Jesuits were intolerant of other religious beliefs and practices, it would have been impossible for Huron to understand the uncompromising theological basis for this attitude.

As frequently happens in such situations, both the Huron and the Jesuits interpreted those portions of each other's beliefs that they could not understand, or that they believed threatened their own interests, as manifestations of evil as each conceived of it. Most Huron became convinced that the Jesuits were malevolent sorcerers who sought to destroy the Huron people. Motives were established why the Jesuits should do this and as the Huron learned more about what the Jesuits believed and did, their actions and possessions were interpreted as proof that they practised witchcraft. This reinterpretation of Jesuit behaviour in terms of Huron stereotypes about witchcraft became so pervasive during the period of the epidemics that the Jesuits felt it necessary to refrain from explaining the more intimate details of their rituals to all but their most promising converts. The Jesuits, for their part, were only too willing to interpet all Huron religious practices as being satanic inventions or perversions of Christian rituals that the devil had foisted upon the Huron. Some Jesuits viewed any opposition to their teachings as the devil's efforts to protect his kingdom. Only in the final years of the Huron mission, when the Jesuits were anxious to baptize as many Huron as possible, did they adopt a more tolerant attitude towards many aspects of traditional Huron culture.

Both the French and the Huron used their own concepts of evil as a means of structuring their respective lack of understanding of each other's ways. It is not surprising that the Huron, who knew little about Europeans and had limited opportunities to observe their culture, should have fallen back upon such explanations. Indeed, this tendency was reinforced by the Jesuits' own policy of keeping the Huron isolated from other Frenchmen. The Jesuits, however, had deliberately set out to study Huron religious beliefs to conduct their mission work more effectively. Their failure to understand Huron beliefs, or to work effectively to change these beliefs from within, must therefore be attributed to the limited and pragmatic nature of their research and to their inability even for strategic purposes to transcend intellectually the values to which they were so fiercely committed. The Jesuits' desire to destroy Huron religion outstripped their search to understand it.

As early as 1640 the Jesuits had become concerned about the threat that was posed to the Huron and to their own missionary work by Iroquois attacks. Yet they remained paternalistic in their efforts to deal with the growing menace of the Iroquois, even after the latter had begun to obtain large numbers of guns. Partly to encourage Huron to convert and partly to assure their own safety, the Jesuits insisted that guns be supplied only to Christian Huron, and even to them in small numbers. At the same time, they advocated that the French should either expel the Dutch from the Hudson Valley or crush the Iroquois. These initiatives proved ineffectual and the scarcity of guns, combined with the larger number of men that were needed to carry on trade with the French by comparison with the number that the Iroquois needed to trade with the Dutch, put the Huron at a serious disadvantage. By the time that the Iroquois launched their final series of attacks on the Huron, Jesuit policy had deprived the latter of the weapons that they needed for their own defence and seriously weakened their will to resist the enemy.

Although the Jesuits had thwarted all efforts to expel them from the Huron country, many traditionalists were too alienated, both from the Jesuits and from the society that they now dominated, to rally to its defence. While some of the Christian Huron fought bravely against the Iroquois, as a group they looked to the Jesuits for a degree of leadership and protection that the latter were unable to provide. It is impossible to demonstrate that the Huron would not have succumbed to Iroquois attack if the Jesuits had never worked among them. It is nevertheless certain that however cunningly and apparently successfully the Jesuits pursued their goal of converting the Huron, the result of their activities was to divide and dishearten the Huron at the very time they needed to pull together for their own defence. The Jesuits therefore unwittingly played a major role in ensuring the Iroquois victory over the Huron.

The Jesuits who undertook to convert the Huron were intelligent men who were prepared to forego comfort and safety in order to save mankind from eternal damnation. The suffering that their policies brought about was an unintentional consequence of their efforts to convert the Huron, even though the Jesuits later seemed to regard these sufferings as worthwhile, or at least far from being in vain. There are, however, more general reasons why attempts such as this to effect coercive change frequently turn out badly. It is recognized as a truism that the consequences of people's actions often end up escaping them, since every undertaking has repercussions upon a vast number of unsuspected relationships within a society (Sartre 1963:47–48). Because of this, actions may have the opposite effect from what was intended. When those who are involved come from different cultural traditions, the dangers of misunderstanding and miscalculation are multiplied, and well-intentioned actions frequently prove disadvantageous, if not disastrous, for all concerned. As a mixture of creativity and destructiveness, all men, no less than the Huron and Jesuits, show themselves to be Ataentsic's children.

Notes

CHAPTER SEVEN

1. Trudel (1966*a*: 526) suggests Manet, Nicollet, or Richer; however, only Richer worked exclusively among the Algonkin in the late 1620s (ibid. 496–500).

2. However, see n. 4, chapter 6.

3. For another version of this incident, see Biggar 1922–36, 5:229–31.

4. See, for example Le Jeune to Richelieu, Thwaites 1896–1901, 7:241–45 and 9:171.

5. Cranston 1949:137–44. For other ideas, see Jurgens 1966:133.

6. For an instance of a household moving from one village to another, see Thwaites 1896–1901, 10:285.

7. Grant 1952:8, based on Laverdière. Campeau (1951–52) vigorously denies this claim.

8. For the latest account of this trip, see Hamelin 1966*b*:517. Lurie (1960:800–801) provides an effective critique of the more extravagant interpretations of his mission.

9. The *Jesuit Relation* of 1642–43 states specifically that this peace was between the Huron and the Winnebago (Thwaites 1896–1901, 23:277); however, in 1636 Le Jeune mentions the Winnebago breaking their truce with the Algonkian-speaking Amikou people (10:83). This suggests that the truce was, in fact, between the Winnebago and the Ottawa or other Algonkian-speaking groups. For a discussion of this point, see Lurie 1960:794.

10. The two other Frenchmen who embarked are said to have gone with the Algonkians. They were probably Nicollet and a companion.

11. Talbot (1956:128) implies that the Jesuits' old cabin was still standing in Toanché. The cabin Brébeuf refers to was clearly a Huron dwelling.

CHAPTER EIGHT

1. If Ihonatiria had 300 inhabitants, about eight deaths per year would have been normal and most of these would have occurred during the winter. Yet in the winter of 1634–35, five people died in one longhouse (of 30 inhabitants?). It is impossible to know if the number for this house was higher than the average for the village as a whole or the average for the village was higher than that for the Huron as a whole.

2. For an exception, see Thwaites 1896–1901, 8:139.

3. In later times, the French *collier* meant a wampum belt and it probably did at this time as well; however, because we have no description of Huron *colliers* for this early period, I have chosen to use the more neutral "collar" to translate this term. For a discussion of the use of these belts in Indian diplomacy, see Vachon 1970 and 1971.

4. Nicolas Rehault, Marquis de Gamache provided the funds for this school (Thwaites 1896–1901, 8:227). This gift, amounting to 16,000 écus of

gold and an annuity of 3000 livres as long as he should live, was given to the Jesuits in support of the Canadian mission after his eldest son joined the order (6:327 n. 9).

5. Le Jeune erroneously describes him as *Ouanda Koca*'s (= Endahiaconc's) son (Thwaites 1896–1901, 12:57). This is another illustration of the trouble the French experienced in discerning genealogical relationships through Huron kinship vocabulary.

6. At first identified only as a town about one league from Ossossané (Thwaites 1896–1901, 14:253). For positive identification as Scanonaenrat, see 15:171.

7. Some seventy of these Indians died (Thwaites 1896–1901, 14:99), which is the same number of dead that the Nipissing took away with them in the spring of 1637.

8. This identification is suggested as Aouandoïé previously had been faced with accusations of witchcraft on several occasions (Thwaites 1896–1901, 8:95).

9. As far as I can determine, E. Jury (1966f: 610) errs in stating that Ondakion and his family were the first Huron to embrace Christianity.

10. For a discussion of the probable archaeological evidence of Wenroronon in the Huron country, see Ridley 1973. Most of the pottery from the small Edwards site, near Ossossané, may be Wenroronon as well as 22 percent of the pottery at Ossossané.

11. Cf. letter of J. Lalemant to Richelieu, 28 March 1640 (Thwaites 1896–1901, 17:219–25) and that of C. Lalemant to E. Charlet, 28 February 1642 (21:269–73).

12. For an assessment of this aspect of his personality by a modern Jesuit, see Talbot 1956:208–9.

13. This interpretation was first advanced by me in 1966b. I did not know at that time that Talbot (1956:221–22) had implied the same interpretation.

CHAPTER NINE

1. In an article published since this book was written, W. Smith (1973) argues that by the 1640s the Huron were being by-passed by the fur trade as a result of the French establishing trading links with tribes living farther into the interior. His main evidence (p. 31) is that by 1633 "the first trading fleet of Ottawa Indians arrived at Quebec." This is based on Hunt 1940:48. Had Smith examined Hunt's references he would have found them (like so many other references of that author) to be in error. There is no evidence of the Ottawa visiting the St. Lawrence prior to the dispersal of the Huron. Here is an example of a clever theory nullified by inadequate standards of historiography.

2. The reference to Indians in the Huron country wanting to settle at Montreal (Thwaites 1896–1901, 24:221) undoubtedly refers to these refugee Algonkin and not to Huron.

3. For further proof, see ibid. 32:289. Note that at Quebec knowledge of the reaction of Huron traders meeting Christian Indians in northern Quebec was based entirely upon reports from missionaries in the Huron country.

4. Grassmann 1966b. Du Creux calls her Chihwatenha's daughter (i.e., brother's daughter ?).

5. It is clear that *petit fils* should be translated "small (i.e. young) son" and not "grandson" as Thwaites (27:91) has done. Elsewhere, this boy is identified as Mathieu, aged two years. He is explicitly stated to be the son of Atironta's wife Caterine (27:113).

6. Estimated at half the total number of skins exported from the colony (Trelease 1960 : 43).

7. Note, however, that the Huron presented the Iroquois with wampum as well as beaver, while the Algonkians gave only skins.

8. Lom d'Arce de Lahontan (1905, 1 : 227) comments on the necessity of the Iroquois obtaining furs to purchase armaments and other trade goods.

9. White (1971a : 31) suggests that these latter enemies from the west may have been the Neutral.

10. White (1972) identifies the Aondironnon (Ahondihronon) with the Ondieronii of Du Creux's map and on this basis proposes to locate them between the Niagara and Genesee Rivers (pp. 69–70). She interprets the phrase *"les plus voisins de nos Hurons"* as referring to the Neutral as a whole, rather than to the Aondironnon specifically. While seventeenth-century grammar is ambiguous enough to make this interpretation a possibility, the fact that Huron warriors pursued an Iroquois raider from the Tionnontaté country to the gates of the Aondironnon village suggests that the conventional interpretation of this passage, which would have the Aondironnon as the closest Neutral group to the Huron, is correct. It may be noted that Desrosiers (1948 : 243) located them in the Niagara Peninsula.

11. For the tribal distributions in southern Michigan prior to *c.* 1650, see Goddard 1972. Archaeologists note a lack of historic sites in this region and on this basis some have concluded that the area was not settled at this time (Fitting 1965).

12. On the map attributed to Bernou of *c.* 1680, central Ontario bears the inscription : " From here the Mahican and Iroquois draw most of the beaver skins

that they carry to the English and the Dutch " (see our plate 51).

13. The Gendron letters were published by Jean-Baptiste de Rocoles in 1660, during Gendron's lifetime. It is curious, however, that much of his first letter describing the tribes who were neighbours of the Huron is copied from the Huron *Relation* of 1648. This raises the question of whether Gendron and Ragueneau both made use of the same document, already in existence at Sainte-Marie. Alternatively, Ragueneau could have transcribed and abridged a copy of Gendron's letter or the letter was composed after the date ascribed to it and was largely based on the published relation of 1648. While much of the information in the Gendron letters seems authentic, his implication that the Huron country was rich in beaver (as distinct from beaver pelts) (p. 13) runs counter to much other evidence.

14. This was also Jogues's opinion (Thwaites 1896–1901, 25 : 47).

15. Hunt 1940 : 78. For the major critique of Hunt's interpretation of this treaty, see Desrosiers 1952.

16. Desrosiers 1947a : 336; based on Tessouat's gift so that " the landmarks and the boundaries of all those countries be removed and that everyone should find himself everywhere in his own country."

17. For a more detailed examination of this problem, see Garrad 1973.

CHAPTER TEN

1. Jones 1908 : 376–79. Forty-six is the number given in Ragueneau's letter to the general of the Jesuit order; however, Jones's *Catalogus Personarum* gives the names of more donnés than the twenty-three that Ragueneau states were there and, even so, omits the name of Gendron.

2. Campeau (1966:551) makes no mention of Poncet de La Rivière's return to the Huron country after he went to Quebec in 1640; however, Jones (1908:346–47) lists him as being in the Huron country from 1645 to 1650.

3. Although attached to the Huron mission, Claude Pijart worked mainly among the Algonkians. Jones (1908:319–98) has him with the Huron mission every year from 1640 to 1650. Monet (1966b:549) implies interruptions during this period.

4. Jones's (1908) *Catalogi* note special skills such as *sutor*, *pharm.*, *faber lign.* Most donnés are described as *ad omnia* (handymen).

5. Jury and Jury (1954:88) state that Tourmente was a donné. Jones (1908:358, 365) lists him among the *domestici et alii*, not the donnés.

6. Oliveau appears to have been sent to Quebec as a miller, but was sent on to the Huron country when he proved not to be qualified. It seems less likely that he was sent from France with the intention that he should go directly to the Huron country. If, however, Russell (1965) is right in conjecturing that the Jesuits were planning to install a grist mill at Sainte-Marie, this conclusion may require revision.

7. For some of these arguments, see also Russell 1965:16.

8. Frank Ridley formulated this interpretation many years ago, although he has not published on this subject (Heidenreich and Ridley, personal communications, 1970).

9. Ragueneau's 1649 statement that the bulk of the Jesuits' food was furnished by the Huron (Thwaites 1896–1901, 34:207) is almost certainly in error (cf. 34:225).

10. For a discussion of the first introduction of European plants and animals into Canada, see R. Saunders 1935.

11. Note, however, that Hamaleinan (1973) suggests that hybrid pottery found at Sainte-Marie was made by the French for their own use.

12. The Neutral settlements used to be believed to extend as far west as Windsor. A clay nodule bearing the date 1640 that was found in Middlesex County has been claimed as a possible relic of the Brébeuf-Chaumonot journey (Thomas 1936). This find now seems more likely to have been a hoax. Thomas mentions that another "Jesuit stone" inscribed "1641" was found in Vaughn township near Toronto about 1895.

13. Thwaites 1896–1901, 23:147 implies that Tsondakwa was the principal headman of the town, suggesting that he might be the same as, or a replacement for, Endahiaconc.

CHAPTER ELEVEN

1. Note, however, that a similar change seems to have been made in mission policy at Sillery at the same time (Thwaites 1896–1901, 32:211). Thus effectively the new policy in the Huron country may have resulted from a general directive from Quebec, issued following or not following prior discussion with Father Ragueneau.

2. 1300 baptisms for 1646?–48 (Thwaites 1896–1901, 33:69) minus 500 for 1646–47 (30:223) gives 800 for 1647–48. These figures probably include Tionnontaté but baptisms of the latter were few in number before 1648.

3. The figures are: 1700 recorded baptisms in the year preceding 1 March 1649 (Thwaites 1896–1901, 33:257); 1300 between 4 July 1648 and 17 March

1649 (34:227); 1400 between 17 March 1649 and August 1649 (34:227); and 1800 in the year preceding May 1649 (34:103). These figures suggest approximately 400 conversions between March and July 1648; 1300 between July 1648 and March 1649; 300 in March and April 1649; and 1100 between May and August 1649.

4. "St. Ignace I" was located in the Sturgeon Valley and was no more than three leagues from Sainte-Marie even by a roundabout route (Thwaites 1896–1901, 23:143). Heidenreich (1966:123) estimates the direct distance to have been two leagues. "St. Ignace II" was two leagues from Sainte-Marie (Thwaites 1896–1901, 34:125–27) and must also have been in the Sturgeon Valley.

5. Heidenreich (1971:46) notes that in a personal communication dated 1967 Frank Ridley has argued that St. Ignace II never existed, but Heidenreich reserves judgement on this theory. In my opinion, Ridley has interpreted the evidence correctly.

6. Hunt has misread Thwaites 1896–1901, 45:243, which states that the Iroquois, rather than the Neutral, carried the Huron who had sought refuge among the Neutral into a harsh captivity.

7. Bressani (Thwaites 1896–1901, 40:49) says there were 400 bags of corn and 400 bags of acorns to feed the Indians, which seems to amount to between 500 and 600 bushels of each food (35:99–101). If we generously assume that acorns and corn are of equivalent nutrient value this would mean the equivalent of 1200 bushels of corn. If 10 bushels are needed to carry a person over the winter (see chapter 2, n. 16), this suggests that the Jesuits had enough to feed only about 120 people.

8. Perrot errs in saying that Jérôme Lalemant was the leader of this party;

evidently he confused Ragueneau with his predecessor.

9. Under the circumstances, it seems unlikely that this was someone who had inherited Ondaaiondiont's name.

CHAPTER TWELVE

1. In this chapter I am not attempting to trace Huron history in as great detail as in the preceding ones. My chief aim is to account for the dispersal of the Huron after 1650. For a detailed analysis of French-Iroquois relations during the latter half of the seventeenth century, see the following papers by Desrosiers (these papers are cited in approximately chronological order): 1953; 1959; 1960; 1961; 1966; 1962; 1955; 1964; 1957; 1958; 1954; 1963; 1956; and 1965. See also Desrosiers 1947b.

2. Hunt (1940:98) interprets Perrot (1911:149–50) to mean that they were later compelled to join the Iroquois, but there is no clear proof of this, since by Detroit Perrot may having been referring to the old Neutral country. Hunt (1940:97) suggests that some joined the Catawba, although the evidence is admitted to be weak. He also suggests (p. 98) that the Negawichi may have been a remnant of the Neutral.

3. Thwaites 1896–1901, 42:179–83. The *Jesuit Relation* of 1655–56 describes this fortified location as a hastily constructed wooden fort.

4. See the note on the Bernou map of 1680 (?) (our plate 50) concerning Lake Erie: "This lake is not Lake Erie as people regularly call it. Erie is part of Chesapeake Bay in Virginia, where the Erie have always lived." Evidently the author of this map mistook the location of these refugees for the original homeland of the Erie.

5. Cf. Hamelin 1966*a*:112. Hamelin has the death of these Huron as the cause of Bourdon turning back.

6. He seems to have come from the village of Arethsi ("Tsawenhohi from Arhetsi," Thwaites 1896–1901, 36:141).

7. For a study of Jesuit power in early New France, see Trudel 1973:230–45.

8. Thwaites 1896–1901, 45:115. For a discussion of Thwaites's translation of this passage, see Donnelly 1967:166.

9. Is this the Aotonatendia mentioned as their destination for the autumn of 1653 (Thwaites 1896–1901, 38:181)? It was located three days journey southwest of Sault Sainte Marie. For a discussion of the archaeology of the Huron-Tionnontaté after 1650, see Quimby 1966:114–16; 130; 134–36.

10. On the identity of Groseilliers's companion, see Nute 1966:224.

11. Reported by D. Lenig according to J. V. Wright, personal communication 1973. I have been unable to confirm this with Mr. Lenig.

References

The following are works cited in the text and notes or consulted in their preparation. In general, works of an ephemeral nature or preliminary reports later superseded by more definitive studies have been omitted.

ABBREVIATIONS

AA	*American Anthropologist*
AARO	*Annual Archaeological Report, Appendix to the Report of the Minister of Education, Ontario*
Am. Ant.	*American Antiquity*
BAE	*Bureau of American Ethnology*
CdD	*Les Cahiers des Dix*
CHR	*The Canadian Historical Review*
DAUTRR	Toronto: *Department of Anthropology, University of Toronto, Research Report*
DCB	*Dictionary of Canadian Biography*
NMC	*National Museum of Canada*
Ont. Arch.	*Ontario Archaeology*
Ont. Hist.	*Ontario History*
Penn. Arch.	*Pennsylvania Archaeologist*
PAPS	*Proceedings of the American Philosophical Society*
RHAF	*Revue d'histoire de l'Amérique française*
ROM-OP	*Royal Ontario Museum, Art and Archaeology, Occasional Paper*
SWJA	*Southwestern Journal of Anthropology*
TRSC	*Transactions of the Royal Society of Canada*
UMAP	*University of Michigan, Anthropological Papers*

ABLER, THOMAS S.

1970   "Longhouse and Palisade: Northeastern Iroquoian Villages of the Seventeenth Century." *Ont. Hist.* 62:17–40.

ADAIR, E. R.

1944   "France and the Beginnings of New France." *CHR* 25:246–78.

ADAMS, A. T.

1961   *The Explorations of Pierre Esprit Radisson.* Minneapolis: Ross and Haines, Inc.

ANDERSON, JAMES E.

1964   "The People of Fairty: An Osteological Analysis of an Iroquois Ossuary." *NMC, Bulletin* 193:28–129.

1968   *The Serpent Mounds Site Physical Anthropology. ROM–OP*, no. 11.

Atlas of Canada

1957   Ottawa: Department of Mines and Technical Surveys, Geographical Branch.

AVERKIEVA, J.

1971   "The Tlingit Indians." *North American Indians in Historical Perspective.* Ed. E. B. Leacock and N. O. Lurie. New York: Random House, pp. 317–42.

BACQUEVILLE DE LA POTHERIE, CLAUDE CHARLES LE ROY, SIEUR DE

1753   *Histoire de l'Amerique septentrionale.* 4 vols. Paris: Nyon fils.

1911–12   "History of the Savage Peoples Who Are Allies of New France." *The Indian Tribes of the Upper Mississippi Valley and Region of the Great Lakes.* 2 vols. Ed. E. H. Blair. Cleveland: Arthur H. Clark Company, 1:273–372; 2:13–136.

BAILEY, ALFRED G.

1933   "The Significance of the Identity and Disappearance of the Laurentian Iroquois." *TRSC*, 3rd Series, 27, ii:97–108.

1937   *The Conflict of European and Eastern Algonkian Cultures, 1504–1700: A Study in Canadian Civilization.* Saint John: New Brunswick Museum. (A second edition of this work with the same pagination was published by the University of Toronto Press in 1969.)

1938   "Social Revolution in Early Eastern Canada." *CHR* 19:264–76.

1972   "Vanished Iroquoians." *Culture and Nationality: Essays by A. G. Bailey.* Toronto: McClelland and Stewart Ltd., pp. 14–28.

BAKER, D.

1972   "Color, Culture and Power: Indian-White Relations in Canada and America." *Canadian Review of American Studies* 3:3–20.

BARBEAU, MARIUS

1914   "Supernatural Beings of the Huron and Wyandot." *AA* 16:288–313.

1915   *Huron and Wyandot Mythology.* Ottawa: *Department of Mines, Geological Survey, Memoir* 80.

1917   "Iroquoian Clans and Phratries." *AA* 19:392–402.

1949   "How the Huron-Wyandot Language was Saved from Oblivion." *PAPS* 93:226–32.

1960   *Huron-Wyandot Traditional Narratives in Translations and Native Texts. NMC, Bulletin* 165.

1961   "The Language of Canada in the Voyages of Jacques Cartier (1534–1538)." *NMC, Bulletin* 173:108–229.

BAWTREE, E. W.

1848   "A Brief Description of Some Sepulchral Pits, of Indian Origin, Lately Discovered near Penetanqueshene." *The Edinburgh New Philosophical Journal* 45:86–101.

BEAUCHAMP, WILLIAM A.

1898   "Wampum Used in Council and as Currency." *American Antiquarian* 20 (1):1–13.

1901   "Wampum and Shell Articles Used by the New York Indians." *New York State Museum, Bulletin*, no. 41:319–480.

1905   "Aboriginal Use of Wood in New York." *New York State Museum, Bulletin*, no. 89:87–272.

BEAUGRAND-CHAMPAGNE, A.

1936   "Les anciens Iroquois du Québec." *CdD* 1:171–99.

1948   "Les origines de Montréal." *CdD* 13:39–62.

BIGGAR, H. P.

1901   *The Early Trading Companies of New France.* Toronto: *University of Toronto Studies in History.*

——, ed.

1911   *The Precursors of Jacques Cartier, 1497–1534.* Ottawa: *Publications of the Canadian Archives*, no. 5.

1922–36   *The Works of Samuel de Champlain.* 6 vols. Toronto: The Champlain Society.

1924   *The Voyages of Jacques Cartier: Published from the Originals with Translations, Notes, and Appendices.* Ottawa: *Publications of the Public Archives of Canada*, no. 11.

1930   *A Collection of Documents Relating to Jacques Cartier and the Sieur de Roberval.* Ottawa: *Publications of the Public Archives of Canada*, no. 14.

BISHOP, M.

1948   *Champlain: The Life of Fortitude.* New York: Alfred A. Knopf.

BLAU, H.

1966   "Function and the False Faces: A Classification of Onondaga Masked Rituals and Themes." *Journal of American Folklore* 79:564–80.

BOUCHER, PIERRE

1664   *Histoire véritable et naturelle des moeurs et productions du pays de la Nouvelle-France, vulgairement dite le Canada.* Paris: F. Lambert (the most recent photographic reprint is by the Société historique de Boucherville, 1964).

BRASSER, T. J. C.

1971   "Group Identification Along a Moving Frontier." *Verhandlungen des XXXVIII Internationalen Amerikanistenkongresses.* Munich, Band II, pp. 261–65.

BROSE, DAVID S.

1970   *The Summer Island Site: A Study of Prehistoric Cultural Ecology and Social Organization in the Northern Lake Michigan Area.* Cleveland: *Case Western Reserve University Studies in Anthropology*, no. 1.

BUTTERFIELD, C. W.

1898   *History of Brulé's Discoveries and Explorations.* Cleveland: Helman-Taylor Company.

CALDWELL, J. R.

1958   *Trend and Tradition in the Prehistory of the Eastern United States.* Washington: *American Anthropological Association, Memoir* 88.

CAMPEAU, LUCIEN

1951–52   "Les Jésuites ont-ils rétouché les écrits de Champlain?" *RHAF* 5:340–61.

1966   "Joseph-Antoine Poncet de La Rivière." *DCB* 1:551–52.

CARMACK, R. M.

1972   "Ethnohistory: A Review of its Development, Definitions, Methods, and Aims." *Annual Review of Anthropology.* Ed. B. J. Siegel. Palo Alto: Annual Reviews, 1:227–46.

CARPENTER, EDMUND

1942   "Iroquoian Figurines." *Am. Ant.* 8:105–13.

CARR, E. H.

1967   *What is History?* New York: Vintage Books.

CARRUTHERS, P. J.

1965   "Preliminary Excavations at the Supposed Site of Ste. Marie II." Ms. in Dept. of Public Records and Archives, Toronto.

CHAFE, W. L.

1964   "Linguistic Evidence for the Relative Age of Iroquois Religious Practices." *SWJA* 20:278–85.

CHANNEN, E. R. and N. D. CLARKE

1965   *The Copeland Site: A Precontact Huron Site in Simcoe County, Ontario. NMC, Anthropology Papers*, no. 8.

CHAPMAN, L. J. and D. F. PUTNAM

1966   *The Physiography of Southern Ontario.* 2nd ed. Toronto: University of Toronto Press.

CHARLEVOIX, PIERRE F. X.

1866–72   *History and General Description of New France.* 6 vols. New York: J. G. Shea.

1923   *Journal of a Voyage to North America.* 2 vols. Ed. L. P. Kellogg. Chicago: The Caxton Club (originally published in French, 1744).

CHARLTON, THOMAS H.

1968   "On Iroquois Incest." *Anthropologica* 10:29–43.

CHAUMONOT, PIERRE J. M.

1869   *Le Père Pierre Chaumonot de la Compagnie de Jésus: autobiographie et pièces inédites.* Ed. A. Carayon. Poitiers: H. Oudin.

1920   (Author uncertain) "Grammar of the Huron Language...translated
        from the Latin by Mr. John Wilkie." *Fifteenth Report of the Bureau
        of Archives for the Province of Ontario.* Toronto: Clarkson W. James,
        pp. 725–77. (Also published in *Transactions of the Literary and
        Historical Society of Quebec* 2 [1831]: 94–198.)

CHURCHER, C. S. and W. A. KENYON
    1960   "The Tabor Hill Ossuaries: A Study in Iroquois Demography."
            Human Biology 32: 249–73.

CLARK, GRAHAME
    1945   "Farmers and Forests in Neolithic Europe." *Antiquity* 19: 57–71.

CLARKE, P. D.
    1870   *Origin and Traditional History of the Wyandotts.* Toronto: Hunter,
            Rose and Company.

COLE, D.
    1973   "The Origins of Canadian Anthropology, 1850–1910." *Journal of
            Canadian Studies* 8: 33–45.

CONNELLY, WILLIAM E.
    1900   "The Wyandots." *AARO*, 1899: 92–123.

CÔTÉ, JEAN
    1956–57 "Domestique séculier d'habit, mais religieux de coeur." *RHAF*
             10: 183–90; 448–53.
    1961–62 "L'institution des donnés." *RHAF* 15: 344–78.

CRANSTON, J. H.
    1949   *Etienne Brûlé: Immortal Scoundrel.* Toronto: The Ryerson Press.

CRANSTONE, B. A. L.
    1971   "The Tifalmin: A 'Neolithic' People in New Guinea." *World
            Archaeology* 3: 132–42.

CROUSE, N. M.
    1924   *Contributions of the Canadian Jesuits to the Geographical Knowledge of
            New France, 1632–1675.* Ithaca: Cornell Publications.

CRUICKSHANK, J. G. and C. E. HEIDENREICH
    1969   "Pedological Investigations at the Huron Indian Village of Cahiagué."
            The Canadian Geographer 13: 34–46.

DAY, GORDON M.
    1971   "The Eastern Boundary of Iroquoia: Abenaki Evidence." *Man in the
            Northeast* 1: 7–13.

DEETZ, JAMES
    1965   *The Dynamics of Stylistic Change in Arikara Ceramics.* Urbana:
            Illinois Studies in Anthropology, no. 4.

DELANGLEZ, J.
    1939   *Frontenac and the Jesuits.* Chicago: Institute of Jesuit History.

DENYS, NICOLAS

1908   *The Description and Natural History of the Coasts of North America.* Ed. W. F. Ganong. Toronto: The Champlain Society (first printed 1672).

DESJARDINS, P.

1966   *La Résidence de Sainte-Marie-aux-Hurons.* Sudbury: *La Société Historique du Nouvel-Ontario, Documents Historiques*, no. 48.

DESROSIERS, LÉO-PAUL

1947*a*   *Iroquoisie.* Montreal: Institut d'Histoire de l'Amérique française.
1947*b*   "Premières missions Iroquoises." *RHAF* 1 : 21–38.
1948   "L'année 1647 en Huronie." *RHAF* 2 : 238–49.
1952   "La rupture de la paix de 1645." *CdD* 17 : 169–81.
1953   "Les Onnontagués." *CdD* 18 : 45–66.
1954   "Préliminaires du massacre de Lachine." *CdD* 19 : 47–66.
1955   "Iroquoisie, terre française." *CdD* 20 : 33–59.
1956   "Négociations de paix (1693–1696)." *CdD* 21 : 55–87.
1957   "L'expédition de M. de la Barre." *CdD* 22 : 105–35.
1958   "Denonville." *CdD* 23 : 107–38.
1959   "La paix-miracle (1653–1660)." *CdD* 24 : 85–112.
1960   "Il y a trois cents ans." *CdD* 25 : 85–101.
1961   "Les années terribles." *CdD* 26 : 55–90.
1962   "Revers et succès (1662–1663)." *CdD* 27 : 77–95.
1963   "Frontenac, l'artisan de la victoire." *CdD* 28 : 93–145.
1964   "La paix de 1667." *CdD* 29 : 25–45.
1965   "Fort Orange (Albany) à l'époque des guerres indiennes." *CdD* 30 : 19–33.
1966   "Guérillas dans l'île de Montréal." *CdD* 31 : 79–95.

Dictionary of Canadian Biography

1966, 1969   Vols. 1 and 2. Toronto: University of Toronto Press.

DIONNE, NARCISSE-E.

1891, 1906   *Samuel Champlain.* 2 vols. Quebec: A. Côté et Cie.

DOBYNS, H. F.

1966   "Estimating Aboriginal American Population: An Appraisal of Techniques with a New Hemispheric Estimate." *Current Anthropology* 7 : 395–449.

DONNELLY, JOSEPH P.

1967   *Thwaites' Jesuit Relations, Errata and Addenda.* Chicago: Loyola University Press.

DOUGLAS, MARY, ed.

1970   *Witchcraft Confessions and Accusations.* London: Tavistock Publications.

DRIVER, HAROLD E.

1961   *Indians of North America.* Chicago: University of Chicago Press.

DU CREUX, FRANÇOIS (CREUXIUS)

1951–52   *The History of Canada.* 2 vols. Toronto: The Champlain Society.

DUFF, WILSON

 1964 *The Indian History of British Columbia*. Vol. 1, *The Impact of the White Man*. Victoria: *Anthropology in British Columbia, Memoir* 5.

DUIGNAN, P.

 1958 "Early Jesuit Missionaries: A Suggestion for Further Study." *AA* 60:725–32.

DUMAS, G.-M.

 1966 "Georges Le Baillif." *DCB* 1:433.

DUNNING, R. W.

 1959 *Social and Economic Change Among the Northern Ojibwa*. Toronto: University of Toronto Press.

DYK, W.

 1938 *Son of Old Man Hat: A Navaho Autobiography*. New York: Harcourt, Brace and Company.

EGGAN, FRED R.

 1952 "The Ethnological Cultures and Their Archeological Backgrounds." *Archeology of Eastern United States*. Ed. J. B. Griffin. Chicago: University of Chicago Press, pp. 35–45.

 1966 *The American Indian: Perspectives for the Study of Social Change*. London: Weidenfeld and Nicolson.

ELTON, G. R.

 1969 *The Practice of History*. London: Collins.

EMERSON, J. N.

 1954 *The Archaeology of the Ontario Iroquois*. Ph.D. Dissertation, University of Chicago.

 1959 "A Rejoinder Upon the MacNeish-Emerson Theory." *Penn. Arch.* 29 (2):98–107.

 1961*a* ed. *Cahiague, 1961*. Orillia: University of Toronto Archaeological Field School. Mimeographed.

 1961*b* "Problems of Huron Origins." *Anthropologica* 3:181–201.

 1967 "The Payne Site: An Iroquoian Manifestation in Prince Edward County, Ontario." *NMC, Bulletin* 206:126–257.

 1968 *Understanding Iroquois Pottery in Ontario: A Rethinking*. Toronto: Ontario Archaeological Society, special publication.

EMERSON, J. N. and R. E. POPHAM

 1952 "Comments on 'The Huron and Lalonde Occupations of Ontario'." *Am. Ant.* 18:162–64.

FENTON, WILLIAM N.

 1940 "Problems Arising from the Historic Northeastern Position of the Iroquois." *Smithsonian Miscellaneous Collections*, vol. 100:159–252.

 1941 "Iroquois Suicide: A Study in the Stability of a Culture Pattern." *BAE, Bulletin* 128:70–138.

 1951 "Locality as a Basic Factor in the Development of Iroquois Social Structure." *BAE, Bulletin* 149:35–54.

1957   *Indian and White Relations in Eastern North America*. Chapel Hill: University of North Carolina Press.

1966   "Field Work, Museum Studies, and Ethnohistorical Research." *Ethnohistory* 13:71–85.

1971   "The Iroquois in History." *North American Indians in Historical Perspective*. Ed. E. B. Leacock and N. O. Lurie. New York: Random House, pp. 129–68.

FENTON, WILLIAM N. and E. S. DODGE

1949   "An Elmbark Canoe in the Peabody Museum of Salem." *American Neptune* 9:185–206.

FIEDLER, L. A.

1968   *The Return of the Vanishing American*. New York: Stein and Day.

FISCHER, D. H.

1971   *Historians' Fallacies: Towards a Logic of Historical Thought*. London: Routledge and Kegan Paul.

FITTING, JAMES E.

1965   *Late Woodland Cultures of Southeastern Michigan. UMAP*, 24.

1968   "Environment Potential and the Postglacial Readaptation in Eastern North America." *Am. Ant.* 33:441–45.

1970   *The Archaeology of Michigan*. New York: The Natural History Press.

1972   "The Huron as an Ecotype: The Limits of Maximization in a Western Great Lakes Society." *Anthropologica* 14:3–18.

FITTING, JAMES E. and C. E. CLELAND

1969   "Late Prehistoric Settlement Patterns in the Upper Great Lakes." *Ethnohistory* 16:289–302.

FLORES SALINAS, BERTA

1964   *México visto por algunos de sus viajeros (siglos XVI y XVII)*. Mexico: Universidad Nacional Autónoma de México.

FORBES, A.

1970   "Two and a Half Centuries of Conflict: The Iroquois and the Laurentian Wars." *Penn. Arch.* 40 (3–4):1–20.

FORBES, J. D., ed.

1964   *The Indian in America's Past*. Englewood Cliffs: Prentice-Hall.

FORD, C. S.

1941   *Smoke from their Fires*. New Haven: Yale University Press.

FOX, W. A.

1971   "The Maurice Site (BeHa-2): Lithic Analysis." *Palaeoecology and Ontario Prehistory. DAUTRR*, no. 2:137–65.

FOX, WILLIAM S. (and W. JURY)

1949   *St. Ignace, Canadian Altar of Martyrdom*. Toronto: McClelland and Stewart.

FREEMAN, J. E., comp.

1966   *A Guide to Manuscripts Relating to the American Indian in the Library of the American Philosophical Society*. Philadelphia: American Philosophical Society. (For Huron grammars and dictionaries, see pp. 185–87.)

FRENCH, M. J.

1949　*Samuel de Champlain's Incursion Against the Onondaga Nation.* Ann Arbor: Edwards Brothers.

GAMST, F. C.

1969　*The Qemant.* New York: Holt, Rinehart and Winston.

GANONG, W. F.

1964　*Crucial Maps in the Early Cartography and Place-nomenclature of the Atlantic Coast of Canada.* With an introduction by T. E. Layng. Toronto: University of Toronto Press.

GARNIER, CHARLES

1930　"Saint Charles Garnier" (letters). *Rapport de l'Archiviste de la Province de Québec pour 1929–30.* Quebec: The King's Printer, pp. 1–43.

GARRAD, CHARLES

1969　"Iron Trade Knives on Historic Petun Sites." *Ont. Arch.* 13:3–15.

1970　"Did Champlain Visit the Bruce Peninsula? An Examination of an Ontario Myth." *Ont. Hist.* 62:235–39.

1971　"Ontario Fluted Point Survey." *Ont. Arch.* 16:3–18.

1973　"The Attack on Ehwae in 1640." *Ont. Hist.* 65:107–11.

GENDRON, FRANÇOIS

1868　*Quelques particularitez du pays des Hurons en la Nouvelle France rémarquées par le Sieur Gendron, docteur en médecine qui a démeuré dans ce pays-là fort longtemps.* Albany: J. G. Shea (originally published Paris 1660).

GÉRIN, L.

1900　"The Hurons of Lorette." *Report of the British Association for the Advancement of Science, 1900,* pp. 549–68.

GIRARD, R.

1948　*Trois Grands Hurons.* Sudbury: *La Société Historique du Nouvel-Ontario, Documents Historiques,* no. 16.

GODBOUT, A.

1942　"Le néophyte Ahuntsic." *Bulletin des recherches historiques* 48:129–37.

GODDARD, IVES

1972　"Historical and Philological Evidence Regarding the Identification of the Mascouten." *Ethnohistory* 19:123–34.

GODEFROY, F.

1938　*Dictionnaire de l'ancienne langue française et de tous ses dialectes.* Paris: Librairie des Sciences et des Arts.

GOLDSTEIN, R. A.

1969 *French-Iroquois Diplomatic and Military Relations, 1609–1701.* The Hague: Mouton.

GRANDSAIGNES D'HAUTRIVE, R.

1947 *Dictionnaire d'ancien français: moyen age et renaissance.* Paris: Librairie Larousse.

GRANT, W. L., ed.

1952 *Voyages of Samuel de Champlain 1604–1618.* New York: Barnes and Noble (originally published 1907).

GRASSMANN, T.

1966a "Pastedechouan." *DCB* 1:533–34.
1966b "Thérèse Oionhaton." *DCB* 1:523–24.
1969 *The Mohawk Indians and Their Valley.* Fonda, N.Y.: Mohawk-Caughnawaga Museum.

GRIFFIN, JAMES B.

1952 *Archeology of Eastern United States.* Chicago: University of Chicago Press.
1961 ed. *Lake Superior Copper and the Indians: Miscellaneous Studies of Great Lakes Prehistory. UMAP*, 17.
1965 "Late Quaternary Prehistory in the Northeastern Woodlands." *The Quaternary of the United States.* Ed. H. E. Wright, Jr. and D. G. Frey. Princeton: Princeton University Press, pp. 655–67.

GUYART DE L'INCARNATION, MARIE

1876 *Lettres de la révérende Mère Marie de l'Incarnation (née Marie Guyard), première supérieure du monastère des Ursulines de Québec.* 2 vols. Ed. P. F. Richaudeau. Paris: Librairie Internationale.

HAGAN, W. T.

1961 *American Indians.* Chicago: University of Chicago Press.

HAKLUYT, RICHARD

1589 *The Principall Navigations Voiages and Discoveries of the English Nation.* Facsimile edited by D. B. Quinn and R. A. Skelton. Cambridge: Cambridge University Press, 1965.

HALE, HORATIO, ed.

1963 *The Iroquois Book of Rites.* Reprinted with an Introduction by William N. Fenton. Toronto: University of Toronto Press (originally published 1883).

HALLOWELL, A. I.

1955 *Culture and Experience.* Philadelphia: University of Pennsylvania Press.

HAMALEINAN, P.

1973 "'Home-made' Pottery from Sainte-Marie I." Ontario Archaeological Society, *Arch Notes* 73, no. 5:10–15.

HAMELIN, J.
  1966*a* "Jean Bourdon." *DCB* 1:111–13.
  1966*b* "Jean Nicollet de Belleborne." *DCB* 1:516–18.

HAMMOND, J. H.
  1905 "North and South Orillia." *AARO*, 1904:77–86.
  1924 "Exploration of the Ossuary Burial of the Huron Nation, Simcoe County." *AARO*, 34:95–102.

HANZELI, VICTOR E.
  1969 *Missionary Linguistics in New France: A Study of Seventeenth- and Eighteenth-Century Descriptions of American Indian Languages.* The Hague: Mouton.

HARPER, J. R.
  1952 "The Webb Site: A Stage in Early Iroquoian Development." *Penn. Arch.* 22 (2):49–64.
  1971 *Paul Kane's Frontier.* Toronto: University of Toronto Press.

HARRIS, MARVIN
  1968 *The Rise of Anthropological Theory.* New York: Thomas Y. Crowell.

HAYES, CHARLES F., III
  1967 "The Longhouse at the Cornish Site." *Iroquois Culture, History, and Prehistory.* Ed. E. Tooker. Albany: The University of the State of New York, pp. 91–97.

HEIDENREICH, CONRAD E.
  1966 "Maps Relating to the First Half of the 17th Century and Their Use in Determining the Location of Jesuit Missions in Huronia." *The Cartographer* 3:103–26.
  1967 "The Indian Occupance of Huronia, 1600–1650." *Canada's Changing Geography.* Ed. R. L. Gentilcore. Scarborough: Prentice-Hall, pp. 15–29.
  1968 "A New Location for Carhagouha, Récollet Mission in Huronia." *Ont. Arch.* 11:39–46.
  1970 "Review of *The Huron: Farmers of the North.*" *CHR* 51:451–53.
  1971 *Huronia: A History and Geography of the Huron Indians, 1600–1650.* Toronto: McClelland and Stewart Limited.
  1972 *The Huron: A Brief Ethnography.* Toronto: *York University, Department of Geography, Discussion Paper* no. 6.

HEIDENREICH, C. E. et al.
  1969 "Maurice and Robitaille Sites: Environmental Analysis." *Palaeoecology and Ontario Prehistory. DAUTRR*, no. 1:112–54.

HELMS, MARY
  1970 "Matrilocality, Social Solidarity, and Culture Contact: Three Case Histories." *SWJA* 26:197–212.

HERMAN, MARY W.
  1956 "The Social Aspect of Huron Property." *AA* 58:1044–58.

HÉROUVILLE, P. D'

1929   *Les Missions des Jésuites au Canada, XVIIe et XVIIIe siècles;*
avec Leymaire, A.-L., *Analyse des documents exposés par la
Compagnie de Jésus et sur les Jésuites.* Paris: G. Énault.

HEWITT, J. N. B.

1894   "Era of the Formation of the Historic League of the Iroquois."
AA, O.S. 6:61–67.

1907   "Huron." *BAE, Bulletin* 30, vol. 1, pp. 584–91.

1910a   "Seneca." *BAE, Bulletin* 30, vol. 2, pp. 502–8.

1910b   "Susquehanna." *BAE, Bulletin* 30, vol. 2, pp. 653–59.

1910c   "Wenrohronon." *BAE, Bulletin* 30, vol. 2, pp. 932–34.

HICKERSON, HAROLD

1960   "The Feast of the Dead Among the Seventeenth Century Algonkians
of the Upper Great Lakes." *AA* 62:81–107.

1962   *The Southwestern Chippewa: An Ethnohistorical Study.* Washington:
American Anthropological Association, Memoir 92.

1970   *The Chippewa and Their Neighbors: A Study in Ethnohistory.*
New York: Holt, Rinehart and Winston.

HICKERSON, HAROLD, G. D. TURNER and N. P. HICKERSON

1952   "Testing Procedures for Estimating Transfer of Information among
Iroquois Dialects and Languages." *International Journal of American
Linguistics* 18:1–8.

HOEBEL, E. A.

1960   "William Robertson: An 18th Century Anthropologist-Historian."
AA 62:648–55.

HOFFMAN, B. G.

1959   "Iroquois Linguistic Classification from Historical Materials."
Ethnohistory 6:160–85.

1961   *Cabot to Cartier: Sources for a Historical Ethnography of
Northeastern North America, 1497–1550.* Toronto: University of
Toronto Press.

HOFFMAN, D. W. et al.

1962   *Soil Survey of Simcoe County, Ontario.* Ottawa and Guelph: *Ontario
Soil Survey, Report* no. 29.

HOMANS, GEORGE C.

1962   *Sentiments and Activities: Essays in Social Science.* Glencoe: The Free
Press.

HUDSON, CHARLES

1966   "Folk History and Ethnohistory." *Ethnohistory* 13:52–70.

HUNT, GEORGE T.

1940   *The Wars of the Iroquois: A Study in Intertribal Trade Relations.*
Madison: University of Wisconsin Press.

HUNTER, ANDREW F.

1889   "French Relics from the Village Sites of the Hurons." *AARO,*
1889:42–46.

1899　"Notes on Sites of Huron Villages in the Township of Tiny (Simcoe County) and adjacent parts." *Appendix to the Report of the Minister of Education*, 42 pp.

1900　"Notes on Sites of Huron Villages in the Township of Tay (Simcoe County). *AARO*, 1899:51–82.

1902　"Notes on Sites of Huron Villages in the Township of Medonte (Simcoe County)." *AARO*, 1901:56–100.

1903　"Notes on Sites of Huron Villages in the Township of Oro, Simcoe County, Ontario." *AARO*, 1902:153–83.

1904　"Indian Village Sites in North and South Orillia Townships." *AARO*, 1903:105–25.

1907　"Huron Village Sites" (including surveys of Flos and Vespra Townships). *AARO*, 1906:3–56.

HUNTER, WILLIAM A.

1959　"The Historic Role of the Susquehannocks." *Susquehannock Miscellany*. Ed. J. Witthoft and W. F. Kinsey III. Harrisburg: The Pennsylvania Historical and Museum Commission, pp. 8–18.

HURLEY, W. M. and C. E. HEIDENREICH, eds.

1969　*Palaeoecology and Ontario Prehistory*. *DAUTRR*, no. 1.

1971　*Palaeoecology and Ontario Prehistory II. DAUTRR*, no. 2.

HURLEY, WILLIAM M. and I. T. KENYON

1970　*Algonquin Park Archaeology*. *DAUTRR*, no. 3.

HURLEY, WILLIAM M. et al.

1972　*Algonquin Park Archaeology*. *DAUTRR*, no. 10.

INNIS, H. A.

1940　*The Cod Fisheries: The History of an International Economy*. New Haven: Yale University Press.

1956　*The Fur Trade in Canada*. Toronto: University of Toronto Press (revised edition; original edition published by Yale University Press, 1930).

IVERSEN, J.

1956　"Forest Clearance in the Stone Age." *Scientific American* 194 (3):36–41.

JAENEN, C. J.

1970　"The Catholic Clergy and the Fur Trade." *Canadian Historical Association, Historical Papers, 1970:* 60–80.

JAMES, C. C.

1906　"The Downfall of the Huron Nation." *TRSC*, 2nd Series, 12, ii:311–46.

JAMESON, J. F., ed.

1909　*Narratives of New Netherlands, 1609–1664*. New York: Charles Scribner's Sons.

JENNESS, DIAMOND

1960　*The Indians of Canada*. 5th ed. *NMC, Bulletin* 65.

JENNINGS, FRANCIS
1966   "The Indian Trade of the Susquehanna Valley." *PAPS* 110:406–24.
1968   "Glory, Death, and Transfiguration: the Susquehannock Indians in the Seventeenth Century." *PAPS* 112:15–53.

JENNINGS, J. D.
1968   *Prehistory of North America.* New York: McGraw-Hill Book Company.

JOHNSTON, RICHARD B.
1968a   *Archaeology of Rice Lake, Ontario. NMC, Anthropology Papers* 19.
1968b   *The Archaeology of the Serpent Mounds Site. ROM-OP*, no. 10.

JONES, ARTHUR E.
1908   "*8endake Ehen*" or *Old Huronia.* Toronto: Fifth Report of the Bureau of Archives for the Province of Ontario.

JOUVE, O.-M.
1915   *Les Franciscains et le Canada.* Vol. 1, *Etablissement de la foi, 1615–1629.* Quebec: Couvent des ss. stigmates.

JURGENS, OLGA
1966   "Etienne Brûlé." *DCB* 1:130–33.

JURY, E. M.
1966a   "Anadabijou." *DCB* 1:61.
1966b   "Atironta (Darontal, Durantal)." *DCB* 1:70.
1966c   "Atironta (Aëoptahon), Jean-Baptiste." *DCB* 1:70–71.
1966d   "Atironta, Pierre." *DCB* 1:71–72.
1966e   "Auoindaon." *DCB* 1:73.
1966f   "Skanudharoua." *DCB* 1:610–11.

JURY, W. and E. M. JURY
1954   *Sainte-Marie Among the Hurons.* Toronto: Oxford University Press.
1955   *Saint Louis: Huron Indian Village and Jesuit Mission Site. University of Western Ontario, Museum of Indian Archaeology, Bulletin* no. 10.

KAPLAN, L.
1967   "Archaeological Phaseolus from Tehuacan." *The Prehistory of the Tehuacan Valley.* Vol. 1, *Environment and Subsistence.* Ed. D. S. Byers. Austin: The University of Texas Press, pp. 201–11.

KENNEDY, J. H.
1950   *Jesuit and Savage in New France.* New Haven: Yale University Press.

KENYON, WALTER A.
1968   *The Miller Site. ROM-OP*, no. 14.

KERRIGAN, ANTHONY, trans.
1951   [Andrés González de] *Barcia's Chronological History of the Continent of Florida.* Gainesville: University of Florida Press.

KIDD, KENNETH E.
1949a   *The Excavation of Ste. Marie I.* Toronto: University of Toronto Press.
1949b   "The Identification of French Mission Sites in the Huron Country: A Study in Procedure." *Ont. Hist.* 41:89–94.

1950   "Orr Lake Pottery." *Transactions of the Royal Canadian Institute* 28 (2):165–86.

1952   "Sixty Years of Ontario Archeology." *Archeology of Eastern United States*. Ed. J. B. Griffin. Chicago: University of Chicago Press, pp. 71–82.

1953   "The Excavation and Historical Identification of a Huron Ossuary." *Am. Ant.* 18:359–79.

KIDD, K. E. and M. A.

1970   "A Classification System for Glass Beads for the Use of Field Archaeologists." *Canadian Historic Sites: Occasional Papers in Archaeology and History*, no. 1:45–89.

KINIETZ, W. V.

1940   *The Indians of the Western Great Lakes, 1615–1760*. Ann Arbor: University of Michigan Press.

KNOWLES, NATHANIEL

1940   "The Torture of Captives by the Indians of Eastern North America." *PAPS* 82:151–225.

KROEBER, A. L.

1939   *Cultural and Natural Areas of Native North America*. Berkeley: University of California, Publications in American Archaeology and Ethnology, vol. 38.

1952   *The Nature of Culture*. Chicago: University of Chicago Press.

LAFITAU, JOSEPH-FRANÇOIS

1724   *Moeurs des sauvages ameriquains, comparées aux moeurs des premiers temps*. 2 vols. Paris: Saugrain l'aîné.

LA MORANDIÈRE, CHARLES DE

1962–66   *Histoire de la pêche française de la morue dans l'Amérique septentrionale*. 3 vols. Paris: G. P. Maisonneuve et Larose.

LANCTOT, GUSTAVE

1930   "L'Itinéraire de Cartier à Hochelaga." *TRSC*, 3rd Series, 24, i:115–41.

1963   *A History of Canada*. Vol. 1, *From Its Origins to the Royal Régime, 1663*. Toronto: Clarke, Irwin and Company.

1964   *A History of Canada*. Vol. 2, *From the Royal Régime to the Treaty of Utrecht, 1663–1713*. Toronto: Clarke, Irwin and Company.

1967   *Canada and the American Revolution, 1774–1783*. Toronto: Clarke, Irwin and Company.

LATOURELLE, RENÉ

1952–53   *Etude sur les écrits de Saint Jean de Brébeuf*. 2 vols. Montreal: Les Editions de l'Immaculée-Conception.

1966   "Jean de Brébeuf." *DCB* 1:121–26.

LATTA, M. A.

1971   "Archaeology of the Penetang Peninsula." *Palaeoecology and Ontario Prehistory II. DAUTRR*, no. 2:116–36.

LAVERDIÈRE, C.-H., ed.

1870   *Oeuvres de Champlain*. 2nd ed.; 3 vols. Quebec: G.-E. Desbarats.

LAWRENCE, JOHN
    1916   "Ekarenniondi: The Rock that Stands Out." *AARO*, 28:40–48.

LEACOCK, E. B. and N. O. LURIE, eds.
    1971   *North American Indians in Historical Perspective.* New York: Random House.

LEBLANC, P. G.
    1968   "Indian-Missionary Contact in Huronia, 1615–1649." *Ont. Hist.* 40:133–46.

LE BLANT, R.
    1972   "Le Commerce compliqué des fourrures canadiennes au début de XVIIe siècle." *RHAF* 26:53–66.

LE BLANT, R. and R. BAUDRY
    1967   *Nouveaux documents sur Champlain et son époque.* Vol. 1 *(1560–1622).* Ottawa: *Publication of the Public Archives of Canada,* no. 15.

LE CLERCQ, CHRESTIEN
    1691   *Premier établissement de la foy dans la Nouvelle-France.* 2 vols. Paris: A. Auroy.

LEE, THOMAS E.
    1959   "An Archaeological Survey of Southwestern Ontario and Manitoulin Island." *Penn. Arch.* 29 (2):80–92.

LEMAY, S. (FATHER HUGOLIN)
    1932–33   *Notes bibliographiques pour servir à l'histoire des Récollets du Canada.* 5 vols. Montreal: Imprimerie des Franciscains.
    1936   "L'Oeuvre manuscrite ou imprimée des Récollets de la Mission du Canada (1615–1629)." *TRSC,* 3rd Series, 30, i:115–26.

LESCARBOT, MARC
    1907–14   *The History of New France.* 3 vols. Trans. W. L. Grant. Toronto: The Champlain Society.

LÉVI-STRAUSS, CLAUDE
    1968   *Mythologiques.* 3, *L'origine des manières de table.* Paris: Plon.
    1971   *Mythologiques.* 4, *L'homme nu.* Paris: Plon.

LIGHTHALL, W. D.
    1899   "Hochelagans and Mohawks: A Link in Iroquois History." *TRSC,* 2nd Series, 5, ii:199–211.

LINDSAY, L. S.
    1900   *Notre-Dame de la Jeune Lorette.* Montreal: La Cie de publication de la Revue Canadienne.

LLOYD, H. M. *See* MORGAN, L. H. 1904.

LOM D'ARCE, [BARON] DE LAHONTAN, LOUIS ARMAND DE
    1905   *New Voyages to North America.* 2 vols. Ed. R. G. Thwaites. Chicago: A. C. McClurg and Company.

LONGLEY, WILLIAM H. and JOHN B. MOYLE
    1963   *The Beaver in Minnesota. Minnesota Department of Conservation, Technical Bulletin,* no. 6.

LURIE, NANCY O.
    1959   "Indian Cultural Adjustment to European Civilization."
          Seventeenth-Century America. Ed. J. M. Smith. Chapel Hill: University
          of North Carolina Press, pp. 33–60.
    1960   "Winnebago Protohistory." *Culture in History: Essays in Honor of
          Paul Radin.* Ed. S. Diamond. New York: Columbia University Press,
          pp. 790–808.

LOUNSBURY, FLOYD G.
    1961   "Iroquois-Cherokee Linguistic Relations." *BAE, Bulletin* 180:9–17.

MACDONALD, GEORGE F.
    n.d.   "Archaeological Survey of the Grand River Between Paris and
          Waterloo, Ontario, 1961." National Museum of Canada, files.

MACFARLANE, ALAN
    1970   *Witchcraft in Tudor and Stuart England.* London: Routledge and
          Kegan Paul.

MCGUIRE, JOSEPH D.
    1901   "Ethnology in the Jesuit Relations." *AA* 3:257–69.

MCILWAIN, C. H., ed.
    1915   Peter Wraxall, *An Abridgment of the Indian Affairs . . . Transacted in
          the Colony of New York, from the Year 1678 to the Year 1751.*
          Cambridge: *Harvard Historical Studies*, volume 21.

MCILWRAITH, T. F.
    1930   "The Progress of Anthropology in Canada." *CHR* 11:132–50.
    1946   "Archaeological Work in Huronia, 1946: Excavations near
          Warminster." *CHR* 27:394–401.
    1947   "On the Location of Cahiagué." *TRSC*, 3rd Series, 41, ii:99–102.
    1949   "Anthropology." *The Royal Canadian Institute, Centennial Volume,
          1849–1949.* Ed. W. S. Wallace. Toronto: Royal Canadian Institute,
          pp. 3–12.

MACNEISH, RICHARD S.
    1952   *Iroquois Pottery Types: A Technique for the Study of Iroquois
          Prehistory. NMC, Bulletin* 124.

MCPHERRON, ALAN
    1967   "On the Sociology of Ceramics: Pottery Style Clustering, Marital
          Residence, and Cultural Adaptations of an Algonkian-Iroquoian
          Border." *Iroquois Culture, History, and Prehistory.* Ed. E. Tooker.
          Albany: The University of the State of New York, pp. 101–7.

MARRIOTT, A.
    1948   *Maria, the Potter of San Ildefonso.* Norman: University of Oklahoma
          Press.

MARTIJN, CHARLES A.
    1969   "Ile aux Basques and the Prehistoric Iroquois Occupation of Southern
          Quebec." *Cahiers d'archéologie Québecoise* (mars), 53–114.

MARTIN, FÉLIX
    1898   *Hurons et Iroquois: Le P. Jean de Brébeuf, sa vie, ses travaux, son martyre.* 3rd ed. Paris: Téqui.

MÉTRAUX, A.
    1948   "Jesuit Missions in South America." *BAE, Bulletin* 143, volume 5:645–53.

MOIR, JOHN S.
    1966   "Kirke, Sir David," *DCB* 1:404–7.

MONET, J.
    1966*a*   "Philibert Noyrot." *DCB* 1:521–22.
    1966*b*   "Claude Pijart." *DCB* 1:549.

MOONEY, JAMES
    1928   *The Aboriginal Population of America North of Mexico.* Washington: *Smithsonian Miscellaneous Collections*, 80.

MORGAN, LEWIS H.
    1852   "Reports on the Fabrics, Inventions, Implements and Utensils of the Iroquois." *Annual Report of the University of the State of New York*, no. 5: 67–117.
    1871   *Systems of Consanguinity and Affinity of the Human Family.* Washington: *Smithsonian Contributions to Knowledge*, vol. 17.
    1904   *League of the Ho-dé-no-sau-nee, or Iroquois.* Ed. H. M. Lloyd. New York: Dodd, Mead and Company (originally published 1851).

MORISON, SAMUEL E.
    1971   *The European Discovery of America: the Northern Voyages.* New York: Oxford University Press.
    1972   *Samuel de Champlain: Father of New France.* Boston: Little, Brown and Company.

MORISSONNEAU, C.
    1970   "Développement et population de la réserve indienne du Village-Huron, Loretteville." *Cahiers de géographie de Québec*, no. 33: 339–57.

MÖRNER, M.
    1953   *The Political and Economic Activities of the Jesuits in the La Plata Region—The Hapsburg Era.* Stockholm: Library and Institute of Ibero-American Studies.

MORTON, W. L.
    1963   *The Kingdom of Canada.* Toronto: McClelland and Stewart.
    1972   "Canada and the Canadian Indians: What Went Wrong?" *Quarterly of Canadian Studies for the Secondary School* 2: 3–12.

MURDOCK, G. P.
    1949   *Social Structure.* New York: The Macmillan Company.
    1959   "Evolution in Social Organization." *Evolution and Anthropology: A Centennial Appraisal.* Ed. B. Meggers. Washington: The Anthropological Society of Washington, pp. 126–43.

MURRAY, J. E.
    1938   "The Early Fur Trade in New France and New Netherland." *CHR* 19: 365–77.

MURRAY, L. W., ed.
    1931   *Selected Manuscripts of General John S. Clark, Relating to the Aboriginal History of the Susquehanna*. Athens, Pennsylvania: Society for Pennsylvania Archaeology.

NAROLL, RAOUL
    1969   "The Causes of the Fourth Iroquois War." *Ethnohistory* 16: 51–81.

NEATBY, L. H.
    1966   "Henry Hudson." *DCB* 1: 374–79.

NEEDLER, G. H.
    1949   "Champlain's Route with the Huron War Party in 1615." *Ont. Hist.* 41: 201–6.

NEWELL, WILLIAM B.
    1965   *Crime and Justice Among the Iroquois Nations*. Montreal: Caughnawaga Historical Society.

NOBLE, WILLIAM C.
    1968   *Iroquois Archaeology and the Development of Iroquois Social Organization (1000–1650 A.D.)*. Ph.D. Dissertation. University of Calgary.
    1969   "Some Social Implications of the Iroquois 'In Situ' Theory." *Ont. Arch.* 13: 16–28. [This work is a summary of Noble 1968.]
    1971   "The Sopher Celt: An Indicator of Early Protohistoric Trade in Huronia." *Ont. Arch.* 16: 42–47.

NOBLE, WILLIAM C. and IAN T. KENYON
    1972   "Porteous (AgHb-1): A Probable Early Glen Meyer Village in Brant County, Ontario." *Ont. Arch.* 19: 11–38.

NUTE, G. L.
    1966   "Médard Chouart des Groseilliers." *DCB* 1: 223–28.

O'CALLAGHAN, E. B. and B. FERNOW, eds.
  1856–87   *Documents Relative to the Colonial History of the State of New York*. 15 vols. Albany: Weed, Parsons and Company.

OTTERBEIN, K. F.
    1964   "Why the Iroquois Won: An Analysis of Iroquois Military Tactics." *Ethnohistory* 11: 56–63.

PARKER, A. C.
    1916   "The Origin of the Iroquois as Suggested by Their Archaeology." *AA* 18: 479–507.

PARKMAN, FRANCIS
    1867   *The Jesuits in North America in the Seventeenth Century*. Boston: Little, Brown and Company (reprinted 1927).

PATTERSON, E. P.
 1972 *The Canadian Indian: A History Since 1500.* Don Mills: Collier-
    Macmillan.

PEARCE, R. H.
 1965 *The Savages of America.* Baltimore: Johns Hopkins University Press.

PENDERGAST, JAMES F.
 1964 "The Payne Site." *NMC, Bulletin* 193: 1–27.
 1965 "Other Ideas on 'The Ontario Iroquois Controversy'." *Ont. Arch.* 8:
    39–44.

PENDERGAST, J. F. and B. G. TRIGGER
 1972 *Cartier's Hochelaga and the Dawson Site.* Montreal: McGill-Queen's
    University Press.

PERROT, NICOLAS
 1864 *Mémoire sur les moeurs, coustumes et relligion des sauvages de
    l'Amérique septentrionale.* Ed. J. Tailhan. Leipzig and Paris: A. Franck.
 1911 "Memoir on the Manners, Customs, and Religion of the Savages of
    North America." *The Indian Tribes of the Upper Mississippi Valley
    and Region of the Great Lakes.* Ed. E. H. Blair. Cleveland: A. H. Clark
    Company. Vol. 1: 23–272.

POPHAM, ROBERT E.
 1950 "Late Huron Occupations of Ontario: An Archaeological Survey of
    Innisfil Township." *Ont. Hist.* 42: 81–90.

POTIER, P.
 1920a "Elementa grammaticae huronicae, 1745." Facsimile of ms. in St.
    Mary's College, Montreal. *Fifteenth Report of the Bureau of Archives for
    the Province of Ontario.* Toronto: Clarkson W. James, pp. 1–157.
 1920b "Radices Huronicae." Facsimile of ms. in St. Mary's College, Montreal.
    Fifteenth Report of the Bureau of Archives for the Province of Ontario.
    Toronto: Clarkson W. James, pp. 159–455.

POULIOT, LÉON
 1940 *Étude sur les Relations des Jésuites de la Nouvelle France (1632–1672).*
    Paris and Montreal: Studia Collegii Maximi Immaculatae Conceptionis,
    V.
 1958 *Le premier retraitant du Canada: Joseph Chihouatenhoua.* Montreal:
    Editions Bellarmin.
 1966 "Jérôme Lalemant." *DCB* 1: 413–15.

PRATT, PETER P.
 1964 "The Question of the Location of the Champlain-Iroquois Battle of
    1615: A Study in Historic Site Archaeology." Mimeographed.

QUAIN, BUELL
 1937 "The Iroquois." *Cooperation and Competition among Primitive Peoples.*
    Ed. Margaret Mead. New York: McGraw-Hill, Inc., pp. 240–81.

QUIMBY, GEORGE I.

    1960   *Indian Life in the Upper Great Lakes, 11,000* B.C. *to* A.D. *1800.* Chicago: University of Chicago Press.

    1966   *Indian Culture and European Trade Goods.* Madison: University of Wisconsin Press.

RAGUENEAU, PAUL

    1925   "Mémoires touchant la mort et les vertus des Pères Jésuites." *Rapport de l'Archiviste de la Province de Québec pour 1924–25.* Quebec: The King's Printer, pp. 1–93.

RANDS, R. L. and C. L. RILEY

    1958   "Diffusion and Discontinuous Distribution." *AA* 60: 274–97.

REDFIELD, ROBERT

    1956   *Peasant Society and Culture: An Anthropological Approach to Civilization.* Chicago: University of Chicago Press.

RICH, E. E.

    1966   *Montreal and the Fur Trade.* Montreal: McGill University Press.

RICHARDS, CARA

    1967   "Huron and Iroquois Residence Patterns 1600–1650." *Iroquois Culture, History, and Prehistory.* Ed. E. Tooker. Albany: The University of the State of New York, pp. 51–56.

RIDLEY, FRANK

    1947   "A Search for Ossossané and Its Environs." *Ont. Hist.* 39: 7–14.

    1952*a*   "The Huron and Lalonde Occupations of Ontario." *Am. Ant.* 17: 197–210.

    1952*b*   "The Fallis Site, Ontario." *Am. Ant.* 18: 7–14.

    1954   "The Frank Bay Site, Lake Nipissing, Ontario." *Am. Ant.* 20: 40–50.

    1958   "Did the Huron Really Migrate North from the Toronto Area?" *Penn. Arch.* 28 (3–4): 143–44.

    1961   *Archaeology of the Neutral Indians.* Etobicoke: Etobicoke Historical Society.

    1963   "The Ontario Iroquoian Controversy." *Ont. Hist.* 55: 49–59.

    1973   "The Wenro in Huronia." *Anthropological Journal of Canada* 11 (1): 10–19.

RITCHIE, WILLIAM A.

    1961   "Iroquois Archeology and Settlement Patterns." *BAE, Bulletin* 180: 25–38.

    1965   *The Archaeology of New York State.* New York: The Natural History Press.

RITCHIE, WILLIAM A. and ROBERT E. FUNK

    1973   *Aboriginal Settlement Patterns in the Northeast.* Albany: *New York State Museum and Science Service, Memoir* 20.

ROBERTSON, WILLIAM

    1812   *The History of America.* 2 vols. Philadelphia: J. Bioren and T. L. Plowman (first American, from the 10th London edition).

ROBINSON, PERCY J.

1942   "The Origin of the Name Hochelaga." *CHR* 23: 295–96.

1948   "The Huron Equivalents of Cartier's Second Vocabulary." *TRSC*, 3rd Series, 42, ii: 127–46.

ROCHEMONTEIX, CAMILLE DE

1895–96   *Les Jésuites et la Nouvelle-France au XVIIe siècle.* 3 vols. Paris: Letouzey et Ané.

ROUSSEAU, JACQUES

1954–55   "L'annedda et l'arbre de vie." *RHAF* 8: 171–212.

RUSSELL, W. A.

1965   "A Mill at Sainte Marie I." *Ont. Arch.*, Series B, 3: 11–17.

SAGARD, GABRIEL

1866   *Histoire du Canada et voyages que les Frères mineurs recollects y ont faicts pour la conversion des infidèles depuis l'an 1615 . . . avec un dictionnaire de la langue huroŗne.* 4 vols. with consecutive pagination. Paris: Edwin Tross.

SALISBURY, RICHARD F.

1962   *From Stone to Steel.* Victoria: Melbourne University Press.

SARTRE, JEAN-PAUL

1963   *Search for a Method.* New York: Alfred A. Knopf.

SAUER, C. O.

1971   *Sixteenth Century North America.* Berkeley and Los Angeles: University of California Press.

SAUNDERS, A.

1963   *Algonquin Story.* Toronto: Ontario Department of Lands and Forests.

SAUNDERS, R. M.

1935   "The First Introduction of European Plants and Animals into Canada." *CHR* 16: 388–406.

SAVAGE, HOWARD G.

1971a   "Faunal Analysis of the Robitaille Site (BeHa-3)—Interim Report." *Palaeoecology and Ontario Prehistory. DAUTRR*, no. 2: 166–72.

1971b   "Faunal Analysis of the Maurice Site (BeHa-2)." *Palaeoecology and Ontario Prehistory. DAUTRR*, no. 2: 173–78.

SCHNEIDER, DAVID M. and K. GOUGH

1961   *Matrilineal Kinship.* Berkeley and Los Angeles: University of California Press.

SERVICE, E. R.

1962   *Primitive Social Organization: An Evolutionary Perspective.* New York: Random House.

SHEA, J. G.

1881   *The First Establishment of the Faith in New France.* 2 vols. New York: J. G. Shea.

SIMARD, ROBERT
    1970   *Le site de Métabetchouan, Lac Saint-Jean; rapport préliminaire.*
          Chicoutimi: Société d'archéologie du Saguenay.

SIMMONS, L.
    1942   *Sun Chief.* New Haven: Yale University Press.

SMITH, ALLAN
    1970   "Metaphor and Nationality in North America." *CHR* 51: 247–75.

SMITH, P. E. L.
    1972   "Land-use, Settlement Patterns and Subsistence Agriculture: A
          Demographic Perspective." *Man, Settlement and Urbanism.* Ed. P. J.
          Ucko, R. Tringham, and G. W. Dimbleby. London: Duckworth, pp.
          409–25.

SMITH, WALLIS M.
    1970   "A Re-appraisal of the Huron Kinship System." *Anthropologica* 12:
          191–206.
    1973   "The Fur Trade and the Frontier: A Study of an Inter-cultural
          Alliance." *Anthropologica* 15: 21–35.

SNYDERMAN, GEORGE S.
    1948   "Behind the Tree of Peace: A Sociological Analysis of Iroquois
          Warfare." *Penn. Arch.* 18 (3–4): 1–93.
    1951   "Concepts of Land Ownership among the Iroquois and Their
          Neighbors." *BAE, Bulletin* 149: 15–34.

SOROKO, O. S.
    1966   "A Soviet Critique of *The Canadian Historical Review.*" *CHR* 47:
          50–58.

SPALDING, H. S.
    1929   "The Ethnologic Value of the *Jesuit Relations.*" *American Journal of
          Sociology* 34: 882–89.

SPENCER, R. F., J. D. JENNINGS, et al.
    1965   *The Native Americans.* New York: Harper and Row.

SPICER, E. H.
    1961   ed. *Perspectives in American Indian Cultural Change.* Chicago:
          University of Chicago Press.
    1962   *Cycles of Conquest.* Tucson: University of Arizona Press.
    1969   *A Short History of the Indians of the United States.* New York: Van
          Nostrand.

STANLEY, GEORGE F. C.
    1949   "The Policy of 'Francisation' as Applied to the Indians during the
          Ancien Régime." *RHAF* 3: 333–48.
    1952   "The Indian Background of Canadian History." *Canadian Historical
          Association, Annual Report, 1952,* pp. 14–21.

STEARN, E. W. and A. E.
    1945   *The Effect of Smallpox on the Destiny of the Amerindian.* Boston: Bruce
          Humphries.

STITES, S. H.

 1905 *Economics of the Iroquois*. Lancaster: New Era Printing Company.

STOTHERS, D. M.

 1970 "The Princess Point Complex and Its Relationship to the Owasco and Ontario Iroquois Traditions." Ontario Archaeological Society, *Archaeological Notes*, March, pp. 4–6.

 1974 "The Glass Site AgHb-5, Oxbow Tract, Brantford Township, Brant County, Ontario." *Ont. Arch.* 21: 37–45.

STRUEVER, STUART

 1968 "Woodland Subsistence-Settlement Systems in the Lower Illinois Valley." *New Perspectives in Archeology*. Ed. S. R. and L. R. Binford. Chicago: Aldine Publishing Company, pp. 285–312.

STRUEVER, STUART and K. D. VICKERY

 1973 "The Beginnings of Cultivation in the Midwest-Riverine Area of the United States." *AA* 75: 1197–1220.

STUIVER, M. and H. SUESS

 1966 "On the Relationship between Radiocarbon Dates and True Sample Ages." *Radiocarbon* 8: 534–40.

STURTEVANT, WILLIAM C.

 1966 "Anthropology, History, and Ethnohistory." *Ethnohistory* 13: 1–51.

SULTE, BENJAMIN

 1907 "Etienne Brûlé." *TRSC*, 3rd Series, 1, i: 97–126.

TALBOT, FRANCIS X.

 1956 *Saint Among the Hurons: the Life of Jean de Brébeuf*. Garden City: Image Books (originally published by Harper and Brothers, 1949).

THEVET, ANDRÉ

 1878 *Les singularitez de la France antarctique*. Ed. P. Gaffarel. Paris: Maisonneuve et Cie (originally published 1578).

THOMAS, H. M.

 1936 "A New Relic of the Jesuit Mission of 1640–41 in Western Ontario." *TRSC*, 3rd Series, 30, ii: 185–92.

THOMAS AQUINAS

 1852–73 *Opera Omnia*. 25 vols. Parma: Tipis P. Fiaccadori.

THWAITES, REUBEN G.

 1896–1901 *The Jesuit Relations and Allied Documents*. 73 vols. Cleveland: The Burrows Brothers Company.

TOOKER, ELISABETH

 1960 "Three Aspects of Northern Iroquoian Culture Change." *Penn. Arch.* 30 (2): 65–71.

 1963 "The Iroquois Defeat of the Huron: A Review of Causes." *Penn. Arch.* 33 (1–2): 115–23.

 1964 *An Ethnography of the Huron Indians, 1615–1649*. Washington: *BAE, Bulletin*, 190.

1970a   *The Iroquois Ceremonial of Midwinter.* Syracuse: Syracuse University Press.
1970b   "Northern Iroquoian Sociopolitical Organization." *AA* 72: 90–97.

TOWNSEND, W. H.
    1969   "Stone and Steel Tool Use in a New Guinea Society." *Ethnology* 8: 199–205.

TRELEASE, ALLEN W.
    1960   *Indian Affairs in Colonial New York: The Seventeenth Century.* Ithaca: Cornell University Press.

TRIGGER, BRUCE G.
    1960   "The Destruction of Huronia: A Study in Economic and Cultural Change, 1609–1650." *Transactions of the Royal Canadian Institute,* 33, no. 68, pt. 1: 14–45.
    1962a   "The Historic Location of the Hurons." *Ont. Hist.* 54: 137–48.
    1962b   "Trade and Tribal Warfare on the St. Lawrence in the Sixteenth Century." *Ethnohistory* 9: 240–56.
    1963a   "Order and Freedom in Huron Society." *Anthropologica* 5: 151–69.
    1963b   "Settlement as an Aspect of Iroquoian Adaptation at the Time of Contact." *AA* 65: 86–101.
    1965   "The Jesuits and the Fur Trade." *Ethnohistory* 12: 30–53.
    1966a   "Amantacha." *DCB* 1: 58–59.
    1966b   "Chihwatenha." *DCB* 1: 211–12.
    1967   "Settlement Archaeology—Its Goals and Promise." *Am. Ant.* 32: 149–60.
    1968a   "Archaeological and Other Evidence: A Fresh Look at the 'Laurentian Iroquois'." *Am. Ant.* 33: 429–40.
    1968b   "The French Presence in Huronia: The Structure of Franco-Huron Relations in the First Half of the Seventeenth Century." *CHR* 49: 107–41.
    1969a   *The Huron: Farmers of the North.* New York: Holt, Rinehart and Winston.
    1969b   "Criteria for Identifying the Locations of Historic Indian Sites: A Case Study from Montreal." *Ethnohistory* 16: 303–16.
    1970   "The Strategy of Iroquoian Prehistory." *Ont. Arch.* 14: 3–48.
    1971a   "Champlain Judged by His Indian Policy: A Different View of Early Canadian History." *Anthropologica* 13: 85–114.
    1971b   "Review of Bailey (1969) and Wallace (1970)." *CHR* 52: 183–87.
    1971c   "The Mohawk-Mahican War (1624–28): The Establishment of a Pattern." *CHR* 52: 276–86.

TRUDEL, MARCEL
    1963   *Histoire de la Nouvelle-France, Les Vaines Tentatives, 1524–1603.* Montreal: Fides.
    1966a   *Histoire de la Nouvelle-France, Le Comptoir, 1604–1627.* Montreal: Fides.
    1966b   "Guillaume de Caën." *DCB* 1: 159–62.
    1966c   "Samuel de Champlain." *DCB* 1: 186–99.

1973   *The Beginnings of New France, 1524–1663.* Toronto: McClelland and Stewart Limited.

TUCK, JAMES A.
1971   *Onondaga Iroquois Prehistory: A Study in Settlement Archaeology.* Syracuse: Syracuse University Press.

TYYSKA, A. E.
1968   "Settlement Patterns at Cahiague." Report submitted to the Archaeological and Historic Sites Board of the Province of Ontario.
1969   "Archaeology of the Penetang Peninsula." *Palaeoecology and Ontario Prehistory. DAUTRR,* no. 1: 61–88.

TYYSKA, A. E. and W. M. HURLEY
1969   "Maurice Village and the Huron Bear." Paper presented at the second annual meeting of the Canadian Archaeological Association, Toronto.

VACHON, ANDRÉ
1966   "Thomas Godefroy de Normanville." *DCB* 1: 341.
1970   "Colliers et ceintures de porcelaine chez les Indiens de la Nouvelle-France." *CdD* 35: 251–78.
1971   "Colliers et ceintures de porcelaine dans la diplomatie indienne." *CdD* 36: 179–92.

VAN DER DONCK, A.
1841   "Description of the New Netherlands." *Collections of the New-York Historical Society,* 2nd series 1: 125–242.

VAN LAER, A. J. F., ed.
1908   *Van Rensselaer Bowier Manuscripts.* Albany: University of the State of New York.
1924   *Documents Relating to New Netherland, 1624–1626, in the Henry E. Huntington Library.* San Marino: Huntington Library.

VIGNERAS, L. A.
1953   "El viaje de Samuel Champlain a las Indias Occidentales." *Anuario de Estudios Americanos* 10: 457–500.
1957–58 "Le Voyage de Samuel Champlain aux Indes occidentales." *RHAF* 11: 163–200.

WALKER, J. W.
1971   "The Indian in Canadian Historical Writing." *The Canadian Historical Association, Historical Papers 1971*: 21–51.

WALLACE, A. F. C.
1958   "Dreams and the Wishes of the Soul: A Type of Psychoanalytic Theory Among the Seventeenth Century Iroquois." *AA* 60: 234–48.
1970   *The Death and Rebirth of the Seneca.* New York: Alfred A. Knopf.

WALLACE, P. A. W.
1966   "Dekanahwideh." *DCB* 1: 253–55.

WARWICK, J.
1972   "Humanisme chrétien et bons sauvages (Gabriel Sagard, 1623–1636)." *XVIIe Siècle* 97: 25–49.

WASHBURN, W. E., ed.
    1964   *The Indian and the White Man.* Garden City: Doubleday.

WHALLON, ROBERT, JR.
    1968   "Investigations of Late Prehistoric Social Organization in New York State." *New Perspectives in Archeology.* Ed. S. R. and L. R. Binford. Chicago: Aldine Publishing Company, pp. 223–44.

WHITE, MARIAN E.
    1961   *Iroquois Culture History in the Niagara Frontier Area of New York State. UMAP,* 16.
    1963   "Settlement Pattern Change and the Development of Horticulture in the New York-Ontario Area." *Penn. Arch.* 33 (1–2): 1–12.
    1971a "Ethnic Identification and Iroquois Groups in Western New York and Ontario." *Ethnohistory* 18: 19–38.
    1971b "Review of *The Bennett Site.*" *Am. Ant.* 36: 222–23.
    1972   "On Delineating the Neutral Iroquois of the Eastern Niagara Peninsula of Ontario." *Ont. Arch.* 17: 62–74.

WILLEY, G. R.
    1966   *An Introduction to American Archaeology.* Vol. 1, *North and Middle America.* Englewood Cliffs: Prentice-Hall.

WILLEY, G. R. and P. PHILLIPS
    1958   *Method and Theory in American Archaeology.* Chicago: University of Chicago Press.

WILSON, DANIEL
    1862   *Prehistoric Man.* 2 vols. Cambridge: Macmillan and Company.
    1884   "The Huron-Iroquois of Canada, A Typical Race of American Aborigines." *TRSC,* 1st series, 2, ii: 55–106.

WILSON, H. C.
    1956   "A New Interpretation of the Wild Rice District of Wisconsin." *AA* 58: 1059–64.

WINTEMBERG, WILLIAM J.
    1926   "Foreign Aboriginal Artifacts from post-European Iroquoian Sites in Ontario." *TRSC,* 3rd series, 20, ii: 37–61.
    1931   "Distinguishing Characteristics of Algonkian and Iroquoian Cultures." *NMC, Bulletin* 67: 65–125.
    1936   "The Probable Location of Cartier's Stadacona." *TRSC,* 3rd series, 30, ii: 19–21.
    1942   "The Geographical Distribution of Aboriginal Pottery in Canada." *Am. Ant.* 8: 129–41.
    1946   "The Sidey-Mackay Village Site." *Am. Ant.* 11: 154–82.

WINTERS, HOWARD D.
    1968   "Value Systems and Trade Cycles of the Late Archaic in the Midwest." *New Perspectives in Archeology.* Ed. S. R. and L. R. Binford. Chicago: Aldine Publishing Company, pp. 175–221.

WITTHOFT, JOHN
    1951   "Iroquois Archaeology at the Mid-Century." *PAPS* 95: 311–21.

1959 "Ancestry of the Susquehannocks." *Susquehannock Miscellany*. Ed. J. Witthoft and W. F. Kinsey, III. Harrisburg: The Pennsylvania Historical and Museum Commission, pp. 19–60.

WRAY, C. F. and H. L. SCHOFF

1953 "A Preliminary Report on the Seneca Sequence in Western New York, 1550–1687." *Penn Arch.* 23 (2): 53–63.

WRIGHT, JAMES V.

1962 "A Distributional Study of Some Archaic Traits in Southern Ontario." *NMC, Bulletin* 180: 124–42.

1965 "A Regional Examination of Ojibwa Culture History." *Anthropologica* 7: 189–227.

1966 *The Ontario Iroquois Tradition. NMC, Bulletin* 210.

1967 *The Laurel Tradition and the Middle Woodland Period. NMC, Bulletin* 217.

1968 "Prehistory of Hudson Bay: the Boreal Forest." *Science, History and Hudson Bay*. Ed. C. S. Beals and D. A. Shenstone. Ottawa: The Queen's Printer, vol. 1, pp. 55–68.

1969 "The Michipicoten Site." *NMC, Bulletin* 224: 1–85.

1972 *Ontario Prehistory: An Eleven-thousand-year Archaeological Outline*. Ottawa: National Museum of Man.

WRIGHT, JAMES V. and J. E. ANDERSON

1963 *The Donaldson Site. NMC, Bulletin* 184.

1969 *The Bennett Site. NMC, Bulletin* 229.

WRONG, G. M., ed.

1939 *The Long Journey to the Country of the Hurons*. Toronto: The Champlain Society.

WROTH, L.

1954 "An Unknown Champlain Map of 1616." *Imago Mundi* 11: 85–94.

YARNELL, RICHARD A.

1964 *Aboriginal Relationships Between Culture and Plant Life in the Upper Great Lakes Region. UMAP*, 23.

Index

The Children of Aataentsic is both a full-scale ethnohistory of the Huron Indian confederacy and a far-reaching study of the causes of its collapse under the impact of the Iroquois attacks of 1649. Drawing upon the archaeological context, the ethnography presented by early explorers and missionaries, and the recorded history of contact with Europeans, Bruce Trigger traces the development of the Huron people from the earliest hunting and gathering economies in southern Ontario many centuries before the arrival of the Europeans to their key role in the fur trade in eastern Canada during the first half of the seventeenth century.

Trigger's work integrates insights from archaeology, history, ethnology, linguistics, and geography. This wide knowledge allows him to show that, far from being a static prehistoric society quickly torn apart by European contact and the fur trade, almost every facet of Iroquoian culture had undergone significant change in the centuries preceding European contact. He argues convincingly that the European impact upon native cultures cannot be correctly assessed unless the nature and extent of precontact change is understood. His study not only stands Euro-American stereotypes and fictions on their heads, but forcefully and consistently interprets European and Indian actions, thoughts, and motives from the perspective of the Huron culture.

The Children of Aataentsic revises widely accepted interpretations of Indian behaviour and challenges cherished myths about the actions of some celebrated Europeans during the "heroic age" of Canadian history. In a new preface, Trigger describes and evaluates contemporary controversies over the ethnohistory of eastern Canada.

Bruce Trigger is a member of the Department of Anthropology, McGill University and author of *Natives and Newcomers: Canada's "Heroic Age" Reconsidered.*

D0022036

$32.00

16

The Children of Aataentsic

A History of the Huron People to 1660

BRUCE G. TRIGGER

McGILL-QUEEN'S UNIVERSITY PRESS   Kingston and Montreal

© McGill-Queen's University Press 1976
Reprinted with a new preface 1987
First paperback edition 1987

ISBN 0-7735-0626-8 (cloth)
ISBN 0-7735-0627-6 (paper)

Legal deposit fourth quarter 1987
Bibliothèque nationale du Québec

Printed in Canada

Printed on acid-free paper

Canadian Cataloguing in Publication Data

Trigger, Bruce G.
    The children of Aataentsic: a history of the
    Huron people to 1660
    First published: Montreal: McGill-Queen's University
    Press, 1976.
    Includes index.
    Bibliography: p.
    ISBN 0-7735-0626-8 (bound) — ISBN 0-7735-0627-6 (pbk.)
    1. Huron Indians – History.   2. Indians of North
    America – Ontario – History.   3. Jesuits – Missions –
    Ontario.   I. Title.
    E99.H9T68 1987   970.004'97   C87-090208-3

Preparation of the manuscript was aided by grants from the Faculty of Graduate Studies
and Research, McGill University: the first edition was published with the help of a grant
from the Social Science Research Council of Canada using funds provided by the Canada
Council.
    This reprint has been published with the help of a grant from the Max Bell Foundation.

To Barbara, Isabel, and Rosalyn

Contents

Illustrations

Maps

Preface to the 1987 reprinting

When *The Children of Aataentsic* was published in 1976 I doubted that, whether its reception was favourable or unfavourable, there would ever be a call to reprint this mammoth work. Indeed I had serious reservations about whether a book of this scale was worthwhile and was greatly relieved when favourable reviews started to appear, beginning with the late Walter Kenyon's "Masterwork" in *Canadian Forum*. In recent months I have received a growing number of inquiries about how copies might be obtained. It was therefore good to learn that McGill-Queen's University Press, with the generous support of the Max Bell Foundation, was planning to reprint it in a handier and more economical format.

Practical considerations alone have dictated that the text and pagination remain unchanged, although in 1982 I had produced a partially revised manuscript version of the text for translation into French. (This translation will be published early in 1988 by Libre Expression.) It is also clear that many readers wanted a copy of the original work which has become of some historical interest in relation to the development of ethnohistorical studies of the Iroquoians. A substantial updating of *The Children of Aataentsic* has already been achieved in *Natives and Newcomers* (1985) which examines more recent developments in the historical and ethnohistorical study of the native peoples of central Canada, with special emphasis on methodological problems.

In *The Children of Aataentsic* my main objective was to demonstrate that it was possible to write a history of a native people that was not focused exclusively on their relations with Europeans. In order to make this work attractive to the general reader, I sought to keep methodological discussions as brief as possible. In my introduction I limited myself to considering the importance of archaeological data for ethnohistorical research, the value of the long-established concept of interest groups for achieving parity in analyses of native and European behaviour, and the necessity of trying to understand native actions as far as possible in terms of the rational pursuit of interests in order to expose the erroneousness of long-standing claims that native people were less rational than Europeans. Unknown to me, the latter goal was simultaneously being pursued by the American historian Francis

Jennings in his remarkable book *The Invasion of America* (1975). In order to keep the introduction as brief as possible, I excised part of my discussion of rationality which I rewrote and published as "Brecht and Ethnohistory" in the journal *Ethnohistory* (1975).

In the decade since *The Children of Aataentsic* was published, the theoretical perspectives of anthropology, history, and ethnohistory have changed dramatically in some respects. In particular, there has been an increasing emphasis on understanding cultural change from what is believed to be a native point of view and explaining change in terms of altering patterns of cognition. There has also been a growing unwillingness to accept economic explanations of human behaviour. As a result of these changes, interpretations of native actions have begun to shift away from those offered in this book. This trend has influenced scholars who praised *The Children of Aataentsic* highly when it first appeared and who have since indicated no disagreement with its basic tenets. I have therefore decided to use this new preface to enunciate these tenets and to try to estimate how well my book has survived its first decade.

In *The Children of Aataentsic* I privileged a rationalist approach. My primary goal was to demonstrate that native behaviour was based on the rational pursuit of desired ends at least to the same extent as that of Europeans. I had concluded that little was to be gained by eliciting sympathy for native people (as various historians had done in the past) if it was not based on respect for their intelligence and self-discipline. I therefore sought to explain native behaviour as far as possible in terms of rational calculations of how desired ends might be achieved. In doing this I eschewed the alternative romantic approach which views the behaviour of each society as determined by its own particular cultural pattern or, as was once believed, by its own specific biological nature. In a relativistic fashion, the romantic view assumes that each culture is a closed system based on its own self-defined rules. Thus the behaviour of one group is unlikely ever to be fully comprehensible to members of another. It is this approach, with its potential for emphasizing the irrational aspects of human conduct, that in various guises has dominated the interpretation of native American behaviour from at least the time of Francis Parkman to the present. Rationalist explanations, by contrast, seek to account for human behaviour in terms of calculations that are cross-culturally comprehensible.

I had no desire, however, to commit myself in a partisan fashion to one side or the other of a simplistic debate between rationalism and cultural relativism. There is clearly not the wide range of variation in cultural behaviour that might be expected if only cultural factors shaped all aspects of

human life. No society, for example, welcomes enslavement or totally ignores its own self-interest. Yet as an anthropologist I was equally aware that individuals or groups can use rational means to pursue culturally defined goals that are themselves often far from rational. The Jesuits' risking of their own lives to rescue the souls of native people from eternal damnation is one example of this. I was also keenly aware of the continuing debates among philosophers and social scientists concerning the relative importance of rational calculations and culturally defined goals as factors influencing human behaviour (see M. D. Sahlins, *Culture and Practical Reason* [1976], Ernest Gellner, *Relativism and the Social Sciences* [1985] and Dan Sperber, *On Anthropological Knowledge* [1985]). These disputes not only remain inconclusive but in many cases appear to centre on highly unproductive questions. It is frequently impossible to distinguish culturally encoded rational experience from "irrational" cultural norms. Religious prohibitions in a hunter-gatherer society may maintain conservation practices in its subsistence pattern, thereby disguising their utilitarian nature and at the same time enhancing people's willingness to practise them. Conversely, many customs that were originally non-utilitarian, if they relate to practical behaviour in any way, may be subject to long-term modification and selection that makes them more "rational." Finally, ethnologists are unable to agree whether statements such as "all men are parrots" are to be understood as intended literally or metaphorically by a particular culture.

As an Ariadne's thread to extricate myself from this labyrinth of confusion, I adopted what I believe to be the most fruitful theory of culture currently available. This theory is based on Karl Marx's assumption that "the mode of production in material life determines the general character of the social, political, and intellectual processes of life." It follows that human beings are likely to be most rational and calculating, and hence least culture-bound, with respect to those matters that relate most directly to their material well-being. Behavioural and conceptual adjustments can be made most easily in human activities such as food production, trade, and competition for material resources. On the other hand, aspects of culture that relate to social status, personal identity, and a sense of psychological well-being, including religious beliefs, values, and ethnic identity, while ultimately influenced by economic factors are by their nature likely to be much more conservative and to respond much more slowly and unpredictably to changing conditions. Traditions of these sorts are not only more tenacious but also less susceptible to rational evaluation. Two principal hypotheses or expectations can be derived from these assumptions: (a) examples of rational calculation are likely to be far more obvious in economic behaviour than in religious beliefs and cultural

values, and (b) when cultures interact, accommodation and change are likely to occur more quickly and easily in economic behaviour than in other spheres. Yet, to the extent that economic change threatens a sense of identity, human groups may seek to solidify and reinforce their traditional religious beliefs and practices as a way of coping with psychological disorientation and this can, in some instances, significantly influence economic processes. Without questioning the sincere altruism with which the Jesuits perceived their missionary work, it is possible to see them as both conscious and unconscious agents of French imperialism. By trying to undermine Iroquoian religious beliefs and traditional social values, they were seeking to eliminate precisely those areas of traditional Huron culture that were most resistant to economic change and maintained the will of native people to resist European domination.

These were the ideas that guided my interpretation of Huron behaviour. Despite their materialist orientation, they are very different from the technological determinism of George T. Hunt (*The Wars of the Iroquois* [1940]) who assumed that European tools quickly and automatically transformed all other aspects of native life. They are also more akin to Alfred G. Bailey's (*The Conflict of European and Eastern Algonkian Cultures, 1504-1700* [1937]) balanced anthropological view of how native cultures responded to European contact than they are to Harold Innis' (*The Fur Trade in Canada* [1930, 1956]) economic determinism. I believe that my underlying assumptions have been evident to most anthropologists, especially those who are sympathetic to any kind of materialist approach to understanding human behaviour. Some historians, however, appear to have interpreted my detailed examination of historical events as the espousal of their own preferred "let the facts speak for themselves" approach. In my view such an approach can never be free from implicit biases which frequently assume a strongly romantic and idealist character.

Every choice has its costs as well as benefits. I cannot claim that my emphasis on rational behaviour has not involved a relative neglect (although I hope only a minor one) of culturally specific factors that shaped the Huron way of life and their responses to changing historical circumstances. Two research projects initiated in recent years are investigating subjects that promise to add significantly to our understanding of Huron behaviour.

The first of these is George Hamell's still largely unpublished analysis of the basic patterns of religious beliefs shared by the Iroquoian, Algonkian, and Siouan-speaking peoples of eastern North America. Drawing upon extensive collections of ethnographic and ethnohistorical data, he has been able, as part of this research, to demonstrate that native copper, rock crystals,

and marine shells were viewed as substances associated with the supernatural underwater world and hence were believed able to confer power, health, and prosperity on their possessors. For over 6,000 years these materials were buried with the dead to enhance the welfare of their souls. Hamell argues that European metal artifacts and glass beads were seen as the equivalents of native copper and quartz crystals and that Europeans initially were viewed as spirits returning from the realms of the dead. Hence the earliest European goods appear to have been valued for their spiritual rather than for their utilitarian qualities. Metal kettles were regularly cut into pieces and fragments widely exchanged from tribe to tribe. These goods turn up far more frequently in native burials than in living sites during early decades of contact. Marine shells also began to be traded into the interior of eastern North America in far larger quantities than before as the availability of European goods stimulated burial ceremonialism and hence a demand for the full range of goods associated with such rituals (C. Miller and G. Hamell, *Journal of American History* 73 [1986]: 311-28). In *The Children of Aataentsic* I observed that in the course of the sixteenth century the arrival of European goods had an impact on Iroquoian societies that was out of proportion to their utilitarian value. What I was not able to do, not having studied native religious beliefs in the detailed and comparative fashion that Hamell is now doing, was to specify what these goods meant to native people during the earliest phases of European contact. Because of this I also failed to explain satisfactorily the fragmentary condition in which this material is found in archaeological sites and to pay as much attention as I might have done to the contexts in which it is being discovered.

Recent ethnosemantic studies by the linguist John Steckley ("The Soul Concepts of the Huron," Master's thesis, Memorial University of Newfoundland, 1978) of manuscript dictionaries, grammars, and religious texts prepared in the Huron language by French missionaries in the seventeenth and eighteenth centuries are also revealing important information about Huron culture and how the Jesuits perceived it. From these texts it is possible to learn far more about how the Hurons viewed the nature of souls than could be gleaned from seventeenth-century missionary accounts. One can also assess how much the Jesuits knew about Huron concepts of the soul at particular periods and to what degree they were linguistically capable of conveying Christian theological concepts to the Huron. More recently Steckley has used knowledge of the terminology that the Jesuits employed at different times to date the Huron carol, "Jesous Ahatonhia," to the early period of the Huron mission and hence to support the traditional attribution of its composition to Jean de Brébeuf.

In recent years the study of Huron dictionaries has helped to clarify the nature of Huron seventeenth-century clan organization and house structures as well as the meaning of place-names. It may be able to shed more light on the nature of the fur trade by revealing how the Huron categorized animal pelts and the phrases commonly used in commercial transactions with the French at different periods. These dictionaries and grammars constitute the largest corpus of relatively unstudied material relating to the Huron culture of the seventeenth century. Its systematic investigation promises to reveal much about Huron culture and how it was understood by the French at different periods. The religious texts that the Jesuits composed in the Huron language should also reveal more about how they tried, and succeeded or failed linguistically, to convey a knowledge of Christianity to the Hurons. The integration of this material into the study of Huron history should amplify and perhaps modify our understanding of many historical issues. It is important that there be more intensive study of the Huron language as a basis for the continuing investigation of these data.

Hamell and Steckley have shown how specific types of systematic study can expand our knowledge of Huron culture. In principle any new knowledge of how native people perceived the world around them and reacted to it ought to improve an understanding of how and why they behaved as they did in specific historical situations. Both approaches necessitate long and detailed study and lexical investigations require specialized linguistic skills. It also remains to be determined to what extent such studies will significantly modify an understanding of Huron history based on the sources that were used to write *The Children of Aataentsic*. The point appears to have been reached in the study of Huron history where increasing effort must be expended to recover each new item of information.

A final development in which the emphasis is on cultural specificities is the explosion in the last two decades of publications that examine how, beginning in the fifteenth century, native Americans were perceived by European scholars and colonists. This research in the field of intellectual history is of particular importance to anthropologists because it reveals in detail the cultural stereotypes, biases, and precedents that shaped the understanding Europeans had of the native peoples with whom they interacted. These studies help ethnohistorians to judge more accurately the biases that coloured European descriptions and interpretations of native peoples as well as to understand the motives that led European colonists to behave as they did. Such studies make intellectual historians such as Cornelius Jaenen (*Friend and Foe: Aspects of French-Amerindian Cultural Contact in the Sixteenth and Seventeenth Centuries* [1976]) and Olive Dickason (*The Myth of the Savage*

and the Beginnings of French Colonialism in the Americas [1984]) indispensable to the study of ethnohistory.

In recent studies of the ethnohistory of eastern North America the pendulum appears to be swinging in the direction of a romantic rather than a rationalistic analysis. There is a growing tendency to reject or ignore economic interpretations of native (or European) behaviour and in their place to adopt an idealist approach. In *The Children of Aataentsic* I opposed the economic determinism of Hunt and Innis, and I continue to believe that culturally specific factors must be carefully considered in any form of historical analysis. Yet I regard the rejection of rationalist and materialist approaches as deplorable and atavistic. In particular, I deplore the failure to distinguish between ecological and economic determinism, which most social scientists — including Marxist ones — find unacceptable, and an appropriate consideration of the constraints which these factors exert on human behaviour. In my opinion the latter provides a solid framework within which to consider the operation of culturally specific factors.

It is still sometimes assumed, as was done frequently in the past, that native cultures were relatively impervious to European influences and that native peoples went on doing what they had done previously until they were overwhelmed by European settlement. The wars of the Iroquois are claimed to be a continuation of long-standing intertribal conflicts with only the scale and intensity increased as a result of the acquisition of guns. D. K. Richter (*William and Mary Quarterly* 43 [1986]: 480-3), Lucien Campeau (*La Mission des Jésuites chez les Hurons, 1634-1650* [1987]), and Conrad Heidenreich important motive for historical Iroquois warfare was the attempt to replace population losses resulting from epidemics of European diseases by capturing and incorporating other native groups in the same fashion that they had made good losses in warfare in prehistoric times. Yet it is by no means clear that this consideration was antithetical to or more important than economic ones. Francis Jennings (*The Ambiguous Iroquois Empire* [1984]), William Eccles (*William and Mary Quarterly* 43 [1983]: 480-3), Lucien Campeau (*La Mission des Jésuites chez les Hurons, 1634-1650* [1987]), and Conrad Heidenreich (*Native Studies Review* 2 [1986]: 140-7) go much further in their rejection of economic motives. They stress political considerations and suggest that the Iroquois were seeking to avenge old injuries or (in Jennings' case with British help) to build an empire in eastern North America. To varying degrees such interpretations mark a return to the position of Francis Parkman.

Eccles portrays native cultures as economically independent, resilient, and able to determine their own destinies until 1760. This is at least in part a reaction (although in my opinion an unjustifiably extreme one) against the

economic determinism of Hunt and Innis which is seen as portraying native peoples as the helpless victims of impersonal economic forces. Superficially this view appears to be supported by Hamell's conclusions about the symbolic rather than the utilitarian value that Indians appear to have attached to European trade goods in the sixteenth century. It is also supported by far more contentious arguments that Indians did not seek to profit from intertribal exchanges and that European goods continued to play a minor role in their lives. Today no one disagrees that trade between native peoples and Europeans was embedded in political alliances in the same fashion as was all intertribal trade. Yet the significance of these alliances appears to have varied considerably (Daniel Francis and Toby Morantz, *Partners in Furs: A History of the Fur Trade in Eastern James Bay, 1600-1870* [1983]). Research by Arthur Ray and Donald Freeman (*"Give Us Good Measure"* [1978]) has also refuted claims by Abraham Rotstein and others that native groups did not seek to maximize returns in exchanges with other tribes and with the Hudson's Bay Company, although the ways in which they negotiated the terms of trade differed from normal European forms of market exchange. In *Natives and Newcomers* I demonstrated that these conclusions also applied to trade between the French and native groups in the early seventeenth century. Despite this, idealist historians such as Eccles continue to maintain that native people did not seek to strike favourable bargains in intertribal trade.

The claim that native people did not become dependent on Europeans is also impossible to substantiate. By the beginning of the seventeenth century the superiority of European axes, knives, and other cutting tools over their native counterparts was universally recognized by the Indians of eastern North America. These were the principal items sought by Huron traders on their long and difficult journeys to the St. Lawrence Valley. Likewise, whatever the respective firepower of bows and arrows and guns, possession of the latter weapons conferred a great military advantage. By the 1630s the Hurons explicitly recognized their dependence on French goods and that this dependence constrained their freedom to deal with French missionaries and to conclude alliances with other tribes. Not all trade was for technologically valued goods and native knowledge of traditional technology disappeared more slowly than Hunt and those who followed him believed. Yet the growing dependence of native peoples on goods they could not learn to manufacture for themselves was a major factor rendering them dependent on Europeans. Their search for furs to exchange for these goods led to the depletion of game and ultimately to spiralling intertribal warfare. This is not to say that other factors, including traditional patterns of intertribal alliances and hostilities, did not play a role in shaping the behaviour of native peoples in

the historical period, although in many cases it is far from clear how far back into prehistoric times particular quarrels and alliances between native groups extended. For example, there are strong reasons to doubt that the Huron were at war with the Oneida and Mohawk prior to the seventeenth century. On the other hand, there is strong archaeological evidence of close contact, and therefore of the possibility of trade, between the Nipissing and the Ontario Iroquoians going back several centuries into prehistory. To ignore the importance of changing economic considerations is to lose sight of a key set of factors that transformed native life. It is also to ignore the intricacy of native responses to the pressures that were affecting their lives at this time. The image of Indians as impervious to European influences seems at variance not only with the facts but also with what is known about European contact with native peoples around the world (Eric Wolf, *Europe and the People without History* [1982]). While Parkman believed that Indians were too primitive and savage to change, his modern successors are romantically inclined to regard these peoples as too self-sufficient to have had to do so.

One of the most powerful manifestations of the neo-romantic bias in current ethnohistorical research is the growing importance ascribed to religious factors in bringing about cultural change. Ironically, however, most of these studies are anthropologically poorly informed, ethnocentric, and contemptuous of the spiritual resources of native cultures. W.H. McNeill in his book *Plagues and Peoples* (1976) and, far more influentially, Calvin Martin in *Keepers of the Game* (1978) have argued that major epidemics of European diseases undermined the faith that native Americans had in their traditional religions, leaving them open to spiritual conquest by Europeans. Martin also argued that the fur trade developed not as a result of native people desiring European goods but as a result of their declaring war on fur-bearing animals and seeking to exterminate them because they held animal spirits responsible for the epidemics. In *Indians, Animals and the Fur Trade* (1981), edited by Shepard Krech III, a panel of experts found little evidence to support the latter claim. This, combined with the weakness of Martin's reply, has done much to counteract widespread acceptance of his thesis of a "war against the animals."

Yet it is now widely believed that, by undermining the faith that native people had in the power of their traditional religions, early epidemics of European diseases played a major role in promoting the spread of Christianity. Christianity's emphasis on personal salvation and life after death are seen as better adapted to a calamitous mortality of this sort than were native religions with their allegedly greater emphasis on life in this world. Yet the research that I did for *The Children of Aataentsic* produced no evidence that Huron faith in their traditional religion was weakened by the epidemics of

1634 to 1640. On the contrary, this was a period of great innovation in terms of curing ceremonies. While individual rituals were abandoned when they proved ineffectual, new ones were invented which ultimately were credited with ending each of the epidemics. Despite the Jesuits' robust health, they and their teachings were not strengthened by the epidemics. The deaths of many baptised as well as unbaptised Hurons, and the missionaries' constant preaching about death, suggested that the Jesuits were sorcerers whose principal aim was to kill the Indians; hence the goal of the Hurons was to find a way to counteract their witchcraft.

The loss of many ritual specialists in the course of these epidemics may have been a serious blow to the Hurons and left them more vulnerable to ideological manipulation. Yet they were no less harmed by a loss of technical skills and political leadership. The main documentable motives for Huron conversions in the decade following these epidemics were economic ones, the promotion of alliances with the French, and the wish to obtain guns which were sold only to converts. Huron traders who were Christians received higher prices from the French for their furs and were treated with more respect than were traditionalists when they came to trade. As the Hurons turned increasingly to the Jesuits for food and protection against Iroquois attacks, many of them were baptised. Yet the Jesuits' experience among both the Huron and later the Iroquois supports A.W. Trelease's observation in *Indian Affairs in Colonial New York* (1960) that the true conversion of Indians depended "on their prior submission to the white man, with the attendant disintegration of their own culture" (p. 172). The Iroquoian data suggest the need for greater caution in assuming that native religions collapsed under the pressure of epidemics, leaving a spiritual vacuum which Christianity could fill. Native cultures appear to have been extraordinarily resilient in responding religiously and psychologically to devastating population loss.

Another trend has been to view conversion primarily as an intellectual process. Lucien Campeau (*La Mission des Jésuites chez les Hurons* [1987]) believes that already in the 1630s the Jesuits were conveying the essential meaning of Christianity to the Montagnais and the Hurons. Kenneth Morrison (*The Embattled Northeast* [1984]) and James Axtell (*The Invasion Within* [1985]) also share a belief in the intellectual and spiritual success of Jesuit conversions. Yet, however assiduously the case is argued, it is very difficult to ascertain what conversion actually meant to native people in the absence of direct documentation from the native side. It can be cynically suggested that what the Jesuits knew of their converts' thoughts and actions was generally only what the converts wished them to know. The Jesuits themselves seem to have been less sanguine about their success as missionaries than

their modern admirers. Even in their *Relations*, which were written to encourage spiritual and financial support in France for their work, their claims of success were frequently highly qualified. They hoped that if native people could be induced through constant persuasion, rewards, and punishments to speak and act like Christians they might eventually think and believe like Christians. Yet they understood the ambiguities involved in such a process of conversion and in their more reflective moments realized that only God could distinguish between true belief and the mere appearance of it. In their missions at Kahnawake and Lorette there were many more women and children than men, and the economic dependence of these Indians on the Jesuits made them anxious to please them. Even Huron and Iroquois chiefs and traders found it politically advantageous to be perceived as Christians since this strengthened their alliance with the French. Yet the Jesuits could never be certain what these Indians did behind their backs or what they actually believed. Gossip even called into question the conduct of Kateri Tekakwitha when she left Kahnawake to accompany a winter hunting party. It is surely significant that in the history of New France no Indian was ordained as a priest and only a few native women became nuns, some on their deathbeds.

There is no agreement about how accurate an understanding of Christian teaching the Jesuits managed to convey to their early converts, although many of them were highly proficient in native languages and had well-developed pedagogical skills. In 1672 the missionary Jean de Lamberville stated that it was impossible to evangelize Indians or to teach them to think like French people because they could not reason properly as do "the Chinese and other civilized nations." The Iroquoians were born into egalitarian societies in which one human being did not have the right to give orders to another, and even parents did not command obedience from their children. Christianity, in contrast, was the creation of monarchical societies and obedience to God and to his earthly representatives within society and the family was central to its teaching. It is by no means certain that the Jesuits or any other Christian missionaries were able to make their doctrines comprehensible to people who lived in self-sufficient tribal societies. It can be argued that the meaning of Christianity only became clear to native people as they were absorbed into the lower echelons of European societies and as a result of this process learned the meaning of concepts such as authority and obedience. Anthropologists such as David Blanchard (*Anthropologica* 24 [1982]: 77-102) suggest that even after this happened the Iroquois at Kahnawake continued for a long time to perceive Christianity largely in terms of their own religious concepts rather than on its own terms. The problem remains that we do not have independent documentation of native perceptions that

would permit a resolution of this problem. In the absence of such knowledge, caution against making exaggerated claims about Jesuit successes or failures seems essential.

One of the best ways available to determine what was happening is to look at the circumstances under which native people converted to Christianity. As documented in *The Children of Aataentsic* and mentioned above, these include economic necessity, the search for economic gain, a desire to secure guns not otherwise available, and a need for protection against enemies. Joseph Chihwatenha, a model convert whose activities are described in the Jesuit *Relations* of the 1630s, may have been seeking to become a sorcerer by acquiring the malevolent powers of life and death which he believed that the Jesuits, as sorcerers or supernatural spirits, possessed. This evidence strongly suggests that spiritual conviction based on an adequate understanding of what Christianity meant to Europeans was not always a primary factor in inducing native people to act as Christians. A sensitive and sensible evaluation of mission work is provided in J. W. Grant's *Moon of Wintertime: Missionaries and the Indians of Canada in Encounter since 1534* (1984).

The essence of historical scholarship is open-mindedness, but not to such a degree that every shift in academic fashion results in new interpretations of the past, whether or not these are warranted by the available data. Since I wrote *The Children of Aataentsic*, scholars such as Hamell and Steckley have pioneered analytical techniques that have produced insights that are relevant for understanding Huron culture. Yet their findings so far do not require major changes in my interpretation of Huron history. The other challenges come not from new sources of data but from changing popular views about the nature of human behaviour. For the most part these interpretations have taken the form either of examinations of specific issues, such as conversion, for specific societies or of broad surveys involving many different native societies. I would attribute what I see as the continuing strength of my interpretation of Huron history not to the theoretical assumptions that I outlined at the beginning of this preface but to my choosing to examine a single, well-documented situation in very great historical detail. In my analyses of what happened to the Huron, I tried to correlate data concerning every aspect of Huron life in an effort to develop a detailed contextual understanding of what was happening. In the course of doing this I discovered repeatedly that what from one perspective seemed to be a solid interpretation of data could not be sustained in a broader context. It is on the basis of this contextual analysis that I continue to feel equipped to defend my interpretations of Huron history against the changing academic fashions of the past decade. I do not claim that my interpretations are immune to change, but at present I do not see

new data or demonstrations of flaws in my arguments that require more than minor adjustments. I further interpret this situation as independent evidence of the usefulness of the theoretical principles that have guided my work. While I believe that I was correct in rejecting the untenable concepts of ecological and economic determinism, I remain convinced of the viability of a more sophisticated materialist approach for explaining important aspects of human behaviour and, in particular, for accounting for the fundamental dynamics of contacts between European and Amerindian cultures.

Finally, one more burgeoning field of research deserves to be noted. In *The Children of Aataentsic* I considered the possibility that epidemics of European diseases had afflicted the Huron prior to 1634 but decided that there was no compelling evidence this was so; hence my estimates of pre-contact populations were based on the reports of Champlain, Sagard, and the Jesuits before 1634. Recently various individuals have challenged this conclusion. In particular Henry Dobyns (*Their Number Become Thinned* [1983]) has argued that beginning as early as 1520 epidemics of European diseases dramatically reduced the population of most of North America, including the Iroquoian region. Attempts are currently being made to determine whether or not this was so through the archaeological study of settlement patterns and the physical anthropological investigation of human remains. While no conclusive answer has emerged, the present archaeological evidence seems to suggest stability in Iroquoian population during the sixteenth century.

All books reflect the era in which they were written and to that extent are hostages to the future. It is evident that I do not regard the past decade as one of undiluted progress in social and humanistic studies. Whether this assessment is correct or I am falling victim to time remains to be determined. I hope that in the future I can continue to welcome solid new evidence, even if it contradicts my own work and the ideas that I cherish.

McGill University   B.G.T.
February 1987

Preface to the First Edition

This book is the product of nine years of intermittent study and research, followed by another five years during which almost all of my time not devoted to teaching and administration has been employed in writing it. My interest in the subject was aroused early in 1960 when, as a newly arrived graduate student at Yale University, nostalgia for Canada led me to write a long paper on French-Huron contact for a course on culture change offered by Professor E. M. Bruner. During my research, I sought to learn as much as possible about the Huron from primary rather than secondary sources. Using the facilities of the Sterling Library, I managed to survey a vast amount of literature in what now seems to have been a remarkably short period of time. The result was a paper titled "The Destruction of Huronia: A Study in Economic and Cultural Change, 1609-1650." On the kind recommendation of the late Professor T. F. McIlwraith of the University of Toronto, this paper was soon published (1960). The favourable reception it received encouraged me to continue my interest in the Huron. While further research has led me to modify many of the ideas I expressed in that paper, it constitutes a brief prototype of all but chapters 1, 3, and 4 of the present work.

During later years as a graduate student at Yale I wrote two more papers that reflected my continuing interest in the Huron. The first was on an ecological theme ("Settlement as an Aspect of Iroquoian Adaptation at the Time of Contact" [1963b]; reprinted in B. Cox, ed., *Cultural Ecology: Readings on the Canadian Indians and Eskimos*. Toronto: McClelland and Stewart, 1973, pp. 35-53) and was written for a course on the prehistory of eastern North America given by Professor Michael D. Coe; the second was "Order and Freedom in Huron Society" (1963a; reprinted in M. Nagler, ed., *Perspectives on the North American Indians*. Toronto: McClelland and Stewart, 1972, pp. 43-56) for a course on the Anthropology of Law by Professor L. J. Pospisil. Both of these papers are essentially ethnographic. About the same time, I wrote a paper on "The Historic Location of the Hurons" (1962a) in which I challenged the traditional idea that the Huron had settled in the north as refugees from the Iroquois. During this period, my awareness of the importance of ethnohistory and of developments in Iroquoian studies was strengthened by my informal contacts with William N. Fenton and Elisabeth Tooker,

both of whom did much to encourage and guide me towards the present study.

Although I turned primarily to other topics in my final years as a graduate student, my interest in the Huron continued and later became more specific when I was asked to read a paper on "The Jesuits and the Fur Trade" (1965) at the Huron Symposium held in Orillia, Ontario, 30 January 1965, to mark to 350th anniversary of Champlain's visit to that region. It was while preparing the final draft of that paper that I conceived the idea of writing a book-length history of the Huron, covering the same general subject matter as the present work.

I was aware, however, that much more research was needed before such a book could be begun. I therefore welcomed the opportunity to collaborate with James F. Pendergast in a major study of the unpublished Dawson site; long alleged to be Cartier's Hochelaga. The principal outcome of this project was the publication of J. F. Pendergast and B. G. Trigger, *Cartier's Hochelaga and the Dawson Site* (1972), to which my own contribution, "Hochelaga: History and Ethnohistory", was a review of what is known about the history of the St. Lawrence Valley during the sixteenth century. This revived an earlier interest that had led to my publication of "Trade and Tribal Warfare on the St. Lawrence in the Sixteenth Century" (1962b). Before the final report appeared I published a number of papers related to this topic: "Who were the 'Laurentian Iroquois'?" (*Canadian Review of Sociology and Anthropology*, 3 [1966]: 201-13); "Archaeological and other Evidence: A Fresh Look at the 'Laurentian Iroquois'" (1968a); "Criteria for Identifying the Locations of Historic Indian Sites: A Case Study from Montreal" (1969b); as well as a general review of Iroquoian prehistory, "The Strategy of Iroquoian Prehistory" (1970). Chapter 4 and sections of chapter 3 are résumés and extensions of the work of this period.

About this time I was also persuaded to write *The Huron: Farmers of the North* (1969a), in which I attempted a functional interpretation of traditional Huron culture. I wrote that book mainly to deepen my own understanding of Huron ways. That book constitutes the basis for the briefer, but even more sharply focused, account of Huron life in chapter 2 of this book. I also published a study of Iroquoian warfare, "Settlement Archaeology—Its Goals and Promise" (1967), and another study of French-Huron relations, incorporating a significant re-interpretation of the later period, "The French Presence in Huronia: The Structure of Franco-Huron Relations in the First Half of the Seventeenth Century" (1968b). The latter paper was a pilot study aimed at planning the historical chapters of this book. During that period, a grant from the French Canada Studies Programme of McGill University permitted

Miss A. E. Clark to carry out some statistical analyses of the *Jesuit Relations* under my direction. These studies were useful in clarifying the extent of Jesuit knowledge of Huron society in each given year of the Huron mission.

Finally, in June 1968 I received sabbatical leave from McGill University and, with the assistance of a Canada Council Leave Fellowship, spent the following year in England and France reading and analysing source material. This period of study and reflection served greatly to advance my understanding of Huron history. After a further year of research, during which I wrote papers on two specialized historical topics, "Champlain Judged by his Indian Policy: A Different View of Early Canadian History" (1971*a*) and "The Mohawk-Mahican War (1624-28): The Establishment of a Pattern" (1971*c*), I began writing the present book in September 1970 and reached chapter 5 by the following summer. During the following twelve months the first draft of the remaining chapters was finished. I was aided at this time by a Killam Award of the Canada Council which permitted me to be on half-time leave from teaching duties at McGill. This allowed a degree of concentration which gave greater continuity to my draft than would otherwise have been possible. During the following year, the final draft of the text was completed.

Since my interpretations of many events in Huron history have altered in the course of writing this book, the present study should be regarded as superseding all my earlier published works whenever the two disagree. In particular, chapters 7 to 12 are not simply expansions of my major 1960 and 1968*b* papers but are often at variance with them. This is largely because of my abandonment of the McIlwain-Innis-Hunt interpretation of the wars of the Iroquois as being a struggle to control middleman positions.

The theoretical orientation of the book is discussed in detail in the Introduction and little more need be said about it here. I stress, however, that my aim has been to write a history of the Huron, not of New France or of French-Indian relations in the seventeenth century. My efforts to explain Huron history have required that I re-interpret the actions of various Europeans in eastern Canada in the sixteenth and seventeenth centuries. These, however, are only a by-product of my research.

In matters respecting the Huron, I do not apologize for detailed citing of the evidence on which I have based my conclusions. Since much of this evidence will be unfamiliar to most readers, its omission seems undesirable. Nor do I apologize for including specific information about Huron individuals whom historians might not consider to be of sufficient importance to merit such treatment. Given the limitations of the data, such information is often of great value for substantiating my arguments.

In chapters 8 to 12 I have restricted my comments about the Jesuits to

what is necessary to understand the influence they exerted on the Huron. I have deliberately eschewed allowing these chapters to become a history of the Jesuit missionaries in the Huron country or enquiring into the broader aims and strategies of the Jesuit Order in international politics. Instead I have tried to understand the motives of the Jesuits who were part of the Huron mission and who were engaged in trying to influence these Indians.

Whatever merit the book has results from the presentation of familiar data from a new point of view. I have not undertaken extensive archival research, but have re-examined the voluminous published sources on the Huron, most of which have been familiar to historians for many years. To attempt to search out the small residue of unpublished documents that might shed light on the Huron would have consumed time better put to other uses and have needlessly repeated the work of skilled archivists.

The decision to write a long book was not taken lightly. Originally, I had planned to write a shorter, more popular work; however, I decided that if detailed explanations were not provided and alternative theories eliminated, the book would offer too many challenges to historians and anthropologists to engage in needless debate. There could only be a proper discussion of my work if I explained my lines of reasoning in detail. I am grateful to Robert Vogel for encouraging me to adopt the longer format and to the press for having been indulgent enough to undertake the publication of a work of this length.

Certain idiosyncrasies deserve explanation. Readers will be surprised to find that the familiar term "Huronia" has been suppressed in favour of "the Huron country." The former term has the disadvantage of implying that what was primarily a tribally constituted unit had a territorial basis. Similar toponyms are not generally applied to corresponding ethnic units among the North American Indians (except the analogous "Iroquoia" for "the Iroquois country"). I have also generally replaced the ambiguous word "chief" with the anthropological term "headman," except when referring to war chiefs. French personal names are given in the form in which they appear in the *Dictionary of Canadian Biography*, even when this departs from common usage. In the absence of a generally recognized authority on Huron phonology, I have not attempted to spell Huron personal names according to any system but have contented myself to sticking to a single form for each name, usually that preferred by the DCB or by R. G. Thwaites. For the sake of consistency I have omitted the diacritics that were sometimes used in writing Huron names, beginning in the 1640s. Where source material is published both in the original language and in English translation in the same volume, I have avoided the affectation of citing pages only in the original. This applies even

to quotations, which are generally my own translation. Care has been taken to check standard translations and any significant discrepancies between them and the originals are noted in the text or notes. While every effort has been made to keep abreast of the burgeoning published literature, the size of the book has made it impossible to do this up to the time of publication. Few references were added after the completion of the final draft of the manuscript in May 1973, while active research, especially on the earlier parts, ended about a year earlier.

In keeping with internationally accepted usage, the term Iroquois refers only to the confederated Five Nations of upper New York State: the Mohawk, Oneida, Onondaga, Cayuga, and Seneca. The term Iroquoian is reserved for the broader linguistic grouping to which they, the Huron, and many other tribes belonged. Likewise, Algonkin refers specifically to the tribal grouping that inhabited the Ottawa Valley and adjacent regions early in the seventeenth century, while Algonkian refers to a more widespread linguistic grouping to which the Algonkin belonged.

For help in clarifying various issues I wish to thank C. E. Heidenreich, A. Cameron, William N. Fenton, C. Garrad, Max Gluckman, K. E. Kidd, R. Klibansky, W. Noble, J. F. Pendergast, P. P. Pratt, M. Trudel, J. A. Tuck, M. E. White, and others. For her assistance with maps and her generous hospitality I wish to thank Monique de La Roncière of the Bibliothèque Nationale, Paris. The theoretical section of chapter 3, dealing with the evolution of Iroquoian social structure, has benefited from the comments of F. G. Lounsbury and others following presentation to a seminar at Yale University 3 May 1971 and to the 1972 Iroquois Conference. For his encouragement, I also owe much to the late Robin Strachan, director of the McGill-Queen's University Press.

I wish to thank Jeanette Fernandez and Sheila Masson for the care and industry with which they typed the final version of the manuscript; H. W. Castner and the Cartographic Laboratory of Queen's University for preparing the final versions of maps; and Sylvia Haugo and A. C. Crouch of the staff of McGill–Queen's Press for editorial and production work. It remains to thank my wife (to whom along with our children this book is dedicated) for bearing patiently with the enormous demands that this book has made on my time ever since we were married.

Chapter 1  Introduction

Aims

When I began this book, I intended to write a straightforward account of the Huron Indians during the early years of their contact with Europeans. The materials for such a study are well known and have provided the basis for numerous biographical and historical accounts, many of considerable merit. These studies have concentrated largely, however, on the activities of European priests, traders, and government officials among the Huron between 1610 and 1650, rather than on the Huron themselves. I believed therefore that these materials offered an exceptional opportunity to make a detailed study of the effects that contact with Europeans had on one of the native peoples of North America. I found, however, that my objectives, although they seemed modest at first, required more work than I had anticipated. This taught me the truth of Léo-Paul Desrosiers's (1947a:8) observation that "of all types of writing, history is the one that requires the most time." It also became apparent that the network of intertribal relations that existed at the period of European contact, and which became more complex and extensive with the development of the fur trade, made it impossible to view French-Huron relations in isolation from, or even merely against the background of, events taking place in other parts of eastern North America. Nor was it possible to fill in the extra information that was required from existing historical studies.

The more I examined the relations between different tribes and different groups of Europeans, the more I became aware of the many aspects of these relationships which historians had not adequately taken into account. Hence this study has become a reassessment of the history of this whole region between 1600 and 1650. It is, however, a reassessment in which events are interpreted from a Huron perspective rather than from a French or Dutch one, as is usually the case. It also became apparent that a study of this sort requires not only the care and thoroughness of a professional historian in the use of written documents, but also new methods to tackle problems of interpretation of a sort rarely encountered by historians and to take account of kinds of data that historians usually ignore. Although the

present study is only one contribution among many to the rapidly developing field of Amerindian history,[1] in some ways it is sufficiently novel that a
general discussion of its orientation and methods seems desirable. This
Introduction is intended to provide a record of the ideas which guided me
in writing this book and of the problems I encountered.

Historians and Canadian Indians

The important role that the Indians have played in Canadian history has
long been recognized. In his influential study of the fur trade, published in
1930, the economist Harold Innis (rev. ed. 1956:392) stated that "the
Indian and his culture were fundamental to the growth of Canadian
institutions," while, the same year, his colleague in anthropology, T. F.
McIlwraith (1930:132), argued that "an accurate interpretation of the first
two hundred years of Canadian history must take cognizance of the Indian
point of view as well as that of the white man." Moving beyond his pro-
grammatic statement, Innis clearly outlined for the first time the importance of the fur trade in the development of modern Canada and investigated
the role that the Indians had played in this trade. Innis's book laid the
foundations of the so-called "Laurentian hypothesis," which was to have
the same kind of impact on Canadian historiography that F. J. Turner's
frontier hypothesis had on that of the United States. Innis viewed Canada
as a political entity originally defined by the fur trade, which had penetrated the northern interior of the continent by way of the St. Lawrence
River and its tributaries.[2]

One of the long-term benefits of this theory was that it stressed the
important role played by the Indians in the European settlement and early
growth of Canada. Historians now generally recognize that long before the
arrival of the Europeans the Indians had adapted to the harsh Canadian
environment; hence, although they lacked the iron tools and elaborate
technology of the newcomers, they were able to teach Europeans many
things. From the Indians, the French learned how to manage and later how
to construct canoes, which made travel through the north possible in
summer. From the Indians they also adopted sleds, snowshoes, and items
of clothing that permitted them to cope with the Canadian winter. Indians
taught the French how to make maple sugar, plant maize and other Indian
crops, recognize what wild plants could be eaten or used for medicine, and

to hunt animals whose habits were unfamiliar to Europeans (Trudel 1966*a*:376–84). Many young Frenchmen went to live and trade with the Indians and, to the dismay of colonial officials, many of them came to prefer this to living amongst their own people.

It is also clear that relations between Indians and Europeans in early Canada were very different from those farther south. In the United States, the most coveted possession of the Indian was his land. The British government's recognition, in 1763, of Indian tribes as independent nations, and its insistence that their land could not be occupied by white settlers unless it had first been voluntarily ceded to the Crown, was one of the major grievances leading to the revolt of the American colonies. After the American revolution, the Indians over whom American hegemony extended were killed, driven westward, or herded onto reservations. Those who became despondent under white tutelage were regarded as hopeless degenerates, while those who fought to keep their land were pictured as blood-thirsty savages whom civilized men had the duty either to tame or to exterminate. For almost a century, scarcely a year went by in which the American army was not engaged in this task of subjugation (Spencer, Jennings et al. 1965:497–506).

Canada, on the other hand, was principally a region of boreal forest, too cold to invite extensive European settlement, but rich in fur-bearing animals and laced with lakes and rivers that made the transportation of furs from the hinterland to coastal markets relatively easy. It was far easier for the white man to buy these furs from experienced Indian trappers than to hunt for them himself; hence, as long as furs remained abundant and fetched a good price on European markets, a symbiotic relationship linked the Indian hunter and the European trader. It is significant that not once was there a case of serious or prolonged conflict between Europeans and Indians living within the borders of Canada.[3] On the contrary, for a long time Indians and white men were allies in the common defence of Canada against first British, then American, invaders. This is not to say that once the Canadian Indians ceased to be a valuable economic asset, the treatment they received was any less shameful than was that meted out to Indians in the United States; one might even argue that, given the nature of earlier relations, it was worse. It is clear, however, that for a long time relations between Indians and whites in the territory on, and bordering, the Canadian Shield were very different from what they were in the United States. This difference is familiar to historians and anthropologists, but has not sufficiently been drawn to the attention of the Canadian public, whose

image of the Indian has been nourished by generations of American news-papers and magazines, and, in recent times by radio, television, and imported textbooks.

Only a few historical studies have as their central theme to explain what has happened to Canadian Indians since the Europeans first arrived in the New World. In 1937, Alfred G. Bailey published his pioneering study of relations between Europeans and Algonkians in eastern Canada prior to 1700. Unfortunately this book did not receive the attention that it deserved and did not stimulate more specific historical research.[4] Professor Bailey's work on the Canadian Indians reflects an interdisciplinary point of view, which was nourished by his contacts with Innis and McIlwraith while he was studying at the University of Toronto. Another important pioneering work was Volume 1 of Léo-Paul Desrosiers's (1947*a*) *Iroquoisie*, which attempts to explain political relations between the Iroquois, the French, and the latter's Indian allies down to 1646. Even in recent decades, titles have not greatly proliferated. George F. Stanley (1952) has published an important paper on "The Indian Background of Canadian History," while Wilson Duff (1964) has published Volume 1 of *The Indian History of British Columbia*, which deals with the impact of the white man. Most recently, E. P. Patterson (1972) has published a general outline of Canadian Indian history, which he argues must be treated as a subject in its own right, rather than as an adjunct of white history.[5] Unfortunately, none of these studies has considered the major methodological problems that are associated with the investigation of Indian history, or attempted to resolve them. Because of this, Indians continue to languish on the peripheries of professional Canadian historiography.

Because so much Canadian historical writing has been in the form of biographies (Soroko 1966), historians have tended to concentrate on well-known Europeans, rather than on the small number of Indians about whom personal data have been recorded. All too often, Indians have been viewed, both collectively and individually, less as actors on the stage of Canadian history than as part of the natural setting against which this action has taken place. Unconsciously, an active role tends to be reserved for the country's European settlers. Nowhere is this tendency better illustrated than in the well-intentioned, but ill-informed and badly integrated, sketches of the Indian tribes of Canada which preface so many general studies of Canadian history. Even when individual Indians, such as Pontiac or Tecumseh, feature prominently in historical accounts, relatively little attention is paid to what motivated them, so that their actions remain incomprehensible and quixotic. Because of this, Indians who acted contrary

to French or English interests are unwittingly rendered sinister and alien, while those who are treated sympathetically turn out suspiciously like the honourable, but imperfect Orientals who serve white interests in the novels of Rudyard Kipling.

Even worse, when careful research has demonstrated the falseness of certain interpretations of events in which the role of Indians has been grossly distorted to accommodate it to European stereotypes, historians often find it impossible to make the clear break with the past that these findings require. Adam Dollard and his companions now may be generally recognized by historians as having died in an effort, not to save New France, but to rob a party of Iroquois hunters of their winter catch. Yet in spite of this, historians continue to argue that this fight was " as heroic and necessary as legend has made it, for without furs New France could not live" (Morton 1963:52).

These deficiencies are not basically the fault of historians, who are accustomed to work with cultures that have long traditions of literacy. Rather, they reflect the difficulties that confront the application of conventional historical methods to the study of the Canadian Indian. These methods were devised to facilitate the use of written documents to study the past history of the society that produced them. In dealing with recent European history, the historian shares enough common cultural background with those he studies that an assessment of their hopes, aspirations, and values can usually be made on the basis of common sense. Occasionally, as, for example, in studies of European witchcraft, historians may seek theoretical guidance for their interpretations from anthropological studies of similar phenomena in contemporary societies (Macfarlane 1970), although some historians entertain doubts about this as a proper mode of analysis. Where specialized knowledge concerning technological, economic, or other matters is required, this can be derived from numerous other disciplines concerned primarily with Western civilization. Even historians who study Chinese, Hindu, or other non-Western, but literate, societies are able from the indigenous literature of these societies to acquire sufficient knowledge of them, or at least of what Robert Redfield (1956) has called their great traditions, to be able to evaluate records and behaviour in a highly informed manner.

When the historian studies the Canadian Indian, however, he is dealing with people who possessed no written records of their own and with ways of life that not only developed totally independently from those of Europe, but which also fall outside the normal range of cultural variation with which he is familiar. The native peoples of Canada were few in number and

mostly lived in small, widely dispersed groupings. As in all small-scale societies, activities of a public nature lacked the highly institutionalized and hierarchical character found in technologically more complex societies. On the contrary, these activities tended to be embedded in, or were extensions of, a basic kinship system.

The differences between large-scale and small-scale societies are sufficiently great that an historian's experience and personal judgement are not enough to permit him unaided to come to terms with the ideas and values that were a part of the Indians' way of life prior to the coming of the Europeans. Unless the historian is able to acquire elsewhere sufficient knowledge of the beliefs and values of the people he is studying, he is unable to evaluate the European sources which constitute the principal record that we have of these people. Lacking such knowledge, he is further unable to transcend the prejudices and limitations of his sources and to evaluate them in the rigorous manner with which historians wish to deal with all written material. It is precisely because most historians lack such knowledge that the Indian does not come alive in their writings, no matter how sympathetic and well-intentioned they may be. The historian's dilemma is thus the lack of a technique which will permit an understanding of Indian ways without having records written by the Indians.

Indeed, in the absence of documents written by Indians, some historians have come to the fatalistic conclusion that white documents make white history. A similar, though more considered pessimism is embodied in E. S. Spicer's (1962:22) assertion that "until well into the nineteenth century the records [in the southwestern United States] are nearly mute on the subject of Indian viewpoints and feelings about the transformation being wrought in their lives." The conclusion that Indian history is not feasible has been reinforced by two further assumptions, which are to some degree interrelated.

The more romantic argument, and one that is now shared only by those who know little about the American Indian, is that Indian cultures changed so little during the centuries prior to the arrival of the Europeans that, in effect, the Indian has no history of his own. The changes that have come about since are held to be the result of white influence and therefore best discussed from the viewpoint of European history. Such ahistorical views of non-Western peoples have been held by many anthropologists, as well as historians,[6] and they have a variety of aetiologies. Anthropologists, in particular, have been prone to what may be called "the Garden of Eden syndrome"; they tend to attribute static qualities to simpler cultures and see in their equilibrium evidence of a successful adaptation to their environ-

ment, and to one another, that contrasts with the conflict and confusion of modern industrial societies. The alternative explanation blamed the static nature of Amerindian societies on the natural inferiority of the Indians. In the last century, it was widely believed that Indians were incapable of acquiring more than a thin veneer of civilization. It was even argued that they would perish under the impact of European civilization, unless they were kept on reservations where, under white supervision, a semblance of their old ways of life could be maintained.[7]

Archaeological evidence demonstrates clearly the degree to which this static view of Indian prehistory is a figment of ill-informed imaginations. Because Canadian Indians lived in one of the harshest environments in the world, they were always relatively few in number and lacked the opportunities for cultural development that in better climes culminated in the brilliant indigenous civilizations that flourished in Mexico and Peru until the Spanish conquest. It is clear, however, that even in Canada there was a gradual improvement in the Indians' adaptation to their environment. The introduction of new items of technology, such as the bow and arrow, permitted hunting bands to exploit game more effectively and the same territory to support larger numbers of people. In the far north, successive waves of Eskimo adapted themselves with remarkable skill to an extremely demanding environment, while along the coasts of British Columbia, Indians harnessed rich, but fluctuating, natural food resources to support a way of life characterized by a concern with social status, elaborate art, and ritual. In southern Ontario, in the centuries preceding the arrival of the Europeans, the Iroquoian-speaking peoples abandoned a hunting and gathering economy in favour of a sedentary way of life based on growing corn, beans, and squash. However imperfect they may be, these archaeological indices provide evidence of social change and, along with evidence of cultural diffusion and population movements, show clearly that the aboriginal cultures of Canada were far from being inherently static prior to the arrival of the Europeans.[8]

Other historians, in particular C. H. McIlwain (1915) and George T. Hunt (1940), have not specifically denied that changes went on in Indian societies prior to the arrival of the Europeans. They have argued, however, that knowledge of such changes is totally irrelevant for an understanding of subsequent events; once Indians depended on trade goods, they became entangled in a network of trading relations and intertribal competition that was fashioned by economic self-interest, rather than by any traditional modes of thought or behaviour. These new economic imperatives transformed the lives of the Indians so thoroughly and so quickly as to make any

understanding of their previous behaviour unnecessary. Hunt argued that anything that the Indians did late enough to be recorded by Europeans can be interpreted in terms of the commercial logic of the fur trade.

Contact with Europeans undoubtedly quickly altered Indian life and Indian policy; on the other hand, old relationships have a powerful habit of influencing events, even when economic and political conditions are changing rapidly. Many anthropologists have objected to Hunt's "economic determinism" and have argued that traditional values and the relationships existing before the time of European contact played an important role in the development of Indian-white relations and of the fur trade (Snyderman 1948; Trelease 1960). These studies have shown many interpretations based upon Hunt's assumptions to be inaccurate and have demonstrated that traditional cultural patterns played as important a role in influencing interaction among the various groups in eastern North America as did economic self-interest. Indeed, economic interests were rarely perceived by such groups independently of these biases. Nancy O. Lurie (1959:37) has suggested that, as a general principle, Indians "made their first adjustments to Europeans in terms of existing native conditions." Recent studies have reciprocally demonstrated that the traditional values of Europeans often hindered their rational economic exploitation of Indian groups. In particular, Raoul Naroll (1969) has argued that the extreme concern of most French soldiers and administrators to safeguard their dignity was responsible for otherwise needless conflict with the Iroquois.

The inability to avoid a discussion of the important role played by the Indians in early Canadian history, combined with the lack of any method that permits this role to be studied adequately, has helped to perpetuate many unsatisfactory practices. Sometimes, well-meaning authors merely repeat the prejudices of their sources or, worse still, those of nineteenth-century commentators. Thus, the Jesuit author of a highly praised biography of Jean de Brébeuf has referred to Huron sexual behaviour as a "sewer of sexual filth" practised by "animalized savages." He also states that Huron women were "drudges from infancy," but nevertheless "were more untamed than the men, quicker to anger, more snarling in their insults, more savage in vengeance, more frenzied in times of trial" (Talbot 1956:67). These descriptions perpetuate stereotypes rather than contribute towards a genuine understanding either of the Huron or of their relations with the Jesuits.

Among the more lamentable results of such an approach is the tendency to judge tribes according to whether or not they served the interests of the particular European group the historian happens to be studying, or for

whom he feels sympathy. Thus, even today, in some uncritical writings the Huron are painted as a docile, peaceful people, almost pre-formed for an exemplary Christian life, while their Iroquois opponents are driven on by an insensate fury and a lust for blood and conquest.[9] In others, particularly those whose authors are staunchly anti-French or anti-Roman Catholic, the Huron have been represented as weaklings and cowards who fell under the influence of the Jesuits, while the Iroquois, though cruel, are admired for their energy and resourcefulness (Parkman 1867). Unfortunately, because stereotypes of this sort can be absorbed so easily, they bulk large in popular histories and school texts. It is disgraceful that in influential works of this type Indian history should be so inadequately treated. Yet, until detailed studies provide the basis for a better popularization of Indian history, one can only hope to eliminate the grossest distortions of this type from such publications.

This simplistic dichotomy between good and bad, brave and cowardly is all the more pervasive because it reflects the two contrasting images of the Indian that have long dominated the white man's thinking about them. The first stereotype, that of the Indian as a bloodthirsty savage who delights in scalping and slaughter, was dominant in the minds of the land-grabbing colonists of the Atlantic seaboard, and was reinforced as the wave of American colonization spread westward. The opposite view, that of the "noble savage" can first be detected in the writings of Michel de Montaigne and, while chiefly popular in the salons of Europe, was shared by at least some of the influential Frenchmen who came to know the Indians firsthand through the Canadian fur trade. In the independence and self-reliance of the Indian, disenchanted Europeans saw a way of life untainted by the ambition, dishonesty, and self-indulgence that they had convinced themselves were the inevitable consequences of civilization (Spencer, Jennings, et al. 1965: 595–97).

While both of these stereotypes continue to affect most writers' views of the Indian, it is perhaps indicative of the current vogue for sentimentality that today it is generally the latter view which prevails. Indeed, this is the view of the Indian past that many Indians, including Indian writers, seem to prefer (e.g., Newell 1965). Nevertheless, it must be remembered that such a view portrays the Indians of the past, not as they were, but according to the white man's ideal of what a "primitive" people should be like. Features attractive to white tastes are emphasized, while others, which are less attractive or even repugnant to them are either glossed over or suppressed. Polygamy, scalping, the torture of prisoners, and the abandonment of elderly and ailing members of a band were all customs practised by

various groups of aboriginal Canadians. They are customs which, when carefully examined, prove not to have been irrational or immoral in terms of the context in which they occurred. Under the influence of white culture, many present-day Indians have been made to feel ashamed of these ancestral practices to the point that they deny they ever existed. Yet surely to ignore or distort important aspects of aboriginal Indian life to make it more acceptable to European tastes is to fail in the understanding of Indian history. The bloodthirsty savage, the noble savage, and all the corollaries that are derived from these stereotypes are products of European imagination and wishful thinking, rather than delineations of real people. While such stereotypes may at one time have been useful as propaganda for or against the Indians, neither view results in an improved understanding of them or of the role they have played in Canadian history. On the contrary, both do considerable harm, because they excuse the historian from attempting to explain the behaviour of individual Indians, or groups of them, in the same detail in which he would attempt to explain the actions of Europeans.

As early as the eighteenth century, attempts were made to explain the behaviour of Indians in biological terms. The reticence among many tribes for men and women to flirt openly, which we now know was part of a general reluctance to display emotions publicly, was once interpreted as evidence of a weak sex drive resulting from unfavourable climatic influences.[10] In the latter part of the nineteenth century there was a marked predilection for racial explanations of cultural differences (Harris 1968:80–107) and such ideas strongly influenced historians' conceptions of the North American Indians. These ideas were discounted, as early as 1862, by the Canadian anthropologist Daniel Wilson (1862, 2:327–90) and today they command no support whatsoever among reputable biologists and anthropologists. Yet in spite of this, antiquated ideas of this sort continue to contaminate historical writing in Canada. Recently, after documenting the valuable role played by the Indians in the European colonization of Canada, Gustave Lanctot (1963:330) commented that the lack of intermarriage between French and Indians during the colonial period "was probably better...for the colony, for the [French Canadian] race grew stronger being free of native cross-breeding." Since then, W. L. Morton (1963:60–61) has stated that "in settled New France there was practically no intermarriage with the Indians, and New France was spared that mixture of blood which led to so many complications in Spanish America." The downgrading of the Indians' natural abilities arises only from a crassly materialistic assessment of their way of life and hence from the inability of

historians to perceive the beliefs and values that motivated them, individually and in groups. We thus return to a problem of method.

Ethnohistory and the Role of Anthropology

The problem is how information recorded by early European colonists can be used to study the history of the Canadian Indians, not merely from a white man's point of view, but with the sympathetic understanding that historians seek to bring to every situation that they investigate. It is clear that insofar as it is possible at all, given the materials at our disposal, the achievement of this kind of understanding requires an interdisciplinary approach in which both history and anthropology play a part. It is also clear that the failure to bridge this gap is largely a result of the general failure, until recently, of Canadian anthropologists to concern themselves with problems that involve using written documents. For the most part, these anthropologists have devoted their energies to the study either of Indian prehistory, by means of archaeology, or of living native peoples within Canada. Significant ethnological research began in 1884, when the British Association for the Advancement of Science appointed a committee to report on the anthropology of the tribes of British Columbia. For fourteen years, grants were provided which enabled studies to be carried out by Franz Boas, A. F. Chamberlain, and others.[11] Most of these early studies were concerned with recording aboriginal ways of life as they were remembered by old people who had grown up in more or less traditional cultures, which they had then seen fall apart as a result of European interference. Even so, their memories rarely took the anthropologist back much before 1850, by which time most Indian peoples had been considerably altered by European contact. More recent ethnological studies are concerned almost exclusively with alterations that have come about since the Indians were first studied by ethnologists, and hence cast little light on the more remote past. The result has been to leave a gap in our knowledge of the Indian between the prehistoric period, studied by the archaeologist, and the recent period, studied by the ethnologist. If either the anthropologist or the historian is to understand how Indian life has changed in the intervening years, this gap is going to have to be filled by means of historically orientated research.

Being trained in the techniques of excavation or interviewing living peoples, most anthropologists have felt themselves ill-equipped to undertake the detailed historical study of changes in Indian life since the first

written records became available. They believe that such work should be done by professional historians; a view that is reinforced by the anthropologist's traditional view of himself as a "field worker" rather than a "library researcher." [12] This is especially true when it comes to locating and handling unpublished archival material, a chore that few anthropologists enjoy and even fewer have been trained to do. In addition, the anthropologist usually knows little about the complex economic and political relationships among the European powers who were in contact with the Indians, and he is thus ill-equipped to understand documentary material. When historical sources are used by anthropologists, it is usually to illustrate or support some particular point they wish to make. This, of course, is exactly the opposite of good historical method. Statements are considered without reference to their immediate context, and no effort is made to assess the biases or abilities of the recorder. The result is a mixture of arrogance and naiveté in the use of this material which frequently repels the professional historian.

Yet, if neither historians nor anthropologists have undertaken the detailed study of Canadian Indian history, it does not mean that such studies are impossible. Recent years have witnessed the development, particularly in the United States, of a new discipline called ethnohistory.[13] The precise objectives of ethnohistory are still rather uncertain. As defined by some anthropologists, the discipline aims to embrace all historical approaches in anthropology. The principal interest of ethnohistorians seems, however, to be using historical documents and oral traditions to study the history of nonliterate peoples. It can be argued quite justifiably that labelling such studies ethnohistory, as opposed to simply history, serves to perpetuate an invidious distinction between so-called primitive and complex societies. The main justification for the term seems to be that it recognizes that the methodology required to study the history of smaller-scale, nonliterate societies is different from, and in many ways more complex than, that of history proper.

The main contribution that anthropology can make to such studies is the wealth of data it provides about the ways of life of non-Western peoples. On the most superficial level, such information makes possible the more precise identification of a host of terms used in connection with Indians in early accounts. The substitution of "wampum" for "porcelain" or "longhouse" for "cabin" may be of little importance, although knowledge of the role wampum played in the northeastern part of the continent, or about the housetypes associated with particular tribes, may add considerable depth to our understanding of these accounts. On the other hand, the

substitution of "chief" or "headman" for "captain" and "spirit" for "devil" not only offsets biases but also sets old descriptions of Indian life into a comparative framework. Only the anthropologist's understanding of Indian life can provide the background needed to assess and understand the behaviour of the Indians as it is recorded in historical records.

A seeming contradiction may, however, be perceived at this point. How can ethnological studies, which began in Canada less than a century ago, be useful for understanding the behaviour of Indians at a still earlier period? This question becomes particularly important when we consider the marked transformations that Indian life has undergone in response to changing conditions since the arrival of the Europeans. Nevertheless, there are many ways in which this more recent information may prove useful. For example, knowledge about the behaviour and customs of modern Indians, even those who have been greatly assimilated into the dominant culture of North America, may provide information about personality types, religious beliefs, and, in some cases, about social and economic practices, that is of value for checking and interpreting historical accounts of these people.

The reliability of such data for historical studies is difficult to establish. It is unreasonable to expect that, even among very conservative groups, prolonged European control and tutelage have not brought about many more changes than the Indians themselves are aware of. In the case of groups like the Iroquois, however, for whom written records are available beginning as early as the seventeenth century, it is possible, by checking information about present customs against progressively earlier accounts, to build up a picture of the main transformations that Iroquois life has undergone during the last three hundred years. Elisabeth Tooker's (1970a) recent study of the Iroquois Midwinter Ceremonial is an excellent example of this kind of investigation, which clearly illustrates the problems involved and the uncertainties that cloud the earlier periods, when even the fullest accounts tend to be fragmentary. This, and other studies, make ethnohistorians increasingly aware of the rapid changes that have taken place in Iroquois culture during the historic period and of the dangers involved in speculatively projecting the culture of any one period farther back into the past. Since Iroquois culture is known, from archaeological data, to have been changing rapidly prior to the arrival of the Europeans, ethnohistorical studies, by themselves, are probably not very reliable for the reconstruction of this culture prior to the seventeenth century.

Indeed, there is one extreme, but in no way disreputable, point of view which maintains that every Indian culture described in early European

sources must be regarded as already radically altered by European influences. T. J. Brasser (1971:261) writes, "The Indian world had been
distorted already in many respects before the first notes of ethnographical
value were jotted down." Developing a long tradition of such interpretation, he argues that the evolution of confederations, and even tribal
structures, as these were understood in the historic period, was a response
to the penetration of European commerce inland. Although building on
existing patterns of kinship, these new units exceeded in scale anything
known or required in pre-contact times. Brasser assumes that the Iroquoian
and Algonkian emphasis on curing rituals was a response to European
diseases and that family-owned trading routes among the Huron developed
because of European trade. He suggests that as coastal groups were driven
inland, they played an important role in disseminating traits such as splint
basketry, ribbon-appliqué, and metal work among the tribes of the midwest, and also introduced prophets who undermined local magical and
religious institutions. Finally, he points out that many anthropologists now
regard religious institutions such as the Delaware Big House, the Ojibwa
Midewiwin, and the sun dance of the Plains Indians, which at one time
were believed to be purely aboriginal, as sociopolitical revitalization movements resulting from the expansion of the frontier.

In the absence of adequate historical or archaeological data, what is
aboriginal and what evolved as a result of contact with Europeans remains
a matter for speculation. Depending on the anthropologist's personal predilection, particular facets of Indian culture can be explained in terms of
one theory or the other. In the past, too many features resulting from
contact or acculturation were uncritically projected backwards into the
prehistoric period; today, however, the opposite tendency appears to be in
the ascendant. Attempts are made to account for the acculturative origins
of many features of Indian culture previously held to be aboriginal. Much
of this development is assigned to the ill-documented, and hence highly
speculative, period between the arrival of the earliest European trade goods
and the first Europeans who have left written records. Except in unusual
cases, where pertinent archaeological or historical data are available, most
of these interpretations remain at the level of unproved or unprovable
hypotheses.

By contrast with the Iroquois, only a much more attenuated and poorly
studied remnant of the Iroquoian-speaking tribes that flourished near the
shores of Georgian Bay in the seventeenth century has survived, in the
form of the Huron of Lorette and the Huron-Tionnontaté mixture, now
called the Wyandot, who live in Oklahoma. Even in this case, however, the

little we know about these groups helps us to reconstruct at least some aspects of Huron life that had no counterpart in European culture and therefore went unnoticed by the early French writers.[14] For example, none of the French who visited the Huron seems to have been aware of the importance of clans and lineages as units of political organization. No special terms were noted for such units and the accounts make it clear that, when the French were interacting with the Indians, they saw themselves dealing with individuals or political leaders of a European type, rather than with representatives of kinship groupings. The little that is known about Wyandot clan structure, as recorded in the last century, helps us to understand at least the broad outlines of how the Huron clan system must have functioned in the seventeenth century (Tooker 1970b). Where specific features cannot be checked out in detail, this information serves to warn anthropologists about the existence of possible lacunae in their knowledge. Finally, it allows them to see the significance of numerous details of Huron behaviour that the French recorded blindly, but which anthropologists, armed with an understanding of Huron culture, may be able to interpret from an Indian point of view.

In many cases where there are few, if any, survivors of a particular tribe, valuable insights can be gained from comparisons with tribes that are known to have had a similar way of life and which have survived. Much that we are told about the Huron makes sense when we compare it with the more substantial information concerning Iroquois culture that begins to become available only a short time after the destruction of the Huron confederacy. Because the data concerning the Iroquois are more complete and better balanced, anthropologists can observe how a culture closely related to that of the Huron functioned as a total system. This provides a framework within which the piecemeal data on Huron culture can be fitted together. There are, of course, serious dangers inherent in this method, and I have severely criticized certain Iroquoianists for treating the Huron prior to 1650 as representing merely an earlier stage in the development of Iroquoian culture generally, or for using illustrations from the Huron and the Five Nations Iroquois indiscriminately to support arguments about the latter (Trigger 1971b:186–87). Significant differences can be noted in written accounts of burial customs, torture patterns, and kinship terminology, while the archaeological record reveals differences in pottery decoration, housetypes, and fortifications, albeit within the same general pattern (Trigger 1969a:121–24). It also remains to be ascertained whether the calendrical rituals, which are now such an important feature of "traditional" Iroquois culture, were established among either the Huron or the

Iroquois before 1650 (Tooker 1960). There is little in the description of Huron religion in the early sources to suggest that these rituals had penetrated this far north prior to the destruction of the Huron confederacy. In spite of these dangers, the considerable knowledge that we have of Iroquois culture can be used, with caution, to gain better insight into the total configuration of Huron culture and hence to understand Huron behaviour as it is reported by the French.

It is also clear that many aspects of Indian life were not confined to a single tribe or even to clusters of closely related ones. Shared cultural development resulted in certain traits being common to many tribes and over vast areas, particularly when the groups involved had adapted in generally similar ways to their environment. These similarities took the form of specific games, housetypes, or rituals, shared mythological themes or a preoccupation with curing rituals, a general pattern of political organization, or similar attitudes towards child-rearing. While they are very difficult to pin down, it is not impossible that certain traits, particularly values and attitudes, may have had a pan-Indian distribution.[15] Similarities of this sort can be used, at least in a very general way, to evaluate and interpret historical records.

Comparisons with later and better documented stages of a culture's development, or with closely related cultures, and a general knowledge of the cultural patterns of aboriginal North America permit the ethnologist to assess historical records and to use them as a basis for reconstructing earlier phases in the cultural development of particular groups. This kind of historical ethnography is so basic to all other ethnohistorical research that it is usually considered to be an integral part of the discipline. Some ethnohistorians, however, choose to regard it as being merely a preliminary to ethnohistory proper, which they would define as being the study of Indian history, or that of any nonliterate people. In either case, it is agreed that as detailed knowledge of a culture as possible is required if the history of that group is to be understood.

Anthropology also contributes to the understanding of Indian history by studying the cultural contacts that have taken place between European and tribal societies during the present century in places such as Africa, New Guinea, or the Canadian Arctic. Insofar as common elements may be observed in such contacts throughout the world, an understanding of these elements may be used to interpret more fragmentary historical accounts, without slighting the obviously distinctive features that pertain to separate historical traditions. The principal danger lies in the erroneous selection of theories to interpret specific situations and the subsequent distortion of

fragmentary evidence to make it conform with these theories; a mistake all too prevalent in some recent studies of Huron society.

So far, we have argued that without the knowledge of tribal life that only anthropology can provide, ethnohistory is impossible. Yet, because the ethnohistorian must deal with historical records, ethnohistory is also impossible without a command of the techniques of historiography, as these have been developed by generations of practising historians.[16] Lacking sufficient knowledge of these techniques, an ethnohistorian will remain a dilettante, however well-trained he may be in anthropology. Among the skills that must be acquired is the ability to evaluate the authenticity and accuracy of primary sources, or at least a sufficient sense of problem to seek the opinion of historians who are competent to pronounce on these matters. Where variant manuscript copies of a work survive, the history of these variations must be investigated and the amateur's sin of choosing the version most congenial to his own interpretation must be avoided. Above all, the ethnohistorian must not fall into the common anthropological error of assuming that a written document necessarily means what it says. Ambiguous wordings, mutilated or ill-copied manuscripts, improperly set type in old printed books, or the editing of manuscripts in such a way as to distort their original meaning all present serious difficulties. Where editors intervene between an eye-witness and the earliest recorded account of what he has seen, as is the case with the *Jesuit Relations*, the possible bias of these editors must be taken into account. Even when what are purported to be Indian speeches survive, they must be treated with caution. Filtered through translators, the recorder's incomprehension, and the general tendency of European authors of the time to embellish and to fabricate whole addresses, it is not always certain that such sources are reliable. All of this makes historical research a painstaking affair.

The ethnohistorian must attempt to assess the experience, ability, and above all the personal biases of the eye-witness from whom a report has been received. An observer's intelligence, his training, and fundamental aspects of his personality all affect his ability to observe the people of another culture and determine those aspects of their behaviour that interest him. Moreover, not all these variations are idiosyncratic. The difficulties encountered in understanding a culture that is radically different, not only in content but also in its basic structure, from the observer's own can result in standard biases, which are reproduced in the accounts of numerous individuals. All Frenchmen experienced difficulty in understanding the nature of Iroquoian religion, which was far more different from their own than were the non-Christian religions of the Near East, India, or East Asia.

Because the Indians lacked the pomp and hierarchy of a church, as the French understood it, their religious beliefs initially were regarded as of little consequence. Later, Indian spirits came to be seen as demons and devils, and shamans were viewed as sorcerers and anti-Christs. In spite of this, individual variations can be detected in French attitudes towards Huron religious beliefs. Some priests and laymen were convinced that the devil was constantly at work, encouraging the Indians in their religious practices, while others dismissed most of their customs as resulting from sheer ignorance. By comparing the writings of these different authors with each other, and against a knowledge of Iroquois religion derived from modern ethnographic sources, it is possible, to some degree, to see through the biases that have shaped these accounts and to extract much reliable information from them.

Self-interest and the differing circumstances under which groups of European explorers, fur traders, and rival orders of priests encountered and interacted with various Indian groups have resulted in accounts of Indian life that differ widely in their attitudes towards the Indians and the kinds of information they provide. These differences are further evidenced when accounts of a particular event were written down by men who were of rival European nationalities. A careful comparison of French and Dutch accounts of their dealings with the Iroquois invariably results in a far more detailed and more complex picture of Iroquois political and economic behaviour than could be obtained if information from only one side were available (Trigger 1971c). Comparing different accounts of a particular event, it is sometimes possible, by a process analogous to surveyors' triangulation, to arrive at some reasonable conclusions about the views of the Indian participants, even in the absence of independent Indian witnesses. Moreover, when conflicting European groups sought to justify their own policies, they occasionally noted Indian reactions to other Europeans that otherwise would have gone unrecorded. Because of the sharply divergent interests of the various groups of Frenchmen who came to Quebec in early times, some extremely unflattering Indian views of certain Europeans have been recorded. The most regrettable shortcoming of the early sources is their failure to record the experiences of the first agents who lived and traded with the Indians: such as Jean Nicollet, Etienne Brûlé, and Nicolas Marsolet. From these earliest *coureurs de bois*, who lived intimately with the Indians and must have known them better than did any other Europeans, much might have been learned about Indian attitudes towards early missionaries and the French generally. In spite of this, it is possible, by carefully comparing the available evidence, to draw reasonable inferences

about the policy and motivations of certain prominent Indians or groups of Indians.

Among some Indian groups, oral traditions are of considerable value for supplementing written records. The Winnebago tribe of Wisconsin, for example, are reported to preserve memories of events that took place soon after their first encounter with a European, which probably occurred in 1634 (Lurie 1960:803). For the Huron, however, and for the Iroquoians generally, oral traditions appear to be of little historical value. The reason for this probably lies in the Iroquoians' attitude towards history. For the most part, the purpose of their traditions was not to preserve a literal memory of the past, but rather to supply them with a guide to the social, political, and moral order in which they lived. For the Iroquois of the seventeenth and eighteenth centuries this moral order was provided by the Dekanahwideh legend, which told of the founding of the Iroquois confederacy (P. Wallace 1966). Since the names of the founders of the league were passed on to future office holders, the legend of the founding of the confederacy was, in fact, a statement concerning its constitution. Apart from this legend, the Iroquois appear to have had only the vaguest traditions about their origins. These were based on a pan-Indian theme that had the first ancestors of their various clans emerging out of caves or holes in the ground (Trigger 1970:14). Early in this century, A. C. Parker (1916) noted that the Iroquois retained no memories of their aboriginal fortifications and housetypes. He also noted that many Iroquois attributed the origin of their confederacy to the religious teacher Handsome Lake, who flourished between 1800 and 1815. Even the ceremonies that had been part of Iroquois culture prior to this time were ascribed to him. Parker (1916:480–81) concluded that the Iroquois conceived of their history in terms of periods of "cultural revolution" and that each new revolution systematically blotted out the memory of a former era.

It is uncertain how far these conclusions apply to the Huron. We have no record of a myth about the founding of their confederacy, but the Jesuits imply that they had knowledge of political events going back two hundred years. Their statement that some Huron claimed to know the locations of their villages over these two centuries suggests some interest in history (Thwaites 1896–1901, 16:227). On the other hand, their inheritance of titles was similar to that of the Iroquois and Peter Dooyentate Clarke's (1870) recording of Wyandot oral history indicates that, in the nineteenth century, the latter group had only the haziest and most inaccurate memory of events prior to 1650, or even for some time subsequent to that date.[17] Hence, one seems safe in concluding that oral traditions do

not provide an independent means for studying the history of Iroquoian-speaking peoples. It is of interest when oral traditions confirm other sources of information about the past, but, except when they do, they should not be used even to supplement such sources.

Ethnohistory is further distinguished from conventional history by its relatively greater reliance on data from auxiliary fields, particularly archaeology, physical anthropology, and linguistics. However, growing awareness of the contributions that colonial and industrial archaeology can make to the study of history suggests that this distinction is not as clear-cut as it used to be. Linguistic data not only provide information about the historical relationships among different ethnic groups; they can also be used to reconstruct various aspects of prehistoric Indian cultures. For example, by means of lexical studies, Wallace Chafe (1964) has provided support for Tooker's (1960) theory that shamanistic healing cults antedate the present emphasis on calendrical rites among the northern Iroquoians, and Lounsbury (1961) has done important work on reconstructing proto-Iroquoian kinship terminology. I doubt that any more productive source of information about prehistoric, or early historic, Iroquoian culture remains to be unlocked than through linguistic studies.

Archaeological data not only provide important information about the development of Indian cultures in prehistoric times, but also furnish supplementary clues about these cultures in the early historic period. Many of these data are complementary to those derived from written accounts, since they illustrate material aspects of Indian life that early accounts rarely describe in detail. Archaeological and historical data are sometimes used in combination to locate the sites of Indian communities mentioned in early historical records. While some of this work has been very slipshod, other identifications of Huron sites are models of scholarly responsibility (Kidd 1949*b*; 1953; Ridley 1947; *see also* Trigger 1969*b*). The accurate identification of such sites invariably permits archaeologists both to verify and to supplement the historical record. Archaeologists have long been aware of the potential of their discipline for investigating changes brought about in material culture by European contact, but in recent years techniques have been pioneered for also studying the social changes that result from such contact (e.g., Deetz 1965). Although still in the experimental stage, these techniques may become exceedingly valuable for studying how Indian tribes were affected by European influences prior to the time of the earliest written records.

As yet, however, the ethnohistorical approach, as practised in North America, has produced only a few major studies of Indian tribes. In my

opinion, the most important published to date is E. H. Spicer's (1962) *Cycles of Conquest*, which traces in detail the impact of successive Spanish, Mexican, and American administrations upon the native peoples of northern Mexico and the southwestern United States. The principal aim of this study was, however, less to provide a history of the native peoples of that region than to examine the range of situations in which North American Indians have been influenced by their contact with Europeans. This theme was explored further by a number of anthropologists in a book edited by Spicer (1961), entitled *Perspectives in American Indian Culture Change*. In this book, the history of six widely separated Indian tribes is traced from the time of contact down to the present. Harold E. Hickerson (1962; 1970) has carefully studied the impact of the fur trade upon the Ojibwa of the upper Great Lakes region, devoting special attention to the effects that trade had upon their social and political organization. More recently, A. F. C. Wallace (1970) has published a history of the Seneca tribe which is, in fact, primarily a biography of Handsome Lake set into an extensive time-and-place description of Seneca culture and the changes it has undergone in historic times. While these studies are major contributions to understanding Indian history, in each of them historical analysis is made secondary to efforts to generalize about cultural processes. Indeed, Hickerson (1970:7) makes this quite explicit when he states that ethnohistory "employs historiographical methods to lay a foundation for the formulation of general laws: in a word, *ideographic* means to *nomothetic* ends." This also appears to be the case with Patterson's *The Canadian Indians*, which has as its main theme to demonstrate similarities between the experiences of the Canadian Indian and those of native peoples in other colonial situations, particularly in New Zealand, Australia, South Africa, and the United States (1972:3–36). While it is impossible ever to separate the explanation of particular events from generalizations about human behaviour, the relative emphasis that is given to these two processes in particular studies varies widely. The present state of ethnohistorical research appears to leave room for the development of a style of presentation in which the detailed explanation of a specific historical situation is pursued as an end that is considered worthwhile in itself.

A Statement of Methods and Assumptions

The availability of data and the willingness of the ethnohistorian to pay attention to them determines the level of specificity at which any study of

Indian-white contact is written. Early studies were generally concerned
with how whole tribes responded to European contact. These studies dealt
mainly with features that entire peoples had in common; what happened
to individuals or to specific groups within a tribe was of interest only in
relationship to the more general process of adaptation. Although attention
was sometimes paid to changes in personality that resulted from these
processes, the aim of such investigations was not to establish a range of
individual variation, but rather to define a limited number of modal
personalities which, at most, took account of differences in age, sex, and
possible economic status. Such studies have contributed to our knowledge
of particular tribes, as well as helping to define types of culture contact and
to sharpen the understanding of this process. By their very nature, however, these studies are essentially structural rather than historical in intent
and execution.

At the other end of the scale is biography, which at its best is a perceptive
examination of the forces at work in a particular situation as they can be
seen in relationship to the life of a well-documented individual. In recent
years, American anthropologists have written biographies, or helped to
write autobiographies, of Indians (Dyk 1938; Ford 1941; Marriott 1948;
Simmons 1942), yet few Indians who lived in the last century, or earlier,
have been the subjects of extensive biographical treatment. Most of the
latter studies have been written by historians who have had only a superficial knowledge of Indian customs; hence their insights into their subjects
are limited, even when the biographer wishes to be sympathetic.[18]

For the early period, a biographical approach is made difficult by the
paucity of material that has been preserved concerning any particular
individual. Information is available about Indians who became outstanding
converts, but little of this concerns their lives prior to conversion. Of the
childhood and life of these converts, as it was lived other than in the
presence of the missionaries, we can learn very little. Moreover, these
exemplary converts were unusual Indians and there is much about their
motives and behaviour that the missionaries either did not understand or
felt it inappropriate to record. For the majority of Indians whose names have
been preserved, only a few isolated events are recorded and even a skeletal
life history of such individuals remains beyond our grasp. That this is so
can easily be ascertained from a perusal of the Indian biographies recently
published in the first two volumes of the *Dictionary of Canadian Biography*
(1966; 1969). We are completely ignorant, or have only the vaguest ideas
about what the majority of Indians thought and felt as individuals and

know little about what they did, except in their dealings with Europeans. Thus our characterization of them can rarely penetrate behind the polite facade that the Indians presented on such occasions. One must therefore accept as a limitation of the material that few studies-in-depth of individuals are possible and that there is little chance of writing large-scale biographies of the Indians who played a major role in our early history.

The weakness of the biographical approach, as far as Indians are concerned, is further illustrated by life histories of prominent explorers and missionaries. Because Indian life can be dealt with in a piecemeal fashion in such works, authors have little incentive to transcend the limitations of their subject's understanding of the Indians. Nevertheless, such ignorance exacts a higher price than might be imagined. By failing to understand those with whom the subject of his biography had dealings, the author ends up with only a partial, and often distorted, understanding of his or her motives and personality (Trigger 1971*a*).

On the other hand, enough isolated information is available concerning the behaviour of individual Indians in certain specific circumstances that a fairly detailed picture can be built up of their differing responses to these situations. Sometimes we can learn enough about the status and family affiliations of individuals that we may infer with some confidence why these Indians behaved as they did. Such data permit the ethnohistorian to steer a middle course between biographies and gross structural analysis, by studying the history of a tribe or confederacy in terms of the behaviour of groups of individuals united by certain common interests. These interest groups are not the abstract social categories established for purposes of comparative research by sociologists and ethnologists; instead, they are groupings that emerge as a result of common interests in real historical situations. Some of them were cliques that had a recognized corporate existence in their own time, others are constructs of the historian. To be a valid interest group, however, its members must have had implicitly shared common goals and supported one another in common action. It may be argued that whatever level of specificity an historian aims to work at, success ultimately must depend in large measure on his understanding of the interactions among such groups.

The nature of interest groups has been examined in detail by many sociologists. They play an important part in the theorizing of George C. Homans (e.g., 1962:182–91), one of the few historically orientated sociologists in the United States, and have been discussed in terms of historical theory in the later writings of Jean-Paul Sartre (1963). Professional

historians, however, have been using this approach in a pragmatic way for a long time (Fischer 1971:216–42). One of the best examples of its application to the study of Canadian history is Gustave Lanctot's (1967) *Canada and the American Revolution*. In this study, Lanctot traces the shifting relations, between 1774 and 1783, among the French-Canadian farmers, clergy, and gentry, the British officers in Quebec, and the British merchants and American rebels in the province. The changing alliances of each group are interpreted as efforts to defend clearly defined, and largely unchanging, interests within the context of a rapidly changing situation. The influence that individual personalities such as Governors Carleton or Haldimand, or Bishop Briand, had on the conduct of affairs is by no means neglected, but it is a matter of some methodological interest to note how these men, along with less famous individuals, are treated, as far as possible, as representatives of specific interest groups.

This approach is particularly valuable for the investigation of social and economic history, especially as it concerns the lower classes. Indians stand in much the same relationship to history as do the working classes, peasantries, and other less literate members of European society in earlier times. The records that we have of both were produced by a relatively small, privileged class that had no personal experience of the ways of life of these people. It is therefore no accident that the techniques developed to study the history of less affluent Europeans resemble so closely those we propose to use for the study of the Canadian Indian.

The technique of studying social interaction in terms of interest groups provides ethnohistorians with a method of approaching as near as the data will allow to an investigation of historical events in terms of their real agents, individual human beings. In particular, it encourages a far more detailed examination of events and processes than does the study of contact as an interaction between two totally different cultural systems. In Canada, Indians and Europeans rarely constituted two homogeneous interest groups, or even lined up as two opposing teams. Groups of European fur traders, government officials, and diverse orders of the clergy often competed with each other more than with the Indians. Likewise, many Indian tribes were noted for their factionalism and internal disagreements even in periods of strength. Not infrequently, common interests gave rise to alliances that cut across ethnic lines and united various Indians and Europeans in opposition to their own people. These sorts of alliances undoubtedly were fraught with more problems than were those between members of the same society. Nevertheless, by the very act of examining how common interests could,

and did, unite members of different ethnic groups, an effort is made to take account of a common humanity transcending cultural differences.

Even when this method has been accepted, however, a major problem remains unsolved. How, when all the data that we have at our disposal have been recorded by Europeans, is it possible for the work of any historian using these data not to be biased in favour of the Europeans, if not in sympathy then at least in terms of insights? Because of the nature of the historical record, we know much more about relations between specific groups of Indians and Europeans than we know about relations between one group of Indians and another. This is true even concerning the fur trade, although one might expect that European interest would have encouraged the collection of large amounts of information about intertribal relations. If so, it was never recorded. Because of this, there is an almost automatic tendency for historians to overemphasize the importance of Indian-white relations in Indian affairs generally. It is also clear that we can learn far more about the general background and personal motivations of the Europeans who are mentioned in our sources than we can about the Indians. If unchecked, the ethnohistorian's natural tendency to make the maximum use of his data can turn the best-intentioned Indian history into nothing more than a restudy of European colonization.

It is undoubtedly true that much of Indian diplomacy "had a way of reflecting" (F. Jennings 1968:23) decisions made in Europe, but to regard Indian history merely as an extension of colonial history, in the manner of some historians, is to confuse what actually happened with the manner in which Indian policy has been recorded. The historian must evaluate the impact of traditional ideas upon the conduct of Indian diplomacy and take into account the patterns of intertribal relations that existed prior to the coming of the whites and that continued to influence Indian politics for a long time afterward. Far greater attention must be paid to the references to intertribal relations that occur, often incidentally, in the historical records. It is also possible that, in the future, archaeological data will be useful in supplementing the information that historians have at their disposal.

To achieve greater equity in writing this history of the Huron, several procedures have been carefully observed. First, while not completely suppressing the individuality of historical figures, I have concentrated on those aspects of people's behaviour that reflect their roles as members of one or more interest groups. Secondly, while the motivations of the members of each interest group have been presented as clearly as possible,

I have tried to do this impartially and in such a manner that the interest of the reader focuses on the total situation rather than on the passions or problems of any one group.

This approach is necessary because, for the most part, we lack the documentation to reconstruct the psychological framework that is associated with Indian behaviour. Hence, by eliminating such considerations, as far as possible, in our evaluation of individual Europeans as well, we achieve something like parity in our treatment of both groups. Secondly, since most of our data concern the dealings of the Huron with various groups of French, by concentrating our analysis on the relationships between groups, rather than on the inner dynamics of the groups themselves, we again tend to utilize the data to best advantage for understanding the Indians.

It should not be concluded, however, that this approach has been adopted only because of the uneven nature of the data. It has also been done for more positive reasons. One can argue that the aim of an Indian history should be to make Indians sympathetic figures. Sympathy, however, does not always imply understanding and, without a clear understanding of people's motives, respect is impossible. All too much has been written about Indians that is well-intentioned and benevolent, yet most of this literature has failed to promote a genuine understanding of the Indians as people who had worthy ambitions of their own and who were, and are, able to conduct their own affairs and to interact intelligently with Europeans. I think it especially important that current ethnohistorical writing should aim to make the behaviour of Indian groups understandable. To do this, Canadian ethnohistorians must investigate, not only the economics of the fur trade, but also the cultural values of the Indians and the full range of problems they have faced. Moreover, and this many anthropologists tend to forget, if we are to understand the total situation, we must attempt to achieve a similar dispassionate understanding of the motives of European groups, such as the Jesuits, who interacted with the Indians. In the long run, this may require as much effort, and even more self-discipline, than does an understanding of the Huron.

Chapter 2   The Huron and Their Neighbours

The Huron Land and Economy[1]

NAME

Huron is not a North American Indian term but is derived from the French *hure*, meaning a boar's head. A popular tradition in New France maintained that this name was invented by French sailors, who were astonished by the bristly hair styles of the Huron warriors who began trading with the French early in the seventeenth century. Yet, this story may be no more than a folk-etymology. Long before the discovery of the New World, *huron* was a slang term meaning ruffian or rustic. No doubt, it would have seemed appropriate for the Huron, who when first encountered by Europeans on the St. Lawrence, and for a long time afterward, must have appeared outlandish by comparison with the coastal peoples, who had been trading with Europeans for over a generation and among whom European food, tools, and items of clothing already played a vital role.[2]

The Huron called themselves *Wendat*, which means "Islanders," or "Dwellers on a Peninsula."[3] This term may refer to the Huron country, which was surrounded on three sides by large bodies of water, or to Huron cosmological beliefs. The Huron imagined their country to be at the centre of the world, which in turn was an island supported on the back of a giant tortoise. *Wendat* was the name, not of a tribe, but of a confederation made up of four tribes. It is therefore analogous to the Iroquois *Hodénosaunee*, or People of the Longhouse, which was a collective term for the five tribes that made up the Iroquois confederacy.

GEOGRAPHY

The Huron country was located at the southeastern corner of Georgian Bay, on a narrow strip of land sandwiched between Matchedash and Nottawasaga Bays on the west and Lake Simcoe on the east (map 1). It was further delineated on its southern boundary by the drainage basin of the Notta-

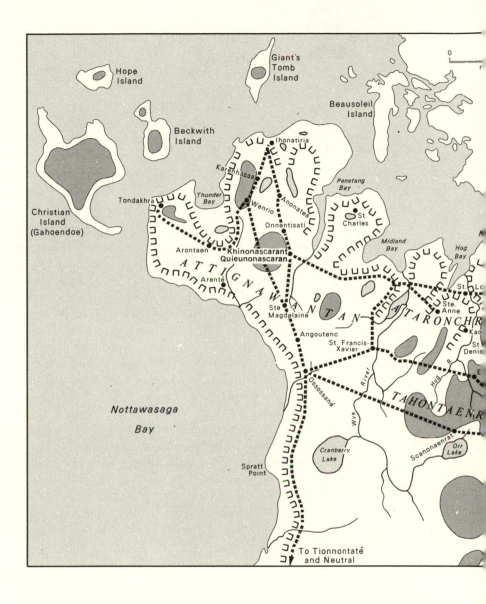

MAP 1. *The Huron Country, c. 1634, showing locations of tribes, settlements, and major trails attested by the Jesuits.*

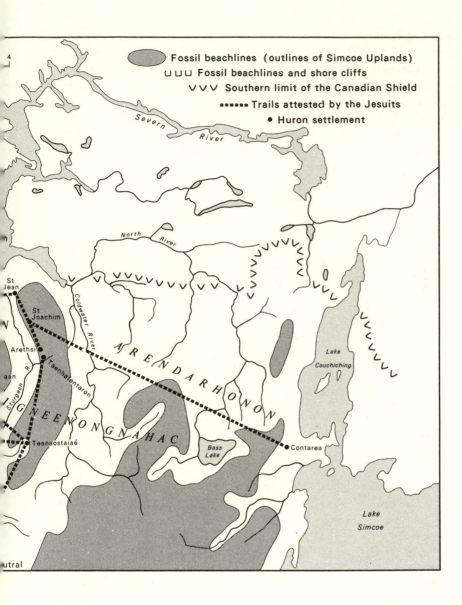

Fossil beachlines (outlines of Simcoe Uplands)
ᴜ ᴜ ᴜ Fossil beachlines and shore cliffs
ᴠ ᴠ ᴠ Southern limit of the Canadian Shield
▪▪▪▪▪▪ Trails attested by the Jesuits
● Huron settlement

wasaga River, which at that time was a vast swamp hindering communication with the south. The Huron villages were concentrated in an area that measured no more than 35 miles east to west and 20 miles north to south. The western part of this region, including the whole of the Penetanguishene Peninsula, was the tribal territory of the largest of the Huron tribes, the Attignawantan, whose name meant "the people of the Bear."[4] In the northern part of the Penetanguishene Peninsula, the land rises quickly from the lake in a series of impressive beach terraces, but, for the most part, the surface relief is only gently rolling. Much of the soil in this area tends to be rather stony and the drier soils supported large stands of oak and white pine. To the south, along the shores of Nottawasaga Bay, there were vast areas covered with sand dunes and stunted coniferous trees, now a densely populated summer resort.

Farther to the east, five short rivers flow north into Matchedash Bay: the Wye, Hog, Sturgeon, Coldwater, and North. Beyond, as the Severn River, the waters of Lake Simcoe follow a circuitous course across the Canadian Shield before entering Matchedash Bay from the north. Between each of these rivers is a ridge of high ground incised with the beach terraces of Glacial Lake Algonquin, while nearer Lake Simcoe the hills rise over 700 feet above Lake Huron. In prehistoric times, the higher ground in this area was covered with maple, beech, and basswood, while cedar and alder grew in the swampy river valleys (Heidenreich et al. 1969:123–27; Heidenreich 1971: map 20). The eastern part of the region was the territory of the Arendarhonon, whose name may signify "Nation of the Rock." The Arendarhonon appear to have been the second largest of the Huron tribes. Between the Arendarhonon and the Attignawantan lived the Attigneenongnahac and Tahontaenrat tribes. Their names have been conjectured to mean "Cord" or "Barking Dogs" and "Deer," "White Thorns," "White Canoe," or "One White Lodge" respectively.[5] Although widely used in recent publications, none of the latter etymologies is more than uncertain speculation; hence I prefer to call all of these tribes by their Huron names. A fifth group, the Ataronchronon, whose name is conjectured to mean "People of the Marshes,"[6] lived in the lower part of the Wye Valley. The existence of this group does not appear to have been recognized in the political organization of the Huron confederacy and it is possible that it was merely a division of the Attignawantan.

Everyone who visited the Georgian Bay region in the seventeenth century was struck by the contrast between the hills and plains of the Huron country, which were covered with luxuriant vegetation, and the rocky inhospitable region to the north.[7] Geographically, the Huron country

is part of southern Ontario. Its bedrock of Palaeozoic limestone is overlaid with deep glacial tills, which in turn support sandy, well-drained soils. Immediately to the north, these formations give way to the metamorphic rock of the Canadian Shield which, while also wooded, is covered with only a thin, broken layer of soil. Although tribes living as far north as Lake Nipissing planted small fields of corn, the fertile soils of the Huron country marked the northern limits of effective corn agriculture in eastern Canada and of the sedentary way of life that was associated with it.

In spite of suggestions to the contrary (Martijn 1969:100 n. 7; Latta in Heidenreich et al. 1969:112), recent detailed studies have produced no evidence of significant climatic changes in this area between A.D. 1600 and the present (Heidenreich et al. 1969:123, 127). The normal frost-free period is 135 to 142 days and the growing season is 195 days. The summers are hot, as in the rest of southern Ontario, and only fourteen to sixteen inches of rain fall during the growing season. In the winter the snowfall is exceptionally heavy: 90 to 110 inches, as compared with 50 to 70 inches in the Toronto area (Heidenreich 1971:56–59; *Atlas of Canada*: maps 21, 23, 28).

Before settlement became extensive, the region must have been rich in non-migratory game, particularly deer, bear, and beaver, although these were fewer in number than in the warmer regions north of Lake Erie. Wild birds, including various kinds of aquatic fowl, were common, except for the turkey, which flourished farther south. Even more important, however, were the trout, pike, sturgeon, and other species of fish, which were spectacularly abundant in the waters that surround the Huron country on every side. Fishing constituted an economic resource for the Huron second in importance only to agriculture (Trigger 1969a:30; Heidenreich 1971:158).

From the Huron country, it was possible to travel northward along the eastern shore of Georgian Bay without ever moving out of sight of land. This water route encouraged the development of ties between the Huron and the hunting peoples of the north, which were lacking among the other agricultural peoples who lived in southern Ontario and New York State (Trigger 1962a).

POPULATION AND SETTLEMENT PATTERNS

The population of the Huron country in the early part of the seventeenth century has been variously estimated to have been between 18,000 and

40,000 people. While it is notoriously difficult to determine the size of
aboriginal American populations, my investigations incline me to favour
the lowest of these figures.[8] The Huron lived in eighteen to twenty-five
villages. Some were very small hamlets, but about six appear to have
contained forty or more multi-family dwellings and were surrounded with
fortified palisades (plate 1). These large villages probably had a population
of 1500 to 2000 people each, and were invariably located in naturally
defensible locations which provided breaks in slope on at least two sides
(Heidenreich 1971:111). The average village occupied four to six acres,
although villages covering up to fifteen acres are reported (ibid. 126). The
Attignawantan appear to have had two large towns, but many members of
this tribe lived in about a dozen small, unfortified villages. The territories
of the three other tribes were more exposed to Iroquois raids; hence their
populations were concentrated in a smaller number of large, fortified
villages.[9]

Most villages were located near streams, which were useful for canoe
travel and close to sandy, well-drained soil that was preferred for growing
corn. Especially in the eastern parts of the Huron country, soil of this type
is found mostly on the sides and tops of hills, rather than in the valley
bottoms. Because of this, many villages were built on old beach terraces,
200 feet or more above the valley bottom, near where springs flowed from
the hillside (Heidenreich 1967:17–18). The villages were joined together
by a network of narrow trails that ran roughly in a north-south and east-
west direction through the forest. Extensions of these trails led southward
to the territory of the Tionnontaté, near Collingwood, and to the Neutral
tribes, who lived in the southwest corner of Lake Ontario. It has been
estimated that there were over 200 miles of trails linking the Huron
settlements (Heidenreich 1971:156–57, map 23).

DIVISION OF LABOUR

In the seventeenth century, the Huron were the northernmost of the
Iroquoian-speaking peoples. They shared with their linguistic cousins to
the south a way of life that was firmly based on corn agriculture and which
supported many thousands of people and some of the highest concentrations of population in eastern North America.[10] Prior to their encounter
with the French, the Huron knew of no culture that they had reason to
believe was materially more successful than their own. They proudly
contrasted the richness of their way of life with the poverty of the numeric-

PLATE 1. *Model of a Huron village based on archaeological and historical data. Courtesy National Museum of Man, National Museums of Canada.*

ally much smaller hunting bands who lived to the north. Because of their subsistence patterns, these groups not only were less sedentary than the Huron but often found themselves dependent on Huron food reserves to carry them over a bad winter. The chronic shortages and narrow margins of surplus on which these bands subsisted contrasted with the large surpluses and far less frequent food shortages that were characteristic of Huron life.

The most basic distinction in Huron society was that made between the sexes (Quain 1937; Witthoft 1959:32–36). Almost every task was considered to be either exclusively men's work or exclusively women's work, and every Huron was expected to be familiar with all or most of the tasks appropriate to his or her sex. For the most part, men engaged in tasks that required considerable physical strength, or which took them away from home for long periods. Women performed tasks of a more routine nature that kept them in, or close to, their villages. Both sexes did much of their work in teams and the differing nature of this work meant that men and women spent much of their time in the company of their own sex and apart from each other. These work habits may explain, in part, the formality and avoidance that generally characterized public relations between the sexes in Huron society.

WOMEN'S WORK

The chief task performed by women was the planting, tending, and harvesting of the crops, which accounted for perhaps three-quarters of all the food that the Huron ate.[11] These crops were limited in number. Corn was the most important by far, but beans, squash, and sunflowers were also grown.[12] Both flour and flint corn were planted, although in this northern latitude the latter was preferred as it matured in 100, as opposed to 130, days.[13] This corn had two to three cobs per stalk, each four or more inches long and bearing 100 to 650 kernels per cob (Heidenreich 1971:171–73). Assuming that corn constituted about 65 percent of the Huron diet, a woman had to produce enough to provide each member of her family with about 1.3 pounds of it per day (ibid. 163).

The Huron women worked the soil with small wooden spades, scraping it up to form hills a foot or more high and several feet in diameter, in which they planted their seeds year after year (plate 2). These hills, which may have numbered 2500 per acre, not only supported the corn stalks but prevented sheet erosion and, by trapping cold low-lying air, reduced the

PLATE 2. *Lafitau's depiction of Huron agricultural practices. This illustration from Joseph-François Lafitau's* Moeurs des sauvages amériquains *(1724) provides a striking example of the ethnographic unreliability of many of the most famous illustrations of Indian life in Canada in the early historic period. While the cornhills faithfully reproduce Lafitau's description of Indian agriculture in Canada, the human figures and their tools (but not their clothes) are copies of T. de Bry's 1591 engraving of Jacques Le Moyne de Morgues's painting of Timucua agriculture done in Florida, 1564–65. W. C. Sturtevant (American Antiquity 33 [1968]: 91 ff.) has further demonstrated that Le Moyne's hoes are of European rather than Indian type. There is no reason to accept the claim that the skyline was intended to be that of Montreal Island. Because of direct copying all the figures produced by Lafitau's artist are left-handed. Courtesy National Anthropological Archives, Smithsonian Institution.*

danger of frost damage.[14] Because only light soils could be worked and these tended to dry out easily, the Huron experienced an average of at least one serious drought every decade, as well as one or two less serious ones during that period (Heidenreich 1971:58–59). The failure of the Huron to add fresh organic matter to their fields also meant that their crops quickly depleted the fertility of the soil. It is estimated that the natural fertility of the types of soil the Huron used was sufficient to grow crops for only four to six years; however, by burning leaves and branches to add ash to the soil, and carefully weeding their fields, the Huron were able to go on using them for eight to twelve years (ibid. 180–89). As the fertility of old fields declined, new ones had to be brought under cultivation in order to maintain levels of production.[15] When nearby fields and sources of firewood had been used up, it was necessary for a Huron village to relocate. This seems to have occurred about once every ten to fifteen years.

Approximately 7000 acres would have been sufficient to feed the Huron population at any one time,[16] but, since the Huron aimed at producing surpluses to trade with other groups, the amount of land under cultivation was probably above this figure. In order to grow and harvest this much food, Huron women had to work hard. Visitors commented on the care they took to weed their fields and to chase away birds and animals that threatened their crops. In areas that were safe from attack, women frequently spent the summer living with their children in temporary cabins near their fields.

Although each woman appears to have tended her own fields, these were of small extent and there was probably a considerable amount of informal cooperation (cf. Snyderman 1951). All of the food produced by women living in the same house was either stored in the porches at either end or hung from the rafters and, while each woman may have intended to use her own, no one was permitted to go hungry as long as any food remained to the household. The corn buried in bark-lined pits either inside or near houses may have been specially protected seed corn (Heidenreich 1971:119).

In addition to growing crops, the women gathered a wide variety of wild roots, nuts, and berries, which added flavour to an otherwise bland diet. Some of the fruit was dried to preserve it for winter. Only when crops failed did wild plants become a major item in the Huron diet. At such times, in addition to the wild foods that were eaten regularly, various kinds of tree bark, mosses, and lichens were consumed. Acorns were repeatedly boiled prior to being eaten to make them less bitter.

Women were also responsible for the time-consuming tasks of cooking,

sewing, and tending children. Food was cooked over an open hearth using dry, relatively smokeless wood that the women collected each spring. This wood came from the limbs of dead trees, which the winter's storms had knocked down. Most of it was a by-product of forest clearance and the depletion of nearby supplies was, as we have noted, one of the reasons for the periodic relocation of Huron villages. The ash from the hearths, along with other refuse, was dumped onto middens located on the periphery of the village. Middens have been found inside only the largest villages, but it appears that in no case did a Huron woman have to walk more than 100 feet from her house to dispose of garbage (Heidenreich 1971:147).

Although Huron cuisine is reported to have included many dishes, most of these were variations on a few themes. Their most common dish was a thin soup made of corn meal, which was ground by the women in a hollowed-out tree trunk, using a wooden pole, six or seven feet long (plate 3). Pieces of fish, meat, or squash were sometimes added to this soup. The fish were boiled whole, then mashed up without removing bones, entrails, or scales, before being returned to the pot. The Huron made unleavened bread, sometimes adding dried fruit and pieces of deer fat to the dough to give it more flavour. Meat was also roasted over the fire. The French complained about the Huron failure to wash their utensils and to observe satisfactory standards of hygiene in their cooking. They also found some Huron delicacies not to their liking; among these was *leindohy* or stinking corn: small ears of corn that had been permitted to ferment in a stagnant pond for several months before being eaten. They also objected to a special bread that was made from fresh corn, which the women masticated, spat out, and pounded in a large mortar before baking it in corn leaves. The Huron regarded both of these as party dishes.

The clothes that Huron women made were of relatively simple design. Most of them were made from the skins of animals. We know little about the preparation of these skins, except that they were fleshed with stone or bone scrapers. Men and women invariably wore loincloths and were much embarrassed by the complete male nudity that appears to have been common in the hotter months among certain neighbouring peoples, such as the Ottawa and the Neutral. In addition, Huron women wore a skirt extending from the waist partway to the knees, although in summer they left their bodies bare from the waist up, the same as men did. Men and women both wore moccasins and, in the winter, they also wore a cloak, long sleeves, and leggings, which were held in place by leather strings tied about their body. These clothes were not sufficiently warm to prevent some people from freezing to death each winter. In spite of their sense of cultural

PLATE 3. *Huron woman grinding corn. From Champlain's Voyages of 1619. Although these illustrations are often assumed to be Champlain's own work, the evidence presented below (see esp. plate 21) suggests they were drawn by a professional draftsman familiar with French and Portuguese traditions of cartographical illustration for the southeastern United States and tropical areas of the New World. Such a draftsman would have attempted to give visual form to Champlain's written or verbal descriptions of the Indians of Canada. Although nothing can be specified as incorrect about this particular illustration, on principle none of the drawings accompanying Champlain's publications can be regarded as having ethnographic value independently of his written work. This engraving and the ones that follow cannot be compared with John White's magnificent and earlier drawings of North American Indians. Courtesy McGill University Libraries.*

superiority, the Huron admired the clothes and camping equipment that were made by the northern hunting peoples and sought these in trade.

Crude as Huron clothes were in design and execution, they were often carefully decorated with painting and with bands of trim made from porcupine quills. Both sexes spent considerable time caring for their hair and greasing their bodies with oil and animal fat to protect them against sun, cold, and insects. On festive occasions, colours were added to these fats and the whole body was painted with representations of men and animals, or with geometrical designs. Some of these paintings were so well done that, from a distance, Europeans mistook them for suits of clothing. On these occasions, a single person might also wear up to twelve pounds of strings and plaques of shell beads. Men habitually wore tobacco pouches, which hung behind their backs and were a repository for their charms and other valued personal possessions. Many of these pouches had been elaborately decorated by the women.

Women fashioned the globular clay vessels used for cooking. These pots ranged from a few inches to a foot or more in diameter and were decorated around the lip and collar with patterns made up of incised straight lines. The Huron made only one functional type of vessel, a soup pot. Stones were used to hold these vessels in place over the hearth.[17]

Women also wove mats out of reeds and corn leaves, which were used to cover the doors and sleeping platforms of their houses. They made cord from Indian hemp (*Apocynum cannabinum*), swamp milkweed (*Asclepias incarnata*), and basswood bark (Heidenreich 1971:200–201) and used the finer cord to make scarfs, collars, and bracelets which were worn by both sexes. They also fashioned baskets out of reeds and birchbark and sewed the latter together to make dishes from which to eat and drink.

Women sometimes accompanied their husbands on the late winter hunting expeditions that travelled for several days to the south or east of the Huron country to slay deer. No doubt these women helped to butcher the game and to carry home the skins and meat. Women do not seem to have participated in the autumn hunts, possibly because warfare was still going on at that time of year, nor did they often travel outside Huron territory, especially when this involved lengthy canoe trips. Only a very few instances are recorded of women travelling between the Huron country and Quebec during the years of the French-Huron alliance. In these respects the Huron differed from the northern Algonkians, who moved as families in their annual cycle, and from the Iroquois, whose women played an important role in hunting activities and also frequently accompanied their husbands on diplomatic visits to Quebec.

Women's work was of an inward looking, familial nature. Their unit of routine association were the females who lived in a single, multi-family dwelling. Beyond that, their loyalty extended to their village, but this appears to have been the broadest focus of their loyalties. Because they did not travel abroad as men did, Huron women tended to be the guardians of family and village traditions and, possibly for this reason, were more conservative than their menfolk.

MEN'S WORK

The earliest French visitors to the Huron country judged Huron men to be the epitome of idleness. Champlain states that he found women doing most of the work, both at home and in the fields, while the men amused themselves hunting, fishing, trading, making war, dancing, and sleeping, the latter being their favourite occupation (Biggar 1922–36, 3:137). To a Frenchman of Champlain's time such a life seemed appropriate to aristocrats or to beggars, but not to common people who were supposed to earn their living by the sweat of their brow.

Such opinions reflect the difficulty that the French experienced in trying to understand even the least esoteric aspects of Huron culture. In Europe, where the fertility of fields was maintained through crop rotation, forest clearance was of minimal importance. Because of this, the French consistently failed to note the extent of this activity among the Huron. Likewise, because every Huron man performed a wide variety of tasks, he tended to organize his time in a less regular way than did contemporary Europeans, especially urban dwellers. To the French, such behaviour appeared to be further evidence of laziness.

In fact, all of the evidence indicates that Huron men worked at least as hard as Huron women did, and that their contribution to the economy was no less important. It was they who cleared new fields. With stone axes they chopped down small trees and girdled the larger ones. Then they stripped the branches off the large trees and burned these branches around their trunks in order to kill them. The women planted their crops between the remaining stumps, which were removed when they became rotten and broke apart easily.

Because the fertility of the soil was soon depleted, new fields constantly had to be cleared around a village in order to keep up with declining yields. It has been estimated that a village of 1000 people would have required at least 360 acres of cleared land to feed itself (Heidenreich 1971:213). New

villages usually were located only a few miles from the old one to make it easy for fields to be cleared well in advance of the move. In addition to the extremely hard work of clearing fields, Huron men grew small quantities of tobacco for their own use, in plots of ground near their houses.[18]

Other male tasks of key importance to the Huron economy were those connected with hunting and fishing. Until recently, the importance of fishing for Huron subsistence has been greatly underestimated. Fish were taken with nets, either on the open water or at weirs constructed across streams and rivers. In the winter, nets were laid through holes cut in the ice. Fish were also caught with wooden spears or with hook and line, although the latter was not a particularly effective method, as lines tended to break easily.

Although fish were caught in great abundance at various times of the year and in different parts of Huronia, the most important fishing expeditions were those for a month or more each autumn to the islands in Georgian Bay to catch the spawning whitefish (*Coregonus culpeaformis*). Parties of fishermen built Algonkian-style round cabins on these islands and proceeded to set their nets a mile or more out in the lake each evening and leave them there overnight. Depending on the weather, the fish were either dried in the sun or were smoked, and then packed in bark containers.

Although hunting was less important than fishing from a nutritional point of view, skins were essential for clothing. Moreover, hunting was a prestigious activity much enjoyed by men. Birds were either captured in nets or shot with arrows, bears were tracked with specially trained hunting dogs, and beaver were driven from their lodges in winter and killed when forced to come up to holes in the ice in order to breathe. In addition, a variety of smaller animals were killed and eaten, including large field mice which infested Huron villages.

The Huron had no domestic animals except dogs, which they kept in great numbers. Many of these dogs appear to have been killed and eaten (Thwaites 1896–1901, 7:223; Savage 1971a), although some were special pets and never killed. The Huron also raised bear cubs whose mothers had been killed by hunters. When they grew older, these bears were slain and eaten in ceremonies resembling those in which dogs were sacrificed.

The principal game animal, and the one the Huron most enjoyed hunting, was the deer. Deer hunting was usually a cooperative activity, in which as many as several hundred men drove the animals into a river, or a specially constructed enclosure, where they could be slain more easily. Sometimes, converging barriers of brush, each up to nine feet high and half a mile long, were used to drive deer into these enclosures (plate 4).

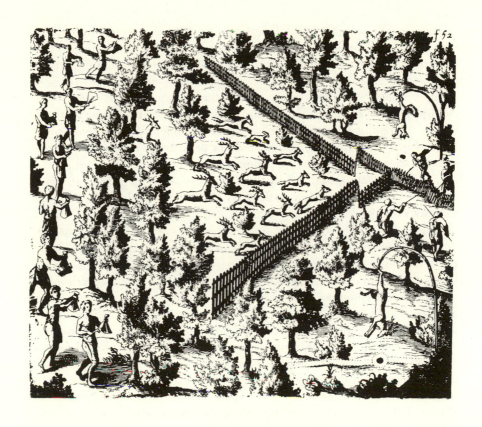

PLATE 4. *A Huron deer hunt. From Champlain's* Voyages *of 1619. On the left hunters with bone clappers drive deer into an enclosure where other hunters kill them with spears. The sides of the enclosure are more elaborate and regular than Champlain describes them as well as much shorter. Courtesy John Carter Brown Library.*

Twenty-five men could construct such a barricade in less than ten days and, by hunting every second day for five weeks, they might be able to kill 120 deer. As already noted, most of this hunting was done in the fall and late winter. This was when the deer gathered in the largest herds and hence could be hunted most easily. Because game was scarce in the vicinity of Huron settlement, deer hunting took place to the south and in the Trent Valley. The skins and fat of the deer were carefully preserved, but only a small amount of the meat could be brought back to the villages to be eaten at celebrations.[19]

The third major group of tasks performed by men was the construction carried on out-of-doors during the summer months. The most arduous activity was the erection of the multi-family longhouses. These were constructed of slabs of bark, preferably cedar, which were tied onto a wooden frame and held down by a network of saplings. Houses were located nine to twelve feet apart to minimize the danger of fire, and many had a narrow end facing into the prevailing wind, to lessen the chances of fire spreading to other houses and to prevent them from being blown down (Heidenreich 1967:18). The standard Huron house was about 90 to 100 feet long and 25 to 30 feet wide. Poles seem to have been dug into the ground along either side of the house and were tied at the top to form an arbour-shaped structure.[20] At one or both ends of the house was an enclosed porch,[21] where corn and firewood were stored, and near the centre were large poles which held racks on which the occupants placed their pots, clothing, and other possessions. A raised platform, four to five feet off the ground, ran along both sides of the house, while down the middle was a row of large hearths, each about twenty feet apart. These may have been used for heating the longhouse and smaller ones on either side used for cooking (Heidenreich 1971:118). A single family lived on either side of each of the central fires. Judging from their construction, Huron houses could have remained in habitable condition only for the average lifetime of a village. When new ones were required, all the men of the village cooperated in their construction.

Another communal activity was the construction of the palisades which protected the larger Huron villages. This work was directed by the village headmen, the labour force being provided by young men from the village and from nearby hamlets that lacked defences of their own. Huron palisades were not like those of a European fort, but consisted of several rows of wooden poles, each three to five inches in diameter and spaced six to twelve inches apart. Only if the palisade consisted of more than two rows, was one of the inner ones made of stakes up to ten inches in diameter

(Heidenreich 1971:140). The rows of stakes were reinforced by inserting large slabs of bark between them and were then woven together with smaller branches to form a kind of rough basket-weave enclosure around the village.[22] It has been estimated that as many as 24,000 poles were required to fortify the largest Huron villages (Heidenreich 1971:154). One or more gates were provided, each of which required an individual to turn several times while entering the village.[23] Watchtowers and defensive galleries were constructed on the inside of the palisades and were reached by ladders made of notched logs. For constructing both houses and palisades, small trees were preferred. The desirability of second growth for such operations was yet another reason for villages remaining in areas that had long been inhabited (Heidenreich 1971:153).

A final outdoor activity was the construction of canoes. Huron canoes, like those of the northern Algonkians, were covered with birchbark. The size of canoes varied. Large ones, which were up to twenty feet long and held as many as six men, were built for travel on Georgian Bay and the major rivers, while smaller ones were used where portages were more frequent. The building of canoes naturally required smaller work teams than did the construction of either houses or fortifications.

Men also manufactured tools and weapons. Scrapers, drills, and small triangular arrowheads were chipped from chert, some of which came from the Niagara Escarpment (Heidenreich 1971:228; Kidd 1952:72). Many tools, however, were manufactured from small nodules of chert or quartz from local glacial deposits. The bipolar technique used to work this material is more similar to that used farther north than it is to the bifacial flaking technique found among the Iroquoians to the south. This seems to reflect the similar raw material used by the Huron and the northern Algonkians (W. Fox 1971). Chisels and rectangular axes and adzes were ground mainly out of a greenish-black chlorite schist, but also out of diorite and other hard stones (ibid. 143–46). Harpoons, projectile points, awls, and needles were made of bone, and ladles were carved out of antler (Kidd 1952:73). Spoons, bowls, arrow shafts, snowshoes, sleds, clubs, and suits of armour were fashioned out of wood, using stone tools. Men also wove fishing nets out of the twine that was manufactured by the women. Many of these tasks may have been performed indoors during the winter.

Men also produced, or obtained through trade, a wide range of ornamental objects: tubular beads made out of bird bones; discoidal ones made from the ribs of imported conch shells; and stone beads, some in the shape of animals made from red slate and perhaps also from catlinite. Combs and small amulets in human form were whittled out of bone and occasionally

pipes were made from stone.[24] It is uncertain whether men or women made the more common clay pipes. The bowls of these pipes were either round or flaring and some were decorated with human or animal effigies. These pipes are clearly the work of talented potters and it seems likely that a few people may have produced the pipes for an entire village.[25]

In addition to hunting and fishing, clearing land, building houses, and manufacturing tools, the major activities that men engaged in were trading, waging war, and government. These activities frequently brought men into contact with Huron from other villages and with foreigners. Particularly as a result of their trading activities, Huron men were more aware of cultural differences than Huron women were, and were accustomed to tolerating such differences. While women were the guardians of family life and its traditions, men were charged with the responsibility for safety and order, which involved maintaining their village's links with the outside world.

The Bonds of Friendship

Every human being, or group of human beings, whose existence was known to the Huron was considered to be either their enemy or friend. A man's enemies might seek to harm him in a variety of ways, and both material and spiritual assistance was necessary to combat them. Friends were those upon whom a person could rely for help under any circumstances. The principal mark of friendship was the willingness of individuals to share whatever goods they had with one another, freely and without complaint. From an enemy, whether known or unknown, one could expect only hostility, injury, or death.

KINSHIP

The basic unit of friendship and cooperation was the extended family, which lived together in a single longhouse. Although the size of longhouses varied considerably, the average one appears to have sheltered six families, each composed of a man, a woman, and their children.[26] There is little precise information about the manner in which the individual families who lived together were related to one another, but it appears that in most cases the extended family ideally consisted of a woman and her daughters,

or a group of sisters, together with their husbands and children (claims to the contrary are discussed in chapters 3 and 6). It also seems likely, from what is known about residence rules in other societies, that even if the Huron preferred matrilocal residence, available space and eccentric preferences of marriage partners often resulted in this rule being ignored in practice.

The Huron did not use kinship terms in the same way that Europeans use them and the failure of French writers to take note of this creates serious ambiguities in their accounts of Huron life. The Huron word for mother (*anan* or *ondoüen*) also meant mother's sister. Sisters referred to each other's children as sons and daughters (*ayein/eyein*), and all their children called each other brother and sister (*ataquen/etaquen*), although there were separate terms distinguishing older brothers and sisters from younger ones.[27] Thus, in an ideal longhouse, all of the women of maternal age would be called mother, and all the children were equally sons and daughters to these women and brothers and sisters to each other. While in no sense obliterating the identity of the nuclear family, the use of these terms must have encouraged a more far-reaching sense of family unity than is apparent using our own system of kinship nomenclature.

On the other hand, although brothers do not appear often to have lived together, in a symmetrical way the Huron used a single term for father and father's brother (*aystan* or *aihtaha*), and brothers referred to each other's children as their sons and daughters, while these children all addressed each other as brother and sister. The terms aunt (*harha*) and uncle (*hoüatinoron*) were thus reserved for father's sisters and mother's brothers respectively, and only the children of such aunts and uncles were called cousin (*earassé*). All blood relatives of the grandparental generation, including great aunts and great uncles, were referred to as grandfather and grandmother. Likewise, all consanguineal relatives of the second descending generation, whether or not they were one's lineal descendants, were called grandsons and granddaughters.

CHILDHOOD

Although children were welcomed in Huron society and were much loved, especially by the women, the average Huron family was small by comparison with seventeenth-century French ones. They appear to have averaged about three children. In part, this may have resulted from a high rate of infant mortality, but births were also less frequent than in Europe

since women abstained from sexual intercourse for two or three years while they breast-fed each child. The births of girls were more rejoiced at than those of boys, because their descendants would be a source of strength to their matrilineage, whereas, once boys had married, the majority of them went to live with their wives' kindred. Yet, in spite of this preference, the Huron clearly wanted many descendants of both sexes to protect and care for them in their old age.

Pregnant women generally worked up to the time of their delivery and tried to be on their feet as soon as possible afterward. A corner of the longhouse was partitioned off for the birth, and the woman either delivered herself or was attended by an elderly female who acted as midwife. Women tried not to cry out for fear of being thought cowardly; apparently, just as a man proved his courage in battle, so a woman proved hers in childbirth. In spite of this stoical approach, a considerable number of women died in the process.[28]

Immediately after birth, a child's ears were pierced and it was given a name, which was probably the possession of an individual lineage or clan and could be given to a child only if it was not already in use. During the day, the child was swaddled in furs and tied to a cradleboard. The latter could be stood on the floor of the longhouse while the mother was working or carried around by her, either suspended against her back by a tumpline or propped up inside her dress so that the child could look forward over her shoulder. These cradleboards were often decorated with small paintings and strings of beads. At night, the child slept naked between its parents.

In view of current ideas about child rearing, it is interesting to reflect that no aspect of Huron behaviour shocked the French more than their refusal to use physical punishment to discipline their children. On general principles, the Huron considered it wrong to coerce or humiliate an individual publicly. To their way of thinking, a child was an individual with his or her own needs and rights rather than something amorphous that must be moulded into shape (Tooker 1964:124 n. 27). The Huron feared that a child who was unduly humiliated, like an adult, might be driven to commit suicide (Thwaites 1896–1901, 14:37; Fenton 1941).

Huron children received no formal training. Girls, however, began at an early age to play games that taught them how to perform household tasks and, in a short time, they were pounding corn and helping their mothers in the fields. As a result, a young girl not only acquired the skills she would need as an adult, but also became accustomed to cooperate with the women of her household, among whom she was likely to spend the rest of her life. When a girl reached puberty, she was not forced to leave the house while

she was menstruating, as Algonkian women were, but henceforth she cooked and ate her food separately at such times, using small clay pots made especially for this purpose.

The training of boys was quite different. Boys were not expected to help their mothers or sisters to perform household tasks and, if asked, would refuse to do so. From an early age, however, they were trained to use weapons and spent their time out of doors shooting arrows, spearing fish, and playing ball games. These activities helped to develop a boy's sense of vision, hearing, and smell, as well as his manual dexterity. They also helped to forge strong and enduring links between boys of the same age, which in many ways became more important to them than those of family and kinship. Boys were encouraged to become brave and self-reliant and to endure misfortune with exemplary fortitude. In order to harden their bodies, they frequently went about scantily clad, even in winter. As evidence of self-control, boys were expected to learn to speak deliberately and to the point, and to curb the expression of violent emotions. Talkativeness and public displays of emotion were viewed with withering scorn as being womanly. They also learned to remember and describe places they had seen and to remember speeches, treaties, lists of names, and other information necessary to conduct business without written records.

At about the age of fifteen, at least some young men went on vision quests. They would remain in the forest without food for a fortnight or longer, until a guardian spirit revealed himself to them and foretold their future. It was also at this age that a youth had revealed to him the personal chant (in Iroquois, *adónwe'*), which he would henceforth sing in times of danger.

In the training of both sexes, much emphasis was placed on the value of good behaviour, discretion, and modesty. In their dealings with one another, Huron were expected to be gentle and considerate and to repress feelings of frustration or hostility, which could only properly be vented against a common enemy. Their repression of hostility, and reticence to express feelings in an uninhibited manner, may explain the seemingly contradictory French assertion that the Huron were cheerful and contented, but always a little taciturn.

COURTSHIP AND MARRIAGE

Men and women were expected to be restrained in each other's presence. Kissing and embracing in public were not permitted and indirect evidence

suggests that even married couples tended to have sexual intercourse in the corn fields or bush outside the village.[29] In spite of such prudery, the Huron considered premarital sexual relations to be perfectly normal and engaged in them soon after puberty. To the astonishment of the French, and the horror of the more prudish of them, girls were as active as men in initiating these liasons. The French were also surprised by the lack of jealousy that characterized such relationships. Young men were required to recognize the right of a girl to decide which of her lovers she preferred at any one time. Sometimes, a young man and woman developed a longstanding, but informal, sexual relationship, in which case the girl became known as the man's *asqua* or companion. This did not prevent either partner from having sexual relations with other friends.

The Huron did not attach the same importance that we do to the distinction between married and not married. Instead, they encouraged various stages of experimentation and growing commitment that did not culminate in a stable relationship until children were born. The Huron were monogamous and are reported not to have married any relations within three degrees of consanguinity, apparently on either the maternal or the paternal sides of their families (Charlton 1968). In addition, they do not appear to have been allowed to marry any member of their own clan.

While parents could not compel their children to marry, they played an important role as marriage brokers. They provided sons with the present used to propose to a girl and approached her parents to seek their support for the match. If the consent of the girl's parents was not forthcoming, usually because they felt the boy was not a good hunter, fisherman, or warrior, the marriage could not take place. If they gave their consent, the boy offered the girl a beaver robe or a wampum necklace. If she took it, they slept together for several nights. After this, the girl was free to accept or reject her suitor, but in either case she could keep the present he had offered her. If she agreed to marry, her father provided a feast for their two families and friends. This feast served to solemnize the union. Hereafter the woman was recognized as the man's *aténonha* or wife. If a young girl who had many lovers became pregnant, it was normal for each of these men to claim the child was his and for the girl to choose from among them the man she wished to marry.

Any marriage could be terminated at the wish of either partner. Prior to the birth of a child, infidelity and divorce seem to have been common and were matters of little concern. Afterwards, couples separated only infrequently, and if they quarrelled or became estranged, friends and relatives would intervene to save the marriage. In spite of the apparent

stability of these mature marriages, even elderly couples continued to take the right of divorce seriously. One of the main reasons that middle-aged men gave for not becoming Roman Catholics was their fear that if their wives left them, they would be unable to remarry.

Perhaps because of the sexual freedom of their youth, physical relations between a husband and wife do not appear to have played a vital role in holding marriages together. Adultery is not recorded as being particularly common, even though husbands spent long periods away from their wives each year.

ADULT AMBITIONS

A Huron wished above all else to be loved and respected by his fellow tribesmen. Men strove to be brave warriors, good hunters, or clever traders and to gain a reputation for giving sound advice when this was asked for. Women sought public approval by looking after their families and guests well. Generosity was an important means of winning the respect of others and, for this reason, whole families worked hard to grow the corn, obtain the meat, and accumulate the presents necessary to entertain their friends and neighbours and to be able to contribute lavishly to communal activities. A Huron's principal aim in acquiring wealth seems to have been to share it with others, social status accruing to those who dispensed their possessions unstintingly.

In particular, the Huron enjoyed giving and attending feasts, and success in any special endeavour was cause for sponsoring a celebration. Visitors were welcomed and a complete stranger had only to sit down in a longhouse in order to be fed and made to feel at home. These attitudes nourished a strong sense of responsibility towards the community. If a house and its contents were destroyed by fire, as happened not infrequently, the rest of the village helped to build a new one and presented its occupants with corn, firewood, and household utensils to repair their losses. Whenever public funds were required, families vied with one another to subscribe to them. In each case, the name of the donor and the value of his present were announced publicly. Gifts were distributed in large numbers at funerals and curing ceremonies, the extent of individual offerings again being public knowledge. A strong overt disapproval of stinginess created feelings of shame, which helped to sustain this tradition of generosity.

These attitudes towards property coloured many aspects of Huron life. There were no markets where people could gather to trade, and even

ordinary barter does not appear to have been the most common means of redistributing goods within the confederacy. Instead, economic activities were largely incorporated within a system of social relations in which hospitality, gift giving, and ceremonial exchange played important parts.

The most important cleavage in Huron society, except for that between the sexes, was between young and old men. Most of the important political, economic, and ritual positions were occupied by mature men, who in their youth had proved their ability, above all as successful warriors. By contrast, young men were viewed as untried and, therefore, as unreliable: an evaluation which they much resented and which gave rise to disputes with the council chiefs.

The hereditary chiefs, in particular, had a vested interest in maintaining good relations with neighbouring tribes, both to save the Huron country from the scourge of war and to ensure that trading activities went on unhindered. In order to acquire prestige, youths were anxious to find some pretext for going to war, and often alleged that the peaceful policies of their elders were designed to prevent young men from having a greater share in the direction of village affairs. Sometimes, the desire to fight led young warriors to ignore the orders of their headmen and to attack tribes with whom the Huron were at peace. This generalized conflict was a factor that greatly complicated the foreign relations of the Huron especially since it was common to all the northern Iroquoian-speaking peoples.

DEATH

The Huron seem to have believed that they had at least two souls. One might eventually be reborn, and this explained why some children resembled their dead ancestors. The other remained with the body until the Feast of the Dead was celebrated. Death was a source of great anxiety to the Huron, who viewed it as cutting off necessary personal contact between people who loved one another. The souls of the dead were believed to be angered by this severance of familiar relationships and, for this reason, they were feared, although at the same time their memory was loved and honoured. Simply to mention a dead person's name, without using an honorific to indicate he was dead, was a serious insult to his family. This is one of the reasons why headmen quickly announced an individual's death throughout the village, and why anyone who had the same name changed it for a while. If fire broke out in a village, the first efforts were directed towards protecting the nearby cemetery.

A Huron was expected to die as bravely as he had lived. Men frequently were dressed for burial prior to death and gave an *athataion* or farewell feast, at which they partook of the best food and sang their personal chant to show that they did not fear death. Specific families, probably belonging to different phratries (or groupings of clans), were mutually responsible for burying each other's dead. As soon as someone died, those whose task it was flexed his body in a crouching position and wrapped it in the finest fur robe that his relatives possessed. Friends and relatives converged on the dead person's longhouse, bringing presents of food with them. The women of the village mourned in a stylized fashion, exciting their grief by painfully recalling the names of their own dead kinsmen. The men did not weep, but assumed a melancholy expression and sat with their heads sunk between their knees. A village notable made a speech, in which he praised the dead man and offered consolation to his relatives.

The deceased was usually buried on the third day after he died. A meal was provided at daybreak for those who had come from a distance, after which the body was carried to the cemetery. There, it was placed in a bark coffin, supported on poles eight to ten feet high (plate 5). Then presents, which had been contributed by the mourners, were presented to dry the tears of his relatives and to thank those who had buried him. Sometimes, sticks were thrown from the top of the coffin into a group of young men and women who had gathered on either side of it, and presents were given to the persons who, after a fierce struggle, gained possession of these sticks.

Not everyone was buried in the same manner. Very young children were interred under paths, in the hope that their souls might be reborn in the womb of a woman passing by. The bones of slain captives, and sometimes of other public enemies, such as witches, found their way into the village middens. Anyone who had died a violent death was immediately buried in the ground, and a small mound, with a bark hut over it, was erected on top of his grave.[30] The bodies of those who drowned or froze to death received even more bizzare treatment. These were cut up in the village cemetery and the flesh and entrails were burned, while the skeleton was buried. Failure to do this was believed to anger the sky, or the spirit of the lake, and would result in further accidents and dangerous changes in the weather.

After the funeral, the husband or wife of the deceased remained lying in a dishevelled state in their house for ten days. During this period, the bereaved spouse kept his or her face pressed against the ground and did not speak to anyone, except to say good-day to visitors. This initial period was followed by a year during which remarriage was not supposed to take place,

PLATE 5. *A Huron village cemetery. From Champlain's* Voyages *of 1619.*
A normal scaffold burial and a specialized inhumation are depicted.
The design of the poles is clearly European as are the chimneys on the
longhouse in the background. The two most elaborate hairstyles are copied
from Le Moyne's Florida illustrations. Courtesy McGill University
Libraries.

and widows and widowers neither greased their hair nor went to feasts. Women often blackened their faces and went about poorly clad and un- kempt during this period.

GOVERNMENT

Among the Huron, the French encountered a system of government based on principles that were completely contrary to their own. For most seventeenth-century Europeans, authority was delegated from a divinely sanctioned king to his subordinates, who had the power to punish dis- obedience to his administration with fines, imprisonment, and even death. The Huron system grew out of their family structure and was so con- structed that not even the smallest units were called upon to surrender any of their rights. No headman could rely on officially sanctioned power to see that his decisions were enforced; instead, he had to depend on public opinion to support his proposals. In Europe, decisions that were not made in an autocratic fashion were usually decided upon by a majority vote; among the Huron, issues were discussed until a general consensus was reached. No man could be expected to be bound by a decision to which he had not willingly given his consent.

The basic unit of Huron political organization appears to have been the clan segment.[31] A clan segment was made up of all those individuals who were members of matrilineal extended families that inhabited a single community and claimed their descent from a common female ancestor. Although there were many of these clan segments within each tribe of the Huron confederacy, each was named after one of eight creatures: Turtle, Wolf, Bear, Beaver, Deer, Hawk, Porcupine, and Snake. Members of clan segments in different villages that bore the name of the same animal recognized a symbolic affinity for one another, similar to that of kinship. Individuals were not permitted to marry either members of their own clan segment or people whose segments bore the same name. Because clan segments with the same name were found among all the Huron tribes, this symbolic kinship provided a sense of unity that cut across tribal divisions and gave additional stability to the Huron confederacy. Later evidence suggests that these clans were grouped together to form three larger divisions or phratries. These appear to have been mainly of ritual signifi- cance, although they too may have been exogamous.[32]

If a village was small, its nucleus might consist of a single clan segment. Large villages were made up of several segments, each of which appears to

have occupied its own section of the village. Archaeological evidence indicates that in some villages, different clan segments, or groupings of these segments, lived in separate palisaded enclosures, which nevertheless were located in close proximity to one another.[33] If the Huron had invariably followed a pattern of matrilocal residence, all of the women and children, but none of the married men, would have lived in the part of a village that belonged to their clan segment. We know, however, that political offices were inherited matrilineally; that is, they passed to one of the incumbent's brothers or a sister's son, rather than to his own offspring. In this way, offices were retained within the same clan segment. Since it is unlikely that men would live outside the clan segment whose headmen they were, boys belonging to chiefly lineages were probably sent to live with their mother's brothers and, when they married, their wives came to live with them. Such a pattern of chiefly avunculocal residence may, in part, explain the Huron longhouses inhabited by male members of a lineage and the many women living in their husbands' villages rather than their own that are reported in the *Jesuit Relations*.[34]

Each clan segment appears to have had two headmen. One was a civil leader, who was concerned with maintaining law and order; coordinating group activities, including feasts, dances, and games; and with all dealings with other groups concerning peace. The other was a war chief, who was concerned exclusively with military affairs. The civil headmen were chosen from a particular lineage within each clan segment. Since there was no rule, such as primogeniture, to specify who this individual should be, the personal qualities of the candidates counted for a great deal. These qualities included intelligence, oratorical ability, reputation for generosity, and, above all, performance as a warrior. In order to assure that he would be able to represent the segment effectively, no one was made head of a clan segment without support from the other Huron headmen. These headmen were invited to a magnificent investiture feast to win their approval for the clan segment's nominee. At this feast, they presented the new headman with gifts on behalf of the clan segments, villages, and tribes they represented. They also symbolically drew him from the grave and conferred his predecessor's council name upon him, so that, in effect, the previous office holder was resurrected. In this manner, the names of civil headmen continued from generation to generation in the same lineage. It is unclear what role women played in the election of headmen, but it is possible that, as among the Iroquois, their opinions were important within their own clan segment.

While the mode of election of war chiefs and their role in government is

not clearly understood, it appears that these offices were also hereditary in certain lineages. Councils of war were held at the village, tribal, and confederacy levels. These headmen planned military strategy and led warriors in battle; only under unusual circumstances do they appear to have played a significant role in other spheres of Huron life.

All of the internal affairs of a clan segment were managed by its civil headman, in consultation with the heads of the various households and lineages that made up the group. The murder of one member of a clan segment by another was a strictly internal matter, and any attempt by outsiders to interfere in the settlement of such a case would have been deeply resented. If a dispute between clan segments living in the same village became too severe, one of the segments might split off and found a separate village of its own, just as, contrariwise, if a suitable opportunity arose, friendly segments might join together to establish a single large village. The physical capacity to opt out of larger units allowed each clan segment to retain a maximum amount of autonomy.

The village, whether made up of one or more segments, constituted a second important unit of Huron society (Fenton 1951). The daily face-to-face interaction of villagers generated a concern for one another that did not exist at higher levels of Huron political organization. Villagers aided one another to build houses, helped those in distress, participated in many feasts and collective rituals, and shared in the common defence of the village. In large villages, intermarriage between clan segments helped to forge strong bonds of community solidarity.

The headmen for each village were the civil leaders of the clan segments. Because they represented clan segments, they could not be removed from office except by their own clansmen, nor could they be compelled against their will to accept any decision arrived at by other headmen. Though all were equal in this sense, one of the headmen appears to have been recognized as spokesman for the entire village. It is uncertain whether the clan segments were ranked in order of importance, so that the head of the senior clan automatically became the principal headman of the village, or if the prestige of individual headmen tended to fluctuate according to the personalities involved.

The village council appears to have met daily in the house of the principal headman, which was larger than the rest so that it could serve various community functions. The civil headmen of each of the clan segments, as well as the "Old Men" of the village, attended these meetings. While the title of the latter suggests that they consisted of all the older men in the village, it was probably conferred only on those who, in their mature

years, had acquired sufficient reputation that their advice was considered to be of value. These men appear to have had considerable influence in village councils.

Often these councils had no specific business to discuss and the meeting was more like that of a social club. Nevertheless, decisions were made that influenced many aspects of village life. The council arranged public feasts, dances, and lacrosse matches, and decided for whom special curing rites requiring village participation would be performed. The council also undertook to see that no one was in need and coordinated communal projects, such as constructing palisades and relocating the village. All legal disputes arising between members of the different clan segments that lived in the village were adjudicated by the council. Any public announcements resulting from its deliberations were made by the principal headman or his deputy, who was a close relative and who frequently accompanied him and made announcements in his name. The political organization of both the clan segments and the village councils shows clearly that, while no Huron had the legal power to coerce another, individuals and lineages were far from equal in social prestige. The dichotomy between egalitarian ideals and the tendencies towards accumulating power and prestige that were part of Huron society was perennially a source of concern to the Huron.

The councils that governed each of the four Huron tribes appear to have been made up of all the civil headmen from each of the tribal villages; although in the case of the Tahontaenrat, who had only one village, village and tribal government were probably identical. Each tribe recognized one of the members of this council as its principal headman and treaties were made in his name. It was apparently his permission that foreign groups had to obtain if they wished to cross tribal territory. The name of the principal headman of the Arendarhonon was Atironta. Endahiaconc, the Attigneenongnahac leader, was also the leading headman of their main village, Teanaostaiaé. Anenkhiondic, who lived at Ossossané, was said to be head of the Attignawantan, but among the part of the tribe that lived in the Penetanguishene Peninsula a man named Auoindaon, and later Aenons, appears to have claimed similar honours.[35] There seems to have been a political cleavage between the northern and southern Attignawantan, of which the rival claims of these two chiefs were probably a reflection.

In spite of the importance that the French and the Algonkians attached to the Huron tribal headmen, their position was not analogous to that of a European head of state. The members of a tribe shared a common territory and common traditions, and were even willing to accept that because of the size of the tribal unit or for historical reasons, the leader of one of their

clan segments should have the right to represent all of them on ceremonial occasions. This did not, however, give any headman the right to interfere in the internal business of any clan segment but his own. The powers of the tribal head were further limited because other members of the council had hereditary responsibilities that were complementary, rather than subordinate, to his own. For example, one of the Attignawantan headmen was responsible for dealing with the tribes the Huron visited by water along the shores of Lake Huron, and messages to these tribes were sent in his name. Presumably, these duties were imagined to have been entrusted to particular headmen when the tribal government was first established.[36]

It appears that any headman could call a meeting about a matter falling within his sphere of concern. Most meetings, however, were called by the tribal headman and met in his village which, in this sense only, was a tribal capital. Meetings were held at any time of the year. If the matter was particularly important, old men were sent as messengers to summon the headmen, as their word carried more weight than did that of younger men. One of the duties of the tribal councils must have been to help settle disputes between people living in different villages, particularly if their clan segments or village councils were unable to resolve them. The tribal councils also discussed matters of interest to the confederacy as a whole, with the aim of formulating proposals that would best serve their respective interests. For various reasons, including their differing geographical location, the views of the four tribes on matters of foreign policy often differed radically from one another.

Very little is known about the composition of the confederacy council, but its membership appears to have consisted of most, if not all, of the civil headmen who sat on the various tribal councils. The confederacy leaders thus represented most of the clan segments in the Huron country. If a similar system prevailed in modern Canadian politics, a single man would simultaneously serve as mayor of Toronto, prime minister of Ontario, and a senior ranking member of the federal cabinet.

The structure of the confederacy council must have been altered by the addition of the Arendarhonon tribe about 1590 and the Tahontaenrat as late as 1610. The Attignawantan and Attigneenongnahac were accorded senior status for being the founding members of the confederacy, and the Attignawantan, because of their size, occupied half the seats on the council. It is possible that the Tahontaenrat were not officially seated on the council even in the late 1630s, although they may have been allowed to attend meetings.[37] The admission of the Arendarhonon shows, however, that the Huron were not as inflexible as the Iroquois were later, when they refused

to disrupt the traditional roster of council chiefs in order fully to integrate the Tuscarora into their confederacy (Hale 1963:79).

While special meetings were called in times of emergency, the main meeting of the confederacy council appears to have been each spring and to have lasted several weeks. On this occasion, new headmen were installed, there was much singing and dancing, and war feasts were held prior to raids being launched against enemy tribes. The main function of these meetings seems to have been to strengthen the confederacy by bringing together the headmen from all the Huron villages and giving them an opportunity to reaffirm old friendships and discuss topics of mutual interest. The main problems confronting the confederacy as a whole were to prevent disputes between members of different tribes from disrupting its unity, to maintain friendly relations with tribes with whom the Huron traded, and, where possible, to try to coordinate dealings with enemy tribes, in particular the Iroquois.

At meetings of the confederacy council the Attignawantan sat on one side of the longhouse, the remaining tribes on the other. The headman who presided over these meetings was an Attignawantan. Meetings began with speeches of welcome and thanksgiving and, after the reason for the meeting was formally announced, the headmen from each tribe and village were asked their opinions in turn. After consulting with his advisors and headmen from the same tribe, each would state his opinion slowly and distinctly, speaking in a special ceremonial style that was full of metaphors, circumlocutions, and other rhetorical devices that were uncommon in everyday speech. Every one listened attentively, politeness and good humour being considered essential. Violent outbursts were rare and, to the surprise of European visitors, were strongly disapproved of, even if the issue was a hotly debated one. Discussion often continued late into the night, until a satisfactory consensus had been reached.

The confederacy, tribal, and village councils all had public funds, which they used to carry on diplomacy, reward friends in other tribes, and make reparations payments. In part, these funds were maintained from gifts the councils received through diplomatic channels or in return for favours they had granted. When more was required, it was a matter of pride for Huron families to donate what was needed.

LAW

The Huron recognized four major categories of crime: murder and its lesser equivalents wounding and injury, theft, witchcraft, and treason.[38] In

theory, murder placed an absolute obligation upon the kinsmen of the dead man to seek revenge by clamouring for the slaying of either the murderer or someone closely related to him. The obligation to do this fell particularly upon the clansmen of a murdered person, that is, upon his sisters, mother's brothers, and sisters' sons. The responsibility of a clan segment to defend its members did not cease when a member was married and living elsewhere. It was also the duty of clansmen to protect a man against death and injury, even when this was in retribution for his own deeds. Depending on the degree of relationship between the murderer and the murdered man, a killing might give rise to a prolonged blood feud between the clan segments, villages, tribes, or even confederacies to which they belonged. Thus, blood feuds varied in scale from family quarrels to major wars. The Huron were well aware that no tribal organization and no confederacy could survive if internal blood feuds went unchecked. One of the basic functions of the confederacy was to eliminate such feuds among its members; indeed, between Huron, they were regarded as a more reprehensible crime than murder itself.

In so doing, however, no effort was made to interfere with the right of a murderer's clansmen to defend him. To have done so would have constituted unwarranted interference with the affairs of the clan segments that made up the confederacy. Instead, it was agreed that within the confederacy, blood feuds would be settled by the payment of reparations from the social group to which the murderer belonged to that of his victim. Both the payment of these reparations and the presents received were shared, to some degree, by all the members of the groups involved. Only if after prolonged discussion, the clansmen of the murderer refused to pay compensation did the relatives of the murdered man have the right to take up arms against them.

The amount of compensation varied according to the rank and sex of the murdered person. If a chief or "Old Man" was slain, the compensation was greater than for someone of lesser importance, and the compensation for a woman was greater than that for a man. The average compensation for a man was about thirty presents and for a woman forty; each present having the approximate value of a beaver robe. After the amount of compensation was determined, a bundle of sticks, indicating the number of presents that were required, was divided among the murderer's tribe, village, or clan segment. It does not appear that his immediate family was asked to provide more presents than were other members; clansmen and fellow villagers often vied with one another to show their public spiritedness in helping the murderer's family. These gifts were presented to the victim's relatives in a

formal ceremony with great expressions of condolence. At the end of the ceremony, the relatives of the dead man gave some small presents to the murderer's kinsmen to indicate that they were forgiven and the matter was closed.

The personal treatment that a murderer received was a matter for his clan segment and lineage to decide. Normally, it took the form of verbal rebukes, rather than physical punishment. Nevertheless, since all members of a group stood to lose through the misbehaviour of any one member, it was in their interest to bring pressure to bear upon a murderer to make sure that he did not kill again. The guilty person knew, moreover, that if he misbehaved repeatedly, he would gradually alienate his clansmen and lose their support. By making tribes, villages, and especially clan segments responsible for the behaviour of their members, the Huron were able to secure order without resorting to capital punishment or interfering with the traditional rights of the various groups that made up their confederacy.

Wounding was a less serious offence than murder and was compensated by presents that varied according to the seriousness of the injury and the status of the person who had been attacked.

The French were frequently critical of the Huron for the lenient attitude they took towards thieves. The simplicity and relative imper-manence of Huron possessions, and the sharing of goods and housing among extended families, probably made ownership intrinsically a matter of less concern to them than it was to Europeans (Herman 1956; Stites 1905). More importantly, however, because of the semi-public nature of Huron dwellings and the lack of any formal policing in their villages, there was little that could be done to protect movable possessions against theft. The main concern of the Huron was therefore to minimize the disruptive consequences of quarrels that might arise from such actions.

This was done by defining theft very narrowly, as the taking of goods forcibly from an individual or from inside a longhouse without per-mission. In theory, a person was entitled to carry off anything he found lying about unattended. In order to protect their valuables, both from fire and thieves, the Huron either carried them around with them or hid them in caches dug into the soil beneath their houses. The Huron did not fine or penalize a thief, nor did they permit a man from whom goods had been stolen to reclaim them without first inquiring how someone else had come to possess them. A refusal to answer constituted an admission of guilt. If a man could prove who had robbed him, he and his relatives were socially sanctioned to go to the thief's longhouse and carry off everything on which they could lay their hands. Hence, relatives of a person who had stolen very

little might find themselves bruised and despoiled. Again, pressure was put on kin groups to enforce good behaviour among their members.

TRADE

So far, we have been examining Huron efforts to curb violence and maintain amicable relations within their own society. Basic to such activities was a concern for a general sort of reciprocity, in which a willingness to redistribute possessions played an important role. A rough kind of reciprocity can also be seen in the hurly-burly of dealing with theft, and even a serious crime, such as murder, could be atoned for with gifts, if they were given in a spirit of contrition and with an evident desire for reconciliation. A murderer might kill in a fit of jealousy or anger, but his crime was not seen as alienating him from his society.

Relations of friendship and material reciprocity were extended beyond the Huron confederacy in the form of trading arrangements. In the historic period, trade was a source not only of luxury goods but of meat and skins which were vital to a population that had outstripped the resources of its nearby hunting territory. Important as these goods were, however, foreign trade was not merely an economic activity. It was embedded in a network of social relations that were, fundamentally, extensions of the friendly relationships that existed within the Huron confederacy.

The Huron traded with both the other Iroquoian tribes of southern Ontario and the Algonkian-speaking peoples who lived to the north of them; however, the nature of the trade was completely different. Almost all of the goods imported from the south were luxury items. One of the most important imports was tobacco, which grew better in the warmer territories of the Tionnontaté and Neutral than it did in the Huron country. From the Neutral country came tobacco and black squirrel skins, which the Huron made into cloaks that were highly prized by themselves and the Algonkians to the north. From the same area originated the so-called "Erie stones," which Gendron (1868:8) informs us the Neutral traded with other tribes. Gendron was later to take some of these stones, which were probably a naturally occurring form of calcium carbonate, back to France, to become the basis of his famous cancer cure (Jury and Jury 1954:106–7). In addition to its own products, the Neutral country was a source of goods from farther south. These included racoon skin robes, which came from the Erie country,[39] wampum beads, which seem to have originated among the Susquehannock, and conch and other shells, which

ultimately came from the Gulf of Mexico and the eastern seaboard of the United States.[40] Gourds, which were used to store oil, also appear to have come from a considerable distance to the south.[41] Occasionally, Huron warriors would visit the Susquehannock in order to consolidate plans to wage war against the Iroquois and to trade with them directly.

A small amount of what the Huron obtained from the north could also be classified as luxury goods. These included charms, clothing, camping equipment, buffalo robes, which came from the west by way of Sault Sainte Marie, and native copper,[42] which was found around the shores of Lake Superior. In return, the Algonkians received tobacco and a few exotic luxuries, such as wampum. The bulk of the trade, however, was in more essential items. The northern hunters were anxious to obtain nets and rope, but, above all, the Huron country was a source of cornmeal, which helped to sustain them over the hard winters. Groups of Nipissing and Petite Nation Algonkin passed each winter in the Huron country, in encampments close to the Huron villages. In the middle of autumn, these groups began to move south, bringing with them the furs they had trapped or purchased from other tribes and catching and drying fish along the way. Both commodities were used to buy corn, tobacco, and nets from the Huron. The Petite Nation appears to have been on particularly good terms with the Arendarhonon and came each winter to live near the village of Cahiagué. The Nipissing wintered in the Wye Valley, among the Ataronchronon or Attignawantan. Each summer, groups of Huron men travelled north to trade for furs. These journeys may have taken some of them as far afield as Lakes Michigan and Superior, and into the central part of Quebec.[43] In winter, the Huron crossed the ice of Georgian Bay to trade cornmeal and nets for dried fish among the neighbouring bands.

In order to sustain this trade, Huron women planted considerably more corn than was required to feed their own families. The trade was highly advantageous to the Huron because it provided them with additional protein, in the form of dried fish, and with skins, which were badly needed for clothing. Because of the size of the Huron population, game in nearby areas was sorely depleted. It therefore seems unlikely that, without this trade, as large a population could have lived in the Huron country for any length of time as was found there in the early historic period (Trigger 1962a; 1963b).

Because the Huron valued their trade and did not wish it to be disrupted, they were careful to cultivate good relations with their northern trading partners. In so doing, they were conforming to well-established conventions that were tacitly understood and accepted by all the tribes in the region.

Trade was embedded in a network of social relations and the exchange of goods was carried out largely in the form of reciprocal gift-giving. Such reciprocity was considered an integral part of any friendly interaction, and ties between individual trading partners were modelled on those between relatives. Visits to foreign tribes for purposes of trade were seen as hazardous adventures that had to be hedged about with many formal courtesies. Before entering a village, all the members of an expedition would paint themselves and put on their best ornaments. Feasts, speech-making, and formal exchanges of gifts between headmen normally went on for several days, both before and after the more commercial trading.

The French could not understand why, although the Huron were clearly skilful in collecting furs, they scorned to haggle over the price of individual items and became annoyed when Europeans tried to do so. The Huron understood the operation of a market economy in the sense that they were aware of the relationship between the scarcity of an item and the price that could be obtained for it; nevertheless, they refused to express a profit motive openly. To haggle about the price of goods was interpreted as a lack of friendship. The success of the Huron as traders depended largely on their skill in maintaining good relations with other tribes, particularly with the northern peoples, who had cultures different from their own. All trading partners were expected to conform to the hospitality, gift-giving, and careful observation of various formalities that made up the conventions of this trade.

Many Huron appear to have had trading partners among each of the tribes they visited (Trigger 1960:23). These were the persons with whom they stayed and exchanged goods. They often referred to these partners as their kinsmen and were probably linked to them through formal bonds of adoption. Some partners seem to have exchanged children as evidence of trust and goodwill and also to provide hostages. Occasionally, Algonkians who came to the Huron country as exchanges married Huron and remained there.

There was always the danger that if a Huron and someone from a group with whom the Huron traded got into a fight and one of them were killed, the demand for blood revenge would lead to war. Because of the disastrous effect this would have on trade, the Huron were anxious to settle such disputes as quickly as possible. They were willing to pay much more to compensate for a murder of this sort than for the murder of one Huron by another. The chief factor which made the settlement of this sort of murder

more difficult than the settlement of ones within the confederacy was the problem of finding a mediator who was acceptable to both sides.

Among the Huron themselves, trade was governed by elaborate rules. The rights to a particular route were said to belong to the family of the man who had discovered it. No other Huron was supposed to trade along such a route without first receiving permission from the head of the family that had legal title to it, and such permission was normally granted only in return for valuable presents. If a man engaged in trade illegally, the master of the route and his followers had the right to seize him and despoil him of his goods as he returned home. In keeping with the desire to minimize the effects of theft, however, once such a man had returned safely to his village, all they could do was to complain about his behaviour.

Although most trading seems to have been done by ordinary men in the prime of life, all of the major trade routes were under the control of leading headmen. Such control must have provided these headmen with an important means of acquiring wealth, which in turn could be used to validate their high status within their tribes. It appears that whoever discovered a new trade route, effective control of it soon passed into the hands of the headman of his clan segment or of an even more influential chief within his tribe. Further control was exercised over this trade by the headmen limiting the number of young men from each village who went out each year to trade.

Finally, in spite of the friendly relations that the Huron strove to maintain with the Algonkians, it is clear that their attitude towards these northern hunters was ambivalent. The uncertainty of their way of life was clearly recognized and they were treated in a condescending manner. When they attended Algonkian feasts, the Huron brought their own food with them and, while Huron men married Algonkian women who came to live in the Huron country, no Huron woman would consent to go and live among the Algonkians.[44] Moreover, in keeping with the key role they played in the trading networks of the region, the Huron did not bother to learn the languages of the northern tribes, but rather expected these peoples to learn theirs (Wrong 1939:86). Foreigners who experienced difficulty in learning to speak Huron were regarded as lacking in intelligence. In the historic period, Huron served as a *lingua franca*, not only in the trade that went on around the shores of Lake Huron, but in trade as far east as the Ottawa Valley and possibly as far west as the Winnebago, a Siouan-speaking group who lived on the shores of Green Bay, Wisconsin.

Enemies

We have already seen that among themselves and in their dealings with their allies, friendliness and reciprocity were important elements of Huron life. It is not to be imagined, however, that the opposite of these qualities was not important also. Although the Huron appeared to be open and friendly in their daily life, they were scarcely less afraid of treachery amongst their own people than they were of foreign enemies. Both kinds of hostile forces were seen as negations of the cooperative reciprocity which alone constituted the basis of trust and confidence among them.

WITCHCRAFT AND TREASON

The most dangerous of the enemies that the Huron believed existed within their own society were witches. Witches were individuals of either sex who used magic to bring death and sickness to people they disliked. Unlike ordinary homicide, witchcraft was an indication that a man or woman was a public enemy in much the same way that groups such as the Iroquois were. Such behaviour was held to be so disgusting and immoral that it put the witch beyond any claim of protection, even from his closest relatives. In theory, anyone had the right to slay a proven witch and the witch's relatives were not permitted to seek compensation or blood revenge for such killings.

Witches were believed to harm people by supernaturally causing charms to enter their bodies. These charms could be any foreign object, such as a tuft of hair, nail parings, an animal's claw, a piece of leather, a feather, or grains of sand. In order to make the object enter a body, it had to be rubbed with the flesh of an *angont*, or mythical serpent that lived under the ground or in the water and which was familiar to witches.

The principal motivation for practising witchcraft was believed to be jealousy. Thus, if anyone had been outstandingly successful in hunting or trading, or if a family's harvest had been particularly abundant, they were careful to share their good fortune with others in order to avoid trouble. Yet, since the slightest offence might arouse a witch's resentment, even the most generous person was in danger.

The Huron had shamans called *aretsan* who specialized in treating diseases caused by witchcraft. These specialists were consulted if any illness did not immediately show signs of responding to natural treatment. Proof of witchcraft could be obtained if the *aretsan* was able to remove one or

more charms, by giving the patient an emetic, sucking the charm from his body, or extracting it with the point of a knife without leaving an incision. Yet, a sick man's dream, a rumour, or merely being seen alone in the woods without reason was enough to incite accusations of witchcraft against certain people. Especially in times of crisis, when tensions ran high or epidemics threatened the village, the fear of witchcraft reached dangerous levels. At such times, whole families who felt threatened by witches might move from one village to another. Those who were suspected of witchcraft were in danger of falling victims to mob violence.

It is clear that almost all accusations of witchcraft resulted from violations of Huron norms concerning cooperation and reciprocity. Overtly antisocial behaviour, such as speaking harshly to people, refusing to give feasts or to be generous with one's neighbours, or simply having an unusual desire for privacy, were enough to arouse suspicion. Likewise, repeated irresponsible actions left individuals open to charges of witchcraft. For the most part, these suspicions led only to veiled threats and accusations, meant to frighten the suspected witch and make him conform to social norms.

On the other hand, no one, even a man who believed that his relative had been killed by witchcraft, would dare to slay a suspected witch unless he was certain that public opinion would sanction his action and compel the kinsmen of the murdered man to accept the verdict. Most, if not all, of the cold-blooded slayings of witches appear to have been sanctioned by headmen or war chiefs, who often judged the victims at secret council meetings before appointing an executioner to slay them without warning. Sometimes, an accused witch was arraigned before such a meeting and tortured, in the hope that names of accomplices would be revealed. On rare occasions, those found guilty were slain in public as a prisoner of war might be.

The second crime that the Huron considered worthy of death was treason. Traitors were men who sought to betray the whole country to its enemies, either in the hope of material reward or out of generalized hostility. It is doubtful that the Huron regarded the latter as different from witchcraft. Fear of information being passed to the enemy was prevalent among the Huron and helped to strengthen everyone's loyalty in the face of potential danger. Those suspected of having dealings with the enemy were watched closely and, if a man was believed to be endangering the security of the confederacy, the headmen would give orders for him to be slain. Such killings were made to look like the work of enemy raiders. The headmen investigated all cases of violent deaths, hence were able to declare that no further inquiry into the nature of a particular case was necessary.

Since headmen could legitimize all slayings of witches and traitors, they

were in a position to coerce individuals whose behaviour was socially disruptive, or who too greatly challenged their authority. They could even
eliminate these people, if necessary. Because such action required the
consent of the head of the clan segment to which their intended victim
belonged, these headmen were likely to act only if they were convinced
that the safety of village or tribe required it. Yet the fact that headmen
were able to perceive such common interests, indicates that, at least to a
limited degree, they saw themselves as a ruling group whose interests
transcended more basic loyalties to their kinship groupings (Trigger 1963a).

Thus witchcraft and fear of treason were more than strong forces
promoting a sense of community responsibility and assuring the realization
of the communal ideals of Huron society. They also served as the basis of a
de facto authority that was needed to manage Huron society, but which the
emphasis on the dignity and rights of individuals and kin groups made
overtly unacceptable to all concerned.

WAR

Foreign tribes with whom the Huron did not have bonds of trade and
reciprocity were automatically not to be trusted. This mistrust generated
hostility which frequently led to open conflict. Similar attitudes prevailed
among the other northern Iroquoian tribes, who were all deeply influenced
by the warfare that prevailed among them (Witthoft 1959; Trigger 1967;
1969a:42–53).

The French who visited the Huron country were accustomed to wars that
were fought for territorial gain or commercial advantage, or because of
religious differences. To their surprise, none of these motives played an
important role in traditional Iroquoian warfare. The major reason that the
Huron gave for waging war was to avenge the injuries that warriors from
other tribes had inflicted upon them (Du Creux 1951–52:102–3; Thwaites
1896–1901, 17:65). Thus, if a Huron were slain, or was believed to have
been slain, by Iroquois raiders, or was killed in battle against the Iroquois,
his relatives clamoured for revenge. This was obtained only when the
Huron had killed one or more Iroquois in retaliation. Since neither side
regarded such killings as anything but fresh injuries, the result was a self-
perpetuating cycle of violence that was broken only at irregular intervals so
that exchanges of prisoners might be arranged.

War was also the principal means by which young men acquired the
personal prestige that assured them the respect of their elders and an

influential voice in the affairs of their village in later life. A reputation for skill and bravery in war gave even a candidate for a civil chieftainship a better chance of obtaining this office. Because of this, young men clamoured for war, and often committed acts of violence which disturbed the fragile peace treaties that the tribal headmen had concluded with their traditional enemies. Only within confederacies, and where strong trading alliances existed, could public opinion hold the young men in check and prevent hostilities from arising in response to an emotional cry for blood revenge.

Among the Huron, every man was a warrior and the virtues of man and warrior were identical. Boys were trained in the use of weapons from an early age and were encouraged to be brave, self-reliant, and stoical. Men sought every opportunity to test their courage; when no danger was present, some would hold burning sticks against their bodies until flesh was burned. In this way they reassured themselves that they still retained the courage necessary to fight the enemy.

The Huron and their neighbours did not normally wage war against each other from late autumn through early spring, when leaves were off the trees and it was hard to find cover. During the rest of the year the Huron were on the alert for enemy raiders and rumours about enemy plans circulated from village to village. The larger villages, especially those located on the exposed southern and eastern flanks of the Huron country, were protected by palisades and the Huron headmen endeavored to keep enough warriors at home during the summer to defend these villages. The Huron headmen also sought to cultivate friends among other tribes, who would provide them with advanced warning of an attack. These informers might be resident foreigners or headmen who had a personal interest in friendly relations with the Huron. Dealings with such men made the Huron fearful of similar traitors in their own midst. War chiefs were circumspect about their plans and visitors who were not trusted had to live in specially assigned houses and were not allowed to travel about unattended.

Military campaigns were organized by war chiefs in response to requests from families who had lost members to the enemy. These chiefs went from village to village explaining their plans, distributing presents to gain support for their expedition, and inciting the young men to join them. When support was won at the village level, a general council was held to confirm the plan. This was followed by a war feast, at the end of which, amidst much singing and dancing, the various war parties left to invade enemy territory.

Every warrior wore a kind of armour made of pieces of wood laced together with cords (plate 6). This armour covered his back, legs, and other parts of his body and was proof against stone-tipped arrows. Warriors also carried shields, some of which were made of cedar bark and covered the whole body, as well as clubs, and a bow and arrows. The same weapons were used in war as were used for hunting. In addition, Huron warriors wore red circlets of moosehair around their foreheads, as well as their finest shell necklaces and other ornaments. This finery emphasized the ritual nature of war. For food, each warrior carried a bag of roasted cornmeal that could be eaten without bothering to cook it or even to soak it in water. This concentrated food would last a man from six to eight weeks, after which he had to forage.

The Huron waged various kinds of campaigns. Occasionally, in retaliation for some serious injury, a band of several hundred warriors would lay siege to an enemy village. Fires were lighted against the palisade, in order to compel the enemy warriors to come out and defend the settlement. When they emerged, both sides lined up and fought a pitched battle, which nevertheless ended when a few deaths or injuries were suffered on either side. After a few of the enemy had been killed or taken prisoner, the Huron would retreat before enemy reinforcements arrived from neighbouring villages.

Usually, however, Huron war parties split into groups of five or six men each, who hid in the fields or along paths in the forest in hopes of surprising a few Iroquois. Sometimes, daring individuals stole into enemy houses at night and tried to kill some of the sleeping inhabitants before making their escape. Such acts won Huron warriors the respect of their comrades.

Nothing, however, was as desirable as to be credited with the capture of an enemy warrior. Women and children who were captured were usually tortured and killed on the spot and their heads or scalps kept as trophies. The scalps were tanned and, in time of war, were fastened onto poles and set upon the walls of villages to frighten attackers. The same fate might befall able-bodied men, if too many were captured or their presence otherwise endangered their captors' security. Usually, however, captured warriors became the victims of a sadistic game, in which hopes of escape or reprieve were balanced off against physical pain and the greater likelihood of a savage, if glorious death. In their treatment of such prisoners the Huron revealed a sinister aspect of the psychological finesse which was an important facet of their culture.

As soon as the Huron had an enemy in their power they tore out his fingernails, cut or bit off his fingers, and slit his neck and shoulders with a

PLATE 6. *Huron warrior wearing slat armour. From Champlain's*
Voyages *of 1619. While the slat armour accords with Champlain's text,*
the solar ornament on the man's helmet is a European touch frequently
applied to representations of Latin American Indians. For a later,
stylistically different engraving of this picture, see Johan de Laet,
L'histoire du Nouveau Monde, *1640, reproduced in W. P. Cumming, et al.,*
The Discovery of North America (*London, 1971*), *p. 272. Courtesy*
McGill University Libraries.

knife. These injuries made it difficult for him to escape from the leather
thong with which his arms were then bound. At the same time, the Huron
reminded him of the cruelties he and his people had practised on them,
saying that he must now be prepared to suffer likewise. They also made
him sing his personal chant, which prisoners often continued to sing all the
way to the Huron country.

The capture of an enemy enhanced the reputation of a Huron warrior,
but did not give him control over the fate of his prisoner. This was decided
by the war chief who had organized the expedition. When a number of
prisoners were captured, they were usually divided among the tribes whose
warriors had participated in the expedition. As these prisoners passed
through each village, they were stripped, bound hand and foot, and slowly
led between two lines of Huron, who tortured them with clubs, thorns,
knives, and firebrands, but were careful not to kill them. Afterwards, the
tribal council assigned them to individual families who had lost members
to the enemy. In this way, the lost relative was ostensibly replaced and the
tears of those who had been bereaved were publicly dried. Since the
number of prisoners who were taken was usually smaller than the number
of Huron slain by the enemy, only the most important families were
presented with such captives.

Every prisoner was adopted by the family to whom he had been given.
Almost invariably, enemy women and children were integrated into these
families and lived the rest of their lives with them, unless an exchange of
prisoners was arranged as part of a peace treaty. If the appearance,
personality, or skills of an adult male were pleasing to his adoptive family,
they might decide to spare his life. So long as he behaved well, he would be
treated kindly and might be given the rank and titles of the dead man he
replaced. Like the women and children, he would gradually become a loyal
member of his new family and in time he might go to war against his own
people. This transformation was psychologically motivated by the captive's
knowledge that the majority of male prisoners were condemned by their
adoptive parents to death by torture. This was the most satisfying revenge
that a family could take for the loss of one of its own members.

Even when an adoptive family condemned a prisoner to die, they continued to treat him with courtesy and an outward show of affection, and for
a time provided him with every physical comfort. By treating the prisoner
as the incarnation of their murdered relative, the family was able to work
up greater enthusiasm to avenge the latter's death. Before his final
torment, a farewell feast was given, similar to that celebrated by a Huron
who knew himself to be on the point of death. Everyone was welcome to

attend this feast and the prisoner was expected to show his courage by inviting those present to amuse themselves killing him. It was also his duty to sing and dance with the Huron at this time. Now, and throughout the gruesome ordeal that followed a prisoner was expected to display the primary virtues of a warrior: courage and the ability to suffer without complaining. If the Huron could not make a prisoner weep and plead for mercy, this was believed to indicate misfortune for them in future wars.

PRISONER SACRIFICE

The torturing of a prisoner took place inside the longhouse of the village's principal war chief.[45] It began in the evening and, while it might last one or several days, it was necessary for the prisoner to die in the open air at sunrise, since the sun was the special witness of the fate of warriors. In addition to being an act of blood revenge, the prisoner's death was viewed as a sacrifice to the sun. The sacred nature of what was about to happen was emphasized by the orders of the headmen that no one in the village should engage in sexual intercourse that night and that, while torturing the prisoner, everyone should behave in an orderly and restrained fashion and should burn only his legs at the beginning. It was also announced to what headmen the main parts of his body would be given after he was dead.

At this point, the prisoner was stripped of whatever clothes he still wore and his hands were bound together. He was then compelled to make his way from one end of the longhouse to the other, while the crowd thrust flaming sticks at him. To increase his torment, the Huron also tried to force him to run through the hearths that were ablaze down the centre of the building. At the ends of the cabin he was made to rest on beds of hot ashes, while the bones of his hands were broken, burning sticks were stuck through his ears, and his wrists were burned or cut through by wrapping cords around them and pulling these cords back and forth fast as possible. Later, fire was applied to the prisoner's genitals and, while the sources are reticent on this point, it appears that some of the torture had strongly sexual connotations (Thwaites 1896–1901, 13:77; 17:65; Du Creux 1951–52:258). Occasionally, while making his way through the longhouse, a prisoner was able to scatter hot ashes from a hearth and set fire to the building. In the resulting confusion, he had a very slim chance of escaping; the dim hope of which must have sustained him up to this point. As the prisoner's strength failed him, however, it became necessary to carry him through the longhouse. At this point, the headmen ordered the people to

stop torturing him, so that he would not die before sunrise. The prisoner was then placed on a mat and allowed to rest, while many people left for a breath of fresh air.

When the prisoner began to revive, he was forced to sing again and his torture was resumed. Hitherto, the aim had been to make him suffer, but not to endanger his life. To that end, punishment had been restricted to the extremities of his body. Now, when he could no longer run about, his tormentors, who were mainly young people, attacked the rest of his body. They made deep cuts into his arms, legs, thighs, and other fleshy parts and quenched the flow of blood by thrusting glowing brands into the wounds. To the horror and disgust of the French, women as well as men eagerly participated in these actions. Each tormentor patiently waited his turn, and showed no sign of anger or lack of self-control while he had the prisoner in his power. Frequently, they addressed him with mock benevolence. One youth would say he was caulking a canoe as a present for the prisoner, while in reality he was pouring burning pitch over the man's body. Others would assert that the prisoner was cold and proceed to warm him by roasting his flesh. From time to time, the Huron gave him something to eat or poured a little water into his mouth so he would last until morning. At the same time, they redoubled their efforts to make him cry out as much as possible.

On the morning the prisoner was to die, fires were lighted around a scaffold six or seven feet high that had been erected in a field outside the village.[46] The prisoner was made to mount the scaffold and was loosely tied to the branch of a tree that passed overhead. In this way, the crowd could watch his contortions. Once the prisoner was in position, the Huron continued to burn his body, but also began to attack his vital organs. He was made to eat pieces of his own flesh and brands were thrust into his throat, eyes, and rectum. Later, he was scalped and burning pitch was poured over his head. When it was clear he was about to die, his head was either cut off or smashed open, while, at the same time, the Huron cut out his heart and chopped off his hands and feet. They eviscerated his corpse and gave the children of the village bits of his intestines to hang on the ends of sticks and carry through the village as symbols of victory.

If the prisoner had been a brave man, his heart was cooked and eaten by the young warriors, who believed that they would acquire his courage in this manner. Others made cuts in their necks and let the prisoner's blood run into them to avoid being surprised by the enemy. Afterwards, the prisoner's body was cut up to be cooked and eaten. Some Huron ate it with horror, while others relished the taste of human flesh, but to all it was an

act of religious significance. After sunset on the day the prisoner was killed, everyone made loud noises to drive his spirit from the village.

The Individual and Society

RELIGION

The Europeans who sought to convert the Huron found themselves combating a religion whose structure was completely different from their own. One indication of this was the absence in the indigenous culture of any office corresponding to that of priest. Like the other native peoples of Ontario and the northeastern United States, the Huron lacked specialists who performed regular religious ceremonies on behalf of the whole community. Moreover, they did not construct special buildings, shrines, or altars for religious purposes. This does not mean that religion was unimportant to the Huron; it merely indicates that instead of having its own institutionally delimited sphere, as it had in European culture, religion was indissolubly a part of all the things the Huron believed and did. The Huron did not perceive religion as being a well-defined set of beliefs that an individual could either accept, or substitute with another, at will. To them, their religion and way of life were one and the same. Many of the most important aspects of Huron religion were embraced by the term *onderha*, which meant the "prop" or "foundation" of a country. This term was used to denote the dances, customs, and ceremonies that bound a people together and promoted friendship, solidarity, and goodwill amongst them.

Collective activities were based upon beliefs that transcended clan and tribal affiliations and also served to bridge the gap between the male and female spheres of Huron life. Specialized knowledge of Huron beliefs and traditions was the property of certain old men, who at feasts were called upon to recite their stories. In this way, the traditions of the past were made known to the younger generation and the solidarity of Huron society, past and present, was reaffirmed.

The Huron lived in a world in which everything that existed, including man-made things, possessed souls and were immortal. Souls that had the power to influence human beings were called *oki*. These included the spirits that resided in the forests, lakes, rivers, and elsewhere in nature and which could bring good or bad fortune to people in such diverse activities as travel, war, and making love. The term was also extended to human beings

who exhibited unusual qualities. These included shamans, witches, valiant warriors, outstandingly successful traders, and even lunatics. Such people were believed either to possess supernatural powers in their own right or to have a companion spirit whose power they could call upon.

Although the Huron had no well-organized pantheon of deities, their most important spirit was the sky, who controlled the weather and assisted human beings in times of need. The sky was invoked whenever an important bargain or treaty was concluded and it was believed that if oaths sworn in his name were broken, he would punish the offender. It was also believed dangerous to mock the sky. Lesser spirits were associated with particular islands or large rocks that the Huron encountered in their travels, and with natural features within the familiar landscape of the Huron country. Some of the spirits associated with these landmarks were friendly by nature, but others sought to hurt or kill human beings and some were ravenous to feed upon human corpses. To propitiate these spirits and secure their aid, offerings of tobacco were thrown into campfires or left in clefts in the rock whenever the Huron passed by their abode.

Observances of a religious nature were associated with every type of Huron activity. In particular, hunting and fishing were structured with many rituals. When Huron men engaged in these activities, they were careful not to permit the fat from their catch to fall into the fire or the bones to be burned or thrown to the dogs. If this were to happen, the souls of the dead animals would be angered and, in retaliation, living animals would no longer permit themselves to be caught. The Huron also believed that fish dreaded contact with the dead. Hence they were careful to keep human corpses out of sight of their fishing nets (which also had souls) and would not go fishing when one of their friends had died. To ensure good catches, some Huron villages married two girls, who had not yet reached puberty, to the spirit of a fishing net. This ceremony is reported to have originated amongst the Algonkians, when the spirit of a net appeared to a man in a dream and asked for a wife to replace the one he had lost. The ritual marriage apparently lasted for one year, during which the families of the two girls received a special share of the catch. These rituals illustrate very clearly the difference between the Huron's view of himself as a part of nature and the traditional European concept of man as having dominion over his environment.

In hunting and war, the Huron paid special attention to their dreams, which, as we shall see, they held in very special regard. Such dreams might give promises of success, or warnings of danger which an individual could then take action to avoid. Huron men are said to have often paid more

attention to their dreams than to the advice of their leaders. This would be in keeping with the emphasis on masculine self-reliance that was so important to the Huron. Often a man's guardian spirit, who became associated with him at puberty, would render him advice and assistance in the form of dreams.

CREATION MYTH

Perhaps because of the absence of specific cults and a professional priesthood, most Huron spirits seem to have been only very meagrely personified. Among the most important and best delineated of which we have knowledge, were Iouskeha and Aataentsic, who were identified with the sun and moon respectively. Both played an important role in the Huron myth of creation.[47]

The Huron believed that Aataentsic, the mother of mankind, had originally dwelt in the sky, where spirits live much as men do on earth. One day, when either chasing a bear or cutting down a tree to obtain medicine for her husband, Aataentsic slipped through a hole in the sky and began to fall. When the great tortoise, who swam in the primeval ocean below, saw this, he ordered the other aquatic animals to dive to the bottom of the ocean and dredge up soil to pile on his back. They did so, and in this way the earth was formed and Aataentsic landed gently upon it.

When Aataentsic fell, she was pregnant. She became the mother, or maternal grandmother, of two boys: Tawiscaron and Iouskeha. It was Iouskeha who created the lakes and rivers, made corn to grow, provided good weather, released the animals from a great cave in which they had been concealed, and made it possible for men to hunt them. He also learned the secret of making fire from the great tortoise and passed this knowledge on to mankind. Iouskeha grew old as men did, but never died, since he was able to rejuvenate himself in old age and become once more like a man twenty-five or thirty years of age. Aataentsic had an evil nature and spent her time trying to undo Iouskeha's good works. It was she who had charge of the souls of the dead, caused men to die, and bred epidemics. While she was by nature an old woman, she possessed the power to turn herself into a beautiful young girl, when it suited her to do so. Tawiscaron appears to have shared many of Aataentsic's evil qualities.

When they grew up, Iouskeha fought with Tawiscaron. In this fight, Iouskeha struck his brother and injured him. As Tawiscaron fled, drops of his blood fell on the ground and were turned into flint (*tawiscara*), which

the Indians used to make their stone tools. After this, Iouskeha and Aataentsic continued to live together; the one seeking to help, the other to harm, mankind. They had a bark cabin surrounded by cornfields in a place far from the Huron country, apparently associated with the villages of the dead. Occasionally, they would visit the Huron and join in their festivals disguised as mortals. If Iouskeha was seen in the Huron cornfields carrying a well-developed stalk of corn, this vision signalled a good harvest, if he was seen gnawing on human flesh, it signified a bad one. It was also he who, as the sun, protected warriors.

It is tempting to see in these myths a fascinating commentary on Huron social structure (Trigger 1969*a*:92–93). The idea that Aataentsic was the mother of the human race and the unimportance attached to paternity are straightforward reflections of the matrilineal bias of Huron culture, but the roles assigned to Iouskeha and Aataentsic are in many ways the opposite of those that were assigned to men and women in everyday life. Among the Huron, men committed most of the real and symbolic acts of violence: chopping down the forests, killing animals, and hunting one another. Women were associated with life-giving pursuits: bearing children, growing crops, and caring for the home. Yet, in Huron myths, it is Iouskeha who makes the crops to grow and protects mankind, while his grandmother seeks to harm human beings whenever she can. It is possible that by conferring certain human characteristics on mythical figures of the opposite sex, these myths aimed at compensating both sexes for the psychological limitations of the roles assigned to them in real life. Women were flattered by being mythically endowed with dangerous and aggressive qualities, while men had their real role as destroyers of life complemented by a symbolic one as sustainers of it. The ambivalence men felt about their aggressive role may be symbolized by Iouskeha's attack upon his twin brother, who seems to have shared Aataentsic's aggressive and destructive nature. It is probably no accident that Tawiscaron's blood turned to flint, the stone used to make instruments of violence. Finally, the fact that Aataentsic and Iouskeha, though so different in nature, were made to live together, stressed the essential complementarity of their roles and, in this way, ultimately served to justify the sexual division of roles in Huron society.

CHARMS

Huron men relied on charms to bring them luck in activities such as hunting, fishing, fighting, gambling, and love. A charm was an object that

had associated with it an *oki*, or spirit capable of helping the person who possessed it. Some charms could confer many types of benefits on their owners; others were useful for only one purpose. Those of proven worth were highly valued and were inherited from one generation to the next. New charms were revealed in dreams or might be found in the entrails of an animal that had been particularly hard to kill. Others were merely stones of curious shapes that had been found in the woods, where it was believed some spirit had made and lost them. Some were purchased at great price from the northern Algonkians who, because of their reputation as hunters and fishermen, were believed to possess very powerful charms. Men carried their charms in their pouches and, from time to time, would speak to the spirits associated with them and offer these spirits beads, or pieces of tobacco, as presents. They also gave feasts that were designed to reinforce the power of their charms.

SHAMANS

From time to time, either individually or as groups, the Huron sought the help of those among them who claimed to control supernatural powers. Most of these *arendiwane*, or shamans, were men and women who had obtained their special potency through visions or dreams in which a powerful spirit had revealed itself to them. Such visions normally required prolonged fasting and the avoidance of sexual intercourse for a period of time. As already noted in connection with the sacrifice of prisoners, sexual abstinence was important for the accomplishment of many activities of a sacred character; however, not even the most powerful shamans ever practised sexual continence for life, or even for long periods, and the Huron had no equivalent of the European concept of religious celibacy.

Some shamans went so far as to claim that they themselves were supernatural spirits who had become incarnate as human fetuses. These appear to have been mainly dwarfs, or people who were afflicted with other physical deformities. Such claims were based on the Huron belief that various mythical beings had such deformities; however, no matter what was the origin of his power, a shaman had to validate his claims by producing satisfactory results. Occasional failures could be attributed to sorcery or other malign influences, but, if a shaman had a notable series of failures, people generally lost faith in him. Hence, we may assume that most men who claimed supernatural powers had relatively short careers.

The powers claimed by shamans varied. Some men and women an-

nounced that they were able to control the weather and, in return for gifts, would offer to prevent frosts, produce rain, or eliminate diseases that were threatening the crops. Often, they would suggest public ceremonies which, if carried out properly, would avert the danger. Still others promised to bring luck in fishing or hunting, predicted the outcome of military ventures, determined by ritual means what was happening to warriors many hundreds of miles away, or undertook to recover objects that had been lost or stolen. All of this was done in return for presents, which were normally paid in advance.

The most important shamans were those who undertook to heal the sick, an activity that was performed by male shamans only. These were of two sorts: the *ocata*, who diagnosed and recommended treatment for all sorts of illnesses, and the *aretsan*, who specialized in extracting spells cast by witches. Both kinds of medicine men were highly esteemed and were well-paid for their services.

CURING SOCIETIES

In addition to these medical shamans, there were curing societies, whose work in healing the sick was considered to be extremely important. Each society had a leader, his office apparently being hereditary. Often these leaders were important headmen, whose ritual position complemented and strengthened their secular authority. Membership in these societies was generally open to those who had been cured by them and thereafter remained hereditary in such an individual's family.

Little is known about individual curing societies, although it appears that each specialized in treating certain types of illness. One of the most important and most general societies was the *Awataerohi*, whose members were held in awe for their ability to handle fire. Some chewed hot charcoal and either showered it over the patient or, after blowing it on their hands to warm them, rubbed the affected parts of his body. Others held glowing coals in their mouths and growled into the patient's ear, while still others danced around him holding red hot stones in their mouths. The power to handle such material, or to plunge their arms into boiling kettles, was said to be acquired supernaturally.

The *Atirenda* was another curing society which, in the 1630s, had about eighty members, including six women. This society was famous for treating ruptures. In their principal dance, the *otakrendoiae*, members of this society pretended to kill one another with charms, whose effects were

then overcome. As they fell under one another's spells, they bit their cheeks so that blood poured from their mouths, or simulated it with red powder. The performance of dances by individuals who were disguised as hunchbacks and who carried sticks and wore wooden masks, suggests the existence of a curing society similar to the Iroquois False Faces. Still other men and women imitated animals or performed with sacks over their faces and straw stuffed around their waists. The sick person's family rewarded the performers of such rituals with food and other gifts.

The prominent role played by shamans and curing societies in Huron life indicates that combating illness was an important focus of Huron religious activity. Its importance is even greater when it is realized that the Huron did not limit the concept of health to physical well-being, but extended it to include anything that affected a person's happiness and sense of personal fulfilment. The latter included what we would call his good or bad luck.

PSYCHOTHERAPY

The Huron recognized three types of illness and mental disequilibrium. The first were those that had natural causes. These were diseases that could be treated successfully by means of herbs, drugs, incisions, poultices, and by profuse sweating. If such treatment did not succeed, the Huron concluded that the disease had a different origin.

The second type were those caused by witchcraft. Such diseases could be cured only if the shaman was able to discover and remove all of the spells that had been injected into a sick man's body. The third type of illness was caused by the presence in a person's soul of unfulfilled desires, of which even the patient himself might not be conscious. To cure illness of this sort, these desires had, in some manner, to be ascertained and fulfilled.[48]

The Huron attached great importance to dreams of all sorts and deliberately sought the answers to many of life's problems in them. It was believed that dreams were the language of the soul and that sometimes hidden desires were revealed to the patient through them. In the case of young children, such desires might be communicated to their parents in this form. Otherwise, it was necessary for the *ocata* to penetrate into the depths of his patients' souls to perceive what these desires were. This might be done by gazing steadily into fire or water, working himself into a frenzy, or sweating for a prolonged period, either alone or in the company of other men. Even when desires were revealed in the form of dreams, the *ocata*'s

advice was required, as dreams sometimes were false and attempts to fulfil them could harm an individual.

Dreams gave promises of success or warnings of danger that could be averted only if certain desires of the soul were fulfilled. Sometimes these desires were for a specific object, such as a dog or a canoe. Among older people, they were not infrequently for socially unsanctioned forms of sexual gratification. Still other individuals believed that their souls commanded them to humiliate or even kill someone else. All of these commands ran directly counter to the Huron norms of generosity, sexual modesty, overt friendliness, and self-control. Still other desires arose from the promise of guardian spirits to confer special powers on an individual in return for ceremonies or presents which required the assistance of other people.

It was believed that failure to satisfy the desires of an individual's soul could result in that person's death. Because of this, the Huron felt obliged, as far as possible, to help to satisfy these wishes. Some desires, however, could not be fulfilled in the form in which they were asked, either because what had been requested could not be obtained or because the desire was destructive to the asker or to other people. In these cases, the *ocata* might suggest a symbolic equivalent that would be just as effective.

When specific objects were desired, villagers vied with one another to oblige the sick person. This was simply another example of the generosity in which the Huron took pride. Such gifts were given without expectation of anything in exchange; rather it was a matter of being able to help those in need. If demands were unreasonable, however, they were scaled down, again with the advice of the *ocata*. When a certain mother asked for one hundred cakes of tobacco to cure her son, ten were given instead (Thwaites 1896–1901, 10:173). In this way, individuals were prevented from making unreasonable demands on the community.

Acts which were self-destructive were also fulfilled symbolically. If a warrior dreamed that the enemy were burning him at the stake, he would seek to avoid this happening in reality by having his fellow villagers go through the preliminaries of torturing him, but a dog would be killed in his place.

A common desire of the soul was for curing rituals to be performed. Often these rituals were on a small scale, but, if the sick person was wealthy or a close relative of a headman, the entire community might participate in them. When the village council pronounced that a person's recovery was a matter of urgent public concern, everyone would join in performing the ceremony exactly as the sick person wished.

Often these ceremonies had sexual overtones. Occasionally, young people were asked to dance without wearing breechclouts, and on one occasion a woman is reported to have asked that during a dance a young man should urinate into her mouth (Wrong 1939:118). At other times, people were requested to eat vast quantities of food, even though they might have to vomit up part of what they had eaten in order to finish the meal; or they might be asked to eat biscuits which swelled their stomachs, although they believed that if they broke wind under such circumstances they would die.

The most sensational of all the curing rituals was the *andacwander*.[49] To perform this ceremony, the unmarried people of the village assembled in the sick person's house and spent the night having sexual intercourse with the partner of their choice, while the patient watched and two shamans shook their tortoise shell rattles and sang. Sometimes a sick man might request a young girl to have intercourse with him. Although this ceremony so shocked the Jesuits that they were hesitant even to mention it, it appears to have been a common one. This indicates the degree to which the Huron's concern for the welfare of members of their own society led them, in well-defined and short-lived contexts, to transgress even the most restrictive norms of their society.

The main Huron winter festival, the *Ononharoia*, belongs to the general category of soul-curing rituals. It was celebrated at least once a year in every large village. The main reason was either that many people in the village felt ill or depressed, or that some important individual was unwell. This boisterous celebration, which lasted three days, began with people breaking into houses, where they proceeded to upset furniture, break pots, and toss firebrands about. Following this, people who felt ill dreamed of objects, then went about the village propounding riddles and seeking to find someone who could guess what these objects were and give them to them. During this period, they were showered with many presents in the hope that one of them would fulfil their dream. If they were finally given what they were looking for, it was a sign that all their troubles were over. After the festival, all presents were returned, except those that were answers to dreams.

Through the medium of soul desires, individuals were able to treat personal frustrations and illicit desires as forces that were neither part of their overt personality, nor subject to conscious control. In a society where there were strong pressures for social conformity and personal restraint, this device provided a necessary outlet for personal feelings. Through their soul desires, individuals who felt neglected, abused, or insecure could indirectly make claims upon the community for psychological support. This

support was given in a manner that in no way compromised the recipient's independence or sense of personal freedom, and which conformed to the general Huron principle of expressing friendship through generosity. From time to time, it also permitted people to relax the norms of their society and gratify themselves by doing, in public, things that normally were impermissible.

GAMES

The three most common Huron games were lacrosse, the dish game, and *aescara*. The dish game was played with five or eight dice made of fruit stones, painted black on one side and white on the other, while *aescara* required several hundred rushes, each about a foot long. Because teams from different villages frequently played against one another, these games provided an opportunity for various groups of Huron to come together in friendly rivalry and to indulge their inveterate passion for gambling. Betting was often for very high stakes, and individuals who had gambled away everything they owned are reported to have wagered their hair or even their fingers on the outcome of a game. Losers were expected to bear their losses graciously, although occasionally men who had gambled away a great deal of their household's property committed suicide, so great was their sense of dishonour.

Games that were played publicly had a strong religious element. Some were played in hope of curing a sick person, others to avert an epidemic, influence the weather, or honour the memory of a dead player. Once a game was decided on, the players from each village fasted, abstained from sexual intercourse, sought dreams that would bring them victory, and exhorted their personal charms to help them win. Lacrosse was played in an open field, but the other games were played inside a longhouse. The spectators supporting both teams seated themselves on either side of the main aisle of the longhouse and sought, by shouting, to attract luck to their side. Each side kept careful score of all points won and lost, and any player who suffered successive losses was replaced. Games might last for several days, with food and hospitality being extended to all present.

FEASTS

The Huron celebrated many events of both a public and private nature. The largest feasts were those that accompanied the annual meeting of the

confederacy council and the investiture of new chiefs. Lesser ones were to celebrate personal good fortune or victories over the enemy, to solemnize life crises, such as marriage and death, and for the curing of the sick.

Invitations to attend feasts were sent out well in advance; sometimes people were invited individually, at other times whole villages were made welcome. It was regarded as an insult for anyone invited to attend a feast to refuse to do so without good reason. Each person who came was expected to wear his finest ornaments and to bring his own spoon and bowl with him. The guests assembled inside the longhouse of their host, the men seating themselves at one end, the women at the other. Once they had arrived the doors were closed, after which no one was supposed to enter. Failure to observe this rule was believed to disrupt the purpose for which the feast was given. Dancing was important to any such occasion. It was led by two older men, who shook rattles and sang, while the rest of the guests danced round them in an oval formation and joined in the refrain. Dancers did not hold hands, but each was expected to move vigorously and to make appropriate facial expressions (plate 7).

If the feast lasted all day, food was served both morning and afternoon. The man who gave the feast announced the contents of each kettle, which were then distributed by servers who went from row to row taking each person's bowl and filling it. Strangers, and those who had come from other villages, were given the best portions of what was available, while the heads of animals were reserved for the highest ranking headmen. Guests were expected to eat heartily, but the hosts ate little and spent most of their time seeing that everyone was entertained. In addition to singing and dancing, feasts were enlivened by various contests and games.

THE FEAST OF THE DEAD

By far the most important of all Huron ceremonies was the Feast of the Dead, which the Huron generally referred to as "the Kettle." At this feast, the bodies of all those who had not died violent deaths were removed from the temporary raised tombs in the village cemeteries and buried with great pomp in a common ossuary. A Feast of the Dead appears to have been held whenever a large village shifted location, the reason for this being that once the village was abandoned it was no longer possible to protect and care for the bodies buried in the adjacent cemetery. This created the regrettable necessity for the living and the dead, who had remained near to one another as long as the village lasted, to part company. The dead from nearby

PLATE 7. *Huron dance. This scene seemingly errs in showing the dance being held out of doors. Dances were normally performed in association with rituals held inside longhouses. The hairstyles are also not Huron. It is possible that the tortoise rattle is accurately represented, although recent Iroquois ones consist of a shell only. Courtesy McGill University Libraries.*

satellite villages were included in this final burial, along with deceased natives from the area who had gone to live elsewhere, and members of other Huron villages who wished to be interred close to a special friend. The significance of the mingling of the bones of the dead from many parts of the Huron country in a single grave cannot be overstressed. The Huron said that because their dead relatives were united in this way, it was necessary for the living to cooperate and be friends with one another. Friendly tribes from outside the confederacy were invited to attend the ceremony as an expression of goodwill, but only very close allies appear to have been asked to mingle the bones of their dead with those of the Huron.[50]

This final burial was believed to release the souls of the dead, who up to then had lived in the village cemetery, and allow them to travel westward to the land where Iouskeha and Aataentsic lived. In that land was a village of souls corresponding to each of the tribes, or major villages, of the Huron. Whether identified with the Milky Way or the trail running along the south shore of Georgian Bay, the journey to the land of the dead was an arduous one. At one point the terrestial route led past a tall standing rock called Ecaregniondi,[51] said to be daubed with the paint spirits used on their faces. Beyond this, a spirit called Oscotarach drew the brains out of the heads of the dead and, still farther along, was a deep ravine into which unlucky souls might fall and be drowned. Because of these difficulties, the souls of very young children and of the very old remained in the Huron country, where they planted their corn in the fields that the living had abandoned. Because the souls of those who had died violent deaths were believed dangerous, they were excluded from the villages of the dead. These included suicides and warriors who had died in battle, the latter forming a band by themselves in the hereafter. Those who reached the villages of the dead continued forever to hunt, fish, till the soil, and attend feasts and dances, much as they had on earth.

A Feast of the Dead was held in each major village once every ten to fifteen years.[52] Arrangements were made well in advance and invitations to attend were sent out through the whole country. The feast lasted ten days, eight of which were spent preparing the bodies for reburial and assembling the participants. In each village where there were bodies to be reburied, the latter were removed from their raised tombs. Then, unless they had died recently, the female relatives of the dead stripped them of any remaining flesh which, along with the mats and robes in which they had been wrapped, was reverently burned. This work is reported to have been done without overt repugnance, although the corpses were often putrid and swarming with worms. After the bones had been cleaned, they were

wrapped in a beaver skin bag, which was decorated with beads and sometimes fashioned to look like a man sitting in a crouching position. The
bodies of those who had died recently were merely wrapped in new skins
and carried on litters. A feast was then given in memory of the dead, at
which the vast array of presents collected in their honour was displayed.
Afterwards, both the bodies and the presents were carried to the village
where the feast was to be celebrated. Here, every visitor was assigned a
host, in whose house he placed the bones of the dead and the gifts that
accompanied them. In general, hosts and visitors appear to have belonged
to clan segments that were named after the same animal.

While continual feasting and dancing went on in the village, and prizes
were offered to the winners of various games, a pit about ten feet deep and
fifteen feet or more in diameter was dug in an open field near the village.
Around the pit, a scaffold was erected, about fifty feet across and ten feet
high, with crude ladders rising up to it on all sides. Numerous cross-poles
were erected on top of the platform (plate 8). On the seventh day, the
undecomposed bodies were brought to the edge of the pit and placed
beneath the scaffold on slabs of bark fastened to stakes several feet high.

The following day, the bundles containing the bones of the dead were
opened and mourned over for the last time. Then they were taken to the
field where the ossuary had been dug. There all the mourners arranged
themselves in groups according to villages and clan segments. The presents
that each group had brought to honour its dead were hung on poles and
remained on show for several hours. This display gave each clan segment
an opportunity to proclaim its affluence and piety towards its dead members, and also served to impress foreigners with the wealth of the country.
Afterwards, all of the packages of bones were taken and hung on the cross-
poles that had been erected on top of the platform, again arranged according
to clan segments. The headmen stood on the platform and announced the
recipients of many of the presents collected in the name of the deceased.
These recipients included his friends, those who had helped to bury him,
and those who were acting as hosts at the Feast of the Dead. In this manner,
a very significant redistribution of property was accomplished.

Towards evening, about fifty beaver robes, possibly one given by each of
the clan segments of the Huron confederacy,[53] were used to line the burial
pit. Then some old kettles were put into the pit for the use of the dead and
the undecomposed bodies were lowered into it. Fires were lighted, meals
cooked, and the mourners spent the night camped around the ossuary.

At sunrise, a signal was given and the crowd mounted the platform and
began emptying the bones of the dead into the pit, retaining, however, the

PLATE 8. *The Feast of the Dead. From Lafitau's* Moeurs des sauvages amériquains *(1724). This is an eighteenth-century artist's attempt to depict Brébeuf's description of the 1636 ritual at Ossossané. The dangling articulated skeletons and unwrapped corpses draped over the mourners' shoulders are the artist's macabre fantasies. Courtesy McGill University Libraries.*

packages in which they were wrapped. At the same time, a great cry of lamentation was raised. A number of men were stationed in the pit, whose duty it was to see that the bones were packed in properly. The effect was to mingle the bones of different individuals together. When all the bones had been deposited, the robes bordering the edges of the pit were turned back and the space in the centre was covered over with mats and bark. Logs, probably scavenged from the platform, were then piled over the mouth of the pit, to prevent animals from burrowing into it, and the sand which had been dug out was used to erect a small mound on top of it. Dishfuls of corn were sprinkled over this mound to provide food for the souls of the dead. During the rest of the morning, further presents were distributed. Most of the fur bundles in which the dead had been wrapped were sliced apart and thrown to the crowd, who scrambled to get hold of them. Other presents were given to reward those in charge of the feast and to thank the headmen who had come from a considerable distance. Still other items that had been displayed were retained by the families who had used them to honour the dead.

Finally, wooden stakes were driven into the ground around the burial pit and a roof was erected on top of them. Similar huts appear to have been erected over the graves of those who had died violent deaths and may have been the sign of a final burial. No attempt was made to rebuild these huts after the original had rotted away. When the hut was finished, the participants feasted once again. Everyone was joyous at this time and returned home pleased that dead friends and relatives had received a fitting burial and been honoured with so many presents.

Important as the economic aspects of this feast may have been, the most important element remained the great affection that each Huron had for the remains of his dead relatives. By joining in a common tribute to the dead, whose memory each family loved and honoured, the Huron were exercising a powerful force for promoting goodwill among the disparate segments of each village, each tribe, and of the confederacy as a whole. The importance of this most sacred of Huron rituals made it, in effect, a microcosm of the structures and values upon which Huron society as a whole was based.

The Iroquoian Cultural Pattern

The Huron way of life was not unique, but was part of a cultural pattern shared by all the Iroquoian-speaking peoples who lived in the general

vicinity of the lower Great Lakes. Although the northern Iroquoians frequently dwelt in settlements that had over 1000 inhabitants, the overall population density of this region was not particularly high. In historic times, the villages making up tribes, and sometimes confederacies, were drawn together in clusters of settlement, each of which was surrounded by vast tracts of hunting and fishing territory. Most of these clusters formed a loose ring around Lake Ontario, while others extended into the St. Lawrence and Susquehanna Valleys, and probably into the Ohio River watershed as well (map 2). Although sharing a common style of life, the inhabitants of each of these clusters generally spoke a distinctive Iroquoian language or dialect, while their customs and the things they made differed from one another in many details.[54]

The entire area occupied by the northern Iroquoians was one of hardwood forests, with increasing coniferous admixture in the north. It was also an area that abounded in fish, particularly whitefish and sturgeon, and in some districts in eels, and where nonmigratory animals were plentiful. The principal game was deer. These animals assembled in large numbers in the late fall and early spring in areas where oak and chestnut mast were abundant. Beaver, which also made good eating, reached densities of between ten and fifty per square mile in suitable country, but, both in numbers and quality of fur, they were inferior to the beaver that inhabited the lakes and rivers of the Canadian Shield.

NEIGHBOURING TRIBES

The nearest neighbours of the Huron were the Tionnontaté, who lived south of the great swamps of the Nottawasaga drainage basin. From Ossossané, a well-marked trail followed the curve of Nottawasaga Bay southward for some thirty miles before reaching their villages. Archaeological evidence indicates that these extended from Mulmer township in Dufferin County into Collingwood township in Grey, below the rugged portion of the Niagara Escarpment now called the Blue Mountain (Garrad 1970:238). It was from their location that the name Tionnontaté, roughly signifying Mountain People, was derived.[55] Their population is uncertain, but it likely numbered no more than a few thousand.[56] Although they are reported to have had nine villages, all but two appear to have been small hamlets, and two more may have been wholly or partly inhabited by the Algonkian-speaking peoples who lived farther to the west (Thwaites 1896–1901, 20:43; 21:125).

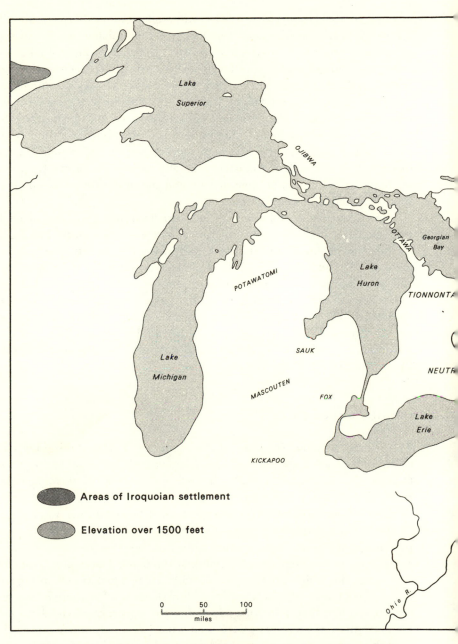

MAP 2. *Distribution of Iroquoian and other tribes in the lower Great Lakes area, c. 1630.*

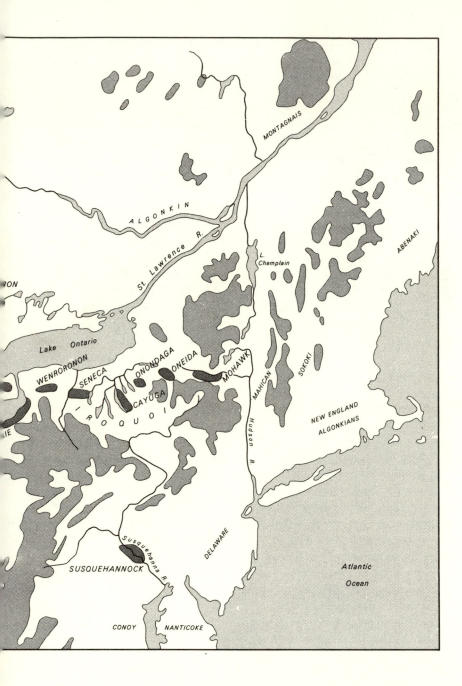

MONTAGNAIS

ALGONKIN

St Lawrence R.

L. Champlain

ABENAKI

Lake Ontario

WENRORONON

SENECA

ONONDAGA

ONEIDA

CAYUGA

MOHAWK

MAHICAN

SOKOKI

I R O Q U O I

Hudson R.

NEW ENGLAND
ALGONKIANS

Susquehanna R.

DELAWARE

SUSQUEHANNOCK

Atlantic

Ocean

CONOY

NANTICOKE

Frequent mention is made of the division of the Tionnontaté into two groups: the Nation of the Wolves and the Nation of the Deer. Some writers have suggested that these were two tribes who made up a Tionnontaté confederacy analogous to that of the Huron, but they seem more likely to have been the names of clan segments that were dominant in particular villages.[57] The Jesuits noted no linguistic differences between the Tionnontaté and the Attignawantan (ibid. 20:43), nor any cultural differences, except that the Tionnontaté were more given to tattooing than were the Huron (38:251). The Huron and the Tionnontaté were differentiated politically, rather than culturally.

The lake plain in the area of Tionnontaté settlement has a longer and more reliable growing season than the Huron country, or many areas farther south. In the seventeenth century, tobacco seems to have been grown there in large quantities. For this reason, the French called the Tionnontaté the Petun, or Tobacco Nation (ibid. 20:43; Biggar 1922–36, 6:248). Much of the better quality flint used by the Huron also may have come from this region (Heidenreich 1971:228). In spite of having these resources, the Tionnontaté did not attempt to go north to trade, since this would have required them to pass by or through Huron territory (Thwaites 1896–1901, 21:177). On the other hand, the Tionnontaté cultivated good relations with the Ottawa bands who lived to the west of them. The latter groups travelled freely and maintained close contacts with other Algonkian groups who lived along the eastern and northern shores of Lake Huron.

From the Tionnontaté villages, a trail led south across the high-lying interior of southwestern Ontario. This region had no permanent inhabitants and served as hunting territory for tribes whose homes were nearer to the Great Lakes. Between the lower part of the Grand River Valley and the Niagara River lived the tribes that made up the Neutral confederacy.[58] This sobriquet was applied to them by the French because, in historical times, they were not at war with either the Huron or the Iroquois, nor did they permit members of these groups to fight within their villages (Biggar 1922–36, 3:99–100; Thwaites 1896–1901, 21:193). The Neutral were not more peaceful, however, than were the other Iroquoian tribes. Instead, they carried on blood feuds with sedentary Algonkian peoples who lived to the west of them, probably in what is now the state of Michigan (Wrong 1939:157–58; Thwaites 1896–1901, 21:195; 27:25–27). In 1641, the Jesuit missionaries who visited the Neutral noted that they had about forty villages and estimated the total population of the confederacy to be about 12,000 people (Thwaites 1896–1901, 20:95, 105; 21:189–91, 223). This estimate was made, however, after a particularly

serious epidemic. It is possible that, at the turn of the century, they had a population as large as that of the Huron.

We do not know for certain the number or names of the tribes that made up the Neutral confederacy. Although they remain to be confirmed archaeologically, French maps from the late seventeenth century seem to record the names and locations of three of them. These are the Attiragen-rega, due west of Lake Ontario near Hamilton, the Antouaronon in the lower Grand Valley, and the Niagagarega, just west of the river that still bears their name.[59] These maps suggest that the Neutral villages were not gathered together in one region, as were those of the Huron confederacy, nor were they dispersed evenly through the Neutral territory. Instead, they were probably gathered in tribal clusters like those of the Iroquois. Most of the Neutral appear, however, to have lived at the west end of Lake Ontario. The Jesuits report that four villages were located east of the Niagara River, but Marian White (1961:25–37) believes this was a temporary occupation between 1630 and 1645.

It is possible that the Neutral subsistence pattern differed in important ways from that of the Huron. They lived in the warmest part of southern Ontario, where the forest cover consisted almost entirely of deciduous hardwoods capable of supporting large numbers of wild animals. Thus it is not surprising that the reports which describe the Neutral attach great importance to hunting and indicate that, by contrast with the Huron, meat was available throughout the year. Skins were among their principal items of trade and Frank Ridley (1961:56) reports that bone refuse is much more common on historic Neutral sites that he has examined than on other sites of similar age in southern Ontario. This suggests that the Neutral may have been more dependent on hunting as a means of subsistence than were either the Huron or the Seneca. Related to this may also be the smaller size of Neutral villages, which the French figures suggest, on an average, were only half the size of Huron ones;[60] however, some villages archaeologists have examined appear to have been of considerable size.

The Huron and Neutral called each other "Attiwandaronk," which means "people who speak a slightly different language" (Thwaites 1896–1901, 21:193). While clearly different, their languages appear to have been more similar to each other than either was to the Iroquois ones. Both may have been derived from a common Ontario Iroquoian proto-language.

The Jesuits reported that the Neutral tortured female, as well as male, prisoners and that they were more inclined to extravagant ceremonialism than were their northern neighbours (21:195, 199–201). These may, however, have been ill-formed impressions, reflecting the rather unsatisfactory

relations that the Jesuits had with the Neutral. Like the Tionnontaté, the Neutral were given to extensive tattooing of the body and, like the Ottawa, men often dispensed with a loincloth in summer (21:197). The Jesuits also report that Neutral burial customs differed from those of the Huron. In particular, they appear to have kept corpses in their houses for as long as possible, prior to giving them temporary scaffold burials (21:199). Neutral ossuaries are considerably smaller than Huron ones and display unusual features, such as clay linings and upper and lower sections divided by layers of clay (Ridley 1961:56). The French also noted that the Neutral were not skilled in the use of canoes and did not travel great distances by water, as the Huron did (Sagard 1866:807). Like other Iroquoian tribes living south of Lake Huron, the Neutral lacked the canoe birch with which the Huron and the northern Algonkians constructed their light and easily manoeuvrable craft; instead they had to make do with coverings of elm or hickory bark.[61]

Even less well known are the Erie, a tribe or confederacy living at the southeastern end of Lake Erie. The Sanson map of 1650 suggests that the territory of this tribe extended from the east end of Lake Erie along the south shore as far as Cattaraugus Creek, or halfway to Lake Chautauqua (White 1961:40–51). This is partially supported by archaeological evidence, which indicates that between approximately 1535 and 1640, two contemporary communities, about eight to ten miles apart, were gradually moving southward through the eastern part of this region (White 1971a:25–27). After that time, the Erie are reported to have moved inland under pressure from their enemies (Thwaites 1896–1901, 33:63). It is unknown how many villages constituted the Erie cluster.

The Huron name for this group, Erieehronon, was construed by the French to mean *Nation du Chat*. They were so-named, it was stated, for the great numbers of wildcats in their country (Wrong 1939:224). It is likely, however, that the Huron word the French translated as "cat" (*tiron*) actually meant racoon (see n. 39, supra). Nothing specific is known about the Erie language. Archaeologically, they appear to share much in common with the Neutral (Wright 1966:83–84; 87–90). Unlike the other northern Iroquoian tribes, they are alleged to have used poisoned arrows (Thwaites 1896–1901, 41:83).

The Wenroronon were a small, probably tribal, group who lived east of the Neutral and "beyond the Erie."[62] They are said to have been allied in some way with the Neutral confederacy prior to their dispersal in 1638, after being decimated by war and disease.[63] No archaeological sites have been positively identified as being Wenroronon, although Hewitt

(1910c:932) suggested that their name, which he interpreted to mean "People of the Floating Scum," indicates that they might have lived close to the oil spring near Cuba, in Allegheny County, New York State. No historic sites have been found in that area and Marian White (personal communication 1973) suggests that they may have lived in the vicinity of Oak Orchard Swamp. Among the Huron, Wenroronon shamans were renowned for their skill in drawing arrows from wounds (Thwaites 1896–1901, 17:213).

South of the Iroquois lived the Susquehannock, or Andaste, about whom again all too little is known. The principal historic sites of these people have been found in Lancaster and York Counties, Pennsylvania, whither, it has been suggested, they had been drawn from the upper parts of the Susquehanna Valley in order to be able to trade more easily with Europeans, who were active in the Chesapeake Bay area at an early date (W. Hunter 1959:13). Susquehannock pottery has its closest stylistic affinities with Cayuga and Seneca (Witthoft 1959:36–42), but too little vocabulary has been preserved to establish the linguistic relationship between Susquehannock and the other northern Iroquoian languages with any degree of certainty.[64] In historic times, the Susquehannock were allies of the Huron against the Iroquois and, like the Huron, they appear to have been energetic traders. Some Susquehannock were reported to be living in the Huron country as late as 1647 (Thwaites 1896–1901, 30:253). They were the last northern Iroquoian people who remained unconquered by the Iroquois.

The *Jesuit Relations* mentions another group, the Scahentarronon, whose name suggests they lived on the Great Flats or Wyoming Plain along the north branch of the Susquehanna in the vicinity of Wilkes-Barre, Pennsylvania (8:115). Hewitt has identified this tribe with the Massawomecke, mentioned by Captain John Smith, in 1608, as being enemies of the Andaste.[65] If Hewitt is correct, the Scahentarronon were probably a tribe consisting of three villages of some importance. The alternative name that is given for this group, Akhrakvaeronon, has been identified as that of a people destroyed by the Iroquois in 1652.[66] It is possible that early writers may have subsumed two different groups, the Andaste and the Scahentarronon, under the general name Susquehannock, or that the two groups federated or became allies after 1608. Because of a lack of archaeological evidence and the ambiguities of our sources, the Scahentarronon remain a shadowy and uncertain entity.

Much more is known about the five tribes that made up the Iroquois confederacy. Unlike the Huron tribes, the Iroquois ones did not live

adjacent to one another, but were dispersed in tribal clusters in a line stretching across upper New York State. The westernmost tribe was the Seneca, who originally lived in two large villages, and several hamlets, in the Genesee Valley. To the east of them, the Cayuga inhabited three villages around Cayuga Lake. The Onondaga had one large and one small settlement southeast of modern Syracuse, while the Oneida had a single village in either the Oneida or Oriskany Valley. The tribe best known to Europeans in the early historic period were the Mohawk, who had three towns and five hamlets located in the central part of the Mohawk Valley (Fenton 1940:200–31).

The five Iroquois tribes were culturally heterogeneous as well as geographically separated. Although the Mohawk and Oneida tongues were very similar, and both were closely related to Onondaga, greater differences separated these three languages, Seneca, and Cayuga.[67] The Seneca, which was the most numerous tribe, may also have been the most dependent on agriculture (Fenton 1940:230). The long separate development of the people making up these tribes is reflected not only in distinctive languages and pottery types but also in significant variations in their clan organization and use of kinship terms. The Mohawk and Oneida used only three clan names, whereas the other tribes resembled the Huron in having eight.

In spite of the difficulties inherent in estimating aboriginal populations, it is frequently stated that, early in the seventeenth century, the Iroquois confederacy had only half the population of the Huron one (Kroeber 1939:133). Some archaeologists have indulged in far-reaching speculations about how this difference might have arisen (Noble 1969:22). Such estimates are based, however, on Iroquois figures that are valid only for the latter half of the seventeenth century, if at all. When we consider the small size of the majority of Huron settlements, the ten large ones the Iroquois are reported to have occupied prior to 1650 do not suggest a population notably smaller than that of the Huron; indeed, it might be argued that the Iroquois were more numerous. The Iroquois, like the Huron, were stricken by serious epidemics beginning in the 1630s, and it can be estimated that prior to that time their population numbered about 20,000. As a result of these epidemics, both confederacies appear to have lost about half their population. Further losses from war and disease may explain the failure of the Iroquois to increase in numbers in spite of the many captives they incorporated into their tribes after 1640.

In the early seventeenth century, the Iroquois confederacy did not have a common policy for dealing with their neighbours. Its main aim appears to have been to suppress blood feuds among its members. Each of the tribes

had an unequal, but fixed, number of headmen on the confederacy council, who, as we surmise among the Huron, may originally have represented the various clan segments of which each tribe was made up. The traditional number of these sachems, or council chiefs, was fifty. The regular meeting of the confederacy council took place each autumn in the principal town of the Onondaga tribe, whose headman, Atotarho, enjoyed ritual precedence on such occasions. Since decisions could only be binding by mutual consent, neither unequal representation nor ritual precedence led to loss of autonomy for any of the member groups. In this respect, and in many details of their political organization, the Huron and Iroquois confederacies appear to have been very similar. Using the metaphor of the longhouse, the Onondaga regarded themselves as the keepers of the hearth for the confederacy, while the Seneca and the Mohawk were styled as its doorkeepers (Fenton 1971:138–39).

In the sixteenth century, a number of groups of Iroquoian-speaking peoples had been living in the St. Lawrence Valley, as far downstream as the Ile aux Coudres. All of these groups grew corn, but those living around Quebec City seem to have been particularly dependent on fishing and to have lacked the large, fortified settlements noted farther inland. The identity and disappearance of these groups will be discussed in detail in chapter 4.

While these groups exhaust the list of Iroquoian peoples known to have been living in the Great Lakes region in early historic times, it is possible that other groups lived to the south and west of the area we have examined. If so, they were dispersed by disease and warfare before they could be identified by European explorers. Seventeenth-century maps record many Iroquoian tribal names in these areas, but since all names, including those of well-known Algonkian tribes, are given in Iroquoian on these maps, it is far from certain that any of them were Iroquoian-speaking. It seems certain that these tribes had no direct influence on the Huron in the historic period and probably little or none at an earlier time.

CULTURAL SIMILARITIES

It is important not to over-emphasize similarities among the northern Iroquoian-speaking peoples. Many presumed similarities may be an illusion resulting from inadequate sources and undue extrapolation. Nevertheless, even granting the existence of important economic, stylistic, and behavioural differences between one Iroquoian tribe and another, it is possible to

define certain general characteristics that form a cultural pattern. These
are:

1. A primary dependence on horticulture as a means of subsistence, with
fishing ranking next in importance as a source of nutrition. The only
groups who may have been an exception to this rule are the St. Lawrence
Iroquoians in the Quebec City area, for whom fishing may have been more
important than horticulture, although this is far from certain. Among
groups such as the Huron confederacy and the Seneca tribe, horticulture
may have accounted for as much as eighty percent of the food eaten. All of
the northern Iroquoians practised a similar form of slash and burn agriculture, although their farming methods were skilfully adapted to local
variations in the environment (White 1963). Also, the same food crops
were grown throughout the whole area—corn, beans, squash, and sunflowers. All of these crops are ultimately of Mesoamerican origin, with the
possible exception of the sunflower, which seems to have been domesticated
in the southeastern United States (Yarnell 1964:118). Corn constituted the
bulk of the food that was produced and eaten.

2. All groups had a similar division of labour. Men cleared the land,
hunted, fished, built houses, carried on long-distance trade, and defended
their communities, while women grew and harvested crops, tended
children, and, in general, cared for their families.

3. The northern Iroquoians all lived in villages that were fortified, if
large or exposed to attack, and in bark-covered longhouses that sheltered a
number of individual families. These families were arranged on either side
of a row of hearths that ran down the centre of the dwelling. The preferred
material for constructing these longhouses seems to have been elm bark
among the Iroquois and cedar bark among the Huron. In historic times,
Iroquois houses had a rectangular floor plan, while Huron ones had
rounded ends. It is also likely that Iroquois longhouses had vertical walls
with an arching roof, while Huron ones were constructed by anchoring
poles in the ground and lashing them together overhead, in the form of an
arbour (plate 9). In spite of these minor differences, Iroquoians from one
population cluster would have had little difficulty understanding the living
arrangements of another.

4. The northern Iroquoian system of kinship varied in only a few details
from one group to another. Membership in clan segments and extended
families was based on matrilineal principles, which also governed the
inheritance of office. Residence appears to have been preferably matrilocal,
although, as we have suggested with respect to the Huron, it is likely that
a boy who was potentially heir to an hereditary position took up permanent

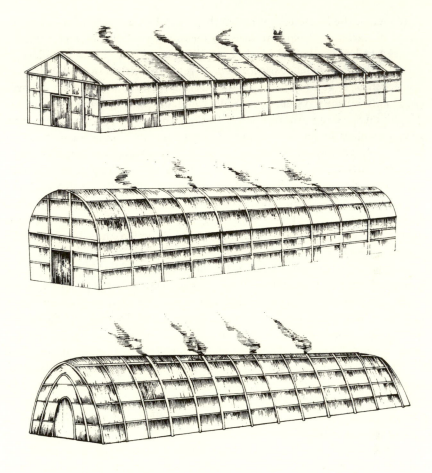

PLATE 9. *Alternative reconstructions of Iroquois (top and centre) and Huron (bottom) longhouses. The top reconstruction is based on an illustration from L. H. Morgan's* Houses and Houselife of the American Aborigines. *The centre one is based on John Bartram's diagram of an Onondaga longhouse of 1743 and is similar to ones depicted farther south along the eastern seaboard of the United States from the late sixteenth century. Below, a tentative reconstruction of a Huron longhouse following J. Lalemant and Antoine Laumet (Cadillac). The rounded ends of Huron longhouses were, in fact, more pronounced than this drawing suggests. From Trigger 1969a, Courtesy Holt, Rinehart and Winston.*

residence in the household of his mother's brother. In spite of these matrilineal preferences, Iroquoian kinship terminology and incest prohibitions seem to reflect a bilateral ideal of social organization. It was forbidden to marry either maternal or paternal blood relatives within several degrees of relationship. Eggan (1952:43; 1966:104) has pointed out that, in general, Iroquoian kinship systems resemble those of neighbouring, patrilineal, Algonkian-speaking groups more than they do the "lineage" systems that were prevalent in the southeastern United States.[68] The latter were of the Crow type, which sharply distinguishes the kinsmen who belong to a man's mother's matrilineal descent line from those who belong to his father's matrilineal descent line. Such systems are associated with highly developed matrilineal institutions. Looked at from an historical perspective, the absence of features of this sort suggests that the northern Iroquoian societies were less evolved in a matrilineal direction than were societies found farther south.

5. Another feature of northern Iroquoian society was the recognition of a bond of affinity between members of clan segments that had the same name or symbol. This relationship was strong enough to prevent intermarriage between members of such groups. The Huron and the three western Iroquois tribes had eight clan names. Six of them (Turtle, Wolf, Bear, Beaver, Deer, and Hawk) referred to the same animals among both the Huron and the Iroquois, but the Iroquois had Snipe and Heron clans in place of the Huron's Porcupine and Snake (Tooker 1970b:94). The extension of kin-type relations to all those whose clan segments were named after the same animal made it possible for travellers to find "relatives" in unfamiliar communities, and constituted a cross-cutting bond that helped to hold tribes and confederacies together. Their unity was further reinforced by the grouping of clans to form three phratries that may also have been exogamous, and whose members had ritual obligations towards one another for burial and other ceremonies.

6. Huron and Iroquois political organization had many common features and these were probably shared by the other, less well-known tribes and confederacies. Each clan segment had its own leaders for civil and military matters. Each of the former was responsible for the internal affairs of his segment and for peaceful dealings with other groups; each of the latter led his fellow warriors. Tribal and confederacy organizations were made to work by having the civil headmen of the various clan segments discuss issues and try to coordinate action. The implementation of the decisions of such councils required securing the consent of all those involved, since no Iroquoian had the right to commit another to a course of action against his

will. In spite of their apparent precariousness, governments of this sort could successfully suppress blood feuds within confederacies having as many as 20,000 members and, up to the tribal level at least, could coordinate their policies when it came to dealing with outsiders.

7. The warfare practised by the Iroquoians in the early historic period conformed to a common pattern. Their aim was not to acquire land or basic foodstuffs. Instead, warfare was the means by which young men could gain prestige, by taking heads or scalps as trophies and capturing prisoners who could be sacrificed in a torture ritual. War was rationalized as blood revenge; warriors of a tribe or confederacy carried out raids to avenge previous killings, presumed to have been committed by members of some neighbouring group. As a side effect, warfare may have served to conserve game animals, since it reduced the amount of hunting in the no man's lands between the groups involved.[69] War was also a minor source of booty, in the form of the clothing and personal ornaments worn by prisoners. In particular, for the Huron, prisoners were a source of wampum, or shell beads, which originated on the coast and were scarce and valued items in the interior.

8. The Huron and Iroquois also shared many of the same religious beliefs and practices. Their creation myths were almost identical and many of the deities they worshipped were the same. So were most of the games they played, their feasts, and their celebrations. In addition, they shared with many of the northern Algonkian peoples a deep interest in healing rituals. Some of these were performed by shamans, but among the Huron and Iroquois others were enacted by healing societies, whose membership cut across the various kinship units. While it has been suggested that these societies developed as a response to epidemic diseases that were introduced by Europeans (Brasser 1971:263), linguistic studies indicate that shamanistic practices are of considerable antiquity in Iroquoian culture. More striking is the lack of evidence at this period for the celebration of calendrical feasts such as Seed Planting, Corn Sprouting, Green Corn, or, except as a healing ritual, Midwinter. Until recently, it was generally believed that the rituals which were associated with the ideal of renewal and which served to mark the annual crises in maize cultivation or natural vegetation were among the oldest and most basic features of Iroquoian culture. While it is possible that these rituals were overlooked by the first Europeans who visited these tribes, Elisabeth Tooker (1960) and W. L. Chafe (1964) have suggested that since the seventeenth century the principal emphasis in northern Iroquoian ceremonialism has shifted away from shamanistic practices and curing ceremonies to calendric rituals. The most important

changes seem to have come about late in the eighteenth century, with the development of the "New Religion" of the Seneca prophet Handsome Lake. The main forces encouraging these developments seem to have been a growing emphasis on plough agriculture and the more sedentary life resulting from acculturation. The similarities to rituals celebrated by tribes in the southeastern United States may result from contacts that the Iroquois had with that area during the eighteenth century.

9. Finally, the northern Iroquoians shared many of the same values and attitudes, which, if difficult to define, nevertheless were, and remain, important features of their way of life. The material culture of the northern Iroquoians was not impressive and for the most part their artistic productions were limited, both in quantity and in quality. Instead, the genius of Iroquoian culture is to be found in their psychological finesse, and the attention they lavished on social relations generally. A fundamental premise of Iroquoian life was a respect for individual dignity and a sense of self-reliance, which resulted in individuals rarely quarrelling openly with one another. Displays of violent emotions were publicly disapproved of and hostility tended to express itself in accusations of witchcraft, neurotic illness, and, more violently, in suicide. More easily definable aspects of Iroquoian behaviour were their love of speeches, their politeness and hospitality to fellow villagers and to strangers, and the kindness and respect they showed towards children.

Chapter 3 The Birth of the Huron

It was long believed that the various northern Iroquoian tribes came into existence when a single people moved apart and became culturally and linguistically differentiated.[1] Earlier in this century, it was speculated that the original Iroquoian culture might have developed in the southeastern United States, where the Iroquoian-speaking Cherokee and Tuscarora were living in historic times (Lloyd 1904; Parker 1916). More recently, archaeological evidence has indicated that following a shift to horticultural production around the lower Great Lakes sometime after A.D. 500, the northern Iroquoian cultures began to evolve from hunting and gathering patterns that had been indigenous to that area (MacNeish 1952). Many of the most characteristic features of Iroquoian culture are now recognized as being the result of shared development in relatively recent times rather than cultural residue from an earlier period.

Glottochronological evidence indicates that the northern Iroquoian languages separated from Cherokee 3500 to 3800 years ago and from Tuscarora 1900 to 2400 years ago (Lounsbury 1961), thus making these linguistic relationships irrelevant for understanding the origins of northern Iroquoian culture. Neither sufficient physical anthropological nor archaeological information is available to reveal when Iroquoian-speakers first appeared in the vicinity of the Great Lakes, nor do we know whether the Iroquoian languages spread from south to north or north to south. All that can be said for certain is that the Iroquoian way of life, like those of their neighbours, was the product of a lengthy, indigenous cultural evolution. For this reason, it seems best to set aside the question of Iroquoian ethnic origins while surveying the developments that gave rise to the northern Iroquoian cultural pattern. It must be stressed that at present it is impossible to correlate any archaeological culture with even a broad linguistic grouping prior to about A.D. 500.

Ontario Prehistory

BEFORE AGRICULTURE

Southern Ontario is located close to the northern limits of the deciduous forests that cover most of eastern North America. Much of the southern part of the province lies in a transitional zone of increasing coniferous admixture, which gives way to boreal forest north of Lake Superior. Although southern Ontario is a rich biotic zone by comparison with the thinly soiled Precambrian Shield to the north, it suffers from long, cold winters. It is also remote from the Mesoamerican heartland, whose cultigens and burgeoning societies exerted a strong, if poorly understood, influence upon the cultural development of the eastern portion of North America. Because of the marginal location of southern Ontario, it is not surprising that hunting and gathering persisted until a late period and that only a few cultigens managed to penetrate that far north.

The earliest evidence of human presence in Ontario does not pre-date the retreat of the Wisconsin glaciation, which began uncovering land in the southwestern portion of the province about 13,000 years ago. The ice retreated in a slow and irregular fashion, which was interrupted by at least one major glacial advance and accompanied by numerous fluctuations in the water levels of the Great Lakes. The whole area south and west of the Ottawa Valley and Lake Nipissing was not irrevocably free of ice much before 6000 B.C. (Quimby 1960:19–26; Griffin 1965:656–58; Hurley and Kenyon 1970:105–8).

There is little evidence of human occupation from this early period. About fifty fluted spear points of the so-called Clovis type have been found across southern Ontario, from Elgin County in the west to Lanark County in the east. Most of these occur just north of Lake Erie (Garrad 1971). Both on the Prairies and in the northeastern United States, these points have been dated between 11,000 and 8000 B.C.,[2] and shown to be associated with a pattern of elephant (i.e., mammoth and mastodon) hunting that was widespread at that time. Quimby (1960:31) argues that no type of stone projectile point was as well suited for hunting these animals as were these large fluted ones.

With the decline of elephant hunting, fluted points gave way to simple lanceolate forms that are associated with the loosely defined Plano tradition. Griffin (1965:660) classifies this tradition among the earliest of the Archaic, or locally adapted hunting and gathering cultures.[3] The principal game animals in southern Ontario at this time are assumed to have been deer,

moose, and barren ground caribou. Although evidence of Plano occupation is found considerably beyond the northern limits of the earliest fluted point traditions, sites are few in number and prior to 3000 B.C., the population seems to have been extremely low (Hurley and Kenyon 1970:107–8). This is not surprising; the boreal forest that was established in southern Ontario at that time seems to have had no greater carrying capacity than modern ones and away from now submerged lake shores probably supported only about one person for every 200 to 300 square miles (Fitting 1968). It is not unlikely that, at least in general principle, the social organization of these early hunters resembled that of Naskapi bands studied in the far north of Quebec early in this century. These bands were made up of thirty to fifty people each. By living off herds of caribou, their members were able to stay together throughout the year. The extremely low population density cut interaction between bands to a minimum and, because of this, individuals tended to marry cross-cousins within their own band. The structure of these bands was therefore neither matrilineal nor patrilineal, but bilateral.[4]

Between 6000 and 3000 B.C., the climate grew warmer and drier. In southern Ontario, pines, which had begun to increase about 7000 B.C., replaced spruce and fir as the dominant forest cover. These, in turn, gave way before hardwoods, which eventually spread northwards onto the southern flanks of the Canadian Shield. From 6000 to 3000 B.C., the Great Lakes stood at very low levels, only to rise again as the isostatic rebound of land recently freed of ice raised their outlets. As essentially present-day conditions came into being over large areas of southern Ontario and New York State, a new pattern of cultural adaptation developed. This pattern, known as the Laurentian Archaic, was appropriate to an area of hardwood forests in which fruit and nuts, as well as heavy concentrations of deer and other non-migratory game, could be found and where fresh-water fish were abundant. The Laurentian Archaic can be differentiated from the contemporary Maritime Archaic pattern, found along the east coast, where caribou, sea mammals, birds, and salt-water fish were major items in the diet, and from the Shield Archaic pattern, found in the boreal forests to the north. The Shield Archaic has been defined in terms of certain rather generalized tool types (bifacial and uniface blades, lanceolate and side-notched projectile points, many kinds of scrapers, and crude chopping and scraping-cutting tools) and by the absence of the more sophisticated artifacts found in Archaic traditions farther south. The Shield Archaic seems to be the continuation of an early Archaic pattern of adaptation to a boreal environment. In some areas it may have persisted into the historic period (Wright 1968:57).

The Laurentian cultures had a wide range of tools that were useful for coping with a hardwood environment. Woodworking tools, such as axes, adzes, and gouges, were pecked and ground out of hard igneous rocks. Such implements appear to have been unnecessary for working softer woods and are absent in earlier cultures. Other diagnostic traits of the Laurentian tradition are ground slate projectile points and knives, including the semi-circular knife known as the *ulu*, simple forms of banner stones, a variety of side-notched and corner-notched projectile points, and barbed bone points (Ritchie 1965:79–80). Banner stones were used as weights on throwing sticks or *atl-atls*, which hunters used to hurl darts prior to the introduction of the bow and arrow.

The earliest date ascertained for a Laurentian Archaic site in New York State is 4610 B.C.; for Ontario, it is 3290 B.C. (Hurley and Kenyon 1970:108). The latter comes from the "Allumette Island I" site on the Ottawa River. While these dates may indicate the later development of a Laurentian Archaic pattern in Ontario, fewer sites of this period have been excavated in Ontario than in the United States; hence information is bound to be more fragmentary and provisional. A distributional study by James V. Wright (1962) of surface finds of Archaic ground stone tools in southern Ontario reveals a greater number of bannerstones and ground axes in the west than in the east, and a greater number of slate points, *ulus*, and gouges in the east than in the west.[5] This division between the eastern and western parts of southern Ontario is of interest, because it crops up repeatedly in later times.

Many copper artifacts have been found in Archaic sites in southern Ontario. These were made from metal that occurs in a pure, or native, state in the rocks of the Lake Superior basin. Thousands of prehistoric mining pits have been located along the Canadian shore of Lake Superior, in the Keweenaw Peninsula, and on Isle Royale. Once the pure copper was extracted from the rock, it was worked into shape by cold-hammering, grinding, and annealing it (Quimby 1960:52–53; Griffin 1961). The copper artifacts found in Ontario and New York State appear to have been obtained by trade from the Old Copper culture, a variant of Laurentian that flourished in the upper Great Lakes region around 2000 B.C. (Ritchie 1965:82). The majority of artifacts were tools, some of which were equipped with socketed attachments. For the most part, these tools are replicas of stone gouges, adzes, and ground slate spear points. In spite of their utilitarian shapes, it seems likely that these copper tools were acquired mainly as prestige items. The presence of conch shell ornaments in Archaic sites in New York State, and of copper artifacts far to the south,

indicates that exotic materials were traded over vast distances during this period (Winters 1968).

The many artifacts found in southern Ontario indicate that the population of this region was considerably larger than it had been previously. Although little is known about patterns of subsistence or settlement at this time, it has been suggested that the Archaic sites in the Ottawa Valley were base camps where groups, who spent the winter hunting in the interior, gathered each summer to fish (Hurley and Kenyon 1970:112–13). This pattern, which enabled maximum exploitation of the dispersed plant and animal resources of the area, was followed by the Montagnais, Ojibwa, and other nonagricultural peoples of Ontario and southern Quebec into the historic period.[6] In view of basic similarities in environment and subsistence patterns in the Archaic period and among these groups in early historic times, it appears that a broader analogy may be drawn.

It may be inferred that in the late Archaic period the population of southern Ontario was divided into hunting bands, each composed of several hundred members. Since the area now lacked herd animals, the members of these bands had to break up each autumn into small groups, that scattered in search of game in different parts of the band territory. Because if a lone hunter were injured or became seriously ill in the course of the winter, his wife and children would starve, these hunting parties were usually made up of two or more brothers, or a father and sons, together with their families. These relatives shared the dangers of the winter together, without expectation of any outside support. In summer, the various segments of the band would gather under the leadership of a recognized headman. Supported by abundant catches of fish, the members of these bands found time to enjoy each other's company, to arrange marriages, and to celebrate rituals, one of the most important of which, by the end of the Archaic period, was the burial of their dead (Ritchie 1965:178). These larger groupings functioned as political units insofar as members cooperated in the defence of a common territory. They were also necessary to regulate the economic exploitation of these areas and to provide long-term support for their constituent family groupings, whose very existence could be threatened by the loss of a single adult member.

Population densities may have approached the one person per twenty-five square miles found in historic times among groups such as the Ojibwa. The territories occupied by individual bands would have been much smaller than they had been previously, and this would have broken down the isolation between neighbouring, and probably multiplying and fissioning, bands. Under these conditions, band endogamy declined in favour of

intermarriage between adjacent groups. In societies largely dependent on hunting, men who grow up together generally prefer to remain a team, hence women leave the band into which they are born to live with their husbands. As a result of such marriages, bilateral bands would have been transformed into clan groups, whose male members tended to claim descent from a real or a fictitious common ancestor. Like the clan segments of the Iroquoians, the vast majority of Algonkian patrilineal groups bore the name of some animal, although most were fish and birds rather than mammals. The word totem, now used by anthropologists to designate a patron animal spirit, is an Algonkian word meaning a local group of consanguines (Hickerson 1970:44). Because of the importance attached to the kinship relation between the male members of these clans, marriage within the group came to be viewed as incest and was forbidden. Cross-cousin marriage continued to play an important role in regulating marriage but cross-cousins were now normally born into different bands rather than into the same one, as they had been previously.[7]

Such marriage patterns forged informal, but nevertheless effective alliances between neighbouring groups. Allied bands frequently shared a common language or dialect, and constituted what have loosely been called tribes. Historic groupings, such as the Algonkin or the Ottawa, seem to have been alliances of this sort, although their members probably had less sense of common identity than European explorers ascribed to them. We have no way of knowing whether any of the tribes in the Archaic period had phratries, or a dual arrangement of patrilineal clans, that formed the basis for rivalry in games and ceremonial activities on the rare occasions when a number of bands might assemble in one place. Alignments of this sort served to strengthen and extend the clan system and are a feature of more densely populated areas (Eggan 1966:83).

Around 1500 B.C., in New York State, the Laurentian Archaic pattern began to pass through a transitional stage which, by about 1000 B.C., had given rise to a new cultural pattern known as Early Woodland. Typical Early Woodland artifacts include tubular smoking pipes, various types of gorgets, birdstones, boatstones, and bar amulets (all three made of polished stone and of uncertain function, although probably ornamental), and, for the first time, copper ornaments, as opposed to copper tools. The latter were mostly beads (Ritchie 1965:178–79). The most distinctive feature of the Early Woodland pattern is the appearance of pottery, which from this time on, is ubiquitous in the archaeological record. The earliest pottery is called Vinette I. These are thick-walled vessels, made with a coiling technique, and decorated with cord markings. Vinette I is far from being the earliest

pottery in eastern North America; a simple, but distinctive, fibre-tempered variety being manufactured in the southeastern United States as early as 2000 B.C. Vinette I pottery is associated principally with the Meadowood culture, found in New York State and the St. Lawrence Valley (ibid. 192–93).

In Ontario, the Early Woodland phase is very poorly understood. While Early Woodland artifacts are widely distributed in surface collections and have been found mixed with later material in a number of sites, no purely Early Woodland assemblages have as yet been identified. Where radio-carbon determinations are available, Vinette I seems to date about 500 years later in southern Ontario than it does in New York State (Hurley and Kenyon 1970:114–15). Moreover, at the East Sugar Island site on Rice Lake, typical Laurentian material was found apparently associated with Middle Woodland pottery types (Ritchie 1965:209). This, and other considerations, have led various archaeologists to propose that the Vinette I ceramics found in Ontario are a late intrusion northwards and that there may not have been a separate Early Woodland period in the province (Wright 1967:131–32). This suggests that a basically Archaic (pre-ceramic) culture survived later in Ontario than it did to the south and east, but was influenced by the stone tool types of the Meadowood culture from about 1000 B.C. on.

Burials resembling those of the Glacial Kame culture have been found in southern Ontario. This culture is dated roughly between 1600 and 1000 B.C. and thus falls into the transitional period between late Archaic and Early Woodland (Ritchie 1965:131–34). The Glacial Kame culture is centred in the midwestern United States, and appears to be derived in some manner from the Old Copper culture. The many parallels between the Glacial Kame and Meadowood cultures include tubular pipes, copper celts and adzes, bar-shaped birdstones, rectangular gorgets, shell disk beads, red ochre in burials, and the practice of cremation (ibid. 198–200). Although both cultures appear to be contemporary, Glacial Kame lacked pottery, as the cultures of southern Ontario seem to have done. The presence of both Glacial Kame and Meadowood traits in southern Ontario may indicate that this area was an important avenue by which ideas, as well as raw materials, were being transmitted at this time. The elaboration of burial rituals in late Archaic and Early Woodland times marks the beginning of a pre-occupation with the honouring of the dead that was to persist, with fluctuations, in the lower Great Lakes area and culminate for the last time in the Huron Feast of the Dead.

The Middle Woodland stage in Ontario dates from some time before

500 B.C. to perhaps as late as A.D. 500. Its pottery is characterized by a much greater range of decoration than existed previously, but nevertheless consists only of sub-conoidal cooking pots made by the coiling method. The principal decorations that appear on Middle Woodland pottery are dentate stamp, pseudo-scallop shell, rocker stamp (dentate and plain), cord-marking, and dragged stamp (ibid. 179). At least three roughly contemporary Middle Woodland cultures have been delineated in Ontario: Laurel in northern Ontario and adjacent parts of Manitoba, Michigan, and Minnesota; Saugeen in southwestern Ontario; and Ontario Point Peninsula in the eastern part of southern Ontario (Wright 1967:95–125). It is possible, however, that as more sites are excavated, the pottery types associated with these three cultures will be shown to intergrade with one another, and with the Point Peninsula culture of New York State, to form a broad continuum of stylistic variation.

In general, pottery types appear to be much more homogeneously distributed throughout this region than are stone tool types and copper artifacts, which often vary considerably within the same "culture." While it was once believed that the Middle Woodland cultural pattern was introduced by a migration of people coming from the northwest, Brose (1970:67–68) has suggested that the pottery complex may have developed locally, possibly in the Illinois area, and from there spread throughout the Great Lakes region. If patrilineal bands were engaging in exogamic marriages, the diffusion of female potters would result in the widespread distribution of similar elements of ceramic design. At the same time, these marriage patterns would encourage artifacts manufactured by men to develop along local lines. Pottery would diffuse very rapidly in this manner and might give the impression of a sweeping occupation of the region by newcomers, when in fact no change of population had taken place.

There is good evidence that the centrally based wandering pattern, which we postulated began in the Archaic stage, was being followed at this period. Yet, it appears that the population was larger than before and that a greater range of food resources was being exploited. While still important, hunting probably accounted for a smaller part of the total diet than it had previously. The members of patrilineal bands seem to have lived together during the warmer months of each year when fishing was productive, catching sturgeon in the spring and whitefish in the autumn. Shellfish were collected in large numbers, and concentrations of sites in areas where wild rice was common suggest that it too was intensively harvested and eaten (Ritchie 1965:207–11). Wild rice may also have played an important role in helping people to survive the winter, although families still appear

to have spent the leanest months hunting in small parties, mainly away from the major lakes and rivers. The artifactual evidence from Middle Woodland sites indicates that men and women lived together throughout the year. There is nothing to suggest that men left their families in order to hunt and fish for long periods elsewhere, as was the case with the Huron and neighbouring horticultural, or semi-horticultural, peoples in early historical times. The ecological adaptation of the people of southern Ontario in the Middle Woodland period appears to have been essentially the same as that of the Ojibwa and related nonagricultural peoples, who lived north of this area into the historical period.

To date, relatively little is known about the settlement patterns of the Middle Woodland period. At the Donaldson site, located near the mouth of the Saugeen River in southwestern Ontario and dated about 500 B.C., James V. Wright (and Anderson 1963) has identified the post mold patterns of at least two roughly rectangular structures measuring twenty-three by fourteen feet and seventeen by eleven feet respectively (plate 10). The larger structure is believed to have had a gabled roof and to have been open at the south end. Near the centre of this cabin was a large circular hearth. Traces of a fireplace were found near the wall of the smaller, and somewhat more elliptical, structure. Nearby were twelve burials, in which beads of copper and marginella shell were found, as well as perforated bear teeth and various stone tools. This site has been interpreted as a fishing station that was occupied in the spring and early summer.

From the other end of the Middle Woodland time span is the Kipp Island No. 4 site in eastern New York State. Dense concentrations of post molds bear witness to the prolonged recurrent occupation of this site. The most clearly defined house outline was a round one, eighteen to twenty feet in diameter, with a doorway facing south. Because of the intensive occupation of the site, no hearths or storage pits could be attributed with any certainty to this particular dwelling. Another, less satisfactorily defined structure was rectangular with rounded corners and measured about nineteen by ten feet. A final structure, only partially outlined, may have been an oblong building over forty feet in length, possibly a prototype of the later Owasco (early Iroquoian) longhouse (Ritchie 1965:247).

Some of the most informative data concerning the nature of Middle Woodland societies come from the Summer Island site in Lake Michigan. There was found a summer fishing camp that had been occupied, at most for a few seasons, sometime in the second or third centuries A.D. The outlines of four cabins, together with their fish and meat drying platforms, were located and two of them were excavated very carefully so that

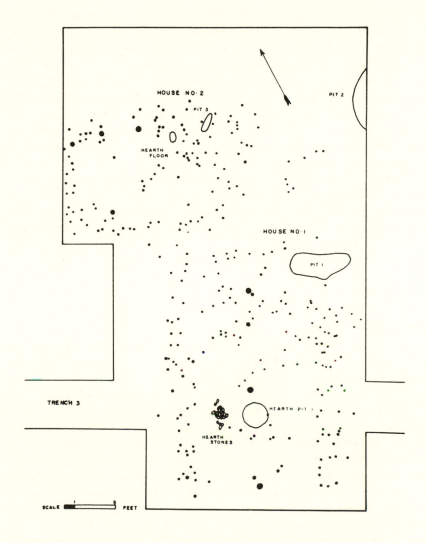

PLATE 10. *Floor plan of house structures 1 and 2 from the Donaldson site near Southampton, Ontario* (C. *500* B.C.). *The post molds suggest two roughly rectangular structures. House 1 is believed to have had a gabled roof and been open at the south end. The Donaldson site was probably a fishing station occupied in the spring and early summer. Courtesy National Museum of Man, National Museums of Canada.*

distributions of artifacts in and around them could be analysed in detail. While three of the four structures appear to have been circular, and at least two of them had a single central hearth, the largest was an elliptical structure twenty-nine by twelve feet, with two hearths along its main axis. The distribution of artifacts within this structure indicated that it had been inhabited by two nuclear families. The careful manner in which sections of the cabin had been allotted to each of its adult inhabitants permitted Brose (1970:53–59) to infer that it had been lived in by two men with one wife each, two sub-adults, and an unknown number of children. A detailed examination of variations in pottery types, within and between houses, strongly rules out the possibility of matrilocal residence and suggests a patrilocal or bilateral pattern with probable cross-cousin marriage.

This clear-cut example of an extended family dwelling from about the beginning of the Christian era underscores what has long been known to Algonkianists, but has been ignored by Iroquoian specialists: that the hunting and gathering peoples of Ontario and Quebec, who have been interpreted as providing a model of what Iroquoian social organization was like prior to the introduction of horticulture, did not necessarily, or even in major part, live in single-family dwellings. It is clear from Le Jeune's description of life among the Montagnais in the seventeenth century that winter hunting parties consisted of two or more brothers and their families, who lived together in large conical tents constructed of poles and covered with portable bark mats (Thwaites 1896–1901, 7:107). The existence of patrilocal extended families among these hunting peoples indicates the shortcomings inherent in explanations that seek to account for the development of Iroquoian extended families out of a primordial nuclear family organization, and which see this development mirrored in a presumed transition from single family dwellings to multifamily longhouses (Noble 1969:18). Everything that is known about the mixed forest region of eastern North America indicates that extended families, and probably exogamic clans, existed there long before the development of a horticultural economy. As we shall see, the major problem concerning the development of Iroquoian social structure is not how these institutions came into being, but how, and under what circumstances, institutions based primarily on patrilineal descent were reshaped to become matrilineal.

The incipient longhouse from the Summer Island site also suggests that this type of dwelling was not necessarily an Iroquoian invention. As long as the number of nuclear families that live together is small and the house that must be supported on a framework of poles does not cover a large area, a variety of shapes is possible. The Montagnais lived in round cabins with a

single fire in the middle and, even at Summer Island, there were round houses that were only fractionally smaller than the "longhouse" we have been discussing. Thus a longhouse is not the only structure suitable to house an extended family. Yet, as the number of families who live together increases, the difficulty of erecting a structure that is more than twenty-five feet across requires that houses be increased in length to provide additional living space. The architectural principles used to build bark-covered cabins were widely known in Middle Woodland times and it is possible that the longhouse is merely an application of these principles to meet the problem of placing more families under a single roof.[8]

In the early historic period, the longhouse was not restricted to the Iroquoian culture area. The normal housetype among the Algonkian speakers living in the vicinity of Georgian Bay was an elliptical structure equipped with two fireplaces and sheltering several families (Wrong 1939:185). This was also the style of cabin that Huron men constructed when they went north on their annual fishing expeditions. The Jesuits state that the Nipissing erected sizable longhouses for ritual purposes (Thwaites 1896–1901, 23:217) and medicine lodges were still being built in this style by the Ojibwa of northern Ontario as recently as the 1930s (Ritchie 1965:283, plate 95). Farther afield, Champlain's description of a fortified Montagnais summer camp at Tadoussac reveals that these Indians were living in longhouses in 1603 (Biggar 1922–36, 1:98–99), while a summer camp containing one longhouse, which was also used for holding village feasts, was observed among the Indians of New Brunswick in 1607 (Lescarbot 1907–14, 2:356).

The proto-longhouse from the Summer Island site indicates that multi-family dwellings, resembling the small early Iroquoian longhouse, may have developed among the northern Algonkians long before the end of the Middle Woodland period. A single dwelling approximately twenty-two feet wide and eighty feet long and dated circa A.D. 1300 has been excavated at the Juntunen site, a stratified fishing station on Bois Blanc Island in the Straits of Mackinac. The pottery from this site shows considerable Ontario Iroquoian influence and the excavator has suggested that the longhouse may be further evidence of contact with that area (McPherron 1967:103). Alternatively it may provide a link between the incipient longhouse of the Summer Island site and the longhouses reported among the historic Nipissing, Ojibwa, and other northern groups. Until strong evidence to the contrary is forthcoming, it seems preferable to view the longhouse as an extension of the smaller multifamily dwellings that were prevalent among the hunting tribes of this area and that only now are being recognized in

the archaeological record. The longhouse may not have been the invention of any one group, but the result of a trend that manifested itself whenever larger houses were required. The greater frequency of longhouses on Iroquoian sites, and their exceptional size, may simply reflect the ability of larger numbers of related families to live together throughout the year once a horticultural economy was introduced.

Ontario and New York State remained relatively unaffected by developments that took place in the central Mississippi, Ohio, and Illinois River valleys between 300 B.C. and A.D. 250. Between these dates, the Hopewell tradition, which drew some of its inspiration from the earlier Adena culture of the Ohio Valley, evolved and flourished in this region. The beginning of Hopewell was marked by significant increases in population and in the size of local aggregations, by the development of a ceremonial and mortuary complex with strong evidence of status differences, and by increased interaction between groups over a wide area of the eastern United States. One feature of this interaction was the extensive trading of exotic raw materials, such as copper, silver, mica, gelena, obsidian, large marine shells, and fresh water pearls; another was the widespread sharing of selected artifact styles (Struever 1968:288). The luxury goods produced in this period, such as stone pipes with bowls in the form of birds and animals, personal ornaments made of copper and mica, and elaborate pottery figurines, marked a high point in the artistic expression of the northeastern United States. Cloth was manufactured by a finger weaving technique and decorated with batik patterns, or with designs worked in copper, pearls, and shell. Pottery also attained an artistic level, both in shape and decoration, that was not to be equalled thereafter in the region. Another spectacular product of Hopewell industry was large numbers of burial mounds and vast geometrical earthworks that seem to have been cult centres. These were usually located on cliffs and other eminences overlooking rivers.

In spite of a high level of cultural development, Hopewell sites are generally confined to the broad bottoms of flat river valleys that lie within the deciduous forest area of the American Midwest. Deer were more common in the broken forests of this region than they were in New York State and Ontario. Vast numbers of birds migrated along the river valleys, and the permanent lakes that dotted the valley bottoms abounded in fish. Hopewell culture was able to develop and flourish, at least in the Illinois area, largely because of an economic pattern based on the intensive collection of certain selected natural plant foods and, probably secondarily, upon floodplain agriculture. The main plant foods that were available were acorns, hickory nuts, and seed-bearing plants such as marsh-elder (*Iva*),

smartweed (*Polygonom*), and lamb's-quarter (*Chenopodium*). All of these plants grew naturally in this area in sufficiently large concentrations that they could be harvested with a small labour input. The local seed plants may also have been grown on the floodplain, along with southern imports, such as gourds, pumpkins, sunflowers, beans, and maize. There is no evidence, however, that these imports, or indeed agriculture as a whole, bulked as large in the Hopewell cultural pattern as they did in the Iroquoian one (Struever and Vickery 1973).

Although Hopewell sites are found as far north as Grand Rapids, Michigan, none are known in southern Ontario. The main evidence of Hopewell influence in Ontario comes from the Middle Woodland burial mounds located in the Trent Valley region, and particularly along the north shore of Rice Lake. These mounds, which date roughly between 100 B.C. and A.D. 300, occur in an area rich in wild rice and which seems to have been one of the major centres of population in Ontario in the Middle Woodland period. Some of the burial mounds, such as the Le Vesconte Mound on the Trent River and the Cameron's Point one on Rice Lake, have yielded grave goods of Hopewellian type, including copper and conch shell pendants, cut mica, perforated sharks' teeth, and panpipe sheaths made out of silver and copper (Johnston 1968*a*). The majority of mounds, however, show few, if any, clear-cut traces of Hopewell connection. The burial mounds, as a whole, may be explained as products of a weak Hopewellian influence on the local Point Peninsula culture of southeastern Ontario. These influences may have arrived in Ontario from New York State, by way of the Squawkie Hill culture, which is itself a local Point Peninsula manifestation influenced by Hopewellian ideas and elements of material culture, many of which appear to be of a religious nature (Ritchie 1965:213–14). The Ontario sites thus occur on the outer fringes of the Hopewellian sphere, and were probably modelled after what were already "attenuated examples of Hopewellian practice" (Johnston 1968*a*:29). It is perhaps no accident that the mounds showing the clearest evidence of Hopewell influence seem to be the earliest in the region. This would indicate the very short-lived and tenuous influence that cultural ideas of southern origin exerted on southern Ontario at this time.

In spite of this, the widespread evidence of native copper artifacts and exotic shells indicates that Ontario was far from isolated during the Middle Woodland period. While these contacts were less extensive geographically than were those of the Hopewell culture, they maintained all of the links with the upper Great Lakes and the southeastern United States that have been noted in the preceding Archaic period. Although the bulk of copper

found in any one site was generally smaller than found in earlier sites, this may reflect the marked increase in the population that was now drawing upon the copper supplies of the Lake Superior region. The rising demand for copper may, in part, explain why it was used increasingly for ornamentation rather than for manufacturing bulky prestige tools (Ritchie 1965:178).

THE EARLY IROQUOIAN PERIOD

Early in the Christian era, cultural change began to quicken its pace both in southern Ontario and New York State. In spite of the presence of some type of horticulture in the Hopewellian tradition, there is no proof, either direct or indirect, that crops were grown farther to the north much before A.D. 500. It has been suggested that tropical flint corn, which was the ancestor of most of the corn grown in the northeastern United States in later times, had not yet been adapted for areas where there were fewer than 150 frost-free days.[9] The flint corn which eventually would be cultivated by the northern Iroquoian-speaking peoples had a growing period of only 100 days, while the less popular flour corn matured in 130 days. These hardier varieties were eventually to grow as far north as Lake Nipissing and the south shore of Lake Superior. Despite the apparent lack of cultigens, pottery vessels generally became larger in the Middle and Late Point Peninsula cultures, possibly indicating a more sedentary way of life (Ritchie 1965:232). Pipes, which were already common in the Kipp Island culture in New York State, grew considerably more so in the succeeding Hunter's Home culture. This suggests that smoking was becoming more popular, but it has not yet been determined whether Indian tobacco (*Nicotiana rustica*) was among the substances being smoked. Ritchie (1965:232) is of the opinion that Hunter's Home marks the point at which *Nicotiana rustica* was introduced into upper New York State as a domesticate, rather than merely as an item of trade from the south, and that corn was probably being grown by this time also. In spite of these changes, the centrally based wandering pattern of Middle Woodland times does not appear to have given way to more sedentary village life anywhere around the lower Great Lakes prior to A.D. 500 (Fitting 1970:143).

In central New York, Hunter's Home evolved into the Owasco culture, which Ritchie (1965:271–72) divides into three phases: Early (or Carpenter Brook), Middle (Canandaigua), and Late (Castle Creek). The last of these phases persisted until about A.D. 1300 and is ancestral to the historic

Iroquois cultures. Throughout the Owasco period, there is evidence of growing dependence on food crops. It has been suggested that, in part, this may have been made possible by a relatively mild climatic phase, the so-called Neo-Atlantic Optimum, which lasted from approximately A.D. 900 to 1200 (Martijn 1969:96–97). Of at least equal importance may have been a crucial but as yet little understood breakthrough in acclimatizing crops to a shorter growing season. Corn, beans, and squash are evidenced in New York State in Early Owasco times (Ritchie and Funk 1973:186).

The introduction of horticulture is commonly believed to have resulted in a marked increase in population during the Owasco period (Ritchie 1965:280; Whallon 1968:236). In New York State many horticultural sites have been found on the second terraces of large streams, above the flood plain where the crops were planted, although others are located a considerable distance from any waterway (Ritchie 1965:273, 280). It has been argued that, in at least some areas, the northern Iroquoians were already inhabiting such sites on a year-round basis, as they did in historic times. Studies of faunal evidence from large sites in western New York suggest, however, that these were occupied only during the warmer months of the year, as fishing camps had been previously (White 1963:8–10). It is therefore possible that a sedentary village pattern developed more slowly than is generally believed, and remained incomplete throughout early Iroquoian times.

Whether or not this is the case, it is clear that these horticultural villages were not the only unit of settlement in Owasco times, any more than in the historic period. Fishing camps along lakes and rivers, hunting camps on the glaciated Allegheny Plateau and, finally, traces of habitation on the flood-plains, which contain mostly pottery and probably were summer houses inhabited by women working in the fields, are all evidence of a variety of sites, which some or all of the inhabitants of these larger villages must have lived in at different times of the year (Ritchie 1965:279–80).

With the Owasco culture, the coiled pottery of earlier times gave way to an improved form of seamless pottery that was shaped out of a ball of tempered clay, using a small wooden paddle. Early Owasco vessels had flat lips; later, they were often sharply splayed out. Vessels gradually became less elongate and more globular and, in the Castle Creek phase, many were collared and had well-marked castellated rims. Pots were up to twelve gallons in capacity, suggesting that food was sometimes cooked for more than a nuclear family (ibid. 289–93). The exterior of these vessels was check-stamped, or cord or fabric impressed. Other decorations were con-

fined to the upper portions of the vessel and were executed with a cord-wrapped stick or paddle edge.

The largest village of the Early Owasco period excavated so far is the Maxon-Derby site, near Syracuse. This site, which is dated about A.D. 1100, covers two acres and does not appear to have been fortified. Within the excavated portion of the site, post molds belonging to seven houses have been uncovered. These houses had parallel sides with rounded ends, and varied in size from twenty by twenty-three feet to sixty by twenty-seven feet. They appear to have been arbour-shaped structures covered with sheets of bark supported on a framework of poles. The latter were from two and a half to three inches in diameter and were spaced six to ten inches apart. The four principal houses show signs of having been repaired and enlarged several times and one of them may have had a vestibule by the doorway for storing provisions and gear. Contrary to late Iroquoian practice, fireplaces were arranged along one or both of the long sides of these houses. The total village is estimated to have contained at least ten houses and to have had a population of 200 to 250 people (ibid. 281–84).

These longhouses were not the only house-types in New York State during the early phase of Iroquoian cultural development. At the Sackett site, farther east in what would later be Cayuga territory, a series of circular houses, twelve to fourteen feet across and with a single hearth in the middle, has been uncovered. This site, which is assigned to the Middle Owasco period and dated about A.D. 1140, covers about three acres and was surrounded by a simple palisade. Its large size and estimated population of some 350 people make it highly unlikely that it was a seasonal hunting or fishing camp (ibid. 286).

The Chamberlin site, located only three miles from Maxon-Derby, but about two centuries later in time (circa A.D. 1290), shows a gradual development in the direction of the historic Iroquoian settlement pattern. Although the hearths remain near the walls of the houses, the houses themselves are now over eighty feet long. Like the Sackett site, Chamberlin was surrounded by a low ridge of earth, which probably once supported the base of a palisade that was set on, but not into, the ground (Tuck 1971:23–34). The fortifications that begin to appear at this site and others may indicate increasing warfare during the Middle and Late Owasco periods. At least some palisades consist of a single line of posts, about three inches in diameter and set three to eighteen inches apart. To be an effective barrier, such posts would have had to be interwoven with vines and smaller sticks (Ritchie 1965:284). Small trees were used to construct houses and

palisades, in part because of the difficulty involved in felling large numbers of big trees with stone axes.

Although there is only slender evidence of areal stylistic variation within the Owasco culture, strings of village sites have been discovered that can be shown to have been inhabited in succession by a single community from Owasco times into the historic period. These studies reveal that the ancestors of the Mohawk, Onondaga, Seneca, and presumably the other Iroquois tribes, were located in their historic tribal territories from at least Owasco times onward, and that no theories of migrations are needed to account for their development (Tuck 1971).

On the whole, villages appear to have been smaller, more numerous, and more evenly spaced in Owasco times than they were later. There is no evidence that the individual tribes known in historic times existed as political entities this early. Nevertheless, such continuity of occupation, in circumscribed areas over long periods of time, provides some clue to the social reality that underlies the longstanding linguistic divisions between most of the tribes of the Five Nations. Since the Iroquois found themselves surrounded by other agricultural peoples, individual groups strove to defend their territories in the face of growing competition, probably over hunting and fishing grounds rather than agricultural land. The effect of such behaviour was not to make one group dominant over another, but to maintain a balanced distribution of groups, each holding on to its own territory. It is possible that, even during the early Iroquoian period, alliances may have embraced more than a single village, although this is far from certain.

The earliest horticultural economy yet known in southern Ontario belongs to the recently defined Princess Point culture or complex, which may have begun before A.D. 500 (map 3a). This culture has been interpreted as an extension of the Early Owasco culture into the southern part of southwestern Ontario, an area generally lying within the same deciduous forest belt as the Owasco sites in New York State. The pottery, pipes, and lithic material from Princess Point sites are said to be very similar to those from Early Owasco ones, although certain attributes, such as the high percentage of exterior punctates on the rims of pottery vessels, suggest affinities with the Black Duck culture in northern Ontario and Minnesota. All of the sites studied so far are located on river flats, small sheltered inlets, or streams close to rivers. The Porteous site, which dates near the end of this culture, has yielded traces of a longhouse, thirty-six feet long and twenty-two feet wide, with a central distribution of hearths inside it (plate 11). Carbonized corn has been found on even the earliest Princess

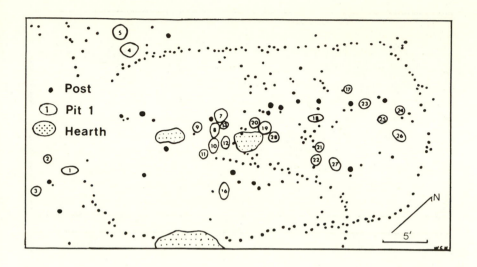

PLATE 11. *Plan of a small longhouse from the Porteous site, near Brantford, Ontario (late Princess Point or early Glyn Meyer culture, c. A.D. 700). This longhouse belongs to an early stage in the development of a horticultural economy in southern Ontario. Two hearths are centrally aligned $5\frac{1}{2}$ feet apart. The structure resembles in many ways the "incipient longhouse" from the much earlier Summer Island site. Courtesy W. C. Noble.*

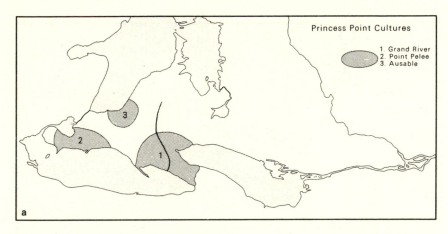

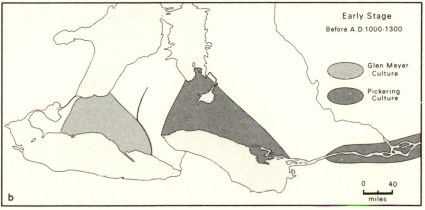

MAP 3. *Current synthesis of the Iroquoian developmental sequence in Ontario (based largely on Wright 1961 and 1972 and Stothers 1974).*

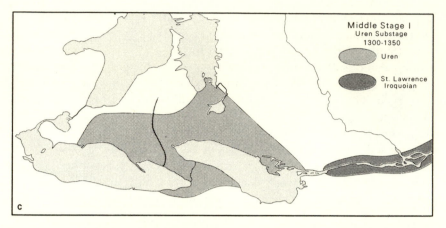

Middle Stage I
Uren Substage
1300-1350

Uren

St. Lawrence
Iroquoian

c

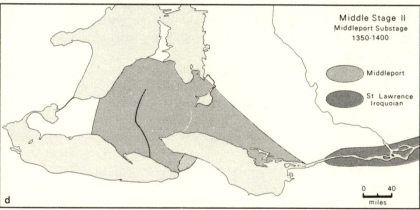

Middle Stage II
Middleport Substage
1350-1400

Middleport

St Lawrence
Iroquoian

0   40
miles

d

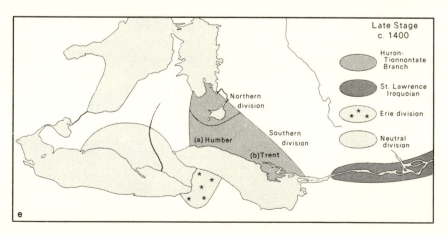

Late Stage
c. 1400

Huron-
Tionnontate
Branch

St. Lawrence
Iroquoian

Erie division

Neutral
division

Northern
division

Southern
division

(a) Humber

(b) Trent

e

Point sites. One carbonized bean has been tentatively associated with this culture, although beans are not attested elsewhere in Ontario until much later (Stothers 1970; Noble and Kenyon 1972).

The Princess Point culture appears to have evolved into what archaeologists call the Glen Meyer culture, which lasted until approximately A.D. 1300. The Glen Meyer culture was confined to southwestern Ontario. Most sites found so far are between Port Rowan, on Lake Erie, and Ipperwash, on Lake Huron; an area containing large tracts of sandy, easily worked soil (map 3b). Because of lack of excavation, little can be said with certainty about the settlement pattern associated with this culture. Villages tended to be located between small ravines or on hilltops, in a manner that indicates a concern for defence. Such sites appear large by Iroquoian standards, many covering five to ten acres. They also occur in clusters, although it is unclear how many sites in any one cluster are contemporary. The size and clustering of village sites and an apparent absence of hunting camps has been claimed as evidence of heavy reliance on horticulture (Wright 1966:22–40; 52–53).

The Glen Meyer culture is distinguished from the contemporary, but possibly later-starting, Pickering culture, which occupied the region lying between Lake Ontario and the Canadian Shield and possibly extended down the St. Lawrence Valley and into New York State (ibid. 40–53; Trigger 1968a:436). Although the general character of the archaeological remains associated with the Pickering (plate 12) and Glen Meyer cultures is the same, they can clearly be differentiated from one another. While many ceramic attributes, including vessel form, paddle and anvil manufacturing, distribution of decoration, and bossing are held in common, the body of the pot was characteristically covered with ribbed paddle or checked stamp impressions in the Pickering culture and the technique of scarification was largely limited to the Glen Meyer culture. Also, pottery gaming discs and cup-and-pin game deer phalanges have so far been found only in Pickering sites, while slate pendants are found only in Glen Meyer ones. Pipes are scarce in both cultures, and are much cruder than those from Owasco sites in New York State (Wright 1966:51, 53; cf. plate 10, 6–16 and Ritchie 1965, plate 100). While it is generally assumed that tobacco was grown in Ontario at this time, its status as a domestic plant remains to be demonstrated. Corn was grown by the Pickering people, but their villages appear to have been smaller and more widely dispersed than were those of the Glen Meyer culture and, in addition to moderate-sized horticultural villages, there were numerous small campsites, usually located near good fishing spots. Because of this, it has been suggested that

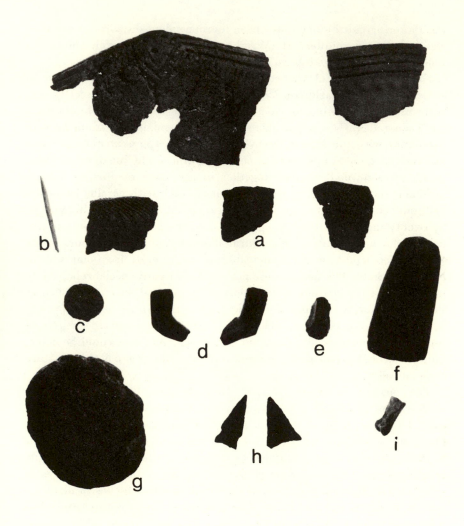

PLATE 12. *Typical early Iroquoian artifacts from Ontario (Pickering culture): (a) broken pottery; (b) bone awl; (c) pottery gaming disc; (d) pottery pipes; (e) stone scraper; (f) adze; (g) anvil stone; (h) arrowheads; (i) deer toe bone altered for unknown purpose. Courtesy National Museum of Man, National Museums of Canada.*

the Pickering culture may have been less dependent on horticulture than was its western counterpart (Wright 1966:22). In general, the larger Pickering villages were located inland, on naturally defensible sites.

Fortunately, two of these habitation sites have been excavated in sufficient detail to yield considerable information about their settlement patterns. The earlier of the two is the Miller site, east of Toronto. This site has been radiocarbon dated about A.D. 1125, and is thus roughly contemporary with the Maxon-Derby site. It covers approximately one acre and was surrounded by a palisade consisting of a single line of small poles, which were no doubt woven together in the same manner as Owasco palisades. Inside the village were five houses, each with parallel side walls and rounded ends (plate 13). These houses varied in size from thirty-eight by twenty to sixty by twenty-eight feet, and the largest of them had five hearths down the centre. This central alignment of hearths occurs in the Middle Woodland Summer Island site, but not in early Iroquoian sites in New York State. The houses were not arranged in any special relationship to one another and there is no evidence of internal structures, such as sleeping platforms running along the walls (although these seem present at the earlier Porteous site). The framework was constructed entirely of small trees, which could be cut and bent easily. As far as could be determined, each house had only a single door, located at one end of the structure (Kenyon 1968).

The partially excavated Bennett site is located about thirteen miles northwest of Hamilton and is dated circa A.D. 1260, near the end of the early Iroquoian stage of development. The village is located on a small knoll, about one mile from the nearest stream, and covers two and a half to three acres. It was surrounded by a palisade which, over much of its length, consisted of two rows of posts, running two to three feet from each other. The individual posts were about two and a half inches in diameter and six inches to one foot apart. The one house that was fully excavated measured fifty-five by twenty-two and a half feet, while other houses, which were not fully excavated, were approximately the same width and even longer (plate 14). Hearths were arranged along the main axes of these houses, as they were at the Miller site, and post molds six inches or more in diameter were found aligned parallel to the walls of the houses but about four feet, eight inches in from the walls. These posts appear to have supported two rows of sleeping platforms. One house had an extension at one end about fifteen feet long, but the absence of hearths or sleeping platforms in this section suggests that it was probably used for storage. Traces were also found of sheds built against the outside walls of these

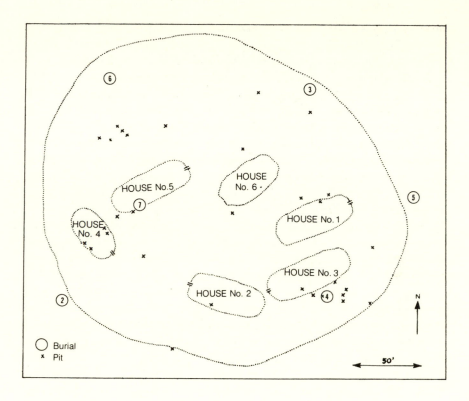

PLATE 13. *Plan of the Miller site showing palisade and outlines of houses (c. A.D. 1125). This site is assigned to the Pickering culture. The palisade is formed of a single line of poles; houses are from 38 feet to 60 feet long. The largest had five hearths down the centre. Courtesy W. A. Kenyon and Royal Ontario Museum, Toronto.*

FLOOR PLAN
Burials
Pits
Shallow Pits
Fire Floors
Posts
Pot Concentrations
Artifact Caches
Disturbed Areas

PLATE 14. *House patterns in a portion of the Bennett site* (c. A.D. *1260*).
*This site is also assigned to the Pickering culture. The palisade consisted,
in parts, of two rows of posts 2 to 3 feet apart. A few large posts inside each
house supported sleeping platforms and sheds were built against the outside
walls of the houses, probably to store firewood. The extension to house 1
lacked hearths and appears to have been a storage area. Courtesy National
Museum of Man, National Museums of Canada.*

houses. They may have been used to store wood. There seem to have been doors at either end of the one house that was completely excavated, but the evidence is not clear on this point (Wright and Anderson 1969).

On the basis of present evidence, numerous similarities can be observed in the development of settlement patterns in the Owasco and Pickering cultures. In both, villages were small and, throughout the early Iroquoian period, there appears to have been an increasing emphasis on their defence. The longhouse had a similar shape in both Ontario and New York State, and appears to have been increasing in length. In Ontario, however, the absence of circular houses and the central alignment of hearths suggest a more rapid development of the house-type of the historic period than is found in New York State.[10] The use of larger timbers to support sleeping platforms also may be a "progressive" feature which first makes its appearance in Ontario. This suggests that at least some features of the Iroquoian longhouse may have originated in the north and did not diffuse into the southern part of the northern Iroquoian culture area until considerably later. The many innovations observed in settlement patterns during the duration of the Pickering culture are in keeping with rapid changes noted in other aspects of this culture (Wright 1966:53).

The Owasco, Princess Point, and Pickering cultures provide evidence of what appears to have been a widespread, and fairly rapid, shift towards a horticultural subsistence pattern and a more sedentary village life amongst the Iroquoian-speaking peoples of the region, beginning before A.D. 500. This was a transition in which the Algonkian-speaking peoples of New England and the midwestern United States also seem to have participated. While, because of an uncertain growing season and limited amounts of soil, horticulture never became a dominant mode of subsistence on the southern fringe of the Canadian Shield, a significant amount of corn appears to have been grown at least as far north as the Straits of Mackinac by A.D. 1200 (McPherron 1967:103).

What caused the widespread adoption of horticulture at this time? The usual explanation has been that horticulture diffused among the hunting and gathering peoples of New England and the lower Great Lakes as soon as cultigens became available that were adapted to the shorter growing season of these regions. Such an explanation assumes that hunting and gathering peoples will inevitably perceive an agricultural economy to be superior to their own and will plant crops as soon as they become available. Today, this is not a position that all anthropologists are willing to accept. Some would argue, correctly I believe, that any explanation of the spread of agriculture must take account, not only of how suitable crops came to be

present, but also of those factors in the recipient cultures that predisposed their members to accept them. It is possible to turn the argument around and to claim that a pre-existing need for new sources of food might have produced a situation in which experimentation took place and which, in turn, led to the development of corn with a shorter growing season.

One hypothesis holds that population pressure was the principal factor leading to the adoption of a horticultural economy. An increasing population in the late Middle Woodland period might have generated a need for new sources of food and created the conditions under which horticulture initially was adopted. The greater sustaining power of food crops led to a rapid increase in population during the Owasco period, which reinforced reliance on domesticated foods. At the same time, increasing competition over natural resources produced greater conflict, which forced scattered groups to band together for defence and, by concentrating the population, increased still further their reliance on horticulture (P. Smith 1972 : 418).

As yet we know very little about population trends immediately prior to the early Iroquoian period. While the evidence from New York State is generally interpreted as indicating a rapid growth in population during the Owasco period, it is unclear how much this evidence reflects real growth and how much it results from the greater ease with which archaeologists can detect larger and more sedentary sites. Nor is it clear whether increasing village size resulted wholly from a growing population or was the result of hitherto separate groups coming together to form larger communities. Until much more evidence is available than has been published to date, any speculations about population trends during this period are bound to be hazardous.

Moreover, even in the historic period, the overall population density of the northern Iroquoian culture area was probably no more than three persons per square mile.[11] The amount of land under cultivation was a minuscule portion of the total of easily workable soil that was available. It has been estimated that even the exceptionally dense population of the Huron country could have increased significantly before any kind of cyclical fallowing system would have been required as a response to pressure on the land (Heidenreich 1971 : 198). More plausible factors keeping overall population densities low might have been the inability of the Iroquoians to increase the amount of fish and meat that could be collected and, more importantly, the limited number of deer and other animals that were available to provide skins for clothing. Deer occur in greatest concentrations in areas where openings border on the edge of forests (ibid. 206). While such clearings would have increased significantly with the advent of

slash and burn horticulture, the deer population was probably kept down by overhunting. Pressures on natural resources could have led to conflict between neighbouring groups, yet it is noteworthy that in historic times the majority of closely neighbouring tribes not only were at peace with one another but, in some cases, even shared their hunting territories. Population control was effected by the lengthy nursing of the young, which resulted in small families, and to a lesser degree by war and by inadequate care of women in childbirth. Thus, whatever demographic trends were like prior to the early Iroquoian period, the adoption of horticulture appears to have created as many, if not more, problems than it solved. Population increase is unlikely to have been exerting strong pressure on fish and game resources prior to the adoption of horticulture and, if it were, the adoption of food crops would have done nothing to remedy a resultant shortage of skins for clothing. The fact that even the historic Iroquoian populations were well supplied with such necessities suggests that natural resources were more abundant in relation to the population at an earlier time than any theory of cultural change resulting from population pressure would require.

My alternative explanation postulates that the seasonal cycle of the hunting and gathering peoples of this area pre-adapted them for horticulture. In modern times it has been noted that, among northern Algonkian peoples, the large summer gatherings at fishing sites are highly valued, as they provide an opportunity for social interaction that extends beyond a small segment of a patrilineage. Thus, when government subsidies or the profits of the fur trade increase the economic resources of a band, there is a strong tendency for its members to continue living together in one place throughout the year.[12] Where European traders or government officials are not present, leadership is provided for such groups by the traditional headman of the band, who formerly maintained order during the summer. Thus, even from a political point of view, these bands appear to have had the basic structures necessary to transform themselves into permanent communities. There is no reason why the Iroquoian-speaking tribes living south of the Canadian Shield should not have been similarly inclined and structured in prehistoric times.

Corn may originally have been experimented with as a substitute for wild rice. It had the advantage that it could be grown more widely and in proximity to a broader range of desirable locations; moreover, the danger of losing a crop was considerably less.[13] As soon as varieties of corn even marginally capable of growing in the north came to hand they would have been recognized as a valuable source of food and the amount grown would

have been increased as a means of extending the length of time that a band could remain together annually. As corn was produced that was still better adapted to a shorter growing season, it gave rise to an economy capable of supporting a sedentary group, which does not appear to have been possible relying only on wild rice. An example of a transitional economy is provided by the Ottawa bands, who, in early historic times, lived along the western border between southern Ontario and the Canadian Shield. Each band had a main village where crops were grown and which was inhabited throughout most of the year by the women, children, and old men. During the summer, parties of both sexes wandered one hundred miles or more from the village to hunt, fish, and dry blueberries, while, in the winter, groups each made up of eight to ten men went on lengthy hunting expeditions, eventually transporting meat back to their villages in a processed form (Fitting and Cleland 1969:295–96).

This explanation suggests that the nuclei of the earliest sedentary villages in this area may have been the hunting bands of an earlier period. The patrilineal bands associated with a hunting and gathering economy ranged in size from about thirty members up to several hundred, the size depending largely on the resources that were available and the efficiency with which they were exploited (Service 1962:70). It is reasonable to assume that the bands living in the lower Great Lakes area in late Middle Woodland times would have been near the upper limits of this range and it may be more than a coincidence that the earliest sedentary villages appear to have had two or three hundred inhabitants. The small size of the early Iroquoian settlements suggests that, while a number of extended families lived at least part of the year in a single village, as previously they had lived together during the summer, separate bands had not yet begun to join together to form larger communities. It also suggests that, unless a rapid fissioning of groups was going on, the increase in population during this period was less than has been assumed. It is reasonable to suppose that these early Iroquoian bands were in some way the basis of the clan segments that made up the larger Iroquoian villages of later times. From the Huron data presented in chapter 2, it is clear that, while clan segments were joined together within larger political structures and larger units of settlement, they retained much of the political and jural autonomy that hunting bands had enjoyed prior to becoming sedentary.

At some point the basis of group membership must have shifted from being patrilineal to being matrilineal, although it is difficult to determine when this happened.[14] Iroquoian archaeologists generally have argued that the development of the matrilineal extended family can be traced in the

development of the Iroquoian longhouse. As we have seen, however, extended families can be based on either matrilineal or patrilineal descent systems, and the mere presence of a longhouse cannot, by itself, determine which method of descent was being followed. Deetz (1965) has predicted that where women make pottery there will be a greater tendency for particular design attributes to cluster on the pottery produced in a matrilocal community than in one with any other rules of residence. This is because women who are matrilineally related to one another will tend to live together and hence pass on particular styles to their daughters, whereas, in a patrilocal household, women from various families will be brought together; hence the girls they train will inherit a more heterogeneous repertoire of designs. In a preliminary study of Iroquoian pottery from New York State, Whallon (1968) has found that the stylistic homogeneity of pottery within villages and the clustering of attributes tend to increase during Owasco times and later, but are already high in the Early Owasco period. This suggests that matrilocal residence was widely practised by then, at least in New York State, even though it may have become more prevalent later on.

Various explanations have been offered for this presumed shift from patrilocal to matrilocal residence. It has been noted that some communities that are heavily dependent on fishing (such as were found among the tribes along the coast of British Columbia) have matrilineal kinship systems and matrilocal, or avunculocal, residence patterns. On this basis it has been suggested that heavy reliance on fishing might have led to a shift from patrilineal to matrilineal descent in the lower Great Lakes region in the later Middle Woodland period. Ritchie (1965:296) and Whallon (1968: 236) have argued, however, that the development of female work groups engaged in horticulture was the chief factor leading to the adoption of matrilocal residence patterns. A general theory of matrilocal residence postulates that it develops when women assume a dominant role in food production, or when horticulture becomes the main source of nutrition and hence women's work becomes more valuable than men's work (Schneider and Gough 1961:660–61; 667). The application of this theory to Iroquoian society assumes that the team that was of the greatest economic importance was a woman and her daughters cooperating to grow crops.

This argument ignores the economic importance of male activities, such as fishing, forest clearance, house building, trade, and defence, all of which are known to have required a considerable degree of teamwork and may have been at least as important in the Huron's estimation as were the planting, tending, and harvesting of crops. Moreover, while the women of

a household may have shared their produce, there is little evidence that they worked together to produce it. The main work team in the fields appears to have been a woman and her young children, the boys being employed to chase away birds and wild animals. The important work teams in Iroquoian society seem to have been principally male ones.[15]

The development of larger extended family households and of their matrilineal bias may best be studied separately. The greater economic security that resulted from the sharing of all kinds of resources within these extended households must have played an important role in their development. Moreover, if feuding has as great an antiquity in Iroquoian culture as it appears to have, growing need for protection, as evidenced by palisades being constructed around villages, may have played an important role in inducing greater numbers of nuclear families to live together in a single house. Such an arrangement would have made a surprise attack more difficult. It is also likely that by this time a new division of labour in Iroquoian society was keeping men away from their villages and in scattered groups for much of the year, while the women remained at home, in daily face-to-face contact with one another. This situation was very different from the older hunting and gathering pattern, in which husbands and wives moved about together throughout the year. This new relationship between the sexes, combined with a higher mortality rate among young men than women because of war and accidents, may have encouraged the formation of matrilocal households as the most stable form of extended family.[16]

Because matrilineal descent generally develops as a response to matrilocal residence, rather than the reverse (Schneider and Gough 1961 : 551–54; 659–60), matrilineal clans and matrilineal inheritance of office could have arisen in response to a growing pattern of matrilocal residence. Yet, as already noted, even in the historical period the Iroquoian kinship system had not evolved a strongly matrilineal pattern. Bilateral tendencies were evident in kinship terminology and in marriage prohibitions, which extended to both the paternal and maternal side of the family. The Huron-Wyandot use of the term "father's sister" (*ahrä'hoc*)[17] to refer to "mother's brother's wife" and the reciprocal use of "mother's brother" (*häwäteno'rä*) for "father's sister's husband" suggests that, at some time in the past, the Huron and their neighbours may have practised cross-cousin marriage. This was something that Fred Eggan (1952:43; 1966:104) suspected about the Iroquoians in general long ago on the basis of other evidence, and which he points out, if true, would link the origins of the northern Iroquoian kinship systems much more closely to those of neigh-

bouring Algonkian peoples, such as the Cree, Ojibwa, and Ottawa. The survival of this usage in Wyandot, but not in the Iroquois languages, suggests greater conservatism in kinship terminology in the northern part of the Iroquoian culture area than farther south. Yet, even among the Huron, cross-cousin marriage, if it ever existed, was suppressed in favour of bilateral marriage prohibitions, possibly in order to diversify marital alliances once multi-clan communities had developed.

More archaeological studies of the sort Whallon attempted are needed, both in Ontario and New York State, as well as the combined efforts of ethnologists and historical linguists, if further work is to be accomplished on the reconstruction and interpretation of early and proto-Iroquoian kinship systems. Until diverse knowledge of this sort is forthcoming, much will remain unknown about changes in Iroquoian social structure and we will be uncertain whether there was a significant time lag in the evolution of new kinship systems from one region to another. It is perhaps significant that while there is evidence for corn, beans, and squash in New York State at the beginning of the Owasco period, corn is the only domestic plant so far demonstrated to be present in either the Glen Meyer or Pickering cultures. The absence of beans would have seriously limited the Ontario Iroquoian subsistence economy. Corn, while rich in carbohydrates and varying in the total amount of protein, is always deficient in the vital amino acids lysine and tryptophane, which are abundant in *Phaseolus* species (Kaplan 1967:202–3). Any diet in which corn and beans are both present has a nutritional value adequate for all but the most protein sensitive members of the population, such as lactating mothers and newly weaned babies. While we know little about the Glen Meyer culture, it is possible that the small and dispersed nature of Pickering villages, and the large number of hunting and fishing camps in that culture, reflect the nutritional limitations of the horticultural complex that was available to them, as compared to the Owasco culture. Until more studies have been made of the ecology of Pickering sites, it can be questioned whether the agricultural villages were occupied throughout the year and whether they had yet become the foci of Iroquoian life that they were in historic times.

Some light may be shed on the role that these villages played by the burial customs of the period. Two well-separated Owasco cemeteries were found at the Sackett site, but most graves of that culture are randomly dispersed throughout the villages. The vast majority of interments are flexed primary burials, that were made soon enough after death that the body had not yet begun to decompose (Ritchie 1965:295–96). At the Miller and Bennett sites, bodies were found buried inside and around houses, and

sometimes even outside the palisades, in pits containing from one to thirteen bodies. While some of these bodies were flexed primary inter-ments, a significant number, particularly where multiple burials were involved, consisted either of bodies that had been dismembered, or of completely decayed ones whose bones had been wrapped in a bundle prior to being buried (Wright and Anderson 1969:11–13; Kenyon 1968:21–23). It is perhaps significant that at the earlier Miller site, only one body out of a total of thirty-two was a primary burial.

The multiple burials, and the varying condition in which bodies were interred, raise important questions. It is possible that during the warmer months individuals were buried soon after death. The disarticulated bodies could have been those who died far from their villages and had been brought back for burial or who had died over the winter and could not be buried until the ground thawed out in the spring. In a village of 250 people, six to nine persons might be expected to die of old age and disease in a normal year, most of them during the winter.

While it is possible that each extended family buried its dead separately, each multiple burial may also represent the dead of a whole village who were available for burial in the spring, possibly after bodies had been brought in from outlying campsites. The burial with thirteen bodies found at the Miller site suggests an unusually high mortality rate (from disease?), but there is no reason to interpret this single occurrence, or multiple burials in village sites generally, as necessarily being an incipient form of ossuary interment. The basic elements of the latter ritual, namely, the temporary interment of all, or most, of the community's dead and their reburial in a common grave when the village was abandoned, seem to be conspicuously missing from the Pickering sites that have been excavated so far. As yet, no rules have been formulated that can explain satisfactorily the pattern in which burials were distributed in relationship to houses and to the village as a whole.

Considerable light has been cast on Pickering burial customs by the discovery at the Serpent Mounds site, on Rice Lake, of three early Iroquoian burial pits, each containing a minimum of fifteen to twenty-nine secondary burials (Johnston 1968b:48–50; Anderson 1968:12–14). These pits were located near an important burial site of the Middle Woodland period, of which perhaps some traditions had survived into early Iroquoian times. There was, however, no evidence of an Iroquoian village site in the vicinity, and only slender evidence of an Iroquoian fishing camp. Here, it would seem, bodies that had decayed over the winter, or possibly over the course of several years, were buried in a site unattached to any permanent

habitation. Such behaviour, which may prefigure the ossuary burial of later times, would nevertheless be distinctly unusual in the historic period, when efforts were made to save the bones of warriors killed in enemy territory, so that these could be brought back to their village for burial. The importance attached to the Serpent Mounds site suggests that, at least in the Pickering culture, villages may have been less of a ritual focus than they were in later times.

Other notable features of burials, in both Ontario and New York State, are the absence of grave goods, except for an occasional clay pipe or pottery vessel, and the apparent simplicity of the burial ritual. Ritchie (1965:179) notes that the mortuary ceremonialism which had played such a con-spicuous role in late Archaic and early Middle Woodland times had waned throughout the late Middle Woodland period. It is also pointed out that there is little indication of long distance trade in Owasco sites and the impression is one of a "provincial, self-sufficient and locally orientated people" (ibid. 293). While this would seem to apply, in general, to the Ontario Iroquoians as well, a limited number of beads made of native copper and marine shell are reported from early Iroquoian sites in the province (e.g., Wright and Anderson 1969:74; Wright 1966:39). This indicates that, at least to a limited degree, contacts with the south and the northwest were providing the same exotic materials that are present in Ontario sites from the Archaic period onwards.

THE MIDDLE IROQUOIAN PERIOD

By about A.D. 1300, the evolving Glen Meyer and Pickering cultures had coalesced to give rise to a single middle Iroquoian culture that was present throughout most of southern Ontario west of Kingston and extended into the extreme northwestern part of New York State, close to the Niagara Frontier (Wright 1966:54–65). Whatever cultural connections may have formerly existed between the rest of southern Ontario and the St. Lawrence Valley were severed at this time. Henceforth, the cultures lying east and west of the Frontenac Axis (the rocky part of the Canadian Shield that extends across the St. Lawrence Valley between Kingston and Brockville) were to develop independently of one another. The middle Iroquoian culture of southern Ontario is divided into two substages: Uren, lasting from about A.D. 1300 to 1350 (map 3c), and Middleport, from 1350 to 1400 (map 3d).

James V. Wright (1966:53; Wright and Anderson 1969:62–77) attrib-

utes the emergence of a single culture in southern Ontario at the beginning of this period, to a conquest of the Glen Meyer people by warriors from the Pickering culture. He argues that some of the Glen Meyer people may have fled westward into Michigan, but, for the most part, the conquest led to the partial assimilation of the Glen Meyer culture by the Pickering one; the result being Uren. Uren pottery, which is best known from sites in southwestern Ontario, combines many of the diagnostic features of the earlier Pickering and Glen Meyer ceramics. To the scarified body treatment, formerly present in the region, ribbed paddle impressing and checked stamping, both characteristic of the Pickering culture, are added as important attributes. Other ceramic traits that appear to be derived from the late Pickering culture are castellations decorated with a chevron motif and pottery gaming discs, which begin to appear in southwestern Ontario at this time (Wright 1966:58; Wright and Anderson 1969:64–71, 74). In general, male-manufactured items of culture (stone and bone tools) show a greater similarity to Pickering antecedents than to Glen Meyer ones, although, since the majority of these items were common to both cultures, these similarities are of a minor statistical nature. The one unique Glen Meyer lithic item to carry over into Uren is the pebble pendant. The Glen Meyer end scraper also remains more popular in western Uren sites than it is in the east and lanceolate, stemmed, and corner-notched arrows continue as minor varieties, although they are not found in late Pickering sites such as Bennett, where the small triangular arrowheads characteristic of later times predominate (Wright and Anderson 1969:71–74).

If the development of a more or less uniform Uren culture throughout southern Ontario had been brought about by the rapid diffusion of only male- or female-manufactured items of culture, it might be explained as a result of the practice of exogamy by communities organized on a matrilocal or patrilocal basis, much as Brose has proposed to explain the rapid diffusion of early Middle Woodland pottery styles. Such an explanation is ruled out, however, by the all-embracing nature of the change that is observed in the archaeological record. In spite of this, no direct evidence of conquest has been produced (White 1971*b*). Such evidence might take the form of destroyed villages or settlement patterns which indicated that victors and vanquished were living side by side after the conquest took place. It is significant that in Wright's judgement the cultural homogeneity of Ontario was greater in the later Middleport substage than it had been in Uren, an odd situation if the fusion resulted from military conquest at the beginning of the Uren period. It is, therefore, necessary to consider alternative explanations for the cultural blending that Wright has observed. For

example, the evolution of Ontario social structure might have reached a saddlepoint between a declining patrilocal residence pattern and an increasing matrilocal one. Unless exceptional hostilities interfered, there might have been a short period during which both male and female cultural items diffused rapidly from one part of southern Ontario to another, breaking down old cultural divisions. Such a process would have been speeded up if there had been an expanding population.

It is also worth noting that in spite of the general uniformity of material culture in southern Ontario during the one hundred years that the middle Iroquoian stage lasted, at the end of this period a new east-west split developed, which produced the Neutral-Erie and Huron-Tionnontaté cultures respectively. Although we have no certain knowledge of the degree of difference between the Huron and Neutral languages, Brébeuf's statement that Neutral was "not a little" different from Huron, and the trouble that the Jesuits took to draw up a lexicon and grammar comparing the two languages, suggest that the split between them was probably older than two hundred years (Thwaites 1896–1901, 20:105; 21:229–31). This, in turn, suggests that the split between the Glen Meyer and Pickering cultures, at least in part, may also have been a split between the Neutral and Huron languages. If this is true, the events which produced the cultural uniformity of middle Iroquoian times in Ontario did not disrupt ethnic patterns in the region.

Between A.D. 1300 and 1400, Iroquoian pottery in Ontario grew progressively more globular, and collars and castellated rims became more pronounced. The more elaborate decorations on the bodies of pots gave way to a plainer ribbed-paddle treatment and incised decoration around the rim gradually replaced decoration impressed with a cord-wrapped stick (Wright 1966:57–61). These developments paralleled, in a general way, ones in New York State, where Owasco was developing into the Oak Hill culture and giving rise to the cultural traditions that led to the historic Iroquois (Ritchie 1965:302–303). In spite of similar developmental trends, the pottery sequences of Ontario and eastern New York were clearly distinguished from one another (plate 15).

Pipes, some made of stone but most of them ceramic, became important in Ontario in the Middleport substage. Hitherto, pipes had been few in number and crude in execution, but from this time onwards they were abundant and occur in a variety of sophisticated shapes. Although some earlier forms persisted, the new types appear suddenly and apparently have no stylistic relationship to earlier local types. It has been suggested that the novel types were borrowed from the Oak Hill culture of New York State,

PLATE 15. *Typical middle Iroquoian artifacts from Ontario*
(c. A.D. 1300–1400): (a) broken pottery; (b) stone and pottery pipes;
(c–h) bone objects: hair piece or comb, awls, netting needle, flute, antler
flaking tool; (i) stone adze; (j) gaming disc; (k) arrowhead; (l) juvenile
model pottery; (m) perforated bear canine; (n) stone scraper.
Courtesy National Museum of Man, National Museums of Canada.

where prototypes appear to have evolved from the already more advanced pipe complex of the Owasco culture (Wright 1966:62–63). Henceforth, although pipes are less elaborate in Ontario than in New York State, there is a steady increase in their variety and complexity. The introduction of the Middleport pipe complex may mark the time when *Nicotiana rustica* began to be grown with any regularity. Although it is suggested that specific pipe designs may have been the property of particular clan segments, there is no convincing evidence to support this claim. Men may have purchased pipes that pleased them and designs, as such, may have had no social connotations.

Throughout the middle Iroquoian period, the population of southern Ontario appears to have lived in a relatively small number of large villages, but made extensive use of numerous, widely scattered hunting and fishing camps (Wright 1966:64). The largest sites cover more than five acres and longhouses began to be purposely aligned parallel to one another within these villages (Noble 1969:19). Such alignments permitted more structures to be located inside a palisade, and the planning involved was a significant response to larger village populations. It is uncertain, from the archaeological evidence, whether more than a single clan segment inhabited a village at this time, but the size of the villages makes it likely that sometimes they did. This would have required the development of town councils, as distinct from the traditional government of clan segments by a headman in consultation with the adult males of his group.

Houses probably continued to increase in length during this period, although the evidence is far from conclusive. Also, storage cubicles seem to have become more common at the ends of houses (Noble 1969:18). The most curious house plans are from the Webb site in Simcoe County, which dates from the Middleport substage. At this site, located on the edge of a marsh about a half mile from Georgian Bay, traces of a series of round cabins, each approximately ten feet in diameter and with a central fireplace, were discovered (Harper 1952). While the excavator thought that these might be single family dwellings which preceded the development of the longhouse, the subsequent discovery of earlier longhouses only a short distance away rules out this interpretation. It is just possible that we are dealing with an Iroquoian hunting or fishing camp, similar to the ones described for the seventeenth century by Gabriel Sagard (Wrong 1939:185).

Although relatively few sites are known for the Uren period, there is a marked rise in the number of villages and camp sites in the following Middleport substage. This suggests an increase in population at this time.

The palisades around villages evidence a continuing concern for defence, but this concern is only minimally expressed in the location of villages. The latter, for the most part, are built on dry ground bordering on streams or rivers (Wright 1966:56–61, 64). There is no proof that squash and beans were being grown, although the charred remains of sunflower seeds from the Uren site, in Oxford County, indicate the presence of one hitherto unattested cultigen (Kidd 1952:75).

Violence, particularly in the form of blood revenge, was undoubtedly a feature of life in the northern Iroquoian culture area from very early times. However, prior to the development of sedentary villages, raiding and blood feuds took place in the context of small, unfortified encampments and the evidence for such behaviour is very limited and often ambiguous. Bodies found riddled with arrows indicate violence, but do not inform us whether the individuals were slain as the result of an in-group quarrel or a pre-meditated act of blood revenge. Occasionally, headless bodies and extra skulls are found in graves of early times and many of these are perhaps best interpreted as evidence that heads were already being sought as trophies (Ritchie 1965:123).

The care taken to build palisades around early Iroquoian villages in Ontario and New York State provides additional evidence of violence for that period, although it is unclear whether violence was increasing or a more sedentary life was encouraging groups to undertake additional efforts to protect themselves. The cause of warfare at this time is also uncertain. Blood feuds were almost certainly a continuing reason and, as in earlier times, they may have served to rationalize other motives.

In the Uren culture there is evidence of a dramatic new dimension to warfare, in the form of cannibalism. The earliest witness of this practice is a small quantity of fragmented human bone recovered from the middens at the Uren site (Wright 1966:56–57). This site also yielded a number of perforated gorgets manufactured out of sections of human skulls. More fragments of human bones were found in the refuse of the Middleport site, and thereafter such remains become increasingly common in Iroquoian sites throughout Ontario (ibid. 60, 64). Some of these bones bear signs of cutting, cooking, and having been split open to extract the marrow (Kidd 1952:74). The small number of males between the ages of sixteen and twenty-five in the early Tabor Hill ossuaries, as compared with men of other ages, suggests that, at this time, many men were being lost through warfare, which would have been the main form of accident from which the body was unlikely to be recovered (Churcher and Kenyon 1960:256–57). Evidence of cannibalism has also been forthcoming in New York State.

In historic times cannibalism was not a simple gastronomic pleasure, but an integral part of a cult in which male prisoners of war were tortured to death as a sacrifice to the god of war or to the sun. While there were many differences between the sacrificial cult as it was practised in the southeastern United States and among the northern Iroquoians, certain elements, including the use of prisoners, the removal of the heart, the killing of the victim on an elevated platform and in view of the sun, and finally the cooking and eating of all or parts of his body, connect the northern Iroquoian ritual with those practised in the southeastern United States and in Mesoamerica. The differences indicate that this cult did not diffuse in its entirety from one region to another, but rather that certain key ideas diffused, probably from south to north like the horticultural complex, and were used by the northern Iroquoians to develop a sacrificial complex of their own.

But if religious ideas, which diffused into the Iroquoian area from elsewhere, account for specific features of prisoner sacrifice, it is apparent that the northern Iroquoians placed less emphasis on the theological justification for what they did than on the much older custom of blood revenge. War was waged, at least in theory, to avenge the killing of a member of one's own confederacy, tribe, and probably originally of one's community, by an alien. In order to retaliate for such an injury, it was necessary to seize a member of the group that was held responsible so that he or she could be adopted as a replacement for the victim or, failing this, to slay an enemy and keep his head or scalp as a trophy. Women and children who were brought home were permitted to live, since they could be more easily enculturated; male prisoners were more dangerous and more likely to run away, hence were frequently slain. In the case of prisoner sacrifice, adoption and revenge were combined, since the prisoner was adopted by the murdered man's family before being killed. Blood revenge was considered a sacred duty and its serious disruptive effects were realistically taken account of by the Iroquoians.

It seems unlikely, however, that blood revenge would have generated the prolonged conflicts that were witnessed in early historic times, had other factors not been operative as well. The main influences promoting conflicts do not appear to have been economic. War was not waged to obtain agricultural land and we have already noted that pressure on hunting territories does not seem to have pitted groups against one another. The chief spur to conflict was that warfare was the principal means by which a young man acquired prestige. Prowess in war was not the only avenue to success, but it was the most general, and this made most young men ready and willing to fight whenever an opportunity arose.

The three themes that motivated Iroquoian warfare—blood revenge, individual prestige, and prisoner sacrifice—were woven together in such a way that each of them complemented and reinforced the other. The acts of daring that warriors performed in enemy territory not only avenged wrongs committed against their society, but provided a supply of captives to replenish its ranks, as well as for sacrifice. The method of sacrifice gave the Huron an opportunity to vent their hatred of the enemy on a particular victim and gave the victim, who was a warrior, a final and glorious opportunity to display his courage.

John Witthoft (1959:32–36) has argued that as corn growing replaced hunting as the dominant mode of subsistence, the resulting decline in the male role as food producers led them to seek to enhance their prestige as warriors. At the same time, women projected their resentment at the lack of male participation in routine tasks, such as planting and harvesting corn, by transforming themselves from being butchers of game into being butchers of male captives. As it stands, this theory has two weaknesses. First, it ignores the importance of fishing to the Iroquoian economy and also the important and arduous work that men performed in clearing new fields. Secondly, men, as well as women, played an important and active role in torturing prisoners.

In spite of these shortcomings, significant insights can be gained from Witthoft's analysis. In early times, when hunting was a major element of subsistence, it probably served as an important test of a man's courage and of his ability to use weapons. Even in historic times, deer hunting remained one of the Huron male's favourite activities. Fishing and clearing fields required energy and dedication, but such activities do not seem to have provided Iroquoian men with a satisfactory means of measuring themselves against one another. Moreover, these were the activities by which they were judged by their wives' matrilineages. It is reasonable to assume that, as hunting grew less important to subsistence, warfare became the principal means by which men acquired personal prestige and established a role for themselves in the life of their communities. The need for this prestige necessitated having an enemy and stimulated the spiralling pattern of bloodshed that was an integral part of the Iroquoian way of life. Under these circumstances, elaborations, such as prisoner sacrifice, were no doubt welcomed as additional excuses for waging war. It was probably as warfare became increasingly important that clan segments acquired war chiefs, in addition to the civil ones, whose office seems to have been a continuation of the traditional leader of a hunting band. While the growing importance of war alone might have led to the creation of such an office, it is worth

noting that the distinction between war chiefs and civil leaders was wide-spread among the Indians in the southeastern United States in early historic times, and is also a trait of Mesoamerican culture (Driver 1961 : 340). Here again, we appear to be dealing with a feature of nuclear American culture that penetrated almost to the northern limits of corn horticulture.

It is also in the middle Iroquoian period that we see in Ontario, at least west of the Trent Valley, the development of an interest in elaborate burial rites which, instead of being of external origin, appears to be the local expression of a repeated focus of interest among the Indians of the north-eastern Woodlands.[18] The ossuaries, or bone pits, that began to appear in the late Pickering culture, mark the first periodic interment of large numbers of bodies in a common grave. Beginning in middle Iroquoian times, the Feast of the Dead developed as a community ritual that was celebrated whenever a sizable village shifted to a new location. This communal reburial of the dead differs from the burial in individual graves that was practised by the Iroquois, Susquehannock, and Iroquoians of the St. Lawrence Valley, and possibly by the proto-Huron of the Trent Valley. The presence of multiple cemeteries in the vicinity of many Five Nations villages suggests that, even in death, their moieties, or clan segments, preferred to remain separate from one another (Noble 1969:23; Wray and Schoff 1953:55).

While most middle Iroquoian ossuaries appear to have been somewhat smaller, the one that has been best studied by a physical anthropologist was found to contain over 500 bodies. This is the Fairty ossuary which was located near the Robb site on the outskirts of Toronto and seems to date from about the end of the Middleport substage. Assuming a mortality rate in keeping with the ages of the skeletons and an average interval of ten years between ossuary burials (Anderson 1964:30–37), a regional popula-tion of between 1500 and 2500 people has been suggested. While this figure seems large for an individual community of this period, the interval of ten years is the probable life span of a large village. Smaller villages exhausted nearby fields and sources of firewood more slowly and probably were inhabited for a longer period. If we double the duration of the village, we derive a smaller population figure that seems appropriate for the medium-sized settlements typical of this period. It is perhaps indicative of the still isolated condition of the Iroquoian peoples of Ontario that few offerings were placed in these ossuaries prior to the historic period. Only a stone scraper and one shell bead were found in the Fairty ossuary (Wright 1966:61).

THE LATE IROQUOIAN PERIOD

The late Iroquoian cultures in Ontario evolved directly from the Middleport one (ibid. 66). New styles of pottery decoration became fashionable during this period, but the principal innovations were modifications based on established conventions. Throughout the remaining years of the Ontario Iroquoian sequence, the only kind of pottery vessel continued to be the large globular pot that served as a soup kettle. Pipes became increasingly varied and, particularly after A.D. 1500, clay ones decorated with human figures grew common (ibid. 71; Noble 1969:24). Soon after A.D. 1400, beans and squash are attested for the first time in the archaeological record in Ontario (Wright 1966:98). This suggests either the late arrival of these two cultigens in Ontario or a long pause before they became popular. In addition to the eight and ten row corn known in Ontario since the early Iroquoian period, four, six, and twelve row corn appears (Noble 1969:21). There is also slight evidence that a greater number of animal species, particularly small animals, were being eaten at this time. This may reflect the growing pressure that increasingly dense population clusters were exerting upon the local fauna (ibid. 21, cited from Emerson 1961*a*).

From the beginning of the late Iroquoian period, there was a tendency for communities to cluster in restricted areas of southern Ontario and for these areas to be separated from one another by wider tracts of uninhabited forest. As parts of Ontario that had hitherto been occupied were abandoned, the most significant cleavage to develop was between the communities living north of Lake Erie and those living north of Lake Ontario (map 3*e*). Clear-cut differences between these two regions can be observed in pottery types and ossuaries (Wright 1966:66–68). Such differences distinguish sequences of development leading to the historic Neutral and Erie peoples on the one hand and to the historic Huron and Tionnontaté on the other (plate 16). Although relatively little is known about the development of the Neutral tribes, they appear to have gradually shifted, or contracted, eastward until, by the historic period, they were living between the Grand River Valley and the Niagara frontier (ibid. 84–87). The generally smaller size of Neutral ossuaries and the discovery of as many as eleven of them around a single site (ibid. 85), suggest that ossuary burial may not have served the same integrative functions among the Neutral that it did among most of the proto-Huron. On the whole, the split between the proto-Neutral and proto-Huron cultures appears to have reopened the division between Pickering and Glen Meyer.

The proto-Huron sites are located in a triangle between the Canadian

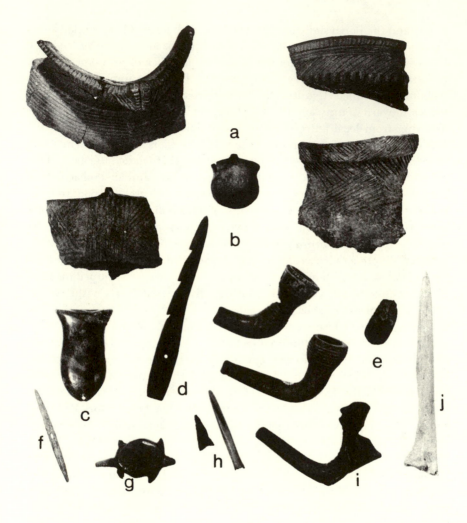

PLATE 16. *Typical Huron–Tionnontaté artifacts: (a–b) broken pottery vessels; (c) stone pipe; (d) antler harpoon; (e) stone scraper; (f) netting needle; (g) tortoise-shaped amulet; (h) stone and bone arrowheads; (i) pottery pipes; (j) dagger made of human ulna. Courtesy National Museum of Man, National Museums of Canada.*

Shield and the north shore of Lake Ontario, with a possible extension along the south shore of Georgian Bay. Even within this area, however, sites are not evenly distributed. Instead they form a number of groupings which, unfortunately, are still very poorly defined. The most important of these seem to be in Simcoe County, the Toronto area, and another farther east in Prince Edward County and the Trent Valley. The sites in each area appear to spring from local antecedents of the middle Iroquoian period, and the clusters themselves may represent the tribal divisions that were to make up the Huron confederacy, or groupings of villages that would later form these tribes. All of these groupings have a generally similar archaeological culture; however, in recent years, a "northern" cultural division, roughly congruent with the Simcoe County sites, has been distinguished from other proto-Huron groups on the basis of two pottery types: Lalonde High Collar and Sidey Notched. Future work may reveal specific, although perhaps less striking, differences between the sites in the Toronto area and those of the Trent Valley. At present, the sites in these two areas are lumped together as parts of a tentatively defined "southern division" culture, within which sites are only distinguished geographically.[19]

During the late Iroquoian period the average house was about twenty-seven feet wide and one hundred feet long. There was, however, considerable individual variation, and houses up to 190 feet long are reported (Heidenreich 1971:115–16). Architecturally, the Huron were more conservative than the Iroquois. Even into the historic period, the designs of their houses remained basically the same as they had been in late Pickering times. The majority tapered gently towards the ends, which were invariably rounded. With the exception of the posts that supported the sleeping platforms, these houses were constructed of slender poles covered with sheets of bark. Likewise, while village palisades had up to seven rows of stakes, most of these stakes were thin and placed up to a foot apart. By contrast, as early as A.D. 1350, in the Chance culture, which is ancestral to the historic cultures of the eastern tribes of the Iroquois confederacy, the round-ended longhouse had been replaced by the square-ended type characteristic of the Iroquois in the historic period. Although most of the poles used to construct the walls of these houses were about three inches in diameter, larger post molds, up to ten inches across, are encountered at regular intervals (Ritchie 1965:314–15; Hayes 1967). The palisade around the Garoga site, a late prehistoric Mohawk settlement, was constructed of two rows of stakes larger than any observed on earlier Iroquois sites, or on historic Huron ones. The individual post molds, placed about a foot apart, were fifteen to twenty inches in diameter and had been sunk approxi-

mately three feet into the ground (Ritchie 1965:318). This provides archaeological confirmation for Champlain's observation that Iroquois fortifications were far stronger than Huron ones (Biggar 1922–36, 3:70) and for Bogaert's description of an Oneida town with three wooden images over one of its gates; which is unparalleled for Huron villages (Jameson 1909:148).

There is more evidence of variation in Huron housetypes in the prehistoric archaeological record than from historic accounts. Four houses were uncovered at the Copeland site in Simcoe County, which dates about A.D. 1500 (Channen and Clarke 1965:5–10). One of these was a conventional longhouse eighty-eight feet long. Another, wider structure measured forty-two feet by thirty feet. While the doors at either end and the traces of sleeping platforms along the walls conformed to the normal longhouse pattern, the seven hearths inside this building were randomly scattered, rather than arranged down the centre. The same was true for the house next to it, which was forty-five feet long, but tapered from thirty feet at one end to twenty feet at the other. In this house, there was only one sleeping platform, which ran along the west wall. The most unusual building on the site was ninety by fifty-eight feet (plate 17). The side walls consisted of two or more rows of poles running parallel to one another, while a row of larger posts, eight to ten inches in diameter, ran down the centre of the building, presumably to support the roof. Twenty-three hearths were discovered inside this structure. These were arranged in no particular order, although most of them were located south of the centre posts.

This structure, which gives every appearance of having been a dwelling, seems to be similar to the central building excavated by Wilfrid Jury at the so-called site of "St. Ignace II," along the Sturgeon River (W. S. Fox 1949). Although the latter building was interpreted as a Jesuit church and mission centre, serious doubts have since been cast on the proposed date and identification of the village (Heidenreich 1966:125). Many of the longhouses at the "St. Ignace II" site are reported to have had a row of poles down the middle, presumably to support a wider roof span. Jury interpreted this as evidence of French influence, but it may be an architectural tradition indigenous to this region, the history of which remains to be unravelled. Similarly, no evidence of sidewall sleeping platforms has been found at the Sopher and Warminster sites (Noble 1969:20). These are both historic sites, apparently belonging to the Arendarhonon tribe. Considerably more work will have to be done on prehistoric sites before we know for certain whether all Arendarhonon houses lacked such platforms. It is

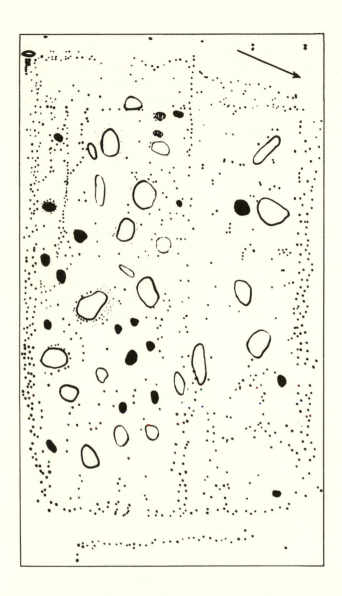

PLATE 17. *House 1 from the Copeland site, Simcoe County* (c. A.D. *1500*).
*This prehistoric site contains a number of structures that depart from the
ideal longhouse style. House 1 is 90 feet by 58 feet and had a row of posts
running down the centre to support the roof. Courtesy E. R. Channen and
National Museum of Man, National Museums of Canada.*

possible that additional work may reveal significant variations in Huron house styles corresponding to ethnic divisions.

In the late Iroquoian period, villages generally tended to grow larger and to be located in defensive positions remote from navigable waters. Some of them also began to cluster close to one another (Wright 1966:91). The increasing size of villages may be the result of population growth, but alternatively it may have resulted from smaller communities, each consisting of a single clan segment, agreeing to live together. The suggestion that the several clans that inhabited each of the large communities in the historic period might have resulted from the growth and fissioning of a single clan segment does not explain why the clan segments in any one town had such a heterogeneous assortment of names. When clans split they usually modified their names only slightly, such as Turtle becoming Mud Turtle and Little Turtle (Tooker 1970*b*:93). It also does not account for the political independence of clan segments in historic times.

The development of tribal clusters has only begun to be unravelled in Ontario, in part because the shifting of certain tribes in the late Iroquoian period makes it difficult to trace such developments from the archaeological record. The evidence for this process is much clearer in New York State, where the groups that made up each of the five Iroquois tribes remained within their tribal territories from at least Owasco times. Archaeological work indicates that originally at least three small communities existed in the later Onondaga territory. These were located some distance from one another, and each community shifted its location at regular intervals within a distinct area; hence it is reasonable to assume that each had its own hunting territory. After A.D. 1400, the three villages were reduced to two, but one of the new villages was now much larger than the other, suggesting that it arose through the fusion of two earlier villages. Sometime between A.D. 1450 and 1475, the two remaining villages relocated within two miles of each other. Although both of these villages were well defended, their greater proximity seems to indicate a friendly relationship. Tuck (1971:214–16) interprets this coming together as the result of a non-aggression pact, which prevented clashes that would have been disastrous for the smaller village, if not for the larger one. He goes on to suggest that this event marks the founding of the Onondaga tribe, although similarities in language and culture may have provided the basis of an Onondaga cultural, if not political, identity in earlier times.

While the actual events leading to the formation of the historic Onondaga tribe may have involved more village sequences than archaeologists have detected, we have here an example of how settlements, originally

consisting of individual clan segments, could be drawn together into larger village units and then into tribal clusters. For the most part, the drawing together of the communities to form tribes led to the abandonment of many formerly settled areas, and produced larger, but more widely separated, clusters of habitation. This created ideal conditions in which homogeneous tribal cultures could develop. In addition, the considerable distances that now separated each tribal grouping favoured the development of distinctive cultures in each tribal area.

The development of tribal organizations required new institutions to maintain their solidarity. One of these may have been the linking together of clan segments named after the same animal to form exogamous clan structures that extended across tribes and later across whole confederacies. As a result of this development, the idea of clan membership became modified. Instead of being restricted to a local unit of kinship organization, it came to be also applied to a larger grouping of ritual affinity that was not geographically restricted. The resulting interdigitation of loyalties to clan and tribe, and to clan and village, constituted the warp and woof which helped to hold expanding Iroquoian societies together. The additional grouping of clans to form phratries, which regulated many aspects of Iroquoian ceremonial life, including burial rituals, further strengthened these ties.

Whether or not they existed earlier, medicine societies also must have played an important role in the integration of Iroquoian society at this time (Tuck 1971:213). Membership in these societies, which was an important aspect of Iroquoian ritualism, was open to those who had been healed by them and was inherited, no doubt matrilineally, upon a member's death. In this way, these societies acquired a membership that cut across lineage, clan, village, and even tribal divisions, thus linking together a wider assortment of people than did the clan organizations.

Games were another source of pleasurable interaction within and between villages. Lacrosse was a rough and dangerous sport, played by young men. It no doubt served to channel some of their aggressiveness and prestige-seeking along peaceful lines. Other activities, such as the dish game, brought the inhabitants of different villages together in friendly rivalry when their teams played against one another. Games of all kinds were accompanied by feasting and revelry. They periodically brought clan segments and the inhabitants of different villages together and reinforced their unity by providing a friendly setting within which aggression and rivalry might be discharged.

Clearly the prehistoric Iroquoian cultures were not static; nor were they totally integrated and harmonious within themselves. Instead, they must

be seen as entities in a process of rapid transition from a subsistence economy based on hunting and gathering to an alternative one based on horticulture. In making this change, the Iroquoians generally showed themselves to be good handymen, capable of using whatever ideas were at hand in order to adapt their way of life to changing conditions. The important role played by shamanistic healing rituals provides one example of the manner in which elements of an older way of life found new roles for themselves in a changing social order; the importance of hunting magic in historic times provides another. While the latter practices were accorded an importance that was out of all proportion to their economic significance, they served to reinforce the prestige of traditional male activities in a way that was important to the harmonious operation of the society as a whole. On the other hand, borrowings, not the least of which was the horticultural complex itself, also came to play an important role in Iroquoian society. These borrowings, which seem to have included prisoner sacrifice and the distinction between war chiefs and civil headmen, were made, however, in a piecemeal fashion and adapted to the special requirements of Iroquoian society. Thus they emerged as distinctive features of the Iroquoian way of life. Evidence can also be found of compromises between old ways and new ones. The tenacity with which clan segments clung to traditional rights reveals the skill with which the Iroquoians managed to preserve older attitudes and institutions, and to use these as foundations for new and more complex structures. This is evidence not so much of conservatism as of a healthy and constructive attitude towards change.

Nevertheless, some of the complications that resulted from the social and economic transformation their society had undergone remained as unresolved tensions in historic Iroquoian culture. As the Iroquoians became more dependent on agriculture, men spent more time away from their villages hunting, fishing, trading, and fighting. Women, on the other hand, tended to remain in their villages throughout the year and became more closely identified with them than the men were. The male's position within his own society was further challenged by the declining economic importance of hunting, which was an activity he much valued and a source of prestige to skilful individuals. We have already argued that this decline may have led to an increase in warfare, as a compensatory avenue of male achievement. The resulting ambivalence that men had about their relationship with their community may also have produced the uneasy relations between men and women that are noted as a distinctive feature of Iroquoian culture. These tendencies were undoubtedly carried much further among the Five Nations Iroquois in historic times, as the growing demand

for furs kept traders and warriors away from their villages for even longer periods. Under these conditions, women probably came to play a far more important role in domestic politics than they had done previously. Later, as the Iroquois fell under European domination, the importance of the male declined with the decreasing emphasis on trade and warfare and they were compelled to adapt, not too successfully, to European methods of agriculture. While the final collapse of male prestige may have led Iroquois women to idealize and exaggerate the power they had exercised in the past, it appears that in prehistoric times, no less than in our own, a changing economy generated social tensions as it altered the traditional roles between the sexes.

The Huron Confederacy

The archaeological record indicates that the region where the Huron were found living in historical times was occupied continuously by horticulturalists from the early Iroquoian period onwards. In the 1640s, the Attignawantan who lived in the extreme west of the Huron country claimed that they could point out the sites their ancestors had inhabited for over two centuries (Thwaites 1896–1901, 16:227–29). There is, therefore, little reason to doubt that this tribe developed in the area between Georgian Bay and Lake Simcoe and that at least some of the many prehistoric sites found there are those of their ancestors.

The Arendarhonon appear to have joined the Huron confederacy late in the sixteenth century.[20] The interest they had in the Trent Valley region, and the presence of many late prehistoric and protohistoric sites east of Lake Simcoe, suggest that they were among the original inhabitants of that area. The oldest sites seem to be near the east end of Lake Ontario and in Prince Edward County. This may indicate a gradual movement up the Trent Valley, beginning about A.D. 1500 (Pendergast 1964:13).

The origins of the two remaining Huron tribes are more ambiguous. Wright has suggested that the Attigneenongnahac may have evolved in the northern part of Simcoe County, no doubt east of the Attignawantan, while the Tahontaenrat developed in the Humber and adjacent valleys in the Toronto area, where numerous late Iroquoian prehistoric sites have been discovered (Wright 1966:78). This might account for the large number of prehistoric sites in the Oro township area of Simcoe County (Heidenreich 1969:23) and accords with the Jesuits' statement that it was both the

Attignawantan and Attigneenongnahac who could point out sites going back two centuries; however, the latter claim seems based on Attignawantan sources, and may not apply in its entirety to the Attigneenongnahac.[21] Moreover, the Tahontaenrat, who were a small group in historic times, may not have been sufficiently numerous to account for the many sites in the Toronto area. They are also stated not to have joined the Huron confederacy before about 1610, while the fusion of northern and southern division traits, that gave rise to the historic Huron culture, appears to have been underway in Simcoe County by about the middle of the sixteenth century (Wright 1966:66). In spite of a preference for matrilocal residence, this blending of ceramic traditions no doubt came about as a result of increasing intermarriage, as hitherto distinct tribes began to live in closer proximity to one another.[22] An alternative theory would have the Attigneenongnahac moving north from the Toronto area, by about 1550, and settling in the eastern part of the Huron country, before shifting to their historic tribal area. Over fifty years later, the Tahontaenrat would have entered the region from either the south or the east. It is possible that the cluster of protohistoric sites reported for Innisfil township in the southern part of Simcoe County (Popham 1950) may have belonged to the Tahontaenrat prior to their final migration northward.

The origins of the Tionnontaté are as obscure as those of the Attigneenongnahac or the Tahontaenrat. Their pottery types, for the historic period, are similar to those of the Huron and have only recently been differentiated on the basis of a few characteristic decorative motifs (Wright 1966:76). Little evidence has been found of prehistoric sites in their historic tribal area, hence it has been suggested that they must have originated elsewhere. Wright (1966:79–80) has proposed that they might represent a breakaway group from the original inhabitants of northern Simcoe County, but his theory is argued on the basis of an inaccurate interpretation of Huron social structure.[23] Garrad and Heidenreich tentatively derive them, along with the Tahontaenrat, from the Innisfil sites (Heidenreich 1971:map 22). Alternatively, future research may reveal them to have evolved from the Iroquoian groups who inhabited Huron and Grey Counties during the Middleport substage. These people disappeared from the shores of Lake Huron in the late Iroquoian period (Wright 1966:66) and may have clustered farther east to become the Tionnontaté.

What was the driving force behind the development of larger settlements and the emergence of tribal coalitions that are observed in the late Iroquoian period? The larger villages are frequently explained as being

the result of a growing population, but this explanation is inadequate. When not confronted by other difficulties, Iroquoian farmers preferred to live in small villages. These exhausted nearby soil and supplies of firewood more slowly than did large villages and therefore they had to be relocated less often. Large villages, on the other hand, quickly consumed their adjacent hinterland and, because of this, women were forced to travel longer distances to and from their fields, which also became ever more fragmented. The increasing inefficiency of such arrangements compelled villages to be relocated more frequently as they grew larger. Relocation was, however, an arduous task for the men of the village and does not seem to have been practical more than about once every decade. These opposing considerations resulted in the largest stable communities having populations of about 1500 people. Even towns of this size seem to have been stretching the regulatory mechanisms of Iroquoian society, and factionalism was rife between clan segments (Heidenreich 1971:129–34). The fact that larger populations settled close to one another in big, adjacent communities indicates that other factors must account for the development of both large villages and tribal alliances.

One of these factors was almost certainly war. Warfare was a feature of Iroquoian culture from earliest times. In the late Iroquoian period, not only were towns surrounded by palisades, but many of the larger ones were located on hilltops or high ground where two streams came together. Evidence of such fortification is noted both in Simcoe County and among the sites from the early part of the late Iroquoian sequence in the Humber Valley. From the middens there are also indications of increasing cannibalism, which Wright (1966:91) estimates reached a peak before A.D. 1550. It is also possible that by promoting the growth of larger communities and settlement clusters, warfare created a situation in which hunting became less productive and thereby produced increasing dependence on horticulture.

The growing destructiveness of such warfare may have compelled friendly neighbouring groups to cooperate for mutual defence. Likewise, the desire of communities to protect themselves may have led them to suppress neighbouring settlements, if these were inveterately hostile. This may have involved incorporating defeated groups into the victorious community, an art at which the Iroquoians excelled in historic times. Any successful coalition left neighbouring communities at a disadvantage, unless they too managed to consolidate themselves into larger groupings. Thus, in one way or another, the need for defence produced larger settlements, until these reached the limits at which Iroquoian slash-and-burn horti-

culture could operate efficiently. Once these limits had been reached, these same forces led to the development of defensive alliances in which friendly villages settled in close proximity. The development of such alliances would have eliminated local blood feuds, which may have been most destructive in terms of people's lives and possessions. While putting an end to local battles, these alliances did not prevent warriors from acquiring personal prestige; but they compelled them to carry their quarrels farther afield.

Data concerning who was fighting whom in prehistoric times are scarce and largely ambiguous. It seems highly likely that proto-Huron villages carried on blood feuds with one another, but we do not know to what degree the individual Huron tribes fought with one another after they had come into existence. It is possible that much of the homogeneity in pottery types that was maintained during this period resulted from the movement from village to village of women who were taken captive in such raids.

There are few references to prehistoric warfare in Ontario in the historical records. The Huron spoke of struggles they had waged against the Tionnontaté not long before the arrival of the first Europeans and, even in the early historic period, war chiefs were attempting to organize raids against the Neutral confederacy (Thwaites 1896–1901, 20:43; Wrong 1939:151). It therefore appears that even in late prehistoric times the tribes of the Huron confederacy waged war against other Iroquoian tribes in Ontario. In the historic period, the Huron's chief adversaries were the Seneca, against whom they appear to have been fighting well before the start of the seventeenth century. They were also at war with the other tribes of the Five Nations, although engagements were more sporadic (map 4).

The most important clue to warfare patterns in prehistoric times seems to be provided by the foreign pottery which is found in many Iroquoian sites. Pottery vessels were frequently carried a considerable distance by canoe, but travel between Iroquoian groups was mostly overland. It is unlikely that on these trips the Iroquoians had any reason to carry such cumbersome and fragile vessels with them; hence, when pottery of a foreign type occurs in an Iroquoian site, it is likely to have been produced by foreign women who were living there. Such women could have arrived as peacefully acquired brides, as refugees, or as prisoners of war. While examples of all three events are found in the historical literature, it seems unlikely that the first of these, intermarriage, was frequent between groups living one hundred miles or more apart, or that, when it did occur, it was normally the woman who moved. When refugees are involved, their

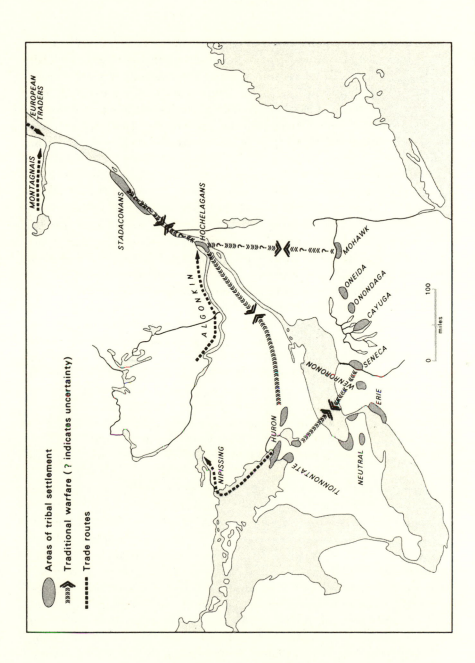

MAP 4.   *Intertribal relations, mid-sixteenth century.*

pottery is found in the sites to which they fled, while their host's pottery is unlikely to be found in the villages from which they came. The same kind of asymmetrical distribution is produced by the forced resettlement of a defeated group in the villages of their conquerors. When dealing with the more normal give-and-take of blood feuds, we can expect to find small to moderate amounts of each adversary's pottery in the sites on either side.

This index of female movement cannot be applied among the various proto-Huron groups, because their material culture was extremely similar to begin with. Moreover, the relative proximity of these groups would make it difficult to decide whether movement was a sign of friendship or hostility. It is also impractical to apply this measurement before the late Iroquoian period, since cultural patterns tended to be very widespread prior to then.

In the published data for proto-Huron sites, the amount of "Neutral-Erie" pottery is always small, and declines from about A.D. 1450 onwards. In part, this may reflect decreasing contact with the Neutral, as the proto-Huron villages located in the Toronto area gradually moved northward. "Cayuga" sherds occur from A.D. 1450 on, but "Seneca" and "Cayuga" ones become increasingly common only after 1550 and reach their maximum in sites of the historic period. Few Huron sherds are reported from Seneca or Cayuga sites much prior to the historic period. A different distribution can be plotted for eastern Iroquoian pottery, which occurs occasionally on proto-Huron sites before A.D. 1500, but increases in frequency after that time, then declines sharply not long before 1600.[24] The majority of eastern Iroquoian pottery types that have been identified could have come either from the Iroquoian tribes who lived in the St. Lawrence Valley or from the three eastern tribes of the Iroquois confederacy. Since Huron sherds occur with some frequency in sixteenth century sites of the St. Lawrence Valley, but rarely on Onondaga, Oneida, or Mohawk sites prior to the next century, it seems more likely that mutual raiding was going on between the tribes who lived west of Kingston and those in the St. Lawrence Valley. The end of this conflict appears to coincide with the disappearance of the St. Lawrence Iroquoians discussed in the next chapter. Until this time, the St. Lawrence Iroquoians seem to have been the main enemies of the Huron, although from 1550 on, "Seneca" and "Cayuga" sherds increase in frequency dramatically, suggesting an important shift in warfare. The archaeological evidence indicates that the brunt of warfare with the St. Lawrence Iroquoians was sustained by the Huron groups who lived in the Trent Valley and the Toronto area, rather than by those in Simcoe County (Wright 1966:74). An increase in "Seneca" and

"Cayuga" sherds in Simcoe County after 1550 seems to result from the shifting of tribal groups north and westward at this time, bringing the hitherto sheltered population of this region into more direct contact with the Iroquois.

On the other hand, it has also been noted that evidence of cannibalism appears to decline in Ontario after 1550 (ibid. 91). This possibly reflects the growth of new friendships and alliances among the proto-Huron. It may also reflect the disappearance of a major foe in the St. Lawrence Valley and the growing distance between the Huron tribes, who were generally moving northward, and the Iroquois, who became their main enemy. The expansion of alliances that seems to have been occurring at this time would have reduced fratricidal struggles among neighbouring groups and initiated a generally more peaceful time in Ontario. It probably also led the Ontario Iroquoians to look for new enemies farther afield against whom their young men could test themselves, when "just causes" gave them a reason for doing so.

So far, we have been discussing only the development of tribal groupings. Sometime, however, before the end of the sixteenth century, both in Ontario and New York State, neighbouring tribes came to be linked together in loose associations aimed at curbing intertribal aggression. The principal feature common to all Iroquoian confederacies appears to have been an agreement among member tribes not to resort to bloodshed to settle grievances among themselves. The suppression of blood feuds was supervised by a confederacy council made up of civil headmen from the member tribes, which gathered periodically for feasts and consultations, judged disputes, and arranged for reparations payments as the need arose. There is no evidence that the member tribes of a confederacy were bound to help one another in case of attack or to aid each other in their wars; often the foreign policies of the member tribes were very different from one another. Nevertheless, the confederacies did serve to restrain violence among neighbouring tribes and to this degree promoted greater security for all their members.

Unfortunately, very little is known about the origin of confederacies and speculation on this subject has been affected by disagreements concerning the influence that European contact had on indigenous institutions. Some anthropologists argue that the Iroquois confederacy was established as early as the middle of the fifteenth century, and even this is seen as the culmination of a series of local alliances between two or more Iroquois tribes (Tooker 1964:3–4 n. 1). It has been proposed that Dekanahwideh's blotting out of the sun, an event that is part of the traditional account of the

founding of the Iroquois league, refers to a solar eclipse visible in upper New York State in A.D. 1451 (P. Wallace 1966:255). It may be noted that Tuck does not date the founding of the Onondaga tribe much earlier than this time.

Other scholars have accepted Iroquois claims that their confederacy was founded a lifetime before the Europeans came to trade as evidence that the league was established sometime between 1559 and 1570 (Hewitt 1894). This and later dates support an alternative line of thought which attributes the origins of all Indian confederacies to European influence. Confederacies are interpreted as tribal groupings formed to be better able to resist European intrusion. Alternatively, it is suggested that tribes living in the interior made alliances in order to break restrictive trading covenants between coastal tribes and the Europeans and to be able to participate in this trade themselves. Once formed, these confederacies were strengthened by the demands of the fur trade, and became mechanisms for dealing with European colonists (Tooker 1964:4 n. 1).

Yet, even if the Iroquois confederacy was strengthened in response to European intrusion, this appears to have happened with considerable ease. Unlike some later, short-lived confederacies that attempted to bring culturally heterogeneous groups together in opposition to European expansion, the Iroquoian confederacies embraced groups of people who were culturally and linguistically related, and who already shared similar political institutions. In many ways, the formation of such confederacies can be viewed as an extension of the same forces that had already created tribal, in place of band, structures. For this reason, it seems doctrinaire and unwarranted to reject the Huron claim that their confederacy began around A.D. 1440, with the Attignawantan and the Attigneenongnahac as its founding members. If both tribes were already living in Simcoe County, the alliance between them would have been little more than an extension of the process of tribal formation that was probably going on at that time. If, however, the Attigneenongnahac were living farther south, this early alliance may have closely resembled those between the tribes of the Iroquois confederacy in later times. For a long while, however, the Huron confederacy seems to have embraced only two of the four Huron tribes.

The Historic Location of the Huron

While the Huron and Iroquois confederacies appear to have had a similar council structure and were established to promote friendship among

member tribes, the two groups differed from one another in certain critical aspects. Even after their confederacy was formed, the Iroquois tribes remained separate from one another, each living in the middle of its ancestral territories. Among the Huron, at least in later times, as tribes joined the confederacy, they moved from their separate territories into the northern part of Simcoe County to form a single population cluster. Each tribe may have retained its old hunting grounds, but this cannot be documented with certainty. The Attignawantan obviously gave up part of their hunting lands, and possibly part of the area where they had lived, as village land for incoming tribes and must have been compensated with rights to hunt elsewhere. The result was a concentration of population in the north of Simcoe County which far exceeded that of any other part of the northern Iroquoian culture area.

This raises two questions: Why did the Huron choose to settle near the shores of Georgian Bay; and why did they, unlike the Iroquois, locate all the settlements of their confederacy so near to one another?

The traditional explanation has been that the Huron retreated into northern Simcoe County because of Iroquois attacks. They were imagined to be cowering on the shores of Georgian Bay, making a last stand against the enemy, when the French arrived. The Huron were obviously concerned about Iroquois raids and carefully fortified their communities that were exposed to attack. Yet theorizing such as this is based on an incorrect evaluation of the military capabilities of the Huron by comparison with those of the Iroquois before 1640. Prior to that date, the Huron were not at the mercy of the Iroquois. Year after year, Huron raiding parties set off for the Iroquois country and usually returned with prisoners for their sacrificial killings. Moreover, the Huron were not at war with the tribes who lived to the north of them, whereas the Iroquois appear to have been at war not only with the Huron, but also with the Susquehannock, who lived to the south, and with various Algonkian tribes to the east and northeast. Yet, in spite of having more enemies than the Huron, no greater numbers, and little, if any, military superiority, the Iroquois tribes were not compelled to settle close to one another for protection. At most, the greater danger to which they were exposed seems to have expressed itself in the stronger defences of their villages. Given the secure nature of their northern frontier, it may be that concern about Iroquois attacks was one of the factors that induced some of the smaller Huron groups to shift northward. This does not explain, however, why a substantial number of Huron had lived in Simcoe County from the earliest stages of Iroquoian development, nor does it explain why the four Huron tribes ultimately

elected to locate their villages close to one another near Georgian Bay.[25]

From an Iroquoian point of view, the historic Huron country had many natural advantages. Light soil, that the Iroquoians were able to cultivate, occurred there more abundantly than anywhere else in the eastern half of southern Ontario (Chapman and Putnam 1966:Summary Map). The region was also surrounded on three sides by lakes and rivers abounding in fish at every season of the year. This proximity of fish and good soil supplied the key elements in the Iroquoian subsistence economy and no doubt explains why Huron had lived there in considerable numbers from an early period.

On the other hand, climatic conditions in northern Simcoe County were less favourable than along the north shores of Lakes Erie and Ontario. Winters were colder, the average snowfall was about 40 inches more, and the growing season was somewhat shorter. While the latter did not seriously affect the cultivation of corn, it compelled the Huron to secure most of their tobacco from farther south. Corn, and all other crops, were also endangered by a low rainfall. While the Huron country had many natural advantages, it was less than ideal from a subsistence point of view. In order to explain why the population of southeastern Ontario chose to live in this area, it is necessary to consider other reasons than war or local subsistence resources.

One of the chief attractions of the historic Huron country seems to have been its location, which had great potential for trade and commerce. A rich agricultural area, capable of supporting a large population and producing food surpluses in most years, this region was located on the margin of the Canadian Shield. Corn could be grown as far north as Lake Nipissing, but a shorter growing season and, what is more important, a scarcity of good soil meant that a sedentary way of life had developed nowhere north of the Huron (Heidenreich 1970). The people of the north were dependent on hunting and gathering, their population density was low, and, in winter, food shortages were common. The Huron country was thus located on the border of two very different ecological zones, whose inhabitants had economies that were complementary to one another. Even among so-called primitive peoples, such a border between two different ways of life is more likely to be a zone of interaction than a barrier to contact.

Moreover, the northern part of Simcoe County was ideally placed for easy contact between the agricultural peoples of southern Ontario and the hunters of the north. By way of Lake Simcoe, the Severn River, and the smaller streams entering Matchedash Bay, people living throughout the Huron country could quickly reach Georgian Bay. While the Huron were

no less skilful in using canoes than were the northern Algonkians, neither liked to travel by water out of sight of land (Biggar 1922–36, 3:45). This was because their bark canoes were fragile, and tended to leak and be damaged easily. Under these conditions, the safest and most direct water route to the north followed the eastern shore of Georgian Bay (map 5). Along this route a traveller would have encountered the Ouasouarini (Fish), Outchougai (Heron?), Atchiligouan (Heron?), and a number of other patrilineal bands, who may have been either Ottawa or Ojibwa. At the mouth of the Nipissing River, a canoe could turn east, passing into the tribal territory of the Nipissing. From there the Mattawa River led eastward to the Ottawa, along which one could travel either northward into the boreal forest, with its maze of interconnecting lakes and rivers, or south through the territory of the Algonkin. Alternatively, turning westward along the shore of Lake Huron, travellers would pass more Algonkian-speaking bands, the Amikou (Beaver), Nikikouek (Otter), Oumisagai (Mississague or Eagle), and the Outaouan, who inhabited Manitoulin Island, until they came to the Baouichtigouian, who spent the summers at Sault Sainte Marie.[26] The latter were certainly among those later known as Ojibwa. From there, further water routes ran north into Lake Superior and hence up various rivers to the north, or south along the shores of Lake Michigan.

Thus it was possible to travel with relative ease from the Huron country over a vast area of the north. In spite of the extensive boundary along which the rich agricultural land of southern Ontario abutted the Canadian Shield, the only comparable artery of travel between these two regions was the Ottawa River, and it was made more difficult by frequent portages. Any group established in the Huron country was also well-situated to deny passage northward to groups who lived farther south and to prevent the northern hunters from making contact with such groups. So long as they were numerically superior, the people living in the Huron country could, if they wished, monopolize much of the trade between southern Ontario and the north.

We have already noted that in historic times the Huron took every advantage of their country's location, trading their own products, as well as acting as middlemen in the exchange of goods between the regions to the south and north. By far the greatest amount of trade was between themselves and the northern Algonkians. So important was Huron corn among the northern hunters that the French referred to the Huron country as the granary of the Algonkians (Thwaites 1896–1901, 8:115). For the northern hunting peoples, corn, and the opportunity to pass the

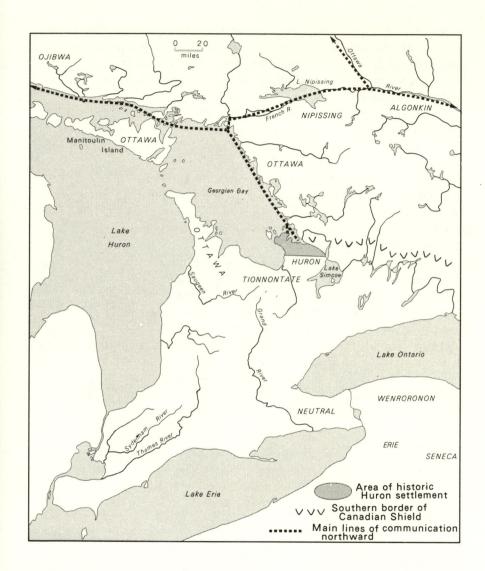

MAP 5. *Major lines of communication onto the Canadian Shield.*

winter among the Huron, meant that their chances of survival were considerably enhanced. This probably resulted in the development of an unusually high population density north of the Huron country. Being supported by imports would also have made these northern hunters increasingly dependent on the Huron.

The Huron depended on furs and meat from the north. Good soil was plentiful in the Huron country; hence, while it required more effort to grow additional crops, corn was the one elastic factor in the Huron subsistence economy. Fishing was highly productive among the Huron, so that the dried fish that the Huron received in barter for their corn may have been something of a luxury. Even so, however, the dried fish received in trade permitted Huron men to divert energy to other tasks. On the other hand, in spite of the tendency for deer to increase wherever there were clearings, the large population of the Huron country had virtually exterminated the deer population near at hand, and hunters had to travel long distances to find game. Difficulties in transportation made meat a luxury among the Huron and skins for making clothing were probably in short supply also. Yet, through trade, it was possible to secure furs and also some meat in return for agricultural products. It is extremely doubtful that without trade the population of the Huron country could have become as densely concentrated as it was in the historic period. Whether or not trade with the Algonkians was an important factor inducing people to settle in the Huron country, it was almost certainly a precondition for their high population density.

Prehistoric Trade

Before the role of trade in shaping the Huron settlement pattern can be assessed, enquiries must be made concerning the antiquity of the trading patterns noted in the historic period. There is no doubt that Huron interaction with the north was greatly intensified by the fur trade. Some scholars, however, view the fur trade as being added onto existing networks of trade, while others are of the opinion that these networks were much smaller in extent and carried only a small volume of trade in prehistoric times (Heidenreich 1971:227–32). Some of the latter would deny that prehistoric trade had any adaptational significance, at least as far as the Huron were concerned. There is also considerable difference of opinion concerning the antiquity of many Huron trading practices, such as recognizing trading

routes as being the possession of individual lineages. Some interpret these as aboriginal institutions; others view them, like hunting territories among the northern Algonkians, as by-products of the European fur trade (Brasser 1971:261–62).

The view that trading was a recent development seems to find archaeological support in the very small quantities of exotic material that occur in Iroquoian sites prior to protohistoric times. There is some questionable evidence of local trade prior to the historic period. Flint from the Niagara Escarpment appears to have been reaching northern Simcoe County; likewise, there seems to have been a trade in the igneous rock used to make stone axes. On the other hand, the material originating outside the region found on prehistoric Iroquoian sites in Ontario usually amounts to only a few beads made from marine shell or from native copper (Wright 1966:99). This suggests that the trade links with the southeast and the upper Great Lakes region remained open, but that trade was limited in volume and possibly indirect. In sheer bulk, the exotic material found in Iroquoian sites is far less than from many sites of the Middle Woodland or Archaic periods. Ossuary burials are also largely devoid of offerings in prehistoric times. The contrast between the abundance of exotic material, both in village sites and ossuaries, during the historic period and the dearth of such material prior to that time supports the view that Iroquoian societies were self-sufficient and tended to be locally orientated prior to the development of the fur trade.

On the other hand, even in historic times, the bulk of trade appears to have been in perishable goods, such as corn, fish, and skins. These items either vanish completely, or are difficult to identify as trade goods, in the archaeological record. Yet, it is possible that the contacts involved in such exchanges have left indirect evidence in the archaeological record. The main evidence of contact between southern Ontario and the north is the pottery of Ontario Iroquoian type, or influence, that is found scattered over a wide area of northern Ontario (Wintemberg 1942; Martijn 1969). So far, this pottery has been studied very inadequately. In many cases, it remains uncertain whether it is of Iroquoian manufacture, or an Algonkian copy of Iroquoian originals (Martijn 1969:90). This problem is particularly severe in the case of a number of sites, as far north as Lake Nipissing, which contain assemblages of pottery that seem to be purely Iroquoian and have been labelled as such, on occasion, by Iroquoian archaeologists (Ritchie 1961:32).

The classic example is the Frank Bay site on Lake Nipissing. In this richly stratified site, Frank Ridley (1954) found Middle Woodland levels

overlain by an unbroken record of occupation from Pickering times into the seventeenth century. The pottery from each level is essentially identical to coeval pottery found north of Lake Ontario. Thus, no matter how the site is interpreted, it provides clear evidence of Ontario Iroquoian influence in the north, beginning in early Iroquoian times. The interpretation of this site is, however, a matter of some controversy. It may have been a campsite visited annually by Iroquoians who were travelling, and possibly trading, this far north. Alternatively, it may have been a summer camp belonging to the Nipissing, who lived in this area in historic times. In support of the latter interpretation, Ridley has noted that the site is located close to the Nipissing village marked on the Gallinée map of 1670. The dog burials, the variety of abandoned European material in the historic stratum, and the presence of an ossuary nearby also suggest that it was a habitation site rather than a way station.[27] Since the Nipissing celebrated their own Feast of the Dead, it is not improbable that the site belonged to them and their ancestors. Small differences in the frequencies of pottery types, and the possible presence of linear stamped pottery from northern Michigan, also provide vague hints of possible non-Iroquoian ethnicity.[28]

If Frank Bay is Nipissing, it suggests that the close contact between this group and the Huron can be traced back into early Iroquoian times. Though the economy of the Nipissing remained dramatically different from that of the Iroquoians, close contact, which historically involved large numbers of Nipissing spending the winter among the Attignawantan or Ataronchronon, might have resulted in the Nipissing either acquiring Iroquoian-style pottery through trade, or learning to make it themselves. It appears that here, as elsewhere where cultural contact cuts across ethnic boundaries, pottery types cease to be reliable indicators of ethnicity.

Other prehistoric sites containing Iroquoian-style pottery have been found in Algonquin Park. These date from early Iroquoian times onward, but the majority of finds seem to be late Iroquoian. The nature of these sites indicates that the area was being exploited during the summer months by hunting and fishing parties who had home bases elsewhere (Hurley and Kenyon 1970:122–25). Some of the hunters may have been Huron, or proto-Huron, from southern Ontario, but it is equally probable that they were Algonkians using Iroquoian-style pottery. The latter may have come from the Lake Nipissing region or the eastern shores of Georgian Bay, but, since pottery resembling that produced by the St. Lawrence Iroquoians is also present, it is possible that some of the intruders may have been Algonkin from the Ottawa Valley.

North of Georgian Bay, Ontario Iroquoian pottery occurs alone only in

small quantities. Such sherds may provide evidence of the passage of Iroquoian travellers, but unfortunately most of the occurrences have not been reported in sufficient detail that they can be interpreted with any confidence. Nor, in most cases, can such sites be distinguished from ones in which Iroquoian sherds occur alongside pottery of non-Iroquoian type and with stone tools that conform to a homogeneous pattern that has been identified as northern Algonkian. Sites of both types extend at least as far west as the Rainy River and as far north as Lake Abitibi (Wright 1965). The eastern extent of prehistoric Ontario Iroquoian pottery is more difficult to determine. Many prehistoric sites in northern Quebec have yielded small quantities of Iroquoian-style pottery (Martijn 1969:76, 85), but most of these occurrences have been shown to represent a transmission of St. Lawrence Iroquoian pottery northward or, when studied more thoroughly, may be expected to do so. One of the most intriguing sites found to date is Matabachouwan on Lake St. John (Simard 1970). This site has produced, along with some St. Lawrence Valley pottery, a few sherds of what appear to be Ontario Iroquoian types that reached maximum popularity in prehistoric times. All but one of these sherds were found in areas of the site that do not appear to have contained trade goods. The absence of the pottery types that were most common among the Huron in the historic period (Huron Incised, Sidey Notched, and Warminster Crossed) suggests that this pottery may be prehistoric and that either proto-Huron or neighbouring Algonkian groups may have travelled as far east as Lake St. John sometime after A.D. 1400[29]. In the sixteenth century, copper from Lake Superior was being traded eastward to the Saguenay region, providing further evidence for such contacts. It is possible, however, that the Nipissing were the main participants in such trade rather than the Huron.

Much of the Ontario Iroquoian-style pottery found in the upper Great Lakes region dates from an early period. At the Juntunen site, after A.D. 1200, the strongest ceramic affinities are with the Pickering culture of southern Ontario. Further evidence of Iroquoian influence at Juntunen, between A.D. 1200 and 1400, is an ossuary containing thirty-four bodies; some fully articulated, others completely disarticulated. This provides an unexpectedly early date for the possible diffusion of the Feast of the Dead among the northern Algonkians. A longhouse was also found at the Juntunen site, but, while its eighty-foot length may suggest Iroquoian influence, we have already noted the antiquity of this housetype in the north. It is of interest that over 770 pieces of native copper were found in the most recent levels of the site (A.D. 1200 to 1400). These ranged from

unworked nuggets to completed awls, beads, and other implements. McPherron (1967:106) concludes that the inhabitants of the site were a marginally agricultural Algonkian group, who played an important role in the copper trade of the upper Great Lakes.

Farther west, at the Pic River site, on the north shore of Lake Superior, over ten percent of the pottery in level III, radiocarbon dated around A.D. 960, has been identified as being Pickering in type (Wright 1965: 203–5). A single Pickering sherd has also been found in the McCluskey site, at the mouth of the Rainy River (ibid. 194). These finds indicate some kind of contact, either direct or indirect, between the Iroquoian peoples of southeastern Ontario and the Algonkians of the Lake Superior region by early Iroquoian times.

These contacts continued throughout the prehistoric period. At the Michipicoten site, on Lake Superior, fifteen percent of the pottery in level III (dated A.D. 1472 ± 75) has been identified as Huron or Tionnontaté, while in level II, which is somewhat earlier, pottery of this type constitutes forty-three percent of the total (Wright 1965:203–5; 1969:49–50). Iroquoian pottery, tentatively dated between A.D. 1500 and 1600, has been reported from Isle Royale in Lake Superior (Griffin 1961:11). These finds provide evidence of extensive and persistent contacts between southeastern Ontario and the southern portions of the Canadian Shield, beginning in early Iroquoian times. There is little reason to doubt that they are indicative of some kind of trade going back to the beginnings of a horticultural economy in southern Ontario. The question that remains to be answered is who was involved in these contacts. Various interpretations have been suggested, which may apply in different cases.

Some of this pottery could have been made by the Huron and carried onto the Shield by Huron hunters and traders. It is known that Iroquoian travellers in the north carried pottery vessels with them on their canoe trips. They used them for cooking and (so Sagard noted) to urinate in when they were far from shore (Wrong 1939:59–60). Bark vessels would have been more convenient to carry, but seem to have had a short lifespan when used as cooking vessels (Martijn 1969:86 n. 5); hence the Huron must have concluded that the greater durability of clay vessels made their transport worthwhile. Some of the Iroquoian potsherds found in remote campsites probably betoken the breaking, or abandonment, of pots of this sort. Yet, even if specific pots were made by Huron women, it is often impossible to determine whether they were carried abroad by Huron or by their Algonkian trading partners. Martijn (1969:91) has suggested that the ownership of pots made by Iroquoian women may have been a status

symbol among the Algonkians. He cites as an example of this a typical Iroquoian pot deposited in an Algonkian grave at Michipicoten.

It also has been proposed that many pots of Iroquoian design, particularly those found alongside other types of pottery, may have been made by Huron women who married Algonkian men. It is argued that, since the Algonkian bands were patrilineal and exogamous, once knowledge of making such pottery had been introduced into the north, it would have spread quickly from one group to another (McPherron 1967:106). While it is impossible to say what kind of relations existed between the Iroquoians and northern Algonkians in early times, in historic times no Huron woman would have consented to live among the Algonkians.

It is possible, however, that Algonkian women acquired pottery-making skills among the Huron and then, through intermarriage, transmitted these skills to groups living farther north. Such knowledge may have been acquired during the winter, when Algonkian bands resided near Huron villages. It is also possible that Algonkian girls may have lived with Huron families as part of a ritual exchange of children between trading partners. These girls would have learned to make pottery from their foster mothers and when they returned to their own people, would have carried these skills with them. Relations of this sort were probably most frequent with the Algonkian-speaking groups who lived closest to the Huron and may, in part, explain the almost identical nature of the pottery of the Nipissing and Ontario Iroquoians, beginning in early Iroquoian times. Unfortunately, the similarity of this pottery creates the possibility that the far-flung Iroquoian traits evident in the pottery of the upper Great Lakes, do not, in fact, indicate direct contact between the inhabitants of that area and those of southern Ontario. Instead, such pottery may have diffused through intermediary Algonkian groups, such as the Nipissing and Ottawa.

The archaeological record thus leaves unresolved the extent of the Huron trading network in prehistoric times. The small amount of copper in prehistoric Ontario Iroquoian sites might be interpreted as evidence that trade with the Lake Superior region was in the hands of Nipissing and Ottawa middlemen, who were diverting only a small part of it southward. Alternatively, it might be argued that as much, or even more, copper was reaching Ontario than had done so previously, but that an expanding population resulted in a thinner overall distribution. This, of course, does not answer the question of whether trade with Lake Superior was direct or indirect.

While the extent of Iroquoian contacts with the north in prehistoric times remains in doubt, by the early Iroquoian period extensive direct

contacts clearly existed between some of the Iroquoian-speaking peoples of southern Ontario and the Algonkian groups who lived around the shores of Georgian Bay and Lake Nipissing. There is little reason to doubt that these relations centred around a reciprocal exchange of corn, nets, and tobacco for skins, dried fish, and meat. Even in earliest times, the northern part of Simcoe County was the agricultural area best suited for contacts with the north and hence had the greatest potential to sustain a large population through a symbiotic relationship. Even in the short run, the inhabitants of this region stood to benefit from limited trade. The degree to which they might wish, or were able, to enforce a monopoly over such trade would depend on their strength relative to neighbouring Iroquoian groups and on the nature of their relationships with these groups.

Unfortunately, we know all too little about the relationships among the various Huron tribes prior to the historic period. Culturally and linguistically, these tribes were more similar to one another than the five Iroquois tribes were; for example, only the Tahontaenrat are said to have spoken a significantly divergent dialect. On the other hand, cultural and linguistic similarities never secured membership in the Huron confederacy for the Tionnontaté, and the Huron never allowed them to share in their trade with the north. Relations between the Attignawantan and the Attigneenongnahac appear to have been friendly for a long time prior to A.D. 1600, but we do not know whether or not this friendship and sharing of trade preceded the arrival of the Attigneenongnahac in north Simcoe County.

Warfare with St. Lawrence Iroquoians and the Iroquois of New York State may have compounded the advantages of moving away from the shores of Lake Ontario, although by itself, it does not appear to have been sufficient to compel such a move. Had conditions to the north not been so favourable, the tribes who arrived latterly in the Huron country might not have been tempted to move and, had they been encircled by a solid ring of agricultural tribes, as the Iroquois were, they would not have been able to do so. The very ability of these tribes to move seems to have been the result of a frontier situation which also promoted peaceful and profitable relations with the north.

The Arendarhonon, Tahontaenrat, and possibly, still earlier, the Attigneenongnahac, seem to have been attracted towards the southeastern corner of Georgian Bay by the trading potential of that region. Once near Lake Simcoe, they were in a position to travel north without difficulty and to trade there, whether the Attignawantan wished them to or not. The Attignawantan and the Attigneenongnahac may have welcomed the gradual approach of the two other tribes, as offering them greater security

against attack from the south and east. If the volume of trade was increasing, the admission of these other tribes may have involved little loss of profit for the original participants.

Moreover, since the Attignawantan had engaged in this trade the longest and were the most skilful at it, they would have been well able to cope with competition. On the other hand, the Attignawantan's inveterate refusal to permit the Tionnontaté, who were less advantageously placed to defy them, to participate in this trade suggests that they resented having to share their commerce with other groups. It may be that in respect of the Arendarhonon and Tahontaenrat the Attignawantan and Attigneenongnahac felt themselves insufficiently strong, and not well enough situated, to prevent this from happening. If the other tribes were growing increasingly anxious to participate in this trade, the Attignawantan may have concluded that it was in their own best interests not to oppose them, except in the case of the Tionnontaté. Hence, the final stages in the growth of the confederacy may have taken place without overt conflict.

As will be made clear in the next chapter, the admission of the Arendarhonon and Tahontaenrat to the confederacy and their resettlement in northern Simcoe County did not take place until European trade goods had begun arriving in Ontario. This makes it highly likely that both events were related to the early development of the fur trade. The evidence suggests, however, that long before this period, native commerce had been playing an important role in drawing the Huron tribes not already living in the north nearer to Lake Simcoe. At the same time, the union of the Attignawantan and the Attigneenongnahac had laid the foundations of the Huron confederacy. Therefore, in both the economic and political spheres, processes that had been influencing the Iroquoian peoples living north of Lake Ontario for many centuries had, by the latter half of the sixteenth century, reached the point where only the elaboration of native trading patterns resulting from the beginnings of the European fur trade was needed to bring about the expansion of the confederacy and the nucleation of population that was observed by the first Europeans who visited the region. The introduction of European goods did not alter the pattern of Huron development so much as it intensified it. The final coming together of the Huron population in northern Simcoe County would have been far more difficult, or even impossible, had trading relations with the north not existed in earlier times and if all the Huron tribes had not already been aware, at least to some degree, of the potential benefits to be derived from a symbiotic relationship with the northern hunting peoples. Many other peoples had their ways of life totally disrupted and transformed by their

early commercial encounters with Europeans or with Indians who had been influenced by Europeans. In the case of the Huron, it seems that several hundred years of development on the edge of the Canadian Shield had prepared them for their historic role as the principal trading partners with the French in this part of North America. In this respect, the Huron though similar to the Iroquois in many other ways, were totally different from them.

Chapter 4  Alien Shadows

Before their earliest recorded encounter with the French in 1609, the Huron had already been heavily influenced by contacts between their eastern neighbours and European traders on the St. Lawrence River. Any discussion of these influences is bound to be highly conjectural and subject to revision as additional archaeological data becomes available. It is, however, a topic that cannot be avoided, if we are to understand Huron society in the seventeenth century. The aim of this chapter is to survey what is known about how the arrival of the Europeans influenced the Indians of eastern Canada prior to 1609 and to examine the responses of the Huron to these influences.[1]

Cartier and Roberval on the St. Lawrence

CARTIER'S FIRST VOYAGE

The first recorded meeting between Iroquoians and a group of Europeans took place in 1534. That year, Jacques Cartier, a master mariner from St. Malo, who had previously visited Brazil and Newfoundland, was commissioned by Francis I to discover new lands in America. Leaving France with two ships on 20 April, he crossed the Atlantic and sailed into the Strait of Belle Isle and along the south coast of Labrador as far as Bonne Esperance Harbour. There, he turned south to chart the unrecorded west coast of Newfoundland, then crossed the Gulf of St. Lawrence and skirted Brion Island, the Magdalens, and Prince Edward Island. From the latter, he sailed north along the coast of New Brunswick and entered Chaleur Bay, which for a time he hoped might be the long sought-for passage leading to the Pacific Ocean and the riches of the Orient. At the north entrance to the bay, a French longboat encountered two groups of Micmac in some forty to fifty canoes. Upon landing, these Indians made a loud noise and held up furs on the ends of sticks to indicate that they wished to trade. The French were alarmed by so many Indians and motioned them to move away.

When the Indians continued to pursue them on the water, the French fired two cannons and scattered fire-lances in their midst to frighten them off (Biggar 1924:48–51).

The Micmac were more experienced traders than Cartier's men seem to have been. The next day, nine canoes appeared near the French ships, obviously wary, but again making signs that they wished to trade. This time the French reciprocated, both parties landed, and a profitable trade ensued. The next day, as the French sailed along the north shore of Chaleur Bay, they spotted signal fires[2] at Tracadigash Point and a boatload of Indians came out and offered them cooked seal meat. As soon as two Frenchmen went ashore bearing trade goods, more than three hundred men, women, and children appeared. These Indians warmly greeted the French and bartered all of their furs for iron kettles, knives, and other wares (Biggar 1924:52–57). The behaviour of the Micmac indicates that they were already used to dealing with Europeans. They had evidently collected furs over the winter and brought them to the coast in the hope that Europeans would turn up with whom they might trade.

Several days later, Cartier was compelled by foul weather to take refuge in Gaspé Harbour, where he remained 16–25 July. There he encountered a party of about three hundred men, women, and children. They wore only loin cloths and a few old skins over their shoulders, had no furs to trade, and possessed nothing of value, except their canoes and fishing nets. In Cartier's estimation these Indians were "the sorriest people in the world" (Biggar 1924:60). One of the distinctive features of this group was that the men shaved their heads, except for a long tuft on top, which they tied into a knot with leather thongs. A word list was compiled which remains the oldest recorded Iroquoian vocabulary (ibid. 80–81; B. Hoffman 1961:157).

These Indians had come from the vicinity of Quebec City and were part of what, for lack of a more distinctive name, are called the St. Lawrence Iroquoians (map 6). On the basis of sixteenth-century accounts, the latter can be subdivided into two groups, who are denominated, after their principal settlements, Stadaconans and Hochelagans (Trigger 1968a:430–31; Pendergast and Trigger 1972:43–45). The Hochelagans, who lived in the upper part of the St. Lawrence Valley, occupied at least one large town surrounded by a triple palisade and extensive cornfields. They were a sedentary, horticultural people and resembled in detail the Iroquoian groups who lived farther inland at this time and in the seventeenth century. Other Hochelagan-type groups had formerly lived farther up the

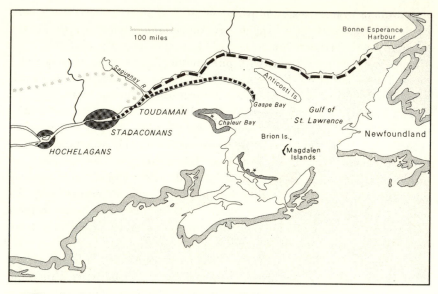

Coastline known to Europeans in 1534 (after Hoffman 1961)

Coastline inferred to be known to European traders by 1634

Location of Iroquoian settlement (by ethnic divisions)

Copper route from Lake Superior

Stadaconan summer fishing expeditions

Inferred Stadaconan summer expeditions

MAP 6.   *The lower St. Lawrence, c. 1533.*

St. Lawrence Valley, although no archaeological sites with trade goods have been found there.

The Stadaconans were quite different. They inhabited about a dozen small, unfortified communities between the Ile aux Coudres and Portneuf, thirty-two miles up-river from Quebec City. They planted corn, but seem to have relied more heavily on fishing and eeling than did the other northern Iroquoian-speaking peoples. Moreover, their villages appear to have been mainly winter camps and places to grow corn. Every summer, groups, each consisting of several hundred men, women, and children, would travel down the St. Lawrence, to fish for mackerel on the Gaspé

Peninsula or to hunt seals and porpoises along the north shore of the Gulf of St. Lawrence (Trigger 1963b:94; 1968a:430; Bailey 1933; Fenton 1940:167–69; Trigger 1962b:242). While the majority of Stadaconan villages were on good terms with one another, there is no evidence of a general tribal structure. In keeping with the economic conservatism of this group, each village may have remained politically autonomous.

The relationship between the Hochelagans and Stadaconans is also obscure. Cartier says the Stadaconans were subjects of the Hochelagans (Biggar 1924:161), but there is no reason to believe this was the case. The distance separating them suggests that they constituted distinct tribes, or groups of villages. The relations that the Stadaconans and Hochelagans had with the Indians living farther inland were quite different from one another (Trigger 1968a:431). It seems likely that, just as between most tribes who were not members of the same confederacy, there may have been rivalry, or even hostility between the two groups.

The identity of the St. Lawrence Iroquoians constitutes a longstanding ethnological problem. Anthropologists and historians have seen in these two groups the ancestors of one or more of the Iroquoian tribes of the seventeenth century. Schemes have been proposed which would have these tribes moving inland, late in the sixteenth century, to become the Tionnontaté, one or more of the Huron tribes, the Seneca, Onondaga, Oneida, Mohawk, or even the Tuscarora (Pendergast and Trigger 1972:63). They have also been viewed by archaeologists as a branch of the Onondaga or Oneida, who allegedly spread out in the St. Lawrence Valley about A.D. 1100, and retreated into New York State after 1542.[3]

All of these interpretations do violence to current knowledge of these groups. Linguists, who have studied the vocabularies that record the language of Hochelaga and Stadacona are agreed that this language, or group of dialects, is closer to Huron than it is to any of the languages of the Five Nations Iroquois.[4] Hence it is impossible that these people are, to any substantial degree, the ancestors of one or more of the Iroquois tribes. Since the Huron tribes were already present in southern Ontario prior to the disappearance of the St. Lawrence Iroquoians and the material culture of the latter, as revealed by archaeology, is different from the Ontario Iroquoian tradition, it is unlikely that these people are the ancestors of any of the Huron tribes. Finally, James F. Pendergast's archaeological studies reveal the development of a distinctive Iroquoian culture in the St. Lawrence Valley, beginning as early as the Pickering culture to the west.[5] The similarities between the later phases of this development and those of the eastern Iroquois cultures in New York State appear to result from cultural

contact between these two regions. The simultaneous discovery that the eastern Iroquois tribes developed *in situ* in their historic tribal territories supports the linguistic evidence and virtually rules out the possibility of any of the Iroquois tribes being descendants of the St. Lawrence Iroquoians.

Prior to the discovery of the antiquity of Iroquoian culture in the St. Lawrence Valley, the Stadaconans were viewed as a typical Iroquoian group who had taken corn agriculture as far north as Quebec, but, finding themselves in an environment that was less favourable to agriculture, had adopted something resembling an Algonkian type of hunting and fishing economy (Fenton 1940:172). Now, the Stadaconans can alternatively be viewed as an Iroquoian group that had not accepted the more complex patterns of intensive agriculture that mark their neighbours to the south-west. If we accept the implications of the *in situ* theory, it is no more surprising to find Iroquoian-speaking peoples who did not participate in all features of the Iroquoian cultural pattern than it is to find Algonkian-speakers who did share many of these features.

The fishing party that Cartier encountered had not come to the Gaspé with the intention of trading with Europeans. They had no surplus skins and, at first, were reluctant to have any dealings with the French. This suggests that, unlike the Micmac, they had little direct experience of Europeans. After the French mingled with them for a while on shore, they began to come in their canoes to the sides of the French vessels, where they were given knives, glass beads, combs, and other inexpensive trinkets (Biggar 1924:60). On 22 July the French again visited the Iroquoians' encampment and were greeted by the men with customary singing and dancing. All but a few of the young women, however, had retired into the woods. When Cartier gave a comb and tin bell to each woman who remained, the men ordered the twenty or so women who were hiding to return, which they did, rubbing Cartier's face and arms in a traditional Iroquoian greeting. Cartier gave each of them a tin ring, after which there was much singing and dancing (61–63). The account of this visit observes that the Indians stole what they could from the French (63). While the Iroquoians did not regard the acquisition of goods that were left unattended as theft, it is likely that these Indians, like many others who lacked the means to trade, took considerable risks to acquire the exotic possessions of Europeans. Elsewhere, this hunger for European goods often resulted in quarrels, followed by violence and bloodshed.

While the Stadaconans who came to the Gaspé were inexperienced in trading with Europeans, this does not mean that they did not know anything about them. Some Stadaconans travelled along the north shore of the

St. Lawrence to hunt seals and porpoises, perhaps occasionally reaching the south coast of Labrador. Some of these may already have met or traded with Europeans. Prior experience of this sort would explain the speed with which the Stadaconans became interested in establishing a trading relationship with the French. It would also explain an otherwise cryptic observation in the account of Cartier's second voyage. There it is stated that the Hochelagans "make their living by horticulture and fishing and the goods of this world mean nothing to them for they do not have knowledge of them and are not nomads like the Stadaconans" (160–61). If we assume that "goods of this world" mean European trade goods, this could be interpreted to signify that the annual visit of the Stadaconans to the north shore of the Gulf of St. Lawrence had already resulted in them having limited dealings with Europeans.

At the end of his stay in Gaspé Harbour, Cartier had a large cross erected, bearing the arms of Francis I. Seeing the religious ceremony that accompanied the erection of the cross, Donnacona, who was the leader of this fishing party, became angry that the French were presuming to use land that belonged to his people without first acquiring the right to do so. He set out in a canoe for Cartier's ship, accompanied by his brother and three of his sons (or nephews). Keeping well away from the French ships, Donnacona pointed at the cross and delivered a harangue, accompanied by many gestures, which made it clear that this region was his and the French had no right to erect anything without his permission. Cartier had an axe held up, pretending that the French wished to barter for the bear skin Donnacona was wearing and thus suggesting to Donnacona that he was willing to pay for the use of the land. As Donnacona warily approached the ship to collect the axe, he was seized by a group of French sailors, who made everyone in the canoe board the French vessel.

Cartier gave the Indians food and drink and attempted to tell Donnacona, again by means of gestures, that the cross was a land-mark and that the French would soon return, bringing him iron ware and other goods. Cartier also stated that he wished to take two of Donnacona's sons to France for the winter. As an expression of goodwill, he had Taignoagny and Domagaya dressed in shirts, ribbons, and red caps and gave each of them a brass chain. Donnacona appears to have understood that Cartier meant to keep the boys, but, rather than becoming angry, he accepted with a show of pleasure the hatchets and knives that were given to him and the two Indians who accompanied him, prior to their being released. Later, six boatloads of Indians came to say goodbye to the prisoners and to bring them a supply of fish. The following day, Cartier set sail (64–67). He

circled the east end of Anticosti Island and returned to France by way of the Strait of Belle Isle.

During his stay in Gaspé Harbour, Cartier probably had learned that the Stadaconans were only visiting the coast and lived farther inland. His aim in kidnapping Taignoagny and Domagaya seems to have been to obtain Indians who could learn French and would later guide him to their villages. It is frequently asked why Donnacona did not try to secure the release of his sons. Some historians have suggested that his decision to cooperate with the French was motivated solely by political or economic considerations (Morison 1971:375). The previous year, two hundred Stadaconans, who were on their way to the Gaspé, had been massacred near the mouth of the Saguenay River by a people called the Toudaman (Biggar 1924:177–78). These were a group living to the south, probably the Micmac (B. Hoffman 1961:203–4). They and the Stadaconans appear to have been fighting for control of the Gaspé Peninsula, and Donnacona may have hoped to win the French as his allies in this struggle. Donnacona also may have wanted to establish trading relations with the French, to have as ready access to European trade goods as did the Micmac and other tribes who were living near the coast.

Alternatively, like the Huron and other Iroquoian tribes in the next century, the Stadaconans may have been in the habit of exchanging children with their trading partners as pledges of good faith. High-handed and unreciprocal as Cartier's actions were, Donnacona could have interpreted them in the light of such a custom and believed that, if he remained friendly, he would see his sons again and acquire a valuable trading partner. On the other hand, an attempt to rescue his sons might have resulted in them being killed or carried off, never to return. In later times, military alliances, trade, and personal goodwill were indissoluble elements of any alliance. Paternal affection, as well as practical political and economic considerations probably motivated Donnacona's restrained behaviour. Finally, Iroquoian politeness and tenacity in suppressing spontaneous emotions were able to add to Donnacona's actions a deceptive appearance of satisfaction and goodwill.

SECOND VOYAGE

In spite of Donnacona's composure, an anxious winter must have followed, which was followed by a still more anxious summer. Not until early September 1535 was Donnacona to learn that his sons had reappeared

aboard three French ships that were sailing towards Stadacona. In October of the previous year, Cartier had been commissioned to sail once more and explore the lands beyond Newfoundland. In addition to searching for a route to the Indies, the stories that Taignoagny and Domagaya had told about the native copper trade had aroused Cartier's hopes of finding jewels and precious metals in the New World (Biggar 1924:105–6). These boys had also promised to lead him to the large settlement of Hochelaga, which lay up the St. Lawrence in the direction of these riches.

Leaving France in May 1535, Cartier reached Blanc Sablon in mid-July and then spent almost eight weeks exploring the St. Lawrence. Directed by his two prisoners, who by now had acquired a working knowledge of French, he slowly made his way up-river, crossing from one side to the other in order to see as much as possible. He may also have been delaying his arrival at Stadacona until Donnacona had returned from his annual trip to the Gaspé Peninsula. Off Tadoussac, Cartier encountered four canoes whose crews had come from the Quebec City area to fish and hunt for seals. These Indians were so frightened by the sight of the French ships that only one vessel came near enough for Donnacona's sons to hail them and invite them to draw alongside (114–15). On 7 September, the French anchored near the western extremity of the Ile d'Orléans, where many Indians were fishing. Seeing that Taignoagny and Domagaya had returned, these people welcomed the French with traditional singing and dancing, and some chief men came out to Cartier's ships bringing him a present of eels, fish, maize, and several large squash. This was followed by numerous deputations of both sexes, to whom Cartier gave small presents in order to ingratiate himself (119–21).

The next day, accompanied by twelve canoes filled with his men, Donnacona came abreast of Cartier's flagship. After sending ten of these canoes a safe distance away, he approached Cartier's ships with the other two. Seeing his sons were safe, he embraced Cartier in an affectionate manner, after which Cartier stepped into his canoe and ordered bread and wine to be brought to the Indians (121–23). Following this reception, Donnacona departed, apparently taking his two sons with him. Cartier travelled up-river in his longboats, in order to search for a good harbour for his ships. As he did so, he began to understand the geography of the Quebec City region (map 7). The Stadaconan settlements were all located along the north shore of the river. Cartier passed the villages of Ajoaste, Starnatam, Tailla, and Sitadin, before catching sight of Stadacona on the flank of Cape Diamond.[6] Just north of Stadacona, where the Lairet flows into the St. Charles River, Cartier found a safe anchorage for his ships.

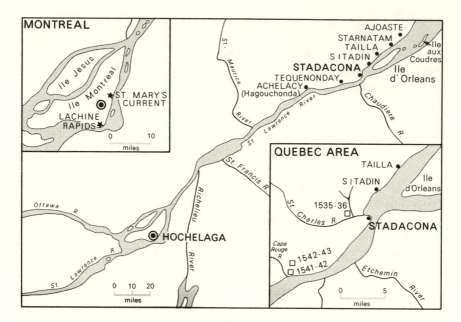

MAP 7. *Approximate location of Iroquoian villages mentioned in the texts of Cartier's voyages.*

The site had the added advantage that the St. Charles River flowed between the proposed encampment and Stadacona, providing the French with additional protection against the Indians. As he left the river, the people of Stadacona thronged to greet him. A headman made a speech of welcome, women danced and, once again, Cartier distributed knives and glass beads (123–25). On 13 September Cartier brought all three of his ships up-river from the Ile d'Orléans, preceded by Donnacona and twenty-five canoes filled with Indians, who came up-river from the east. Once again, the Indians swarmed about the ships to welcome the French (127).

Many historians have noted that the days that preceded Cartier's docking on the St. Charles River marked the highpoint in his relations with the Amerindians. The Stadaconans were delighted that Donnacona's sons had

been returned to them and Donnacona must have believed that he had acquired a powerful ally and trading partner. When, however, Donnacona came to greet Cartier on the way to Stadacona, Cartier noted that Taigno-agny and Domagaya, who had hitherto shown themselves to be friendly, were now reluctant to associate with the French and refused to board his ship, even when pointedly asked to do so (127–28). Although they assured Cartier that they intended to keep their promise to travel with him to Hochelaga, it is often assumed that Taignoagny and Domagaya began to avoid the French when they learned that their father did not wish Cartier to travel up-river (Morison 1971:406–7). This explanation seems inade-quate, however, since Donnacona was still going to great lengths to mani-fest his goodwill towards Cartier. If Donnacona was willing to dissemble his feelings about the projected journey, there is no reason why his sons should not have done the same.

Taignoagny and Domagaya had personal reasons for behaving as they did. They had been kidnapped, made to endure an ocean voyage to an unknown destination, and to learn, by trial and error, a language the structure of which was totally alien to them. In addition, they had been compelled to eat strange food and, in France, were exposed to a wholly unfamiliar way of life and many customs that must have frightened and disgusted them. There is no reason to doubt that Cartier wished to treat them well; since both young men were endowed with Iroquoian self-reliance, they probably accepted most of what happened to them as an adventure and a challenge. They even acquired a taste for European clothes, which they continued to wear after their return home, and for some varieties of European food.[7]

They had, however, been brought up in a society in which young people enjoyed great freedom and were never physically punished or forcibly restrained by their elders. In the opinion of sixteenth and seventeenth century Europeans, physical coercion was essential for dealing with young people and Cartier probably did not hesitate to chastise them when he judged their behaviour merited it. Moreover, while we do not know their ages, Iroquoian attitudes towards sexual behaviour may have got them into situations that resulted in even more severe disciplinary action. Indian youths who had been to Europe rarely expressed the desire to return there. We may therefore assume that, even if Cartier believed that he treated Taignoagny and Domagaya fairly, his behaviour often must have seemed cruel and arbitrary. The Stadaconans were, no doubt, surprised by Taignoagny's and Domagaya's stories about their experiences in France,

but tended at first to view them as the complaints of young people and not as a serious impediment to an alliance.

The following day, when Cartier was marking the place to dock his ships he noticed that, while many Indians were swarming about, Donnacona, his sons, and those who were with them (their clansmen?) kept apart. Seeing this, Cartier ordered a number of Frenchmen to go with him to find out what was the matter. Taignoagny informed Cartier that Donnacona was angry because the French were carrying their weapons while the Indians did not do so. Although vexed at being challenged, Cartier replied that it was the custom for Frenchmen always to bear arms, as Taignoagny knew well. Following this, Cartier and Donnacona again greeted one another warmly and the Indians who were present gave three loud shouts of approval (Biggar 1924:128–30).

This incident provides an example of the subtle and indirect way in which Iroquoian diplomacy was conducted. The complaint about the French carrying arms was undoubtedly a rebuke to behaviour that Donnacona interpreted as signifying a lack of trust in his people, but it also expressed displeasure over two other matters. Firstly, Cartier was beaching his ships, and thus again he was using land without obtaining permission to do so from its owners. Secondly, by now Donnacona had learned from Taignoagny and Domagaya that Cartier was planning within a few days to travel up-river to visit the Hochelagans. It has been suggested that Donnacona was opposed to the French travelling up-river because he wished to protect the Hochelagans, but nothing about his behaviour suggests that this is so (Fenton 1940:171).

On the contrary, it seems clear that Donnacona wanted to keep the commercial and political advantages of an alliance with the French to himself and did not wish Cartier to travel inland to make a separate alliance with potential competitors. Lacking a formal treaty with the French, Donnacona may have feared that Cartier sought to conclude such an alliance with the Hochelagans, to the detriment of the Stadaconans. Also, by travelling up-river without obtaining his permission, Cartier was infringing still further on Donnacona's territorial rights. Looked at in Iroquoian terms, Donnacona's opposition to Cartier's visit to Hochelaga seems to have been motivated by a reasonable mixture of fear, pride, and self-interest. It is unwarranted to dissect social, economic, and political motives among the Indians of eastern North America at this period, not because the Indians did not have such motives, but because the activities associated with them were so clearly interrelated that such motives cannot

be compartmentalized as easily as they can be for Europeans. Nevertheless, interpreted strictly from an economic point of view, Donnacona's objection provides the first example of an Indian group in eastern North America attempting to establish a middleman position in the trading of European goods with the interior. Tribes that could secure and hold onto such a position were able to profit by exchanging furs they did not trap for European goods they did not have to manufacture. As a result, the role of middleman was to become a highly coveted one among some tribes.[8] The idea of informing himself about native customs occurred to Cartier no more than it did to most other early navigators. He had no idea what his actions signified to the Indians and failed to appreciate the reasons for Donnacona's complaint. He also began to fear that Taignoagny and Domagaya were plotting against him for no good reason. In the latter, we see further evidence of the deep-seated mistrust of the Indians that had led Cartier to fire on the peaceful Micmac a year earlier.

The next day, Cartier beached his two large ships, leaving his pinnace anchored in the St. Lawrence ready for his trip up-river. Donnacona and his sons appeared, accompanied by more than five hundred men, women, and children—most likely the entire population of Stadacona. A delegation of about a dozen leading Indians were entertained by Cartier on board ship and presents were given to them. This time, Taignoagny, as interpreter, informed Cartier that Donnacona was angry about his plan to visit Hochelaga and that he would not let his sons accompany the French. He added that the river was dangerous above Quebec. Cartier replied that he would press on, with or without Taignoagny and his brother, since he had to obey the orders of his king. He offered Taignoagny a rich present if he would go along, which the latter refused. At this point, the Indians withdrew to their settlement (Biggar 1924:131–32).

The next day, Donnacona sought again to persuade Cartier not to visit Hochelaga, or, if that were impossible, at least to conclude a formal alliance with the Stadaconans before doing so. Arriving at Cartier's ships, Donnacona gave the French leader a lavish present of fish and eels, after which the Indians sang and danced to express their goodwill. Then Donnacona invited the principal French and Indians to sit in a circle on the beach and made a long speech in the course of which he offered to "give" Cartier a girl about ten years old and two younger boys. Taignoagny explained as best his knowledge of French allowed that these prestations were to dissuade Cartier from going to Hochelaga. Donnacona's actions cannot be interpreted as the permanent surrender of these children. One of the boys was his own son, while the girl was his sister's daughter, who, as a clans-

woman, stood in an especially close relationship to him. It is clear, from what happened next, that by offering to let these children live with the French, Donnacona was seeking to conclude a formal alliance with the newcomers.

When Cartier said he would not accept the children if, in return, he had to promise not to go up-river, Domagaya assured him that they were offered as tokens of goodwill and that he was prepared to accompany Cartier. By this, Domagaya appears to have meant that, if Cartier was determined to go up-river, Donnacona would be content if only Cartier would first formally assure him that a special relationship existed between them. At this point, Taignoagny and Domagaya exchanged some harsh words and Cartier was convinced that Taignoagny was rebuking his brother for offering to help the French. While Domagaya seems to have been a pliant individual, who was anxious to curry favour with the French and consequently often revealed things he should not have, there is no reason to believe that he liked the French any better than his brother did. What Cartier failed to perceive was that Taignoagny's and Domagaya's offers represented two stages in Donnacona's negotiations with him. Already suspicious of his two former victims, Cartier now suspected that each in his own way was trying to deceive him further. In return for the children, whom Cartier retained as hostages, Donnacona was presented with two swords and two brass wash basins. A salute of twelve guns was also fired from the ship, which much astonished the Indians. A rumour spread that two Indians had been killed by a similar volley from the pinnace that was anchored near Stadacona, whereupon all of the Indians fled. Cartier suspected Taignoagny of starting this rumour (132–35).

Donnacona was obviously not content with the response he had received from Cartier, and must have grown increasingly mistrustful of him as a result of this meeting. Nevertheless, he did not cease to try to dissuade Cartier from travelling up-river. The next day he sent three shamans, with blackened faces and wearing dogskin pelts and long horns, to paddle around Cartier's flag-ship, while one of them delivered a long speech. The shamans landed and were carried into the woods by Donnacona and his men, where they continued their harangue. About half an hour later, Taignoagny and Domagaya appeared, their caps under their arms and their hands folded in imitation of French acts of devotion they had witnessed. They said that one of their deities had informed these shamans that, if the French proceeded to Hochelaga, they would all perish from ice and snow. When Cartier laughed and said his priests revealed the contrary, Taignoagny and Domagaya returned to the woods and soon the other

Indians appeared before the ships expressing pleasure at the good news
(136–40). Here we see another aspect of Iroquoian behaviour that was
often to puzzle the French in the next century: the assumption that it is
improper to question the beliefs of other people.[9] Although the French
laughed at the Stadaconan shamans' not unreasonable warning, the
Stadaconans felt obliged to respect and show pleasure about the French
shamans' pretended divination.

In a final effort to establish a proper alliance, Donnacona offered that
Taignoagny or Domagaya might go to Hochelaga with the French, if, in
return, Cartier would agree to send a Frenchman to live with him. Cartier
was convinced that the two youths were rogues and announced that he
would give no hostage and that he was going up-river even though he had
neither a guide nor an interpreter (140). Not understanding the nature of
Iroquoian diplomacy, Cartier had unwittingly spurned the alliance that
Donnacona was hoping to establish with the French. He also appeared to
be threatening to form an alliance with Donnacona's rivals. Whether, if
Cartier had understood what was going on, he would have behaved any
differently remains an open question.

On 19 September Cartier began moving up-river. Passing the village of
Tequenonday, which was perched atop a hill, he arrived at Achelacy,
which lay at the foot of the Richelieu Rapids, near the modern community
of Portneuf. The headman of this village, who was apparently delighted
to see Cartier by-passing Stadacona, presented him with a girl eight or nine
years old and a boy who was less than three. In so doing, he was no doubt
hoping to emulate Donnacona and to seal an alliance with the French.
Cartier accepted the girl, but returned the boy because he was too young
(142–44). Slowly, because of the shoals and dangerous currents, Cartier
made his way up the St. Lawrence. Along the banks of the river, he noted
the cabins of many Indians who had come there to fish. At the west end
of Lake St. Peter, he traded some knives and beads for a pile of muskrat
skins (147). It was there that he decided to leave his pinnace and make his
way up-river in two longboats. Being shown the correct channel by friendly
Indians, Cartier arrived off the south shore of Montreal Island on 2 October
(13 October, New Style).[10]

Cartier's visit to Hochelaga the following day is too well known to
require repetition here (plate 18). The Frenchman's arrival at the palisaded town, his reading of the gospel to the Indians, who brought their
sick to him to be healed, and his afternoon climb to the summit of Mount
Royal, from which he accurately surveyed the view on every hand, have
become part of Canadian folklore. Less frequently commented on is the

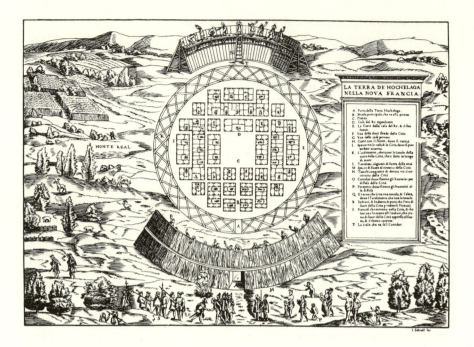

PLATE 18. *Ramusio's Plan of Hochelaga. This engraving that
accompanied Giovanni Ramusio's 1556 Italian translation of the Cartier
voyages frequently has been accepted as an eye-witness drawing.
W. D. Lighthall ("The False Plan of Hochelaga," Transactions of the
Royal Society of Canada, 3rd series, vol. 26 [1932], sec. 2, pp. 181 ff.)
convincingly refutes this belief. In particular, the groundplan of the houses
can be shown to be based on a misleading description of these houses in the
Cartier relation. Ramusio's plan thus becomes the first in a long list of
illustrations of early Canada that are of little or no ethnographic value.
Courtesy McGill University Libraries.*

brevity of Cartier's visit and the rapidity with which the sighting of the Lachine Rapids caused him to abandon his attempt to push farther up-river. Throughout the day, Cartier was apprehensive about his longboats and anxious to return to them by nightfall. He was also worried about the pinnace, which he had left with a small crew down-river (172). The speed with which he visited the town of Hochelaga and his obvious relief when the visit was over can only have communicated a sense of his mistrust to his hosts. Likewise, because the French did not like the taste of food cooked without salt, they refused to join in a magnificent feast that the women of Hochelaga had prepared for them (167). In spite of the knives, hatchets, beads, and tin trinkets that Cartier gave to the people of Hoche-laga, his behaviour must have seemed inexplicable and discourteous to them. While Cartier left amidst every sign of goodwill, he had failed to achieve anything that would contribute towards future good relations with the Hochelagans, or make this area a useful base for the exploration of the interior. Cartier not only lacked knowledge of how to deal with the Indians (which is understandable) but, convinced of his own superiority, he did not perceive the need for such knowledge. Nor can it be argued that his apprehensiveness on this occasion resulted mainly from the lack of an interpreter. Given his attitude, the lack of an interpreter probably neither helped nor adversely influenced his relations with the Hochelagans. It did, however, reduce the amount of cartographical information that he was able to collect.

While Cartier was away, the sailors who had been left on the St. Charles River built a small fort in front of the two ships and mounted artillery on the ramparts in order to cover the approaches (Biggar 1924:174). This was a still greater infringement on land belonging to the people of Stada-cona, and indicated that the French were intending to remain for the winter, if not to establish a permanent base there. Donnacona was happy to learn that Cartier had returned from Hochelaga and may have had his mind further set at ease by advance reports of what had transpired there. Soon after Cartier returned, Donnacona and some of the other headmen visited the French settlement to welcome him back. Cartier entertained them, although his chronicler observed sourly that the Indians were insincere and did not deserve such good treatment (175).

The next day, Cartier, the gentlemen of his crew, and some fifty sailors made their first formal visit to Stadacona, a mile or so away. They were greeted, as they had been at Hochelaga, outside the village. After speeches of welcome had been delivered and the French had distributed knives, tin rings, and other gifts (again stressed to be of little value), they entered the

village and visited the houses in which Donnacona and Taignoagny lived, which they found to be well provisioned for the winter (175–78).

In the relatively friendly, but very brief, period that followed, the people of Stadacona came to the French fort to trade fish and eels for knives, awls, beads, and other ornaments. At this time, the French had an opportunity to observe how the Stadaconans hunted and fished, to experiment with tobacco, and to gather some curious information about Stadaconan sexual behaviour (179–87). Some of the French harangued the Indians concerning the supposed follies of their religious beliefs. The Indians listened politely, almost certainly understanding little of what was being said. Unable to conceive of an exclusive religion, the inhabitants of Stadacona decided to benefit from whatever rituals the French could teach them and came *en masse* to ask for baptism. Cartier was able to turn aside this request by saying that he lacked holy chrism, which he falsely assured them was necessary to perform this sacrament (180–81).

Soon, however, Cartier was annoyed to discover that Taignoagny and Domagaya were telling their people that the French were cheating them by exchanging for food goods that were worthless or of little value in their own country. The Stadaconans were not disinterested in such information. All the evidence from the next century indicates that the Indians of this region were experienced traders, who understood how to make the rules of supply and demand work to their own advantage and who could fully utilize knowledge of this sort (Biggar 1924:187–88; 1922–36, 2:171).

Cartier's fear of Donnacona and his two sons was nurtured by the headman of Achelacy,[11] who was jealous of Donnacona's proximity to the French. It was also sustained by Stadaconan individuals or lineages who seem to have been currying favour with the French (Biggar 1924:188). Cartier became especially alarmed when Donnacona's niece escaped to her own people, apparently after she had been beaten by a French youth. Fearing that Donnacona was planning to attack the French settlement, Cartier added wide ditches and extra scaffolding to his fort and strengthened the night-watch. Donnacona and his sons came several times to the bank of the river opposite the fort, but Cartier refused even to speak with them. Finally he accused them of numerous acts of bad faith, including having carried off the girl they had given him. Donnacona's people protested that the girl had run away of her own volition and a few days later they persuaded her to return to the French (188–92). For a time, this served to relieve the tension between Cartier and the Stadaconans, and the Indians again came freely to the French fort.

The *Bref récit* of Cartier's second voyage implies that the brittle truce

between the supporters of Donnacona and the French lasted throughout
the winter. For part of the winter, however, Cartier ordered the Iroquoians
to stay away from his ships, because of a severe illness that had broken out
among the Indians (204). When contact resumed, these Indians put
Taignoagny's and Domagaya's advice to good use. Knowing that French
provisions had run short, they demanded larger amounts of European
goods in return for fish and venison. If the French refused to pay, they
carried their food home, stating that they could easily use it themselves
(217). A grimmer picture of relations between the French and the Indians
is supplied by André Thevet (1878:422), who claimed to have interviewed
Donnacona. He reports that, over the winter, the French amused themselves by robbing the Indians and cutting their flesh to test the sharpness
of their swords. The truth probably lies somewhere in between. Among
Cartier's crew, there were undoubtedly frightened or malicious individuals,
who were ready to attack the Indians at the least provocation; men such as
these were to cause trouble enough at Quebec in the early part of the
seventeenth century. Likewise, the Indians' habit of carrying off things
that were left lying about unattended, in the belief that the French no
longer wanted them, was inevitably viewed as theft by the Europeans, and
this occasionally led to violence. Finally, Taignoagny and Domagaya appear
to have been only too willing to exacerbate whatever grievances arose
against the French. A variety of unrecorded incidents must have kept both
Cartier and the Indians on guard, whenever they met throughout the
winter.

In the month of December, Stadacona was stricken by an illness which
killed over fifty people (Biggar 1924:204). The French believed it to be
scurvy, although this seems unlikely, since the Stadaconans are reported
to have had a highly effective cure for that disease. Later, however, no
doubt from a lack of fresh meat, almost all of the French contracted scurvy
and twenty-five of them died from it. Fear of Indian attack led Cartier to
take elaborate precautions to disguise the desperate condition of his men.
In March, Cartier noted that Domagaya had recovered from what seemed
to have been an attack of scurvy. When he told Domagaya that his servant
was ill from the same disease, Domagaya did not hesitate to send two
women to gather the fronds of the common white cedar (*Thuja occidentalis*)
and to show the French how to brew a curative drink from it. According to
Cartier, all of his crew recovered within a week of taking this cure. Some
who were suffering from syphilis found that it relieved that ailment as
well.[12]

In February, Donnacona, Taignoagny, and many others went hunting

and were gone for about two months. In the seventeenth century, the Iroquoians hunted in the late autumn and the early spring, rather than in midwinter; however, among less horticultural groups, such as the Ottawa, men left their villages for extended winter hunts, and it is not unlikely that the Stadaconans followed this pattern. Cartier feared that the Stadaconans were collecting a force to attack him and became alarmed when Donnacona returned on 21 April, accompanied by many unfamiliar faces. Domagaya visited Cartier to inform him that his father had brought back a lot of venison, but even this visit aroused Cartier's suspicions because Domagaya refused to cross the river. Cartier believed that this was because Domagaya found the fort too well guarded (216–19). Cartier sent his servant, Charles Guyot, who was better liked by the Stadaconans than anyone else, to see what was happening there. He found Donnacona apparently ill and the house of Taignoagny full of strangers, but was not allowed to visit the other houses. It appeared that a political struggle was going on in Stadacona, since Taignoagny sent word to Cartier that, if he wished to please him, he should seize a man named Agona and take him back to France with him (219–20).

Cartier, and most modern historians, have interpreted this as a power struggle between Donnacona and Agona as to which man, or clan segment, should control Stadacona (Trudel 1963:110–11; Morison 1971:420); however, from what we know about Iroquoian political organization, a personal struggle of this sort seems highly unlikely. Among the Iroquoians, a headman could exercise power only by gaining the support of his followers for each decision that he made. No headman could force anyone to obey him against that man's will, nor would a headman retain the respect of his clan segment, if he were to betray one of its members to strangers. Headmen were elected to manage the affairs of their clan segment and could not, in their own right, control what went on in other clans or communities. Under these conditions, no additional personal power was to be gained by eliminating one of the protagonists. More likely, a dispute had broken out in the village, whether within or between clan segments makes little difference, about what policy should be pursued with respect to the French. The strangers that Guyot observed in the village were probably men who had come from neighbouring communities to join in the debate.

There were individuals in Stadacona who had reported Donnacona's hostility to Cartier (or so Cartier, with his defective understanding of the language, believed) (Biggar 1924:188). These men may have been urging a more conciliatory policy for dealing with the French than the one Donnacona and his sons wished to see followed. Divisions of this sort were the

rule rather than the exception in Iroquoian politics, especially when it came to dealing with an enemy. If Agona were the leader of the conciliatory faction, Taignoagny's message to Cartier may have been more than the inexperienced scheming of a Machiavellian youth. Taignoagny (or his father) may have guessed that Cartier was planning to kidnap more Indians before he returned to France and hoped that, if he could incite him to try to seize Agona or even were able to spread a convincing rumour that Cartier was planning to do this, he could convince Agona of the need to oppose the French. Such a plan seems more in keeping with what we know about Iroquoian political behaviour than does the conventional interpretation of this request.

During the winter, Cartier had been fascinated by reports of a "Kingdom of the Saguenay," which he was told lay somewhere in the interior of the continent. Donnacona claimed to have visited this place and he described it, through his interpreters, as a land rich in gold, rubies, and other precious things and inhabited by white men who dressed in woollen clothing (200–202; 221). Some historians have speculated that this story may reflect knowledge of Spanish settlements far to the south, and it has been suggested that Indians from the St. Lawrence might even have visited these settlements (Trudel 1963:109). Yet Donnacona also claimed to have visited lands where men had only one leg or where they lacked anuses and ate no solid food (Biggar 1924: 221–22). This has led other historians to dismiss the Kingdom of the Saguenay as yet another of these imaginary lands. Viewed in terms of archaeological data, however, the bulk of the information about this so-called Kingdom of the Saguenay makes sense. The only metal that the Indians were familiar with, prior to the arrival of the Europeans, was native copper. Hence, one may conclude that it was either the greedy imagination of the French or the romanticizing translations of Taignoagny and Domagaya that led Cartier to believe that the Indians were talking about gold.

It is evident from Cartier's account that the Stadaconans were participating in a trade that had begun in the Archaic period. From the vicinity of Lake Superior, copper nuggets and artifacts diffused from tribe to tribe over much of eastern North America. Some of this copper was clearly reaching the Stadaconans. For example, when Donnacona left for France his people presented him with a large knife made of red copper (233).

Historians have been puzzled by seemingly contradictory accounts of how this copper was reaching the St. Lawrence. The Hochelagans indicated that one route lay along the Ottawa River, but that this route was blocked by *agojuda*, or "evil men," who were armed to the teeth, wore slat

armour, and waged continual war (170–71). Some commentators have identified these people as the Iroquois, although this is geographically improbable, unless the story refers to Iroquois attacks on groups living in the Ottawa Valley. Others have suggested that they were the Ottawa Valley Algonkin (Lighthall 1899 : 204; B. Hoffman 1961 : 204; Fenton 1940 : 172). The latter were somewhat acculturated to Iroquoian ways, at least in the seventeenth century, and may have worn slat armour. They were, however, only a marginally horticultural people and, because of this, they and the Hochelagans should have been on good terms and had a symbiotic trading relationship, resembling that between the Huron and the Algonkian peoples who lived around the shores of Georgian Bay. This leaves the Huron. In the last chapter we presented archaeological evidence which suggests that, in prehistoric times, there may have been prolonged conflict between the Huron and the St. Lawrence Iroquoians. It is also noteworthy that Huron influence seems particularly strong in late sites on the upper St. Lawrence, suggesting a considerable amount of warfare between the two groups at this time (Pendergast and Trigger 1972 : 284). This warfare may have prevented the Hochelagans from travelling northward to trade with the Algonkians of the upper Great Lakes.

On the other hand, both the Hochelagans and Stadaconans agreed that the normal route by which copper was reaching the St. Lawrence Valley was down the Saguenay River (Biggar 1924 : 106, 171). This suggests that the copper was moving along the major auxiliary trade route of the historic period, which ran from Georgian Bay, across Lake Nipissing and the upper Ottawa Valley, into the network of lakes and rivers in central Quebec, finally reaching Lake St. John and the Saguenay Valley. This explains how the name Saguenay came to be applied both to the river and to the sources of copper much farther inland. It also provides the source for Cartier's description of the Saguenay and Ottawa Rivers coming together to form an island (201–2). It is even possible that Donnacona's description of a civilized people living in the interior was a vague reference to the Huron, who, although they may not have engaged directly in the copper trade with Quebec, would have been sufficiently different from the Algonkian-speaking peoples of the north to be noteworthy. The finds at Matabachouwan, described in the last chapter, may bear witness to this roundabout trade between the St. Lawrence Valley and the upper Great Lakes. The importance that the Indians attached to this trade was out of all proportion to its utilitarian value and this may have aroused undue expectations of wealth in the minds of the Frenchmen who listened to Donnacona.

From Donnacona, Cartier also learned that the Richelieu River led south to lands where there was neither ice nor snow, and whose inhabitants waged continual war against one another (202–3). These stories were embroidered by Taignoagny and Domagaya with references to oranges and other tropical produce, but seem based on a knowledge of New England. The Stadaconans and Hochelagans had considerable quantities of shell beads, with which they used to make "collars." Although Cartier tells a curious story about how these beads were drawn from the river after they had formed on the mutilated bodies of prisoners or criminals (158–60), it seems likely that they were obtained from the south, either through trade or as booty. Beads made from marine shells appear in prehistoric Iroquoian sites in Canada, but only in small quantities, and the development of the wampum trade is generally believed to post-date the introduction of metal tools, which permitted the Indians of Long Island and adjacent regions to manufacture large numbers of these beads. The reference to shell collars suggests that the wampum trade, or at least a trade in beads closely resembling wampum, may have begun earlier and that shell beads were more common by the early sixteenth century than the archaeological data suggest (Beauchamp 1898 : 3–4; 1901 : 329, 342, 354).

The stories that Donnacona told, together with Cartier's belief that Agona should be made the ruler of Stadacona to strengthen the position of the French in the St. Lawrence Valley, led the French leader to make a ruthless decision: he would not return to France without taking with him Donnacona, his sons, and his principal supporters (Biggar 1924 : 220–21). In this way, he believed, Agona would be free to rule in the Quebec City area and Donnacona could be made to tell his stories to the king, in order to enlist the latter's support for future voyages. Cartier also may have hoped that, once Donnacona had learned to speak French, more information could be obtained from him concerning what he had seen in the interior (Carleill, cited in Hakluyt 1589 : 723). Donnacona would be promised that, if he cooperated, he could return to Canada, but, in fact, Cartier feared his ill will and was planning never to allow him to return (Trudel 1963 : 113, 142; based on Biggar 1924 : 231).

To lure his intended victims, Cartier hinted that, if Taignoagny conducted Donnacona and Agona to the ships, the latter would be kidnapped; however, none of the Indians trusted Cartier and for two days not a single person from Stadacona came near the ships (Biggar 1924 : 222–23). This suggests that signs of Cartier's impending departure had given rise to speculation about more kidnappings. It also suggests that the divisions in policy among the Stadaconans were not as great as Cartier had hoped. The

Stadaconans were lured to the French fort, when news spread that Cartier had abandoned one of his ships and was permitting the people of Sitadin to remove the iron nails from it (223). Donnacona and his sons accompanied the rest of their people, but Donnacona refused to cross the river, while Taignoagny and Domagaya hesitated for over an hour before doing so. Cartier reassured Taignoagny that he only intended to take a few children to France but, as a favour, said he would seize Agona and maroon him on some island. Taignoagny promised to lead Donnacona and all the people of Stadacona to visit the French ships (223–24).

The next day, 3 May, the French erected a large cross by the river. In the afternoon, Donnacona and his two sons arrived, accompanied by a large number of men and women. Significantly, there is no mention of Agona being part of this group, which suggests that Donnacona had warned him to keep away from the French. Donnacona and his sons were uneasy and refused to enter the French camp. Instead, they lit a council fire outside it. After unsuccessfully urging Donnacona to enter the fort, Cartier instructed his men to be prepared to seize him, his sons, and two other headmen, and to drive the other Indians away. Seeing mischief afoot, Taignoagny ordered the women to flee, but, while he was doing so, his father and brother were lured into the fort. Taignoagny rushed after them to make them come out, but at this point the French seized the men Cartier had designated and took them on board their ships. Frightened and uncertain of French intentions, the other Indians sought the protection of the forest (225–27).

That night, the Stadaconans recovered from their shock and assembled on the bank of the river, shouting war cries and demanding to see their headman. In the meanwhile, Cartier promised Donnacona that if he cooperated and went to see the king of France, he would be given a fine present and returned to his people the following year. By noon the next day, a vast number of Indians had gathered, apparently from Stadacona and the surrounding villages, but most of them were hiding in the forest. Perceiving no alternative, Donnacona showed himself to these people and assured them that all was well and that he would return the next year. He added many other things that the French could not understand. A number of headmen presented Cartier with twenty-four shell bead collars to urge him to treat Donnacona well and said they would bring Donnacona food for the impending voyage. Cartier gave Donnacona two brass kettles, eight hatchets, and some knives and beads, which the headman sent to the women and children of his family (228–30).

At dawn the next day, four women came in a canoe to bring Donnacona

large quantities of corn, meat, and fish. Cartier and Donnacona reassured
these women that they would be returning the next year, after which each
of the women gave Cartier another shell bead collar. Meanwhile, all of the
people of Stadacona gathered by the river to say farewell to Donnacona
and the other prisoners. As Cartier's ship made its way down the St.
Lawrence several boatloads of Indians came up to the ship to present
Donnacona with three bundles of beaver and seal skins and a copper knife.
The bundles of skins suggest that these Indians were already aware of
European interest in the fur trade. They also offered Cartier shell collars
for Donnacona's safe return (231–33). These formalities must have hidden
the deep anxiety and bitterness which the Indians, both aboard Cartier's
ship and along the river, felt about what had happened. Taignoagny does
not seem to have been allowed to speak publicly after he was captured,
which suggests that he was being kept under physical restraint (229, 231,
233).

Cartier left twenty-five members of his crew dead in the New World
and had aboard his ship ten Indians. These were Donnacona and his two
sons, once more fated to return to France against their will; his niece ten
to twelve years old; two younger boys, one of whom was a close relative
of Donnacona; a younger girl from Achelacy; and three other Indians,
two of whom were headmen (249). None of these Indians was ever to
return to Canada. When Cartier reached France, he found the country at
war with Spain. The war lasted until 1538, and was followed by three
years of preparations and diplomatic difficulties before a new expedition
could be launched. By the end of this period, all but one of the Indians
had died from European diseases against which they had little or no immunity. The survivor was a young girl.

Not much is known about the lives of these Indians in France. By the
time they landed, they appear to have been pacified by Cartier's promises
that they would soon be returning to Canada with much wealth (Kerrigan
1951:20). It seems that most lived in St. Malo and in 1538 Cartier was
reimbursed by Francis I for providing them with board and lodging
(Biggar 1930:69–70). On 25 March 1539, three males were baptized
(ibid. 82), apparently *in articulo mortis*. Donnacona eagerly performed his
role of raconteur, obviously hoping that arousing the greed of the French
would increase his chances of returning home. He appears to have learned
French and studied the mentality of his captors carefully. When he was
interviewed by the king, he spoke of mines rich in gold and silver and of
lands where there was an abundance of spices. Donnacona promised that
he and his people would help the French to reach these lands and embel-

lished his stories with fashionable marvels, including men who had wings on their arms and flew like bats. He seems to have completely won Francis I's confidence, for, when the Portuguese ambassador questioned the veracity of these tales, the king replied that Donnacona's stories never varied and that even under pain of death he swore they were true (ibid. 77–80). Donnacona was interviewed by other important individuals, including the historian André Thevet (1878:407). Unfortunately, his cunning availed him nothing, since he died a Christian, so we are told, after being in France for four years (Hakluyt 1589:723). The fact that the Indians were not baptized for several years after they were brought to France suggests that they were under little pressure to conform to French ways and were regarded mainly as political prisoners or potential interpreters.

CARTIER AND ROBERVAL

Cartier's third voyage was to be one of colonization as well as exploration (plate 19). A French sailor stated that one of its goals was to subjugate the lands of the Indians (Biggar 1930:461). While the potential profit from this colony was seen to lie mainly in its mineral wealth, Francis I was also hoping for considerable profit from the fur trade (Lanctot 1963:79). In 1540, Cartier was made captain-general of a proposed expedition and was licensed to recruit fifty prisoners from the jails of northern and western France for his colony. The following January, however, there was a change in plans and Jean-François de La Rocque, sieur de Roberval was placed over Cartier and granted vice-regal powers in the New World. In Roberval's commission, much emphasis was placed on the conversion of the heathen, but this was to placate Pope Paul III and to counteract Spanish and Portuguese protests that the French were ignoring the decree of Pope Alexander VI, which had divided the New World between their two countries. In the spring of 1541, Roberval was having financial difficulties and decided to spend the following year raising money by practising piracy in the English Channel. Cartier was dispatched to Canada with five ships loaded with various domestic animals and a substantial number of male and female colonists. The colonists included some alleged members of the nobility, as well as condemned felons (Trudel 1963:119–43).

Cartier departed from St. Malo on 23 May, but his fleet had a rough passage and he did not arrive at Quebec for three months. Surprised that the French had returned after such a long interval, the inhabitants of

PLATE 19. *Canada in the Harleian map of* c. *1542. The delineation of the St. Lawrence is based largely on data collected during the Cartier voyage of 1535–36. That Hochelaga is located north of the St. Lawrence River indicates that Cartier was not aware of the existence of the Rivière des Prairies north of Montreal Island. The landscape painted south of the St. Lawrence seems to portray the region between Mount Royal and the Monteregian hills to the east. The Europeans and European settlement making up part of this scene probably reflected plans for French colonization along the St. Lawrence* c. *1642. Courtesy Public Archives of Canada.*

Stadacona rushed to the banks of the St. Charles River, expressing their joy and hoping to welcome back Donnacona and his compatriots. Cartier had no interpreter with him. He had decided not to bring the only surviving Indian for fear she would reveal that the others were dead. Hence he could communicate only by gestures and with the limited Iroquoian vocabulary that he and the other sailors had acquired on their previous visit or from their captives.

Agona enquired of Cartier what had become of Donnacona and the others and was informed that Donnacona was dead, but the rest had married and were living in France as great lords, for which reason they did not wish to return to Canada. Cartier imagined that Agona was pleased, because Donnacona's death confirmed his own position as "lord and chief of the country" (Biggar 1924:251–52). Yet, with so many Frenchmen about and his own people unaware of what had happened, it is unlikely that Agona would have quarrelled with Cartier on the spot and risked being carried off by him. His later actions make it clear that he neither believed the whole of Cartier's story nor was pleased to learn of Donnacona's death. Nevertheless, he placed the beaded headband he was wearing on Cartier's head, gave him two shell-bead bracelets, and embraced him. Cartier distributed presents to Agona and the women who were with him and the two men parted on what seemed good terms.

Although Agona and his people were outraged by Cartier's failure to honour his promise to return Donnacona and the other Indians, Cartier was soon to provide them with even more cause to hate him. Cartier no longer wished to live near Stadacona, but wanted a base farther inland, from which he would be free to explore up-river.[13] For this purpose, he selected a site near Cape Rouge, nine miles upstream from Stadacona, and had all five of his ships brought there. He unloaded cattle and supplies, planted crops, and set his men to work building a colony, which he named Charlesbourg-Royal. This consisted of a fortified habitation by the river, and for additional protection a fort on top of the steep cliff behind it. In Cartier's view, no better place for a settlement could be found. The soil appeared fertile, the forests abounded in useful trees and vines, a rich source of iron was at hand, at the base of the cliff there was a thick vein of rock containing "gold" and "silver," while on top of the cliff he found "diamonds." Two ships were dispatched to France with specimens of the mineral wealth of the new colony (254–55).

Cartier's behaviour was a serious provocation to the Indians. Without asking their permission, or acquiring use of the land from them, he had brought in settlers, erected buildings, and planted crops. He had also come

with women as well as men, and with greater numbers than before, so that it was clear he intended to settle the land he occupied. Such behaviour constituted a challenge to all the Indians in the district. Furthermore, Cartier had denied the Stadaconans' right to control traffic along the river by locating his colony farther inland, thus reviving all the fears that Donnacona had experienced about an alliance between the Hochelagans and the French. Even if Agona had not resented the failure of the French to honour their promises to return his tribesmen, such behaviour would have left him with no alternative but to view Cartier as his enemy.

On 7 September Cartier left most of his people at work on Charlesbourg-Royal and went with a small party to explore the Lachine Rapids, prior to a major exploration into the interior the following spring. On his way up-river, Cartier visited the headman of Achelacy, whose daughter was among the Indians he had taken to France. Remembering this headman's former antagonism to Donnacona, Cartier presented him with a fancy red cloak, two bronze basins, knives, and hatchets, and persuaded him (again without benefit of an interpreter) to take two French boys into his household to learn his language (256–57). Cartier's experience with Taignoagny and Domagaya had obviously convinced him that Indian youths who were taken to France did not make trustworthy interpreters. Sending French boys to learn Indian languages was an action that the French were to repeat many times, and with much success, in the next century. The natives of Achelacy may have regarded the boys as an exchange for the girl who had not come back, but whom they hoped would be returned at a later date. This made Cartier's action appear to them to be one of courtesy and trust. The people of Achelacy may also have been pleased to see that Cartier was ignoring the Stadaconans. In spite of this, their headman must have been perplexed and grieved not to see his daughter and he may have been alarmed by news of the kind of settlement that the French were erecting not far from his village.

Arriving at Montreal Island, Cartier failed to navigate through the St. Mary's Current and spent the day following an Indian trail as far as the foot of the Lachine Rapids. Along the way, he passed through two fishing villages, but did not bother to visit Hochelaga.[14] Having learned a little more about the geography of the rapids from the Indian fishermen he encountered, he returned to his boats, where some four hundred Indians had gathered. They greeted him in a friendly manner and Cartier, in return, gave axes and sickles to the headmen and combs, tin and copper brooches, and similar ornaments to the rest. As on his previous visit, however, he did not trust the Hochelagans and, rather than staying to explore

the Lachine Rapids properly, he set off down-river the same day (257–59). Curiously enough, though he had passed through two Indian settlements, he gave as one of his reasons for returning to his boats that he had spent the day without food and drink (258). His refusal to eat Indian food was evidently not limited to his first visit to Hochelaga.

On the way back to his settlement, Cartier revisited Achelacy, but found that the headman and his warriors were absent from the village. The headman's son told Cartier that his father had gone to Maisouna, which appears to have been a settlement or region south of the St. Lawrence.[15] When Cartier reached Charlesbourg-Royal, he was informed that the Indians were no longer visiting the settlement to barter their fish and game, but were prowling about in a suspicious manner. It also appeared that the headman of Achelacy had gone to Stadacona to confer with Agona, and that, in spite of his apparent friendship, he too was conspiring against the French (259). We have no information about what happened to the boys who were staying with the Indians at Achelacy, but circumstantial evidence would suggest they were withdrawn soon after Cartier's return from Hochelaga.

Very little information has been preserved about what happened thereafter. The Indians appear to have concluded that Charlesbourg-Royal was too strong to be attacked directly and had decided on a war of attrition. They invested the settlement, first killing some Frenchmen who had gone to cut wood and then others who ventured outside the fort. In the course of the winter, thirty-five Europeans are reported to have been killed by the Indians.[16] In 1542, news of these hostilities reached Europe, by way of Spanish fishermen who claimed to have obtained their information not only from French sailors but also from Indians who had come down the St. Lawrence from Canada to trade deer and wolf skins for axes, knives, and other items (Biggar 1930:462–63). Although the latter story has been dismissed as improbable, it is possible that some of the Iroquoian-speaking peoples from the Quebec City area were already in the habit of trading with European fishermen as far east as the Strait of Belle Isle, in conjunction with their annual hunt for porpoises (B. Hoffman 1961:204–9). These Indians were evidently on good terms with the Spaniards and, knowing them to be a dependable source of European goods, may have felt all the more confident in attempting to expel the French intruders, who were trying to seize possession of their land.

It is uncertain how widespread this dissatisfaction with the French had become. The village of Achelacy may have feared Cartier's intrusion on its land and seems to have joined in the attack. At some point, the Hoche-

lagans also seem to have turned against the French (Biggar 1924:259). It has been suggested that the latter turn-about indicates that Cartier explored up-river the following spring, but, in view of the hostility of the Stadaconans, such a venture seems unlikely. By June 1542, Roberval had not arrived and Cartier judged that his small band was unable to resist the Indians, who were harassing the colony daily (264–65). Thus he set sail with his cargo of supposed gold and diamonds. In St. John's Harbour, Newfoundland, Cartier encountered Roberval, who was headed for the St. Lawrence with three ships. Roberval ordered him to return to Canada. Cartier, however, believed his ships to be laden with riches and had crews on board that might well have mutinied rather than spend another winter on the St. Lawrence. Hence he stole off in the night, setting a direct course for St. Malo. There, his diamonds became a byword for falseness and Cartier was never again entrusted with the command of an important expedition.

Yet, if the Stadaconans were rid of Jacques Cartier, their troubles with the French were not over. In July, they saw Roberval's three ships sail past Quebec without stopping and come to anchor off Cape Rouge. No mention is made of Cartier's settlement, which may have been dismantled either by Cartier or by the Indians after he had left. Whatever had happened to Charlesbourg-Royal, Roberval had to build, or rebuild, a settlement for the approximately one hundred and fifty people who were with him (Morison 1971:448). He named the new settlement France-Roy. Much more is known about Roberval's settlement than about the earlier one. The main habitation was built on the hill, probably where Cartier's lookout had been. It was surrounded by a palisade and equipped with barracks, mess halls, bedrooms, a mill for grinding corn, and an outdoor oven. At the base of the hill was another lodging, with a tower two stories high, used mainly for storage (Biggar 1924:266).

In the winter, rations ran short and, because Roberval lacked Cartier's knowledge of how to control scurvy, more than fifty people died. The Indians do not appear to have attacked the habitation and in the meagre references that survive there is no mention of hostility. In the spring, the Indians brought large quantities of shad, which they traded with the French (267). This change of attitude has been attributed to the stronger military forces and defence works with which Roberval had equipped his colony. It is possible, however, that much of the Iroquoian resentment was directed against Cartier and his companions personally. Although Roberval, no less than Cartier, was intruding on Indian land, the new leader enforced strict discipline among his settlers (268), and this may have led to

better relations with the Indians. Even so, however, while the few accounts connected with this voyage describe the Indians as gentle people, their failure to mention any individual suggests that the latter may have kept their distance (268; 295–96).

By the spring of 1543 Roberval had decided that his colony would return to France. Before departing, he made an effort to reach the fabled Saguenay by way of the Ottawa River. He travelled up the St. Lawrence with sixty-nine people, apparently reaching Montreal Island.[17] There is no evidence that Roberval attempted to establish a colony on the island, as Beaugrand-Champagne (1948) has suggested, and the only statement that might suggest conflict with the Indians is the one hundred and twenty pounds of grain he is reported to have sent down-river to his settlement (Biggar 1924:270). This might have been stolen from the Indians of the upper St. Lawrence, as René de Laudonnière later stole Indian corn for his hard-pressed colony in northern Florida and as Champlain was planning to plunder it from the Iroquois in 1628–29 (Biggar 1922–36, 5: 304–5). It is equally possible, however, that Roberval purchased this corn from the Hochelagans. One boat was lost, causing the death of eight men, but there is no proof that this happened while Roberval was shooting the Lachine Rapids (Trudel 1963:162 n. 70). It would seem to have been on the way to Canada that Roberval's pilot, Jean Alfonse, had explored the lower part of the Saguenay River, without, however, reaching the falls at Chicoutimi.[18]

A hostile climate, bad relations with the Indians, the failure to find gold, and the inability of a nascent fur trade to support a colony were to give the St. Lawrence Valley a respite from colonization that was to last until 1600. We have no means of knowing what memories of these earliest attempts to transplant Europeans and a European way of life to this region survived among the Indians, or how far inland tales of these events spread. It is unlikely, however, that the Huron failed to learn something about what was happening and to become aware, for the first time, of the unsettling, alien forces that were eventually to engulf their society.

French efforts at colonization continued, but, between 1555 and 1560, they were directed towards Brazil and, between 1562 and 1565, to the southeastern seaboard of the United States. These colonies, even more ill-fated than those of Cartier and Roberval, were destroyed by the Portuguese and Spanish (Trudel 1963:177–212). Throughout this period, the Indians of eastern Canada must have continued to hear rumours about the activities of Europeans along the east coast of North America, about Hernando De Soto's savage expedition through the southeastern United States (1538–43),

and about the epidemics that were decimating the Indian populations to the south. Whether or not these reports had sufficient clarity or immediacy to be of more than passing interest to the Huron is unknown. They must, however, have served as continuing portents of a changing world.

Trade on the St. Lawrence 1543–1600

The failure of French efforts at colonization by 1543 did not mean that European interest in the St. Lawrence had come to an end. After 1550, growing English competition in Newfoundland caused many French fishermen to frequent the shores of Nova Scotia and the Gulf of St. Lawrence. Moreover, the decline in Spanish fishing during that country's wars with England in the latter half of the century opened up for the French a new export market that preferred dry rather than wet processed cod, and this too encouraged the movement into the Gulf (Innis 1940:46). There, French sailors began to interact with increasing regularity with the Micmac of Nova Scotia and New Brunswick and the Montagnais of southern Labrador. These were peoples who were willing and able to trade large numbers of furs for European goods. By returning to the same place each year, French fishermen established a lasting trading relationship with particular bands of Indians.

Gradually, this trade brought about a major shift in the subsistence patterns of the Indians of the Maritimes. Previously, they had passed most of the year exploiting the abundant food resources of the coast, while only the winters were spent hunting in the interior. The desire for more trade goods led them to spend a longer period each year hunting in the forests. Because of this, they had to supplement their diet with biscuits, dried peas, and other preserved foods purchased from the French. While such food helped to compensate for the declining utilization of coastal resources, it made these Indians increasingly dependent on their European trading partners.[19] There is also evidence that, at least by the beginning of the seventeenth century, the Indians of the Maritimes were exchanging European goods for agricultural produce, and possibly for deer skins, with the Indians of Massachusetts (Biggar 1922–36, 1:395–96). The latter region was visited by Europeans only occasionally and, since a horticultural economy was well-established there, the tribes of that region were willing to supply part of the growing demand for additional food supplies among the non- or semi-agricultural Indians of the Maritimes in return for

European trade goods. It has been argued that, prior to British settlement in Virginia, the Indians from that far south were exchanging deer skins northward, in return for European goods from the Maritimes (McIlwain 1915:xxxii).

As the demand for furs increased in Europe, the relative profits to be derived from the fur trade, as compared with fishing, increased. Eventually this resulted in expeditions being sent to Canada whose primary goal was to trade for furs (Biggar 1901:32). At first, furs of all kinds were in demand: deer, marten, bear, otter, seal. In the latter part of the century, however, an old process for making hats out of felted beaver fur began to revive. The pelts best suited for this process had been taken in winter and worn by the Indians, with the fur next to the body, for some fifteen to eighteen months. The latter caused the long guard hair to drop out leaving on the pelt only fine, but barbed, underhair, about an inch long. This odoriferous product took time to produce and, as the fashion of wearing beaver hats grew more popular in Europe, fishermen and traders extended their operations farther into the Gulf of St. Lawrence to keep abreast of the demand (Innis 1956:12–14).

Sealing, walrus hunting, and whaling also attracted growing numbers of Europeans to the St. Lawrence. The Basques, who were already whaling off Newfoundland by 1527, gradually pushed their hunts into the St. Lawrence and established stations for rendering oil from their catch in harbours as far west as Tadoussac, at the mouth of the Saguenay River. Les Escoumins, which was not far away, was said to have been the centre of the whale fisheries. By 1578, twenty to thirty vessels seem to have been engaged in whale hunting in the St. Lawrence, and it may have been some of these whalers who, by 1550, had begun trading for furs with the Indians at Tadoussac.[20]

Traders and fishermen do not appear to have travelled beyond Tadoussac before 1580. According to a report of Captain C. Carleill, the kidnapping of Donnacona, and the bad manner in which Cartier had treated the Stadaconans, had caused the Indians of the Quebec City area to so dislike the French that they refused to have any dealings with them before 1580, when trade on the upper St. Lawrence was resumed (Hakluyt 1589:723). Carleill, however, had his information at second hand; hence his story is open to a number of different interpretations. It seems unlikely that, even if the Iroquoians were hostile to French, or European, intrusion into their territory and had been sufficiently powerful to compel whalers and fishermen to remain down-river, they would have refused to trade with them at a convenient and neutral place such as Tadoussac. A. G. Bailey (1933:

103) has suggested that the resumption of trade on the upper St. Lawrence did not result from a new attitude among the Stadaconans, but from their annihilation by the Algonkians, who inhabited the St. Lawrence Valley in the following century. In a period for which there is so little documentation, it is tempting to try to read a maximum amount of significance into the few data we have.

There is no doubt that European travel up the St. Lawrence resumed around 1580. About 1585, Cartier's nephew, Jacques Noël, ventured as far as Montreal Island and climbed Mount Royal in order to study the view to the west (Trudel 1963:222). Further trips are known to have been made that were involved with trade. In 1599, François Gravé Du Pont went as far as Three Rivers, possibly contributing the place names that replace those of Cartier on the Levasseur Map of 1601 (ibid. 249–52; plate 20). Basque whalers anxious for extra profits may also have been making their way up-river before 1600, but no record has been preserved of these voyages.

Until 1608, however, the main trading centre in the St. Lawrence Valley remained at Tadoussac, which became a port of call for professional fur traders, as well as for fishermen and whalers. The professionals did not succeed in their attempts to drive the part-time traders out of business. The latter were still active along the lower St. Lawrence River in the 1620s, in defiance of monopolies that had been granted to the professional traders by the French government.

Little is known about the early development of the professional fur trade on the St. Lawrence River. It appears to have started when a small French ship was sent to the St. Lawrence in 1581. This voyage was sufficiently profitable that the next year a larger ship was sent, followed by three ships in 1583 (Biggar 1901:32). That year Richard Hakluyt saw in Paris a depot containing furs estimated to be worth 5000 crowns that had come from the St. Lawrence (ibid. 33). In 1584, the merchants of St. Malo sent five ships to the St. Lawrence and were planning to send twice the number the year after. By 1587, rival traders were battling on the river.

In 1585, Jacques Noël and Etienne Chaton de La Jannaye managed to obtain a twelve-year trading monopoly embracing the St. Lawrence and adjacent regions, in return for undertaking to establish a colony there. This monopoly was relinquished almost immediately, after the other merchants of St. Malo secured cancellation of the monopolists' exclusive right to control the lucrative fur trade on the St. Lawrence (Trudel 1963: 221–26). This was clearly the only resource from which there was a hope of deriving substantial profits.

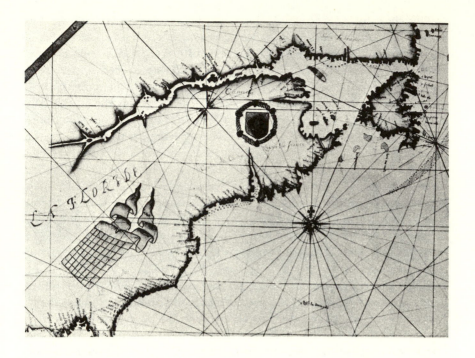

PLATE 20. *Part of the Levasseur map of 1601. On this map the toponymy of Cartier and Roberval is replaced for the first time by names such as Gaspé, Québec, Trois-Rivières, which have endured to the present day. These changes reflect a new era of French interest in the exploitation and colonization of the St. Lawrence Valley. Courtesy Public Archives of Canada.*

This short-lived monopoly is significant because it marked a revival of French interest in colonization in this part of the New World. In 1598 and 1599, Troilus de La Roche de Mesgouez and Pierre Chauvin were granted similar monopolies in New France and La Roche established a short-lived colony on Sable Island.[21] Thus began a long struggle between the proponents of free trade and those who sought authority to monopolize the fur trade of the St. Lawrence and the Maritimes in return for establishing colonies there.[22] Although most historians are sympathetic towards the colonizing point of view, both policies were riddled with inconsistencies and neither offered much hope for the long-term survival of French interests in Canada. The fur trade required only a small resident population for its effective management, as the Hudson's Bay Company was later to demonstrate. Yet, as the most eloquent advocate of colonization, Samuel de Champlain, pointed out, without strong colonies (and, he might have added, sufficient naval power) to enforce their hold on this part of North America, the French were unlikely to hold their trading posts against foreign competition (Biggar 1922–36, 6:361–74). On the other hand, monopoly holders correctly argued that the profits of trade were not enough to support colonization on the scale that was required. Lucrative as the fur trade was, by itself it was insufficient to support a thriving European colony on the edge of the Canadian Shield.[23] For such a colony to develop, either a more diversified economic base was needed or else massive support from the mother country. As Champlain and his successors were to learn, any scheme to build a colony solely on the resources of the fur trade was doomed to failure.

By 1584, the merchants of St. Malo appear to have been on good terms with the Indians who traded at Tadoussac. About that time a number of Indians were brought to France as visitors, at least one of whom came from the St. Lawrence Valley.[24] We are informed that these Indians spent the winter in France to increase the friendship between the French and the Indians (Trudel 1963:215, 223). It is unknown whether those from the St. Lawrence were Iroquoian or Algonkian-speakers, although circumstantial evidence suggests they were Algonkian. They travelled to France under very different circumstances from the Indians whom Cartier had seized several decades earlier. Like many Indians who were taken to France in the seventeenth century, they were probably the sons of headmen who already were on good terms with the French and could be confident that their sons would be returned to them the following summer. The traders from St. Malo hoped that these Indians would learn to speak French, so they might serve as interpreters when it came to discussing

matters of policy. Already, however, a *lingua franca* was developing along the lower St. Lawrence that was made up partly of European and partly of Algonkian words, and was used for trading and elementary communication (Biggar 1930:453–54; Lescarbot 1907–14, 2:24).

The pre-eminent role that Tadoussac played in the fur trade into the early part of the seventeenth century was no accident. As we have already seen, even in prehistoric times, the Saguenay River was the terminus of a trade route stretching across central Quebec and westward to Lake Superior. Although the St. Lawrence Iroquoians travelled down-river beyond Tadoussac, they did not claim this region as their own territory. Its original inhabitants were probably Montagnais, an Algonkian-speaking, hunting and gathering people.

In 1603, Champlain observed that Tadoussac was a focal point for various groups who gathered there in the summer to trade. These included the Etchemin or Malecite, a Maritime group that was on good terms with the local Montagnais. By then the Etchemin were already hard-pressed by the Micmac who were expanding their hunting territories westward as their dependence on the fur trade was increased (Biggar 1922–36, 1:295–96). Since the Micmac had steadier access to iron hatchets, they were generally successful in their wars. By the 1620s, many Etchemin were forced to settle north of the St. Lawrence on a permanent basis (Sagard 1866:149–50). Once European traders began to visit Tadoussac, the hope of obtaining hatchets must have attracted these Indians northward, first to trade and later as settlers. It is also possible that in the early days the Stadaconans came there to trade, but this is purely hypothetical.

Of greatest importance, however, was the trade that passed through the hands of the Montagnais who lived in the Saguenay Valley. Unlike the Micmac and Malecite, these bands did not sacrifice their freedom to exploit the abundant food resources of the St. Lawrence Valley in order to devote more time to hunting in the northern forests.[25] Instead, they used their position astride the Saguenay River to obtain furs from Indians who already lived in the interior. The latter were not permitted to travel down the Saguenay to trade with the Europeans and, as competition became more intense, some were killed for attempting to do so (Thwaites 1896–1901, 8:41). The Indians from the interior were encouraged to visit the Montagnais of the Saguenay region and to barter their beaver skins for goods the Montagnais had purchased from the French. Thus the Montagnais established for themselves an important role as middlemen who profited by exchanging trade goods supplied by the French for furs they did not have to trap. The extent of this trade in the late sixteenth century

is revealed by geographical information that Champlain was able to collect on his first visit to this area. By means of intermediaries, European trade goods were reaching Hudson Bay and furs were coming south from there (Biggar 1922–36, 1:123–24). It also seems likely that this trade had extended westward along the old copper route to the headwaters of the St. Maurice and Ottawa Rivers.[26] The key location in this trading system was Lake St. John, which was the hub of a far-flung network of inter-connected lakes and rivers.

Advantageous as the position of middleman was for the Montagnais of Tadoussac, it should not be imagined as an *ad hoc* development. The rules underlying this trade appear to have been as old as trade in eastern Canada. Of fundamental importance was a general agreement that one tribe did not have the right to travel, without permission, across the territory of another. Groups who lacked experience trading with Europeans often preferred to allow dealings with these strangers to remain in the hands of Indians who already had an alliance with them. By spreading rumours about how dangerous the Europeans were, and, at the same time, preventing the Europeans and the Indians from the interior from meeting one another, the Montagnais both retained the friendship of these tribes and profited by giving them fewer European goods for their furs than they in turn received from the French for them.

The Disappearance of the St. Lawrence Iroquoians

Sometime between 1542 and 1603, not only the Stadaconans but all the Iroquoian-speaking inhabitants of the St. Lawrence Valley vanished. It is uncertain when this happened, and how it came about has been the subject of much tenuous and often misleading speculation. Many hypotheses have been based on assumptions about the ethnic identity of these people that now are either abandoned or rendered very doubtful. One thing is certain: in the seventeenth century no tribe, or portion of a tribe, was explicitly identified as being descended from these peoples.

No eye witness accounts of the St. Lawrence Iroquoians are available after Roberval ceased his efforts to colonize the St. Lawrence Valley. Marc Lescarbot, in his *History of New France*, attributed the disappearance of the Hochelagans to an Iroquois invasion around 1600.[27] Denis Jamet, a Recollet writing from Quebec in 1615, gave a similar explanation for the disappearance of the St. Lawrence Iroquoians, but dated the event nearer

the time of Cartier's visit. He also claimed to know of an aged Huron who remembered seeing their villages prior to their destruction.[28] Later tales interpreted as accounting for the fate of the St. Lawrence Iroquoians have, however, received more attention from historians and anthropologists. Nicolas Perrot (1911:42–47), writing between 1680 and 1718, stated that the Iroquois were the original inhabitants of the St. Lawrence Valley and had been driven out by the Algonkians.[29] Perrot does not give the source for this story, which may be based on Mohawk or Algonkian oral traditions concerning the struggle for control of the St. Lawrence Valley that was going on between these groups early in the seventeenth century. The Iroquois were not, however, living in the St. Lawrence Valley at that time or, as the archaeological evidence shows, at any earlier period; hence they cannot be identified with the St. Lawrence Iroquoians. Thus, the claim must be rejected that Perrot's story, or a similar suggestion by Charles Aubert de La Chesnaye (cited by Bailey 1933:106), has any connection with the fate of the St. Lawrence Iroquoians. Similarly, a Jesuit record that certain Algonkin who were living in the lower Ottawa Valley in the first half of the seventeenth century claimed to have been driven from Montreal Island by the Huron has been interpreted as proof that the St. Lawrence Iroquoians were dispersed by the Huron (Thwaites 1896–1901, 22:215–17; 29:173).

There are serious doubts concerning the accuracy with which both the Perrot and Jesuit traditions were recorded. It has been suggested that Perrot confused the terms Iroquois and Iroquet and that his story is merely another version of Charlevoix's tale about how the Algonkin group known as the Petite Nation, or Nation of Iroquet, was driven into the lower Ottawa Valley by other Algonkian-speaking peoples. It has also been suggested that, in their story, the Jesuits inadvertently wrote Huron when they meant Iroquois (Pendergast and Trigger 1972:79, 80). Elsewhere, I have presented an extended critique of all the material from the seventeenth and eighteenth centuries that has a bearing on the fate of the St. Lawrence Iroquoians and have argued that none of it provides a reliable basis for reconstructing the history of the St. Lawrence Iroquoians in the late sixteenth century (ibid. 71–92). Instead, any study of this period must be based on an attempt to determine the general processes that were at work in the St. Lawrence Valley between the visits of Cartier and Champlain. This requires a detailed consideration of the effects that the growth of the fur trade, and of European influence generally, may have had on intertribal relations in this area.

In 1930, Harold Innis (1956:12–15) proposed that the Iroquoians were

expelled from the St. Lawrence Valley by the Montagnais and neighbouring Algonkian tribes. He argued that, because of their geographical position
and easy access to furs, the Algonkians were the first to receive iron axes
and thus they were able to wage war against the agricultural tribes living
up-river. Innis suggested that they attacked the Iroquoians in order to
control the St. Lawrence River as a trade route. Although this updating
of Perrot's theory won the support of Bailey (1933), Fenton (1940:174–75),
and others, it has serious weaknesses. It overlooks the fact that relations
between adjacent horticultural and hunting peoples in eastern North
America were generally friendly, since such groups were able to exchange
surplus corn for skins and dried meat. As the Algonkians living in the
interior spent more time hunting in order to participate in the fur trade,
they would have become more dependent on the Iroquoians for agricultural
produce and in this way the Iroquoians would have been able to secure
more furs to trade with the French. Thus, with the development of the fur
trade, relations between these two groups should have become friendlier,
rather than more hostile. Under these circumstances, it seems unlikely that
the St. Lawrence Iroquoians would have prevented the Algonkians from
using the river.

In the sixteenth century, large numbers of Stadaconans used to travel
to the Gaspé and the north shore of the Gulf of St. Lawrence, where they
were able to secure European goods. It is possible that easier access to iron
weapons enabled the Micmac to expel the Stadaconans from their fishing
grounds in the Gaspé Peninsula, but, at best, only vague memories of the
struggle for control of this region may be preserved in Micmac legends
concerning their wars with the Kwedech, a hostile tribe that used to live
along the St. Lawrence (Fenton 1940:174–75). The Montagnais around
Tadoussac could have been drawn into the wars that the Micmac may have
waged against the Stadaconans late in the sixteenth century. On the other
hand, these wars seem to have had a very specific objective: control over
hunting and fishing rights in the Gaspé Peninsula. There is therefore no
reason to believe that such a struggle would have culminated in the
destruction of the Stadaconans.

More recently, Bernard Hoffman (1961:202–14) has attempted to
explain the disappearance of the St. Lawrence Iroquoians in terms of
economic developments similar to those that were at work in the Maritimes.
He noted that the Stadaconan subsistence economy was heavily based on
the resources of the St. Lawrence, but ignored the horticultural orientation of the Hochelagans. Because of this, he erroneously assumed that
his analysis of the Stadaconans would apply to the whole of the St. Lawrence

Valley. Hoffman argued that, as the fur trade spread up the St. Lawrence Valley, the Indians grew increasingly dependent on hunting. Thus, when fur-bearing mammals became depleted near the river, they were forced to move inland in search of game. This led to a still further decline in time spent fishing, and hunting became the basis of their subsistence economy, as well as a source of furs. Because hunting was less productive than fishing, this change resulted in "social disorganization," which, in turn, made these Indians fall easy prey to the Iroquois who invaded the St. Lawrence Valley around 1600.

Hoffman's theory has several major weaknesses. It does not take account of the historical fact that the fur trade developed in the Saguenay Valley and then spread westward across central Quebec some time before the St. Lawrence became a major artery of trade. It does not explain why the Iroquois attacked the Indians in the St. Lawrence Valley or why the Stadaconans and Hochelagans disappeared as groups, as opposed to being forced from their tribal territories. The process of social disorganization is neither defined nor explained and, finally, Hoffman's reconstruction of events in the St. Lawrence Valley does not correspond with what is known about conditions there early in the seventeenth century. While it is true that, up-river from Tadoussac, the valley was largely deserted, this was not because its inhabitants had moved inland to hunt for fur-bearing mammals. As the fur trade grew, groups who lived along the St. Lawrence tended to become middlemen rather than hunters. The latter process has already been documented for the Tadoussac area and is later attested along the St. Maurice and Ottawa Rivers. There is thus no reason to believe that trade alone would have been sufficient to cause the Indians living near the St. Lawrence to abandon their prosperous riverine economy. On the contrary, it would have encouraged them to remain close to the St. Lawrence.

Other hypotheses have been proposed to help explain the disappearance of the St. Lawrence Iroquoians. It has been noted that the St. Lawrence Valley lies close to the northern limits for growing corn and many writers have suggested that a series of bad harvests might have prompted these tribes to move farther south (Lloyd 1904:189; Fenton 1940:175; Barbeau 1949:228–29; Martijn 1969:96–101). There is evidence of a period of colder climates in North America beginning around A.D. 1550, but it is unclear whether the fluctuation was of sufficient amplitude to have affected the Stadaconans, who, in any case, were less dependent on horticulture than were their neighbours to the south. There is also no evidence that Iroquoian cultural development in the St. Lawrence Valley was adversely affected in any way by the cooler weather postulated between A.D. 1200

and 1450 (Martijn 1969:97). Finally, the theory of climatic deterioration does not explain why the St. Lawrence Iroquoians disappeared, as opposed merely to moving elsewhere as identifiable groups.

Fenton (1940:175) has suggested that the Indians in this region may have been decimated by European diseases in the latter half of the sixteenth century. While there is no direct evidence to support this suggestion, it is not impossible that European diseases were a factor contributing to their disappearance. In the next century, Father Pierre Biard attributed many deaths and illnesses to the European food and drink that the Indians con-consumed while gathering at the ships to trade (Thwaites 1896–1901, 3:105–7). Fenton (ibid.) has also speculated that, in order to trade more easily, the Stadaconans may have abandoned their hilltop forts and settled nearer the river, thus exposing themselves more to the attacks of their enemies. While each of these suggestions is worth considering, more aggressive hypotheses are required to bring the period we are discussing into line with the historical realities of the better documented period that follows.

It is clear from the writings of Samuel de Champlain that early in the seventeenth century no tribe was living in the St. Lawrence Valley above Tadoussac. Algonkian fishing parties visited the river for short periods, but the Algonkians stood in mortal terror of the Iroquois, who dominated the region. Champlain is emphatic that they were unable to travel along the St. Lawrence for fear of the Iroquois war parties that were infesting the banks of the river (Biggar 1922–36, 1:137). These reports add weight to those of Lescarbot and Jamet and suggest that the depopulation of the region was the result of warfare, which, by the beginning of the seventeenth century, had given the Iroquois, or more specifically the Mohawk, control of the upper St. Lawrence Valley. They also suggest that the St. Lawrence Iroquoians were either annihilated or dispersed in these wars, as the early traditions maintain was the case.

The course of events leading to the destruction of the St. Lawrence Iroquoians and to the Mohawk domination of the valley is more difficult to reconstruct. At present, we can no more than suggest a number of alternative hypotheses. It is possible that the Stadaconans and Hochelagans were destroyed at the same time by the same enemy, but it is also possible that they met separate ends. The Stadaconans may have been destroyed by their traditional enemies, the Toudaman, but, as already noted, the arguments in favour of this theory are not entirely convincing. If we assume that the Stadaconans were eliminated separately, the most attractive hypothesis is that they were destroyed by the Hochelagans. Rivalry over trade was

already evident between these two groups in 1535, and it may have been the Stadaconans' desire to control trade with the interior, more than their hatred of the French, that led them to oppose Europeans travelling beyond Tadoussac after 1542. As the Hochelagans came to want more European goods, they may have grown increasingly hostile to Stadaconan claims. Unable to bribe the partly horticultural Stadaconans with their surplus corn, it is possible that the Hochelagans attacked and dispersed them around 1580, thus making it possible for Europeans again to travel up-river. If so, this event provides one of the earliest examples of the difficulties encountered by small tribes when they attempted to maintain an exclusive position as middlemen between European traders and more powerful tribes living farther inland.

The fate of the Hochelagans is equally problematical. Conceivably, they might have been attacked by the Algonkian-speaking peoples of central Quebec and the Ottawa Valley who desired more direct access to French traders below Quebec. Yet, the northern Algonkians are unlikely to have destroyed a horticultural group living adjacent to them. The Huron are another possibility and some antiquarians have interpreted the Ottawa Valley Algonkin tradition of a Huron attack on Montreal Island as having significance for the disappearance of Hochelaga (Lighthall 1899). Of still greater importance is the archaeological evidence that suggests a long tradition of warfare between the proto-Huron and the Iroquoians of the upper St. Lawrence Valley. This warfare came to an end late in the sixteenth century. The Huron may have conquered the Hochelagans, with the victorious tribes incorporating some of the vanquished into their own ranks.

Yet, even if the proto-Huron and the St. Lawrence Iroquoians had been enemies for a long time, what reason did they have for expanding their traditional warfare to the point of annihilation? The Hochelagans may have sought to control trade with the interior and this may have prompted the Huron to attack them. The use of iron weapons could also have given the Hochelagans an advantage, which caused the numerically superior Huron to unite and eliminate them as an act of self-defence. While the latter argument must be given some weight, neither of these explanations is particularly convincing. By themselves, the Hochelagans could not deprive the Huron of European goods, since such material came from the Saguenay along the old copper route. Moreover, the archaeological and early historical evidence does not suggest that the Huron were deeply involved in trading for European goods much before 1600, or that they were seeking to make direct contact with European traders prior to 1609.

Under these conditions, it is highly unlikely that the Huron were sufficiently motivated, either by an unsatisfied desire for trade goods or by fear of the Hochelagans, to attempt to eliminate the latter as middlemen. Because they lived so far inland, the Huron were relatively protected from the challenges that were transforming the lives of their neighbours nearer the coast.

In the late sixteenth century, the Mohawk found themselves in very different circumstances. In the north, their most productive hunting territories were directly adjacent to those of the tribes that lived in the St. Lawrence Valley. Because they were more dependent on hunting than were the entreprenurial Huron of Simcoe County, the Mohawk were seriously threatened by any change in the balance of power between themselves and their northern neighbours. Moreover, by comparison with these tribes, the Mohawk were very poorly located for trade with Europeans. The most direct water route to the St. Lawrence ran north through Lake Champlain and along the Richelieu River, but this was a route that could be barred by the St. Lawrence Iroquoians whenever they wished to do so. The Mohawk were also at a disadvantage by comparison with the coastal tribes of New England, who could obtain goods from occasional European ships or, on a more regular basis, from the Micmac and Malecite. Farther south, European ships appeared less frequently off the coast, but, even there, three short-lived European colonies were founded north of Florida between 1526 and 1590 (Trudel 1963:277). These colonies and irregular coastal trade seem to have aroused the interest of the Susquehannock in acquiring European goods, well before the beginning of the seventeenth century.[30] Verrazzano had viewed the mouth of the Hudson River in 1524, but no Europeans are known to have sailed up the river prior to 1609. Moreover, the Mohawk did not have direct access even to this potential artery of trade, since Mahican territory intervened. Instead of the tribes who lived nearest the sources of European goods being the friends of the Mohawk, they mostly seem to have been peoples with whom the Mohawk had been at war for a long time.

In spite of this, European goods appear in Iroquois sites as far west as the Seneca by the late sixteenth century. Most of the early material is found as offerings in individual graves. In the earliest sites, a few iron axes and large iron knives have been found, and occasionally some round or oval glass beads. Brass kettles and beads made from fragments of such kettles are also reported. The influx of European goods increased rapidly and soon such goods begin to appear in village refuse. Charles F. Wray and Harry L. Schoff (1953:54–55, 62–63) date the earliest European goods between

A.D. 1550 and 1575 and are convinced that, before 1590, stone axes and flint knives had given way to European equivalents as far west as the Seneca tribe. Yet, their dates for these sites, which are based on the estimated periodicity of the removal of villages to new sites, may be twenty-five to fifty years too early (W. Noble, personal communication 1970). Even so, the likelihood that small quantities of European goods were reaching the Seneca prior to 1600 suggests that all the Iroquois tribes must have been obtaining such goods.

Some of this material may have been obtained through trade, although items that were useful in war, such as iron axes, would probably not have been exchanged willingly by rival groups living nearer the St. Lawrence. When Champlain was accompanying his Algonkian allies in 1609, he encountered a party of Mohawk warriors at the southern tip of Lake Champlain. When they saw the enemy, the Mohawk are said to have erected a barricade with poor axes which they sometimes acquired in war or with ones made of stone (Biggar 1922–36; 2:96). The poor axes are clearly cheap iron ones, manufactured for trade with the Indians. Champlain's statement indicates that, as late as 1609, the main way the Mohawk acquired European axes was by capturing them in war. It also suggests that the earliest "trade goods" found among the four western tribes either were gifts from the Mohawk or were captured by warriors from these tribes fighting alongside the Mohawk against the Indians who lived in the St. Lawrence Valley. Once the Ottawa Valley Algonkin started to obtain European goods, the Oneida and Onondaga probably emulated the Mohawk and raided these groups in their home territory. By crossing Lake Ontario and following the Rideau River northward, it would have been easier for these tribes to attack the Algonkin than to wage war on the St. Lawrence.

The Iroquois may have been forced to fight to obtain trade goods, because the Hochelagans sought to treat them in the same manner as the Stadaconans had treated the Hochelagans. Possibly, the Mohawk and Hochelagans were traditional enemies. If so, the latter may not have wanted European goods to reach the Iroquois, or at least attempted to prevent them from getting knives and hatchets, which would have been useful in war. Such a situation would have put the Mohawk at a serious disadvantage and made obtaining European knives and hatchets seem a matter of life and death to them. The desire for unrestricted access to trading stations on the St. Lawrence, or to secure iron tools in war, may have led to an all-out attack on the Hochelagans resulting in their destruction not long before A.D. 1600, the date suggested by Lescarbot (map 8).

Yet, by invading the St. Lawrence Valley as far down-river as Tadoussac,

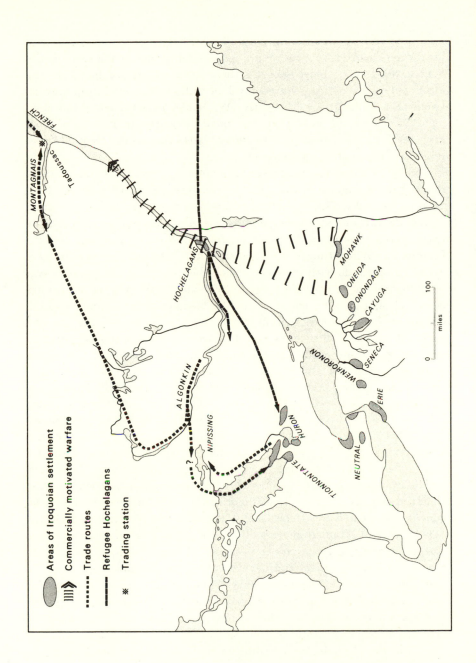

MAP 8. *Intertribal relations, late sixteenth century.*

the Mohawk seem to have encountered more difficulties than they had anticipated. Whether the Stadaconans were dispersed by the Iroquois, or had disappeared earlier, the Iroquois' attack on the lower parts of the St. Lawrence brought them into conflict with the Montagnais, who had always lived around Tadoussac and who were now laying claim to the Quebec City area. This generated a conflict, the first phase of which lasted until about 1610.

The climax of Iroquois power on the St. Lawrence seems to have been about 1600. Sagard reported that in 1625 the remains of an Iroquois fortification were visible at Quebec, which they had built after they had seized the spot from the Montagnais (Sagard 1866:271–72). The "Montagnais" mentioned in this story could be the St. Lawrence Iroquoians, especially since Sagard states that they had worked the soil prior to being driven away and forced to wander in the forests. It must be remembered, however, that, even in the seventeenth century, the Algonkians who lived in the St. Lawrence Valley planted limited amounts of corn, when conditions were peaceful enough to suggest a reasonable return for their effort.[31] The fortification that Sagard refers to was probably a temporary war camp, such as the Mohawk erected elsewhere in the valley, and it is not unlikely that the people they attacked were the Montagnais, who had settled at Quebec after it was abandoned by the Stadaconans. The fort does not indicate Iroquois settlement in the valley, but it does suggest that war parties had penetrated at least as far downstream as Quebec City. Significantly, however, Sagard states that the Iroquois were not able to hold onto this position and therefore ceased to frequent the region.

If our interpretation of these events is correct, we have in these early conflicts on the St. Lawrence the first evidence of the Iroquois becoming involved in wars that were not of a traditional type. The motive for this conflict was clearly economic and was connected with the fur trade. Instead of seeking to take individual prisoners, the Mohawk sought to annihilate or disperse whole populations whose activities were felt to be a threat to their well-being. In traditional warfare, the aim was to preserve one's enemies as a group in order to be able to go on fighting with them indefinitely. Wars may have been fought in prehistoric times to eliminate an enemy completely, but all known wars of this sort are in some way connected with trade with Europeans.

This war turned the St. Lawrence Valley above Tadoussac into a no-man's land, traversed by Iroquois raiding parties and generally avoided by the Montagnais and Algonkin, even though this meant losing some of their best fishing stations. At the same time, by having attacked the Montagnais

and failed to secure control of the river as far as Tadoussac, the Mohawk had lost an important objective. Their principal short-term benefit was probably to secure European goods from groups they had either defeated or frightened into abandoning their settlements. Champlain was able to travel up-river as far as Montreal Island in the summer of 1603, but he wrote that a French settlement at Three Rivers would be a great boon for the freedom of tribes who dared not come that way for fear of the Iroquois. At the very least, such a settlement would permit the Algonkian-speaking tribes to trade in peace (Biggar 1922–36, 1:137). He added that it might also make friends of the Iroquois, no doubt because they would then have a place to trade.

I have already stated that it is unclear when, and under what circumstances, the Iroquois confederacy developed. Although it reveals nothing about relations among the five Iroquois tribes at an earlier date, the distribution of the earliest European goods among all five tribes may indicate a considerable degree of friendship in the latter part of the sixteenth century. It is possible that a common desire for such goods led to growing cooperation, which greatly strengthened the Iroquois confederacy, if it did not bring it into existence (Tooker 1964:3–4 n. 1). It is also possible that warriors from all five tribes participated in the initial attacks on the St. Lawrence.

The Iroquois confederacy does not appear, however, to have been designed as an offensive coalition; instead, it functioned to suppress blood feuds and to promote friendship among member tribes. Moreover, for several decades, it was the Mohawk who were to undertake aggressive action to secure trading privileges with Europeans, while the four other tribes were to play a more passive role in such endeavours. The main motives underlying the formation of the confederacy, or its development, may have been the desire of the four western tribes to secure trade goods and the reciprocal wish among the Mohawk for peace with their western neighbours in order to be able to pursue their warlike policies on the St. Lawrence more effectively. Moreover, as trade spread inland, peace among the Iroquois permitted the western members of the confederacy to campaign against the northern Algonkians and ultimately against the Huron, and, by plundering these groups, to secure increasing amounts of European goods. The simultaneous development of an enlarged Huron confederacy and the increasing amounts of trade goods becoming available to the Susquehannock and other tribes to the south must have served to maintain and reinforce the Iroquois alliance during the decades that followed.

Survivors

Even if the St. Lawrence Iroquoians were dispersed in one of the ways outlined above, their ultimate fate remains uncertain. Lescarbot, apparently
one of our more knowledgeable sources, speaks summarily of extermination, while Jamet states that they were dislodged by their fierce wars
and retreated one after the other farther inland. Conceivably, some were
taken prisoner by the Iroquois and absorbed into one or more of their
tribes. Yet no historical, archaeological, or linguistic evidence affirms this.
Some ethnologists have speculated that the St. Lawrence Iroquoians fled
inland to join the Huron confederacy and are the ancestors of the Arendarhonon, Tahontaenrat, or both (Tooker 1964:3 n. 1). Archaeologically,
this does not seem to be possible. Two other suggestions deserve more careful consideration.

The first is that remnants of the Hochelagan population survived among
the Algonkin who lived in the lower part of the Ottawa Valley in the
seventeenth century and that it was their presence which led these Algonkin to claim they had once lived on Montreal Island (Lighthall 1899). The
main arguments in support of this theory concern the identity of a group
known as the Onontchataronon. It is generally believed that Onontchataronon was merely the Huron name for the Weskarini, or Petite Nation,
an Algonkin group that lived in the vicinity of the Rouge, Petite Nation,
and Lièvre Rivers. The two names are equated on the Sanson Map of 1656
and Sagard states that Onontchataronon (which he transcribes *Quieunon-
tateronon* and is the same name he gives to the Tionnontaté) was the
Huron name for the Petite Nation.[32] It is also significant that while one
of the principal headmen of the Onontchataronon was called only by the
Iroquoian name of Tawiscaron, the Jesuits regarded their mission to this
tribe as one that required an Algonkian-speaking priest (Thwaites 1896–
1901, 27:37). The Huron gave Iroquoian names to all the tribes and important headmen with whom they had dealings; hence it can be argued
that it is nothing more than coincidence that Iroquoian names were applied
so often to this group and to its leaders.

On the other hand, the Petite Nation and the Onontchataronon are nowhere explicitly identified as being the same people in Jesuit documents
from the first half of the seventeenth century. Only the Onontchataronon
are said to have lived on the Island of Montreal and, on a number of
occasions, when lists of tribes are given, the Onontchataronon and Petite
Nation are enumerated separately (18:229; 21:117; 24:269; 29:145).

While all of the sources agree that the Petite Nation lived east of the Ottawa Valley, the *Jesuit Relation* for 1640 suggests that the Onontchataronon lived to the west of the river (18:229). Finally, Percy J. Robinson (1942) has argued that the name of the group contains the Iroquoian root *onnonta*, signifying hill or mountain. He has also attempted to demonstrate that Onontchataronon and Hochelaga are the same name, but less convincingly in my opinion. Nevertheless, it is at least possible that the Onontchataronon were an independent tribe, or a branch of the Weskarini that contained considerable numbers of Hochelagan refugees. If the group was either wholly or partly of Iroquoian origin, all of its members must have been heavily Algonkianized by the early seventeenth century, since the Algonkian language seems to have been used alongside, or in place of, Iroquoian as its working language. It must be remembered, however, that any hypothesis concerning this group is highly speculative and that even a small number of refugees might have given rise to the claim that there was an historical connection between the Onontchataronon and the former inhabitants of Montreal Island. It may also be noted in passing that, if there is any truth to the Onontchataronon claim to include Hochelagan refugees, there may also be some truth to their claim that other Hochelagan refugees moved south to join the Abenaki (Thwaites 1896–1901, 22:215).

The second suggestion is that some of the St. Lawrence Iroquoians may have found refuge among the Huron, not as a single tribe, but as remnants who became members of already existing tribes. Until recently, however, the evidence to support this theory has been highly circumstantial. For example, Jamet's claim that in 1615 a Huron reported having seen a village along the St. Lawrence many years before has been interpreted as proof that this man and his people had migrated from there to the Huron country (Le Blant and Baudry 1967:350 n. 3). In view of the propensity of Iroquoian men to travel, this interpretation is at best hazardous.

In recent years, however, archaeological evidence has indicated that, sometime in the late sixteenth century, large amounts of St. Lawrence Iroquoian pottery began appearing among the Tionnontaté (at the Sidey-Mackay site) (Wintemberg 1946) as well as in Huron sites along the Trent waterway. In particular, this appears to be so at the Trent site, which has been partially excavated as of 1971. Peter Pratt (personal communication 1971) is of the opinion that the evidence from the Trent Valley indicates the absorption of groups of refugees from the St. Lawrence. Like the Wenroronon refugees of 1638, these people were adopted into several Huron villages to avoid economic hardship and the political complications

that would ensue had they founded their own village or villages in Huron territory. If we are correct in believing that it was the Arendarhonon who were living in the Trent Valley prior to A.D. 1600, they may have absorbed most of the people who fled westward from the St. Lawrence.

While it may be objected that the St. Lawrence Iroquoians were unlikely to seek refuge among their traditional enemies, this objection is not insuperable. In later times, a whole Huron tribe was to settle among the Seneca, after the Iroquois had inflicted far more serious injuries on the Huron than would have resulted from the traditional warfare between the Huron and the St. Lawrence Iroquoians. Having been decimated by a Mohawk attack that went far beyond the limits of traditional warfare, the St. Lawrence Iroquoians may have been happy to seek refuge among former foes. With the Iroquois becoming more aggressive, the Arendarhonon and the other Huron may have been equally pleased to see their own ranks reinforced by newcomers.

If this reconstruction is accurate, it explains a number of isolated, but nevertheless significant, pieces of information that can be gleaned from the early records. First, it accounts for the Arendarhonon's special interest in the St. Lawrence Valley and the close relationship they had with the Onontchataronon and, possibly through them, with the Algonkin of the Ottawa Valley generally. Throughout the first half of the seventeenth century, large numbers of Onontchataronon were in the habit of spending each winter in Arendarhonon territory. This would be more easily explained if remnants of the St. Lawrence Iroquoians had become attached to both groups and were working to promote contacts between them.

It would also explain Champlain's belief that, at some time in the past, the Iroquois had driven the Ottawa Valley Algonkin out of the St. Lawrence Valley (Biggar 1922–36, 2:280–81) and had caused the Huron living in the Trent Valley to abandon their tribal territory and seek refuge in Simcoe County (3:59). While Champlain interpreted this information, gathered through inexperienced interpreters, as evidence of a massive Iroquois offensive sometime in the sixteenth century, it seems more likely that these traditions refer to the dispersal of Iroquoian refugees from the St. Lawrence Valley about twenty years before. Champlain also recorded an ambiguous claim to the effect that in the past either the Entouhonoron (a term which appears to mean the four western Iroquois tribes) were forced to flee some forty or fifty leagues, or that they had forced the Huron to remove that distance.[33] This has been interpreted as support for the now discredited theory that the St. Lawrence Iroquoians were the ancestors of one or more

of the historic Iroquois tribes. More likely, it refers either to yet other St. Lawrence Iroquoians moving south to join their conquerors or to the Iroquois forcing such groups to flee westward to join the Huron and Tionnontaté.

The interpretation of events in the late sixteenth century outlined above has the advantage of explaining many hitherto enigmatic and apparently contradictory statements in a more satisfactory manner than so far has been achieved. Many other examples can be found of events which have happened to only a small number of people being expanded by oral traditions, to embrace much larger groupings to which these people belonged or became attached. It would appear that Sauk and Fox legends about origins on the east coast of the United States and a later flight inland, in fact refer to these groups accepting Sokoki and Mahican refugees from the Atlantic seaboard in the historic period (Brasser 1971:263).

The Birth of the French-Algonkian Alliance

The Mohawk attacks on the Montagnais living around Tadoussac and Quebec were to have an important and lasting influence on the history of the St. Lawrence Valley, because they occurred at the same time that French merchants were hoping to expand the fur trade. The conflict that ensued was to provide these merchants with the means by which they could extend their trading network along the St. Lawrence and the major tributaries flowing into it.

In the autumn of 1599, Pierre de Chauvin de Tonnetuit, a wealthy merchant of Honfleur, obtained a ten-year monopoly over the fur trade of New France, in return for a promise to settle 500 people there. The following spring, he set sail for Tadoussac with his partner, François Gravé Du Pont, and Pierre Du Gua de Monts, a native of Saintonge. Against the advice of these two men, who preferred a settlement up-river, Chauvin decided to establish a token colony at Tadoussac to serve as a trading post. He constructed a house twenty-five feet long and eighteen feet wide, which had a fireplace in the centre and was surrounded by a weak palisade and ditch. Throughout the summer, Chauvin carried on a brisk trade in beaver and other furs, before departing for France. He left behind sixteen men, who were to maintain his monopoly and begin trading as soon as possible the following spring. As a result of sickness, quarrelling, and lack of provisions, only five of these men lived through the winter. The sur-

vivors owed their lives to the Indians, who fed and cared for them. This disastrous experiment temporarily put an end to efforts at colonization along the St. Lawrence (Biggar 1901:42–44; Trudel 1963:235–42).

The following year, Chauvin apparently sent out only one ship and, in 1602, he sailed for the New World with two. In 1602, Chauvin's monopoly was altered to include certain other traders from St. Malo and Rouen. When he died early in 1603 the monopoly passed to Aymar de Chaste, who sent three ships to the St. Lawrence to trade and survey the region to find a more suitable location for settlement (Biggar 1901:44–50). An account of this voyage was published by Samuel de Champlain, who was an acquaintance of de Monts. Born at Brouage, in Saintonge, around 1570, Champlain had fought in the French wars of religion and afterwards claims to have travelled in the West Indies. His main qualification for accompanying this expedition seems to have been his skill as a painter and map-maker.[34]

The monopoly holders who were now spending the summers at Tadoussac were more anxious to establish a firm alliance with the Montagnais than the casual traders of an earlier period had been. They had to protect their monopoly against illegal competition, and particularly against the Basque whalers who continued to frequent the St. Lawrence. It was also in their interest to expand trade as rapidly as possible, which meant developing new ties, either directly or indirectly, with the northern hunting peoples. General outlines of a policy for dealing with the Indians had emerged as early as 1602.[35] This policy was based on three observations which embodied the considerable experience that had already been gained from trading with the Indians.

The first was the realization that it was more important to maintain good relations with the Indians living north of the St. Lawrence than with tribes living to the south. This was because the furs coming from the north were superior in quality to those coming from the south. Moreover, because of the extensive network of rivers in the north, furs could be accumulated and brought to the St. Lawrence in greater quantities from that direction.[36] This put the Iroquois at a serious disadvantage and guaranteed that in any quarrel in which it was believed necessary to choose between them and the northern Algonkians, the French would opt for an alliance with the Algonkians.

The second observation was that good trading relations depended upon broadly based alliances between the French and their Indian partners. The Montagnais of the Saguenay area were at war with the Mohawk and for some time appear to have been hard-pressed by them. Because of this, it was necessary to help them in their wars, both to free them to engage in

trade and to maintain their goodwill. Although the French were primarily interested in increasing trade, nothing won the confidence of these Indians more than did an offer of military assistance. Chauvin therefore promised the Montagnais that the French would settle among them and either compel the Iroquois to make peace or destroy them (Biggar 1922–36, 1:100).

The settlement in 1600 may already have been explained to the Indians as the fulfilment of such a promise, although we know nothing specific about Chauvin's relations with the Montagnais at that time. In 1602, two Indians from Tadoussac were taken to France and, while there, were presented to Henri IV. These Indians returned to Tadoussac the following spring to assure their people that the French king supported Chauvin's promises. This prompted Anadabijou, the headman of the Tadoussac band, to say the French would be welcome to settle there in order to help the Montagnais wage war on their enemies (1:101). In practice, however, the aim of the fur traders appears to have been to assist the Montagnais by supplying them with knives, hatchets, and other weapons that would give them an advantage over the Iroqouis. While not engaging directly in an Indian war, the French thereby showed their concern for the welfare of their Indian trading partners and were establishing a basis for closer cooperation and eventual settlement with a finesse that was lacking in Cartier's day. Although these fur traders are frequently condemned by historians for their reluctance to advocate the colonization of New France, in general their behaviour was admirably realistic and demonstrated a desire to get along with the Indians that did not exist among other Europeans who came to the New World.

The third observation was the need to encourage contact with tribes who lived in the interior. Until this time, most of the trade with the west had been channelled along the old copper route and thus was controlled by the Montagnais who lived around Tadoussac. Only a limited number of French ships travelled farther up-river, and those that did found few of the more westerly peoples coming to the banks of the St. Lawrence. Under normal circumstances, the Montagnais would have preferred to have these arrangements remain as they were; however, the Iroquois threat also made them anxious for allies who would help them to drive the Iroquois from the St. Lawrence. By 1603, or possibly earlier, they had drawn into an alliance not only some Etchemin, but also the Indians who lived north of the St. Lawrence as far west as the Ottawa Valley (1:103). The bands who lived to the east of Three Rivers were Montagnais, while those who lived to the west into the Ottawa Valley, were Algonkin (Thwaites 1896–1901, 23: 303–5). Although both groupings were Algonkian-speaking, they were

differentiated linguistically. The Algonkin also shared a number of cultural traits with the Algonkian and Iroquoian peoples who lived in the less rigorous environments to the south and west of them and they were marginally horticultural, while the Montagnais planted crops only very infrequently. In return for a military alliance against the Iroquois, these bands seem to have been free to come to Tadoussac and trade with the French (map 9).

The demand for European goods may have been expanding rapidly enough in the region north of Tadoussac to minimize the economic sacrifice that was involved for the Montagnais in granting such a privilege. Nevertheless, the trouble that Champlain had to go to a decade later to expand trade as far west as Lake Huron suggests that even at this early date the French may have been encouraging the development of an alliance that would open the St. Lawrence, both militarily and diplomatically, as an artery of trade for the Algonkian-speaking peoples of the interior. This goal appears to have been achieved harmoniously, because both the French and the Montagnais stood to gain from it, though in different ways. By introducing the more westerly Montagnais and the Algonkin to the French as their military allies, Anadabijou and his people not only made it easier for these Indians to establish contact with the French but also were enhancing their own prestige within the new alliance. Later, Anadabijou's grandson was to list as his ancestor's chief accomplishment that he had maintained the peace between these confederated Indian bands and the French (Biggar 1922–36, 5:64). Presumably this had become a traditional role in this family, beginning in his grandfather's day.

By 1603, the Algonkian alliance was beginning to hold its own against the Iroquois. When the French arrived at Tadoussac in May of that year, they found that over one thousand Montagnais, Algonkin, and Etchemin had gathered there. These Indians had erected a series of longhouses and were celebrating, with a scalp dance, a victory that they had probably gained over the Iroquois the year before (1:107–9). Among those who were present to meet the French was Tessouat, the headman of the Kichesipirini, or Islander Algonkin, whose summer camping ground was on Morrison Island, in the upper part of the Ottawa Valley.[37] In later years, because of their strategic location, Tessouat and his people were destined to exercise an important influence over the development of the fur trade. In order to reaffirm his friendship with the Algonkin and gain their support for a new foray against the Iroquois, Anadabijou presented them with French axes, swords, kettles, ornaments, and with food (1:109). Later, when he was travelling up the St. Lawrence River to Montreal Island,

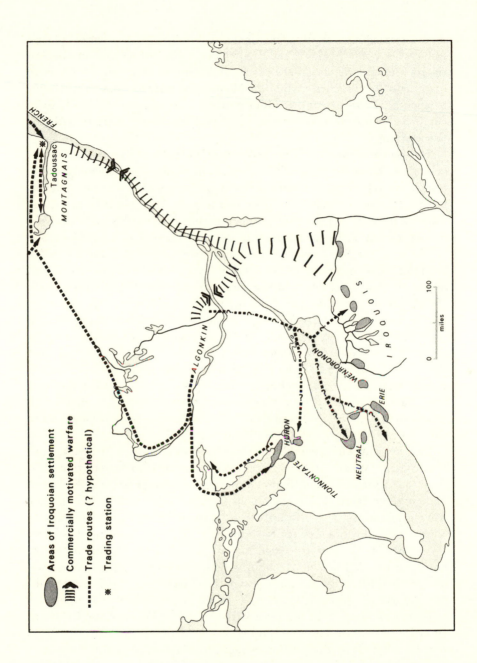

MAP 9. *Intertribal relations, 1603.*

Champlain encountered this confederated war party in a fortified camp at the mouth of the Richelieu River (1:141). They defeated three Iroquois canoes on Lake Champlain and returned to Tadoussac with the heads of the people they had killed. Before the French departed in mid-August, Begourat, the Montagnais leader of this party, entrusted his son to Gravé Du Pont, so that he might spend the winter in France. Begourat did this on the recommendation of Anadabijou, who was pleased by reports he had heard about the good treatment that the two Indians had received who had accompanied Gravé Du Pont to France the year before (1:188). Although the French do not appear to have reciprocated by leaving French youths to winter among the Montagnais, they had won the Indians' trust to the point that the latter were expressing their friendship in one of the most solemn ways known to them. They also expressed their sense of obligation for what they conceived of as being a military alliance with the French, by giving Gravé Du Pont an Iroquois woman captive to take back to France with him (1:188). Among the Iroquoians and Algonkians, the sharing of captives was the sign of a military alliance.

The trip which in 1603 took Champlain and Gravé Du Pont to within sight of the Lachine Rapids was for these men a valuable reconnaissance. From an ethnological point of view, it is of interest because it reveals that the St. Lawrence Valley was almost completely deserted for fear of the Iroquois, although it was a time of year when many people would normally have been using the river. Apart from the Algonkian war party already mentioned, only a few groups were encountered fishing, and most of these were below Quebec. Also of interest is the geographical information that Champlain collected from the Montagnais who accompanied him and from certain Algonkin he encountered on the way. Although Champlain misconstrued what he was told about Lake Huron to sustain his hopes of finding a short route to the Pacific Ocean, it is clear that these Indians had a good working knowledge of the lower Great Lakes and had travelled on them. They described the St. Lawrence River in detail, as well as Lakes Ontario, Erie, and parts of Lake Huron. All of Champlain's informants mentioned Niagara Falls and some were familiar with the Trent River flowing into Lake Ontario. The Montagnais had never been much farther than Lake Erie, but some of the Algonkin claimed to have travelled on Lake Huron, although none had been to the west end of the lake (1:153–161). It is not known whether such extensive travel was common among the Algonkin and Montagnais in prehistoric times, but it seems likely to have been stimulated, at least in part, by the fur trade. That the St. Lawrence Valley and the lower Great Lakes were open for travel at this

time suggests that warfare between the four western Iroquois tribes, on the one hand, and the Huron and Algonkin, on the other, was not nearly so fierce as it was to become later.

In the course of his visit to the New World in 1603, Champlain became fascinated with the Maritime region of Canada. He saw it as a region with a milder climate than the St. Lawrence, potentially rich in mines, and possibly nearer an easier passage to the Far East than the St. Lawrence appeared to be. In 1603, Aymar de Chaste died and his monopoly passed to Pierre Du Gua de Monts. No doubt, Champlain's advice played an important part in de Monts's decision that while trading vessels would continue to be sent to the St. Lawrence, further efforts at colonization would be directed towards Acadia. A colony was established, first at the mouth of the Sainte Croix River in New Brunswick, and then at Port Royal in Nova Scotia. By 1607, however, it had become clear that it was impossible to enforce a monopoly along the winding and indented coasts of the Maritimes. Because of this, de Monts could not support a colony and compete on equal terms with those who were trading illegally. In 1607, the king, acting under pressure from the Paris hatters' corporation and from the merchants of St. Malo, who favoured free trade, had de Monts's privileges revoked, leaving him with a monopoly for only one more year. At this point, and again under Champlain's influence, de Monts began to turn his attention to the St. Lawrence, where furs were obtained at only a few critical points that could be policed more easily against rival traders. In the spring of 1608, Champlain was dispatched to the St. Lawrence to found a new settlement (Biggar 1901:51–68; 1922–36, 4:27–30).

On 3 June Champlain arrived at Tadoussac which, because of navigational hazards farther up the St. Lawrence, was for many years to remain the head of navigation. There he must have renewed his acquaintance with Anadabijou and the other Indians he had met five years earlier. By reminding them of the benefits that they had agreed would flow from French settlement, he secured their consent to found a new colony up-river. Travelling beyond Tadoussac in a pinnace, he selected a site for the new trading post at the narrows of Quebec, a location that would allow the occupants to prevent illicit traders from passing up-river. A patch of forest was cleared and a storehouse and three buildings erected. This "Habitation" was surrounded by a palisade and a ditch fifteen feet wide. To test the soil, gardens were prepared and wheat, rye, and other European crops were sown.

Shortly after arriving at Quebec, Champlain barely escaped a plot, which he claimed was led by a locksmith named Jean Duval, to kill him and

destroy the colony. Duval was said to be hoping for a reward from the Basque traders, whose commerce on the river was threatened by de Monts's monopoly (Biggar 1922–36, 2:25–34). By their action, he and his fellow conspirators also may have hoped to avoid a dangerous winter at Quebec. As a result of this conspiracy, the Indians were treated to what, to them, must have been the inexplicable sight of Duval's severed head being exposed by his own people from the most conspicuous point in their settlement.

During the summer of 1608, and the following disease-ridden winter, Champlain had ample opportunity to assess the situation on the St. Lawrence. In 1603, the Montagnais and their allies had been holding their own against the Iroquois and had been victorious in isolated skirmishes. Five years later, these Indians were still holding their own, but remained very much afraid of the Iroquois, who outnumbered them. The intervening period seems to have been largely one of inconclusive struggle. Although many Indians came to Quebec from mid-September to mid-October to fish for eels, they camped close to the French settlement and, on numerous occasions, their fear of the Iroquois was so great that they came to the habitation to spend the night. Champlain permitted the women and children to enter the habitation, but made the men stay outside, under French protection. These Indians expressed gratitude for the French presence and said that if the French remained at Quebec, they would learn to protect themselves (2:50–51). Later in the winter, the Indians left to hunt beaver and then elk. In February, they returned starving from the south shore of the river to beg food from the French, their supply of eels having run out long before (2:53–56). These Indians may have simply been enduring a hungry period in the early spring, or the weather that year may have produced a spell of bad hunting. More likely, however, Champlain was witnessing the disruption of a traditional subsistence pattern, resulting from fear of the Iroquois.

Since 1603, the Indians who lived in the valleys of the Batiscan, St. Maurice, and Ottawa Rivers had grown more accustomed to dealing with Europeans. An increasing number of Europeans may also have been travelling up the St. Lawrence to trade with them. In order to put an end to the Iroquois menace, so that these Indians could trade freely along the St. Lawrence, and to reinforce the prestige of de Monts's traders in the face of competition from freebooters, it was decided that a new policy was needed. Instead of merely supplying their Indian allies with weapons, henceforth armed Frenchmen would offer to travel with them on raids against the Iroquois, in an effort to defeat the enemy. We do not know

whether this idea originated with Champlain or Gravé Du Pont, who was de Monts's deputy. Since de Monts's monopoly was about to expire, any action that would strengthen his company's ties with the Indians of the St. Lawrence must have seemed desirable. In addition, both Gravé Du Pont and Champlain were keen to promote the exploration of the interior and this would be achieved by Champlain accompanying his Indian allies into regions that no European had yet visited. Early in 1608, Champlain and Gravé Du Pont discussed plans for military aid to their Indian allies. Later that year, Champlain seems to have agreed to accompany a Montagnais expedition up the Richelieu River the following summer (2:63–64). In August, he conferred with the son of Iroquet, one of the most important headmen of the Onontchataronon. Champlain declared that he wished to help the Onontchataronon in their struggle against the Iroquois and seems to have arranged a general rendezvous for the following year (2:69). This meeting was to have important consequences, since the Onontchataronon were in the habit of wintering among the Arendarhonon.

Whether or not Champlain had conceived of the idea, he was carrying out a masterful piece of diplomacy. Up to this time, the French had sought to maintain the goodwill of the Indians by arming them so they could better fight their enemies, but they had only partly succeeded in their objective of opening the St. Lawrence as a trading route. For a long time, the French had hoped to arrange a peace between the Iroquois and Algonkians, so that both groups would be free to trade with them (1:100, 137). Yet, the French lacked the contacts, and their Indian allies the will, to bring this about. By introducing themselves and their guns into the struggle, de Monts's men hoped not only to drive the enemy from the St. Lawrence but to confirm the goodwill of their allies. By this time, they must have realized that among the Indians no better proof of goodwill could be offered to trading partners than to join them in fighting their enemies.

The Huron and the Early French Fur Trade

Historical and archaeological evidence both indicate that the Huron were obtaining European trade goods before they were in direct contact with the French. It is more difficult, however, given the limited amount of archaeological evidence available, to determine when European goods began to arrive in the Huron country. Sites containing small amounts of such goods are found to the south and east of the area that the Huron occupied when

they were first described by Europeans in 1615. These sites extend into the southern part of Simcoe County and eastward into the Trent Valley system (map 10). Within the historic Huron country, a limited number of sites have been found that contain only small amounts of European goods. These contrast with a much larger number of historic sites, which occur only in this area and yield much larger quantities of European goods.

It is therefore clear that sometime prior to 1615, but after European goods had begun to reach this part of Ontario, Huron settlements extended over a considerably more extensive area than they did in the historic period. Either the population was larger or villages were less compactly clustered. While the possibility of population decline as a result of European diseases in the late sixteenth century cannot be ruled out, the scattered distribution of the villages containing small amounts of trade goods suggests that the population was, in fact, more dispersed.

Although the relative proportion of sites containing large quantities of European goods, as opposed to those containing small amounts, might be used to calculate when these goods began to arrive in the Huron country, this method is open to numerous objections and any conclusions derived from it must be treated with great caution. We do not know exactly when European goods began to reach the Huron in large quantities, although it was probably after direct contact was established with the French in 1615. While all of the sites outside the region known to have been inhabited in 1615 had been abandoned by this date, the distinction that is made between sites with large and small amounts of European goods within the area of historic settlement is based on very limited evidence (map 11). Finally, the areas outside the historic Huron country are less well surveyed, from an archaeological point of view, than are those inside it, and even certain parts of the historic region, particularly in the Penetanguishene Peninsula, have received more cursory treatment than the rest (Heidenreich, personal communication, 1970). Since we are dealing with shifting populations, this too may bias the results.

Nevertheless, approximately 117 sites containing large quantities of European goods are presently recorded within the area of Huron settlement in historic times.[38] If we assume that all these sites date after 1610 and that villages shifted on an average of once every ten years, this gives a total of twenty-nine sites per decade. This is more than the eighteen to twenty-five villages estimated to be in existence at any one time by the French,[39] although it is possible that this discrepancy reflects shortcomings in the historical data. Many small villages may have gone unrecorded, particularly in the eastern part of the Huron country, which was regularly visited by

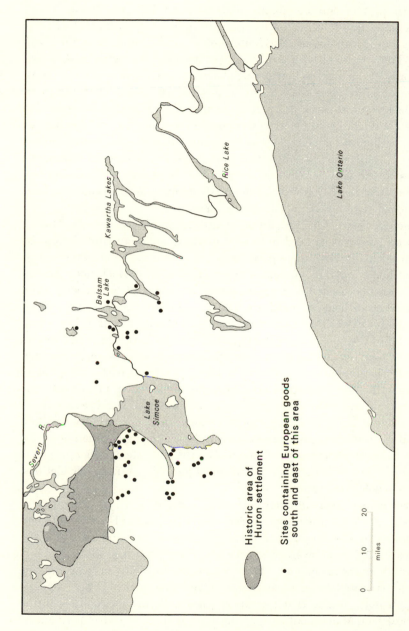

MAP 10. *Distribution of Huron sites containing small quantities of trade goods to the south and east of their area of settlement from 1615 onwards (after Heidenreich 1971: map 22).*

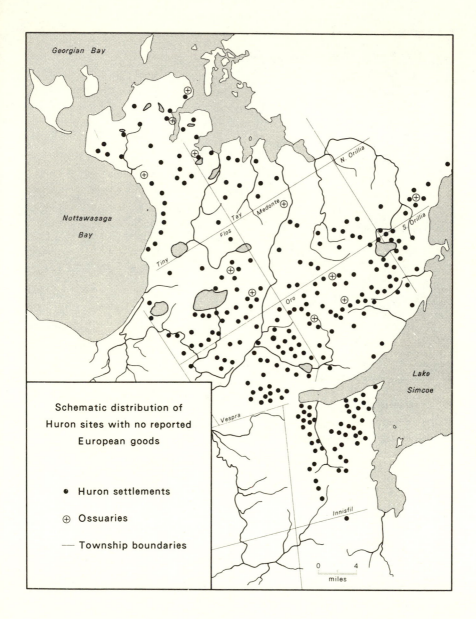

MAP 11. *Maps showing contraction of area of Huron settlement from prehistoric times into the historic period (sites dated in terms of quantities of European trade goods).*

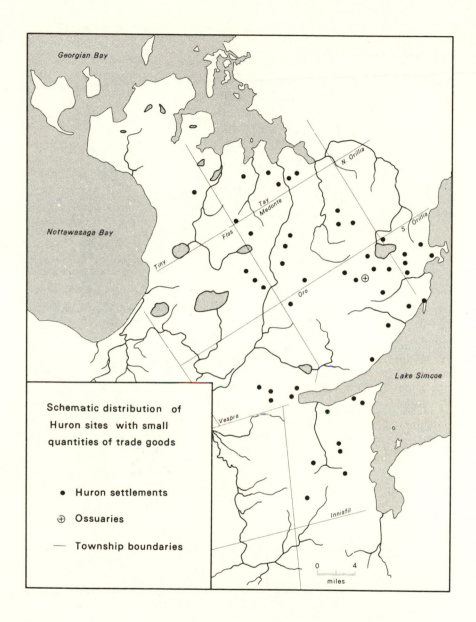

Georgian Bay

N. Orillia

Tay
Medonte

Nottawasaga Bay

S. Orillia

Tiny

Flos

Oro

Lake Simcoe

Vespra

Innisfil

Schematic distribution of
Huron sites with small
quantities of trade goods

● Huron settlements

⊕ Ossuaries

— Township boundaries

0   4
miles

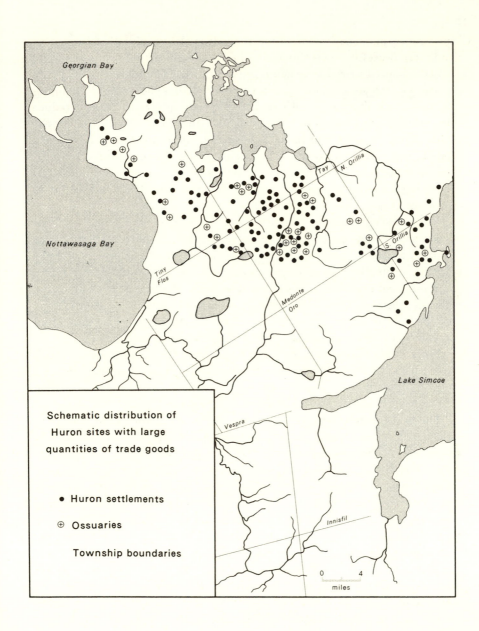

Georgian Bay

Nottawasaga Bay

Tay
N. Orillia

Tiny
Flos

Medonte
Oro

S. Orillia

Lake Simcoe

Vespra

Innisfil

Schematic distribution of
Huron sites with large
quantities of trade goods

● Huron settlements

⊕ Ossuaries

Township boundaries

0   4
miles

the French missionaries only after 1640. It is also possible that in earlier, and more peaceful, times this region had a more dispersed population, and hence produced more sites, than it did after 1640. The high mortality rate in the late 1630s is known to have resulted in some villages changing location twice during that decade; if this were general, it would reduce the number of villages in existence at one time to twenty-three. On the other hand, it is unrealistic to believe that all historic sites have been found, hence site counts are likely to go higher in the future. It must, therefore, be concluded that the archaeological enumeration includes out-lying hamlets and temporary stations that the French did not count as settlements.

Of the sixty-three sites that have been found to contain small amounts of European trade goods, thirty-six occur in the northern part of Simcoe County, fourteen in the south, and another thirteen to the east of Lake Simcoe. Estimating twenty-nine sites per decade, this would date the first appearance of European goods in the late 1580s or, using a lower site ratio, possibly a little earlier. While this argument is a highly circumstantial one, it is perhaps more than a coincidence that, on the basis of his study of an archaeological sequence of late Huron sites, William C. Noble (1971) has estimated that European goods did not appear in the Huron country much before 1580.[40] This suggests that the first appearance of such goods on a regular, though still limited basis, may correlate with the intensification of European trade on the St. Lawrence that began in 1580.

The earliest sites have yielded only very small quantities of European trade goods. The Sopher, Benson, and McKenzie sites each contained only a few items. These include one iron celt, an iron awl, a copper knife, sheet brass, and beads made out of rolled sheets of brass and copper. No glass beads have been reported from these sites. Metal beads were probably manufactured from broken kettles, which the Huron, or their trading partners, had cut up. The only trade item that has been described in detail so far is an iron celt that was associated with a bundle burial in the Sopher site ossuary. It was 113 millimetres long and was manufactured by the malleated fusion of two thin slabs of iron (Noble 1971). It had no socket and was evidently made in imitation of an Indian stone celt. It has been speculated that celts of this sort may have been hurriedly manufactured aboard ship in accordance with native specifications; however, it is equally probable that such tools already were being produced in Europe for barter with an Amerindian clientele. Slightly later but still probably dating around 1615, are the McMurchy, Graham-Rogers, and Warminster sites. These have produced a richer and more varied selection of trade goods,

including brass rings, awls, and beads, iron hatchets, and glass beads. Numerous scraps of iron are also found on these sites. This indicates that, by the start of the historic period, increasing amounts of European material were reaching both the Huron and the Tionnontaté.

There is, however, no evidence that the Huron were trading directly with the French prior to 1609. In 1603, Champlain was informed that the Huron, who were called the "good Iroquois," were in the habit of bartering for French merchandise with the Algonkin. It was also from their Huron trading partners that Champlain's informants claimed to have heard about a copper mine to the north and from whom they had obtained some copper bracelets that they showed him (Biggar 1922–36, 1:164). One may assume that, by this time, the Huron had become interested in European goods, at least as novelties. Unlike the Iroquois, however, they had little trouble in obtaining what they wanted. The Algonkian traders were at best only marginally horticultural and were more than happy to exchange French goods for Huron corn, just as the Indians of the Maritimes exchanged European tools for corn with the Indians of Massachusetts. The Algonkians' role as middlemen in this trade became grafted onto an older exchange of meat and skins for Huron agricultural products. There is no direct evidence that the Nipissing and Ottawa engaged in trading European goods with the Huron much before 1615, although it is almost certain that they did. European goods must have been reaching these bands for some time, either up the Ottawa River or across central Quebec. Once they began receiving such goods, it would have been almost impossible not to share them with their Iroquoian trading partners in southern Ontario. The Nipissing and the Ottawa were probably the main suppliers for the Attignawantan, Attignee-nongnahac, and possibly for the Tionnontaté. The Arendarhonon possibly got most of their trade goods from the Onontchataronon, who may have begun visiting them while they were still living in the Trent Valley. The arrival of St. Lawrence Iroquoian refugees who had been accustomed to receiving trade goods may have helped to stimulate the Arendarhonon's interest in such items. The interaction between the Arendarhonon and the Onontchataronon probably led to broader trading connections between the Huron and other Algonkian-speaking groups in the Ottawa Valley.

The quantity and type of European goods that were reaching the Huron do not appear significantly to have altered their daily life during the late prehistoric period. In particular, the technological impact of these goods must have been negligible. The most obvious change that can be observed in the archaeological record is the inclusion of trade goods and other valued items in ossuaries for the first time. This parallels the burial of European

goods with the dead among the Iroquois and seems to indicate a growing interest in mortuary ceremonialism among both groups.

On the other hand, the influence of this early trade seems to have been considerably more far-reaching in its political consequences. It is not unreasonable to assume that a growing desire to trade with the northern Algonkians, by way of the long, but relatively easy Georgian Bay route, led the Arendarhonon and Tahontaenrat to settle in the northern part of Simcoe County as new members of the Huron confederacy, the former about 1590 and the latter about 1610 (Thwaites 1896–1901, 16:227–29). From about 1610 on, all the Huron tribes were living close to the shores of Georgian Bay and along minor waterways that allowed them to reach the bay easily. Whether the Tionnontaté were getting their European goods from the Huron or from their own northern Algonkian trading partners, their position was such that the Attignawantan were able to prevent them from travelling north. Moreover, with the formation of an expanded confederacy, the Attignawantan attained a political ascendancy that made it even easier for them to prevent the Tionnontaté from ever using this route (21:177).

The developments associated with the growth of the St. Lawrence fur trade broke down much of the localism that hitherto had been a feature of Iroquoian life. The disappearance of the St. Lawrence Iroquoians led to more intimate contacts between the Huron and Ottawa Valley Algonkin. As a result of these contacts, the Algonkin soon came to appreciate the value of Huron corn no less than did older trading partners, such as the Nipissing. The Iroquois also emerged as the main enemies of the Huron. Neither the Huron nor the Iroquois yet were as well-equipped with iron weapons as were the Algonkian allies of the French, nor did they have more than traditional motives for attacking one another. It is likely, however, that the new trade links between the Arendarhonon and the Onontchataronon caused Huron warriors to become involved in the hostilities of their allies; which resulted in growing conflict with the Onondaga, Oneida, and Mohawk. As more tribes joined the Huron and Iroquois confederacies and ceased to fight with one another, the young men of these confederacies would have found it necessary to direct their hostilities farther afield. Increasing warfare between these confederacies would have been an additional factor promoting their internal consolidation.

The development of trade in European goods also may have stimulated an expansion of trade generally. More interaction with the south is indicated by increasing amounts of marine shell in Huron sites. The first contacts between the Huron and the Susquehannock may date from this

period, when the Susquehannock were also being stimulated to trade as a result of their own initial contacts with Europeans (W. Hunter 1959). The major changes, however, took place in southwestern Ontario. Huron control over goods coming from the north seems to have led to a cessation in their blood feuds with the Iroquoian tribes who lived to the south and west of them. The wars that the Huron had with the Tionnontaté in the late prehistoric period may reflect the latter's desire to share in this trade, but eventually such conflict seems to have given way to a mutually satisfactory trade, in which tobacco was exchanged for European goods (Thwaites 1896–1901, 20:43). The Neutral who were mainly suppliers of fancy furs and exotic goods from the south, were in a position to barter for European goods with both the Huron and the Iroquois and this may explain why they were friendly with both confederacies. The Neutral also seem to have been trading with the Algonkin at this period. Trading visits to the Neutral may have been one of the ways in which the Algonkin and Montagnais acquired their detailed knowledge of the lower Great Lakes.

It may be objected that I am exaggerating the influence of the still nascent fur trade. It must be remembered, however, that in the Indian history of this region, trading in exotic goods has often played a role that was out of all proportion to its utilitarian significance. It is therefore not surprising that, while the Huron were little affected technologically during this period of indirect trade, their political organization and foreign relations underwent extensive changes in response to it. What appears in the archaeological record as a few scraps of metal seems in fact to have been a sufficient catalyst to realize certain potentials for development that were inherent in prehistoric Huron society, but which otherwise might never have come to fruition.

Chapter 5   Forging an Alliance

The Huron on the St. Lawrence

THE FIRST ENCOUNTER

Although no detailed Huron account has been preserved concerning their first contact with the French, scraps of information recorded by the Jesuits in the 1640s reveal something about how the Huron remembered this event in later years. According to these accounts, the Huron first learned that European ships were coming to the St. Lawrence from neighbouring tribes, and, on the basis of this information, some Huron men decided to meet these newcomers for themselves (Thwaites 1896–1901, 39:49). The first who accomplished this were members of war parties, who, in the course of their excursions against the enemy, visited places where the French were trading with the Indians. Following these initial contacts, the Huron decided to secure a safe route to use to trade with the French every year (16:229). The first Huron to meet the French were members of the Arendarhonon tribe (20:19). Atironta, the principal headman of that tribe, was the first headman to go to Quebec to conclude an alliance with the French (20:35; 23:167).

It is tempting to assume that the war parties mentioned in these Huron traditions are the same ones that Champlain records as coming to the St. Lawrence in 1609 (Biggar 1922–36, 2:67–68). Nevertheless, two objections may be raised against the identification of these Huron stories with Champlain's account. First, the Huron dated their initial encounters with the French around A.D. 1600, rather than in 1609. Second, the first Huron headman to have dealings with Champlain was named Ochasteguin, not Atironta (ibid. 2:68).

The chronological objection is not a serious one. The Huron often referred to events taking place twenty, forty, or two hundred years into the past. These figures must be interpreted as signifying general periods of time, rather than a precise number of years; hence "forty years ago" may easily refer to an event that took place in 1609. The different names given for the Huron headman who first had dealings with the French are a greater

difficulty. Names of individual Indians appear in a variety of forms, even in accounts by the same authors, and Champlain often confused the issue further, by failing to mention that Indian leaders with whom he had dealings were ones that he had written about earlier.[1] In spite of this, Ochasteguin and Atironta are both mentioned in the account of his voyage of 1615, so they cannot be merely variants of the same name. Ochasteguin does not appear in Champlain's accounts after 1615, whereas Atironta, the principal headman of the Arendarhonon, was a prominent figure throughout the whole segment of Huron history that we are considering.[2] It is possible that Ochasteguin was the name of an individual who later inherited the principal chieftainship of the Arendarhonon, in which case he would have been a close relative of the Atironta Champlain met in 1615. On the other hand, he may have been a less prominent Arendarhonon and eventually the Arendarhonon, for political or ritual reasons, may have chosen to pay less attention to his early encounters with the French. Atironta's visit to Quebec in 1616, which immediately followed Champlain's journey to the Huron country, seems to have been remembered by the Arendarhonon as marking the conclusion of a formal alliance between them and the French (Thwaites 1896–1901, 20:35; 23:167). On this basis, we may conclude that the first direct contact between the Huron and the French took place in 1609, while a formal alliance was concluded between them seven years later. This allows us to offer the following reconstruction of the events leading up to this alliance.

THE BATTLE OF LAKE CHAMPLAIN

In chapter 4, it was mentioned that in the summer of 1608 the son of Iroquet, one of the important headmen of the Onontchataronon, came to Quebec. There he was much impressed by the newly constructed French habitation and told Champlain about the conflict that his people were having with the Iroquois. Champlain said that he and Gravé Du Pont were anxious to help the Onontchataronon in their wars and invited them to join the French and the Montagnais on a military expedition up the Richelieu the following summer.

This novel French offer to fight alongside their Indian allies seems to have particularly interested the Onontchataronon, since the latter were anxious to avenge an act of treachery that the Iroquois had committed against them during a period of truce (Biggar 1922–36, 2:69). In the autumn, Iroquet and some of his people no doubt made their way up the

Ottawa River and travelled by way of Lake Nipissing and Georgian Bay to the territory of the Arendarhonon, where they camped for the winter near one of the large Arendarhonon villages, probably Cahiagué. While there, Iroquet seems to have invited some of his Arendarhonon trading partners to accompany him on the raid that was planned for the following summer. A small group of warriors, led by Ochasteguin, agreed to do this. They were anxious to meet the French and possibly to trade with them. Primarily, however, they seem to have been interested in winning renown by going to war alongside these strangers, who possessed a limitless supply of metal tools and powerful weapons that made a noise like thunder. In the company of the Onontchataronon, they would experience no difficulty travelling down the Ottawa River. Had they been alone, it might have been difficult to secure rights of passage, particularly if middlemen, such as the Kichesipirini, did not wish them to contact the French.

On the way down the Ottawa, this nucleus of Huron and Onontchataronon warriors was joined by many Algonkin men and women, who were interested only in trading with the French. By mid-June, this group, now swollen to some two to three hundred people, reached St. Eloi Island, near the mouth of the Batiscan River. There they heard rumours that the French did not intend to help them against the Iroquois, but were interested only in their furs (2:71). These rumours were probably started by the Montagnais, or possibly by Algonkin groups, who were angry that Iroquet was planning to introduce his Arendarhonon allies to the French.

Despite a cruel winter, during which most of his men had died from scurvy and dysentery, Champlain was enthusiastically awaiting the opportunity to explore the Richelieu River. On 5 June 1609, he learned that Gravé Du Pont had arrived at Tadoussac and, two days later, he set out to meet him there. The two men proposed that Champlain should embark on his proffered expedition, accompanied by twenty armed Frenchmen, while Gravé Du Pont would attend to the affairs of the settlement and supervise the trading at Tadoussac (2:63–64). Champlain returned to Quebec and had a shallop fitted out for his trip up-river. He left Quebec on 12 June in the company of his Montagnais allies, and a few days later reached St. Eloi Island, where he found the Algonkin and Arendarhonon waiting for him.

Two days were spent exchanging information and greetings. Iroquet explained that he and his men were there to fight the Mohawk and that he had solicited Indians who had never before seen a European to make an alliance with the French and join the federated Algonkian tribes in their war against the Iroquois. Iroquet and Ochasteguin both presented Champlain with gifts of furs and asked him to have guns fired for the benefit of

those who had never encountered them before. Champlain did this and noted the astonishment of the newcomers when they heard them. The Indians also asked if they might visit Quebec before they set off for war, both to gratify their curiosity about the buildings that had been erected there and so that those who had brought furs might trade them. Champlain agreed, pointing out that he had brought no merchandise with him, since his sole aim was to help his Indian allies in their wars. He specifically repudiated the now familiar rumour that he was interested only in trade. The Algonkin and Arendarhonon, for their part, denied that they ever had heard such accusations made against him (2:71).

Champlain and the Indians returned to Quebec, where five or six days were spent eating, dancing, and trading. Gravé Du Pont was summoned from Tadoussac and arrived with two shallops full of French traders. To create additional goodwill, Champlain announced that Gravé Du Pont was sending some of these men to fight alongside his Indian allies and might come himself. On 28 June both men set off up the St. Lawrence but, by the time they had reached Point Platon, Gravé Du Pont seems to have decided that, since the trading was over, his time would be spent better elsewhere (2:73). Accordingly, Champlain was dispatched up-river, but with only nine Frenchmen to fight alongside him.

At the mouth of the Richelieu River, Champlain was surprised when most Algonkin men who, unknown to him, had never intended to accompany his expedition, continued up-river with their wives and the European merchandise they had obtained (2:76). This left sixty warriors who were prepared to do battle with the Iroquois. The war party was composed of Ochasteguin and Iroquet and their men, and some Montagnais (2:104, 105). It is doubtful that any Arendarhonon chose to return home at this time; from the beginning, Ochasteguin's followers had probably numbered no more than twenty.

On reaching the Chambly Rapids, Champlain found it impossible to move his shallop farther up-stream. He scolded the Indians for not warning him about this barrier, although it was no barrier to them. He was also acting unreasonably, since he had personally experienced difficulty when he had attempted to explore the Richelieu River in 1603 (1:141–42). He decided to send the shallop and most of his men back to Quebec and to continue south by canoe, in the company of the Indians and two French volunteers (2:80–81; map 12).

After the arduous portage around the Chambly Rapids, Champlain had an opportunity to begin observing the methods of waging war that were customary among the Indians of eastern North America. However much

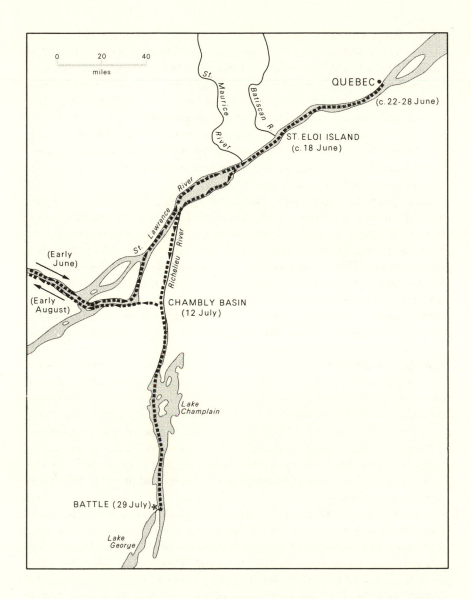

MAP 12. *Route followed by the Huron and Algonkin who accompanied the 1609 expedition against the Mohawk.*

the conflict between the Iroquois and the Algonkians had been heightened by Mohawk attacks on the St. Lawrence, techniques of warfare remained largely traditional on both sides. For seventeen days, the Indian war party travelled south along the Richelieu River and the west side of Lake Champlain. During the daylight hours, they split into three groups. Scouts went ahead to look for signs of the enemy, while the main body of warriors remained some distance behind, well-armed and prepared to give battle. The hunters, whose job was to provide game for the band, stayed in the rear (Biggar 1922–36, 2 : 85).

Every evening, the warriors hauled their canoes up along the shore, erected their temporary bark cabins, and felled trees to form a barricade around their camp on the landward side. This work took about two hours. Scouts were sent out, and, if they reported everything safe within several miles of the camp, the entire war party went to sleep for the night. Champlain criticized the lack of a night-watch, but was told by the Indians that they would be unable to work all day without a good night's sleep. He also observed shamans performing an Algonkian shaking tent ceremony each evening, in an effort to divine the movements of the enemy. Champlain states that he spared no effort to expose the folly of such practices and the general deceitfulness of shamans (2 : 86–88). No doubt, these harangues were almost incomprehensible to the Indians, which was fortunate, since, if they had been understood, they would almost certainly have offended his hosts. On the other hand, Champlain was impressed by the manner in which headmen discussed strategy and repeatedly drilled their men, so that no confusion would arise in battle (2 : 88–89). In a composite force of this kind, such drill was particularly necessary.

As the Indians moved south, Champlain collected a considerable amount of misinformation, which in part reflects the linguistic difficulties he was having. He was probably told that, because of the wars between the Mohawk and the Algonkin, the no man's land around Lake Champlain was no longer safe for hunting. He interpreted this to mean that, because of these wars, a formerly sedentary population had been driven from this area (2 : 90). He also believed that the Iroquois were living east as well as west of Lake Champlain at this period (2 : 93).[3]

Farther south, the Indians travelled only at night, and spent the days hidden in the forest. To escape detection by the enemy they did not light fires, and their main food was corn meal soaked in cold water to make a kind of porridge. As the chance of encountering the enemy increased, they became more attentive to dreams and other forms of divination, and

eventually even Champlain began to report favourable dreams in order to encourage his companions (2:95).

Around ten o'clock on the evening of 29 July, Champlain's party spotted about two hundred Iroquois warriors. Both sides were intent on fighting, but, in accordance with their common traditions, neither wished to fight at night. This was a practice that the Iroquoians justified by saying that they desired the sun to witness their valour. The Iroquois landed and erected a strong barricade on the shore of the lake, near Point Ticonderoga, while the Algonkians and Arendarhonon spent the night on the lake, with their boats tied together so as not to become separated in the darkness. Throughout the night, the Iroquois danced and sang, and the protagonists on both sides boasted about their courage and shouted insults at their foes. Charges and countercharges were exchanged, suggesting that the leading warriors on both sides knew one another personally. The French remained under cover, so that their presence would come as a surprise to the enemy once the battle had begun. After preparing their arms, they separated, each going with a different canoeload of Montagnais, whom they recognized in this manner as being their oldest and most important allies (Biggar 1922–36, 2:97).

At dawn, the Algonkians and Arendarhonon landed and the Iroquois came out of their fort. Both sides lined up and prepared to do battle. Champlain regretted that his allies could not understand him, since he believed that if they had he could have led them in such a way as to exterminate the enemy (2:98). As it was, Champlain found himself participating in a traditional encounter, in which he could only hope to show his courage and goodwill. As soon as the Arendarhonon and Algonkians landed, they began to run toward the enemy, who remained near their fort. Nearer the Iroquois, they parted ranks in the centre and Champlain advanced some twenty paces ahead of the rest. They continued to move forward in this formation until Champlain was within fifty feet of the enemy. The Iroquois, astounded to see an armoured Frenchman, stood motionless for a time, gazing at him. Then, as they were preparing to fire a volley of arrows, Champlain raised his musket and aimed it towards the three headmen who were their leaders (plate 21). These men, each of whom wore wooden body armour, had been pointed out to Champlain by the Montagnais. When he fired, two of these headmen fell dead and another Mohawk was mortally wounded. This unexpected development caused great alarm among the Iroquois, which was intensified when another Frenchman fired at them from behind the trees. The Iroquois and the allied Indians began shooting arrows at each other, but the former quickly

PLATE 21. *Battle of Lake Champlain, 30 July 1609. From Champlain's
Voyages of 1613. This engraving shows Champlain and two French
musketeers assisting the Algonkians and the Huron in a skirmish with the
Iroquois. On the right is shown the temporary camp in which the Iroquois
had spent the night. The canoes look like French riverboats and the nudity
of the Indians and their erroneous hairstyles undermine the credibility of
the picture. The hammocks and palm trees are borrowed from scenes of
Latin America. Under these circumstances it is difficult to accept
S. E. Morison's (1972: 110–11) claim that Champlain drew this picture,
quixotically borrowing the exotic elements from de Bry and other sources.
Courtesy Public Archives of Canada.*

lost courage and fled into the woods, whither they were pursued by Champlain and his companions. Ten or twelve Iroquois were taken prisoner and perhaps fifty more were slain. By contrast, Champlain's Indians suffered only a few wounds. A large amount of Indian corn was plundered from the camp that the Iroquois had abandoned, as well as some suits of slat armour that the Iroquois had learned was not bullet proof (2:98–101).

After feasting and celebrating for several hours, the victors rapidly withdrew northward. That evening, they began torturing one of the prisoners. Eventually, his screams led Champlain to rebuke his allies for their cruelty and, since the prisoner was already almost dead, he offered to shoot him to put an end to his suffering. When the Indians refused to permit this, saying that they did not wish the Iroquois to have an easy death, Champlain walked away in anger. Seeing this, the Indians gave him permission to shoot the prisoner, which he did immediately (2:101–3). While one may wonder why Champlain waited so long before intervening, to his credit it must be noted that the ritual torture practised by the Indians did not disgust most seventeenth-century Europeans to the extent we imagine it should have done. Mutilations and prolonged and brutal forms of execution were part of the hangman's art in all parts of Europe at this time; so that Europeans who came to the New World were generally familiar with the sort of cruelties that the Indians practised. Champlain's anger was less an emotional revulsion against cruelty than the result of his conviction that his allies were acting unfairly in so treating a prisoner of war. It is doubtful that he would have objected to the torturing of someone who was guilty of treason, heresy, or sexual deviancy. Because he abhorred cannibalism, Champlain was also angered by efforts to compel the other Iroquois prisoners to eat the heart of the dead man.

When they reached the Chambly Rapids, the Algonkin and Arendarhonon departed for their own country. They travelled due west to the St. Lawrence River, thereby avoiding a long journey to the mouth of the Richelieu River and up the St. Lawrence to Montreal Island. No doubt, they took home with them their share of Iroquois prisoners and scalps, as evidence of their success. Before they left, Champlain promised that he would meet them the following summer at the mouth of the Richelieu River to assist them further in their wars. The Arendarhonon and the Algonkin, for their part, promised that as many as four hundred men would come with them and that, after their annual raid against the Iroquois, they would take Champlain inland and show him the Huron country, as well as some of the copper mines farther north (2:104–5; 119; 121–22). Such prospects for exploring the interior and establishing trading links

between de Monts's company and tribes living north and west of the St. Lawrence must have greatly encouraged Champlain and justified the policy of personal involvement in Indian wars.

After the Arendarhonon and Algonkin had departed, Champlain travelled down the St. Lawrence River with the Montagnais. They stopped briefly at Quebec, where Champlain gave his companions bread and dried peas, as well as some beads they had requested to decorate the severed heads of their enemies. Then they continued down-river to Tadoussac, where the Montagnais were greeted by their relatives. Following local custom, the Montagnais women undressed themselves and swam out to the canoes to claim the heads of their enemies, which they later suspended around their necks for their dances. Numerous ceremonies followed, in the course of which the Montagnais promised that next year they would take Champlain up the St. Maurice River and show him the Northern Ocean (2:118–19). Thus, from the point of view of exploring, Champlain added another string to his bow. Several days later, a group of Algonkin from the upper Ottawa Valley arrived at Quebec, expressing regret that they had not been present at the recent victory and presenting Champlain with furs as a token of their appreciation for the help he had given to their friends (2:107). While gifts were expected in return as evidence of reciprocal goodwill, these presents were further proof that the new policy was success-ful as a means of gaining influence among the northern peoples and estab-lishing trading alliances with them.

In September, Champlain and Gravé Du Pont returned to France leaving Pierre Chauvin, a Huguenot merchant and sea captain from Dieppe, in command at Quebec. Champlain reported on the success of his expedition to de Monts and described his voyage to the king, whom he presented with an Indian girdle made of porcupine quills (2:110). During the winter, Champlain must have watched with anxiety the increasing hopelessness of de Monts's efforts to secure a renewal of his monopoly over trade along the upper St. Lawrence. The hopes that both men had for maintaining the settlement at Quebec and exploring the interior depended, at the very least, on securing such a monopoly. Free trade won the day, however, and, until 1613, no new monopoly was granted. The old mon-opoly had already lapsed prior to the trading in 1609, but during that year there had been little competition for furs.

The threat of competition for the following year was, however, much greater and, faced with it, traders were unwilling to bear the additional costs involved in maintaining a permanent settlement at Quebec. De Monts was anxious to continue the settlement and, by hard persuasion, managed

to form a company with some Rouen merchants, on condition that the settlement function as a warehouse for the fur trade. Yet, in the face of continuing free trade, even this arrangement had little hope of surviving for long (Biggar 1901:74).

THE BATTLE OF THE RICHELIEU

When Champlain arrived at Tadoussac on 26 May 1610, he found sixty Montagnais warriors awaiting his return. A few days later, when these Indians visited Quebec, Champlain was informed that some of the Basques and merchants from St. Malo, who had come to trade, were promising the Indians that they too would send men to fight alongside them. The Indians said that they regarded these promises as false ones that were designed to lure them into trading, and they ridiculed these traders as women who only wanted to make war on their beavers (Biggar 1922–36, 2:121). While the Montagnais were anxious to convince Champlain that their greatest friendship was reserved for him and Gravé Du Pont, their behaviour suggests that they were interested in obtaining good prices for their furs and would sell them, whenever possible, to the highest bidder. Their expressions of scorn for the other European merchants were intended mainly to curry favour with Champlain. Nevertheless, their desire for an alliance with Champlain probably gave de Monts's traders some advantage in their dealings with the Montagnais, especially when they were in a position to observe the latter having dealings with rival European traders.

While still at Tadoussac, Champlain was annoyed to learn that the Montagnais insisted on deferring their promise to show him the St. Maurice River until the following year (2:119). Already once, in 1608, these same Indians had been unwilling to let him, or any other Frenchman, accompany them up the Saguenay River beyond Tadoussac (2:19). The Montagnais obviously remained anxious to prevent the French from making direct contact with their trading partners in the interior of northern Quebec. Champlain still had hopes of travelling inland with the Arendarhonon; therefore, although he had been deceived by the Montagnais, he decided to ignore the slight.

Since speed was essential, if rival traders were not to carry off most of the furs from the upper St. Lawrence, Champlain left for Quebec two days after he arrived at Tadoussac. At Quebec, he found the French colony in good health and provided a feast for Batiscan, the headman of the Three Rivers area, who, in return, honoured him with another feast (2:120).

After the Montagnais arrived from Tadoussac, both groups of Indians decided to go up-river to await the arrival of the Onontchataronon and Arendarhonon at the mouth of the Richelieu River. Champlain promised to follow them and to send four shallops loaded with merchandise to trade with the Indians from the interior (2:121–22). He seems to have had two reasons for having arranged this rendezvous so far up the St. Lawrence River the previous year. First, it was to ensure that it would be within any new monopoly zone. Unfortunately, no monopoly had materialized, nor was Champlain able to prevent other traders from following de Monts's boats up-river to the appointed meeting place. Second, by establishing a trading centre on the upper St. Lawrence, Champlain hoped to develop more direct relations with the Algonkin and Arendarhonon who, although friends of the Montagnais, had to come as their guests when they traded at Tadoussac or Quebec. By establishing a trading station within Algonkin territory, Champlain hoped to forge a direct, rather than an indirect, bond between the Algonkin and the French. In this endeavour, he was completely successful. From this time on, trade took place separately at Tadoussac and on the upper St. Lawrence. Much as the Montagnais may have resented this arrangement, their fear of the Iroquois and need for an alliance in which they could rely on the support of the French and the Algonkin were sufficient to suppress overt opposition. Relations with the Arendarhonon remained indirect, inasmuch as they were still meeting the French as guests of the Onontchataronon, just as the Algonkin had previously traded with the French as allies of the Montagnais.

Champlain left Quebec to go up-river on 14 June. About twenty miles from Quebec, he encountered a canoe containing a Montagnais and an Algonkin, who were coming to tell him that in two days two hundred Arendarhonon and Algonkin would be arriving at the Richelieu River and that another party, led by Iroquet and Ochasteguin, would be arriving a little later. The Algonkin, who was a headman, presented Champlain with a piece of native copper a foot long, that he said he had obtained on the bank of a river where there were more pieces like it (2:123).

At the mouth of the St. Maurice River, Champlain found the Montagnais and the four shallops that had gone up-river waiting for him. The Montagnais entreated Champlain to recognize them as the oldest allies of the French by continuing to travel in their canoes when they went to war. Champlain promised to do this (2:124). The next day, the whole group travelled up Lake St. Peter and arrived at St. Ignace Island, directly opposite the mouth of the Richelieu River. There, the Montagnais began felling trees to clear a space for their camp, while they awaited the arrival of the

Huron and Algonkin, who were travelling to the rendezvous by way of Chambly. Soon, a canoe arrived at the Montagnais camp bringing word that the Huron and Algonkin had fallen in with a hundred Iroquois who had erected a fortified camp about four miles up the Richelieu River.

The Montagnais immediately decided to help their allies and asked Champlain to accompany them, which he agreed to do. He departed, taking with him four other Frenchmen who were under his command. The independent traders who were at the mouth of the Richelieu refused to join in this battle, except for Captains Thibaut and Des Prairies and their crews. The French and Indians made their way to the south shore of the St. Lawrence and proceeded across the narrow neck of land between the St. Lawrence and Richelieu Rivers to the Iroquois encampment. Marshes and dense woods hindered the French, who were wearing pike-men's armour and, because of this, the Montagnais reached the site of battle well ahead of them. There, the Montagnais and the Indians from the Ottawa Valley were repulsed in a premature assault on the fort, in the course of which several headmen were slain; however, the arrival of the French revived the spirits of the survivors. Both sides began firing swarms of arrows, one of which pierced Champlain's ear and entered his neck. The French fired on the Iroquois, but while, at first, the noise of the guns frightened them, they soon began to drop to the ground while the guns were being discharged, to avoid being struck by the shot.[4] Seeing that he was running out of ammunition, Champlain requested his Indian allies to take cover behind their shields and attach ropes to the logs that supported the barricade around the Iroquois fort (plate 22). The French covered the Indians with musket fire while they did this. Then, reinforced by Des Prairies's men, the French and their allies stormed the fort, swords in hand, and killed all but fifteen of its occupants. The rest were taken prisoner (2:125–34).

The only booty found inside the camp were some beaver skin robes and the blood-stained fur clothing worn by the dead. The Indians did not bother to plunder the latter and derided the French who did so. This shows that, while the Indians valued European goods, the desire or necessity of obtaining them had not yet eroded traditional values, which included scorn for an act of greed of this sort. The Indians scalped the dead or cut off their heads as trophies, and returned to St. Ignace Island, taking their prisoners with them. The next day was spent trading with the French and torturing several prisoners, whose flesh was fed to the dogs (2:135–37). The other prisoners remained in the possession of the Montagnais and Algonkin, who reserved a similar fate for them in their villages. Champlain claimed as his

PLATE 22. *Battle of the Richelieu River, 19 June 1610. From Champlain's Voyages of 1613. Although there are no hammocks or palm trees in this engraving, the depiction of the Indians suggests that it was produced in the same manner as the preceding illustration. Courtesy Public Archives of Canada.*

share of the booty an Iroquois prisoner, whom he hoped would be useful for promoting peace among the warring tribes of the region.

The battle of 1609 on Lake Champlain has been studied by historians more carefully than has this one. In particular, it has been debated whether or not Champlain should be censured for arousing the fury of the Iroquois, by attacking them without provocation at that time (Trudel 1966a:165–67). The battle of the Richelieu was a more important event, however, because it marks the last time that the Mohawk were to be a serious threat in the St. Lawrence Valley until 1634. Desrosiers (1947a:47) estimated that, in the major defeats the Mohawk had suffered on the St. Lawrence since A.D. 1600, they had lost 250 warriors and argued that it was these losses which compelled them to cease their attacks. While the figures on which Desrosiers's estimate is based are probably inflated, it cannot be doubted that these raids had been extremely costly for a tribe whose total population was probably no more than 5,000 and which, throughout much of this period, seems also to have been at war with the Susquehannock.[5] The loss of at least two of their headmen at Ticonderoga had been a serious blow to the Mohawk and this bloody defeat on the Richelieu, combined with knowledge that the Europeans were now actively and consistently aiding their Algonkian opponents, must have made them dread the prospect of further campaigns on the St. Lawrence. While the Iroquois quickly developed techniques to avoid being killed by French musketfire, guns continued to frighten them for a long time. Iroquois raiders continued to operate along the Ottawa River until the early 1620s, when they were frightened away by armed Frenchmen, who had begun to travel up that river in larger numbers (Wrong 1939:261).

Yet, serious as these losses may have been, they do not by themselves explain the Mohawk's decision to cease their attacks on the St. Lawrence Valley. For the preceding thirty years, that region had been the sole source of iron tools for the Mohawk. In 1609, Henry Hudson, an Englishman in the pay of the Dutch East India Company, ascended the Hudson River as far as the Albany area, thereby discovering the trading potential of that portion of the river. By a strange coincidence, this happened only about five weeks after Champlain had engaged the Iroquois at Ticonderoga, a mere eighty miles away. While the initial Dutch contacts were with the Mahican, who lived along both banks of the river, trade quickly developed with the Mohawk, whose territory lay to the west (O'Callaghan 1856–87, 1:14). Although intermittent conflicts with the Mahican may have disrupted these early contacts, the Mohawk eventually found peaceful trade with the Dutch a preferable alternative to their increasingly costly struggle

on the St. Lawrence. The opening up of an alternative source of European trade goods is probably no less important than the defeats they suffered on the St. Lawrence for explaining the Mohawk's decision to abandon their attacks on that area.

The day after the first Mohawk prisoners were killed, Iroquet and Ochasteguin arrived. Both of them regretted not being present for the battle. They were accompanied by about eighty men, which brings the total number of Huron and Algonkin who descended the Ottawa River that year to about three hundred. About two hundred of these are said never to have seen a European before. Since the tribes from the upper Ottawa Valley had been visiting Tadoussac since at least 1600, this suggests that a large portion of these Indians were from the Huron country. The Indians remained on St. Ignace Island for three more days, engaging in trade while their leaders continued to confer with the French (Biggar 1922–36, 2:138).

SAVIGNON AND BRÛLÉ

Champlain wished to have a young Frenchman who had already survived two winters at Quebec learn the Algonkin language, and for this purpose he proposed to have him spend the winter with Iroquet and his people. The man he had in mind appears to have been Etienne Brûlé, who was then about eighteen years old.[6] Brûlé had already expressed a desire to live with the Indians and Champlain and Gravé Du Pont believed that, in addition to learning to speak a native language, he could gather valuable information concerning the geography and peoples of the interior.

Iroquet agreed to take Brûlé, but the other Algonkin headmen objected to this arrangement. They argued that if an accident were to befall him while he was in the care of the Indians, the French might seek blood revenge. Champlain conferred with these headmen and informed them that, by refusing to take this man, they were incurring his displeasure. He said that to accept Brûlé would strengthen their ties with the French and that if Brûlé perished from illness or enemy attack, the French would not hold his hosts accountable. Eventually, the headmen accepted Champlain's proposal, but insisted that Champlain reciprocate by taking a young Indian to France for the winter so that he could report to his people what he had seen there. Champlain agreed to the exchange and was given custody of Savignon, who was the brother of a Huron headman named Tregouaroti (Biggar 1922–36, 2:138–42, 186).

This is the first record of a Frenchman and an Indian being exchanged and sent to live for a time with each other's people. By conforming with a custom that Indian trading partners used to express goodwill and to guard against treachery, de Monts's traders took another step towards establishing an enduring relationship with the Indians of the interior. Such exchanges between French and Indian trading partners were to become the basis on which, in later years, many Frenchmen (who were all considered by the Indians to be tribesmen and therefore, in some sense, relatives of one another) were to live in security in the Huron country. Sending young Frenchmen to live with the Indians would also produce a proficient staff of interpreters and trading agents. By dwelling with the Indians, these men were to learn the customs of different tribes and become successful intermediaries in the dealings that these tribes had with the French.

The three-cornered exchange that was arranged between French, Huron, and Algonkin is understandable only if we assume that Iroquet was planning to spend the following winter among the Arendarhonon, as he and some of his people seem to have been doing regularly at this period. Officially, he and his followers would have provided the Arendarhonon with the required assurance for Savignon's return. In practice, however, the security was probably even more direct. Brûlé likely spent the winter living with a Huron, rather than an Algonkin, family, since, for the rest of his life, he worked as an interpreter among the Huron rather than among the Algonkin. Champlain did not explain, and probably never knew, how or why Iroquet and Ochasteguin arranged this complicated exchange. The Arendarhonon were probably anxious to have one of their young men live with the French, in the hope that this would establish closer ties between their peoples and eliminate the need to rely on Algonkian interpreters; however, since Iroquet had introduced these two groups, the Onontchataronon were still officially viewed by the Huron as intermediaries between themselves and the French. The exchange was therefore arranged so as to recognize, at least in a nominal way, this prior relationship.

Champlain does not say why he did not attempt to travel up the Ottawa River, as he had originally planned to do. Certainly, he would have been a welcome visitor among the Huron. It is likely, however, that he was deterred by his wound and, even more so, by a desire to return to France quickly. Competition from the independent traders had been severe, both at the mouth of the Richelieu River and at Tadoussac, and Champlain must have been worried that de Monts's associates would again be threatening to withdraw their support. It is also possible that Algonkin groups such as the Kichesipirini, who wished to remain intermediaries in the trade with

the Huron, were opposed to Champlain visiting the Huron country. Their opposition may have played a part in his decision not to attempt a journey into the interior at that time. Champlain promised the Arendarhonon and Algonkin that he would meet them the following year at the foot of the Lachine Rapids. He hoped that by again moving the trading station up-river, de Monts's traders might be able to outstrip their competitors.

Champlain returned to Quebec with Savignon and the Iroquois prisoner he had claimed as part of his spoils. While he was supervising the fortification of the French settlement, the prisoner escaped. Champlain states that he fled from fear of being tortured, in spite of the assurances given him by a woman of his tribe whom the French had living at Quebec (2:143). This woman was probably the Iroquois prisoner the Montagnais had given to Gravé Du Pont in 1603, and whom he had taken back to France with him. It is a sad commentary on the inadequacy of our sources concerning the Indians that we know nothing about what this woman was doing at Quebec in 1610, or what eventually became of her.

Jean de Godet Du Parc was left in command at Quebec when Champlain departed for France on 13 August. He was accompanied by Savignon, who became the first Huron to travel to Europe and to be presented at the French court. Because of Sagard and Lescarbot, we know more about his stay in France than we do about the Indians who were taken there in earlier times. Savignon seems to have been about the same age as Brûlé. He probably had participated in military expeditions and, while he lacked the political maturity and ritualistic knowledge of older men, he would have had an adult's knowledge of Huron customs and a corresponding pride in them. Sagard's comment that he was too old to learn well (1866:331) merely indicates that he was not as amenable to being taught French ways as the priests would have liked; which may explain why they do not seem to have baptized him. Lescarbot (1907-14, 3:22) saw Savignon in Paris, and described him as a tall, sturdy youth who enjoyed ridiculing Frenchmen whenever he saw them quarrelling without coming to blows. Huron men did not engage in verbal disputes and were not supposed to interrupt one another; hence to Savignon verbal quarrels appeared effeminate. When he returned to his people, Savignon praised the excellent treatment he had received in France, but never expressed any serious desire to return there (Sagard 1866:332). Like most Indians, he was appalled by the capital and corporal punishment that was a conspicuous feature of life in the French capital. He was also disturbed to see Europeans beating their children and physically restraining them. In later years, Savignon told his people that the French killed and hurt individuals without distinguishing the innocent

from the guilty (ibid. 320). He said that if Huron children were allowed to go to France they were in danger of being beaten or killed there.

Someone unfamiliar with the Huron might dismiss such sentiments as the idealized reactions that a European author put into the mouth of an unsullied "noble savage," whom he wished to portray encountering the corruptions of civilized life. Knowledge of the Huron indicates, however, that these passages represent the authentic reactions of an Indian, reared in a tradition of personal liberty and blood feud, to European concepts of legal and parental authority. Sagard, who recorded these reactions, was fully convinced of the folly and immorality of Huron notions about child-rearing and dealing with crime.

As Savignon learned more French, he must have told Champlain and Gravé Du Pont a great deal about his people. A growing awareness of the size of the Huron confederacy and of the extent of their trading relations seems to have indicated to these men, for the first time, the important role that this confederacy could play in the development of the fur trade. As a result, a trading alliance with the Huron must have been recognized as a useful way to cope with the increasing competition for furs, now that the St. Lawrence had been thrown open to unrestricted trade.

TRADE AND TALK IN 1611

Champlain and Savignon set out for Canada on 1 March 1611 but, because wind and ice delayed their passage, they did not reach Tadoussac until 13 May. There were already several vessels in harbour when they arrived, but the Montagnais refused to trade for more than a few items that they required for their immediate needs. Instead, they were waiting for more boats to arrive, so that increased competition for furs would force the traders to exchange more goods for them (Biggar 1922–36, 2:171). By drawing increasing numbers of European traders to the St. Lawrence, free trade had terminated the artificial scarcity of European goods that a monopoly situation had created and which had made it possible for the French traders to demand a high price in furs in return for their stock. Champlain admired the sagacity with which the Montagnais were exploiting the European traders, but it was in his own interest to eliminate as quickly as possible a situation which played into the hands of the Indians.

Champlain continued on to Quebec, where he found that by eating fresh meat throughout the winter, the problem of scurvy had been overcome for a second season. He had planned to send two or three Frenchmen to explore

the St. Maurice River, but once again Batiscan demurred and the expedition was put off for another year (2:173-74). Following this, Champlain and some of de Monts's employees travelled up the St. Lawrence to Montreal Island, which they reached 28 May. Finding that no Indians had arrived, Champlain went above the Lachine Rapids and explored the west end of the island. He then ordered a patch of forest to be cleared at Pointe à Callières (in the present harbour area) and planted crops to test the soil (plate 23). He also had an earth wall built on Market Gate Island, to see whether this site remained above water in the spring flood (2:175-79). Champlain contemplated establishing a settlement on Montreal Island, although it is doubtful that such a plan could have secured any backing in France, given the unfavourable conditions of trade at that time. On 1 June Gravé Du Pont arrived, followed by numerous other Frenchmen who hoped to share in the expected trade.

On 5 June Savignon and another Indian were sent up-river to try to hasten the arrival of their people, but they returned on the ninth, having sighted no one. They did, however, report seeing large numbers of herons on an island in the middle of the Lachine Rapids. Later Savignon, a Frenchman named Louis, and Outetoucos, a Montagnais headman, went hunting on the island. On the way back, their canoe capsized. Louis, who was hampered by his bulky clothing and who, like most Frenchmen of this period, did not know how to swim, panicked and was drowned. Outetoucos, a powerful man, abandoned the canoe and tried to swim to safety, but lost his life as he made his way towards the shore. Only Savignon managed to save himself by clinging to the canoe. He returned reluctantly to the French, fearing that they would blame him for Louis's death and avenge themselves by killing him (2:181-84). While he had strong opinions about French justice, Savignon had failed to observe that it did not operate on the principle of blood revenge.

Finally, on 13 June Iroquet and Ochasteguin arrived with two hundred companions, amongst whom was Savignon's brother, Tregouaroti. These Indians had with them Etienne Brûlé who had been entrusted to their care the year before. Champlain and Savignon went in a canoe to meet them, and speeches and shouts of approval from the Indians were met with a salute of gunfire by the French. The Indians then requested that there be no more firing since many who had come had never seen Europeans before and were frightened by the noise. Savignon and Brûlé both confirmed that they had been well-treated during the winter. The Huron were particularly glad to see Savignon, since the Montagnais had told them he was dead. They also told Champlain that several hundred more Indians

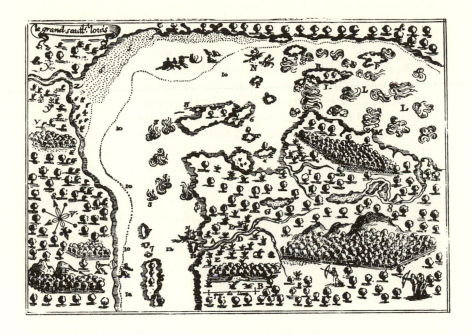

PLATE 23. *Champlain's map of a portion of Montreal Island. From Champlain's* Voyages *of 1613. L indicates the Lachine Rapids; D the St. Pierre River near the present Lachine Canal. A indicates land that Champlain cleared in 1611 to test the fertility of the soil, and E an opening in the forest where the Indians camped when they came to trade with the French. Courtesy Public Archives of Canada.*

had planned to come down-river, but had decided not to when they heard that Champlain had secretly freed the Iroquois prisoner he had acquired the year before and had told him to encourage his people to exterminate the Algonkin (Biggar 1922–36, 2:189–90). It is possible that Champlain had discussed the likelihood of peace with his prisoner, since it had long been the desire of the French traders to reconcile the Iroquois and the Algonkian-speaking peoples. Champlain denied, however, that he had released the prisoner and the version of the story that reached the Algonkin and the Huron has all the earmarks of being a rumour spread by the Montagnais in order to sow distrust amongst the tribes of the interior. The aim of these rumours was to disrupt the developing relationship between these tribes and the French, without endangering the alliance that the Montagnais had with these tribes against the Iroquois.

The next day, the leading Huron and Algonkin consulted with Champlain about where they should locate their temporary encampment. They also had Brûlé, who could now speak Huron, inform him that they were concerned about the large number of Frenchmen who had come up-river and whom they knew would trade but would refuse to help them in their wars. Champlain assured the Indians that all the traders were subjects of the French king and that, even though each group was trading on its own, the Indians had nothing to fear from them (2:189). While these speeches may have been designed to flatter Champlain, it seems more likely that the tribes from the interior, particularly the Huron, were genuinely alarmed to see so many Europeans, especially when the latter were commercial rivals of one another. Hence, in seeking assurances for their own safety, the Huron may have been acting without ulterior motive. Champlain assured them that he had had no dealings with their enemies and, in return for one hundred beaver skins, he distributed trade goods among the Indian leaders who were present. Being reassured of his goodwill, the Indians told Champlain that in five or six days, another three hundred Indians would be coming to trade and to fight the Iroquois. These were presumably Algonkin, who had held back because they were afraid that Champlain had allied himself with their enemies. The next two days were spent trading, but the French traders quarrelled among themselves and various fights broke out among them. In the course of these quarrels, several Indians were attacked. Instead of using this situation to their own advantage, as the more experienced Montagnais would have done, the Huron and Algonkin were frightened and began fortifying their camp (2:192–93).

On the evening of the second day, Savignon was asked to come to the Indians' camp, and later Champlain and Gravé Du Pont were invited also.

There, they found the Huron headmen holding council. These headmen presented them with four strings of shell beads and fifty beaver skins, explaining that these presents had been sent by headmen who had not been able to come down-river, but who, like themselves, wished for an alliance with the French (Biggar 1922–36, 2:194–95). Presumably, the fifty beaver skins represented the major clan segments whose headmen sat on the confederacy council, while the four strings of beads represented the four Huron tribes. The Huron said they knew Champlain wanted to visit their country and that in the future they would take him there, even at the risk of their lives. They added that if other Frenchmen wished to winter with them as Brûlé had done, they would be made welcome. Champlain interpreted this as an invitation to join them in their wars and said that he would ask the French king for forty or fifty men and come the following year to meet their headmen and to help the Huron against their enemies. He also assured them that if their country proved suitable, Frenchmen would settle there. Champlain believed that the Huron approved of this, because they hoped the French would help them to fight the Iroquois and protect their settlements from attack. The Indians promised to provide Champlain and his men with provisions if he should visit their country, and the meeting came to an end at daybreak (2:195–96).

This meeting was attended only by Huron. Its purpose seems to have been to take the first steps towards a treaty of friendship between the Huron and the French that was no longer dependent on the Arendarhonon's special relationship with Iroquet and the Onontchataronon. The conclusion of such an alliance required that Champlain visit the Huron country, where he could meet the headmen who had been unable to travel down-river. Clearly, all fifty of the council chiefs could not leave home at the same time to go to the Lachine Rapids. Champlain's visit would also demonstrate that in the opinion of the French, the Algonkin were no longer intermediaries between themselves and the Huron, although the Algonkin would retain the right to levy tolls on the Huron for use of the Ottawa River. The impression that is gained from this meeting is that the question of an alliance with the French had rapidly become an important issue within the Huron confederacy.

On 17 June the Indians finished their trading and divided into small groups. They left Savignon and their camp under French protection and said they were going to hunt for more beaver. In fact, they established a new camp some distance above the Lachine Rapids, where the French shallops could not follow them. The next day, Iroquet and Tregouaroti returned to fetch Savignon and to invite Champlain and Brûlé to visit

them. Savignon took leave of Champlain the following day, and the next day Champlain was conducted to their encampment. The journey involved a long trek across the island, probably to the shores of the Lake of Two Mountains. There, Champlain was invited to attend a feast at which, although he had already eaten, he ate again so as not to offend local custom. He then attended a meeting, where he was told that the Indians had abandoned their original camp because they had heard that the other French traders intended to kill them and they feared that Champlain would not be able to prevent this from happening (2:199–200). While Champlain's published emphasis on the Indians' distrust of the independent traders may have been partly to discredit these traders and partly a repetition of Indian blandishments designed to flatter him, it seems likely that, to some degree, the Huron and Algonkin were genuinely afraid of the French traders.

Nevertheless, they also informed Champlain that an independent trader named Bouyer was offering them valuable presents to allow a young Frenchman in his employ to spend the winter with them. The Indians said that they would not grant this request, unless it were acceptable to Champlain, since they were under special obligation to him for the help he had given them in their wars. Champlain replied that he did not object to them taking a boy who worked for a rival trader, but they must demand a large number of presents for doing so, and make sure that he remained in the care of Iroquet (2:201–3). This probably meant not only that he should not be allowed to live with a Huron family as Brûlé seems to have done, but that he was to remain in the lower part of the Ottawa Valley. Iroquet may have been planning not to winter in the Huron country, or alternatively Champlain may have been asking him to leave the young Frenchman among a branch of his people who remained in their tribal territory over the winter.

The Onontchataronon seem to have kept their promise; Marcel Trudel (1966a:178 n. 91) has identified Bouyer's young man as Thomas Godefroy de Normanville, who in later years worked as an interpreter, not among the Huron but among the Algonkin. It was also decided that Brûlé, whom Champlain refers to in an impersonal way as "my young man" should return to the Huron country with Tregouaroti (Biggar 1922–36, 2:205). After this was arranged, Champlain was requested to try to convince an Indian who had been captured three times by the Iroquois and cruelly tortured by them, that he should not set off with a small band to try to avenge his sufferings (2:203–4). Although Champlain was unsuccessful in this, the request that he intervene indicates the growing confidence that

the Indians had in him. On his return to the French boats, Champlain shot the Lachine Rapids in a party of eight canoes, thus further enhancing his reputation among his Indian allies (Trudel 1966a:178). Since Champlain was unable to swim, this was an admirable act of courage, especially as Louis had drowned in these rapids only a short time before. Soon afterward, the Huron and Algonkin departed for the interior.

Following the departure of these Indians, the traders waited impatiently for the three hundred Algonkin who were still supposed to be coming down-river. Finally, on 5 July a canoe arrived bearing news that only twenty-four canoes would be arriving, since many Algonkin had died of a fever that had broken out amongst them, and others had already left to go to war. These Indians, who probably numbered about sixty, arrived on 12 July. Before trading, they gave a present to the son of Anadabijou, who was with the French, to express their regret concerning the recent death of his father.[7] They also offered ten beaver skins to the captains of each of the trading vessels to express their friendship and goodwill. Champlain assured them that the French traders would give them presents in return and that they would be allowed to barter in peace. This was followed by a successful trading session (Biggar 1922–36, 2:209).

The next day, these Indians brought Champlain a personal gift of forty beaver skins and expressed their pleasure at the reports they had received concerning his dealings with the first groups of Indians that had come down-river. They also stated that Champlain should found a settlement at the Lachine Rapids to protect this region from the Iroquois and to make trading with the French easier. The principal motive that the Algonkin had for approving this project was to have a permanent trading post that was in their own territory and therefore free from Montagnais influence. In this, and in other ways, the Algonkin were striving to free their trading relationship with the French from dependence upon their alliance with the Montagnais. Champlain gave them presents and assured them that he wished to found a settlement on the island. They then disinterred the body of Outetoucos and buried it with great ceremony on St. Helen's Island, where they felt it would be safe from Iroquois desecration (2:210–11).

On 15 July Tessouat, the powerful chief of the Kichesipirini, arrived with fourteen canoes. He too exchanged greetings with the French and the next day his people traded with them. Meanwhile, Tessouat gave Champlain a valuable present of thirty beaver skins. He spoke with him about possible travels in the north and said that, if any of Champlain's companions wished to go with him, they were welcome to come along. Champlain agreed to send a young man named Nicolas de Vignau with

the Kichesipirini and instructed him on what he was to observe. The Kichesipirini did not have many furs to barter, possibly because they were still
trading most of them eastward along the northern route to Lake St. John
and Tadoussac (2:211–12). On 18 July some of the Algonkin set off to raid
the Iroquois, while the rest returned up-river. It was decided that Champlain should return to France to report to de Monts.

THE NEW MONOPOLY

The continuation of free trade on the St. Lawrence had produced an
economic crisis for the European traders. De Monts's partners no longer
wished to support the settlement at Quebec and it was increasingly obvious
that Champlain's efforts to develop trading contacts in the upper part of
the St. Lawrence Valley were benefiting the free traders more than they
were his own employers. Without a monopoly, exploration would cease and
the chance would be lost to discover mineral wealth and the still anticipated
route to the Far East, both of which were expected greatly to benefit the
prosperity of New France. Without settlement, the St. Lawrence Valley
was without protection and the French claim to it remained ineffectual.

Champlain had long believed it necessary to plan the development of
New France in broad terms. Therefore, as de Monts's modest efforts
foundered, Champlain began to promote his own more grandiose proposals
for a colony on the St. Lawrence. The basis of Champlain's plan, as spelled
out in his two proposals written in 1618, was for a colony with a diversified
economy. Not only furs, but also fish, timber, gum, ashes, tar, dye roots,
hemp, silver, lead, clothing, gems, vines, and livestock were to constitute
the exports of the colony. In addition, it was hoped that revenue could be
derived from tolls charged for the use of a route to China that would
eventually run up the St. Lawrence. To ensure control of the St. Lawrence,
Champlain proposed to found a town in the valley of the St. Charles River
that would be as large as St. Denis in France, and would be named Ludo-
vica, after the new king, Louis XIII. Fifteen priests, three hundred families
of four persons each, and three hundred soldiers would be settled in the
colony, and forts would be built at Tadoussac, Cape Diamond, and on the
south shore of the St. Lawrence to protect it (Biggar 1922–36, 2:326–45).

Two features of Champlain's proposal deserve special notice. The first is
that furs would account for only a small fraction of the total revenue of the
colony, and the second is that one function of the colony, and a means by
which it would increase its population, was to convert Indians to the Chris-

tian faith and teach them to live like Frenchmen. Champlain believed that assimilation of this sort would not be difficult; once the Indians could speak French, they would quickly learn to think and feel like Frenchmen (3:6). He also argued, however, that European colonists were essential so that force could be brought to bear, when needed, to make the Indians abandon their "filthy habits, loose morals, and uncivilized ways" (4:320–21). None of these ideas was new for Champlain. As early as 1603, he had argued that it was essential, for their own good, that the Indians be compelled to adopt French ways, and that colonization was the best way of bringing this about (1:117).

The practical key to the realization of Champlain's dreams of empire continued, however, to reside in the despised and intractable fur trade. In the summer of 1611, he told the Huron that the next time he returned to the St. Lawrence he would be accompanied only by his friends (2:200). His aim was to have the fur-trade monopoly re-established on a more secure basis by grouping the more respectable traders, who annually visited the area, into one large company and by protecting the monopoly that would be granted to these partners by having a powerful nobleman offer the company his patronage, in return for an annual salary. In order to be permitted to join the company, the merchants would have to agree to support Champlain's plans for colonization and exploration (Biggar 1901:85–86).

At some cost to himself, de Monts secured a temporary respite for the settlement at Quebec. When, in the autumn of 1611, his partners refused to continue to support it, de Monts bought them out and agreed to maintain the settlement on an interim basis at his own expense. Meanwhile, Champlain won the patronage of Charles de Bourbon, Comte de Soissons. The count had himself appointed Lieutenant-General in New France and secured a twelve-year monopoly over the fur trade from Quebec westward. He, in turn, appointed Champlain to be his lieutenant in the New World. This empowered Champlain to administer justice, conclude treaties with the Indians, wage war, restrain illegal traders, and continue searching for mines and for a route to the Indies. When de Soissons died, his monopoly was transferred to his nephew, Henri de Bourbon, Prince de Condé. Condé also acquired the more exalted title of Viceroy of New France. On 22 November 1612, he confirmed Champlain in his new office, which made him governor of New France in fact, but not in title. Because of the delay caused by the death of the Comte de Soissons, there was not enough time to organize a new company before trading began in 1613. It was, therefore, announced that Condé would grant a limited number of passports that

would entitle their bearers, and them alone, to send their vessels up-river past Quebec. All traders, whether operating above or below Quebec, were forbidden to pilot foreign vessels into the St. Lawrence or to sell firearms to the Indians (Biggar 1901:88).

Because Champlain was occupied throughout most of 1612 with his efforts to re-establish a monopoly for the fur trade, he was unable to visit Canada that summer. He did not send either the soldiers he promised would aid the Indians or anyone qualified to deal with the Indians in his place. As had happened the year before, many independent traders travelled up-river to Lachine. These were, for the most part, men in whom the Indians had little confidence and who seem to have lacked even the most rudimentary working knowledge of the intricacies of Indian trading relations. Growing competition generated conflicts among them that must have made trading difficult for the Indians. One account states that, in 1612, two hundred Indians turned up at the Lachine Rapids, another gives the number as 2000 (Biggar 1922–36, 2:217, 285). The latter figure is likely a misprint, although two hundred seems unusually low, considering the numbers that had come to trade the previous year.

The Indians were angry that Champlain failed to keep his promise to aid them in their wars. Even more importantly, however, they were alarmed that the principal European whom they trusted, and with whom their leaders had an alliance, was not there. They must have been further confused when some of the independent traders assured them that Champlain was dead, while de Monts's traders stoutly maintained the contrary (2:217–18). None of the French seemed willing, or able, to take Champlain's place and none was prepared to accompany them to war. In the absence of a leader who could represent the French traders and negotiate with the Indians, quarrels broke out, and some of the Indians seem to have been robbed. Because of this, the Indians announced that they would no longer come to the Lachine Rapids to trade. While Champlain may have exaggerated the unpleasant side of these events, his description of what happened illustrates the important role that traditional forms and personal relationships continued to play in the fur trade, at least among the Huron and Algonkin. Neither group was sufficiently dependent on European goods that they could not afford to break off trading with the French for one or two years. In any case, both groups could have continued to obtain such goods by trading with the Montagnais. The latter, as we have already noted, were seeking in subtle ways to undermine the confidence that these tribes had in the French, in hopes of recovering control over the flow of trade goods between the French and the tribes that lived farther inland.

So far, we have been viewing Champlain mainly as an agent of de Monts's trading company. He was obviously brave and adventurous, and apparently well suited to win the support of Indian trading partners by accompanying them on expeditions against their enemies. His criticisms of their religious beliefs might have offended the Indians, but, as Lescarbot (1907–14, 2:179) pointed out, because of difficulties of translation, and particularly because of the absence of the equivalents of many Christian theological terms in Indian languages, much of what Champlain said on this topic must have been totally incomprehensible to his listeners. As a man of action, Champlain impressed the Indians far more than did any of the traders, who came only "to make war on their beavers." Because of this, it has generally been assumed that Champlain was a man who understood the Indians and got along with them. He has been praised for his desire to see the French and Indians intermarry and become one people, although such sentiments indicate merely a lack of racial, as opposed to cultural, prejudice. Trudel (1966c:197) rather extravagantly lauds him for treating the Indians with consideration and for making them laugh and forgiving their offences, and Morris Bishop (1948:113) has argued that, because Champlain was horrified by the enslavement of the Indians in the West Indies, he was opposed to using force to convert them in Quebec.

Yet, beginning in 1612, another side of Champlain's personality became apparent. With increasing emphasis, he presented himself as a colonizer and a vice-regal official, rather than as the agent of a trading company. As he did so, the Indians, with whom as a trader he had established a relationship of trust, became a small part of larger plans. His writings indicate that he came to regard the Indians, and even most Europeans with whom he had dealings, less as individuals than as means whereby he could advance his own career. It is not surprising that, at this stage, Champlain should have been concerned about his future. He was now in his early forties, not wealthy and, except for his work for de Monts, had little to show for his life. Under such circumstances, he must have felt that his own destiny had become inseparably linked with that of Quebec and been desperately anxious to advance the welfare of his unpromising colony. Whether the personal plight of this insecure and ambitious man can excuse the cynical use he made of those around him is, of course, another matter.

In general, Champlain appears to have been extremely ethnocentric and inflexible. Since neither of these characteristics would have been particularly helpful when it came to interacting with Indians, it is likely that Champlain's early successes were the result more of the situation than of the man. It also appears that he pursued the Indian policies that he or his

employers had formulated with less understanding of their ways, and less sympathy, than the majority of historians have imagined. Many of Champlain's personal weaknesses become clear in the dealings that he had with the Huron and Algonkin after 1612.

THE VIGNAU AFFAIR

In 1612, Nicolas de Vignau, who had spent the previous winter living among the Kichesipirini, returned to Paris and reported to Champlain that he had travelled with a relative of Tessouat to the territory of the Nipissing and from there had journeyed northward with them to a body of salt water, where he had seen the wreckage of an English ship. He said that he had been shown the scalps of eighty seamen, who had been slain when they tried to steal corn and other necessities from the Indians. He also reported that these Indians were holding captive a young Englishman. Vignau stated that it was possible to travel from the Lachine Rapids to this northern ocean and return again, by way of the Ottawa River, in seventeen days (Biggar 1922–36, 2:255–57). Champlain had heard from the Indians about this Northern Ocean, and had guessed the existence of Hudson and James Bays, beginning with his first visit to Canada in 1603 (Crouse 1924: 139–40). He therefore determined to make a journey to this ocean the primary objective of his trip to Canada in 1613 (for his knowledge of Canadian geography in 1612, see plate 24).

Champlain left Honfleur on 5 March and arrived at Tadoussac 29 April. There, the Montagnais were dying from hunger, since the winter had been mild and, because of the lack of snow, hunting had been poor (2:249). Champlain remained from 7 to 13 May at Quebec, where again there had been no scurvy; then he set out for the Lachine Rapids, arriving on 21 May. There the traders encountered only a few Algonkin. Some of these were returning from the south with two Iroquois prisoners; others had come down the Ottawa River to trade. The latter informed the French that, because of the bad treatment they had received the year before, many Indians had decided not to come down-river. Instead, 1200 of them had embarked on a campaign against the Iroquois (2:253–54). While we do not know the details of this campaign, it appears to have been directed against the tribes who were raiding the Ottawa Valley to obtain European goods. Because of the large number of warriors involved, it is likely that Huron, as well as the Algonkin, were taking part in it.

The news that most of their Indian trading partners had gone to war

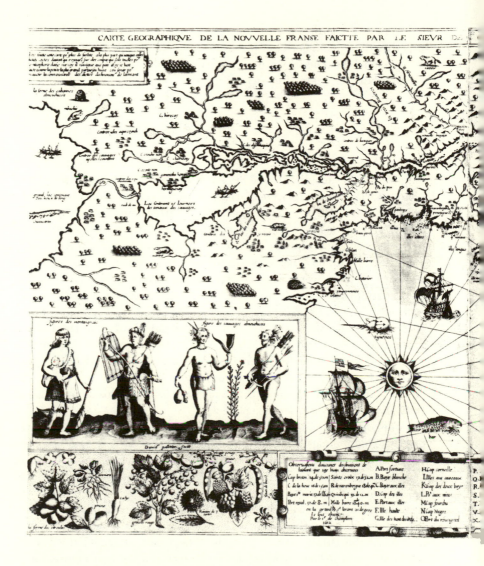

PLATE 24. *Champlain's* Carte géographique de la Nouvelle France, *dated 1612. From Champlain's* Voyages *of 1613. This map is remarkable for its detailed and accurate portrayal of the eastern half of Lake Ontario. The large islands at the head of the St. Lawrence are noted, as well as Prince Edward County, the Bay of Quinte, the Trent River flowing into the Bay of Quinte, and Lake Oneida* (lac des Irocois) *flowing through the Oswego River into Lake Ontario. This map appears to be based on a*

description of the interior collected by Champlain from an Indian informant in 1603 (Biggar 1922–36, 1 : 159–61). Champlain apparently decided not to use this hearsay evidence on his small map of 1613. His representations of the east end of Lake Ontario on his maps of 1616 and 1632 are also far less accurate than on this one, although he personally visited the area in 1615. Courtesy Public Archives of Canada.

greatly discouraged the French who had been granted licences to trade. Since Champlain was once again responsible for relations with the Indians, he decided to travel up the Ottawa River to make a new alliance with the Algonkin and encourage them to trade. He left St. Helen's Island on 27 May, travelling with four Frenchmen and one Indian in two canoes. The French included Vignau and Thomas Godefroy, whom Captain Bouyer had formerly sent to live with the Onontchataronon. As far as the Chaudière Falls, each night was spent within barricades erected against the Iroquois warriors who were reported to be frequenting this region (2:260). Beyond the Long Sault Rapids, Champlain's party encountered fifteen canoes belonging to an Algonkin band known as the Quenongebin. These Indians had heard that Champlain was back and were travelling down-river to trade with the French. True to the Algonkin policy of seeking to retain control over trade passing along the Ottawa River, they attempted to dissuade Champlain from continuing his journey. Yet, after much persuasion, they agreed to provide him with an experienced canoeman to take charge of his second craft. In return, one of Champlain's French companions was ordered to accompany them down-river to protect them from the Iroquois (Biggar 1922–36, 2:264–65). Farther up the Ottawa, Champlain passed the mouth of the Petite Nation River, along which the Algonkin band called the Weskarini, or Little Nation, lived (map 13). He was informed that it was possible to travel across the interior of Quebec to the headwaters of the St. Maurice River by way of the Gatineau and that the Algonkin sometimes followed this route to avoid the Iroquois (2:266–67). Champlain also observed the offerings of tobacco that the Indians made to the spirit of the Chaudière Falls every time they portaged around it.

Farther upstream a long portage had to be made around the Rapides des Chats. This required the French to abandon some of their food and clothing in order to lighten their loads. Two more falls were passed before entering Lac des Chats, into which the Madawaska River was seen flowing from the south. The valley of this river was the territory of the Matouweskarini Algonkin, from which the name of the river has been derived. Above Lac des Chats, a dispute broke out between Vignau and the Indians, concerning whether it was preferable to follow the river to Morrison Island or to travel there over land. Champlain chose to follow the Indians' advice. The route, which was obstructed with fallen pine trees, took him past a series of small lakes until he reached Muskrat Lake, where a group of Algonkin, whose headman was named Nibachis, had its summer camp (2:275). These were probably the Keinouche (Pike) Algonkin, or Quenongebin. Circumstantial evidence indicates that Champlain lost his astrolabe near Green Lake. An

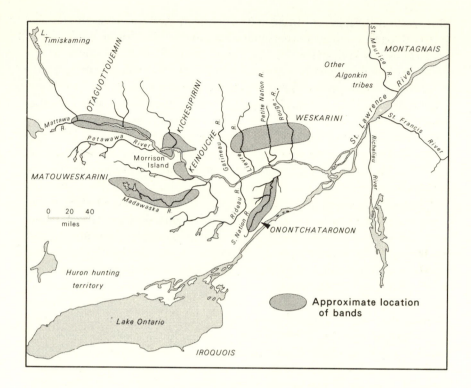

MAP 13. *Location of Algonkin bands definitely attested as living in the Ottawa Valley in the first half of the seventeenth century.*

astrolabe inscribed with the date 1603 was found near there in 1867. While it cannot be proved that this was Champlain's instrument, it seems almost certain that it was.[8]

Nibachis was surprised to see Europeans in his territory, but welcomed Champlain and offered to him and his companions tobacco and fish. He also showed Champlain the small fields where his people were growing corn. Champlain noted that the soil was poor and for that reason the Algonkin did not depend as heavily on agriculture as did the Huron. Nibachis had two canoes fitted out and, after seven leagues travel by water and an easy portage, Champlain arrived on the shores of the enlarged section of the Ottawa River that lies south of Allumette Island. There he was met by Tessouat, who had been forewarned of his coming. Tessouat conducted his guests across the river to Morrison Island, where the Kichesipirini had their summer camp. This small island, which was covered with oak, pine, and

elm trees, had rapids at either end. Champlain believed that the Kichesipirini lived there to avoid their enemies, but the real reason appears to be
that the island lay astride the main trade route along the Ottawa River.
Indians travelling in either direction had to land at this point, and thus
could be forced to pay for rights of passage (Wrong 1939:255). This island
gave the Kichesipirini control over the river such as no other Algonkin
tribe enjoyed and this explains, to a large degree, the special jealousy with
which they guarded their rights to tax and regulate trade in the upper part
of the Ottawa Valley. Sagard was later to describe the Kichesipirini as the
most arrogant and uncivil, but also the richest and best clothed, Indians he
had seen (ibid. 257–58).

Champlain examined the Kichesipirini village and visited their cemetery, where he found the graves to be covered with wooden structures and
adorned with carved representations of the deceased. He was informed that
the Kichesipirini buried with their dead all the things they had possessed
in life, in the belief that their spirits were able to use these objects. When
Champlain asked the Kichesipirini why they lived in this barren location,
they replied that, if Champlain kept his promise to establish a French
settlement at the Lachine Rapids, they would move south and join him
there (Biggar 1922–36, 2:280–81). It seems highly unlikely, however, that
the Kichesipirini would have abandoned Morrison Island, which would
have meant relinquishing their control over commerce along the Ottawa
River. I therefore interpret this reply as encouragement to the French to
found a trading settlement within Algonkin territory, similar to the one
they had founded in 1608 among the Montagnais. Later developments suggest that the Kichesipirini also may have thought of establishing a satellite
village on Montreal Island, both to develop closer relations with the French
and to be able to cultivate corn under more favourable conditions (Thwaites
1896–1901, 29:145–47). Champlain repeated his promise that he would
establish a colony there the following year.

The next day, Champlain was invited to attend a feast that was held in
the house of Tessouat, the headman of the Kichesipirini. All the men of the
settlement were present and the food consisted of corn soup, boiled fish, and
roasted meat. Champlain did not eat any of the soup, which he observed
was dirty, but asked for fish and meat to prepare in his own fashion. As was
the custom among the Huron, Tessouat did not eat, but spent his time
entertaining his guests (Biggar 1922–36, 2:282). Iroquoian influences can
be observed in this and in other details of the Algonkin cultural pattern.
When the feast was over, the young men withdrew and a half-hour was
spent smoking in silence in order to clear the brain. Champlain then assured

the Kichesipirini of his friendship and of his desire to help them in their wars. He explained that he had men for this purpose at the Lachine Rapids and had come to invite the various Algonkin bands to wage war. He also mentioned his desire to see the Northern Ocean. He then asked for four canoes to take him up-river, so that he might invite the Nipissing to accompany the French to war (2:283–84).

The Kichesipirini had no desire to make themselves the instruments by which Champlain would be able to contact the Nipissing and conclude an alliance with them. After conferring with his council, Tessouat replied that, as a result of the bad treatment the Algonkin had experienced at Lachine the previous year, their young men had already gone to war. It would therefore be better to postpone a French military expedition until the following year. He stated that Champlain could have four canoes, but warned him that the Nipissing were dangerous sorcerers and, for that reason, the Kichesipirini were not their friends. Tessouat added that the Nipissing were cowards and therefore of little value in any military campaign (2:284–86). He obviously hoped that Champlain would respect the Kichesipirini's disapproval of his plan to visit the Nipissing and would decline his offer of canoes. Champlain, however, was extremely anxious to visit the Northern Ocean and wished to contact the Nipissing, who travelled there. He therefore replied that he did not fear the dangers of the journey and thanked his hosts for their canoes (2:286–87).

A few hours later, while Champlain was examining the crops that the Kichesipirini had planted, Thomas Godefroy reported that Tessouat and his council had concluded that Champlain's expedition would have to be postponed until the following year. Enough Kichesipirini would then be available to ensure that the Nipissing did not harm him (2:287). This was all too clearly another case of Algonkians attempting to thwart Champlain's plans to travel north of the St. Lawrence. Champlain was angered by this news and told the Kichesipirini that if they failed to honour their promise to provide him with canoes, he would no longer regard them as his allies; but he added that if the journey were an inconvenience for them, he could make do with two canoes. He said that he was surprised that the Kichesipirini should object to him visiting the Nipissing, since they had already taken Vignau there and he had not found the route as difficult, nor the people as unfriendly, as they described them (2:288).

The Kichesipirini looked angrily at Vignau, and Tessouat asked him if he claimed to have been among the Nipissing. After some hesitation, Vignau replied that he had been there. Some Indians leapt upon the young man and Tessouat called him a liar. Tessouat added that he was not sur-

prised that Champlain was importuning the Kichesipirini, after he had been told such fables. Champlain was also told that Vignau had passed the entire winter living with Tessouat. Champlain managed to rescue Vignau from his assailants, whereupon Vignau once again swore that it was true that he had been to the Northern Ocean (2:288–90).

At this point, Godefroy came to tell Champlain that the Kichesipirini had secretly sent, or were planning to send, a canoe to notify the Nipissing of his arrival. The aim of this expedition was, no doubt, to attract some Nipissing down-river so that Champlain would have no excuse for travelling to their country. Champlain returned to the council and announced to his hosts that it had been revealed to him in a dream that they planned to send a canoe to the Nipissing without telling him. He added that this angered him since he wished to go there in person. He also recounted to them Vignau's story of his trip north. When they had heard this story, the Kichesipirini demanded that Vignau prove he had been there, saying that if he could not do so, he should be killed. Vignau became very frightened, especially when Champlain threatened that if they should go farther and the story prove false, he would have him strangled. After some reflection, Vignau told Champlain that he had never been beyond Morrison Island and that all he had said concerning the Northern Ocean was untrue. Hearing this, Champlain became so angry that he could no longer tolerate having Vignau in his presence. Vignau told Godefroy that he had not thought Champlain would attempt the journey and had invented the story in hopes of a reward. To atone for what he had done, he offered to remain there and attempt to find the Northern Ocean. Champlain was determined, however, to take him back to Lachine, where he would compel him to face justice (Biggar 1922–36, 2:290–96).

Champlain now despaired of ever seeing the Northern Ocean and regretted that he had been wasting his time and had annoyed the Kichesipirini. He told Tessouat that he was convinced that Vignau was a liar. The Kichesipirini smugly admonished Champlain that he should have shown more confidence in their headmen, who were his friends and always spoke the truth, rather than in a mercurial young man like Vignau. They added that they were convinced that on the way up-river Vignau had tried to kill him, thus planting a further seed of suspicion, which quickly took root in Champlain's mind. The Indians said that if Champlain gave them leave to do so, they would kill Vignau; and they were about to lay hands on him when Champlain intervened, saying that he personally would see that he was punished.

Champlain informed the Kichesipirini that there were four French

vessels at the Lachine Rapids and invited them to come there to trade. He also promised Tessouat that if he were able, next year he would return prepared to go to war with his Indian allies (2:298). On 10 June Champlain and Tessouat exchanged farewell presents and Champlain asked him to protect the wooden crosses he had erected to mark the stages of his journey up-river. Then, accompanied by forty Kichesipirini canoes loaded with furs, Champlain began to make his way down-river. As Champlain departed from Morrison Island, he was filled with trust and goodwill for the Kichesipirini, and especially for their "good old headman" Tessouat (2:298).

Champlain's plans to travel northward came to an embarrassing end, once he became convinced that Vignau was a liar. It is unclear, however, to what extent Vignau lied and whether or not his later confession was a true one. Trudel (1966a:200–1) believes that Vignau probably visited James Bay in 1612 and that it was only by threatening to kill him that the Indians frightened him into denying that his story was true. He points out that if Vignau had not believed what he said, he would not have offered to risk his life to search for the Northern Ocean. Trudel concludes that Champlain was the dupe of the Kichesipirini, and Vignau a victim of their machinations to control trade with the interior.

There is much to suggest that Vignau's original story contained at least an element of truth. When Tessouat first took Vignau to live with him, he spoke of a journey to the north and promised that Vignau would accompany him (Biggar 1922–36, 2:211–12). Champlain recorded this promise in the account of his voyage of 1611, but seems to have forgotten about it by 1613. The Nipissing were active traders and, in later years, one of their most important trade routes took some of them from Lake Nipissing to James Bay and back again once each year. That they offered to take Champlain north with them in 1616 (3:104) is evidence that this trade route was already established by that time, and it may have been a prehistoric trade route of some importance. Finally, Henry Hudson had spent the winter of 1610–11 on Hudson and James Bays and, the following June, he, his son, and six other men were forced into a shallop and cut adrift on James Bay by his mutinous crew (Neatby 1966:377).

There are, however, some serious objections to Vignau's story. It is possible, as Champlain feared, that Vignau had heard rumours about Hudson's misfortunes and had based his story on these rumours. The total of eighty men he reported were killed is an impossible figure; yet Trudel (1966a:200–201) has argued in Vignau's defence that eighty may be a misprint for eight, in which case the number would be almost correct. Also, the Cree who lived in the vicinity of James Bay did not grow corn,

or any other crop; hence the statement that the English tried to rob them of their agricultural produce indicates a lack of personal knowledge of northern Ontario. Again, however, it could be argued that the corn Vignau refers to had been brought as trade goods from the south. It is not impossible that the Nipissing were carrying corn meal this far north, although the difficulties involved in transporting it would have meant that it was being traded in only very small quantities.

The most serious objection to Vignau's story is, however, his chronology. In 1641, Father Jérôme Lalemant reported that each spring a group of Nipissing went to trade with the tribes that gathered along the shores of James Bay. The journey northward, which probably followed the north shore of Lake Superior and down the Missinaibi River, lasted about thirty days, after which they travelled along the bay for about ten days. The journey home, by way of the Abitibi River and Lake Timiskaming, must have taken at least another month.[9] A statement that in the summer the whole tribe gathered on the shores of Lake Nipissing suggests that they returned from this journey sometime in early July, which would be possible if they had set out in late April (Thwaites 1896–1901, 21:239). Since the trade at Lachine was normally over by mid-July, Vignau and his Kichesipirini hosts would have had to follow a very tight schedule for Vignau to have been able to return to France in 1612. Yet it was not an impossible one. What gives the lie to Vignau's account is his claim that the journey took only seventeen days.[10] There is also the question of whether or not, even if the Nipissing and Kichesipirini were better friends than the latter wished Champlain to think they were, the Nipissing would have allowed the Kichesipirini and a French youth to explore one of their important trading routes, especially one that could be exploited from the Ottawa Valley.

There is no doubt that Vignau had some accurate information about the north. What is less certain is whether he had actually seen James Bay or merely had heard an account of the Nipissing's journey north in 1611. If they had stayed at James Bay long enough that year, they might have learned what happened to Hudson and his party after they had been abandoned by their shipmates. This explanation would account for Vignau's later offer to search for a route to Hudson Bay, which implies that he had not travelled such a route, although he was confident that it existed. It might also explain why Vignau, at no point, attempted to retract his confession of having lied; although his refusal to divulge more detailed information about his contacts with the Nipissing is a good indication that the Kichesipirini had frightened him into silence, as Trudel claims.

In any case, Vignau's confession cannot be accepted as a complete explanation for Champlain's hasty decision to cancel his journey northward. Champlain knew, from English reports, that there was a sea to the north and numerous Indians, from Tadoussac westward, had confirmed that it was possible to reach this sea from the St. Lawrence Valley. It was, therefore, illogical for him to conclude that, because of some geographical barrier, the people living in the Ottawa Valley had no knowledge of this sea (Biggar 1922–36, 2:293). Both the Montagnais and the Algonkin had already repeatedly thwarted his plans to travel northward. Therefore he ought to have been suspicious of further efforts to prevent his movement up-river. His credulousness towards the Kichesipirini suggests that he was intimidated as well as deceived by them; while the vehemence with which he turned on Vignau indicates that he was not the best judge of character, of either Indians or Europeans.[11] Considerable naiveté about the Indians is evident in Champlain's failure to take account of their policies, as is a patronizing attitude in his under-estimation of their ability to devise stratagems to deceive him.

After Champlain left Morrison Island, he travelled directly down the Ottawa River, thus having a chance to see the stretch of river that the portage by way of Muskrat Lake had enabled him to avoid. There were six or seven falls in this area, which made it more difficult to go up the river than to go down. Before they reached Lachine, the forty Kichesipirini canoes that accompanied Champlain were joined by nine large Weskarini ones, carrying forty men, and by twenty more Kichesipirini canoes that had set out ahead, each heavily laden with merchandise. Champlain arranged with the Indians that none of them should begin trading until he gave the word. In this way, he hoped to make sure that independent traders could not get a share of the trade (2:303).

Once Champlain returned to the Lachine Rapids, Vignau was made to confess his lies in the presence of both the French and his Kichesipirini accusers. He asked to be pardoned and promised that if he were allowed to stay in Canada, he would search for the Northern Ocean. When none of the Indians present would agree to take him, Champlain decided to abandon Vignau "to God's keeping" (2:307). This is the last that is heard of Vignau. If a French trader did not take pity on him and help him to return to France, it is likely that he was left at the mercy of the Kichesipirini who, seeing him abandoned by his people, probably killed him, as they had threatened to do, for revealing their secrets.

After trading was over, Champlain asked the Algonkin to let two young men stay with them for the winter. At first they objected, pointing out the

trouble that Vignau had caused. Finally, however, when Champlain vouched for the behaviour of these men and insisted that the Indians take them as a pledge of friendship, they agreed to do so (2:307). Champlain left Montreal Island on 27 June, while the traders remained to await the return of the Indians from their wars. No Huron had arrived by this time and there is no evidence that any turned up later in the year. The Huron were not yet so dependent on European goods that they had to come annually to obtain them and, in view of the troubles they had experienced the year before, they may not have bothered. On the other hand, the many Algonkin who came to trade, in spite of a major military campaign, indicate the increasing organization of trade amongst the Indians of the Ottawa Valley.

CHAMPLAIN'S NEW COMPANY

In the course of the trading season of 1613, several boats belonging to privileged traders were waylaid and robbed on their way from Quebec to Tadoussac. This was apparently done by independent traders, who were still permitted to operate on the lower part of the St. Lawrence River. The attacks gave the Prince de Condé an excuse to ask for, and obtain, an extension of his monopoly as far as the Matane River in the Gaspé Peninsula. He was thus able to bring the lucrative trade at Tadoussac under his control and to enrich and enhance the prestige of his company (Le Blant and Baudry 1967:307–9). In the spring of 1614, the articles of the new *Compagnie du Canada* were agreed on. The shares of the company were to be divided into three portions; one held by traders from Rouen, the other two by those of St. Malo and La Rochelle; however, the merchants from La Rochelle refused to sign the contract and finally the shares were divided between the merchants from Rouen and St. Malo. These traders agreed to pay the Prince de Condé one thousand crowns annually and to take out six families each year as colonists. Champlain, as Condé's lieutenant, was to receive a substantial salary and to have at his disposal four men from every vessel that traded on the St. Lawrence. The settlement at Quebec became the property, and therefore the responsibility, of the new company (ibid. 310–21).

In 1614, the trade carried on by the *Compagnie du Canada* must have been considerable, since over 25,000 skins were exported from New France.[12] Champlain did not return to Canada that summer and his second failure to fulfil promises to build a trading post near Lachine and to help his Indian allies in their wars must have puzzled and annoyed them. If

they had counted on Champlain joining them in a campaign that year, they were compelled to revise their plans.

It is unclear why Champlain did not visit Canada in the summer of 1614. It may have been partly for personal reasons. The previous autumn he had been having problems with his sixteen-year-old wife, whom he had married four years earlier, mainly for her dowry.[13] More importantly, however, he seems to have remained in France to promote the work of colonization. As yet, his governate was nothing more than a trading post, and previous experience had taught him not to trust the promises that traders made to promote settlement. Champlain was seeking allies who were as interested as he was in seeing French settlements established in Canada. One perhaps minor way he hoped these settlements could be made to grow was by encouraging Indians to adopt French ways and to settle down as French subjects. It therefore seemed worthwhile to encourage the clergy to undertake missionary work among them. Champlain lacked the resources to support such a project. Nevertheless, he persuaded Louis Houel, sieur de Petit Pré, to find three or four Recollet friars who were willing to go to Canada and to try to raise funds to support them. This man was a secretary of the King and Controller-General of the salt works in Champlain's home town of Brouage. Although Houel's initial efforts were not successful, at the meeting of the Estates-General that took place in the autumn of 1614, the cardinals and bishops approved Champlain's project and raised 1500 livres to sustain four missionaries. The following March, the associates of the *Compagnie du Canada* agreed to transport six missionaries to Canada without charge each year and to support them there (Trudel 1966a : 210–12). Soon after, Champlain embarked for Quebec in the company of four Recollets: Fathers Denis Jamet, Jean Dolbeau, and Joseph Le Caron, and lay brother Pacifique Duplessis. Jamet was the superior of the mission, but it was Le Caron who chose to begin his mission work among the Huron. Le Caron, born about 1586 near Paris, had been chosen as chaplain and tutor to the Duc d'Orléans. When the Duke died, Le Caron joined the Recollets, making his profession in that order in 1611.

Sealing the Alliance

TRADE AND POLITICS IN THE HURON COUNTRY

The six years that had elapsed since the Arendarhonon first made contact with the French had brought about many changes within the Huron confederacy. The only Frenchman to witness these changes was the young

Etienne Brûlé, who seems to have been living among the Huron since 1610. Already in the spring of 1611 Brûlé was wearing Huron dress and was well on his way to becoming a skilful interpreter and intermediary in the fur trade. Unfortunately, he left no account of these years, or of his life generally. His career is known only through the writings of Champlain and various priests, all of whom hated and despised him.

Nevertheless, from what has been recorded it is possible to gain a general idea of what happened among the Huron during these years. According to the Jesuits, since the Arendarhonon was the first tribe to contact the French, Huron law granted this tribe the sole right to carry on trade with them. Yet, because of the importance of this trade, the Arendarhonon decided that it was best to share it with the other tribes of the confederacy. Of their previous right, they retained only the distinction of being the oldest and closest allies of the French (Thwaites 1896–1901, 20:19). Decades later, the Arendarhonon were willing to offer protection to Frenchmen who were having difficulties with the other Huron tribes.

This sharing of trade among all the tribes of the confederacy took place before 1615, since by then the Attignawantan were actively engaged in both the diplomatic and economic activities that were associated with it. In later years, it became clear that even if the Attignawantan were willing to let the Arendarhonon claim the honour of being the oldest Huron allies of the French, they were careful to monopolize important contacts, and possibly the bulk of the trading between the Huron and the French. What happened among the Huron was probably as follows.

In the winter of 1608–9, Ochasteguin had been invited to accompany the Onontchataronon on an expedition against the Mohawk and to visit the settlement that the French had recently established on the St. Lawrence. Ochasteguin accepted and, with a small band of Arendarhonon, he became the first Huron to travel down the Ottawa River and meet the French. According to Huron law, as a result of having opened up a new trade route, Ochasteguin and the members of his clan segment became the masters of that trade. This meant that they acquired full rights to determine who would be allowed to participate in it. Since such permission was normally granted only in return for gifts, or a share of the profits, Ochasteguin was theoretically in a position to acquire immense wealth by Huron standards, and, by redistributing it, to assume a dominant role in Huron politics. Yet that control of this trade was assumed by Atironta suggests that, because of its importance, the principal headman of the tribe soon took charge of it, regardless of the clan segment to which the actual discoverer of the route belonged.

While this usurpation may seem autocratic, it is in keeping with the political realities of a society lacking centralized control. There was no way to police trade routes; therefore, if the rest of the Arendarhonon were determined to trade with the French, Ochasteguin's clan segment would have been unable to enforce their theoretical monopoly. If conflict was to be avoided, the Arendarhonon had to agree how this trade was to be shared amongst the clan segments that made up the tribe and, at the same time, they had to stand together as a tribe to guard against claims by outsiders. This could not be accomplished if serious disputes were to break out between rival claimants. Hence, once it was decided that the trade was sufficiently important that all Arendarhonon should share in it, the principal headman of the tribe seems to have been recognized as its rightful master. By being empowered to collect the fees associated with this trade, Atironta would have been able to secure large quantities of European goods. The prestige that he derived from redistributing these goods among his own people not only protected his traditional authority, but permitted him to enhance his prestige.

Such an arrangement was particularly important for preserving the power of traditional headmen, once other traders began to acquire personal influence and renown from their enhanced ability to provide their fellow tribesmen with European goods. The ability of these headmen to acquire wealth from their formal control of the fur trade, without having to engage in trade themselves, probably explains the sobriquets *atiwarontas*, *atiwanens*, and *ondakhienhai* (big stones, elders, and stay-at-homes) which the Jesuits report were applied to them in later times (Thwaites 1896–1901, 10:231–33). Huron mechanisms for the control of trade seem to have been such that the opening of new trade routes enhanced the power of traditional office holders, rather than bringing about a major reorganization of the political structure.[14]

The same process was repeated at the level of the confederacy. Trade with the French could not help but be of vital interest to all Huron; hence the other Huron tribes were anxious to claim a share in it. While the Arendarhonon were the second largest tribe in the confederacy, the Attignawantan were more numerous. Moreover, the Attignawantan were the original inhabitants of north Simcoe County, and had received the Arendarhonon into their territory; hence they had the Arendarhonon at a psychological disadvantage. The great influence of the Attignawantan within the confederacy is reflected in the fact that their headmen occupied half of the seats on its council. They also referred to the Arendarhonon as cousins or offspring, rather than as sisters or equals. If the Arendarhonon

had chosen to ignore the Attignawantan's wishes to trade with the French, conflict might have ensued which would have disrupted trade, exposed the Huron to the attacks of their enemies, and perhaps led to the break-up of the confederacy. Rather than risk these consequences, the Arendarhonon chose to share their trade with the other members of the confederacy. This seems to have meant granting the headmen of the other tribes permission to trade with the French without requiring them to pay the Arendarhonon for doing so. By appearing to do this willingly, the Arendarhonon were able to convert an act of political necessity into one from which they were able to derive honour and prestige. In this way, they also managed to obtain official recognition as being the special allies of the French.

The formal sharing of this trade, and a general discussion of future relations with the French, seems to have taken place at the annual meeting of the confederacy council held in the spring of 1611. No doubt, the redefinition of trading privileges that was worked out at this meeting made the Huron council chiefs anxious to conclude a treaty with the French, in which the latter would recognize these newly acquired rights. It is therefore likely that traders from tribes other than the Arendarhonon travelled down-river in 1611. I have already suggested that the fifty beaver skins and four strings of wampum that were presented to Champlain and Gravé Du Pont at that time appear to have been the first ritual exchange between the entire confederacy and the French.

The broader composition of the Huron trading expedition of 1611 also may explain why Champlain began to refer to the Huron as Charioquois, instead of Ochasteguin, and why both of these names appear on his small map of 1613 (plate 25). Champlain may have used Ochasteguin to refer specifically to the Arendarhonon, while by Charioquois he meant either the other Huron tribes, or the Huron in general. Although we do not know the origin of Charioquois, or many other names that Champlain used, its general significance is clear, since in the 1632 edition of his writings the more familiar term Huron is consistently substituted for it (Biggar 1922–36, 2:186 n. 2).

Hereafter, trading relations with the French appear to have been pursued most actively by the northern branch of the Attignawantan. Sagard reported that in the 1620s men from neighbouring villages came to Quieunonascaran to seek permission from the headman, Onorotandi, to trade along the lakes and rivers leading to the Saguenay and from his brother (i.e., fellow headman), Auoindaon, to go to Quebec (Wrong 1939:99). While neither was the principal headman of the Attignawantan (that was the prerogative of Anenkhiondic of Ossossané), the cleavage

CHAMPLAIN'S SMALL MAP OF 1613.

PLATE 25. *Champlain's small map of 1613. From Champlain's* Voyages *of 1613. Drawn late in 1613, this map is an improvement of another map by Champlain probably dating from the winter of 1612–13. The main difference is a more detailed portrayal of the Ottawa River resulting from his visit to that area in the summer of 1613. Both maps locate the Hochataigains (Ochasteguin's Huron) and the Charioquet (later called Huron) indeterminately north of the St. Lawrence and west of the Ottawa Rivers. This may reflect Champlain's growing awareness of a distinction between the Arendarhonon and the rest of the Huron after 1611. He later lost sight of this distinction. Courtesy Public Archives of Canada.*

between the northern and southern Attignawantan was such that this arrangement is not necessarily an objection to a general argument that control over major trade routes fell into the hands of the principal headmen in each tribe.

Unfortunately, we do not know enough about Brûlé to be certain where he was living during this critical period; however, by the 1620s, he was no longer with the Arendarhonon. Instead, he seems to have been domiciled at Toanché, which was the Attignawantan's chief point of departure for the St. Lawrence (Jurgens 1966:132). Brûlé may have been prized away from his original hosts by the Attignawantan, or he may have decided on his own to move to Toanché. In either case, his action is indicative of the degree to which trade with the French had fallen into the hands of the most powerful of the Huron tribes.

In terms of distance, it would have been easiest for the Huron to have traded with the French by way of the Trent Valley and the St. Lawrence River. This route was already known to the Algonkin, and presumably had been used by them in the preceding decade. For two reasons, however, it was not the route that the Huron chose to follow. First, it took them into Iroquois-controlled territory, which made it too dangerous for commercial purposes. Secondly, it went through an area that was uninhabited; hence the Huron would not have been able to acquire furs from traditional trading partners on their way to the St. Lawrence. While the route by way of Georgian Bay and the Ottawa Valley was a longer one which required making over fifty portages, it had definite advantages and, for all practical purposes, was the only one available to the Huron. This route gave the Attignawantan, and possibly the Attigneenongnahac, an advantage over the other Huron tribes, since it passed through the country of the Nipissing, who had long been their trading partners. On the other hand, the Arendarhonon were intimate with the Onontchataronon; hence, they had a compensating advantage when it came to travelling along the lower part of the Ottawa River.

CONFLICT ON THE OTTAWA RIVER

Increasing trade along the Ottawa River had attracted Iroquois raiders to that area. Their aim was to obtain trade goods, by robbing them from the Huron and Algonkin who were using the river. It is possible that some of these raiders were Mohawk, who stepped up their attacks along the

Ottawa once they decided that it was too dangerous to continue raiding on the St. Lawrence. Yet, the Mohawk were now also able to rob Indians nearer home, who were trading with the Dutch along the Hudson River. Such robberies may account for why the Mohawk were reported to have been fighting the Mahican in 1614 (Jameson 1909:47). The same year, the Dutch built a trading post called Fort Nassau, on Castle Island, near Albany, where they left ten or twelve men to trade with the Indians. This post remained in operation until 1618. It was probably during this period that the Mohawk began trading with Europeans. By as early as 1616, Dutch traders were being employed among both the Mohawk and the Mahican (O'Callaghan 1856–87, 1:14).

The tribes that had the most to gain from attacking the Ottawa Valley were the Oneida and Onondaga, who still lacked easy access to European trading posts. Such raids inevitably exacerbated any existing conflicts between them and the Huron and Algonkin. They also gave the latter peoples a common interest in freeing the Ottawa River, so that it could be used as a safe trading route, as they were now accustomed to use the St. Lawrence River. By 1612, conflict between these rival blocs had grown to the point where over one thousand warriors set out to attack the offending Iroquois. As a result of these raids, the Huron were drawn into a conflict with the Onondaga and Oneida that had probably not existed, or at least had been much less serious, prior to the development of the fur trade. The initial stages of this conflict continued until at least 1615.

Yet, if economic motivations were expanding the scale of warfare, they do not seem to have influenced its conceptualization. These expeditions remained primarily matters of blood revenge. Their aim was to discourage the Iroquois from attacking Indians in the Ottawa Valley, rather than to annihilate them as a people. In this respect, the warfare in the Ottawa Valley was more traditional than were the assaults that the Mohawk had launched against the former inhabitants of the St. Lawrence Valley several decades earlier. This warfare did, however, make it possible for the Huron to secure trading rights in the Ottawa Valley. Without the need for allies, it is unlikely that the Algonkin would have been willing to permit the Huron to travel down-river to trade with the French. The Algonkin now found themselves in the same situation that the Montagnais had been in earlier. To secure allies to fight the Iroquois, it was necessary for them to grant the right to visit the French to their former clientele to the west. By so doing, they risked losing their ability to maintain a middle-man position in respect to trade with the interior (map 14).

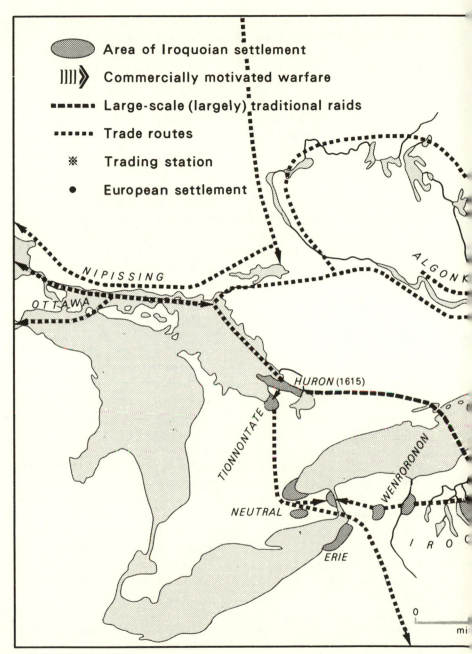

MAP 14. *Intertribal relations, c. 1615.*

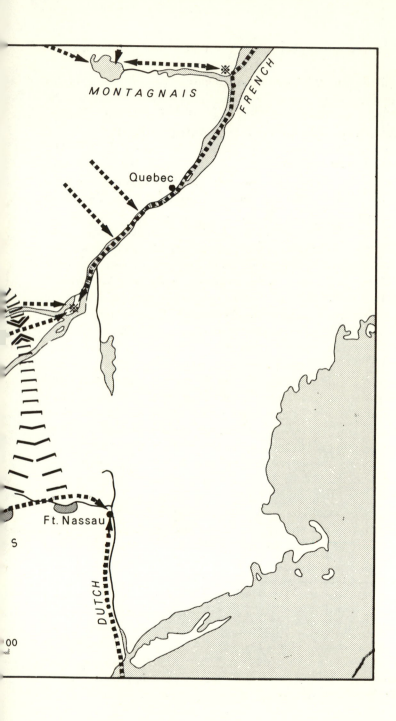

MONTAGNAIS

FRENCH

Quebec

Ft. Nassau

DUTCH

LE CARON AND CHAMPLAIN JOURNEY TO THE HURON COUNTRY

Champlain and the Recollets arrived at Tadoussac on 25 May 1615. As soon as the shallops were ready, Le Caron went up-river to meet the Indians who had come to trade. That year, the Huron and Algonkin gathered at the Lachine Rapids, but were also frequenting the mouth of the Rivière des Prairies, which flows north of Montreal Island.[15] The latter river provided an easier passage from the Ottawa River to the St. Lawrence since none of its rapids was so difficult to negotiate as were those at Lachine. It was also more sheltered from Iroquois attack than was the St. Lawrence.

After he had met the Indians, Father Le Caron decided to spend the winter in the Huron country. He hoped to study the Huron language and way of life and to see what hope there was of converting these Indians to Christianity (Biggar 1922–36, 3:26). The Huron do not seem to have had any objection to taking him and no doubt believed that by having an older, and therefore more responsible, Frenchman living amongst them, their alliance with the French would be strengthened. On 20 June Le Caron returned to Quebec to obtain provisions for the winter. On the way, he met Champlain, who was travelling up-river to meet the Indians. Champlain advised Le Caron not to visit the Huron that year, but to spend the winter at Quebec and go there the following spring. He argued that at Quebec Le Caron would have the companionship of his fellow priests and other Frenchmen, while little satisfaction could be hoped for if he dwelt among the Indians (3:28–31). At this time, Champlain had no intention of wintering among the Huron himself; hence his advice may partly have been motivated by jealousy that someone else would gain ascendancy over them. In any case, he regarded living with the Indians as something fit only for wild young men such as Brûlé. Le Caron believed that he could adapt to life among the Huron and silenced Champlain's objections by announcing that he was prepared to suffer hardship to accomplish his mission.

When Champlain arrived at the Rivière des Prairies, the Indians greeted him enthusiastically. The Huron requested that he honour his promise to return with them to their country with a number of armed Frenchmen, so that he could help them against their "old enemies," the Iroquois. They also reminded Champlain of his failure to fulfil his former promises to assist them in their wars (3:31). The Algonkin did not object to this visit and were themselves sending warriors to the Huron country to join a military expedition against the Iroquois. It would thus appear

that by inviting the Algonkin to join in yet another major raid against their common enemy the Huron had manoeuvred them into dropping their overt opposition to letting Champlain travel inland to meet the Huron headmen and conclude an alliance with them.

Gravé Du Pont concluded that even though Champlain had not planned to accompany the Huron, it was necessary that he do so at this time in order to assure their continued goodwill. The two men also felt that this voyage would provide Champlain with an opportunity to explore the interior, since, if he were travelling with the Huron, the Kichesipirini could not oppose him ascending the Ottawa River (3:31–32). When Champlain agreed to help the Huron in their wars, they promised that 2500 men would accompany him on an expedition into the heart of the Iroquois country and that, before the end of the autumn, they would return him to Quebec. Champlain then explained to them the strategy by which he hoped to defeat the Iroquois. Finally, he returned to Quebec for four or five days to make arrangements for the journey. On the way down-river, his route again crossed that of Father Le Caron, who was returning to the Rivière des Prairies (3:32–33).

Champlain was absent for ten days. As he was headed back to the Rivière des Prairies, he met Gravé Du Pont and Father Jamet, who were returning to Quebec. They told him that because of his long absence, the Indians had decided that he was not returning and had set off for home with Father Le Caron and twelve other Frenchmen whom Gravé Du Pont had sent to spend the winter with them (3:34–35). A rumour had spread that Champlain had been killed by the Iroquois, but the speed with which the Huron departed seems more likely a measure of their lack of trust in his promises. No doubt, the Huron hoped that the four or five Frenchmen who were acquainted with handling firearms would help them in their wars.

Instead of blaming himself for his delay, Champlain expressed annoyance that he was unable to arrange his expedition properly and that so few armed men were available to accompany him. Nevertheless, on 9 July he set out to follow the Huron. He was accompanied by his servant, an interpreter, and ten Indians, all travelling in two large canoes of the sort the Huron used for long journeys on relatively smooth bodies of water. The Indians were probably Huron who had remained behind to see if Champlain would return.

We know little about Le Caron's journey to the Huron country. Sagard and Le Clercq state that he had to help paddle his canoe and suffered greatly (Sagard 1866:41; Le Clercq 1691:72). Both sources, however, are

fond of exaggerating the hardships that were endured by the Recollets, and this may be another instance of this type of hagiography. Frenchmen were sometimes asked to paddle if their Indian companions were ill, but with twelve other Frenchmen on route it is unlikely that Le Caron would have suffered abnormal hardships, unless his behaviour had seriously annoyed his Indian companions.

Le Caron was well-received among the Huron and was induced to settle, not amongst the Arendarhonon, but at the Attignawantan community of Carhagouha. This village, which Heidenreich (1966:120–21; 1968), following Bressani, locates near Midland Bay, was palisaded and seems to have been the principal town of the northern Attignawantan. It was the predecessor of Quieunonascaran, which was founded in 1623 and was the residence of Onorotandi and Auoindaon, who controlled the northern Attignawantan trade with the Saguenay and St. Lawrence Rivers. Prior to 1623, these headmen had probably lived in Carhagouha, which was therefore a community of key importance for trading with the French. Huron families tried to persuade Le Caron to live with them and to be adopted, with a view to strengthening their relationship with the French (Sagard 1866:41).

Le Caron's religious scruples led him to request permission to live in a separate cabin outside the village. We do not know whether he would have done this in any case, or if he was led to make this request by aspects of Huron life that were morally objectionable to him. The Huron built him a cabin, where he lived until the following May. He is not reported to have converted any Huron, although he learned something about the Huron language and way of life. He also began work on a Huron dictionary, which Le Clercq (1691:88, 327–28) reports survived to his own day. The bulk of this dictionary seems, however, to date from his second visit to the Huron in 1623, especially the sections dealing with rules and principles.

Champlain and his small band travelled up the Rivière des Prairies and ascended the Ottawa River past Morrison Island. Beyond this island, he found a large number of rapids in the river, while the terrain on both sides was rocky and hilly. The area was thinly inhabited by a group of Algonkin known as Otaguottouemin, who lived by hunting, fishing, and drying blueberries for the winter.[16] When Champlain's party reached the Mattawa River, they made their way westward to Lake Nipissing, which they reached on 26 July. Champlain spent two days in the principal village of the Nipissing, whose headman entertained him with banquets, and took him hunting and fishing. Champlain observed that the area was rich in

fish and game and estimated that seven hundred to eight hundred people were spending the summer there (Biggar 1922–36, 3:40). The Nipissing headmen told Champlain that they would be willing to take him north with them the following spring on a journey that would last for forty days and require an equal amount of time to return (3:101–5). Although Champlain did not plan to spend the winter in the Huron country, this promise to take him to James Bay revived his hopes of being able to extend his knowledge of the geography of North America in that direction. No doubt, the Nipissing made this promise because they were anxious to establish trading relations with the French. Champlain must have had some second thoughts concerning his treatment of Nicolas de Vignau, but in his writings he remained silent about them.

Champlain proceeded down the French River and into Georgian Bay. Throughout this region, he found only a little corn being grown and the country impressed him as being particularly desolate. Near the mouth of the French River, Champlain met three hundred Indians, whom he called Cheveux Relevés, because they wore their hair very high and carefully arranged. These belonged to the group of northern Algonkian bands that were later known as the Ottawa. The men tattooed their bodies and, unlike the Huron, they did not bother to wear loincloths. Their faces were painted, their noses pierced for ornaments, and many wore earrings. Champlain was given to understand that the people he had met were visiting this area to dry blueberries and that their principal villages were located to the west of those of the Tionnontaté, along the south shore of Georgian Bay. In later years, the Ottawa were active traders, particularly in the Lake Michigan area. The men Champlain encountered carried shields made of dressed leather from an animal like the buffalo (*bufle*), which suggests that their trading connections may already have been well-established in that direction. European goods, however, were still rare and highly valued. When Champlain presented the leader of this band with an iron hatchet, he regarded it as a rich present (3:43–45).

From the mouth of the French River, Champlain followed the traditional Huron canoe route south along the eastern shore of Georgian Bay. While doing so, he had a chance to observe the Thirty Thousand Islands and the rocky, thinly wooded coastline of Muskoka. On 1 August, as he crossed the mouth of Matchedash Bay and passed Beausoleil Island, which the Huron called Skionechiara, he observed a great change in the landscape. To the south, he beheld the hills of the Huron country, with its rich forests, extensive clearings, and beautiful river valleys (Biggar

1922–36, 3:46). After a five-hundred-mile journey across the Canadian Shield, he was approaching a fertile and well-cultivated land, where a Frenchman might feel at home.

The Indians Champlain was travelling with brought him first to Otoüacha (Toanché), which appears to have been the main Attignawantan point of departure for their journeys to Quebec. This village was located near Thunder Bay, on the Penetanguishene Peninsula (Heidenreich 1966:118–20). He remained in Otoüacha for several days, and while there also visited the village of Carmaron, two miles away. The headman of Carmaron celebrated Champlain's visit with a feast and entreated him to stay there (3:47). Champlain was unable to do this, however, since he had to reach Cahiagué, the Arendarhonon town that was the rallying place for the expedition against the Iroquois. Champlain returned to Otoüacha, where he waited two more days while arrangements were made for him to visit all the Huron settlements and to meet the leading Huron headmen as he travelled to Cahiagué.

In Otoüacha, Champlain had his first personal encounter with Huron sexual mores. One evening, when he left the house in which he was staying to escape its fleas, a Huron girl offered to have intercourse with him. She apparently believed that this was what he wanted, since he was wandering about the village after dark for no other apparent reason. This girl was, no doubt, very surprised when Champlain not only refused, but gave visible signs of his disapproval before retreating to the company of his male companions (3:47).

From Otoüacha, Champlain proceeded to Touaguainchain, an otherwise unknown village located somewhere between Otoüacha and the next settlement that he visited, Tequenonquiaye. At both of these villages, Champlain was received with great courtesy and entertained with feasts. Tequenonquiaye was the predecessor of Ossossané, and was the largest and most important town of the Attignawantan. The community that Champlain visited seems to have been located slightly farther south than the Ossossanés of later times.[17] Having visited the main town of the southern Attignawantan, Champlain was free to meet the less prestigious leaders of the northern Attignawantan. To do this, he made a considerable detour northward, travelling along the high ground lying to the west of the Wye Valley, as far as Carhagouha, where Father Le Caron was already living. Here on 12 August Le Caron celebrated a mass and a wooden cross was erected near the small house that was being built for him (3:48–49).

Meanwhile, Champlain learned that because the Huron had believed that he was not coming to their country, they had abandoned their plans

for a major raid against the Iroquois. Now they were attempting to assemble a large war party but this was proceeding slowly. Because of this, Champlain remained at Carhagouha until 14 August before spending three days travelling to Cahiagué. In the course of this journey, he visited four or five important palisaded towns.[18] While his itinerary is unknown, it probably took him to the main settlements of the Attigneenongnahac and the Tahontaenrat, and then into the territory of the Arendarhonon (map 15). Champlain states that this circuitous journey was his own idea, but the Huron probably wished that before he went to war, he should meet the major headmen of the confederacy who had sent him presents in 1611. Many years later, Le Clercq claimed that Champlain visited all the Huron settlements to raise the arms of the King of France in them, to conclude close alliances with their headmen, and to prepare their young men for war (Le Clercq 1691:78). There is no reference, in Champlain's account, to the erection of crosses bearing royal arms and it is unlikely that the Huron would have responded favourably to such action. On the other hand, Le Clercq seems to have grasped the political significance of what Champlain accomplished. By visiting each village, he concluded treaties of friendship with individual Huron headmen, in which he promised to help them in their wars, and they, in return, promised that they would trade with the French (Biggar 1922–36, 3:226–27). Henceforth, these agreements would constitute the basis for closer cooperation between the French and the Huron.

The effectiveness of Champlain's diplomacy depended largely, however, on the interpretation the Huron gave to what he did. Champlain viewed his tour of the Huron villages more as an accidental ramble than as a round of serious negotiations. Although he visited every part of the Huron country, his ignorance of their political organization remained astonishingly great. He recorded the names of only a few Huron headmen in his writings and there is no evidence that he understood what role they played. He also referred to all Huron as Attignawantan, thereby revealing that he remained unaware of the nature of Huron tribal organization. His description of the operations of government is extremely vague and attributes to them an ad hoc quality that again indicates gross lack of information. Champlain concluded that the Huron had no punishment except vengeance, and that by acting on the basis of passion rather than reason, they generated more quarrels than they suppressed. Moreover, the Huron did not have any god or believe in anything supernatural whatever and, for this reason, lived like brute beasts (3:143). Champlain was a good observer of Huron economy and daily life, but, as a soldier and an aspiring

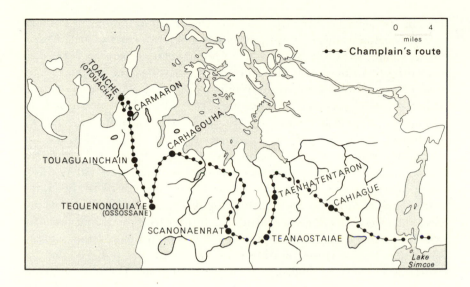

MAP 15. *Reconstruction of Champlain's route through the Huron country to Cahiagué, and beyond.*

vice-regal official, he was unwilling to see in their noncoercive social organization anything but chaos and barbarism.

Champlain arrived at Cahiagué on 17 August. This settlement was located three leagues from the Narrows of Lake Couchiching, in the general vicinity of Bass Lake (3:56). In recent years, it has been identified with the Warminster site, which is located on a long, gently sloping interfluve northwest of Bass Lake, in Medonte township.[19] The eastern and western borders of this site are protected by steep valleys containing running water. To the north it terminates at the edge of a post-glacial shore-line, beyond which lies a swampy tangle of cedar and alder, while on the south it extends nearly to the heads of the two boundary valleys. The cornfields of this village must have covered more than 1000 acres and appear to have been laid out south of the site, in a semicircular pattern (map 16). At Warminster, two Huron villages, covering nine and a half and five acres respectively, have been found within six hundred feet of one another. They appear to have been contemporary and to have constituted a single large double village. Each section of the village was surrounded by a massive palisade made up of three to seven rows of staggered posts. The two settlements are estimated to have contained a total of one hundred houses and

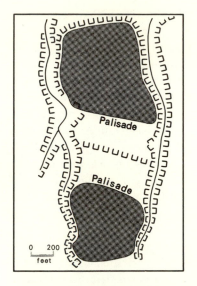

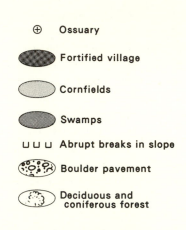

Ossuary

Fortified village

Cornfields

Swamps

ᴗ ᴗ ᴗ Abrupt breaks in slope

Boulder pavement

Deciduous and
coniferous forest

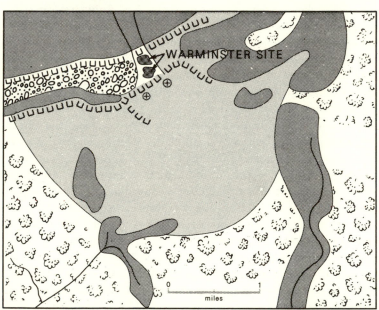

MAP 16. *Reconstruction of field pattern and natural setting of the Warminster site after ten years of occupation (Lot 10, Conc. XIV, Medonte Twp.). The expanded section shows outline of palisades in greater detail (both maps after C. E. Heidenreich).*

a population of about 3000 people (Cruickshank and Heidenreich 1969: 37–38).

Champlain described Cahiagué as being the principal Huron village, by which he probably meant that it was the largest. He also stated that it contained two hundred large cabins.[20] Champlain frequently over-estimated, but, even if he more than doubled the actual number of houses, there is no doubt that Cahiagué was a large settlement. The Warminster site is large by Huron standards; it is located in Arendarhonon territory; and, although the archaeological evidence has not yet been published in detail, it appears to date from the early historic period. Thus strong arguments can be presented in favour of identifying this site as Cahiagué. On the other hand, it is strange that Champlain would not have mentioned such an unusual feature as the village being divided into two separately palisaded units.

Sagard reports that when Cahiagué changed location, sometime before 1623, two new villages were founded in place of the single old one (Wrong 1939:92). This has generally been interpreted to mean that, as a result of quarrels between clan segments, the inhabitants of Cahiagué separated and founded new villages located some distance apart. It is possible, how-ever, that Sagard is describing the formation of a double village and that the Warminster site is, in fact, the successor of Cahiagué, rather than the village Champlain visited. Until more details are published and the precise date of the Warminster site has been established, it will be impossible to decide which of these alternatives is correct. At present, we do not know the volume or nature of European goods that were reaching the Huron country in the decade that followed Champlain's visit, as opposed to what had been arriving in the preceding decade. If Cahiagué was abandoned soon after 1615, it will be especially difficult to determine whether the Warminster site was occupied shortly before or after that date.

Champlain remained at Cahiagué for two weeks, while the war party that was to proceed against the Iroquois was drawn together from all parts of the Huron confederacy. The number of warriors that finally assembled is not stated but, if it resembled the average large Huron war party, there may have been about five hundred. In addition to Huron warriors, Iroquet and his men joined the expedition as well as other Algonkian-speakers who were wintering among the Huron. Champlain, who viewed himself not as the Huron did (as an ally), but rather as the leader of this war party, chafed at the delay in assembling these warriors. As each group arrived, there was a succession of dances and feasting, in which the warriors vaunted their prowess and expressed their certainty of victory.

Then, the newcomers would go to live with the clan segment in Cahiagué that had the same name or which belonged to the same phratry as their own. Champlain imagined that these ceremonies were intended to welcome him alone, but they seem to have been the usual ones meant to confederate warriors from different tribes, villages, and clan segments for a campaign against a common enemy (Biggar 1922–36, 3:53, 56). Among those who were preparing to accompany the expedition was Atironta, the principal chief of the Arendarhonon and now the paramount Huron ally of the French. Champlain, as a new and powerful friend, was obviously an important part of the campaign, but he seems to have overestimated the military importance that the Huron attached to his participation. Mainly, it was interpreted as an expression of goodwill towards the Huron.

BRÛLÉ'S VISIT TO THE SUSQUEHANNOCK

While he was at Cahiagué, Champlain learned that the Susquehannock were interested in joining the proposed expedition against the Iroquois and were hoping that, by doing so, they would be able to meet him and form an alliance with the French. Champlain was also told that the Susquehannock had captured three Dutchmen, who had been helping their enemies to wage war on them; however, they alleged (probably untruthfully) that they had released these prisoners, thinking them to be French (3:54–55; for more about these prisoners, see chapter 6).

The Huron decided to dispatch a dozen warriors to carry the plans for their impending attack to the Susquehannock and to invite them to join the expedition. Brûlé asked Champlain for permission to accompany these warriors, which Champlain readily granted, since the journey would permit Brûlé to observe the country to the south (3:58). In so doing, however, Champlain deprived himself of the only interpreter who understood the Huron language well. Henceforth, he had to communicate with the Huron in a circuitous fashion, relying on Frenchmen to translate what he said into Algonkin and on Algonkin to translate it in turn into Huron. The route followed by Brûlé's companions is not described in detail and has been the subject of much controversy. The dotted line on Champlain's map of 1632 (plate 28) suggests that they travelled south to the Neutral country along the trail that ran westward through the Tionnontaté settlements and then south through the Beaver Valley and down the Grand River. Yet, the urgency of their mission, and Champlain's statement that the group started out, not from Cahiagué, but from the Narrows

at Lake Couchiching, make it more probable that they travelled across Lake Simcoe to the Neutral country.[21] It is implausible that they travelled around the west end of Lake Ontario before pushing south between the Niagara and Genesee Rivers (cf. Cranston 1949:81–83; Jurgens 1966: 131). More likely they crossed southwestern Ontario to Lake Erie and made their way along its eastern shore, being careful to avoid the Iroquois. From there, they skirted south of the Iroquois settlements to the Susquehannock village of Carantouan. Throughout the latter part of their journey, the Huron travelled through bogs and thick forests to avoid Iroquois war parties (Biggar 1922–36, 3:214–15).

Nevertheless, the Huron encountered a small group of Iroquois who were returning to their village. They killed four of them and captured two others (3:215). These prisoners assured the Huron a particularly enthusiastic welcome in Carantouan, where the prisoners were probably tortured to death. A council was held and, after it was confirmed that Champlain was accompanying the Huron, the Susquehannock decided to send a war party north to join in the attack on the Iroquois village, which was only three days away (3:216). War was, however, an occasion for ritual among the Susquehannock, no less than among the Huron. Hence, while Brûlé fretted at the delay, the Susquehannock slowly made ready. They set out to join the Huron, but did not reach the appointed rendezvous until two days after the Huron had left for home. Learning that the Huron had departed, the Susquehannock returned to Carantouan, where Brûlé, lacking guides for his return to the Huron country, was obliged to spend the winter. It is not stated what happened to the Huron who accompanied him, but some of them may have slipped north to carry news of the Susquehannock's plans to their compatriots who were attacking the Iroquois (3:217).

During the winter, Brûlé visited the lower reaches of the Susquehanna River and the islands of Chesapeake Bay, possibly accompanying Susquehannock who went there to trade. In the spring, he set off with five or six Indians to return to the Huron country. It is uncertain whether these were Huron returning home or Susquehannock on their way to visit the Huron. On route, they were attacked by the Iroquois and in the ensuing fight Brûlé became lost in the forest. He grew very hungry and finally decided that it was better to surrender to the Iroquois than die of starvation. Brûlé followed a footpath until he encountered a Seneca or Cayuga fishing party returning to their village. He shouted at them and, after some initial hesitation, both sides laid down their arms and the Iroquois took Brûlé to their homes, where they offered him something to eat

(3:217–21). Some of Brûlé's companions who had escaped from the Iroquois reached Cahiagué by 22 April. In order to account for Brûlé not being with them, they euphemistically reported that they had left him on the trail when he had decided to return to Carantouan (3:168).

After he had eaten, the Iroquois took Brûlé to the longhouse of one of their principal headmen, who interrogated him. Brûlé denied that he was an *Adoresetoüy*, or man of iron, which was the Iroquois name for the French, but since he spoke Huron, they did not believe him. A dispute broke out about what should be done with him. The war chiefs and younger men regarded him as an enemy and began torturing him. They tore out his fingernails and part of his beard, burned him, and dragged him to the torture scaffold which the Iroquois erected in the middle of their villages. Brûlé attributed his salvation to divine intervention. Seeing himself in mortal danger, he recited a brief prayer; following which, as one of the Iroquois was seizing his *agnus dei* medal, a violent thunderstorm broke out. This so terrified the Iroquois that they desisted from torturing him further (3:221–24).

It has been suggested that Brûlé invented this pious story to please Champlain and the Recollets (Trudel 1966a:227–29). Whether or not there actually was a thunderstorm, it is clear that the Iroquois council chiefs, who generally exerted a moderating influence in intertribal relations, managed to rescue Brûlé from his tormentors. Hereafter, Brûlé was treated kindly by the Iroquois and invited to their feasts and celebrations. His knowledge of an Iroquoian language and his familiarity with Iroquoian customs seem to have quickly made him as popular among the Iroquois as he was among the Huron. The headmen, however, had a practical reason for befriending Brûlé. Neither the Seneca nor Cayuga were as well situated for trade with the Dutch, or for raiding the Ottawa Valley, as were their allies to the east. Hence the council chiefs were interested in exploring the possibility of establishing a trading relationship with the French. Brûlé knew what they wanted and saw an opportunity to expand existing trade networks. He promised his hosts that when he left them, he would do what he could to promote a three-way peace between them, the Huron, and the French and that he would return to them soon (3:224). After he had remained some time with the Iroquois, the latter conducted him to the borders of the Neutral country. He does not appear to have arrived in the Huron country in time to see Champlain, before the latter's departure on 20 May.[22] We do not know if Brûlé remained in contact with the Iroquois or if the promises he made to them were lies told to secure his release. There is, however, evidence that Brûlé had

dealings with the Seneca around 1630. This suggests that in the intervening years he maintained contact with the western Iroquois, possibly
in the course of his visits to the Neutral country.

THE EXPEDITION AGAINST THE IROQUOIS

On 1 September the Huron war party set out from Cahiagué and travelled
along the shore of Lake Couchiching to the Narrows. There, Champlain
saw the great weirs that the Huron had erected to catch fish as they moved
between Lakes Simcoe and Couchiching (3:56–57). The Huron remained
at the Narrows for about a week, while they waited for still more men to
arrive. From Lake Simcoe, they made their way eastward to the Kawartha
Lakes, portaging either to Balsam Lake or directly to Sturgeon Lake
(Needler 1949). After passing through these lakes, which lie along the
southern margin of the Canadian Shield, they followed the Otonabee
River to Rice Lake and went along the Trent River to the Bay of Quinte.
The journey through the Trent Valley was a slow one, with the Indians
stopping at frequent intervals to hunt and fish. They hunted deer com-
munally; driving them into the water where they killed them with arrows
and spears. Some spears, possibly belonging to Algonkin, were made by
fastening French sword blades onto the end of poles (Biggar 1922–36,
3:61; Sagard 1866:414). The French shot the deer with their muskets.
During one of these hunts, they wounded an Indian, who accidentally
wandered into their line of fire. The affair was quickly settled, however, in
the traditional Indian manner, by satisfying the wounded man with
presents (Biggar 1922–36, 3:61). The main purpose of this hunting and
fishing was to feed the army, although the deer skins were taken back to
the Huron country to be used for clothing. Champlain noted that in
former times the Trent Valley had been inhabited and that it had been
abandoned through fear of the enemy (3:59; 6:246). This provided him
with more grist for one of his favourite themes—the great war that he
imagined the Iroquois had waged in past times against the Huron and
Algonkin.

From the mouth of the Trent River, the Huron made their way down
the Bay of Quinte, then travelled among the islands at the east end of
Lake Ontario until they were south of the St. Lawrence. There they
landed on a sandy beach and hid their canoes in the forest. The precise
route that the Huron followed after they left the Bay of Quinte is uncertain.[23]

After carefully hiding their canoes, the Huron travelled on foot for some ten or twelve miles along a sandy beach. This was part of the nineteen miles of sand that stretches along the eastern shore of Lake Ontario from about a mile south of Little Stony Creek to two and a half miles south of the Little Salmon River. Peter Pratt (1964:31) identifies the three bodies of water that Champlain has drawn east of this section of his route on his 1632 map with North Pond, South Pond, and Little Sandy Lake. Somewhere along the beach, the Huron turned inland, travelled through the forest for four days, and crossed either the Oneida or Oswego Rivers, which flow from Lake Oneida into Lake Ontario (Biggar 1922–36, 3:64). On 9 October, when the Huron were about four leagues from their destination, they captured an Iroquois fishing party, consisting of three men, four women, and four young people. When Iroquet began to cut off a finger from one of the women, Champlain said that such behaviour was an act of cowardice and threatened that, if it continued, he would be unwilling to give his allies any further help in their wars (3:64–65). Iroquet replied that it was customary to torture prisoners, and at this point, one of the Kichesipirini accompanying the expedition seized an Iroquois child by its feet and broke its head against a rock or tree (Thwaites 1896–1901, 9:259–61). Champlain does not state what followed, but since the Onontchataronon had two female prisoners the following winter, it is possible that at least some of these women escaped their usual fate.

The next afternoon, the Huron and their allies came within sight of the community they were planning to attack. It was a large town, located near a pond or small lake and, if the drawing accompanying Champlain's account can be trusted, there was a stream on either side of it (plate 26). It was enclosed by a far stronger palisade than any Champlain had observed among the Huron. The wall was constructed of four rows of large stakes interlaced with each other and topped by galleries faced with large slabs of wood. Gutters ran between the posts, which allowed the defenders to extinguish any fires that might be lighted against the palisade (Biggar 1922–36, 3:70).

The location of this village has been hotly debated for over a century. From the information contained in Champlain's account, it could have been located near any large body of water in the central part of upper New York State. The three locations that have received the most support are the north end of Canandaigua Lake; Onondaga Lake in Onondaga County; and the Nichols Pond site in neighbouring Madison County (Pratt 1964: 35–41). In recent years, however, excavations at the Nichols Pond site

PLATE 26. *The Iroquois settlement under attack by Champlain and his allies in 1615. The schematic ground plans and distribution of houses, the geometrical plan of the fortifications and their curious construction, and the dress of the Indians leave no reason to trust the fidelity of this scene. Courtesy Public Archives of Canada.*

have shown it to be prehistoric, while no archaeological evidence of any sort has been forthcoming to support the other two locations (ibid. 41–50). A recent review of this problem has concluded that Champlain's account is not sufficiently detailed to permit the precise reconstruction of his travels in New York State and that the site of the town he attacked remains unknown (ibid. 50–51).

Nor is it any easier to ascertain the tribal identity of this town. Various authors have ascribed it to the Seneca, Cayuga, Onondaga, or Oneida, the latter two being the most popular candidates. Unfortunately, Champlain was no better informed about the tribal structure of the Iroquois confederacy than he was about the Huron one, and the term he uses to denote the enemy, Entouhonoron or Antouhonoron, cannot be identified as the name of any tribe known in historic times (ibid. 11). Biggar and his co-workers have led many readers astray by their unwarranted substitution of Onondaga for Entouhonoron in their translations of Champlain's writings.

Champlain seems to have been vaguely aware of the separate identity of the Seneca, whom he calls the Chouontouaronon (Biggar 1922–36, 3:55). This is a variant of Tsonnontouan, which was the standard French name for the Seneca. Yet, throughout this period, Champlain appears to have applied the term Iroquois only to the Mohawk, while by Entouhonoron he meant the four western tribes of the confederacy, including the Seneca. This corresponds to early Dutch usage, which distinguished between the Mohawk and the Sinnekin (the four western tribes), while the French made a similar distinction between the Lower Iroquois (Mohawk) and the Upper Iroquois (the other four tribes) throughout most of the seventeenth century (Hewitt 1910a:503–4). On his map of 1632, Champlain located the Entouhonoron west of the Iroquois and, in the index to this map, he stated that they lived in fifteen settlements, fought with the Iroquois against all other tribes, and denied passage along the St. Lawrence to all foreigners (Biggar 1922–36, 6:249–50). From his description of the route, Champlain and his allies might have attacked an Oneida, Onondaga, or Cayuga settlement. Since it seems to have been the Oneida and Onondaga who were harassing the Huron and Algonkin in the Ottawa Valley at this period, it was most likely one of these tribes that was being attacked. The Oneida normally had one settlement, the Onondaga two. The fact that the beleaguered town received no help suggests that there was no other community nearby. This in turn suggests that the town was Oneida rather than Onondaga.

THE BATTLE

As soon as the Indians who accompanied Champlain were near the Iroquois village, they constructed a fortified war camp, in which they were to live for the next ten days. Champlain did not wish his allies to let the presence of the French become known until the following day; however, the Huron and Algonkin were anxious to open fire on their enemies and, in their desire to secure prisoners, some of them pursued the Iroquois too near their village, where they themselves were in danger of being captured. To rescue these men, Champlain and several of his companions approached the enemy and opened fire on them. These Iroquois had never experienced gunfire before and speedily withdrew into their town, carrying their dead and wounded with them (Biggar 1922–36, 3:66).

Angered by what had happened, Champlain addressed harsh and angry words to his Indian allies. He stated that if everything were directed according to their wishes and the guidance of their council, the result was bound to be disastrous (3:67). We have no idea what the Huron and Algonkin headmen thought of Champlain's address, or how much of it they understood. Champlain believed that as a former soldier of France, he was infinitely better trained in the art of war than were the Indians, and that this alone gave him natural authority to command them and to censure any aspect of their conduct of which he did not approve. The Indians believed that Champlain had the right to express an opinion, like anyone else, but if he wished his advice to be followed, he had to convince them, either by his arguments or by his example, that it was good advice. The concepts of command and obedience, on which Champlain was to rely so heavily in the days that followed, were not ones that had meaning for the Huron or Algonkin.

Champlain did, however, persuade the Indians to construct a *cavalier*, or wooden platform with an enclosed area on top, which would hold four or five musketeers. This platform was to be positioned near the town and, from it, the French could fire over the palisades and prevent the Iroquois from using their galleries to defend themselves. Champlain also ordered a number of large wooden shields to be constructed, under cover of which the Huron could approach the palisades and prevent the Iroquois from extinguishing the fires that were to be lighted against them (3:67–69). Champlain was determined to breach the walls of the town and, having done so, to destroy it, as he had destroyed the Mohawk war camp in 1611. What he did not understand was that the principal aim of the Huron was to harass the village and, by threatening to set fire to its defences, to force

the Iroquois warriors to come out and engage in hand to hand combat, as had happened during the battle on Lake Champlain.

The Huron hoped that Champlain's plans would draw the Iroquois from the town; therefore the next morning they set about cutting wood and building the platform and shields, as Champlain had directed. At the same time, the Iroquois strengthened their defences. The Huron and Algonkin were waiting for the Susquehannock to join them, but Champlain believed that they were strong enough to storm the town and that delay would be dangerous. He therefore urged an attack. Two hundred men carried the platform to within a few feet of the village walls and three Frenchmen began to fire from it. They soon forced the Iroquois to abandon the ramparts, from which they had been shooting arrows and hurling rocks at the Huron. Instead of carrying the shields forward, the Huron began shouting insults at the enemy and shooting arrows into the settlement. They also either set fires so that the wind would blow them away from the palisades or piled up so little wood that, when they set it ablaze, it did little damage. Champlain began to shout at the Indians that they were behaving badly and urged them to follow his orders (3:72–73). Given Champlain's inability to speak either Huron or Algonkin, it is unlikely that any of this advice, given in the heat of battle, was understood by the Indians. Champlain had regretted his linguistic deficiencies at the battle on Lake Champlain, but on this occasion he seems to have been totally oblivious of them. Eventually, he saw he could do nothing to control the situation, although with his own men he continued to fire on such of the Iroquois as he could see. The French on the firing platform are reported to have killed many of the enemy. The latter, however, returned to brave the French gunners. While some poured water through the palisades to extinguish the fires, the rest kept up a hail of arrows that wounded two Huron headmen, Ochasteguin and Orani, and hit Champlain in the knee and leg. Although only fifteen other men were injured after a three-hour battle, when the Huron saw that their headmen had been wounded they retreated in a disorderly manner into their fort (3:73–74).

When they had assembled within the fort, Champlain again upbraided them for their undisciplined behaviour. He noted, however, that his words had no effect on them and concluded that the Huron were no warriors; because headmen had no absolute authority over their men and there was no "concert of action" among them, all their undertakings were bound to come to a bad end. Champlain urged them to attack the Iroquois again, but they refused, explaining that many men had already been wounded and would have to be cared for on the way home. Therefore, they did not

wish to risk more casualties. The Indians were willing to wait a few days longer, to see if the Susquehannock would arrive. They agreed that, if the latter came, they would launch another attack on the town and try to carry out Champlain's directions (3:75).

In spite of Champlain's persistent pleading that they set fire to the Iroquois fortifications, the Huron refused to do so. Instead, until 16 October they continued to skirmish with the enemy, who from time to time came out of the town to fight with them. If the Iroquois appeared to be gaining an advantage, Champlain's men would cover the withdrawal of their allies with their muskets. The Iroquois greatly feared these guns and retreated as soon as they saw them. The Iroquois protested that the French should not interfere in their conflict with the Huron and taunted the Huron for being cowards, since they required French assistance before they dared to attack them (3:76–77).

Finally, seeing that the Susquehannock had not arrived and that the weather had turned bad, the Huron and Algonkin decided to return home. They also must have feared that Iroquois reinforcements would arrive soon from nearby villages. They fashioned a number of baskets and bound the wounded in a crouching position so that they could be carried on the backs of other Indians. Champlain was impressed by the order with which the Indians withdrew. The older men and wounded were placed in the centre of the column, with well-armed warriors to the sides and in the rear. This order was maintained for three days, during which the Indians covered the twenty-five to thirty leagues back to the spot where their canoes were hidden. Because of his wounds, Champlain was among those who had to be carried on this march, an experience which caused him much agony. Everyone's discomfort was increased by a strong wind and a heavy fall of snow and sleet (3:77–79).

No doubt, Champlain's suffering added to his general feeling of disappointment. In his opinion, the campaign had been a disastrous failure. It also convinced him that his Indian allies had no natural ability as warriors and were unable to follow the most elementary instructions (3:72, 78–79). Because of this, he seems to have decided that he would never again accompany the Indians on such a campaign. Historians have generally agreed with Champlain. They describe this battle as the first triumph of the Iroquois over the French. Trudel (1966a:223) sees it as a turning point in the history of the Iroquois and the first of a series of victories that within forty years were to give them control of the lower Great Lakes.

Even if it were possible to speak collectively about the Iroquois at this

period, such an assessment would be a serious misinterpretation of what happened. There is no evidence that any of the Iroquois were less frightened of the French after this battle than before. Many villagers had been killed by French gunfire and, as news of this spread, fear of the French must have increased rather than diminished. Nor is there evidence that any of the Indians who participated in this battle regarded it as a defeat for the Huron. The battle was not the equivalent of a European siege (Trudel 1966*a*:222). Its primary aim was not to capture an enemy town, but to challenge the enemy to fight, in the hope of killing or capturing some of them. We do not know how many prisoners the Huron captured, aside from the eleven that were taken at the start of the siege, but since a considerable number of the enemy were killed, it must have been a reasonably satisfactory campaign from the point of view of blood revenge. Moreover, the assistance of the French seems to have kept their allies' losses low, although their presence may also have been viewed as disadvantageous, since it deterred the Iroquois from engaging in as much hand-to-hand combat as the Huron and Algonkin might have liked. Champlain nowhere mentions that the Indians were dissatisfied with the campaign, and it seems likely that he alone regarded it as a disastrous defeat. The Huron probably viewed it as a major, but not an atypical, bout in a continuing blood feud with the Iroquois. They probably also hoped that by inflicting injuries on the latter, it might make them less able, or willing, to continue their attacks in the Ottawa Valley.

As a former soldier, Champlain was knowledgeable about European warfare. Yet, he made no effort to understand the nature of Indian warfare or even to determine why particular wars were being fought. He assumed that raids were made for the same general reasons that wars were fought in Europe and that any differences were a result of the technological inferiority and tactical ineptitude of the Indians. He also had no understanding of the important ritual implications of warfare in this region or of the Indians' treatment of their prisoners. For all these reasons, Champlain misjudged the aims of the expedition he accompanied. Because of this, he not only failed to understand the role that he was expected to play, but was unable to judge whether it had been a success or failure in the estimation of his Indian allies.

A WINTER AMONG THE INDIANS

When the Huron returned to where they had left their canoes, Champlain reminded them of their promise to take him down the St. Lawrence River

to Quebec. Thereupon, he began to experience the usual vacillations with which the Indians were accustomed to turn down an unacceptable request made by a friend. At first, no one was willing to take him; then four volunteers were found; finally, no one would provide a canoe for the expedition (3:80). Champlain soon realized that the Indians had no intention of taking him home and that he would be forced to spend the winter in the Huron country. At first, he feared that the Huron might be planning to do him some injury, because the battle had not gone as they wished. Later, however, when he found himself well-treated, he decided that they were keeping him and his companions to protect them against Iroquois counter-attacks and so that he could participate in their councils and determine what they should do in the future to defend themselves against their enemies (Biggar 1922–36, 3:81). Much about Champlain is revealed by this immodest appraisal.

The Huron had different reasons for behaving as they did. The Iroquois frequented the St. Lawrence Valley above Montreal and to travel along that portion of the river was very dangerous. Because of this, one might question whether the Huron or Algonkin had been serious when they promised to return Champlain to Quebec along this route. To give them the benefit of the doubt, it is necessary to assume that they believed that if they were accompanied by musketeers, they would be relatively safe from attack.

Thus, while safety was a factor, the Huron had other important reasons for refusing Champlain's request. They and their allies probably mistrusted Champlain and feared that he wished to travel through Iroquois-controlled territory in order to make contact with their enemies. Only a few years before, rumours had circulated about Champlain having dealings with the Iroquois and the memory of these rumours could easily have given rise to such suspicions (Bishop 1948:240–41). His frequent criticism of his allies and his outbursts of rage during the campaign may have created additional doubts about his professed friendship for the Huron. Friendly contact between Champlain and the Iroquois was the last thing that either the Huron or the Algonkin wished to occur. Moreover, it would almost certainly have proved fatal for the Indians who accompanied him. For this reason, the most prudent course was for the Huron to refuse to take Champlain to Quebec by way of Iroquois-controlled territory. Had Champlain inspired more trust and striven to have better rapport with his allies, some of them might have been willing to risk their lives to take him to Quebec.

The return to the Huron country from the east end of Lake Ontario was

even slower than the journey down the Trent Valley had been. On 28 October the war party split into small bands. Some headed for home, others remained north of Lake Ontario for the autumn hunt. It was decided that Champlain should go hunting with Atironta, either because by now the latter had replaced Ochasteguin as Champlain's official host or because Ochasteguin's wound made it impossible for him to go hunting. From the east end of Lake Ontario, Atironta and twenty-five of his men appear to have travelled up Cataraqui Creek and portaged the short distance to Loughborough Lake.[24] About twenty-five miles from there, they erected some bark cabins and constructed a large enclosure into which they drove and killed deer. In thirty-eight days, the Huron killed 120 deer, keeping the fat, skins, and a little of the meat to take home with them. While hunting with the Indians, Champlain became lost and was forced to wander in the forest for several days before he perceived the smoke of his host's camp. Hereafter, Atironta made certain that Champlain did not leave camp without an Indian companion. He said that if Champlain had not returned, the Huron should never again have dared to visit the French for fear the latter would hold them responsible for having killed him (Biggar 1922–36, 3:91).

In early December, Atironta's party set out for home. Each of the Huron had to transport one hundred pounds of skins and meat, while Champlain carried a burden of twenty pounds. As long as the ground remained frozen, most of these loads were transported on improvised sledges, but, as the weather turned warmer, it became necessary to travel on foot, sometimes through swamps of knee-deep water. At last, either on 20 or 23 December they returned to Cahiagué.[25] Champlain remained there for several weeks. He discovered that the Onontchataronon were wintering in an encampment near the village, where their wives and children probably had lived while the men had gone to war against the Iroquois. Iroquet was having his son treated by Huron shamans for injuries he had received while trying to kill a bear (3:94).

On 4 January Champlain left for Carhagouha, where he spent over a week living with Father Le Caron and discussing with him a proposed visit to the Tionnontaté. They set out together on 15 January and arrived in the first Tionnontaté village on the seventeenth, probably spending one night at Tequenonquiaye and another on the trail. The total length of this part of their journey was about thirty-five miles (Garrad 1970:237). Champlain and Le Caron visited seven Tionnontaté villages, two of which were in the process of being relocated. Champlain states that he and Le Caron were welcomed by the Tionnontaté and that at each village he

contracted a treaty of friendship with its inhabitants and persuaded them to come to Quebec to trade (Biggar 1922–36, 3:95–96). Sagard, on the other hand, reports that Le Caron was not well received, possibly because he incurred the hostility of the Tionnontaté shamans, and that he was soon forced to return to the Huron country (1866:42). This story was repeated and slightly elaborated by Le Clercq (1691:87).

It is possible that Champlain and Le Caron were treated differently, although both of them returned to the Huron country at the same time. Champlain, however, has little concrete to say about the Tionnontaté. This suggests that, like later French visitors, Champlain and Le Caron incurred the wrath of the Huron by attempting to conclude a trading alliance with the Tionnontaté. This may have led to a Huron campaign of slander, in which the latter attempted to convince the Tionnontaté that the French were dangerous people with whom it was unsafe to have dealings. Such campaigns were frequently successful among both the Tionnontaté and the Neutral, and this one may have turned the Tionnontaté against Champlain. It is understandable that Champlain would not have wished to mention a humiliation of this sort. It is also noteworthy that, because of Huron opposition, Champlain's dream of trade between the Tionnontaté and the French was never realized. Charles Garrad (1970: 238), who has made a special study of Tionnontaté historic sites, suggests that the first village visited by Champlain was probably Ehwae, which was their principal, and most southerly, one. From there, he made his way north and west towards Craigleith, before entering the territory of the Cheveux Relevés.

Champlain devoted more space to describing his visit to the Cheveux Relevés. He was delighted by the warm reception they gave him and describes them as being the cleanest Indians he had yet encountered and the ones most given to celebrations and feasting (Biggar 1922–36, 3:98–99). Among his hosts were the Indians he had encountered at the mouth of the French River the previous summer and whom he had probably promised that he would visit some time in the future. He found that the main Cheveux Relevés settlements were located west of the Tionnontaté villages. It was there that they planted their crops and spent the winters; however, like the Stadaconans, they were more dependent on hunting and gathering than were their Iroquoian neighbours and both in summer and in winter they ranged extensively in search of food. In the summer, such travels were frequently combined with trade.

The Cheveux Relevés appear to have been on good terms with the Tionnontaté. Like the northern Algonkians among the Huron, some of

them spent the winter living in, or on the outskirts of, Tionnontaté villages, engaging in trade with their inhabitants. They were also on good terms with the tribes of the Neutral confederacy. All these peoples were allies against the Assistaronon, which in this instance was probably a collective term for the Algonkian-speaking tribes of the Michigan Peninsula. It is uncertain how far westward the Cheveux Relevés settlements extended, but it is clear from Champlain's map of 1632 that he did not travel as far west as the Bruce Peninsula (Garrad 1970:238). It is possible that the Assistaronon dominated, if they did not inhabit, the southeastern shores of Lake Huron. The Bruce Peninsula and the region to the south may have been a no man's land between these two groups.

The Cheveux Relevés asked Champlain for military aid against the Assistaronon. Champlain replied that any assistance would have to wait until he made another trip to this region, since he currently lacked necessary supplies (Biggar 1922–36, 3:99). Knowing about the alliance between the Cheveux Relevés and the Neutral confederacy, he expressed a desire to visit the Neutral. The Cheveux Relevés declined to take him south into the Grand Valley, alleging that a Frenchman had accidentally killed a Neutral who was visiting the Iroquois village Champlain had attacked the previous autumn. Since this killing had not been atoned for with presents, the Neutral were likely to seek satisfaction by killing the first Frenchman who fell into their hands. Champlain realized that, once again, his plans were being thwarted by the reluctance of the Indians to promote contact between the French and the more remote tribes with whom these Indians traded. He must have been particularly aware of it in this instance, because some Cheveux Relevés, wishing to encourage his goodwill, assured him that no harm would befall him were he to visit the Neutral (3:100–101). Champlain had wished to use the Cheveux Relevés country as a point of departure for a trip south because of its geographical proximity to the Neutral, but also because his Huron hosts had already shown themselves reluctant to help him to establish contact with the Neutral. Unable to accomplish anything further in this region, Champlain and Le Caron retraced their steps towards Carhagouha, arriving there in mid-February.

DISCORD AT CAHIAGUÉ

When Champlain returned to the Huron country, he set off to visit the Nipissing, who habitually wintered in the lower part of the Wye Valley,

not far from Carhagouha. His aim was to find out when they were planning to leave for James Bay so that he might travel with them. Before Champlain reached the Nipissing, however, he began to hear reports of a quarrel that had broken out between the inhabitants of Cahiagué and the Onontchataronon who were living near that village. According to Champlain, this quarrel had arisen over a male Iroquois (Entouhonoron) prisoner, whom the Huron had given to Iroquet in the expectation that he would torture him to death. The event Champlain refers to was probably a division of the prisoners that had been captured the previous autumn. In that case, as one of the participants in this raid, Iroquet would, by right, have received some of the prisoners as his share of the spoils. What angered the Huron was that, instead of killing the prisoner, Iroquet had found him to be an excellent hunter and had exercised his right to keep him alive as his adopted son. If Iroquet's injured son had died, he may have been anxious to find someone to replace him.

Either on general principles, or because this prisoner had injured one of their number, some of the inhabitants of Cahiagué felt aggrieved and determined to kill the prisoner themselves. One man was appointed to carry out this task. Coming upon the prisoner without his intention being suspected, the Arendarhonon slew him in the presence of the Onontchataronon headmen. The latter, indignant at such an act, and feeling obliged to avenge the murder of an adopted kinsman, slew the Arendarhonon on the spot. When the Arendarhonon learned what had happened, they armed themselves and fell upon the Onontchataronon. In the ensuing skirmish, Iroquet received two arrow wounds and some of the Onontchataronon cabins were pillaged. Unable to resist the Arendarhonon, the Onontchataronon offered them fifty wampum belts and a large number of shell beads, as well as various kettles, iron axes, and two female prisoners. The Arendarhonon remained hostile and the Onontchataronon feared that in spite of their efforts to restore goodwill, the Arendarhonon were planning to murder all of them (Biggar 1922–36, 3:101–3).

Champlain was soon met by two or three Indians from Cahiagué, who asked him to hurry back to their village to effect a reconciliation between them and the Onontchataronon. They declared that otherwise a general war would break out between the Huron and Algonkin. If this happened, the Huron, who still regarded the Algonkin as being closer allies of the French than they were themselves, would no longer be willing, or able, to come down-river to trade with the French (3:103). Threatened by the loss of lucrative trade, Champlain hurried to Cahiagué to use his influence to stop this quarrel. On the way, he visited the Nipissing to discuss with

them their plans for their journey northward. They informed him that this journey had been broken off. Champlain was told that Iroquet had visited the Nipissing searching for him. In the course of this visit, he had given the Nipissing wampum and requested them to abandon their plans, so that they could come to Quebec in the spring and help to reconcile the Huron and the Algonkin (3:104). It is doubtful, however, that Iroquet's principal motive was to prevent the Nipissing from travelling north, or that the Nipissing would have abandoned the opportunity for some of their people to traverse their annual trade route to James Bay, which was an important source of furs for them. More likely, they gave Champlain the impression that they were not travelling north that year as a polite way of refusing to take him with them.

It would appear that the Algonkin and possibly the Huron had persuaded the Nipissing that it was not in their own interest to permit Champlain to make contact with their northern trading partners. The suggestion that some of the Nipissing should go to Quebec the following summer may have involved a promise that the Algonkin would help the Nipissing form a trading alliance with the French, in return for a Nipissing pledge not to assist the French to explore the interior. If so, this was a major shift in Algonkin policy, since, only two years before, the Kichesipirini had actively been opposed to Champlain making direct contact with the Nipissing. It is this opposition which originally may have induced the Nipissing to offer to take Champlain with them.

Champlain attempted, but was unable to persuade the Nipissing to change their mind. Although he was greatly disheartened by this news, he was now used to the Indians failing to keep their promises to introduce him to their trading partners. He consoled himself with the thought that, in the future, he might find the means of travelling north, as he had eventually found the means to visit the Huron. He concluded, however, that where there was no expectation of his help in warfare, the Indians tended to impede, rather than to facilitate, his exploration of their trading routes (3:31–32).

Champlain set out for Cahiagué with six of his men on 15 February. His arrival greatly pleased both the Huron and the Onontchataronon. Two days were spent hearing from both sides what had happened. It is indicative of the importance attached to Champlain's new alliance with the Huron that he stayed with Atironta, while one of his interpreters, possibly Godefroy, was sent to the Onontchataronon to gather their side of the story (3:106). On the third day, the headmen and other prominent men of Cahiagué went with the French to the Onontchataronon encampment,

where the leaders from both sides gathered in a cabin. These leaders agreed that they wished to resolve their dispute peacefully and invited Champlain to act as an arbitrator (3:107).

We know from other sources that both the Huron and their Algonkin trading partners were especially concerned about disputes that arose as a result of murder or injury between different peoples. If not resolved, these disputes could transform a friendly trading relationship into bloody discord. Within a tribe or confederacy, there was always a headman or a council that had as one of its functions to mediate disputes of this sort when they arose within the group. The arbitration of disputes between the Huron and other groups was made more difficult because there was no statutory mediator of this sort. Hence, both the Arendarhonon and the Onontcha-taronon turned to a common ally for help in resolving their quarrel.

Nevertheless, Champlain's view of the role to be played by a mediator and that held by the Indians were significantly different. The Indians regarded mediation as they did any exercise of leadership, as a matter of persuasion; a mediator should listen to both sides and then make sure that they discussed their differences until a mutually satisfactory solution was reached. Champlain saw the position as conferring much greater authority on him. He claimed that by asking him to mediate their quarrel, the Indians had submitted themselves to his arbitration and he implied that they thereby recognized themselves as subjects of the French king. He asked them to promise in advance that they would follow his advice and to acknowledge that henceforth, as a vice-regal official, he might arrange their affairs as he thought best (3:107–8). While both sides verbally assented to this, they had no concept of authority that could confer such power on Champlain. It is therefore certain that they did not know what they were approving. Champlain interpreted their agreement as signifying that he was gradually acquiring the leadership over these tribes to which he believed his governorship of New France and his natural superiority as a Frenchman entitled him.

Champlain warned both the Huron and the Onontchataronon that, if their quarrel led to war, they would be greatly weakened when it came to resisting their common enemies. He also pointed out that if such warfare prevented one or both parties from coming to trade with the French, the French would be obliged to look for allies and trading partners elsewhere (3:109). This threat to conclude a trading alliance with the Iroquois was certain to intimidate the Huron and Algonkin, but, by exacerbating existing fears that Champlain was carrying on negotiations with the Iroquois

behind their backs, it did little to cement the still-evolving relationship between the French and their Huron and Algonkin trading partners.

Champlain then proceeded to tell the contending parties that their blood feud was unworthy of reasoning men, and was characteristic, as he phrased it, of brute beasts. He took the opportunity to denounce again the individuality and lack of coordination in Indian warfare and to argue that greater cooperation was needed to oppose the common foe and to avoid a disastrous defeat at their hands. He argued that the Huron who had been slain had committed a serious crime in killing the Iroquois prisoner and that the Onontchataronon who had avenged the crime were a small minority who had been carried away by passion. He added that the Onontchataronon were not angry at the Huron as a whole, but only at the slain Huron for what he had done (3:109–11). In so arguing, Champlain remained totally oblivious of the principle of collective responsibility for kinsmen that was the basis of Huron and Algonkin justice. Champlain added that when the Iroquois had been attacked, he had retaliated by stabbing his assailant, prior to the latter being attacked by the Onontchataronon. Because of this, it was impossible to tell whether or not the Huron had been slain by the Onontchataronon (3:111–12). Whether this story was true or had been invented in self-defence by the Onontchataronon, it provided a far superior basis for reconciliation than did Champlain's other arguments. He also claimed that the Onontchataronon did not love the prisoner as much as the Huron believed and that after he was dead they had eaten him (3:112), presumably because they once more regarded him as an enemy for having wounded a Huron ally. This seems improbable and, in my opinion, the claim was likely invented, either by Champlain or by the Onontchataronon to assuage the Arendarhonon.

Champlain also argued that the Onontchataronon very much regretted what had happened and to prevent it gladly would have sacrificed their prisoner. He reminded the Arendarhonon of the large compensation they had received for their own tribesman who had been killed, even though he himself was guilty of murder. Champlain admonished both sides to forget what had happened and to live in friendship as before. If they did, the French would continue to trade with them and assist them in their wars. To assure that the summer's trading would not be interrupted, he advised them that if they were still not satisfied, all the groups involved should come to the St. Lawrence. There, in the presence of all the captains of the trading vessels, the French would renew their friendship with each of these tribes and plan new measures to protect them from their enemies

(3:113). By holding out this promise, Champlain hoped to assure not only that there would be trade the following summer, but that both sides would be reconciled within the broader framework of an alliance with the French that was based on military cooperation, trade, and ritual ties.

The Arendarhonon seemed pleased with Champlain's proposals and returned happily to their homes. The Onontchataronon, on the other hand, announced that because of this incident they would not come again to Cahiagué, although in future years they were still wintering among the Arendarhonon (3:114). Champlain returned to the longhouse of his host, Atironta, and continued to do all he could to cultivate his goodwill and encourage him to trade (3:114). By now, the French were well aware of the Huron's ability to amass furs in return for horticultural produce. They also realized how much their success in promoting trade depended on maintaining good relations with the Huron. Because of this, the relative importance of the Algonkin was rapidly declining.

While Champlain prided himself on the role he played in settling this dispute, it seems that, at least to a limited degree, he had again been tricked by Indian diplomacy. The Arendarhonon and Onontchataronon undoubtedly appreciated his assistance as a mediator, but because of the strong economic and political ties that linked them together, it is highly likely that, even without Champlain, they would have been able to resolve their differences. A major concern of both groups was to prevent Champlain from journeying northward with the Nipissing. The dispute that arose between them, while at first real enough, offered them an excellent opportunity to divert Champlain's attention, by convincing him that his services as a mediator were required if the alliance he had made with the Huron headmen was not to be disrupted. Champlain was clearly flattered by this request, as well as fearful that the Huron trade might be lost to the French. Thus, it was not difficult to convince him that he would have to abandon his plans to join the Nipissing, in order to accompany the Huron and Onontchataronon down-river and to see that both sides observed the peace and had free access to French traders. It seems most likely that, by the time Champlain returned to Cahiagué, the dispute between the Huron and Onontchataronon had become a charade that was being played out for his benefit (Trigger 1971a:93).

It is unclear where Champlain spent the rest of the winter. The Arendarhonon later claimed that he stayed most of the time with them (Thwaites 1896–1901, 20:19). This suggests that he remained with Atironta, although he visited Father Le Caron from time to time and met various other Huron headmen (Biggar 1922–36, 3:145). During the

winter, Champlain was able to observe Huron customs and to formulate his own ideas about how relations between the French and the Huron should develop. In particular, he was convinced that priests alone would not be able to convert the Huron, unless French families were settled amongst them. These families would set an example for the Huron and also, by taking control of the country, would compel the Huron to behave properly (3:145).

The long-term policy that Champlain wished to see applied to the Huron was one that would make them not only Christian in religion, but French in language and culture (3:6). Although his appeal for French settlers to help in this project was phrased in terms of religion, it was clearly devised to promote his general plan for colonization in Canada. As a first step towards realizing this plan, Champlain and Le Caron discussed with the Huron headmen the possibility of French settlers coming to live among the Huron. Champlain was delighted by the ready agreement that the headmen gave to his proposals. They stated that while they did not understand many aspects of what he was talking about, they would be happy to have French families living in their country. They said that in return they would send some of their own children to live with the French (3:146).

The headmen seem to have interpreted Champlain's offer as an extension of the exchange of young men that had begun in 1609. Such an exchange would provide them with hostages to ensure the safety of the Huron who went to trade with the French. Since French, as well as Huron, would be endangered by enemy attacks on the Huron country, they would also ensure that the French would help to retaliate against such attacks. Finally the Huron hoped that if a limited number of French were to settle in their midst, they would be able to learn how to manufacture many items that they now had to purchase from Europeans. New plants and agricultural skills might also be acquired from them (3:146). This extremely practical attitude indicates that even at this early stage in French-Huron relations, the Huron were critically appraising European technology and believed themselves able to benefit by adopting selected items from it.

When, however, Champlain quoted the Huron as saying that their way of life was miserable by comparison with that of the French and, for this reason, it would be easy for them to abandon their old ways and learn to live like Frenchmen, he was either indulging in wishful thinking or quoting his own sentiments, which Huron headmen were echoing in an effort to be polite to him. The Huron had no intention of giving up their own way of life and probably had no idea that this was what Champlain expected

them to do. Even when they expressed interest in adopting Christian religious practices, they no doubt had in mind rituals that they could adopt in addition to their own, as they regularly added rituals from neighbouring groups. The evidence that Champlain presents indicates overwhelmingly that the Huron were mainly interested in the material advantages to be derived from closer association with the French. Champlain's comment that "their words seemed to me to be good common sense, because they show the desire they have to gain a knowledge of God" (3:146) can only be interpreted as an invention to gratify readers who were interested in supporting mission work in New France.

ATIRONTA VISITS QUEBEC

In May 1616 the Huron began to make preparations for their annual trip down the Ottawa River to trade with the French. On 20 May Champlain and Le Caron set out from Otoüacha, or the vicinity of Carhagouha, in the company of Atironta (Biggar 1922–36, 3:168). It is uncertain whether all the French who had been in the Huron country returned to the St. Lawrence at this time, or whether some remained behind to help the Huron defend their settlements and to encourage them to trade the following year. It seems likely that this was Atironta's first trip down-river and that he had joined the expedition because he wished to demonstrate that among the Huron he, rather than Ochasteguin, was now the principal ally and trading partner of the French. His visit to Quebec was also intended to reciprocate Champlain's visit to the Huron country. The descent to Montreal Island took forty days and appears to have been an exceptionally pleasant one. A large number of fish and game were caught on the way and these added to the abundance and variety of the provisions that the Huron had brought with them.

On arriving at the Lachine Rapids, Champlain found Gravé Du Pont in a state of despair, having heard that Champlain was dead (3:169). While such a rumour may have been based on a report that Champlain had been wounded, the Montagnais or Kichesipirini had exaggerated this report in an effort to undermine, even briefly, the confidence that the French traders had in the Huron. Trading took place in 1616, as in previous years, on Montreal Island; however, once official greetings had been exchanged Champlain set out for Quebec on 8 July, taking Atironta with him. Before leaving, Champlain promised the Huron and Algonkin that he would continue to assist them in the future as he had done in the past.

He urged them to remember their promise to remain reconciled and assured them that if they kept this promise, he would bring them valuable presents in future years (3:170).

Champlain reached Quebec 11 July and Atironta remained with him for four or five days, examining the French settlement and observing how the French lived. Atironta expressed admiration for what he saw and repeated his earlier wish to have Frenchmen live among the Huron and for Huron youths to be sent to live among the French. He also requested that Champlain honour his proposal to establish a settlement on Montreal Island, in order to secure that part of the river against Iroquois attack. He stated that if Champlain did this, Huron would come and live there. No doubt, by making this promise, Atironta was hoping to develop even closer relations with the French. In view of Champlain's program to promote settlement on the St. Lawrence and to expand these settlements through the assimilation of Indians, it was a very welcome request. Before Atironta left to rejoin his companions, Champlain gave him valuable presents and asked him to return again to visit Quebec (3:171–72). Atironta must have interpreted his visit to Quebec as an indication that the French recognized his function as their principal ally among the Huron. The presents that Champlain gave him would likewise have been interpreted as a response to those that the Huron headmen had sent down-river in 1611.

Conclusion

The years 1609 to 1615 saw the development of a Huron trading relationship with the French, which gradually became free of the ties that either of them had with the Algonkin. By 1611, the Huron headmen seem to have agreed that all the tribes of the Huron confederacy had a right to engage in this trade. They also agreed that control of trade should be vested in the hands of the traditional council chiefs, with Atironta, the principal headman of the Arendarhonon, being recognized as the special ally of the French. These arrangements, which protected the Huron confederacy against internal discord and which also reinforced its traditional political organization, were to remain in effect until the dissolution of the confederacy in 1649.

Despite Algonkin opposition, the French and Huron succeeded in establishing direct contact with each other. At first, the Huron travelled down-river only in the company of their Onontchataronon allies, but by

1611 they had secretly sent presents to Champlain which expressed their desire for a separate alliance with the French. Yet, although the Algonkin were growing increasingly dependent on the Huron both for corn, which they could exchange for furs among the northern hunters, and for military assistance against the Iroquois, the Huron were anxious not to offend them by overtly challenging their rights as middlemen. Moreover, since the headmen who controlled trade could not all leave their country at one time, the conclusion of a formal treaty depended on Champlain travelling inland to meet these leaders in person and to confer with them.

Champlain's visit to the Huron country and Atironta's return visit to Quebec fulfilled Huron expectations concerning the manner in which a trading alliance should be concluded. Champlain visited all the major Huron villages and assured their headmen of his friendship and of the desire that the French had to trade with them. In addition, by accompanying a Huron war party, Champlain was able to impress his hosts with the general concern he had for their well-being. The Jesuits were to report, many years later, that the memory of Champlain's visit was still cherished by the Arendarhonon, who recalled his many good qualities and commented on his continence with regard to women (Thwaites 1896–1901, 20:19).

In spite of his success, Champlain was not aware of many Huron customs nor did he understand the significance that many of his actions had for them. He had, of course, little experience in dealing with the Arendarhonon prior to his visit to their country and Brûlé, who had lived amongst them for a number of years, was almost certainly regarded and treated by the Huron as a young man. Because of this, Champlain could have acquired little knowledge of the inner workings of Huron politics. In particular, Champlain seems to have placed undue emphasis on the role of war in making an alliance with the Huron. Such an alliance, in his opinion, consisted of a sworn friendship, in which an Indian tribe agreed to trade with the French in return for him agreeing to help them in their wars (Biggar 1922–36, 3:226–27). No doubt, the Huron were pleased that Champlain wished to accompany them on a raid, as they were pleased that he should hunt with them, but they were not particularly hard-pressed by their enemies. Military alliances were not a necessary part of their trading relations with the Algonkian-speaking peoples and long periods were to pass during which they received no military assistance from the French, yet continued to trade with them. What the Huron headmen did want was an assurance that their people would be well treated if they came to trade with the French on their own, rather than in the company of Algonkin. This assurance, amongst others, they received from Champlain.

On the other hand, Champlain's repeated criticism of Huron customs and his interference with their torturing of prisoners must have annoyed and troubled them. One can only imagine that such translations as the Indians had of what he said softened his remarks and made them more acceptable. More serious were Champlain's threats to abandon the Huron and Algonkin and to seek his allies elsewhere if things did not go as he wanted. The Huron tended to be suspicious of groups they did not know well and such threats must have served to heighten their fears that the rumours they heard about Champlain's dealings with the Iroquois were true.

Champlain's success in concluding a treaty with the Huron seems to have been achieved in spite of the broad gulf of mutual misunderstanding that separated him from the Arendarhonon. Each assumed the other's behaviour to be more like their own than in fact it was and each therefore interpreted the other's actions in terms of their own code. That such misunderstanding did not lead to serious difficulties must be attributed to the nature of the situation. Champlain's actions in the Huron country in the winter of 1615–16 do not reveal him as a man who understood the Indians and knew how to deal with them, as many historians have claimed. Instead, they show him to be a man who not only understood very little about Indian ways but was too inflexible in his opinions to learn about them. That a treaty was concluded at all seems to have been largely the result of Champlain accommodating himself, haphazardly and unwittingly, to the Huron conventions that had to be observed if such a treaty were to be made. It is therefore more accurate to speak of the Huron headmen concluding a treaty with Champlain than of Champlain concluding a treaty with them.

Once formulated, however, this treaty was the basis of all future relations between the Huron and the French. Hereafter, in spite of Algonkin and Montagnais intrigues, the Huron felt confident to undertake the journey to the St. Lawrence and to trade with the French on their own account. Frenchmen were now free to live among the Huron as allies, and henceforth the Huron would feel more secure in sending their people to live with the French. Aid in warfare and the activities of the French missionaries would be seen, not as the basis of the French-Huron alliance, but as an extension of the friendship and goodwill that was ritually established at the time of Champlain's visit and was renewed thereafter by repeated exchanges of gifts and formal expressions of good faith between the two groups.

Significantly, the only casualty of Champlain's visit to the Huron country appears to have been Champlain himself. He had not intended to

spend the winter among the Huron and their refusal to return him to Quebec had frightened and angered him. The very thought of spending a winter among the Huron had been distasteful to him before his visit and there is no reason to believe that the actual experience changed his mind. In later years, Champlain was to find one excuse after another not to accompany the Huron, or any other Indian group, on their military excursions against the Iroquois and diplomatic missions to the Indians were entrusted to priests or trading agents. Perhaps Champlain now felt too old for such travel; more likely, however, he was determined never again to subject himself to Indian control. The winter that Champlain was compelled to spend among the Huron seems to have enlarged a basic fear and mistrust of the Indians, which hitherto had been concealed by a sense of superiority and of his ability to control them (Trigger 1971a:87–93).

Chapter 6 　The Quiet Years

Introduction

The years 1616 to 1629 constitute a well-defined period of Huron history. It is indicative of the important role that trading relations with Europeans had come to have for the Huron that this period began with the conclusion of a trading alliance between the Huron and the French and ended with the latter's first expulsion from Quebec. Unfortunately, the documentation for this period is neither as abundant nor as varied as the historian might wish. One very obvious gap is the lack of material dealing with the Huron in Champlain's writings after 1618. Champlain never returned to the Huron country and his later writings are preoccupied with the administration of the tiny and ill-supported colony at Quebec, on whose success he saw his own future now depending. Even his interest in exploring the interior, and possibly discovering a route to the Pacific Ocean, appears to have declined in the face of this overriding concern. For example, the delineation of the Great Lakes region in his map of 1632 shows no advance over what was recorded by him in a map drawn up immediately after his return to France in 1616 (Wroth 1954) (plates 27 and 28). Gross inaccuracies in the representation of parts of the interior explored by Brûlé and others suggest little effective consultation with these men.

The only Indians with whom Champlain was in regular contact after his return from the Huron country were the Montagnais who lived around Quebec. Other tribes are referred to only in so far as Champlain found it necessary to confer with their headmen. Regular trading with the Indians was carried on by representatives of whatever company held the monopoly at Quebec. It is perhaps indicative of the smooth course of French-Huron relations during these years that none of the available documents suggests that Champlain had personal dealings of any consequence with the Huron after 1618.

A still more serious shortcoming is the failure of any other layman to record his experiences in the Huron country between 1616 and 1629. Everything that we know about such men who visited the Huron country at this time was recorded either by Champlain or by the clergy, both of

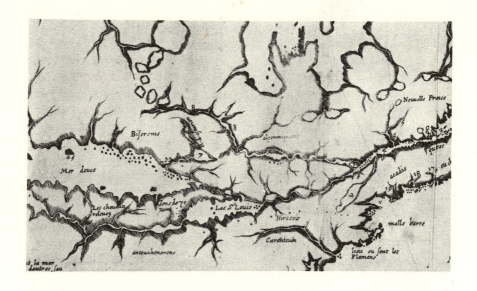

PLATE 27. *Detail of Champlain's map of New France, 1616. This map, probably a proof from an unfinished plate, embodies the cartographic knowledge that Champlain acquired from his visit to the Huron country in 1615–16. The St. Lawrence Valley and Georgian Bay are now brought into reasonable alignment though the geography of the lower Great Lakes remains poorly understood. The existence of Lake Erie is unsuspected and most of southwestern Ontario is eliminated. This map is valuable mainly because a comparison with Champlain's* Carte de la Nouvelle France *of 1632 indicates that his knowledge of the interior was unaffected by the important explorations of Brûlé, Daillon, and others in the intervening sixteen years. This may indicate that after 1616 Champlain lost his burning zeal to unravel the geography of the interior. Courtesy John Carter Brown Library.*

whom violently disapproved of the lives that many of these men led there. Yet these laymen often lived among the Huron for extended periods, helped to defend their villages, learned their language, and in some cases became members of Huron families. Even an illiterate description of their adventures would have provided more information about daily life among the Huron than do the writings of priests who refused to live in Huron villages. They might also have provided information about activities such as trade, war, and intertribal politics, about which the missionaries evinced only marginal interest.

The major sources of information concerning the Huron at this time are the writings of the Recollet missionaries who worked among them from 1623 to 1628. Contemporary Jesuit documents are few in number and the little that is known about Jean de Brébeuf's three-year stay among the Huron has been gleaned largely from his later writings. The most important Recollet sources are the two books written by Gabriel Sagard, a Recollet lay brother and former secretary to the provincial of the Recollets of Saint-Denis. These are *Le grand voyage au pays des Hurons*, published in 1632, and his longer *Histoire du Canada*, published in 1636. In the first of these books, Sagard described his stay in the Huron country during the winter of 1623–24. This book contains the best general account of Huron life by a single author and recounts miscellaneous incidents that happened while he was there. Sagard was anxious to enhance his own reputation by playing down the role of Father Joseph Le Caron, who was in charge of the Recollet mission to the Huron; indeed throughout his book, the humble but vain lay brother liked to give the impression that he was the *de facto* leader of the expedition. An annotated version of the *Grand Voyage* was reproduced in Sagard's *Histoire*, and to it was added an introductory part describing the activities of the Recollets in Canada from 1615 to 1625, and a final section covering the period from the arrival of the Jesuits in 1625 to the abandonment of Quebec by the French in 1629.

The *Histoire* was a semi-official piece of propaganda, protesting Cardinal Richelieu's refusal to allow the Recollets to return to Canada in 1632. While it was by no means an extravagant polemic, it was disapproved of by the Jesuits. It is not surprising therefore that the eighteenth-century Jesuit missionary and historian, Pierre Charlevoix (1866–72, 1:78), attacked Sagard's work on the grounds that he neither understood the Huron language nor took the trouble to verify what he reported. Charlevoix's comments have misled some later historians into believing that Sagard was an untutored and credulous person, whose work is not to be taken seriously. On the contrary, allowing for his self-importance and a

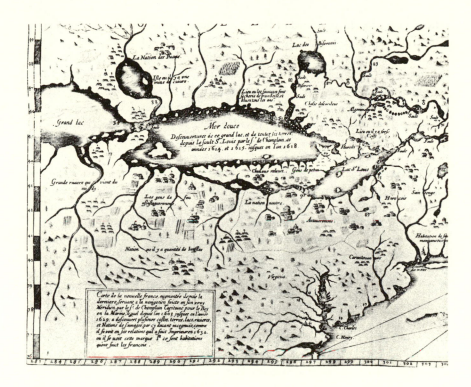

PLATE 28. *Detail of Champlain's* Carte de la Nouvelle France, *1632.*
From Champlain's Voyages *of 1632. The geography of southwestern
Ontario remains poorly understood and the Neutral are shown living south
of the Great Lakes between the Assistaronon and the Iroquois (whose western
tribes are called Antouoronon). Lake Simcoe (unnamed) and the Huron
country are more accurately outlined than on the map of 1616. Dotted lines
indicate the routes Brûlé followed to the Susquehannock (Carantouanais)
and of Champlain's expedition against the Iroquois. The Lac des Biserenis
is Lake Nipissing. Courtesy Public Archives of Canada.*

tendency (not uncommon for that period) to embellish his narrative with stories surreptitiously borrowed from other sources, Sagard's *Histoire* constitutes a valuable record of French-Huron relations.

Also of value is Chrestien Le Clercq's *Premier établissement de la foy dans la Nouvelle-France*, published in 1691. This was yet another piece of propaganda, but unlike Sagard's relatively even-tempered book, it attempted explicitly to discredit all of the work that the Society of Jesus had done in Canada. Although Le Clercq's facts are often inaccurate, the book reproduces in whole, or in part, numerous manuscripts dealing with the Recollet mission that have since been lost. These include parts of a relation written by Le Caron, Father Daillon's account of his visit to the Neutral country in 1626–27, and records of meetings at which missionary policy was discussed. For all of its shortcomings, Le Clercq's narrative provides a more balanced picture of Recollet activities in Canada than does Sagard and allows us to correct some of the distortions that Sagard's personal vanity introduced into his writings. Le Clercq's generalizations also help to clarify certain aspects of Recollet policy.

Archaeological work carried out in the Huron country, particularly in recent years, has begun to yield evidence which, in the future, will contribute to a more complete understanding of changes in Huron life at this period.[1] While the results obtained so far are interesting, the evidence remains too fragmentary to permit general conclusions. It appears, however, that further work will amplify and confirm, rather than revise, the general outline of Huron cultural development as it has been derived from written sources and is presented in this chapter.

Given the nature of the sources, it is impossible to discuss this period in simple chronological order. In the first part of this chapter, I will examine various facets of Huron external relations chronologically. In the second part, I will examine the evidence for changes in Huron life at this time, which cannot be treated chronologically. Many of the trends undoubtedly began prior to this period and became intensified later. This section is thus a general discussion of the effects of European contact, in the absence of deliberate efforts by the French to bring about change.

Trade with the French

VOLUME

The most striking feature of this period was the trade that was carried on between the Huron and the French. Every year after the Huron had con-

cluded their alliance with Champlain, Huron traders came to the St. Lawrence to exchange their furs for European goods. Before long, the Huron, though not irreversibly dependent on these goods, were accustomed to obtaining them on a regular basis. In order to win a clear idea of the impact that this trade had on the Huron, it is necessary to determine the type and amount of goods that were being exchanged between the Huron and the French. Because detailed records of this trade are not available, this is not something that can be done in precise detail. Nevertheless, from the evidence that is available, it is possible to make some useful, if rough, estimates.

During this period, the French continued to trade for a variety of fancy furs such as moose, lynx, fox, otter, marten, badger, and muskrat (Thwaites 1896–1901, 4:207). As a sideline, they also purchased beaver glands, which they sold in France for medicinal purposes.[2] As already indicated, however, even before the turn of the century, beaver skins had become the main item of trade between the Indians and the French. Lescarbot states that in 1558 a beaver skin sold in France for only fifty sous ($2\frac{1}{2}$ livres). By 1611, the growing demand for skins had raised the price to eight and a half livres, and, by 1618, ten livres, a price that remained roughly constant for many decades (2:127; 4:207; 15:159; 28:235).[3] Most of the pelts that the Huron brought to Quebec were beaver skins.

The number of skins that came from the Huron country is less certain. Charles Lalemant, writing in 1626, said that 12,000 to 15,000 skins were exported through Tadoussac each year; however, on one occasion, as many as 22,000 skins had been exported (4:207). Even more skins may have left New France in 1627, which was described as the best year for the fur trade in a long time (Biggar 1922–36, 5:232). In 1630, 30,000 skins were exported, but this was probably because, during the two previous years, the French had lacked supplies of trade goods and hence had been unable to trade with the Indians.[4] A much smaller number of skins were exported from New Netherland at this time: 4700 in 1624 and 7685 in 1628 (Trelease 1960:43).

There is no direct evidence concerning how many of these furs were obtained from the Huron, rather than from the Algonkin or Montagnais. Champlain states that, in 1623, sixty Huron and Algonkin canoes came down the Ottawa River (Biggar 1922–36, 5:100–101), of which the majority appear to have been Huron. Le Clercq (1691:258) affirms that the following year sixty Huron canoes followed Le Caron down-river. Estimates of this sort are likely to be somewhat low, however, since at this period the Huron were coming in small groups to trade. Their canoes held

from two to six people and, in general, larger ones were preferred for travelling on the Ottawa River (Wrong 1939:56, 246). In spite of the scarcity of data, Heidenreich's (1971:280) estimate of sixty Huron canoes each year, in all carrying about 200 traders, seems accurate. Sagard states that each canoe could carry about a hogshead of cargo (Wrong 1939:101), which appears to be equivalent to 200 skins weighing about a pound each.[5] This suggests that the Huron supplied the French with about 10,000 beaver skins annually, which was a high percentage of the total number of furs that they obtained. It may be noted, however, that the Huron traded corn for furs with the Algonkin on their way down the Ottawa River. Thus, by the time they reached the French trading stations, they had in their possession many furs collected by the Ottawa Valley tribes. The other principal suppliers of the French were the Montagnais at Tadoussac, but while the latter's trade network stretched as far north as Hudson Bay, because of the low population density in central Quebec, considerably fewer furs were collected by them than by the Huron. Also, by this time, intensive hunting had probably reduced the number of beaver in the Saguenay region. It seems likely, therefore, that the Huron supplied about two-thirds of all the furs that were traded along the St. Lawrence at that time. In particularly good years, or when the Huron had been unable to trade with the French the year before, the number of furs they brought probably exceeded 10,000. Considering the importance of the Huron trade, it is not difficult to understand why the clerks who traded with the Indians had to be as skilled in the Huron language as they were in Montagnais or Algonkin (Biggar 1922–36, 6:62–63).

TRADE ON THE ST. LAWRENCE

In the early days, expeditions in which Champlain fought alongside the Huron and Algonkin had proved a potent means of attracting Huron traders to the St. Lawrence. These expeditions had also blunted the power of the Mohawk and made the St. Lawrence River an important artery of communication. Moreover, by having Champlain accompany an expedition that was launched against the Iroquois from the Huron country, the Huron headmen had been able to circumvent Algonkin opposition and conclude a treaty with the French. Once the Mohawk were driven from the St. Lawrence and the French-Huron alliance was firmly established, expeditions of this sort became less important for encouraging the Huron to visit the St. Lawrence.

Champlain stated that in 1617 he had planned to assist the Huron and Algonkin, but had been prevented from doing so by the small number of warriors who turned up that year.[6] It seems that few Huron visited the St. Lawrence Valley that year because they anticipated Oneida reprisals, once the latter learned that Champlain and most of his musketeers had left the Huron country. Having obtained sufficient trade goods to satisfy their needs when they had visited the St. Lawrence in 1616, many Huron probably decided to stay home and guard their villages the following year, rather than join a campaign south of the St. Lawrence.

In 1618, Huron traders attempted to persuade Champlain to return to the Huron country with them. They stated that they were being harassed by their enemies and wished his help to defend their villages. Champlain had been angered by the failure of the Indians to turn out in force the previous year, and also by the Montagnais' murder of two Frenchmen, whose bodies had been discovered in the spring of that year. Because of this, he declined to help the Huron. Instead, he pointed out that he had intended to assist them the previous year, but they had failed to turn up; now he lacked the men and supplies to do so. He promised that he would return in 1619 to give them the victory that they wanted over their enemies (Biggar 1922–36, 3:210–11). Champlain states that he made this promise in order to make certain that the Indians would return to trade the following year; however, his promise to Brûlé that he would return to reward him and to aid his Indian friends in their wars (3:226) seems to indicate that, at least for the moment, he may seriously have been considering another expedition.[7] He can scarcely have intended to take part in any prolonged campaign, since he was planning to return to Quebec in 1619 with many settlers and the materials to establish his long hoped-for colony (3:229). In order to avoid the expense involved in such an enterprise, over the following winter the partners in the trading company sought to strip Champlain of his command at Quebec. While they failed to do this, they prevented him from sailing for the New World until 1620.

The Huron do not appear to have been particularly troubled by Champlain's failure to return. Twice before, in 1612 and again in 1614, he had not turned up for a rendezvous, hence his not doing so again can scarcely have surprised them. By this time, the Huron were sufficiently anxious to trade with the French, and sufficiently confident of their relations with company officials, that Champlain's failure to keep his promise did not cause them to cease visiting the French. They would only have done that if Champlain had openly expressed hostility towards them, or if they were convinced that he was planning to harm them in some way. In time, it

must have become apparent to the Huron headmen that Champlain was no longer willing to accompany his Indian allies. Yet, they seem to have accepted Champlain's excuses for his inactivity and ceased to expect his personal assistance in their wars. They may have realized that his enforced sojourn amongst them had made him reluctant to entrust himself to them for a second time. More likely, they interpreted his unwillingness to travel as an indication of advancing age and status. They may have concluded that, as with their own council chiefs, official duties kept him at home.

This did not mean that the Huron ceased to expect military assistance from the French. Henceforth, however, they were satisfied with the armed Frenchmen who came with the authorization of the fur traders to winter, or to stay longer, in their country. By living in, or near, the Huron villages, these men helped to guard these villages against Iroquois raiding parties. The fear that French musketeers continued to inspire in the Iroquois at this period is likely to have resulted in fewer Iroquois invading the Huron country. This permitted the Huron men who normally remained to guard their villages to engage in trading activities. While we have no record of Frenchmen joining Huron raiding parties after 1615, in 1624 a number of Frenchmen volunteered to fight alongside the Huron in a projected war against the Neutral (Wrong 1939:157). More important, the French who travelled to and from the Huron country were able to protect the Huron from Iroquois attack in the lower part of the Ottawa Valley. Sagard records that once the Iroquois learned that Frenchmen were travelling with the Huron, they ceased raiding the Ottawa Valley, just as they had formerly ceased attacking the St. Lawrence Valley (ibid. 261).[8]

This apparently voluntary cessation of raids by the eastern tribes of the Iroquois confederacy indicates how completely the Mohawk and their neighbours had been intimidated by the French. As trading opportunities opened up along the Hudson River, they appear to have abandoned any serious attempt to obtain either furs or European goods by stealing them from trading expeditions that were likely to be accompanied by Frenchmen. Not enough was to be gained to make it worthwhile to risk a possible encounter with the French. The western Iroquois tribes continued to raid the Huron country, despite the presence of some armed Frenchmen. This was probably in part because they had less easy access to European trade goods than did the Mohawk or Oneida and because the number of French who wintered among the Huron was limited. Thus the chance of obtaining such items in raids against their traditional enemies encouraged them to continue these raids in the face of new dangers.

INTERTRIBAL POLITICS IN THE OTTAWA VALLEY

Once the Ottawa Valley was safe from attack, the Huron no longer had to travel in large war parties, as they had done on their earliest trading expeditions. Instead, small groups of traders could journey to and from the Huron country independently of one another. Sagard's descriptions indicate that over much of the route only one or two canoes might stay together (Wrong 1939:56, 255), although in some cases six or more did so (247). Frenchmen who set out for the Huron country at the same time, but in different canoes, were likely to encounter one another only once or twice en route, and then only accidentally (56). While little is known about the composition of trading parties, each group was probably made up of men from a single village. In 1624, Brûlé is reported to have travelled down the Ottawa River with five or six canoes from Toanché (247). Sagard mentions that as a sign of their passing the members of a trading party often erected a piece of birch bark painted with the symbol of their village (251–52). Travelling companions from large villages were probably further subdivided according to clan.

A trip to or from the Huron country took three to four weeks. Although only one watershed was crossed, forty to one hundred stretches of rough water had to be negotiated. Many of these necessitated unloading the canoes and carrying them and their contents overland for considerable distances. Others required crews to get into the water and guide the loaded canoes through the rapids by hand (264). At its highest point, the canoe route rose 677 feet above sea level. By comparison, the Huron country was at an altitude of about 580 feet, and the French trading stations were almost at sea level. Both the greater climb and the direction of the current made the homeward journey more difficult than the trip to the St. Lawrence (Latourelle 1952–53, 1:59).

The aim of the Huron was to reach the St. Lawrence between mid-June and mid-July. This was when other tribes from the interior gathered to trade for goods that had arrived from France a few weeks earlier. The trip down-river was generally a hurried one, for fear the French would depart before their arrival. By contrast, the journey home was more leisurely, with time taken out to fish and visit other Indians along the way (Wrong 1939:60, 63). The Huron approached the trading stations by way of both the Lachine Rapids and the Rivière des Prairies north of Montreal Island. As the trading stations were moved down-river, the Lachine route became less popular, although some Indians continued to use it throughout the first half of the seventeenth century (264–65). At first, the Huron may

have preferred to use the Rivière des Prairies because it was more sheltered from Iroquois attack. Later, however, they preferred it because none of its rapids was nearly so formidable as were those at Lachine.

The decline of the Iroquois threat in the Ottawa Valley also eliminated the urgent need for cooperation between the Huron and their Algonkian-speaking allies along the St. Lawrence and Ottawa Rivers. These Algonkians begrudged the loss of their role as middlemen between the French and the Huron; however, for numerical reasons, and because they wished to barter for Huron corn, neither the Kichesipirini, nor any other Algonkin group, was prepared to resort to violence to try to disrupt trade between the Huron and the French. The Huron acknowledged the Kichesipirini's right to collect tolls in return for allowing other Indians to pass along their section of the Ottawa River. The Kichesipirini collected these tolls by compelling the Huron to give them presents and to barter corn meal for furs at rates that were highly favourable to the Kichesipirini. Thus the question of a right of passage did not lead to open hostility.

In spite of this, the cessation of Iroquois raids resulted in increasing friction between the Algonkin and the Huron traders. When the various tribes assembled to trade with the French in 1623, the Huron complained that the Algonkin had maltreated them, by robbing them and levying heavy tolls on their goods (Biggar 1922–36, 5:103). Although the French attempted to restore friendly relations, the next year Sagard reported the continuing high-handed behaviour of the Kichesipirini. The latter did not allow Huron canoes to travel down the Ottawa River individually, but held them back until a considerable number had gathered, in order to obtain corn meal more cheaply (Wrong 1939:255). Sagard witnessed the crews of his own and other canoes being compelled to trade their corn on terms set by the Kichesipirini. The Huron dreaded these annual encounters but recognized themselves bound, both by prudence and by intertribal law, to treat the Algonkin with respect. While the Huron were anxious to avoid having to trade with the Kichesipirini, they assumed, no doubt correctly, that the Kichesipirini would cause serious trouble if the Huron attempted to ignore the latter's right to regulate the trade that passed through their territory.

The Kichesipirini were able to create the most difficulties for the Huron, because their summer camp lay astride the Ottawa River. Algonkin groups who lived down-stream located their summer camps along the larger tributaries of the Ottawa River, possibly originally to avoid Iroquois attacks. There is no evidence that any of these groups attempted to levy tolls on goods passing through their territories in the systematic way that

the Kichesipirini did. Nevertheless, they too caused trouble for Huron traders. In 1624, the Petite Nation told the first Huron who came down-river that year that the French fleet had been lost at sea and that it was a waste of time for them to continue their journey. Although the ships had been late reaching Tadoussac, the French were no doubt correct when they assumed that this report was being spread in the hope that the Huron would resume trading with the Algonkin, rather than continuing on to trade with the French (262–64).

The same year, when the Huron passed a Montagnais encampment near Sillery, the latter attempted to compel them to surrender a portion of their corn meal in return for a right of passage (268). The Montagnais were prevented from doing this by the French, who refused to recognize the territorial claims of the Montagnais in such matters and sent an armed shallop to assist the Huron. This episode nevertheless indicates that the Montagnais, like the Kichesipirini, demanded rights of passage from interior tribes who were passing through their territory to trade with the French. No doubt these were partly claimed as compensation for the monopolies over trade with the interior that had been lost, in turn, by both of these groups.

The Algonkin and Montagnais used rumours to frighten the Huron as well as to discourage them. When Sagard and Brûlé attempted to persuade the Huron traders to continue down-river to Quebec in 1624, the Algonkin and Montagnais who had gathered at Cape Victory, near the mouth of the Richelieu River, told the Huron that the Mohawk had given them twenty wampum belts to inform them of the Huron's arrival, so that they might come and kill them. The fact that the French had been negotiating a peace treaty with the Mohawk, which was to be formally ratified only a few weeks later, lent an air of plausibility to the story; nevertheless it was a fabrication designed to frighten the Huron and prevent them from going to Quebec. Sagard also suggests that by reminding the Huron of their dependence on their allies' goodwill, the Algonkin and Montagnais hoped to get presents from them. In fact, the Huron offered a considerable quantity of tobacco, corn, and fishing nets to the Algonkin and Montagnais headmen, to counteract the presents that these headmen claimed the Mohawk had given them (265–66).

There is no evidence of trading between the Indians and the French at Lachine after 1616. Thereafter, trading took place at Three Rivers or near the mouth of the Richelieu River, either at St. Ignace Island or Cape Victory (otherwise Cape Massacre, or in Huron Kontrandeen [Anthran-déen]). The latter spot was so named after the victory that Champlain and his Indian allies had won near there in 1610. While the accounts suggest that

each of these places was a major trading station in different years, trading may have gone on at all three locations in the course of a single season.

The French were responsible for the removal of the trading place down-river. The earlier shifts up the St. Lawrence, from Quebec to Saint Ignace Island and then to Montreal Island, had resulted from rivalry between de Monts's men and the independent traders to whom the fur trade had been thrown open in 1609. The monopoly granted to the *Compagnie du Canada* in 1614 ended the competition for furs on the upper St. Lawrence and, once regular trading relations had been established with the Huron, the French traders no longer wished to journey from Quebec to the Lachine Rapids. It was convenient for them to centralize all of their trading with the Indians at Quebec, in so far as this was possible. This eliminated many disadvantages, including the cost of transporting goods up-river and the dangers of passing through the Richelieu Rapids (Biggar 1922–36, 5:97). In 1623, Gravé Du Pont, who was the chief factor at Quebec, went up-river to urge the Indians to come to Quebec. He only managed, however, to persuade sixteen canoes to venture down-river and, once again, French traders were forced to travel to Cape Victory (5:100). The next year, when Brûlé and Sagard tried to coax the Huron to Quebec, the latter were persuaded not to go by the Montagnais and Algonkin. The Algonkin realized that if no Indians went down-river, the French would have to come to Cape Victory to trade. This would spare them having to travel with their wives and children to Quebec, where, in any case, there was no food for them (Sagard 1866:753).

The Algonkian-speaking peoples who brought their families with them to trade were as anxious to avoid the long journey to Quebec as the French were to avoid having to transport their goods up-river. The French preferred to trade at Quebec; the Algonkin preferred Montreal. The stations at either end of Lake St. Peter, where the trading actually took place, were compromises between these conflicting interests. They were compromises that also pleased the Algonkians who lived in the Batiscan and St. Maurice Valleys. Not having women and children with them, the Huron traders were less burdened than were their Algonkian-speaking allies, and, because of this, they were probably less opposed to going to Quebec than the Algonkin were. Nevertheless, the farther downstream they travelled, the more intertribal difficulties they encountered. Hence, like the Algonkin, they probably preferred to trade at Montreal rather than at Three Rivers, and at Three Rivers rather than at Quebec.

A small number of Huron went to Quebec from time to time. Mostly, they visited the French settlement on business. They came in 1628

because, as a result of the French trading vessels not arriving in Canada that summer, the traders at Quebec did not bother to meet the Indians at the accustomed trading stations (ibid. 853). In the case of Sagard, the obligation to return a visiting friar to the Recollet house seems to have been the sole reason that his Indian companions agreed to travel down-river (Wrong 1939:267).

Curiosity about the French settlement probably also caused some Huron traders to visit Quebec, as Ochasteguin and Atironta had done earlier. These would have been headmen, who wielded enough influence to persuade their companions to accompany them. Such visitors returned home to report the wonders they had seen at Quebec. These included the tides in the river, a phenomenon that the Huron had never seen before. Sagard reports that, because of these tides, the Huron believed the St. Lawrence River to be controlled by a more powerful water spirit than any in their own country (Sagard 1866:470–71).

Unfortunately, little is known about the Huron who wintered at Quebec in 1625 (Le Clercq 1691:343). They may have been the Attignawantan families whom Le Caron is alleged to have persuaded to "settle" at Quebec, when he visited the Huron country in 1623–24 (ibid. 257). Yet, these Indians remained at Quebec only for a single winter, and it is unlikely they saw themselves as potential settlers there. Atironta, the principal headman of the Arendarhonon, and the successor of the first Atironta who had visited Quebec, spent the winter of 1645–46 living there with his relatives (Thwaites 1896–1901, 27:103). As the principal Huron ally of the French, Atironta no doubt felt he had the right to stay at Quebec at the expense of his allies, in the same manner that Huron extended hospitality to the French who visited their country. It is therefore probable that the Huron who visited Quebec in 1625 did so to satisfy the curiosity of their headman and to promote better relations between the Huron and the French. Since Father Daillon travelled to the Huron country in the company of these Huron in 1625 and was taken to Toanché rather than Cahiagué, it is likely that the leader of this group was a headman of the northern Attignawantan, who by this period seem to have replaced the Arendarhonon as the principal trading partners of the French.

PEACE WITH THE MOHAWK

The use of the St. Lawrence River was made even easier by the peace treaty that was concluded, in 1624, between the French and their Algonkian allies on the one hand and the Mohawk on the other.[9] The French

first became aware of the possibility of peace in June 1622, when two Mohawk appeared at Three Rivers and proposed to put an end to the war that had gone on for fifty years between their people and the Montagnais (Biggar 1922–36, 5:73–80). They stressed that they were there unofficially and that their aim was to visit and eventually to recover relatives and friends who had been taken prisoner by the Montagnais; however, they also revealed to the French that tentative peace talks had been going on between the Mohawk and Montagnais for some time. Champlain was in favour of such a peace, since he believed that the French would derive many benefits from it. It would guarantee to everyone the free use of the St. Lawrence River and open up new opportunities for trade in the interior. It would also make it possible for both the Algonkians and the Iroquois to hunt in the vast no man's land that lay between the St. Lawrence River and the Iroquois country. This area, which embraced Lake Champlain and the Adirondacks, was particularly rich in game, since for a long time the conflict between the Iroquois and the Algonkin had permitted only sporadic hunting there. Finally, a peace treaty with the Mohawk might allow the French to persuade the entire Iroquois confederacy to trade with them (5:74).

Peace between the Mohawk and Montagnais had been a goal of French policy as early as 1603. Now for the first time, there seemed to be an opportunity to conclude such a treaty. Seizing the opportunity, Champlain invited these two Mohawk to visit Quebec, where they were entertained with feasts and dances. The Montagnais were also persuaded to have their spokesmen accompany the Mohawk when the latter returned to their country. These envoys invited the Mohawk headmen to come to Quebec and discuss a formal peace treaty. To indicate the goodwill of the French, Champlain sent a valuable present of beaver skins to the Mohawk headmen (5:80).

The Mohawk had reasons that were unknown to the French for wanting peace at this time. Since these reasons are important for understanding the whole structure of relations between Indians and Europeans in eastern Canada and the northeastern United States at this period, a brief explanation of them is required. We have already noted that, prior to 1609, the Iroquois had been forced to obtain European goods from the St. Lawrence Valley and that competition for these goods had generated a series of conflicts into which the French were drawn, and which ultimately proved very costly for the Mohawk. Because of this, the Mohawk welcomed the arrival of Dutch traders on the Hudson as an opportunity to disengage themselves from a losing struggle on the St. Lawrence.

The Dutch soon were trading with the Mohawk as well as the Mahican. The Mohawk appear to have been free, at least most of the time, to travel through Mahican territory to the Dutch trading post at Fort Nassau and later at Fort Orange. Their landlocked position put them at a disadvantage, however, in comparison with their eastern neighbours, whose tribal lands stretched along both banks of the Hudson River. In the first years of the fur trade, when the Dutch were anxious to promote good relations wherever possible, they were attentive to the Mohawk. This helped to offset the Mohawk's geographical disadvantage. We even learn that, in 1615, three Dutch traders, led by a man named Kleynties, accompanied a Mohawk raid against the Susquehannock. This suggests that the Dutch were willing to provide their trading partners with the same sort of military assistance that the French were extending to theirs. Unlike Champlain's expeditions, however, this one ended in total disaster; the three Dutch were captured by the Susquehannock, who tortured but did not kill them. The following year they were ransomed from their captors by Cornelis Hendricksen who was exploring and trading on the Delaware River.[10] No doubt, this early misadventure was, in part, responsible for the later reluctance of the Dutch to become directly involved in the wars of their Indian allies.

As the Dutch began to develop a more far-sighted trading policy, the landlocked Mohawk were of only marginal interest to them. The Dutch knew that in the northern hinterland of the St. Lawrence and Ottawa Valleys, the French had tapped a source of furs which, in both quantity and quality, exceeded what could be hoped for from the Indians of New York State. Henceforth, the principal ambition of the Dutch was to find a way to divert this trade from the French trading stations into their own hands (Van Laer 1924:55, 104). The most promising lead in such a venture initially seemed to be the friendship that existed between the Mahican and the Algonkian-speaking peoples to the north. The latter were accustomed to trade for wampum with the Mahican and, at various times in the past, both groups seem to have been allies against the Mohawk. The wampum beads, which the northern Algonkians valued very highly, were produced in the Long Island region so that the Dutch now controlled the supply of them (Van Laer 1924:223–24; Trelease 1960:48; J. Murray 1938:368–69). The French had no wampum to trade with their allies at this time, so it seemed possible that the Dutch could use this advantage to lure some of the northern Indians to their posts.

In spite of having free access to the Dutch traders, the Mohawk must have viewed with alarm the latter's efforts to court friendship with their powerful enemies to the north. There was always the danger that if

hostilities broke out and the Dutch had to choose between the Mohawk and the northern Algonkians, the Mohawk would once again find themselves cut off from a regular supply of European goods. Under these circumstances, the Mohawk appear to have decided that rather than risk finding themselves in the same position they had been in prior to 1610, it was in their best interest to drive the Mahican from the vicinity of Fort Orange. By taking control of the river, they could compel the Dutch traders, who were few in number, to make an alliance with them on their own terms. In this way, the Mohawk could ensure that their own trade with the Dutch would not be interrupted and, at the same time, they could prevent the Dutch from making alliances with potential enemies to the north.

Casting their diplomatic net widely, as they did whenever relations with the Dutch or the English became strained in later years, the Mohawk moved to transform the detente they had with the French and the northern Algonkians into a genuine, if short-lived, peace. Their aims were to cover their northern flank while they attacked the Mahican and also to have an emergency source of European goods, lest either their war with the Mahican or Dutch sympathy for the latter were to result in their usual supply being cut off. It was no accident that the Mohawk ratified a formal treaty with the French and their Algonkian allies at Three Rivers in July 1624, the same year that war broke out between them and the Mahican (map 17). Six Mohawk headmen were present for this ceremony, which Le Clercq (1691:260) says was a solemn ritual, attended by representatives of all the Indian trading partners of the French, including the Huron. Trudel (1966a:370) argues that because Champlain does not describe such a ceremony, the treaty-making must have lacked the speeches, feasts, and dancing that normally characterized such events. The total absence of ceremony is highly unlikely, however, since without it the treaty would have had no meaning to the Indians. Even though Champlain played a major role in the negotiations that led up to the treaty, he may have been prevented by illness or some other reason from attending the ceremony, and, if Gravé Du Pont represented the French, Champlain may have overlooked the ceremony when he came to write his memoirs. Le Clercq reports that the Mohawk who concluded this treaty were accompanied by twenty-five canoes loaded with furs. The French must now have regarded the Mohawk as normal trading partners.

The role of the Huron in these negotiations is uncertain. Le Clercq (1691:260) implies that Huron traders participated in the ratification of this treaty. These traders would have had the authority to do this only if the issue had been discussed by the Huron the previous winter and the

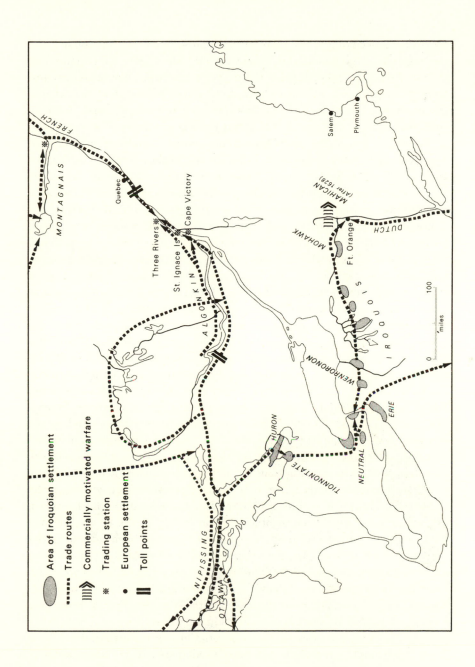

MAP 17. *Intertribal relations, c. 1625.*

headmen who were coming to trade had been empowered to make peace in the name of the whole confederacy. There is, however, no evidence that the Huron were more than passive beneficiaries of a peace in whose making they had little part. Whether or not they made peace with the Mohawk, the Huron continued to wage war against the Seneca and the three other western tribes of the Iroquois confederacy.

The new Mohawk policy towards the French and their allies seems merely to have confirmed the peaceful use of the St. Lawrence River that the French had already established by force of arms. There are, however, two pieces of evidence which suggest that prior to these negotiations the Mohawk may have been challenging the hegemony of the French. Le Clercq states that the missionary Guillaume Poulain and some companions were captured by the Iroquois on their way to the Nipissing country in 1621; however, the Iroquois agreed to exchange these prisoners for some of their own men who had been captured by the French (207, 219). Le Clercq also reports that, in 1622, about thirty Iroquois canoes appeared at Quebec, whose crews proceeded to attack the habitation and the Recollet house. Seven or eight Iroquois are said to have been killed and, in revenge, the Iroquois tortured and killed two Huron, whom they had taken prisoner (208–11). Both of these stories rest on insecure foundations. Le Clercq based his account of the attack on Quebec on information imparted to him by Guillemette Couillard, who was then about seventy years old and was recalling what had happened at Quebec in her youth. Trudel (1966a:369) doubts the accuracy of both stories and suggests that the silence of contemporary documents is more convincing than Le Clercq's evidence.

While it is certain that Couillard's story is much exaggerated, there is, however, a small amount of evidence which suggests that it might contain a kernel of truth. In 1624, Huron headmen extracted a promise from Sagard that he would ask the French to build a house below the Lachine Rapids, in order to protect them against their enemies (Sagard 1866:760). This request recalled a promise Champlain had made years before, but the fact that the Huron raised the issue again at this time perhaps indicates that renewed Mohawk attacks along the St. Lawrence were causing them some anxiety. If a couple of Huron had been killed in 1622, this might also explain why relations with the French were strained the following year. Given the independent behaviour of individual Iroquoians, renewed attacks do not indicate that all, or even most, of the Mohawk were spoiling for a fight. If there had been renewed attacks in the early 1620s, it would, however, have made the peace that followed seem all the more attractive to the French.

SOURCES OF HURON FURS

What made the Huron such valuable allies of the French was their ability to accumulate vast quantities of beaver pelts and transport them to the trading stations each year. During the period we are discussing some of these pelts were undoubtedly taken by Huron hunters; yet it is clear that hunting was never as important among the Huron as fishing. Moreover, the Huron hunting territories were not as rich in beaver as were certain other parts of southern Ontario. Their most productive beaver grounds were probably in the Holland Marsh near the south end of Lake Simcoe, although the Huron may have shared the southern part of this area with the Neutral. While beaver were no doubt plentiful in the Trent Valley, the Tionnontaté and the Neutral shared still richer areas in the swamps at the headwaters of the Grand River, while the Neutral and the tribes of southeastern Michigan vied for control of the swampy areas around Lake St. Clair and along the Thames and Sydenham Rivers (Heidenreich 1971:208). All of these areas were limited in extent and capable of rapid depletion, if heavily exploited by the relatively dense Iroquoian populations of southern Ontario. The unusually large number of beaver bones found in the Sidey-Mackay site, which is probably Tionnontaté, has been interpreted as evidence for the more intensive hunting of beaver by the Ontario Iroquoians as a result of the early fur trade (Wintemberg 1946: 155). Unfortunately, faunal remains from very few relevant sites are available for comparison with these data. It may be significant, however, that thirteen percent of the identified bone elements from the Maurice site, which is in the Penetanguishene Peninsula and approximately coeval with Sidey-Mackay, turned out to be beaver, as opposed to seven percent from the later Robitaille site (Savage 1971a:167; 1971b:176). This suggests an increase in local beaver hunting in the early contact period, followed by a decline, as beaver supplies became depleted. Beaver were still plentiful in the Neutral country as late as 1626, when Iroquet and a band of twenty men trapped 500 of them (Sagard 1866:803). It is of interest that the Neutral were prepared to let the Onontchataronon hunt their beaver. Probably Iroquet paid for this privilege by presenting European goods to Neutral headmen.

By around 1630, however, beaver seem to have become extinct within the Huron hunting territories. In his *Histoire du Canada*, Sagard (1866: 585) recorded that the Huron had overhunted the beaver within their country and were now finding none there. In 1635, Paul Le Jeune noted that the Huron had exterminated their own beaver and had to obtain from

other Indians all the skins they traded with the French (Thwaites 1896–1901, 8:57). The latter statement makes it clear that depletion was not limited to the immediate vicinity of the Huron settlements. Some beaver hunting continued; for example, a Huron named Tsondihwané and his son left Ossossané to hunt beaver in the autumn of 1642 (26:249–51). Such hunting was probably done on the Canadian Shield and use of this territory would have required permission from the Algonkians. Continued hunting in this area may explain Gendron's (1868:13) otherwise anomalous comment that the Huron country was still rich in beaver in the 1640s.

There is no reason to believe that the Huron, even in the earliest days of the fur trade, trapped a large percentage of the furs that they traded with the French. Yet, as the fur trade grew in volume, they must have acquired increasing numbers of furs from trading partners. It probably came as little surprise to the Huron and created few problems for them when their own beavers became extinct. The Huron were already on good terms with Algonkian hunting groups who inhabited a vast area rich in beaver and laced with rivers that made the collection of pelts relatively easy. By tapping this source more intensively, the Huron were able to assure themselves of an almost inexhaustible supply of furs to trade with the French. Moreover, since the Algonkians would have used most of these pelts for clothing prior to trading them, either for corn or for European goods, this mode of acquisition saved the Huron the trouble of wearing these furs until the guard hairs had fallen out and they were of prime quality to trade with the French.

From the writings of Gabriel Sagard it is possible to gain a fairly clear picture of the extent and nature of Huron trade in the 1620s, although it is impossible to determine how many furs were coming from any one source (map 18). A number of the Huron's furs were obtained from the Ottawa Valley Algonkin and the Montagnais, who also traded with the French on a regular basis. Each year, when the Huron travelled downriver, they carried corn, cornmeal, tobacco, fishing nets, and black squirrel skins, the latter being an exotic luxury much prized among the Montagnais. The Huron's exchange with the Kichesipirini was, as we have seen, of a quasi-compulsory nature, with low prices being paid in furs for Huron corn, but among other groups the trading appears to have been more profitable. None of these groups had to trade with the Huron for European goods, but they were interested in obtaining corn, which only the Huron could supply to them in bulk.

The Huron's control of the fur trade, both in the Lake Huron region and to a lesser extent in the Ottawa Valley, depended on their ability to produce

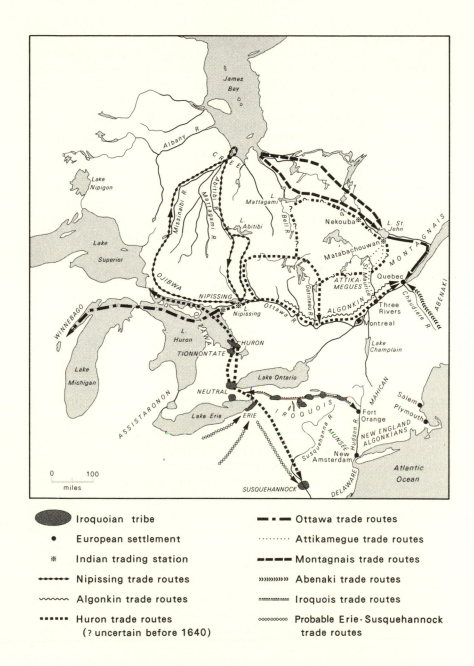

MAP 18. *Major trade routes in the first half of the seventeenth century.*

large surpluses of corn on a regular basis. Some groups of northern Algonkians appear to have already been dependent on Huron corn in pre-historic times. With the development of the fur trade, however, the northern hunting peoples were compelled to spend more time either trading or trapping beavers, in order to obtain sufficient quantities of European goods to satisfy their wants. Because of this, the amount of time spent fishing and hunting for subsistence declined and these groups became increasingly dependent on agricultural produce to make up the deficit. The Montagnais purchased much of their food from the French, but for the more westerly tribes the Huron were a more reliable and less expensive source.

The influence exerted by this growing demand for corn on the develop-ment of trading networks is clearly illustrated by the trade that the Huron carried on with the Nipissing and Ottawa. By the 1620s, some Nipissing were travelling down the Ottawa River to trade with the French (Biggar 1922–36, 5:129), although this was a fairly recent develop-ment and the Nipissing did not trade with the French either as extensively or as regularly as did their Algonkin neighbours. In spite of this, every summer when the Huron traders returned from the St. Lawrence, the Nipissing met them as they passed through Nipissing tribal territory and exchanged furs for European goods. So vital was corn to the Nipissing economy that they preferred to focus most of their trading cycle on the Huron, rather than seek an extensive separate relationship with the French.[11]

Even more specialized were the Huron's relations with the Ottawa (Cheveux Relevés) bands, who lived around the shores of Georgian Bay, and with the Nation de Bois, which was probably a branch of the Ojibwa. The Ottawa controlled extensive trade networks which ran westward along the shores of Lakes Superior and Michigan. They were also famous, in Sagard's time and later, for their acumen as traders (Sagard 1866:192). Although French trade goods played as important a part in their trade with the west as they did in the Nipissing's trade with the north, there is no evidence that the Ottawa traded directly with the French prior to 1653. Instead, each summer they met the Huron traders returning from the St. Lawrence near the mouth of the French River. There, they exchanged furs, shell beads, pigments, and possibly native copper which they had obtained farther west, for the European goods that the Huron had brought back from the St. Lawrence. Sagard reports that trading sessions lasted over several days, while the Ottawa and Huron bargained over the terms of trade (Wrong 1939:66–67; Sagard 1866:192).

The furs that the Huron obtained by barter with other tribes on their way to and from the St. Lawrence each year accounted for only part of their total intake. More furs were obtained from northern Algonkians who wintered in the Huron country. During the winter, the Attignawantan and Ataronchronon bartered corn with the Nipissing, which the latter either consumed on the spot or kept for trade the following summer. In this way, the Huron were able to secure most of the furs that the Nipissing trapped themselves and which they collected on their annual trading expeditions to the shores of James Bay. Although they traded with the French more extensively than did the Nipissing, the Onontchataronon were also an important source of furs for their Arendarhonon hosts. While it is unlikely that the Onontchataronon brought many pelts from their beaver grounds in the lower Ottawa Valley, the 500 beavers that Iroquet trapped in the Neutral country were probably intended for trade with the Arendarhonon.

There is no record of Ottawa wintering among the Huron. Many had their villages to the west of the Tionnontaté and obtained their corn from them. Yet, if the Ottawa were less dependent on the Huron for corn than were the Nipissing and Algonkin, they were more dependent on them for European goods. By limiting themselves to receiving such goods from other Indians, the Ottawa were able to concentrate on trading with groups that had less access to these goods than they had and among whom relatively small amounts of trade goods were valued more highly than they were farther east.

The hazards of the latter form of trade are exemplified, however, by the difficulties that the Ottawa experienced with the Winnebago, a populous and sedentary Siouan-speaking people who lived in the vicinity of Green Bay, Wisconsin. The Winnebago are reported to have slain some Ottawa who may have been attempting to initiate trade with them. They perhaps did this to steal the Ottawa's trade goods and because they did not appreciate the military superiority that access to iron weapons had conferred on the Ottawa, whom they scorned as a weak and nomadic people, just as the Huron did. Whatever the reason, it is clear that the Winnebago did not yet appreciate the desirability of securing a regular supply of European goods. When war broke out as a result of these killings, the Ottawa and their allies, who were better armed with iron weapons, gained the upper hand. This led to a division of opinion between those Winnebago who wished to continue the war and those who argued that trade goods were useful and the killing of the Ottawa envoys had been a mistake. Bacqueville de La Potherie (1911–12, 1:293–95) reports that the Winnebago

were forced in self-defence to found a single large village, where epidemics and other disasters carried off thousands of people and reduced the tribe to a few hundred individuals (Lurie 1960: 797–803). While the chronology for these events is not entirely certain, the epidemics were probably the ones that began in the upper Great Lakes area in 1634, which suggests that the war between the Winnebago and the Ottawa had begun in the previous decade. The main problem bedevilling the Winnebago was the difficulty that a people primarily dependent on agriculture and who were unused to trading with hunting peoples had in adjusting to the requirements of the fur trade. These were problems that the Huron were able to avoid by building on pre-existing trading networks. By intensifying long-standing relations with the Nipissing and Ottawa, the Huron could tap trade routes leading north to the salt waters of the Arctic and deep into the watersheds of Lakes Superior and Michigan.

The Huron traders did not leave the centre of this vast network, however, only to transport their goods to the French trading stations. Every spring and autumn, Huron traders carried European goods to the Tionnontaté and Neutral villages. There they visited their trading partners and exchanged these goods for furs, tobacco, wampum, and other luxury items of southern origin. While few details of this trade have been recorded, the journeying of Huron traders to Tionnontaté and Neutral villages, and of Tionnontaté and Neutral traders to Huron villages, must have been an important activity at this period.

Huron traders were also active on Georgian Bay, visiting the various Algonkian-speaking bands that inhabited its eastern and northern shores. The statement that the Huron travelled in winter across the ice of Georgian Bay to trade corn for fish with neighbouring Algonkian groups shows that the origins of this trade were not entirely forgotten as the fur trade grew more important (Thwaites 1896–1901, 13:249). Summer expeditions took the Huron at least as far west as Sault Sainte Marie and possibly into the Lake Superior region. There is no evidence that the Huron journeyed into northern Ontario along the routes of their Nipissing trading partners, although they may have travelled westward along Ottawa trade routes. In 1639, François Du Peron listed the Winnebago as one of the tribes with whom the Huron traded (ibid. 15:155), and even earlier, Sagard had affirmed that Huron was a lingua franca that was used to trade with this tribe (Wrong 1939:9). It has also been suggested that seven Huron accompanied Jean Nicollet to the Winnebago country in 1634 (Hamelin 1966b:517).

In general, however, Sagard implies that it was the Ottawa, rather than

the Huron, who traded with the Winnebago (cf. Wrong 1939:67; Sagard 1866:194). Moreover, while Nicollet is said to have left the Huron when he began his journey to Lake Michigan, his companions are identified only as Indians, and not specifically as Huron (Thwaites 1896–1901, 23: 277). Evidence of trade and contact between the Huron and the Winnebago is therefore tenuous. Barthélemy Vimont states specifically that Nicollet's aim was to make peace between the Winnebago and the Huron (ibid.) and Bacqueville de La Potherie (1911–12, 1:293) affirms that in their war with the Winnebago, the Ottawa were aided by other tribes as well as by the French weapons they received. Vimont may, however, have been using the term Huron loosely to refer to any tribe served by the Huron mission (Lurie 1960:794). It is also possible that while the Huron did not regularly trade this far west, some of their warriors may have accompanied the Ottawa when they waged war against the Winnebago.

Although it has been suggested that the Huron did not begin to trade in the interior of Quebec before about 1640 (Heidenreich 1971:277, 279), it is clear that this is not so. According to Sagard, control of trade with the Saguenay was a carefully guarded prerogative of certain Huron headmen (Wrong 1939:99), and elsewhere he explained that this trade was one of the most profitable for both the Montagnais and the Huron (87). It is certain that the term Saguenay refers to the interior of Quebec and that Huron were following the old copper route eastward in order to trade with the hunting bands of that region. This is confirmed by Sagard's eyewitness observation that a party of Huron who were on their way to the Saguenay turned north along the Ottawa River instead of south, after they had reached the mouth of the Mattawa River (249, 253–54). From there, they may have made their way into the interior of Quebec by way of Lake Timiskaming and the Belle River, possibly as far as Lake Mattagami. Since there is no evidence that Huron ever came to Tadoussac, they then may have made their way eastward along the Ashuapmuchuan River to the headwaters of the St. Maurice, although they did not travel down this river either. Alternatively, their travels may have taken them no farther than the Cabonga region, whence they made their way back to the Ottawa Valley along the Gatineau River. Unfortunately, given the present state of the evidence, it cannot be determined whether or not, or to what degree, the Huron traded in that region in prehistoric times. If they did not trade into Quebec in prehistoric times, their routes may have developed from the relatively short Gatineau trip to much longer ones that by 1642 were taking them as far as Matabachouwan ("Maouatchihitonnam") in the Lake St. John region (Thwaites 1896–1901, 24:155).

If the Huron did trade along the copper route in prehistoric times, this developmental scheme may be totally invalid.

It seems inevitable that once trading had begun between the Huron and the French, the Europeans' growing demand for beaver pelts would have led to a considerable and rapid increase in the volume of Huron trade. If 200 to 300 Huron were carrying furs to the St. Lawrence each year, an even larger number must have been involved in collecting the pelts, and in Indian trade generally, in southwestern Ontario, around the shores of Georgian Bay, and eastward into central Quebec. While many of the same individuals may have been trading with other tribes and with the French, it is possible that 300 to 400 Huron were engaged in intertribal trade, in addition to those who did business with the French. As we have seen in chapter 4, archaeological evidence indicates that in prehistoric times the Huron traded at least with the Nipissing and with the Algonkian bands who lived around the shores of Georgian Bay. It may be that as the fur trade developed, the Huron gradually expanded their trading network. Alternatively, this network may already have existed in prehistoric times and the Huron may simply have intensified their contacts with these more remote areas after 1600. Whichever happened, it is clear that the Huron were experienced traders prior to their initial contacts with the French. It also may be that the historic trade routes that belonged to the Ottawa and Nipissing are intensifications of earlier trading systems. If regional trade was largely built upon pre-existing relationships, this would help to explain the rapidity and apparent ease with which the Huron were able to expand the volume of this trade to meet the demands of the French fur traders.

By the early 1620s, the fur trade appears to have penetrated as far north and west as it was to reach until after the dispersal of the Huron. Even in the late 1650s, the Sioux who lived at the west end of Lake Superior lacked iron weapons and, for this reason, were regarded as easy prey by the displaced tribes who crowded into their territory from the east (Perrot 1911:159–63). About the same time, when the Iroquois began raiding the lower part of the Ohio Valley, they encountered Algonkian-speaking groups who still used only stone hatchets and knives "and the other things that the Indians used before they began to trade with the French" (Thwaites 1896–1901, 44:49). As late as the 1670s, the tribes living south and west of the Illinois had no access to European trade goods, either from the east or from the Spanish settlements to the south (59:127). The limited capacity of the Huron and their trading partners to convey European goods into the interior hampered the spread of these goods until the Europeans established their own trading posts in the upper Great

Lakes region in the 1690s. The Huron may have reached the limit of their carrying capacity in the 1620s, although this seems doubtful. More likely, however, they increased their intake of furs after this period by more intensive collecting within the areas where they already traded. Such a procedure had the advantage of increasing trade without requiring the expansion of trade routes or the pioneering of trading relations with wholly unfamiliar peoples.

While changes were undoubtedly brought about by an increasing emphasis on trade, trading activities probably had less impact on Huron daily life than is generally imagined. If we assume that 250 men spent three months each year travelling to and from Quebec and another 350 spent two months each year trading with other Indians, this would mean that only about one adult male in six was engaged in external trade. This is about the same number that Sagard reports went each year to wage war on the Iroquois. Heidenreich (1971:153) has estimated that it took the Huron about three months to build and fortify a settlement for 1000 inhabitants. If a town was relocated every 12 years, this would have required an average of 1500 man days of work per year (although all the labour would have been concentrated in a much shorter period). Considerably more time had to be spent clearing fields. Using the figures worked out above, the men from Heidenreich's village would have spent only 2416 days each year trading. A large percentage of the furs collected by the Huron may have been brought to the Huron country by others, and one cannot necessarily equate the importance of trade and the time that was spent on it. Nevertheless, between 1615 and 1629 the male Huron still spent far more time waging war and performing domestic tasks than he did trading.

FRENCH IMPORTS

It is impossible to determine accurately the amount of French trade goods that the Huron were importing into southwestern Ontario at this period. De Caën, who held the trading monopoly, sent two ships to Tadoussac each year loaded with freight valued at 4800 livres (Thwaites 1896–1901, 4:207; Trudel 1966a:431). Charles Lalemant enumerates the cargo of these vessels as made up of cloaks, blankets, night caps, shirts, sheets, hatchets, iron arrowheads, large needles, swords, ice picks, knives, kettles, prunes, Indian corn, peas, crackers, sea biscuits, and tobacco (Thwaites 1896–1901, 4:207). Most of the food, tobacco, and clothing seems to have

been destined for trade with the Montagnais and the Indians from the Maritimes (3:75–77; 5:25). The Huron had no need for more corn, and even nonindigenous specialities, such as prunes and biscuits, which the French took to the Huron country for their own use, seem to have been purchased by the Huron in limited quantities, if at all. These foods remained rare in the Huron country because of the difficulty involved in transporting them there, rather than because the Huron did not enjoy them. Sagard reports that when he set off for the Huron country he took along a small box of sea biscuits, hoping that it would last him until he reached his destination. When the Huron with whom he was travelling found out that he had these biscuits, they compelled him to share them with the whole group in accordance with their traditional norms of generosity. Thereafter, Sagard had to accustom himself to eating corn soup, for which his hosts encouraged him to overcome his initial distaste (Wrong 1939:56–58).

Although Louis Hébert arrived at Quebec in 1617, and began farming there under a contract that obliged him to sell his surplus produce to the trading company, the total amount of food available to the French for trade was insufficient to undercut the Huron. Throughout this period the Algonkin, although better located for trade with the French than with the Huron, continued to rely on the latter for supplies of corn. The cost of transporting goods to the New World ensured that French trading in agricultural produce was only with hunting groups, like the Micmac and Montagnais, who lived too far away to make the large scale transport of corn from the horticultural tribes living in the interior a practical proposition. The Huron country remained the granary for the Ottawa Valley Algonkin, as well as for the semi or nonagricultural peoples of the upper Great Lakes and central Quebec (Thwaites 1896–1901, 8:115).

The Huron do not appear to have bartered for large quantities of cloth or clothing, although they did not fail to appreciate these items. Blankets, capes, and shirts are listed among the things that they sought (5:265; 12:249), and these items were given as presents to leading Huron traders (Sagard 1866:797; Thwaites 1896–1901, 8:75). The Huron also requested stockings and shoes as presents from the French who visited their villages (Wrong 1939:245) and Sagard reports that women asked to borrow his cassock for travelling in the rain (ibid. 146). The general impression, however, is that European clothing remained relatively unimportant among the Huron. The Montagnais, on the other hand, began wearing French clothes at an early period, and it is likely that at least some of the Algonkin did also (Thwaites 1896–1901, 5:25; 7:9–11). It may have been their

traditional style of dress, more than anything else, that won the Huron their French name, which implies that the French regarded them as rustics or hillbillies.

Huron traders were primarily interested in obtaining metal ware. This preoccupation is reflected in the Huron name for the French, which was Agnonha, meaning "Iron People" (Wrong 1939:79). The most common iron objects found in Huron sites are the blades of table, butcher, and jack-knives (Garrad 1969:3; Latta 1971:127). Often iron knives outnumber the combined total of all other metal objects. Awls, either round or square in cross-section, are also common, as are trade axes. So many axe heads are reported to have been ploughed up when Simcoe County was cleared for settlement in the last century, that scrap dealers found it profitable to travel from farm to farm collecting them (Hunter 1902:67; Jury and Jury 1954:53). These three implements were popular because their cutting edge was superior to that of stone or bone tools.

The metal arrowheads that were manufactured from iron, copper, and brass for trade with the Indians could pierce Iroquois slat armour. The stemmed metal points found at some sites appear to be specimens of such trade goods (Latta 1971:127). Kettles made out of thin sheets of brass or copper bent around iron hoops were also favourite trade items and, when worn out, the Huron cut them up to make arrowheads, as well as pendants and other decorations. These decorations were often pierced and appear to have been sewn on to clothing.

In addition to these common items, the ossuary at Ossossané, which dates from 1636 (only slightly later than the period we are considering), contained scissors, iron bracelets, metal rings, a key, and a burning glass (Kidd 1953:367–69). The Huron may have carried the key off from some sailor's chest; Sagard states that they hung such keys as ornaments around their children's necks (Sagard 1866:380). In addition, Huron sites of this period contain numerous red, blue, white, and polychrome glass beads. These beads occur in a variety of shapes, such as round, tubular, and twisted, and while some are in solid colours, others are striped or have cores that are a different colour from the exterior (Kidd and Kidd 1970). Kidd (1953:367–69) suggests that one type imitates native beads of red slate that were much prized by the Huron. The glass is a dull red that can be differentiated from slate only on a fractured surface. Moreover, the shapes of these beads imitate tubular, square, and triangular native beads. Kidd's suggestion that the French produced these beads especially for the Indians is perhaps supported by the marketing skill embodied in

Sagard's observation that every tribe, except the Nipissing, made more of red beads than of any other kind (Wrong 1939:250).

The fragmentary archaeological evidence suggests a marked increase in the amount of European goods reaching the Huron country by the second decade of the seventeenth century. The annual trade seems to have been somewhat larger after 1634 than it was from 1616 to 1629 and the per capita annual inflow of European goods was certainly greater after the population decline of 1634 to 1640. On the other hand, trade does not appear to have been disrupted any year prior to 1628, although it was frequently disrupted after that date; therefore, the total increase in goods reaching the Huron was probably not as great after 1634 as might be inferred from trade figures referring to individual years. At no period did the flow of European goods into the Huron country keep pace with the demand for these items. The Huron frequently objected that they were short of things they needed (ibid. 245), and besieged Frenchmen who were visiting the trading posts with personal requests to return with beads, awls, and other items.

The Huron were also notorious for their thieving when they visited Three Rivers and Quebec. Sagard (1866:379) states that the French traders were unable to avoid loss, even when they watched the Huron carefully. This accusation was made at a time when complaints about the Indians living nearer to Quebec seem to have been diminishing. The French also complained that the Huron stole from Frenchmen living in the Huron country, if the latter had not entered into a kinship relation with them (Wrong 1939:81). It must have been obvious to the Huron that taking goods in this manner angered the French, even though much of what they did was probably not wrong by Huron standards. It must therefore be concluded that trade alone was unable to satisfy the Huron's craving for European goods and that they were willing to annoy the French and to risk injury in order to obtain more.

The Huron's desire for European goods did not mean, however, that they had become totally dependent on these items. The economic relationship between the Huron and the French can best be brought into focus by a comparison with coastal peoples, such as the Micmac and Montagnais. The culture of these groups had undergone extensive modification as a result of the fur trade and their reliance on their European trading partners was much greater than that of the Huron. By 1623, the Montagnais who lived around Tadoussac and Quebec were spending so much time trapping and trading that they were unable to manage without supplies

of peas, corn, and sea biscuits. By contrast, the Huron were not dependent on the French, or any other Indian group, for their subsistence (Biggar 1922–36, 5:251, 267).

The Montagnais were also no longer cooking in birchbark baskets (Wrong 1939:108; Thwaites 1896–1901, 5:97)[12] and were so committed to the use of copper kettles that the French were uncertain whether or not they had formerly made clay pots (Sagard 1866:271). They had also ceased to make, or use, stone axes (ibid. 271). The Huron continued to manufacture and use pottery, birchbark vessels, and stone axes (Wrong 1939:61). The Montagnais had also been able to obtain guns, not from the official traders at Quebec, but from others who were operating illegally below Tadoussac (Biggar 1922–36, 5:3; Le Clercq 1691:194–95). It is suggested that these traders hoped that by arming the Montagnais and encouraging their resentment over the high prices that the official traders were charging for their goods, they could incite the Montagnais to attack Quebec. The sale of guns to the Indians was illegal at this time and their obtaining them was a source of anxiety to the French at Quebec, because the Indians were opposed to the monopoly that the officials there were attempting to enforce. Since the Huron lacked any contact with traders other than those at Quebec, they were unable to obtain firearms. It is also reported that while the Montagnais continued to build canoes, they bought longboats from the French so that they could travel more safely along the lower St. Lawrence River (Sagard 1866:251).

The gradual loss of major items from Montagnais traditional culture, and their replacement by European goods that the Montagnais did not know how to manufacture, resulted in a degree of dependence on European traders that was as yet unknown among the Huron. The Huron's larger population and greater remoteness from the French trading stations were sufficient to ensure that not enough European goods could be transported to the Huron country to satisfy the demand for them. These limitations in supply compelled the Huron to rely more heavily on their own products.

The Huron not only were less dependent on trade with the French than were the Montagnais, but also were less sophisticated about it. Below Tadoussac, monopolies were difficult to defend and the Montagnais were accustomed to doing business with rival European traders. In spite of efforts to enforce a monopoly, clandestine trade continued. Early in the 1620s, Protestant merchants from La Rochelle erected a stockade to protect themselves while bartering with the Indians (Biggar 1922–36, 5:50–51). They are also reported to have directed a stream of anti-Roman Catholic propa-

ganda at the Montagnais, in an effort to make the French at Quebec seem more odious to them (5:4). The experience that the Montagnais gained encouraged them to drive hard bargains with Europeans. Where rival traders were known to be operating, the Montagnais would refuse to trade until a number of rivals were present, to enhance their own bargaining position. When the Montagnais headman, Erouachy, was offered too small a present by the captain of one of the company ships that arrived at Tadoussac in 1623, he threw the present into the river and ordered his men to board the ship and carry off whatever they needed, leaving only what they wished in exchange. Rather than risk a blood feud, the French stood by as the Montagnais plundered their ship. They considered themselves fortunate when the Montagnais returned that evening and sought to restore normal relations (Wrong 1939:45–46). According to Sagard, the French were considerably more frightened of offending the Montagnais than the Montagnais were of offending them (ibid. 46).

The Montagnais were extremely angry when the enforcement of the trading monopolies at Tadoussac and Quebec led to a rise in the price of trade goods at these key centres after 1614. Although they had welcomed French settlement at Quebec as protection against the Iroquois and a year-round source of food, the adverse effects of the monopoly soon produced mixed feelings. Collective resentment against the official traders resulted in personal quarrels between French and Indians, leading to the killing of two Frenchmen in 1617 and two more in 1627. Evidence from elsewhere indicates that if the Montagnais and the traders at Quebec had been on generally good terms, these murders would not have occurred. Moreover, the heavy-handed, but vacillating manner in which the French reacted to these murders produced further resentment among the Montagnais (Trigger 1971a:94–100). By 1624, Champlain's worst suspicions about the Montagnais seemed justified when he learned that they were boasting that if they were to kill all the French at Quebec, other vessels would come and they would get their goods more cheaply (Biggar 1922–36, 5:124–25).

The Huron, by contrast, had known free trade only between 1610 and 1612 and, being inexperienced in dealing with Europeans, had been frightened by the competition for their furs. The effective exclusion of rival traders from the upper St. Lawrence after 1613 allowed Champlain to establish a trading relationship with the Huron which, in the latter's eyes, closely approximated the kind of intertribal trading relationship to which they were accustomed. Each year when they came to the St. Lawrence, several days were devoted to speeches, feasts, and the exchange

of valuable presents, both before and after the bartering took place. These
c   es reaffirmed the treaty of friendship between the Huron and
t.   .ch, without which the Huron would have felt uneasy about
returning to the St. Lawrence the following year. So long as their treaty
was reaffirmed, the Huron traders remained confident that they would be
well-received and expected the French to have the same trust in them.
Not having close contact with the Montagnais, and sometimes being on bad
terms with them, the Huron probably remained unaware of events down-
river and accepted the prices charged by the company for its goods as fair.

In addition to their general treaty, the Huron were anxious to establish
relations of real or fictional kinship with individual Frenchmen who
visited their country. In this and in other ways, they hoped to elicit the
support of these individuals as intermediaries when they traded with the
French. Huron traders were anxious to have Le Caron accompany them to
the St. Lawrence in 1624 (Le Clercq 1691:258) and Sagard reports that
before he left, the people of Quieunonascaran asked him to keep the
French traders well disposed towards the Huron and to do all he could to
see that Huron traders got what they wanted from the French at a reasonable price. In return, the Attignawantan promised to provide the French
traders with furs of the best quality (Wrong 1939:244). The Huron traded
with the French, as with other tribes, in the Huron language. They did not
bother to learn the jargon that was spoken at Quebec, which Le Jeune
describes as an amalgam of French and Indian words that the French
believed was Indian and the Indians believed was French (Thwaites
1896–1901, 5:113–15). This jargon appears to have employed words
derived from French and from various Algonkian dialects.

All of this shows that the Huron were still able to view their trade with
the French in terms of a traditional system of intertribal friendship and
alliance. The Huron wished to receive as many European goods as possible
for their furs, but, instead of haggling over individual pelts, a request for
more trade goods was phrased as an appeal for further proof of friendship.
The Huron regarded generosity to friends and allies as an obligation; therefore, if the French traders really were their friends, they would treat the
Huron who came to Quebec generously. This embedding of marketing
within a framework of political and social relations puzzled the French
traders. The Huron, like the Montagnais, knew how to bargain, but
instead of trying to negotiate directly, or to play different traders off
against one another, they insisted on bargaining within the framework of
a political alliance. The Huron expected the French to share the same

values that they did and were appalled when merchants haggled over the price of individual skins (Wrong 1939:140). Unfortunately, few details have been recorded about this encounter between tribal and bourgeois values.

The evidence suggests that in spite of the important role that the Huron played in the fur trade, their contacts with the French were essentially of a traditional type. In part, this reflects the low frequency and specialized nature of these contacts. It also indicates, however, that although the Huron were highly successful as fur traders, their economy was still largely independent of that of the French and they remained a tribal people. The role they played in the fur trade was an extension of prehistoric trading relations that provided the Huron with a model for their dealings with the French.

The French in the Huron Country

Direct contact with the French was limited in one direction to the brief visits of 200 to 250 Huron men who went annually to the St. Lawrence Valley to trade. Between 1615 and 1629, only one woman is reported to have made this journey. In the other direction, it was limited to a small number of priests, traders, and other Frenchmen who went to live among the Huron and were welcomed by them as tangible evidence of French goodwill. The Huron regarded it as an essential condition of their alliance with the French that they treat these guests well, and individual Huron traders were anxious to establish special personal relations with them. In particular, they hoped to adopt or conclude matrimonial alliances with these visitors, either of which meant that the French entered into kinship with a particular Huron family (Wrong 1939:70-71). Sagard reports that when he was taken into the home of Oonchiarey, the Huron who had brought him to the Huron country, he was treated as a member of the family and called son, brother, cousin, and nephew by different members (71). Efforts to persuade priests to marry Huron women caused the former considerable embarrassment and resulted in the Recollets drawing the erroneous conclusion that Huron men were anxious to debauch and prostitute their women (133-34). Like many tribal peoples, the Huron viewed all social relations as an extension of kinship; hence they were behaving quite normally in attempting to establish such relations with the French, not only symbolically but also in the most literal way possible.

Although the Huron knew and frequently used (albeit in a phonetically altered fashion) the Christian names of the French who lived in their midst, sometimes they gave these people specifically Huron names (Thwaites 1896–1901, 16:239–41). Some of these became hereditary titles of respect. Achiendassé, Father Jérôme Lalemant's name, was later used to designate all the superiors of the Jesuits at Quebec, in the same way that Huron council names were passed from one office-holder to the next. In a more personal way, Pierre Chaumonot, who seems to have been called Aronhiatiri ("Heaven-Bearer") at the time of the Huron mission (Jones 1908:371–74), later was given the name Echon (Jean ?), which had been Brébeuf's Huron name. Other names appear to have been more in the nature of sobriquets; Sagard reports that a French boy who lived with the Recollets in the Huron country was called Auhaitsique, after a small fish, while another Frenchman was called Houaonton, "a quarreller." There was probably an element of irony in the name Garihouanne, "Big Chief," which Sagard says the Huron gave him either because of his bravery or because of the respect that the officials of the trading company had shown him when he embarked for the Huron country. More likely, it was invented to make fun of his self-importance.

Because of the Huron's remoteness from Quebec, Champlain did not attempt to assert his authority as a vice-regal official over them. Although he appears to have employed priests as his emissaries to the Huron, his aim was to retain the friendship of the confederacy rather than to try to regulate its activities. This contrasts with his treatment of the Montagnais, whom he regarded as an integral part of his colony and wished to subject to his authority. In particular, he tried to bring pressure to bear on the Montagnais to force them to settle down as horticulturalists and to recognize themselves as French subjects. Champlain was, however, unable to control the Montagnais, in large part because neither the headmen nor their followers had any understanding of the European concept of authority, which was a first requirement if Champlain's schemes were to work. He also lacked the physical power to force the Indians to obey him, and his aim to have the Montagnais become sedentary was directly opposed by the fur traders, who had more influence among the Indians than he had. Because of this, Champlain grew increasingly frustrated and callous in his dealings with the Montagnais; to the point where his behaviour, which at first must have seemed merely incomprehensible and erratic, greatly angered them. Eventually, Champlain was to call the Montagnais his worst enemies (Trigger 1971a:102–4).

TRADERS

The most influential Frenchmen who lived in the Huron country between 1616 and 1629 were sent there by the trading company. Of greatest importance were the highly salaried individuals known as *truchements* or interpreters. Brûlé may have been the only Frenchman who properly held this title among the Huron (Trudel 1966a:390). His duties were to encourage Huron to trade with the French and, if necessary, to travel with them when they came to trade so that he might act as an intermediary. Other men were paid smaller salaries and allowed to trade for furs in return for living among the Huron and helping to guard their villages and annual journeys to the St. Lawrence. Most of these men bore muskets. By sending them to live among the Huron, the French traders retained the Huron's goodwill and encouraged the Huron to trade with them.

Although individual Frenchmen reacted to the Huron differently, the majority of these traders appear to have adapted fairly easily to the circumstances in which they found themselves. While some lived in their own cabins on the outskirts of Huron villages, others followed Brûlé's example and went to live with Huron families. Sagard (1866:166) was among the first to record how much more easily the average European could adapt to Indian ways than Indians could adapt to European ways. From this he concluded that it was dangerous to encourage Europeans to live among the Indians. These early coureurs de bois wore Huron items of clothing; indeed, the young Brûlé was dressed entirely in Indian fashion when he first returned from the Huron country in 1611 (Biggar 1922–36, 2:188). They also hunted with Indian men and joined them in their ritual steam baths without embarrassment or religious scruples (Sagard 1866:611). Like secular Europeans in similar situations elsewhere, most of them were delighted by the frankness of native sexual relations and enjoyed seducing Huron women and being seduced by them. In spite of their reservations about the physical appearance of the French, Huron girls appear to have made themselves available to these visitors, whom they no doubt found interesting because of their novelty, as well as because they were able to give them European goods as presents. It appears that some Frenchmen persuaded Huron girls to live with them as *asqua* or companions, thus giving rise to Sagard's charge that the French had established "brothels" in various parts of the Huron country (Wrong 1939:134). The popularity of the French did not elicit expressions of jealousy from Huron men, since promiscuity was characteristic of youth

and the Huron frowned on the public expression of jealousy and on men trying to restrict the sexual freedom of unmarried women. Promiscuous behaviour was therefore not incompatible with good relations between the French traders and the younger men with whom they lived and worked in the Huron country.

A more serious consequence of such behaviour was the tension that it created between traders and missionaries. The Recollets accused all but a few traders of subverting, by their actions, the moral teachings that the missionaries were trying to impart among the Huron. At first, the traders must have viewed the exhortations of the missionaries with some amusement, but this gave way to hostility when the priests accused them of deliberately seeking to undermine their missionary work for fear that it might put an end to their carnal pleasures. The traders were specifically accused of informing the Indians that French women were not chaste, as the priests claimed (Sagard 1866:327), and of telling them other unspecified lewd tales (Wrong 1939:137). This clash between Christian ideals and normal European behaviour amused the Huron but embarrassed the Recollets because it undermined their credibility. It also needled the Recollets because it revealed that they lacked sufficient influence either among the Huron or with the traders to put a stop to such behaviour. The trading company protested that it was unable to control employees who were stationed hundreds of miles from its nearest trading post, and in any case its representatives at Quebec were hostile to the Recollets. Since the Huron subjected the Recollets to the same temptations, it is little wonder that these celibates viewed Brûlé and his associates as the devil incarnate.

The priests, who are our only source of information for this period, never admitted the validity of native marriages between French men and Huron women. In spite of this, it is certain that such marriages took place. In 1637, when the Jesuits attempted to discuss the terms by which their lay employees might contract Christian marriages with native women, the Attignawantan headmen expressed surprise and said that the French who formerly had married Huron women had done so without discussions in a general council (Thwaites 1896–1901, 14:17–19). Some men who remained in the Huron country for long periods probably developed genuine attachments for particular Huron women and lived with them and their families on a more or less permanent basis. If marriages were contracted with women from influential families, they would have enhanced the prestige of individual French traders. When it became necessary for a Frenchman to leave the Huron country, the break-up of a marriage would not necessarily cause ill-will, provided that he gave appropriate presents as

compensation to his wife and to her family. It would appear, however, that not all traders did this (ibid. 14:19–21).

These permanent and temporary alliances with Huron women served to bind French traders and their Huron hosts together in ways that were readily understandable to the Huron. By accepting Huron hospitality in all its forms, the French came to understand the Huron better, and gradually found themselves ensnared in a web of obligations and kinship which made it difficult to refuse to aid them. These traders were strengthening the secular relationship established by Champlain in 1615 by living with the Huron on a more long-term and often more intimate basis than Champlain would have countenanced.

The earliest and most important of these traders was Etienne Brûlé. As already noted, he appears to have arrived in the Huron country in 1610. The following winter, Brûlé made good progress in learning the Huron language and adapting to Huron ways. Because he was liked by the Huron, Champlain decided that he should return to the Huron country for another year. As he grew older, he seems to have demonstrated effective qualities of leadership and, as these became apparent to his Huron hosts, he won their respect as an intermediary with the French. Eventually, he was hired by the trading company to live and work among the Huron as their agent. The French traders were especially anxious that he should prevent the Dutch from contacting the Huron to persuade them to trade at Fort Orange. So important was Brûlé's work judged to be that he was paid over 100 pistoles a year, which was many times the wage of an ordinary employee of the company, and almost equal to Champlain's official salary (Biggar 1922–36, 5:132; Thwaites 1896–1901, 4:209).[13] In addition to encouraging the Huron to trade, Brûlé was expected to inform Champlain and the trading company as he learned about the geography and peoples of the interior (plate 29).

Brûlé normally travelled to the St. Lawrence in the company of Huron traders from the village of Toanché where he lived, but once there he acted as an interpreter and intermediary for all the Huron who traded with the French. Brûlé had begun to live with the Huron while he was young and spent most of his adult life among them. It was therefore not difficult for the French to view him as being half Indian. Sagard states that he was as credulous as any Huron when it came to believing the lies that the Algonkin told to prevent the Huron from going to trade (Wrong 1939:266). This has suggested to some commentators that because he had lived so long among the Huron he had come to think like them. Brûlé understood and approved of many Huron customs and, as the years passed, his personal

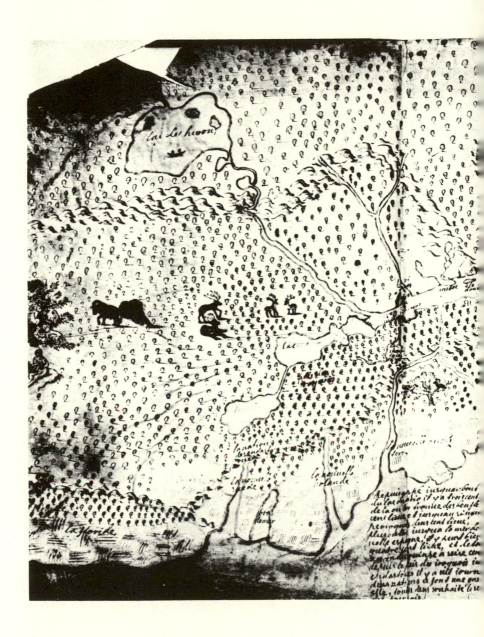

PLATE 29. *Early manuscript map of the Great Lakes. The reference to New Sweden indicates that it is no earlier than 1638; on the portfolio page on which it is mounted 1665 is pencilled in a modern hand. The authorship of the map is uncertain. Its representation of the Great Lakes differs considerably from Champlain's maps of 1616 and 1632 and is based on better knowledge of parts of southwestern Ontario than Champlain possessed. Yet it reveals less knowledge of the Great Lakes than the Jesuits acquired soon after their return to the Huron in 1634. The references to the Susquehannock, Lake Superior, and to copper deposits are noteworthy. The prototype may have been based on information supplied by Brûlé. Brûlé's exploration of the upper Great Lakes and to the Susquehanna Valley may have led him to visualize Lakes Ontario and Erie on the one hand and Huron and Superior on the other as two diverging systems. Map 4040B of de la Roncière 1907 (Album 66, Bibliothèque Historique de la Marine), no. 1. Another copy is numbered 4044B (= Album 67), no. 2.*

relations with the Huron probably seemed more real to him than did the memories of his youth among his own people. Even in a situation of extreme danger, the only Christian prayer he could remember was the ordinary grace said before meals. It is also likely that once he was adopted by a Huron family and began to live like them, the Huron came to regard Brûlé as one of themselves (Jurgens 1966:131). It will become clear, however, that although Brûlé lived for many years in the Huron country, he viewed his role as a trading agent separately from his friendship for the Huron and was willing to sacrifice Huron interests to benefit his employers, whoever they might be. Like many others in his situation, Brûlé seems to have felt little genuine attachment to his identity either as a Frenchman or as a Huron, but was capable of sacrificing either in order to accomplish whatever duties he was hired to perform.

It is uncertain how many Frenchmen were resident in the Huron country throughout most of this period. Fifteen had accompanied Champlain there in 1615, but most of these returned to Quebec the following year. Five or six Europeans are said to have been living among the Huron when the French who were sent there in 1623 arrived (Le Clercq 1691: 248). Du Vernay, who was reputed to have been of noble birth and who had formerly been in Brazil, arrived in Quebec by 1621 (Biggar 1922–36, 5:364) and is known to have spent the winter of 1622–23 in the Huron country (5:101). It has been assumed that a man named Grenole was resident there before 1623, since he travelled with Brûlé to Sault Sainte Marie before Sagard returned to France in 1624. Butterfield (1898:99–108) has dated this trip between 1621 and 1623, but Trudel (1966a:229) more prudently puts it "around 1623," thus leaving open the possibility that Grenole did not arrive in the Huron country prior to that summer.

In 1623, eleven French laymen were dispatched to the Huron country. They were to spend the winter there to help defend Huron villages and ensure that Huron traders would come to the St. Lawrence the following spring. In addition to Brûlé and Du Vernay, who had been in the Huron country the previous winter, other members of this group were Guillaume Chaudron and La Criette, both of whom appear to have been servants of Champlain;[14] Grenole, already mentioned; La Montagne, who was almost drowned on his way back to Quebec the following year (Sagard 1866:744); and La Vallée. There also seems to have been at least one Frenchman who had arrived in the Huron country previously and had not come downriver in 1623 (Biggar 1922–36, 5:129).

The majority of Frenchmen who went to the Huron country in 1623

were also there during the winter of 1624–25 (ibid. 5:129). One of these was Auhaitsique, who was drowned on his way back to Quebec in 1625. When Father Nicolas Viel returned to Quebec that year, he is reported to have left his books with some French who were remaining in the Huron country (Jones 1908:282–83), and Charles Lalemant is explicit that there were traders among the Huron in the winter of 1625–26 (Thwaites 1896–1901, 4:197). Grenole and La Vallée are known to have been among the Huron in 1626–27 (Sagard 1866:800). Some laymen were in the Huron country the following winter, since a number of them accompanied Father Daillon to the trading station in 1628 (Jones 1908:294). Among these may have been a young man named La Marche, whom Le Jeune states had visited the Huron before 1629 and had nearly been abandoned by them on the way back to Quebec (Thwaites 1896–1901, 8:85). Finally, in 1628, twenty Frenchmen were sent to the Huron country when no supplies of food or trade goods came from France. Since they bore arms, they were undoubtedly welcomed by the Huron as previous lay visitors had been (Biggar 1922–36: 6:41).

The evidence indicates that, throughout this period, a number of traders lived among the Huron, not all of whom travelled down-river to Quebec each year. In addition to the salaries they were paid, men who were sent to the Huron country were given the right to trade with the Indians for a limited number of skins each year (Thwaites 1896–1901, 4:209), which they were obliged to sell to the company at a fixed price. Sagard (1866:902) states that some of the French who returned from the Huron country in 1629 had 700 to 800 livres worth of furs with them.[15] Undoubtedly, the opportunity to trade was a powerful incentive for men to seek permission to live among the Indians (Le Clercq 1691:329). Anyone arriving in the Huron country with trade goods was certain to be welcomed and, after living with the Huron for even a short time, it was no doubt possible to acquire a vocabulary sufficient for trading purposes. More influential relations must have depended, however, on the acquisition of linguistic skills and the building up of personal relations, such as only Brûlé and a few other Frenchmen were able to accomplish.

We know regrettably little about the specific activities of these traders. In 1623, some of them were residing with Huron families in Ossossané (Sagard 1866:602). At the same time, Le Caron discovered that other Frenchmen were using his old cabin near Carhagouha (Le Clercq 1691: 249), and later that year Du Vernay, who was one of the few traders of whom the Recollets approved, appears to have lived with them at Quieu-nonascaran (Wrong 1939:193). It may be that we only have records of

traders living among the Attignawantan because the priests who came to the Huron country lived only with that tribe. On the other hand, Brûlé's apparently early move from Cahiagué to Toanché suggests that the Attignawantan may have used their influence to make certain that not only the priests, but also most or all of the French traders came to live with them. We know, however, that these men travelled considerably, so that even if their formal ties were with Attignawantan families, they probably visited all parts of the Huron confederacy.

Even making allowances for the extreme bias of Recollet accounts, it is clear that relations between individual traders and the Huron were not always without incident. Given the cultural differences between the Huron and the French, it is inconceivable that they would have been. In 1623–24, a Frenchman stole a quantity of wampum beads from the village of Toanché but became frightened and fled to the Recollet cabin at Quieunonascaran when he learned that a shaman had been hired to detect the thief. The Recollets learned what had happened only after they had accepted him as their guest (141). In the estimation of the Huron, a more disgusting example of European behaviour was exhibited by a number of Frenchmen on their way to trade with the Neutral. As they were passing through the Tionnontaté country, a servant of Champlain named Guillaume Chaudron became seriously ill. Rather than stop to take care of him, his companions left him among the Tionnontaté, stating that if he died the Indian who was looking after him was to bury him, but could keep his clothes in payment for his services.[16] The Tionnontaté were shocked by the callous way in which the young man had been abandoned by his companions. News was sent to Chaudron's Indian host who lived in Ossossané. He hastened to the young man and, with the help of the Tionnontaté who was taking care of him, carried Chaudron back to his longhouse, where he died after being confessed by Father Le Caron (194–95). It is clear that the Huron were horrified by the manner in which the French traders had put gain ahead of responsibility to one of their own people. Stories of this sort do not mean, however, that the Huron did not welcome these traders; on the contrary, they much preferred them to the priests. This was largely because they were able to carry firearms, but also because their behaviour generally accorded more closely with the Huron's own standards than did that of the priests.

The confidence that the Huron had in these traders is evidenced by their letting them travel with them or even alone to visit many of the tribes with whom the Huron carried on trade, in spite of their suspicions that the French wished to conclude separate trading treaties with these

groups. The first known of these journeys occurred when Brûlé was allowed to accompany the Huron envoys to the Susquehannock country. Brûlé's description of the Neutral country, which was influential in persuading Father Daillon to go there in 1626 (Sagard 1866:800), may date from this time, although his biographers speculate that he made another visit around 1625 (Butterfield 1898:110–12). He may well have visited the Neutral several times after 1615, since Frenchmen who lived among the Huron often went there to trade. One example was the journey discussed in the preceding paragraph, which took place in 1623, and Grenole and La Vallée are reported to have visited them in the autumn of 1626 (Sagard 1866:800). It is interesting that two or more traders set out on both of these trips and that they travelled south through the Tionnontaté country, as Champlain had hoped to do in 1616. This means that they set out from Ossossané, rather than from Teanaostaiaé, which was their departure point later, and may be another indication of the control that the Attignawantan were exerting over the activities of the French at this time. Evidently, French traders were permitted to visit both the Neutral and the Tionnontaté and did so freely.

Around 1623, Brûlé and Grenole were also permitted to travel northward. It is uncertain, however, whether they accompanied Huron or Ottawa who were going to trade. As a result of this trip, Brûlé reported the existence of the rapids at Sault Sainte Marie, which were named the Sault de Gaston in honour of Louis XIII's brother (589). He was also able to show the Recollets a bar of native copper that he had obtained from Indians who lived about eighty or one hundred leagues from the Huron (212–13). These Indians were probably the same group that Grenole said obtained copper from a mine, and among whom he had seen women who had the tips of their noses cut off as punishment for promiscuous behaviour (328). This punishment was later reported among the Miami and some other tribes living in the upper Great Lakes region (Kinietz 1940:184–85). It is possible that Brûlé and Grenole went no farther than Sault Sainte Marie and that their knowledge of Lake Superior was based on hearsay. The fact that Brûlé gave a slightly different estimate for the size of Lake Superior from the one he claimed was given by the Indians has been interpreted as evidence that he travelled as far west as where the cities of Duluth and Superior now stand (Butterfield 1898:108). This, however, is highly speculative.

The French who visited the Huron were thus permitted to trade with neighbouring tribes in the same way that individual Huron were. Perhaps they could do this even more easily, since it is nowhere mentioned that

they had to buy the right to carry on such trade from the headmen who controlled the trade routes, as ordinary Huron had to do. No doubt, however, they gave various presents to their hosts and to prominent headmen, so that even in this respect they may have appeared more like ordinary Huron traders than the records suggest. The French traders were subject, however, to a number of special restrictions. Sagard reports that they were not allowed to travel along the "Saguenay" routes (Wrong 1939:87), obviously because the Huron feared that the French would attempt to exploit the trade of that region from Three Rivers, once they made contact with the Indians who lived there. It is also stated that Frenchmen were not allowed to winter among any of the tribes with whom the Huron traded, for fear they would encourage them to trade with the French (Sagard 1866:809–10). The Huron believed that while there was little danger in a short visit, in the course of a winter it might be possible for a Frenchman to win the confidence of a tribe and organize them to visit the St. Lawrence. Thus, while it is a measure of their confidence in these men that the Huron permitted the French to visit their trading partners, their restrictions are a measure of their prudence and the degree to which they valued their monopoly control over the trading networks of the interior. It may also be an indication of the mutual respect that existed between the Huron and the French traders that the one attempt that was made to undermine the Huron monopoly during this period was the work not of a French trader, but of a priest.

RECOLLET POLICY

Although the Recollets had judged the Huron country to be their most promising mission field after Father Le Caron returned to Quebec in 1616, the Recollets did not resume work among the Huron until 1623. Father Guillaume Poulain wintered among the Nipissing in 1621–22, but the handful of priests who were resident at Quebec at any one time devoted almost all their efforts to converting the nearby Montagnais (Trudel 1966a:330–33). Although the Recollets blamed this cutback on the poverty of their order and lack of support by the trading company (Sagard 1866:783), it is clear that they had additional reasons for not continuing Father Le Caron's work. Until they had the manpower and financial support to launch a major effort, they preferred to work among smaller groups, especially since these groups lived near to Quebec and their behaviour was of crucial importance to the French settlement.

Nevertheless, in the intervening years, the Recollets worked hard to establish at Quebec a base that was adequate for their projected operations. In 1619, aided by their old benefactor, Louis Houel, as well as by the Archbishop of Rouen and others, they secured a dozen workers and began building a residence on the south bank of the St. Charles River. There they constructed a small stone house equipped with a chapel, kitchen, and lodgings for workmen on the ground floor, and rooms for the missionaries and that could be used for the care of the sick on the floor above. Underneath was a cellar seven feet deep. The residence was fortified with wooden bastions, and a palisade and ditch surrounded the courtyard. The ditch may, however, have been intended more to keep the cellar dry than for protection. The chapel was later moved into a stone tower that guarded the entrance to the establishment. The Recollets had a barn stocked with pigs, poultry, and a pair of donkeys they had brought from France. By 1622, they were growing enough grain that, supplemented by hunting and fishing, their farm was able to support twelve people without receiving any provisions from France. In 1623, the Recollets received letters patent conferring on them the ownership of 200 arpents of land around this establishment (Trudel 1966a:318–23). The rapid progress made on this project and the wonders associated with it, not least of which were the donkeys, must have been a source of intense interest to Huron and other Indians who visited Quebec.

During this period, the Recollets had an opportunity to elaborate a general policy for carrying out their mission work. The outlines of this policy had been adumbrated at a meeting held at Quebec in July 1616, following Le Caron's return from the Huron country (Le Clercq 1691: 91–100). This meeting was attended not only by the Recollets but also by Champlain and six other "well-intentioned" people. The Recollets' policy closely resembles the missionary program that Champlain had been advocating since 1603. Le Caron may have been influenced by discussions that he had with Champlain the previous winter (Biggar 1922–36, 3:145) but, in general, the approach that the Recollets advocated for New France was similar to that adopted by Franciscan orders in other parts of the world (Stanley 1949); thus it seems more likely that Champlain enlisted Recollet support because he knew their policies to be in keeping with his own aims. Since the program laid down by the Recollets was to influence over two decades of missionary work among the Huron, and was to become one side of a prolonged controversy over Indian policy in New France, it is necessary to examine it in some detail.

On the basis of their missionary experiences elsewhere, the Recollets

were convinced that in Canada they faced special difficulties. It was generally agreed that civilized non-Christians such as Hindus or Buddhists were easier to convert than were Amerindians. The former already understood the nature of religious dogma and of an organized religious hierarchy; therefore, conversion consisted largely of substituting one set of religious beliefs for another. The Indians, on the other hand, had no more idea of religious authority, as opposed to personal beliefs, than they had of a coercive political hierarchy. The individual freedom that was fundamental to Indian culture ruled out both the idea of heresy and of subordinating one's will to priestly guidance. That a priest alone might have the authority to perform certain rituals was understandable, since Indian shamans claimed such privileges, and even ordinary people had exclusive rights to sing certain songs or to perform specific rituals in healing societies. Nevertheless, the idea that an individual might, in the name of such beliefs, claim the right to judge another man's actions, or tell him what he had the moral right to say and do, was something that no Indian who was encountering Europeans for the first time could have imagined possible. The concept of authority and the respect for it that was inculcated into all civilized peoples provided the missionary and the civilized non-Christian with a common basis of understanding that was totally lacking between the missionary and the Indians of eastern Canada (Le Clercq 1691:515). The fundamental problem that the Recollets saw impeding their work was that the Indians were too "primitive" to be converted. From this they drew the devastatingly simple conclusion that if they were to convert the Indians they had first to find ways of "civilizing" them.

As early as 1616, the Recollets had assumed that it would be a simpler task to convert sedentary peoples than nonsedentary ones. Thus the Huron were assumed to be easier to convert than the Indians of the Maritimes or those who lived along the shores of the St. Lawrence (ibid. 91; Sagard 1866:793). In the name of religion, these latter groups had to be compelled to become sedentary. Even those individual nonsedentary Indians who had lived with the French for a considerable period and had been instructed by them, tended to lose their Christianity when they went back to their own people (Sagard 1866:166).

The Recollets did not believe that even sedentary Indians could be converted satisfactorily, unless they were first made to adopt standards of behaviour that were more in keeping with Christian practice. Specifically, this meant learning to live like Frenchmen. In the eyes of the Recollets, the Indian way of life was synonymous with the total absence of discipline, law, and government. One could therefore not hope to convert an Indian

before he had been changed, as they put it, from a "savage" into a "human being" (Le Clercq 1691:96, 143). Le Caron believed that the latter task would be harder to accomplish than conversion (ibid. 264).

To teach a sedentary group how to live like Frenchmen, it was envisaged that French colonists would have to be settled in their midst who could instruct them and, at the same time, provide the coercion that the Recollets, like Champlain, believed would be necessary to make them give up their old ways. Farmers and artisans were especially desired and, since the settlers were to be a model of religious devotion as well as of secular habits, Protestants were to be rigorously excluded from any such enterprise (Sagard 1866:167; Le Clercq 1691:96–99). The Recollets viewed nothing short of the total replacement of Huron culture by the French way of life as a necessary prerequisite for the conversion of the Huron. Among other things, this involved the ultimate suppression of the Huron language and its replacement by French. It is curious to find Sagard (1866:340), who responded so sensitively to many aspects of Huron life, digressing in his *Histoire du Canada* to advise authorities that they should do all in their power to eliminate native languages and force the Indians to speak French, since priests should not have to waste their time learning difficult languages spoken by only small numbers of people. These were probably expressions of general Recollet policy that Sagard was instructed to insert into his book and it is not certain to what degree Sagard personally espoused this policy. It is perhaps significant that Sagard left the order a few months after his *Histoire* was published.

While the Recollets wished to convert Indians, they were firmly opposed to early or easy baptism. They realized that Indians asked to be baptized without understanding the significance that this rite had for the French. They did so to obtain presents, or because baptism appeared to cure ailments, or to establish a ritual relationship between themselves and the French. After consulting with theologians at the Sorbonne, it was decided that only converts who were dying should be baptized immediately. Others were to be baptized only after prolonged instruction and careful trial of their faith, or if they agreed to live like Frenchmen (Le Clercq 1691:147). As a result of this ruling, few Indians were baptized, except those who on their deathbed had recourse to baptism as yet another healing ritual.

Since the Recollets lacked the resources to undertake a massive program of assimilation among either the Montagnais or the Huron, they laid considerable emphasis on having Indian boys live with them, in the hope that these boys could be indoctrinated with French culture and Christian

beliefs and later would be helpful for mission work among their own people (ibid. 99). In 1621, they sought royal subventions to found a residential school for fifty boys at Quebec, but efforts to finance an institution of this size received their final setback when their chief supporter, the bishop of Rouen, died. At no time did the Recollets have more than one or two pupils living with them and only six boys were ever sent to France for further study (Trudel 1966a:323–30). Another ambition that was never realized was to train some of these boys for the priesthood. The Recollets hoped that Christianity would appear more attractive to the Indians if they could see their own people serving as priests (Le Clercq 1691:225).

The view that the Recollets had of conversion made them zealous guardians of French culture in the New World. If the Indians were to be persuaded to become French in culture and Roman Catholic in religion, it was necessary that nothing other Frenchmen did should be allowed to compromise the authority of French institutions or Christian beliefs. For this reason, the Recollets were violently opposed to accepting reparations payments from the Montagnais for the two Frenchmen who were killed near Cape Tourmente in 1617 (or 1616). To do so, they argued, would be to sell the lives of Christians for skins and to authorize murder (Sagard 1866:56–57).

Such policies inevitably made the Recollets bitter foes of the trading company. Their desire to promote French colonization as an integral part of their mission work was in accord with Champlain's wish to increase the settled population of New France and to diversify its economic base. This policy was squarely opposed by the traders, both because of the expense involved and because they feared that European settlers would eventually seek to control the fur trade. The company was also opposed to the suggestion that Indian trappers should be encouraged to become sedentary. When the Recollets sought to persuade a number of Montagnais families to settle near Quebec and grow corn, they were warned that if they persisted, the traders would drive these Indians away (ibid. 165).

The Recollets' firm stand about punishing offences committed by the Indians and their desire to compel them forcibly to adopt French ways were also in keeping with Champlain's desire to gain control over the Montagnais. The company, on the other hand, was interested in furs and therefore was satisfied with the Indians remaining as they were. Realistically appraising the situation, the traders preferred good relations with the Indians to having control over them. Finally, Champlain and the Recollets

had a common interest in seeking peace with the Iroquois, since such an arrangement would promote exploration and further mission work. It appears that from the beginning, the traders foresaw the dangers to trade that were inherent in such plans and either opposed them or approached them more cautiously than Champlain and the Recollets did.

The Recollets soon began to assume responsibility for promoting Champlain's plans to develop New France. In 1616, Joseph Le Caron and Denis Jamet accompanied him back to France to lodge complaints with the directors of the *Compagnie des Marchands de Rouen et de St. Malo* about the behaviour of their agents, whom they accused of hindering mission work. Le Caron returned to France again in 1625, where he published two tracts attacking the *Compagnie des Marchands*, hoping thereby to influence the king's council. Meanwhile, in 1620, another Recollet, Father Georges Le Baillif, had been sent to Quebec to investigate conditions there. On his return to France, he submitted to the king a list of the needs of the colony, which summarized all the demands hitherto made by Champlain and by the Recollet order. These included building fortifications, forbidding Protestant religious observances in the colony, founding a residential school for Indian children, harsher punishments for wrong-doers, and an increase in Champlain's salary and authority (Dumas 1966). Both priests were well-connected, Le Caron having been tutor to the Duc d'Orléans and Le Baillif a member of a noble French family. They were particularly hostile to Guillaume de Caën, the Protestant ship owner who held the trading monopoly in New France from 1621 to 1627—accusing him of neglecting the colonization of New France and being openly hostile to Roman Catholicism. While it is true that like all traders in New France, he neglected his promises to develop the colony, there is no evidence that de Caën was ever hostile to the Recollets. Sagard described him as a "polite, liberal, and understanding man" and there are frequent references to the good services he provided for the missionaries (Trudel 1966*b*: 160). In spite of this, the Recollets' activities resulted in de Caën being forbidden to travel to New France in 1626 and his monopoly being cancelled the following year in favour of a new program of intensive and exclusively Roman Catholic colonization. While the anti-Protestant fanaticism of Le Caron and Le Baillif may have been their own, their efforts to secure support for the program of colonization and mission work that they and Champlain had devised together, made these two men Champlain's most valuable allies. Through these activities, the Recollet missionaries became important agents and champions of New France.

LE CARON'S MISSION TO THE HURON

In 1623, the Recollets had an opportunity to expand their diplomatic activities and mission work. That spring, the French at Quebec became worried about their alliance with the Huron. Le Clercq states that they feared that the Huron were about to make an alliance with the latter's enemies (1691:246–47). The French knew that the Dutch were attempting to expand trade and believed that any peace between the Huron and the Iroquois would soon lead to trade between the Huron and the Dutch (Sagard 1866:811). To reinforce their ties with the Huron, Champlain decided to send a large party of French to visit them that year, including a number of Recollets.

This decision indicates the importance that the French attributed to their trade with the Huron and their nervousness about the state of the French-Huron alliance at that time. What precipitated this particular crisis? Historians have mostly treated the fears of the French as if they were justified (Trudel 1966*a*:364–66), although they have almost certainly erred in doing so. The French may have been alarmed by rumours concerning one of the periodic peace treaties that Huron and Iroquois tribes negotiated in the hope that families on both sides would be able to recover kinsmen who had been taken prisoner but not yet killed. Yet, in spite of fulsome protestations of good faith, such truces usually lasted no longer than was needed to repatriate these relatives. Moreover, if there was talk of peace between the Huron and the Seneca, fighting had resumed by the time the missionaries arrived in the Huron country; another possible truce between the Huron and the Iroquois, to be discussed below, seems to have been a later response to a Huron victory in the autumn of 1623. The French miscalculated if they believed that any treaty of this sort would last, let alone lead to a diversion of trade southward.

The Dutch were undeniably attempting to divert trade from the St. Lawrence Valley to their own posts. They were doing this, however, by seeking closer ties with the Montagnais and the Algonkin. Their traders appear to have had only very limited knowledge about the interior of North America, to the extent that the structure of the Iroquois confederacy was still unknown to them. It is likely that they knew about the Huron from Champlain's published accounts, but this does not mean that they knew precisely where the Huron lived or how they might contact them. Furthermore, it is inconceivable that the Mohawk, or any other Iroquois tribe, would have permitted the Huron or the Dutch to travel through their territory to trade with one another. The Mohawk were

already fearful that an alliance between the Dutch and the northern Algonkians would disrupt their supply of trade goods if intertribal wars were to break out again. The Huron could supply more and better quality furs than could the Mohawk; hence there was the added danger that if trade developed the Dutch would favour the Huron rather than them in any future conflict. The only terms on which the Mohawk might have accepted a trading arrangement centred on Fort Orange would have been if they retained the exclusive right to act as intermediaries. It is impossible to imagine, however, that at that time the Huron would have considered breaking off trade with the French only to make themselves totally dependent on their traditional enemies for supplies of European goods.

Finally, while some historians have stressed French fears that the Huron were geographically closer to Fort Orange than they were to Quebec and therefore would naturally be inclined to trade with the Dutch, this argument does not survive closer scrutiny. Irksome as the long journey down the Ottawa River may have been, it was a water route. The alternative route, down the Trent Valley, across Lake Ontario, up the Oswego Valley to Lake Oneida, and then down the Mohawk Valley, was far more difficult to traverse, even if no political complications had beset its use. For all these reasons, it is unlikely that there was any danger of Huron trade being diverted to New Netherland or that either the Huron or the Iroquois had yet considered the possibility of such a thing happening.

The French undoubtedly had other reasons for wanting to renew their ties with the Huron at this time. The Huron were annoyed about the ill-treatment that they were receiving from the Kichesipirini, who were older allies of the French than they were. Also, if two Huron were killed at Quebec in 1622, their compatriots may have blamed the French for letting this happen. More importantly, however, the French were in the process of arranging a peace between themselves, their Algonkian-speaking allies, and the Mohawk. Not long before, the Mohawk had been attacking Huron traders in the Ottawa Valley and, in any case, they were members of the Iroquois confederacy and therefore enemies of the Huron. This put the French in a very difficult position. On the one hand, they did not wish a tactical arrangement with the Iroquois to undermine relations with their most important trading partners—who probably mistrusted their motives far more than did the Algonkians who were helping to negotiate the treaty. On the other hand, the French did not want the treaty to promote good relations between the Huron and the Mohawk, lest this should serve Dutch interests. Apprehension over the consequences of their own actions may have made the French uncertain of their relations with the Huron,

and hence anxious to strengthen their alliance with them. There is no contemporary evidence to support the suggestion that the priests who were sent to the Huron country had specific instructions to disrupt whatever treaties the Huron might be negotiating with the Iroquois (cf. Le Clercq 1691:258; Charlevoix 1866–72, 1:34–35).

The Recollet party, which was made up of Fathers Joseph Le Caron and Nicolas Viel, Gabriel Sagard, and possibly two secular assistants who had come to serve the Recollets in New France in 1619, set off with the eleven armed Frenchmen who were being sent to defend the Huron villages (Jones 1908:276). One of the two Recollet assistants was probably the young man known only by his Huron name, Auhaitsique. It is uncertain whether the Recollets merely accompanied the laymen as a way of getting to the Huron country, or whether Le Caron travelled there as Champlain's personal representative, as Le Clercq later maintained (1691:246). Considering the similar policies of Champlain and the Recollets, Champlain could have relied on Le Caron much more than on any trader to pursue objectives that were in keeping with his own plans for the development of New France. It is also certain that Le Caron would have been willing to act, at least informally, as Champlain's emissary. Even if he did not receive a specific commission from Champlain, Le Caron may well have regarded himself not only as a missionary but also as a servant of the French government.

The request that the Huron traders take three members of a French religious order home with them must have come as a surprise. Although Le Caron had lived among the Huron seven years before, the traders at first refused to accept the missionaries. They said that they wanted men who could bear firearms and help them to fight their enemies. They were, however, mollified when they were informed that the priests had supernatural powers that would be useful to them in their wars. Three canoes were finally made available, after Guillaume de Caën generously donated a quantity of axes, knives, beads, and other trade goods that were given to the Huron to encourage them to accept the missionaries. These presents, supplemented by additional gifts of fish and meat that the missionaries obtained by barter from passing Algonkin, assured them the goodwill of the Indians and eventually they arrived safely in the Huron country (Sagard 1866:170–96).

Because each missionary travelled with a different group of Huron, they did not all arrive at the same time or in the same place. Le Caron was taken back to Carhagouha, where he had lived previously, while Viel probably landed at Toanché. Sagard travelled with Huron from Ossossané who were

led by a man named Oonchiarey. They landed along the shores of Matchedash Bay and travelled overland to their village. Sagard lived for a time with Oonchiarey's family, who treated him kindly and gave him a compartment of his own within their longhouse. He describes Ossossané as a well-fortified town, containing thirty or forty longhouses and 200 to 300 families. Sagard called this town Quieuindahian or Tequeunonkiaye, the latter being similar to the name Champlain used (Wrong 1939:70). The new name may indicate that the location of the community was changed between 1623 and 1634. Other evidence suggests that Sagard visited the Ossossané that was abandoned in 1636. The latter has been identified with a high degree of probability with an archaeological site on lot 16, Concession 7 in Tiny township (map 19). The site is located on a well-defined promontory bounded on the west by an abrupt escarpment and on the south by a somewhat less precipitous streambed. Below the promontory, one and a half miles of swampy dunes lie between the site and Nottawasaga Bay. The cornfields of the village must have been located above the promontory and surrounded the village to the east in a large semi-circle (Ridley 1947; Heidenreich 1971:fig. 11). Both Viel and Sagard followed Le Caron's example in naming the village they were first associated with after their patron saint. Thus Carhagouha, and later Quieunonas-caran, became St. Joseph, while Ossossané became St. Gabriel, and Toanché was St. Nicolas (Sagard 1866:296).

If Heidenreich (1966:120) is correct, Le Caron must have returned to Carhagouha while that village was being relocated. Shortly afterwards, he was living in the relocated village, which was called Quieunonascaran. After a time, Father Viel and a number of other Frenchmen arrived in Ossossané and Sagard was ordered to accompany Viel to Quieunonascaran. To ease his departure, Sagard informed his hosts that he had possessions belonging to Le Caron that he had to take to him (Wrong 1939:76). Out of necessity, the three missionaries lived for a time at Quieunonascaran with one of the principal headmen, but Le Caron requested the village council to build a separate cabin for them outside Quieunonascaran to replace the abandoned missionary residence at Carhagouha. The council tried to persuade the Recollets that they should live with one or more families in the village. Le Caron replied that it was "not possible to receive enough enlightenment from heaven to instruct them in the bustle of their lodges," and that the Recollets did not want to show more preference for one family than for another (ibid. 77–78). Because they already attributed shamanistic powers to the Recollets, the Huron must have concluded that they wished to live alone in order to exercise these powers.

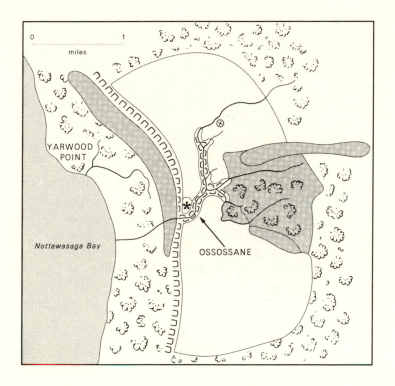

Cornfields

Swamp

Fortified village

Break in slope

Ossuary

Deciduous and coniferous forest

MAP 19. *Reconstruction of the field pattern and natural setting of Ossossané prior to 1634 (Lot 16, Conc. VII, Tiny Twp.) (after C. E. Heidenreich).*

Seeing that Le Caron could not be persuaded to change his mind, the council agreed to build a cabin for the priests. A site was chosen in a ravine only a few hundred feet from the town. There the men of Quieunonascaran erected a lodging about twenty feet long and covered it with tree bark; but because the bark had not been gathered in the spring it soon split, letting in rain and cold. The Recollets had their workmen divide the interior of the building in two, in order to separate their chapel from a general living area. Between these two rooms was an enclosed space used to store their vestments and other valuable possessions (ibid. 81; Sagard 1866:214). Around the cabin the Recollets planted a small herb garden, which they fenced off in order to keep out children. The garden did poorly, allegedly because the soil was poor, but more likely because it was planted too late.

Le Caron's decision not to live with the Huron was based mainly on his conviction, formulated as early as 1615, that the so-called "lewd" habits of the Huron were incompatible with the spiritual requirements of a priest. The clergy could at most venture into such an environment in an attempt to change it; they could never agree to live in it (Sagard 1866: 41–42). By isolating themselves in this way, the Recollets were, in effect, rejecting the hospitality that the Huron wished to extend to them. As adopted members of the community they continued to enjoy the same rights as every other household. A communal work force helped to construct their house and they were given a share of *auhaitsique*, small fish that were collectively harvested in seines by the villagers (ibid. 694). On the other hand, because they lived by themselves, they were compelled to barter with the Huron for food, whereas, if they had lived with Huron families, they would have been fed without charge (Thwaites 1896–1901, 4:197; Wrong 1939:71–72). The Recollets did not understand why the Huron charged them for food and complained that the latter gave nothing to strangers without demanding payment for it (79). They also protested that Huron who came to visit them frequently stole things. These included not only items that were left outside their house but also objects from their living room (84). By contrast, Sagard states that his hosts at Ossossané took special care to guard his possessions and warned him to beware of thieves, particularly among the Tionnontaté who came as visitors to the town (71). This clearly indicates that the thieving at Quieunonascaran resulted from the lack of integration of the Recollets into that community. This lack of solidarity was also reflected in the complaint of a Huron youth who was helping to build the Recollets' cabin to the effect that such work was unnecessary since the priests were not relatives (78). Relations with the

inhabitants of Quieunonascaran were made more difficult by the frequent refusal of the priests to attend feasts to which they were invited. In part, they did this for religious reasons, but Sagard states that they also did it because they lacked the resources to reciprocate (84). This refusal of the priests to join in communal activities must have puzzled the Huron and hampered the effectiveness of the Recollets' work.

The Huron had much difficulty when it came to categorizing the Recollets. Unlike other Frenchmen, they did not carry arms and insisted on living apart from the Huron. They refused to participate in friendly activities, such as attending feasts or joining Indian men in sweat baths (198). In addition, they refused to consider marrying Huron women or to respond to their sexual advances (125–26), and they reproved women for proposing sexual liaisons either with them or with other Frenchmen (134). That the Recollets were some variety of shaman had been confirmed by the assurances that the French had given the Huron traders to the effect that their supernatural power would help the Huron to defeat their enemies. Fasting and sexual abstinence were necessary to become a shaman and teams of Indian men acquired supernatural power in these ways before engaging in intervillage athletic contests and games of chance. Priestly celibacy must have been interpreted as evidence that the Recollets sought, or possessed, supernatural powers of extreme potency. Such powers could, of course, be used for good or evil, but the secretiveness and unsociable behaviour of the Recollets must have made the Huron fear that they were engaging in some form of witchcraft that was designed to harm them.

The Recollets were willing to try to perform many of the same tasks that the traditional shamans did in the hope of supplanting them. They did not doubt that God would be willing to grant their prayers to help promote their missionary work. When the Quieunonascarans agreed to build a cabin for the Recollets in 1623, they asked the priests to stop the rain, which was excessive at that time. Sagard notes with satisfaction that after they had spent the night praying, the rain stopped and fine weather prevailed until the cabin was finished, after which it began to fall again. The Huron are reported to have regarded this as a proof of supernatural power and to have proclaimed everywhere the greatness of the spirit whom the Recollets invoked (78).

The priests who lived in the Huron country had remarkably good luck in such endeavours if we are to believe their accounts. Sagard reports that the rains were very heavy in April and May 1624. After trying all of their own rituals in vain, the headmen of Quieunonascaran held a council, where it was decided that they would offer the Recollets a cask of corn if they would

produce fair weather. Sagard was sent to the council where, after pointing out that God did not always answer men's prayers, he agreed that the Recollets would intercede for the people of Quieunonascaran. The Recollets had no sooner started to pray and to march around their cabin reciting the litany than the rain ceased, after which the skies remained clear for about three weeks (178–81). Sagard believed that such activities greatly strengthened the influence of the Recollets in Quieunonascaran; for example, the village council is reported to have resolved that henceforth they would call the priests their "spiritual fathers." The Recollets' apparent success in controlling the weather was also given as one of the reasons why, following a drought in the summer of 1626, the Huron were anxious to have the priests return after a year's absence (Thwaites 1896–1901, 4:223). Such activities did not, however, advance an understanding of Christianity; they merely enhanced the Recollets' reputation as shamans.

Because of their religious scruples, the Recollets were not always so obliging. One day, after Sagard had been making shadow pictures with his fingers, his Huron companions caught an especially large number of fish. Although they implored him to perform more of this magic, Sagard refused so that he would not encourage "such superstition" (Wrong 1939:187–88). Baptisms, although rarely performed, appear to have been viewed by the Huron primarily as healing rituals. In Quieunonascaran, the wife of Ongyata, a headman of some importance (Sagard 1866:395), was baptized as she was about to die. To everyone's surprise, she rallied and remained in good health for some time. In spite of the pious Christian sentiments that are attributed to this woman, it would appear that both she and her husband continued to regard baptism as a curing ritual. Her request to be rebaptized shortly before her death indicates her hope that another baptism would restore her health (Wrong 1939:175–76).

The supernatural powers that the Recollets either claimed or had attributed to them further heightened the Huron's awe of them and of the clerical equipment they had brought with them. The Huron and the Algonkin attributed magical powers to their scarlet damask chasuble and believed that if they could carry it into battle, or hang it from their battlements, they would overcome their enemies (Sagard 1866:411). The Kichesipirini were sufficiently convinced of this that they offered the Recollets eighty beaver skins in exchange for it (Wrong 1939:155). The mass chalice, which the Huron called a kettle (*anoo*), is also reported to have been an object of fear (Sagard 1866:476), although it is unknown whether the Huron already interpreted the doctrine of transubstantiation as implying that the Roman Catholic mass was similar to their own rites

involving cannibalism. Many Huron believed that the carved wooden skull that Sagard carried on his rosary had been the skull of a living child (Wrong 1939:146). A woman is reported to have stolen a priest's garment from the Recollets, but whether she valued it as an item of clothing or for its presumed magical properties is unknown. She returned it to the Recollets, claiming that a Tionnontaté had stolen it (Sagard 1866:476).

The Recollet missionaries interfered in Huron affairs whenever they felt that their own interests, or those of the French generally, were being threatened. Sagard recounts their strong opposition to a war with the Neutral that certain Huron headmen were advocating. He reports that after considerable effort the Recollets managed to dissuade the Huron from attacking the Neutral. Although the Recollets claimed that they were opposed to the war because they believed the odds were against the Huron winning, their real concerns seem to have been that the war would be a barrier to their projected conversion of the Neutral and would interfere with the fur trade (Wrong 1939:157). On the other hand, Sagard abandoned his idea of trying to promote peace between the Huron and the Iroquois. He had thought that such a peace would help to spread the gospel to the Iroquois and would promote commerce. The French traders warned him, however, that it was more likely to lead the Huron to trade with the Dutch, which would be a theological as well as an economic disaster (Sagard 1866:811).

During the winter of 1623–24, the Recollets frequently met the Nipissing, who were living about three leagues from Quieunonascaran, and persuaded them to allow Father Viel to go to James Bay with them the following spring. Sagard boasted that this was something the Nipissing had never agreed to before, since they feared to reveal the sources of their furs to Europeans (Wrong 1939:86–87, 269). In fact, a similar promise had been made to Champlain. Arrangements were also made for Sagard to travel some 200 or 300 leagues beyond the Huron country in a southerly direction, possibly to visit the Susquehannock (ibid. 269). According to Sagard, both journeys had to be called off when he and Le Caron were unable to return to the Huron in 1624. On the basis of earlier experiences, it seems doubtful that the Indians would have kept their promises with respect to either of these journeys.

There was an unpleasant encounter between the Recollets and the Huron headmen at Ossossané concerning the burial of Guillaume Chaudron. The Recollets insisted on an inhumation burial in a special, presumably consecrated, location away from the Ossossané cemetery. The Huron joined in the funeral and the women of the village did their tra-

ditional mourning on orders from their headmen. In spite of this, the French did not distribute any presents to honour the bones of the deceased and to express their gratitude to the mourners. This annoyed the Huron, who said that, because of this, the dead man would have to share the goods that the Huron gave to the spirits of their dead relatives. A shaman who attended this funeral was ordered to leave by the French, on the orders of the priests. He had previously been refused permission to try to cure Chaudron, although he had asked to be allowed to do so (ibid. 195; Sagard 1866:603).

Arrogant behaviour of this sort may explain an incident that happened in the Recollets' cabin at Quieunonascaran in the winter of 1623-24. Many Huron were in the cabin and one of them, who did not have a place to sit, tried to push aside a Frenchman who already had one. We are not told why the Huron acted as he did, but a legitimate principle of rank or seniority likely was involved. When Le Caron told the Huron to be quiet, the latter became angry and struck at the priest with a stick. The French who were present prevented the priest from being hit, but, as a result, a brawl broke out between the French and the Huron youths (Wrong 1939: 164; Sagard 1866:394). Sagard ran to the village to secure the intervention of the principal headman, Auoindaon, as well as other prominent people (Onorotandi, Yocaisse, Ongyata, and Onnenianetani). A general council was held the next day, at which the French were asked to forget what had happened and were presented with some bags of corn and invited to a general feast (Wrong 1939:165–66). This incident reveals some of the tensions that were generated by the inability of the Recollets either to understand Huron culture or to accept it on equal terms with their own. Because of this, the Recollets were more feared than loved by the Huron, although not sufficiently feared to be fully protected from the supreme insult of being attacked in public.

The Huron who courted the friendship of the Recollets were men who traded with the French. Foremost among these was the aged headman, Auoindaon, who, at least among the northern Attignawantan, claimed to control the trade route leading to Quebec. Auoindaon is reported to have visited the Recollets often and to have shown great solicitude for them. If he found them at prayer, he would get on his knees and imitate their gestures until they had finished. When Sagard was left alone in the Recollets' cabin, Auoindaon offered to spend the night with him to protect him from the Iroquois or against evil spirits that might trouble him (ibid. 174–75). He also asked for baptism, no doubt hoping that this might lead to a closer alliance with the French (Sagard 1866:478). Many Huron who

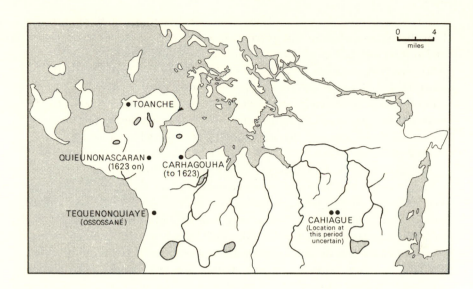

MAP 20. *Huron settlements mentioned by name for the period 1623–29.*

associated with the priests did so in the hope of receiving small presents in
return either for services or for expressions of interest in their teachings.
The headmen and traders were, however, clearly interested in promoting
closer relations with the French in hopes of improving their trading
relations with them. Specifically, this meant persuading the Recollets to
report the good treatment they had received and to intercede with French
traders so that the Huron could get their goods from these traders at a
reasonable price (Wrong 1939:244). The desire of the Huron traders to
preserve and strengthen their alliance with the French guaranteed that
all Frenchmen who were living in the Huron country would be well
treated, so long as the Huron traders who had dealings with the French
were treated in the same way.

   The Recollets often went out from Quieunonascaran to visit other groups
(Le Clercq 1691:250). Undoubtedly they visited most, if not all, of the
northern Attignawantan villages, none of which was far from their headquarters (map 20). Le Caron was in Ossossané for Chaudron's funeral, and,
at some point during his stay in the Huron country, Father Viel struck up
an important friendship with Soranhes, a prominent trader from Teanaostaiaé (Sagard 1866:795). We do not know, however, whether the
Recollets travelled in the eastern part of the Huron confederacy. Sagard

was able to report that the town of Cahiagué had been relocated and split into two parts since Champlain's visit (Wrong 1939:92), but it is unclear whether the Recollets had visited the new town or had merely been told what had happened. There is also no evidence of any missionaries visiting either the Tionnontaté or the Neutral settlements at this time. An otherwise cryptic reference to the slight work they had started among the Neutral (Sagard 1866:408) suggests that possibly one or more of their lay workers may have visited these people disguised as traders.

One of the Recollets' principal aims was to continue the study of the Huron language that Father Le Caron had begun in 1615. They realized that unless they could speak the Huron language fluently any effort to inculcate a satisfactory knowledge of Christian teaching was bound to be unsuccessful. Le Caron continued to work on his dictionary and added to it various notes on Huron grammar. He was assisted in this work by Father Viel, who continued to send him material after Le Caron had returned to Quebec. Le Caron's dictionary appears to have been finished by 1625, when Father Georges Le Baillif presented a copy of it to the king (Le Clercq 1691:327–28). Another product of the linguistic studies of this period was Sagard's list of Huron words and phrases which he called *Dictionnaire de la Langue Huronne* and published as an appendix to his *Grand Voyage*. This is the only one of the Recollets' linguistic studies that is known to have survived to the present.

Sagard noted that one of the more serious obstacles to the eventual explanation of Christian beliefs to the Huron was the absence in their language of many necessary theological terms. The Huron had no single words by which it was possible to express concepts such as sacrament, kingdom of heaven, trinity, holy spirit, angels, resurrection, or hell. Even apparently more universal concepts, such as temptation, faith, and charity, seemed to have no precise equivalents in Huron. The explanation of the simplest religious texts thus required elaborate periphrasis (Wrong 1939: 73–74), and there was no way of being certain that the intended meaning had been adequately conveyed.

The problem of communication was, in fact, more serious than Sagard, or any of the Recollets, realized. All of the basic teachings of Christianity had, from the earliest days, been tailored for a complex society in which ideas of authority, hierarchy, and punitive justice were taken for granted. To express Christian doctrines in a way that was compatible with the beliefs of people whose whole way of life was founded on exactly the opposite principles required more than linguistic skills which could translate the Christian message. It required the remoulding of Christian teach-

ings to fit a different social code. This was something that the Recollets were incapable of perceiving and would have been opposed on principle to doing.

On the contrary, their second major objective was to try by precepts and teaching to begin to Europeanize Huron attitudes as a necessary first step towards eventual conversion. The low priority accorded to conversion at this time was given as the reason why the lay brother Sagard was added to the party rather than a third priest (Le Clercq 1691:246). Because the Recollets had already determined that Indians should be baptized only after a severe trial of their faith, they tended to assess all protestations of interest in Christianity with scepticism. They recognized that the Indians often showed an interest in their instructions in hopes of specific material gain (ibid. 280). What they did not realize was that other Huron sought their friendship for fear of falling victim to the Recollets' witchcraft.

Many Huron came to visit the Recollets in order to exchange corn, squash, beans, and smoked fish for awls, iron arrow heads, or a few glass beads (Wrong 1939:84); in brief, they treated the Recollets as petty traders. When families gave feasts but did not have enough metal kettles of their own, they asked to borrow the Recollets' kettles but never returned them without food in them (84). Huron men visited the Recollets in order to obtain enough tobacco for a smoke. Much of the tobacco that was consumed by the Huron was imported from the south, hence was a valuable commodity. Because of this, Huron men accepted it from the French as evidence of their hospitality (85).

It was also realized that the Huron's desire not to contradict anyone resulted in their appearing to agree with what the missionaries were saying, when in fact they did not understand or agree with them. This made it difficult for the missionaries to determine whether or not individual Huron were sincerely interested in their teachings. Knowledge of this practice did not, however, prevent the Recollets from criticizing Huron religion. Huron beliefs and customs were consistently mocked and abused, and the refusal of the Huron to defend their views aggressively was misinterpreted by the triumphant priests as indicating a lack of religious conviction. Women were rebuked for their personal behaviour for reasons that must have been totally incomprehensible to them. Although these reproofs appeared to be accepted in a lighthearted manner (Sagard 1866:327), it is clear that the Huron were often annoyed by such behaviour and, in very trying circumstances, their anger sometimes showed through. For example, on their return to Quebec, Sagard's companions were unable to convince him that a rocky hill they were passing was the home of an

important guardian spirit. Because of this they remained sullen for a long time.

Only three conversions are reported for the period 1623–24: Ongyata's wife and a man and his daughter (Le Clercq 1691:257). In keeping with Recollet policy, efforts were made to persuade families that seemed inclined to be converted to move to Quebec, where they were told they could settle on the Recollet estate (ibid. 257). The Recollets mainly sought, however, to persuade a number of Huron familes to allow boys to be taken to Quebec, or to France, where they might receive instruction. In order to prepare for this, Le Caron ordered Sagard to teach some elementary reading and writing to a group of Huron children, but his efforts came to naught because the children lacked sufficient discipline (Sagard 1866:330). Many adults came to observe these classes and asked Sagard to teach them some French words. Sagard also attempted to explain such things as the European view of the relationship between the sun and the earth (462). Although Sagard persisted with his efforts to prepare five or six boys to accompany the Recollets to France, their families refused to let them go. These families might have been expected to act differently on the grounds that they were thereby sealing a closer trading alliance with the French; however, Savignon, by recounting his own experiences, convinced them that the French were too cruel and unjust to be trusted with Huron children (320).

FATHER VIEL'S "MURDER"

In 1624, both Le Caron and Sagard returned to Quebec. Sagard shared a canoe with a war chief named Angoiraste and two of his companions, Andatayon and Conchionet (Wrong 1939:244). Le Caron remained at Quebec, but Sagard, who had expected to return with supplies for the Huron mission, received a letter from the Provincial, Father Polycarpe Du Fay, ordering him to return to Paris. This left Nicolas Viel as the sole missionary among the Huron during the winter of 1624–25. We know little about his life there, except that he continued to study the Huron language and expressed the wish that he might be allowed to continue working among the Huron for the rest of his life. In the spring of 1625, he decided to come down-river to make a brief spiritual retreat. As he was passing through the Sault-au-Récollet, in the Rivière des Prairies, his canoe overturned and he was drowned. His body was recovered from the water a few days later and was buried at Quebec.

The generally accepted version of Viel's death maintains that for some unknown reason he was murdered by his Huron companions who in order to hide their crime also murdered a Huron boy named Auhaitsique, who had become his disciple and was travelling to Quebec with him. This story was widely believed in the latter part of the seventeenth century and was recorded by Le Clercq, who presented Viel and Auhaitsique to his readers as "the first two martyrs of Canada" (Le Clercq 1691:322). In recent years, however, Archange Godbout (1942) and Marcel Trudel (1966a:340–42) have shown this story to be a tendentious fabrication. Auhaitsique was not a Huron, but the nickname the Huron had given to a young Frenchman who was probably a servant of the Recollets. Likewise, none of the contemporary accounts of Viel's death describe it as anything but a simple accident (Sagard 1866:789, 794; Thwaites 1896–1901, 4:171). It was only in 1634 that Paul Le Jeune claimed that Viel had died as a result of foul play (7:233). Two years later, Brébeuf wrote that the Kichesipirini had informed him that the Huron had murdered not only Etienne Brûlé but also Viel and his companion (10:79). He had been told this story, however, in an effort to persuade the Jesuits to stop living among the Attignawantan. Although Sagard popularized this claim of martyrdom in his *Histoire du Canada*, the desire of the Kichesipirini to undermine the renewed friendship between the Attignawantan and the French seems reason enough for them to have invented the claim that Viel had been murdered. When travelling down-river, Huron traders not infrequently preferred to shoot rapids, rather than to make an excessive number of portages. Canoes sometimes overturned in these rapids, and it is not surprising that in such an accident the Indians might swim to safety, while the French, who wore bulky clothes and mostly did not know how to swim, drowned. Sagard reports that when he came down-river in 1624, the Huron let him remain in their canoe while they got into the water and guided it through the Lachine Rapids. Under such circumstances, an accidental drowning is not improbable, and the absence of any suspicion of foul play for nine years after Viel's death makes later charges seem unlikely.[17]

Because of Father Viel's death, two missionaries who had planned to return to the Huron country with him had to postpone their journey. One of these was a Recollet: Father Joseph de La Roche Daillon, the son of a nobleman from Anjou. The other, Jean de Brébeuf, was a Jesuit. The scion of petty Norman aristocracy, Brébeuf had entered the Jesuit novitiate at Rouen at the age of twenty-four. He taught for several years at the College at Rouen and at the age of thirty-two the Jesuit Provincial, Pierre Coton,

had chosen him to go to New France, where he arrived in April 1625.[18] Charles Lalemant stated that the journey to the Huron country was called off because, with Viel dead, there was no cleric there who knew the Huron language or who could help the newly arrived missionaries to establish themselves (Sagard 1866:789). Considering the general lack of goodwill between missionaries and French traders at this time, the lack of direct contacts with the Huron may have been reason enough to call off the journey. The Huron traders were undoubtedly frightened by Viel's death, since, according to the terms of their alliance with the French, they were charged with responsibility for his safety and well-being. Therefore, in the absence of strong pressure from the French traders, the Huron may have wanted to consult with other headmen, or even with the confederacy council, before agreeing to take any more priests home with them. The clerks of the trading company no doubt understood the Huron's anxiety and helped to dissuade the priests. There is no need to invoke suspicion of foul play in order to explain the behaviour of either the French or the Huron at this time.

The most important accomplishment of Father Viel's two years in the Huron country was gaining Soranhes's permission that his fifteen-year-old son Amantacha might be educated in France. Soranhes lived in Teanaostaiaé and was therefore an Attigneenongnahac (Trigger 1966a). He was also an early and active participant in the fur trade. Throughout his life, his dealings with missionaries seem to have been motivated largely by a desire to court favour at Quebec. There is, therefore, little reason to doubt that, however much Soranhes may have liked and trusted Father Viel, this unusual promise was prompted by his wish to establish a special relationship with the French. Even so, Soranhes appears to have hesitated. He had promised Father Viel that he would send Amantacha to Quebec in the spring of 1625, but neither Soranhes nor his son travelled down-river that year.

Nevertheless, after Viel's death Soranhes kept his promise and, in 1626, he came to Quebec, where he is said to have entrusted Amantacha specifically to the care of Father Le Caron. To the latter's delight, Amantacha was a handsome and intelligent youth, who, from the start, got on well with the French (Le Clercq 1691:367). Soranhes was, however, an ambitious trader who was anxious to contract many alliances with the French, and who probably believed that by doing so he was helping to ensure Amantacha's welfare. He therefore accepted friendship presents not only from the Recollets but also from the Jesuits and from Emery de Caën, who was in command at Quebec in Champlain's absence (Sagard 1866:796–97). A three-cornered dispute about the boy's guardianship

broke out, in which de Caën appears to have discreetly supported the Jesuits (Le Clercq 1691:372; Sagard 1866:796). It was finally decided that Amantacha should travel to France on Emery de Caën's ship and that his education should be entrusted to the Jesuits. He travelled in the care of the Jesuit priest, Philibert Noyrot, and was accompanied by Etienne Brûlé, who was returning to France that year and whom Amantacha is said to have loved like a father.[19]

Amantacha went first to Rouen, where he lived with Emery de Caën and his uncle, Ezéchiel. He was then taken to meet the Jesuits of Paris who, along with the new Viceroy of New France, the pious Henri de Lévis, Duc de Ventadour, undertook to pay for his education. Amantacha's schooling proceeded slowly, however, because Brûlé was the only man in France who knew how to speak Huron and the Jesuits found him too coarse and uneducated to assist them adequately (Thwaites 1896–1901: 4:213–15). It was probably for this reason that the Jesuits decided not to keep their promise to return Amantacha to his father in 1627, in spite of an agreement that if Soranhes were satisfied with the treatment his son had received in France, he would let him return there for several more years (4:225).

During his stay in France, Amantacha learned to speak and write French (5:245) and was sufficiently well instructed in the principles of Roman Catholicism that the Jesuits decided to baptize him publicly in December 1627. To draw attention to their achievement, a special stage was erected in the Cathedral of Rouen for the benefit of onlookers (Du Creux 1951–52:34.) The service was conducted by the Archbishop, François de Harlay, while two members of the nobility stood as Amantacha's godparents (Trudel 1966a:329). Amantacha was given the Christian name Louis de Sainte-Foi. A rumour, spread by the sailors, that Amantacha was the son of the King of Canada caused numerous townspeople to flock to the ceremony (Sagard 1866:798). Du Creux (1951–52:34) reports that in spite of the cold weather there was a flash of lightning during the ceremony and a flame seemed to play about the stage that had been erected for it. It was not until the spring of 1628 that it was decided to send Amantacha back to his people.

DAILLON'S NEUTRAL FIASCO

During the winter of 1625–26, Father Daillon studied the Huron language at Quebec with the aid of Le Caron's dictionary and the Huron who were

spending the winter there (Le Clercq 1691:344–45). In order to gain the latter's goodwill and to persuade them to take him to the Huron country, Daillon supplied them with food (ibid. 343). Thus, when the Huron came to trade the following summer, Daillon had no trouble securing a place in one of their canoes. He probably travelled with the people he had befriended over the winter. This may also explain why Daillon settled at Toanché rather than at Quieunonascaran, where the Recollets formerly had their headquarters (Jones 1908:292).

The effect this change had on relations between Quieunonascaran and Toanché is not known. After Viel had drowned, the people of Quieunonascaran may not have wanted to be responsible for another priest. Alternatively, Quieunonascaran is known to have declined in importance between 1623 and 1637 and it is possible that some of the clan segments from that village moved to Toanché. If so, the change may simply reflect the differing fortunes of these two villages. Since the people of Toanché had brought Viel to the Huron country, it may be that by securing another priest they felt they were regaining what had doubly been lost to them, first by Viel moving to Quieunonascaran and then by his death. Daillon was accompanied to the Huron country by Brébeuf and Father Anne de Nouë, both of whom were Jesuits.

More than any other missionary who visited the Huron confederacy, Daillon felt charged with a political as well as a religious mission. This feeling was increased when, before setting out for the Huron country, he received a letter from Le Caron ordering him to visit the Neutral. On 18 October, Daillon left the Huron country with the traders Grenole and La Vallée, who were going to trade with the Neutral. Passing through the Tionnontaté villages, they were on the road for five days before they reached the first Neutral village (Map 21). They then visited four more settlements before they reached Ounontisastan, where lived Souharissen, the principal headman of the Neutral. Through an interpreter, Daillon announced that he wished to conclude a treaty of friendship between the Neutral and the French and to make the two peoples trading partners. He also offered presents to Souharissen as a pledge of his sincerity. In return, Souharissen granted Daillon his protection and agreed that he could remain among the Neutral over the winter. At this point, Grenole and La Vallée returned to the Huron (Sagard 1866:800–802).

Daillon's actions not only were aimed at weakening the Huron's role as middlemen but also violated their rule that Frenchmen living in the Huron country should not winter among the tribes with whom they traded. It is not known whether Daillon was acting on his own in seeking

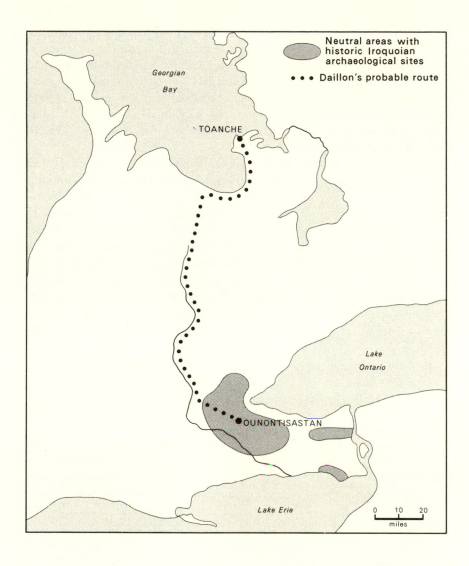

MAP 21. *Daillon's route to Ounontisastan (partly based on information supplied by W. Noble and M. E. White).*

an alliance with the Neutral, or whether the Recollets were cooperating with either Champlain or the French traders in an effort to undermine the Huron monopoly. No doubt, the traders would have been pleased to pit the Huron and Neutral against one another in order to get furs more cheaply. Nevertheless, this was a sufficiently dangerous game that the French traders who were living among the Huron did not wish to play it themselves. It is possible that a scheme of this sort might have been worked out between the higher echelons of the Recollet order and the trading company in France. The Recollets may have been hoping to prove to the company that they could be more useful in Indian diplomacy than were the hated interpreters.

Eventually, Daillon persuaded the Neutral to promise that they would send four canoes to trade with the French. The Neutral were evasive, however, and pleaded that because they did not travel extensively by canoe, they did not know the route from their country to the St. Lawrence. Daillon knew that this route led along the north shore of Lake Ontario, and from the Huron and Algonkin he had learned that by following it a person could reach the French trading stations in about ten days. When Daillon tried to learn the details of the route from Iroquet, who was in the Neutral country hunting beaver, the latter refused to tell him anything (803). It is likely that Iroquet soon headed north to inform his Huron allies what Daillon was doing.

The Huron did not delay in counteracting Daillon's influence. They began spreading rumours that Daillon was an evil sorcerer and that the French were monsters who ate thunder and lived on serpents. Because the Neutral knew little about the French, these rumours soon produced the intended effect. Individual Neutral who fell ill accused Daillon of bewitching them and he was beaten and had his baggage pillaged. As long as Daillon remained under the personal protection of Souharissen he was, however, relatively safe. To circumvent this, Huron agents appear to have persuaded, or bribed, some men fron Ouarorono (either a Neutral village near the Niagara River or the Wenroronon tribe) to slay him. These men invited Daillon to Ouarorono but, when he would not come, they waited until Souharissen and his men had gone hunting, then came to Ounontisastan with the intention of killing him. When their first hatchet blow failed to hit him, fear of Daillon's supernatural powers overcame them and they contented themselves with pillaging his possessions. Later, perhaps under pressure from Souharissen, they agreed to return some of these. By this time, however, rumours were reaching the Huron country that Daillon had been murdered. Fathers Brébeuf and de Noué persuaded

Grenole to go to Ounontisastan and retrieve Daillon, if he were still alive. In spite of the humiliating circumstances from which he was rescued, Daillon continued to maintain that Frenchmen should be sent to live among the Neutral (807).

Daillon's mission ended in failure and served to confirm the Huron's fears that the missionaries were living in their midst for no good purpose. Daillon's attempts to undermine their trade, while ably counteracted by the Huron, were probably interpreted as further evidence of the malevolent sorcery that they feared lay behind the professed goodwill of the missionaries. This, even more than the apparent confirmation that the missionaries were commercial rivals, must have troubled the Huron in the years to come.

Yet, it is unlikely that Daillon's mission ever had any chance of success. The Neutral were reluctant to trade directly with the French and their claim not to know the route to the St. Lawrence was probably a polite way of rejecting Daillon's proposal. No doubt they feared that any attempt to develop their own trade would lead to war with the Huron. Since they were also receiving European goods from the Iroquois, the latter probably would not have allowed them to use the St. Lawrence River. Indeed, to protect their trade and to prevent the Neutral from receiving French military assistance, the Seneca might have gone to war with them more readily than the Huron would have done. Faced with the threat of war on two or more fronts, the Neutral probably concluded that an independent trading alliance with the French was not worthwhile.[20]

In spite of the anger he had created among the Huron, Daillon remained in the Huron country for another year. He returned to Quebec in the summer of 1628 and lived there over the following winter. In 1629, he left for France with the other priests who were in the colony. Daillon was the last Recollet to visit the Huron.

THE JESUITS RETURN TO NEW FRANCE

Daillon's departure from the Huron country foretold the general waning of the Recollets' fortunes in New France. After 1625, they were no longer the only missionaries in Canada. While they later claimed that they had invited the Jesuits to join them because they lacked the resources to exploit their mission field adequately (Le Clercq 1691:297), it is doubtful that they would have been able to resist the designs of the politically astute and ambitious Society of Jesus for long, even if they had been inclined to try.

Instead of seeking an alliance with Champlain, as the Recollets had done, the Jesuits undertook to control the highest echelons of the colonial administration in France itself, in order to ensure that no traders, officials, or other religious orders in New France could oppose them. This operation was carried out with great discretion and required both tact and a willingness to come to terms with vital trading interests. Bitter experience had taught the Jesuits the need for compromise on this score.

The Society of Jesus had been involved in mission work in Canada before the Recollets arrived at Quebec in 1615. In 1610, through the influence of Pierre Coton, who was Henri IV's confessor, and other prominent people, the Jesuits secured a royal command that their order should accompany Jean de Biencourt de Poutrincourt to his colony at Port Royal, in Nova Scotia. Prior to making this choice, they had turned down Champlain's proposal that they come to Quebec and share in the fur trade there, in return for an investment of 3600 livres (Bishop 1948:155). Poutrincourt objected to having the Jesuits and it was only the following year that Fathers Pierre Biard and Enemond Massé arrived in Nova Scotia. Their subsequent bitter quarrels with Poutrincourt and Samuel Argall's destruction of the colony that the Jesuits attempted to establish on Mount Desert Island off the coast of Maine brought an end, in 1613, to their first round of activity in New France. The supporters of Poutrincourt denounced Biard as a traitor for having accompanied Argall to Port Royal, and hereafter nearly everyone concerned with trade and colonization agreed that the Jesuits should be kept out of New France. Champlain turned to the Recollets, when he again sought missionaries for his colony at Quebec. In spite of these inauspicious beginnings, the Jesuits did not lose interest in New France. Father Massé, in particular, hoped to return to New France and, as a teacher in the Jesuit college at La Flèche, he inspired many of his students with a wish to go there (Trudel 1966a:94–149).

Following his release from prison in 1619, the Duc de Condé yielded his rights as Viceroy of New France to his brother-in-law, Henri II, Duc de Montmorency, in return for 30,000 livres. Montmorency confirmed Champlain as his lieutenant and, like his predecessors, committed himself to a policy of developing the colony. He withdrew the fur trading monopoly from the associates of St. Malo and Rouen and granted a fifteen-year contract to a new company directed by Guillaume de Caën and his uncle Ezéchiel. The *Compagnie de Caën*, headed by both Protestant and Roman Catholic members of an important shipowning family of Rouen, was formally obliged, among other things, to settle six families each year at Quebec and to construct five houses. After a bitter struggle with the old

company, the shareholders in the latter were given permission to join the *Compagnie de Caën* as individual members. Although criticized for failing to promote settlement, Montmorency accomplished much during the five years that he was viceroy of New France. The habitation was rebuilt, the first fort was built on Cape Diamond, and the Recollets' mission house was constructed. Louis Hébert was formally possessed of the land on which his house and farm were located, and Guillaume de Caën was granted a seigniory at Cape Tourmente, where he built a habitation and began to pasture some cattle (ibid. 297).

In 1625, Montmorency seems to have been compelled by Cardinal Richelieu to relinquish some of the many offices he had acquired. His impending resignation led the Jesuits to persuade his young nephew, Henri de Lévis, Duc de Ventadour, to acquire his uncle's rights in New France in return for 100,000 livres. Both the Duc de Ventadour and his wife were extremely zealous Roman Catholics. In 1630, the Duke was to found the Compagnie du Saint-Sacrement and, in 1643, following the death of his wife, he became a priest. From 1624 onwards, his confessor was the Jesuit Philibert Noyrot, who seems to have persuaded his patron to purchase the office of viceroy (Du Creux 1951–52:26–27).

In the spring of 1625, Ventadour arranged, at his own expense, to send three Jesuits to Quebec: Charles Lalemant, Enemond Massé, who had formerly been in Nova Scotia, and Jean de Brébeuf. Neither Louis Hébert nor the traders at Quebec were happy to see the Jesuits, since they feared that with Ventadour's backing, they would soon be interfering in the affairs of the colony. The Jesuits therefore encountered open hostility and efforts were made to persuade them to return to France. Champlain and the Recollets were probably equally worried about Jesuit interference in their own activities; however, being aware of the powerful backing that the Jesuits had acquired, the Recollets received them with a show of friendliness. When the Jesuits were refused permission to stay at the habitation, the Recollets offered them accommodation in their own house on the banks of the St. Charles River.

It soon became clear that the Jesuits had not come to New France simply as missionaries. Instead, they were armed with special powers to curb the interpreters, whom the Recollets had long complained were interfering with their mission work, but whom they had been helpless to do anything about. The Jesuits had the authority to send these interpreters back to France, where they might be broken of their independent and seemingly immoral ways. Almost immediately, Brûlé and the Montagnais interpreter, Nicolas Marsolet, were ordered to return to France, although this decision

was bitterly opposed by Emery de Caën. Marsolet won a reprieve by expressing contrition and promising to teach the Jesuits the Montagnais language if he were allowed to remain. He is reported to have kept his promise faithfully, although for ten years he and the other interpreters had refused to teach the Recollets anything (Thwaites 1896–1901, 4:209–13; 5:113). Brûlé seems to have been more recalcitrant and, in spite of de Caën's efforts to prevent it, he was ordered to sail for France. Before the ships left, however, he conveniently became ill and was forced to spend the winter of 1625–26 in the care of the Jesuits. He too was persuaded, in due course, to teach the Jesuits to speak Huron (4:213–15).

However successfully the Jesuits may have asserted their control over these men, once they had extracted the desired linguistic information from them, they ordered both of them to return to France in 1626. Brûlé was sent, in part, to accompany Amantacha and to provide linguistic assistance to his tutors (4:225). The reason for Marsolet's exile in spite of his apparent reform, is unknown. Marsolet was back in New France in July 1627, when he helped a Recollet lay brother to baptize the dying Algonkin shaman Napagabiscou (Sagard 1866:522); Brûlé may have returned the same year, but it is not clear if he was allowed to resume living among the Huron. The bitterness that these two men felt towards the Jesuits is evident in their behaviour after the capitulation of Quebec, when both were in the employ of the English.

In 1626, with the help of some workers from the habitation and a carpenter borrowed from the Recollets, the Jesuits erected a four-room house, to which an outbuilding containing a hand-mill was added. The same year additional missionaries arrived, bringing twenty workmen and confirmation of a concession of land stretching northward from the mouth of the St. Charles River. These workmen seem to have been lodged in the original house the Jesuits had built, and although they were able to stay in Canada for only one year, they cleared land and built a new residence called Notre-Dame-des-Anges at the confluence of the Lairet and St. Charles Rivers.[21]

In 1625, Father Brébeuf was prevented from setting out for the Huron country by the death of Father Viel. His missionary zeal led him, however, to spend the winter living with a band of Montagnais. While this allowed him to experience Indian life, it prevented him from studying the Huron language as intensively as Father Daillon did and also from winning the confidence of the Huron who were wintering at Quebec. He did, however, manage to pick up some knowledge of the Huron language (Thwaites 1896–1901, 4:221). In the summer of 1626, Brébeuf and Father Anne de

Noüe, who had just arrived from France, were ordered to accompany Daillon to the Huron country. Daillon quickly obtained passage with the Huron, although they were reluctant to accept the Jesuits (Le Clercq 1691:344). In general, this probably reflected the Huron's lack of enthusiasm to embark any white man who did not bear arms; however, the Jesuits' heavy boots and wide-brimmed hats made them more dangerous to have in canoes than were the grey-robed and sandalled Recollets, and Talbot (1956:56) suggests that their unfamiliar black robes also may have caused the Huron to be wary of them. It was only after many presents were offered to compensate the Huron for extra paddling and loss of cargo that two crews agreed to provide space for them.

Brébeuf, de Noüe, and Daillon settled in Toanché, where they had a cabin erected on the outskirts of the village, as the Recollets formerly had done at Carhagouha and Quieunonascaran. The Jesuits remained there, while Daillon made his infamous journey to the Neutral country. They appear to have had no distinctive missionary program, but attempted to follow that of the Recollets, which meant applying themselves to the study of the Huron language and not baptizing anyone for fear it would prove premature. Brébeuf baptized only one person during the three years that he remained in the Huron country. This was a baby who appeared to be dying, but who recovered and was alive in 1635 (Thwaites 1896–1901, 8:135–37). Like the Recollets, he and de Noüe exhorted the Huron to live in conformity with Christian standards and attempted to exemplify these standards in their daily life. They also came to share the Recollets' distaste for the traders and, in particular, their hatred for Etienne Brûlé.

By early 1627, it was clear that Father de Noüe was unable to learn the Huron language and it was decided that he should return to Quebec. No missionaries came to the Huron country that year, so that Brébeuf and the discredited Daillon were alone in Toanché. Alarmed by Daillon's flirtation with the Neutral, the Huron brought an unusually large number of furs to the French trading stations (Biggar 1922–36, 5:232). A highly successful trade, accompanied by a suitable reaffirmation of the French-Huron alliance, may have helped to repair the damage that Daillon had done, and this, in turn, may have made it possible for Daillon to trust his life to the Huron and return to Quebec the following year. In any case, Daillon left the Huron in 1628 and Brébeuf became the sole missionary among them.

1628 was a year of drought in the Huron country, and Toanché was among the places hardest hit. When Tehorenhaegnon, who was one of the most famous shamans in the region, failed to make rain, he announced that

this was because the red painted cross that had been erected in front of Brébeuf's cabin was frightening the thunderbird and causing the rain clouds to divide as they approached the village. This charge has been interpreted as evidence that, even at this time, the shamans felt hostile towards the priests for encroaching on their traditional domain. More likely, however, Tehorenhaegnon was genuinely concerned about the effect that this fiery symbol had on the behaviour of the thunderbird, and his jealousy was merely the professional rivalry one shaman felt towards another, without involving any specific malice towards Brébeuf as a foreign interloper. The seriousness of Tehorenhaegnon's charge lay in the belief already prevalent among the Huron that the French priests might be practising witchcraft, of which causing famine was one possible manifestation (Thwaites 1896–1901, 10:43–49).

When the headmen of Toanché sent for Brébeuf and asked him to take down his cross or to hide it for a time in his cabin or in the lake, Brébeuf refused. He threatened the Huron with supernatural punishment if they removed the cross themselves and, at the same time, decried their ignorance in believing that the thunder was a spirit. In order to turn the argument to his own advantage, Brébeuf agreed to paint the cross white, but stated that if it did not rain immediately thereafter, Tehorenhaegnon would be exposed as an impostor. When several days passed and it did not rain, Brébeuf went to the village council and demanded that its members paint the cross red again and, to restore its honour and ensure a harvest, that they each bring a dish of corn as an offering, which he would then redistribute among the "needy families" of the village. Anxious to try whatever shamanistic rite Brébeuf was proposing, they did what was asked and followed Brébeuf's example by kneeling down and kissing the cross. In Brébeuf's words "they did so well that the same day God gave them rain and in the end a plentiful harvest" (10:49). This victory over Tehorenhaegnon emphasized the superiority of Brébeuf's magical powers and also demonstrated his goodwill towards the people of Toanché. It conformed, however, to traditional Huron religious beliefs and, while enhancing Brébeuf's authority, did not contribute to a better understanding of Christian teaching.

The goodwill of the Attignawantan was especially valuable that summer since the French trading vessels did not get through to Tadoussac that year. Because of this, the French had little to trade. The Huron had to pay higher prices for what there was and, even so, returned home with many skins unbartered. In addition, Amantacha had not been returned to his father. Huron annoyance was partly offset by twenty Frenchmen being

sent to live with them for the winter. This was the largest contingent of armed Frenchmen that had ever arrived in the Huron country. Although they were sent mainly because there was not enough food for them at Quebec, they served to retain the goodwill of the Huron at a difficult juncture.

During the three years Brébeuf was in the Huron country, in the Huron's estimation he gained a better working knowledge of their language than anyone who had been there before (Biggar 1922–36, 6:46). By the end of this period, he was able to recite Bible stories, to explain simple theological matters (Thwaites 1896–1901, 5:191), and had translated Father Ledesma's catechism into Huron. The latter was appended to the 1632 edition of Champlain's *Voyages* (Latourelle 1952–53:18–19).

With the situation at Quebec becoming increasingly uncertain, all Frenchmen living in the Huron country were ordered to return to the St. Lawrence in 1629. This included a command from Father Massé that Brébeuf should return. Thus, in the spring of 1629, Brébeuf took his leave of the Huron. He was present at the surrender of Quebec in July and subsequently had to return to France with the other missionaries.

Huron Life

The main problems that the Huron faced were adjusting to European goods rather than to the Europeans themselves. Trade goods had become available to the Huron in moderate quantities, but, as we have seen, contacts with white men were still limited and nondisruptive. During this period no more than twenty to thirty Europeans lived among the Huron at any one time and often there were less than ten. Most of these men were traders who had no desire to challenge the Huron way of life, and in many ways were assimilated with it. No French officials lived among the Huron, and the priests who were there after 1623 had neither the skills nor the coercive power to challenge the Huron way of life or to interfere in their affairs to any significant degree.

An initial period during which political and cultural initiatives remain in the hands of indigenous groups has been a feature of contact between Europeans and tribal peoples in many parts of the world. The introduction of iron tools frequently reduces the time required to perform certain important routine tasks and permits energies to be directed elsewhere. The

result is not a disruption of the indigenous culture or a breakdown in existing social relationships, such as may occur when direct European intervention is involved. Instead, this period witnesses the realization of potentials that existed in the native culture. Particularly, one finds the elaboration of social status, increasing emphasis on ceremonialism (especially involving conspicuous consumption), greater artistic endeavours, and heightened competition to control scarce resources (Averkieva 1971; Salisbury 1962).

TECHNOLOGICAL CHANGE

The data on trade already presented indicate that the Huron were primarily interested in obtaining iron tools with sharp cutting edges and copper and brass kettles. While stone artifacts are not particularly abundant on prehistoric sites (Emerson 1967:137), preliminary reports of research carried out in the Penetanguishene Peninsula suggest a rapid decline in these artifacts in the historic period. In respect of the Robitaille site, it is claimed that "lithics seem to have been almost abandoned" (Latta 1971: 130). As the Huron acquired iron knives and axes in considerable numbers, these replaced their traditional stone adzes and cutting tools. Indeed, Sagard's observation that the Huron fashioned arrow shafts with a knife or, when they had no knife, with sharp-edged stones (Wrong 1939:98) suggests that, already by 1623, iron tools may have been used more commonly than stone ones for this purpose. Sagard's comment refers to the Attignawantan, from whose territory most of the published archaeological evidence has been recovered. Only more research can determine whether the other Huron tribes were as well supplied with iron tools at this time.

Iron awls are common in Huron sites of the historic period. At least some of them were probably used to punch holes in scraps of brass and copper (Latta 1971:127), but it seems likely that metal awls were used mainly as drills and for working wood and bone. As such, they fall into the general category of Huron cutting tools. The popularity of iron knives and axes is not difficult to explain. The knives had an edge that was superior to that of stone scrapers or other Huron cutting tools. They were, moreover, fairly lightweight objects; hence large numbers of them could be transported with little difficulty. Iron axe heads were considerably heavier and more difficult to transport. As we shall see, however, they were more effective for felling trees than were their stone counterparts. It also prob-

ably required less effort to carry an iron axe from the St. Lawrence Valley to the Huron country than to chip and grind a stone one out of a block of chlorite schist.

It is equally certain, however, that in spite of the popularity of iron cutting tools, the knowledge of how to make stone ones was not about to be lost. The Robitaille site has yielded numerous examples of triangular stone projectile points, that are reported to be extremely well made, as well as a number of stone adzes (Latta 1971:129). A major factor keeping a knowledge of stone-working alive was, no doubt, the inability of traders to satisfy the demand for European goods. While this is not surprising in view of the size of the Huron population and its distance from the trading stations, the situation contrasts sharply with the apparent abandonment of a lithic industry among the Montagnais at this time.

Considerable numbers of bone artifacts are found in historic Huron sites. Projectile and harpoon points are fairly common; awls and netting needles abundant (Kidd 1952:73). The relative commonness of bone tools suggests that the advantages of metal implements over their bone counterparts were not great enough to stimulate a strong demand for the former, so long as iron cutting tools remained in short supply. Faced with the need to choose what was most essential, iron axes, knives, and awls were preferred, especially since these tools made it easier to manufacture the traditional bone ones.

It has been suggested that women's tools remained largely unchanged, either because of greater conservatism on their part or because male traders habitually chose items that were useful to themselves rather than to their womenfolk (Latta 1971:130–31). It must be remembered, however, that bone tools were produced by men, hence they would have been interested in replacing them with metal ones if they had been especially difficult or time-consuming to manufacture. Bone netting needles and bone or stone arrowheads were made and used by men and are more common than metal imports. This reinforces the argument that, given the difficulties involved in obtaining and transporting goods to the Huron country, European items that replaced ones which were difficult to manufacture, or which performed markedly better than their Huron counterparts, were preferred to those that replaced ones that could be manufactured relatively easily. It may also be noted that in spite of the importation of glass beads, native beads were still manufactured in considerable quantities out of bone and marine shell. The Huron's red slate beads may have been imported from elsewhere, since unworked fragments of this material are missing from Huron sites (Latta 1971:128–29; Kidd 1952:73).

The glass beads at the Robitaille site are generally in poor condition, probably indicating that they were kept until wear or breakage made it impossible to string them (Latta 1971:128).

Although the Huron purchased large numbers of copper and brass kettles, there is no evidence of a decline in pottery-making. Broken pottery vessels occur in even the latest Huron sites in quantities that suggest little curtailment in manufacture as a result of trade with the French (Kidd 1950). There is no evidence that pottery was "definitely on the way out" as has been claimed was happening among the Seneca at this time (Wray and Schoff 1953:56–57). Once again, it is clear that the number of metal kettles that could be imported by the Huron was insufficient to supply their needs and this ensured the survival of the native product.

Another factor preventing the accumulation of large numbers of metal kettles by the Huron was the ease with which they wore out. Like the axes that were supplied to the Indians, poor quality kettles were foisted by the Europeans on their inexperienced and goods-hungry trading partners. We have noted that the Huron in Quieunonascaran were in the habit of borrowing kettles from Europeans when they had feasts (Wrong 1939:84).

Aside from their prestige value and supernatural powers, one of the practical advantages of metal kettles was for travelling by canoe, since they were lighter and broke less easily than the clay pots that the Huron normally carried with them. The Huron were also interested in these kettles because they provided them with a supply of scrap metal. There is extensive evidence that worn out kettles were cut into pieces, which were used to make arrowheads, beads, plaques, and pendants. The arrowheads that the Huron made were triangular in outline, like their stone ones, while tanged arrowheads appear to have been obtained ready-made (Latta 1971: 127). The copper and brass pendants normally had holes bored through them that would have served either for suspension or for sewing them onto clothes. A sheet of brass recovered at the Robitaille site had been cut into the outline of an animal standing on its tail (ibid. 128).

The Huron also reworked iron artifacts. Notches were filed into knife blades to turn them into harpoon points, knives having handle and blade made of a single piece of metal being preferred for this purpose (Garrad 1969). The reworking of all types of metal was done by filing, grinding, and hammering—techniques that for millennia had been used by the Indians of this region to work native copper. There is no evidence that the Huron acquired any additional metal-working skills at this time. They did not know how to mend items that were broken or worn through, and repeatedly asked Sagard and other Frenchmen to perform such services for

them. The Huron must have viewed scrap metal as the equivalent of native copper. Its abundance resulted in the florescence of an old, but hitherto restricted, technology.

It has been assumed that the introduction of iron knives and axes reduced the amount of time that men had to spend performing essential tasks, such as clearing fields and manufacturing other tools. Technologically, this argument appears to be sound, although the amount of time saved by using iron tools remains problematical. The iron knife must have speeded up the working of bone and wood, and fewer stone axes would have had to be manufactured than formerly. Yet, considering the many hours that were spent cutting trees, both to clear fields and to erect houses and fortifications, it seems likely that the greatest saving was made through the use of iron axes. Experiments carried out using flint axes mounted in the traditional European fashion, in ashwood handles through a rectangular hole in the haft, have demonstrated that an oak tree over a foot in diameter can be felled in less than half an hour (Iversen 1956), while a conifer seven inches in diameter can be cut through in five to seven minutes (Clark 1945). To employ such axes effectively, however, the user must chip at the tree with short, quick strokes, using mainly the wrist and elbow. In New Guinea, experiments and observations have shown that a stone adze fitted into an elbow haft is about one-third to one-quarter as efficient for forest clearance as a European steel axe. A man who is experienced in using both types of implement can chop down a tree (species unstated) just under thirteen inches in diameter in twenty-four minutes with a stone adze, while a tree of the same species fifteen inches in diameter can be cut down in eight minutes using a steel one (Salisbury 1962:219–20; Townsend 1969; Cranstone 1971).

In spite of the close agreement of these figures from Europe and New Guinea, they cannot be applied automatically to the Huron data. The iron axes that the French supplied were manufactured specially for the fur trade and were made of metal that was much inferior to the steel ones that are in use today. They also lacked the large, heavy head above the socket which accounts to no small degree for the efficiency of modern axes (Kidd 1949a:115). The Huron probably used them in the same way that they used stone axes, that is, cutting with short, quick strokes. Even if a trade axe used in this manner was not as inefficient as it looks, it was probably less time saving than a modern one. Yet, if such axes speeded up forest clearance by only a factor of two, instead of three or four, they would have resulted in a considerable saving of energy.

The acquisition of iron axes also made it easier for the Huron to cut

down larger trees than they had been accustomed to previously. The novel manner in which such logs were used to construct walls and supports for sleeping platforms in houses of the historic period can be illustrated by a comparison of the plan of a house from the Robitaille site with another from the earlier Maurice site, both of which are similar in size and shape (Tyyska 1969:76; plate 30). It must be noted, however, that, even in prehistoric times, the Iroquois frequently used large posts to construct their houses and palisades. It therefore appears to have been technologically feasible for the Huron to have handled larger logs at an earlier period, had they been convinced that the investment of energy was worthwhile. Iron axes simply made it possible to use larger logs without expending additional energy to cut them down.

In spite of this, it is questionable whether Huron men spent less time clearing forests than they had done previously. Expanding trade with the northern hunting peoples must have markedly increased the demand for Huron corn, which, in turn, necessitated increased production. In the first of what has become a succession of bizarre and overblown theories about the effects of the fur trade on Huron life, Hunt (1940:59) suggested that as the Huron grew increasingly preoccupied with trade, they ceased to produce food of their own and imported all they required for their own needs and for trade from the Neutral and Tionnontaté. This suggestion is without foundation. There are frequent references to Huron being engaged in horticultural activities up to, and including, 1649 and 1650. Moreover, it is ludicrous to imagine that the numerically much smaller Tionnontaté population could have produced enough food to supply Huron requirements, or that it would have been economically feasible to transport large amounts of corn northward from the Neutral country. Carrying this corn overland would have consumed too much time and energy to make it worthwhile.

It seems likely that much of the time saved by greater efficiency in forest clearance was lost through the need for increased production. Part of the demand for more corn may have been met by the annual export of surpluses that formerly were reserved to offset years of drought or crop pestilence. This would explain the apparent vulnerability of the Huron to crop failures in the later historic period, even though they were still reported to be producing surpluses to protect themselves against such failures. In addition, however, larger crops must have been grown. Since women's tasks were not influenced by the new technology, the amount of time they spent tending crops must have increased sharply. Thus one of the results of the fur trade seems to have been the very opposite of what Hunt believed. Trade did not become a substitute for food production; on the

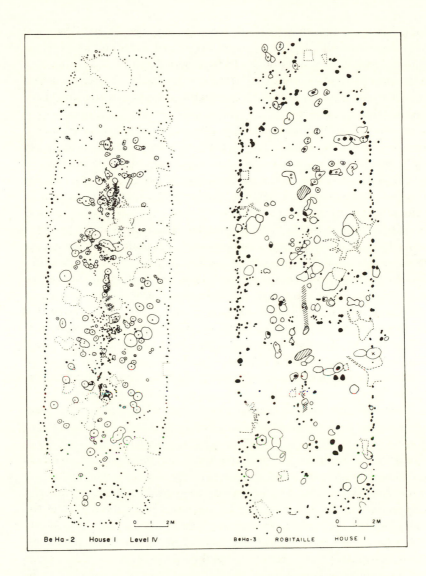

BeHa-2   House I   Level IV   BeHa-3   ROBITAILLE   HOUSE I

PLATE 30. *Plans of longhouses from the Maurice (BeHa-2) and Robitaille (BeHa-3) sites. Both sites are in the Penetanguishene Peninsula. The first is dated* A.D. *1570–1620, the second is later. The large post molds in the house from the Robitaille site indicate that bigger trees were being felled in later times to construct houses. Courtesy C. E. Heidenreich and W. M. Hurley.*

contrary, increasing food production became the basis of expanding Huron trade.

The Recollets who lived among the Attignawantan in 1623 planted a small kitchen garden with peas, herbs, and "other trifles" (Wrong 1939: 81). In spite of this, contacts with Europeans do not seem to have influenced Huron methods of cultivation or their choice of crops. Sagard reports that a Huron trader from Toanché planted a few peas and that these produced seeds twice as big as Sagard had seen growing in France or at Quebec (ibid. 91). In view of the dominant role conventionally ascribed to Iroquoian women as horticulturalists, it is interesting that in this case it was a man who was experimenting with new crops. This is scarcely surprising, however, since men also grew the Huron's one speciality crop, tobacco. We may be seeing here an example of how, in prehistoric times, geographically mobile warriors and traders played an important role in diffusing crops throughout the Iroquoian culture area. The balanced repertoire of crops already being grown by the Huron may explain their failure to adopt new crops at this time, or it simply may be that not enough time was available for European crops to become established prior to the destruction of the Huron confederacy.

It has been suggested that hunting declined in importance as trade developed. As evidence, it is pointed out that stone artifacts are scarce in historic Huron sites, while few of the metal tools are suitable for hunting (Latta 1971:130). It is also argued that, at least in the late northern Attignawantan sites, considerable amounts of dog bone (*Canis* sp.) are found, but few bones of deer or other wild animals. This, it is claimed, indicates that, by historic times, the Huron obtained little meat by hunting or trading, but were dependent on horticulture and fishing, supplemented by dog meat (Savage 1971a:148).

It must be noted, however, that none of the northern Iroquoian cultures has left distinctive hunting kits in the prehistoric archaeological record and that hunting was probably never as important as fishing from at least Owasco times onward. Moreover, as the population in northern Simcoe County increased in late prehistoric times, many types of game must rapidly have become depleted, particularly in areas such as the Penetanguishene Peninsula. The apparently high percentage of wolf, as opposed to domestic dog, bones at the Maurice site (c. 1570–1620) (Savage 1971b) may represent a continuing shift in local hunting patterns that began with the depletion of local stocks of deer, followed by that of other wild animals. This does not mean, however, that the Huron did not range farther afield for their hunting. The meat from such hunts was fleshed from the bone

and would leave no trace in Huron middens. It is known that the traditional spring hunts continued as late as the winter of 1647–48 (Thwaites 1896–1901, 33:83–85) and that Huron men were skilled hunters at a much later date. The relatively minor role of hunting in prehistoric times and the decline in local supplies of game as the Huron population became more concentrated suggest that the diminution of wild animal bones that can be observed in village middens may not have resulted from more time being spent trading. Indeed, since the fur trade led the Huron to exhaust the beaver within the entire range of their hunting territories by 1630, it may be argued that, for a time, the fur trade produced more intensive hunting, which continued into the period we are discussing.

A notable feature of all Huron settlements at this time is their location either near the shores of Georgian Bay, or close to rivers that flow directly into it. By crowding nearer the lake, these villages came to occupy an even smaller total area than they had previously. Their distribution, which differs from the more inland one of earlier times, no doubt reflects a continuing adjustment of population to the geographical requirements of the fur trade, as well as the growing effectiveness of the confederacy council in promoting unity among the member tribes.

On the other hand, the largest settlements continued to be stoutly defended and were constructed in naturally fortified locations. The reason for this was continuing hostilities with the Iroquois, and particularly with the Seneca. As we have already noted, the traditional prestige system of the Huron and Iroquois made endemic warfare, at least on a limited scale, essential for both groups. Sagard reports that in the early 1620s, about 500 men set out each year to raid the Iroquois. This must have been at least as many as at any other time in Huron history (Wrong 1939:152). It seems that as the growth of trade made peaceful relations with neighbouring tribes more desirable, the Huron directed their raids against their remaining enemies, the Iroquois. Also, the Iroquois may still have hoped to capture European goods from the Huron, just as the Huron captured shell beads from them.

Iroquois raiders were reported to be active in the Huron country in the summer and autumn of 1623 (ibid. 175). The same year, a raiding party led by a young man from Quieunonascaran won a signal victory over the Iroquois south of Lake Ontario. In a single engagement, they captured about sixty Iroquois, slaying most of them on the spot. The others were brought back to the Huron country to be tortured to death. These prisoners were divided among a number of villages, including Ossossané and Toanché, whose warriors had taken part in the raid (ibid. 152; Sagard

1866:423–24). This was a major victory by Iroquoian standards and demonstrates that at this time the Huron were more than holding their own against the Iroquois. Perrot (1911:148), although scarcely a reliable source for this period, reports that there was a truce between the Huron and the Iroquois in 1624, but it is not known which Iroquois tribes were involved. Conceivably, however, the truce was related to the Huron victory of 1623.

In general, relations between the Huron and the other Iroquoian tribes of Ontario were peaceful. The Huron and Tionnontaté seem to have been on particularly good terms and only the continuing refusal of Huron headmen to let the Tionnontaté trade with the French seems to have prevented them from becoming part of the confederacy. Relations with the Neutral were more strained, no doubt because the Neutral also traded with the Iroquois and were less dependent on the Huron for European goods. In 1623, a dispute seems almost to have led to war between the two groups. Fear of a Neutral attack-in-strength prompted even the northern Attignawantan to dismantle isolated houses and move into Quieunonascaran, which they heavily fortified (Sagard 1866:416). At the same time, weapons were made ready, provisions stockpiled, and warriors held councils to coordinate their plans for defence (Wrong 1939:156–57). An alliance was planned with the Assistaronon, who were sworn enemies of the Neutral. As soon as some Neutral had been captured, three or four Huron were to daub themselves with their blood and visit the Assistaronon (Wrong 1939: 157–58). Although the Assistaronon were enemies of the Tionnontaté and the Ottawa as well as of the Neutral, the Huron evidently did not regard an alliance with them as out of the question. In spite of these preparations and the eagerness of certain war chiefs, peace prevailed. This seems to indicate that already by this time considerations of trade weighed more heavily in relations between the Neutral and the Huron than did those of blood revenge.

Between 1616 and 1629, new offensive capabilities seem to have been altering the pattern of Iroquoian warfare, although the nature and reason for these changes have been misunderstood in previous studies.[22] It was at this time that the Huron and Iroquois were beginning to obtain and to manufacture arrowheads of iron, copper, and brass (Wray and Schoff 1953: 56–57). The strongest of these arrowheads were able to pierce the wooden Iroquoian body armour that had hitherto protected warriors. This seems to have discouraged the traditional form of encounter, in which both sides lined up in the open and shot arrows at each other until one side gave way. Sagard's description of Iroquoian warfare suggests that, by 1623, both the

Huron and the Iroquois preferred to maraud each other in small groups. Warriors would remain hidden until they could rush upon the enemy and engage them in hand to hand combat prior to any arrows being discharged. Armour continued to be worn because it helped to protect the body against blows sustained in close combat and because it afforded protection against stone and bone-tipped arrows, which continued to be used.

Throughout this period, the Huron probably enjoyed a slight advantage over the Iroquois. This may have been, in part, because they were able to obtain more metal arrowheads than could the Seneca. The armed French who lived in some of the Huron villages were also an asset that the Seneca did not have. While the French did not prevent the Seneca from raiding Huron territory, they compelled them to be more wary of approaching Huron villages than they would have been otherwise. Yet, while the traditional modes of warfare were altered, it is clear that the concepts that animated Iroquoian warfare in the past remained alive and that the balance of power between the Huron and Iroquois that had emerged several decades before was basically unaltered.

Another change that the introduction of European goods brought about was the supplementing of traditional forms of torture with techniques that involved the use of metal implements. These included searing and piercing the flesh with red hot iron objects and placing glowing hatchets strung on willow swathes around the necks of prisoners.

SOCIAL CHANGE

In recent years there has been much speculation about changes in Huron society between 1615 and 1629. Wallis M. Smith (1970) claims that this was a period of rapid social change which was a reaction to a crisis situation. He argues that a growing emphasis on trade strengthened the role that men played in Huron society, effectively undermined the matrilineal kinship system, and led married women to live with their husbands' families. While this "social disruption" was incomplete, even by 1629 it had "radically alter[ed] Huron social organization."

Smith's analysis is based primarily on data presented by Cara Richards (1967) which attempt to demonstrate that in the majority of Huron and Iroquois households that were described in detail in the seventeenth century, women were living with their husbands' relatives. Smith differs significantly from Richards in interpreting her case studies as evidence for the partial breakdown of a prehistoric pattern of matrilocal (uxorilocal)

residence, rather than for a prehistoric pattern that was itself other than strictly matrilocal. He overlooks published critiques of Richards's paper in which it has been pointed out that a goodly number of the situations she interprets as evidence of non-matrilocal residence may be nothing more than Frenchmen treating Huron kinship terms as if they were being used in the same way that French ones were (Abler 1970:28–29; Trigger 1969a:55–56). Occasionally there is clear evidence of sons and nephews being confused, and it seems likely that the French misunderstood many of the relationships that were described to them by the Huron. That the seventeenth century Jesuit writers never understood what a lineage or clan segment was, must dispel any illusion that we can find in the writings of this period a knowledgeable description of Huron social organization.

I have also suggested that young men who were eligible to inherit clan offices may have gone to live permanently with their mothers' brothers, since in a traditional matrilineal system this is one way in which a headman can continue to reside with his own clan segment (Trigger 1969a:56). If the Huron followed this custom, it would explain much of Richards's evidence, since it was precisely these important families with whom the Jesuits had the most to do. Chiefly families were probably also the ones that intermarried most frequently with women from other villages, tribes, and ethnic groups, which would also explain why such women feature so prominently in Richards's analysis.

In view of all of these possibilities for a contrary interpretation of the evidence, the small number of case studies that Richards has assembled do not bulk very large against some important evidence that both she and Smith have overlooked. Pierre Boucher (1664:103) stated explicitly that among the Huron, men went to live with their wives. Boucher worked in the Huron country for four years and may have had a better opportunity to experience Huron family life firsthand than did the Jesuits. Du Creux (1951–52:98) also seems to have been referring to the Huron when he wrote in his *History of Canada* that among the Indians a man generally moved into his wife's lodgings. Because of Boucher's explicitness, it seems rash to postulate a shift away from matrilocal residence patterns at this time on the basis of evidence that is at best equivocal.

Moreover, it can be shown that the theoretical basis for such a position is inadequate and possibly completely erroneous. Smith has accepted the conventional argument that matrilocal residence existed among the Huron in prehistoric times because of the important role played by women in food production. He argues that as trade became more important, male influence increased and this tended to undermine traditional residence patterns.

In chapter 3, I cast serious doubt on the theory that Huron matrilocal residence can be explained as resulting from the role played by women in horticultural activities. I argued that, on the contrary, it resulted from men being absent from their villages and scattered in small groups for much of the year, whereas women remained in the villages in permanent face-to-face association. This made it more practical for extended families to be structured on a matrilineal than on a patrilineal basis. Since I first published this interpretation, Mary Helms (1970) has shown that matrilocal residence was reinforced among a number of Amerindian peoples as a result of men being drawn away from their communities with increasing frequency in early historic times. Helms suggests that long-term male absence from a sedentary community may be a general factor promoting the development of matrilocal residence among basically bilateral groups, of which the Huron would count as one example. Whether this theory will supplant Schneider and Gough's explanation, based on the relative economic importance of male and female work teams, or whether it will become merely an additional explanation remains uncertain.

Alternatively, it can be argued that if matrilocal residence among the Huron were a reflection of the important role women played in food production, the development of the fur trade should have strengthened, rather than weakened, this pattern. This is because the basis of expanded trade was increased corn production, which could come about only as a result of increased labour by Huron women. If men had formerly been dependent on women for most of the food they ate, they were now also dependent on them for their key item of trade. Far from being subordinated to men, the power of women should have increased under such conditions. Either explanation of the origins of matrilocal residence suggests that such patterns should have been strengthened among the Huron as a result of the fur trade. In view of these theoretical considerations and the flimsy nature of the evidence, I find it impossible to accept the argument that a breakdown in matrilocal residence patterns was taking place among the Huron at any time prior to 1650. If alternative forms of residence were prevalent at this period, these are likely an indication of the incompleteness of the shift away from the earlier patrilocal forms of residence that were associated with the organization of hunting bands.

Smith also has argued that, with the enhancement of the male role, the traditional powers of descent groups were eroded and matrilineal succession to office became less important than it had been previously. The basis for this argument is Brébeuf's statement, in 1636, suggesting that at that time the Huron were no longer paying as much attention to the selec-

tion of their headmen as they had done previously and thus they no longer called them *Enondecha*, "as if a good headman and the country were one and the same" (Thwaites 1896–1901, 10:231). This is admittedly a difficult passage, but it may be yet another example of a concept of progressive moral degeneration that often guided the Jesuits' interpretation of history. It is noteworthy, for example, that Brébeuf said precisely the same thing about the *arendiwane* or shamans (10:199). The major arguments that Smith advances to demonstrate a decline in the corporate strength of descent groups are based on the untenable view that the Huron confederacy was a single tribe and the Huron tribes were clans; hence these arguments do not prove what Smith intends. All they demonstrate is that the Huron tribes were not clans or descent groups. There is no evidence that clan segments were losing their corporate function at this time or that the matrilineal principles which governed the inheritance of offices were being weakened; indeed, a careful reading of the *Jesuit Relations* indicates the contrary (e.g., 26:297).

It has also been suggested that the reduction in the overall length of houses that has been observed at the Warminster site and other sites of the historic period provides additional evidence of the breakdown of matrilineal extended families as a result of the influence of the fur trade. Such influences are also allegedly evident in a greater variety of house types and the breakdown of traditional patterns of arranging pits and hearths inside of houses (Tyyska and Hurley 1969). Tuck (1971:221), however, has demonstrated that a similar reduction in the length of Onondaga houses began long before the earliest evidence of European trade goods and thus must be related to indigenous changes in Iroquoian social structure. In chapter 3 I suggested that larger longhouses may have evolved as one means of defence during the early Iroquoian period. It is therefore possible that a decline in the size of longhouses, and an accompanying decrease in the size of extended families, may reflect either the greater security of the late Iroquoian period or the transformation of protection from being both a lineage and a village concern into being a purely village one. The evidence from New York State demonstrates the danger of indiscriminately attributing every change in the archaeological record to the impact that contact with Europeans was having upon Indian life.

This does not mean, of course, that the fur trade did not bring about important changes in Huron social organization. I have already suggested that it probably enhanced the power and prestige of the council chiefs, who were able to profit from their control of trading networks and use these profits to play a more important role in the traditional redistributive sys-

tem. Such activities would have heightened the distinctions between headmen and other members of Huron society, while the control of major trade
routes, such as the one leading to Quebec, by tribal leaders must have produced greater inequalities not only between lineages within clans, but also
between clan segments belonging to the same tribe. Such developments
would explain how Bressani came to speak of Huron society as being made
up of nobles and plebeians (Thwaites 1896–1901, 38:247). They may also
account for allegedly new epithets, such as "big stones" or "stay-at-
homes," that were being applied to Huron headmen in the 1630s (10:
231–33). A desire to obtain goods in order to enhance their individual
prestige could also explain the alleged corruption of the "Old Men and
notables of the country" who are reported to have "secretly taken
possession" of a considerable number of fur robes at the Feast of the Dead
held at Ossossané in 1636 (10:303). There is, however, no confirmation
that in doing this, these headmen were behaving contrary to traditional
norms. Brébeuf's claim that in such ceremonies the poor lost all they had,
while the rich lost little or nothing (10:303–5) may be a condemnation of
a non-Christian religious custom that is without foundation.

Privileged individuals were given the best portions of food at feasts and
they and their families had access to communal healing ceremonies that
were not performed for persons of lesser importance. While this hierarchy
of prestige accorded with a hierarchy of wealth, it would be wrong to
assume that position was derived from wealth. It seems more likely that
the opposite was true: that a man's ability to derive wealth from the fur
trade largely depended on his traditional position in the Huron political
structure. Tensions may have developed between the numerous Huron
who engaged in trade and the headmen who controlled the trade routes.
There is, however, no evidence, even in later and more troubled times, of
nouveau riche traders attempting to challenge the power of traditional headmen through the conspicuous distribution of European goods, as is reported
among the West Coast Indians. This potential conflict was probably muted,
in part, because the headmen and the traders under them often belonged
to the same, still-functioning clan segments and therefore shared a common interest in enhancing the prestige of their group. The remoteness of
the trading stations also helped to inhibit individual initiative. It would be
unwise to imagine that inequalities did not exist in Huron society before
the start of the fur trade, especially since we know that at least some of the
Huron tribes engaged in trade, as well as farming, long before European
goods had begun to arrive in their midst. The changes that the fur trade

brought about in social stratification were therefore changes in degree, rather than a revolution in Huron political organization.

Archaeological evidence from the Warminster site provides additional information about the distribution of goods in Huron society at this period. While Huron items appear to be fairly evenly distributed, the amount of European goods found in the pits in different houses at the site varied considerably. Two of the nine houses that were excavated contained by far the most goods, and one house contained none at all. It was also noted that in the two "richest" houses, the cluster of pits around one hearth was rich in European goods at the expense of other clusters. This suggests marked discrepancies not only between extended families but also between individual nuclear families (Tyyska 1968). Considerable caution is needed, however, in interpreting such data. House pits were used for storage and, except when a village was destroyed, contain only items that became lost or were not thought worth carrying off when the settlement was abandoned. It may be questioned therefore whether the material recovered from these pits provides an adequate indication of their owners' wealth. While it seems likely that most wealth would remain in the hands of the head man and woman of a longhouse, the varying distribution of European artifacts between houses raises certain problems. Men vied to accumulate material possessions, but their aim was ultimately to gain prestige by redistributing such goods to other members of the community. There may have been a growing tendency for traders to try to retain possession of European goods, particularly if these were useful for production, and it could be this sort of accumulation that is represented in the varying amounts of goods found in the different houses at the Warminster site. On the other hand, the distribution of goods in a village after a major redistributive ritual such as the Ononharoia, was almost certainly different from what it was immediately before such an event, when particular individuals were seeking to accumulate as many items as they could. It is therefore possible that the Warminster data represent the accumulative phase of a redistributive cycle, rather than permanent differentials in individual access to scarce commodities.

For a redistributive economy to withstand changes of the sort we have been describing it must be able to reinforce its norms which encourage and require redistribution against the growing desire of successful entrepreneurs to retain a larger share of the wealth that pours into their hands. Among the Huron, traders must have been especially tempted to hang on to productive tools that were useful and in short supply. If a way could have

been found to validate retaining possession of such goods, the result would have been the erosion of the Huron ethic of redistribution and its replacement by an ethic that rationalized acquisitiveness and conspicuous display.

A redistributive ethic seems clearly to have prevailed in Huron society. Even in succeeding decades, when reparations had to be paid, everyone vied in making contributions so that they might appear solicitous for public welfare (Thwaites 1896–1901, 28:51). The Ononharoia continued to be celebrated in the traditional manner, and Sagard tells of a headman giving up a domestic cat that Le Caron had given him, when a sick woman dreamed that she would be cured if the cat were presented to her. To underline the extent of this sacrifice, Sagard adds that the headman's daughter loved this cat so much that she died of grief when it was taken from her, in spite of her desire to help her neighbour (Wrong 1939:118–19).

An indirect, but nevertheless effective, measure of the strains that the fur trade was posing for the traditional redistributive system may be found in the pattern of Huron witchcraft accusations after 1615. As is the case in many societies where the majority of human relations are close personal ones, witchcraft accusations tend to mirror the changes that occur as traditional obligations become modified. Many instances of witchcraft, especially those recorded after 1634, reflect breakdowns in traditional relationships resulting from culture change. Though the evidence is not susceptible to statistical treatment, the frequency of such accusations also seems higher than it had been earlier. Many of the cases that have been recorded reflect the effects that conversion to Christianity had on the obligations particular Huron owed to their society. Others seem to have had primarily economic causes. One instance is reported of a "rich" Christian convert being accused of witchcraft and then threatened with death, presumably because he was no longer willing to participate in the redistributive activities that were associated with the Huron religion (Thwaites 1896–1901, 30:19–21). Another Huron expressed relief, after he had been converted, at no longer having to bear the expense of participating in such rituals (23:129). These examples show that by the 1640s some prominent Huron who had access to trade goods were happy to escape from these obligations. In spite of this, the use of accusations of witchcraft to force such men to live up to their traditional obligations tells us something about the operation of Huron society at this time.

Witchcraft accusations can function in one of two ways. On the one hand, they can be directed by the beneficiaries of traditional obligations against those who fail to discharge their duties towards them. Alternatively, they can be made against the traditional recipients of such obli-

gations by those who are anxious to avoid them, but who feel guilty about neglecting kinsmen or fellow villagers. In the latter case, the guilt is projected on to the very persons who are being wronged: at once intimidating them and soothing the conscience of the defaulter for his break with tradition (Macfarlane 1970; Douglas 1970). The former response is characteristic of traditional societies, while the latter seems to be associated with ones in which the traditional social order is breaking down and change has become the norm. It seems highly significant that no witchcraft accusations of the latter sort are recorded, or even hinted at, for the Huron. This indicates that the basic pattern of Huron economic and social relations remained essentially the same as it had been in late prehistoric times. While the control of particular lines of trade, most probably by traditional headmen, served to intensify status differences already existing among the Huron, this did not result in a crisis in Huron society or a breakdown in traditional structures or values.

CULTURAL FLORESCENCE

The fur trade also stimulated the elaboration of certain Huron crafts and other forms of artistic expression. We have already discussed the florescence of metal working at this time. It needs only to be stressed that the aim of much of this metal working was to produce plaques and more elaborate effigy ornaments that could be sewn on to clothing or worn in other ways. Ornamental bone carving also appears to have become more common and elaborate among the Huron, although this is a craft that still requires careful study. It is generally asserted that combs with decorated handles, human face plaques, and small bone figurines are considerably more common in historic sites than in prehistoric ones (Kidd 1952:73). These figurines may have had a religious function, like the so-called "bone dolls" of the Seneca and Cayuga, which were meant to avert witchcraft or to warn their owners of approaching danger (Carpenter 1942:111).

Both stone and clay pipes became more numerous and varied in the historic period. While ring bowl pipes remained the most common type, mortice and coronet, as well as effigy pipes grew increasingly popular. Among the human effigy pipes is the so-called blowing face type, on which a face with pursed lips and often an entire crouching body is depicted. Some of these bodies are represented in a skeletalized fashion. At one site, bodies but no heads were found in the middens, suggesting that the breaking of these pipes had ritual significance (Latta 1971:125–26). Other

clay effigy pipes had bowls depicting the heads of human beings, wolves, ducks, owls, and other animals. Stone pipes were most frequently whittled out of limestone and then polished. It has been suggested that the elaboration of pipes among the Huron may reflect the acquisition of new wealth, which permitted the purchase of more or better tobacco from the Neutral and Tionnontaté (ibid. 130).

Two observations can be made about the elaboration of metal working, bone working, and pipe manufacture. The first is that this elaboration was not confined to the Huron, but can be observed among the Iroquois and other Iroquoian tribes between 1600 and 1650 (Wray and Schoff 1953: 56–57). This suggests that new tools and materials, and possibly greater wealth generally, were stimulating a higher level of artistic expression. Specific explanations for developments among the Huron therefore bear little weight unless they also explain similar developments elsewhere. Equally important, however, is that each of these developments represents the elaboration of skills that had been a part of the Iroquoian cultural pattern for a long time. In particular, the steady increase in the variety and elaborateness of Huron pipe types throughout late Iroquoian times and the appearance of most of the new effigy types by the early contact period (Emerson 1967:189) indicate that what happened in historic times was the florescence of an already dynamic tradition, rather than any radical departure from it. Similar antecedents can be demonstrated for bone carving and metal working had been limited in earlier times mainly by the scarcity of raw material.

In spite of this, the material manifestations of Huron culture remained unspectacular. The most remarkable impact of the wealth produced by the fur trade was on ceremonialism, and particularly on those rituals that involved the redistribution of goods. These developments can be traced most clearly in connection with the Feast of the Dead. While originally a community ritual, by historic times the Feast of the Dead had become one of immense importance for promoting unity within the expanded Huron confederacy, and between the Huron and many of the Algonkian peoples with whom they traded (Hickerson 1960). Whenever such a feast was celebrated, the representatives of all these peoples were invited to attend and they both contributed and received gifts at various stages in the ceremony. Brébeuf states that over 1200 presents, which were either to be buried with the dead or redistributed to honour their memory, were exhibited at the Feast of the Dead held at Ossossané in 1636. At the end of the ceremony, twenty beaver skin robes (in all containing 200 skins)

were reserved by the Master of the Feast to thank the headmen of the other tribes for attending (Thwaites 1896–1901, 10:303).

A striking characteristic of historic ossuaries is the numerous offerings they contain by comparison with prehistoric ones. Forty-eight robes, of ten beaver skins each, were used to line the Ossossané ossuary, and each undecomposed body that was interred in it was wrapped in one or more such robes. The artifacts which occurred throughout this ossuary were mostly items intended for the personal use or adornment of the dead. Objects of North American origin included marine shell beads, projectile points, pigments, textile fabrics, and pipes. One complete conch shell, no doubt intended as raw material for manufacturing beads in the afterlife, was found near the bottom of the pit. Nevertheless, European goods made up a large portion of the offerings. In addition to glass beads, iron knives, rings, and similar items, two or three badly decomposed copper kettles were found (plate 31). These last seem to have been intended for the collective use of the dead (Kidd 1953:364). Nor was this the most splendid of Huron interments. As many as twenty-six French kettles have been discovered in a single ossuary, as well as up to sixteen conch shells and miscellaneous iron axes, copper bracelets, glass beads, metal arrowheads, and iron cups (Bawtree 1848; Hammond 1924). While many of the kettles appear to have been damaged and incomplete prior to burial, the loss of scrap metal, as well as of many other valuable items, through interment would periodically have removed a moderate amount of European goods from circulation. This would have increased the Huron's demand for such goods, which was already high because of intense use and a rapid rate of attrition (Innis 1956:17).

The elaboration of the Feast of the Dead gave ritual expression to the expanding network of relationships on which the Huron had come to depend. It was also a practical means for promoting social interaction and reinforcing goodwill among the peoples who made up this trade network. The Feast of the Dead not only was an old ritual among most of the Huron tribes but also was their key ritual for expressing solidarity. This aspect of the ritual appears to have been unique among the Huron, rather than a feature shared by all Iroquoians. It was noted in chapter 3 how an increase in the size of ossuaries appears to have paralleled the development of Huron social and political integration in prehistoric times. The final elaboration of this ritual, under the influence of the fur trade, was therefore the florescence of a traditional feature of Huron culture rather than a radical departure from it.

PLATE 31. *Copper kettle* in situ *in the Ossossané ossuary of 1636.*
Because K. E. Kidd has convincingly correlated this ossuary with the
Feast of the Dead that Brébeuf described for the spring of 1636, the
material it contains constitutes a valuable base line for determining the
variety of European goods in circulation among the Huron at this time.
Courtesy K. E. Kidd and Royal Ontario Museum, Toronto.

It is significant that the Huron chose to elaborate a ritual that depended so heavily on redistribution and making offerings to the dead. This provides further evidence that they did not view either their beaver skins or the wealth that was derived from the fur trade solely as items of commerce. Instead, they viewed them as a means of realizing the traditional values of their society. The continuing importance of these values is indicated by the fact that the Huron should have chosen to make a ritual that was already a microcosm of these values an anchor point to which their developing trade, and the new relations associated with it, might be tied.

The Huron View of the French

No detailed information has been preserved concerning what the Huron thought about the French or how they perceived the specific items of culture they adopted from them. What has been transmitted to us is seen through the distorting optic of French culture. In spite of this, it is possible to delineate some general ways in which the Huron reacted to the French.

The Huron admired the trade goods that the French sold to them and were aware of the technological superiority of certain French tools over their indigenous counterparts. Because Savignon had seen craftsmen at work in France, the Huron knew that these tools were made in Europe, rather than obtained elsewhere. Since the Huron lacked any division of labour, except by sex and age, it was difficult for them to understand that not every Frenchman was capable of making or repairing everything that the French sold to the Huron. The Huron frequently asked French visitors to mend broken kettles and to provide other services for them (Wrong 1939:183) and did not understand why their requests usually went unanswered.

The Huron were also not equipped to understand the hierarchical structure of French society or a lack of correlation between authority and technical skills, that was so different from their own ways. They believed that only the oldest and most experienced French headmen were capable of making things as complicated as iron knives and kettles and that the king made the largest kettles. For this reason, they asked only seemingly important Frenchmen to do the more complicated jobs of mending and altering European goods (183). It may also be, although there is no direct proof of this, that the Huron attributed much of the technological skill of the French to magic. Thus the ability of the French would have seemed

connected less to technological superiority than to the luck they had in acquiring magical arts. Since supernatural powers were believed to be inherent in nature, the possession by the French of a particular kind of magic was no indication of their intrinsic cultural superiority. There is little evidence that the Huron regarded the French as superior to themselves, while there is much evidence that they regarded them as inferior.

The Huron were curious about many things they saw the French doing or using, but which they were not motivated to try themselves. Huron are said to have taught Sagard their language in order to watch him writing down what they said; the expression that they used for writing was "marking it with a snowshoe," a neat phrase likening the marks a pen leaves on paper to the imprint of a snowshoe (73). The Huron also understood that writing could be used to make a person's meaning understood at a distance, which must have been interpreted as a supernatural quality (173). Yet, in spite of the Recollets' efforts to teach Huron children how to write, it was not a skill that any Huron had the initiative to try to acquire.

The Huron were also fascinated by the missionaries' books. Some were said to spend whole days counting their pages and admiring the letters and the pictures they contained (ibid.; Sagard 1866:330). The magical power of these books was suggested by the missionaries and by the illustrations they contained. European pictures and images were far more detailed and realistic than any representations the Huron had ever produced or seen. Because of this, the Huron seem to have believed that some, if not all, of these representations were alive. Le Jeune reports that they called certain saints' statues at Quebec *ondaqui* (sing. *oki*) or spirits and believed them to be living things. The Huron asked if the tabernacle was their house and if they dressed themselves in the ornaments seen around the altar (Thwaites 1896–1901, 5:257). Similarly, Sagard's wooden death's head was considered to be the head of a real child.

The Huron accepted on trust many things that the French told them and which they could not check for themselves. They were, for example, informed that French women had beards the same as men and, according to Sagard, only learned differently when they met Hélène de Champlain, who came to Quebec in 1620 (Wrong 1939:137). If true, this story provides further evidence that the Huron visited Quebec only infrequently prior to 1620, since Louis Hébert's wife had been there since 1617.

In the process of trying to understand the French, the Huron not unnaturally tended to overestimate, as well as to underestimate, the newcomer's abilities. They wanted to know whether the French ate thunderbirds and requested, on occasion, that the French use their guns to shoot a

thunderbird in order to divert a storm (183). Likewise, seeing that the dogs at Quebec had ears which hung down, unlike their own that had pointed ears, the Huron asked the Recollets to cause their dogs' ears to bend in a similar manner. Once they knew that the French could not perform specific miracles, they revised their estimates of their abilities in a realistic fashion. On the other hand, when the Recollets demonstrated that they were at least as able to heal the sick and to control the weather as Huron shamans were, the Huron continued to make use of, and further test, their abilities. In this respect, the Huron treated the French priests just as they treated any person who claimed shamanistic powers (173).

Individual Huron also expressed a faddish interest in isolated facets of French culture. Almost everyone wanted to try on the clogs worn by the Recollets, and many attempted to persuade the Recollets to make such shoes for them (146). The Huron were also interested in sampling French food, lemon rind being one of the delicacies that particularly pleased them (Thwaites 1896–1901, 5:257). On the other hand, they invariably refused to eat corn soup if the French had added salt, spices, or wild herbs to flavour it. This, they said, made it smell bad (Wrong 1939:82). One young man of foppish temperament is reported by Sagard to have refused to go hunting and to have amused himself cooking in the French manner (124). Unfortunately, this story is so similar to one Marc Lescarbot (1907–14, 2:247–48) told about a young Micmac that it seems likely that Sagard stole the story from him. French fashions did, however, produce cultural innovations. After the Recollets arrived in 1623, several women gave their children clerical haircuts (Sagard 1866:363).

The Huron showed great interest in domestic cats, which they believed were possessed of reason since they came when called. This they interpreted as evidence that they were controlled by a powerful spirit. The chief source of these cats was the Recollet house at Quebec, and giving them as presents was a potent method of cultivating good relations with Huron headmen. There was already at least one cat in the Huron country by 1623, which was a gift from Father Le Caron to an important headman (Wrong 1939: 118). Another was given to the war chief, Angoiraste, after he had brought Sagard back to Quebec (ibid. 270; Sagard 1866:761). The Huron were used to keeping tame animals as pets; thus the novelty of these cats was the species, rather than tame animals as such.

While the Huron admired selected items of European culture, they were far from uncritical of the French. Some of this criticism reflected the opposing cultural ideals of the two groups. The Huron were offended by Frenchmen gesticulating with their arms, talking all at once, and inter-

rupting one another, and for this reason they jokingly called them women (Wrong 1939:140). The Huron likewise despised French merchants for haggling over the prices of individual pelts, which they felt was contrary to the spirit of the alliance that existed between them (ibid.).

Other criticisms of the French seem to reflect the high opinion that the Huron had of themselves and the general condescension with which they treated their Algonkian neighbours. They regarded the difficulties that the French had in learning to speak Huron as evidence of their stupidity, and thus explained all difficulties the French had in acquiring skills that the Huron held to be commonplace (138). The Huron also ridiculed beards as unnatural and disfiguring, and Huron men feigned amazement that women would look favourably on a man who had one. They claimed that beards were the cause of the intellectual deficiencies of the French (137). The Huron fancied themselves as being superior to the French, not only because they were taller but also because they were glabrous and therefore more intelligent.

Specific events served to discourage respect for the French. Because of Recollet opposition, the French had been unable to accept reparations payments for the two Frenchmen who had been slain by the Montagnais in 1616 or 1617; however, the growing hostility of the Montagnais forced the French to pardon the killer officially when the Indians gathered to trade at Three Rivers in 1623. As testimony of this pardon, the French threw a sword into the river and distributed presents among the assembled tribes (Trigger 1971*a*:95–98). The Huron, who had come to trade, watched this ceremony in silence, but the following winter they joked among themselves that it cost little to kill a Frenchman (Sagard 1866:226). They were also shocked by the callous manner in which the French traders treated one another, and were horrified when they were told that in France the poor had to beg for food (Wrong 1939:89).

Individual personality traits played a major role in determining how well any particular Frenchman got on with the Huron. The most important test that he faced was how well he behaved on his journey to the Huron country. The reputation that he gained at that time spread rapidly and strongly influenced other Huron's opinions of him (74). A traveller was expected to be generous and to share what food he had with his travelling companions (57). He was also expected to bear hardships without complaint and to maintain a cheerful disposition, so as to encourage the rest of his party (58). Once in the Huron country, a willingness to participate in Huron activities was a decided advantage.

There is no reference to the Huron drinking, or attempting to obtain alcoholic beverages, at this time. While they may have consumed a small amount of alcohol when they visited the trading places along the St. Lawrence, they evidently did not think it worth the trouble to carry wine or spirits home with them. Indeed, the only wine that is known to have been transported to the Huron country at this time was taken there by the Recollets to celebrate communion and entertain occasional French visitors.

The Huron's lack of interest in alcohol correlates with their unbroken self-esteem. In their relations with the French, the Huron were still their own masters. Their role in the fur trade was built on earlier trade relations and the cultural florescence which this trade made possible was a realization of tendencies that had been inherent in their traditional culture, rather than a disrupting or degrading process. All of these developments contributed to a sense of achievement and well-being. The Huron had no reason to resent the French or to feel inferior to them. On the contrary, they seem to have felt more justified than ever in regarding other peoples as being inferior to themselves. Sagard summed up the general feeling of the Huron when he wrote that Auoindaon, the principal headman of the northern Attignawantan, asked to be spoken of as the brother or cousin of the French king and expressed his equality with the king by pressing the two forefingers of his hands together (149). While this may be another colourful story stolen from Lescarbot (1907–14, 2:355), it faithfully represents Huron sentiment at this time. The most distinctive feature of this period was its freedom from the negative aspects of European contact that were to become so prominent in the grim decades that followed.

Notes

CHAPTER ONE

1. Among recent books dealing with Amerindian history and Indian-White relations, the following are of major importance: Fenton 1957; Fiedler 1968; J. Forbes (ed.) 1964; Hagan 1961; Leacock and Lurie (eds.) 1971; Spicer 1969; Washburn (ed.) 1964.

2. For a critique of the role of this theory in Canadian historiography, see A. Smith 1970.

3. A partial exception are the Beothuk of Newfoundland, who were denied access to their coastal hunting and fishing grounds by Europeans. In the middle of the eighteenth century, exasperated by their petty thieving, the French offered a bounty for Beothuk heads (Jenness 1960:266–67).

4. See also Bailey 1938.

5. For other recent publications that suggest a growing interest in Canadian Indian history, see Walker 1971; Baker 1972; Morton 1972.

6. "Anthropologists have customarily conducted studies of cultural change as if change did not exist until Europeans appeared on the scene" (Gamst 1969:6).

7. For an analysis of the view that efforts to civilize the Indians would destroy them, see Pearce 1965. For a typical statement of the view that the Indian was doomed as a result of European contact, see C. Lavollée, cited in Harper 1971:41.

8. For general summaries of North American prehistory, see J. Jennings 1968; Willey 1966; Willey and Phillips 1958; Caldwell 1958; Griffin 1952.

9. For a critique of these stereotypes, see Hunt 1940:3–12.

10. Robertson 1812. For an appreciation of his work, see Hoebel 1960.

11. For summaries of the development of anthropology in Canada, see McIlwraith 1930, 1949, and Cole 1973.

12. For notable examples of the use of written documents by anthropologists, see Kroeber 1952; Hallowell 1955; Eggan 1966; Fenton 1940. Recent work on Indian land claims in the United States has also resulted in more anthropologists using primary documents (Hickerson 1970:2).

13. For discussions of the scope of ethnohistory, see Sturtevant 1966; Hudson 1966; Fenton 1966; Hickerson 1970:5–7.

14. For a comparison of what is known about Huron culture prior to 1650 with what is known about Wyandot and Iroquois culture more recently, see Tooker 1964.

15. For basic traits, see Driver 1961. Claude Lévi-Strauss (1968, 1971) has drawn attention to pan-Indian traits in Indian mythology. These, he believes, suggest the existence of pan-Indian themes at a "deep-structural" level. Anthropologists working with American Indians are profoundly aware of widespread similarities in values and attitudes. It is unclear, however, to what degree these are an aboriginal heritage or a more recent reaction to similar acculturative pressures.

16. For discussions of historical method, see Carr 1967; Elton 1969; Fischer 1971. A more extensive bibliography is in Hickerson 1970:3–4.

17. For more detailed comments, see Trigger 1970:13–14.

18. For Canadian efforts to write biographies of this sort, see Girard 1948 and Pouliot 1958.

CHAPTER TWO

1. The main primary sources on which this description of the Huron is based are the writings of Samuel de Champlain (Biggar 1922–36); Gabriel Sagard (1866; Wrong 1939); and the annual relations and other documents of the Jesuits published in Thwaites 1896–1901. For corrections and additions to the latter, dealing mainly with details of Roman Catholic theology, ritual, and organization, see Donnelly 1967. For ethnological information Grant's (1952; originally published 1907) partial translation of Champlain is in some respects preferable; for maps and illustrations many prefer Laverdière 1870. For a discussion of the works of Sagard, see Warwick 1972. For a critical study of the *Jesuit Relations*, see Pouliot 1940; also Spalding 1929; McGuire 1901.

Minor primary sources that have been consulted include Boucher 1664; Chaumonot 1869; Gendron 1868; and original documents reproduced in Le Clercq 1691. An English translation of the latter work, not cited because it does not include the French text, is Shea 1881.

Later sources consulted include: Charlevoix 1866–72 and 1923; Du Creux 1951–52; and Lafitau 1724.

Detailed and comprehensive studies of Huron culture have been published by Kinietz 1940:1–160; Tooker 1964; Trigger 1969a; and Heidenreich 1972. In Tooker's publication, all the material concerning the Huron in the main primary sources has been collated and paraphrased. Footnotes correlate these data with what is known about the related Wyandot and Iroquois cultures. Because Tooker's work has been designed to serve as a guide to the ethnographic data concerning the Huron, I am able to omit a plethora of references documenting my description of Huron life. The main use of notes in this chapter is to draw the reader's attention to more detailed studies of various facets of Huron life and to indicate, where necessary, on what basis controversial interpretations are offered.

2. The earliest reference to this etymology occurs in Jérôme Lalemant's account of the Huron mission for the year 1638–39 (Thwaites 1896–1901, 16:229–31). Lalemant expresses reservations about the authenticity of the story. Godefroy (1938, 4:532) states that in Old French Huron was a "*qualificatif méprisant, désignant un personnage grossier.*" Grandsaignes d'Hautrive (1947:357) lists "*rustre*" and "*vilain*" among its original meanings. For a more detailed discussion of this term, see Hewitt (1907:584). For comments relevant to understanding differences in the degree of acculturation of the coastal peoples and the Huron, see Sagard 1866:251, 271.

3. Hewitt (1907:584) has accepted this etymology. Alternative interpretations have Wendat meaning "speakers of a common language" (Jones 1908:419–20) or the "Villagers" or "One Village" (Heidenreich 1971:300–301). French translations of Huron speeches referring to their country as an island (Thwaites 1896–1901, 15:21; 33:237–39) and the Jesuit gloss "quia in insula habitabant"